The
Devil's
Redemption

Volume 2

The
Devil's
Redemption

**A NEW HISTORY
AND INTERPRETATION
OF CHRISTIAN
UNIVERSALISM**

Michael J. McClymond

𝕭

BakerAcademic
a division of Baker Publishing Group
Grand Rapids, Michigan

© 2018 by Michael J. McClymond

Published by Baker Academic
a division of Baker Publishing Group
PO Box 6287, Grand Rapids, MI 49516-6287
www.bakeracademic.com

Paperback edition published 2020
ISBN 978-1-5409-6338-3

Printed in the United States of America

The Library of Congress has cataloged the hardcover edition as follows:
Names: McClymond, Michael James, 1958– author.
Title: The devil's redemption : a new history and interpretation of Christian universalism / Michael J. McClymond.
Description: Grand Rapids : Baker Publishing Group, 2018.
Identifiers: LCCN 2017051460 | ISBN 9780801048562 (cloth)
Subjects: LCSH: Universalism. | Salvation—Christianity. | Salvation after death.
Classification: LCC BX9941.3 .M33 2018 | DDC 234—dc23
LC record available at https://lccn.loc.gov/2017051460

Appendix D was originally published as Michael McClymond, "*Origenes Vindicatus vel Rufinus Redivivus*? A Review of Ilaria Ramelli's *The Christian Doctrine of* Apokatastasis (2013)," *Theological Studies* 76, no. 4, pp. 813–26. Copyright © 2015 Michael McClymond. Reprinted by permission of SAGE Publications. https://doi.org/10.1177/0040563915605264

This book is dedicated to my teachers at Yale University Divinity School:

Sydney Ahlstrom, Brevard Childs, Hans Frei, Rowan Greer,
Richard Hays, Lansing Hicks, Paul Holmer, Timothy Jackson,
Robert K. Johnston, David Kelsey, Bonnie Kittel, George Lindbeck,
Jaroslav Pelikan, and Lamin Sanneh;

and to my teachers at the University of Chicago Divinity School:

Jerald Brauer, Brian Gerrish, Langdon Gilkey, W. Clark Gilpin,
Martin Marty, Bernard McGinn, Frank Reynolds, Susan Schreiner,
and David Tracy.

Contents

Abbreviations

ANF   *The Ante-Nicene Fathers: Translations of the Writings of the Fathers Down to A.D. 325.* Edited by Alexander Roberts and James Donaldson. 10 vols. 1885–87. Reprint, Grand Rapids: Eerdmans, 1950.

ca.   *circa*, about

CCSL   Corpus Christianorum: Series Latina. Turnhout: Brepols, 1953–.

CD   Barth, Karl. *Church Dogmatics.* 14 vols. Edited by G. W. Bromiley and T. F. Torrance. Edinburgh: T&T Clark, 1956–69.

cent.   century

ch(s). chapter(s)

CSEL   Corpus Scriptorum Ecclesiasticorum Latinorum. 101 vols. Vienna: Verlag der Österreichischen Akademie der Wissenschaften, 1864–2011; Berlin: de Gruyter, 2012–.

d.   died

DR   *The Devil's Redemption;* cross-references by chapter and section number to the present work

ET   English translation

FC   Fathers of the Church

fl.   flourished

GCS   Die griechischen christlichen Schriftsteller der ersten drei Jahrhunderte, herausgegeben von der Preussischen Akademie der Wissenschaften. 40 vols. Leipzig: J. C. Hinrichs, 1897–1936.

GNO   Gregorii Nysseni Opera; auxilio aliorum virorum doctorum edenda curavit Wernerus Jaeger. 19 vols. Leiden: Brill, 1952–.

KD   Barth, Karl. *Kirchliche Dogmatik.* 13 vols. Munich: Kaiser, 1932; Zurich: EVZ, 1938–65.

KG   Evagrius, *Kephalaia gnōstika*

LCL   Loeb Classical Library

NPNF[1] *A Select Library of Nicene and Post-Nicene Fathers of the Christian Church.* First Series. Edited by Philip Schaff. 14 vols. 1886–89. Reprint, Grand Rapids: Eerdmans, 1979.

NPNF²   *A Select Library of Nicene and Post-Nicene Fathers of the Christian Church.*
        Second Series. Edited by Philip Schaff and Henry Wace. 14 vols. 1890–1900.
        Reprint, Grand Rapids: Eerdmans, 1983.
PA   Origen, *Peri archōn. In Origenes vier Bücher von den Prinzipien.* Edited by
        Herwig Görgemanns and Heinrich Karpp. Darmstadt: Wissenschaftliche
        Buchgesellschaft, 1976.
par(s).   paragraph(s)
PG   Patrologia Graeca [= *Patrologiae Cursus Completus.* Series Graeca]. Edited by
        J.-P. Migne. 161 vols. Paris, 1857–86.
PL   Patrologia Latina [= *Patrologiae Cursus Completus.* Series Latina]. Edited by
        J.-P. Migne. 217 vols. Paris, 1844–55.
PO   Patrologia Orientalis. Edited by René Graffin et al. 53 vols. Turnhout:
        Brepols, 1904–.
SC   Sources chrétiennes
sec(s).   section(s)
ST   Aquinas, Thomas. *Summa Theologica* [*Summa Theologiae*]. Translated by
        Fathers of the English Dominican Province. New York: Benziger, 1947–48.
        (Cited using part, question, and article numbers.)
TD   Balthasar, Hans Urs von. *Theo-drama: Theological Dramatic Theory.* 5 vols.
        San Francisco: Ignatius, 1988–98.

7

German Thinkers

KANT AND MÜLLER, SCHLEIERMACHER
AND HEGEL, SCHELLING AND TILLICH

What can I know? What should I do? What may I hope?

—Immanuel Kant[1]

There is a threefold primitive condition of man, his primitive state in
the eternal ideas, his primitive state in the extra-temporal existence
of every Ego, and his primitive state in the temporal beginning of
his earthly development.

—Julius Müller[2]

This may perhaps be the state in which hell ceases to exist; and it is
in these periods of eternity that the restitution [*Wiederbringung*] of evil
takes place, which is something we must necessarily believe in. Sin
is not eternal, and hence its consequences cannot be so either. This
last period within the last is that of the entirely perfect fulfillment—
that is, of the complete becoming man of God—the one where the
infinite will have become finite without therefore suffering in its

---

1. Kant, *Critique of Pure Reason*, 677 (A805 / B833).
2. J. Müller, *Christian Doctrine of Sin*, 2:425.

infinitude. Then God is in all actuality everything, and pantheism will have become true.

—Friedrich W. J. Schelling[3]

Hegel . . . showed the world evolving dialectically through a succession of "forms of consciousness," each stage superseding the one before until they all rise up sublimely into "Absolute Spirit." Hegel's *Phenomenology of Spirit* leads us to a climax as grand as that of the biblical Book of Revelation, but instead of ending with everyone divided between heaven and hell, it subsumes us all into cosmic consciousness. Kierkegaard countered Hegel with typically awkward questions: what if I don't choose to be part of this "Absolute Spirit"? What if I refuse to be absorbed, and insist on just being *me*?

—Sarah Bakewell[4]

The world of nineteenth-century German philosophy and theology after Immanuel Kant—as represented by Fichte, Hegel, Schleiermacher, Schelling, Schopenhauer, and Nietzsche—is extraordinarily complex, and much of this development is not obviously related to the theme of Christian universalism. Among the authors just named, only Schleiermacher and Schelling explicitly engaged the question of a final salvation that would encompass all human beings. Yet the tightly connected and continually expanding set of ideas and concepts in German thought had many foreseen and unforeseen implications for Christian theology, including the theme of eschatology. Nineteenth-century German thought has been a living legacy among twentieth- and twenty-first-century authors.

The moral philosophy of Immanuel Kant in some surprising ways pushes beyond the realm of the earthly and mundane and in an otherworldly direction. This claim regarding Kant is counterintuitive, since he is generally regarded as having severely limited the realm of human knowing to *phenomena* and so as having shifted a number of perennial questions—God, freedom, immortality—into the realm of the *noumena* (i.e., the things-in-themselves) where no definitive knowledge is possible. In one sense this is true. Kant's skepticism regarding the supersensible realm left its imprint on Schleiermacher among others.

3. Schelling, *Stuttgart Seminars*, 243; Schelling, *Sämtliche Werke*, 7:484.
4. Bakewell, *At the Existentialist Café*, 18–19.

Yet in another sense, Kant's *Religion within the Limits of Reason Alone* (1793) invoked the concept of a so-called transcendental self that involved a bold leap beyond the realm of the space-time-material universe. As we will see below, there are parallels between Kant's transcendental selfhood and the Origenist idea of preexistence (see *DR* 3.5).[5] In the period after Kant, it is usually Hegel—and then Nietzsche at the century's end—drawing the lion's share of scholarly attention. Yet the theme of human autonomy develops through a line defined by Kant, Fichte, and Schelling as much as or more than through Hegel.[6] Schelling's ideas became important for twentieth-century Christian theology through Paul Tillich (*DR* 7.8) and within the more recent kenotic and relational theologies (*DR* 9.12).

7.1. The Kantian Legacy of Transcendental Selfhood

Kant's philosophy gave expression to a problem that lay at the very core of any notion of the moral self's autonomy and responsibility.[7] His starting point was the perceived condition of the human self as *inclined to evil* yet *culpable for evil*. On the one hand, every human is entrammelled by evil impulses and desires. On the other hand, according to everyday assumptions, every human is responsible for his or her own wrongdoing and cannot shift blame to someone or something else. The conjunction of these two propositions creates a philosophical dilemma: Can the self in the present life be held accountable not merely for individual acts of sin or wrongdoing but also for the underlying evil disposition that gives rise to these wrongful acts? Let us imagine that a certain pill, once ingested, creates an overpowering urge to steal. Would then

5. Alfons Fürst has linked Origen with Kant in relation to the themes of human autonomy, dignity, and self-determination. See Fürst and Hengstermann, *Autonomie und Menschenwürde*, esp. 9–10. These concepts underlie modern ethical discussions and democratic forms of governance (9). For Kant and Origen alike, human reason possesses a logos-character and so is autonomous—a law-to-itself. Human beings thus give the law to themselves and do not receive the law from without, in heteronomous fashion.

6. Loncar writes: "If Idealism's crucial role in modernity is appreciated at all, it is often only with reference to Hegel, for the traditions that run through Feuerbach and Marx, Kierkegaard and Existentialism, and Schopenhauer and Nietzsche are associated with reactions to Hegel. Yet Kant, Fichte, and Schelling also played central roles in defining, defending, and advancing some of the distinctive ideas of modernity, not least the idea of freedom as autonomy, a peculiar and radical understanding of free agency that now pervades our culture and, one could add, modern theology" ("German Idealism's Long Shadow," 100). Terry Pinkard, in *German Philosophy, 1760–1860*, underscores autonomy as the central and unifying concept of German idealism.

7. One text that is important for the idea of transcendental selfhood is Kant's *Religion within the Limits of Reason Alone*. Christopher Insole reexamines Kant's notion of moral selfhood in a series of recent writings: Insole, "Irreducible Importance of the Religious Hope"; Insole, "Kant's Transcendental Idealism"; Insole, *Kant and the Creation of Freedom*; Insole, "Kant and the Creation of Freedom"; Insole, "Thomistic Reading."

a six-year-old child be responsible for shoplifting in the local supermarket if
the mother of the child had deliberately given this pill to the child to swallow,
saying that it was medicine? In this case, would the responsibility not rest with
the mother rather than with the child? And what of human beings born into the
world with inclinations toward wrongdoing? Are not all of us something like
the kleptomaniac child—that is, often acting on the basis of an evil disposition
present with us from our earliest years and yet not chosen by us?

Western Christian theology since the time of Augustine has highlighted
the doctrine of original sin, asserting that Adam and Eve's fall into sin in the
garden of Eden resulted in an inclination to sin among all later human beings.
Martin Luther and other early Protestant thinkers had, if anything, intensified
Augustine's stress on human depravity. While Immanuel Kant rejected notions of hereditary sin or guilt, in certain respects his view of human nature
remained Augustinian and Lutheran. On an empirical level, he agreed with the
biblical presumption that all humans are sinners from birth, and he thought
that this was a general truth confirmed by observation. Having set aside the
Adam explanation, Kant was forced to think along different lines, and this led
him toward a notion of transcendental selfhood and transcendental moral
agency—an initial choice that takes place apart from the space-time-material
conditions of the empirical self and that creates the context within which the later
deliberations and choices of the empirical self will occur. In *Religion within the
Limits of Reason Alone*, Kant traced "the propensity to evil" to a trans-empirical
or nonsensible source. The "propensity" derived from an "intelligible action,
cognizable by means of pure reason alone, apart from every temporal condition."[8]
The evil inclination came from an "action" that did not happen in the space-
time-material universe.

As Kant's thought developed from the 1750s to the 1770s, his attention turned
more and more toward finding a philosophical basis for human autonomy.
During the 1740s and into the 1750s he was a compatibilist—that is, he held
that divine determination and human choice or responsibility were compatible
with one another.[9] In Kant's earlier thinking, God alone enjoyed a full transcendental freedom. He held this philosophical position until around 1762. At this
point, writes Christopher Insole, Kant sought "such divine freedom for human
beings also." It may have been Kant's reading of Jean-Jacques Rousseau's *Émile*
(1762) that led him to become unhappy with his earlier compatibilist account
of human freedom. "A will that is subject to another," he wrote, "is imperfect

8. Insole, "Kant and the Creation of Freedom," 120, citing Kant, *Religion within the Limits of
Reason Alone*, 26–27 (*Gesammelte Schriften*, 6:31).

9. For Kant's compatibilist views, see his lesser-known, early writings in Kant, *Theoretical
Philosophy*.

and contradictory." The autonomy theme, powerfully expressed in the late, brief essay "What Is Enlightenment?" (1784), began to take over Kant's thought from this point.[10]

The emergence of Kant's transcendental idealism was linked to his preoccupation with human freedom. In the *Critique of Pure Reason* (1781), Kant wrote that "if appearances are things in themselves, then freedom cannot be saved."[11] Because Kant conceived of space and time along Newtonian lines and as deterministic, he feared a "fatalism of actions."[12] Yet this was not all. It was not just man versus the machine, so to speak, but there was also a dynamic of creature versus Creator. Kant's critical philosophy had perhaps as much to do with an essentially theological issue as it did with the question of materialistic or mechanical causation.[13]

Kant in his *Critique of Practical Reason* (1788) does not officially surrender the doctrine of creation. He states that God as "the universal original being" was the cause "of the existence of substance." Divine creation is an idea, Kant says, "that can never be given up." Noumenal selves (i.e., things-in-themselves, apart from their being known or perceived) are among the "substances" created by God and are "finite things in themselves."[14] Yet in his later critical philosophy, there is a shift from the divine mind to the human mind as "creative." Though previously Kant held that God was the creator of substances, he later made the transcendental human self the *creator of relations* among substances. If the noumenal world were spatial and temporal, Kant reasoned, then God's creative power would in effect wipe out all human freedom. In such a case, "a human being would be a marionette or automaton . . . built and wound up by the supreme artist."[15] In his "Reflection" (1778–80), Kant wrote that "space is nothing in itself and is not a thing as a divine work, but rather lies in us and can only obtain in us. . . . The appearances are not actually creations, thus neither is the human being; rather he is merely the appearance of a divine

10. Insole, "Kant's Transcendental Idealism," 624. See Kant, "What Is Enlightenment?," 85–91; Kant, "Beantwortung der Frage: Was ist Aufklärung?," 481–94.

11. Insole, "Kant and the Creation of Freedom," 112–13, citing Kant, *Critique of Pure Reason*, 535 (A536 / B564).

12. Kant, *Critique of Practical Reason*, 85.

13. "The doctrinal question is whether . . . our freedom is . . . made possible only by God's withdrawal" (Insole, "Kant and the Creation of Freedom," 113). "At least part of the motivation, for Kant, is a need to solve a crisis about human freedom in relation to divine action" (ibid., 115). What we might here call the logic of divine withdrawal is also reflected in other thinkers and schools of thought treated in this book: Kabbalah (*DR* 2.5), Schelling (*DR* 7.7), Bulgakov (*DR* 8.6), Moltmann (*DR* 9.10–9.11), and contemporary kenotic and relational theologies (*DR* 9.12).

14. Insole, "Kant's Transcendental Idealism," 617, citing Kant, *Critique of Practical Reason*, 84–85.

15. Insole, "Kant's Transcendental Idealism," 609, 616, citing Kant, *Critique of Practical Reason*, 85.

creation."[16] The medium for the reciprocal interaction of noumenal selves was "the divine omnipresence."[17] Kant's philosophy during the 1770s thus presents *a split self: determined and yet undetermined.* Despite the mechanistic web of causation that surrounds the empirical human being, Kant "insists that the phenomenal appearance of the determinism of our actions does not conflict with our genuine transcendental freedom."[18] The noumenal self enjoys "absolute spontaneity" or "self-activity from an inner principle according to the power of free choice."[19]

Kant in the 1770s was struggling with the entire idea of human beings as created, and at some points he acknowledges the dilemma posed by affirming both the createdness and the freedom (as he conceived it) of humans. He wrote: "Freedom is the capacity to produce and effect something originally. But how original causality and an original capacity for efficient causation obtain in a created being is not to be comprehended at all." In 1776–78, as the American Revolution was fought on the other side of the Atlantic, Kant was struggling to define his idea of human freedom. He called this the "only unsolvable metaphysical difficulty."[20] Createdness seems to conflict with Kant's idea of human causal and moral originality. In *The Metaphysics of Morals* (1797) he acknowledged that he could not reconcile his own notion of human freedom with the idea of humanity's creation by God: "No concept can be formed of how it is possible for *God to create* free beings, for it seems as if all their future actions would have to be predetermined by that first act, included in the chain of natural necessity and therefore not free."[21]

Robert Brown comments that "the doctrine of a transcendent [or transcendental] fall seeks to formulate in a philosophically more rigorous way the Christian belief in a fallenness of human nature [and] to preserve free will and responsibility by removing the fall entirely from the interlocking causal network of events in space and time."[22] Yet the notion of the transcendental

16. Insole, "Kant's Transcendental Idealism," 615, citing Kant, *Gesammelte Schriften*, R6057.

17. Insole, "Kant's Transcendental Idealism," 616.

18. Ibid., 625.

19. Ibid., 626, citing Kant, *Lectures on Metaphysics*, 81.

20. Insole, "Kant's Transcendental Idealism," 627, citing Kant, *Gesammelte Schriften*, R4221, R5121. Insole argues that Kant's philosophy became less coherent over time as his stress on human autonomy increased: "In the 1750s Kant's metaphysics of causation and analysis of freedom were not only compatible, but one led ineluctably to the other. In the 1770s it seems that Kant does not quite know how to reconcile divine and human freedom, except to insist that transcendental freedom must be somehow accessible to both us and to the divine mind" (ibid.).

21. Insole, "Kant and the Creation of Freedom," 120, citing Kant, *Metaphysics of Morals*, 6 (*Gesammelte Schriften*, 6:280n). Elsewhere Kant says, "God cannot concur in the causality of freely acting beings . . . for he must not be regarded as the *causa* of their free actions" (Insole, "Kant and the Creation of Freedom," 121, citing Kant, *Gesammelte Schriften*, R6167).

22. R. F. Brown, "Transcendental Fall," 49. Cf. Loncar, "German Idealism's Long Shadow."

fall renders unnecessary the historical Adam, Eve, and garden of Eden.[23] At the same time, the transcendental fall preserves the idea that humans are "fallen beings" throughout their earthly lives and that human society bears the imprint of this "fallenness." It was in *Religion within the Limits of Reason Alone* that Kant first propounded his idea of the transcendental fall. In this work Kant sought to preserve human responsibility: "Man *himself* must make or have made himself into whatever, in a moral sense, whether good or evil, he is or is to become. Either condition must be an effect of his free choice; for otherwise he could not be held responsible for it."[24] Since human beings as moral agents have made themselves what they are, Kant insisted that "we must not . . . look for an origin in time of a moral character for which we are to be held responsible." According to Kant, the ultimate ground for the will's determination as good or evil is ultimately inscrutable: "The rational origin of this perversion of our will whereby it makes lower incentives supreme . . . remains inscrutable to us." For Kant, "this propensity itself must be set down to our account."[25] The general implication of Kant's ethical argumentation is that humans have somehow given to themselves the moral dispositions that they possess.

It is possible to interpret Kant's metaphysics in more than one way. Some see what Kant called noumena and phenomena as two different realms existing in parallel with each other. This interpretation raises multiple problems. If choices made in the noumenal realm *do not lead* to any causal consequences in the phenomenal realm, then the noumenal realm seems irrelevant. Yet if the noumenal choices *do lead* to causal consequences, then the phenomenal realm is no longer self-contained but is causally disrupted by noumenal agencies. Kant scholars differ in their interpretations of Kant's thinking on this point and over whether Kant's thinking was self-consistent.[26]

Kant's transcendental or noumenal self is reminiscent of the Origenist tradition. Even the term "noumenal" is a point of contact. For Origen and his followers, what God created was not the material world but the spiritual, intelligible, or

23. In *Religion within the Limits*, Kant writes that "however the origin of moral evil in man is constituted, surely of all the explanations of the spread and propagation of this evil through all members and generations of our race, the most inept is that which describes it as descending to us as an *inheritance* from our first parents" (35). Even though Kant regards the traditional doctrine of original sin as "inept," he presupposes a pervasive sinful inclination in speaking of an "evil" present in "all members . . . of our race."

24. Kant, *Religion within the Limits*, 40.

25. Kant, *Religion within the Limits*, 38.

26. R. F. Brown, "Transcendental Fall," 50–52. Some have proposed to think of Kant's noumenal/phenomenal distinction as applying not to two worlds but to *one world* under *two aspects*. Yet it is not clear that this proposal resolves the issue regarding the reciprocal cause-and-effect relationship of noumena with phenomena.

noumenal world of "rational natures" (Greek *noes*). For Origenists, the material world was a secondary creation. Kant's reasoning on noumena and phenomena was analogous to this. What is more, the trajectory Kant sketched with his transcendental fall bears on the question of human fulfillment. If freedom exists only in the transcendental or noumenal state, then it would seem to follow that the restoration of freedom can only come about by a return to the transcendental or noumenal state. Kant did not carry this line of thought to its logical conclusion, yet the possible implications are clear enough. A transcendental or noumenal condition for humanity in the future would require a state of *dematerialization* of the sort that both Schelling (*DR* 7.7) and Solovyov (*DR* 8.3–8.4) later proposed.

Kant's transcendental human self was the starting point for Johann Gottlieb Fichte's *Ich-philosophie* ("I-philosophy" or "ego-philosophy"). Fichte (1762–1814) was among the first commentators on Kant to suggest that the spirit of Kant's system was best served by simply eliminating all references to the unknowable realm of the noumena. In 1799 Kant himself rejected Fichte's rereading, though Fichte continued in his new direction.[27] Fichte's *Ich-Philosophie* of "I = I" holds that the human being is self-conditioning or self-creating. The self throws up a field within which action occurs and within which it realizes itself. Fichte's philosophy severs the bond linking the self to an external world. While Kant had qualms about the implications of divine creation for human freedom, Fichte took a more radical line, calling the doctrine of divine creation "the absolute, fundamental error of all metaphysics and the teaching of false religion."[28] If there were to be such a thing as creation in Fichte's thought, then it would have to operate in the reverse direction, as indicated in the terse statement attributed to him, "I create God every day."[29] Fichte's philosophy functioned as a starting point for later philosophies of self-will and self-assertion.[30]

Kant's thought became foundational for later German thinkers in their conceptions of human selfhood, the origin of evil, and the possibilities for an overcoming of evil. The idea of a human self that acts in perfect freedom, beyond the limits of finite experience, proved seminal in the further development of idealism. Ironically, the Kantian philosophy that transcendentalized humanity also de-transcendentalized God, turning the deity into a mere

27. Insole, "Kant and the Creation of Freedom," 119.
28. Fichte, *Die Anweisung zum seligen Leben*, 479, cited in Brito, "Création et temps," 386 (my translation).
29. Cited in Mead, *Movements of Thought in the Nineteenth Century*, 95. This saying is widely reported in secondary literature, but I have not been able to find it in Fichte's own writings.
30. While Friedrich Nietzsche comes at once to mind, a philosophy of the absolute self found an early advocate in Stirner, *Ego and Its Own*. For a critical review of Fichte, Stirner, and Nietzsche, see Santayana, *Egotism in German Philosophy*.

postulate of human moral self-awareness. At first glance, Kant's reasoning had finitized all human knowledge and understanding, and yet on a deeper level—by postulating a transcendental selfhood unconstrained by matter, space, and time—Kant did much to expand the idea of human power and potential. Later idealist thinkers overstepped the narrow limits of Kantian epistemology. Both Fichte and Hegel conceived of the human self, in its willing or thinking, as all but infinite. The so-called absolute idealism of Schelling and Hegel involved a more dynamic and process-oriented approach to idealism, a shift due in no small part to Hegel's and Schelling's appropriation of Böhme and Böhmist thinkers (see *DR* 7.4; 7.7).[31]

Like Aristotle and Aquinas before him, Kant presumed that our moral intuitions are veridical—that is, that they tell us something about the world. In this sense Kant was more optimistic than Arthur Schopenhauer (1788–1860). For a pessimistic thinker such as Schopenhauer, human moral intuition—or the inclination toward justice, truth, and meaning—does not imply that justice, truth, or meaning can or will be attained. Such intuition or inclination may be deeply implanted or innate in human nature, yet may be constantly frustrated and so become a source of human misery rather than human fulfillment.[32] Augustine and Aquinas both believed that human aspirations could and would be fulfilled, but they grounded their confidence of this in the character of God as the Creator of all and the Guider of history. Schopenhauer rejected the Creator and the doctrine of creation because he recognized that these ideas conflicted with his pessimism.[33] Kant lay betwixt Aquinas and Schopenhauer, since he insisted on the real correlation of human moral intuitions with the nature of

---

31. Böhme's impact in shaping German idealist notions of a developmental deity and historical process is clearly set forth in D. Walsh, *Mysticism of Innerworldly Fulfillment*.

32. One of the ideas to be taken up in the conclusion (*DR* 12.6) is the *utopian strand* in Kant's idea of hope. The notion that wickedness goes unpunished and virtue goes unrewarded—i.e., that there is finally no just proportion between virtue and happiness—offends our moral sense, according to Kant. Rather than accepting the apparent injustice of the world, Kant presumed that the offended moral sense tells us something about *how the world really is*. Belief in a God who rectifies everything by bringing morality and virtue into proper alignment or proportionality is a moral postulate for Kant. As Insole explains Kant in "Irreducible Importance of the Religious Hope," 340: "We are not moral *because* of the promise[d] future happiness, but as it ought to be the case that being moral leads to happiness, we *should* believe in this connection. . . . The 'highest good' is the necessary highest end of a morally determined will—that is to say, it is what ought to happen—and so it is a 'true object of that will.'" The logic of Kant's reasoning on religious hope is: "The world *ought* to be X, therefore I *ought to hope or believe* it to be X." This way of approaching religious hope ties into the "hopeful universalism" of Barth (*DR* 9.3) and Balthasar (*DR* 10.9), who both seem Kantian in their way of approaching the question of hope for the salvation of all. We call this a utopian strand because it rests on the presumption that our moral intuitions will not be consistently violated by the world we see around us.

33. Brito, "Création et temps," 362.

reality, and yet, in positing the transcendental self, he moved away from the self as created by God toward a notion of the human self's self-creation.[34]

7.2. Müller's Quasi-Origenist Non-universalism

In *Religion within the Limits of Reason Alone*, Kant was preoccupied with "radical evil" in human life. Julius Müller (1801–78) carried forward this Kantian preoccupation. Yet Müller went further than Kant in his thinking on the transcendental self. As we saw above, Kant's view of human nature and moral action was deeply split into an empirical realm where the self is governed by necessity, and a transcendental realm of utter freedom. Müller commented:

> However decidedly we may feel obliged to reject the natural necessity of that predeterminism which Kant regarded as insurmountable in the empirical sphere, we cannot nevertheless conceal from ourselves that every successive moment is in some way conditioned by the preceding. If therefore there is to be maintained, in relation to human life, an unconditioned freedom in the inner self-determination, a pure procedure of the self-decision from the state of indecision, it must be capable of being shown in that commencing point.[35]

Once an evil habit is acquired, there is a blending of freedom with unfreedom. So freedom at the later stage must be "grounded in that original act of free self-determination."[36] One might presume that such an "original act" of the self would occur in a *preexistent state*—that is, a time chronologically prior to earthly and bodily life. Müller instead proposed a *trans-temporal* or *omni-temporal existence*—comprising past, present, and future together—that empirical, earthly, bodily human existence does not intersect or interrupt.

None of us are able to remember a first evil action in our lives, argues Müller, and this weighs against the notion that we are all determined by such a first action. Such a first moment cannot be recalled because it does not exist—at least not in our present lives. It would be hazardous to imagine that the all-important

---

34. Kant's thought could be described as a partially secularized Thomism. See Insole, "Irreducible Importance of the Religious Hope," 346:

> With Aquinas, contemplating the ultimate end leads intrinsically to happiness. Kant's moral thought has an identical structure: there is an ultimate end, and although that end is not itself happiness, it is accompanied intrinsically with happiness and delight. Kant envisages a relationship between happiness and morality not so very different from the one that Aquinas envisages. . . . Aquinas is unlike modern and contemporary thinkers in having (as he sees it) no problem at all in accounting for our motivation towards the good: this is just the structure of creation.

35. J. Müller, *Christian Doctrine of Sin*, 2:76–77.
36. Ibid., 2:77. See the discussion of Müller in Givens, *When Souls Had Wings*, 233–36.

choice of good or evil would be entrusted to us when we are only children. So we search in vain for "an original self-decision," since it is only this that will explain our moral lives at the present time. We need to find "a pure beginning by self-determination."[37] Müller concludes that "the course of our investigation compels us to step beyond the region of the temporal, in order to find the source of our freedom of the will." For "if . . . God is not the author, but the enemy of sin, then the freedom of man must have its beginning, in a sphere beyond the domain of time, in which alone pure, unconditional self-determination is possible."[38]

Müller suggests that this line of argument confirms beyond all doubt the doctrine of personal immortality, since human beings definitely make choices beyond the bounds of their bodily life. No event in earthly history can reverse or cancel out the trans-temporal choice. Plato developed this idea, yet only in a mythological way. Origen made trans-temporal choice subject to "temporal conditionality" by situating it prior to the present life, as Müller says he did not do.[39] What is more, Müller objects that Origen interpreted the human self as divine: "For it does not content him to denominate it a perfectly holy and blessed life: but he makes these spirits, in their primitive condition, share in the very essential substance (*Wesenheit*) of God."[40] Because of this elevation of the preexistent self to quasi-divine status, Müller says that "the difficulty of conceiving of the fall of the spirit-world is enhanced to impossibility."[41]

37. J. Müller, *Christian Doctrine of Sin*, 2:78–79.
38. Ibid., 2:80.
39. Ibid., 2:79–83. Here he objects to Origen's idea of trans-temporal choice as "temporally preceding the earthly life."
40. Ibid., 2:83. On the essential divinity of the human spirit or self in Origen, Müller cites Origen, *Peri archōn* 2.9.6; 2.1.1; 1.8.2; 4.4.36. On this question in Origen, see the documentation in *DR*, 267n141, 421. Müller follows the general view of Origen's teaching expressed in Jerome's *Letter to Avitus* and Pierre-Daniel Huet's massive 1688 study of Origen. In support of his view, Müller cites Gottfried Thomasius, *Origenes*, where Thomasius argues that Origen attributed a quasi-divine status to the human self. Thomasius writes that Origen's intelligible world "besteht aus einer bestimmten Zahl vernünftiger Wesen . . . durch die Gemeinschaft mit ihm selber göttlicher Nature sind" (consists in a definite number of rational essences . . . which exist through communion with God's own divine nature). He adds: "Ihr Sein und Leben ist wesentliche das göttliche; denn sie existieren eben dadurch, das sie an dem absoluten Sein participiren" (Their being and life is actually divine, for they exist in this way, that they participate in the absolute Being). In Origen's thought, argued Thomasius, there is an identification of essence and nature (*Substanz und Natur*) between that which participates (i.e., the human self) and that which is participated in (i.e., God). See Thomasius, *Origenes*, 154–55; cf. 160. One is struck at how often this question of the metaphysical status of the human self in Origen has appeared in the literature on Origen—in Jerome (fourth–fifth century), Pierre-Daniel Huet (seventeenth century), and in Gottfried Thomasius and Julius Müller (nineteenth century).
41. J. Müller, *Christian Doctrine of Sin*, 2:83–84. Müller sees a problem in grounding earthly evils in a nonearthly realm: "If now the universality of evil is also transferred to the sphere of the

Müller explicitly links Kant to Origen, saying that the German philosopher took up where the ancient author had left off. Kant's notion of "noumenal" or "intelligible freedom" gave a basis for the "moral imputation of evil" that the limited notion of an empirical selfhood could not supply.[42] Yet Müller had problems with Kant:

> How singularly strange is the result of this [i.e., Kantian] philosophy! It exposes to man, and opens his eyes to view, the nothingness of his empirical world, but at the same time reveals to him how fast bound he is to this nothingness. Beyond, in the heavenly region of the intelligible, it proclaims, truth must reside, but with the same breath, it announces to him, his inability to elevate himself into this region of the true. Thus poised he oscillates between heaven and earth, by both reciprocally attracted and repulsed, only conscious of his forms of cognition and their subjectivity.[43]

Even as Müller sought to find the roots of human free will in a trans-empirical and trans-temporal realm, he recognized that neither Kant nor Schelling had ever been able to resolve this issue.[44]

Expressing his own view, Müller writes: "There is a threefold primitive condition of man, his primitive state in the eternal ideas, his primitive state in the extra-temporal existence of every Ego, and his primitive state in the temporal beginning of his earthly development."[45] Only near the end of his two-volume work does he directly address the origin of the soul:

> That a mere nature-process should bring that into existence, which is qualitatively distinct from nature and exalted above it, the spiritual principle in the individual, must appear to us a perfect contradiction. Much rather personality as such, at the commencement of its temporal existence, proceeds from its own time-less ground, and that nature-process furnishes it [with] the basis of its temporal development.[46]

In the end, Müller's position is not all that different from Origen's. The soul has no preexistence per se, yet it has a kind of trans-temporal existence that comprises past, present, and future—not interrupted or disrupted by empirical, bodily existence. The roots of earthly, human choice lie in this trans-empirical

---

intelligible primitive decisions, then that necessity directly makes its appearance where it should be overcome and transformed into pure freedom" (2:409).

42. Ibid., 2:84, 87.
43. Ibid., 2:93.
44. See ibid., 2:93–111, for Müller's critique of Kant and Schelling.
45. Ibid., 2:425.
46. Ibid., 2:440.

and trans-temporal realm. One is reminded of Plotinus's doctrine that the soul is only partially "descended" into the body, with one aspect still in the heavenly realm and another in the earthly, physical realm.[47] In reference to the unfallen angels, Müller states that we can well believe "that a part of the spirit-world has by its primitive decision grounded itself [in] a moral existence in undisturbed union with God, in order in continuous development to exalt its creational purity to free holiness." Here the likeness to Origen is obvious. There is no basis, he writes, for "denying the possibility, that another portion of those spiritual beings have decidedly and entirely turned away from God," so that "in time every inclination to good" passes from them.[48]

Müller's arguments raise numerous questions. What does it mean to "choose" within an atemporal realm? Müller seems no more to have come to a resolution of this problem than Kant did. And why should anyone believe in such a trans-empirical self that by definition cannot be observed? Is this trans-empirical self simply a necessary deduction, to explain the reality of human moral responsibility? How might one juxtapose or combine the transcendental self with the empirical self and still assert that these two constitute the same person? And if the trans-empirical self does not interrupt or disrupt the empirical self—which goes on choosing as before—then what is the point of positing the trans-empirical self? Müller interpreted Kant's transcendental self not in terms of atemporality but rather in terms of what we might call pan-temporality or omni-temporality. The transcendental human self possesses the whole of its existence—past, present, and future—in a kind of eternal now. Müller thus attributed to the human self the kind of pan-temporality that traditional Christian theology had ascribed only to God.[49] So, at least in this respect, the human self

---

47. John Dillon notes that "in Plotinus we have his doctrine of the 'undescended' status of the highest part of the soul, which he conceives as remaining 'above,' in the intelligible realm" ("Plutarch, Plotinus and the Zoroastrian Concept of the Fravashi," citing Plotinus, *Enneads* 4.8[6].8; 5.1[10].10; 3.4[15].3). Likewise, in medieval Catharist teaching, some texts assert that the human spirits "remain in the other world during the state of descent, and only the souls are fallen" (Duvernoy, *La religion des Cathares*, 67: "restés dan l'autre monde lors de la chute, et le âmes seules sont tombeé"). On this point, we see continuity between Plotinus, ancient Zoroastrianism, medieval Catharism, and Müller's German idealism.

48. J. Müller, *Christian Doctrine of Sin*, 2:409–10.

49. Traditional Christian thinkers—from the early Middle Ages onward—generally attributed to God the property of "eternity," which they defined as God's simultaneous possession of the whole of his existence, past, present, and future. In the sixth-century CE, Boethius wrote: "So let us consider the nature of eternity, for this will make clear . . . the nature of God. . . . Eternity, then, is the complete, simultaneous and perfect possession of everlasting life; this will be clear from a comparison with creatures that exist in time . . . for it is one thing to progress . . . through everlasting life, and another thing to have embraced the whole of everlasting life in one simultaneous present" (*The Consolation of Philosophy* 5.6, cited in Helm, "Eternity"). Boethius attributed "eternity" in this sense to God and not to any creature.

in Müller became quasi-divine in a way that was only implicit in Kant but that became explicit in Fichte.

On the question of final salvation, Müller rather surprisingly did not develop his quasi Origenism in the direction of universalism. "God will certainly realize his idea of the world according to all its moments," yet "whether a given individual will enter into this completed realization as a living member of the same cannot *a priori* be decided." Because of his emphasis on human choice, he judges, "That some *are capable* of perishing, is certainly grounded in the mystery of human freedom." What is more, present-day experience shows the reality and the stubbornness of resistance to God's love: "When now experience shows, that many do really resist the most holy work of Divine Love, why is it to be impossible, that this resistance against God should again renew itself in the life hereafter and continue to do so through endless ages[?]"[50] Perhaps because of its quasi divinity and its boundless freedom, Müller's self is quite capable of utterly rejecting God's love and thus making itself utterly miserable.

God's punishment will not continue, argues Müller, without the existence of continuing sin. For "punishment is only intelligible under the presupposition of the continuing existence . . . of the sinful condition." This means that "the accusations on the ground of [in]humanity, which modern adversaries of Christianity have raised against the doctrine of eternal damnation[,] refute themselves."[51] Müller rejects purely intellectualist accounts of human sin and waywardness, and insists that "no one overcomes the sin which is in him by mere reflection."[52] He comments on habituation in sin and the self-chosen character of hell:

> As . . . the most perfect self-hood, is at the same time the highest freedom, so the development of evil completes itself in a condition, in which the not-willing the good has become at the same time a perfect non-ability, in which personality persistently averted from God has become as it were a petrifaction in sin. This is the worm which dies not, the fire which is not quenched—self-hood, which will not bow in order to become truly exalted, which will not die in order to live, nothing but hatred and yet completely powerless, incessantly raging against God, whom it is nevertheless compelled to cognize as the almighty Creator of being.[53]

In summary, Müller's theory of the trans-empirical choice helps to explain God's justice in a world in which human beings begin their lives in unequal

50. J. Müller, *Christian Doctrine of Sin*, 2:484–86.
51. Ibid., 2:486.
52. Ibid., 2:489.
53. Ibid., 2:488.

states and with unequal opportunities for moral and spiritual development. The disparity of moral aptitude among human beings, from their very birth, may be attributed to atemporal and transcendental choices that human selves make apart from the visible, material, temporal world. In this aspect of his thinking, Müller expresses a quasi-Origenist perspective in the idiom of German idealist philosophy. With regard to final destinies, though, Müller parts company with Origen and the Origenists. He insists on the responsibility of human individuals to choose rightly and suggests that some persons will never find their way out of a closed cycle of selfishness and resistance to God's love. Eternal hell is an actual state and a fully culpable condition for those who choose it and remain within it. Müller's arguments show that Origen's attempted explanation for evil and vindication of God may be divided into two components—namely, a theory regarding a primal fall of creaturely selves and a doctrine concerning the restoration of fallen selves. Müller himself believed that only one of these elements in Origen's theodicy was either necessary or worthwhile.

7.3. Schleiermacher on Universal Election and Human Solidarity

Often referred to as the father of modern (or modernist) theology, Friedrich Schleiermacher (1768–1834) is well known for his novel thinking, first signaled in his *Speeches on Religion* (1799) and continuing into his major work of dogmatics, *The Christian Faith* (1821–22 [1st ed.]; 1830–31 [2nd ed.]).[54] Among his doctrinal innovations, Schleiermacher is known for teaching universal rather than particular election. Universal election would seem to make universal salvation a certainty, though Schleiermacher hedges his language at points, speaking of final salvation for all as a possibility and hope rather than an ensured outcome.[55] In affirming universal election, Schleiermacher in the nineteenth century anticipated Karl Barth in the twentieth. On this theological theme,

54. Works by Schleiermacher in English translation include *On Religion: Speeches to Its Cultured Despisers*; *Dialectic; or, The Art of Doing Philosophy*; *The Christian Faith*.

55. Daniel Pedersen, in "Eternal Life in Schleiermacher's *The Christian Faith*," acknowledges that there are ambiguities in Schleiermacher's eschatology and that some scholars question whether Schleiermacher held to a doctrine of individual immortality or continued consciousness after death. Pedersen argues, though, that personal immortality is necessary to "Schleiermachers's system" (357), for otherwise his "dogmatics is incoherent" (341). The idea of personal immortality is, however, more of an inference in Schleiermacher's theology than an assertion. Schleiermacher shows a "modest agnosticism" (352) about our ability at the present time to describe postmortem existence. See the discussion of David Congdon (*DR* 9.13), who follows the lead of Karl Barth and Eberhard Jüngel on the afterlife and yet seems to be more skeptical on postmortem life than Schleiermacher, Barth, or Jüngel.

Barth is more indebted to Schleiermacher than is generally recognized.[56] The fulminations against Schleiermacher that were characteristic of Barth's earlier years led many interpreters to see discontinuity between the two thinkers and to ignore areas of continuity such as the doctrine of election.[57]

Before turning to Schleiermacher's position on divine election, we should briefly consider some of the debates on his notion of God's relationship with the world, a theme overshadowing his whole theology. In his early years, Schleiermacher intensively studied the philosophies of Kant and Spinoza, and Spinoza's influence gave shape to his thinking on the God-world relation. This is evident in the *Speeches on Religion*, where Schleiermacher presents a monistic view and shies away from depicting God in personal or anthropomorphic terms. Here he argues that theism and pantheism are equally valid and claims that religious piety can function without any God-idea at all.[58] The early speeches reveal a cosmic religiosity akin to that of Spinoza.[59] Schleiermacher's letters show that he was also reading and learning from Schelling during the first decade of the nineteenth century. Schleiermacher's idea of God as Absolute is analogous to Schelling's first philosophical system—namely, what is generally referred to as the identity philosophy (*DR* 7.7). This gave rise to many tensions in Schleiermacher's philosophical and theological reasoning about God.[60] The *Dialectic* (1811)

56. Schleiermacher, *Christian Faith*, 536–60 (secs. 117–20), treats election. In addition he wrote a monograph, *On the Doctrine of Election*. See also Göckel, *Barth and Schleiermacher*; Hagan, *Eternal Blessedness for All?*

57. Barth declared Schleiermacher to be "disastrously dim-sighted in regard to the fact that man as man is not only in *need* but beyond all hope of saving himself" and declared—again with reference to Schleiermacher—that "one can *not* speak of God simply by speaking of man in a loud voice" (*Word of God and the Word of Man*, 195–96). Yet Göckel comments: "Barth revised the doctrine of election not once but twice. The understanding of the doctrine in his early dialectical theology shows a remarkable resemblance to the reconstruction by Friedrich Schleiermacher. Thus, the famous christological revision of the doctrine in *Church Dogmatics* II/2 is not only a revision of traditional views but also a modification of his earlier position that already included a critical stance vis-à-vis the tradition . . . through a lens provided by Schleiermacher" (*Barth and Schleiermacher*, 198). To be sure, there are differences. For Schleiermacher, Christ is the universal redeemer and mediator of salvation but does not determine as such the divine decree of election. Schleiermacher's view remains theocentric, while Barth's is Christocentric (ibid., 102–3).

58. Richard B. Brandt (*Philosophy of Schleiermacher*, 233) notes that the *Speeches on Religion* indicate that "the object in which religion is interested is the universe as a whole" and "the idea of God occupied a very secondary place."

59. Julia Lamm argues that Schleiermacher "maintains his affinities with Spinoza through his refusal to assign personality to God, his suspicion of anthropomorphism, and his emphasis on the whole." At the same time he "departs from Spinoza in his claim that only love expresses the essence of God and . . . his identification of redemption through Christ with the goal of the eternal divine decree" (*Living God*, 218).

60. The most important early work by Schelling is his *System of Transcendental Idealism* (1800). Brandt argues for both Spinoza and Schelling as precursors of Schleiermacher: "In the *Discourses on Religion* his central concept of the universe of the Infinite is strongly suggestive of Spinoza; and after

provides a link between the *Speeches* (1799) and *The Christian Faith* (1821–22) and a yardstick against which to measure and interpret the later statements regarding God and the world.[61] In his *Dialectic*, Schleiermacher writes something concerning the Absolute akin to his later position in *The Christian Faith* on the "antithesis" of sin and redemption: "In the Absolute, there is a falling apart into a totality of antitheses from the primary life, in which all actions are reduced to and grounded in it, and through which the Absolute and the total coexistence of all single objects are one and the same."[62] Absolute identity is the ground of everything, and it transcends all conceptual distinctions. God develops out of himself the subordinate oppositions that we perceive in the world. Antitheses appear in history yet disappear again as they are resolved into unity.[63]

The publication of Hegel's *Logic* (1812) may have provoked a reaction in Schleiermacher—namely, to articulate further his distinction between God and the world. Yet the distinction is hard to specify. Schleiermacher's God might be regarded as a *genus* (with the world as the species), a *unity* (with the world the corresponding plurality), or a *ground* (of the world in its totality). It is clear that God is not a *cause* in the ordinary sense. Schleiermacher argues that God—as absolute identity—cannot be imagined, so to speak, as the first domino to fall—that is, as the topmost link in a chain of finite causes and effects. To be sure, God must somehow be related to the world. In the *Dialectic*, Schleiermacher argues that if God were fully independent of the world, then the world would be merely accidental—which cannot be. But creation cannot be conceived as God's free act, for that would involve God in an antithesis (i.e., not creating versus creating). As ultimate unity, God lies beyond all such antitheses.[64] The overcoming of antitheses was one of Schleiermacher's basic

---

1805 he held a form of identity philosophy very like that of Schelling" (*Philosophy of Schleiermacher*, 37). Schleiermacher's diaries and letters from 1801 to 1805 show a theory of the Absolute like that of the early Schelling (155). Schleiermacher asks: "Is then the whole world anything but an individuation of the Identical?" (157, citing Schleiermacher, *Aus Schleiermachers Leben . . . Briefe*, 4:94). Brandt thinks that the implied answer is no and that "Schleiermacher to a large extent . . . shared Schelling's views about the absolute identity, [and] its self-manifestation in the worlds of nature and of mind" (*Philosophy of Schleiermacher*, 158). Brandt argues that Schleiermacher was not a nature Romantic (like, e.g., William Wordsworth), had relatively little appreciation for natural beauty, and did not confuse appreciation of beauty or the sublime with religion as such. His interest, as he wrote to his sister, lay in "the inward and higher" (131). The Infinite was more clearly revealed in the mind than in nature as such (133). Schleiermacher "continually stresses the agnostic side of his philosophy," and "consequently he often excuses himself from making positive statements" (232; cf. 229).

61. On Schleiermacher's *Dialectic*, see Thandeka, "Schleiermacher's *Dialektik*"; Thandeka, *Embodied Self*.

62. Brandt, *Philosophy of Schleiermacher*, 236, citing Schleiermacher, *Dialektik*, 325.

63. Brandt, *Philosophy of Schleiermacher*, 238, 161.

64. Ibid., 236–37, 241–42. On Schleiermacher's critique of divine creation, see the *Dialektik*, 300–307, esp. 300–302.

philosophical principles. It helps to explain his rejection of the traditional view of election that distinguished "elect" from "reprobate" persons.

In *The Christian Faith*, Schleiermacher discusses election in the context of ecclesiology, or the study of the church. Previously he had authored a treatise comparing the Lutheran and Calvinistic views of the election doctrine.[65] His view may be summarized in terms of two propositions: first, that election is not twofold but unitary or singular; and, second, that election has as its object not individual human beings but the whole of humanity. Schleiermacher was critical of earlier models of election that correlated divine mercy and divine righteousness with two distinct groups of people. In affirming *universal* election, Schleiermacher set himself against the entire Western theological tradition, including Augustine, Aquinas, later Thomism, Luther, Calvin, and early Protestantism. The Catholic Jesuits and Molinists and the Protestant Arminians and Wesleyans—who affirmed the role of human free will in salvation and God's election according to foreknowledge of human merits or faith (*praevisa merita*; *praevisa fides*)—did not teach universal election. So Schleiermacher's account of divine election was both novel and trendsetting.[66]

To avoid relating the divine attributes (e.g., mercy and justice) to different people in different ways, Schleiermacher sought to relate the attributes of mercy and righteousness to both groups of people—that is, to both the elect and the reprobate. In this way he stood against a traditional doctrine that he thought had shattered the essential unity of God's will. The election Schleiermacher had in mind pertained to final salvation. "The election of those who will be justified is a divine predestination to salvation in Christ," since there is "only one eternal and general decree of the justification of humankind for the sake of Christ."[67] In this "undivided decree of election . . . those who in this way are

65. The Lutherans and Calvinists found themselves in an anomalous situation, since King Frederick William III of Prussia had combined them in 1817 into a single church, the *Unionskirche*, which Schleiermacher served. So he stressed the congruity of his teaching on election with both Lutheran and Calvinist theology: "In that I would confess to holding this view [i.e., universal election], I advance it as a sign of my impartiality in not asserting that the Calvinian theory drives us any more strongly to this view than does the Lutheran theory" (Schleiermacher, *On the Doctrine of Election*, 79). "Both theories of election relate to . . . the indispensability of divine grace in connection with . . . conversion" (24).

66. Prior to Schleiermacher, it seems that the only major figure who may have taught a single divine election of all human beings to salvation was John Scotus Eriugena, in his *Treatise on Divine Predestination*. In opposing Gottschalk's *gemina praedestinatio* ("double" or "twofold predestination"), Eriugena insisted that God elected no one to hell or eternal suffering. Yet Eriugena in the *Treatise on Divine Predestination* retained much of Augustine's position while stressing the role of free will. Only in the later *Periphyseon* (see *DR* 4.10) did he move decisively toward universalism. Schleiermacher may thus have been without precedent in proposing a doctrine of universal election to salvation.

67. Schleiermacher, *Christian Faith*, 231 (sec. 119), 178 (sec. 109.3).

taken hold of by the power of the Word are quickened and born again, each as God has ordained one's mode of being and time."[68] In this decree "through divine power, yet in a natural way, the human race is to be transformed into the spiritual body of Christ."[69]

Schleiermacher rejected what he called the "down-grading of our God-consciousness to particularism."[70] He ruled out in advance any special, particular, or individual relation of God with just one creature, one human being, or one event of history (e.g., a miracle). Such assertions were incompatible with his construal of the God-world relationship. The implication was that neither election nor reprobation involved any individual relationship with God. Bluntly stated, God did not elect human individuals; God elected humanity.[71] Schleiermacher objected to "the constantly perplexing notion of a particular divine decree with reference to the individual person."[72] His logic implied that original sin was part of God's all-encompassing plan. Schleiermacher writes, "I cannot see how the *ordinavit* [he ordained] with regard to the fall can be denied . . . for otherwise, redemption, which is God's greatest work, must merely be based on an act of permission."[73] This means that Adam fell because God ordained humanity to *sinfulness* as well as to *redemption*. Universal sinfulness in Adam is the necessary prelude to universal redemption in Christ.[74]

To be sure, there is in Schleiermacher's thought a historical dissemination of the gospel, which means that not all people in the world have at any given time embraced the Christian message and been included in the Christian community. Nonetheless, this "antithesis" is temporary. "Within the same human race," says Schleiermacher, "no section . . . is definitely distinguished from any other in respect to the divine activity of Christ," for "at each particular point this antithesis is merely a vanishing one, so that everyone still outside this fellowship will [at] some time or another be . . . brought within it."[75] The distinction between the regenerate and the unregenerate is what Brian Gerrish calls "a

68. Schleiermacher, On the Doctrine of Election, 75.
69. Ibid., 76.
70. Schleiermacher, Christian Faith, 224 (sec. 118.1).
71. Göckel (Barth and Schleiermacher, 35–36) notes that Schleiermacher "rejects not merely the idea of a positive decree of reprobation, as Lutheran theologians did by positing a twofold divine will, but the idea of a divine decree in regard to individual persons altogether."
72. Schleiermacher, On the Doctrine of Election, 44.
73. Ibid., 96n133.
74. Edwin Chr. van Driel comments: "Since everything falls within the scope of divine causality, including sin, Schleiermacher does not construe sin as opposition to the divine initiative, but as part of it. Sin and redemption are the means by which God connects all humankind to Christ, through whom the divine impartation enters the world" ("Schleiermacher's Supralapsarian Christology," 269–70).
75. Schleiermacher, Christian Faith, 540 (sec. 118).

transient corollary of history."[76] Those outside the Christian community need not—and, for Schleiermacher, will not—remain outside. Because the proclamation of the gospel is an ongoing, dynamic process, everyone will be regenerated "when his time is fully come."[77]

Annette Hagan explains that Schleiermacher's "solution to the ancient dilemma of the separation into two groups consisted in explaining that separation as a temporary state of development. Allowing for the *post mortem* working of grace, he argued that the kingdom of God would be completed eschatologically through the universal restoration of all human beings."[78] Reprobation is not a final condition for anyone but an indeterminate state destined to disappear.[79] It is simply a matter of earlier versus later membership in God's kingdom. Reprobate persons might be compared to slow runners who lag behind and finish the race later on. What is more, death does not determine one's final status with God. Death is but a stage in the ongoing development, showing a progressive realization of the divine decree over time.[80] "Damnation," he wrote, "is taken to be a necessary stage, [and] it must also be a stage of development."[81] Regarding particular versus universal salvation, Schleiermacher said simply that he preferred universalism: "I would gladly take the latter [universalist] road in that it is easier for my feelings to bear not only the thought of people without faith dying but also the thought of those who are already forgiven at this point and of all those who are blessed but whose blessedness would nevertheless have to be disturbed by the thought of those who have forever been excluded."[82]

76. Gerrish, *Tradition and the Modern World*, 118, cited in Hagan, *Eternal Blessedness for All?*, 146.

77. Schleiermacher, *Christian Faith*, 540 (sec. 118).

78. Hagan, *Eternal Blessedness for All?*, 2.

79. Sounding much like Schleiermacher, Karl Barth argued in *Church Dogmatics* II/2, 350, that no strict line of division separates believers from nonbelievers and that a believer cannot regard unbelief as a final condition: "We have every reason to consider the elect and others together for all their opposition. We cannot, at any rate, regard their opposition as absolute. For all its distinctive sharpness, the opposition between them [and believers] can only be relative, because both are in the absolute hand of God."

80. Inspired perhaps in part by Schleiermacher, the idea of possible postmortem spiritual development caught on in British theology of the later nineteenth century. A vivid expression of this idea appears in H. B. Wilson, "Séances Historiques de Genève," 205–6 (quoted in Rowell, *Hell and the Victorians*, 116–17): "We must rather entertain a hope that there shall be found, after the great adjudication, receptacles suitable for those who shall be infants, not as to years of terrestrial life, but as to spiritual development—nurseries as it were and seed-grounds, where the undeveloped may grow up under new conditions—the stunted may become strong, and the perverted restored. And . . . all, both small and great, shall find a refuge in the bosom of the Universal Parent, to repose, or be quickened into higher life, in the ages to come, according to His Will."

81. Schleiermacher, *On the Doctrine of Election*, 77.

82. Schleiermacher, *On the Doctrine of Election*, 78. In Suzanne McDonald's explanation, Schleiermacher rejects "eternal separation from God" because he argues that our "self-consciousness" (of absolute dependence) is "not purely individual." Instead, "it is also relational and universal: it

He thought that both positions could be supported from Scripture and that universalism had fewer systematic problems.[83]

By way of critique, we should note that Schleiermacher's concept of God creates difficulties for his universalism. The traditional doctrines of divine grace, love, and redemption lose much of their meaning and pertinence if one interprets God as an impersonal or nonpersonal Absolute. What would it mean to be redeemed by a nonpersonal God? What form would final salvation take? While the God-language of The Christian Faith remains ambiguous, it is possible that Schleiermacher during the 1810s abandoned his earlier notion of God as the Absolute (per the Speeches and Dialectic) and adopted a more orthodox view of God. "In his later years," as Richard Brandt notes, "Schleiermacher became quite anxious to be as conciliatory as possible to the church." He conceived that the office of the Christian theologian was to depict the content of Christian conviction and not to portray philosophical truth as such. For this reason, Schleiermacher's theological utterances might not be an accurate gauge of his philosophical views, and vice versa.[84]

Schleiermacher's early view of God as the Absolute would be difficult if not impossible to square with the doctrine of the incarnation. From the standpoint of the Absolute, one cannot conceive of God as engaged in discrete, temporal actions, and so it is hard to make sense of the gospel claim that "the Word became flesh" (John 1:14). Many of Schleiermacher's friends and foes have alike agreed that his Christ is neither fully divine nor absolutely unique.[85] His

---

is a race-consciousness . . . [and] embraces the entire human race." McDonald adds, "This means that for our self- and God-consciousness to be perfect, it must include the corporate solidarity of race-consciousness. Since each individual is part of the whole, if some individuals were excluded from salvation, then the blessedness of those who are saved would be impaired" ("Calvin's Theology of Election," 127).

83. Göckel states that "Schleiermacher's doctrine of election does not lead to an outright espousal of the idea of universal salvation, beyond the eternal salvation of those who die in fellowship with Christ" (Barth and Schleiermacher, 102). Yet this claim goes against the whole line of argument on divine election in The Christian Faith. Schleiermacher clearly did not believe in an eternal hell, never hinted at any sort of a temporary hell, and, beyond this, asserted that "everyone still outside this fellowship will some time or another be . . . brought within it" (Christian Faith, 540 [sec. 118]). Göckel seems to be attributing to Schleiermacher a tentativeness about universal salvation that is actually more characteristic of Barth.

84. Brandt, Philosophy of Schleiermacher, 232. He adds: "Dogmas expressive of Christian experience may not coincide with the affirmations about God which Schleiermacher himself believed to be theoretically justifiable" (245). So while The Christian Faith sounds "more theistic" than his other writings, it is not clear that Schleiermacher's views on God had actually changed during the 1810s (ibid.).

85. Hugh Ross Mackintosh—coeditor of the English translation of The Christian Faith—claims that Schleiermacher "puts 'archetypal humanity' rather than the personal incarnation of God at the center of his view of Christ" (Types of Modern Theology, 90). Most interpreters see Schleiermacher's Christ as an exalted human but not as divine. Some perceive a docetic tendency, so that his Christ

rejection of the doctrine of the Trinity might be seen as one of the repercussions of a conception of God as undifferentiated unity beyond all distinctions.[86]

Despite the language of divine immanence in Schleiermacher, one comes away from reading *The Christian Faith* with a sense of distance between God and humanity. A single, unconditional decree of God determines everything everywhere. God's "activity" is always general and never particular. The universe in its totality is God's one and only "activity." The individual relates to God only through the cosmic whole. Iain Nicol and Allen Jorgenson explain that, for Schleiermacher, "our apprehension of God's action as temporal and so contingent . . . does not gainsay the essentially eternal foundation and consequent singularity of God's decree."[87] Another passage reads: "The human race . . . redeemed from the power of sin through the appearance of the divine Son, belongs to the idea of the world and so holds an indispensable place within it which was foreseen and ordained by God."[88] Note the sequence of argument here: the human race "belongs to the idea of the world" and for that reason is ordained by God. One has to ask: Is this a doctrine of *grace* or instead some form of *fatalism?* Schleiermacher's notion that human beings relate to God through their being part of the world suggests that he is offering a kind of *cosmic piety* that subsumes human individuality, and humanity in its entirety, within some larger whole.[89]

---

is *neither* fully divine *nor* fully human. See Macquarrie, *Jesus Christ in Modern Thought*, 206–7; Gunton, *Yesterday and Today*, 89–99; Barth, *Theology of Schleiermacher*, 103–4. All are cited in Hector, "Actualism and Incarnation," 307–9. Hector, it should be noted, opposes this general view concerning Schleiermacher's Christology.

86. Thinkers affirming God's undifferentiated unity—e.g., Eriugena (*DR* 4.10), Eckhart (*DR* 4.12), Böhme (*DR* 5.3), Solovyov (*DR* 8.3–8.4), and Tillich (*DR* 7.8)—generally maintained God's *threeness* as well as God's *oneness* by speaking of God on two different planes: at a lower level at which one might speak of three persons, and at a higher or more ultimate level (*Gottheit, Ungrund*, "God beyond God," etc.) wherein the distinction of persons vanishes. Schelling (*DR* 7.7) and Bulgakov (*DR* 8.6) tended to assimilate ultimate unity to the person of the Father, so that the Father represents undifferentiated and unknowable unity, while the Son and Spirit are concrete manifestations of divinity. In the *Speeches* and *Dialectic*, Schleiermacher affirms God as undifferentiated unity. Yet Schleiermacher adopts *neither* the two-levels view of God *nor* the assimilation of the Father to undifferentiated unity. His position on God in *The Christian Faith* thus remains ambiguous.

87. Nicol and Jorgenson, introduction to *On the Doctrine of Election* (Schleiermacher), 17.

88. Schleiermacher, *On the Doctrine of Election*, 74.

89. One might compare Schleiermacher's cosmic piety with that of ancient Stoicism. Marcus Aurelius (121–80 CE) with his *Meditations* might be considered a parallel (cited by book and section number, then by page number). "This thou must always bear in mind, what is the nature of the whole, and what is my nature" (2.9; 145). "Constantly regard the universe as one living being, having one substance and one soul; and observe how all things have reference to one perception, the perception of this one living being; and how all things act with one movement; and how all things are the co-operating causes of all things which exist; observe too the continuous spinning of the thread and the contexture of the web" (4.40; 172). "All things are implicated with one another, and

We might ask further: What meaning does election carry if those who do not display any prescribed Christian traits (e.g., faith, love, obedience) are nonetheless said to be elected by or with Christ and elected for the Christian community? In this theology, the distinction between church and nonchurch fades in importance, and one might as well emphasize *human solidarity* rather than *Christian solidarity*, since on Schleiermacher's account these two circles of solidarity will increasingly overlap and finally coincide.[90] This presumption of a progressively increasing human solidarity might be jarring for a minority church that finds itself sharply separated from the nonchurch. What could Schleiermacher's teaching on election mean for Christian believers not in Germany but in today's North Korea or Saudi Arabia? In asserting that "all other fellowships of faith are destined to pass into the Christian fellowship," Schleiermacher's theology represents a form of Christian triumphalism.[91] As a product of nineteenth-century European Christendom, its relevance for the twenty-first century may be rather circumscribed.

7.4. Hegel as Rationalist and Esotericist

Georg Wilhelm Friedrich Hegel (1770–1831) is among the best-known thinkers of all time, and his writings have been interpreted in varied ways during the last two centuries. Among professional philosophers, there is a reading of Hegel as the last figure in a series of German idealists that runs from Kant through Fichte and Schelling. Hegel has thus been understood as the culminating figure of German idealism—before its later nineteenth-century decline and replacement by empiricist and scientific perspectives in Germany. This reading sees Hegel's thought as chiefly preoccupied with technical questions of metaphysics, epistemology, and ethics, the traditional subdisciplines for those in today's university-based departments of philosophy.

---

the bond is holy; and there is hardly anything unconnected with any other things. . . . For there is one universe made up of all things, and one god who pervades all things, and one substance, and one law" (7.9; 208–9).

90. Simone Weil (1909–43) was a modern saint of human solidarity, perhaps illustrating how Schleiermacher's election doctrine and idea of human solidarity might be put into practice. Leslie Fiedler writes in the introduction (3–39) to Weil's *Waiting for God* that Weil was "blending Christianity and Stoicism" or "the love of God" with "filial piety for the city of the world." Though attracted to Roman Catholicism, she sought a faith "catholic enough to include the myths of . . . a world untouched by the Churches" (8). Weil—of Jewish descent—refused baptism as a personal act of solidarity with non-Christians, explaining to her Catholic interlocutor, "I have . . . the vocation to move among men of every class and complexion, mixing with them and sharing their life and outlook . . . merging into the crowd and disappearing among them" (*Waiting for God*, 48).

91. Schleiermacher, *Christian Faith*, 536 (sec. 117).

Yet a cursory glance at Hegel's corpus of writings and the writings of his followers shows that such an interpretation is too circumscribed to encompass all that he thought and wrote. A number of Hegel's followers made their chief contributions in the fields of church history (Ferdinand Christian Baur, 1792–1860) or dogmatic theology (Philipp Marheinecke, 1780–1846; Hans Martensen, 1808–84). Another disciple took an anti-theological stance and established a systematic theory of atheism (Ludwig Feuerbach, 1804–72). The best-known follower of all propounded a revolutionary new political ideology that came to political fruition in the twentieth century (Karl Marx, 1818–83). It should be clear that there is more to Hegel than philosophy alone, understood in the narrower sense. Hegel carries importance for political theory, aesthetics, literary theory, cultural studies, religious studies, and other disciplines. Literary and hermeneutical theorists have been constantly returning to Hegel's writings for decades. The old man has a habit of dying and rising again, after his departure has been prematurely announced. Hegel is here to stay.

Some secular or secularizing interpreters have propounded a "non-metaphysical reading" of Hegel. Klaus Hartmann led the way in a 1972 article, identifying Hegel's system as a "hermeneutic of categories." Along similar lines, David Kolb wrote, "I want most of all to preclude the idea that Hegel provides a cosmology including the discovery of a wondrous new superentity, a cosmic self or a world soul or a supermind."[92] Yet on this account it is hard to know what to make of Hegel's elaborate discussions of "Spirit" or the "Absolute" in The Phenomenology of Spirit, Lectures on the Philosophy of History, and Lectures on the Philosophy of Religion. These non-metaphysical readings of Hegel scrub away whatever might be troubling to contemporary secular readers. Such anti-theological revisionism often ends with some left-wing politics tacked on. The non-metaphysical readers may be seen as heirs of the early nineteenth-century Young Hegelians. They leave out of account the so-called early theological writings—long left unpublished—that attest to the importance of religious themes in the development of Hegel's thought during the 1790s.[93] Hegel delivered his Lectures on the Philosophy of Religion no less than four times (1821, 1824, 1827, and 1831), and the sheer magnitude of his reflection on religion is readily apparent.

Support for both a metaphysical and theological reading of Hegel comes from an unlikely source, Friedrich Nietzsche (1844–1900), who commented near the end of his writing career: "Germans understand me immediately when I say that philosophy has been corrupted by theologian blood. The Protestant

92. Hartman, "Hegel," 124; Kolb, Critique of Pure Modernity, 42–43; both cited in Magee, Hegel and the Hermetic Tradition, 14–15.
93. The German edition of these writings appeared as Hegel, Hegels theologische Jugendschriften; the partial English translation is Hegel, On Christianity.

minister is the grandfather of German philosophy, Protestantism itself is its *peccatum originale* [original sin]. . . . You only need to say 'Tübingen seminary' to understand just *what* German philosophy really is—an underhanded theology."[94] Historians of philosophy inform us: Kant begat Fichte, Fichte begat Schelling, and Schelling begat Hegel. But this is not the only way of understanding Hegel's intellectual lineage. One recent writer speaks of the "uniquely Swabian [i.e., south German] *theosophical*" undercurrents swirling through Schelling and Hegel alike.[95] Nineteenth-century interpreters soon after Hegel's death had no difficulty in seeing Hegel's thought as religiously inspired or motivated. As we will see below, the familiar contrast between theological readings of Hegel (right-Hegelian) and anti-theological readings (left-Hegelian) is likely too simplistic, and there is in fact a third way of reading Hegel. The religious dimension of Hegel's thought is a matter not of Christianity *reaffirmed* or Christianity *secularized* but Christianity *esotericized*.[96]

There are numerous reasons to regard Hegel as an esoteric thinker, and the case for this claim is strong, once one has weighed all the evidence. Hegel's personal associations, his background of reading, and his continuing intellectual development—not only in his early years but also into his later years—show his immersion in Western esoteric thought. The fundamental character of Hegel's thought may be the weightiest argument of all. As Glenn Magee notes, if "philosophy" is defined as a "love of wisdom," then Hegel by his own account did not qualify. "He is no lover or seeker of wisdom," says Magee, since "he believes he has found it." As Hegel wrote in the well-known preface to his *Phenomenology of Spirit*, "To help bring philosophy closer to the form of Science, to the goal where it can lay aside the title of '*love* of knowing' and be actual knowledge—that is what I have set before me."[97]

By the end of the *Phenomenology of Spirit*, Hegel claims to have arrived at *absolute knowledge*. So we might ask, how can any human being, of whatever intelligence or genius, claim to possess such absolute knowledge? This is the sort of assertion that, prior to Hegel, one associated with theosophers such as Böhme (*DR* 5.2–5.3). After Böhme in his inaugural vision observed the sun reflecting off of a pewter dish, he later claimed that he was given a central

94. Nietzsche, *The Anti-Christ*, 9 (par. 10).

95. R. J. Foster, "Creativity of Nature," 13.

96. An esoteric reading of Hegel finds support in a number of secondary works, including Baur, *Die christliche Gnosis*; Noack, *Die christliche Mystik*; R. Schneider, *Schellings und Hegels schwäbische Geistesahnen*; d'Hondt, *Hegel secret*; Benz, *Mystical Sources of German Romantic Philosophy*; Voegelin, "Hegel"; O'Regan, *Heterodox Hegel*; Hanratty, "Gnostic Synthesis"; Mitscherling, "Identity of the Human and the Divine"; Magee, *Hegel and the Hermetic Tradition*. Particularly helpful for this study have been Baur, Benz, Voegelin, O'Regan, Hanratty, and Magee.

97. Magee, *Hegel and the Hermetic Tradition*, 1, citing Hegel, *Phenomenology of Spirit*, 3.

vision or glimpse (*Zentralschau*) into the heart of all reality whatsoever. Esoteric thinkers since the Renaissance had long been associated with a kind of
intellectual Titanism, a quest for total knowledge of and control over all things.
Recall that Pico della Mirandola, at only twenty-three years of age, announced
publicly that he would expound all existing knowledge in terms of nine hundred
propositions of his own devising (*DR* 4.12). Theosophy—the vision of divine
Wisdom—was commonly connected with *pansophia*, a universal wisdom that
connected all areas of knowledge. As we will see below, the intellectual context
of the south German province of Württemberg, where Hegel lived for his first
eighteen years, makes the link between Hegel and esotericism during his Jena
period not only possible but also plausible.

There are abundant references to esoteric traditions in Hegel's texts and
in firsthand accounts of Hegel's life, showing their influence on him.[98] In his
writings, early and late, Hegel approved of Eckhart, Bruno, Paracelsus, and
Böhme. Jakob Böhme presents the most striking case. In his *Lectures on the
History of Philosophy* (delivered 1819–31), Hegel devoted more space to the
German cobbler than to many other noteworthy philosophers. Hegel's library
included Hermetic writings by Heinrich Cornelius Agrippa (1486–1535), Paracelsus (Philippus von Hohenheim, 1493–1541), Giordano Bruno (1548–1600),
and Jakob Böhme.[99] What is more, Hegel associated with known esotericists
such as Franz von Baader (1765–1841). In correspondence, Hegel discussed
with colleagues the nature of magic. In his lectures, Hegel stated that he used
the term "speculative" to mean the same thing as "mystical"—striking support
for the claim that Hegel's idealist philosophy was a kind of mysticism carried
into a new genre. Informally, Hegel aligned himself with initiatory societies
such as the Freemasons and the Rosicrucians.[100] Even the doodles drawn in his
manuscripts contained Hermetic shapes, such as triangles, circles, and squares.
The very structure of his thought seems to have been indebted to esoteric ideas
regarding "correspondences."[101]

Glenn Magee sees links between esotericism and particular writings of Hegel.
He finds a Masonic subtext of "initiatory mysticism" in Hegel's *Phenomenology
of Spirit* (1807), a Böhmean subtext to the *Phenomenology*'s famous preface, a
kabbalistic and Böhmean influence in the *Science of Logic* (3 vols., 1812–16),

98. The paragraphs that follow are based on Magee, *Hegel and the Hermetic Tradition*, 2–5.
99. On the terms "Hermetism" and "Hermeticism," see *DR* appendix A. The adjective "Hermetic" is ambiguous, but here is used in its wider sense to refer to esoteric thought generally,
of the sort that one finds in the *Corpus Hermeticum* and other works of ancient gnosis, alchemy,
Kabbalah, and so forth.
100. See d'Hondt, *Hegel secret*. On the Rosicrucians, see *DR*, 557n428.
101. See Brach and Hanegraaff, "Correspondences."

alchemical and Paracelsian elements in the philosophy of nature within the *Encyclopedia of the Philosophical Sciences* (1816, 1827, 1830), alchemical and Rosicrucian imagery in the *Philosophy of Right* (1820), and an influence of kabbalistic and Joachimite millennialism in the *Lectures on the Philosophy of History* (1822–30). To flesh out Magee's claim: Hegel's *Phenomenology of Spirit* represents an initial stage of Hermetic "purification" that raises the mind above the level of the sensory and the profane, while the *Logic* is equivalent to the Hermetic ascent to the realm of pure form or Universal Mind. Hegel's philosophy of nature describes the emanation or "othering" of Universal Mind in the form of the spatiotemporal world. Its categories then accomplish a transfiguration of the natural world, so that the world is now a reflection of the Universal Mind. Hegel's philosophy of Spirit achieves a return of created nature to the divine by means of humanity, rising above the level of the natural and actualizing God in the world through such concrete forms of life as the political state, religion, and speculative philosophy.

Hegel's theorizing as a whole is evocative of the esoteric tradition of *pansophia*, especially as exemplified by Friedrich Christoph Oetinger (1702–82). Before Hegel made the statement, Oetinger declared that "the truth is a whole."[102] This theme is a major link between Hegel and esotericism. If we begin from the premise that human beings live a finite life and see reality from a particular or partial perspective, then to have access to "the whole" requires a kind of cosmic vision. One must be lifted above temporal circumstances and see things from a divine vantage point. Almost by definition, the Hegelian thinker has to be a theosopher. Alternatively, if we start from theosophical premises—as Oetinger evidently did, and as Hegel arguably did—then the obscure saying that "truth is the whole" makes complete sense.

In several periods of his life, Hegel was exposed to esoteric thought. During his boyhood in Stuttgart, from 1770 to 1788, Württemberg was a major center of esotericism, with much of the Pietist movement there influenced by Böhmism and Rosicrucianism. Leading Pietist authors, such as Johann Albrecht Bengel and especially Friedrich Oetinger, were strongly influenced by Böhmean theosophy and Kabbalah.[103] These cultural influences surrounding Hegel's formative years are not more widely known in part because of academic specialization. Few

---

102. Oetinger wrote, "The truth is a whole [*die Wahrheit ist ein Ganzes*]; when one finally receives this total, synoptic vision of the truth, it matters not whether one begins by considering this part or that" (*Sämtliche Schriften*, 5:45, cited in Magee, *Hegel and the Hermetic Tradition*, 67). The expression "the true is the whole" (*das Wahre ist das Ganze*) appears in the preface to Hegel's *Phenomenology of Spirit*, 11 (par. 20).

103. Oetinger was a declared disciple of Böhme, wrote his first book as a commentary on Böhme, and was learned in Christian Cabala; his holistic idea of truth was both pansophic and theosophic. See Magee, *Hegel and the Hermetic Tradition*, 64–68. Cf. Weyer-Menkhoff, "Friedrich

scholars are aware of the complexities of religious life and thought in eighteenth-century Germany. Those familiar with these complexities are generally found in academic disciplines other than philosophy. Yet a contextualized reading of Hegel's earlier life ought to begin with late eighteenth-century Württemberg, which was permeated with a local form of theosophical Pietism.

A second esoteric period for Hegel lasted from 1793 to 1801, when he worked as a private tutor, first at Berne and then Frankfurt. Hegel's biographer Karl Rosenkranz sees the writings of this early period as having a "theosophical character," as Hegel was becoming acquainted with the writings of Böhme, Eckhart, and Johannes Tauler and involving himself in Masonic circles.[104] During his years in Jena (1801–7), Hegel's interest in theosophy continued. He lectured at length and approvingly on Böhme and Bruno. Several pieces he composed—which have come down to us only in fragmentary form—use esoteric language and symbolism. His lectures on the philosophy of nature during this time reflect an ongoing interest in alchemy. When Hegel came to Jena, it seems likely that Schelling introduced him to his circle of friends who had interest in esoteric writings. Schelling himself was an avid reader of Böhme and Oetinger.

The final period of esoteric interest in Hegel's life lasted from 1818 until his death in 1831. The later texts contradict the notion that Hegel toyed with esotericism in his youth but cast it aside as he matured. Hegel's esoteric interests were not an aberration due to youthful enthusiasm. In fact, the evidence points in the opposite direction. In Berlin, Hegel formed a friendship with Franz von Baader, the premier theosopher of the day, and together they undertook a study of Meister Eckhart. The preface to the 1827 edition of the *Encyclopedia of the Philosophical Sciences* makes prominent mention of both Böhme and Baader. In the final period of his life, Hegel's interest in esotericism seems not to have diminished but to have grown, and he was more overt in publicly aligning himself with esoteric thinkers of the past and present.

Hegel's ties to esotericism were not particularly controversial in the early decades after his death. Soon after Hegel's death, F. C. Baur published a major work, *Die christliche Gnosis* (1835), conjoining Hegel to ancient gnosis as well as to the modern theosophy of Böhme. During the 1840s, Schelling publicly

Christoph Oetinger." On esoteric and Böhmist influences in Württemberg Pietism, see Groth, *Die "Wiederbringung aller Dinge"*; Benz, *Mystical Sources of German Romantic Philosophy*.

104. Rosenkranz comments that Hegel's early writing "hat wesentliche einen theosophischen Charakter" (had actually a theosophical character) ("Hegels ursprüngliches System 1798–1806," 153–242, citing 258). On the young Hegel's philosophy, see Rosenkranz, *Hegels Leben*, 80–140. Rosenkranz was by no means favorable toward this aspect of Hegel, commenting in a letter, "Wie Schade doch, das Hegel so theosophische Schrullen nährte" (What a shame indeed, that Hegel thus nourished the theosophical cranks). See Rosenkranz, *Hegel: Sendschreiben*, 73.

claimed that Hegel borrowed much of his philosophy from Böhme. One of Hegel's disciples, Friedrich Theodor Vischer, posed the question, "Have you forgotten that the new philosophy came forth from the school of the old mystics, especially from Jacob Böhme?" The nineteenth-century Danish churchman Hans Martensen—a Hegelian, a Böhmean, a student of Eckhart, and nemesis of Søren Kierkegaard—maintained that German mysticism prepared the way for German philosophy.[105] More recently, Georges M.-M. Cottier called Hegel's philosophy *une Gnose christologique* (a christological gnosis).[106] Generally speaking, European scholars have been better acquainted with modern esotericism than have English or American interpreters of Hegel. This may be one reason that the interpretation of Hegel as an esoteric thinker has not been considered outré among Europeans.

Hegel's sustained dialogue with Franz von Baader in the winter of 1823–24 regarding Meister Eckhart seems to have had a pronounced impact on the Berlin philosopher. Hegel was especially struck by Eckhart's saying "The eye in which I see God is the same eye in which God sees me. My eye and God's eye are one eye and one seeing, one knowing and one loving."[107] According to a story generally accepted as authentic, Hegel responded with a breathless "Da haben wir est ja, was wir wollen" (Here we have indeed what we are wishing for).[108] Baader's view defined the line of interpretation of Eckhart taken in German Romanticism. Eckhart's sermons, for Baader, established the infinite worth of the individual by relating the finite to the infinite. Eckhart's critics and appreciators alike have agreed that his theology broke down divisions between God and creatures. In one sermon Eckhart wrote, "I am so changed into him [i.e., God] that he produces his being in me as me, not just similar. By the living God this is true. . . . There is no distinction."[109] Yet there may have been a divergence in the ways in which Hegel and Baader interpreted Eckhart. For Hegel, in contrast to Jacobi, Schleiermacher, and Romanticism generally, the relation of the finite to the infinite was realized on the level of

---

105. Benz, *Mystical Sources of German Romantic Philosophy*, 2.

106. Cottier, *L'atheisme du jeune Marx*, 20–30, cited in Magee, *Hegel and the Hermetic Tradition*, 5n6.

107. Eckhart, *Teacher and Preacher*, 270.

108. Franz von Baader recounted: "Ich war mit Hegel in Berlin sehr häufig zusammen. Einstens las ich ihm nun auch aus Meister Eckart [sic] vor, den er nur den Namen nach kannte. Er war so begeistert, dass er den folgenden Tag eine ganze Vorlesung uber Eckhart vor mir hielt und am Ende sagte: 'Das haben wir est ja, was wir wollen'" (I was very frequently with Hegel in Berlin. Once I read to him from Meister Eckhart, whom he knew only by name. He was so enthusiastic that the following day he held forth in a whole lecture on Eckhart before me and said in the end: "Here we have indeed what we are wishing for"). See Baader, *Sämmtliche Werke*, 15:159. Cf. Nicolin, *Hegel in Berichten seiner Zeitgenossen*, 261.

109. Eckhart, *Essential Sermons*, 188.

knowledge or cognition, not on the level of feeling or experience.[110] Without doubt, though, Hegel rated Eckhart's work very highly, and Eckhart—among the earlier thinkers surveyed in Hegel's lectures—is almost unique in escaping any kind of censure by Hegel."[111] Cyril O'Regan argues that Hegel saw Eckhart's mysticism as encapsulating Hegel's own vast philosophico-theological program.[112]

Hegel followed Eckhart in positing a totally realized eschatology, in which the present mystical breakthrough experience did not so much anticipate the eschaton as substitute for it. For Eckhart, heaven was not "there and then" but "here and now." This presentist emphasis was so strong that it raises the question of whether one might speak of personal immortality.[113] The mystical experience was not a foretaste; it was the thing sought. In this sense, Eckhart was a gnosticizing thinker whose arguments concurred with those of the ancient Valentinians, who viewed the resurrection not as a future hope but as a realized state already attained in human awareness. In this particular respect Hegel was much like Eckhart. The knowledge described in his philosophy *was* the final attainment. It was knowledge in its final state and not a matter of "see[ing] through a glass, darkly" (1 Cor. 13:12).

In Eckhart's words, "My eye and God's eye are one eye"; the mystic's vision was God's own vision and vice versa. One implication might be that the usual categories of time and duration no longer applied in describing this experience. Eternity, in Eckhart and later in Hegel, was a transcendence of time itself and not a duration or extension of time. The time-eternity distinction appears to be set aside in the final sections of *Phenomenology of Spirit*, dealing with "revelatory religion" and "absolute knowledge," as well as in the conclusion to Hegel's *Encyclopedia*, where the self undergoes a kind of apotheosis.[114] For Hegel, the durative notion of immortality is merely a representation—in other words, picture-thinking—and not the final conceptual truth. Hegel comments that "this absoluteness and infinitude of self-consciousness is represented in the doctrine of the immortality of the soul" and that "eternity is not mere duration.

110. O'Regan, *Heterodox Hegel*, 250–51.

111. Ibid., 94.

112. Ibid., 129, citing Hegel, *Lectures on the Philosophy of Religion*, 1:347n166 (1824 version); note by Peter C. Hodgson.

113. O'Regan comments (*Heterodox Hegel*, 255): "Hegel thought . . . that he had found in Eckhart Christian intratextual warrant for a way of understanding immortality that would not be as vulnerable to critical rationality as the standard Christian view." This shift involved "a dismantling of the absoluteness of the distinction between this life and the next life," "a radicalization of the soteriological function of the mystical union," and "a revisionist and critical understanding of the durational representation of immortality."

114. Ibid., 256.

. . . It is knowing."[115] Absolute knowledge is itself an apotheosis of finitude into infinitude. O'Regan notes that, in both Eckhart and Hegel, "the thoroughgoing devaluation of time and history obviously leads to the erasure of the eschatological dimension of Christianity."[116] When one of Hegel's hearers asked for his opinion on life after death, it is said that Hegel simply pointed toward a Bible and said nothing—an uncharacteristic silence, to be sure.[117] It is not clear that Hegel believed in personal or individual immortality as generally understood. Yet he did believe in a cognitive realization in which the finite knower and Absolute Spirit would cease to be distinct from each other.[118]

There is a conundrum in linking Hegel to authors and thinkers regarded as mystical. Hegel is generally considered to be the ultimate philosophical rationalist, who strove in his writings for a kind of total conceptual transparency. During his mature period, his prose was scrubbed clean of the contaminating presence of concrete objects, leaving behind a pure, imageless inwardness. Nothing seems further from the traditional reading of Hegel than to link him with mysticism. Cyril O'Regan suggests the helpful notion of an "apophatic erasure." In his writings, Hegel took the thought-forms of mysticism and then utterly erased all traces of transcendence that might cling to them. We end up with a paradoxical transcendence—that is, an immanental transcendence.[119]

---

115. Hegel, *Lectures on the Philosophy of Religion*, 1:195 (1821 version); Hegel, *Lectures on the Philosophy of Religion*, 3:386 (fragments), cited in O'Regan, *Heterodox Hegel*, 256.

116. O'Regan, *Heterodox Hegel*, 257.

117. Desmond, *Hegel's God*, 16, citing Pinkard, *Hegel*, 577. Desmond adds: "I rather think he had no conviction concerning personal immortality, since when he does speak at all of immortality it is with reference to the immortality of *cognition*: not of the singular but of the universal; not of the human person but of general humanity."

118. Hegel did not follow Eckhart in all major respects. As O'Regan has noted, Hegel differed from Eckhart in maintaining the uniqueness of Jesus. Eckhart equalized every self with Jesus (or with Mary), so that Jesus Christ was no longer indispensable. Instead, divinization took place in a nonmediated event in which the self played the role of Virgin or Mother of God (*Theotokos*) by giving birth to the Word (cf. Eckhart, *Deutsche Werke* 2.22). Jesus was merely an exemplar of this divinization. Early on, Hegel abandoned a purely exemplarist Christology and stressed Jesus's uniqueness (O'Regan, *Heterodox Hegel*, 259). It was Eckhart who set the context for the later exemplarist Christologies of Böhme and the Böhmists. Eckhart was also not a sophiologist, in that he did not distinguish Wisdom from Word but identified these two (ibid., 94). The roots of Russian Sophiology run not through Eckhart but through Böhme and Schelling. Yet in Eckhart as in later Sophiology, there was a confusion of creating and begetting. In his exegesis of the Johannine Prologue, the birth (*Geburt*) of the Trinity was closely tied to creation. Creation and begetting were two sides of one and the same action (ibid., 110). O'Regan (ibid., 399n82) references Eckhart's *Defense*, excerpted in Eckhart, *Essential Sermons*, 71–76. Cf. Blakney, *Meister Eckhart*, 278.

119. On "apophatic erasure," see O'Regan, *Heterodox Hegel*, 43, 104, 106, 134, 382n41. O'Regan states: "I define 'apophatic erasure' as the operation whereby apophatic vocabulary, and thus the implications of such a vocabulary, are excised from a religious or theological proposal, leaving only a positive nonmysterious content to be appropriated. Practically this means that Hegel relates

Hegel's philosophy is a mystery in broad daylight. With effort, one can read the texts and grasp the broad meaning. Yet in reading, one has the sense of an undefinable something that remains unexpressed in the text, lurking just beyond the edge of the page.

A close consideration of the texts shows that Hegel's mystery in broad daylight is nothing other than the divinity of humanity. Until recently, the interpretations have been dichotomous, as Louis Dupré notes: "Studies tend to result in all-or-nothing conclusions. Either Hegel was orthodox, occasionally somewhat original, Christian, or he was thoroughly secular."[120] Yet a third alternative exists, fully explored in O'Regan's impressive study. On this view, Hegel was not a secularist in terms of intent or outcome, nor was he traditionally Christian, but might be classified in terms of a different religious genre. This third alternative is explored below, and we will ask what Hegel's thought might imply regarding the question of a universal human destiny or outcome.[121]

7.5. Hegel and the Consummation of Absolute Spirit

History itself, for Hegel, was a process of self-constitution on the part of God, Spirit (*Geist*), or the Absolute. Hegel employed images of development through time, such as the embryo or seed. He also used the motif of exile and return from exile. In the well-known preface to his *Phenomenology of Spirit*, Hegel makes reference to the Greek hero Odysseus and his wanderings that begin and end at the island of Ithaca—a lengthy yet cyclical journey. God or *Geist* by nature goes out and then returns to itself again.[122] Some have compared this with the literary genre of the *Bildungsroman*. *Phenomenology of Spirit* might thus be seen as Hegel's audacious attempt to write God's coming-of-age story. In the *Lectures on the Philosophy of Religion*, he states that "this Logos has already itself the characteristic of return within itself. . . . The resolution consists in the fact that Spirit is the Totality."[123] The final state reintegrates finitude within infinity. The externality of the finite is overcome through the "inwardization of the object."[124]

---

positively to such mystics as Boehme and Eckhart only to the degree to which he ignores, or better, systematically represses, the apophatic vocabulary and the suggested limits of cognition" (382n41).

120. Dupré, foreword to *Heterodox Hegel*, by Cyril O'Regan, ix.

121. The citations of Hegel's writings below refer to standard English translations of many of the major works: *Lectures on the History of Philosophy*; *Lectures on the Philosophy of History*; *Lectures on the Philosophy of Religion*; *Letters*; *Logic*; *Phenomenology of Spirit*; *Philosophy of Mind*; *Philosophy of Nature*; *Philosophy of Right*; *Reason in History*.

122. O'Regan, *Heterodox Hegel*, 63, 46, 48–49, 59.

123. Hegel, *Lectures on the Philosophy of Religion*, 3:86 (1821 version).

124. O'Regan, *Heterodox Hegel*, 63. Alfredo Ferrarin notes that Hegel's "inwardization" equally transcends "externality" and "interiority": "Spirit is the inwardization of externality and of all otherness

Hegel was an important modern critic of divine impassibility. He rejected the idea of God as self-involved and self-enclosed, a *Deus incurvatus* (God curved in on himself). Such a view, he argued, would make God irrelevant and obliterate the meaning of finite existence by reducing it to the level of a mere accident. Hegel explains in his *Lectures on the Philosophy of Religion*:

> Eternal being-in-and-for-itself is what discloses itself, determines itself, divides itself, posits itself as what is differentiated from itself, but the difference is at the same time constantly sublated. Thereby actual being in and for itself constantly returns into itself—only in this way is it spirit. . . . A play of love with itself . . . does not arrive at the seriousness of other-being, of separation, of rupture.[125]

Hegel uses the language of "play" or "sport" to denote an impassible God and refers to the "seriousness" of his own passibilist divinity. A God who does not suffer is deficient. Thus Hegel built divine suffering into his notion of God—a point already expressed in the *Phenomenology of Spirit*:

> Thus the life of God and divine cognition may well be spoken of as a disporting of Love with itself; but this idea sinks into mere edification, and even insipidity, if it lacks the seriousness, the suffering, the patience, and the labor of the negative. . . . This *in-itself* is abstract universality, in which the nature of the divine life *to be for itself*, and so the self-movement of the form, are altogether left out of account. . . . But the life of the Spirit is not the life that shrinks back from death and keeps itself untouched by devastation, but rather the life that endures it and maintains itself in it. It wins itself truth only when, in utter dismemberment, it finds itself.[126]

The final outcome is defined as knowledge, the pure concept (*Begriff*) known to God and humanity alike. Hegel explicitly linked divine to human knowing, as stated in the *Encyclopedia*: "God is God only so far as he knows himself: his self-knowledge is, further, a self-consciousness in man and man's knowledge of God, which proceeds to man's self-knowledge in God."[127]

This emphasis on divine and human knowledge leads Hegel to take a stand against the tendency of the German Romantics to substitute emotion for thought, or intuition for knowledge. He wrote, "That one can know nothing at all of God is an empty standpoint," for according "to the whole nature of the Christian religion . . . we should know God cognitively, God's nature and essence, and

---

and the externalization of interiority" (*Hegel and Aristotle*, 237; cf. 38, 74, 136, 252, 289, 300, 311, 314). On "inwardization," see also Generchak, *Sunday of the Negative*, 34; Greene, *Hegel on the Soul*, 37, 46.

125. Hegel, *Lectures on the Philosophy of Religion*, 3:291–92 (1827 version).

126. Hegel, *Phenomenology of Spirit*, 10, 19 (pars. 19, 32).

127. Hegel, *Hegel's Philosophy of Mind* (1894 ed.), 176 (par. 564).

should esteem this cognition above all else."[128] The Romantics were worshiping at the altar of an unknown god (cf. Acts 17:23). Christianity, as Hegel often repeated, is a *revealed* religion.[129] Hegel did not, however, accompany or qualify his statements about God's self-revelation with any acknowledgment of mystery or of what God might not have revealed. Hegel's God thus seems to have been revealed *exhaustively*. One of the ironies in Hegel's system is that his concept of revelation did not correlate with faith in God but led into rationalism.

In attacking those who did not share his views on God's knowability, Hegel did not distinguish between Jacobi, Schelling, and Schleiermacher. He faulted all of them for failing to affirm true knowledge concerning God as he understood it. Schelling's early identity philosophy comes in for criticism in the *Phenomenology of Spirit*. While he does not overtly name his erstwhile friend and colleague, Hegel's earliest readers understood him to be referring derisively to Schelling in speaking of the philosophy of "the Absolute, the A = A" as "the night in which . . . all cows are black."[130] On Hegel's view, Schelling left the infinite God hidden, so that there was no knowledge and only ignorance. Elsewhere in his writings he took a swipe at Schleiermacher's *Speeches on Religion*, with their celebration of a "feeling" (*Gefühl*) that displaced knowledge or thought from its rightful centrality. The section on "Revelatory Religion" in the *Phenomenology of Spirit* was Hegel's counterproposal. A memorable assault on Schleiermacher came in the foreword to H. F. W. Hinrichs's *Die Religion in inneren Verhältnisse zur Wissenschaft* (1822), where Hegel wrote that if Schleiermacher's theology were correct, then "a dog would be the best Christian for it possesses the feeling of its dependence in the highest degree and lives merely in feeling."[131]

One interpretive question in Hegel pertains to the distinction between natural and revealed theology. Did Hegel turn natural theology into revealed theology? Or revealed theology into natural theology? Or does the distinction still apply? The answers are unclear. Hegel generally tended toward an overcoming of distinctions, so that "the objects of philosophy . . . are upon the whole the same as those of religion."[132] Hegel has puzzled interpreters because his thought might be described as either rationalistic or mystical. Frederick Copleston writes of

128. Hegel, *Lectures on the Philosophy of Religion*, 1:266 (1824 version), 1:88 (1821 version).
129. Hegel, *Hegel's Philosophy of Mind* (1894 ed.), 175–76 (par. 564).
130. Hegel, *Phenomenology of Spirit*, 9 (par. 16).
131. Hegel's foreword, translated in A. V. Miller's appendix to *Beyond Epistemology*, by Frederick G. Weiss, 238, cited in O'Regan, *Heterodox Hegel*, 36.
132. Hegel, *Logic*, 3 (no. 1). O'Regan comments that "it could be asserted that Hegel heals the split between natural theology and theology of revelation" (*Heterodox Hegel*, 21). Yet, with respect to such doctrines as the Trinity and the incarnation, such *healing* might be considered as a *confusing* of human reasoning with divine revelation, and vice versa. Hegel's failure to distinguish theology from philosophy is reminiscent of Eriugena (see *DR* 4.10).

Hegel's "rationalization of mysticism."[133] As Glenn Magee notes, Hegel was not like other thinkers who were seeking wisdom, for Hegel had *already* arrived. He had *already* glimpsed the panorama of cosmos, nature, humanity, and history from what seems like an impossibly exalted God's-eye and end-of-days vantage point.[134] The philosophical writings are simply transcriptions of what Hegel *had seen*, and the presentation is "pansophic" in its effort and ambition to incorporate everything. To be sure, Hegel's rationalized mysticism inverts the usual understanding of mysticism. It no longer implies something unknown regarding God but consists rather in definite knowledge: "For the mystical is not concealment of a secret or ignorance, but consists in the self knowing itself to be one with the divine being."[135] Absolute Spirit realizes itself in a church of knowledgeable mystics, and Hegel may have regarded himself as the church's first or foremost member.[136]

All of Hegel's thought about God revolves around the doctrine of the Trinity. Each of the major Christian doctrines—incarnation, redemption, the spiritual community, and so on—is subservient to and indeed seems to be absorbed in or subsumed under the doctrine of the Trinity. In this sense the trinitarian dogma mushrooms into a trinitarian theosophy or pansophy, since all that is known about God or about the world is somehow included within this single concept.[137] Hegel declared that the Trinity is not a mystery: "What is for reason is not a secret. In the Christian religion, one knows; and this is a secret only for the finite understanding, and for the thought that is based on sense experience."[138]

133. Copleston, "Hegel and the Rationalization of Mysticism."

134. Glenn Magee comments:

Hegel writes in the preface to the *Phenomenology of Spirit*, "To help philosophy come closer to the form of Science, to the point where it can lay aside the title of 'love of knowing' and be actual knowledge—that is what I have set before me" [par. 3]. By the end of the *Phenomenology*, Hegel claims to have arrived at Absolute Knowledge, which he identifies with wisdom. Hegel's claim to have attained wisdom is completely contrary to the original Greek conception of philosophy as the love of wisdom, that is, the ongoing pursuit rather than the final possession of wisdom. His claim is, however, fully consistent with the ambitions of the Hermetic tradition. (*Hegel and the Hermetic Tradition*, 1)

135. Hegel, *Phenomenology of Spirit*, 437 (par. 722).

136. In his preface to A. V. Miller's translation of the *Phenomenology of Spirit*, J. N. Findlay writes that "the path traced in the Phenomenology . . . was the path that had been taken by the World Spirit in past history, and that had been rehearsed in *the consciousness of Hegel, in whom the notion of Science first became actual*" (vi; emphasis added). Hegel's acolytes sometimes take Hegel as seriously as he took himself! For a critique of Hegel's intellectual ambition and pomposity, see Santayana, *Egotism in German Philosophy*, esp. 84–98.

137. In CD I/1, 295, 347, Karl Barth's trinitarian exposition of God as "Revealer" (Father), "Revealed" (Son), and "Revealedness" (Spirit) has Hegelian overtones to the extent that it highlights salvation as a form of knowledge, and the doctrine of the Trinity expands and absorbs the content of other Christian doctrines (see DR 9.1; 9.3; 9.6).

138. Hegel, *Lectures on the Philosophy of Religion*, 3:192 (1824 version).

Hegel was thus far removed from the eighteenth-century rationalists and deists who were embarrassed by the doctrine of the Trinity—in their view an offense against human reason. Hegel's approach contrasted with Schleiermacher's too, since the latter marginalized the Trinity by consigning it to a final, halfhearted treatment at the very end of *The Christian Faith*.[139]

Yet this speculative revival or retrieval of the doctrine of the Trinity is not quite as it appears to be. To the casual or inattentive reader, Hegel's writings are often like a hall of mirrors. Hegel tended toward a modalistic view of the Trinity, just as Schleiermacher did. In the *Phenomenology of Spirit*, Hegel ends up with three interconnected moments in the unfolding of Spirit rather than a Trinity of mutually relating persons. To cite Hegel's abstract language: "There are thus *three distinct moments*: essence, being for-self which is the otherness of essence . . . [and] the knowledge of itself *in the 'other.'*" While "this immanent movement [of three moments] proclaims the absolute Being as *Spirit*," by contrast "the picture-thinking of the religious community . . . brings into the realm of pure consciousness the natural relationships of father and son." The religious community errs in that it "takes the moments of the movement which Spirit is, as isolated and immovable Substances or Subjects instead of transient moments."[140] In the dense section on revealed religion in the *Encyclopedia*, Hegel likewise defines three "moments" rather than three "persons" in God—an episodic or epochal notion of God. The three moments are those of divine self-manifestation (Father), divine differentiation (Son), and divine return (Spirit). The second moment is associated with the creation and the world as well as the Son, and the third with the universal community.[141]

On a surface level, Hegel was committed to the doctrine of creation from nothing, or *ex nihilo*. Yet ultimately Hegel's position was that of creation *ex Deo*. One does not find creation from nothing discussed where one might expect it in the *Phenomenology of Spirit*, in the *Encyclopedia*, or in the third volume of the *Lectures on the Philosophy of Religion*. Passing references to this doctrine appear in *The Difference between Fichte's and Schelling's System of Philosophy* and the *Science of Logic*.[142] Yet in the *Difference* essay, creation from nothing is equated with creation from the abyss of the Father. Cyril O'Regan suggests that when Hegel speaks of creation from nothing, what he actually means is creation *ex Deo*. Such a reading of Hegel on creation is also supported, as we

139. Schleiermacher, *Christian Faith*, 738–51 (secs. 170–72).

140. Hegel, *Phenomenology of Spirit*, 465–66 (pars. 770–71); emphasis added to "three distinct moments"; other emphasis original. Cf. 465–78 (pars. 770–87).

141. Hegel, *Hegel's Philosophy of Mind* (1894 ed.), 175–80 (pars. 564–71).

142. See Hegel, *Difference*, 93–94; Hegel, *Science of Logic*, 84, cited in O'Regan, *Heterodox Hegel*, 146.

will see, by Hegel's heterodox account of Lucifer's fall and the emergence of the material world.[143] Hegel's notion of creation *ex Deo* echoed the earlier accounts by Eriugena (*DR* 4.10) and Böhme (*DR* 5.3) and anticipated that of Sergius Bulgakov (*DR* 8.6), who much like Hegel identified the "nothing" in "creation from nothing" as a divine nothingness.[144] Hegel's profession of creation from nothing seems disingenuous, just as his affirmation of the Trinity conceals a triadic modalism, and his account of Christ and creation is idiosyncratic. In one passage Hegel appears to assert an ontological identity between God the Son and the created world.[145] "Creating" for Hegel did not refer to "causing." He stated that God did not "cause" the world to be, a view at odds with the mainstream perspective (e.g., Aquinas and Luther) that "creation" means "causing something to exist."[146]

From the standpoint of Christian orthodoxy, Hegel's deviations on Christ are just as significant as those regarding the Trinity and divine creation. In identifying the Son of God with the world, he inclined toward something like Arianism. Like ancient Arians, Hegel did not clearly distinguish God's begetting the Son from God's creating the world: "Nature is the Son of God. . . . Nature is alienated spirit."[147] Hegel's Christology expanded the biblical idea of kenosis (see Phil. 2:7) to refer not to the self-humbling of the eternal Son but to a broader metaphysical principle of divine self-manifestation through self-negation and outpouring into otherness. Hegel's thought is one of the entry points for kenosis theology in modern theology, though as we will see below, he might need to share the credit with Schelling, who through his teaching at

143. Hegel affirms creation from nothing in *Logic*, 163–69 (no. 88) (cited in O'Regan, *Heterodox Hegel*, 411n19), and yet the identification elsewhere of "nothing" with the abyss of the Father gives a hermeneutical clue as to what Hegel might mean. How else might one interpret the *Phenomenology of Spirit* (468–69 [par. 776]) in identifying Lucifer as an aspect of God (i.e., the evil side), and Lucifer's fall as tantamount to the creation of the material world, *except* on the presupposition of creation *ex Deo*? On creation *ex Deo* in Hegel, see Declève, "Schöpfung, Trinität und Modernität bei Hegel"; Min, "Trinity and the Incarnation," esp. 175n2.

144. Whether Origen held to creation *ex nihilo* or creation *ex Deo* is difficult to say, and a case might be made either way (see *DR* 3.6).

145. Hegel writes, "God the Father (this simple universal, being-within-itself), giving up his solitude creates nature (the self-external, being-outside-itself), begets a son (his other I), but by virtue of his infinite love beholds himself in this Other, recognizes his image therein and in it returns to unity with himself" (*Hegel's Philosophy of Mind* [2007 ed.], 13; no. 381 Zusatz).

146. Hegel writes, "'Creating' is not a 'grounding' or a 'causing': it is something higher than these limited thought-categories" (*Lectures on the Philosophy of Religion*, 1:248–49 [1821 version]). Schleiermacher (*DR* 7.3) basically agreed with Hegel in distinguishing "creating" from "causing," and so too did Bulgakov (*DR* 8.6).

147. Hegel, *Hegel's Philosophy of Mind*, no. 247 Zusatz, cited in O'Regan, *Heterodox Hegel*, 152. This problem of confusing God's begetting the Son with God's creating the world recurs in late nineteenth- and twentieth-century Russian Sophiology, as John Meyendorff showed and Georges Florovsky implied (*DR* 8.7). See Meyendorff, "Creation in the History of Orthodox Theology."

Erlangen University influenced the Lutheran theologian Gottfried Thomasius (1802–75), who is generally associated with the rise of kenotic theology.[148]

In the *Phenomenology of Spirit*, one finds a kenotic motif as Hegel speaks of the Word or Son that is emptied as representing the emptying of the Father in uttering the Word.[149] In the 1821 *Lectures on the Philosophy of Religion*, the Trinity as a whole is understood on the model of self-emptying (*Selbstablassen*). Kenosis in the first instance refers to the self-emptying of the Father, yet kenosis applies also to the second moment of the Son, while the third moment of the Spirit results from a double kenosis of Father and Son. One of the most striking features in Hegel's Christology is its dismantling of any notion of a self-sufficient or independent deity. O'Regan draws the conclusion that "Hegel's use of the theologoumenon [of kenosis] . . . tends to critique hypostatic autonomy and subvert the Christian theological tradition from within."[150]

The theme of the death of God first appears in Hegel's early text *Faith and Knowledge* (1802) and was later developed in greater detail.[151] The most famous reference comes at the very end of the *Phenomenology of Spirit*, which contains

148. Thomas R. Thompson ("Nineteenth-Century Kenotic Christology," esp. 78–79) assigns the rise of nineteenth-century Lutheran kenotic theology to Gottfried Thomasius (1802–74). David L. Law ("Kenotic Christology") argues that "*kenosis* was in the air in the 1840s" (253) and that a number of thinkers anticipated the rise of Lutheran kenoticism. Thomasius studied under Friedrich Schelling at Erlangen University (ca. 1821–ca. 1823) and likely was exposed to the philosophical exposition of Phil. 2 that Schelling later published in his *Philosophie der Offenbarung* (*Philosophy of Revelation*) (1841–42). See Schelling, "Exegetischer Nachweiss aus Phil. 2,6–8." Schelling thus may be regarded as a hidden source of German kenotic theology. This was already recognized by Paul Wapler, in "Die Theologie Hofmanns" (1905): "Schelling muß ein Genie des persönlichen Wirkens und der Repräsentation gewesen sein. Vor allem ist uns wichtig, daß Thomasius den Erlanger Jahren Schellings einen unmittelbaren Einfluß auf die Entstehung der neuen theologischen Anschauungen zuschreibt, wie sie sich zu eigentümlicher historischer Gestalt in dem Kreis der Erlanger Theologen damals herauszubilden begannen" (Schelling must have been a genius in personal influence and self-presentation. For us it is above all important that Thomasius attributed the origin of his new theological views to the immediate influence of Schelling's years at Erlangen [University], which began at that time to establish the circle of Erlangen theologians in their characteristic historical form; 702). For more on Schelling's connection with Thomasius, see Breidert, *Die kenotische Christologie*, 113. Breidert further treats Schelling's influence on kenoticism generally (278–91). See also Becker, *Self-Giving God and Salvation History*, 112 (on Schelling's influence on Thomasius); D. L. Law, *Kierkegaard's Kenotic Christology*, 140–44 (on Schelling's influence on kenotic Christology generally). I am indebted to James Lee for supplying several of these references.

149. Hegel, *Phenomenology of Spirit*, 465 (par. 770).

150. Hegel, *Lectures on the Philosophy of Religion*, 3:83 (1821 version). The passage cited above from Hegel's *Phenomenology* on the Father's self-emptying seems to anticipate Hans Urs von Balthasar's idea of the Father's *Urkenosis* in begetting the Son (*DR* 10.7). The kenosis, or self-emptying, of the Spirit appears in Bulgakov (*DR* 8.6; 8.8) and Moltmann (*DR* 9.10–9.11). Twentieth-century theology thus was built on a kenotic foundation laid by Hegel and Schelling. The Spirit's self-emptying is the theme of a dissertation written under Moltmann: Dabney, *Die Kenosis des Geistes*.

151. Hegel, *Faith and Knowledge*, 40–41.

the phrase "the Calvary [or Golgotha] of Absolute Spirit" (*die Schädelstätte des absoluten Geistes*).[152] The death of God in Hegel carries a twofold meaning. On the one hand it means the disappearance of Jesus as a historical human being. "Disappearance" is the right word because Hegel thinks of Jesus as passing out of view and as replaced by the spiritual community. In Hegel, there is no doctrine of the resurrection per se. At the same time, this death is God's self-divestiture of independence. God no longer exists in separation or self-sufficiency. At this point in Hegel's exposition of the gospel story, divergent interpretations of his thought appear. Some affirm an atheistic Hegel, others see Christ's death as simply a moment in the unfolding of Spirit, while still others affirm a dialectical interplay of theism and atheism. The debate is complex, but for the present it may suffice to say that Hegel's perspective cannot be identified with that of traditional Christianity. Nonetheless, the reductively atheistic view cannot make much sense of what Hegel writes about the spiritual community that finds its consummation in God, Spirit, or the Absolute.

Death for Hegel is nothing other than a full explication of the finitude implied in the incarnation. The theme of death sometimes moved Hegel to flights of eloquence: "Death is . . . finitude in its highest extreme. The temporal and complete existence of the divine idea in the present is envisaged only in Christ's death." The repeated refrain is: "Gott selbst ist tot" (God himself is dead). God himself enters into pathos and death. Hegel teased out the radical implications: "The human, the finite, the fragile . . . are themselves a moment of the divine . . . [and] are within God himself." This means "that finitude, negativity, otherness are not outside of God . . . and do not, as otherness, hinder unity with God."[153]

Hegel interpreted the cross metaphysically rather than morally. There is no atonement theology, no representative or substitutionary death, no focus on sin or guilt as such, and no doctrine of forgiveness, justice, payment, or merit. At times Hegel used the language of "satisfaction for sin," but he turned the meaning in a new direction: "In this death, therefore, God is satisfied. God cannot be satisfied by something else, only by himself. The satisfaction consists in the fact that . . . God come[s] to be at peace with himself."[154] The cross means that God is reconciled to God. Hegel's position at this point is wholly consistent with earlier gnostic, kabbalistic, and esoteric thinkers. Jesus's cross is a self-involving action. God suffers for his own sake—not for the sake of sinful humanity.[155] The cross is no longer about grace. God is faithful to himself,

---

152. Hegel, *Phenomenology of Spirit*, 493 (par. 808).

153. Hegel, *Lectures on the Philosophy of Religion*, 3:326 (1827 version).

154. Hegel, *Lectures on the Philosophy of Religion*, 3:219 (1824 version).

155. O'Regan writes, "Hegel recalls the satisfaction theory of atonement only to subvert it. . . . The rendering of satisfaction does not appear to be for the sake of human being but, oddly, for the

not to creation or creatures. Yet through the cross, Christ establishes a model for finite spirit. O'Regan calls this the "exemplarist" view of Christ in Hegel, a pattern seen earlier in Eckhart, Böhme, and the Böhmists.

Conspicuously absent from the gospel according to Hegel is any significant engagement with Christ's resurrection. Instead, Christ's death gives way to spiritual community, which fills the space ordinarily occupied by the resurrection. Jesus's death means disappearance, and the community replaces him.[156] In biblical terms, one might say that Pentecost displaces Easter or that the church's emergence into history replaces Christ's emergence from the empty tomb. One implication of this displacement is that Christ's significance becomes transient rather than permanent. In Hegel's modalistic trinitarianism, the flesh-and-blood Jesus is left behind as *the Spirit surpasses Christ*. Because Jesus moves from a limited to an unlimited condition, he must transcend his own historically determinate mode of existence. It does not seem possible to reconcile Hegel's philosophy with the orthodox notion of Jesus as a living, continuing, resurrected, glorified, reigning, returning, and eternal mediator between God and humanity.[157]

The third epoch—the spiritual community—receives emphasis in Hegel's system. In this teleological scheme, everything points toward the final outcome. "Spirit is thus posited as the third element, in *universal self-consciousness*, it is in *community*."[158] The state of actualization that Hegel describes is one in which totality conditions individuality. The relations of individuals to one another are determined by the whole.[159] At the end of his discussion of "revealed religion" in the *Phenomenology of Spirit*, Hegel refers to the spiritual community as a "universal divine Man" (*der allgemeine göttliche Mensch*).[160]

Hegel's extensive reflections in the *Phenomenology of Spirit* on the "unhappy consciousness" (*das unglückliche Bewusstsein*) are directly related to his

sake of the divine itself" (*Heterodox Hegel*, 207). "Reconciliation refers to the divine, healing its own breach" (ibid., 209). O'Regan perceives in Hegel an exaggerated emphasis on *divine agency* in Christ's death together with a de-emphasis on atonement as such (ibid., 208). This may be true of Moltmann as well (*DR* 9.10–9.11): an emphasis on God's action in this event masks a change in its underlying meaning.

156. O'Regan writes, "Resurrection could be said, not only to be marginalized, but to be effectively excised altogether" (*Heterodox Hegel*, 214).

157. Ibid., 191, 195. Emilio Brito judges that Hegel's Christology cannot be reconciled with catholic orthodoxy. See Brito, *Hegel*, 48–49. Origenism presented its own conception of the transience of Christ's mediatorship and the notion (cf. 1 Cor. 15:28) that the kingdom of Christ would finally pass away and be replaced by a kingdom of the Father alone. For discussion, see *DR* 296n245, 384, 408, 826.

158. Hegel, *Phenomenology of Spirit*, 473 (par. 781).

159. O'Regan, *Heterodox Hegel*, 239.

160. Hegel, *Phenomenology of Spirit*, 478 (par. 787). Hegel's consideration of the entire community as one man—and a divine Man—is reminiscent of the *Adam Qadmon* or Primal Man motif discussed in connection with Jewish Kabbalah and Christian Cabala (see *DR* 2.5–2.6; 2.11). Almost certainly this passage should be read as an echo of that earlier tradition.

conception of the spiritual community.[161] He describes as futile any search for the reality of the incarnation in a realm beyond oneself—that is, in the domain of the past, wherein one seeks to find a historical Jesus. Such a historical quest is mistaken, for it fails to recognize the *passing away of Jesus* that is a precondition for *the presence of Spirit.* Hegel thought of autonomy as essential to any fully realized spiritual community. Here Hegel depends on and develops Enlightenment notions of human self-determination. The root of human fulfillment lies in human nature itself: "Man, finite when regarded from himself . . . [has] a foundation of infinity in himself. He is the object of his own existence—he has in himself an infinite value, an eternal destiny."[162] Hegel's thought is focused less on incarnation than on apotheosis. "The presence of the divine," O'Regan writes, "transforms the human into the divine."[163] One finds here not a theology of the divine image in humanity but a theology of the demigod. The "unhappy consciousness" of the finite self in its separation and yearning must and will be overcome, and this outcome involves an identity-in-difference (as Hegel explains it), in which the finite spirit both is and is not equated with Absolute Spirit. It is an open question whether Hegel's spiritual community allows finite spirits to remain as discrete individual entities, and, if not, whether the spiritual community abolishes finite spirits. In some passages in Hegel's writings, the *Aufhebung* (sublation) of Spirit seems more like a pathway to human annihilation than to human fulfillment.[164]

161. Some of the key passages on the "unhappy consciousness" are Hegel, *Phenomenology of Spirit*, 126 (par. 207), 130–31 (par. 216), 322 (par. 528), 410 (par. 673), 455 (pars. 752–53), 476 (par. 785).

162. Hegel, *Lectures on the Philosophy of History*, 333. Søren Kierkegaard, in *Philosophical Fragments*, criticizes Hegel's view of human fulfillment—dubbed as "Religion A" or "Religion in the Sphere of Immanence"—for presuming that human beings contain within themselves the resources for their own salvation. "Religion B" or "Religion in the Sphere of Transcendence"—Kierkegaard's alternative to Hegel—requires a Savior and salvation that are external to the human self.

163. O'Regan, *Heterodox Hegel*, 241. Fyodor Dostoyevsky and Vladimir Solovyov criticized this aspect of Hegelianism, saying that Hegel's man-God had replaced Christianity's God-man. The man-God ideal appears strikingly in the *Corpus Hermeticum* (41, bk. 11.20; ed. Copenhaver), where the author aspires to know God by first becoming God: "Unless you make yourself equal to god, you cannot understand god; like is understood by like. Make yourself grow to immeasurable immensity, outleap all body, outstrip all time, become eternity and you will understand god. Having conceived that nothing is impossible to you, consider yourself immortal and able to understand everything. . . . Collect in yourself all the sensations of what has been made . . . [and] then you can understand god." Pico's *Oration on the Dignity of Man* (ed. Borghesi, Papio, and Riva) was almost as audacious in suggesting that God, after creating human beings, had left them as the gods of this earth. The titanic ambition of Hegel's philosophical project becomes more readily understandable against this Hermetic and Renaissance backdrop.

164. Hegel, *Lectures on the Philosophy of Religion*, 1:431 (1827 version): "There are finite spirits but the finite has no truth; for the truth of finite spirits and its actuality is instead just the absolute spirit. The finite is not genuine being . . . and its negation is affirmation as the infinite, as the universal in and for itself." If one reads Hegel in this particular way—as an "annihilationist" of

Hegel departs markedly from the mainstream Christian tradition by asserting that finitude itself is evil. The origin of this evil of finitude does not lie in human choices (i.e., the fall of Adam and Eve) but in God himself. Here Hegel follows earlier precedents, and this becomes explicit in the way that his writings recapitulate the specific ideas of Jakob Böhme on the fall of Lucifer. Like Böhme (*DR* 5.3), and like the earlier Kabbalah (*DR* 2.5), Hegel identifies divine wrath with evil and vice versa. The fall of Lucifer is part of mainstream Christian teaching. Yet distinctive to Böhme and Hegel is the association of Lucifer's fall with the origin of finitude, finite spirits, and the material world. In the *Phenomenology of Spirit* Hegel writes, "The becoming of Evil can be shifted further back out of the existent world. . . . It is the very first-born Son of Light [Lucifer] himself who fell because he withdrew into himself or became self-centered."[165] A similar statement appears in the *Encyclopedia*, in a passage where Hegel approvingly names Böhme and so indicates the source of his ideas: "God's first born is Lucifer . . . [who] centred his imagination on himself . . . [and] became evil . . . who is otherness within the divine love."[166] Another statement occurs in the *Lectures on the Philosophy of Religion*: "The first only begotten one was Lucifer . . . not the Son but rather the external world, the finite world, which is outside the truth."[167] The material world of finitude is false and Luciferian. It is spirit in congealed form, in Hegel's thought no less than in Böhme's.[168]

Böhme and Hegel thus present a tragic vision of the everyday, material world. Evil came to birth when one aspect of the divine reality split itself off from the rest of the divine milieu. This process within God engendered an aggressive antitype standing over and against God—a "no" that answers back to the divine "yes." Schelling sniped that Hegel's version of the fall was indebted to Böhme, implying that Hegel's philosophy was heterodox and thus seeking to tarnish Hegel's reputation. Given Schelling's own debt to Böhme, this was a rather hypocritical objection to make.[169] The larger implication of Hegel's view of the fall and the origin of evil, as O'Regan explains, is that "Luciferian involution is not identified as the act of the *other* of God, but rather as the act

---

sorts—then the dissolution of human beings is not a punishment for some but the fate of all. No one can or should seek to escape this outcome.

165. Hegel, *Phenomenology of Spirit*, 468 (par. 776).

166. Hegel, *Encyclopedia*, no. 248 Zusatz, cited in O'Regan, *Heterodox Hegel*, 152.

167. Hegel, *Lectures on the Philosophy of Religion*, 3:293 (1827 version), cited in O'Regan, *Heterodox Hegel*, 154.

168. O'Regan, *Heterodox Hegel*, 155.

169. Ibid., 152. A number of Hegel scholars have acknowledged Hegel's heterodoxy regarding the doctrine of creation and fall and Hegel's dependence on Böhme. See Koslowski, "Hegel"; Harris, *Hegel's Development*, 186–88, 406–7.

of the *othering* of God."[170] Satan's fall is not against God's purpose but is part of it. The plan for divine self-unfolding includes the fall.[171] What is more, the fall did not precede the material world but is identified with its emergence. Finite reality is evil per se, and this includes finite spirits as well as finite matter. Self-centeredness is both the originating and defining characteristic of finite spirit. It is unsurprising therefore that social philosophies based on Hegelian premises have often painted a bleak picture of society, in which power conflicts determine human relations.[172]

What sort of theodicy is possible on Hegelian premises? The brief answer is that evil becomes fully rationalized, along with everything else in Hegel's system. Just as Lucifer's fall is a forward step for the Absolute, so too the Adam story depicts a "fall upward." Innocence means ignorance and so is something to be gotten rid of. The serpent speaks truth in telling Adam and Eve that if they eat the fruit they will be "like God." Hegel's inverted interpretation of Genesis 3 echoes that of ancient gnosis. The serpent is not a deceiver but a bringer of wisdom.[173] Hegel's theodicy is—to use the terminology of George Bataille and Jacques Derrida—a "restricted economy." This means, in O'Regan's words, that "there is no expenditure without reserve, no suffering that is not a way station to a higher order of being and enjoyment, no sacrifice that does not recoup its gift, and, in this case, add to the store of the divine self."[174] Jacques Derrida writes, "A determination is negated and conserved within another which reveals the truth of the former. . . . The *Aufhebung* is included within the circle of absolute knowledge, never exceeds its closure, never suspends the totality of discourse, work, meaning, law, etc. . . . The Hegelian *Aufhebung* thus belongs to restricted economy."[175] Schelling's nineteenth-century critique was not unlike that of Derrida. According to Schelling, Hegel's supposed drama was specious,

170. O'Regan, *Heterodox Hegel*, 156.
171. "It cannot be said any longer that human being falls, but rather the divine falls in or as human being" (O'Regan, *Heterodox Hegel*, 322). Because God completes himself in history, "Christ now appears to be . . . the Redeemed Redeemer of the Gnostic sects" (ibid.). On "the redeemed Redeemer" of ancient gnosis, see Thomassen, *Spiritual Seed*, 69–71, 75, 171–75.
172. Alexandre Kojève (1902–68), a founder of French postmodernist thought, was well known for his *Introduction à la lecture de Hegel leçons sur la Phénoménologie de l'esprit* (*Introduction to the Reading of Hegel: Lectures on the "Phenomenology of Spirit"*; 1947, French; 1980, English). These lectures highlight the parts of Hegel's *Phenomenology* centering on the master-slave relationship (111–19 [pars. 178–96]) and human relations as a "life-and-death struggle" in which each seeks to destroy the other (114 [par. 187]). Kojève's actions matched his theories. He was later exposed as having been for three decades a secret Soviet agent in France who idolized Joseph Stalin and justified Stalinist brutality.
173. O'Regan, *Heterodox Hegel*, 156, 162, 170, citing Hegel, *Encyclopedia*, no. 24 Zusatz.
174. O'Regan, *Heterodox Hegel*, 234.
175. Derrida, "From Restricted to General Economy," 348.

a dance of disembodied ideas, a repetitious cycle without freedom or novelty. The Hegelian story had nothing in common with everyday life, with its many contingencies and uncertainties.

Hegel may come closest to writing a theodicy in his *Lectures on the Philosophy of History*. Here he refers to history as a "slaughter bench" and poses the question, "To what final aim [have] these enormous sacrifices . . . been offered?" At the end of the lectures, the answer turns out to be that the sacrifices are for the sake of the outcome—namely, the spiritually realized community: "All the sacrifices that have ever and anon been laid on the altar of the earth [are] justified for the sake of this ultimate purpose."[176] The moral justification is thus wholly teleological. War with all its miseries is part of a process eventuating in a worthwhile outcome. The famous aphorism in the *Philosophy of Right*—"The rational is the real and the real is the rational"—means that evil is disguised goodness.[177] Hegel will not admit the evilness of evil. Ultimate rationality requires total rationalization.

What makes this outcome yet more galling is that in Hegel this vast sum of human suffering is not for some greater human good. In this sense Hegel differs from Leibniz, who stays closer to the Christian tradition by keeping human interests in the foreground. For Hegel, human suffering is simply the price that must be paid for the Absolute to realize itself.[178] Yet no one can raise any moral objection to this state of affairs. In *Reason in History* Hegel writes, "For the history of the world moves on a higher level than that proper to morality."[179] So Hegel pulls out the rug from under the objector. While the biblical sufferer Job answered back to God, to *Geist* there is no answering back.[180] The Absolute is amoral, and through "the cunning of reason" it works to attain its end by whatever means are necessary. The individual person possesses no intrinsic or ultimate value in Hegel's philosophy. One's value depends instead on one's place in the larger whole.

Twentieth-century thinkers such as Theodor Adorno, Emmanuel Levinas, and Jacques Derrida were all sharply critical of Hegel.[181] In no area was this

176. Hegel, *Lectures on the Philosophy of History*, 21, 477, cited in O'Regan, *Heterodox Hegel*, 311.
177. Hegel, *Philosophy of Right*, 10.
178. Peter Koslowski discusses Hegel's idea of "the meaning of world history as sacrifice" (*die Deutung der Weltgeschichte als Opfer*) and links this to a heartlessness and amoralism at the core of Hegel's thought ("Der leidende Gott," 27).
179. Hegel, *Reason in History*, 82–83, cited in O'Regan, *Heterodox Hegel*, 313.
180. O'Regan notes that the effect of Hegel's reasoning is "a neutralization of all claims whose origin is the finite partial perspective" (*Heterodox Hegel*, 317). Objections by finite persons are "egocentric."
181. Derrida notes Hegel's vast influence: "Misconstrued, treated lightly, Hegelianism only extends its historical domination, finally unfolding its immense enveloping resources without

critique more pointed than with regard to the "closed" character of Hegel's narrative. Postmodernists insisted on "openness" and repudiated the authoritative, authorial voice of the man behind the lectern in Berlin. Jean-François Lyotard's famous definition of postmodernism as "incredulity" toward metanarratives was implicitly a swipe at Hegel.[182] This "incredulity" was in the first instance not directed toward the biblical narrative but rather toward the Hegelian narrative, with its imposing and seemingly totalitarian character, calling not for faith or for discussion but for intellectual submission.[183]

7.6. A Theological Critique of Hegel's Thought

A Christian theological critique of Hegel might concur with certain aspects of the postmodernist critique and yet invoke a different set of criteria. It might begin from the recognition that Hegel's philosophy is not based on acknowledged theological authorities. While Hegel's philosophy of religion follows superficially the contours of the gospel story, there is no substantive engagement with Scripture, and Hegel himself refers to the Bible as a "wax nose" that can be twisted to mean anything at all.[184] Hegel is more receptive toward heterodox authors such as Eckhart and Böhme than toward either Scripture or traditional theological authorities. We see this especially in his account of Lucifer's fall and the Luciferian nature of the material universe. In presenting the doctrine of the Trinity, Hegel makes no use of early church councils, creedal definitions, patristic authors, scholastic formulations—not even the Protestant confessions that, as a professed Lutheran, he might be thought to accept as normative. Instead he expounds the Trinity with appeals to Plato, Aristotle, Hinduism, gnosticism, Neoplatonism, and Kant.[185] Hegel thus seems to provide an apologia for a nonstandard or gnostic-esoteric Christianity. O'Regan sees *subversiveness*—a discrepancy between surface and reality—in Hegel's writings. Robert Solomon sees a discrepancy as well and views Hegel's professed

---

obstacle. Hegelian self-evidence seems lighter than ever at the moment when it finally bears down its full weight" ("From Restricted to General Economy," 317–18). One response to Hegel's rationalization of human suffering has been a call for a solidarity of memory with victims who have lost everything—including, on Hegel's premises, even the right to speak on their own behalf (O'Regan, *Heterodox Hegel*, 315).

182. Lyotard, *Postmodern Condition*, xxiv–xxv: "Simplifying to the extreme, I define *postmodern* as incredulity toward metanarratives. . . . The narrative function is losing its functors, its great hero, its great dangers, its great voyages, its great goal. It is being dispersed in clouds of narrative language elements. . . . Where, after the metanarratives, can legitimacy reside?"

183. O'Regan, *Heterodox Hegel*, 11–14, 375nn35–44.

184. Ibid., 65.

185. Ibid., 133.

adherence to Christianity as masking the genuinely humanistic and nontheological character of his thought.[186] Yet Hegel's heterodoxy need not be a sign of
hidden secularity or religious insincerity. For reasons already given, it is more
plausible to follow Baur, O'Regan, Voegelin, Walsh, and Magee in categorizing
Hegel as an esoteric religious thinker.

Hegel's God develops through time and so is not the same God at the end
of the world-historical process as at the beginning. If God is understood in
classical theistic terms as maximal in goodness, wisdom, and perfection—or
"that than which nothing greater can be thought"—then Hegel's God at the
beginning must be judged as deficient.[187] By definition, a God with unrealized
potential is less than maximally good, and Hegel's presentation of an imperfect
deity has religious as well as philosophical repercussions. During the twentieth
century, process thinkers proposed a dipolar God with two aspects (antecedent
and consequent), according to which God's essential nature does not change,
even as another aspect of God (e.g., knowledge or relationality) undergoes
change. To account for a developmental God, one needs to indicate what does
and does not change in God's character and in God's involvement with the
world. In Hegel's writings, this issue remains ambiguous.

As shown already, Hegel's philosophy is not genuinely trinitarian but is instead a form of triadic and sequential modalism. While some divergence exists
among Hegel scholars, no one seems to think that Hegel held to trinitarian
orthodoxy, and the question is how best to describe his deviation. Perhaps the
surest statement is that Hegel was a modalist, like his predecessors Eckhart and
Böhme. Like other modalists, Hegel could not do justice to biblical salvation history. The personal distinctions and relations of Father, Son, and Spirit, and with
them the entire trinitarian sequence of redemptive history, disappear in Hegel's
philosophy. Moltmann, Pannenberg, and Splett all attribute to Hegel a "Spirit
monism" (*Geistesmonismus*) whose basic model is that of the self-origination
of subjectivity through self-awareness. Pannenberg calls this "a projection of
finite categories into the divine reality."[188] Because Hegel's God lacks transcendence, Hegel made God conform to a human model. In this *Geistesmonismus*,

186. Solomon, *In the Spirit of Hegel*, 62–63, writes: "Hegel scholars have taken his Christian
ambitions, however unorthodox, to be the very heart of his philosophy. But the spirit of the times
was going the other way. . . . Hegel, of all philosophers, was a self-conscious spokesman for his
times. The problems of religion were now corollaries to the ideals of humanism, and if the language of Christianity still pervaded German philosophy, the substance had long ago been altered
beyond recognition."
187. Anselm, *Proslogion*, chs. 14–15, "that than which nothing greater can be conceived" (*aliquid
quo maius nihil cogitari potest*) (Fairweather, *Scholastic Miscellany*, 83–84).
188. O'Regan, *Heterodox Hegel*, 128, referencing Moltmann, *Trinity and the Kingdom*, 17–18,
citing and translating from Pannenberg, "Subjectivité de Dieu," 184.

the Father and Christ fade from view as the Spirit surpasses them both. Father and Son are two stages along the way to the reality of the Spirit.

William Desmond refers to the self-serving or erotic character of Hegel's deity. Even at the moment of the cross, perhaps the most profound moment of the entire Christian story, God is not acting on the basis of unconditional love or out of compassion for sinful creatures. Instead God is making use of creation as a foil for his own self-development. The Hegelian narrative that begins in *eros* cannot end in *agape*. Hegel's God never confers grace in the sense of unmerited favor. A dark passage in Hegel—fraught with meaning when we think of the violent twentieth century—refers to history as a "slaughter-bench" and urges us to accept this outcome as necessary to the self-development of Spirit. An erotic deity cares for himself, not for others, and so Hegel's philosophy subverts the biblical picture of God's other-regarding love. Hegel sets aside grace in his necessitarian depiction of divine activity. Hegel rejects the merely contingent or accidental and wishes to absorb everything into the sphere of the necessary. There is a third category, though, which Hegel does not consider, and this is the category of gift. A gift may be neither accidental nor necessary. Classical Christian theology views creation and redemption as divine gifts, but Hegel cannot incorporate gift or grace into his conceptual system.

What, then, of universalism in Hegel? In reflecting the esoteric tradition, Hegel does not straightforwardly affirm a doctrine of *apokatastasis*, as Schelling does (*DR* 7.7). Hegel clearly expresses the narrative sequence of *identity-alienation-reconciliation* that has appeared in many Böhmist thinkers. The question is whether Hegel's thought allows for a futuristic eschatology and whether this would be on the social or the individual level. Generally speaking, Hegel seems to immanentize the eschaton and to identify it with a state of knowledge or perhaps with a visionary or mystical unity with the Absolute. The distinction between the already and the not yet, the here and now and the there and then, this life and the afterlife, the present age and the coming age, is blurred, if not obliterated. Eschatological realization is subjectivized. Humanity does not enter the eschaton, but rather the eschaton enters humanity.

Another and even deeper question in Hegel's thought is whether finite reality endures or is absorbed into Absolute Spirit. Hegel wishes to say that the final state stands higher than the initial state, as something richer and fuller. Hegel wants us to believe that all the stages of the journey are somehow preserved in arriving at the journey's destination. Yet Hegel's polemic against the "unhappy consciousness" of duality, separation, or twofoldness makes it difficult to imagine how any meaningful distinctions remain. Is not the final stage like a gurgling pot of molten metal, dissolving everything thrown into it? Once distinctions disappear, then what difference would the prior history make? Melted objects leave no trace of what they once were.

The underlying metaphysical problem in Hegel is rooted in his shift away from the doctrine of creation from nothing in the direction of a creation from God (ex Deo). This move carries profound implications for eschatology. Creatio ex Deo does not guard the creature's integrity and otherness. Ironically, the effort to exalt the creature by denying creation from nothing may lead to the creature being finally lost. Hegel's nineteenth-century Catholic critic Franz Anton Staudenmaier highlighted this point. O'Regan notes that Staudenmaier perceived "the subversion of the ontological difference between infinite and finite consequent upon denial of . . . the normative creation view." So Staudenmaier was "as much (if not more) concerned with the destruction of the finite that this position involves as with the reduction of the infinite to the finite."[189] Hegel's philosophy manifests the dual danger of the degradation of God to the condi-tions of finite and creaturely existence, on the one hand, and the dissolution of creation and creatures into the divine Infinity, on the other hand. In our reading of his philosophy, Hegel veered toward Charybdis rather than Scylla—that is, toward a whirlpool of cosmic dissolution rather than the shipwreck of atheism. Hegel's exaltation of finite creatures to infinite status turned into a denial of the world—a form of acosmism.[190]

This way of interpreting Hegel places him closest in the ancient church to Evagrius of Pontus and Stephen bar Sudaili (DR 3.10; 4.5). In describing the eschaton, Evagrius used the analogy of freshwaters flowing into the ocean that lose their fresh character and become saline. Evagrius's concrete image captures the basic idea that we find in Hegel's reference to finite objects losing their finitude in union with the Infinite. Bar Sudaili presented the trinitarian distinctions of Father, Son, and Spirit as themselves finally ceasing, and Hegel's prioritization of Spirit over Father and Son could be read in this way too. In the third epoch of the Spirit, it is not clear that the language of "Father" or "Son" any longer applies. The radical Origenists of the early church held that the Son and the Spirit in the eschaton would be subordinated to the Father, according to their interpretation of the Pauline assertion "When all things are subjected to him [i.e., the Son], then the Son himself will also be subjected to him who put all things in subjection under him, that God may be all in all" (1 Cor. 15:28). In ancient Origenism, if Christ's kingdom must be abolished, it is removed in favor of the Father's reign. In modern Hegelianism, the dissolution of the

---

189. O'Regan, Heterodox Hegel, 172.

190. "Left Hegelians"—e.g., Ludwig Feuerbach and Thomas J. J. Altizer—sought to dissolve God into the world. "Right Hegelians"—e.g., Philip Marheinecke and perhaps Karl Barth—tended to dissolve the world into God.

Father's reign and the Son's reign makes way for a final reign of the Spirit, who becomes "all in all."[191] Pannenberg seems to be correct in attributing to Hegel a *Geistesmonismus* in which "Spirit" (*Geist*) refers not so much to the Third Person of the Trinity as to Hegel's Absolute in its final overcoming of dualities and distinctions.

Emilio Brito, in his penetrating treatment of Schelling, draws a number of contrasts between Schelling and Hegel. Hegel's philosophy, he argues, has no resurrection of the body. The body for Hegel is merely a limitation to be removed. In a manner of speaking, then, Jesus was "raised" through the irreversible dissolution of his body. For Hegel, there was no exaltation of Christ after his death. Moreover, the difference between resurrection and parousia vanishes. In Hegel's speculative account of the gospel story, the material world's value became concentrated in the body of Jesus, and at the time of his death on the cross this value was finally and permanently transcended. In Jesus's descent to the dead, the glory of the world was eclipsed. For Hegel, the only heaven that exists is a state of inwardness (*Innerlichkeit*). Heaven is the eternal homeland of infinite subjective spirit. The only beatific vision is the invisible enjoyment of the eternal Idea. Everything natural must succumb to the fire of negativity, so that the spiritual substance of the Absolute may break free from all limitation. This final judgment will not be a renewal of all things but an overcoming of finitude and of human history by an Absolute that gives no grace. The spiritual community and its vocation finally disappear into the Absolute. In this way Hegelian eschatology exhausts itself in timeless philosophical presence.[192]

7.7. Schelling's Speculative Reinterpretation of Creation, Fall, and Redemption

Schelling is a difficult author and one whose thought passed through a number of phases, including an earlier period of the so-called identity philosophy, a middle period typified by the publication of the *Essay on Freedom* (1809), and a later phase in which the philosopher showed strong interest in world mythology and Christian revelation, culminating in the publication of the *Philosophy of Revelation* (1841–42) and the *Philosophy of Mythology* (1842). Not all are convinced that Schelling's philosophy can be divided into three distinct phases. Generally

191. Hegel's model for history is sometimes loosely called "Joachimite," after Joachim of Fiore (1135–1202). Yet while Joachim held that Father, Son, and Spirit reigned successively, in three epochs, he did not abolish the personal distinctions in the Trinity, as Hegel did. On Joachim's "posterity" in modern European thought, see de Lubac, *La postérité spirituelle de Joachim de Fiore*; Gil, "Zeitkonstruktion"; Daniel, *Abbot Joachim of Fiore*.

192. Brito, "Création et eschatologie," esp. 264–65. Cf. de Lubac, *La postérité spirituelle*, 359–77.

there is agreement that the 1809 work on freedom represents a decisive break with what preceded, though the distinction of a third from a second period is harder to make out.[193]

Despite his conflation of faith with knowledge, Schelling in his later years brought his eschatology more into accord with the Bible and normative Christian eschatology than Hegel ever did. He slowly arrived at a view that was more in accord with mainstream theology. By the final phase of his life, Schelling, unlike Hegel, affirmed individual immortality and the resurrection of the body. His later thinking shows a genuine eschatological openness rather than an inevitable outworking of a prearranged pattern. Like the Catholic Jesuit thinker Teilhard de Chardin (DR 10.3), Schelling thought of the cosmic redemptive plan as a process of re-creation.[194]

Schelling's early philosophy of identity involved a complete rejection of the doctrine of creation.[195] In this earliest period, Schelling followed Fichte, who not only rejected the Christian doctrine of creation but also spoke of it scornfully, calling it "the absolute and fundamental error of all metaphysics and the teaching of false religion."[196] The driving metaphysical question for the young Schelling was this: How does the Absolute pass out of itself and set itself in opposition to the world? The answer lay in a "defection" or "fall" (Abfall)—nontemporal and inexplicable—from the realm of the Absolute. This "fall" demarcated a distinction between infinite and finite. Yet the fall was a necessary moment in God's self-revelation.[197] This "fall" in Schelling was more of a metaphysical than a moral idea, and so it should not be regarded as the functional equivalent of the sin of Adam and Eve.

For Schelling in his earliest period, philosophical knowledge was itself a way of salvation. The human spirit could only escape the empirical prison of sense experience and multiplicity by a kind of "leap." This "leap" counteracted the primal "fall." Intellectual intuition of reality corrected the "fall" and so brought reunification with God. In Philosophy and Religion (1804), Schelling taught that the soul in being connected with the body was devoted to annihilation. The true reality of the soul lay in its idea or eternal concept in God, which was the basis for eternal knowledge. The eternal principle of selfhood remained forever

193. Works by Schelling in English translation that are relevant to this chapter are Of Human Freedom; Stuttgart Seminars; The Ages of the World; and the online translation of Initia Philosophiae Universae. The German lecture interpreting Christ's kenosis in Phil. 2 was published as "Exegetischer Nachweiss aus Phil. 2,6–8" in Schelling's Sämtliche Werke.

194. Brito, "Création et eschatologie," 247. The next several pages are indebted to Brito's excellent analysis.

195. Ibid., 248.

196. Fichte, Die Anweisung zum seligen Leben, 479, cited in Brito, "Création et temps," 362.

197. Brito, "Création et eschatologie," 248–49.

self-identical. This archetype (*Urbild*) is not altered by temporal existence. It neither gains nor loses through the existence or disappearance of bodily life. Temporal appearances were not fully real. The human spirit was like the Absolute Spirit—that is, an eternal reality disconnected from temporal existence. On this basis, it was not possible to speak of the earthly soul as having immortality in the sense of individual persistence. Therefore the younger Schelling did not anticipate a continuation of the present sort of selfhood but rather a liberation from it. To desire immortality was to seek the soul's separation from the body. To desire immortality was to embrace true philosophy.[198]

The younger Schelling agreed with Hegel that immortality inhered as a quality of the soul and was something already existing.[199] Schelling's initial assumptions were thus rather Platonic. The doctrine of immortality meant little more to Schelling at this early stage than the tautological statement that the soul's eternal element is eternal. Since this eternal element was thought to be supra-individual, there was no individual survival after death. Identity with God was the supreme goal of rational being. Yet identity with God was eternal and unknowable in any empirical way. This identity with God negated time and established eternity in the midst of time. This eternity amid time could be interpreted as peace with God, the disappearance of the past, or—in another sense—the forgiveness of sins. The soul's union with the body was a form of punishment for the soul. Human life was a return to the self's archetype in God by means of intermediate stages, culminating in the complete union of the self with the idea of the self. The eschaton would bring complete liberation from all manner of association with matter. The return of souls to their original condition implied a dissolution of the material world.[200]

Schelling's middle period, represented by the *Essay on Freedom*, brought in a notion of becoming or development that was not present in his earlier thinking. Only a metaphysics of becoming, he believed, could adequately depict a changing world. God must be "living," for "God fashions himself."[201] The process of creation was nothing other than the personalization of God, in which God surmounts his original condition. Drawing on Böhme's conception of the *Ungrund* (*DR* 5.3), Schelling held that God was at first divided into conscious and unconscious aspects. The creation of the world came about from God's

198. Ibid., 249–50.

199. Ibid., 249n21, citing Rosenkranz, *Schelling: Vorlesungen*, 264.

200. Brito, "Création et eschatologie," 250. The final disappearance of material reality was a theme in radical Origenism and in modern thinkers influenced by Schelling, such as Vladimir Solovyov. See O. Smith, *Vladimir Solovyov and the Spiritualization of Matter*, and *DR*, 226–27, 265–66, 295–96, 416–17, 885.

201. Brito, "Création et eschatologie," 251, citing Schelling, *Sämtliche Werke*, 7:432.

action to overcome this division. One way to read Schelling's *Naturphilosophie* would be to regard the material world as a form of unconscious deity, needing to be awakened to awareness of itself as divine. Schelling in the 1869 treatise embraced the notion of "God all in all" (1 Cor. 15:28) in a way that was reminiscent of Origen and the Origenists.

The *Stuttgart Seminars* (1810) gave fuller expression to eschatology than Schelling's earlier writings did. Just as before, Schelling differentiated the inner from the outer man and held that only the inner man was genuine. At the same time, he altered his understanding of death, seeing it not simply as a separation of spirit from body but as a separation of good from evil. In death, human beings undergo a reduction to the essential—*reductio ad essentiam*.[202] No longer did Schelling think of human nature as purely spiritual, but he saw the spiritual and corporeal aspects as conditioning one another, so that there was a spirituality of the physical and a physicality of the spiritual.[203] The human soul after death was said to be "aerial" and more robust than it was prior to death. The spirit world, existing apart from human beings, was as certain as the world of nature. Yet the spirit world and the natural world would finally become one world. All "potencies" functioned toward unification. Through a process that might be called alchemical, evil will be separated from good. Evil, or nonbeing, will be set below nature, into a profound depth, where there will be consuming fire. This fire is called hell, and it consumes creaturely egotism just as it had previously devoured all divine egotism. Evil, or being-for-itself, will be separated from God and consumed in the fire. By this division in nature, each of the cosmic elements will come into rapport with the world of spirits.[204] At this stage, the final end of creation will be realized. God will be rendered totally effective and visible, the lowest will be joined to the highest, and all that was at first only implicit will become explicit. Humanity—already in the process of divinization—will be universally divinized, just as nature is fully divinized. Because sin is not eternal, its consequences will not be eternal, and they will cease to exist.[205] In the conclusion to the *Stuttgart Seminars*, Schelling makes explicit his idea of the *apokatastasis*.[206] The eschaton allows for a full realization of the incarnation, which Schelling calls "the perfect incarnation of God" (*der völligen Menschwerdung Gottes*). In this

202. Schelling interpreters sometimes refer to this as "essentification," while Schelling's disciple Paul Tillich called it "essentialization" and gave it a central place in his theology (see *DR* 7.8).

203. Schelling's idea of spiritual corporeality is reminiscent of that of Swedenborg, whose work Schelling read, as well as Mormonism, which came later than Schelling but presented this idea in a vivid form (*DR* 2.9 and *DR* appendix K).

204. Brito, "Création et eschatologie," 253–54, with n. 41.

205. Ibid., 254–55.

206. Xavier Tilliette (*Schelling*, 1:555) writes that Schelling "envisage l'apocatastase" (envisions the *apokatastasis*—i.e., the final salvation of all), cited in Brito, "Création et eschatologie," 255n48.

final state, the infinite will have become completely finite without detracting from its own infinity. Schelling writes at the very end of the *Stuttgart Seminars*: "Then God is truly all in all, then pantheism is true."[207]

In his final writings, Schelling emphasized the theme of revelation, and in this sense he turned in a different direction than Hegel. The philosopher's task, he believed, was to expound the truths of revelation as truths of reason.[208] This stress on revelation set Schelling at odds with the increasingly materialistic approach to science and philosophy that was becoming dominant in Germany from the 1840s onward. Absent from Schelling's approach to revelation was the Old Testament, since he rejected the notion that the God of the Israelites is the true God. He argued that the God of the Israelites bore some relation to the true God without being the true God, a view that opened the door to the developmental view of God that became common in the emerging German liberal tradition.[209]

In his treatment of God, Schelling emphasized the doctrine of creation and insisted on God's freedom to manifest himself in creation.[210] He also held that God was already perfectly actualized in himself prior to the world. In *Philosophy of Revelation*, as in the *Essay on Freedom*, Schelling cited 1 Corinthians 15:28. Here he called these words "the most profound in the New Testament."[211] Sin, he argued, created a tension between the Father and the Son and separated the Son from the Father. In time the Son will renounce his independence from the Father and submit himself to the Father. The Son's final subordination will

207. Schelling, *Sämtliche Werke*, 7:484, cited in Brito, "Création et eschatologie," 255. Schelling speaks not of *panentheism* but of *pantheism* as being the final, eschatological truth. Panentheism, or all-in-God, may be only a step toward pantheism, or all-as-God. In traditional theism, such a final identification of creatures with God is impossible. Gregory of Nyssa posited an eternal progress in heaven (*DR* 3.9), as did Jonathan Edwards, as discussed in P. Ramsey, "Appendix III." Yet this idea of endless progress ipso facto rules out any *identity* of Creator and creature.

208. James Gutman, introduction to *Of Human Freedom*, by Friedrich Schelling, xxvi.

209. Kaplan, *Answering the Enlightenment*, 91. Kaplan recounts Schelling's gnosticizing interpretation of Gen. 22, whereby the true God is not the one who commands Abraham's offering but the angel who interrupts it. Yet for Schelling the Old Testament tales of sacrifice and other rituals do "inform us of the same kenotic act of God's love . . . that happens in the Incarnation" (92).

210. "The doctrine that God created the world is a pillar of genuine faith. The labor of this present work would be adequately rewarded had it only made this thought comprehensible and intelligible" (Schelling, *The Ages of the World*, 80). Schelling's position on divine freedom in creating does contain a tension, in that he asserts that "God is . . . necessarily self-revelatory being (*ens manifestativum sui*)" (79). In Schelling's subtle logic a being that acts according to its own nature can be said to be both acting necessarily and acting freely. In another passage in *Ages of the World*, he seems to present a kabbalistic doctrine of divine withdrawal or *tsimtsum*: "Every single system acknowledges that the force of contraction is the real and actual beginning of every thing. The greatest glory of development . . . is expected from what has been excluded and which only decides to unfold with opposition" (107).

211. Schelling, *Sämtliche Werke*, 14:64, cited in Brito, "Création et eschatologie," 256–57.

not be the same as the former subordination, for at the end he will renounce
all independent autonomy. At this point the Son will be able to give the Spirit.
In the beginning, One was All or perhaps, the Father was All. In the end,
All will be One. Then all the persons of the Trinity will be One. Reality in its
multiplicity will become One.

In *Philosophy of Revelation*, Schelling views the three persons as three sover-
eigns over three successive epochs. The time before creation was in a special
way the era of the Father. The present is the time of the Son. Eternity will be
the time of the Spirit. Schelling made reference to the "everlasting gospel" of
Joachim of Fiore and the words of the poet Johannes Scheffler (or Angelus
Silesius; 1624–77):

> *Der Vater war zuvor, der Sohn ist noch zur Zeit, der Geist wird endlich seyn am Tag*
> *der Herrlichkeit.*
> The Father was before, the Son but for time's story; the Spirit will forever be,
> upon the day of glory.[212]

Simply put, the Father is before time, the Son is in time, and the Spirit is after
time.

One of the later sections (no. 32) in Schelling's *Philosophy of Revelation* was
wholly devoted to a discussion of the final end. Here he elaborated his distinctive
idea of "essentification." Human death for him was something like the extrac-
tion of an essence from a plant, in which the plant's strength remained in the
extract.[213] The *Philosophy of Revelation* repeated much of what was said earlier
in the *Stuttgart Seminars*. Jesus after his crucifixion was dead according to the
flesh but made alive in the spirit. Schelling proposed three stages in human

---

212. Schelling, *Sämtliche Werke*, 14:72–73, cited in Brito, "Création et eschatologie," 258.
213. Schelling writes: "The death of man is not so much a separation as an essentification, in
which only the contingent is destroyed, while the essence, that which is most truly man, is preserved.
For no man in his life appears wholly as he is, but after death he remains purely himself. . . . This
essentified being . . . must be an extremely real being; yes, in truth, it must be far more real than
the actual body" (*Philosophie der Offenbarung*, in *Sämtliche Werke*, 14:207, cited in Benz, "Theogony,"
234). Ernst Benz notes that "Schelling did not invent this concept of essentification but took it over
from [Friedrich Christoph] Oetinger. In Oetinger we find a whole complex of concepts developed
from the word 'essence': to essentify, essentiation, essentification, essentiator. By 'essence' Oetinger
meant something's whole being and not merely an image or idea" ("Theogony," 234–35). Oetinger
often referred to God as "the Essentiator." And he viewed the human soul as quasi-divine: "The
soul is not material, for it is of divine origin; it is essentified, not composite. The essentification
or essentiation of the soul is accomplished by the derived word of God that flows into it" ("Von der
Sünde wider den heiligen Geist," in *Sämtliche Schriften*, 6:454, cited in Benz, "Theogony," 236).
Oetinger himself acknowledged that Böhme's notion of "tincture" lay behind his own idea of "essence" (Benz, "Theogony," 238–39). The lineage for this idea of "essentification" thus runs from
Böhme to Oetinger, then to Schelling, and finally to Tillich.

existence: the purely natural, the purely spiritual, and then a synthesis of natural and spiritual. Natural life exists with spiritual life in an indissoluble unity. As Jesus died on the cross he sacrificed his ego-ness, and the Holy Spirit became the Spirit of Christ. Jesus died and rose again in the power of the Spirit. Admittedly, Schelling had trouble with the orthodox doctrine of Christ's resurrection. He generally thought of the resurrection as a collective reality affecting the community rather than an event pertaining to Christ as an individual.[214] At the same time, in his later years he showed concern about whether his philosophy was theologically orthodox.[215]

During the eschaton, according to Schelling, the interior world will become exteriorized. Not only humanity but nature as a whole will possess a "spiritual body" (1 Cor. 15:44) and will be transfigured into the condition in which it existed prior to the fall.[216] Christ's final glory will be a received glory, a new glory, rather than a glory that he had had formerly. Taking a subordinationist view of Christ, Schelling argued that the Father gave authority to Christ (cf. Matt. 28:18), and so Christ's glory was not that of the Father. Christ therefore is not God as such but is Lord.[217] At the present time, Christ's glory remains hidden, and it will be manifested only at the end. Christ's exaltation effects a reconciliation with the world, so that the interior world is exteriorized and made visible.[218] Unlike Hegel, Schelling did not propose that the spiritual community will be absorbed into an act of absolute knowing. In this way Schelling also avoided Hegel's acosmism.[219]

At the end of the *Philosophy of Revelation*, Schelling mentions Saints Peter, Paul, and John as symbolically representing the Catholic Church, the Protestant Church, and the Eschatological Church, respectively.[220] Schelling sought

214. Brito, "Création et eschatologie," 259–61.

215. Benz ("Theogony," 64–65, with n. 64) cites a letter written to Schelling on May 26, 1833, informing him of an orthodox German Protestant theologian who in 1735 had written a book defending something like Schelling's essentification idea. Schelling responded that "hitherto I had supposed that my similar position had *aliquid heterodoxi* [something heterodox] about it; but now I see that it was long ago put forward by well-known theologians without prejudice to their orthodoxy."

216. Brito, "Création et eschatologie," 262. The "spiritual body" teaching is reminiscent of Origenism. The exteriorization of the interior appears as a motif in the *Gospel of Thomas* 22 (Meyer, *Nag Hammadi Scriptures*, 142–43): "When you make the inner like the outer . . . then you will enter the kingdom."

217. Brito, "Création et eschatologie," 263.

218. Ibid., 265–66.

219. Ibid.

220. Ibid., 263–64. Despite Schelling's Protestant context, as Brito notes, he relativized the Church of Paul (i.e., Protestantism) and did not set it above the Church of Peter (i.e., Catholicism). Thus he was more pro-Catholic than most other Protestants of his day (266n122). Moreover, Schelling recognized more than Hegel did the indispensable role of worship in the community of faith (266n124).

to eliminate—in his final or Johannine Church—all manner of externality and authority and all "possession of things."[221] This final state, he thought, will surpass human comprehension. Emilio Brito suggests that Schelling was not antihierarchical in his views of the historical church, though some critics read him this way.[222] Yet it is not surprising that Schelling's theory of an ideal church that is utterly nonhierarchical would fall afoul of those concerned to uphold church authority.

7.8. Tillich's "Half-Way Demythologization" of the Fall and Restoration of Souls

Paul Tillich (1886–1965) acknowledged his debt to Schelling. In a lecture given on the hundredth anniversary of Schelling's death, Tillich spoke of Schelling as his "great teacher in philosophy and theology" without whom his own "work on problems of systematic theology would be unthinkable."[223] He wrote not one but two academic dissertations on Schelling's thought.[224] In a rare autobiographical paragraph in *A History of Christian Thought* (1968), Tillich recalled his first encounter with the writings of Schelling and the decisive impact that they had on his own development:

> I recall the unforgettable moment when by chance I came into possession of the very rare first edition of the collected works of Schelling in a bookstore on my way to the University of Berlin. I had no money, but I bought it anyway, and this spending of nonexistent money was probably more important than all the other nonexistent or sometimes existing money that I have spent. For what I learned from Schelling became determinative of my own philosophical and theological development.[225]

221. One finds again an analogy with radical Origenism, in which authority itself passes away, when Christ "delivers up" the kingdom to the Father, and God becomes "all in all" (1 Cor. 15:28).

222. Brito expresses surprise at the nineteenth-century Catholic authors adamantly opposed to Schelling's idea of the Eschatological Church—in which external authority would no longer exist—even though Schelling indicated that this church would not come to exist in history as such. Brito ("Création et eschatologie," 266n124) cites Kuhn, "Die Schelling'sche Philosophie," esp. 29–32, and Döllinger, "Die Schelling'sche Philosophie."

223. Tillich, "Schelling," 197, quoted in Loncar, "German Idealism's Long Shadow," 99.

224. Tillich, *Die religionsgeschichtliche Konstruktion in Schellings positiver Philosophie: Ihre Voraussetzungen und Prinzipien* (1910); Tillich, *Mystik und Schuldbewusstsein in Schellings philosophischer Entwicklung* (1912). Both works were translated into English: Tillich, *The Construction of the History of Religion in Schelling's Positive Philosophy: Its Presuppositions and Principles* (1974); Tillich, *Mysticism and Guilt-Consciousness in Schelling's Philosophical Development* (1974).

225. Tillich, *History of Christian Thought*, 438. In this work, Tillich emphasizes Schelling's points of difference from Hegel (437–48).

Tillich followed not only Schelling but also Jakob Böhme, whose insights, he wrote, were "profound in comparison with much theism in modern theology." Tillich judged that Böhme had exercised "an astonishing influence on the history of Western philosophy."[226] According to one interpreter, if the "Boehmist elements" were removed from Tillich's theology, then his theological system would simply "evaporate."[227] Böhmism was essential to Tillich's account of the vitality and inner life of the Godhead, which Tillich variously described as a unity, harmony, coincidence, or transcending of such polar oppositions as being and nonbeing, eternity and temporality, and freedom and destiny.

In what follows, we will point out some of the systematic interconnections within Tillich's thought, especially in relation to eschatology. Tillich himself noted the way that his own ideas were systematically related: "It has always been impossible for me to think theologically in any other than a systematic way. The smallest problem, if taken seriously and radically, drove me to all other problems and to the anticipation of a whole in which they could find their solution."[228] Sizable books have been written on Tillich's "system," so only a brief sketch appears here, with emphasis on ideas pertaining to the theme of universal salvation.

Tillich's theology rested on *a series of negations*. He rejected analogies for God drawn from the realm of everyday experience. One of his best-known points was that God is not merely "a being" but is "being-itself." To get this point across, Tillich quipped that "God does not exist."[229] Tillich dismissed any "personal God," since this designation implied the limited notion of God as "a person."[230] In *The Courage to Be* (1952), Tillich refers to "the God above the God of theism."[231] Any identification of anything finite and conditional as infinite and unconditional would be "idolatrous."[232] Natural theology in the traditional sense was impossible, since it "deprive[d] God of his divinity."[233] God cannot be identified as the "cause" of anything happening in the world.[234] Affirming "everything we say about God is symbolic," Tillich in his thinking oscillated between an emphasis on divine transcendence and a countervailing stress on the value of religious symbols.[235]

226. Tillich, foreword to *Jacob Boehme*, 8; and Tillich as quoted in D. J. Peterson, "Jacob Boehme and Paul Tillich," 225.

227. Morrison, "Paul Tillich's Appropriation of Jacob Boehme," quoted in D. J. Peterson, "Jacob Boehme and Paul Tillich," 225.

228. Tillich, *Systematic Theology*, 1:vii.

229. Ibid., 1:238; 2:6–12, 235, 237.

230. Ibid., 1:245.

231. Tillich, *Courage to Be*, 186–90. Cf. Tillich, *Systematic Theology*, 2:12.

232. Tillich, *Systematic Theology*, 1:13.

233. Ibid., 1:131.

234. Ibid., 1:238.

235. Ibid., 2:9. Ancient esotericism held to an inconceivable and unnameable God, to whom nonetheless a plethora of names and symbols were applied. The *Corpus Hermeticum* (5.20) states

In Tillich's theology, there are no "revealed words" (i.e., a literal or written word of God) nor any "revealed knowledge," but instead a "knowledge of revelation."[236] There are no miracles, in the sense of physical events that violate natural laws. Instead there are occurrences that we might call "sign-events" because persons come by them to a new understanding of God.[237] Tillich diminished the importance of the historical Jesus in rejecting what he calls "a Jesus-centered religion and theology."[238] When Jesus died on the cross, nothing new came to pass. Jesus's death was simply a manifestation of God's eternal conquest of the element of nonbeing within his own divine life.[239] Tillich rejected the idea of petitionary prayer—that is, prayer to God that would bring about a change in one's physical environment or external circumstances.[240]

Methodologically speaking, Tillich's theology rested not on an exegesis of Scripture but on an interpretation of symbols. Religious symbols exist, yet theology can neither confirm nor negate them and so must simply interpret them.[241] For Tillich, "revelation" was a subjective event of new insight or understanding rather than something that happens objectively.[242] Sometimes Tillich used the word "manifestation," which conveyed much the same meaning. When Tillich wrote that there has been "continuous revelation in the history of the church," he seems to have had in mind this subjective process of coming to new insight.[243] "Revelation" is an ongoing human realization of knowledge and participation in the divine life.

On the subject of Jesus, Tillich's views diverged from those of mainstream Christianity. The word "Jesus," he held, was not interchangeable with the word "Christ."[244] He did not believe in "incarnation" in the orthodox sense, for "God does not become something that is not God." The idea of divine beings transmuted into human beings was essentially pagan. The word "became" in the

---

that God "has no name" yet "has all names" (Copenhaver, *Hermetica*, 20). Tillich too embodies this esoteric "no names" / "all names" paradox. On this theme, see the earlier discussion of Pseudo-Dionysius (*DR*, 341n77), Kabbalah (*DR*, 160n114), and Böhme (*DR*, 479).

236. Tillich, *Systematic Theology*, 1:123, 129n6.

237. Ibid., 1:115–17; 3:114.

238. Ibid., 1:134.

239. Ibid., 2:173–76.

240. Ibid., 1:267.

241. "Theology as such has neither the duty nor the power to confirm or to negate religious symbols. Its task is to interpret them according to theological principles and methods" (ibid., 1:240). Sometimes Tillich writes as though symbols themselves engender new symbols: "Religious symbolism has produced three main symbols for unambiguous life: Spirit of God, Kingdom of God, and Eternal Life" (3:107).

242. Ibid., 1:111, 128.

243. Ibid., 1:132.

244. Ibid., 3:150.

phrase "the Word became flesh" (John 1:14) did not imply a change in God. This language instead symbolized the paradox of divine participation in history. Jesus had no "divine nature" according to Tillich. Instead he accepted the idea of an "eternal God-man-unity" or "Eternal-God-Manhood"—phrases with an esoteric resonance.[245] Tillich called Christ "Son of God," "Spiritual Man," or "Man from Above." He did not identify "Logos" with Jesus but saw "Logos" as a principle of divine self-manifestation: "God is manifest in a personal life process as a saving participant."[246] Regarding the resurrection, Tillich referred to this doctrine as "highly symbolic." He rejected the phrase "resurrection of the flesh," though he accepted a "resurrection of the body," understanding "body" as something "spiritual."[247]

Among Tillich's favorite words were "ambiguity," "ambiguous," and "ambiguously." Indeed, much of volume 3 of the *Systematic Theology* centers on the notion of "ambiguity." The ambiguity of human experience was almost an obsession for Tillich. Human beings are lost in a world that offers only hints and suggestions but no satisfying answers to their deepest questions. No answer they obtain is clear or understandable. All revelation, he writes, is necessarily ambiguous.[248] The threat of meaninglessness hangs over humanity at every moment. Karl Barth's comment on Tillich's theology was simply that "Man is alone."[249] For Tillich, humanity may speak about God, yet God does not speak to humanity. Any notion of divine speaking would imply an "idolatrous" or "demonic" identification of some element of finite and conditioned existence with the infinite and unconditioned reality of God. Even more sobering is the consideration that language itself represents a form of alienation. The word spoken "opens up a gap" between the object named and the meaning intended by the speaker. "The inherent ambiguity of language is that in transforming reality into meaning it separates mind and reality."[250] To be sure, Tillich at times speaks of the *logos* that inheres in the human mind, linking it to the world and to God. Yet there is a vein of skepticism that casts doubt on the project of finding meaning in the world. The final volume of Tillich's *Systematic Theology*, as noted, seems to be the most skeptical of all, with its focus on ambiguity.

245. Ibid., 2:148–49.

246. Ibid., 2:94–95; cf. 2:149.

247. Ibid., 3:412.

248. Ibid., 3:48. The chapter headings and subheadings in the table of contents for vol. 3 of the *Systematic Theology* use the word "ambiguity" and its variants no less than thirty-five times.

249. R. K. Anderson, "Barth on Tillich," 1478. Barth states: "In Tillich's theology man is alone. There isn't another who meets him, of which it might be said: 'He stands for me. He is above me; I am below him, I obey him.' I can find nothing in Tillich comparable to the biblical story: man as creature meeting God his creator. . . . His theology is something of a gnostic system."

250. Tillich, *Systematic Theology*, 3:69.

The language Tillich used for human existence had a gnostic tinge to it. He often spoke of "alienation," "estrangement," and "imprisonment," and the second volume in the *Systematic Theology* includes an extended discussion of "estrangement."[251] Through self-reflection "man discovers the finitude in which he is imprisoned."[252] He appeals to nineteenth-century thinkers—Kierkegaard, Marx, Schopenhauer, and Nietzsche—in support of the idea that "existence is estrangement."[253] In a passage describing existentialism yet also summarizing Tillich's own views, he writes:

> New reality presupposes an old reality; and this old reality . . . is the state of the estrangement of man and his world from God. This estranged world is ruled by structures of evil, symbolized as demonic powers. They rule individual souls, nations, and even nature. They produce anxiety in all its forms. It is the task of the Messiah to conquer them and to establish a new reality.[254]

In broad strokes, Tillich's thought discloses the triadic pattern that we have already encountered—namely, unity-diversity-unity, or identity-alienation-reconciliation. For Tillich, this triad is typified as *essence, existence*, and *(recovered) essence* (or the "New Being"). Many accounts of Tillich's thought stress the central importance for him of "essence" and "existence." Whether regarded philosophically or theologically, the triad essence-existence-essence undergirds the whole structure of the *Systematic Theology*.[255] The triad traces two metaphysical movements and an intervening condition between the two. The first movement is from essence to existence. The second movement leads from existence back to essence, a process that Tillich names later on in his *Systematic Theology* as "essentialization." Human life in all of its fragmentary and ambiguous character sits in the middle of these two movements. Tillich writes, "So we can distinguish three elements in the process of life: self-identity, self-alteration, and return to one's self. Potentiality becomes actuality only through these three elements in the process which we call life."[256] In analogy to the essence-existence distinction, Tillich saw a tension in intellectual history between what he called "essentialism" and "existentialism" and wished for his part to avoid the pure

251. Ibid., 2:44–59.
252. Ibid., 1:82.
253. Ibid., 2:25.
254. Ibid., 2:27.
255. Allen O. Miller and Donald E. Arther compress Tillich's entire system into several pages in *Paul Tillich's Systematic Theology*. They note that Tillich expounded "the problem of being human" in terms of "the interplay between essential being and existential being" and that "life is the actualization of essential humanity in the particularity of concrete existence" (3). See also Eisenbeis, *Key Ideas*.
256. Tillich, *Systematic Theology*, 3:30.

"essentialism" of such thinkers as Plato and Hegel as well as the pure "existentialism" of Kierkegaard.

Tillich's most frequent references to the triad appear in his discussion of Plato's myth of the soul, a motif with constitutive importance for his theology:

> Existence for Plato is the realm of mere opinion, error, and evil. It lacks true reality. True being is essential being and is present in the realm of eternal ideas, i.e., in essences. In order to reach essential being, man must rise above existence. He must return to the essential realm from which he fell into existence. In this way man's existence . . . is judged as a fall from what he essentially is.[257]

In another passage Tillich again outlines Plato's myth of the fall of the soul and its later ascent, emphasizing the epistemological aspects of the myth:

> Knowing is a form of union. In every act of knowledge the knower and that which is known are united. . . . But the union of knowledge is a peculiar one; it is union through separation. . . . The unity of distance and union is the ontological problem of knowledge. It drove Plato to the myth of an original union of the soul with the essences (ideas), of the separation of the soul from the truly real in temporal existence, of the recollection of the essences, and of reunion with them through the different degrees of cognitive elevation. The unity is never completely destroyed; but there is also estrangement. The particular object is strange as such, but it contains essential structures with which the cognitive subject is essentially united and which it can remember when looking at things. This motif runs through the whole history of philosophy.[258]

As we will see, Tillich's brief account of Plato's myth is also an account of his own myth, which is analogous and homologous to that of Plato.

Despite the ambiguity and limitedness of present life, human beings for Tillich possess "the power of infinite self-transcendence," which is "an expression of man's belonging to that which is beyond nonbeing, namely, being-itself."[259] Human nature itself bears the imprint of its transcendent origin. While human reason is finite, "reason is not merely finite."[260] Humans have what Tillich calls "potential infinity."[261] They are in "a pre-eminent position"

257. Ibid., 2:22.
258. Ibid., 1:94–95.
259. Ibid., 1:191.
260. Ibid., 1:82. Tillich cites Kant in support of his idea of humanity's capacity for infinite self-transcendence (1:82n7). He reads Kant not as shutting the door to transcendence but as open to transcendence in viewing the "categorical imperative" as a "doctrine of the unconditional element in the depth of practical reason."
261. Ibid., 1:206.

because they have "self-awareness" and ask "the ontological question."[262] He writes that "man alone is *microcosmos*," "participates in the remotest stars and the remotest past," and "potentially there are no limits he could not transcend."[263] For "man . . . is free to transcend every given reality."[264] On the other hand, human existence in its present state has undergone an "irrational" transition from essence to existence.[265] The result is that human beings are not in their essential state and are instead in a state of alienation. Tillich defines "sin" as a state in which "the holy and the secular are separated, struggling with each other and trying to conquer each other." Stated otherwise, "sin" is "the state in which God is not 'all in all'" (cf. 1 Cor. 15:28).[266] "Sin" implies the ideas of separation and fragmentariness, while "God" implies the ideas of reconciliation and unity. Humans in a finite, earthly, and "fallen" state nonetheless long for restoration and return. Along these lines, Tillich's theology mimics Plato's myth of the fallen soul as well as the gnostic modifications and intensifications of this myth.

In expounding on the human condition, Tillich offered a nontraditional reading of *creatio ex nihilo*. He rejected the idea of preexisting matter and so agreed with earlier Christian teachers. Yet Tillich sought a deeper meaning in *creatio ex nihilo*, inspired, it seems, by Böhme and Schelling. His idea was that creatures, being made "out of nothing," continue to have "nothingness" remaining with them as a "heritage of nonbeing." For this reason, "there is an element of nonbeing in creatureliness."[267] In Tillich's thought, both being and nonbeing are constitutive elements of human existence.

Tillich's "fall" was not that of traditional theology. There was no "before" in any strict sense nor will there be any "after." He rejected the "biblical literalism" that attached itself to the story of Adam and Eve.[268] He explained: "Creation and the Fall coincide in so far as there is no point in time and space in which created goodness was actualized and had existence. This is a necessary consequence of the rejection of the literal interpretation of the

262. Ibid., 1:168.
263. Ibid., 1:176.
264. Ibid., 1:186. Despite the emphasis on estrangement and ambiguity, Tillich's thought often breathes a confidence in human nature and human capacities that reminds one of *Corpus Hermeticum* (41; 11.20), discussed above in connection with Hegel and the demigod or man-God motif (see *DR*, 649, with n. 163).
265. Tillich, *Systematic Theology*, 2:3.
266. Ibid., 1:218.
267. Ibid., 1:253–54.
268. "Biblical literalism did a distinct disservice to Christianity in its identification of the Christian emphasis on the symbol of the Fall with the literalistic interpretation of the Genesis story" (ibid., 2:29).

paradise story. There was no 'utopia' in the past, just as there will be no 'utopia' in the future. Actualized creation and estranged existence are identical."[269] One might wonder why Tillich clung to the traditional Christian language of "creation" and "fall" while interpreting this in a nontraditional way. The answer seems to be that this language, for Tillich, communicated something profound concerning human experience. It underscored the contrast between what is and what should be. Secular naturalism could not do justice to humanity's sense of alienation and the persistent longing for a pristine and ideal existence. "Creation" and "fall" were revelatory ideas in personal and existential terms.

There is still the dilemma of how to interpret Tillich's "fall." Because he rejected a chronological "before" and "after," one could understand essence and existence in a nontemporal way. The result might be a purely conceptual distinction that has nothing to do with the time dimension. Yet to interpret it in this fashion is to go against Tillich's own account, which relies on what he calls a "half-way demythologization" that removes the element of "once upon a time" and yet does not altogether remove the time dimension. Tillich states explicitly that "the phrase 'transition from essence to existence' still contains a temporal element."[270] Tillich, the theologian of ambiguity, offers a decidedly ambiguous doctrine of creation and fall. His account seems to hover in between a strictly literal reading of the book of Genesis and a purely symbolic interpretation.

Tillich's "half-way" mythologized and "half-way" demythologized interpretation draws as much from Plato as from the book of Genesis. Plato's "fall of the soul" was not a logical deduction but a narrative that could not be fully explained. If existence had been simply a logical implication of essence, then human existence would have appeared as essential. Sin would then appear as something created and as a natural consequence of humanity's essential nature. "But sin is not created, and the transition from essence to existence is a fact, a story to be told and not a derived dialectical step. Therefore, it cannot be completely demythologized."[271] Tillich criticized Hegel's attempt at total demythologization. He set *both stories*—the biblical story of Adam and Eve, and the Platonic myth of the soul—over against Hegel's essentialism and rationalism. Here Tillich follows Schelling's emphasis on myths and stories (*DR* 7.7), in contrast to Hegel's effort to free philosophical concepts from all connection with symbols and sense experience (*DR* 7.4).

269. Ibid., 2:44.
270. Ibid., 2:29.
271. Ibid.

One question for Tillich, as for Schelling, is this: Why does the transition from essential to existential being take place at all? Tillich claimed that no reason can be supplied. "The way from essence to existence is 'irrational' . . . [and] cannot be understood in terms of necessity."[272] Tillich's persistent critique of Hegel was that the latter construed this transition from essence to existence as a necessary development—a process inherent to the self-realization of *Geist* (Spirit). Tillich would have none of this. In this respect he was closer to anti-Hegelians such as Kierkegaard, who with his "leap of faith" refused to regard human experience in terms of any necessary development or sequence.

Tillich presents his account of "the fall" at considerable length in the second volume of his *Systematic Theology*.[273] Because "sin is not created," Tillich looked to both the Platonic "fall of the soul" and the Genesis account of "Adam's fall" as illuminating stories that convey truth regarding the human condition. He rejected Hegel's idea that the fall of humanity was not a rupture, but only an "imperfect fulfillment." He equally rejected claims of naturalistic philosophers that "man has no predicament."[274] "Taken as a myth," the story of Genesis 1–3 "can guide our description of the transition from essential to existential being."[275] Because Tillich did not think that the Genesis story could be "completely demythologized," he lingered in an uncomfortable middle ground between biblical literalism and the spiritualizing exegesis (e.g., that of Hegel) that turned biblical stories into abstract truths.[276] Tillich wanted to affirm opposing interpretations and to mediate between them.

For Tillich, the story of the fall of Adam is not the story of any human individual. Instead the story points toward what he calls a "universal transition from essence to existence." He writes, "There is no individual Fall. In the Genesis story the two sexes and nature, represented by the serpent, work together. The transition from existence is possible because finite freedom works within the frame of a universal destiny."[277] Tillich's "Adam" represents mythically all humanity in its "state of essential being." While this state is not an actual stage in the life of any human individual—past, present, or future—"the essential nature of man is present in all stages of his development, although in existential distortion." Essential humanity exists always-already. Tillich interprets essential humanity psychologically in terms of what he calls "dreaming innocence," a condition

272. Ibid., 2:3.
273. Ibid., 2:29–44.
274. Ibid., 2:30.
275. Ibid., 2:31.
276. Ibid., 2:29.
277. Ibid., 2:32; cf. 2:38.

characterized by potentiality rather than actuality.[278] For Tillich, "dreaming in-nocence" was a nonmoral or premoral state, since Adam does not "know good and evil." He rejected the orthodox insistence on Adam's "perfection . . . before the Fall," which he says "makes the Fall completely unintelligible." Adam is imperfect because Adam is undefined. Adam is a bundle of potential, not an actual human being. Since Adam enters into the moral sphere only in and through his transgression, it was hard for Tillich to escape the slippery slope leading toward Hegel, for whom Adam's fall was a "fall upward"—a necessary stage toward self-realization. Tillich evidently wished to avoid this conclusion, yet it is not clear whether he did so.

Tillich also linked the loss of innocence to sexuality, so that "sexual conscious-ness is the first consequence of the loss of innocence."[279] This line of reasoning brought Tillich close to gnostic and esoteric thought on Adam and Eve. The esoteric tendency was to relocate the fall of humanity in Genesis 2 rather than Genesis 3. As soon as humanity existed in material form as male and female, there was already separation, and for esoteric thought separation itself is evil and has to be overcome (DR 2.11).

There was another way in which Tillich retrojected the fall from Genesis 3 to Genesis 2. Not only the sexual polarity of male and female but also the con-trast between the commanding God and the commanded creature was a sign of imperfection. Tillich wrote, "The divine prohibition presupposes a kind of split between creator and creature. . . . For it presupposes a sin which is not yet sin but which is also no longer innocence." He called this state "aroused freedom," which was somehow neither "innocence" nor "sin." Tillich came near to saying that the divine law itself was sin, a common theme in ancient gnosis. Paralleling this was an appreciation for the serpent, which Tillich said "represents the dynamic trends of nature."[280] In Böhme and Tillich—in contrast to Christian orthodoxy—*good* appears to be static, while movement, dynamism, and life arise only through the emergence of *evil*. Evil can thus be said to be dynamic, because the birth of evil is also the origin of movement and of life.[281]

---

278. Ibid., 2:33. Tillich's account echoes that of Jakob Böhme, which shifted "the fall" from Gen. 3 to Gen. 2—as Adam slept and as Eve was fashioned. Adam fell asleep in a spiritual paradise and awoke in a material and fallen world. Having lost the Heavenly Sophia—his true spiritual bride—he now found himself with a flesh-and-blood woman (DR 5.3). For Tillich and Böhme, sleeping and dreaming are images of the human state that precedes the fall.

279. Tillich, *Systematic Theology*, 2:34. "Again it is sexual innocence which psychologically gives the most adequate analogy" (2:36).

280. Ibid., 2:35, 37.

281. In Milton's *Paradise Lost* (1674; 2nd ed.), Satan's agency drives the plotline, so that the devil rather than God or Christ seems to come off as the true protagonist. William Blake declared that Milton wrote fittingly of Satan because he "was of the devil's party without knowing it," while

Yet Tillich adds that "alone, the serpent is without power" and that "only through man can transition from essence to existence occur."[282] Dynamism requires a conjunction of opposites.[283]

Tillich's eschatology involved what we might call a nontemporal ending.[284] Origen, he thought, anticipated his own teaching that the eschaton is included in every moment of human experience:

> The last point in Origen's theology is the doctrine of the final end of history and the world. He interprets this end spiritualistically. The primitive imagery is interpreted in spiritual terms. The second coming of Christ is the spiritual appearance of Christ in the souls of the pious. He comes back to earth again and again, not in a dramatic appearance in physical terms, but into our souls. The pious people are fulfilled in a spiritual experience. The "spiritual body" of which Paul speaks is the essence or the idea of the material body. . . . The punishment for sin is hell. Hell is the fire which burns in our conscience, the fire of despair because of our separation from God. This, however, is a temporary state of purging our souls. At the end everyone and everything will become spiritualized; the bodily existence will vanish. This famous doctrine of Origen is called *apokatastasis tōn pantōn*, the restitution of all things.[285]

Time is a slippery concept in Tillich's thought. He writes, "The eternal is not a future state of things. It is always present, not only in man (who is aware of it), but also in everything that has being within the whole of being."[286] As Tillich proposed a nontemporal "fall" of humankind from the state of essence into existence, so too he held a nontemporal conception of the eschaton. Such considerations led Tillich to what he called his "Platonizing answer": "Being, elevated into eternity, involves a return to what a thing essentially is; this is what Schelling has called 'essentialization.'"[287] For "eternal Life . . . includes the positive content of history, liberated from its negative distortions and fulfilled in its potentialities." "Life in the whole of creation . . . contributes

---

Percy Bysshe Shelley said that Satan was the "Hero of *Paradise Lost*" (quoted in Bryson, *Tyranny of Heaven*, 20).

282. Tillich, *Systematic Theology*, 2:39.

283. The proverbs in William Blake's *The Marriage of Heaven and Hell* (1793) encapsulate many of the themes in Tillich's account of the fall: "Without Contraries is no progression. . . . Love and Hate are necessary to Human existence. From these contraries spring what the religious call Good & Evil. Good is the passive that obeys Reason. Evil is the active springing from Energy" (xv–xvi [caption to plate 3]).

284. Tillich, *Systematic Theology*, 3:420.

285. Tillich, *History of Christian Thought*, 63–64.

286. Tillich, *Systematic Theology*, 3:400.

287. Ibid. See *DR* appendix J for an analysis of differing notions of time and eternity.

in every moment of time to the Kingdom of God and its eternal life. . . . And since eternal life is participation in the divine life, every finite happening is significant for God."[288] So too "an immanent judgment . . . is always going on in history."[289]

Tillich's *Systematic Theology* interprets the eschaton in terms of "essentialization":

> The world process means something for God. He is not a separated self-sufficient entity who, driven by a whim, creates what he wants and saves whom he wants. Rather, the eternal act of creation is driven by a love which finds fulfillment only through the other one who has the freedom to reject and to accept love. God, so to speak, drives toward the actualization and essentialization of everything that has being. For the eternal dimension of what happens in the universe is the divine life itself.[290]

The idea of "essentialization" has universal scope and includes "everything that has being." All existence finds a place in the final fulfillment.

Often Tillich speaks of the ambiguities of faith and unfaith. No one can declare himself wholly on the side of faith or of unfaith. Each person contains both elements, so that there is a hidden believer in the unbeliever and a covert atheist in the saint.[291] In Tillich's dialectical account, there is a yes and a no for each person. Certain elements in each human being pass into the final fulfillment while other elements are filtered out. All existing things come finally to fulfillment. But to the extent that an existing entity contains elements of nonbeing, that entity undergoes a metaphysical winnowing process separating out being (undergoing essentialization) from nonbeing (destined to pass away). This is Tillich's "doctrine of universal essentialization."[292] One finds multiple lines of reasoning in Tillich's system that all converge toward the final consummation, in which every good entity or good aspect in the universe will be conserved and preserved.[293]

In the first volume of his *Systematic Theology*, Tillich propounds what seems like a doctrine of final *apokatastasis*:

288. Ibid., 3:397–98.
289. Ibid., 2:164.
290. Ibid., 3:422.
291. "No one can say of himself that he is in the situation of faith. . . . He is always in faith *and* in doubt . . . and he is never certain which side really prevails" (ibid., 1:10).
292. Ibid., 3:408.
293. "Participation in the eternal life depends on a creative synthesis of a being's essential nature with what it has made of it in its temporal existence. In so far as the negative has maintained possession of it, it is exposed in its negativity and excluded from eternal memory. Whereas, in so far as the essential has conquered existential distortion its standing is higher in eternal life" (ibid., 3:401).

Fulfillment is universal. A limited fulfillment of separated individuals would not be fulfillment at all, not even for these individuals, for no person is separated from other persons and from the whole of reality in such a way that he could be saved apart from the salvation of everyone and everything. One can be saved only within the Kingdom of God which comprises the universe. But the Kingdom of God is also the place where there is complete transparency of everything for the divine to shine through it. In his fulfilled kingdom, God is everything for everything.[294]

Tillich here sounds like Schleiermacher (*DR* 7.3), who in his doctrine of universal election laid emphasis on humankind's inherent solidarity in salvation. Yet Tillich is even more emphatic than Schleiermacher in stating that not one person will ever be saved except in connection with the salvation of all other persons. Either no one is saved or else everyone is saved.

Tillich saw truth in universalism, since "absolute judgments over finite beings or happenings are impossible." Moreover, "from the point of view of the divine self-manifestation the doctrine of twofold eternal destiny contradicts the idea of God's permanent creation of the finite as something 'very good.'" So "the doctrine of the unity of everything in divine love and in the Kingdom of God deprives the symbol of hell of its character as 'eternal damnation.'"[295] "Eternal damnation" did not exist for Tillich. He appealed to a notion of the human-as-microcosm to argue that each human being is implicated in the destiny of others: "In the essence of the least actualized individual, the essences of other individuals and, indirectly, of all beings are present. Whoever condemns anyone to eternal death condemns himself, because his essence and that of the other cannot be absolutely separated."[296] This is so because "no individual destiny is separated from the destiny of the universe."[297]

Tillich acknowledged that the church rejected Origen's notion of the *apokatastasis* because it seemed to undermine the "absolute seriousness" of the threat to "lose one's life." On Tillich's view, the concept of essentialization mediates between traditional eschatological views and universalism.[298] Judg-

---

294. Ibid., 1:147. "God is everything for everything" seems to be Tillich's retranslation of the scriptural phrase to which Origen and Origenists often appealed: "that God may be all in all" (1 Cor. 15:28).

295. Tillich, *Systematic Theology*, 3:407–8.

296. Ibid., 3:409.

297. Ibid., 3:418–19.

298. Tillich's eschatology is generally much closer to universalism than opposed to it. Yet sometimes his words are dialectical, ambiguous, or simply confusing. On the theme of "eternal death," he asks, "How can we reconcile the seriousness of the threat of death 'away' from eternal life with the truth that everything comes from eternity and must return to it?" (ibid., 3:415). He considered Origen's view that "everything temporal returns to the eternal from which it comes" (ibid.). Yet

ment means "the despair of having wasted one's potentialities" combined with an assurance of "the elevation of the positive within existence . . . into eternity."[299] Within his universalist framework, Tillich incorporated the theme of divine judgment, for "the Christian assertion of the tragic universality of estrangement implies that every human being turns against his *telos*, against Eternal Life, at the same time that he aspires to it." So "essentialization" is a "dialectical" truth.[300] As with Origen's cleansing fire (*DR* 3.7), Tillich did not reject God's "wrath" but identified it as a form of the divine love. For him "wrath" is "the emotional symbol for the work of love which rejects and leaves to self-destruction what resists it."[301] References to God as fire are meaningful in this way: "The appearance of evil as positive vanishes. . . . God in his eternal life is called a 'burning fire,' burning that which pretends to be positive but is not."[302]

Tillich's approach to creation, fall, and consummation seems to be in tension with itself. He held that "the transition from essence to existence is a fact, a story to be told." Yet Tillich's "story" involves no "before" and "after," and it would seem that "story" in any form requires temporality, a series of events taking place through time. Tillich uses the word "fact" in a problematic way to refer to something that does not happen observably or empirically (i.e., "essentialization").[303] Because he denies any necessary transition from essence to existence ("the fall"), it would seem that he ought to deny any necessary transition ("fulfillment," "essentialization") in the reverse direction from existence to essence. So the rationale for Tillich's claim of "universal essentialization" remains obscure. This point is asserted but is not justified. Tillich held to his triadic framework (i.e., essence-existence-essence) without committing himself to any temporal or before-and-after schema. By taking the notion of the soul's preexistence more literally, Tillich's theology could be reconstrued in a more overtly Platonic or esoteric way, and it might then be easier to make sense of

---

Tillich would not commit to Origen's view and writes instead that "both have to be denied—the threat of eternal death and the certainty of the return [to God]" (3:416).

299. Tillich, *Systematic Theology*, 3:407.

300. Ibid., 3:406.

301. Ibid., 1:284.

302. Ibid., 3:399.

303. Tillich writes: "The transition from essence to existence is the original fact. . . . It is the actual fact in every fact. We do exist and our world with us. This is the original fact. It means that the transition from essence to existence is a universal quality of finite being" (ibid., 2:36). Here Tillich identifies a "fact" of "transition" with a "quality of finite being." It is hard, though, to see how a "transition" undergone by some finite being can also be a "quality" of that same being—unless, of course, one is examining all finite beings sub specie aeternitatis—i.e., under an eternal and nontemporal aspect. Yet such a de-temporalizing or eternalizing of human beings is what Tillich says he wishes to avoid, and so Tillich's meaning remains obscure at this point.

678 The Devil's Redemption

his teaching. On a Platonic or esoteric account, the soul's longing (*eros*) in its present condition of estrangement is its desire for return to what it once had but then lost.

As things stand, Tillich affirms a universalist outcome on the basis of multiple considerations (i.e., God's love for creatures, human solidarity, the unity of the cosmos, etc.), yet he lacks a single decisive argument for universalism that is congruent with the presuppositions of his own system. Tillich is not ready to embrace a straightforward Platonic argument for universalism—namely, that souls desire to return to the former condition that they once enjoyed with God in a premortal state. He might have had a stronger foundation for his doctrine of universal salvation if his Christology had not been so weak and underdeveloped. Christ functions for Tillich as a symbol of general human participation in the New Being, and yet, in this exemplarist Christology, it is not clear why Christ is needed to mediate between human beings and the New Being. Altogether absent from Tillich's theology is the gospel note of "It is finished" (John 19:30)—a salvation already accomplished through the death and resurrection of Jesus, to which such twentieth-century theologians as Bulgakov (*DR* 8.6), Barth (*DR* 9.1–9.8), Balthasar (*DR* 10.4–10.9), and Moltmann (*DR* 9.10–9.11) have all borne witness in varied ways.[304]

So we may conclude that Tillich was an inconsistent or halfhearted Platonist who wanted to embrace the full myth of the soul's fall and restoration but could not bring himself to do so. Tillich found deep truths embedded in Plato's myth, and the myth provided the framework for the double transition from essence to existence and then from existence to essence. Tillich's reading of the book of Genesis revises the biblical story in the direction of Plato's myth, taking Adam as a symbol of all humanity and collapsing creation and fall into one. Life in the space-time, material universe is life amid dualities: good versus evil, freedom versus destiny, and so on. Not only did creation and fall coincide for Tillich, but so did law and sin. The giving of the moral law was itself an event bringing alienation or division. Tillich's dualities are only overcome beyond the bounds of space, time, and matter, as human persons are finally united with God's life. In Tillich's system there are many echoes of Platonic and esoteric thought and hints at a Platonic or esoteric consummation beyond the earthly life, yet these ideas are not fully articulated or elaborated.

304. In Barth's comments to his students in 1959, he spoke of Tillich as having a "very docetic Christology, because the Word . . . didn't become flesh." Tillich taught that "Jesus had to die that Christ may live. Jesus had to disappear so that Christ could appear. . . . Not so! Jesus doesn't disappear. That's docetism." Barth added that "at a certain point he [Tillich] ceased to go forward and ever since he has been going round and round in his Schelling philosophy." See R. K. Anderson, "Barth on Tillich: Neo-Gnosticism?," 1478.

7.9. Summary and Conclusions on German Thinkers

In a broad sense, the German thinkers surveyed in this chapter share something with Christian Platonists of all ages, whether universalist or not.[305] Material reality, empirical observation, and historical events occupy a secondary position, subordinate to a spiritual, nonempirical, or eternal realm of being. The German thinkers discussed here distinguish ideal human existence from concrete and empirical human life. Beginning with Kant, and continuing among Kant's followers, one finds a split vision of human life in which the transcendental self takes on greater importance than the empirical self. Metaphysically speaking, this transcendental self might be situated in the past, present, or future, or perhaps in a timeless realm that lies beyond our categories of past, present, and future. As in Origen and Origenist thought (DR 3–4), the transcendental self could be referred to the realm of human origin, or to that of human destiny, or perhaps to both.

Many of these issues seem rather hazy, as in the "half-way demythologization" of Paul Tillich, involving a kind of preexistence of souls, a bodily life, and a process of essentialization that might imply an eternalization of selfhood. Julius Müller for his part resists any equation of his teaching on the transcendental self with traditional forms of Origenism that he disavowed. However one interprets Müller, though, there remains a split in the human self, so that one aspect of the self remains rooted in eternity while the other finds expression in the space-time-empirical realm. Though Müller held many ideas in common with Schelling and Tillich, he rejected the idea of *apokatastasis*, or universal return to God, and so showed that it was possible in principle for a thinker to begin from the premises of German idealism and not end up as a universalist.

Like Kant, Müller was concerned with theodicy, though not in the same way as Kant. To establish a morally responsible self was Kant's driving concern, and Kant thought that this was impossible if the self received the moral law in a heteronomous way. The human self had to give the moral law to itself. It had to be self-legislating. Kant was forced to postulate a free and untrammelled human choice that—on his own premises—could not take place within a spatial-temporal-material universe that is dominated by fixed causal laws. On

---

305. Schelling wrote his first major philosophical treatise in 1793 on Plato's *Timaeus*. About a decade later, when he wrote *Philosophy and Religion* (1804), Schelling's cosmology was still "more Platonic than Christian," and he developed his argument by citing Plato rather than the book of Genesis (Kaplan, *Answering the Enlightenment*, 63). Schleiermacher too was very much the Platonist. Not only did he read Plato but "Schleiermacher was himself a masterful translator, whose German translations of Plato are still widely used and admired today, nearly two hundred years after they were done" (Forster, "Friedrich Daniel Ernst Schleiermacher").

this basis, Kant posited a transcendental self and its transmundane choice or choices as the foundation for the temporal self and its choices.

Building on Kant's premises, Müller traced back all human choices to their root and concluded that there must be some primal, transcendental choice for which the human self is accountable and which explains the moral character that human selves presently possess. Yet Müller was more like Origen in his preoccupation with the essential question of the fairness or unfairness of life. What Müller refers to as humanity's "primitive state in the eternal ideas"[306] has everything to do with explaining the moral contours of the present life. It is not just that people are born in different *material conditions*, one in wealth and another in poverty. It is that people seem to be born with different *moral temperaments*. Since the doing of good or evil, with the attendant punishments or rewards, seems itself to be dependent on one's moral temperament, it does not seem fair or just that moral temperaments would differ from the time of birth. So Müller hypothesizes that moral temperaments are not a *given* of human life but rather are an *outcome* of extramundane choices.

Schleiermacher's tentative assertion of universal salvation is based largely on his doctrine of a singular rather than a twofold divine election—in other words, an election of all human beings to salvation. Historically speaking, this novel approach to the doctrine of divine election had considerable influence on later thinkers, especially in German-speaking Protestantism. Schleiermacher's theology was not only foundational for the German liberal tradition but was also pivotal for Karl Barth's teaching on election (*DR* 9.3–9.5). Substantive engagement with Scripture is hard to find in Schleiermacher's writings, including his teaching on divine election. As far as the Old Testament is concerned, this view of election falls short, since it implies that *all peoples are chosen* and that there are no nonchosen peoples or nonelect persons. Neither the Old Testament in its treatment of Israel, nor the New Testament in its representation of the church, provides support for the assumption that every person without exception is part of God's "chosen people." From the outset of his discussion of final salvation, Schleiermacher assumes a single divine decree of salvation for all and then argues that—in light of the empirical situation—since not all persons die in faith, postmortem grace or salvation must be available. Yet this line of argument begs the question—that is, it presupposes the point that needs to be proved. Schleiermacher's line of inquiry should not first ask, How can we reconcile God's singular decree for all to be saved with the observed lack of faith or conversion among many people? Rather, it should ask, Is there a singular decree of God for all to be saved?

306. J. Müller, *Christian Doctrine of Sin*, 2:425.

Schleiermacher's singular decree of divine election seems to be a corollary of his doctrine of God, which does not allow for *particular divine election* because it does not allow for *particular divine action* of any sort. In many respects, Schleiermacher's God resembles a philosophical Absolute that is cut off from the world, that cannot be grasped in ordinary conceptual categories (e.g., God as "knowing," "willing," "acting," "communicating"), and that, in all logical consistency, should not be said to have *elected anything*.[307] If Schleiermacher's God-concept undermines the idea of particular or twofold election, then this God-concept appears to rule out other forms of election as well. To the extent that Schleiermacher's teaching on universal salvation is grounded in his doctrine of election, and his doctrine of election is founded on his doctrine of God, then the whole edifice rests on a shaky foundation. The doctrine of God is among the most contested areas of Schleiermacher's theology.

Among the thinkers surveyed in this chapter, Hegel is the one who differs most from all the others. In Hegel, it seems that eschatology as such is dissolved into a pure moment of absolute cognition and that this pure moment is already realized in the present time in some kind of mystical or intellectual experience. That, at least, is one way of interpreting Hegel. If there is a universal return in Hegel's thought, it would be difficult to identify this with the ancient doctrine of *apokatastasis*. Hegel seems to affirm a final self-overcoming or self-transcendence of finitude itself. Hegel's eschaton—like that of Evagrius (*DR* 3.10) or bar Sudaili (*DR* 4.6)—might thus involve a dissolution of all distinctions between the finite and the infinite.

Yet this doubtful verdict on Hegel as a universalist should not obscure Hegel's larger significance for twentieth-century Christian theology, which drew on his speculative reinterpretation of Christ's crucifixion, evoking powerful echoes in such later thinkers as Karl Barth (*DR* 9.3–9.7), Eberhard Jüngel, and Jürgen Moltmann (*DR* 9.10–9.11), and perhaps—in unacknowledged ways—even in Hans Urs von Balthasar (*DR* 10.7). To twentieth-century theology, Hegel bequeathed the fertile notion that Jesus's crucifixion was not merely a payment of the just penalty due to sin but a dramatic, world-shattering event involving and altering the intratrinitarian life of Father, Son, and Spirit. It would be hard to overestimate the range of theological thought—and atheological reasoning (in, e.g., Friedrich Nietzsche and Thomas Altizer)—provoked by Hegel's rendition of Jesus's death. Hegel's legacy to twentieth-century universalism comes not

---

307. Just over a century ago, Arthur McGiffert commented on Schleiermacher's view of God, noting that it did not allow for any particular or individual relation with God: "We become conscious of our oneness with the absolute, not through immediate vision of it, but only through our relation to the phenomenal universe, and as a result of the impression of the world upon us" ("Modern Ideas of God," 13).

through any overt adherence to a doctrine of *apokatastasis* but through his account of Good Friday and the later universalistic interpretations of that account.

In the general contours of his thought, Schelling stands near to Origen and
the Origenists. There is a broad movement in his thought from humanity's
origin in God, its movement into earthly and material existence, and its final
and universal return to God. Schelling writes, "Man was created at the center
of the godhead, and it is essential for him to be at the center, for that alone
is his true place."[308] Schelling's devaluation of the material as such—and his
notion of a dematerializing or spiritualizing of material reality in the form
of a "spiritual body"—is also reminiscent of Origenism. At the same time,
Schelling preserves a place for material reality in his account of the final condition. His teaching on the passing away of the Son's kingdom also shows an
affinity with radical Origenist eschatology, which took its point of departure in
reflections on 1 Corinthians 15:28. Schelling was pleased to find in Joachim of
Fiore a teaching on the connection of the immanent Trinity with the history
of God's self-revelation and self-manifestation in history. In this account, the
Spirit will attain to sovereignty over creation, achieved as the creation returns
to the Father. For Schelling, the glory of the Father and the Son will not cease,
but the glory of the Spirit will be added to these. The day of glory is a time of
glorification for Father, Son, and Spirit together.[309] Seen in twentieth-century
retrospect, Schelling in some respects anticipates Teilhard de Chardin (*DR*
10.3). Yet, to a greater degree than Teilhard, Schelling proposes that the final
state of the world will not come without a crisis, bringing separation as well
as union. This will involve a separation of evil from good, and the interpen-
etration of nature and spirit.[310] Teilhard for his part had relatively little to say
regarding evil and perhaps even less to say regarding God's judgment on or
destruction of evil.

Schelling has had an enormous influence on twentieth- and twenty-first-
century Christian theology, yet not primarily—as in Hegel—with respect to
his account of Jesus's life and death. It is Schelling's account of divine creation
that resonated among later authors. Where Hegel was staurocentric (i.e., cross-
centered), Schelling was cosmocentric. As noted above, Schelling, as a teacher
of the youthful Gottfried Thomasius, aided the emerging idea of a *kenotic Christ*.
Beyond this, though, Schelling was arguably even more influential and innovative in his doctrine of a *kenotic God*. In this novel way of thinking, the doctrine
of kenosis was applied not only to the incarnation of God's eternal Son in

308. Schelling, *Philosophie der Mythologie*, in *Sämtliche Werke*, 11:85, cited in Benz, "Theogony," 211.
309. Brito, "Création et eschatologie," 258.
310. Ibid., 266–67.

taking on human flesh (Phil. 2:7) but also to the event in which God created the world. In creating, God had to choose to be self-limited and so to withdraw himself spatially (to establish space for creatures) along with his omnipotent power and agency (to make room for creaturely will and initiative). Schelling's notion of the self-limited God has clear affinities with kabbalistic and Lurianic teaching on the divine withdrawal (*tsimtsum*) in creating (*DR* 2.5–2.6) as well as with later elaborations and refinements of this notion in Böhme and the Böhmists. Contemporary kenotic-relational theologies and so-called open theism are deeply (if often unselfconsciously) indebted to the kenotic approach to the God-world relationship that was largely inaugurated in the later writings of Schelling. Our later discussion (*DR* 9.12) will show how kenotic conceptions of God align with and support the idea of universal salvation.

In earlier Christian theology, divine creation had always been considered an expression of power—indeed, an act of immense and inconceivable power. In Schelling, by contrast, divine creation was an abandonment of power. In the competitive God-world relation that Schelling envisaged, the sheer fact of an existing world logically implied that God was already self-limited. Divine omnipotence was largely an abstraction, since the concept applied only when one was considering God apart from the world that God made. Given the theological trends of the last two to three decades, it would seem that Schelling's intellectual children today are becoming more numerous than Hegel's progeny and that the cross-centered theologies of the mid- to late twentieth-century (e.g., Barth, Balthasar, Moltmann) are increasingly being replaced by creation-centered theologies of a kenotic sort.[311] Correspondingly, the possible arguments for

---

311. A word is in order on Schelling's influence, as related to and yet distinct from Alfred North Whitehead's influence on contemporary theology. While both Schelling and Whitehead offered a challenge to traditional theological notions of divine omnipotence, they did so in different ways. Many Christian thinkers were uncomfortable with replacing traditional views of an infinite and omnipotent God with an essentially limited or finite deity, and so they often opted for the notion of God as *voluntarily* self-limited. Schelling's philosophy suggested that God, in creating a world of free and autonomous creatures, limited his own power and agency as an indispensable precondition for such a world coming into existence. Once a universe of free, autonomous creatures came to be, God from that point onward was forever self-limited. This limitation of divine power and agency was not essential or eternal to God but was chosen by God. Philip Clayton might be seen as a contemporary Schellingian, and he argues that human suffering—and even innocent suffering—is "a necessary consequence of God's creating a universe in which autonomous beings can evolve" (Clayton and Knapp, *Predicament of Belief*, 65). Cf. Clayton's sympathetic analysis of Schelling's God-concept in *The Problem of God in Modern Thought*, 467–508. Alfred North Whitehead, and the process theologians indebted to him, opted for a more radical rejection of traditional Christian theism in which there is no event of God's creating the world, and God and the world are eternally correlative, as luminously expressed in Whitehead's famous phrasing: "It is as true to say that God is permanent and the World fluent, as that the World is permanent and God is fluent. It is true to say that God is one and the World many, as that the World is one and God many. . . . It is as true to say that God

universal salvation have also migrated—from reasons centering on the life
and death of Jesus to reasons centering on the metaphysics of the God-world
relationship

---

transcends the World, as that the World transcends God. It is as true to say that God creates the
World, as that the World creates God" (*Process and Reality*, 348). A distinction between Schellingian
and Whiteheadian views of God may be in the background of Thomas Oord's *Uncontrolling Love
of God* (2015), in which he critiques Clayton's idea that "God is voluntarily self-limited" (89–94)
and proposes instead that "God is essentially kenotic" (94–95; cf. 105, 155, 164, 175, 180). Taken
literally, the idea of God as "essentially kenotic" seems to be self-contradictory, since the biblical
idea of kenosis requires a "before" (i.e., "prior to emptying") and an "after" (i.e., "subsequent to
having been emptied"). God could only be "essentially kenotic" if God had forever been "emptied
out" or had been eternally "empty"—a notion that interprets "emptying" as a state rather than as
a process and so generates conceptual confusion. Less literally and more charitably interpreted,
Oord's "essentially kenotic" understanding of God amounts to a Whiteheadian position in which
God is eternally and essentially finite and correlative to and conditioned by the space-time-material
universe. On the Whiteheadian view, God's finitude or limited power is not subject to divine choice
or will but is simply how God is. On kenotic-relational theologies, see *DR* 9.12.

8

Russian Thinkers

SOLOVYOV, BERDYAEV, FLOROVSKY, AND BULGAKOV

Final destinies! But who does not know that nearly every soul is now infected with a more or less vulgar Origenism, with the secret belief that one will ultimately be "forgiven" by God? . . . One begins to think that there is some sort of internal inevitability here.

—Pavel Florensky[1]

Eschatology . . . is the last word of Christian ontology.

—Sergei Bulgakov[2]

Being is not "all-unity," it is not "organic whole"; it is marked by the abyss between the absolute and the creature; and these two worlds are causally united by way of freedom.

—Georges Florovsky[3]

It is remarkable how little people think about hell or trouble about it. This is the most striking evidence of human frivolity. Man is

1. Florensky, *Pillar and Ground of the Truth*, 153.
2. Bulgakov, *Bride of the Lamb*, 379.
3. Florovsky, "V mire iskanii i bluzdanii," 204, as quoted in Gavrilyuk, *Georges Florovsky*, 105.

capable of living entirely on the surface, and then the image of hell does not haunt him.

—Nicolas Berdyaev[4]

No one addressed the question of Christian universalism in quite the way that the Russian thinkers did. Vladimir Solovyov (1853–1900), Sergius (or Sergei) Bulgakov (1871–1944), Nicolas Berdyaev (1874–1948), and Georges Florovsky (1893–1979) all had something to say on the questions of divine judgment, heaven and hell, and final salvation.[5] Berdyaev's reflections on hell are exceptionally complex. He approached the topic not as a dogmatic theologian but as an independent thinker, free to speculate and to vacillate. Sergei Bulgakov's account of Christ's return, divine judgment, the eschaton, and heaven and hell occupies one hundred and fifty pages of closely argued text in his posthumously published *The Bride of the Lamb* (1945). Unlike Berdyaev, Bulgakov sought to approach eschatology in a comprehensive way, to arrive at definite conclusions and to leave no stone unturned. He discussed such arcana as the nature of the resurrection body, the question of annihilationism, and the possible repentance of Satan and the demons.

Though many Russian thinkers adopted nontraditional views on eschatology, they nonetheless all believed in hell. None of them denied hell altogether, regarded the topic as off-limits, or treated it with silence. The distinctiveness of Russian thought on this topic could have something to do with the historical and cultural context. The twentieth-century encounter with suffering and evil began for most Western nations during World War I and yet did not reach its climax until the evils of Fascism, Stalinism, and the Jewish Holocaust fully emerged in the 1940s. In contrast, the Russians had experienced the untold miseries of war, death, famine, civil war, revolution, and political repression already by the 1920s—the Jazz Age for many in the West. In 1939, when the Western powers at last came to see where Adolf Hitler was leading Germany, Russia had already passed through its forced starvation in the Ukraine and the Stalinist "Great Terror."[6] It is not surprising then that Russian thinkers were deeply pondering God, history, good, and evil during the interwar years.[7] The meaning of the

4. Berdyaev, *Destiny of Man*, 266.
5. On the spelling of names, I will here abide by Paul Gavrilyuk's convention: "I followed the life-time western spelling of the author's name on the assumption that such a spelling accorded with the author's own intention" (*Georges Florovsky*, x).
6. See Conquest, *Great Terror*; Conquest, *Harvest of Sorrow*.
7. As shown in a later chapter (*DR* 10.5), Berdyaev's *The Meaning of History* (1923, Russian; 1936, English) played a seminal role in Hans Urs von Balthasar's 1930 doctoral thesis at the University of Zürich, *Geschichte des eschatologischen Problems in der modernen deutschen Literatur* (History of

Russian Revolution became an all-important question to exiled Russian intellectuals, even if they did not all agree on how to answer that question.

In 1922, about a hundred scholars were exiled from the Soviet Union on direct orders from Lenin. This group included Bulgakov and Berdyaev. One religious intellectual who stayed behind was the polymathic priest, mathematician, and philosopher Pavel Florensky, who died in 1937. In the 1920s, many Russian religious intellectuals ended up in Paris, where, as Paul Gavrilyuk comments, "the Paris School of Russian theology was Orthodox theology in exile. This theology was permanently marked by the trauma of Russian intellectual uprooting and the resulting spiritual homelessness."[8] A thriving Russian intelligentsia continued in exile, bearing the marks and the mentality of an exilic community.

The understanding of the historical process that one finds in Solovyov stood in contrast with that of later Russian thinkers—for example, Berdyaev and Bulgakov—whose intellectual coming-of-age occurred either during World War I or just after the war. Absent from the latter is the sense of confidence and expectation of historical progress that appeared in Solovyov's earlier writings. When Solovyov died in 1900, his hope for social progress had diminished, though he still had no marked sense of radical evil. By contrast, Bulgakov's intriguing reflections on the Luciferian mind-set featured some of his most eloquent prose. Perhaps only C. S. Lewis's *The Screwtape Letters* (1942), written at almost the same time, comparably captured the devil's mentality.[9] Yet where Lewis sometimes drew back, Bulgakov gazed vertiginously downward, straight into the abyss.

Solovyov, Berdyaev, and Bulgakov shared a background in German idealist thought—including especially Kant (*DR* 7.1) and Schelling (*DR* 7.7)—as well as exposure to esotericism and especially the Russian interpretations of the writings of Jakob Böhme (*DR* 5.13). Paradox or antinomy played a major role in these Russian thinkers. This meant that hell could "exist" without a proper foundation for "existing." Among these three, Berdyaev was most clearly influenced by Böhme's notion of the *Ungrund* (Abyss) that logically precedes the personal God and can only be understood as a chaotic, formless freedom, or blind striving. Hell's irrationality was thus not anomalous for Berdyaev. It was what one might have expected, on the basis of metaphysical postulates taken over from Böhme. Ultimately Berdyaev gives a yes-no or "antinomic" position on hell that is difficult to fathom and perhaps deliberately so. Solovyov was an

---

the Eschatological Problem in Modern German Literature), and so set the tone for Balthasar's ambitious, three-volume *Apokalypse der deutschen Seele* (1937–39).

8. Gavrilyuk, *Georges Florovsky*, 132, 134.

9. C. S. Lewis's *The Screwtape Letters* were originally published in newspaper format in 1941, while Bulgakov's *The Bride of the Lamb* was finished by 1939, though "the great cataclysm experienced by the world caused a long delay in its publication" (Bulgakov, *Bride of the Lamb*, xvii).

exceptionally eclectic thinker who drew on Christian Cabala, Böhme, Emanuel Swedenborg, German idealism, and Russian occultism. Solovyov's universalism was something like that of ancient gnosis (*DR* 2.3), as we will see below.

As dean and theology professor at the St. Sergius Theological Institute in Paris, Bulgakov was more concerned than Solovyov and Berdyaev with justifying universalism vis-à-vis the claims of Scripture and tradition. Bulgakov delved at length into issues of eschatology in his final and culminating work, *The Bride of the Lamb*. Georges Florovsky, the patristics professor at St. Sergius whom Bulgakov had recruited, began his career as an ardent admirer of Solovyov's thought. Yet in the 1920s, Florovsky underwent a volte-face that set him at odds with his mentor and superior, Bulgakov. Bulgakov's Sophiology and Florovsky's opposition to it were on full display during the 1930s as Russian Orthodox bishops both inside and outside the Soviet Union became gravely concerned about what some took to be Bulgakov's unorthodox Orthodoxy. Because of the bishops' internal divisions, the theological judgment (*ukase*) issued against Bulgakov was unenforceable as a church decision. Yet this 1930s "sophiological controversy" has shaped the contours of Russian theology over the last eight decades.

8.1. The Russian Background, I: Orthodoxy, Idealism, and Böhmism

To comprehend Russian thinkers such as Solovyov, Berdyaev, and Bulgakov, one ought to consider Russian Orthodoxy generally, as well as the currents of thought swirling through Russia at the end of the nineteenth century. "Silver Age" Russia (ca. 1880–ca. 1920) was a time of cultural ferment that brought an enhancement of interest in religious thought.[10] In Russian religious thought, as Judith Deutsch Kornblatt and Richard Gustafson write, "we see in philosophical form doctrines of sin and salvation, of God and grace, of humanity, history, and culture, that arise from a Christian experience markedly different in its values and piety from both Roman Catholicism and Protestantism." Despite differences of approach, "the predominant dual focus of most Russian religious thought [was] on the doctrines of Incarnation and Deification."[11]

10. Nicholas Zernov's *The Russian Religious Renaissance of the Twentieth Century* made this movement better known in the English-speaking world. For further bibliography on the Russian religious renaissance, see Gavrilyuk, *Georges Florovsky*, 272–90; Kornblatt, *Divine Sophia*, 277–87.

11. Kornblatt and Gustafson, introduction to *Russian Religious Thought*, 4–5. Beatrice de Bary comments that "in Orthodox doctrine there is a sense in which humanity's rootedness in God already exists 'logically prior' to the individual's particular journey to deification" (ibid., 11–12). This rootedness derives from the image of God in humanity and from the implications of Christ's incarnation, who is seen as assuming not just an individual human nature but the entirety of human nature. See the discussions of Gregory of Nyssa in *DR* 3.9 and Maximus the Confessor in *DR* 4.8.

Russian Orthodoxy was and is less centered on concepts of sin, guilt, atonement, forgiveness, and justification than Latin or Western Christianity. Instead there appears to be—at least to Westerners—a metaphysical focus. In the foreground is the relationship of God to world, or infinite to finite, while particular interest lies in defining the way in which creatures come to share in the divine life. The dual foci of incarnation and deification may be linked with a concern regarding religion and culture—what one might call the "incarnating" of the Christian message or ethos into society and the "deifying" of social and cultural forms through the divine presence. In thinking about salvation, the focus lies not on isolated individuals but on the human community in general. Salvation assumes a cosmic aspect. Russian religious thinkers have sometimes spoken of a holy materialism (not to be confused with atheistic materialism) and called for the humanizing or spiritualizing of the animal, plant, and inorganic world through human exertion.[12]

German idealism greatly influenced nineteenth-century Russian thought. This influence extended both to the religiously oriented thinkers such as Solovyov and to the atheistic and materialistic *Narodniks* ("people-ists," "populists") who contributed to the growth of Marxism. Russian religious thinkers with their holy materialism and focus on the nonhuman world found themselves at odds with the anthropocentrism of Kant (*DR* 7.1) and Hegel (*DR* 7.4–7.6). Many therefore turned to Schelling (*DR* 7.7), whose *Naturphilosophie* (philosophy of nature) treated not only the God-humanity relation but also the three-way relation of God, natural world, and humanity. Nineteenth-century Russians wanted to forge their own intellectual tradition, yet they had to start somewhere, and Schelling seemed to offer the best point of departure.[13] Though Solovyov's thought drew on many sources, his debt to Schelling is especially conspicuous.[14] Bulgakov's first major work, *The Philosophy of Economy* (1912), was in many respects a Russian Orthodox adaptation of Schelling's *Naturphilosophie*.

Russian religious thinkers adopted many theological ideas, while shifting their meanings. In Solovyov and Bulgakov, for instance, the early church's Chalcedonian Definition (451 CE)—according to which "Jesus Christ . . . must be

---

12. See O. Smith, *Vladimir Solovyov and the Spiritualization of Matter.*

13. Peter Chaadaev in his *First Philosophical Letter* (1836) spoke for many in stating, "We [Russians] have nothing that is ours on which to base our thinking. . . . We are . . . a culture based wholly on borrowing and imitation." Ivan Kireevsky in 1856 proposed that "Schelling's last system could serve us as the most convenient point of departure" for an indigenous Russian philosophy, together with "religious thought" from "the ancient Holy Fathers" (Kornblatt and Gustafson, introduction to *Russian Religious Thought*, 7, citing Edie, Scanlan, and Zeldin, *Russian Philosophy*, 1:111–13). Kireevsky (1806–56) also called Russians to study the early church writers (Gavrilyuk, *Georges Florovsky*, 124).

14. On Solovyov's indebtedness to Schelling, see Valliere, "Solov'ëv and Schelling's Philosophy of Revelation"; Seiling, "From Antinomy to Sophiology," esp. 75–98.

confessed to be in two natures, unconfusedly, immutably, indivisibly, inseparably [united]"—took on an expanded significance.[15] No longer was it an assertion simply about Jesus; it became a cosmic principle, by which God or Sophia (or Wisdom) "incarnates" in humanity as a whole and perhaps within the entire created universe. In the 1930s, the heresy charges brought against Bulgakov by Russian churchmen centered on such creative theological reinterpretations. The so-called sophiological controversy set the parameters for much of Russian Orthodox theologizing during the twentieth century.[16] Other theological or christological doctrines that Russian religious thinkers readapted were duothelitism (two wills in Christ) and synergism (divine-human cooperation)—ideas that might be used to describe the relationship between divine and human activity in the historical process.

Russian religious thinkers in the modern era were often laymen rather than clergymen. Neither Solovyov nor Berdyaev were ever ordained to ministry. Bulgakov was not ordained until 1918 and had composed his early philosophical writing while still a layperson and an economics professor. Bulgakov's friend and mentor, Pavel Florensky, received ordination but was a polymath primarily known for his work in mathematics. During this era, most members of the intelligentsia believed that the Russian Church was not amenable to new ideas or to intellectual exploration. The talented and youthful philosopher Solovyov raised eyebrows in university circles when he enrolled for classes at an Orthodox seminary.

As noted above (DR 5.13), one author with unusual influence in nineteenth-century Russia was Jakob Böhme.[17] In the Silver Age from 1880 to 1914, Russian culture was eclectic and fluid, in part because of the dominance of laypersons in intellectual life. No sharp line separated Orthodox Christianity from esoteric spirituality or teaching. Even dedicated lay church members and Russian clerics were open to Freemasonry and to the esoteric thought of Jakob Böhme. France and Russia both underwent an occultic revival, which in France took off in the late 1700s and in Russia during the late 1800s. Cosmological and otherworldly speculations gave way to a more down-to-earth concern with casting spells, reading horoscopes, and obtaining tangible results through connection with the spirit world. The occultic revival in Russia has been well documented.[18]

15. "The Definition of Faith of the Council of Chalcedon," NPNF² 14:264–65.

16. A 2005 issue of St. Vladimir's Theological Quarterly reexamined the sophiological controversy: Geffert, "Charges of Heresy against Sergii Bulgakov"; Klimhoff, "Georges Florovsky and the Sophiological Controversy."

17. Z. David, "Influence of Jacob Boehme on Russian Religious Thought"; O. Smith, "Russian Boehme."

18. DR 5.11–5.12 charts the rise of Martinism as a less theoretical and more ritually centered form of Freemasonry in France during the late 1700s. On Russian occultism, see Carlson, "Fashionable

8.2. The Russian Background, II: Freemasonry and Esotericism

Konstantin Burmistrov has underscored the importance of Russian Freemasons as carriers of new currents of thought from the late 1700s to the time of the Bolshevik Revolution. Even as "Russian theological thought suffered a deep intellectual decline," the latter half of the eighteenth century was "an epoch when freemasonry permeated the whole of Russian society and gave rise to a Russian intelligentsia—i.e., the leading social force of subsequent Russian history."[19] The words "freemasons" and "intelligentsia" were more or less synonymous. To be sure, the Russian Masons did not leave Orthodoxy behind, and they sought salvation within the church. Yet *their* church did not correspond to the limits of the official church but was an "interior" or "mystical" church beyond the walls. The Russian Masons' worldview was complex and combined elements from multiple esoteric streams. On their view, a true, pristine, and ancient tradition could be found embedded in almost every religious, esoteric, or philosophical school of thought, yet only the Jewish Kabbalah preserved these elements in their purest form.[20] While nineteenth-century Russian religious thinkers did not generally belong to Masonic lodges, Burmistrov notes that "many of their ideas and pursuits were almost identical with those of Russian Masons of the late eighteenth century." Like the earlier Masons, the Silver Age thinkers were caught in a double bind, sandwiched between Orthodox traditionalism on the one side and a secular intelligentsia on the other.[21]

One of the borrowings of the Russian Masons from Kabbalah was the notion of *Adam Qadmon*, which they interpreted as universal humankind, Christ, or a primal, prototypical humanity that existed prior to the material world.[22] One of the more intricate questions related to the kabbalistic *Sefiroth* emanating from *En Sof*, the ultimate, inconceivable, and nameless reality. Earlier Christian

Occultism"; Carlson, "Gnostic Elements"; Kornblatt, *Divine Sophia*, 1–97. On the definitions of "occultic" and "esoteric," see *DR* appendix A.

19. Burmistrov, "Christian Orthodoxy," 25. See also Burmistrov, "Place of Kabbalah."

20. Burmistrov, "Christian Orthodoxy," 27–28. A document supposedly composed in Hebrew—*A Letter of the Rabbi of Lisbon to the Rabbi in Brest*—spoke of how modern European Freemasons descended from an ancient "Society of Righteous Men," to which Jesus belonged and which was established among the Israelites after the Babylonian captivity. In fact, a Polish Mason, Prince Michal Dluski, wrote this treatise in 1817. How this positive view of Jewish religious tradition among the Russians was compatible with widespread anti-Semitism is an open question. Note that Western esotericism featured any number of documents alleged to be much older than they actually were—e.g., *Corpus Hermeticum*, the *Corpus Dionysiacum* (i.e., writings of Pseudo-Dionysius), and the *Zohar*.

21. Burmistrov, "Christian Orthodoxy," 30–32.

22. Ibid., 38: "Adam Kadmon became one of the basic ideas in the Christian kabbalah of the sixteenth through eighteenth centuries. This concept was interpreted in various ways, but the identification of Adam Kadmon with primordial Christ, the prototype of creation, was the keynote in the works on kabbalah written by Christians starting with Pico della Mirandola." Cf. ibid., 30.

Cabalists had identified the three higher *Sefiroth* (*Keter, Hokmah,* and *Binah*) with the three persons of the Christian Trinity.[23] Yet Russian Masons departed from this interpretation and instead identified the transcendent *En Sof* with the first *Sefirah* and also with God the Father. This idea of an ultimately transcendent and unknowable Father later reappeared in Bulgakov's writings.[24] An unpublished text by Ivan Elagin, a leading Russian Mason, was called *Explanations of the Mysterious Meaning [of the Text] about the Creation of the Universe in Holy Scripture* (1780s). It commented on the chaotic matter preexistent with God and the internal processes in God prior to the creation. Elagin regarded "God the Father eternally comprising the Wisdom-Sophia—as a set of archetypes of creation—and emanating the Son-Word and the Wisdom in the form of Spirit."[25] Elagin's anticipation of Sophiology was remarkable; he seems to have been a Sophiologist *avant la lettre*.

The kabbalistic view of Jesus Christ differed from that of church doctrine. For the Masons, neither *Adam Qadmon* nor the primordial Christ were to be identified with the historical Jesus. Ivan Elagin reserved the title of "Savior" for the primordial Adam-Christ, while Jesus of Nazareth was merely a "hieroglyph" or "acting representation" of Adam-Christ.[26] Burmistrov argues that Solovyov held to a similar view. For Solovyov, both Christ and Sophia emanated from *En Sof*, yet "Christ" in this context meant not "Jesus" but the "Primal Man" (or *Adam Qadmon*). Solovyov's draft treatise on Sophia includes a Tree of *Sefiroth* diagram, with "Christ" and *Adam Qadmon* presented as synonymous and placed near the top of the tree, while "Jesus" is located at the bottom. In another passage Solovyov identifies *Adam Qadmon* with Logos-plus-Sophia, and, in still another, he identifies *Adam Qadmon* with the World Soul.[27] Missing from these passages is any identification of Christ or Logos with the flesh-and-blood

23. See Coudert, *Impact of the Kabbalah*, 125–26.

24. See the epilogue, "The Father," in Bulgakov, *Comforter*, 359–94. Bulgakov thought this epilogue might serve as a prologue to his own major trilogy of books. He asked, "Is the Father not the Absolute, which is hidden from us in the obscurity of absoluteness and which is separated from us by the glaciers of transcendence?" (359). Bulgakov's thinking on God the Father was thus congruent with kabbalistic premises.

25. Burmistrov, "Christian Orthodoxy," 36. "According to Ivan Elagin, Ein-Sof is a repository of eternal ideas and potentialities which, taken together, constitute the divine Wisdom-Sophia. . . . According to his scheme, at the beginning of the creation Ein-Sof/God the Father generates the Son and the Spirit-Sophia" (35).

26. This view of "Christ" as a spiritual principle—not to be identified with the earthly Jesus— was common teaching in second- and third-century gnosis (*DR* 2.3). Burmistrov comments that Russian Masons embraced "a Gnostic concept of the Savior." Yet he stresses that "Russian religious thinkers were unique because they were able to reconcile extreme religious conservatism with an unusual receptivity to alien systems and doctrines" ("Christian Orthodoxy," 50).

27. Burmistrov, "Christian Orthodoxy," 39–41, citing Solovyov, *Collected Works*, 2:57, 172, 382.

Jesus of Nazareth.[28] While using the customary doctrinal terminology, Solovyov seems not to have held to church teachings on Jesus's divinity.

In Christian Cabala, the doctrine of universal salvation follows more or less directly from the identification of *Adam Qadmon* with Christ. Burmistrov writes, "It was on such an interpretation of this relationship that the idea of a Universal Church rested: since all human souls were initially contained within the primordial man (Adam Kadmon / Christ), Christ is always present in each soul. Hence follows the idea of the *apokatastasis*, or universal salvation." He adds, "The doctrine of the universal restoration, rejecting the eternal nature of hell, became the basis of the soteriology of [Christian] Knorr von Rosenroth . . . and the Sulzbach circle of Christian kabbalists."[29] As we saw earlier (*DR* 2.11), final salvation in ancient gnosis and among modern Western esotericists was often seen as the restoration of a primal unity that souls or spirits had once had with God, or in this case with primordial man.

8.3. Vladimir Solovyov and the Roots of Russian Sophiology

The writings of Vladimir Solovyov are generally regarded as the starting point of the Russian religious renaissance at the end of the nineteenth century.[30] He has been called "the first systematic Russian religious thinker."[31] There is a growing secondary literature on his thought.[32] Yet scholars differ on how to classify Solovyov and construe his thought. There are at least three different starting points for interpretation: "Sophia," "Godmanhood" (*bogochelovechestvo*), and "all-unity" (*vseedinstvo*). On analysis, these three concepts intertwine, so that a full elaboration of each one includes the other two.[33] Despite the obscurity of

28. Wil van den Bercken judges that Solovyov evinces "remarkable abstraction" in presenting Christ: "Solov'ëv seldom speaks about the concrete Jesus of Nazareth. Christ is a divine connecting link, the centre of the world, the pivot of history. The biblical Jesus is lost in a philosophical Christology, to which a doctrine on Divine Wisdom, Sophia, is added" ("Macrochristianity," 66).

29. Burmistrov, "Christian Orthodoxy," 39. Cf. Coudert, *Impact of the Kabbalah*, 120–32.

30. Works by Solovyov in English translation include Solovyov, *Russia and the Universal Church*; Solovyov, *Lectures on Divine Humanity*; Kornblatt, *Divine Sophia*. The first and third of these were published first in French rather than in Russian, as *La Russie et l'église universelle* (1889) and *La Sophia et les autres écrits français* (1978).

31. Kornblatt and Gustafson, introduction to *Russian Religious Thought*, 10.

32. Secondary literature includes Florovsky, "Seductive Path"; Gustafson, "Solovyov's Doctrine of Salvation"; Carlson, "Gnostic Elements"; van den Bercken, de Courten, and van der Zweerde, *Vladimir Solov'ëv*; de Courten, *History, Sophia and the Russian Nation*; Kornblatt, *Divine Sophia*, 3–97; O. Smith, *Vladimir Solovyov and the Spiritualization of Matter*.

33. Evgeny Rashkovsky notes that *vseedinstvo* was Solovyov's neologism, a term he introduced to summarize his own thought ("Three Justifications," 34). Paul Valliere, in *Modern Russian Theology*, makes Godmanhood central for interpreting Solvyov and Bulgakov. Evert van der Zweerde claims

much that he wrote, Solovyov is a systematic thinker whose metaphysics connects with his understanding of Godmanhood, his politics, his social program, and his historical and eschatological vision. Some compare Solovyov with Origen because of his systematizing tendency and his understanding of salvation as an encompassing and cosmic process.[34] Others cite Schelling's influence, while Richard Gustafson points to both Origen and Schelling: "What Solovyov does . . . is to restate Origen's theory of Creation and Redemption in modified Neoplatonic terms he borrows from Schelling." For Solovyov and Schelling alike, "the positive is always the whole or unity and that which is contrasted with it is division of the whole. . . . The identical units which existed in the unified whole are in the divided whole; the matter in both is the same . . . but the formal aspect of the two is totally different."[35]

As Solovyov's writings show, he used the term "Sophia" in varied ways. In the *Lectures on Godmanhood*, after he first uses "Sophia," we find a bewildering array of different explanations for the term: "Christ," "God's body," "the matter of Divinity," "soul of the world," "Godmanhood," "Divine-Humanity," "Humanity of God," "the principle of humanity," the "divine or ideal world," "perfect humanity," "the all-one humanity," "archetypal humanity," "the realization of the divine principle," "form of divinity," "one and all," "absolute unity of Divinity," and "mediator" between God's unity and created multiplicity.[36] From this list it should be obvious that "Sophia" in Solovyov's thinking carries an exceptionally wide range of meanings. Broadly, there seem to be three foci—namely, God's nature in himself, Christ or divine humanity, and God's

by contrast that "the central principle of Solov'ëv's thought [is] All-Unity" ("Deconstruction and Normalization," 54). Richard F. Gustafson, in "Solovyov's Doctrine of Salvation," 31, identifies two central principles: on the *philosophical level* "total unity," and on the *theological level* "divine humanity." In "The World Soul and Sophia in the Early Work of Solov'ëv," Wendy Helleman emphasizes Sophia: "Many recognize Sophia as the single most important key to the work of Vladimir Solov'ëv . . . [since] Sophia certainly was crucial for assuring unity, whether in nature, the church, or the state. . . . In nature Sophia represented the inner organic unity of the world as World Soul. She provided the solution to the 'estrangement' or fragmentation characteristic of his time" (164). Since Sophia's role is "assuring unity," this leads one back to "all-unity," and because Solovyov did not clearly distinguish Sophia from Godmanhood, these three concepts all seem to imply one another.

34. Helleman ("World Soul," 166) notes that "Solov'ëv's . . . fall of the World-Soul [is] a primordial event with enormous repercussions. The influence of Origen is evident here as well as in his view of the genesis of our world as the *consequence* of this fall."

35. Gustafson, "Solovyov's Doctrine of Salvation," 33, quoting Schelling, *Of Human Freedom*, 46.

36. Solovyov's definitions of Sophia are summarized in Kornblatt, *Divine Sophia*, 8–9. Boris Jakim—the translator into English of Russian works by Solovyov, Florensky, and Bulgakov—has enumerated the meanings of Solovyov's "Sophia." In his "Translator's Introduction" to *The Bride of the Lamb* (ix–xvi), Jakim offers five meanings of "Sophia": (1) World-Soul, (2) humanity's prototype, (3) a principle of trinitarian self-revelation, (4) a creaturely Sophia in the form of humanity, and (5) a creaturely Sophia in the cosmos as a whole (xii–xiii).

relation to the created world. Ultimately, these three aspects are linked. For Solovyov, God is God only in connection with the world, humanity cannot be understood except in relation to God, and the created world is "in" God and so reflects and manifests God. Solovyov does not identify Sophia as strictly divine or as strictly created, and so Sophia straddles the Creator-creature divide. While this may be problematic for theological orthodoxy, for Solovyov it is part of a deliberate effort to unite God and the world within a single, encompassing whole.[37]

Taking a developmental approach to Solovyov, Wendy Helleman charts his shifting uses of the term "Sophia." In *La Sophia* (1876), Solovyov identified "soul" as "spirit" that has entered the world and functions as a principle of unity for sensible or material being. Here he also posited an anti-divine principle with a tendency toward materiality. *La Sophia* equated the World Soul with the anti-divine principle, the demonic, and Satan. From Helleman's account, we see that Solovyov's earliest writings were "gnostic." He presented a bleak world dominated by Satan and by materiality, from which the soul must escape to find its way to liberation. In the *Lectures on Godmanhood* (1878), the picture became less gloomy. Solovyov identified Sophia with the World Soul and identified both with the ideal humanity that mediated between the plurality of the created world and absolute divine unity. The cosmogonic process was a theogonic process, with the perfect divine-human organism as its goal. The World Soul became united with the divine Logos in consciousness, enabling it to comprehend how all things are interconnected. In the *Lectures on Godmanhood*, the World Soul had some degree of freedom but was not anti-God as such. In *Russia and the Universal Church* (1889), another shift occurred, with a new emphasis on the fallenness of the World Soul. At this point Solovyov abandoned the identification of Sophia with the World Soul. The World Soul was a force of chaotic energy and once again an antitype or antithesis to Sophia. In *Russia and the Universal Church*, the extra-divine realm became fragmented and anti-divine. Solovyov described Sophia as the accomplished unity of God, and, in kabbalistic terms, as *Malkuth* or the kingdom in which God is all in all.[38]

37. John Meyendorff, in "Creation in the History of Orthodox Theology," argues that Sophiology, beginning with Solovyov, resembled ancient Origenism in confusing God's creating of the world with God's begetting of Christ. Origenism and Sophiology, he holds, both treated God's creating as an eternal activity akin to God's begetting. This had the effect of elevating creatures to quasi-divine status. Arianism moved in the opposite direction by assimilating God's begetting to God's creating, so that Christ became the first entity created by God. Athanasius clearly differentiated God's begetting (of Christ) from God's creating (of the world), and so he upheld Christ's eternal Sonship and full divinity as well as the crucial Creator-creature distinction.

38. Helleman, "World Soul," 165–80, based in part on Zen'kovskiĭ, *History of Russian Philosophy*, 2:504–10.

How does one make sense of Solovyov's changes of view and his conceptual abundance? How many "Sophias" were there? Some say that Solovyov was simply inconsistent. Frederick Copleston warns that "we cannot find one single consistent use of the word Sophia, or Wisdom, even in the writings of Solovyev, who is credited with being the first Russian philosopher to develop the subject."[39] Those expecting analytical clarity may be starting with the wrong assumptions. A different question may be in order: Is it possible to locate Solovyov in an intellectual tradition that allows us to make sense of his seemingly disparate statements on Sophia? Maria Carlson demonstrates that ancient gnostic traditions show just the sort of variation in speaking of Sophia that one also finds in Solovyov's writings. According to this interpretation, the semantic scattershot associated with "Sophia" is not something odd or anomalous but is what one might expect to find. The two Sophias—one unfallen and divine and the other fallen and cosmic, separated from one another yet destined to reunite—were a central motif of ancient gnosis. The gnostic-esoteric motif of union-separation-reunion seems thus to have been a driving force in Solovyov's thought.

Solovyov's syncretic impulse also makes sense against a gnostic or esoteric backdrop. He wrote of an emerging "universal religion" that he expected to transcend the limitations of Christianity and all other existing religions.[40] As a proponent of syncretic gnosis, Solovyov's thinking was inherently eclectic and ambiguous. The patchwork appearance of Solovyov's writings on Sophia reflects his presumption of final unity, which allowed him to attempt an integration of all possible religious ideas within a single, overarching system.[41] He accumulated religious ideas and symbols and then blended them together without feeling the need to explain the connections that made this synthesis possible. Solovyov was more an associative than an analytical thinker. He would have needed to rewrite his works to render them fully self-consistent.

Some interpreters resist the identification of Solovyov as a modern gnostic.[42] Yet one should consider Solovyov's life circumstances during his formative

39. Copleston, *Russian Religious Philosophy*, 82.

40. Pico della Mirandola, with his *Nine Hundred Theses* (1486), was another brilliant young man, from an earlier century, who was seeking a comparably ambitious synthesis of all existing religions and philosophies (*DR* 4.12).

41. Solovyov's Christ-centered yet incipiently multireligious universalism recalls the thinking of Guillaume Postel (*DR* 2.7) and Pico della Miradolla (*DR* 4.12), as well as many more thinkers in the twentieth century. L. M. Blanchard, in *Will All Be Saved?*, offers an excellent short account of Protestant pluralistic or plurocentric versions of universalism (181–99) and Catholic pluralistic or plurocentric versions (230–57).

42. See Robert Slesinski, "Solovyov's 'Gnosticism.'" Balthasar acknowledged that Solovyov drew "from Valentinus by way of the Kabbala to its baroque representatives—Boehme, Gichtel, Pordage, Rosenroth, and Arnold—to Swedenborg and to Franz von Baader." In Solovyov, though, this "muddy stream" became "disinfected waters" (*Glory of the Lord*, 3:291–92). In light of the

period in 1875–78: his journey to London to study gnostic and esoteric literature, his purported vision of Sophia, his trip to the Egyptian desert at Sophia's
beckoning, his alleged message from a deceased professor of his, and Sophia's
message to him that he had a great mission to fulfill. In the early Sophia writings, we find references to reincarnation among animals, humans, and demons;
temporary hell states wherein demons expiate their sins and receive salvation;
transformations of humans into angels; assertions of the divine status of the
human self; descriptions of the material world as tainted or evil; discussions of
Satan as controlling the material world; and alchemical and astrological symbolism and vocabulary.[43] Just as decisive for categorizing Solovyov as a gnostic
or esotericist is Solovyov's self-evaluation. He intended to be a successor to
past esotericists: "The only substantial individuals in this context turn out to
be Paracelsus, Boehme, and Swedenborg, so the field remains wide open for
me."[44] Solovyov drew a number of ideas from Böhmists—including Böhme
himself, Johann Georg Gichtel, John Pordage, and Gottfried Arnold—as both
Konstantin Burmistrov and Hans Urs von Balthasar have noted.[45]

In 1875 Solovyov applied for permission to travel to London to study, as he
said, "Indian, Gnostic, and medieval philosophy" and, in the words of Judith
Kornblatt, "to participate in the English occult scene." He attended séances in
London and engaged in automatic writing, during which spirits—principally
Sophia herself—communicated to him through his own pen. At this time
Solovyov famously claimed to have experienced a vision of Sophia while in the
reading room at the British Museum. At the time that this happened, he had
been immersed in the study of gnostic, occultic, and kabbalistic texts. Solovyov's
later journey into the Egyptian desert, in search of further spiritual experiences,
was in response to this pivotal experience with Sophia.

The chronology of Solovyov's occultic activity is also important, since it coincided with the time that he delivered his celebrated *Lectures on Godmanhood*.
Manon de Courten comments, "In a revelation found in automatic writing,

---

Sophia texts, this judgment seems surprising, though Balthasar may not have read them. Balthasar
himself showed his deep appreciation for one of the twentieth century's foremost esotericists
in his afterword to Valentin Tomberg's *Meditations on the Tarot*, 659–65. Cf. Mongrain, "Rule-
Governed Christian Gnosis." Yet a significant number of secondary authors—Paul M. Allen, Maria
Carlson, Manon de Courten, Samuel D. Cioran, Georges Florovsky, Judith Deutsch Kornblatt,
and Dmitry Merzhkovsky—have all identified gnostic elements in Solovyov and made this a part
of their interpretation.

43. See Kornblatt, *Divine Sophia*, 109–63. After completing the essay on Sophia, Solovyov wrote
in a letter to his father in May 1876, "As for my essay, I absolutely must publish it, since it will
be the basis of all my future endeavors, and I can do nothing without referring to it" (109, citing
Solovyov, *Pis'ma*, 2:28).

44. Kornblatt, *Divine Sophia*, 75, citing Solovyov, *Pis'ma*, 2:200.

45. Burmistrov, "Christian Orthodoxy," 36; Balthasar, *Glory of the Lord*, 3:291–92.

Sophia even showed Solov'ev a precise year for what we may understand as her [i.e., Sophia's] actual incarnation: 'I will be born in April 1878.' Out of this last indication we can deduce that the last stage of history was to start in a very near future. We also can see Solov'ev's direct belief in the concrete advent of 'Incarnate Sophia' and possibly his own role in it." The timing of the predicted event (April 1878) was just one month after Solovyov completed his *Lectures on Godmanhood* (January–March 1878). Solovyov's intimate relationship with Sophia becomes apparent in the words transcribed in automatic writing, in which Sophia commands him: "I am that what you are, I am your essence. You are only my subject, my *hypokeimenon*—the thing upon which I lean my feet, my *hypostasion*, this must be your supreme ambition. But I do not want to put my feet on a vulgar object. This is why you have to work and produce great things."[46] Besides Sophia, the deceased Professor Jurkevic, who introduced Solovyov to Böhmism and theosophy, is said to have given a message in automatic writing through and to Solovyov as well, in which he disputed with Sophia over what diet Solovyov ought to be following.[47]

Solovyov's early notebooks contain a remarkable prayer, inspired by the reading he did in the British Museum library:

> Prayer of the Revelation of the Great Secret. In the name of the Father and of the Son and of the Holy Spirit An-Soph, Jah, Soph-Jah.
>
> By the unutterable, awesome, and omnipotent Name, I call upon gods, demons, humans, and all that lives. Gather into one the rays of your power. . . . Most holy Divine Sophia . . . the one empress [*tsaritsa*] of souls, I beseech you by the unutterable depths and grace of your first son, the beloved Jesus Christ: Descend into the prison of the soul, fill our darkness with your radiance . . . appear to us in visible and concrete form, incarnate yourself in us and in the world, restoring the fullness of the ages . . . and may God be all in all.[48]

The prayer is revealing in many ways, containing kabbalistic terminology (*An-Soph*; more often *En-Sof*) and showing Solovyov's eclecticism ("I call upon gods, demons . . ."). "Jesus Christ" is here denoted as the "first son" of "Divine Sophia,"

---

46. De Courten, *History, Sophia and the Russian Nation*, 225–26, 231–33, 236–38. De Courten adds: "In automatic writing, Solov'ev wrote not only under the influence of Sophia, but also of his professor Pamfil Jurkevic, who had recently died. . . . There is almost no trace of the automatic writing fragments in the discursive texts, which suggests that Solov'ev carefully concealed the information that he had received in trance" (226n69). Solovyov's automatic writing is treated in Kornblatt, "Who Is Sophia?"; Kornblatt, "Spirits, Spiritualism, and the Spirit."

47. Kornblatt, *Divine Sophia*, 73, 172. Solovyov's diet was no trivial matter; the physician in 1900 attributed his death in part to self-imposed malnutrition.

48. Kornblatt, *Divine Sophia*, 61. This prayer was discovered by Solovyov's nephew and first published by him, being later republished by Bulgakov (61n96).

suggesting a theologically atypical view of God and Sophia's preeminence over Christ. Also interesting is the appeal for Sophia to "incarnate" herself "in the world" and "in us." The phrases "fullness of the ages" and "God . . . all in all" suggest an eschatological mind-set and perhaps an Origenist vision of universal salvation. The prayer anticipated a number of themes of Solovyov's later writings.

8.4. Solovyov's Universalist Vision of "All-Unity"

Solovyov did his thinking in triads. Everything in reality was to be understood as moving through opposition and a process of reconciliation into unity. While Solovyov criticized Hegel, his triadic dialectic recalls that of Hegel. One difference is that Hegel played it safe by applying his dialectics to the past but not to the future. To the extent that an eschatological element remains in Hegel's system, it is a present tense or realized eschatology and is not futuristic as such (DR 7.4–7.5).[49] Solovyov adopted a more forward-looking stance, and this was a point of contact between Solovyov and the later Russian Marxists. The more obvious influence on Solovyov was not Hegel but Schelling, whose doctrine of "three potencies" involved a process of division or distinction and reunion like that of Hegel. The first and second potencies implied division, while the third potency brought reunion on a higher level. One critic calls it a "trinitarian trick" that "bestows a certain holiness upon everything."[50] Yet Solovyov saw this triadic pattern everywhere. Progress happens: the later state of things is greater and fuller than the earlier. While difference or distinction challenges the inherent, immanent drive toward unity, difference will not in the end prevent "all-unity" from being achieved.

Solovyov's thought raises a question regarding the respective roles of human and divine agencies. He seems never to have resolved the question. Eastern Orthodoxy departed from the general approach taken in the Western church, where Augustine was the most influential theologian in defining the divine-human relationship. Orthodox thinkers appealed to a *synergeia* (synergy, cooperation) of God and humanity, and Solovyov in some broad sense fits into this tradition. Van der Zweerde comments that in Solovyov "Godmanhood is the final cause of history, but humanity is not the efficient cause of Godmanhood."[51] Surprisingly, Solovyov affirmed synergy where one might least expect it—namely, in

---

49. Hegel's philosophy helped inspire the "end of history" discussion that took place with the fall of the Berlin Wall in 1989 and the end of Soviet and Eastern European Communism. See Fukuyama, *End of History*. Living in the aftermath of the Napoleonic Wars, Hegel supposed that Western society was entering a period of final realization or consummation.

50. Van der Zweerde, "Deconstruction and Normalization," 58.

51. Ibid.

his doctrine of the coming of God's kingdom. Human will, effort, and action were needed not only in individual lives but also in order to usher in the collective and cosmic reality of God's kingdom. This seems to be one area in which Solovyov was indebted to Kabbalah. In Jewish Kabbalah, every action of each individual Jew in obedience to the Torah somehow contributes to *tiqqun*, or the cosmic restoration. God's kingdom does not fall into this world, like a stone from the sky. Instead the kingdom is more like a house, built from below, brick by brick. This aspect of Solovyov's thought was easily secularized. The Soviet and Marxist notion of an ideal society created through collective human effort might be seen as a modification of Solovyov's ideas. His stress on human effort suggests that he conceived the kingdom in this-worldly terms and as attainable through humanistic and naturalistic processes.[52]

Solovyov's treatment of the coming kingdom of God as a human task may also be a reflection of his affinity with or borrowing from Russian Cosmism, a school of thought led by Nikolai Fedorovich Fedorov (1829–1903), having as its "main themes . . . the active human role in human and cosmic evolution; the creation of new life forms, including a new level of humanity; the unlimited extension of human longevity to a state of practical immortality; [and] the physical resurrection of the dead."[53] As Solovyov was in the process of delivering his celebrated *Lectures on Godmanhood* in early 1878, he first learned of Fedorov's ideas in conversation with Fyodor Dostoyevsky—though he was not then told whose ideas they were. In 1881, Solovyov met Fedorov in person at the Moscow apartment of Leo Tolstoy. In Fedorov's view, the shared work that ought to unite all living human beings was the scientific and technological task of resurrecting the dead.[54] Mortality, for the Cosmists, was like a disease that needed to be cured.[55] In their exchange of ideas, Solovyov came to agree with Fedorov that the resurrection of the dead was to be a human achievement, but Solovyov held that this would come about by spiritual advancement rather

52. Bertrand Russell, one of the earliest Western critics of the Russian Bolshevist regime, complained that Bolshevism was not merely "a political doctrine" but also a "religion, with elaborate dogmas and inspired scriptures" and characterized by "militant certainty about objectively doubtful matters" (*Theory and Practice of Bolshevism*, 8). One of these terrible certainties concerned the final victory and vindication of the Communist system of philosophy and government—a certainty that could be viewed as a secular adaptation of Christian eschatologies like that of Solovyov. With its this-worldly orientation, Solovyov's later philosophy seems to stand halfway between Christianity and Bolshevism.

53. G. M. Young, *Russian Cosmists*, 4.

54. Ibid., 97–98.

55. The Russian Cosmists anticipated the contemporary transhumanist movment in proposing that human nature is not fixed and that extending human longevity and even attaining physical immortality are legitimate scientific aims. For an overview, see Tirosh-Samuelson, "Engaging Transhumanism."

than by scientific progress.[56] It was to be, in George Young's words, a "resurrection by love."[57] Like Solovyov, Bulgakov too held that human beings would
help to usher in the coming of God's kingdom, including even the event of the
resurrection of the dead (*DR* 8.8). Several key figures in the Russian religious
renaissance of the late 1800s and early 1900s, writes Young, "shared enough of
the concerns of Fedorov's thought that in Russia today their works are usually
included in discussions of Russian Cosmism."[58]

While Solovyov's early Sophia notebook of 1876 displayed a gnostic strain,
his later thinking increasingly embraced the material world. His developed
doctrine of "all-unity" was not some ghostly thing but was meant to include all
realities on all planes of existence. He upbraided Platonist and idealist thinkers of the past who had written of immaterial or otherworldly realities yet had
neglected the material world. When Solovyov lectured in 1898 on the secular
thinker Auguste Comte (1798–1857), his vision of the future had become decidedly this-worldly. Indeed, some see in this late lecture more congruence with
secular philosophy than with Christian theology. While Bulgakov stressed the
theological aspects, other more recent interpreters of Solovyov see his rejection of traditional dogmas and his panreligious and pancultural aspirations as
leading him away from all of the historical religions, including Christianity.
Like Hegel, his philosophical vision straddled the divide between religious and
secular, and pointed toward a final consummation that might be considered as
religiously secular or as secularly religious.

In the 1898 essay on Auguste Comte, Solovyov came near to identifying his
own aspirations for human history with those of the well-known secularist.[59]
"Godmanhood," in Solovyov's own view, was akin to Comte's "religion of posi-
tivism." Like Hegel, Solovyov's writings admit of left- and right-wing readings.
A left-Solovyovian view would eliminate the specifically theological or religious
elements. The Comte lecture is the clearest indication that this interpretation might be compatible with Solovyov's later views. Van den Bercken sees a
basis for collectivist salvation in Solovyov's collectivist rather than individual-
ist Christology: "In Solov'ëv's Christology . . . the historical Jesus of flesh and
blood is turned into the abstraction of a universal symbolic being. In this way
Solov'ëv already anticipates a collectivist interpretation of redemption."[60] Here
we find another parallel to Hegelianism, in which left-wing followers (e.g.,

56. G. M. Young, *Russian Cosmists*, 101.
57. Ibid., 104.
58. G. M. Young, *Russian Cosmists*, 92. Young discusses Solovyov (92–108), Bulgakov (108–19),
Florensky (119–34), and Berdyaev (134–44) as "Religious Cosmists."
59. Solovyov, "The Idea of Humanity in Auguste Comte," in Kornblatt, *Divine Sophia*, 211–29.
60. Van den Bercken, "Macrochristianity," 68.

Ludwig Feuerbach) reinterpreted the doctrine of the incarnation as applying
not to an individual human being (i.e., Jesus of Nazareth) but to humanity
collectively. Clinton Gardner follows this line of thought vis-à-vis Solovyov,
asserting that he universalized the incarnation. No longer limited to Jesus or
to Christendom and Western culture, "'Sophia' was the name Solov'ëv gave
to the fact or phenomenon of God's incarnation in *all* humanity . . . [in] that
God had been progressively revealing Himself throughout history."[61] Solovyov
on this reading sounds much like Schelling—and Schelling's later disciple,
Paul Tillich—for whom the entirety of human history was an unfolding divine revelation. So too, Evert van der Zweerde argues that Solovyov's central
conception of "all-unity" required that he go beyond the boundaries of any
particular religious tradition, including Christianity. For all-unity "excludes
the very idea of orthodoxy."[62]

If Solovyov may be seen as a secularizing thinker, then it is also possible to
view him as syncretic. The early notebooks in 1876 speak of "the true universal
religion" as "a tree with countless fruit-laden branches that spreads its tabernacle
over the entire earth and over the worlds to come . . . the real and spontaneous
synthesis of all religions." This "synthesis," he wrote, "takes nothing positive
away from them [i.e., the individual religions], and instead gives them something
more than they had had. The only thing destroyed . . . is their narrowness, their
exclusivity." He continued: "The universal religion is not only the positive synthesis of all religions, but also the synthesis of religion, philosophy, and science,
and thus of the spiritual or internal sphere in general with the external sphere,
with political and social life. In becoming universal, religion loses its exclusive
character."[63] Here we have a kind of Hegelian *Aufhebung* (sublation) of religious
life into the social, cultural, scientific, or philosophical spheres. Whether this
is a religious or a secular vision is an open question. In either case, it should
be clear that Solovyov's vision points beyond historic Christianity and toward
a more universal human community.

61. C. C. Gardner, "Vladimir Solov'ëv," 112. The nontraditional term "Sophia" conveys the idea
that "*all* civilizations would be evidence of the divine becoming incarnate in the human" (113).
Solovyov cited Comte's idea of collective humanity as "the Great Being" and added that this same
was "unquestionably . . . [the Sophia] that our forebears, pious builders of temples of Sophia,
wholly felt but were not conscious of at all" (113, citing Solovyov, "The Idea of Humanity in Auguste Comte"). The claim here is that Comte's philosophy articulated more perfectly an idea that
the Christian builders of Hagia Sophia only imperfectly grasped. If the atheist Comte understood
eternal Wisdom better than the devout church builders, then it seems that we are rather close to
Hegel's conception of religion as subordinated to philosophy.

62. Van der Zweerde, "Deconstruction and Normalization," 54. "All-Unity implies that any
position, any interpretation may, and in fact must contain valuable elements, the only real sin
being exclusiveness and abstraction."

63. Kornblatt, *Divine Sophia*, 122. The final sentence is italicized in the original.

Solovyov did not present an argument as such for universalism. As noted above, "all-unity" comes about by the joining of Sophia with the World Soul. This raises the question: What does this have to do with human individuals? In the early wisdom writings, Solovyov spoke of Sophia's "children" and how Sophia exists in and through them: "Sophia herself has no material existence except by her children."[64] Yet if Sophia has no existence apart from "her children," then the opposite also applies, and "her children" exist only in and through Sophia. On the one hand, Solovyov's philosophy sought to preserve individuality, as he wrote: "False negative unity tends to suppress or to swallow up all its constituting elements and thus leads to emptiness. But real unity preserves and strengthens its elements coming true in them as the plenitude of being."[65] On the other hand, Solovyov regarded individuality as something that needed to be included and incorporated within a larger whole, and this raised the issue of whether individuals per se were to be regarded as good. Van der Zweerde speaks of Solovyov's "permanent struggle against all kinds of . . . particularism" (*partikuljarizm*). Solovyov commented that "the idea of a nation is not what it thinks of itself in time, but what God thinks of it in eternity."[66] Such a high-altitude style of philosophizing did not leave much room for particular human lives. Despite the theme of "all-unity," Solovyov in fact said little on the question of individual human destiny. He wrote of a final reunification yet offered no unambiguous answer regarding how the reunification would occur. The general emphasis lay on collective rather than individual salvation.[67]

Without doubt, Solovyov contributed to Russian thought a legacy of intellectual *synthesis*—a theosophy, cosmosophy, or pansophy incorporating all truth, whether divine, human, natural, social, or cultural. The pansophic impulse appeared also among other modern Russian intellectuals.[68] A brilliant and widely read young man, convinced of his intellectual and spiritual mission to join together what the historical religions and philosophies had put asunder,

64. Helleman, "World Soul," 171, citing Solovyov, *La Sophia*, 51.

65. Solovyov, *A First Step towards Positive Aesthetics* (1894), cited in Rashkovsky, "Three Justifications," 33.

66. Van der Zweerde, "Deconstruction and Normalization," 44. Van der Zweerde insists that Solovyov was not a "pantheist" as such. While "in the (created) world, there are no other than relatively independent things," Solovyov's point was "not to deny the independent existence of entities . . . but [to deny] the absolutization of anything relatively independent into something self-subsistent and substantial."

67. Helleman ("World Soul," 175) compares Solovyov with Plotinus: "Solov'ëv's free and fallen World-Soul is . . . reminiscent of Plotinus' individual soul, described as ego-centric, focused on the partial, and thus weakened through its attraction to bodies."

68. Consider the not-so-humbly titled books by the Russian esotericist P. D. Ouspensky [Uspenskiĭ] (1878–1947): *A New Model of the Universe* and *Tertium Organum: The Third Canon of Thought, a Key to the Enigmas of the World*.

Solovyov set out first to gather material for his grand synthesis. In contrast to the empiricist tradition, which began with respect for and observation of particulars, he began with a profound conviction of the hidden unity of that which seemed to be separate. One of Solovyov's major legacies was Russian Sophiology itself, which might never have emerged at all apart from Solovyov's writings and influence. Yet Solovyov also bequeathed a legacy of controversy to twentieth-century Christian Orthodoxy. Kornblatt and Gustafson comment that "Solovyov failed . . . to make a dogmatically acceptable description of Sophia's relationship to the Trinity, a problem that he passed on to the other sophiologists."[69] Bulgakov's theology equally displays the unresolved issue of relating the Trinity to Sophia and vice versa. It is not clear that Bulgakov was any more successful than Solovyov was in providing a consistent account of Sophia. Those who followed neither Solovyov nor Bulgakov—Florovsky, Lossky, and Meyendorff—mined the riches of patristic thought and shaped twentieth-century Orthodox Christian theology, without relying on or appealing to Solovyov's distinctive conception of Sophia.

Solovyov's ideas were not well received by philosophers and theologians of his own day. His writings appealed instead to poets, artists, and writers.[70] Some of Solovyov's followers were an embarrassment even to him—for example, Anna Schmidt (1851–1905), the visionary schoolteacher who came in the last year of Solovyov's life to meet him, declaring that she was the incarnation of Sophia and informing Solovyov that he was the incarnation of the Logos.[71] Solovyov regarded her as mentally ill, though Florensky took time to study her writings. Bulgakov followed Florensky's precedent and also studied Schmidt's writings for a time, alongside those of Solovyov.

So far as everyday affairs were concerned, Solovyov might be described as an impractical dreamer. His plan for reuniting the divided world of Christendom was for the pope to serve as the spiritual leader and the Russian czar as the temporal or political leader. Pope Leo XIII, hearing of it, called it a "beautiful idea" but added that it would require a miracle to happen.[72] Yet one interpreter comments that while "there is ample reason for being critical of the pompous and utopian character of his vision, it remains Solov'ëv's great merit, from a Christian point of view, that he stripped the vision of the church of Russian national narrow-mindedness."[73] In this way he helped to "de-Russify" and to universalize Christian Orthodoxy during the twentieth century.

69. Kornblatt and Gustafson, introduction to *Russian Religious Thought*, 13.
70. Klimhoff, "Georges Florovsky and the Sophiological Controversy," 68.
71. Gavrilyuk, *Georges Florovsky*, 117.
72. Ibid., 110–11.
73. Van den Bercken, "Macrochristianity," 63.

8.5. Nicolas Berdyaev and Hell's Irresolvable Paradoxes

Berdyaev was a celebrated thinker and author in the middle decades of the twentieth century and yet is largely forgotten today.[74] When Hans Urs von Balthasar wrote his early work on eschatology, he compared Berdyaev to Tillich and stated that he preferred the former. Today Tillich (*DR* 7.8) is still read while Berdyaev lies neglected on the shelf. In the 1930s and 1940s, the Paris meetings of Berdyaev's Religious-Philosophical Society were celebrated events among the exiled Russian intellectuals, drawing more auditors than the gatherings at St. Sergius Orthodox Seminary. The reasons for the decline of interest in Berdyaev are not hard to identify. From his early years, Berdyaev opposed the Russian Church. He had an anarchistic or anti-institutional streak, and so would not likely have joined any church or organized religion. One early essay was so critical of the Russian Church and its leaders that it led to legal charges of blasphemy against him.[75] Berdyaev wrote as an independent religious intellectual, not as a church member, let alone as an acknowledged church teacher. As intellectual fashions shifted after World War II, there were no followers to speak of nor any church leaders to continue his legacy. There may also be a philosophical reason for the neglect, and this lies in Berdyaev's break with classical Christian views of God. Embracing Jakob Böhme's "Abyss," or *Ungrund*, he held that human and even divine freedom were rooted in something that transcended God. As Paul Gavrilyuk states, "Berdyaev went to the extreme of making freedom a metaphysical principle ontologically prior to God." Freedom had an "uncreated nature."[76] This subordination of God to something not-God

---

74. Secondary works consulted include Spinka, "Berdyaev and Origen"; O. F. Clarke, *Introduction to Berdyaev*; Tsambassis, "Evil and the 'Abysmal Nature' of God," 114–38; Calian, *Significance of Eschatology*; Deak, "Apokatastasis," 20–59; Finkel, "Nikolai Berdiaev." For the analysis in this chapter, the following primary sources by Berdyaev are important: "Studies concerning Jacob Boehme: Etude I"; "Studies concerning Jacob Boehme: Etude II"; *Destiny of Man*, 266–98; *Divine and the Human*, esp. 22–35; *Beginning and the End*, esp. 229–54.

75. Berdyaev's "Quenchers of the Spirit" [Gasiteli Dukha] (1913) was an attack on the worldliness of the Russian Church during the 1912 *imyaslavie* ("name-glorifiers") controversy:

How tormentingly horrible our Orthodox life is. The Orthodox Church does not point to any ways of life, any ways of spiritual development. In Khar'khov *gubernia* they call "*shkopets*" ("castrate") anyone, who is not drunken and who lives a little more spiritually, than what the national traditional manner of life requires. . . . The gates of hell have long ago prevailed over the Synod Church, just as they prevailed over the papist Church. And this signifies, that the Synod Church is not the authentic Church of Christ, against which the gates of hell cannot prevail. The [present] tragedy . . . unmasks the lie of the official ecclesialism, the absence in it of the Spirit of Christ.

After writing these words, Berdyaev escaped punishment in Siberia only because of the political turmoil that descended on Russia soon after publication of the essay.

76. Gavrilyuk, *Georges Florovsky*, 108. In *The Destiny of Man*, Berdyaev states that "freedom springs from an abysmal, pre-existential source" (297).

was so drastic a move that it seems to have undermined sympathy for Berdyaev among most Christian thinkers.

Berdyaev was like Bulgakov in having been attracted to Marxism in his early life, prior to becoming a religious thinker. The watershed volume *Vekhi* (Sign posts) (1909) included essays from younger Russian intellectuals sympathetic to the West but who professed disillusionment with materialistic views and sought to return to religious faith or at least to idealist philosophy. Berdyaev and Bulgakov both contributed to the volume, as former "legal Marxists" who came to affirm the priority of the spiritual over the material. Berdyaev had always had a spiritual understanding of human life and found the materialism of Marxism off-putting.[77] During their exile from the 1920s through the 1940s, Berdyaev and Bulgakov did not overtly challenge the Soviet regime. Instead they pursued a "philosophy of inner spiritual development and self-perfection as indispensable preconditions for genuine political change."[78] After the 1922 expulsion, the exiled Russian intellectuals at first ended up in various European cities, but during 1923–24 the exiles began moving from Berlin to Prague, and then to Paris as their primary abode. With the help of American money and the YMCA organization, which funded the initial Russian-language publications of Bulgakov's works, Berdyaev set up his Religious-Philosophical Society and Bulgakov his Brotherhood of St. Sophia.

To understand Berdyaev's philosophizing, one has to consider everything he had to say rather than focus on isolated statements. The theme of hell or eternal punishment drove Berdyaev into spasms of impassioned yet often obscure utterance. Sentence by sentence, the arguments oscillate dizzyingly, without reaching resolution but generating some fascinating ideas. It is hard to summarize his views on hell, and it may be best to call it a yes-no or dialectical position rather than a simple negation, as one might conclude at first glance. Berdyaev's hell problem derived from his fundamental principles. Instinctively he loathed anything resembling a notion of legal or forensic justice in God's dealings with humankind. Hell, defined as God's justice in punishing sinners, evoked Berdyaev's raging cri de coeur. Yet alongside this was Berdyaev's fundamental commitment to freedom as an irreducible principle. Metaphysically speaking, the *Ungrund* preceded even God, and both human beings and God were defined in relation to this primal, uncontainable freedom. It would thus have been impossible for Berdyaev to subscribe to anything like Barth's doctrine of universal election, since such an idea would directly have contradicted

77. Ironically, the more committed Marxist of the two, Bulgakov, later returned to the Orthodox faith of his childhood and was ordained a priest, while Berdyaev remained in an ambivalent relation to the Russian Church.

78. Finkel, "Nikolai Berdiaev," 347.

his idea of freedom. On the basis of his own premises, then, Berdyaev could neither straightforwardly affirm nor decisively deny the doctrine of hell. He spoke eloquently of a radical and freely chosen independence from God, so that the doors to hell—as in C. S. Lewis's analogy—remained "locked on the inside."[79] Yet he also insisted that hell could not be the last word or an eternal state, and for this reason he expressed some hopefulness regarding the prospect of universal salvation. Berdyaev offered his views on hell with virtually no reference to the Bible. His arguments were conceptually driven rather than exegetically based. In this respect Berdyaev differed from Bulgakov, who in *The Bride of the Lamb* (1945) presented elaborate scriptural arguments to support his views.

Berdyaev begins *The Destiny of Man* (1937) by saying, "Hell is not only the final but the fundamental problem of ethics and no thoroughgoing system of ethics can dispense with it." He adds, "It is remarkable how little people think about hell or trouble about it. This is the most striking evidence of human frivolity. Man is capable of living entirely on the surface, and then the image of hell does not haunt him."[80] Berdyaev's teaching on hell was not that of Orthodoxy, since he treated it not as an established doctrine but as a troubling problem—and a problem without resolution: "We come here upon a moral antinomy which . . . cannot be solved rationally. The soul conducts an inner dialogue with itself about hell, and neither side has the final say. This is what makes the problem so painful."[81] Insofar as hell might be regarded as a moral incentive or an expression of divine justice, Berdyaev was wholly dismissive and sounded like earlier rationalists. "The justification of hell on the grounds of justice," he writes, "is particularly revolting." Both Aquinas and Dante were mistaken. "It is impossible to be reconciled to the thought that God could have created the world and man if He foresaw hell." Such an "objectified hell," he argues, is "incompatible with faith in God," since it would mean that "creation is a failure." For "a God who deliberately allows the existence of eternal torments is not God at all but is more like the devil. Hell as a place of retribution for the wicked . . . is a fairy tale."[82]

Berdyaev judges that the notion of a retributive hell is "borrowed from our everyday existence with its rewards and punishments." He sums up by saying, "From the objective point of view, from the point of view of God, there cannot be

79. C. S. Lewis, *Problem of Pain* (2001 ed.), 130: "The damned are in one sense successful, rebels to the end. . . . The doors of hell are locked on the inside . . . just as the blessed, forever submitting to obedience, become through all eternity more and more free."

80. Berdyaev, "Hell," in *Destiny of Man*, 266–83, citing 266.

81. Ibid., 266.

82. Ibid., 267–68.

any hell. To admit hell would be to deny God."[83] Human beings—especially the self-righteous types—invented hell as an expression of their own vindictiveness: "The 'good' create hell for others. For centuries the 'good' who found salvation affirmed and strengthened the idea of hell. . . . That evil work of the 'good' was done chiefly in Western Christian thought, beginning with St. Augustine and culminating in the writings of Thomas Aquinas and Dante." The result was that "the idea of hell has been turned into an instrument of intimidation, of religious and moral terrorism."[84]

In Berdyaev's reckoning, good actions inspired by fear are lacking in ethical value: "We cannot seek the Kingdom of God and the perfect life out of fear of hell. . . . Such fear is morbid emotion robbing our life of moral significance and preventing us from reaching perfection."[85] While the idea of rewards and punishments—including the idea of hell—appear often in the New Testament and especially in Jesus's teachings, these statements ought not to be taken literally.[86] Berdyaev simply asserts that it is wrong to obey moral rules with regard to punishments or rewards. Neither heavenly rewards nor infernal punishments are valid ethical motives, for "ideas of everlasting bliss and everlasting torments" are part of "a religion adapted to the herd-mind," which "always contains a utilitarian element."[87] On the one hand, while "hell is torture, and torture may force man to do anything . . . [the] things done under torture . . . are not a moral and spiritual achievement." On the other hand, "mysticism which rises to the heights of disinterestedness" has no utilitarian aspect. "The mystics who expressed consent to suffer the torments of hell out of love for God were actuated by a deeply moral feeling." Here he mentions the apostle Paul, the Quietists, and François Fénelon (1651–1715). "Paradoxical as it sounds, hell is the moral postulate of man's spiritual freedom," and

83. Ibid., 268; cf. 297. Like Berdyaev, Bulgakov also attacks the traditional view of hell and for many of the same reasons: "The final accomplishment therefore includes an ontological failure, precisely in its dualistic character: alongside the eternity of the kingdom of God, one affirms the equal eternity of hell. The world is therefore a failure. . . . Such are the stupefying conclusions to which penitentiary theology leads" (*Bride of the Lamb*, 483).

84. Berdyaev, "Hell," 272, 278.

85. Ibid., 278–79. This is another idea in Berdyaev that finds a later echo in Bulgakov: "To frighten theologically is a fruitless and inappropriate activity. It is unworthy of human beings, who are called to free love for God" (*Bride of the Lamb*, 483).

86. Berdyaev writes that "all official courses of theology" speak of hell but do so "based upon Gospel texts which are taken literally, without any consideration for the metaphorical language of the Gospel or any understanding of its symbolism" ("Hell," 272).

87. That morally right actions must be done for duty's sake, and not to gain rewards or avoid punishments, is an idea associated with Kant's philosophy (*DR* 7.1). Yet because Kant viewed the unity of virtue with happiness as the *summum bonum* (highest good; see the discussion of hope in *DR* 12.6), Berdyaev seems even more adamant than Kant in separating ethics from teleology, or good actions from good outcomes.

"in a certain sense man has a moral right to hell—the right freely to prefer hell to heaven."[88]

Berdyaev sharply distinguishes "subjective" from "objective" points of view: "Everything is changed the moment we take up the subjective point of view, the point of view of man." From this standpoint "hell becomes comprehensible, for it is given in human experience." Thus "hell exists in the subject and not in the object, in man and not in God. There is no hell as an objective realm of being . . . [yet] hell exists in the subjective sphere and is part of human experience." "The bad infinity of torments may exist in the self-contained subjective realm. In his own inner life a man may feel that his pain is endless, and this experience gives rise to the idea of an everlasting hell." Berdyaev explains: "The experience of unending torments is that of being unable to escape from one's self-centred agony. There is no hell anywhere except in the illusory and utterly unreal sphere of egocentric subjectivity powerless to enter eternity. Hell is not eternity at all but endless duration in time."[89] He adds, "Hell will not come in eternity, it will remain in time. Hence it cannot be eternal."[90]

Like Isaac the Syrian (*DR* 4.9) and many of the Böhmists (e.g., William Law and George MacDonald; *DR* 5.9), Berdyaev seems to have conceived of hell as a state or condition in which God's love (and not anger) causes suffering for alienated souls: "The torments of hell are not inflicted on man by God but by man himself, by means of the idea of God. The divine light is the source of torments as a reminder of man's true calling."[91] If God's justice sends no one into hell, then why, we might ask, would anyone send himself into such an illusory state? Berdyaev asserts, "It is not God's objective justice that dooms man to the experience . . . but man's irrational freedom which draws him to pre-existential non-being."[92] A mystery remains, yet the mystery lies not in God but in the sphere of the absurd human reaction against God.

On examining Berdyaev's position, a number of difficulties appear. His description of hellish suffering as caused by God's loving presence—"the divine light . . . the source of torments"—seems to oppose his own statement that "hell . . . is the absence of any action of God upon the soul . . . [and] nothing other

---

88. Berdyaev, "Hell," 266–67. Known as the *resignatio ad infernum*, the willingness to be "damned for the glory of God" found a place in the mystics Madame Guyon and François Fénelon and may be foreshadowed in the New Testament in Rom. 9:1–3.

89. Ibid., 268–69.

90. Ibid., 278.

91. Ibid., 270. Berdyaev approvingly quotes from Marcel Jouhandreau's *Monsieur Godeau intime*: "L'Enfer n'est pas ailleurs qu'à la place la plus brulante du Coeur de Dieu" (Hell is nothing other than the most brilliant place in God's heart; 274).

92. Berdyaev, "Hell," 269.

than complete separation from God."[93] If the human self experiences suffering because of God's presence, then it is hard to see how hell can be defined as due to God's absence or separation from God. The objective-subjective distinction might not help Berdyaev at this point, since he seems to be speaking from the objective side (i.e., God's side) and saying two different things. We might also pose a question that Berdyaev does not answer—namely, whether those in the hell state know why they are suffering. If not, then it is unclear how self-correction occurs among those experiencing hell. Berdyaev's inconsistent position on God's relation to those in hell—absent and inactive or present and active—underscores another problem: Does hell as Berdyaev presents it have anything to do with God? From God's view, hell does not even exist, and so hell might operate as a kind of "karma," without God's intentionality or agency. Perhaps the point is simply that those who egoistically withdraw into themselves are bound to suffer until they learn their lesson. In this reading we are dealing with what we might call a soul doctrine, with only a loose relationship to traditional theological notions (e.g., God, sin, forgiveness, Christ, atonement, salvation, heaven, and hell). While there are references to God in the chapter on hell in *The Destiny of Man*, there is an almost total absence of references to Jesus Christ or to redemption. Christ's relationship to hell remains unexplored. Christ's role as the deliverer from hell is not clearly enunciated.

One might say that Berdyaev's position on hell is theologically underdetermined. His discussion of this doctrine has three foci—namely, denying the Western juridical idea of hell (e.g., in Aquinas and Dante); affirming "hell" as a subjective, self-chosen state of egoistic isolation; and affirming that this subjective "hell" could not be eternal. Yet many questions are unresolved. What is the nature of the postmortem condition? Does human egoism alone—apart from God—sufficiently explain "hell"? And how do people exit this state of "hell"? Striking by its omission in Berdyaev is any purgationist idea of postmortem moral or spiritual improvement. Berdyaev states that God's love may be experienced as torment. Yet in most other thinkers who make this claim (e.g., Isaac of Syria, William Law, and Gregory MacDonald), the human self as it suffers undergoes purification or purgation. Berdyaev never says this. This could be because he is so resolutely opposed to all legal or forensic ideas of justice, reward, punishment, or repayment in the relationship between God and humankind. A punishment that someone must undergo for the sake of purification, or to escape from hell, sounds a lot like a debt to be paid. We end up, then, with something inexplicable: a bare affirmation of a hellish soul state that people experience with no apparent reason for it, though it is somehow

93. Ibid., 270, 276.

linked to freedom. Since Berdyaev does not develop a doctrine of human sin or erring, we cannot understand how or why anyone would choose hell. Since no process seems to transpire in the hellish soul state, one cannot say how, when, or why anyone, once in this state, would later leave it behind. Berdyaev seems to assert this to be so, but does not tell us why. His writing on hell is provocative, yet it also fails to answer a number of basic questions regarding human destiny.

Berdyaev is critical of Origen, stating that "Origen's doctrine of apocatastasis contradicts his own doctrine of freedom."[94] Others have made the same point concerning Origen's theology (e.g., Augustine [DR 4.3] and Maximus Confessor [DR 4.8]), yet it is not clear how Berdyaev himself escapes the same objection when he affirms that "hell . . . cannot be eternal."[95] If this is so, then how does this comport with Berdyaev's own radical doctrine of freedom, which he affirms even more emphatically than Origen does? Another issue pertains to ethics. On Berdyaev's view, the final consummation in God transcends human categories of good and evil. "The Kingdom of Heaven," he writes, "lies beyond good and evil and is free both from our good and from our evil."[96] On this basis, the ordinary moral categories do not apply to God's kingdom. And since the categories do not apply, Berdyaev seemingly has no basis on which to offer a moral critique of the traditional doctrine of hell.

The argument deriving hell from human vindictiveness also falls short. First, it is a form of the genetic fallacy—that is, the attempt to dismiss an opinion by giving an unfavorable account of its origins. Unworthy motives might lead someone to embrace the doctrine of hell or else to reject it, and so the issue cannot be resolved by imputing motives to the person with whom one disagrees. Moreover, the vindictiveness argument does not work because it requires that we think of hell as a condition that pious people imagine for other people. Yet history shows that many people who thought about hell spent much of their time thinking about how hell *might apply to themselves* rather than to other people. Rather than thinking about their enemies, they were concerned about whether they themselves—or their family members or friends—were candidates for hell.[97] The idea that belief in hell is simply a

---

94. Ibid., 273.

95. Ibid., 278.

96. Ibid., 293. Berdyaev appeals to a "morality of the transcendent good," which does not "imply indifference to good and evil," and yet this line of thinking remains unexplored and unexplained. Semen Frank, another Russian exile, saw a "Christianized Nietzscheanism" in Berdyaev's effort at going "beyond good and evil" (Finkel, "Nikolai Berdiaev," 359).

97. A poignant account of those who live in fear that they might go to hell appears in "A Tradition of Acquiescence and Anxiety," in Bonda's book *One Purpose of God*, 26–33. Bonda's discussion shows that not everyone who believed in hell employed the doctrine "vindictively" (i.e., against

reflex of human vindictiveness fails as a catchall explanation, since it cannot easily account for the troubled consciences of those who believed that they themselves may have been destined for hell.

Because Berdyaev wrote of hell as purely "subjective" and as something that "will remain in time," it is possible to see him as claiming that hell is essentially an illusory state that exists for certain people during the earthly life and ends at their death.[98] He does not explicitly state this, yet such a way of reading Berdyaev might help to make sense of some of his otherwise inexplicable and seemingly contradictory statements.

8.6. The Metaphysical Foundations of Sergius Bulgakov's Dogmatics

Bulgakov's stature is apparent from Paul Gavrilyuk's claim that he "was the author of the most monumental theological system in Orthodox theology since John of Damascus"—who lived in the eighth century.[99] Bulgakov's writings have had a complex publication history; now seven of his most important volumes are in English translation.[100] He has inspired a steadily

---

other people) and that many applied the doctrine "penitentially" (i.e., in reference to themselves and their own unworthiness before God). A number of Christian mystics, as noted above, declared that even if God were to send them to hell, they would still love God. This seems to be another "nonvindictive" way in which the doctrine of hell has functioned "existentially" among believers.

98. Berdyaev, "Hell," 278.

99. Gavrilyuk, *Georges Florovsky*, 145. One twentieth-century Orthodox thinker who might rival Bulgakov is the Romanian Dumitru Stăniloae (1903–93), who wrote a multivolume dogmatics that has been translated into English.

100. Bulgakov is best known for a collection of early writings followed by two different "trilogies" of works, the former called the "little trilogy" and the latter known as the "great trilogy." The little trilogy includes *The Friend of the Bridegroom* (1927 [in Russian]; on John the Baptist), *The Burning Bush* (1927 [in Russian]; on the Virgin Mary), and *Jacob's Ladder* (1929 [in Russian]; on the angels). The great trilogy appeared under the general heading *O Bogocheloviechestvie (On Divine Humanity)*, and these volumes were first published in Russian by YMCA Press in Paris: *Agnets Bozhii (The Lamb of God)* (1933), *Utieshitel' (The Comforter)* (1936), and *Neviesta Agntsa (The Bride of the Lamb)* (1945). French translations of the first two volumes (by Constantin Andronikof) appeared before the English translations did: *Du Verbe Incarné (The Incarnate Word)* (Paris: Aubier-Montaigne, 1943); *Le Paraclet (The Comforter)* (Paris: Aubier-Montaigne, 1946). Boris Jakim translated one volume in the little trilogy and all three volumes in the great trilogy, all published by Eerdmans: *The Bride of the Lamb* (2002), *The Friend of the Bridegroom* (2003), *The Comforter* (2004), and *The Lamb of God* (2008). Bulgakov's early writings (published in Russian in 1917) appeared in an English translation by Thomas Allan Smith, *Unfading Light* (Eerdmans, 2012); Smith also translated the books on Mary and on the angels: *The Burning Bush: On the Orthodox Veneration of the Mother of God* (Eerdmans, 2009); *Jacob's Ladder: On Angels* (Eerdmans, 2010). Also worth noting is the brief work *Sophia, the Wisdom of God: An Outline of Sophiology* (London: Lindisfarne, 1993). On eschatology, *The Bride of the Lamb* is the most important of these works and will be the focus below.

growing secondary literature and serves as a stimulus to contemporary theological reflection.[101]

Bulgakov was a speculative thinker. In his own words, he "never had a taste for the concrete and the mundane."[102] He never limited himself to expounding official doctrines but rather sought to explore questions that had little relationship to daily experience or church affairs. In Bulgakov, Origen's ancient *zetetic* style (i.e., "searching," "investigating") found a modern exemplar. From the time of *The Unfading Light* (1917) his driving question was, "What is the nature of the God-world relationship?"[103] In inquiring into the God-world relationship, he questioned the metaphysical implications of the incarnation, and the human and cosmic dimensions of Christ's divine-human union in the eschaton. Gavrilyuk writes that Bulgakov was "a metaphysician whose sophiological system postulated . . . unity as a matter of ontological necessity, as already obtaining in the realm of the ideal humanity."[104] This top-down way of thinking is apparent throughout Bulgakov's sophiological reasoning.

To understand Bulgakov, one must take into account his "antinomic" reasoning. On any given page, Bulgakov seems to offer his definitive view on a subject, yet on the next page, one may find a conflicting position. This pattern repeats itself throughout his writings. "Antinomic" is the term Bulgakov applied to himself, derived immediately from Pavel Florensky, though its roots went back to Immanuel Kant's discussion of the "antinomies" of reason.[105] "Antinomic" reasoning in many ways resembles so-called dialectical reasoning. It is a way of thinking through one's intellectual position by means of opposition. Yet there are differences between Hegel's and Schelling's "dialectics" and Florensky's and Bulgakov's "antinomics." While the German thinkers were likely to propose a "third" that mediated between the "first" and the "second," the Russian thinkers

---

101. Important works on Bulgakov include Gorodetzky, *Humiliated Christ*; Evtuhov, *Cross and the Sickle*; Gavrilyuk, "Kenotic Theology"; Arjakovsky, "Sophiology"; Geffert, "Charges of Heresy"; Klimhoff, "Georges Florovsky and the Sophiological Controversy"; Gavrilyuk, "Universal Salvation." De La Noval, in "Fork in the (Final) Road," 318, refers to Bulgakov as "that remarkable twentieth-century Russian theologian who can often be found lurking behind [David Bentley] Hart's theological work."

102. Bulgakov, "Piat' Let," 85, cited in Gavrilyuk, *Georges Florovsky*, 118. Compare this with the comment by Berdyaev, that during childhood he always had the impression that the empirical world around him was a hallucination.

103. Gavrilyuk, *Georges Florovsky*, 145.

104. Ibid., 123.

105. See Gallaher, "Antinomism." "Antinomic" does not mean "antinomian"—a quite different idea. "Antinomism" in Russian theology, according to Bulgakov, first began with Florensky (Gavrilyuk, *Georges Florovsky*, 145n46). On Kant's antinomies, see Kant, *Critique of Pure Reason*, 459–550 (A405–A567 / B432–B595). At least in later life, Bulgakov held that antinomies do not apply to the Logos per se but only appear in probing theological issues from the human side.

typically allowed the "first" and "second" to stand alongside one another in unalleviated tension. This Russian approach may have been more faithful to Kant's original idea of the antinomy, according to which human reason because of its limitations could not break through certain apparent contradictions. Hegel and Schelling both threw off the notion of the finitude of human reason and attempted to do what Kant thought was impossible—namely, to resolve antinomies in terms of an unfolding dialectic of reason that incorporated seemingly contradictory elements in synthesis with one another.

For Bulgakov, the doctrine of the incarnation is not a particular, contingent truth of salvation history, or a specific moment in God's relationship to the creation. Instead, in Gavriluk's words, "the divine incarnation is a universal paradigm of any divine action in the world. On this assumption, an act of creation is an instance of God's uniting himself to his other, to the non-God, to the world."[106] This expanded concept of incarnation has far-reaching ramifications. It implies that God is already united with the world and in some sense is already is incarnated in the world, in and through the act of creation itself. So the question arises: Does the coming of Jesus as the God-man complete or perfect a preexisting God-world union? Or might the God-man be a symbolic representation of a larger, more encompassing God-world union? Such a symbolic view of Jesus might describe Solovyov's thinking but not that of Bulgakov, who held that Christ's coming does not merely symbolize the God-world union but completes it. At the same time, Bulgakov's conception of the God-world relationship is consistently panentheistic, and in this sense Bulgakov is a faithful disciple of Solovyov and perhaps of Schelling as well.

As a panentheist, Bulgakov's tendency was to identify rather than to distinguish Creator and creation. Moreover, asserting that God could not have failed to create a world—and even this particular world—meant that Bulgakov, like Schelling and Solovyov, was ambiguous in his affirmation of God's freedom and graciousness in creating.[107] Lev Zander held that Bulgakov's theological system had its center in the notion that God creates the world out of himself— that is, out of the eternal divine world that preexisted the temporal or material world.[108] Zander's critique coheres with that of Bulgakov's younger colleague

106. Gavrilyuk, Georges Florovsky, 145–46.

107. Bulgakov rejected the idea of "possible worlds," and this heightened his difficulties in affirming divine freedom. Since one could not speak of other possible worlds or alternative worlds, when Bulgakov said that God had to create a world, he meant in effect that God had to create this world. To reconcile this assertion with divine freedom, he argued—like Schelling—that God's nature was inherently creative and that when God acted in accordance with his nature God was acting freely. For further elaboration on this theme, see DR, 833n367, and Gallaher's Freedom and Necessity in Modern Trinitarian Theology.

108. Gavrilyuk, Georges Florovsky, 146, citing Zander, Bog i mir, 1:276.

and critic, Georges Florovsky, who turned the patristic doctrine of creation into a conceptual bulwark in opposing Bulgakov's thought. Florovsky's seminal essay "Creation and Creaturehood" (1928), originally presented in Berdyaev's Paris seminar, did not explicitly name Bulgakov. Yet that may have been due to personal factors: Bulgakov, after all, was Florovsky's boss at the seminary. Moreover, Bulgakov had recruited Florovsky for the seminary post in patristics, so any public criticism of Bulgakov by Florovsky might have reflected poorly on Florovsky himself. Though "Creation and Creaturehood" was couched as a treatise in patristic interpretation, the piece clearly rebutted sophiological views of the God-world relationship. John Meyendorff's 1983 essay on creation in Orthodoxy extended this line of thought from Florovsky's 1928 essay, and the later essay targeted Bulgakov, Florensky, and Russian Sophiology for criticism.[109]

Like Solovyov before him, Bulgakov offered a wide range of statements regarding "Sophia." "Divine Sophia" is "the eternal proto-ground of the world," while "creaturely Sophia" is "the divine force of the life of creation."[110] "Sophiology," he wrote, "is not only a doctrine of ideas as the prototypes of things but primarily a doctrine of the self-revelation of the Holy Trinity, and only subsequently of the revelation of the Holy Trinity in creation."[111] Bulgakov's thinking on God began from the speculative notion that God must reveal himself to himself, even apart from creation. This self-revelation of God—by God, to God, and for God—occurred through the medium of the nonhypostatic divine Sophia. This way of thinking is not a part of traditional trinitarian theology, nor required by it, and seems to emerge from the esoteric tradition of an ultimately abstract and unknowable God-beyond-God (e.g., Eckhart's *Gottheit*) that becomes revealed and hence knowable by a process of self-delimitation. Böhme—whom Solovyov and Bulgakov both read intensively—may be in the background with his idea of Sophia or Wisdom as the "spotless mirror" in which God is reflected to God, and becomes knowable and known to God (*DR* 5.3). Schelling too (*DR* 7.7), greatly influenced by Böhme, spoke of God as positing himself beyond himself, in order to become known by himself.

Bulgakov's doctrine of God thus sat uneasily alongside the trinitarian theology of the trihypostatic deity. He wrote, "The Absolute becomes God, and God is a relative conception: God is such for another, for creation, whereas in itself the Absolute is not God. This self-relativization of the Absolute is the sacrifice

---

109. Meyendorff, "Creation." Florovsky noted that his encounter with Pavel Florensky drove him to focus on the doctrine of creation (Gavrilyuk, *Georges Florovsky*, 146).

110. Bulgakov, *Bride of the Lamb*, 19.

111. Ibid., 26.

of God's love for this *other*, which He himself creates."[112] God (as Absolute) had to become God (as relative), and this took place through God's creating. The logical starting point was the abstract impersonal principle that Bulgakov calls "the Absolute." Kabbalistic thought (*DR* 2.5) also started from a divine principle that was nonhypostatic (i.e., impersonal) rather than hypostatic (i.e., personal). Bulgakov's epilogue on "the Father" at the end of his treatise on the Holy Spirit traces out the logic of transition from abstract divinity to concrete God, or impersonal to personal deity, with particular clarity.[113] Speaking of the impersonal, abstract deity as "the Absolute" and linking this to the first hypostasis, the appendix begins by propounding "the Father" as nonhypostatic. The appendix ends by reversing this and declaring, "The Absolute *loves*. He is the Father."[114] An "Absolute" that "loves" is, by definition, no longer "Absolute." It is related to something beyond itself.

Bulgakov was thus preoccupied with defining an antinomics of the Absolute—what Brandon Gallaher and Irina Kukota refer to as "the dialectic of God-in-himself and [God] in revelation to himself."[115] Throughout his corpus, he struggled to bring together God's impersonal and personal aspects, or, as he termed them, the "hypostatic and nonhypostatic." This became a crucial and controversial issue in his Sophiology. In his earlier writing *The Unfading Light* (1917), Bulgakov identified Sophia as a "fourth hypostasis."[116] Later on, in defense of his own views, he engaged in some metaphysical hairsplitting by distinguishing "hypostasis" from "hypostasicity," where the latter term denoted not hypostatic existence as such but the capacity to become hypostatic.[117]

112. Bulgakov, *Comforter*, 219. This particular quotation could have come from Schelling; it closely follows the thinking of the German philosopher.

113. Ibid., 359–94.

114. Ibid., 394.

115. Gallaher and Kukota, "Protopresbyter Sergii Bulgakov," 7. For more on this translated essay, see n. 117 below.

116. Bulgakov, *Unfading Light*, 217–18. Bulgakov writes concerning Sophia: "Of course she is *different* from the Hypostases of the Holy Trinity, and is a special hypostasis, of a different order, a fourth hypostasis. She does not participate in the inner-divine life, *she is not God*, and that is why she does not convert the trihypostaseity into a tetrahypostaseity, the trinity into a quaternity. But she is the beginning of new, creaturely, multihypostaseity" (217). He also states: "'The fourth hypostasis,' by taking into itself the revelation of the Divine mysteries, introduces *through itself and for itself*, a distinction, an order, an internal sequence in the life of the Divine Triunity" (218). These statements and others in Bulgakov's writings generated confusion among Bulgakov's readers, since he used the phrase "fourth hypostasis" while also denying that Sophia is divine. The second quotation is equally puzzling, inasmuch as it suggests that Sophia (though not divine) introduces "distinction" or "order" into the Triune God.

117. A revised and annotated version of A. F. Dobbie Bateman's 1932 translation of Bulgakov's metaphysically intricate essay "Hypostasis and Hypostaticity" is provided by Brandon Gallaher and Irina Kukota in "Protopresbyter Sergii Bulgakov." As Gallaher and Kukota indicate, the essay "was primarily produced as a dogmatic clarification of the controversial expression 'fourth hypostasis,'

The concept of "hypostasicity" remains obscure and scholars have not agreed on how to render Bulgakov's Russian term into English.[118] Bulgakov's early Russian readers often said they did not understand his theology. Professional theologians in England were baffled. In 1935, the Oxford University scholar B. J. Kidd commented that "it all seems so weird and mystifying," while N. P. Williams, holder of a theology chair at Oxford, commented that Bulgakov's language "about Sophia certainly seems very wild and semi-gnostic in sound."[119]

One might ask: What is the point? Why did Bulgakov find it necessary to complement traditional trinitarian theology with a new set of sophiological concepts—"Sophia," "divine world," "hypostaticity," and so on? The answer seems to be that Bulgakov needed these additional concepts in order to mediate between God as Trinity in traditional terms and his nontraditional idea of God as Absolute/Relative, which was a legacy of both esoteric (e.g., Böhme) and idealist (e.g., Schelling) thinkers. For idealist thinkers like Schelling the essential question concerning God is how the infinite relates to the finite, or how the absolute becomes relative. Traditional Christian thinkers speculated on different questions such as how or why God became human (Anselm). Yet this is not the same question as how or why the Absolute became relative. The superadded concepts in Bulgakov's theology were necessary because of his prior commitment to a view of God that included the absolute-to-relative transition as key to defining God's relation to the world. If Bulgakov had abandoned his initial premise—God as the Absolute—this theology might have been much simpler. But he did not.

In the opening section of *The Bride of the Lamb*, Bulgakov lays down an ontological foundation for his eschatology by first reviewing past thinkers from ancient times onward in terms of their conception of the God-world

---

that he had used to describe Sophia in his 1917 work of philosophical theology . . . *The Unfading Light*" (5–6). They add that "Bulgakov was also responding to the general bafflement of readers when they encountered his 'system'" (6–7). Yet Bulgakov's clarifying essay did not add much clarity, for "with its dizzyingly dense passages" it "fails miserably as a 'catechesis'" (7).

118. Gallaher and Kukota render the Russian term as "hypostasicity," while theologian Rowan Williams uses "hypostaseity," and translator Boris Jakim favors "hypostatizedness" ("Protopresbyter Sergii Bulgakov," 14, citing R. Williams, *Sergii Bulgakov*, 165; Jakim, "Translator's Introduction," xvi). The translations by Gallaher and Kukota and by Jakim seem to be opposed in meaning. If Sophia has "hypostasicity" (à la Gallaher and Kukota), then this term suggests the capacity for Sophia to become a hypostasis or hypostasized. Conversely, if Sophia has "hypostatizedness" (à la Jakim), then this term suggests that Sophia has already become a hypostasis. Part of the confusion in interpreting Bulgakov may lie in the fact that he presented Sophia as both intra-divine and extra-divine. The primary theological objection was to a "fourth hypostasis" in God, and not so much to Sophia as a created or creaturely hypostasis.

119. Gallaher and Kukota, "Protopresbyter Sergii Bulgakov," 10–11.

relationship.[120] Bulgakov generally preferred Plato to Aristotle. Yet he also wished to reconcile Plato with Aristotle. Taken together, Platonism and Aristotelianism were what Bulgakov called "the old testament in paganism." Both Plato and Aristotle were sources to be read and absorbed into Christian theology and Sophiology in particular.[121] Rather audaciously, Bulgakov evaluates all his predecessors in terms of their relation to his own sophiological project. "Aristotle's philosophy turns out to be . . . tangled in sophiological contradictions." Origen too showed only "the beginnings of sophiology" since he mistakenly identified Sophia with the Logos. "The fundamental sin of his [Origen's] theology" was "the failure to differentiate Sophia in God."[122] On this basis, Bulgakov judges that all previous theologians were in error. "Patristic sophiology is unfinished" since there existed "a kind of sophiological ambiguity." Even Gregory Palamas's "doctrine of energies" was "essentially an unfinished sophiology."[123] Bulgakov wishes, then, to complete what Plato, Aristotle, Origen, Gregory of Nyssa, Gregory Palamas, and other thinkers before him left incomplete. He admits that he differs from the church fathers generally in distinguishing Logos from Sophia: "Logos as the second hypostasis is not identical with Sophia, the nonhypostatic divinity in God. Sophia here is the self-revelation of the entire Holy Trinity."[124]

Bulgakov's *The Bride of the Lamb* contains an attack on the idea of God as "cause" and on those thinkers, especially Aristotle and Aquinas, who promoted this error. "God is *not* the cause of the world," asserts Bulgakov.[125] Rather than an idea of creation, Aristotle presented "the idea of God's all-permeating causality."[126] Thomas Aquinas is blamed for continuing Aristotle's tradition on divine causality. Bulgakov prefers Platonic notions of participation to Aristotelian conceptions of causality. He argues that Aquinas took over Aristotle's deity but did not essentially modify it in light of the Christian doctrine of creation.[127] He even accuses Aquinas of pantheism: "The creative act is . . . defined in the spirit of emanative pantheism, while . . . subsumed under the category of causality."[128]

120. Bulgakov, *Bride of the Lamb*, 3–123 ("Creator and Creation").
121. Ibid., 14. In the fifteenth century, Pico della Mirandola (*DR* 4.12) attempted his own reconciliation of Plato and Aristotle in *Of Being and Unity* (*De ente et uno*).
122. Bulgakov, *Bride of the Lamb*, 13, 15.
123. Ibid., 18.
124. Ibid., 16.
125. Ibid., 35.
126. Ibid., 11.
127. Ibid., 19–24.
128. Ibid., 27. See also p. 21: "This purely pantheistic, Aristotelian definition of the relation between God and the world." Part of the disagreement with Aquinas may derive from Bulgakov's idea that effects remain immanent to their causes—a view one finds in Proclus: "Every effect remains in its cause, proceeds from it, and reverts upon it" (*Elements of Theology*, 39 [prop. 35]). Yet

Bulgakov finds hints of Sophiology in Aquinas, in a notion of a "proto-source in God" that is distinct from "the multiplicity of ideas in creation"—that is, a rudimentary distinction of divine Sophia from creaturely Sophia.[129] In the end, though, Aquinas was a failed sophiologist, just like Plato, Aristotle, Origen, and Gregory Palamas.[130]

Along with his attack on ideas of causality in relation to God, Bulgakov also rejects the notion of unrealized ideas within God. Aquinas's principle of *scientia Dei causa rerum* (the knowledge of God is the cause of things) implied that all these possibilities or ideas of possible worlds would need to be realized.[131] Bulgakov's underlying problem is with God's *contingency* in creating: "Scholastic theology . . . affirms that the existence of this world is only *one* of the possibilities, alongside which other worlds or other states of this world are possible. The element of accident or divine arbitrariness is brought into the very heart of the dogma of the creation of the world." He calls it "this dishonorable doctrine of accident and arbitrariness in God."[132] One implication of Bulgakov's argumentation is that creatures have always existed. If they did not always exist, then there would necessarily be some kind of transition in God, from not being a Creator to being a Creator—and for Bulgakov this is unthinkable. When Jesus in his final (or "high-priestly") prayer spoke of being with the Father "before the world was" (John 17:5), this "cannot be understood literally" since "that would introduce time into the divine being."[133] Bulgakov adopts Origen's view that God always was and that creatures always were as well.[134]

Bulgakov strikes an odd note in charging Aquinas with pantheism, especially since Bulgakov himself so often describes the God-world relationship in unitive terms.

129. Bulgakov, *Bride of the Lamb*, 25.

130. Bulgakov came down hard on the French Thomists, some of whom were his contemporaries in Paris during the 1930s and 1940s. He mentions Reginald Garrigou-Lagrange's *Dieu, son existence et sa nature: Solution thomiste des antinomies agnostique* (Paris: Beauchesne, 1914) and Théodore de Regnon's *La métaphysique des causes d'après Saint Thomas et Albert le Grand* (Paris: Retaux-Bray, 1886) (*Bride of the Lamb*, 34n16). Bulgakov attacks Aquinas for enmeshing God in the sphere of "mechanistic" causality. Yet since Bulgakov argues that God made himself "correlative" with the world, so as to be affected by it, it is not clear how Bulgakov escapes the criticisms he directs against Thomas Aquinas and the Thomists.

131. Bulgakov, *Bride of the Lamb*, 26.

132. Ibid., 29–30.

133. Ibid., 397.

134. Origen insists that creatures existed eternally (see DR 3.6), for "we cannot even call God almighty if there are none over whom he can exercise his power. Accordingly, to prove that God is almighty we must assume the existence of the universe." Origen rejects the idea of a temporal creation, implying something "non-existent at first but coming into existence afterwards." See Origen, *On First Principles* 1.2.9 (PA 142–44; Butterworth, 23); cf. *On First Principles* 1.4.3 (PA 188; Butterworth, 42).

What Bulgakov proposes instead of causality and divine choice is a doctrine of necessity in God. He states that "God's creative act . . . is just as necessary a self-determination of God as His being. . . . If God created the world, this means that he would not have refrained from creating it. . . . Having in himself the power of creation, God cannot fail to be the Creator."[135] This is because "creation enters into the divine life with all the force of 'necessity,'" so that "freedom . . . in God is completely identical with 'necessity.'"[136] This view appeared earlier in Hegel and Schelling. "Freedom" is the fulfillment of one's own nature. To follow the dictates of one's nature—and even to do so necessarily—is to act freely. On this basis, God has no "will" in the usual sense. In God "there is no place for acts of willing and therefore a willing will," since "for the divine fullness and autonomy of God's will *there is nothing to desire*, for this will has all."[137] Like Origen, the Origenists, and esoteric thinkers generally, Bulgakov distinguishes two phases in God's creating. The primary creation was the intelligible sphere of creation, while the secondary creation pertained to the bodily realm. In Genesis 1:1, where we read that "God created the heavens and the earth," the term "heaven can mean not only the angelic world as a specific *part* of creation but also the intelligent world of creaturely proto-essences."[138] Bulgakov often affirms that spirit holds primacy over matter. In "a healthy ontology . . . the true substance of matter as universal reality is spirit."[139]

As a professed *panentheist*, Bulgakov seeks to maintain both unity and distinction between God and the world. In some sense he insists that unity has priority over distinction, or, at any rate, that the theologian's first task is to seek out unity before inquiring into diversity, as he states in *The Bride of the Lamb*. This approach contrasts with that of many other theologians, less speculative in character, for whom the Creator-creature distinction is foundational in character.[140] Brandon Gallaher and Irina Kukota raise the question of the God-world relationship in Bulgakov by referring back to Solovyov's "divine world" idea: "The notion of a 'divine world' or nature in God comes from Vladimir Solov'ev . . . but the idea ultimately is a development of the notion (found in Eckhart, Boehme, and Schelling) that identified . . . an *Urgottheit* and *Urgrund* out of which arises

135. Bulgakov, *Bride of the Lamb*, 31.
136. Ibid., 32.
137. Ibid.
138. Ibid., 17.
139. Ibid., 447.
140. Christian theologians who might be classified as antispeculative include Irenaeus, Athanasius, John Chrysostom, Augustine, John of Damascus, Aquinas, Luther, Calvin, John Henry Newman, Karl Barth (for the most part), Thomas Torrance, and—among the Russians—Georges Florovsky, Vladimir Lossky, and John Meyendorff.

both God and the world."[141] The idea of an emerging or evolving God is foreign to historic Christian teaching. Even more alien is the notion that something exists beyond the personal or trinitarian deity—for example, "nature," "divine world," "God beyond God," *Gottheit*, or *Ungrund*—from which the personal or known God emerges. In esotericism, however, this idea is familiar.

When Bulgakov wrote of the "divine world," he was invoking a cohesive set of esoteric ideas, drawn from a number of authors who influenced him, including the Kabbalists (*DR* 2.5), Böhme (*DR* 5.3), Schelling (*DR* 7.7), and Solovyov (*DR* 8.3–8.4). If we equate "divine world" with a preexistent *plērōma*, then Bulgakov's theology begins to look gnostic. Alternatively, this teaching might be viewed as pantheistic if we view creatures as identical in essence with their corresponding ideas in the "divine world." How do the creatures subsist? If the answer is to point to the "divine world" and to see the idea of each creature in that realm as true reality, then the ideal world of divine ideas overshadows and eclipses the material world. Everything genuinely real is actually divine and vice versa. Another question arises: How different are the personal God and the created world from each other if both the personal God and the created world are derived realities and both of them have a common source (i.e., the Absolute)?

In *The Bride of the Lamb*, Bulgakov touches on polytheism and yet does not condemn it outright. Instead he distinguishes a legitimate from an illegitimate form, commenting that "when polytheism is understood as creaturely hierarchies or as an intelligent heaven it receives a relatively legitimate interpretation."[142] Such tolerance toward polytheism suggests that Bulgakov was willing to accept plurality in the sphere of the divine. Yet some other Russian thinkers may have gone further than Bulgakov himself did in embracing divine plurality. Bulgakov criticized Florensky not simply for attributing plurality to God but also for affirming that divine ideas are themselves living entities, which Bulgakov saw as a form of rank or overt polytheism. Pavel Florensky's notion of "ideas as living beings" made "the world of ideas into an Olympus" and so introduced "polytheism."[143]

8.7. Bulgakov and Florovsky in the Sophiological Debate

The sophiological controversy of the 1930s did much to set the terms of twentieth-century Orthodox theology. Many works by prominent Russian

---

141. Gallaher and Kukota, "Protopresbyter Sergii Bulgakov," 26n36.

142. Bulgakov, *Bride of the Lamb*, 5.

143. Ibid., 8n2. As we will see, Bulgakov's assertion of the divinity of the human self suggests that he too may have attributed plurality to God.

Orthodox thinkers—including Georges Florovsky, John Meyendorff, and Vladimir Lossky—were composed either directly or indirectly in response to Bulgakov. Meyendorff claimed that Florovsky in his earlier career wrote very little that *was not* implicitly directed against Bulgakov.[144] Vladimir Lossky, who opposed Bulgakov in the midst of the sophiological debate, later published a midcentury classic called *The Mystical Theology of the Eastern Church* (1957). Lossky's arguments that God is known only to the extent that God reveals himself to humanity, and that the essence of God remains ultimately unknowable, might seem like theological abstractions. Yet these points were directed against what Lossky saw as the illegitimate overreach of the sophiologists in probing into the inner mysteries of God. Florovsky was not openly critical of Bulgakov and Sophiology generally, as were Lossky in midcentury and Meyendorff a generation later. Yet all these figures shared an antipathy to what they saw as the speculative excesses in Sophiology. Before considering Bulgakov's views on eschatology, we will examine the course of the sophiological controversy. The larger question of Sophiology is directly pertinent to an assessment of Bulgakov's theology as a whole, so a brief account of the controversy will be presented here.[145]

Following the exile of Russian intellectuals from the Soviet Union in 1922, St. Sergius Orthodox Theological Institute opened its doors in Paris in 1925. This institution—where Bulgakov was dean and Florovsky taught—became the locus of an unspoken, implicit tension between Bulgakov's and Florovsky's ways of doing Orthodox theology. In 1924 Bulgakov had proposed that Florovsky teach patristics and apologetics in the school. Bulgakov had to implore the reluctant Florovsky to take a position in patristics, since Florovsky's training had been chiefly in the field of philosophy. While in Paris, though, Florovsky discovered patristics to be his true vocation—an outcome due, ironically, to the support and mentorship of the theologian whose theology he would soon come to oppose.[146] Vladimir Lossky and others formed a rival institute, which they called St. Denis, after the French patron saint, and a name that was a variant of Dionysius, the early church writer. Those at St. Denis would have nothing to do with the St. Sergius Institute, especially during the time that Bulgakov was dean there. Also in Paris, Berdyaev ran a Religious-Philosophical Society that was better attended than its Russian

---

144. Meyendorff, "Creation," 33: "It can be said that practically the entire oeuvre of Florovsky dealing with Greek patristic thought and published in the prewar period [i.e., before World War II] was directed against the sophiological postulates of Sergius Bulgakov."

145. See Lialine, "Le débat sophiologique" (covers the earlier period); Klimhoff, "Georges Florovsky and the Sophiological Controversy"; Gavrilyuk, *Georges Florovsky*, esp. 114–58.

146. Gavrilyuk, *Georges Florovsky*, 128–30.

counterparts, drawing hundreds and sometimes almost a thousand attendees to its events.[147]

The sophiological debate was rooted in ideas that long preceded the 1930s. Solovyov's *Lectures on Godmanhood* (1878) and *Russia and the Universal Church* (1889 [in French]), Pavel Florensky's *The Pillar and Ground of the Truth* (1914), and Bulgakov's *Unfading Light* (1917) all sounded many sophiological themes. The social and political chaos in Russia before, during, and after the 1917 revolution, and the continuing travails of the church in the 1920s, got in the way of a careful doctrinal examination of Sophiology. By the time that the Russian Church got down to examining the issues, there were bitter jurisdictional disputes and divided loyalties among the Russian Orthodox Christians.[148] Supporters of Bulgakov viewed the condemnation of Bulgakov's views in 1935—by the Moscow patriarchate and, independently, by the Russian Orthodox Church Outside Russia—as emanating from nontheological motives. Because of internal divisions in the church, the condemnation of Bulgakov's views, once enunciated, could not be enforced.[149] Something Bulgakov had in common with Solovyov was a sense of personal mission in the teaching and propagating of his message concerning Sophia. Solovyov, as noted above, had purportedly received communication from the spirit world that Sophia herself was to be "born" in 1878. Less apocalyptic, but no less resolute, was Bulgakov, who wrote in his diary for September 21, 1921: "God has chosen me, a weak and unworthy man, to be a witness to the Divine Sophia and to her revelation."[150] Bulgakov's firmness in maintaining and defending his Sophiology, amid repeated challenges, reflected this sense of mission. While Bulgakov had a sense of mission regarding the teaching of Sophiology, those opposing him were nonetheless no less adamant.

147. Ibid., 136.

148. Klimhoff, "Georges Florovsky and the Sophiological Controversy," 69.

149. In the aftermath of the Bolshevik Revolution, the leader of the Russian Orthodox Church, Patriarch Tikhon (Vasily Ivanovich Bellavin, 1865–1925), in 1920 issued an *ukase* (official decree) to the Russian Orthodox residing outside of Russia, instructing them to organize themselves. A synod was formed in Serbia, known from 1922 as the Karlovsky Synod. In 1927, it declared its own authority to represent Russian Orthodox abroad, while also claiming to be the voice of a Mother Church that, because of Soviet Communist persecution, could no longer speak for itself. During this period, a schism developed between the Moscow patriarchate and the Russian Orthodox Church Abroad (ROCA), which was not healed until a reunion in 2007. Since 1927, the Russian Orthodox Church Abroad has generally been referred to as the Russian Orthodox Church Outside of Russia (ROCOR). In North America, the situation was complex, in that some Russian Orthodox congregations were affiliated with ROCOR and others with the Moscow patriarchate. My thanks are due to Fr. Dr. Delas Oliver Herbel for explaining these intricacies.

150. Bulgakov, *Vestnik RKhD* 170 (1994): 32, cited in Klimhoff, "Georges Florovsky and the Sophiological Controversy," 68n6.

Florovsky's 1925 letter to Bulgakov made no secret of his opposition to Solovyov, whose cause Bulgakov promoted. Florovsky declared, "By renouncing Solovyov we will be liberated from the whole shadowy tradition, which leads from Masonry to the extra-ecclesial mysticism of the false contemplatives in bad taste. I feel that it is this tradition that has held our creative forces in shackles. . . . As for Solovyov, instead of singing him panegyrics or even hymns of praise, we should instead offer prayers for his troubled and half-broken soul."[151] Florovsky had written a glowing essay on Solovyov in 1912, at the age of nineteen, yet his enthusiasm soon waned. The esoteric and occultic philosophy in the background of Solovyov's writings made Florovsky uneasy. His essential objection, in Gavrilyuk's words, was that "idiosyncratic forms of western mysticism were not a valid source of Orthodox theology."[152] Berdyaev, himself no traditionalist, complained that among his contemporaries in 1923 "one has an impression that Sophia has replaced Christ."[153]

Bulgakov outlined his Sophiology in *The Wisdom of God* (1935, Russian; 1937, English). Yet because of the persistent difficulties of readers in understanding Sophiology, Bulgakov prepared an even more succinct summary—just three and a half pages—for an Anglican-Russian theological conference in England in 1936.[154] In 1935, the head of the Russian Orthodox Church—the Moscow patriarch, Metropolitan Sergius Stragadorsky—launched an investigation into Bulgakov's teaching. The patriarch appointed Alexsei Stavrovsky to prepare a summary and analysis of Bulgakov's teachings and called on Vladimir Lossky to offer a critique of the recently published *The Lamb of God* (1933). After reading these reports, Metropolitan Sergius issued an *ukase* (or *ukaz*, an official warning to the faithful) to the effect that Bulgakov's theology contained significant distortions of Orthodox theology. Bulgakov's teaching on Sophia, in the words of the *ukase* from Metropolitan Sergius, was "a novel and arbitrary (Sophianic) interpretation frequently distorting the dogmas of the Orthodox faith, in several of its points also openly repeating false teachings already condemned by the conciliar Church." What is more, "in the possibilities from its logical consequences it is capable of being even dangerous for the spiritual life," and so "the teaching is deemed alien to the Holy Orthodox Christian Church, and warning [is given] against enthusiasm for it."[155]

151. Gavrilyuk, *Georges Florovsky*, 98, citing Florovsky, letter to Bulgakov, December 30, 1925.
152. Gavrilyuk, *Georges Florovsky*, 102.
153. Berdyaev, "Mutnye liki," 448, cited in Gavrilyuk, *Georges Florovsky*, 103.
154. See Bulgakov, "Summary of Sophiology," in Gallaher and Kukota, "Protopresbyter Sergii Bulgakov," 43–46.
155. Gallaher and Kukota, "Protopresbyter Sergii Bulgakov," 10–11n12, citing Metropolitan Sergius, Ukaz no. 1651.

Without formally charging Bulgakov with heresy, Metropolitan Sergius called on him to retract his most controversial sophiological opinions. Yet the 1935 *ukase* landed in a canonical limbo, since Bulgakov, formerly under Metropolitan Sergius, was at that time under Metropolitian Evlogy Georgievsky, who, to avoid schism, had placed himself under the authority of the patriarch of Constantinople. What is more, the *ukase* did not rely directly on Bulgakov's own writings but on prepared extracts from them. Beyond this, Bulgakov had not been granted an in-person hearing with Metropolitan Sergius or any opportunity to defend himself and his views. The situation grew yet more complicated when the Russian Orthodox Church Outside Russia (ROCOR) broke ties with both Metropolitan Sergius and Metropolitan Evlogy and then, within weeks, issued an even more damning statement against Bulgakov's theology.[156]

Passions among the Russian exiles ran high. During one of Berdyaev's academic meetings, one debater over Sophiology struck another in the nose. Metropolitan Evlogy appointed his own theological commission to investigate Bulgakov, drawing on professors from the St. Sergius Institute. This commission, drawn from Bulgakov's own institution, acquitted their academic dean of heresy but raised a few theological concerns.[157] When professors from St. Sergius were asked to sign the report, Florovsky said he could not do so because the statement did not express his sentiments. This action alienated many other professors. As Gavrilyuk notes, however, "the immediate result of the Sophia Affair was inconclusive and further inquiries into the matter collapsed."[158] Alexis Klimhoff calls attention to the inherent ambiguities involved in the definitions of key terms in the debate: "Sophia . . . has however never received a clear definition and has for this reason been open to charges of incompatibility with accepted orthodox teaching."[159] The point is well taken: ambiguous teachings might be interpreted in an unorthodox way. Metropolitan Sergius's *ukase* said as much. Whenever the point at issue remains vague or undefined, theological discussion cannot attain closure. On essential issues, Bulgakov could be read in more than one way. This may have been because, in antinomic fashion, he spoke and wrote in more than one way on a given issue.

Florovsky thought he knew what was wrong with Sophiology, and he traced the problem back to Solovyov and beyond, to Solovyov's heterodox sources. One

156. Gavrilyik, *Georges Florovsky*, 137–38, citing the ROCOR document "On the Decision of the Council . . . on the New Doctrine of Archpriest Sergius Bulgakov concerning Sophia, the Wisdom of God [October 1935]," 23–34.

157. Geffert, "Charges of Heresy," includes both the majority and minority reports from Metropolitan Evlogy's commission.

158. Gavrilyuk, *Georges Florovsky*, 139–40.

159. Klimhoff, "Georges Florovsky and the Sophiological Controversy," 67.

of his most striking statements on Sophia appears in a 1926 letter written to Bulgakov on Solovyov:

> There are . . . two images of Sophia: the true and real one and the false one. The holy temples in Byzantium and Russia were built in the name of the first image of Sophia. The second image inspired Solovyov and his Masonic and Western teachers, going all the way back to the Gnostics. . . . Sol[ovyov] did not know the *ecclesial* Sophia at all: he knew the Sophia according to Boehme and his followers, according to Valentinus and Cabbala.[160]

When mentioning Solovyov, Florovsky often made reference to the Masons, who, as noted above, have been a focus of recent scholarship, linking them to Solovyov.[161] Florovsky saw an unholy succession that started with ancient gnosis and proceeded to Böhme, the Masons, Solovyov, and, by implication, to Bulgakov as Solovyov's disciple.

The seemingly interminable debate between Bulgakov and Florovsky on Sophiology was thus also a debate over Solovyov. In his early years, Bulgakov stated that the study of Solovyov's thought was the chief task for Russian religious thinkers.[162] In his later years, Bulgakov's mature dogmatic theology bears the impress of Solovyov. For Bulgakov, Solovyov's thought was unlike that of the German idealist philosophers in being wholly centered on Christ. Florovsky saw things differently. For him, Solovyov was altogether lacking in a true centeredness on Christ.[163] Bulgakov tried to dissuade Florovsky from his "anti-Solovyovism" but never succeeded.[164] In the end, Solovyov was a polarizing figure in the relationship between Bulgakov and Florovsky. The two men agreed that Solovyov mattered, but they disagreed entirely about why he mattered.

Florovsky rejected Solovyov's "all-unity," stating that "being is not 'all-unity,' it is not 'organic whole'; it is marked by the abyss between the absolute and

160. Gavrilyuk, *Georges Florovsky*, 103, citing Florovsky, letter to Bulgakov, 22 July (4 August, New Style) 1926.

161. See the section above (*DR* 8.2) on Solovyov and the Russian Masons, drawing on the writings of Konstantin Burmistrov.

162. Bulgakov wrote in 1905: "To understand, master, and absorb Solovyov is the first and ensuing task set before contemporary Russian thought" (Bulgakov, "Po povodu," 367, cited in Kornblatt, *Divine Sophia*, 4).

163. Recent critical scholarship on Solovyov has tended to support Florovsky's opinion rather than Bulgakov's on Solovyov's Christology. The weaknesses of Solovyov's position on the historical Jesus have been noted in scholarship of the last two decades by Manon de Courten, Konstantin Burmistrov, Wil van den Bercken, and Evert van der Zweerde (see *DR* 8.3–8.4). See also Gallaher, "Christological Focus."

164. Gavrilyuk, *Georges Florovsky*, 117.

the creature; and these two worlds are causally united by way of freedom."[165] During the 1920s Florovsky was struggling toward what he would later call the "intuition of creaturehood." The essay on creation and creaturehood came out in 1928, and in time the "intuition of creaturehood" was a defining idea in Florovsky's neo-patristic synthesis. In his view, Solovyov's "panentheism was indistinguishable from pantheism." In some later writings, Florovsky implied that Solovyov had fallen into "demonic delusion." His philosophy, in any case, led to "dead ends."[166] Under the influence of German idealism, Solovyov made God incomplete apart from the world, so that God and the world were codetermining factors. Bulgakov himself sometimes made statements that conveyed this impression: "One cannot think of God without the world; the existence of the world is included in the concept of God."[167] Moreover, Bulgakov's idea of the coexistence of freedom and necessity in God had, in Florovsky's eyes, compromised God's freedom.

Florovksy insisted that the spatial terms "inside" and "outside" bred confusion when applied to God's act of creating. The world was not made out of something existing "inside" of God (e.g., a divine world, preexisting ideas) nor out of something existing "outside" of God (e.g., preexisting matter, *prima materia*). Instead it was made out of nothing. In other words, it was not made out of anything that "existed" prior to God's creating. For Florovsky, Arius and Origen both went astray on the doctrine of creation by confusing God the Father's begetting of God the Son with God's creating of the world, though they fell into error in two different ways. Arius assimilated begetting to creating, so that begetting became a kind of creating, and Christ became the first created entity. Origen's thought moved in the opposite direction, as he assimilated creating to begetting, so that creating became a kind of begetting. This meant that the entire creation was prearranged, and in a sense preexisted, within a divine sphere or a divine Wisdom. Athanasius avoided both errors by clearly distinguishing these two—that is, begetting and creating.[168]

Florovsky held that "German Idealism was a teaching about Godmanhood without the Godman."[169] Godmanhood distracted attention away from the historical Jesus. Much as Florovsky differed from Bulgakov and Solovyov, so he differed from their shared interpretation of Schelling, whom he did not see as helpful

165. Florovsky, "V mire iskanii bluzhdanii," 204, cited in Gavrilyuk, *Georges Florovsky*, 105.
166. Gavrilyuk, *Georges Florovsky*, 105.
167. Ibid., 107, citing Bulgakov, *Agnets Bozhii* (*The Lamb of God*), 159.
168. Gavrilyuk, *Georges Florovsky*, 147–48. Gavrilyuk says simply, "Florovsky regarded sophiology as a species of Origenism" (141).
169. Ibid., 110.

in interpreting the life and significance of Jesus.[170] Florovsky also criticized the political dimension of Solovyov's Sophiology, centered on the historical goal of a "free theocracy" and conceived as a plan to have all of Christendom under the czar as political leader and the pope as spiritual leader. Florovsky questioned how the supernatural end—humanity's union with God—could be achieved by any political means. The philosophy of history that Florovsky embraced was that of "historical singularism," according to which it was only human individuals who had causal influence in historical affairs and not abstract or collective entities.[171] A feet-on-the-ground thinker like Florovsky could never see eye-to-eye with a view-from-on-high speculator like Solovyov or Bulgakov.

Florovsky also differed from Bulgakov on church tradition. In Bulgakov's view, there were only two binding doctrines or dogmas of the church—the doctrine of the incarnation and the doctrine of the Trinity.[172] In *The Lamb of God*, Bulgakov appropriated aspects of Apollinaris's Christology, though this figure had been rejected as a heretic in the early church.[173] Bulgakov held that the Orthodox Church had no definite doctrines concerning eschatology, and he believed that this allowed him to speculate in this area in *The Bride of the Lamb* (1945). Florovsky, in contrast, held to a more constraining notion of early church teaching, and accepted—among many other things—the consensus of the church fathers on the eternity of hell. He wrote, "According to the contemporary views, shared by Berdyaev, the acceptance of an eternal hell smacks of obscurantism. But in my view the denial of the possibility of an eternal hell cancels human freedom and deprives it of seriousness."[174]

8.8. Bulgakov's *The Bride of the Lamb* and the Arguments for Universalism

"Bulgakov's deeply original and controversial eschatology," writes Gavrilyuk, "remains largely unexplored in modern scholarship." Generally Bulgakov was

170. "In Schelling, Godmanhood stood for the divine-human communion that was eternally realized in God. Godmanhood was also an eschatological goal of the ultimate union between God and humanity, to which world history was ineluctably moving. For Solovyov and Bulgakov, Schelling was simply drawing out the metaphysical implications of the divine incarnation" (Gavrilyuk, *Georges Florovsky*, 109–10).

171. Ibid., 118.

172. Ibid., 141.

173. "Bulgakov . . . took the claim that the hypostasis of the Son was divine to mean that the Son only had a divine center of self-consciousness and did not have a human center, since the human rationality of Christ constituted the ideal humanity, the aspect of the divine Sophia" (Gavrilyuk, *Georges Florovsky*, 142).

174. Ibid., 143n34, citing Florovsky, letter to Iu. Ivask, 13 May 1967, in *Vestnik RKhD* 130 (1979): 48. Cf. Florovsky, "Darkness of Night," in *Collected Works*, 3:82–83.

"following the universalist insights of Origen and Gregory of Nyssa" so that he "construed hell as a state of self-inflicted torment necessary to purify the resurrected individual from evil."[175] Yet there is much in Bulgakov's eschatology that is both original and idiosyncratic. Compared with Solovyov or Berdyaev, Bulgakov offered more discussion of particular themes in eschatology. He analyzed specific biblical passages as neither Solovyov nor Berdyaev did and showed himself to be a dogmatic theologian who took seriously both the biblical foundation of Christian teaching and the need to interpret the historical theological tradition. The structure of *The Bride of the Lamb* might seem curious, since this work on ecclesiology and eschatology devotes its first one hundred pages or so to the God-world relationship. A clue about what is happening lies in the brief comment that "eschatology . . . is the last word of Christian ontology."[176] The coming age will heal the wound of being—a wound inflicted by a fissure between Creator and creatures. Bulgakov's eschatology rests on an ontological foundation.

Bulgakov may not have changed his views, yet he seems to have become more overt in his later writings in affirming universalism. In *The Orthodox Church* (1935), he writes, "God does not punish; he forgives. Sinful creatures may refuse His forgiveness. This refusal (which may be unending since human free choice can never be destroyed) makes hell to be hell. In a word, God has mercy on all, whether all like."[177] Here he seems to say that hell might be eternal for some, because of "free choice," and yet that God's mercy applies to all, "whether [or not] all like." So we have an antinomy here, in which salvation does and yet does not depend on human choice. The antinomic approach should be seen against the backdrop of the 1930s sophiological debates. At this time, any overt assertion of universalism would only have been fuel to the flame, heightening suspicions of Bulgakov's "Origenism." It is thus not surprising that the later works, especially the posthumous *The Bride of the Lamb*, present Bulgakov's universalism most clearly.

Generally speaking, Bulgakov's eschatology is "a doctrine originating in Origen and stabilized in the teaching of St. Gregory of Nyssa"—a viewpoint whose opponents are not "equal in power of theological thought."[178] Often mentioned

175. Gavrilyuk, "Universal Salvation," 110.
176. Bulgakov, *Bride of the Lamb*, 379.
177. Bulgakov, *Orthodox Church*, xiii.
178. Bulgakov, *Bride of the Lamb*, 380. Later he claims, "Origen and especially St. Gregory of Nyssa . . . are virtually the only ecclesiastical writers (besides Augustine with his rigorism) who made questions of eschatology an object of special inquiry" (482). This is not factually true, as one can easily see by examining Daley, *Hope of the Early Church*, which surveys the wide range of patristic authors who treated issues of eschatology. Bulgakov also seems not to acknowledge Gregory of Nyssa's differences from Origen. See *DR* appendix D, on Ramelli.

alongside Origen (*DR* 3.4–3.7) and Gregory of Nyssa (*DR* 3.9) is Isaac the Syrian (*DR* 4.9), who might be regarded as the third major authority for Bulgakov's eschatological views. The theological doctrine that appears in the standard, modern Orthodox textbooks, Bulgakov writes, "only expresses the opinion of the majority" and represents teaching that has been "infected" by the "dogmatic maximalism" of Roman Catholicism. For this reason "it would be erroneous to maintain that the dogmatic doctrine expounded in the scholastic manuals represents the authoritative and obligatory dogmas of the church."[179] This is so because "the Church has *not established a single universally obligatory dogmatic definition in the domain of eschatology*." Instead there is room for "free theological investigation," as one sees in *The Bride of the Lamb*.[180] Bulgakov calls his own work "sophiological eschatology" and aligns himself with Florensky and Berdyaev (*DR* 8.5). Bulgakov argues that eschatological statements have a transcendent character, since "by its essence, eschatology deals with a domain of being that transcends the present world and is not measurable solely by the measure of this world."[181] This is an intriguing argument, yet one that could cut both ways, against Bulgakov's novel assertions as well as against more traditional claims.

Sounding like Berdyaev, Bulgakov argues against anthropomorphism in eschatology, and what he especially has in mind is the application of juridical or penal ideas of postmortem rewards or punishments. In too many accounts of Christian eschatology, "the ontological statement of the problem is replaced by a juridical one, and the mysteries of God's love are measured according to the penal code." God's wisdom is "reduced to a manual of instruction for organizing an exemplary prison where the confinement is without end." Aware that some readers will appeal to Scripture in applying penal and juridical ideas to eschatology, Bulgakov insists that "eschatology must see as its task an authentically ontological exegesis of the relevant texts, a search for their inner coherence and theological meaning."[182] From the outset, he reads biblical texts in an "ontological" way, and in practice this means that he uses philosophical reasoning in arriving at his interpretations. He rejects a literal interpretation of Old and New Testament statements on "punishment," "penalty," "vengeance," "reward," "recompense," and other terms that might carry a juridical or penal meaning.

From Solovyov, Bulgakov carries over the idea of synergy in eschatology. "A sort of 'synergism' is manifested here between the originally created world and the divine

179. Bulgakov, *Bride of the Lamb*, 380.
180. Ibid., 379 (emphasis in the original). Though pursuing "free theological investigation," Bulgakov did not always extend this freedom to others. He dismissed Catholic reflections on St. Joseph, husband of the Virgin Mary, by saying that "there is no basis for these dogmatic fantasies" (416n28).
181. Ibid., 380–81.
182. Ibid., 382.

power that renews it."[183] How does humanity help to establish the kingdom of God? It is not clear that Bulgakov embraced the nineteenth-century liberal belief that human beings were themselves building the kingdom of God in efforts toward social justice or social betterment. Nonetheless Bulgakov appeals to synergism where it would seem to have the least pertinence—namely, in relation to his doctrine of resurrection, where there is a "human aspect of synergism, according to which different people await it [i.e., the resurrection] and are prepared for it to different degrees."[184] Much remains unclear in Bulgakov's reasoning regarding the "how" of this synergy and whether it happens through faith, obedience, or social action. As noted above in connection with Solovyov (*DR* 8.4), the idea that human effort is instrumental not only in social amelioration but also in overcoming death and even in resurrecting the dead is an echo of Russian Cosmism, as represented by Nikolai Fedorovich Fedorov (1829–1903). While the Cosmists generally believed that scientific advancement would eventually make human immortality attainable, Bulgakov focused instead on human spiritual advancement, and so he might be considered as an exponent of "Religious Cosmism."[185]

In *The Bride of the Lamb*, Bulgakov does not offer any systematic analysis of the Olivet Discourse (Matt. 24; Mark 13), perhaps because this apocalyptic passage conflicts with his "ontological" approach to eschatology. "The cosmos is . . . not abolished but transfigured," and for this reason, in some sense, "the creation called to being by God is indestructible and endless." The ontological approach meant that Bulgakov approached the future not as something radically new but as emerging from the existing world. He writes that "an ontological connection is thus affirmed between our world and the world to come. They are one and the same world in its different states." Bulgakov qualifies this assertion by stating that a "chasm" separates the world's two states, so that there is no "evolutionary transition" from one to the other.[186] In writing this, he may have sought to circumvent the criticisms raised against Solovyov and the other eschatological optimists who flourished prior to World War I. Yet Bulgakov stresses continuity, not discontinuity. Through its ending, "the world becomes harmonious with its [own] idea."[187]

183. Ibid., 383.

184. Ibid., 438. "All resurrected bodies will rise incorruptible and spirit-bearing. But how is this spirituality realized with regard to . . . creaturely freedom? Does the principle of synergism operate here? Yes, it does, and the judgment and separation are accomplished precisely through this principle" (207).

185. On Bulgakov as a Cosmist, see G. M. Young, *Russian Cosmists*, 108–19. See *DR*, 1121n59, for a discussion of Bulgakov's unusual argument that creatures give advance permission to God to create them—an indication of how strongly Bulgakov emphasized divine-human synergism.

186. Bulgakov, *Bride of the Lamb*, 382–84.

187. Ibid., 402.

In his eschatology, Bulgakov struggles to articulate a consistent perspective on whether Christ's return is an event in time. In *The Bride of the Lamb*, he denies what we might call the "event character" of the second coming: "The net of time is torn, and a supertime suddenly shines through it—not as a calendar event but as something that transcends our time."[188] This statement seems clear-cut. No one can point forward to a date on the calendar—or, for that matter, point back to it, after the fact—and say that this is when Christ returned or when God inaugurated his kingdom on earth.[189] He states, "Christ will not appear within the limits of this world. He will not appear beneath this sky and upon this earth and before this humankind. Humankind will see him in a new world."[190] Even more bluntly he remarks that "the present world, this heaven and this earth, will not see Christ again."[191] There is no hope for the world as we know it, and this suggests that Bulgakov drew close to the view that he said he rejected, according to which the present world will somehow be destroyed or replaced. The reference to the "new world" stands in tension with the earlier statement that "the cosmos is . . . not abolished but transfigured."[192]

Bulgakov at times seems to forget what he wrote elsewhere about the kingdom's coming not being a datable event. This becomes apparent when Bulgakov expounds his idiosyncratic doctrine of Mary's second coming—"for the parousia of the Son is also necessarily the parousia of the Mother of God."[193] For this reason, "the parousia should be understood as the return of Christ *and* of the Mother of God into the world."[194] He asks, "When does this parousia of the Mother of God occur?" and answers his own question by stating, "It is probable that it occurs . . . not later than the parousia of Christ . . . [and] may even precede the parousia of Christ." In this discussion, Christ's return must be a

188. Ibid., 384–85.
189. Cf. the further statements: "The end of the world is not physical but metaphysical" (ibid., 401). "The universal resurrection is a result of Christ's resurrection. . . . The universal resurrection is outside or above earthly time" (432). Bulgakov draws the odd conclusion that, because of our lack of understanding of Christ's ascension into heaven, "there cannot be a clear doctrine of the parousia [i.e., the second coming of Christ], for the two are indissolubly linked" (389).
190. Ibid., 395.
191. Ibid., 396.
192. Ibid., 383.
193. Ibid., 409. In support of this novel doctrine, Bulgakov appeals to icons showing the Mother of God sitting at Jesus's right hand, without being judged herself, as the "seed of a dogmatic doctrine" regarding Mary's return (410).
194. Ibid., 411. Since Christian icons and artwork often show the heavenly saints—i.e., those now with Christ—alongside Christ in the judgment, one might ask whether these saints, along with Mary, come again when Christ comes again (cf. Rev. 19:11, 14). Bulgakov seems to have accepted a parousia of the church as well as of Mary, though he does not develop the idea: "According to revelation, the glorified Church, the angels and the saints [accompany] Christ who comes in glory" (412).

datable event, since another event "precede[s]" it or comes "later."[195] It becomes clear that Bulgakov does not present a consistent picture of the relationship of Christ's coming to human time.

Bulgakov had difficulty accounting for the day of Pentecost, because Scripture presents it as a divine event and perhaps a divine intervention into history (Acts 2). Since Bulgakov's doctrine of God ruled out notions of causality in favor of divine manifestation and human participation, the notion of God as acting in history was foreign to Bulgakov's dogmatics. He needed to interpret Pentecost in a new way. So he tended to assimilate Pentecost to Christ's parousia, as an image of cosmic transmutation: "The Pentecost's fiery tongues become the flame of the world fire, not consuming but transmuting the world."[196] Bulgakov's interpretation of Pentecost (like his exegesis of other biblical passages) is often only tangentially connected to the text he cites. In the context of Acts 2, the "tongues of fire" have nothing to do with "transmuting the world" or with Pentecost-as-parousia. Bulgakov links Acts 2 not to speaking in tongues but to silence: "The fiery tongues of the Holy Spirit were dissipated in space as if extinguished, and the Spirit's tumultuous breath became silent, as if dissipated in the air."[197] Needless to say, this interpretation of Pentecost is idiosyncratic. The underlying problem may have been that Bulgakov could not figure out what to do with Pentecost. It had no obvious relation to a final divine self-manifestation wherein "the net of time is torn, and a supertime suddenly shines through it."[198]

In *The Bride of the Lamb*, Christ's resurrection is the resurrection and salvation of all: "In his glorious resurrection all humankind is raised."[199] Bulgakov states, "The God-man is the all-man, and his resurrection is ontologically the universal resurrection."[200] In his exposition, Bulgakov asserts a "resurrection of life" but no "resurrection of judgment," and for this reason resurrection and salvation become interchangeable terms.[201] The word "resurrection" means

195. Ibid., 412.
196. Ibid., 400. In Bulgakov's reading of Scripture, "fire" consistently refers to some kind of transmutation. "This is the power of the Fire that burns, melts, transmutes, illuminates, and transfigures" (421). This is true of his interpretation of hellfire, as we will see below.
197. Ibid., 399.
198. Ibid., 384–85.
199. Ibid., 433.
200. Ibid., 429. "To be a human being and therefore to belong to Christ's humanity is the sole basis for the resurrection. . . . This same human nature is, by virtue of Christ's Incarnation, also divine-human" (438). "This action of God is applied not only to every individual human soul but also to the integral Adam. . . . For resurrection to occur singly in individuals, without that inner connection that unifies the entire human race, would contradict the multi-unity of the latter" (440).
201. Bulgakov cites John 5:25: "They that hear shall live" (ibid., 436). To his credit, he later cites John 5:28–29, which contrasts the "resurrection of judgment" with the "resurrection of life," yet

"communion with eternal life."[202] Bulgakov says little about the human body or human flesh as such, which is generally the first thing that comes to mind when discussing the doctrine of the resurrection. Instead he presents the "spiritual body" as a sign of "a healthy ontology, according to which the true substance of matter as universal reality is spirit."[203] Bulgakov's resurrection might almost be regarded as a wholly spiritual event, lacking any fleshly or material dimension.

Bulgakov writes that "the resurrection is not a new creation in the strict sense, but only a restoration (*apocatastasis*) of the original creation, which is raised to its highest and ultimate being."[204] In another passage, he adds that "resurrection in glory is therefore the definitive sophianization of man through the manifestation in him of his proto-image."[205] Resurrection is a manifestation of what was already the case: "Resurrection is an *apocatastasis*; a human being is re-created in his original form."[206] Christ's manifestation at the second coming *is* the universal resurrection, which *is* the manifestation of the human proto-image, which *is* universal salvation. The biblical idea of resurrection—as something new, unprecedented, or unimagined—cannot be reconciled with Bulgakov's ontologically oriented eschatology. *Newness* in the strict sense plays no role. The divine declaration from the throne, "Behold, I am making all things new" (Rev. 21:5), could be rephrased as "Behold, I am manifesting all things as they truly always were."

Various lines of argument in *The Bride of the Lamb* all converge toward universalism. Bulgakov does not speak of the divine nature of the human self in *The Bride of the Lamb* as often as he does in the earlier *The Lamb of God*. Instead he generally appeals to the universal effect of Christ's incarnation or the universal resurrection as the basis for universal salvation. Regarding the biblical text on being "changed" into Christ's image (2 Cor. 3:18), Bulgakov writes that "this applies . . . to *all* humanity without any exception, for the Lord, having become the new Adam, assumed humanity in its entirety. . . . The image of the heavenly will shine upon all resurrected human bodies, clothed in *glory*."[207] Having mentioned Ephrem the Syrian's opinion that the bodies of the wicked

he reinterprets the judgment mentioned in this biblical passage as part of the process of salvation (see below).

202. Ibid. In his doctrine of the resurrection Bulgakov is indebted to Gregory of Nyssa (*DR* 3.9), who not only affirmed bodily resurrection but also assigned it soteriological centrality, so that *anastasis* is *apokatastasis*, and resurrection is restoration.

203. Ibid., 447.

204. Ibid., 430. The term *apocatastasis* appears elsewhere in *The Bride of the Lamb*, and it always bears a positive connotation (422, 435).

205. Ibid., 451.

206. Ibid., 435.

207. Ibid., 450.

will differ from those of the righteous in the resurrection, Bulgakov argues that "such ideas . . . presuppose the ultimate failure of God's creation, the impotence of God's image in man, [and] man's loss of his original sophianicity."[208] This cannot be, he writes, because "ignorance of God and total separatedness from eternal life are impossible."[209]

In the final section of *The Bride of the Lamb*, Bulgakov deals with questions of judgment and separation and the significance of biblical and traditional language regarding hell and its torments. Bulgakov's approach is to interpret the biblical language of "separation," "fire," and "torment" as denoting a process that in all cases leads toward final salvation. What results is a kind of universal purgatory. Bulgakov roundly rejects the notion of "free grace," insisting that all persons must "expiate" their own sins. The postmortem meeting of human beings with God is unavoidable: "This encounter with God, this entering into the realm of the divine fire, is not something optional for human beings. It is inevitable." While "for some this is the time of liberation . . . for others it is a time of fear and horror." He asks, "What is this fire that burns the chaff?" Bulgakov's answer is to identify fire with the Holy Spirit, and the Holy Spirit with the manifestation of truth: "This 'exposure' by the Spirit of truth is already the judgment. By virtue of the truth this judgment becomes for everyone a self-judgment, a shedding of the veils of falsehood."[210] Bulgakov preferred such a self-judgment to a divinely imposed judgment, and this reflected his rejection of legalistic or juridical categories. Even so, as we will see below, juridical or legalistic ideas of salvation return with a vengeance in Bulgakov's idea of a necessary, individual "expiation" for sins.

For Bulgakov, judgment and separation are both contained within the single encounter of the human self with Christ: "The judgment and the separation consist in the fact that every human being will be placed before his own eternal image in Christ, that is, before Christ. And in the light of this image, he will see his own reality, and this comparison will be the judgment."[211] Bulgakov thus transforms the human self's encounter with Christ into the human self's encounter with itself, or rather, with its own higher, better, or truer self. This line of thinking echoes Origen's ancient conjecture that the "fire" of judgment in Scripture is the sinner's own conscience and that postmortem judgment is a form of self-judgment (see *DR* 3.7).

Bulgakov rejects a literal interpretation of the New Testament texts on judgment—for example, the teaching on the sheep and the goats (Matt.

208. Ibid., 453, with n. 47.
209. Ibid., 469.
210. Ibid., 455–56.
211. Ibid., 457.

25:31–46). He insists instead that "every human being finds himself and the judgment upon himself," so "this judgment is therefore not transcendent but immanent." The criterion of judgment is not God's or Christ's holiness, regarded externally, but rather "Christ's presence in every human being." Bulgakov thinks that resistance to this final manifestation of truth is impossible in principle. Because this judgment is a self-judgment, it is also "self-evidently persuasive."[212] The outcome will be that all human beings will come to love Christ: "A human being cannot fail to love the Christ who is revealed in him . . . [and] there is no longer any place for anti-Christianity, for enmity toward Christ."[213] To the extent that each human comes to agree with the truth about himself or herself, one might say that there will be a postmortem conversion of heart and mind for everyone not already converted during his or her earlier life. Later on, Bulgakov says the opposite—namely, that human rejection of God may occur in the afterlife—and so his position on the postmortem life seems to be inconsistent.[214]

To escape the duality of outcomes in the New Testament, Bulgakov appeals to the "fundamental antinomies of the kingdom of glory" that "cannot be grasped." This leads him into a wide-ranging reinterpretation of biblical eschatological language:

> In the form of a parable, the discourse on the Last Judgment [Matt. 25] applies this final separation to different objects: to sheep and to goats, to those who go

212. Bulgakov, *Bride of the Lamb*, 458. "Is it possible to reject this ontological self-judgment upon oneself as inappropriate and unconvincing? No! It is not possible, for one is judged by one's own being, by one's own truth" (459).

213. Ibid., 459. These statements raise the question of human freedom. And if the final revelation of truth is so definitive and compelling, then one wonders why God does not grant this vision to all human beings during the present life. Moreover, some people might wait to make a decision regarding Christ in response to the postmortem manifestation—so much clearer and convincing than its earthly analogue. Perhaps to preserve the persuasive rather than coercive character of the postmortem encounter with Christ, Bulgakov states that Christ will then "come as He was on earth: meek and humble in heart, though now in glory" (459).

214. Bulgakov writes of a temporary hell that brings purification, wherein human beings make "expiation" for their wrongdoings. This hell state, he argues, is based on the creature's rejection of God: "The state of hell is, in essence, antinomic, because it combined the revelation of God and the abandonment by God. . . . God himself does not reject creation. It is creation that, in its desolate emptiness, rejects God" (*Bride of the Lamb*, 488). It seems difficult to reconcile this and other statements on hell with earlier statements about the persuasive and self-evident character of that self-judgment that overrules the possibility that people reject God's judgment and the truth about themselves. Perhaps in Bulgakov's account the persuasive judgment comes later in time for some people, after an earlier phase of self-imposed suffering through the rejection of the truth about themselves. If this is Bulgakov's position, then it has some resemblance to James Relly's view (see *DR* 6.4) that all humans, without exception, are objectively saved by God through Christ and yet that some persons will pass through a postmortem period of subjective affliction due solely to the fact that they will continue—perhaps for a lengthy period in the afterlife—to remain ignorant of their own objectively accomplished salvation.

on the right and to those who go on the left. One could deduce from this that human beings are separated into the sinless and those who are subject to sin. But no one is perfectly sinless except the "Sole Sinless One" and the Most Pure Mother of God, just as no human beings are so utterly sinful that no trace of good can be found in them. . . . In the final separation, evil itself will be known only in conjunction with, even if in conflict with, good. In this sense, hell is a function of heaven. . . . It follows that the separation into sheep and goats is accomplished (of course to different degrees) within every individual, and his right and left sides are bared in this separation. To a certain extent all are condemned and all are justified. . . . The difference between the two states can here be only a quantitative one. . . . It is precisely to this ontological condemnation, which is also the metaphysical annihilation of what is condemned, its transformation into a phantom, into a nightmare vision, that the Scripture's pitiless words about death, perdition, annihilation, destruction, and disappearance refer. They refer not to personal being, not to every human being's immortal life, but to his mortal, illusory content, which is consumed by the divine fire. . . . The judgment of God . . . is not the execution of any external laws and norms whose violation entails punishment. That is only a figurative, anthropomorphic manner of expressing the idea that the life of immortality is in conformity with man's divine, sophianic image. Everything that is not in conformity with this image falls into the outer darkness, into nonbeing. . . . This is the "eternal fire." . . . This partial nonbeing, the dark shadow of being, is experienced as fire, torment, punishment, immersion in the lake of fire.[215]

This remarkable passage encapsulates many of the key themes in Bulgakov's eschatology. Here he does not set aside the text of Scripture, though he interprets it "ontologically." The "figurative, anthropomorphic" language in the Bible—sheep versus goats, wheat versus tares, justification versus condemnation, heaven versus hell—calls forth Bulgakov's reinterpretation. To uncover the ideas that Bulgakov finds in the text, a "sophianic" key has to be used. Otherwise, one is stuck with the literal sense, and the Bible will remain a closed book.

What Bulgakov offers in this passage is a kind of Hegelian or Schellingian mediation between heaven and hell—that is, a transcending of opposites in terms of a new synthesis. The mediation alters both sides in the contrast. No longer are there "sheep" and "goats" but now only a *tertium quid*. No longer are there "heaven" and "hell" but now a condition incorporating the traits of both.[216] "Hell is a function of heaven," as Bulgakov writes, and the converse applies as well. Since heaven is a function of hell, not only does hell partake of heavenliness

215. Ibid., 462–63.
216. To neologize—in terms that Bulgakov did not use—one might say that the "sheep" and "goats" are replaced by "geeps," and "heaven" and "hell" by "hellven."

but also heaven partakes of hellishness. In Bulgakov's teaching, everyone is to some extent condemned. No one at death is good enough for heaven.

Bulgakov's reinterpreted eschatology is not good news for those who might have thought that they themselves, or some other people, will go immediately to heaven. If, to the wicked, the message is that heaven lies in store, then, to the righteous—and apparently even to the most saintly of human beings—the message is that a temporary hell lies ahead. "The *many* mansions in His Father's house . . . can be composed of different combinations of hell and heaven, life and death. . . . This union of opposites is the fundamental *postulate* of eschatology."[217] Hell has been beatified and heaven infernalized: "The idea that one can avoid with impunity the consequences of sin is insane, craven, and false. . . . Every person bears within himself the principle of gehennic burning, which is ignited by the power of the parousia of Christ in glory."[218] Such a statement seems to invert the "blessed hope" (Titus 2:13) of the joyful Christian, so that Christ's return becomes a mournful, dolorous affair—a prelude to universal condemnation for everyone's moral shortcomings, followed by either a longer or a shorter period of fiery torments in Bulgakov's temporary hell.[219] Bulgakov goes so far as to say that there will be suffering in heaven on account of those who are not yet in heaven: "The righteous, too, in their edenic habitations suffer from the hell of sinners." While "it is true that the Gospel expressions . . . do not mention this idea," hell is "an affliction of all humanity,"[220] for "this must be said without circumlocution—heaven does not exist in its fullness as long as and insofar as hell exists."[221]

A disconcerting aspect of Bulgakov's eschatology lies in its inadvertent moralism and juridicalism, which becomes increasingly apparent as one nears the conclusion of *The Bride of the Lamb*. Just as Bulgakov's heaven becomes hellish, so grace itself ceases to be fully gracious (*DR* 12.3). For no one will go immediately to heaven at death because, as Bulgakov writes, "no one is

217. Bulgakov, *Bride of the Lamb*, 465. "The fundamental antinomic postulate of eschatology is that the eternal life of incorruptibility and glory can coexist with eternal death and perdition" (477). "The *mixture* of good and evil that is proper to the overwhelming majority of human beings compels us to postulate not a simple but a complex sum total of God's judgment, which unites blessing and condemnation" (476). This coincidence or union of opposites is what one finds in gnostic-esoteric writings (e.g., William Blake's *The Marriage of Heaven and Hell*).

218. Bulgakov, *Bride of the Lamb*, 484.

219. Bulgakov says there will be sadness after the resurrection has occurred: "Those who are justified are not without contamination by sin and bear the sorrowful memory of sin even after resurrection" (ibid., 497).

220. Ibid., 488.

221. Ibid., 489.

perfectly sinless."[222] Because Bulgakov does not accept the notion that Christ bore the penalty or responsibility for human sins, he seemingly has no choice except to say either that God simply sets aside the punishment for sins or that there will be some kind of self-satisfaction for one's sins. The abrogation of divine punishment is to him a horrifying idea, and so he opts for a doctrine of self-satisfaction, described under the terminology of "expiation." He rejects any notion of "simple forgiveness" as something "sentimental" and perhaps as naive or simpleminded:

> One must reject every pusillanimous, sentimental hope that the evil committed by a human being and therefore present in him can simply be forgiven, as if ignored at the tribunal of justice. *God does not tolerate sin, and its simple forgiveness is ontologically impossible.* Acceptance of sin would not accord with God's holiness and justice. Once committed a sin must be lived through to the end, and *the entire mercilessness of God's justice must pierce our being* when we think of what defense we will offer at Christ's Dread Tribunal.[223]

Now we see the flip side of Bulgakov's rejection of legal reasoning regarding God's final judgment and the doctrine of the atonement. The exorcised demon of juridicalism comes back to haunt his theology. Astonishingly, he writes of "the entire mercilessness of God's justice." Divine justice is wholly separated from divine mercy. Here Bulgakov's theological reasoning seems to be harsher than that of predestinarian and confessional Protestants, who believe that the Savior bore the penalty for the sins of the elect and in sheer grace granted them forgiveness. Bulgakov will not allow this.

Bulgakov seems to have been aware of the problem created by his theology of "expiation." He tries to preserve a doctrine of grace, writing that "it is God's power that saves, the redemption by Christ's blood, the forgiveness of the sin." Yet in the same context we read: "One must indisputably admit the full validity of the axiom that every evil of which a human being is guilty must be fully and totally expiated by him, even if he is forgiven. Sin cannot be remitted *for free*, without suffering, for that would not be mercy but a denial of justice."[224] Bulgakov never explains how it is that forgiveness by Christ's expiation of sins

---

222. Ibid., 462. "Since no human being is without sin, there is no one who does not have the burning of hell within himself, even if only to a minimal degree" (465).

223. Ibid., 475–76; emphasis added.

224. Ibid., 484. "For sin must be suffered through and expiated to the end" (489). "They are saved, but they fully expiate this sinfulness" (497). "Sinners experience to the end and fully expiate the evil they received into themselves, this expiation excluding remission 'for free'" (493). The last quotation, regarding evil as "received into themselves," makes evil appear to be quasi-physical, like a toxic substance that people swallow down but then have to purge from their system.

on the cross is consistent with self-expiation by one's own sufferings. His purported system of self-expiation for sins might function efficiently apart from Jesus Christ almost like a law of karma.

"Salvation" in Bulgakov means that those who live wickedly in this life will, after death, confront their true self and so *suffer much* before entering heaven, while those who live righteously in this life will come to a realization of their true self and yet still *suffer somewhat*. Hell itself, for Bulgakov, is an opportunity for those suffering to achieve their own salvation: "Creative human effort will be needed to livingly overcome human perversion and the emptiness of hell by experiencing them to the end," for "the judgment . . . requires from all human beings that they do their duty. A duty is not done by others, and the one who has not done his duty is deprived of his gift and cast into outer darkness." Then "he must then overcome his emptiness by expiating it, by experiencing it to the end . . . [for] these torments are salvific for the spirit."[225] We must ask, what does any of this have to do with Jesus or with biblical teachings on eschatology? "Christ" is Bulgakov's name for ideal humanity. As ideal humanity, "Christ" is a yardstick for measuring human shortcomings. Yet, beyond this, there seems to be no functional doctrine of redemption to explain how Christ's birth, life, death, and resurrection bring about the salvation of all human beings.

Bulgakov raises an objection to his own position that will naturally occur to Orthodox or Catholic Christians, from a consideration of the honor paid to the saints. Is St. Athanasius suffering for his sins? And what of St. Francis of Assisi or St. Teresa of Ávila? Bulgakov asks, "Does the dogma of the veneration of the saints and their canonization not exclude the notion of the relativity and compatibility of heaven and hell?"[226] This objection does not dissuade Bulgakov, and he reaffirms instead that "every human being has need of forgiveness," adding that "the saintliness glorified by the Church signifies not sinlessness but righteousness as the sum total of pluses and minuses, experienced as a synthesis of bliss and suffering. This confirms that, for human beings, there is neither absolute heaven nor absolute hell."[227]

Once again, Bulgakov's position is surprisingly moralistic and juridical, as he evaluates someone's "righteousness as the sum total of pluses and minuses." In fact it is not clear what Bulgakov means by "forgiveness." Since, as he says, "simple forgiveness is ontologically impossible," we have to ask what sort of forgiveness is possible. Is it *complex* forgiveness? Or perhaps some form of

225. Ibid., 499.
226. Ibid., 479.
227. Ibid., 480.

conditional forgiveness—perhaps the idea that once we suffer enough then God will forgive us? At points it seems that Bulgakov is near to abandoning the notion of forgiveness as inconsistent with his theological system. The most compassionate Mary, he writes, "pleads at the tribunal [of God] for universal *mercy, not for the forgiveness of sins* (which is impossible, for sins must be completely expiated and suffered through)."[228] Given all the different "mixtures"—as Bulgakov calls them—of good or of evil, to accommodate all the different levels of sin and righteousness, the Russian theologian would need to develop a kind of calculus to weigh and evaluate each person and assign the appropriate amount of suffering for each.[229]

Bulgakov repeats a number of arguments found in earlier thinkers regarding the non-eternity of hell. He writes that "'eternal torment' . . . with 'eternal life' . . . cannot be abstractly identified as forms of equally infinite time," since "eternity is not a temporal but a *qualitative* determination."[230] He goes on to say that "an exhaustive experiencing, or living out to the end, of extra-divine, creaturely freedom . . . presupposes an indefinitely long process whose result is given ontologically." What, then, of a possible relapse into sin, after one has been restored to God? Bulgakov insists that this will not happen: "A new falling away from God is now and forever impossible for man, just as it is for the holy angels. The dispute between the Creator and creation inevitably ends for creation when it [i.e., creation] recognizes that it is defeated."[231] It nonetheless remains unclear why a future fall from grace could not or should not occur.[232]

228. Ibid., 488.
229. Because of purgatorial sufferings, argues Bulgakov, "evil loses its attractiveness." When "lived to the end" it "loses its savor" (ibid., 481). After mentioning Gregory of Nyssa, Bulgakov writes: "Evil does not have eternity; the latter is proper only to good. On the contrary, evil is destined to be 'annihilated.' The assertion of the infinite presence of evil in the world is a kind of Manichaeanism. . . . Evil does not have the creative power of eternity and therefore cannot extend into infinity" (486). "Evil is empty and impotent; it is finite" (490). This idea concerning the ontological weakness of evil is a minor motif in *The Bride of the Lamb* and more of a focus in Bulgakov's brief essay "On the Question of the Apocatastasis of the Fallen Spirits," 7–30. It should be noted that this metaphysical argument for the impermanence of evil seems to prove too much—that is, that evil simply defeats itself apart from God's activity or any work of Christ. Bulgakov's argument seems to have been inspired by the analogous argument in Gregory of Nyssa (see *DR*, 284–86).
230. Bulgakov, *Bride of the Lamb*, 470. Bulgakov's references show that he knows of the nineteenth-century debates; he cites (468n52) E. B. Pusey's *What Is of Faith as to Everlasting Punishment?* (1880). For further discussion on time and eternity, see *DR* appendix J.
231. Bulgakov, *Bride of the Lamb*, 492.
232. Bulgakov does not explicitly develop any account of the creature's confirmation in grace such as we find in Augustine and Aquinas. Since all depends on the creature's will and decision, as in Origen, Bulgakov seems liable to the objection that Augustine (in *The City of God*) and Maximus Confessor (in his *Ambigua*) both made against Origen—namely, that in asserting universal salvation he had destabilized heaven and opened the door to future falls from grace and restorations to grace. See *DR* 4.3; 4.8.

Perhaps because of his emphasis on human freedom and his debt to Origen and
Gregory of Nyssa, Bulgakov later reverses himself on just this point, affirming
that the last judgment by God is merely a new starting point—the very point
on which Augustine had so sharply criticized Origen:

> The Last Judgment does not put an end to the changeability of creaturely being.
> . . . Rather, the Last Judgment makes the beginning of a new time, of new ages,
> of a new becoming. . . . Heaven and hell are therefore abstractions to a certain
> degree. Let us not forget that, besides the sharp distinction between light and
> darkness, heaven and hell, there exists a series of indeterminate intermediate
> states corresponding to the state of the souls of children (the "limbos" of Catholi-
> cism), of pagans uninitiated into Christianity, and, in general, of non-Christians,
> the mentally ill, severely retarded, and so forth. Truly, "in my Father's house are
> many mansions." And not less important is the fact that this is not a static but a
> fluid multiplicity, with transitions from one state to another.[233]

"Last Judgment" here has become more like "First Chapter." Note the appeal to
the future as a state of "fluid multiplicity" and to "heaven and hell" as "abstractions." Bulgakov speaks of "the sharp distinction between light and darkness,"
but his eschatology generally is devoted to overcoming such a contrast within
a union of opposites.

One of the contrasts set aside in Bulgakov's account is the contrast between
this present age as a time of good and evil in conflict and the age to come as the
time of good triumphing over evil. Instead, Bulgakov states that Christ's second
coming and the final judgment inaugurate not only the temporary though real
sufferings of humanity for their sins but also a new round of conflicts of Satan
and the demons with God. Bulgakov takes somewhat literally the biblical statements regarding Satan and the demons being "cast out" of the world—though
rejecting the "lake of fire" as Satan's final destination (Rev. 20:10). Once "cast
out" in this way, the real battle only begins: "After this expulsion of the prince
of this world, Satan's duel with God begins."[234] Since Bulgakov apparently links
Christ's parousia to the casting out of Satan, it follows that the second coming
of Christ is not God's final victory but the commencement of a new round in
the battle of good and evil. As Christ returns, the battle with the devil begins
in earnest.

In a lengthy discussion of Satan and the demons' salvation, he concludes that
"Satan's very being, his createdness by the omniscient God, is, so to speak, an
ontological proof of the inevitability of his future salvation." This is so because

233. Bulgakov, *Bride of the Lamb*, 500.
234. Ibid., 508.

"even Satan in his madness does not have the power to overcome the fact of his own being, its divine foundation . . . by virtue of which 'God will be all in all.'"[235] An attentive reader will not be surprised by this conclusion, which seems to be an outworking of Bulgakov's initial premises. The salvation of the demons simply reflects the solidarity of all creatures in the event of final salvation: "The torments of hell inevitably extend not only to those who are condemned but also to the entire Church, to all humankind. . . . All are saved with all, just as all are condemned with all and all are responsible for all. . . . Even for the righteous, heavenly bliss comes only after the expulsion of hell from the world. . . . All perish and are saved together.[236] For "this is God's inalienable gift to creation, the completion of His work on the world."[237]

8.9. Summary and Conclusions on Russian Thinkers

Chapter 8 examined a series of Russian thinkers—Solovyov, Berdyaev, Florovsky, and Bulgakov—against the backdrop of Russian church and intellectual history. As we showed previously, Jakob Böhme was a key figure in the development of modern Russian thought, including that of the Russian Freemasons and of Vladimir Solovyov (DR 5.13). On the basis of an analysis of his sources, as well as his esoteric arguments and occultic practices, Solovyov seems to belong in the Western esoteric tradition. This might be one reason for the murkiness and lack of clear definition in Russian Sophiology from its earlier phases onward. Moreover, this also helps to explain the low Christology that one finds in Solovyov, who speaks much of "Christ" as a spiritual principle but little of "Jesus" as a historical figure. Florovsky remained highly critical of Solovyov and regarded him as a "gnostic," despite Bulgakov's efforts to bring Florovsky to an appreciation of Solovyov. Solovyov affirmed a final restoration or *apoka-tastasis*, yet the relation of the eschaton to the process or progress of history is unclear—a problem that Solovyov shares with Moltmann (DR 9.10–9.11). Berdyaev closely followed Böhme in making the utter and even chaotic freedom of the *Ungrund* the foundation of his thought. An ardent universalist of the modern era, Berdyaev denounced the traditional doctrine of an eternal hell as an expression of human vindictiveness. Yet his response to hell was dialectical

---

235. Ibid., 517. Bulgakov devotes almost twenty pages (501–19) to the salvation of Satan and the demons, which is plainly no minor issue for him. Regarding the demons, he writes that "the restoration of this 'dark' part" takes place "through the express intercession of the Forerunner [John the Baptist] in prayer" and "through the intercession of the Queen of Heaven and Earth [Mary]" (417n29).
236. Ibid., 516.
237. Ibid., 472.

rather than dismissive. Berdyaev held that the traditional doctrine enshrined a fundamental truth regarding the experience of alienation from God and the human power to say no to God. Since the mid twentieth century he has had few disciples. Not many of Berdyaev's contemporaries or successors were ready to accept his notion that the principle of chaotic freedom or the *Ungrund* had metaphysical priority over the personal or trinitarian God.

Bulgakov in *The Bride of the Lamb* offers what may be the most ambitious attempt ever in defending the doctrine of Christian universalism in systematic fashion and addressing all the issues evoked by this doctrine. Ultimately Bulgakov's teaching removes the principle of grace by insisting that every individual "expiates" all his or her own sins through purgatorial and penitential suffering. Neither a pure heaven nor a pure hell exists, according to Bulgakov. Heaven becomes somewhat hellish, because everyone bound for heaven still contains some bit of hell within themselves. Hell in turn becomes rather heavenly, since the infernal denizens are ultimately on their way out of hell and into heaven. Bulgakov's universalism comes at a heavy price, which is the loss of grace, and he is only able to defend his views by taking liberties with the biblical text.

There are differing ways of understanding the relations among the thinkers treated in this chapter. At first glance, perhaps the most obvious contrast is between the progressivism and optimism of Solovyov (or at least the early Solovyov) and the more cautious attitude toward historical progress in Berdyaev and Bulgakov. Of the three, Berdyaev seems the least hopeful and the most ready to embrace a vision of the world and of history as essentially tragic. Salvation, such as Berdyaev understands it, is a self-transcendent experience of passing from the historical into the realm of eternity. Apparently he saw little hope for lasting change in the earthly realm, let alone for some tangible manifestation of a kingdom of God on earth. One might range the three in line, with Solovyov the most optimistic, Berdyaev the least, and Bulgakov somewhere in the middle.

Yet there are other, deeper differences, in that Solovyov and Bulgakov are both ontological thinkers while Berdyaev is meontological—that is, one who bases himself on a theory of nothing. In this way of comparing the three, Solovyov and Bulgakov stand on one side and Berdyaev on the other. Drawing from Jakob Böhme, Berdyaev posited a principle of unbounded freedom or ultimate irrationality (the Abyss or *Ungrund*) that had logical priority even over God. Berdyaev was not strictly speaking a theist but a dualist, affirming both a God-principle and a nothing-principle—and an eternal and unresolved tension between the two. This is why Berdyaev's account of hell was ultimately so antinomic, if not contradictory. Rationality could resist but never eliminate irrationality, and hell was itself an expression of irrationality.

In our discussion of the Russian background, and especially the little-known Russian Freemasons, it became clear that Russian Sophiology in the writings of Solovyov, Florensky, and Bulgakov did not appear out of nowhere but had precedents in earlier esoteric ideas and doctrines. Solovyov's vision of the Jesus of history does not seem to have gone beyond that of the Freemasons. What this meant for Solovyov's eschatology is that he did not conceive the final restoration—regarded as an *apokatastasis*—as a personal reign and rule of the God-man, Jesus Christ, but as the outcome of an immanent, historical development. Solovyov's focus on "synergy," or the human exertion involved in the coming of God's kingdom, attests to this immanental way of thinking. Also apparent in Solovyov is the difficulty he had in reconciling his idea of the two Sophias (divine and creaturely) and their final reconciliation in the eschaton with a bona fide trinitarian view of God. There was friction between his idea of Sophia and his idea of the Trinity. Solovyov never resolved this problem, nor did Bulgakov. The problem might be endemic to Sophiology as generally construed.

Orthodox clergy and laity in the 1930s rejected Bulgakov's early proposal in *Unfading Light* of regarding Sophia as a "fourth hypostasis." Henceforth Bulgakov had to struggle conceptually with newly invented concepts of his own devising, such as "hypostatizedness," by which he denied that Sophia was a "fourth hypostasis" and yet held that Sophia was not a mere figure of speech but had ontological status vis-à-vis the Father, Son, and Spirit. Bulgakov insisted that the trihypostatic, personal God found expression—and even self-revelation—through the nonhypostatic Sophia. Needless to say, Bulgakov's assertion is metaphysically odd, for one would not imagine that a trihypostatic, trinitarian God could or would be expressed through that which is nonhypostatic. One line of objection is that Sophiology creates more theological problems than it resolves and that the difficulties will disappear if one simply eliminates the unnecessary Sophia-hypothesis. Father, Son, and Spirit are named and identified as God in Sacred Scripture and play definite roles in redemptive history. By adding Sophia to his account of God, Bulgakov introduced many difficulties, without any clear-cut theological benefit.

In Bulgakov's *The Lamb of God*, the Sophia theology does not add clarity. At points it seems as though Christ is not regarded as one person possessing divine and human natures, but instead is a union of the divine Sophia and the creaturely Sophia. By hypothesis, the divine and creaturely Sophia are not fully distinct from each other but are two aspects of one and the same reality. The idea that Jesus was the incarnation of the divine Sophia was a tenet of certain ancient gnostic thinkers, and this notion in any case falls short of the full incarnation doctrine—centered on the eternal Logos or divine Son—that the Christian church defined as its central dogma. As if this were not enough, there is also in Bulgakov another speculative development, and this lies in his embrace of an unhelpful philosophical notion of "the Absolute," which he assimilates to God the Father and then valiantly struggles to incorporate into his system by denying the Absolute's absoluteness and affirming the Absolute's relativity. But this raises the question: Would it not be easier at the outset to avoid such a recalcitrant philosophical principle as "the Absolute"?

Of the four thinkers who are the focus of this chapter, Bulgakov is the only one who affirmed "universalism" in a more or less straightforward way. In the case of Solovyov we have something else, which seems to be an expectation of personal-social-cosmic development, apparently not involving any direct, divine intervention into the world. This cosmic advancement, as Solovyov imagined it, means that a God-world union that already exists—in some sense—will later find a more complete fulfillment. Is this "universal salvation"? In some sense yes, but in another sense no. A partial parallel to Solovyov may be found in Teilhard de Chardin's notion of the Omega Point (*DR* 10.3).

In the case of Berdyaev, the existentialist tone of his writing and thinking meant that he had almost nothing to say regarding a concrete social hope or outcome. His focus was on the individual human being, and here he was quite preoccupied with the issue of hell. On the question of the human will, Berdyaev was no determinist, nor was he a straightforward libertarian. One might say he was an irrationalistic libertarian, or one who thinks that human beings make choices that are perhaps not explainable or traceable to definite motives of action. In Berdyaev, the Abyss is deep indeed—and this Abyss that is utter, irrational will is the final principle, which precedes even God. In the beginning was the Void. Berdyaev railed against the notion of hell, yet his own assumptions suggest that hell not only exists but that it might continue to exist indefinitely. This would be the sort of hell envisioned by C. S. Lewis, in which the doors to hell remain "locked on the inside."[238] Despite the passion and panache with which Berdyaev attacked the traditional doctrine of the eternal hell and called it blasphemous, he could not quite banish the specter of the eternal hell from his own doorstep. Hell overshadowed him even as he denounced it.

In Bulgakov there is a christological dilemma: If Jesus's human rationality was of an ideal or sophianic character, then was Jesus "human" in the sense of being "one of us"? When interpreted as "humanness," the Savior is humanity-in-general and not any particular human being. Bulgakov also transposed what is traditionally the human nature of Christ into the divine nature—that is, human rationality understood *as divine Sophia*—as Paul Gavrilyuk notes. It seems then that there is no union of Godhood with anything creaturely. Perhaps there is

---

238. C. S. Lewis, *Problem of Pain* (2001 ed.), 130.

only a union of two divine principles with one another. Compounding the difficulty is that Bulgakov at times insisted on the sophianicity of both the divine and human in Christ. The "incarnation" then becomes a union of two wisdoms: divine Wisdom and creaturely wisdom. It seems that the two-natures doctrine concerning Christ has been translated into alien categories.[239]

As suggested by the chapter epigraph by Bulgakov, his idea is that *eschatology* follows from *ontology*. But how can this be? From our observation of the world and an analysis of what exists in terms of metaphysical categories, it is not clear how one ever arrives at anything radically new. Yet is not eschatology just this—a sphere of the radically new and the completely unprecedented? The world around us remains in "bondage to corruption," and yet ahead there lies "the freedom of the glory of the children of God" (Rom. 8:21). "For in this hope we were saved," and "who hopes for what he sees?" (8:24). Eschatology is not ontology, and ontology is not eschatology. Bulgakov's problem is that he wished to extrapolate the eschaton from his philosophical system. Another way of putting this would be to say that Bulgakov's universalism flowed from his metaphysical assumptions. There is not much distance between the initial assumptions and later conclusions. He affirmed, especially in *The Lamb of God*, that the human self in its innermost nature is divine. This ontological assumption more or less dictates that all will finally be saved. The idea of a final reunion of divine Sophia with creaturely Sophia is another universalist motif built into the structure of Bulgakov's theology. The question "How do divine Sophia and creaturely Sophia come into their final union?" might be seen not as a deep philosophical puzzle worthy of careful reflection but as a pseudoproblem derived from questionable initial assumptions.

Bulgakov's universalist position required him to engage in creative exegesis of the New Testament. His extended discussion of the sheep and the goats in Matthew 25 might be summarized in three points: that each of us is both "sheep" (in part) and "goat" (in part); that we all as "sheep-goats" must pass into the fire; and that, while the fire is said to be "eternal," it actually is only temporary and lasts only until the impure or vicious "goat" nature burns away and a pure or virtuous "sheep" nature is left behind. It might have been better if Bulgakov had not offered any exegetical arguments at all rather than such doubtful ones as these.

---

239. Another theological innovation in Bulgakov pertains to his understanding of Christ's redemptive work, as Gavrilyuk explains: "Bulgakov's view [was] that the psychological anguish of Christ in Gethsemane was more soteriologically important than his physical suffering on Golgotha. As far as Florovsky was concerned, such a speculation was an inadmissible 'psychologism,' not sanctioned by scripture or tradition" (Gavrilyuk, *Georges Florovsky*, 156). We thus have in Bulgakov a *Holy Thursday theology*, and in Balthasar a *Holy Saturday theology* (*DR* 10.6–10.7), while what we ought to have is a *Good Friday theology* and an *Easter Sunday theology*. Friday and Sunday, not Thursday and Saturday, are the focal days in Holy Week.

9

Debating Universal Election

KARL BARTH, BARTH'S INTERPRETERS, JÜRGEN MOLTMANN,
AND THE POST-1970S KENOTIC-RELATIONAL THEOLOGIES

Apokatastasis [is] a doctrine which the Church as a whole has recognized as a heresy.

—Emil Brunner[1]

I do not teach it, but I also do not not teach it.

—Karl Barth[2]

In the Elect, He negated in advance the rule of evil. . . . In the Elect, He revealed evil only as a power already vanquished, a kingdom of darkness already destroyed.

—Karl Barth[3]

Should the teaching about hell be a part of the gospel proclamation? No, no, no! The proclamation of the gospel means, rather, the proclamation that Christ has defeated hell, that Christ suffered hell

1. Brunner, *Christian Doctrine of God*, 252.
2. Karl Barth, as quoted in Jüngel, *Karl Barth*, 44–45.
3. Barth, *CD* II/2, 142.

in our place, and that we are allowed to live with him and so to have hell behind us.

—Karl Barth[4]

The cross of the Son divides God from God to the utmost degree of enmity and distinction. . . . To comprehend God in the crucified Jesus, abandoned by God, requires a "revolution in the concept of God": *Nemo contra Deum nisi Deus ipse* [No one opposes God except God himself].

—Jürgen Moltmann[5]

The theological career of Karl Barth (1886–1968) spanned half a century (1918–68). Barth might well be regarded as Europe's—and the world's—most influential Christian thinker throughout this period. From the mid-1940s onward, one of the more controversial and much-discussed aspects of his theology was his teaching on God's universal election of humanity in Christ. Related to this was the question of whether Barth's universal-election teaching did or did not imply final salvation for every human being. To this day, opinions are divided as to whether Barth should or should not be considered a universalist. Some scholars assert that Barth's theology contained a universal thrust or dimension but not an assertion of universal salvation as such. They point to Barth's assertion that the early Christian term *apokatastasis* did not accurately describe his position. Other interpreters argue that a careful consideration of Barth's argument regarding divine election, especially in *Church Dogmatics* II/2, indicates that universal salvation is the only conceivable outcome for all humanity. No other conclusion, it is argued, is consistent with Barth's premises. Still others charge that Barth spoke in inconsistent or conflicting ways or that he deliberately maintained a dialectical or paradoxical position—as might be suggested by the epigraph above: "I do not teach it [i.e., universalism], but I also do not not teach it."[6] Among those who hold to a universalistic reading

4. Barth, "Fragebeantwortung bei der Konferenz," 111 (my translation). "Soll die Belehrung über die Hölle Teil der Evangeliums-Verkündigung sein? Nein, nein, nein! Die Verkündigung des Evangeliums heisst doch die Verkündigung, dass Christus die Hölle besiegt hat, dass Christus die Hölle erlitten hat an unserer Statt und dass es uns erlaubt ist, mit ihm zu leben und so die Hölle hinter uns zu haben."
5. Moltmann, *Crucified God*, 152. The Latin quotation is attributed to Johann Wolfgang von Goethe (1749–1832).
6. Relevant literature—to be discussed below—includes Brunner, appendix to *The Christian Doctrine of God*, 340–53; Berkouwer, *Triumph of Grace*; Bettis, "Is Karl Barth a Universalist?"; Bloesch, *Jesus Is Victor!*; Hunsinger, *How to Read Karl Barth*, esp. 128–35; Colwell, "Contemporaneity of

of Barth, many of the earlier interpreters (especially from the 1940s through the 1960s) took Barth's apparent universalism to be a serious mistake.[7] More recently, those affirming that Barth taught universalism have tended to see his universalism in a positive rather than a negative light. What was once a reproach—namely, "Barth the universalist"—has become for many recent readers of Barth a commendation.

Before turning to the question of Barth and universalism, it seems fitting to say something about Barth's interpreters, who are the subject of this chapter almost as much as Barth himself. From the 1930s through the 1960s, as Barth was adding successive tomes to his massive *Church Dogmatics*, there were any number of figures who mingled their deep appreciation for Barth's theology with sharp criticism. Their number included Emil Brunner, Hans Urs von Balthasar, G. C. Berkouwer, Dietrich Bonhoeffer, Gustav Wingren, Hans Küng, Reinhold Niebuhr, and Barth's own editors and translators, Geoffrey Bromiley and Thomas F. Torrance. The general result was a mixed view of Barth. Because Barth was so strong an influence on Christian theologians everywhere in the mid-twentieth century, those who only partially agreed with Barth's positions felt the need to engage his teachings and speak on the record regarding their interpretation.[8] From the 1980s onward, the situation shifted. Once Barth's influence had lessened, the field of Barth studies tended to be dominated by those with positive views of Barth. Those opposed to Barth tended not to write about him. By contrast, Barth's defenders, partisans, and apologists have been intensely active and often have taken issue with one another. The positive result has been a proliferation of new positions and innovative arguments. A less-than-positive outcome in the new situation is that some secondary authors adopted a more-or-less uncritical stance, seeking to explain and to defend the

the Divine Decision"; J. C. McDowell, "Learning Where to Place One's Hope"; Crisp, "On Barth's Denial of Universalism"; Greggs, "'Jesus Is Victor'"; Greggs, *Barth, Origen, and Universal Salvation*; Greggs, "Pessimistic Universalism"; McCormack, "So That He May Be Merciful to All"; P. D. Jones, "Hopeful Universalism"; B. Burton, "Universalism."

7. The anti-universalist objections of Emil Brunner, Thomas F. Torrance, and G. C. Berkouwer are fully treated below, with references (*DR* 9.8). An early affirmation of universalism that was based on Barth's theology was that of John A. T. Robinson, *In the End, God* (1950). Yet *DR* 9.9, on Barth's legacy, shows that Robinson was by no means alone in the 1950s through the 1980s in viewing Barth as an ally in affirming universalism.

8. On the complexities of the Barth-Brunner relationship, see J. W. Hart, *Karl Barth vs. Emil Brunner*. On Barth and Bonhoeffer, see Pangritz, *Karl Barth in the Theology of Dietrich Bonhoeffer*. On criticisms of Barth by Brunner, Bultmann, Bonhoeffer, Niebuhr, Tillich, and Thielecke, see the excellent study by Gary J. Dorrien, *The Barthian Revolt in Modern Theology*, 81–167. Critical appraisals of Barth appear in Berkouwer, *Triumph of Grace*; Wingren, *Theology in Conflict*; Küng, *Justification*; Balthasar, *Theology of Karl Barth*; Bromiley, *Introduction to the Theology of Karl Barth*; Torrance, *Karl Barth: Biblical and Evangelical Theologian*.

great man's every utterance. Barth himself was said to have prayed, "God save me from the Barthians!"[9] Perhaps the late professor from Basel is smiling down on his followers and the theological battles waged in his name [10]

In what follows, we will first consider the complexities of Barth scholarship since 1970 as a context for interpreting Barth's texts (DR 9.1), with a sidelong glance at Barth's encounter in 1916 with a fire-and-brimstone preacher (DR 9.2). We then turn to consider Barth's statements and arguments as they impinge on the question of universalism (DR 9.3–9.5), to a number of critical questions—especially of a metaphysical character (DR 9.6–9.7)—and then to Barth's interpreters (DR 9.8) and the question of Barth's legacy in European Protestantism from the 1950s through the 1980s (DR 9.9). Later we will treat Jürgen Moltmann's universalistic theology (DR 9.10–9.11). The final portion of this chapter—on recent kenotic-relational theologies (DR 9.12) and David Congdon's Barth-inflected, neo-Bultmannian view (DR 9.13)—will connect with the first section of this chapter on Barth scholarship. The chapter is like a parabola—beginning with interpretive issues in Barth scholarship and concluding with interpretive issues in constructive theology—showing that debates on Barth's theology have deeply informed the contemporary theological debates on the doctrine of God.[11]

9.1. Interpretive Prologue: Post-1960s Interpretations of Barth's Theology

The theology of Karl Barth might be compared to a complex mathematical equation that yields expected and unexpected results. By analogy, one might think of Albert Einstein's relativity postulate (i.e., that the speed of light in a

9. Karl Barth, as quoted in Percesepe, Future(s) of Philosophy, 193. Though Paul Tillich was well known for his disagreements with Barth, he paid him a high compliment in stating, "Barth's greatness is that he corrects himself again and again in the light of the situation, and that he strenuously tries not to become his own follower" (Systematic Theology, 1:5).

10. Hans Frei comments: "Barth possesses astonishing descriptive powers. But then, as one tries to restate it afterwards the material dies on one's hands. It can be done, but there is nothing as wooden to read as one's own or others' restatements of Barth's terms, his technical themes and their development. It is as though he had preempted that particular language and its deployment. For that reason, reading 'Barthians,' unlike Barth himself, can often be painfully boring" (Types of Christian Theology, 157).

11. My critique of one aspect of Barth's theology, universal election, should not be taken as a general interpretation or statement regarding Barth's theology, which is both vast in scope and profound in insight. I cannot improve on Flannery O'Connor's remark: "I distrust folks who have ugly things to say about Karl Barth. I like old Barth. He throws the furniture around" (O'Connor, Correspondence of Flannery O'Connor and the Brainard Cheneys, 180–81). Thomas F. Torrance wrote that "it will take many generations, if not centuries, to evaluate his [Barth's] service adequately" (Karl Barth: An Introduction, 179). Both quotations are taken from S. N. Williams, Election of Grace, 179.

vacuum is always constant as measured in an inertial reference frame). This postulate was found over time to contain all sorts of surprising implications—for example, that when approaching the speed of light, bodies increase in mass, distances shorten, and time slows down. While Einstein went wherever his reasoning led him, it took some time before others agreed or even understood what he was claiming. Karl Barth's theology, embodied in the fourteen-volume, six-million word *Church Dogmatics* (1932–67), has likewise led to all sorts of expected and unexpected theological conclusions. In Anglo-American scholarship, the "Neo-Orthodox" interpretation largely prevailed until 1995, when Bruce L. McCormack's *Karl Barth's Critically Realistic Dialectical Theology: Its Genesis and Development, 1909–1936* made waves in the placid pond of Barth scholarship. Even more controversial was McCormack's suggestion in a 2000 essay ("Grace and Being") that divine election *logically precedes* God as Trinity, so that, in a manner of speaking, one might legitimately say that the Trinity is "constituted" by the divine act of election or self-determination in Christ.[12]

To understand the significance of Barth's doctrine of universal election, with its implications for contemporary universalism, it may be helpful to ponder the German-language critique of Barth in the 1970s and 1980s, especially as initiated by Wolfhart Pannenberg and Trutz Rendtorff, and then to consider McCormack's arguments and his defenders and opponents in the expanding field of English-language Barth scholarship in the 2010s. These proliferating debates regarding Barth have touched on multiple themes: the question of divine and human autonomy; the issue of analogical versus dialectical thinking; the issue of German idealism—particularly Hegelianism—in Barth's theology; the relationship between God's being and God's decision vis-à-vis divine election; the issues of separation, conflict, or suffering in God; and finally the issue of what has been called a "historicized" Christology either in Barth or in Barth's followers. In the background of this discussion is the question of how Barth fits

---

12. See also McCormack, *Orthodox and Modern*. George Hunsinger's *How to Read Karl Barth* (1991) advocated a more conservative reading of Barth. Rather than being resolved, the issues in the debate surrounding McCormack have become increasingly complex. Contributions to this debate—in chronological order—include McCormack, "Grace and Being"; Molnar, *Divine Freedom*; O'Neil, "Karl Barth's Doctrine of Election"; Hector, "God's Triunity and Self-Determination"; Molnar, "Trinity, Election and God's Ontological Freedom"; Molnar, "Can the Electing God Be God without Us?"; van Driel, "Karl Barth on the Eternal Existence of Jesus Christ"; McCormack, "Seek God Where He May Be Found"; Hunsinger, "Election and the Trinity"; Cassidy, "Election and Trinity"; A. T. Smith, "God's Self-Specification"; Molnar, "Can Jesus' Divinity Be Recognized as 'Definitive, Authentic and Essential'?"; McCormack, "Election and the Trinity"; McCormack, "Let's Speak Plainly"; McCormack, "Doctrine of the Trinity after Barth"; Scheuers, "Some Aspects of Karl Barth's Doctrine of Election"; Dempsey, *Trinity and Election*; Hector, "Immutability, Necessity and Triunity"; Kantzer Komline, "Friendship and Being"; B. D. Marshall, "Absolute and the Trinity"; Molnar, "Response: Beyond Hegel"; Molnar, *Faith, Freedom, and the Spirit*.

into the trajectory of modern theology, whether as an antimodern thinker, as a "revelational positivist," as a Nicene or Protestant traditionalist, as a modified German idealist, as an anticipation of Moltmann and current relational theologies, or as none of the above. That Barth can be read in so many different ways attests to the complexity and richness of the *Church Dogmatics*.

To a greater extent than English-language authors, German-language scholarship on Barth in the 1970s and 1980s was preoccupied with the issues of human agency and autonomy and the question of whether Barth's theology made due allowance for these. In the words of John Macken, "Are our being and our acts genuinely ours or are we merely passive instruments of the divine pleasure and insubstantial reflections of the divine activity?"[13] Prompted by this general line of inquiry, Trutz Rendtorff proposed that Barth's theology was not antimodern as such. Instead it was a creative redeployment of the logic of the autonomous self, using the captured weapons of the Enlightenment against the Enlightenment. In this way, Barth replaced the freedom and autonomy of humanity with the freedom and autonomy of God. In the *Church Dogmatics*, Barth made Jesus Christ the preeminent expression of God's autonomy, and for this reason it was necessary for Barth to reinterpret the whole content of Christian theology in terms of Christology. In Rendtorff's critique, Barth's election doctrine was a way of avoiding the problem of evil. Election and reprobation became indistinguishable from God's own act of divine self-determination, and so they were removed from the sphere of human life. Barth's references to sin and evil as an "impossible possibility" showed his inability to concede full reality to sin and evil (*DR* 9.7).

The disappearance of sin and evil as bona fide realities followed a certain logic, because in Barth's way of thinking there simply were no self-subsistent agencies other than God to accomplish acts of sin and evil. Indeed, Barth had difficulty accounting for how there could be any properly human subjects capable of action in distinction from God or in opposition to God. In its ultimate outcome, Barth's election doctrine, though focused on God, showed a striking affinity to the axiomatic victory of good over evil within Enlightenment philosophy.[14] Rendtorff also criticized Barth's theology for diminishing and even dissolving the church. While the world would be lost without Christ, the world would not

---

13. Macken, *Autonomy Theme*, viii. The next paragraphs will draw on Macken's excellent summary of German-language debates on Barth. The critical literature on Barth in German included Rendtorff, *Die Realisierung der Freiheit*; Menke-Peitzmeyer, *Subjektivität und Selbstinterpretation*; Holtmann, *Karl Barth*. The best known of the Barth critics was Jürgen Moltmann, whose arguments were in line with those in the 1975 volume edited by Rendtorff. See Moltmann, *Trinity and the Kingdom*, esp. 53–56, 139–44.

14. On this point regarding sin and evil, Trutz Rendtorff's reading of Barth's theology was broadly in agreement with G. C. Berkouwer's "triumph of grace" idea, discussed below (*DR* 9.8).

be lost without the church. Neither the world nor God himself truly needed the church, since God's activity in the world was not tied to the church. A door was thus thrown open to a "religionless," "secular," or "churchless" interpretation of Christianity, foreshadowed in the later writings of Dietrich Bonhoeffer (1906–45) and further elaborated during the 1960s.[15]

Critics of Barth were concerned with what they saw as his inattentiveness to observable realities. His theology seemed up in the air rather than down on the earth. Wolfhart Pannenberg was among the first to express such reservations and to link this to a German idealist hangover or survival in Barth's theology. In Pannenberg's argument, the derivation of the Trinity from the idea of revelation in *Church Dogmatics* I/1 was a reflection of Hegelianism in Barth, mediated possibly through Hegel's theological follower, Philip Marheinecke (1780–1846).[16] Along similar lines, John Macken opined that "the Idealist-inspired demand for a unique principle on which to reconstruct all reality, haunts Barth's thinking."[17] For idealist thinkers, human history was simply the unfolding of an "Idea." While the opening volume of the *Church Dogmatics* makes revelation the dominant "Idea," the later volumes focus on the "Idea" of reconciliation in Jesus Christ. Christophe Freyd's 1978 dissertation compared Barth with Hegel and argued that Barth's theology can be understood as an idealist system built from the premise of God's radical autonomy. The difference between Barth and Hegel was simply a matter of emphasis. The primary conceptual problem within Barth's "system," for Freyd, was whether or not Barth succeeded in reconciling divine freedom with the existence of human freedom.[18]

Another Barth interpreter, Wilfried Härle, judged in 1975 that Barth's ontology was essentially "dogmatic" in the sense that it was wholly dependent on theological premises. In this "ontology of grace," the creature's being was

---

15. Macken, *Autonomy Theme*, 125–29. On the Christian embrace of secularity, see Bonhoeffer, *Letters and Papers from Prison*; H. Cox, *Secular City*; and, in a more radical vein, Altizer, *Gospel of Christian Atheism*. Macken summarizes Rendtorff's provocative claim regarding a covert link between Barth and the Enlightenment: "Far from attaining his aim of reversing the Enlightenment, Barth became the instrument by which the Enlightenment, with its boundless moral optimism and its separation of Christianity from the Church, pursued its conquering advance into the heart of Christianity. To adopt radical autonomy in a Christological form was to end the traditional opposition between dogmatic theology and modern autonomy. But it could do so only by a radical revision of traditional Christian theology" (*Autonomy Theme*, 127–28, citing Rendtorff, *Theorie des Christentums*, 175).

16. Pannenberg wrote that "only in the philosophy of German idealism do we first find the thought of a self-revelation of God in the sense of a strict identity of subject and content" (*Systematic Theology*, 1:222–23).

17. Macken, *Autonomy Theme*, 166. Gary Dorrien judges that "the large matters of doctrinal ambition and logic" were where Barth "closely resembled Hegel" (*Kantian Reason and Hegelian Spirit*, 13).

18. Freyd, "Gott als die universale Wahrheit von Mensch und Welt," as discussed in Macken, *Autonomy Theme*, 135.

identical to its act of relationship to God.[19] Härle argued that this way of thinking
made creation a mere epiphenomenon of reconciliation. Nature itself remained
shadowy, insubstantial, or ghostly. Härle's deepest objection to this "ontology of
grace" was that Barth did not sufficiently allow for the contingent character of
both sin and reconciliation. In Barth, "the being of the creature . . . exists only
insofar as it is the recipient of grace and corresponds to grace. Even nothingness
[i.e., Barth's notion of evil] exists only insofar as it is a contradiction of grace,
and thus the contradiction must be thought of as being posited by grace itself."[20]
The final phrase in the quotation sets Barth remarkably close to German idealist
thought (*DR 7*) and perhaps also to the Böhmist tradition, with its valorization
of conflict or contradiction within the Godhead itself (*DR 5*). Böhmism and German idealism attributed to God an internal dialectic of self-differentiation and
self-reconciliation. To the extent that Barth's account of evil (*das Nichtige*) makes
God the ultimate source of negativity and the final resolver of negativity, we see
something like a German idealist system operating within the *Church Dogmatics*.[21]

Reading Barth in a quasi-idealistic way offers a different vantage point for approaching the question of universalism. The most theologically helpful element
that Barth found in German idealism was the affirmation of the freedom and
subjectivity of God himself. As Barth's thinking developed from the 1930s to the
1960s, however, he came to see that divine subjectivity could not remain aloof as
the inscrutable will of an arbitrary deity. God's self-revelation had to show God
as the God of humanity.[22] As Wilfried Härle argued: "Once God's eternal free
decision for universal reconciliation had been made, pure transcendence was
no longer possible and the Incarnation, the Resurrection and universal salvation
(*apocatastasis panton*) were a logical necessity." In this way, "God takes the 'other,'
takes contradiction and death into his own being."[23] The doctrine of universal
election, as Barth presented it in *Church Dogmatics* II/2, was thus the consistent outworking of an underlying idealistic logic. From another angle, Barth's
repeated statements affirming that humanity could only be considered in relation
to Christ underscored "the ontological character of Barth's language about the
reality of man in Jesus Christ." Such language, Macken noted, suggested "that

19. Härle, *Sein und Gnade*, as discussed in Macken, *Autonomy Theme*, 166.
20. Summary of Härle in Macken, *Autonomy Theme*, 153 and 152.
21. While Pannenberg and Freyd viewed Hegel as a possible point of contact between Barth
and German idealism, Kurt Lüthi (*Gott und das Böse* [1961]) found a point of contact between
Barth and Schelling. As Lüthi showed, Barth's doctrine of evil made his affinities to the idealist
tradition rather obvious. Macken rightly noted the "anti-Idealist and non-systematic elements in
Barth" (*Autonomy Theme*, 138). Yet Barth's universalist tendencies are linked to idealist elements
in the *Church Dogmatics*.
22. Macken, *Autonomy Theme*, 166, 169.
23. Summary of Härle in ibid., 137.

Barth affirms of the relationship between Christ and other men something akin to the hypostatic union between the humanity of Christ and his divinity."[24] If one accepts this reading of Barth, then Christ's attainment of ultimate vindication and glory *must* be that of everyone else. This full union of Christ with humanity requires universal salvation as the outcome for every human individual.

We turn now from the 1970s and 1980s German-language discussion to the English-language debate over Barth's theology since the year 2000. The provocation for the latter came from Bruce McCormack.[25] Basic to McCormack's reconstruction of Barth's thought, as well as to McCormack's own theological agenda, is the notion that Barth presented two different doctrines of the Trinity in the *Church Dogmatics*.[26] In *Church Dogmatics* I/1, the "root" of the doctrine of God as Trinity lay in the concept or idea of revelation—a derivation of the Trinity that McCormack judged to be "far from a rousing success." At this stage, writes McCormack, Barth's "Christology . . . is controlled by the needs and requirements of his doctrine of revelation rather than by soteriological considerations, as would be the case later."[27] The earlier Barth equated God's Lordship with the divine essence—an "abstract conception of lordship . . . not controlled . . . by God's gracious decision to be God 'for us' in Jesus Christ." This meant that "power in the abstract" in Barth was "not defined by the humility, lowliness, and obedience of the Son."[28] In *Church Dogmatics* IV/1 and following, however, one finds "a completely altered landscape."[29] Here Barth derived the doctrine of the Trinity from the historical person of Jesus Christ and allowed Christ's historical reality to shape his understanding of God's eternal nature. The pivot between these two conceptions of the Trinity lay in *Church Dogmatics* II/2 (the volume on divine election), which, on McCormack's interpretation, was the point in Barth's theological development when he first clearly articulated the view of God as Trinity that would later typify *Church Dogmatics* IV. By carrying through in *Church Dogmatics* IV what he began in *Church Dogmatics* II/2, Barth attained and elaborated a deeper insight into God.[30]

24. Macken, *Autonomy Theme*, 59.

25. In "Grace and Being" (2000), McCormack drew on Eberhard Jüngel's interpretation of Barth. See Jüngel, *God's Being Is in Becoming*. Jüngel nonetheless maintained that the Trinity has logical priority over election in Barth's doctrine of God—a prioritization that McCormack inverted. Kantzer Komline notes that "this difference alone justifies speaking of a major 'shift' in Barth interpretation" ("Friendship and Being," 16n21), a shift initiated by McCormack.

26. McCormack's views are summed up in the earlier essay, "Grace and Being," and the more recent "Doctrine of the Trinity after Barth" (2011).

27. McCormack, "Doctrine of the Trinity after Barth," 97, 92.

28. Ibid., 94, citing Barth, *CD* I/1, 349.

29. McCormack, "Doctrine of the Trinity after Barth," 103.

30. In support of his view of *two different* doctrines of the Trinity in Barth's *Church Dogmatics*, McCormack points out that Rowan Williams, the former archbishop of Canterbury, drew a similar

On the basis of this reconstruction of Barth's development, McCormack made a number of striking statements. First, he claimed that divine election *logically precedes* the divine being as Trinity, so that God as Trinity is "constituted" as such by the divine self-determination in Jesus Christ.[31] More recently, McCormack has asserted that "election and triunity are equally primordial in God" and yet that "election has a logical priority over Trinity—because decision has logical priority over being."[32] What McCormack calls the "actualization" of God is an eternal decision enacted in history: "'Actualization' means that the being of the one God-human which is constituted eternally in an act of divine self-determination is made concretely real in this world."[33] For "if the incarnation is not a new event when it takes place in time, that is because the condition of its possibility is already found in an eternal act of willed receptivity." McCormack boldly states, "There is no such thing as an 'eternal Son' in the abstract. The 'eternal Son' has a name and his name is Jesus Christ." Just as boldly he comments that "the immanent Trinity is already, in eternity, what it will become in time."[34] On the theme of suffering, McCormack writes that "suffering and death do not change God because they are *essential* to him." While McCormack admits that this assertion will "*sound* quite Hegelian," he points out some differences between Barth and Hegel.[35] Touching on the theme of Christ's obedience, Mc-

---

distinction in an essay published during the 1970s. Williams wrote concerning Barth: "The Man Jesus has already a part in God's eternal being. . . . From all eternity, God's self-differentiation as Son or Word is directed toward the human and worldly object of election, Jesus of Nazareth" ("Barth on the Triune God," 178). Williams's account of the intra-divine life in Barth is more dramatic and more conflictual than is McCormack's, and Williams affirms that the way of the Son of God "into the far country" ends "in an experience of death that introduces a contradiction into the being of God—a situation of 'God against God'" (McCormack, "Doctrine of the Trinity after Barth," 112n69, summarizing Williams's views). Williams's reading of Barth is reminiscent of the conflictual understanding of God that one finds in Böhme (see *DR* 5.3). In fact, the phrase "God against God" (*Gott wider Gott*) appears in Böhme's account of the origin of evil in the fall of Lucifer (Böhme, *Aurora* 14.101 [*Works* I/1:142]).

31. See esp. McCormack, "Grace and Being." McCormack's position finds broad support in Heltzel and Collins Winn, "Karl Barth, Reconciliation, and the Triune God"; Myers, "Election, Trinity, and the History of Jesus." Paul Dafydd Jones (*Humanity of Christ*, 212–13) speaks of how God "transforms" and "organizes" himself by way of election and incarnation.

32. McCormack, "Doctrine of the Trinity after Barth," 115.

33. Ibid., 105, 107n57.

34. Ibid., 111. Along similar lines, Robert Jenson views the Trinity in eternity as determined *eschatologically*, by what will happen later: "Truly, the Trinity is simply the Father and the man Jesus and their Spirit as the Spirit of the believing community. This 'economic' Trinity is eschatologically God 'himself,' an 'immanent' Trinity. And that assertion is no problem, for God is himself only eschatologically, since he is Spirit" (*Triune Identity*, 141). In a later work, Jenson writes, "In that Christ's Sonship comes 'from' his Resurrection, it comes from God's future into which he is raised." For "the way in which the triune God is eternal, is by the events of Jesus' death and resurrection," so that "his individuality is constitutive of the true God's infinity" (*Systematic Theology*, 1:142).

35. McCormack, "Doctrine of the Trinity after Barth," 105. Hegel and the Hegelians asserted that the man Jesus *simply was* the Second Person of the Trinity, while, according to McCormack,

Cormack adds that "to make obedience essential to God is to lift freely willed activity—and the suffering that is its goal—into the very being of God."[36]

Paul Molnar, in *Faith, Freedom, and the Spirit* (2015) and other writings, offers a sharp critique of Bruce McCormack, Robert Jenson, and others who developed Barth's theology in the direction of what he calls a "historicized christology."[37] Taking aim at McCormack's claim that the doctrine of election logically precedes the doctrine of the Trinity, Molnar insists that "the order between election and triunity cannot be logically reversed without in fact making creation, reconciliation and redemption necessary to God. It is precisely this critical error that is embodied in McCormack's proposal."[38] With the phrase "historicized christology," Molnar refers to a view in which there is a confusion or blurring of boundaries between the eternal, ontological, or immanent Godhead of Father, Son, and Spirit and the economic Trinity of Father, Son, and Spirit as manifested in history and for the redemption of humanity. Some such distinction is necessary, argues Molnar, for otherwise the implication might be that God "needs" the world, "must" create the world, becomes fully "realized" through the world, and so cannot "exist" apart from the world. Haunting this discussion of the "historicized" Trinity is the specter of G. W. F. Hegel, the progenitor of most versions of historicized Christology in the twentieth and twenty-first centuries.[39] Molnar argues that Moltmann offers an overtly Hegelianized theology, while Jenson's and McCormack's views have gradually converged toward those expressed by Moltmann during the 1980s and perhaps even earlier.[40] In asserting

---

Barth avoided this with his two-natures doctrine of Christ. In response to McCormack: the idea of an eternal Godmanhood, which McCormack seems to accept, plays havoc with Chalcedonian Christology and with the two-natures doctrine and so makes Barth's later Christology resemble Hegel's Christology.

36. Ibid., 109–10.

37. Molnar, *Faith, Freedom, and the Spirit*, esp. 225–59 on McCormack and Jenson. Molnar extensively engages Moltmann in his earlier work *Divine Freedom*, 197–234.

38. Molnar, *Divine Freedom*, 63.

39. In treating kenotic-relational theologies below (*DR* 9.12), we will entertain the possibility that Schelling's ideas and theological constructs have been at least as influential as Hegel's on recent authors such as Philip Clayton (*Adventures in the Spirit*) and Thomas Jay Oord (*Uncontrolling Love of God*). The idea of a "voluntary kenosis" of God in creating the world—or perhaps even an "essential kenosis" in which God is necessarily limited in relation to creatures—harks back to Schelling's philosophy. See the documentation on Schelling and the rise of nineteenth-century kenotic theology in *DR*, 646n148. If Hegel is the progenitor of twentieth-century "historicized christology," to use Molnar's phrase, then Schelling may be the progenitor of the "cosmicized" or "correlativized deity" in contemporary theology. The former applies to Christ as Redeemer, and the latter to God as Creator.

40. Hans-Luen Kantzer Komline supports Molnar's argument, stating that "McCormack, then, defends Barth not only by introducing a Barth hospitable to Moltmann's positive concerns but also by showing how Moltmann's critiques and concerns become Barth's own" ("Friendship and Being," 14n14). In support of this judgment, Kantzer Komline cites McCormack, "God *Is* His Decision,"

that the historical life, suffering, and death of Christ *define* God's eternal being, McCormack's theology has evolved from an earlier Barth-inspired doctrine of God's transcendence vis à vis the world and toward a Hegelianized doctrine of God as necessarily related to the world.

To adjudicate this issue in Barth interpretation, one must consider evidence on both sides in Barth's writings. From the opening volume of the *Church Dogmatics*, up through Barth's final years, there are statements that assert God's independence vis-à-vis the world and God's freedom with respect to creating and the decision to become incarnate: "'God for us' does not arise as a matter of course out of the 'God in Himself.' . . . It is true as an act of God, a step which God takes towards man."[41] In speaking his word, God is free: "The Word of God is properly understood only as a word which has truth and glory in itself and not just as spoken to us. It would be no less God's eternal Word if it were not spoken to us."[42] Another early statement links the freedom of God in creating with the freedom of God in the incarnation: "In His Word becoming flesh, God acts with inward freedom and not in fulfillment of a law to which He is supposedly subject. His Word will still be His Word apart from this becoming, just as Father, Son and Holy Spirit would be none the less eternal God, if no world had been created."[43] Barth adds further, "The Word is what He is even before and apart from His being flesh. Even as incarnate He derives His being to all eternity from the Father and from Himself, and not from the flesh."[44]

In Barth's volume on the divine perfections, *Church Dogmatics* II/1, the theme of divine independence continues to be asserted: God "could be everything only for Himself (and His life would not on that account be pointless, motionless and unmotivated, nor would it be any less majestic or any less the life of love)."[45] So too Barth writes in relation to the doctrine of creation: God "could have remained satisfied with the fullness of His own being. If He had willed and decided in this way, He would not have suffered any lack. He

---

63–64. George Hunsinger's analyses of Moltmann's and Jenson's theologies further support Molnar's view that the theologies offered by both Moltmann and Jenson are problematic. See Hunsinger, review of *The Trinity and the Kingdom*; Hunsinger, "Robert Jenson's *Systematic Theology*."

41. Barth, *CD* I/1, 172.

42. Barth, *CD* I/1, 171–72.

43. Barth, *CD* I/2, 135.

44. Barth, *CD* I/2, 136.

45. Barth, *CD* II/1, 280–81. God's aseity or self-sufficiency in Barth is the focus of the recent work by Brian D. Asbill, *The Freedom of God for Us* (2015), which argues that "the doctrine of divine aseity is among the most central themes in Barth's theology," both in the earlier and later periods. When, in his mature writings, Barth becomes "increasingly christocentric," his commitment to divine aseity is "not lessened but reoriented," thus establishing that "true human identity and action can only arise from the freedom of God" (177).

would still be eternal love and freedom. But . . . He has willed and decided otherwise."[46] Even in the later volumes of the *Church Dogmatics*, this theme continues: "The divine essence does not, of course, need any actualization. On the contrary, it is the creative ground of all other, i.e., creaturely actualizations. Even as the divine essence of the Son it did not need his incarnation, his existence as man . . . to become actual."[47] "God loves, and to do so He does not need any being distinct from His own as the object of His love. If He loves the world and us, this is a free overflowing of the love in which He is and is God and with which he is not content, although He might be, since neither the world nor ourselves are indispensable to His love and therefore to His being."[48] In his late work *The Humanity of God*, Barth comments, "Why should God not also be able, as eternal Love, to be sufficient unto Himself? In His life as Father, Son, and Holy Spirit He would in truth be no lonesome, no egotistical God even without man, yes, even without the whole created universe."[49]

Shifting to the other side—that is, to McCormack's position—one also finds texts that support an alternate reading of Barth. If one were to presume, for the sake of argument, that Barth in some way supported what Molnar calls a "historicized christology," then how might one detect this in Barth's writings? One might expect that Barth would be reluctant to speak of any Word other than the Word incarnate—in other words, that he would be ambivalent about the *Logos asarkos* (i.e., unfleshed or disincarnate Word). One might further expect that Barth would speak of the humanity of Jesus Christ as being eternal and that he would ascribe agency to divine humanity on the eternal level. This is in fact what one finds in some statements. Barth writes, "In this free act of the election of grace . . . the Son of the Father is no longer just the eternal Logos, but as such, *as very God from all eternity He is also the very God and very man He will become in time.*"[50] After citing this passage, Molnar admits that "[Barth's] thinking here unfortunately opens the door to a confusing idea, namely, the idea that Jesus Christ humanly existed before he actually came into existence by the power of the Spirit from the Virgin Mary."[51] At least in this statement and in a few others like it, Barth affirms a notion of eternal Godmanhood.

46. Barth, *CD* III/1, 69.

47. Barth, *CD* IV/2, 113.

48. Barth, *CD* IV/2, 755.

49. Barth, *Humanity of God*, 50.

50. Barth, *CD* IV/1, 66 (emphasis added). See *KD* IV/1, 70: "In diesem freien Akt der Gnadenwahl ist der Sohn des Vaters schon night mehr bloss der ewige Logos, sondern als solcher, also wahrer Gott von Ewigkeit zugleich schon der wahre Gott und der wahre Mensch der er in der Zeit sein wird."

51. Molnar, *Faith, Freedom, and the Spirit*, 346.

Elsewhere in his writings, Barth refers to the doctrine of an eternal Son of God as an "abstraction."[52] In an interview, he rejected the notion of the *Logos asarkos* and in the same context argued: "From eternity the Son (as God and man) exists in God. But until the incarnation this has not happened. Nevertheless, this must be made clear. Otherwise you have a fourth member of the Trinity."[53] Barth's reasoning here is unclear, since it does not seem possible to claim that God the Son "from eternity" exists as "God and man" and then to say that "until the incarnation this has not happened." These two statements might be reconciled by interpreting "incarnation" as an eternal event or timeless reality. On the basis of this statement, Jenson's and McCormack's interpretations of Barth seem to have some validity. This becomes yet clearer when Barth attributes agency not only to the "Son of God" but also to "Jesus Christ" as "the beginning of all the ways of God."[54] Often cited by scholars is Barth's repeated assertion that "Jesus Christ is the electing God," which supports the claim that the eternal Son *as God-man* has transmundane agency (i.e., in electing), and thus that *Church Dogmatics* II/2 presupposes throughout its argumentation an eternal Godmanhood.[55]

McCormack's critics Hunsinger and Molnar argue that it is conceptually untenable, or perhaps logically unintelligible, to make the doctrine of election logically prior to the Trinity or to affirm a "historicized christology" in which the eternal being of the Son of God is constituted by the earthly life of Jesus. They claim that this is something that Barth either *did not say* or *could not have said*. In the recent debate, it is sometimes unclear whether this is an argument over historical theology (i.e., what Barth believed) or systematic theology (i.e., what should be believed). It becomes fuzzy as to whether the question is to be resolved *exegetically* (i.e., by appeal to Barth's statements) or *normatively* (i.e., by showing what is theologically credible). One possibility would be to say that McCormack is correct in one respect, while Hunsinger and Molnar are correct in

52. Barth, *CD* III/1, 54.
53. Godsey, *Karl Barth's Table Talk*, 49, 52. On the *Logos asarkos*, see also *CD* IV/1, 52.
54. Barth, *CD* IV/1, 66.
55. Barth, *CD* II/2, 103, 115, 145, 148, 154. George Hunsinger not only opposes McCormack's and Jenson's views of God but also claims that these views are not based on Barth's writings, and so he seeks to qualify the statement that "Jesus Christ is the electing God," in his essay "Election and the Trinity": "When Barth states that Jesus Christ is 'the subject of election' is he not speaking without qualification (*simpliciter*) but only in a certain respect (*secundum quid*). . . . Strictly speaking . . . only the Son *incarnatus* is identical with Jesus Christ. . . . The eternal Son . . . is necessarily the eternal Son; he is only contingently *incarnandus*" (182–83). Hunsinger has good theological grounds to reject an eternal Godmanhood. Yet to make such an argument *from Barth's texts*, Hunsinger has to import distinctions into those texts that Barth himself did not employ. Taken at face value, certain statements support McCormack's view, just as a different set of texts from Barth, taken at face value, do not.

another respect. As we have shown, McCormack's view is supported by at least some of Barth's texts. At the same time, the blurring of distinctions between the ontological and the economic Trinity may be just as theologically problematic as Hunsinger and Molnar think it is. According to this interpretation, McCormack is *exegetically correct* in his reading of the evidence (or part of the evidence) from Barth's writings, while Hunsinger and Molnar are *normatively correct* in pointing out the theological problems entailed by the ideas that McCormack discovers in Barth's writings. Simply put, Barth is inconsistent. The two sides contending over Barth's legacy are both able to find at least some support in Barth's writings for the views that each side wishes to advocate. While this interpretive debate might seem rather recherché, the remainder of this chapter will show that the doctrine of God in twentieth- and twenty-first-century Christian theology took the path it did at least in part due to the ambiguities contained within Barth's theology.

9.2. Biographical Prologue: Barth and the Hellfire Preacher in 1916

After almost all his former professors had signed a document to endorse the German war effort in 1914, Karl Barth found that he could no longer endorse the liberal theology that, in his view, led to such ethically deplorable results.[56] During this period Barth was seeking a new theological path and pressing into what he called "the strange, new world within the Bible."[57] Intensively studying Paul's Epistle to the Romans, he was also reading through classic commentaries by such German Pietist authors as Johann Albrecht Bengel, Johann Tobias Beck, Friedrich A. G. Tholuck, and C. H. Rieger. Just before Barth began to write his influential commentary on Romans, he told his theological confidante Eduard Thurneysen (1888–1974) that the time was drawing near to "strike the great blow against the theologians"—meaning the German liberals who in Barth's view had led Protestant theology to a dead end.

At just this time, as recounted in Barth's correspondence, Barth with his congregation got a dose of popular pietistic, judgment-and-grace preaching from an itinerant preacher named Jakob Vetter (1872–1918). In November 1916, the evangelist conducted a weeklong series of revival meetings at Barth's church in Safenwil, after being invited by members of Barth's

56. David Congdon clarifies Barth's break with liberal theology, noting that this intellectual shift—reorienting Barth toward what became known as dialectical theology—was triggered not only by the "Appeal of the 93" in October 1914 but also (and perhaps more overtly) by the "Appeal of the 29" published in September 1914. See Congdon, *Mission of Demythologizing*, 240–60.

57. Barth, "Strange New World within the Bible," in *Word of God and the Word of Man*, 28–50.

congregation.[58] As a tent revival preacher (*Zeltmissioner*), Vetter was something like a German counterpart of the American evangelist Dwight L. Moody.[59] While some of Barth's congregants appreciated Vetter, Barth did not. As Barth wrote, Vetter told of "the blood of Christ . . . as medicine for the soul" yet spoke also of "the open jaws of hell," thus creating "an atmosphere of fear as though the ship were sinking and there were no rescue ship." Barth added, "Last night he really let himself go; it was very bloody, and again it went very badly with the human race. We listen very patiently."[60]

One might wonder why Vetter spoke so explicitly about hell. Was this simply the way that German Pietists of that day preached and won converts? It turns out that Vetter was engaged in a battle against the universalist teaching that was spreading in German-language churches just prior to and during World War I. Several decades earlier, the Englishman Andrew John Jukes (1815–1901; see *DR* 5.9) had published *The Second Death and the Restitution of All Things* (1867), which had just appeared in German translation in 1912. Jukes, like many modern universalists, had been influenced by Böhme (*DR* 5.2–5.4). Though little known today, Jukes had a major impact in the German-language context, and Wilhelm Michaelis called him "a very influential and significant man."[61] Perhaps even more important during these years than the translation of Jukes's book was a work on "universal reconciliation" by the German Methodist theologian Ernst Ferdinand (E. F.) Ströter, *Das Evangelium von der Allversöhnung in Christus* (1915).[62] On Ströter, Michaelis states that "the influence that this extensive book had in the German-language context, in circles holding to universal reconciliation, cannot be overemphasized."[63]

58. Dorrien, *Barthian Revolt in Modern Theology*, 50. See Barth, letter of November 20, 1916 [to Eduard Thurneysen], in Smart, *Revolutionary Theology*, 39–41.

59. Bruns's biography, *Jakob Vetter: Der Gründer der Zeltmission*, highlights Vetter's heartfelt preaching, evangelistic effectiveness, and role as "founder of tent missions" in Germany (*der Gründer der Zeltmission*).

60. Barth, letter of November 20, 1916 [to Eduard Thurneysen], in Smart, *Revolutionary Theology*, 39–41.

61. Concerning Jukes's *The Second Death and the Restitution of All Things*, Michaelis wrote: "Dies Buch hat wie auch die meisten anderen Bücher dieses sehr einflussreichen und bedeutenden Mannes viele Auflagen erlebt" (This book went through many editions, like most other books by this very influential and significant man). See Michaelis, *Versöhnung des Alls*, 17.

62. Ströter moved in the same biblical-Pietist-evangelical circles that Vetter did, though they opposed one another on the question of universalism. Ströter also wrote *Die Judenfrage und ihre göttliche Lösung nach Römer Kapitel 11* (1903); *Das Königreich Jesu Christi: Ein Gang durch die alttestamentlichen Verheissungen* (1909); *Die Herrlichkeit des Leibes Christi: Der Epheserbrief* (1910).

63. "Der Einfluss, den dies umfangreiche Buch im deutschen Sprachgebiet auf die Kreise gehabt hat, die die Allversöhnung vertreten, kann nicht hoch genug eingeschätzt werden" (Michaelis, *Versöhnung des Alls*, 16–17; my translation). A German-language Wikipedia essay gives background on Ströter: http://de.wikipedia.org/wiki/Ernst_Ferdinand_Ströter. Ernst Ferdinand

At the time that Vetter visited Barth's church, universalism was on the up-surge. In response to the trend, Vetter published a treatise in 1911 entitled *Warum ich die Lehre von der Wiederbringung aller Dinge ablehne* (*Why I Reject the Teaching on the Restoration of All Things*), which included the following passage:

> We see that the teaching on the universal restoration of all things has its origin not in Holy Scripture or in the Christian ethos, but rather in heathen philoso-phy. . . . According to Origen, the soul is good, as an efflux from God, and sin is only weakness and actually something defective. He believed that the natural human will had the power of self-improvement, while divine grace played the role of encouraging and supporting the human will. Yet if the soul is good and it already has the nature of God's Spirit, then rebirth is no longer necessary, and both the manifestation of God's Son in human flesh and the work of the Holy Spirit are pointless. On this basis, the soul is certain of its own eternal blessedness, for this is simply the natural evolution of its own nature. The fact of redemption is thereby uprooted, Christ is sidelined, and the whole of Chris-tianity is placed under a question mark. The message of the gospel becomes superfluous, and the teaching of self-redemption has an opportunity to develop in place of the doctrine of redemption through the work of Christ on the cross [*am Fluchholz*].[64]

Universalism, for Vetter, was thus linked to "heathen philosophy," a false understanding of the human self as "an efflux from God," confidence in the power of human nature, and a notion of returning to God through self-redemption. Vetter most likely has in view the German Böhmist or Philadel-phian form of Christian universalism (*DR* 5.8). Given the timing of Vetter's visit to Barth's congregation, he may well have felt the need to preach against universalism and to do so by warning of the danger of hell for those who reject Christ.

On the Sunday of Vetter's weeklong visit, Barth had the opportunity once again to address his congregation from his pulpit, which for days he had ceded to Vet-ter. To Thurneysen he wrote the following day, on Monday, November 20, 1916:

Ströter (1846–1922) had lived in the United States, preached in Philadelphia; St. Paul, Minnesota; and parts of Texas, and was a professor at Central Methodist College in Warrenton, Missouri, and later at the University of Denver. After first learning the dispensationalist theology of John Nelson Darby, the reading of Andrew Jukes's book drew him toward universalism. After some three de-cades in the United States, he returned to Germany, and from 1912 to 1922 was living in Zurich. Between 1898 and 1908 he attended the Blankenburger Konferenzen (Evangelische Allianz), but his universalist views became controversial in that context.

64. Jakob Vetter's treatise was reprinted in 1917, after Ströter's *Das Evangelium von der All-versöhnung in Christus* appeared in 1915. I am here translating from Vetter's 1911 treatise, reprinted in Daniel Werner, *Warum ich die Lehre der Allversöhnung verwerfen* (privately published, 1978), 8.

I let go no sharp blast but spoke comfortingly to Jerusalem. In contrast to all the
. . . gruesome thundering about sin, I asserted calmly that there is joy with God
(e.g., little angels with harps and sheets of music) and that the kingdom of God
begins with joy. In the evening [i.e., the Sunday night service] the man of God set
me right by describing the conditions which must precede joy in the soul. But he
was somewhat confused with his heavenly ladders and was unable to set forth
his scruples very convincingly.[65]

Barth set himself in contrast to Vetter. Where Vetter preached alarm, Barth
preached consolation. Where Vetter fulminated against sin, Barth emphasized
redemption. In light of Barth's opposition to Vetter's bad-news / good-news
preaching and Barth's later citation of writings by Ströter, one wonders whether
the debates over universalism in the 1910s might have had some lingering
influence on Barth.[66] Yet whatever Ströter's influence on Barth may or may
not have been, a clear pattern becomes apparent throughout Barth's career. He
would speak "comfortingly to Jerusalem."

9.3. Barth on Election: An Overview

Barth acknowledges the novelty of his teaching on election in *Church Dogmatics* II/2, stating that "we part company with all previous interpretations of the
doctrine of predestination."[67] Not touting his own theological innovativeness, he
indicates that he would have preferred to have found support in earlier Christian thinkers.[68] John Calvin and the Calvinists prior to Barth understood God's
eternal choice (i.e., predestination) as applying to a discrete group of persons
that included some but not all human beings. Conversely, God's rejection (i.e.,
reprobation) applied to all human beings who had not been elected. Barth's view
of election emerges out of traditional Calvinism, though it represents a major
departure from it. For Barth, as for Calvin, the doctrine of election is double-
sided. It includes both predestination (acceptance) and reprobation (rejection),

65. Barth, letter of November 20, 1916 [to Eduard Thurneysen], in Smart, *Revolutionary Theology*,
40–41.
66. Bruce McCormack has noted the exegetical importance of Eph. 1 and Rom. 11 in Barth's
thinking on the universal scope of divine election. See McCormack, "So That He May Be Merciful
to All," esp. 242, 248. It may be significant that the universalist E. F. Ströter wrote and published
specifically on Ephesians and on Rom. 11 and then published his 1915 defense of universal salvation
while living in Zurich, only about 50–60 km. from Barth in Safenwil. Barth named and interacted
with Ströter's work on Rom. 11 in a long excursus in *Church Dogmatics* II/2, and there he called the
work "*extremely useful* in spite of its glaring mistakes" (*CD* II/2, 267 [emphasis added]; cf. 279).
67. Barth, *CD* II/2, 146. "We have broken with dogmatic tradition" (308).
68. Barth, *CD* II/2, x.

but in Barth these two sides of the doctrine of election no longer apply to two different groups of people. No longer is there any division within humankind, so that one division of humanity is "elect" while the other is "reprobate." Instead, the doctrine of election is entirely good news rather than both good and bad news. Barth takes as a starting point "the general Reformation assertion that Christ is the *speculum electionis* [mirror of election]," and yet he says that this assertion "obviously stands in need of more profound and comprehensive treatment."[69] He finds fault with what he takes as the spirit and ethos of Calvin and early Calvinism, that "in face of this mystery we ought to be silent and to humble ourselves and to adore." Barth wants nothing to do with "the mystification of an unknown God and an unknown man."[70]

For Barth, election is God's divine "Yes" to humanity as a whole, universally chosen in Christ: "The doctrine of election is the sum of the Gospel."[71] On the basis of Ephesians 1:4, Barth insists that God "chose us in him" (i.e., "in Christ").[72] Barth's doctrine of election is Christocentric. At the center of the teaching is Jesus Christ himself rather than the individual human beings who are chosen in Christ. Barth's programmatic statement at the beginning of his five-hundred-page account of divine election in *Church Dogmatics* II/2 is the assertion that "Jesus Christ . . . is both the electing God and elected man in One."[73] Barth is deliberate in speaking of "Jesus Christ." Divine election is *not* an eternal decision of the unfleshed or disincarnate Son of God (which Barth calls the *Logos asarkos*) but that of Jesus Christ or the God-man. If we take Barth at his word, the God-man is eternal not only with respect to divinity but also with respect to humanity. Barth tells us that "trust in the divine decision" of God's grace requires that this decision "is manifested to us as the decision of Jesus Christ."[74] For outside of Jesus Christ—"the name and person to which the whole content of the Bible relates as to the exhaustive self-revelation of God"—there is no true knowledge of God.[75]

69. Barth, *CD* II/2, 155.
70. Barth, *CD* II/2, 147. Barth seems to have exaggerated the theme of God's inscrutability in Calvin's theology and Calvin's understanding of the Christian life. In referring to Christ as "the mirror of election," Calvin taught something more like Barth's view than Barth acknowledges. In looking to Christ—to Christ alone, and not to oneself—one attains assurance of salvation. For Calvin, though, this assurance came only to those who believed in Christ. See Beeke, *Quest for Full Assurance.*
71. Barth, *CD* II/2, 3.
72. Recent interpreters of Barth have not spent much time assessing the exegetical foundation of Barth's claim for universal election, based especially on the "in Christ" statement in Eph. 1:4 and various passages from the Gospel of John. See below (*DR* 9.4–9.5) for a brief assessment of Barth's New Testament exegesis pertaining to universal election.
73. Barth, *CD* II/2, 3.
74. Barth, *CD* II/2, 107.
75. Barth, *CD* II/2, 153.

Christ-centered election implies that Jesus Christ himself is both the Elect One and the Reprobate One. Christ is the Reprobate in the suffering on the cross that he willingly endured for humankind. Christ is the Elect through the vindication that took place when he rose from the dead. Christ thus stood under the divine "No" as well as the divine "Yes." Barth's theology often refers to "decision" (*Entscheidung*), a term that captures the very nature of God. He goes so far as to say that "Jesus Christ is the decision of God" and that "the divine-human person of Jesus Christ . . . is identical with the eternal purpose of the good-pleasure of God."[76] Barth first considers the abstruse Calvinist debates between seventeenth-century infralapsarians and supralapsarians.[77] Following this, he settles for what he calls a "purified Supralapsarianism" and stresses that "the divine attitude is not a matter of chance. It is not revocable or transitory."[78]

Barth's logic of election is substitutionary. Despite the debates among modern theologians over the idea of substitutionary suffering, Barth's understanding of election and of the cross of Christ clearly involves substitutionary suffering.[79] Christ "fulfills this judgment by suffering the punishment which we have all brought on ourselves."[80] Barth writes that "the election of the man Jesus is specifically His election to suffering."[81] Barth does not shrink from speaking of God's wrath, inflicted on Christ in his suffering on the cross. Christ bore the divine judgment, condemnation, and wrath due to human sin: "The wrath of God, the judgment and the penalty, fall, then, upon Him. And this means upon His own Son, upon Himself; upon Him, and not upon those whom He loves and elects 'in Him.'"[82] It is in fact Barth's substitutionary logic that evokes the question of universalism. Christ's rejection by God was the rejection of all human sinners and sin. Christ's vindication is the vindication of all. God's verdict of "No" against human sin has already been spoken. The rejection of Christ on the cross means that rejection no longer remains—that rejection itself is rejected.

Contrary to what some critics have charged, Barth does not fail to mention faith in *Church Dogmatics* II/2. He states that "the complement of election is faith," that "election and faith belong together," and that "in respect of those who are elected 'in Him,' it follows that their election consists concretely in their

76. Barth, *CD* II/2, 7, 108.
77. Supralapsarianism held that God's decrees of election and reprobation logically preceded God's decree to permit the fall of humanity into sin, while infralapsarianism held the reverse position. For further discussion, see Fesko, *Diversity within the Reformed Tradition*, and Goudriaan and van Lieburg, *Revisiting the Synod of Dordt (1618–1619)*.
78. Barth, *CD* II/2, 142, 6.
79. On the idea of substitution in Barth, see Menke, *Stellvertretung*, 168–93.
80. Barth, *CD* IV/1, 253.
81. Barth, *CD* II/2, 120.
82. Barth, *CD* II/2, 124.

faith in Him."[83] Yet ambiguity arises at just this point. Inasmuch as all human beings without exception are elected in Christ—and this election is linked to faith—the empirical fact that not all believe calls for explanation. How is one to understand the contrast between those who believe in Christ and those who do not? Barth describes the contrast in more than one way. At certain points, he uses the terms *de jure* and *de facto* to express this difference: "The sanctification of all humanity and human life . . . has already taken place *de jure* in Jesus Christ."[84] There is a problem, though, with this formulation. Describing redemption as *de facto* for some people but not for others conflicts with other passages in which Barth stresses the actuality or factuality of redemption for all. More characteristic than the contrast of *de jure* versus *de facto* is Barth's contrast of knowing versus non-knowing. Thus interpreted, the line of division within humanity is epistemic. Everyone is redeemed, but not everyone knows this. In his essay "The Humanity of God," Barth writes, "The so-called 'outsiders' are really only 'insiders' who have not yet understood themselves and apprehended themselves as such."[85] On the basis of this late essay by Barth, one would have to say that redemption is not merely *de jure* for all but *de facto* for all, though many remain unaware of their own *de facto* redemption.

For Barth, there are not only apparent "outsiders" who are "insiders" without knowing it but also apparent "insiders" who are "outsiders." "Even the most persuaded Christian," Barth explains, "in the final analysis, must and will recognize himself ever and again as an 'outsider.' So there must then be no particular language for insiders and outsiders."[86] Barth tends to think of salvation in terms of expanding circles—like the ripples when a stone is thrown into a pond. Yet this is only part of the picture. The other aspect is a blurring of boundaries, as in *Church Dogmatics* II/2, where in Barth's account the biblical King Saul (generally interpreted as wicked) looks rather righteous, and King David (generally interpreted as righteous) looks somewhat wicked. Barth's treatment of Judas as Jesus's disciple is another case in which the boundaries between righteous and unrighteous, or church and nonchurch, become fuzzy.[87] The rejection of "outsider" versus "insider" language raises questions regarding Barth's ecclesiology, to which we will return below.

In the *Church Dogmatics*, Barth offers a strident critique of the universalism contained in Ernst Troeltsch's posthumously published *Glaubenslehre* (1925). For Barth, Troeltsch was important as a final and culminating figure in a line

83. Barth, *CD* II/2, 113, 161, 126. Cf. *CD* II/2, 244, 327, 556; *CD* IV/1, 93.
84. Barth, *CD* IV/2, 620.
85. Barth, *Humanity of God*, 59.
86. Ibid.
87. See McGlasson, *Jesus and Judas*.

of German liberal Protestant development that began in Schleiermacher. Barth
writes, "With him [Troeltsch] the doctrine of faith was on the point of dissolution into endless and useless talk." In Troeltsch's reflections on ultimate human
fulfillment, Barth identifies a "gnostic and mythological dualism" according
to which the human spirit is trapped in "flesh" and struggles to escape. In
Troeltsch, as Barth explains, "this dualism . . . must be followed right back into
the divine being itself . . . in which we have to accept a conflict . . . between
the aims of the spiritual world and the aberrations of the spirit." The further
implication, writes Barth, is that God must himself undergo redemption: "In
the last analysis redemption is the 'self-redemption of God, the return of God
to himself.' . . . We can speak of a self-amelioration, self-multiplication, and
self-enrichment of God through the finite processes of life, interrupted by our
opposition . . . and completed in the return of finite spirits to the essence of
God, with perhaps a dissolution of their individual existence, an end in which
the moments of truth in theism and pantheism converge."[88] Barth then asks
two questions, both calling for an affirmative answer: "Does this mean that
we are back at Jacob Boehme and Master Eckhart?" and "Was this, then, the
final word of Neo-Protestantism?" Barth clearly repudiated Troeltsch's version
of universalism.

In various passages Barth seems to affirm—and in other passages to deny—
what sounds like a doctrine of universal salvation. Some passages apparently
supportive of universalism are as follows:

The witness of the community of God to every individual man consists in
this—that this choice of the godless man is void; that he belongs eternally to
Jesus Christ and therefore is not rejected, but elected by God in Jesus Christ
. . . and that he is appointed to eternal life with God on the basis of the righteous, divine decision.[89]

This, then, is the message with which the elect community . . . has to approach
every man—the promise, that he, too, is an elect man. . . . It [the elect commu-
nity] knows that God . . . has taken upon Himself the rejection merited by the
man isolated in relation to Him; that on the basis of this decree of His the only
truly rejected man is His own Son; that God's rejection has taken its course and
been fulfilled and reached its goal, with all that that involves, against this One,
so that it can no longer fall on other men or be their concern. . . . It cannot now
be their [i.e., unbelievers'] concern to suffer the execution of this threat, to suffer the eternal damnation which their godlessness deserves. . . . [Damnation] is

88. Barth, CD IV/1, 385–86.
89. Barth, CD II/2, 307.

the very goal which the godless cannot reach because it has already been taken away by the eternally decreed offering of the Son of God to suffer in the place of the godless.[90]

The exchange which took place on Golgotha, when God chose as His throne the malefactor's cross, when the Son of God bore what the son of man ought to have borne, took place once and for all in fulfillment of God's eternal will, and it can never be reversed. There is no condemnation—literally none—for those that are in Christ Jesus. . . . Man is not rejected. . . . When we look into the innermost recesses of the divine good-pleasure, predestination is the non-rejection of man. . . . We are not called upon to bear the suffering of rejection because God has taken this suffering upon Himself. . . . We can believe in our own non-rejection and the non-rejection of all men.[91]

He [i.e., the unbeliever] may let go of God, but God does not let go of him. . . . The choice which he thus makes is eternally denied and annulled in Jesus Christ. . . . The decision about the nothingness of his negative act has been eternally made in Jesus Christ.[92]

The believer cannot possibly recognize in the unbelief of others a final fact. How can he even establish it with any certainty as their unbelief? . . . We cannot—essentially—believe against unbelievers but only for them.[93]

Is it only for those who have recognised their election, and not for those who have not yet recognised it, that the lordship of Satan was broken . . . ? Was this to be effectual for some, and not for others?[94]

This much is certain, that we have no theological right to set any sort of limits to the loving-kindness of God which has appeared in Jesus Christ. Our theological duty is to see and understand it as being still greater than we had seen before.[95]

On the other hand, there are apparent denials of universalism on Barth's part:

It is from an optimistic estimate of man in conjunction with this postulate of the infinite potentiality of the divine being that the assertion of a final redemption of each and all, known as the doctrine of the *apokatastasis*, usually draws its

90. Barth, *CD* II/2, 318–19.
91. Barth, *CD* II/2, 167–68. Cf. *CD* IV/3/1, 354.
92. Barth, *CD* II/2, 317.
93. Barth, *CD* II/2, 327.
94. Barth, *CD* II/2, 333.
95. Barth, *Humanity of God*, 62.

inspiration and power. Paul does not start from this point and therefore he does not get the length of this assertion.[96]

It is His [i.e., God's] concern what is to be the final extent of the circle [of salvation]. If we are to respect the freedom of divine grace, we cannot venture the statement that it must and will finally be coincident with the world of man as such (as in the doctrine of the so-called *apokatastasis*). No such right or necessity can legitimately be deduced. Just as the gracious God does not need to elect or call any single man, so He does not need to elect or call all mankind.[97]

The Church will not then preach an *apokatastasis*, nor will it preach a powerless grace of Jesus Christ or a wickedness of man which is too powerful for it. But without any weakening of the contrast, and also without any arbitrary dualism, it will preach the overwhelming power of grace and the weakness of human wickedness in the face of it.[98]

It [i.e., salvation] can only be a matter of the unexpected work of grace and its revelation on which we cannot count but for which we can only hope. . . . To the man who persistently tries to change the truth into untruth, God does not owe eternal patience. . . . We should be denying or disarming that evil attempt . . . to postulate a withdrawal of that threat and in this sense to expect or maintain an *apokatastasis* or universal reconciliation as the goal and end of all things. No such postulate can be made even though we appeal to the cross and resurrection of Jesus Christ. Even though theological consistency might seem to lead our thoughts and utterances most clearly in this direction, we must not arrogate to ourselves that which can be given and received only as a free gift. . . . There is no good reason why we should forbid ourselves . . . openness to the possibility [of] . . . the super-abundant promise of the final deliverance of all men. . . . Does it [God's reality] not point plainly in the direction of the work of a truly divine patience and deliverance and therefore of an *apokatastasis* or universal reconciliation? . . . We are surely commanded the more definitely to hope and pray for it.[99]

The final quotation puts Barth's dialectics on full display. We cannot, he says, "expect or maintain an *apokatastasis*," while he states that God's reality seems to "point plainly in the direction of . . . an *apokatastasis* or universal reconciliation." He advises us not to "maintain" this doctrine but to have "openness" toward it—not "to expect" it but to recognize that God's reality "point[s] plainly"

96. Barth, *CD* II/2, 295.
97. Barth, *CD* II/2, 417.
98. Barth, *CD* II/2, 477.
99. Barth, *CD* IV/3/1, 477–78.

toward it. Barth talks and walks a fine line. Is it surprising, then, that Barth's readers have interpreted him in conflicting ways?

9.4. Barth on Israel's Election and the Jewish People

The biblical exegesis that comprises a large part of Barth's *Church Dogmatics* II/2 is quite complex and yet reflects certain broad tendencies. In general, one might say that Barth *blurs boundaries*, including the boundaries between church and Israel, believers and nonbelievers, and the righteous and unrighteous characters in the Bible. Israel, says Barth, has an "enigmatic dual existence . . . as Isaac and Ishmael, as Jacob and Esau, as Moses and Pharaoh, as the Church and the Synagogue."[100] At times Barth's reasoning is tortuous, as in the following passage: "The community, too, is as Israel and as the Church indissolubly one. It, too, as the one, is ineffaceably these two, Israel and the Church. It is as the Church indeed that it is Israel, and as Israel indeed that it is the Church."[101] Rereading this does not add clarity, and so one is still left asking: Are the church and Israel two entities or one? And what is going on here? The macroscopic view is that Barth, from the beginning of *Church Dogmatics* II/2, has announced his view that all human beings are elect in Christ. As noted above, Barth wrote that Christ was the "only rejected" human being. In light of his doctrine of universal election, Barth has no choice but to blur the boundaries between God's people and all other people in the Old Testament and New Testament alike—though the Old Testament seems more resistant to this exegesis than the New. In the Hebrew Bible or Old Testament, Israel is described as the "chosen people" and set over and against other nations. Barth's election theory cannot readily accommodate the idea of a unique people (i.e., Israel) who for centuries were set apart from other peoples through their faith in and worship of the true God.

To maintain his theory of universal election, Barth is obliged to deny that Israel's history might be a story of *Israel's faithfulness to God*. Their history for Barth is instead a history of failure, unbelief, and rejection of their own election. He writes summarily, "Israel is the people of the Jews which resists its divine election."[102] While the New Testament indeed speaks of Israel as "hardened" in resisting God (Rom. 11:7), Barth develops this theme in a lopsided way, focusing almost exclusively on unfaithfulness instead of faithfulness.[103] Barth identifies

100. Barth, *CD* II/2, 240.
101. Barth, *CD* II/2, 198.
102. Barth, *CD* II/2, 198. Cf. *CD* II/2, 199.
103. In his "Why Was and Is the Theology of Karl Barth of Interest to a Jewish Theologian?," the Orthodox Jewish thinker Michael Wyschogrod comments: "There is nothing more important that I have learned from Barth than the sinfulness of Israel. . . . But, to turn from confession to

Israel with disobedience: "Israel as such and as a whole is not obedient but disobedient to its election."[104] In comparison with what Barth has to say about Israel, his language on the church is often highly idealized. "The Church is the perfect form of the elected community of God."[105] Barth speaks of Israel's corporate responsibility for Jesus's death: "Israel in itself and as such is the 'vessel of dishonor.' It is the witness to the divine judgment. It embodies human impotence and unworthiness. For by Israel its own Messiah is delivered up to be crucified."[106] And again: "What happens is that Israel's promised Messiah comes and in accordance with His election is delivered up by Israel and crucified for Israel."[107]

The problem is that Barth compresses the history of Israel into the single episode of Israel's rejection of Jesus. He ignores the Jews who were faithful to Israel's God prior to the coming of Jesus and misses the positive note on which Paul begins his great exposition of Israel's place in redemptive history in Romans 9–11: "They are Israelites, and to them belong the adoption, the glory, the covenants, the giving of the law, the worship, and the promises. To them belong the patriarchs, and from their race, according to the flesh, is the Christ" (Rom. 9:4–5). Barth's comments on the Jewish rejection of Jesus imply that the betrayal, trial, and delivering up of Jesus to the Roman authorities were actions undertaken by the Jewish people as such. This is one of the persistent misunderstandings that appears in Christian anti-Semitism and is a view contradicted by a close analysis of the New Testament Gospels themselves.[108] Moreover, Barth's interpretation of the Jews as those who betrayed Christ is deeply ahistorical. What of the centuries of Jewish faithfulness to Yahweh, Torah, and covenant? Does not the New Testament in certain passages underscore Israel's history as precisely a history of faith and faithfulness (e.g., Heb. 11), affording spiritual role models for later gentile Christians?[109] This element is missing from *Church*

---

comment, it is not the whole truth. . . . Along with the unfaithfulness, there is also Israel's faithfulness, its obedience and trust in God, its clinging to its election, identity, and mission against all the odds" (223–24). I am indebted to Mark Nussberger for calling my attention to this essay.

104. Barth, *CD* II/2, 208.

105. Barth, *CD* II/2, 227.

106. Barth, *CD* II/2, 224.

107. Barth, *CD* II/2, 208.

108. On Jesus's death as a historical event and the question of New Testament anti-Semitism, see McClymond, *Familiar Stranger*, 120–28.

109. An online essay in *Kesher: A Journal of Messianic Judaism*, entitled "'Salvation Is from the Jews': An Assessment and Critique of Karl Barth on Judaism and the Jewish People," by an author identified only as "R. R.," makes this point:

To paint Israel and Israel's witness in such unequivocally negative terms reveals one of Barth's most significant blind spots. . . . Barth fails to recognize that Israel's history is not merely a history of disobedience, but also includes within it periods of blissful obedience and faithfulness. In fact, "the history of Israel, as of old and so now, is the recounting of

Dogmatics II/2, as indeed it must be, because Barth's theory of universal election cannot readily incorporate any notion of a distinct and "elect" people—even prior to Christ's coming—who are conspicuously set apart from others. The ahistorical character of the exegesis becomes clear when Barth baldly states: "Strictly speaking, He alone [i.e., Jesus] is Israel."[110] Historical reality has here been subsumed into Barth's transmundane and transhistorical election idea. Like a minnow gobbling a whale but not getting larger, Jesus's history has swallowed up Israel's history without remainder.

Although the Hebrew scriptures attest that Israel was God's "elect" or "chosen people" prior to the coming of Jesus, Barth tells us that this divine election of Israel was only a "veiling" and not the truth of God's election. He asks rhetorically, "Is it not that the special calling of Israel was only the veiling of the divine calling of man and this veiling only the preparation for the unveiling to all peoples as the calling of God's community affecting the whole cosmos?"[111] For Barth, Israel seemed to be God's uniquely chosen people, but this was only the "veiling" of the truth of universal election. The whole Old Testament doctrine of election is thus placed under the category of appearance. Even more distressing in *Church Dogmatics* II/2 than the radical recasting of Israel's identity as the "chosen people" is the pejorative language. We read of the "unbelieving Synagogue," "stubborn Israel," "refractory Synagogue," "spectral form of the Synagogue," "synagogue of death," and "dwellers in the ghetto."[112] Barth writes that "the existence of the Jews . . . is an adequate demonstration of the depths of human guilt. . . . The Jews of the ghetto give this demonstration involuntarily, joylessly and ingloriously, but they do give it." Again he says, "It is a wretched testimony, but in its very wretchedness it is also a usable and powerful testimony."[113]

Barth's discussion veers in a dangerous direction. He writes, "Israel cuts itself off from God's community and goes into the ghetto."[114] It is jarring to

---

this people's seeking to do the Lord's will, to follow in his paths, to meditate on his Law, day and night, to honor his precepts, ordinances and statutes and to bind them before their eyes and write them on their hearts."
The quotation within the quotation is from Katherine Sonderegger's essay "Barth's Christology and the Law of Israel," presented at the 2009 Karl Barth Conference at Princeton Theological Seminary. See also Sonderegger, *That Jesus Christ Was Born a Jew.*
110. Barth, *CD* II/2, 214.
111. Barth, *CD* II/2, 229.
112. Barth, *CD* II/2, 216, 237, 218, 221, 209, 264.
113. Barth, *CD* II/2, 209, 263.
114. Barth, *CD* II/2, 214. Barth's anti-Judaism appears when he speaks of Israel's faith in God as centered on "the glory of good works done by man" (*CD* II/2, 217), and "this wrong choice of self-righteous and work-righteous wandering instead of the confessing and believing in correspondence to the divine mercy" (*CD* II/2, 247).

realize that Barth's lectures on election were offered in 1941–42 and published in 1942, just as the Nazi regime developed its euphemistically named "Final Solution" (die Endlösung, die Endlösung der Judenfrage), or plan for killing the Jews.[115] To his credit, Barth wrote in strident opposition to "Christian anti-Semitism" in *Church Dogmatics* II/2.[116] Yet his position against anti-Semitism does not reverse the fact that his biblical interpretation compromises Israel's claim to be God's "chosen nation" in a distinctive sense. For Barth, the church preexisted in the form of Israel: "This means that the Church is older than its calling and gathering from among Jews and Gentiles which begins with the ascension or the miracle at Pentecost. It is manifested at this point, but it has already lived a hidden life in Israel."[117] If, as just argued, Jesus's history has gobbled up Israel's history, then Barth's concept of the church has likewise absorbed his concept of Israel.[118]

To maintain his doctrine of universal election, Barth had to run the exegetical gauntlet of Romans 9–11, three chapters that hardly seem favorable to his views. To account for the text's seeming dualism of the elect and the nonelect, Barth presents the "vessels of wrath" and "vessels of mercy" (Rom. 9:22–23) not as two distinct groups but rather as two stages in a single redemptive process. Barth seems to have had no other choice. As the apostle Paul's words stand, they seem flatly to contradict universal election. Barth writes, "The meaning of its history cannot, then, be perceived in a juxtaposition of the two different purposes of God. . . . God's sentence of rejection on Israel is not a final word, not the whole Word of God, but only the foreword to God's promise of His glory later to be revealed."[119] Here Barth might be compared with Origen, for whom God had no duality of purposes but rather a single purpose being worked out

115. On the timing of *Church Dogmatics* II/2, see Busch, *Karl Barth*, 315. The plan systematically to kill all Jews is often traced to the Nazis' Wannsee Conference in January 1942, though the policy seems to have evolved and become more radical over time, beginning with the September 1939 invasion of Poland and then again in the spring of 1941, during the preparations for the invasion of Russia. See R. Hilberg, *Destruction of the European Jews*; Breitman, *Architect of Genocide*; Browning, *Origins of the Final Solution*.

116. Barth, *CD* II/2, 269, 288–90, 305. Barth underscores the self-contradictory character of Christian anti-Semitism: "Whoever has Jesus Christ in faith cannot wish not to have the Jews. . . . Otherwise with the Jews he rejects Jesus himself" (*CD* II/2, 289).

117. Barth, *CD* II/2, 211. Cf. *CD* II/2, 265.

118. Lohr, in "Taming the Untamable," suggests that there is a larger problem, one that goes beyond Barth's exegesis, in Christian interpretations of Israel's election by God. He comments that "contemporary ways of thinking about exclusion and particularism have profoundly affected contemporary interpretations of the Bible" (24). Christian commentators "inappropriately [read] a universal agenda" into the Old Testament, yet "a better approach is to accept the exclusive, particularistic nature of . . . the Old Testament generally" (24). For "skewed readings" of the Old Testament are "at the cost of Israel's irrevocable—and thus enduring—election" (24).

119. Barth, *CD* II/2, 227.

differently in different people.[120] Barth's idea of reprobation as a stage toward election found its antecedent in Schleiermacher (*DR* 7.3), whose election doctrine is closer to Barth's than is generally recognized.[121]

Barth's exegesis of Romans 9–11 becomes strained because of the assumptions that he brings to the text. He cites the text "For they are not all Israel which are of Israel" (Rom. 9:6) and gives this explanation: "They are not the true Israel, i.e., the Israel which realizes Israel's determination by accepting its proper place in the Church."[122] Barth interprets "true Israel" or the faithful Israelites prior to Jesus as part of "the Church" or what Barth calls "the preexistent Church in Israel."[123] Whereas the apostle Paul was drawing a distinction among the Israelites under the old covenant, Barth does not follow Paul's logic by affirming *an election within the election* (i.e., a faithful subset among the otherwise unfaithful Israelites) but instead reinterprets the division among Israelites as *a division between Israel and church*. Barth writes, "God has from the first chosen, differentiated and divided in Israel. He has from the very beginning separated the Church and Israel."[124] One phrase in Romans 11:5, "election of grace" (*eklogē charitos*), causes Barth no end of difficulty, as he himself admits: "The degree of logical difficulty in this concept is apparent. 'Election of grace' does not seem to be a concept we can well relate to the 'remnant' of a people which is in any case elected by grace."[125] The problem here arises not from the argument of the apostle Paul but from the presuppositions that Barth brings to the text and that do not allow for an election within the election, or remnant within the nation of Israel.

Another exegetical difficulty for Barth is that some Israelites in Romans 11:1–7 are called the "remnant" inasmuch as they rejected the temptation to idolatry and remained faithful to Israel's God—the "seven thousand" who had not bowed the knee to Baal (1 Kings 19:18; Rom. 11:4). Barth admits what seems to be the

120. Origen used the analogy—later repeated by many others—of the sun that shines both on wax and on clay, making the wax softer and the clay harder. One divine activity, like the shining of the sun, has diverse effects (*On First Principles* 3.1.11). What makes the Origen-Barth analogy apt is that Barth in *Church Dogmatics* II/2 discusses God's agency through *both* Moses *and* Pharaoh, which is precisely the point of the shining sun analogy in Origen. For further comparison of these two thinkers, see Greggs, *Barth, Origen, and Universal Salvation*.

121. See Göckel, *Barth and Schleiermacher on the Doctrine of Election*; Hagan, *Eternal Blessedness for All?* The idea that reprobation may be a step toward election seems to have appeared first in Philadelphian universalism (*DR* 5.7–5.8) and then in John Tyler's *Universal Damnation and Salvation* (1798), Schleiermacher's theology (*DR* 7.3), Andrew Jukes's *The Second Death and the Restitution of All Things* (1867) (*DR* 5.9), and so-called ultra-dispensational universalism (*DR* appendix I).

122. Barth, *CD* II/2, 214.
123. Barth, *CD* II/2, 239.
124. Barth, *CD* II/2, 216.
125. Barth, *CD* II/2, 271.

literal meaning of Paul's comments on the "remnant" of the people who were faithful to Yahweh: "'Remnant' of the chosen people—this makes one think rather of a remaining portion of this people which by action and conduct has made itself worthy to be left, to be withdrawn from the judgment which passes over the whole." Yet Barth chooses not to interpret "remnant" in this way, by diverging into the question of free grace versus works-righteousness: "But Paul knows nothing whatsoever of any such worthiness on the part of some in Israel." Barth continues, "Paul will not tolerate that the courageous attitude of the seven thousand . . . should in any sense be regarded as a justifying work which imposes an obligation upon God."[126] Here Barth misses the larger point—that the continuance of faithful Israelites (versus the unfaithful) is a human sign of God's covenant faithfulness. Going against the grain of Paul's argument in Romans 11, Barth identifies the "remnant" and the "rest" with the "whole" of Israel, and then equates "Church" with "*all* Israel" plus "*all* the Gentile world."[127] Another unusual move appears in the comments on Romans 9:7–8, where Barth comes to the exegetically nonobvious conclusion that both Isaac and Ishmael are "children of the flesh" and that both are "children of the promise."[128]

Much as Barth blurred the boundaries of Israel and church, so too, on an individualistic level, he smudged the lines between biblical heroes and anti-heroes, or believers and unbelievers. To some extent, Barth's exegesis repristinates the familiar Protestant theme of a church of sinners saved by grace. Yet Barth goes further when he states that the God of Abraham, Isaac, and Moses is equally "the God of Ishmael and Esau, even as the God of Pharaoh."[129] "In their own way," writes Barth, "even the reprobate and those whom God merely uses are elected."[130] Reprobation, for Barth, thus becomes a form of election, and "Pharaoh is still in the same sphere as Moses. . . . God's purpose in the

126. Barth, CD II/2, 271–72.

127. Barth struggles with Rom. 11:7 (see CD II/2, 275), where the biblical text states that "Israel failed to obtain what it was seeking. The elect obtained it, but the rest were hardened." On Rom. 11, Barth says that "in the *leimma* [remnant] of v. 5 and the *loipoi* [rest] of v. 7 he [Paul] sees the whole of Israel" (CD II/2, 280). This statement is ambiguous, since it might mean that "remnant" = "the rest" = "the whole of Israel." Barth explains the statement just quoted with an even more impenetrable comment: "Regarded christologically and eschatologically the Church is always both *all* Israel—not only the seven thousand but also the hardened rest—and *all* the Gentile world, those who have already become believers and those who are yet to become so" (ibid.). The adverbs "christologically" and "eschatologically" are a signal that Barth is leaping over inconvenient exegetical and historical details and affirming what he wanted to affirm all along: that all humanity is elect in Christ. So he makes another set of equations: "Church" = "*all* Israel" = "*all* Gentiles." In light of Barth's presuppositions, this line of reasoning makes sense; in light of Rom. 11, it does not.

128. "Both Isaac and Ishmael are 'children of the flesh.' . . . It is as 'children of the promise' that they are children of God and holy children of Abraham" (CD II/2, 215).

129. Barth, CD II/2, 231.

130. Barth, CD II/2, 149.

election of His community is executed through Pharaoh, too, and not through Moses only." The biblical text "So then he has mercy on whomever he wills, and he hardens whomever he wills" (Rom. 9:18) means for Barth that "in different forms, God wills one and the same thing . . . the one purpose of God in the election of His community."[131] In Barth's exegesis, David and Saul or Peter and Judas share a common election and stand together as instruments of God's purposes.[132]

What happens, then, in Barth's theology, to the election of individuals—or, for that matter, the salvation of individuals? The approach to this theme in *Church Dogmatics* II/2 is double-sided. Barth comments on "the discovery and estimation of the individual, which has dominated the so-called modern age," and he generally views individualism not as an implication of biblical teaching but as an expression of secular culture.[133] At times Barth seems categorically to reject the notion of individual election: "We have to remove completely from our minds the thought of an individual purpose in predestination."[134] He later backtracks by saying that "the classical doctrine [of election] certainly did not err in speaking so emphatically and assiduously of the predestination of individual human beings."[135] There seems to be some inconsistency on this point. In discussing Gregory of Nyssa (*DR* 3.9), we noted the criticism that Gregory all but eliminated individual salvation. A salvation of humanity-in-general was perhaps what Gregory had in view, and on this basis it is hard to affirm the decisive significance of individual responses of faith or obedience. Similar issues arise in Barth. The ambiguity concerning individual salvation in Barth is a sign of his tendency to regard human beings corporately. It also reveals Barth's affinity with ancient Greek Christian thinkers (e.g., Gregory of Nyssa and Maximus the Confessor [*DR* 4.8]) for whom humanity in its ideal, corporate form had logical or theological priority over individual humans.[136]

131. Barth, *CD* II/2, 220–21. To support his affirmation of "the one purpose of God," Barth refers to Rom. 11:32: "that he [i.e., God] might show mercy to all." He interprets this in the universalistic way that E. F. Ströter does (cited by name in *CD* II/2, 267). Yet in Rom. 11:32, the "all" likely refers to the many nations that are included and incorporated into the "olive tree" that Paul in Rom. 11 uses as a figure for the people of Israel.

132. "There is something of Saul in David, just as there is something of David in Saul" (Barth, *CD* II/2, 372). "Saul and David were therefore hewn from the same wood. In fact, they were sinful types of the same sinful people" (*CD* II/2, 383). "Judas Iscariot is undoubtedly a disciple and apostle . . . no less so than Peter and John" (*CD* II/2, 459).

133. Barth, *CD* II/2, 306.

134. Barth, *CD* II/2, 143.

135. Barth, *CD* II/2, 310. "For the Bible is, in fact, everywhere concerned with the election of individual men" (*CD* II/2, 341).

136. Charles T. Waldrop notes Gordon Kaufman's doubt "that Barth understands the human nature of the Logos as an individual person, even though that human nature is described in the

9.5. Barth on Election in the New Testament and Christian Tradition

The most important New Testament passage for Barth's doctrine of universal election is the first chapter of the Pauline Epistle to the Ephesians, where we read that "He [i.e., God] chose us in Him [i.e., Christ] before the foundation of the world" (Eph. 1:4). The text raises the question: Who is denoted by "us"? The context in Ephesians does not favor Barth's presumption that "us" refers to humanity generally. Ephesians 1:11–14 speaks in the first person of "we who were the first to hope in Christ" (v. 12), and it seems reasonable to identify the "we who . . . hope in Christ" with the "us" and "we" of several verses earlier, whom God chose in Christ. Later verses shift to the second person—"you also, when you heard the word of truth, the gospel of your salvation, and believed in him" (v. 13)—and the phrasing delimits a group of persons who have heard the gospel, responded to it in faith, and received the "seal" of the Holy Spirit. Nothing in Ephesians 1 indicates that the "we" and "us" of Ephesians 1:4 refer to humanity generally, while the "we" and "us" of Ephesians 1:12 clearly carry a different meaning—namely, believers in Christ.[137] Unless one wants to argue that *everyone* has heard the gospel, *everyone* has believed in the gospel, and *everyone* has received the gift of the Holy Spirit, there is no reason to interpret the "us" of Ephesians 1:4 as referring to all human beings. The idea that the text refers to humanity without exception is not a result of Barth's exegesis but is a presupposition that Barth brought to the text regarding an all-inclusive unity of humanity in Christ.[138]

When one examines the whole of New Testament teaching on divine election, a problem appears for Barth's idea of universal election. In many biblical

---

Church Dogmatics as having its own personality and will" (*Karl Barth's Christology*, viii). Waldrop concludes that "it is not clear to what extent Barth can say that Jesus Christ is an ordinary man as other men are" (172). "Jesus Christ is a man, but he is a man in a unique sense . . . [as] the one man who is the true actualization of human essence and in whom all other people have their true being. Other people do not exist so much alongside of Jesus Christ as within him." This may "mitigate the significance of the existence of other people [i.e., other than Jesus]" (176). Barth's German-language critics from the 1970s and 1980s (see DR 9.1) often claimed that Barth's theology left little conceptual space for individual human beings other than Jesus Christ.

137. An analysis of Barth's problematic exegesis of the Epistle to the Ephesians, the Gospel of John, and other New Testament texts, could easily fill a chapter. For a searching critique of Barth's exegesis in support of universal election, with reference to biblical scholars and theologians of the 1950s and 1960s who offered analyses of Barth's views, see S. A. Hayes, "Emil Brunner's Criticism," 12–45.

138. In Barth, CD IV/2, 59, we find the principle that may underlie Barth's reading of Eph. 1: "The human nature elected by Him and assumed into unity with His existence is implicitly that of all men. In His being as man God has implicitly assumed the human being of all men. In Him not only we all as *homines*, but our *humanitas* as such—for it is both His and ours—exist in and with God Himself." This stress on human nature as such (*humanitas*) rather than on individual human beings (*homines*) seems to be a part of the Platonic and Idealist philosophical background that Barth brought to the biblical text. Gregory of Nyssa anticipated Barth's teaching Christ's adoption of *humanitas* (see DR 3.9).

passages, what we might call predestinarian reasoning emerges as a way of understanding human sin, stubbornness, and unbelief. Of all New Testament texts on election, Ephesians 1 may be the one that is most amenable to Barth's top-down interpretation, linking God's eternal being to election and to the unfolding process of redemptive history. More often than not, though, the New Testament predestinarian passages function in a bottom-up fashion. God's Word is preached and human beings hear it. Because the preached word is God's Word, one might expect a response of repentance, faith, and obedience. Instead there is rejection, hostility, unbelief, and impenitence. *Why?*

A number of New Testament texts answer this question by telling us that those who reject grace were "not chosen." When many of Jesus's hearers fail to understand the significance of Jesus's parables in Matthew 13, Jesus tells his disciples: "To you it has been given to know the secrets of the kingdom of heaven, but to them it has not been given" (Matt. 13:11). "Has been given" is a so-called divine passive, meaning that God gave understanding to some people and not to others. Though words like "election" and "predestination" do not appear in Matthew 13, the idea of election seems to be implied.[139] So, too, at a pivotal point in the narrative of the Fourth Gospel, as the multitudes are "grumbling" and are soon to reject Jesus, we read Jesus's statement: "No one can come to me unless the Father who sent me draws him" (John 6:44). Once again the idea of election—being "drawn" by the Father—emerges in the context of widespread unbelief in God's spoken Word. Later in the Gospel of John there is an even more startling passage that links together the rejection of Jesus with God's elective purposes: "Though he had done so many signs before them, they still did not believe in him, so that the word spoken by the prophet Isaiah might be fulfilled: 'Lord, who has believed what he heard from us, and to whom has the arm of the Lord been revealed?' [Isa. 53:1]. Therefore they could not believe. For again Isaiah said, 'He has blinded their eyes and hardened their heart, lest they see with their eyes, and understand with their heart, and turn, and I would heal them' [Isa. 6:10]" (John 12:37–40).[140]

These are all hard texts, and they remind one of passages in Exodus in which God is said to "harden" Pharaoh's heart. The point is that predestinarian thinking appears in contexts where there is sin and hardheartedness. These passages may

---

139. This idea of a particular divine election of certain individual human beings but not others—appearing in biblical texts even where the terminology of "election" does not—could be explained either in terms of God's conditional choice (e.g., Molinism, Arminianism) or else an unconditional choice (Thomism, Calvinism). Whether in its Calvinist or Arminian forms, the doctrine of particular election differs from Barth's doctrine of universal election.

140. For a study of this biblical theme, with special attention to the Gospel of John, see Carson, *Divine Sovereignty and Human Responsibility.*

be termed "bottom-up" rather than "top-down" because the line of reasoning begins not with God's eternal will but with human impenitence. The unbelief of those who ought to believe raises the question of where God is, and what God is doing, in the situation. In certain texts the answer seems to be that *not everyone* has been chosen.[141] While this bottom-up reasoning repeatedly appears in the New Testament, it is conspicuous by its absence from *Church Dogmatics* II/2, where Barth's line of thought moves relentlessly in a top-down direction.[142]

Barth's election teaching is striking for the way that it removes all mystery or inscrutability from the divine willing. In the *Church Dogmatics*, the hiddenness or mysteriousness of election disappears. As Bromiley and Torrance state in their preface, there is no "dark and unknown area of the divine will."[143] The inscrutable deity of Luther and Calvin is gone, for God has chosen all in Christ. In Barth there is still a mystery of the Trinity and of the incarnation, but no more mystery of election. Barth is not normally thought of as an Enlightenment thinker, and yet, as Bromiley and Torrance imply, has he not illuminated a theological "dark . . . area"? The upshot of *Church Dogmatics* II/2 for the history of theology is rather clear: the debate on divine election was misguided all along. Oceans of ink were spilled over mountains of paper, through a fifteen-hundred-year-long debate over divine election, from the time of Augustine to that of Barth. Yet all this was in vain. The predestination debates among Augustinians, Pelagians, Semi-Pelagians, Thomists, Jesuits, Lutherans, Calvinists, and Arminians were wrong not only in their outcome but also in their assumptions. The presupposition underpinning the entire Western Christian discussion, and binding together those who otherwise disagreed—namely, the presumption of particular rather than universal election—was simply mistaken. Augustine, Aquinas, Luther, Calvin, Bellarmine, and Jonathan Edwards were all arguing about nothing. Barth correctly noted that in *Church Dogmatics* II/2 he had chosen "to leave the framework of theological tradition."[144] One is led to ask: If Barth's universal election is a legitimate and compelling interpretation of the New Testament, then why was it not proposed by anyone prior to Barth? Is Barth so eminent as an individual thinker that everyone is supposed to listen to and follow him even when the whole Western theological tradition contradicts him?[145] The choice here is either to follow the mainstream tradition or to become devotees of a solitary genius.

141. Without providing a full list, some other texts that point in the same direction are Acts 13:48; 1 Thess. 2:16; 2 Thess. 2:11–12; 1 Pet. 2:8–9; Rev. 13:5–8.

142. See *DR* appendix L for a discussion of Christ's union with humanity in Barth's and Bultmann's exegeses of Rom. 5—a theme closely related to the top-down reasoning on election.

143. Geoffrey Bromiley and Thomas F. Torrance, "Editor's Preface," in Barth, *CD* II/2, vii.

144. Barth, *CD* II/2, x.

145. While it is true that Orthodoxy and Eastern Christianity generally did not follow the Western, Augustinian precedents on divine election, most Orthodox authors simply did not spend much

9.6. Barth on the *Logos Asarkos* and Eternal Godmanhood

The universalistic thrust in Barth's theology is intertwined with his notion of Jesus Christ as an eternal God-man, a *Logos ensarkos* (enfleshed Word) rather than a *Logos asarkos* (disembodied or non-enfleshed Word). Early Christian thinkers conceived of the incarnation *as an event* happening at a particular point in time, and as suggested in the first chapter of the Gospel of John, "the Word *became* flesh and dwelt among us" (John 1:14; emphasis added). Some scholars have argued (*DR* 9.1) that Barth rejects this way of thinking about the incarnation—that is, as a contingent, historical event or occurrence (see *DR* appendix L, on Christ and Adam). The recent debate over Barth is ironic, in that during the 1950s and 1960s the "Neo-Orthodox" reading of Barth held that the great thinker was staunchly antimetaphysical. It comes as something of a surprise in the more recent literature to learn that Barth is a speculative thinker after all. (Barth's treatment of "nothingness" [*das Nichtige*] in *Church Dogmatics* III/3 might long ago have removed all doubt about Barth's willingness to speculate.)

Ontological or metaphysical readings of Barth appear in works by Eberhard Jüngel and Bruce McCormack. Yet these two scholars are by no means alone in their assessment of the ontological dimension of Barth's thinking.[146] The notion of Barth as a metaphysical thinker has a lineage that extends back several decades. The terms used at that time were "actualism" or "actualistic."[147] By making the category of "act" or "event" more fundamental than that of "being" or "substance," one ends up with an antimetaphysical metaphysics. Yet it is metaphysics all the same. McCormack's voluntaristic reading of Barth might be seen as a further refinement of earlier notions of "actualistic ontology." God must be understood as "event," as Barth declares: "To its very deepest depths God's Godhood consists in the fact that it is an event—not any event, not events in general, but the event of His action, in which we have a share in God's revelation." God himself *is* the event of being God-for-humanity. Barth links his idea of God as "event" with the notion of God as the "living God."[148]

---

time discussing the theme of election. With the possible exception of John Scotus Eriugena (*DR* 4.10), it is difficult to think of any theologian before 1800—whether Eastern or Western—who offers any historical precedent to Barth's teaching on universal election.

146. A more "metaphysical" or "ontological" reading of Barth appears in Jüngel, *Doctrine of the Trinity*; Jüngel, *Karl Barth*; McCormack, *Karl Barth's Critically Realistic Dialectical Theology*; McCormack, *Orthodox and Modern*. George Hunsinger's *How to Read Karl Barth* also touches on ontological implications in Barth (117, 129, 136, 164, 228, as cited in van Driel, *Incarnation Anyway*, 83–84). Barth himself said that "we must not yield to a revulsion against the idea of being as such" but should instead "take up the concept . . . with complete inpartiality" (*CD* II/1, 260).

147. Hartwell, *Theology of Karl Barth*, 32–36, 52, 66.

148. Barth, *CD* II/1, 263. Gary Badcock writes, in agreement with McCormack: "For Barth, God is in himself the event in which he chooses to be open to fellowship with humanity in Christ. Or, to put

Something new in the more recent Barth interpretations is the willingness to link Barth to Hegel (*DR* 7.4–7.7). Barth once said, "I myself have a certain weakness for Hegel and am always fond of doing a bit of Hegelling."[149] In Hegel's thought, said Barth, "truth and with it knowledge [is] most strictly understood as a movement, as a history." This implies that "God himself is this event—not anything outside this event." Barth says that what he himself asserts in the *Church Dogmatics*—namely, the notion of God as "event"—is what Hegel asserted before him. What is more, Barth speaks positively of Hegel's "living God" and notes that Hegel "saw God's aliveness well, and saw it better than many theologians."[150] The prominence that Barth gave to the doctrine of revelation, especially in *Church Dogmatics* I/1 and I/2, is another possible line of connection to Hegel and to the Hegelianizing theologians of the nineteenth century (e.g., Philip Marheineke).[151]

To grasp Barth's ontology, the appropriate starting place is Barth's God-man. At a few points in his writings, Barth suggests that the notion of the nonincarnate or preincarnate *Logos* is a theological placeholder, with some limited function to play: "The whole conception of the *logos asarkos*, the 'second person' of the Trinity as such, is an abstraction. It is true that it has shown itself necessary to the christological and trinitarian reflections of the Church. Even today it is indispensable for dogmatic enquiry and presentation, and it is often touched upon in the New Testament, though nowhere expounded directly."[152] Yet this one passage is drowned out by Barth's repeated assertions of the eternality of Jesus, the God-man. "The man Jesus already was even before He was."[153] "The Logos is Jesus."[154] "The Johannine Logos . . . was identical with Jesus and . . .

the same thing another way, God is the event of election in which he chooses from all eternity not to be who he is without humankind" (Badcock, "Hegel, Lutheranism, and Contemporary Theology," 154).

149. Busch, *Karl Barth*, 387.

150. Barth, *Protestant Theology in the Nineteenth Century*, 398–99, 405.

151. Hegel's omnipresence in Continental Western thought since the mid-1800s is a truism. Michel Foucault said that philosophers for the last century and a half have been "doomed to find Hegel waiting patiently at the end of whatever road [they] travel" (quoted in Rorty, *Essays on Heidegger and Others*, 96).

152. Barth, *CD* III/1, 54. By saying that the *Logos asarkos* "in the New Testament" is "nowhere expounded directly," it is evident that Barth does not think that New Testament passages such as John 1 or Phil. 2 speak to the question of a preincarnate or nonincarnate Logos. For a contrary reading of the Pauline texts, see Byrne, "Christ's Pre-Existence," which argues that "Paul's writings do not support playing down Christ's pre-existence in the interests of a Christology supposed more firmly anchored in his historical human life. On the contrary, the rhetorical effect of central Pauline texts is seriously eroded if Christ is not affirmed as the Father's pre-existent Son. At stake here is Paul's acute sense of God's love for humanity made vulnerable to the world in the costly gift of the Son" (308, quoting the summary). Cf. K. Giles, *Eternal Generation of the Son*.

153. Barth, *CD* III/2, 464.

154. Barth, *CD* II/2, 97.

was in the beginning with God."[155] "The basic passage in John 1:1–2 speaks of the man Jesus."[156] "The name and person of Jesus Christ was in the beginning with God."[157] "Jesus Christ is the electing God."[158] "The reality of the divine-human person of Jesus Christ [was] before the foundation of the world and all other reality."[159] "In the beginning with God was this One, Jesus Christ."[160] Barth in an interview setting offered the unusually blunt statement that "the incarnation makes no change in the Trinity" and that "there is only and always a *Logos ensarkos*."[161] Some have suggested that what Barth meant in affirming the eternal God-man is that "Jesus Christ" preexisted Mary's womb only as an idea in God's mind. Yet this reading of Barth would make nonsense of Barth's central claim in *Church Dogmatics* II/2 that "Jesus Christ is the electing God"—a statement that attributes not only virtual or notional existence but also personal decision and effective agency to Christ.[162] The thrust of Barth's statements is twofold. On the one hand, there is a rejection of the *Logos asarkos*. On the other hand, there is an embrace of an eternal Jesus Christ or God-man.

The defining statement of *Church Dogmatics* II/2, that "Jesus Christ is the electing God," may be glossed as follows, in the words of Bruce McCormack:

155. Barth, *CD* II/2, 110 (mentioned in reference to Athanasius but with Barth's approval).

156. Barth, *CD* II/2, 117.

157. Barth, *CD* II/2, 175.

158. Barth, *CD* II/2, 103 (repeated verbatim in *CD* II/2, 145).

159. Barth, *CD* II/2, 108.

160. Barth, *CD* II/2, 145.

161. Godsey, *Karl Barth's Table Talk*, 49. Here the questioner asks Barth, "Does the incarnation make a change in the Trinity?" Barth replies:

No, the incarnation makes no change in the Trinity. In the *eternal decree* of God, Christ is God and man. Do not ever think of the second Person of the Trinity as only *Logos*. That is the mistake of Emil Brunner. There is no *Logos asarkos*, but only *ensarkos*. Brunner thinks of a *Logos asarkos*, and I think this is the reason for his natural theology. The *Logos* becomes an abstract principle. Since there is only and always a *Logos ensarkos*, there is no change in the Trinity, as if a fourth member comes in after the incarnation.

162. Charles Waldrop notes that Barth's primary concern is "to point out the defects of the concept" (i.e., the *Logos asarkos*) (*Karl Barth's Christology*, 47). "Because the *logos asarkos* is an abstraction . . . it has no form and content; it is an empty concept. Therefore, even when we are considering the eternal Word of God who precedes the activity of God in time and who participates in all God's work, it is 'pointless' and 'impermissible' to refer to the *logos sarkos*" (ibid.). One possible interpretation, suggested by Waldrop, sees Jesus Christ as eternally existing in God's plan, so that "Jesus exists in the mode of God's intention" (46)—which would make Barth's view like that of Gregory of Nyssa. There is a problem though with seeing Jesus as "existing" eternally in the "mode of God's intention." Jesus is not only eternally intended but also eternally intends, as the "electing God." An analogous debate has appeared among Origen interpreters, regarding whether the "rational natures" are simply ideas in God's mind from eternity or else have agency of their own (*DR* 3.5). Yet Origen's narrative of the fall and restoration of these "rational natures" implies some measure of independent agency on their part, which would not be the case if they were merely ideas in the divine mind.

"There is no mode of being or existence in the triune life of God above and prior to the eternal act of self-determination in which God 'constitutes' himself as 'God for us.'" The consequence following from this is that "there is no such thing as an 'eternal Logos' in the abstract." For "the triunity of God is a function of the divine election," or, as McCormack says, "the eternal act of self differentiation" in which God as trinitarian is *given* in the eternal act in which God elects himself for the human race. The *decision* for the covenant of grace is the ground of God's triunity."[163] McCormack adds:

> The tendency to historicize . . . comes more strongly to the fore in the later volumes of the *Church Dogmatics*—after Barth's revision of the doctrine of election in CD II/2. The central idea here is that God's eternal election of himself to be God "for us" in Jesus Christ is an act in which God constitutes his being as a being for historical existence (i.e., the incarnate life, death, and resurrection of Jesus of Nazareth). In CD IV especially, his thinking about Christology began to draw nearer to Hegel. Barth thereby established both the relative validity and the proper limits of the historicizing tendencies of the previous century and a half. The relative validity lay in God's determination that God's being should be a being in becoming that is the history of Jesus. The limit—and this is significant—lay in the fact that this act of Self-determination was a *free* act on the part of God, not a necessary one.[164]

McCormack offers a very thorough exegesis of Barth's writings, and his interpretation suggests that Barth's overall theological vision not only took a new turn in *Church Dogmatics* II/2, but that this new turn in Barth's thinking also continued to unfold from the 1940s through the 1960s, as Barth wrote the volumes contained in *Church Dogmatics* III and IV.

In the early volumes of the *Church Dogmatics* (I/1, I/2, II/1)—as both McCormack and McCormack's critics would agree—Barth presented God's engagement with the world as a contingent function of God's own essential trinitarian life. From eternity, God already enjoyed perfect fellowship within himself as Father, Son, and Spirit. God did not "need" to create the world, nor did God "need" to become incarnate in Jesus Christ. According to McCormack, Barth's view of God began to shift around 1939–40 as he worked on his doctrine of election.[165] Now the Trinity became a function of the divine election and tantamount to *God's choice to be God-for-us*. McCormack acknowledges that his interpretation of Barth's doctrine of election is not Barth's interpretation of his own doctrine.

163. McCormack, "Seek God," 66; McCormack, "Grace and Being," 103, cited in van Driel, *Incarnation Anyway*, 90–91.
164. McCormack, *Orthodox and Modern*, 13.
165. McCormack, "Seek God," 63–66.

Yet he found himself driven to this "critical correction" in an attempt to remove inconsistency from Barth's thought.[166] Hunsinger and Molnar have both been highly critical of McCormack's reading of Barth (DR 9.1). My own view, suggested above, is that McCormack and Hunsinger are *both correct*, though correct in differing respects. That is, McCormack is *exegetically correct* in his interpretion of Barth's *Church Dogmatics*, while Hunsinger is *normatively correct* in pointing out the theological problems entailed in Barth's position as reconstructed by McCormack.

Regarding Barth's idea of God's self-constituting choice, there seems to be a logical problem if we conceive of divine choosing as analogous to human choosing.[167] The idea of a "self-constituting choice," as implied in Barth, is confusing if not self-contradictory. If one says that "X chooses Y," and if "Y" (the outcome of the choice) is God as Trinity, then what value should we assign to "X"? If the Trinity *follows* this choice—logically though not chronologically—then what *precedes* the choice? In short, how can the Trinity be the subject of choosing if the existence of the Trinity is the outcome of the choosing? Edwin van Driel concludes that "the notion of divine self-constitution is incoherent."[168] Just as problematic as the notion of the self-constituting choice is the idea of the eternal God-man. If creatures are the outcome of God's free choice to create, then how could a creature be the one eternally making the decision to create? If creatures *follow*—logically or chronologically—the choice to create, then how could a creature (i.e., the God-man) *precede* the choice? Once again we end up with a statement that is not so much false as it is unintelligible.[169]

166. See van Driel, *Incarnation Anyway*, 92–95.

167. I am here bracketing out the strictly philosophical questions of what "choosing" or "choice" might mean for an agent regarded as "eternal," and the further question of how to understand the nexus or interplay between choices or actions made in eternity and choices or actions made in the temporal sphere.

168. Van Driel says—perhaps rightly—that "the problem lies . . . not so much in McCormack's reading as in an ambiguity in the formulations of Barth himself" (*Incarnation Anyway*, 101). On Böhmist premises (DR 5.3), there is something that precedes the Trinity—namely, the *Ungrund*, which has no "choice" per se but does express a kind of blind, undirected impulse or striving (*Trieb*). Yet Barth has no such entity in his doctrine of God, and so his position seems logically untenable.

169. Given that the Fifth Ecumenical Council (553 CE) rejected the idea of Christ's preexistent soul (i.e., prior to the conception in Mary's womb), the position that Barth has taken on the eternal God-man might be considered as formally heretical—at least by the standard of the early ecumenical councils. See DR appendix C on anti-Origenist declarations in the early church. A preexistent yet soulless "Jesus Christ" would not be one and the same with the divine-human Savior who was born in Bethlehem; alternatively, a preexisting "Jesus Christ" possessing a soul would seemingly violate the strictures of the Fifth Ecumenical Council. Yet my emphasis here is on the incoherence, rather than the heterodoxy, of this line of reasoning in Barth.

9.7. Barth on Nothingness (*das Nichtige*) and the "Impossibility" of Sin

We turn now to another metaphysical issue in Barth—namely, the ontological status of evil. Recent analysis of Barth's early intellectual development has suggested that Neoplatonic, Kantian, and Hegelian notions played a key role in his evolution as a thinker. So it is perhaps not surprising that when confronting the mystery of evil, Barth should distinguish different degrees or levels of reality or being in a way that corresponds to Neoplatonic or idealist thought. Barth's "nothingness," as he says, is not equivalent to "nothing." If it were, then Barth would not need to take eighty pages to discuss it.[170] What we find in Barth is a variation on the familiar distinction between *ouk-ontic* "nothing" (i.e., sheer nothingness) and *mē-ontic* "nothingness" (i.e., reality as depleted in some fashion).[171]

Barth's account of "nothingness" matters for the discussion of universalism because it implies that God, Christ, faith, and goodness have an ontological advantage over Satan, unbelief, and evil. At times Barth sounds much like the ancient Christian author Gregory of Nyssa, who insisted that God and goodness are destined to outlast evil. Confronted by God and goodness, evil will not thrive and will not even survive but will eventually pass away. Evil, for Gregory, has no staying power (*DR* 3.9).[172] On this point Barth agrees: "The existence of the uncalled, the godless, is false witness. It is quite inconceivable that this false witness should have the permanence of the true witness. Where can it find the necessary strength in a world in which it has been objectively overcome by the death and resurrection of Jesus Christ?"[173] Barth defines *das Nichtige* (translated as "nothingness") in a way that associates it with evil. "Nothingness," he says, "is inimical to the will of the Creator and therefore to the nature of His good creature." The realm of creation is "continually confronted by this menace." "What is real nothingness?" asks Barth. He answers that "nothingness is neither

---

170. Barth treats "nothingness" (*das Nichtige*) in *CD* III/3, 289–368. Secondary literature includes Lüthi, *Gott und das Böse*; Hick, "Karl Barth"; Wolterstorff, "Barth on Evil"; Rodin, *Evil and Theodicy*; J. C. McDowell, "Much Ado about Nothingness"; Krötke, *Sin and Nothingness*.

171. Generally we think of Paul Tillich as the twentieth-century thinker whose theology most clearly involved this sort of metaphysical thinking about being versus nonbeing. Yet Barth's *Church Dogmatics* III/3 shows that he too incorporated this element. For a comparative study of *mē-ontic* nothingness in twentieth-century religious thought, see Tsambassis, "Evil and the 'Abysmal Nature' of God." Lüthi's *Gott und das Böse* (1961) shows the affinity of Barth's notion of *das Nichtige* to Schelling's account of evil (see *DR* 7.7).

172. The subtlest response to this idea of evil's inherent transience may be that of Augustine, who rejected and refuted Gregory of Nyssa's premise that everything that has an origin in time must have an end in time. As noted in the discussion of Augustine, Gregory Nazianzen and Maximus the Confessor on this point both agreed with Augustine against Gregory of Nyssa (see *DR* 4.3; 4.8).

173. Barth, *CD* II/2, 350.

God nor His creature." Yet "nothingness is not nothing." For "nothingness is real in this third fashion peculiar to itself" and so has "ontic peculiarity."[174]

God is opposed to nothingness: "Jesus Christ . . . has set Himself in opposition to nothingness, and in this opposition was and is the Victor." In fact, "conflict with nothingness . . . is the cause of God." The "day and night" set in opposition in Genesis 1 are an image of the "twofold character and aspect of creaturely existence." Barth refuses to see nothingness as part of some "higher unity" or to "ascribe to it a certain goodness, a certain participation in good." Such a view would then include "the devil . . . as the last candidate for a salvation which is due to him too by reason of a general *apokatastasis*." Nothingness has its place within Barth's doctrine of election. What God has *not elected* or rejected is nothingness: "God elects, and therefore rejects what He does not elect. God wills, and therefore opposes what He does not will. . . . Nothingness is that which God does not will."[175] Because God has not willed nothingness, it cannot continue indefinitely: "Nothingness has no perpetuity. God not only has perpetuity but is Himself the basis, essence and sum of all being. And for all its finiteness and mutability even His creature has perpetuity . . . in fellowship with Himself. . . . Nothingness, however, is not created by God, nor is there any covenant with it. Hence it has no perpetuity."[176] Barth concludes that "if Jesus is Victor, the last word must always be . . . that nothingness has no perpetuity."[177] Satan and the demonic realm, which Barth discusses only briefly, are connected with nothingness.[178] This dark realm has already been defeated by Christ and set at nought: "In the Elect [i.e., Jesus], He negated in advance the rule of evil. . . . In the Elect, He revealed evil only as a power already vanquished, a kingdom of darkness already destroyed."[179]

Barth's doctrine of *das Nichtige* is interwoven with his account of human sin, for God fulfills "this judgment on sin . . . by delivering up sinful man and sin in His own person to the non-being which is properly theirs, the non-being, the nothingness to which man has fallen victim as a sinner and towards which

174. Barth, *CD* III/3, 289, 296, 349, 350, 353. The "third fashion" refers to the existence of *das Nichtige* as neither Creator nor creature.

175. Barth, *CD* III/3, 290, 359, 295, 300, 351–52.

176. Barth, *CD* III/3, 360.

177. Barth, *CD* III/3, 364.

178. "Angels and demons are related as creation and chaos, as the free grace of God and nothingness" (Barth, *CD* III/3, 520). "What is the origin and nature of the devil and demons? The only possible answer is that their origin and nature lie in nothingness. . . . Their being is neither that of God nor that of the creature" (*CD* III/3, 522). Barth rejects the idea that Satan and demons are "fallen angels," for "the devil was never an angel" (*CD* III/3, 531).

179. Barth, *CD* II/2, 142. Cf. "The whole kingdom of evil . . . is the shadow which accompanies the light of the election of Jesus Christ" (*CD* II/2, 122).

he relentlessly hastens."[180] When Barth writes that "sin is that which is absurd, man's absurd choice and decision for that which is not," he sounds much like Gregory of Nyssa (DR 3.9) and other Greek fathers, who regarded human sin as a turning away from God's being or as an inclination toward nothingness.[181] Yet Barth went quite a bit further than the Greek fathers in his repeated descriptions of sin as "impossible": "It has, therefore, no possibility—we cannot escape this difficult formula—except that of the absolutely impossible. How else can we describe that which is intrinsically absurd but by a formula which is logically absurd?"[182] An even stronger statement is the following:

> With the divine No and Yes spoken in Jesus Christ, the root of human unbelief, the man of sin, is pulled out. In its place there is put the root of faith, the new man of obedience. *For this reason unbelief has become an objective, real and ontological impossibility and faith an objective, real and ontological necessity for all men and every man.* In the justification of the sinner which has taken place in Jesus Christ these have both become an event which comprehends all men.[183]

Barth interprets the Origenists' key verse—1 Corinthians 15:28—as follows:

> All the future glory of His work in the realm of redemption consists in the fact that in them He will be "all in all," as 1 Corinthians 15:28 says, and therefore again in a new way Himself. That which has nothing to do with God's reality, that which withstands it . . . is an unreal and demonic reality, and any capacity for it is an unreal and impossible possibility—impossible because it is a possibility excluded by the divine possibility, which is the standard of everything possible.[184]

Connected with this doctrine of nothingness is the idea that not only sin but the sinner too is bound to disappear. Because of Christ, says Barth, the sinner ceases to exist. Barth writes that "man is no longer the transgressor, the sinner, the covenant-breaker that God has found him." Instead, "man the covenant-breaker is buried and destroyed. He has ceased to be. The wrath of God which is the fire of His love has taken him away and all his transgressions . . . just as a whole burnt offering is consumed on the altar with the flesh and skin and bones and hoofs and horns, rising up as fire to heaven and

180. Barth, *CD* IV/1, 253.
181. Barth, *CD* IV/1, 410.
182. Barth, *CD* IV/1, 410.
183. Barth, *CD* IV/1, 747; emphasis added. Cf. *CD* II/1, 503: "Sin is when the creature avails itself of this impossible possibility in opposition to God and to the meaning of its own existence." See also the references to the "impossible possibility" or "ontological impossibility" in *CD* IV/3/1, 174, 178.
184. Barth, *CD* II/1, 532.

disappearing."[185] Taken literally, one might call this an annihilationist view of salvation. God saves us by annihilating us: "He has removed us sinners and sin, negated us, canceled us out. . . . The man of sin, the first Adam . . . was taken and killed and buried in and with Him on the cross."[186] How one might apply Barth's dramatic language of negation or cancellation to the human situation remains an open question. Sinners and sinning remain in our everyday experience as an obvious, empirical reality, even though they are said to be "canceled . . . out" in the cross of Christ.[187]

9.8. Barth's Interpreters on the Question of Universalism

The first major response to Barth's election doctrine was perhaps the sharpest critique that he ever received. The author was Emil Brunner, Barth's friend and colleague of the 1920s who became his nemesis in the nature-grace debate of the 1930s.[188] In 1946, in the appendix of the first volume of his *Dogmatics*, Brunner surveyed the history of Christian teachings on predestination, and then assaulted Barth's teaching. The brevity of the appendix belies its importance, since this short response anticipated most of the later lines of criticism directed against Barth's doctrine of election by various authors.[189] Noting that Barth's *Church Dogmatics* II/2 is "the most detailed and comprehensive discussion of the problem [of election] in modern theology," Brunner says that nonetheless

185. Barth, *CD* IV/1, 93–94.

186. Barth, *CD* IV/1, 253–54.

187. See *DR* 12.5 for a discussion of Barth's tendency toward illusionism in his treatment of the problem of evil.

188. Brunner, *Die christliche Lehre von Gott* (1946), translated into English as *The Christian Doctrine of God*, vol. 1 of *Dogmatics* (1950). Brunner also discussed universalism in *The Christian Doctrine of Church, Faith, and the Consummation* and *Eternal Hope*. In addition to Brunner's own writings, secondary works on Brunner's eschatological views include Buis, *Doctrine of Eternal Punishment*, 105–7; S. A. Hayes, "Emil Brunner's Criticism"; Cumming, "Problem of Universal Salvation."

189. Brunner's historical survey of predestination, in the appendix to vol. 1 of his *Dogmatics* (340–46), is integral to his criticism of Barth on election. Brunner states that "before Augustine, there was no doctrine of Predestination" (*Dogmatics*, 1:340), and he traces Augustine's influence on Aquinas, who asserted divine predestination of the elect versus divine foreknowledge of the nonelect (*ST* I, q. 23, a. 7). Twofold or double predestination (*praedestinatio gemima*) emerges in Gottschalk, the early Luther (*The Bondage of the Will* [1525]), John Calvin (*Institutes* 3.21.5), and Theodore Beza. The later Luther "now emphasizes the truth that God in Christ offers us, as His sole will, the Gospel of Grace . . . and to this he adds that whoever speculates upon the will of God outside of Christ, loses God" (*Dogmatics*, 1:342, citing Luther, *Werke*, 40/1:256). While the later Luther taught that not all respond in faith to God's grace, Luther's stress on God's single gracious purpose brings this view, in some ways, closer to Barth's than to Calvin's. For Luther "the true doctrine of Predestination is simply the knowledge of Election in Jesus Christ through faith" (*Dogmatics*, 1:344). Though Barth is usually read in light of Calvin, Brunner shows that Luther may be just as important as a backdrop to Barth's election doctrine.

it contains "some entirely new ideas." Brunner professes his agreement with the main tendency in Barth—namely, "to state the doctrine of Election . . . in harmony with revelation and the thought of the Bible as a whole." Like Barth, Brunner wishes to reject the "speculative doctrine" of election as inaugurated in Augustine and brought to full expression in Calvin.[190] Yet regarding Jesus Christ as "the eternally Elect Man," Brunner states that "no special proof is required to show that the Bible contains no such doctrine, nor that no theory of this kind has ever been formulated," for "if the eternal pre-existence of the God-Man were a fact, then the Incarnation would no longer be an *Event* at all." In Barth's teaching, writes Brunner, the event of the incarnation "is now . . . torn out of the sphere of history, and set within the pre-temporal sphere, in the pre-existence of the Logos." Barth's doctrine of the "pre-existent *Divine Humanity*" is an "*ad hoc* artificial theory" that Barth propounded to "carry through his argument that the Man Jesus is the Only Elect Human being."[191]

Barth's approach to election is both "valuable" and "confusing" in Brunner's view. Inasmuch as Barth's aim is "the exact opposite of Calvin's doctrine of the Double Decree," Brunner finds it "very strange that Barth continually constitutes himself the champion of Calvin's doctrine." For Barth sets Calvin on his head. Along the same lines, Brunner objects to the way that Barth appears to defend Calvinist supralapsarianism against infralapsarianism, since Barth's position had little in common with the supralapsarianism of earlier Calvinists.[192] Brunner develops the idea—echoed by Thomas Torrance around the same time—that Calvinistic double predestination and universalism are flip sides of the same coin: Barth "finally reaches exactly the opposite pole from the doctrine of double predestination. But in spite of the contrast, there is also an affinity between the two: in both cases everything has already been decided beforehand, and there remains no room or man to make a real decision."[193]

Brunner comes to the nub of his objection to Barth:

But what does this statement, "that Jesus is the only really rejected man" [*KD* II/2, 350] mean for the situation of Man? Evidently this, that there is no such thing as being "lost," that there is no possibility of condemnation, thus that there is no final Divine Judgment. . . . [Barth states] "The Church ought not to preach Apokatastasis" [*KD* II/2, 529]. Thus Barth's doctrine is not that of Origen and his followers. Rather, Barth goes much further. For none of them ever dared to maintain that through Jesus Christ, all, believers and unbelievers, are saved from the wrath of

190. Brunner, *Dogmatics*, 1:346.
191. Ibid., 1:347.
192. Ibid., 1:348. Barth discusses infra- versus supra-lapsarianism in *CD* II/2, 127–45.
193. Brunner, *Dogmatics*, 1:351.

God and participate in redemption through Jesus Christ. But that is what Karl Barth teaches; for Jesus Christ is, as the only Elect, so also the only Reprobate man. Thus, since Jesus Christ appeared, and through Him, there are no longer any who are rejected. Not only for those who are "in Him" through faith, but for all men, Hell has been blotted out, condemnation and judgment eliminated. This is not a deduction which I have drawn from Barth's statement, but it is his own. Since Jesus Christ has taken the condemnation of sin upon Himself, "rejection *cannot* again become the portion of man" [*KD* II/2, 182]. "He cannot undo the decision made by God in eternity . . . he cannot create any fact which takes away the Divine choice" [*KD* II/2, 348].[194]

Brunner underscores Barth's claim that Christ is "the only really rejected man" and shows that this teaching stands in direct contradiction to the notion of a "final Divine judgment." If Christ is the only Rejected One, and that rejection was fully effected when Jesus died on the cross, then what possibility of future rejection still remains? The threat is removed, and the final judgment has already occurred.

Traditional Christian theology, based on Jesus's parables, Paul's Letters, and the book of Revelation, taught that individual human beings will pass through a postmortem judgment that will involve a genuine threat of final separation from God as well as a genuine promise of final salvation. Barth's view of election will not allow for this, and so Brunner states that Barth has "dared to throw on the scrap-heap the idea of a final divine Judgment."[195] In Barth's interpretation, God's eschatological judgment was already effected when Jesus died. Divine judgment and rejection fell on Jesus in such a way that judgment and rejection no longer remain. Christ's death *is* the Last Judgment. Barth's verbal hedging— offering hope for universal salvation but not a definite affirmation—made no sense to Brunner. Barth seemed to be at war with himself, affirming that Christ definitely is the only Rejected One while affirming that Christ might not be the only Rejected One.

Brunner found the root problem in Barth's "objectivism"—that is, "the view that, in comparison with revelation, with the objective Word of God, the subjective element, faith, is . . . on a much lower plane." In the New Testament, as Brunner reads it, "justification and faith . . . belong together, and are on exactly the same level, so that we may say: 'Where there is no faith, there Christ is not; where there is no faith, there, too, there is no salvation in Christ.'" Yet "Barth does not admit that this correlation exists," and Barth says that "it is not possible to place him [i.e., the believer] absolutely over and against the one who . . .

194. Ibid., 1:348. References in the text are to Brunner's citation from Barth's *Kirchliche Dogmatik*.
195. Brunner, *Dogmatics*, 1:349.

does not make real and visible the attitude of faith." This *objectivism* of God's work in Christ implies a *relativization* of the importance of faith in Christ. The believer in Christ, writes Barth, "cannot possibly recognize in the unbelief of others, an *ultimate* given fact."[196]

Brunner continues his critique by noting how Barth's election doctrine removes any element of genuine danger associated with unbelief and so empties human choices of their significance:

> The real decision only takes place in the objective sphere, and not in the subjective sphere. Thus: the decision has been made in Jesus Christ—for all men. Whether they know it or not, believe it or not, is not so important. The main point is that they are saved. They are like people who seem to be perishing in a stormy sea. But in reality they are not in a sea where one can drown, but in shallow water, where it is impossible to drown. Only they do not know it. Hence the transition from unbelief to faith is not the transition from "being-lost" to "being-saved." *This* turning-point does not exist, since it is no longer possible to be lost. But if we look at this view more closely, we see also that the turning-point in the historical Event is no real turning point at all; for Election means that everything has already taken place in the sphere of pre-existence.[197]

Brunner concludes with the suggestion that Barth had "not yet said his last word" on the question of the final scope of salvation.[198]

Brunner's focus on the theme of "decision" (*Entscheidung*) echoed one of the key themes of the earlier dialectical theology of the 1920s, inspired in part by the philosophy of Søren Kierkegaard (1813–55). Barth and Brunner—then thought to be comrades with Rudolf Bultmann and Friedrich Gogarten—viewed the Christian message as essentially *a summons to human decision*. Brunner never abandoned this emphasis, which recurred throughout his later writings. In contrast to this, Barth increasingly focused his theological reflection on *the divine decision in election*, which he viewed as encompassing or including the human decision. As Barth's theology evolved, the interplay between the divine decision in Christ and human decisions receded into the background, while the divine decision all but absorbed the human decision.

Where, then, does Brunner come down regarding the possibility of final loss or separation from God in hell? Despite his sharp critique of Barth's tendency toward universalism, Brunner's stance on divine judgment in later life also

196. Ibid., 349–50, quoting Barth, *KD* II/2, 360 (CD II/2, 327): "Gerade der Glaubende kann in Unglauben Anderer unmoglich eine letzte Gegebenheit erkennen."
197. Brunner, *Dogmatics*, 1:351.
198. Ibid., 1:352.

inclines toward universalism. In his book *Eternal Hope* (1954), Brunner writes that the "sheep" and the "goats" of Jesus's parable in Matthew 25 are not to be regarded as symmetrical or set on the same plane. He comments: "This static symmetry picturing the two opposites, apparently in complete conformity with the words of Jesus about a last universal judgment, is somehow essentially false. While the picture-symbol shows inevitably this symmetry, the intention of the words of Jesus is quite different. The picture suggests: there are these two alternatives, the one and the other, the salvation of the blessed, the damnation of the accursed; but the Word of Jesus is a summons calling for a decision, a Word exhorting to penitence and promising grace."[199]

Brunner's focus on human choice deflects attention away from the objective issue (Do some people go to hell?) and toward the subjective or existential issue (What does the proclamation regarding the sheep and goats imply regarding me, my life, my choice, my standing with God?).[200] By highlighting the subjective impact of the Bible's threatening language, Brunner diminishes interest in the question of objective realities. In an existentializing interpretation of eschatological language, the seemingly objective references in Jesus's teaching—for example, "outer darkness" and "eternal fire" versus "reclining at table" or "kingdom of God"—denote present-day human choices, experiences, or possibilities. The purpose of the biblical teaching of the final judgment is thus not to describe future realities but to provoke contemporary decisions of faith. Brunner's *Eternal Hope* (1954) goes on to argue that God's purposes cannot be thwarted by human choices and that the Greek word *aiōnios* means "eschatological" rather than strictly "eternal"—two common universalist tropes. Harry Buis wrote, "We are forced to conclude that here we have what appears to be double talk which, however, lands us in as complete a universalism as any position which ignores judgment completely. . . . While Brunner appears to be basically a universalist, he severely criticizes Barth for his apparent universalism."[201] This

199. Brunner, *Eternal Hope*, 180.
200. Kierkegaard's philosophy, as Jack Mulder Jr. comments, has much the same implication: "Stop working on metaphysical questions and start working on yourself!" Kierkegaardian reasoning, according to Mulder, resists the conclusion that "all individuals must experience everlasting happiness" (Mulder, "Must All Be Saved?," 1–2). See also J. Mulder, *Kierkegaaard and the Catholic Tradition*, esp. 125–52. Some passages in Kierkegaard's journals seem to support universalism, yet his dialectics make it hard to interpret these texts straightforwardly. "They argue about whether God intends the salvation of all or only of some—almost forgetting the far more important theme." "You, O God, intend my salvation; would that I myself might intend it also." "The terms of salvation differ for every individual, for every single solitary human being." "The old bishop once said . . . that I spoke as if the others were going to hell. No . . . if the others are going to hell, then I am going along with them. But I do not believe that; on the contrary, I believe that we will all be saved, I, too, and this awakens my deepest wonder" (*Søren Kierkegaard's Journals and Papers*, 4:530; 6:577).
201. Buis, *Doctrine of Eternal Punishment*, 105, 107.

seems a fair assessment. Brunner's sharp rejection of Barth's election doctrine in the first volume of his *Dogmatics* in 1946, in the name of the human decision regarding Christ, is weakened in the approach to eschatology Brunner took in his later book on hope. Brunner's settled position, by the early 1950s, is rather hard to differentiate from universalism.

John A. T. Robinson succeeded C. F. D. Moule as the dean of Clare College, Cambridge University, and his universalism first found expression in his 1946 doctoral thesis.[202] Soon thereafter, in 1949, Robinson and Thomas F. Torrance sparred with each other in the pages of the *Scottish Journal of Theology*.[203] In Robinson's highly dialectical and existentialist approach to the New Testament, the seeming twofold outcome of the "sheep" and the "goats" in Jesus's parable (Matt. 25) referred to alternative human possibilities that apply to each individual. Both heaven and hell were *true as human possibilities*, even though *only one of these possibilities*—salvation rather than damnation—would ever be realized. As Robinson said: "To the man in decision—and that means to all men, always, right up to the last hour—hell is in every way as real a destination as heaven. Only the man who has genuinely been confronted with both alternatives can be saved."[204]

Thomas F. Torrance was unconvinced by Robinson's arguments and roundly condemned universalism, stating that "the voice of the Catholic Church . . . throughout all ages has consistently judged universalism a heresy for faith and a menace to the Gospel." He added that "at the very best universalism could only be concerned with a hope, with a possibility, and could only be expressed apocalyptically." When made into a "dogmatic statement, which is what the doctrine of universalism [is]," then such a dogmatic statement destroys "the possibility in the necessity."[205] Paul Molnar sums up Torrance's view by stating that "universalism, in his mind . . . is a form of rationalism which ignores the need for eschatological reserve and reads logical necessities back into the gospel of free grace."[206] In his much later work *The Atonement: The Person and Work of Christ* (2009), Torrance insists that universal salvation and limited atonement are twin errors, because both of them interpret the effect of Jesus's

202. Fairhurst, "'Dare We Hope,'" 373.
203. For Robinson's views, see his writings "Universalism: Is it Heretical?"; *In the End, God*; "Universalism: A Reply." See also the following secondary studies: K. S. Harmon, "Finally Excluded from God?," 133–218; T. Hart, "Universalism"; T. Hart, "*In the End, God*." For Torrance, see his "Universalism or Election?"; "Atonement, the Singularity of Christ, and the Finality of the Cross." See also Watts, "Is Universalism Theologically Coherent?"; Molnar, "Thomas F. Torrance and the Problem of Universalism."
204. John A. T. Robinson, *In the End, God*, 118; cf. 123.
205. Torrance, "Universalism or Election?," 310, 313.
206. Molnar, "Thomas F. Torrance and the Problem of Universalism," 166.

death on the cross in terms of a principle of absolute divine causality. He states firstly that "if the nature of God is only to love some and not to love others . . . then the nature of God is attacked." This is the error of limited atonement. Conversely, "if the nature of God is absolute causality and if atonement flows out of that divine nature, then an atoning death for all means the necessary salvation of all."[207] This is the error of universalism. In one of his strongest statements, Torrance writes that the "logico-causal explanation" of the atonement in universalist theology amounts to "a form of blasphemy against the blood of Christ."[208] So Torrance rejects these two polar views, stating that "if a sinner goes to hell, it is not because God rejected them, for God has only chosen to love them, and has only accepted them in Christ." If some people go to hell, "they go to hell, only because, inconceivably, they refuse the positive act of the divine acceptance of them."[209] Even though there is "objective revelation," "objective forgiveness," and an "objective Christ," people may still pass by these things and remain blind to them.[210] Torrance's position on universalism clearly builds on that of Barth and yet interprets Barth in a fashion opposing the interpretation of Robinson.

Gustav Wingren, in *Theology in Conflict* (1958), was one of Barth's early opponents. In Wingren's strident critique, Barth had so reinterpreted sin, evil, and Satan as to render them irrelevant. The result was that there is no genuine struggle of good and evil—nor could there be—on Barth's premises:

> The Devil, or active power of evil, or the force of sin which keeps man in slavery, all these are absent from Barth's theology: there is no Christus Victor story to be told. The human predicament is ignorance. And Barth, by taking this as axiomatic, aligns himself with precisely that liberal theology which he is concerned to attack; what he and the liberals have in common is a lack of any sense of human bondage.[211]

Rowan Williams, the former archbishop of Canterbury, agrees with Wingren's assessment.[212] Their charge is that Barth's theology does not take sin, evil, or Satan with full seriousness, and that human beings are not in bondage to sin but are ignorant of what God in Christ has already accomplished on their behalf.

---

207. Torrance, *Atonement*, 186–87. Cf. Torrance, *Karl Barth: Biblical and Evangelical Theologian*, 239–40. See the discussion in Molnar, "Thomas F. Torrance and the Problem of Universalism," esp. 169–73.

208. Torrance, "Atonement, the Singularity of Christ, and the Finality of the Cross," 248.

209. Torrance, *Atonement*, 156–57.

210. Torrance, *Doctrine of Jesus Christ*, 96.

211. Wingren, *Theology in Conflict*, 24–25, quoted in R. Williams, *Wrestling with Angels*, 127.

212. See R. Williams, *Wrestling with Angels*, 126–28.

A respectful yet critical reading of Barth appeared in G. C. Berkouwer's *The Triumph of Grace in the Theology of Karl Barth* (1956). This book is gentler than Brunner's and is also one of the most thorough early analyses of Barth's theology. Barth responded to Berkouwer in a later volume of the *Church Dogmatics*, indicating his dislike for the title of Berkouwer's book (*The Triumph of Grace*) and proposing an alternative: *Jesus Is Victor*.[213] "Barth's theology bears a pronouncedly *triumphant* character," according to Berkouwer, and "the triumph of grace is most intimately related to the cross."[214] While Barth's early stress in the *Epistle to the Romans* (1922) was on the divine "No," later his emphasis shifted to God's "Yes."[215] Berkouwer comments, "We must therefore not see here a strange and peculiar dialectical 'balance' between Yes and No, but a conquest of the Yes *in* and *through* the No because the triumph of the Yes becomes manifest exactly at that point where judgment is pronounced." This means that "God's Yes resounds *in* and *through* the judgment" and that "Barth's theology must *from its inception* be characterized as triumphant theology which aims to testify to the overcoming power of grace."[216] In Barth's *Epistle to the Romans*, Berkouwer finds an element of "crisis" but a "crisis" that brings judgment and forgiveness together. In Barth's "*synthesis* of comfort and despair . . . there is no question or uncertainty or tension as to whether comfort or despair will emerge as the victor."[217] Berkouwer's interpretation from the 1950s seems to echo Barth's early choice in the 1910s to speak "comfortingly to Jerusalem" (*DR* 9.2).

Related to Berkouwer's "triumph of grace" idea is the question of law and gospel in Barth. In an oft-cited 1935 lecture, Barth rejected the traditional Lutheran teaching that God's law precedes the gospel. He replaced this with the idea that *gospel precedes law*.[218] In *Church Dogmatics* II/2, he wrote, "The Law

213. Barth, *CD* IV/3/1, 173–80. In this passage, Barth discusses the eschatological optimism of Johann and Christoph Blumhardt (see *DR* 5.8), who were important sources in the development of Barth's theology—and, arguably, in Jürgen Moltmann's as well. See Collins Winn and Heltzel, "'Before Bloch.'" On Blumhardt's kingdom theology, see Sauter, *Die Theologie des Reiches Gottes*; Macchia, *Spirituality and Social Liberation*. On Blumhardt's influence on Barth, see Berkouwer, *Triumph of Grace*, 45–46; Collins Winn, *"Jesus Is Victor!"* As Collins Winn shows, the watchwords of the Blumhardts—"Jesus is victor" and "Your kingdom come"—pointed toward a victory of Christ *here and now*, a form of realized eschatology that found an echo in Barth's theology.

214. Berkouwer, *Triumph of Grace*, 18–19.

215. Ibid., 24.

216. Ibid., 33, 39, 37.

217. Ibid., 41. See also Barth, *Epistle to the Romans*. An analogy for the preaching of judgment and forgiveness together might be the following: imagine telling someone that a meal just consumed contained deadly poison and yet the appropriate antidote as well. The second part of the message would annul any fear or anxiety caused by the first part.

218. Barth, *Evangelium und Gesetz*, translated as "Gospel and Law." Barth wrote that "because the law is in the gospel, comes from the gospel, and points to the gospel, we must first know about the gospel in order to know what law is, and not the other way around" ("Gospel and Law," 72). So

is completely enclosed in the Gospel. It is not a second thing alongside and beyond the Gospel. It is not a foreign element which precedes or only follows it. It is the claim which is addressed to us by the Gospel itself."[219] In light of a statement like this, we must ask, how does one understand God's giving of the Old Testament law and the subsequent centuries during which Torah-observant Israelites and Jews have lived under it? If "Law" is "completely enclosed in the Gospel," then it is not clear that "Law" has much of anything to say that is not already—and better—said by "Gospel" itself. Barth has not only reordered law and gospel (from law-gospel to gospel-law) but has gone further by nullifying the dialectic between these two. There is no longer any tension or contrast in need of resolution but only grace and more grace, or gospel and more gospel. Even the spectacular rhetoric of Barth's early commentary on Romans, which carries within it a strong element of "Law," becomes difficult to understand on this account.[220] Brunner said that Barth had removed the "tension of life grounded in the dialectic between God's holiness and His love."[221]

Berkouwer discusses nothingness (*das Nichtige*) and Barth's insistence that it has already been defeated in Christ. Its existence is only apparent: "With an eye to Jesus Christ it is not possible to say that the chaos still has objective reality in any sense, that it has existence other than that which our as yet covered sight ascribes to it, that it is really to be feared, that it is still a danger or can still do damage."[222] The evil that Barth calls "nothingness" *seems* dangerous but *is not*. Salvation is then only an epistemic change, a seeing of what is already the case. The battle against evil is already won. Berkouwer asks the question of "how . . . the chaos can still play a role in the affairs of men."[223] The answer for Barth is that people do not recognize that the chaos is unreal. It has "only the force of a dangerous appearance," is "a kingdom of unreality," and is "nothing and not-dangerous."[224] Yet some people—indeed many people—do not see this. Because evil for Barth is *appearance and not reality*, one is able to understand certain

also in his *Ethics*, Barth wrote that "this revelation of God's love in the givenness of the command is the *gospel*. . . . Only through it does the law acquire truth and weight" (92). See M. S. Johnson, "Gospel and Law."

219. Barth, *CD* II/2, 557.

220. Barth acknowledged what he called the philosophical "Kantian and Platonic conceptions" in both the first and second editions of his commentary on Romans (cited in Berkouwer, *Triumph of Grace*, 21n29). Barth's positing of "eternity" against "time" in the commentary has a Platonic aspect to it (ibid., 26) and suggests a law-gospel dialectic in which God's eternity is the judgment of human time and the works of time-bound humanity. On the verbal fireworks of Barth's commentary, see Webb, *Re-figuring Theology*.

221. Brunner, *Dogmatik*, 2:366, cited in Berkouwer, *Triumph of Grace*, 12n6.

222. Barth, *KD* III/3, 419, cited in Berkouwer, *Triumph of Grace*, 74.

223. Berkouwer, *Triumph of Grace*, 75, citing Barth, *KD* III/3, 424.

224. Berkouwer, *Triumph of Grace*, 78, citing Barth, *KD* III/3, 613–14.

assertions that might seem contradictory. Barth speaks of the "powerlessness" of unbelief and yet of its "deathly danger."[225] There is danger, but only for those who do not recognize the unreality of unbelief or the unreality of sin.

Berkouwer points out that Barth does not sharply distinguish God's triumph in creation (over nothingness) from God's triumph in reconciliation (over human sin). These are two aspects or phases of one triumph.[226] The demons, aligned as they are with nothingness, have already been defeated and overcome. Satan's defeat by Jesus Christ is, for Barth, not merely preliminary but something definitive and complete. The consistent shift toward realized eschatology in Barth becomes clear in his account of Adam and Christ. Human history begins in the pride and fall of Adam, and so "there was never a golden age."[227] Barth will not allow that Adam comes prior to Christ either chronologically or logically. Though Scripture calls Christ "the last Adam" (1 Cor. 15:45), Barth reverses the sequence so that Christ comes first rather than second. It is not Adam but Christ who defines humanness. The figure of Adam is almost as unreal as is Barth's nothingness.[228]

At a conference in 1936 in Debreczen, Hungary, Barth was asked, "Does not the universal grace which desires to save all men eliminate reprobation?" He answered, "We can be certain that God's lordship is and will be total in all, but what this signifies for us we must leave to God. And therefore we dare not say that in the universal grace damnation is eliminated. The Holy Scriptures speak of election and of rejection."[229] Berkouwer writes in response to Barth's comments: "In view of Barth's emphasis on the factuality of Christ's rejection, it is not possible to close the door to the *apokatastasis* doctrine by pointing to the fact that the Bible speaks of rejection as well as election, and then entrust everything *eschatologically* to the hand of God."[230] Here Berkouwer arrives at a core issue: Can Barth really assert an *eschatological uncertainty* in light of *the gracious certainty* of the divine election of all human beings in Christ and in the face of the completed work of redemption in the cross of Christ?

225. Berkouwer, *Triumph of Grace*, 114.
226. Ibid., 76n8.
227. Ibid., 83–84, citing Barth, *KD* IV/1, 567.
228. See Barth, *Christ and Adam*, where Barth writes that "man's nature in Adam is not, as is usually assumed, his true and original nature; it is only truly human at all in so far as it reflects and corresponds to essential human nature as it is found in Christ" (43). "Adam . . . can only be the forerunner, the witness, the preliminary shadow . . . of the Christ who is to come. . . . For Christ who seems to come second, really comes first, and Adam who seems to come first really comes second. . . . Our relationship to Adam depends for its reality on our relationship to Christ" (24).
229. Berkouwer, *Triumph of Grace*, 114, quoting Barth, *Gottes Gnadenwahl*, 50. Bruce McCormack notes that the lectures that Barth gave at this 1936 conference were the foundation for the much more extensive exposition of election in *Church Dogmatics* II/2 (McCormack, *Karl Barth's Critically Realistic Dialectical Theology*, 458–63).
230. Berkouwer, *Triumph of Grace*, 115.

In a 1967 essay, Joseph Bettis sought to defend Barth against the charge of universalism.[231] He pointed to Barth's explicit repudiation of universalism. Bettis also pointed toward the radical nature of God's freedom in Barth and interpreted universalism as implying the final salvation of all as a necessary outcome—a view that Barth did not maintain. Yet Bettis in his essay rarely cited Barth's own language to support his claims. He seems also to have misunderstood Barth, claiming that Barth did not understand the atonement in objective terms, nor understand grace as something based on an eternal decree.[232] In *Jesus Is Victor!* (1976), Donald Bloesch read Barth's election doctrine in a way that might be described as antinomic. According to his interpretation, Barth did not endorse either of the two polar views—that is, either universalism or particularism. Bloesch wrote, "Barth transcends the polarities between universalism and particularism in that he denies both of these as rational principles or even as necessary conclusions of faith."[233] By the 1980s, the Catholic theologian Hans Urs von Balthasar came to agree with the critics who held that Barth's rejection of universalism was only "rhetorical." Balthasar wrote, "All protestations that he [Barth] does not mean *apokatastasis panton*, 'for a grace that, in the end, would automatically have to include and reach each and all would certainly not be free or a divine grace,' remain, as W. Kreck says, 'ultimately rhetorical.'"[234] What made this an interesting critique is that Barth had welcomed Balthasar's *The Theology of Karl Barth* (1951) and found it to be one of the very best books in expounding his theology.

In *How to Read Karl Barth* (1991), George Hunsinger discusses the universality of Christ's work.[235] Hunsinger writes that "the 'ontological connection' that establishes our being in Christ pertains not just to believers, but to all other human beings and to every human being as such."[236] On the basis of Barth's theology, he argues that the difference between believers and unbelievers pertains only to knowledge or ignorance of one's situation, not to the ontological state that one is in: "Believers and unbelievers are bound together . . . by a solidarity in grace. What distinguishes Christians from non-Christians is not their ontic but their noetic situation. Christians will know, that is, in a way that non-Christians will not, of their own perilous situation in sin and of their all the more protected situation in Christ."[237] The implication is that "salvation is

231. Bettis, "Is Karl Barth a Universalist?"

232. Ibid., 433–35.

233. Bloesch, *Jesus Is Victor!*, 70.

234. Balthasar, *Dare We Hope?*, 94. The references here are to Barth, *Die Botschaft*, 8; Kreck, *Die Zunkunft des Gekommenen*, 144.

235. Hunsinger, *How to Read Karl Barth*, esp. "The Universality of Salvation in Christ" (128–35).

236. Ibid., 129, citing Barth, *CD* IV/2, 275.

237. Hunsinger, *How to Read Karl Barth*, 134, citing Barth, *CD* IV/3, 342 and 715.

not essentially manifest but hidden, not essentially a process but an event, not essentially a transformation in us but a transformation in Christ, not essentially something we undertake but something we undergo."[238]

Hunsinger writes that "the salient difference between Barth's position and more traditional views has primarily to do with the locus of mystery." The theme of mystery in Augustinian and Calvinistic teaching on election revolves around God's restrictive decree for salvation. In contrast to this, Barth holds that "the dark mystery is that human beings inexplicably (i.e., 'inexplicably' within the terms of Barth's theology) are by all appearances actually capable of rejecting the divine disposition, decision, and work in their favor." While this might not seem like such an enigma (are not all people sinners?), in Barth's theology there is indeed an enigma in that the "human will to reject the divine grace, while actual, would appear to be truly impossible." Barth's apparent puzzle is not that God seems to be inconsistent with himself (as in traditional Calvinism) but rather that human beings engage in the "ontological impossibility" of opposing God.[239] Hunsinger claims that "despite his objectivist soteriology, Barth stops short . . . of unequivocally proclaiming universal salvation." In the end, "Barth therefore makes a very strong move in the direction of universal salvation while leaving the question open." While Hunsinger acknowledges the universalist direction in Barth's theology, he concludes that Barth is agnostic about the final scope of salvation.[240]

John Colwell's 1991 essay "The Contemporaneity of the Divine Decision" addresses the question of universalism in Barth. With regard to Barth's verbal rejection of universalism and the interpreters' repeated reassertions of universalism, Colwell sees two options: "Either Barth remained blissfully oblivious to the most obvious implication of a fundamental tenet of his theology; or there must be some factor in his doctrine of election that has been overlooked by his critics."[241] Colwell opts for the latter option—a more charitable way of interpreting Barth. What Barth rejects is a universalism that is "necessary and guaranteed." The main point is that any external or a priori necessity for God to save humanity would violate the freedom of God.[242] The novel claim in Colwell's essay is that Barth's election doctrine must be understood with regard to Barth's reworking of the doctrine of eternity. Eternity cannot be understood as a static reality for God, for this would violate the freedom of the living God. This means that "when Barth's doctrine of election is considered in the context of this

238. Hunsinger, How to Read Karl Barth, 130.
239. Ibid., 131.
240. Ibid., 132–34.
241. Colwell, "Contemporaneity," 139.
242. Ibid., 141.

understanding of eternity the divine decision to elect is seen to be contemporaneous with the human history of those elected."[243] Colwell concludes: "Barth can avoid the charge of universalism without logical contradiction because he understands the decision of election in dynamic rather than static terms . . . as an event of God's eternity which includes human history rather than as a timeless abstraction or an event of the infinite past which would invalidate the authentic futurity of God's eternity."[244] Colwell's meaning is not entirely clear here, though there is little question that Barth's construal of the nature of time and eternity shapes his account of election.[245] On the question of universalism in Barth, Colwell writes, "While Barth consistently rejects universalism as a doctrine, he certainly does not reject the possibility that all men and women may ultimately be saved."[246] Since universalism is generally defined as the doctrine that all will finally be saved, Colwell seems to be operating with a nonstandard definition of the term—namely, a doctrine that *all must (in principle) be saved* versus a doctrine that *all will (in fact) be saved*. Colwell is claiming that Barth denied universal salvation as a necessary outcome but allowed for it as a contingent outcome. Yet this idea of a contingent outcome sits uneasily alongside Barth's emphatic assertions of God's completed work of redemption in Christ, which cannot—from the human standpoint—be regarded as contingent, since redemption was already long ago accomplished in the life and death of Jesus.

Undefined terms cause problems, and this applies to the word "universalism" itself. The statement that "Barth denies 'universalism'" will mean different things, depending on the meaning attached to the term itself. Colwell may be following the precedent of Barth, who used such words as *apokatastasis* and "universalism" not merely to refer to a final outcome but to denote a *necessary or inevitable outcome*. Along these lines Barth wrote: "If we are to respect the freedom of divine grace, we cannot venture the statement that it must and will finally be coincident with the world of man as such (as in the doctrine of the so-called *apokatastasis*). No such right or necessity can legitimately be deduced. Just as the gracious God does not need to elect or call any single man, so He does not need to elect or call all mankind."[247] It is important to note Barth's precise language: that "no such right or necessity can legitimately be deduced." What Barth specifically denies is *the "right or necessity"* of final salvation for all, not *the result or outcome* of final salvation for all. Many of Barth's readers miss the *narrowness* of what Barth is denying. It may be only the gnostic-esoteric

243. Ibid., 152–53.
244. Ibid., 159.
245. See Hunsinger, "*Mysterium Trinitatis*"; Langdon, "God the Eternal Contemporary."
246. Colwell, "Contemporaneity," 140.
247. Barth, *CD* II/2, 417.

universalists (*DR* 2) who have generally held universal salvation to be a *necessary outcome*, since universal salvation for them is based on the very nature of the human spirit or self. In employing Origen's and the Origenists' key term *apokatastasis* and then explaining this in terms of a necessary outcome, Barth may have given the misleading impression that Origen conceived of salvation as necessary. In fact Origen highlighted the contingency of final salvation for all, as something depending on innumerable human choices, whereas Barth saw it as dependent on a singular and irrevocable divine choice. If there is a theologian who has a problem with soteriological necessitarianism, it is arguably Barth rather than Origen, as Brunner discerned in his early critique of Barth's election doctrine.

In 2003, Oliver Crisp wrote "On Barth's Denial of Universalism." The upshot of Crisp's essay is to show that Barth's appeal to divine freedom does not allow him to escape the universalist implications of his own theological reasoning. Crisp construes the basic logical structure of Barth's doctrine of election as follows: (i) "Christ's atonement is universal in scope and efficacy." (ii) "Christ is the Elect One and therefore the sole member of the set 'elect,' in whom all human agents are elected." (iii) "Christ is the Elect One whose atonement for the sin of human agents is universal in scope and efficacy, and all human agents are members of the set 'elect-in-Christ.'" Barth's appeal to divine freedom can be represented as follows: (iv) "Because God is free, the eschatological destiny of all humanity is uncertain." Crisp concludes, "If all humanity have been (derivatively) elected and efficaciously atoned for by Christ (as per (i)–(iii)), then their soteriological status simply cannot be uncertain, as per (iv). This seems fatal to the consistency of Barth's position."[248]

In a 2006 essay, Alister McGrath sees more continuity between Barth and nineteenth-century German liberalism than most Barth scholars do. He finds in both Barth and the German liberals a "lack of interest in human bondage to sin." As a result of this, "the theological drama which constitutes the Christian faith is thus held to concern humans and their knowledge of God, rather than the salvation of sinful humans, caught up in the cosmic conflict between God and sin, the world and the devil." What is more, "such a conflict is an impossibility within the context of Barth's theology, in that Barth shares with Hegel the difficulty of accommodating sin within an essentially monistic system." The only struggle is with "ignorance" or "misunderstanding," on an epistemic level, and "we find only talk about God making himself *known* to humanity."[249] For McGrath, the problem lies in Barth's theological method, which gives primacy

248. Crisp, "Barth's Denial," 129–30.
249. A. E. McGrath, "Karl Barth's Doctrine of Justification," 181–82.

to "the fact of revelation" over soteriology as such. He construes humanity's fundamental problem as the lack of the knowledge of God. Rejecting human-centeredness in theology, "Barth has essentially inverted the liberal theology" and yet has done so "without fundamentally altering its frame of reference." With his post-Kantian fixation on "how God may be known," Barth was per-haps unwittingly "perpetuating the theological interests and concerns of the liberal school."[250]

To support this claim, McGrath quotes from Barth's *Church Dogmatics* IV/1:

> In the mirror of Jesus Christ, who was offered up for us, and who was obedient in this offering, it is revealed who we ourselves are, that is, the ones for whom he was offered up, for whom he obediently offered himself up. In the light of the humility in demonstration of which he acted as true God for us, we are exposed, made known and have to acknowledge ourselves as the proud creatures who ourselves want to be God and Lord and redeemer and helper, and have, as such, turned away from God.[251]

McGrath concludes that "Barth's account of the justification of humanity, while not inattentive to traditional soteriological issues, appears to be redirected to focus on the epistemic situation of humanity." McGrath connects this emphasis on knowing and knowledge with the doctrine of election: "Barth's frequently observed emphasis upon salvation as *Erkenntnis* [knowledge] is easily understood in light of his doctrine of election. Given that all people will be saved eventually . . . the *present knowledge* of this situation is clearly of enormous importance."[252]

In a 2007 essay, Tom Greggs seeks to take seriously both the seeming logical necessity of universalism in Barth's theology and Barth's disavowals of universal-ism.[253] To do this, he looks closely at Barth's response to Berkouwer's *The Triumph of Grace in the Theology of Karl Barth*. Greggs's ultimate conclusion is that Barth is indeed a universalist in that ultimately he believes that hell will be empty and all will enjoy fellowship with God. This outcome follows logically from Barth's doctrine of election. Yet Barth's rejection of universalism is not without signifi-cance. It seems to Greggs that Barth understood "universalism" as implying an abstract principle that would *necessitate* God's action and so undermine divine freedom: "That Barth rejects *apokatastasis* is not because of a limitation of his hope for humanity or his belief in the all-encompassing nature of election and

---

250. Ibid., 185–86. Key elements in McGrath's critique echo those of the 1970s German-language critics of Barth (*DR* 9.1).

251. Barth, *CD* IV/1, 574–75, quoted in A. E. McGrath, "Karl Barth's Doctrine of Justification," 186.

252. A. E. McGrath, "Karl Barth's Doctrine of Justification," 186–87.

253. Greggs, "'Jesus Is Victor.'"

the objective nature of salvation. It is rather a rejection of a principle. In Barth's own words: 'I don't believe in universalism, but I do believe in Jesus Christ, the reconciler of all.'"²⁵⁴ Stated otherwise, Greggs explains that "for Barth to place his faith in universalism would be to place his faith in something which was greater than Christ and undermined the sovereignty of God."²⁵⁵

In 2007, Bruce McCormack gave a succinct summary of Barth's view of election:

> All human beings are, for Barth, elect in Jesus Christ. All human beings are "in" Jesus Christ by virtue of their election. Because they are *already* "in him" *even as* he becomes incarnate, all that takes place in him (as a consequence of the divine humiliation and the exaltation of the royal human) is effective for them in that it takes place: justification, sanctification, vocation. No further work need take place in order to make this work of Christ effective. The work of the Holy Spirit does not make effective a work of Christ that would otherwise be ineffective. The work of the Holy Spirit in awakening human beings to faith and obedience is a work of awakening them to the fact that the work of Christ is already effective for them, thereby enabling them to live in correspondence to their true humanity in him.²⁵⁶

In McCormack's view, the divine act of electing is effective for all humanity regardless of any external factor. The role of the Holy Spirit, says McCormack, is not to make effective what God in Christ has accomplished but is simply to accomplish "a work of awakening" humanity to what already is the case. What God accomplished through Christ is already effective. McCormack's epistemic interpretation of Barth's soteriology comports with McGrath's interpretation— though what McGrath criticizes in Barth, McCormack affirms.

In this section we have surveyed more than a dozen authors who address the question of whether Barth was a universalist. What is rather surprising is the extent to which they agree. To be sure, they differ on what aspects of Barth's theology of election and salvation they emphasize and on how they evaluate these aspects. Yet there is broad agreement regarding Barth's position on many points—for example, that God in Christ has elected all humanity for salvation, that in the life and death of Christ salvation is already achieved, that among human beings there is an epistemic difference (some of whom know what Christ has accomplished on their behalf and some of whom do not), and that God's election must not be seen as necessitated, or as the outworking of an abstract principle, but rather as God's free decision. The authors we have

254. Ibid., 210–11, quoting Busch, *Karl Barth*, 394.
255. Greggs, "'Jesus Is Victor,'" 211.
256. McCormack, "Seek God Where He May Be Found," 69.

examined suggest that Barth's denial of being a "universalist" or of holding to *apokatastasis* should be narrowly construed. It is not a denial of the proposition that all might finally be saved—and certainly not an affirmation that some will finally be lost—but is merely a negation of there being any *necessity* in an outcome in which all are finally saved.

The divergence among Barth's interpreters centers on the larger implications of what we have termed the *epistemic difference* and the significance of *God's free decision*. Several of Barth's critics (including Brunner, Wingren, Williams, and McGrath) interpret the epistemic difference as implying that sin, the threat of punishment for sin, and evil are less than fully real or illusory in Barth's account. Because the great turning point in God's overcoming of sin, evil, and punishment occurred nearly two millennia ago in the death of Jesus, any contemporaneous threat, danger, or power connected with sin, evil, and punishment is *merely apparent*. Brunner uses the analogy of the person in shallow water who believes that he or she will drown but who in fact cannot possibly drown. Here is the *epistemic difference* at work: some people may believe that they are at risk of punishment and rejection by God, but no such risk exists for anyone. For Christians who hold that Jesus's teaching in the Gospels implies a genuine threat and danger to those who knowingly reject Jesus, this implication of Barth's theology may be unsettling. Is there any way to avoid this implication and to banish Brunner's image of the person mistakenly afraid of drowning?

To answer this question, one must turn to the theme of *God's free decision* in electing all human beings for salvation. On a pastoral and homiletic level, God's decision must somehow be coordinated with human faith and human decision. Traditional Calvinist teaching on predestination—that God from eternity has chosen some but not all for salvation—presents its own set of difficulties and leads ineluctably toward the question: How might I know whether I am among the elect? Barth's reasoning has its own logic and leads ineluctably toward a different question: Does my own faith in Christ (or lack thereof) play any role in determining whether or not I am saved?

Colwell moves in an interesting direction by probing Barth's understanding of divine eternity and human temporality. His emphasis on the "contemporaneity" of God's elective decision with human choices is an attempt to prevent the divine choice from engulfing or obliterating human choices. Yet what might "contemporaneity" mean, when Barth tells us that God's gracious, elective "decision" (*Entscheidung*) is irrevocably fixed from all eternity? The word "decision," with its cognates "decided" and "decisive," implies something determinate rather than contingent. To preserve God's gracious decision in all its decisiveness and to open up some conceptual space for human deliberation and contingent decision-making, one seemingly must resort to some form of perspectivalism, so that what is (from God's perspective) already fixed and determinate is also (from the human perspective) open, indeterminate, and contingent. This brings us back once again to the *epistemic difference*. If there is a discrepancy between God's perspective and the human perspective on salvation, then it is difficult to escape the conclusion that God's view is objective and finally true, while the human view is subjective and merely apparent. Once again we come back to the critique of Brunner and some others that the apparent human choice regarding salvation (as we observe it happening) is either illusory or insignificant. It seems, then, that Barth's doctrine of universal election is difficult if not impossible to square with the idea of genuine contingency or personal meaningfulness in human faith-decisions.[257]

9.9. Barth's Ambiguous Legacy: From the 1950s to the 1980s

In the middle decades of the twentieth century—from the 1940s through the 1960s in German-speaking countries and from the 1950s through the 1980s in the Anglophone world—Barth's influence in Christian theology was at its apogee. Academic theology after World War II has been in many respects an ongoing dialogue with Barth. Protestants of all stripes and—to a lesser but discernible degree—Catholic and Orthodox thinkers too were affected by the Swiss theologian.[258] Gotthold Müller, who published an extensive bibliography on Christian universalism, pointed to Barth as the one figure who had decisively shifted the discussion: "An entirely new perspective in this history of *Apokatastasis* emerged in the theology of Karl Barth." Müller perceived a change

257. The traditional Calvinistic doctrine of particular election—precisely because it maintains particular and not universal election—does not present a problem as acute as that of Barth. In the doctrine of particular election, one needs to account for how the eternal divine choice of particular persons is compatible with contingent, human faith-choices to believe in and to follow Christ. Yet one does not have to account for how an eternal divine choice of all persons without exception is compatible with contradictory, human faith-choices, as Barth seemingly must do.

258. On Barth and Catholicism, see Wigley, *Karl Barth and Hans Urs von Balthasar*; Dahlke, *Karl Barth, Catholic Renewal, and Vatican II*; Long, *Saving Karl Barth*; Norwood, *Reforming Rome*. Barth's influence on Balthasar is well known. The latter's reading of Barth's account of God's beauty played a role in the emergence of his theological aesthetics, while the multivolume *Theo-drama* was a project in part inspired by Barth's redemptive-historical approach to dogmatics (*DR* 10.5–10.9). Hans Küng in an early work, *Justification: The Doctrine of Karl Barth and a Catholic Reflection* (1964), sought to show that Barth's account of justification was compatible with Catholic theology. Even more importantly, the Vatican II constitutions showed certain "Barthian" traits or aspects. Peter Kuzmic (of Gordon-Conwell Theological Seminary) indicated (in conversation with the author) that the great twentieth-century Orthodox theologian Dumitru Stăniloae acknowledged that reading Barth had inspired his own theological work, though Stăniloae remained publicly silent regarding Barth's influence.

in Barth's approach to universalism between the time of his *Credo* (1935) and the *Church Dogmatics* II/2 (1942), the volume dealing with divine election.[259] Esteban Deak argued that twentieth-century theological positions on the question of universal salvation might be divided into three categories: *pre-Barthian*, *Barthian*, and *post-Barthian*. Because of World War II and the social disarray that lingered in the aftermath of war, Barth's views on election did not exert their full effects until the 1950s and 1960s.

In Deak's analysis, a *literalist approach* to exegesis of the relevant scriptural texts was characteristic of pre-Barthian discussions of universalism. This included not only the opponents of universalism but also such tentative or assertive proponents as Otto Rieman, Ferdinand Ströter, Karl Geyer, Paul Althaus, Reinhold Seeberg, Wilhelm Kümmel, and Albert Fünning.[260] In contrast to this, the Barthian discussion showed a *dialectical approach* to the issue, beginning with Barth himself and continuing in the writings of Wilhelm Michaelis, Gotthold Müller, Heinrich Ott, Heinz Schumacher, the Norwegian Lutheran bishop Harald Krabbe Schjelderup, the Anglican bishop and theologian John A. T. Robinson, and Ernest Stähelin.[261] The third or post-Barthian perspective might be termed an *immanentist approach*. It had "little in common with the first two approaches" because it was either "not asking the question of heaven and hell at all" or treating it "just peripherally." Into this category one might place Paul Tillich, Jürgen Moltmann, and "the 'third world' theologians of revolution."[262] Characteristic of the third group are interpretations of biblical eschatological language in immanentist or anthropological terms.[263]

259. G. Müller, "Idea of an *Apokatastasis ton Panton*," 50–51, in reference to Barth, *Credo*. Cf. G. Müller, *Apokatastasis Panton: A Bibliography*.

260. Reflecting the pre-Barthian position and arguments, see Riemann, *Die Lehre von der Wiederbringung*; O. Schrader, *Die Lehre von der Apokatastasis*; Ströter, *Das Evangelium Gottes*; Seeberg, *Christliche Dogmatik*, 2:606–77; Geyer, *Ewiges Gericht und Allversöhnung*; Fünning, *Das feste, prophetische Wort*. Esteban Deak notes that Ströter—a German-American Methodist—"was greatly influenced by the English theologian Andrew John Jukes" (Deak, "Apokatastasis," 146). Jukes's works were translated and published in German from the 1880s into the 1920s. Regarding Jukes, see the analysis of his theology in *DR* 5.9 and his influence on German universalism in the 1910s in *DR* 9.2.

261. In Deak's analysis, "Barthian" texts of the 1950s and 1960s dealing with universalism included Michaelis, *Versöhnung des Alls*; John A. T. Robinson, *In The End, God*; Ott, *Eschatologie*, esp. 68–71; Schumacher, *Das biblische Zeugnis von der Versöhnung des Alls*; Stähelin, *Die Wiederbringung aller Dinge*. The 1953 Norwegian Lutheran controversy on hell, involving Ole Hallesby and Bishop Schjelderup, is documented (in texts translated into German) in Schauer, *Was ist es um die Hölle?* The hell debate pitted Ole Hallesby and Bishop Schjelderup—and with them two different theological faculties—against one another. For discussion of the Norwegian debate, see https://en.wikipedia.org/wiki/Ole_Hallesby; Deak, "Apokatastasis," 174–80; Iverson, "Debate on Hell in Norway"; Barnhouse, "Hell in Norway"; Vorgrimler, *Geschichte der Hölle*, 317–20.

262. Deak, "Apokatastasis," 142–99, esp. 143–44.

263. See the brief survey of universalism over forty-odd years in Fairhurst, "'Dare We Hope.'"

Barth's doctrine of election did not stand alone, but had larger implications for how Barth and post-Barthian thinkers approached the question of God and salvation generally. *Church Dogmatics* I/1, I/2, and II/1 all insisted strongly on the freedom, sovereignty, and independence of God. Barth's deity was *the God-who-is*. A shift began to occur, however, with the appearance of *Church Dogmatics* II/2 and its affirmation of universal election in Christ. God's graciousness became, so to speak, structured or built into the doctrine of God. One might say that God was no longer *the God-who-is*, but rather *the God-who-is-for-us*.[264]

In retrospect, one can perceive a trajectory leading from the theology of Barth to that of Jürgen Moltmann, which intensified some of the underlying tendencies of Barth's later dogmatics. God's identification with humanity, and especially with human suffering, was a dominant theme in Moltmann's theology. *The Crucified God* (1972, in German; 1973, in English) made God's participation in human suffering fundamental; *God in Creation* (1985) presented a panentheistic view of God's relation to the world that Barth had rejected; and *The Coming of God* (1996) made Moltmann's universalism more explicit than ever before (*DR* 9.10–9.11). The rise of "kenotic," "open," and "relational" theologies during the 1980s and 1990s meant that the doctrine of God shifted yet further in the direction of the God-who-is-for-us, with the immanent Trinity (God-in-himself) sometimes seeming to disappear in the face of the God-for-us. For many kenotic-relational theologians, the only God that is knowable or worthy of discussion is the God manifested to us in the economy of salvation (*DR* 9.12).[265]

Theologians laid hold of Barth's theology and legacy in multiple ways, affirming or disputing particular aspects of Barth's massive synthesis. In 1946, Emil Brunner emerged as the leading early critic of Barth's election doctrine, which Brunner took as implying the "heresy" of universalism. Yet Brunner's considered position on election and eschatology had many of the same emphases as Barth's did. Before his early death, Dietrich Bonhoeffer briefly touched on the theme of universal salvation, but he did so dialectically by neither simply affirming nor denying the doctrine: "Although we are speaking here of a double issue [i.e., outcome] we must not do so without at the same time emphasizing the inner necessity of the idea of *apocatastasis*. We are not in a position to resolve this antinomy."[266] John A. T. Robinson, in his book *In the End, God* (1950), drew

---

264. In discussing Bruce McCormack's views, Han-Luen Kantzer Komline distinguishes "a divine ontology that logically prioritizes God's 'being-for' *ad extra* and one that logically prioritizes God's being *in se*" ("Friendship and Being," 12). A similar distinction is drawn here.

265. See the critique of the late twentieth-century trend away from an immanent Trinity (i.e., God in himself as free and transcendent) and toward a purely economic Trinity (i.e., God as known and as related to the world) in Molnar, *Divine Freedom*.

266. Bonhoeffer, *Communion of Saints*, 201.

out the universalist implication from Barth, not to criticize it but to advocate it. Wilhelm Michaelis—who like Robinson asserted universalism as such, rather than a hopeful attitude—published his major work, *Versöhnung des Alls*, in the same year. As noted above, Robinson's work provoked a strident response from Thomas Torrance, one of the editors of Barth's *Church Dogmatics* and a custodian of Barth's legacy in the English-speaking world. Adolf Köberle was so concerned about the impact of Barth's theology that he visited the aging Barth in Basel to express concern that his doctrine of election might undermine the church's missionary enterprise. Unfortunately, there seems to be no surviving record of that conversation with Barth.[267]

By placing the doctrine of universal election at the center of his imposing *Church Dogmatics*, Barth gave greater legitimacy and prestige to universalist styles of theology. The Cambridge New Testament scholar C. F. D. Moule wrote a slender book entitled *The Meaning of Hope* (1953), in which he wrote, "I cannot believe that such [divine] love does not pursue us even in hell. If *we* cannot rest without knowing our loved ones are right with God, is it conceivable that God can be content to let them go?"[268] Christian hope was the main theme in 1954 at the Second Assembly of the World Council of Churches (WCC). In 1959, the United Church of Canada produced a study of eschatology, which was not definitive on the question of universalism but stated that "we may hope that He will find a way whereby all men may eventually come to repentance and eternal salvation," when "the imperfections of the universe and man's failure and tragedy are swallowed up in the victory of God."[269] John Hick, in *Evil and the God of Love* (1966), affirmed universal salvation to be a "practical certainty," for "we do not as Christians hope simply for our own salvation, but equally for that of any man and therefore of all men."[270]

In Roman Catholic thought, the focus on Christian hope in the early 1960s found support at the Second Vatican Council (1962–65), whose closing coincided with the appearance of the first German edition of Moltmann's *Theology of Hope* (1965). The participation of the Christian church in the hopes and fears of humanity as a whole was a major theme in the pastoral constitution *Gaudium et Spes* (1965). As early as 1953, Jean Daniélou commented on Christian hope and the theme of human solidarity before God: "Too often we think of hope in too individualistic a manner as merely our personal salvation. But hope essentially

267. Köberle, *Universalismus*, 81, cited in Schulz, "Universalism," 91–92.
268. Moule, *Meaning of Hope*, 52–55, cited in Fairhurst, "'Dare We Hope,'" 373.
269. Fairhurst, "'Dare We Hope,'" 373, citing A. G. Reynolds, *Life and Death*, 54, 107.
270. Hick, *Evil and the God of Love*, 381. Hick expressed his commitment to universalism more pointedly in *Death and Eternal Life*, 242–61, where he sought to show that universalism could be reconciled with human freedom.

bears on the great actions of God concerning the whole of creation. It bears on the destiny of all humanity. It is the salvation of the world that we await. In reality hope bears on the salvation of all men—and it is only in the measure that I am immersed in them that it bears on me."[271] The publications of Teilhard de Chardin in the 1950s (*DR* 10.3) did not affirm universalism as such but nonetheless offered a cosmic optimism, embodied in the dictum that "everything that rises must converge."[272] Karol Wojtyła—the soon-to-be Pope John Paul II—in his Vatican Lenten retreat in 1976 wrote: "Will God be all in all if in the final consummation . . . there is to be this division, this contradiction? . . . Perhaps, in the light of the truth that 'God is love' . . . they [i.e., Origen and other universalists] were tentatively reaching out towards some later phase of the history of salvation—not disclosed in revelation and the scriptures—which might put an end to this separation between those who are saved and those who are damned."[273] In 1984, Hans Küng, appealing to Moltmann's theology, insisted that hell does not have the last word over Christian hope. Though rejecting any facile universalism, Küng addressed divine judgment by saying, "Neither in one way or the other can we tie God's hands or control him. There is nothing to be known here, but everything to be hoped."[274]

9.10. Jürgen Moltmann and the God-with-Us in Suffering

Jürgen Moltmann (1926–) might be today's most widely known living Protestant theologian. His oeuvre is many-sided. For an author such as this, the question arises of where to begin in the analysis of his writings.[275] One interpreter highlights one of Moltmann's early life experiences, which, though not strictly a conversion to Christ, was nonetheless a conversion to theological reflection, in which he did not "decide" for Christ but Christ "decided" for him. The text

271. Daniélou, *Essai sur le mystère de l'histoire*, 340, as quoted in Balthasar, *Dare We Hope?*, 11.

272. Teilhard de Chardin, *Future of Man*, 186.

273. John Paul II [Wojtyła], *Sign of Contradiction*, 153–54, 180, cited in Fairhurst, "'Dare We Hope,'" 374.

274. Küng, *Eternal Life?*, 178–79, cited in Fairhurst, "'Dare We Hope,'" 374.

275. Among the works by Moltmann cited here are, in chronological order, *Theology of Hope*; *The Crucified God*; *The Church in the Power of the Spirit*; *The Trinity and the Kingdom*; *God in Creation*; *The Way of Jesus Christ*; *The Spirit of Life*; *Jesus Christ for Today's World*; *The Coming of God*, esp. "The Restoration of All Things," 235–55; *Sun of Righteousness, Arise!*; "The Presence of God's Future: The Risen Christ." Among the secondary sources on Moltmann are Meeks, *Origins of the Theology of Hope*; Molnar, "Function of the Trinity"; Spence, "Von Balthasar and Moltmann"; Bauckham, *Theology of Jürgen Moltmann*; Farrow, "In the End Is the Beginning"; Bauckham, *God Will Be All in All*; Müller-Fahrenholz, *Phantasie für das Reich Gottes*; Molnar, *Divine Freedom*, 197–233; J. W. Cooper, "Moltmann's Perichoretic Panentheism," in *Panentheism*, 237–58; Ansell, "Annihilation of Hell"; N. G. Wright, "Universalism in the Theology of Jürgen Moltmann"; Ansell, *Annihilation of Hell*.

of Scripture occasioning this experience was Jesus's cry of dereliction on the cross: "My God, my God, why have you forsaken me?" (Matt. 27:46; Mark 15:34). This experience—against the backdrop of the horrors of World War II and its concentration camps—caused Moltmann to realize that in the post-Auschwitz era "only a suffering God can help."[276] The starting point for Moltmann's reflection was thus a sense of the theological necessity of affirming God's solidarity with human pain, suffering, and victimization. He realized that God suffers for, with, and from human suffering. In some respects Moltmann's whole theology could be seen as an answer to the question implied in Jesus's cry from the cross: *God, where are you?*[277] For Moltmann, this question lies at the center of the contemporary clash between religious faith and secularism. From the beginning, Moltmann's theology has been acutely attuned to the issue of theodicy, or God's justice in the face of innocent suffering. His understanding of the cross does not resolve the problem of suffering, but it does address the issue of abandonment in suffering by showing us a God who suffers with us.

Alongside this personal experience, one must pay attention to Moltmann's social and cultural context in post–World War II Germany, where there was a surge of hope for Germany's renewal and reconstruction, though not without disappointments along the way.[278] In his preface to *The Coming of God*, Moltmann recalls the motivations that underlay his earlier theology: "At that time [1964] I was trying to find a new fundamental category for theology in general: the theology of love in the middle ages and the theology of faith at the Reformation was to be followed in modern times by the theology of hope."[279] Speaking broadly, Moltmann's theology has done much to reemphasize the importance of eschatology in Christian theology, not as a kind of appendix tacked on at the

276. This phrase—"Only a suffering God can help"—appeared in Bonhoeffer's *Letters and Papers from Prison*, 11. The idea often appears in Moltmann, and occasionally Moltmann uses the exact phrase in his own writings (*Open Church*, 25).

277. Geiko Müller-Fahrenholz writes:
Moltmann hat immer gemeint, ein Bekehrungserlebnis im engen pietistischen Sinne habe es in seinem Leben nicht gegeben. Er habe sich nie für Christus "entschieden." Aber er kennt doch den Moment, in welchem er den deutlichen Eindruck bekam, dass sich dieser Christus für ihm "entschieden" und ihn "im schwarzen Loch" seiner Seele gefunden habe. Dieser Moment ist ein Satz aus dem Markus-Evangelium: "Mein Gott, warum hast du mich verlassen?" Es gibt kein Wort der Heiligen Schrift, dem eine ähnlich zentrale Bedeutung für Moltmanns Leben und für seine Theologie zukommt. [Moltmann always said that he had had no conversion experience in his life in the narrow pietistic sense. He had never "decided" for Christ. But he knows the moment when he had the clear impression that Christ had "decided" for him and found him "in the black hole" of his soul. This moment came with a sentence from the Gospel of Mark: "My God, why have you forsaken me?" There is no saying of Holy Scripture that is of a similar central importance for Moltmann's life and for his theology.] (*Phantasie für das Reich Gottes*, 17 [my translation])

278. Meeks, *Origins of the Theology of Hope*, 4.

279. Moltmann, *Coming of God*, xii, cf. 158.

end but rather as a determining aspect in all the major theological topics and themes. Though some in the liberal tradition thought that eschatology was a stumbling block to modern people, Moltmann took the contrasting position that eschatology would help to make the Christian faith credible once again. He writes that "from first to last, not merely in the epilogue, Christianity is eschatology, is hope."[280] Yet Moltmann's eschatology is dialectical in the sense that it recognizes a contradiction between the cross and the resurrection, so that God's promise defies present reality. This implies that the eschatological kingdom is a radically new future. God's promise is not for another world but for the present world—a restoration of the whole creation, subject though it now is to sin and to death.[281]

When looking back at his first three major works, *Theology of Hope*, *The Crucified God*, and *The Church in the Power of the Spirit*, Moltmann commented that, though he had not intended it at the time, his thought moved in sequence from Easter (hope) to Good Friday (suffering) to Pentecost (church).[282] While the most important or "controlling theological idea" in Moltmann's early work was "his dialectical interpretation of the cross and the resurrection of Jesus," this later gave way to a "particular form of trinitarianism which becomes the over-arching theological principle of his later work."[283] According to Moltmann's dialectic, the cross represents God's absence while the resurrection represents God's presence. Beginning with *The Crucified God*, Moltmann developed his theology in a strongly trinitarian way, since he interpreted Jesus's death on the cross as an event that transpired between the Father and the Son. Moltmann has also sought to overturn the frequent subordination of pneumatology to Christology, and instead sought to develop both Christology and pneumatology in mutual relationship and within a trinitarian framework.[284]

Moltmann's theology has an orientation toward praxis. *Theology of Hope* proclaims the church's mission to transform the world in anticipation of God's promised eschatological transformation of the world. The task of theology is not merely to interpret the world but to change it, an idea that recalls a famous saying of Karl Marx.[285] Moltmann's theology took shape from this sense of a calling to change the world, and this played a role in fertilizing the soil of Latin America during the emergence of liberation theology there. Yet Moltmann has

280. Bauckham, *Theology of Jürgen Moltmann*, 9.
281. Ibid., 9–10.
282. Ibid., 3.
283. Ibid., 4.
284. Ibid., 6.
285. Karl Marx, *Theses on Feuerbach*, no. 11: "The philosophers have only interpreted the world, in various ways; the point is to change it" (https://www.marxists.org/archive/marx/works/1845/theses /theses.htm).

resisted any effort to define theology solely as a reflection on praxis. His writings from the 1970s onward have been shot through with a stress on the elements of contemplation, celebration, and doxology. What is more, he resists the notion of closure implied in speaking of a theological "system." By contrast, he insists that his thinking is characterized by ongoing and open-ended dialogue. The church is to be faithful to what it knows of Christ and so to question others outside the church, and yet to acknowledge the openness of the future, which allows others to question the church.[286]

The sources of Moltmann's theology are varied, and they include Karl Barth's writings, the Marxist and futurist philosophy of Ernst Bloch, the theology of Hans Joachim Iwand, and the radical sociopolitical Schäbean Pietism of Johann Christoph Blumhardt and his son Christoph Blumhardt.[287] It is the thought of Bloch that seems to be in the foreground of Moltmann's *Theology of Hope*, while the Hegel-influenced reflections concerning Jesus on the cross stand in the background of *The Crucified God*. A long line of Moltmann interpreters, including the sympathetic as well as the unsympathetic, have highlighted the Hegelian character of Moltmann's theology, especially his account of Jesus's death on the cross. Richard Bauckham, a meticulous and sympathetic interpreter of Moltmann, states that "both Hegel and Iwand contributed significantly to the development of Moltmann's dialectical interpretation of the cross and the resurrection."[288] John W. Cooper,[289] M. Douglas Meeks,[290] and Brian

286. Bauckham, *Theology of Jürgen Moltmann*, 6–7.

287. On the Blumhardts' influence on Moltmann, see Collins Winn and Heltzel, "'Before Bloch.'" Both Blumhardts were universalists (*DR* 5.8), and Karl Barth was strongly influenced by the theology of the elder Blumhardt, while the younger Blumhardt was a personal friend and mentor to the young Barth.

288. Bauckham, *Theology of Jürgen Moltmann*, 2.

289. J. W. Cooper, in *Panentheism*, posits a double-sided relationship between Hegel and Moltmann:

Moltmann proceeds from the analysis of the crucifixion in Hegel's account of Christianity in *Lectures on the Philosophy of Religion*. . . . Moltmann, however, reverses Hegel in a crucial way. Hegel posits the negation of the Father in the incarnation of the Son and then the negation of the Son in the crucifixion. Both Father and Son are dialectically transformed or "sublated" into the Spirit that lives in the church and Christendom. The three persons do not coexist in communion but are successive modes of Absolute Spirit's relation to the world. Moltmann, in contrast, affirms the ongoing community of three distinct persons, making them the primary reality of God. (242)

If one accepts Cooper's analysis, then Moltmann avoided Hegel's trinitarian problem but perhaps had a trinitarian problem of his own. By beginning with the three distinct persons, Moltmann seems to have evaded the danger of modalism but to have drawn dangerously near to—or perhaps embraced—a tritheistic view of God.

290. Meeks goes so far as to claim, "If we are looking for the single most important source for what is new and unique in Moltmann's theology, it is undoubtedly the thought of Hans Joachim Iwand. The whole of Moltmann's theology of hope is cast by the temper of Iwand's theology" (*Origins of the Theology of Hope*, 30). Others have pointed toward Ernst Bloch as a crucial early

John Spence[291] have all underscored Moltmann's Hegelian affinity and lineage. Hans Urs von Balthasar, despite the Hegelian undercurrent in some of his own thinking, made Hegel's perceived influence on Moltmann's theology a matter of reproach.[292]

Moltmann's writings from the 1980s onward show the influence of a series of Jewish and especially Jewish kabbalistic authors: Isaac Luria, Gershom Scholem, Franz Rosenzweig, and Walter Benjamin. Moltmann's *God in Creation* appeals to the kabbalistic and specifically Lurianic doctrine of *tsimtsum* (*DR* 2.5). According to this doctrine, in order for there to be space for creation to emerge, God had first to withdraw, thus establishing a Godforsaken region for creatures. Following Kabbalah, creation and fall are *linked* (if not *identified*), so that what one normally thinks of as redemption in some sense represents a reversal of what first took place in creation. There is creation/fall—the divine withdrawal. Then there is uncreation or unfall—the divine expansion. As at least one interpreter has recognized, Moltmann's doctrine of creation seems itself to imply universal salvation. From the way in which Moltmann has sketched his account of the origins of the universe, as well as from the way that he speaks of Jesus's cross, it is hard to imagine any other outcome.[293]

---

influence on Moltmann. Meeks explains Moltmann's close yet critical stance vis-à-vis Hegel: "Following his teacher Iwand, Moltmann everywhere holds to the problems of the God-question as stated by Hegel while consistently refusing the premature and rigid solutions of the Hegelian system" (35). Following Hegel and Iwand, Moltmann asserts "that forsaken men are already taken up by Christ's forsakenness into the divine history" so that "God is in us, God suffers in us, where love suffers," and "we participate in the trinitarian process of God's history" (38, citing Moltmann, *Crucified God*, 255). Something else that may have come to Moltmann through Hegel is the sense that modern people have "a qualitatively new experience of God" (*Origins of the Theology of Hope*, 35).

291. Brian John Spence ("Von Balthasar and Moltmann") claims that Hegel's theology set the questions for Moltmann's theology but that Moltmann's answers were not exactly those of Hegel, whose Christology was much weaker and less developed than that of Moltmann. Spence makes a similar claim regarding Balthasar's thought.

292. In Moltmann, who is "nearer to Hegel" than Rahner was, "God is entangled in the world process and becomes a tragic, mythological God" (Balthasar, *TD* 4:321–22). "Moltmann . . . endeavors to reinterpret Hegel" and yet "has arrived at Hegel's view in his *Phenomenology*" (*TD* 5:227–28).

293. Douglas Farrow recognizes this point regarding Moltmann's universalism. In reference to Moltmann's kabbalistic doctrine of *tsimtsum*, he explains: "This divine reoccupation of the God-forsaken territory in which creatures are given their existence is from the very beginning the overcoming of a contradiction. Hence the claim that from the standpoint of the cross *creatio ex nihilo* already means forgiveness, justification and resurrection, while from the standpoint of creation the cross 'means the true consolidation of the universe'" ("In the End Is the Beginning," 437, citing Moltmann, *God in Creation*, 91). This leads Farrow to conclude that Moltmann's actual reasons for embracing universalism may be different from his stated reasons. In the note to the comment above, he adds: "It is this that secretly determines Moltmann's universalism (contra *CoG* [*Coming of God*], p. 245), for there can be no consolidation without resolving the contradiction entirely" ("In the End Is the Beginning," 446n59).

Not to be ignored in Moltmann's background, though, is the obvious and unmistakable impact of the theology of Karl Barth, who makes an "odd couple" when taken alongside Ernst Bloch.[294] As noted above, Barth shifted in his early writings from a notion of God-who-is toward a God-who-is-for-us. Moltmann may be seen as carrying this process a step further, with a God-who-is-for-us-in-suffering. The phrase "in suffering" refers not only to human suffering but also to God's own suffering. This divine suffering is by no means limited to the brief time during which Jesus was nailed to the cross. Instead, for Moltmann, suffering has become a constitutive principle of God's own being. What underlines Moltmann's universalism is the divine suffering that belongs to God's creating the world as well as to God's redeeming work.

Moltmann's universalism has been apparent throughout his career and in his many books. In *The Crucified God*, Moltmann writes, "Theology of the cross . . . is the true Christian universalism. There is no distinction here, and there cannot be any distinctions. All are sinners without distinction, and all will be made righteous without any merit on their part by his grace." That "God's Son has died for all," says Moltmann, "must undermine, remove, and destroy the things which mark men out as elect and non-elect."[295] Yet Moltmann differs from both Karl Barth and Hans Urs von Balthasar with respect to his *explicit* (rather than *implicit*) support for universalism. While the two Swiss thinkers were both hesitant to assert universal salvation or *apokatastasis*, Moltmann shows no such reservations. In *The Coming of God*, Moltmann interprets the Pauline Letters to affirm that "not only all human beings and earthly creatures, but the angels too—evidently the disobedient ones, since for the others it is unnecessary—will be reconciled through Christ." He affirms that "true hope must be universal, because its healing future embraces every individual and the whole universe. If we were to surrender hope for as much as one single creature, for us God would not be God."[296] This idea that no single creature can ever be lost comes up repeatedly in Moltmann's writings.[297]

Moltmann's universalist theology cannot be reduced to any single denominator. Richard Bauckham notes that "Moltmann's theology . . . always tends to broaden its base and to integrate perspectives."[298] At least three different

294. Meeks, *Origins of the Theology of Hope*, 16–19, on Barth's and Bloch's influences on Moltmann.
295. Moltmann, *Crucified God*, 194–95.
296. Moltmann, *Coming of God*, 240, 132.
297. See Moltmann, *Coming of God*, 70, 251, 265; Moltmann, *Way of Jesus Christ*, 239, 303; Moltmann, *Jesus Christ for Today's World*, 104. Richard Bauckham ("Eschatology in *The Coming of God*," 12n8) draws a parallel between Moltmann and Alfred North Whitehead, who stated that God manifests to the world "a tender care that nothing be lost" (*Process and Reality*, 346).
298. Bauckham, "Eschatology in *The Coming of God*," 9.

strands of argumentation appear in Moltmann's eschatology, and each of them leads him in the direction of universalism. For simplicity's sake, these might labeled as *Christocentric-crucicentric*, *kabbalistic-cosmological*, and *trinitarian-processive*. Moltmann himself has acknowledged three different elements in his eschatology, referred to as "christological," "integrative," and "processive."[299] The threefold distinction here builds on Moltmann's comments regarding his own eschatology.

In the *Christocentric-crucicentric strand*, Moltmann's key claim is that all judgment and hell were exhausted and completed in Jesus's death on the cross. The background of this claim could be seen as Hegelian or perhaps Barthian. In *The Coming of God*, Moltmann makes it clear that his basis for believing in universal salvation lies in his interpretation of the cross: "The true Christian foundation for the hope of universal salvation is the theology of the cross, and the realistic consequence of the theology of the cross can only be the restoration of all things."[300]

The *kabbalistic-cosmological strand* derives from Moltmann's adherence to Lurianic Kabbalah, with particular reference to Isaac Luria (*DR* 2.5–2.6). The key claim is that God had to withdraw to "make space" for creation but will later expand to fill, complete, and restore all things. The most striking and dramatic aspect of the *tsimtsum* doctrine is the idea that God's withdrawal created a field of nothingness, a *nihil*, that Moltmann identifies as Godforsakenness and even as hell itself. This nothingness is a "partial negation of the divine Being, inasmuch as God is not yet creator. The space which comes into being and is set free by God's self-limitation is a literally God-forsaken space. The *nihil* in which God creates his creation is God-forsakenness, hell, absolute death."[301] Moltmann blends Kabbalah with insights from gnostic and Neoplatonic teaching on emanation, which, in his view, contains "elements of truth which are indispensable for a full understanding of God's creation."[302] Moltmann's cosmology also insists on the solidarity of humanity with the whole creation, including, as he says, "animals, plants, stones, and all cosmic life systems."[303] Since "stones" too are included, this may suggest a panvitalist philosophy. Moltmann asserts that "human life is participation in nature. . . . The redemption of humanity is aligned toward a humanity whose existence is still conjoined with nature."[304]

299. See Moltmann, "World in God or God in the World?," 36.
300. Moltmann, *Coming of God*, 251.
301. Moltmann, *God in Creation*, 87. Molnar (*Divine Freedom*, 216n88) comments on this passage: "The result of making the *nihil* something . . . is the incorporation of *nihil* itself directly into the Godhead," so that "God-forsakenness, hell and absolute death are part of God before creation."
302. Moltmann, *God in Creation*, 83.
303. Moltmann, *Way of Jesus Christ*, 258.
304. Moltmann, *Coming of God*, 260.

The *trinitarian-processive strand* has to do with what Moltmann calls a "trinitarian process,"[305] or an "inner-trinitarian process."[306] As Moltmann understands it, this process began with the resurrection of Jesus and extends until the goal of the new creation of all things is achieved. This is what he also calls the "trinitarian history of God."[307] According to Moltmann, "the process of resurrection" is equally "the new process of creation" as well as "the great process of giving life to the world, and the new creation of all things." These are all correlative notions.[308] The "process" that Moltmann envisages is like a cosmic rebirth or cosmic regeneration. In stressing the themes of new life, the giving of life, resurrection, or regeneration, Moltmann has very little to say about sin or the forgiveness of sins. One is reminded of the early Böhmist thinkers, such as William Law (*DR* 5.9), who reinterpreted Christian salvation in nonlegal terms as a matter of regeneration or the impartation of divine life from God to the creature. Moltmann's trinitarian-processive understanding of salvation moves along similar lines. The most important biblical text that Moltmann cites in connection with the divine trinitarian process may be 1 Corinthians 15:22–28. This passage is cited or discussed in *The Crucified God, The Future of Creation, The Trinity and the Kingdom, The Way of Jesus Christ,* and *The Coming of God.*[309] For Moltmann, this passage points to a process "which the resurrection of the crucified One has irrevocably set going."[310]

9.11. Evaluating Moltmann's Universalist Theology

In evaluating Moltmann, we might first note the shifts that occurred in the course of his theological development. His first major work, *The Theology of Hope,* offers in effect an eschatological theodicy. Moltmann does not seek to justify or explain evil as contributing to the greater good. The promise given in Jesus's resurrection does not explain evil and yet does provide hope for God's final triumph over all evil and suffering. When we turn to *The Crucified God,* the emphasis has altered, and there is a greater stress on God's suffering in solidarity with the world in its suffering.[311] By the time that Moltmann published

305. Ibid., 335.
306. Moltmann, *Crucified God,* 264; Moltmann, *Trinity and the Kingdom,* 92; Moltmann, *Coming of God,* 335.
307. Moltmann, *Church in the Power of the Spirit,* 50.
308. See Moltmann, *Way of Jesus Christ,* 242; Moltmann, *Coming of God,* 77, 198, 335; Moltmann, *Trinity and the Kingdom,* 91; Moltmann, *Future of Creation,* 123.
309. Moltmann, *Crucified God,* 246–66; Moltmann, *Future of Creation,* 123–25; Moltmann, *Trinity and the Kingdom,* 91–93; Moltmann, *Way of Jesus Christ,* 319; Moltmann, *Coming of God,* 110, 196, 335.
310. Moltmann, *Way of Jesus Christ,* 310.
311. Bauckham, *Theology of Jürgen Moltmann,* 10–11.

God in Creation, the emphasis has shifted still further and in the same general direction. God's solidarity with the world has now moved from the realm of redemption—Jesus's death on the cross—and includes the realm of creation as well. Explicitly embracing the Jewish esoteric teaching of Kabbalah, Moltmann insists that creation itself implies a form of suffering within the Godhead. By this point, Moltmann no longer accepts a clear-cut distinction between the creaturely and the divine realms. Creation itself is a kenosis or self-emptying of God. As Richard Bauckham summarizes, "Moltmann abandons the traditional distinction between the immanent and the economic trinities, between what God eternally is in himself and how he acts outside himself in the world. The cross (and, by extension, the rest of God's history with the world) is *internal* to the divine trinitarian experience."[312] Paul Molnar's *Divine Freedom and the Doctrine of the Immanent Trinity* (2002) offers an extensive critique of Moltmann that highlights what Molnar regards as Moltmann's basic confusion of the world process with God's inner life.[313]

Bauckham points out another trend in the course of Moltmann's development: "Moltmann's theology has become more and more strongly pneumatological."[314] There are different ways of thinking about this, but one might see this as a kind of creeping Hegelianism in Moltmann, in which Spirit (*Geist*) becomes the dominant category for interpreting God's interaction with the world, and in which Christ's role is modalistically confined to the career of the earthly Jesus. In such a modalist account, the era of Christ gives way to the era of the Spirit, that time in which we find ourselves today (*DR* 7.5–7.6). What is more, the Spirit does not merely come to glorify Christ but is radically free in such a way as to leave the future open-ended. Bauckham comments that this "attention to pneumatology . . . corresponds to his growing stress on the immanence of God in creation, as his eschatological panentheism (the hope that God will indwell all things in the new creation) has been increasingly accompanied by a stress on the coinherence of God and the world already."[315]

Bauckham notes that Moltmann's idea of the reciprocity between God and the world has far-ranging effects on Moltmann's theology.[316] Divine suffering is subsumed under a broader notion of divine self-limitation or kenosis, and it becomes embedded in the act of creation as such and so becomes characteristic of all of God's relations with his creation. God allows creation to be itself—and so to be other than himself—and so gives it a measure of freedom. Yet divine

312. Ibid., 16.
313. Molnar, *Divine Freedom*, 197–233.
314. Bauckham, *Theology of Jürgen Moltmann*, 21.
315. Ibid., 22.
316. Ibid., 59–60, citing Moltmann, *Trinity and the Kingdom*, 98–99.

suffering, in the sense of pain, seems to be implied in God's willingness to be self-limited. What Moltmann sees as positive here is that God's self-limitation allows God's goodness to be expressed.[317] God's love evokes the free response of creatures. God's capacity to suffer and God's actual suffering are thus closely linked to the foundational issues of divine and human freedom and to God's entire relationship with creation.[318] Yet there is much in Moltmann's line of thinking that might be called into question, such as the suggestion that creating itself brings suffering to God and the implication that there is a trade-off between divine omnipotence and divine goodness.

A serious deficiency in Moltmann's eschatology is the substantial absence of Christ's return (parousia) from his account of "the coming of God." As Bauckham observes, one finds a lack of attention to Christ in his "eschatological role, as redeemer and judge, at his *parousia*," and, quite strikingly, "the *parousia* . . . is scarcely a central feature or itself a subject of discussion." Christ's coming for Moltmann is associated not with the final state but rather with a transitional or intermediate state that Moltmann interprets as "millennial." This Christ-centered and millennial kingdom passes away in time, and so, as Bauckham writes, "generally this book [i.e., *The Coming of God*] speaks of the eschatological coming of God in a non-christological way."[319] Such an ambiguous stance toward Christ suggests that Moltmann's "coming" is more a "coming of God" than a "coming of Christ." This might be related to the Jewish messianic and kabbalistic roots of Moltmann's teaching. According to Kabbalah, the *Shekhinah* is presently in exile with Israel and remains in a state of suffering until the time of fulfillment comes. In Kabbalah generally, there is nothing quite like the "already but not yet" kingdom inaugurated by Christ's first coming but still unfulfilled prior to Christ's second coming. Moltmann introduces a sequential or partial-fulfillment aspect to his eschatology by invoking a temporal and temporary kingdom under Christ that he calls "millennial." Yet the appeal to a "millennium" seems ad hoc and does not fit well into Moltmann's framework.[320] The earthly life of Jesus for Moltmann was primarily a sign of God's identification with suffering people. This vision of history matches Kabbalah better than

317. Moltmann, *Trinity and the Kingdom*, 108–11, 118–19; Moltmann, *God in Creation*, 86–90.

318. Moltmann, *Trinity and the Kingdom*, 52–60, 105–8, 191–222; Moltmann, *God in Creation*, 79–86.

319. Bauckham, "Eschatology in *The Coming of God*," 4–5.

320. In relation to Moltmann's millennialism, Miroslav Volf—a prominent theologian and Moltmann's former student—argues that "understood as transition, the millennium is not only unnecessary but *detrimental*" ("After Moltmann," 243; emphasis original). If Volf is correct, and the millennium is extraneous to Moltmann's eschatology—while equated with Christ's reign—then this might lend support to a kabbalistic interpretation. Moltmann's eschatology, that is, would be simpler and more cohesive if one simply eliminated Christ's return and Christ's millennial reign.

it does the New Testament: there is a present time of suffering, and a coming time of divine presence, fullness, and freedom from suffering. The idea of an inaugurated kingdom here and now, present partially but not fully, appears in some sense through Moltmann's stress on the "process of resurrection." Yet the overall historical template that Moltmann employs is kabbalistic, and this may help to explain the stress on "the coming of God" rather than "the coming of Christ."

Bauckham offers some penetrating reflections on the role of *transience* in Moltmann's account of the God-world relationship. God in his faithfulness, argues Moltmann, could not and would not allow anything once created to vanish. He asserts in *The Coming of God* that if God redeemed only some parts of creation, while leaving others to perish, God would no longer be God.[321] Thus *everything* in the universe—perhaps even uninhabited planets, stars, and galaxies, underwater mountains, and so on—must be preserved forever. Moltmann writes that "resurrection has become the universal 'law' of creation, not merely for human beings, but for animals, plants, stones and all cosmic life systems as well."[322] Moltmann does not so much *argue* this point as *presuppose* it, as Bauckham explains: "If eschatological hope rests on God's faithfulness and grace to his creation, then the eschatological act of new creation in which God completes and redeems his creation, giving it eternal life, must be as comprehensive as the creative act which gives creation its present, transient existence." Moltmann's assumption is that "transience" is "per se an imperfection which can be a characteristic of God's good creation only if God redeems all transient creatures from their transience." Yet Bauckham asks whether "transience cannot be evaluated in a more discriminating way."[323] Is God truly obligated through creation to preserve every single entity that was part of the original creation? If so, then it would seem that God lacks freedom vis-à-vis the created world. While God can shuffle the deck of cards, so to speak, God cannot discard any cards.

Nik Ansell's favorable approach to Moltmann's eschatology in *The Annihilation of Hell* (2013) is also sharply critical at points. Ansell writes that Moltmann reasons from the standpoint of an "eschatological monism" that "makes universalism look like a foregone conclusion," and this applies especially with respect to "his handling of Scripture." This means that Moltmann is "vulnerable to the charge that he has simply imposed the 'template' . . . of his own theology upon the biblical writings," thus "subordinating apocalyptic material (which would in his framework, refer to an ending in the penultimate, historical direction of

321. Moltmann, *Coming of God*, 269–70.
322. Moltmann, *Way of Jesus Christ*, 258.
323. Bauckham, "Eschatology in *The Coming of God*," 12.

time) to more universal-redemptive historical voices (which reveal the ultimate eschatological direction of time, in his view)." In the process, "the pronouncements on 'Hell' attributed to Jesus in the gospels are more or less brushed aside."[324] Ansell faults Moltmann for ignoring the biblical motif of repentance, which may be essential in any theology that wishes to assert universal salvation.[325] He also shows little attention to the question about motives for living a righteous life.[326] Moreover, Ansell has "serious problems with the eschatological eclipse of the gift of creation that characterizes Moltmann's theology."[327]

We may now respond specifically to the three strands of Moltmann's universalist reasoning mentioned above (*DR* 9.10). With respect to the *Christocentric-crucicentric strand*, Moltmann asserts that all divine judgment and hell itself ended at Jesus's cross. The most obvious problem with this claim is that it goes against Scripture and Christian tradition. Woven throughout the New Testament Gospels and Epistles and the book of Revelation is a many-sided picture of a last judgment by God that is always portrayed as future from the standpoint of present-day human life. Only if Moltmann could make a case to reject this biblical language and imagery—and the corresponding church tradition—would his case begin to be plausible. The sequence of the Apostles' Creed—"from thence he shall come to judge the living and the dead"—situates the judgment that Christ performs after Christ's earthly life and ascension into heaven. Nothing in the New Testament or early Christian tradition suggests that Christ's death on the cross somehow abolished all expectation of a future judgment or reckoning before God. In support of his view that all judgment ended at Jesus's cross, Moltmann quotes and yet misinterprets Luther, and neglects the fact that Luther himself believed that all human beings would individually pass through a last judgment before Christ.[328] Moreover, Moltmann's own theology of the cross

324. Ansell, *Annihilation of Hell*, 361. The idea of a multistage sequence of ages or epochs, leading to the final salvation of all, was characteristic of German Philadelphian universalism (*DR* 5.8) as well as hyper-dispensational universalism (*DR* appendix I). Here Moltmann followed earlier precedents.

325. Ansell, *Annihilation of Hell*, 361–62. On Moltmann's interpretation of Scripture, Richard Bauckham cuttingly comments that "what little exegesis he [i.e., Moltmann] offers tends to be remarkably ignorant and incompetent" ("Time and Eternity," 179).

326. Ansell, *Annihilation of Hell*, 364.

327. Ibid., 378.

328. In "The Logic of Hell," Moltmann quotes Luther's "Sermon on Preparing for Death" (1519) and claims that "for Luther, hell is not a place in the next world, the underworld: it is an experience of God" (46). He quotes Luther's words: "Thou must look upon hell and the eternity of torments, not in themselves, not in those who are damned. . . . Look upon the heavenly picture of Christ who for thy sake descended into hell and was forsaken by God as one eternally damned. . . . See in that picture thy hell is conquered and thy uncertain election made sure" (ibid.). Luther speaks here in the context of faith in Christ ("Look upon . . . Christ"), and there is nothing to indicate that Luther denied that "hell is . . . a place in the next world." On Luther's idea of "the Last Day" as a future event, see Althaus, *Theology of Martin Luther*, 226, 417–25.

does not adequately account for the salvation of Satan and the demons. While he explicitly attributes salvation to evil spirits, as Bauckham comments, "the extension . . . to include the devil and the fallen angels . . . is something of a non sequitur, since Moltmann has not suggested (and seems never to suggest) that Christ suffered and died in solidarity with (fallen) heavenly beings as well as with earthly beings."[329] What Moltmann asserts as the basis for universal *human* salvation—namely, the solidarity of Christ as man with all humanity—would not imply *demonic* salvation as well.

One of the curious things about Moltmann's theology of the cross is that he seems not to associate Jesus's cross with sin or with salvation—in the traditional sense—but simply with suffering. What Moltmann sees on the cross is God's suffering in solidarity with suffering humanity, but not any sort of atonement in the classical sense. In *The Crucified God*, Moltmann uses the ambiguous expression "the godless and the godforsaken" to gloss over the distinction between those who willfully turn from God and those who find themselves the innocent victims of the world's cruelty.[330] The two groups are not distinguished in Moltmann's writing. While he rightly considers the problem of the *innocent sufferer*, his silence regarding the *guilty sufferer* is telling. Or are there no guilty sufferers? What about sin? Guilt? Forgiveness? Grace? Faith? Justification? Atonement? The substantial absence from Moltmann's writings of such crucial soteriological themes raises the question of whether we really have Christian theology in Moltmann's writings or else a philosophy of hope or secularized eschatology (along the lines of Bloch), reconstrued and rephrased with reference to biblical terminology and motifs. Karl Barth wrote to Moltmann in 1964 asking whether *Theology of Hope* was simply a "baptized" Ernst Bloch.[331] One might ask whether Moltmann has a doctrine of grace or whether some kind of naturalistic process has displaced and replaced the idea of grace.

The *kabbalistic-cosmological strand* in Moltmann involves a number of serious difficulties, particularly with respect to the competitive relationship

329. Bauckham, "Eschatology in *The Coming of God*," 13n9. Moltmann asserts the salvation of demons in *The Coming of God* (254–55) and *God in Creation* (169). The notion that Christ suffered for the demons—or will be crucified for the demons—was one of the rejected views held by certain early followers of Origen. See the eighth point in the synodical letter of Theophilus (400 CE) and anathema 7 in the Fifteeen Anathemas of 543 CE (see *DR* appendix C).

330. Bauckham, *Theology of Jürgen Moltmann*, 11. See Moltmann, *Crucified God*, 192, 242–44, 276. "He humbles himself and takes upon himself the eternal death of the godless and the godforsaken, so that all the godless and the godforsaken can experience communion with him" (276).

331. Barth asked, "Ist Ihre 'Theologie der Hoffnung' etwas Anderes als das getaufte 'Prinzip' Hoffnung des Herrn Bloch?" (quoted in Müller-Fahrenholz, *Phantasie für das Reich Gottes*, 33, with reference to E. Bloch, *Das Prinzip Hoffnung* [1959]). An even more serious charge against Moltmann comes from R. E. Otto in the claim that "Moltmann's God is the idea of human community" (*God of Hope*, 11, cited in Bauckham, *Theology of Jürgen Moltmann*, 24n6).

that it establishes between God's presence and activity and creaturely presence and activity. According to the problematic theory of *tsimtsum*, God *must* withdraw before the creature can either come to exist or act on its own. It is like pouring water into a glass. When I fill the glass with water, I displace the air that used to be there. When I empty the water from the glass, the air rushes in to fill the space. The same space cannot simultaneously hold both air and water. Yet if this is how it is with the God-creation relation, then a question arises regarding the supposed final expansion of the previously contracting God: Would not the expansion of God *annihilate* all creatures? If not, then what was the point of God's withdrawal in the first place, which was supposed to be necessary for creation to occur? To be sure, Moltmann denies explicitly that God's presence ever could or would annihilate creatures.[332] Yet Catherine Keller judges that Moltmann's eschatology is ultimately destructive because he advocates the final end not only of evil and injustice but also "of finitude itself."[333]

The basic problem is that Moltmann's idea of creation and his idea of creation's fulfillment are at odds with one another. In creating the world God had to restrict his presence, because the creation could not otherwise endure it.[334] In the eschaton, however, God will interpenetrate all things in a "perichoresis which does not destroy created beings but fulfills them."[335] Then "we shall be able to look upon his face without perishing."[336] But why should this be? Why is God's presence a *threat* to creatures at the moment of creation, and seemingly during the present time, but *not a threat* in the eschaton? Perhaps an even deeper problem with the kabbalistic-cosmological strand in Moltmann's argument lies in the implication that the world takes its origin in a "God-forsaken space" that Moltmann in some passages associates with hell. Despite Moltmann's insistence on the importance of ecology and the value of materiality in *God in Creation*, his reliance on the theologically suspect idea of *tsimtsum* pushes his cosmology dangerously near to an essentially gnostic idea of a creation inherently alienated from God.

In his *trinitarian-processive strand* of reasoning, Moltmann teaches that "God acquires through history his eternal kingdom," but this does not mean that

332. Moltmann writes, "Even the end of the world cannot be total annihilation and new creation. It can only be a transformation out of transience into eternity" (*Coming of God*, 271). This issue of infinite Spirit (*Geist*) perhaps engulfing or annihilating finite reality appears as a problem in Hegel too (*DR* 7.5–7.6). The reappearance of the same problem in Moltmann's eschatology might be a sign of his affinity with Hegel.

333. C. Keller, *Apocalypse Now and Then*, 18.

334. Moltmann, *Coming of God*, 306.

335. Ibid., 318.

336. Ibid., 317; cf. 295.

Christ's kingdom is eternal or lasts forever.[337] Following 1 Corinthians 15:22–28 rather literalistically, Moltmann teaches that Christ rules until he has subjected all things to himself, and then he transfers his kingly rule to the Father.[338] In *The Trinity and the Kingdom*, Moltmann explains that the rule of Christ is in two phases: the present messianic rule and the millennial rule.[339] The millennial reign is "a transitional kingdom leading from this transitory world-time to the new world that is God's." The millennial reign is not yet the kingdom of glory, which only comes about when Christ hands back the kingdom to the Father.[340] Moltmann is explicit in stating that Christ's reign comes to an end: "With this transfer [to the Father] the lordship of the Son ends. . . . All Jesus' titles of sovereignty—Christ, kyrios, prophet . . . are *provisional* titles, which express Jesus' significance for salvation in time. But the name of Son remains to all eternity."[341] The teaching that Christ's kingdom will be transient was proposed by Marcellus of Ancyra in the fourth century, but majority opinion in the early church stood against this opinion.[342] The eternal honor and dignity of Christ—as well as various biblical statements—seemingly make it impossible to think that Christ's reign will ever end, whatever interpretation one might attach to the puzzling statement in Scripture that Christ will "deliver up" the kingdom to the Father (1 Cor. 15:24). Moltmann's reading of 1 Corinthians 15:22–28, while literalistic in some ways, is inattentive to the text in other respects. This passage centers on the theme of God's dominion over creation. It speaks of the subjugation of God's enemies, who are then made "a footstool" for God's "feet." Yet Moltmann leaves no place in his theology for God's dominion as such or for the subjugation of God's enemies.

Having evaluated three distinct strands in Moltmann's universalist theology—*Christocentric-crucicentric, kabbalistic-cosmological*, and *trinitarian-processive*—we

337. Ibid., 225.

338. Bauckham, "Eschatology in *The Coming of God*," 21–22.

339. Moltmann, *Trinity and the Kingdom*, 235n41.

340. Moltmann, *Coming of God*, 195. On the millennial rule generally, see Moltmann, *Coming of God*, 195–99; Moltmann, *History and the Triune God*, 96.

341. Moltmann, *Trinity and the Kingdom*, 92. "The kingdom of God is therefore transferred from one divine subject to the other" (93). Problematic here is not only the ending of the Son's lordship but also the idea that the three persons are three separate subjects—a viewpoint that seems tantamount to tritheism. Again in *The Trinity and the Kingdom*, we read, "The Son is not identical with God's self. He is a subject of his own" (86–87). The divine persons "have the divine nature in common; but their particular individual nature is determined in their relationship to one another" (172). On Moltmann's apparent tritheism, see Hunsinger, review of *The Trinity and the Kingdom*.

342. Marcellus of Ancyra maintained that the kingdom of Christ would eventually come to an end, and the phrase "whose kingdom [i.e., Christ's] will have no end" in the Niceno-Constantinopolitan Creed was formulated in response to Marcellus's view. See Lyman, "Marcellus of Ancyra."

may now consider the question of Ernst Bloch's influence and then return to the question of Moltmann and Kabbalah.

The "esoteric Marxism" of Ernst Bloch, especially that contained in his major work, *Das Prinzip Hoffnung* (1959), had a seminal influence on Moltmann. The result of reading Bloch, said Moltmann in 1970, was that "all at once the loose threads of a biblical theology, of the theology of the apostolate and of the kingdom of God, and of philosophy, merged into the pattern for a tapestry in which everything matched." Moltmann stated that Bloch's "principle of hope" is more appropriate than any other philosophy for conceptualizing the Christian doctrine of hope and for giving it a plan and a mode of action.[343] Moltmann's theology not only builds on Bloch but also replicates some of Bloch's weaknesses. Leszak Kolakowski, the eminent historian of Marxism, comments on Bloch's futuristic "daydreams" and adds that "throughout his life . . . [he] remained a literary man deeply versed in books, dreaming of a perfect world yet unable to explain how it was to be created, or even what form its perfection was to take."[344] According to Bloch, human beings are "essentially Utopia-minded, believing in a perfect world and anticipating the future with undying hope." All aspects of culture are pervaded with "irresistible utopian energy." Moreover, Bloch rejects the need to establish a factual basis for his project of hope, dismissing what he calls the "fetishism of facts" as well as "shallow empiricism." What Marxism offers to humanity, says Bloch, is a "concrete Utopia" rather than an abstract one—a dream rooted in the historical process itself. As an atheist, Bloch denied that God exists, but he held that God might come to exist in the future—with "God" here understood as the *Ens perfectissimum* (most perfect being) emerging from the evolution of Communist society. Bloch thus provides a theogony or account of the birth of God, a fantastic projection of the God-who-is-yet-to-be, commenting that "the true Genesis is not in the beginning but at the end."[345]

Bloch views matter itself as the *Urgrund* (primal source or foundation), an indeterminate realm from which anything might conceivably take shape. In this way Bloch's writings contain "echoes of Giordano Bruno . . . Böhme and Paracelsus." By way of summary, Kolakowski writes: "What disqualifies Bloch's philosophy is not that it is wrong but that it lacks content. There is certainly no harm in fantasies about a better future or dreams of invincible technology used to promote human happiness. The trouble with his fantastic projections is not that we cannot tell how to bring them about, but that we are not told in what they consist." Using the example of the flying machine,

---

343. Meeks, *Origins of the Theology of Hope*, 16, citing Moltmann, "Politics and the Practice of Hope," 289; Moltmann, *Perspektiven der Theologie*, 174.

344. Kolakowski, "Ernst Bloch," 428, 426.

345. Ibid., 429–30, 432, 438–39, citing E. Bloch, *Das Prinzip Hoffnung*, 1628.

Kolakowski notes that this was dreamed of and imagined long before there was any technology to make it possible. In this sense, utopian dreams play a constructive role. We dream before we construct. Yet Bloch's utopia is quite different, since it is a perfect world whose perfection remains unexplained. Bloch emphasizes Marx's "soteriological strain" and so mediates "the neo-Platonic gnostic tradition that found its way into Marxism through Hegel."[346] When one juxtaposes Bloch with Moltmann's little book on eschatology, *Sun of Righteousness, Arise!* (2010), one gets the nagging feeling that Bloch's Marxist dream has become Moltmann's theological hallucination. As Douglas Farrow comments, this seems to be an eschatology in which Jesus does not truly come again. What is more, Moltmann's desire for a final state that is strictly communitarian and nonhierarchical seems to have obliterated any consideration of the pervasive evil in the world and how it might be overcome.

When one turns from the Hegel-influenced argument of *The Crucified God* to the Kabbalah-driven argument of *God in Creation*—published some twenty years later—one finds that Moltmann emphasized even more emphatically than previously the connection and continuity of God and the world. John Cooper calls Moltmann's thought "the most extensive explicitly panentheistic Christian theology of the late twentieth century."[347] This continuity of God with the world might be seen—in kabbalistic terms—as a continuity of suffering between creatures and Creator. The creatures' suffering is the Creator's suffering. Paul Fiddes points out that the issue in speaking of divine suffering is to talk coherently about "a God who suffers universally and yet is still present uniquely and decisively in the sufferings of Christ." In Fiddes's view, Moltmann does not successfully navigate this issue, and so there is a danger that Christ's suffering is not unique in any way but becomes simply an outward symbol of God's eternal suffering.[348] As Moltmann says, "The pain of the cross determines the inner life of the triune God from eternity to eternity," and "the history of the world is the history of God's suffering."[349] Many texts—and an increasing number in the later publications—show that Moltmann did not confine God's suffering to the event of Jesus's death on the cross. So it remains unclear how Moltmann can meaningfully connect God's suffering in creation

---

346. Kolakowski, "Ernst Bloch," 440, 447–48.

347. J. W. Cooper, *Panentheism*, 237. Paul Molnar is blunt: "Moltmann literally cannot distinguish creatures from the creator in any recognizable way. Thus, he argues that, although creation *ex nihilo* means God is *free*, still God makes room within himself by fashioning the nothingness from which he then creates the world. . . . A God who makes nothingness in order to create and then makes this part of his being is not the Christian God" (*Divine Freedom*, 200).

348. Fiddes, *Creative Suffering of God*, 3. See also 4–12.

349. Moltmann, *Trinity and the Kingdom*, 161, 4.

and for creation to the suffering that occurred historically in the particular event of Jesus's death.[350]

If one views Moltmann through the lens of the kabbalistic tradition, then his arguments make sense. It is not just that human beings in this world and in their suffering exist in a state of exile. More than this, God himself goes into exile, according to the kabbalistic teaching on the *Shekhinah*. The first origin of the universe came about not only through *tsimtsum* or a divine withdrawal—as Moltmann asserts, in agreement with Kabbalah—but also through a "breaking of the vessels," which is a change affecting the very nature of God. It is not just that God withdraws but that a change takes place within God that must later be resolved. This is at the heart of kabbalistic teaching on God and the world.

While one aspect of kabbalistic teaching affirms God's continuity with the world, another side stresses the internal tension, conflict, and suffering within God. This element is conspicuous in Moltmann's theology. Ansell's interpretation of Moltmann accentuates this theme of intra-divine conflict or division—"the fundamental *tension* that evil creates within the divine life, a tension that necessitates (in his [i.e., Moltmann's] striking phrase) the 'overcoming of God by God.'"[351] The origination of evil *within God* was a key idea in Jewish Kabbalah (*DR* 2.5), and Ansell is identifying kabbalistic themes that Moltmann assimilated into his own theology. Moltmann says that God himself is in need of redemption. He writes, "God has to give himself. . . . It is only in this way that he is God. He has to go through time; and it is only in this way that he is eternal. . . . It was necessary for God to be Man, for only so could He be truly God."[352] In another passage we read: "God himself becomes free in the process [of redemption]. . . . Even God himself will only be free when our souls are free."[353] God stands in need of redemption, and conversely, human suffering is God's suffering—and not merely in the sense of empathy or compassion. Paul Molnar raises the crucial objection that Moltmann's "God cannot overcome

---

350. See the discussion in Bauckham, *Theology of Jürgen Moltmann*, 56–57, with n. 11. God's suffering is generalized beyond the cross in Moltmann, *Church and the Power of the Spirit*, 62–64; Moltmann, *Trinity and the Kingdom*, 118; Moltmann, *God in Creation*, 15–16, 69, 210–11. Even in Moltmann's earlier work, *The Crucified God* (270–74), there is a discussion of the Jewish thinker Abraham Heschel (1907–72) and his notion of divine pathos in the Old Testament prophetic literature, along with the rabbinic understanding of the *Shekhinah* in relation to the sufferings of Israel. For the view that God suffers in and through all creaturely suffering, see Rashdall, *Idea of the Atonement*, 450–54; F. Young, "A Cloud of Witnesses," in Hick, *Myth of God Incarnate*, 36–37. On this theme, see also Fretheim, *Suffering of God*; Merkle, "Heschel's Theology of Divine Pathos"; Weinandy, *Does God Suffer?*

351. Ansell, *Annihilation of Hell*, 365.

352. Moltmann, *Trinity and the Kingdom*, 32–33.

353. Ibid., 39.

suffering since suffering itself is the principle that encompasses his very being and love."[354] Since Moltmann's God forever continues to love, God must forever continue to suffer, inasmuch as these two things are inseparable. As Moltmann writes, "A God who cannot suffer cannot love either. . . . Only that which suffers is divine."[355]

9.12. The Rise of Kenotic-Relational Theologies since the 1990s

Since the 1990s, a growing number of Christian thinkers have constructed a conception of God centered on such notions as kenosis, relationality, and perichoresis. While some refer to the newer understandings of God as panentheistic, this term does not have a single, unambiguous definition.[356] Moreover, the term does not capture the multiple ways of speaking of God among recent thinkers. It may thus be more fitting to refer, as does Kevin Vanhoozer, to a "kenotic, relational, perichoretic ontotheology."[357] It should be obvious that this combination of terms represents an umbrella designation, so that there are many individual variations among those who might be categorized in this way. At the same time, a broad pattern is apparent, as David Cunningham comments:

> Most recent writers seem convinced that the language of relationality has something important to contribute to Trinitarian doctrine. This term is central for a number of authors, including Leonardo Boff, Colin Gunton, Robert Jenson, Elizabeth Johnson, Walter Kasper, Catherine Mowry LaCugna, Jürgen Moltmann, and Alan Torrance. While these writers are not unified in their understanding and their assessment of relationality, they all endorse its importance in the construction of Trinitarian theology.[358]

354. Molnar, *Divine Freedom*, 203.
355. Moltmann, *Trinity and the Kingdom*, 38.
356. The term "panentheism" was first used by Karl Krause (1781–1832) in the early nineteenth century. John Culp explains the word this way:
  "Panentheism" is a constructed word composed of the English equivalents of the Greek terms "pan," meaning all, "en," meaning in, and "theism," meaning God. Panentheism considers God and the world to be inter-related with the world being in God and God being in the world. It offers an increasingly popular alternative to both traditional theism and pantheism. Panentheism seeks to avoid either isolating God from the world as traditional theism often does or identifying God with the world as pantheism does. Traditional theistic systems emphasize the difference between God and the world while panentheism stresses God's active presence in the world. Pantheism emphasizes God's presence in the world but panentheism maintains the identity and significance of the non-divine. (Culp, "Panentheism")
See also Hartshorne and Reese, *Philosophers Speak of God*; J. W. Cooper, *Panentheism*.
357. Vanhoozer, *Remythologizing Theology*, esp. 81–178.
358. David Cunningham, "Participation as a Trinitarian Virtue," citing the article abstract.

"Kenotic panentheism," as Vanhoozer explains, is a form of "voluntary meta-physical relationality," according to which God chose to create the world, and to make it in a particular way, in which God's own existence would be affected and conditioned by the existence of the world and the individual creatures in it.[359] Moltmann set a precedent for many other contemporary thinkers in conceiving of a kenosis that was essential to God's self-communication of love and that began with creation itself. In *The Trinity and the Kingdom* (1980 [in German]), Moltmann wrote, "The divine kenosis which begins with the creation of the world reaches its perfected and completed form in the incarnation of the Son. . . . The outward incarnation presupposes inward self-humiliation."[360] The idea of creation-as-kenosis has wide-ranging implications, as Ted Peters explains: "The relationality God experiences through Christ's saving relationship to the world is constitutive of Trinitarian relations proper. God's relations *ad extra* become God's relations *ad intra*."[361]

Vanhoozer expounds the basic assumptions of the kenotic-relational view as follows:

> Kenotic panentheists conceive God both as the Ground or principle of creativity of the universe, and as one who responds to entities and events as he experiences them in world history. While God could exist without the cosmos, however, there is nevertheless a certain consequent necessity to God's dependence on the world that follows from his decision to create. Why should this be so? Because, says the panentheist, love demands it. For love, if it is to be genuine and interpersonal, must be mutual, reciprocal, and non-coercive. Love that forces is not love. On the contrary, love hurts, and never more than when it is unrequited. But this is precisely the possibility that kenotic panentheism opens up: that God, in creating a world with free creatures, graciously gives the world the power to codetermine at least some aspects of the divine experience, perchance to frustrate God's loving purpose. Panentheists see God's love generally in God's self-limitation vis-à-vis the cosmos and more particularly in the self-limitation of the incarnate Christ. With regard to the cosmos, God limits his power and knowledge so that the diverse systems of the natural world can develop with a degree of autonomy.[362]

According to the panentheistic conception, God's being is thought in some way to include everything else, and so there is a tendency to gloss over the metaphysical disruptions between God and creation caused by sin and evil. Vanhoozer writes that "the new orthodoxy [of the kenotic-relational God] causes

---

359. Vanhoozer, *Remythologizing Theology*, 130.
360. Moltmann, *Trinity and the Kingdom*, 118–19.
361. T. Peters, *God as Trinity*, 96, cited in Vanhoozer, *Remythologizing Theology*, 71.
362. Vanhoozer, *Remythologizing Theology*, 133.

other doctrinal dominoes to fall as well," and this includes the traditional doctrine of hell, for "hell is actually a place or possibility that God opens up inside
himself." Vanhoozer explains:

> The type of relation that ultimately matters . . . is *ontological*. . . . There seems to
> be no room for properly covenantal relations, however, in kenotic-perichoretic rela-
> tional ontotheology, no room for Jesus the Messiah in the panentheistic "in." That
> human beings have become alienated from the God in whom they live and move
> and have their being—that sin can remove us from God's presence—is difficult,
> if not impossible, to articulate within a panentheistic participatory framework.

In presenting his own version of Christian panentheism, Philip Clayton comments: "I find no place within emergent theology for substitutionary atonement,
ransom metaphors, or the focus on the need for a sacrifice to propitiate the
wrath of an angry God."[363]

The theological idea of kenosis originated in the sphere of Christology, and
in relation to a particular New Testament passage, where in Paul's account of
God's eternal Son we read that "he emptied [*ekenōsen*] himself" (Phil. 2:7).[364]
Yet contemporary theological accounts of kenosis have applied the term and
concept beyond its original sphere of reference. For example, the biologist-cum-
theologian Arthur Peacocke proposed a connection between creation-as-kenosis
and the pain of childbirth: "The processes of creation are immensely costly to
God in a way dimly shadowed by the ordinary human experience of the costli-
ness of creativity in multiple aspects of human existence."[365] Nothing along
these lines appears in Philippians 2, since the text does not discuss creation
as such. In Romans 8:22 one finds reference to creation's "groaning together"
and "travailing together" (Greek *systenazei, synōdinei*), though in this case it is
not a *primal* but an *eschatological* "groaning and travailing," a forward-oriented
impetus toward final fulfillment. Contemporary kenotic thinkers use biblical
terms and imagery in creative ways. Moltmann himself tied his theory of world
origin to gender concepts by suggesting that creation from nothing—which he
rejects—is analogous to the male procreative act, while creation as a kenotic act
in God "must rather be called a feminine concept, a bringing forth."[366]

Because of God's self-emptying in creating the world, God is said to experience the evil and suffering of the world *from the inside*. The panentheistic

363. Ibid., 154–55, citing Clayton, *Adventures in the Spirit*, 113.
364. Kenosis as a modern philosophical and theological motif seems to have originated not
with Gottfried Thomasius but in the writings of Friedrich Schelling, and specifically Schelling's
exegesis of Phil. 2. See *DR* 7, n. 148.
365. Peacocke, "Cost of New Life," 37, cited in Vanhoozer, *Remythologizing Theology*, 132–33n245.
366. Moltmann, *Trinity and the Kingdom*, 109.

view of the God-world relationship displays some analogies to the ancient pre-Christian notion of God as the World Soul. In this conceptuality there is a question of whether the world becomes necessary to God. Kenotic-relationalists will generally answer this question in the negative and so seek to differentiate their views from those of process theologians. Yet much depends on how one defines such terms as "necessity" and "freedom." If divine "freedom" means simply that God consistently acts in accordance with God's own character, then for kenotic-relationalists it is possible to say that there "must" be a world and yet that the world is made "freely" by God.[367]

Another characteristic of kenotic-relational theologies lies in an extended application of the doctrine of *perichoresis*. In traditional trinitarian doctrine, "perichoresis" refers to the co-inherence of the Father, Son, and Spirit in one another, and not to a general metaphysical principle applying to God and the world alike. Philip Clayton writes, "Panentheist trinitarians support a participation of the created order in God in a manner that is at least analogous to the co-participation of Father, Son, and Spirit in the one Godhead."[368] In this line of thinking, as in others, Moltmann was a forerunner. In *The Trinity and the Kingdom*, he sharply distinguished Father, Son, and Spirit, in a way that some critics thought tended toward tritheism, but then reconnected the three persons of the Trinity through appeal to the doctrine of perichoresis.[369] In *God in Creation*, Moltmann applied the doctrine of perichoresis more directly to the mutual relation of God and creation. Along similar lines, Denis Edwards writes that "all creatures participate in the life of trinitarian communion."[370]

---

367. Brandon Gallaher offers an intricate and wide-ranging analysis of this issue in *Freedom and Necessity in Modern Trinitarian Theology*, with specific applications to Bulgakov, Barth, and Balthasar. For Gallaher, "God's eternal free perichoretic life of love" as Father, Son, and Spirit implies that the persons of the Godhead are "freely *dependent*" on one another (20). This construal of the immanent Trinity shapes Gallaher's account of the economy of salvation. While he acknowledges notions of unfettered divine freedom vis-à-vis creation (which he calls "F1"), his emphasis is on the way that God freely acts in accord with his own fixed moral charater ("F2"); God freely enters into dependence on and action on behalf of some other ("F3"; 12–41). Gallaher states, "We shall contend that God, insofar as He has freely bound himself to the world in Christ and has made its joy and sufferings to be His very own, is in need and cannot do otherwise than He has in fact chosen to be: God for us in Christ. . . . He lays upon himself an external necessity of the world in His love for it in Christ" (37). Gallaher's general perspective matches that of most contemporary kenotic-relational theologians, though he has elaborated his arguments on freedom and necessity in much greater detail. Gallaher stands closest to Bulgakov (*DR* 8.6) and other Russian thinkers when he adopts the "antinomic" position that God's actions "*could have been otherwise*" and also yet "*could not have been otherwise*" (41; emphasis original).

368. Clayton, "Panentheist Internalism."

369. See Hunsinger, review of *The Trinity and the Kingdom*.

370. Denis Edwards, "Relational and Evolving Universe," 204, cited in Vanhoozer, *Remythologizing Theology*, 152.

Cosmic perichoresis appears as a theme in some contemporary Orthodox authors as well—for example, Alexei Nesteruk, who insists that the world is "in" God because the entire universe subsists in the person of the Logos and thus exists in God through perichoretic participation.[371] This use of the doctrine of perichoresis reconstrues the God-world relationship in the direction of divine immanence rather than divine transcendence.

Vanhoozer refers to a "doctrinal migration" that has affected the doctrines of perichoresis and kenosis: "As relational theists have lifted the concept of perichoresis out of its original Trinitarian context and made it a general principle, so panentheists have lifted kenosis out of its proper christological context, exalting it into a broader metaphysical principle." By an "illegitimate Trinitarian transfer," these thinkers are "applying categories that properly pertain to christology and the doctrine of the Trinity respectively to the God-world relation per se."[372] Vanhoozer sees a danger here—attributing to creation the necessity that strictly applies only to the intra-trinitarian relations: "To take perichoresis as the root metaphor for the God-world relationship is to conceive creation no longer in terms of the triune economy (i.e., a contingent relation) but rather of the triune essence (i.e., a necessary relation). To affirm a perichoretic relation between God and the world is to claim that God would not be who he is apart from this relation."[373] Just as it would be a mistake to assert that God the Father "begat" the world as he "begat" God the Son, so it would seem equally misguided to say that God is "perichoretic" with the world as God is with himself as Father, Son, and Spirit. Miroslav Volf raises another sort of objection, noting the mistaken way in which mutual indwelling or perichoresis is affirmed among creatures: "Another human self cannot be internal to my own self as a subject of action. Human persons are always external to one another as subjects."[374]

Kenotic-relational theologians generally interpret Jesus's cross not as a redeeming or atoning event but as a revelation of God's self-chosen weakness. Moltmann comments that "if Christ is weak and humble on earth, then God is weak and humble in heaven."[375] Moreover, Jesus's cross expressed not only weakness but also a devastating crisis in which "God abandoned God."[376] The

371. Nesteruk, "Universe as Hypostatic Inherence."
372. Vanhoozer, *Remythologizing Theology*, 131, 150. The first quotation is partially italicized in the original.
373. Ibid., 149–50.
374. Volf, *After Our Likeness*, 210–11, cited in Vanhoozer, *Remythologizing Theology*, 153. Cf. Otto, "Use and Abuse of Perichoresis."
375. Moltmann, *Trinity and the Kingdom*, 31.
376. Moltmann, *Crucified God*, 244: "What happened on the cross was an event between God and God. It was a deep division in God himself, insofar as God abandoned God and contradicted himself, and at the same time a unity in God."

cross for Moltmann is an "event" in the divine history, so that "the pain of the cross determines the inner life of the triune God from eternity to eternity."[377] This means that suffering is inherent and eternal in God. In *The Trinity and the Kingdom*, Moltmann goes so far as to speak of "the tragedy in God," an idea that he seems to have taken over from Nicolas Berdyaev (*DR* 8.5).[378] Along with the co-suffering of the Father with the Son, there is also "the suffering of God's Spirit in the birth-pangs of the new creation."[379] Following Moltmann, Paul Fiddes interprets the expression "God died" in terms of *relationlessness*, of "separation entering into the heart of God's relationships with himself."[380]

While Moltmann's view of the cross of Christ has evoked criticisms, certain kenotic-relational authors stress more than Moltmann did the world's essentially tragic character. Edward Farley writes that "in a very real sense God Godself is implicated in the tragic character of world process."[381] On this basis Farley elevates empathy as a root metaphor for understanding God's activity in the world—though this divine empathy occurs without evoking joy or expectation of a better world to come. Wendy Farley offers a "tragic vision" centering on a world mired in suffering. Divine compassion is "a mode of relationship and a power that is wounded by the suffering of others." Yet sympathetic suffering brings comfort: "This communion with the sufferer in her pain . . . mediates consolation and respect that can empower the sufferer to bear the pain." Her theodicy focuses on suffering rather than sin. She assumes that suffering cannot be eradicated and so is a tragic, unavoidable by-product of finitude and freedom. For Farley, "love is a *kenosis* of the plenitude of power." She goes so far as to say that the "savagery of history is testimony to this long defeat of God by humanity." The only alternative to this sort of empowering power is some notion of dominating power, which she does not accept: "Any power that is causally absolute, even if motivated by a good will, necessarily deprives other creatures of any real activity, participation, or uniqueness."[382] For Wendy Farley, God is not a Mighty Savior but a Cosmic Anodyne. God never overcomes suffering or evil but simply helps humanity to endure or to cope with it.

In contrast to classical theistic accounts of God, kenotic-relational theologies depotentiate God or diminish divine power. From the moment that God creates the world—or, at least, a world that includes intelligent, volitional

377. Moltmann, *Trinity and the Kingdom*, 161.

378. Ibid., 42.

379. Moltmann, *Way of Jesus Christ*, 179.

380. Fiddes, *Creative Suffering of God*, 201.

381. E. Farley, *Divine Empathy*, 311, cited in Vanhoozer, *Remythologizing Theology*, 438.

382. W. Farley, *Tragic Vision and Divine Compassion*, 69, 81, 98, 110, 93, cited in Vanhoozer, *Remythologizing Theology*, 438–39.

creatures—God is necessarily self-limited so as to make "space" for creatures
such as ourselves to choose and to act. If relational metaphysics is the starting
point, and if one's metaphysical categories must apply to all of reality, then it
follows that the only sort of God that can exist at all is a relational God.[383] God
cannot be providential or omnicausal, as this is traditionally understood. In
creating the world, God must "back off" so that human beings "have space."
The question here is whether the kenotic-relational view has finitized God by
drawing God down to the level of creatures, so that God competes with them
for space and vies with them for mastery, and either God is in control or else
creatures are in control.[384] Another question is whether kenotic-relational theologies, in a hidden fashion, serve an Enlightenment agenda of upholding human
autonomy. The concern that human beings occupy a "space" where God does
not or cannot intrude and interfere makes it seem that creaturely autonomy is
the implicit goal in view.

Vanhoozer asks where the good news is in this account of God: "What is the
gospel according to panentheism? Perhaps that God 'makes room' for us?"[385]
If one begins from Enlightenment assumptions of human autonomy and the
presumed efficacy and goodness of human agency, then a God who "makes
room" and gets out of the way is just what one might desire. This was the
general attitude that gave birth to deism—a kind of compromise position, in
which Western intellectuals professed a willingness to believe in God but only
so long as God did not interfere in their lives.[386] Despite all the emphasis on
relationality, the current kenotic-panentheistic view has something in common
with the God of the deists, inasmuch as their God is strictly *a noninterfering
deity*.[387] There is an irony here, because the remoteness of the deistic God seems
to be poles apart from the closeness of the panentheistic God. Yet the nearness

383. Molnar expresses this point by way of critique, saying with reference to Moltmann that
"relationality is the subject and God is the predicate instead of the other way around" (*Divine
Freedom*, 227).

384. John W. Cooper contrasts the kenotic-relational notion of God as "a large disembodied
human person relating to much smaller beings," with the more traditional, "infinite Other who
has graciously made us finite analogies to himself" (*Panentheism*, 344).

385. Vanhoozer, *Remythologizing Theology*, 134n256.

386. Blaise Pascal saw this grudging attitude toward God in the philosophy of René Descartes:
"I cannot forgive Descartes. He would willingly in all his philosophy have done without God, if he
could; but he could not get on without letting him give the world a fillip to set it agoing: after that,
he has nothing more to do with God" (cited in Tulloch, *Pascal*, 177).

387. Vanhoozer explains why some affirm the world is a "closed" system: "Panentheists consider
the classical theist response—that God intervenes in the world as a substance outside it—to be a
dead end. If God were external to the world, his actions in the world would necessarily be interventions and hence unintelligible in terms of this-worldly explanations, assuming that the world is a
closed causal nexus" (*Remythologizing Theology*, 134).

of God in panentheism does not imply that God is active everywhere, as is the traditional theistic God.

Arguing that divine interventionism would undermine the ability of science to explain the natural world, Philip Clayton has sought to formulate an alternative, *noninterventionist* model of special divine action. Scientific explanations, Clayton writes, presuppose that nature is a closed, autonomous physical system.[388] The analogy here to deism is apparent. To be sure, there is talk of relationality, and yet nothing happens in the world that is in any specific way the outcome of God's agency. As a personal agent, God fades from view. Moreover, if we presuppose that human beings are sinners, then the message that God "makes room" for us is not good news. This would not be the *solution*; this would be the *problem*. As fallen creatures, we human beings use and abuse our freedom, harm one another, and are powerless to break out of self-imposed vicious cycles. Whatever autonomy we might possess will do us little or no good in the long run.

The denial of divine transcendence or aseity in kenotic-relational theology is not supported by argument but is built into the initial assumptions. The metaphysical starting point casts doubt on God's freedom and makes it seem that God has suffered a kind of metaphysical imprisonment. At risk is the freedom of God to act or not to act, to act in one particular way or in another way, to create or not to create. Furthermore, there is the issue of God's freedom to be in relation (or not to be in relation) with creation in general and with particular creatures. Contemporary kenotic-relational theologies at first appear to be based on a biblical picture of God, but on closer examination their metaphysical foundation appears to be more like that of earlier esoteric thinkers (*DR* 2; 5), for whom God has no choice but to be in relation with the world. With God's freedom in question, the love of God and the grace of God also come into question. This is an unexpected consequence in kenotic-relational theologies and in other Christian universalist theologies (*DR* 12.3).

The kenotic-relational definition of God's relation to creatures as fully reciprocal rules out the sort of unconditional and unconditioned love ascribed to the God of the Bible, which is not a reciprocal or creature-dependent love. The insistence on reciprocity is antithetical to Jesus's biblical teaching on unconditional love: "But I say to you, Love your enemies. . . . For if you love those who love you, what reward do you have?" (Matt. 5:44, 46). While in the Bible and in Christian tradition, the unconditional love of God is represented as the highest form of love and as the model for earthly love, nonreciprocal love does not even count as love in the kenotic-relational paradigm. What the Bible regards

---

388. Vanhoozer, *Remythologizing Theology*, 134–35n259, citing Clayton, *Adventures in the Spirit*, 219.

as the paradigm instance of love—that "Christ died for the ungodly" (Rom. 5:6)—is ruled out. Because relational theology rejects the idea of nonreciprocal relationships, this way of thinking about God, to be logically consistent, would need to exclude the idea of God's unconditional love in Christ.

There seems to be something metaphysically incoherent in the kenotic-relational notion of God as "making space" for creation. In the biblical view, if God were to "back off" from creatures, then creatures would simply cease to exist. There are a few biblical passages that envisage just this possibility. "If he [i.e., God] should set his heart to it and gather to himself his spirit and his breath, all flesh would perish together, and man would return to dust" (Job 34:14–15; cf. Ps. 104:27–30). One might say: "The world – God = 0." On this basis it does not make sense to affirm a causal self-limitation in God's creating the world. Instead, we might ponder again the implications of the doctrine of creation *ex nihilo*. This doctrine is crucial for Christian thinking about God, because it shatters any lesser notion of deity that one might set up in place of the biblical God. Kenotic-relational theology, to be self-consistent, must reject creation from nothing.[389] Yet if one rejects this doctrine, then only two options remain: *creatio ex Deo* or else *creatio a materia*. If the former is true, then all creatures are made of "God stuff," and a whole series of theological consequences follow from that assumption. If the latter is true, then the world is made of something that God did not create, and likewise another series of theological consequences would ensue.[390]

Kenotic-relational theologies substitute a newer form of metaphysics based on relationality for older forms of metaphysics based on substance. Both approaches run the risk of infringing on God's freedom. This does not mean that there can be no place for metaphysics in Christian theology. Yet a "good metaphysics" takes its cues from God's self-revelation in Scripture and in the person of Christ, while a "bad metaphysics" does not. Perhaps there should be some place for *both substance and relation* as philosophical and theological categories.[391] In response to the current emphasis on "relations," one must pose

389. Creation from nothing is currently under debate not only among process thinkers but also in wider theological circles. For contrasting views, see Oord, *Theologies of Creation*; McFarland, *From Nothing*; Webster, "'Love Is Also a Lover of Life.'"

390. On creation from nothing, see Desmond, *Hegel's God*; Desmond, *God and the Between*. The Creator-creature relationship in creation from nothing—as the conferral of existence itself—is utterly unlike any relationship that might exist between creatures. The act of creation carries what William Desmond calls "T3 transcendence": a hyperbolic transcendence that is entirely nonobjectifiable and non-analogical in character. See Desmond's analysis of "Transcendences" in *Hegel's God*, 2–7. In contrast to this, contemporary kenotic-relational theologians appear to be both limiting and objectifying God in what they propose regarding the God-world relationship.

391. Traditional Christian theology affirmed both relation and substance in God. See Emery, "Essentialism or Personalism?"

the question: "Relations *between what?*" Are there simply relations as such, or relations between relations, or must there be *things* between which relations exist? Contemporary notions of relations and relationality might not be able to pass philosophical muster without relying on implied yet unarticulated notions of things, substances, or realities.[392] Those affirming relationality, as noted above, are in fact affirming a particular sort of relation—namely, *the reciprocal or codetermining relation, seen as defining all relations.* This metaphysical presumption of codetermination precludes the most distinctive of all Christian affirmations about God's relation to the world—namely, the doctrine of creation from nothing.

Alister McGrath warns against the danger of "Trinitarian inflation." It is simply unwarranted to argue that because God as Trinity has a certain trait, X, therefore human beings, created in God's image, must also have the same trait, X.[393] Paul Molnar comments, "The idea that God's relations *ad extra* will become God's relations *ad intra* indicates a confusion and reversal of reason and revelation, which follows if Christ is not seen as God's grace and if faith and revelation become the products of human experience in the form of a relational ontology."[394] Though Richard Bauckham has been sympathetic to Moltmann, he faults him for making trinitarian relationality or perichoresis his model for human social life, noting that "this view of our relationship to the Trinity has no biblical basis."[395]

Vanhoozer summarizes his objection to kenotic-relational theologies by stating that "the panentheist paradigm appears seriously to hobble God's capacity to work his will," for "insofar as one's model of God fails to do justice to God as a personal divine agent, it revises what the Bible is primarily about. Put differently: if God is not an ascriptive agent, then the Bible is no longer about what God has done in creating, reconciling, and redeeming human beings. As to sounding the gospel, then, panentheism is an uncertain trumpet."[396] Furthermore, "to suggest that creatures enjoy union and communion with

---

392. See Vanhoozer, *Remythologizing Theology*, 141. On this question of the metaphysical status of relationships, see Speidell, "Trinitarian Ontology"; David Cunningham, "Participation as a Trinitarian Virtue"; Levering, *Scripture and Metaphysics*, 199–212. Moltmann himself resists reducing everything to relations: "There are no persons without relations, but there are no relations without persons either" (*Trinity and the Kingdom*, 172). Moltmann views the reduction of the concept of person to that of relation as ultimately modalistic.

393. A. E. McGrath, "Doctrine of the Trinity," 30–31, cited in Vanhoozer, *Remythologizing Theology*, 157n83.

394. Molnar, *Divine Freedom*, 144.

395. Bauckham, "Jürgen Moltmann and the Question of Pluralism," quoted in Vanhoozer, *Trinity in a Pluralistic Age*, 160.

396. Vanhoozer, *Remythologizing Theology*, 139–40, 134; quotation partially italicized in the original.

God simply by virtue of being . . . evacuates the history of salvation of salvific significance, makes light of sin, and encourages skepticism about the necessity of the cross. Salvation history becomes no more than the story of how creatures come to realize that God only appears to be distant."[397] Vanhoozer points out that human beings do not relate to each member of the Holy Trinity in the same way. The Spirit indwells us and is "in" believers, and yet believers are not said generally to be "in" the Spirit. The Spirit enables the relationship with the Father and Son, but the Spirit is not "an 'other' in his own right."[398] Just as importantly, believers are not said in Scripture to mutually indwell one another. The presentation of perichoresis in contemporary theology often glides over such nuances in the biblical texts.

In his *Church Dogmatics*, Karl Barth clearly expressed the problems endemic to panentheism: "God does not form a whole with any other being either in identity with it or as compounding or merging with it to constitute a synthesis—the object of that master-concept, so often sought and found, which comprehends both God and what is not God." In the same passage, Barth spoke of God as the one who loves in freedom: "God is who He is in independence of them [the creatures] even in this relatedness. He does not share His being with theirs. He does not enter with them into a higher synthesis. . . . Even in His relationship and connexion with them, He remains who He is. He creates and sustains the relationship."[399] Barth's emphasis is in line with the thinking of such authors as William Desmond, Paul Molnar, Kevin Vanhoozer, and John Webster. The question ultimately is whether being "in Christ" is *cosmological* or *covenantal*—determined in creation itself or else through God's free grace given to fallen creatures.

In expounding the theology of the cross, Hans Urs von Balthasar offered a verdict on Moltmann that might apply to some of the more recent kenotic-relational theologies: "Interpretations of this kind, like all talk of God's suffering, become inevitable wherever the internal divine process, 'procession,' is lumped together with the process of salvation history. God is entangled in the world process and becomes a tragic, mythological God."[400] What truly matters in Jesus's death is not merely suffering but the covenantal context of this suffering. Vanhoozer writes that "the cross is not a symptom of God's general metaphysical relationship to the world but the climax of God's particular relationship to Israel that

397. Ibid., 150. Vanhoozer refers here to Paul Tillich, "The Two Types of Philosophy of Religion," in *Theology and Culture*, 10–29, comparing one type of philosophy to "meeting a stranger" and another to "overcoming estrangement" (*Remythologizing Theology*, 150n54).

398. Vanhoozer, *Remythologizing Theology*, 158.

399. Barth, *CD* II/1, 311–12.

400. Balthasar, *TD* 4:322.

began with a divine promise to Abraham."[401] Oswald Bayer comments on the modern emergence of "a natural theology of the cross," according to which God needs the world to become fully God.[402] Such a naturalized and Hegelianized interpretation of the cross inevitably deemphasizes faith. What happens at the death of Jesus simply happens, and happens for everyone, whether they believe it or not. This false objectivization of the cross removes the subjective correlate to God's objective work—namely, faith, repentance, and obedience—and so it leads into universalism. Moltmann and the kenotic-relational thinkers interpret Jesus's cry of dereliction, "My God, my God, why have you forsaken me?" (Matt. 27:46), as an event of separation within the Godhead. Yet this moment may instead be seen as the climax of Jesus's obedience. Jesus's death was an *active* passion. P. T. Forsyth wrote, "The perfection of the Son and the perfecting of his holy work lay, not in his suffering but in his obedience." This is also the view of Colin Gunton, for whom the cry of dereliction was the climax of the Son's obedience, not a breach between Father and Son.[403] David Bentley Hart insists that the Son's very Godforsakenness, exemplified in the cry of dereliction, "is enfolded within and overcome by the ever greater distance and always indissoluble unity of God's triune love," and that this is clearly shown in the words of self-commitment: "Father, into your hands I commit my spirit" (Luke 23:46).[404]

9.13. Apocalypse Now: Congdon's Neo-Bultmannian Universalism

One of the most recent works of Christian universalist theology is David Congdon's *The God Who Saves* (2016), which develops the implications of arguments contained in Congdon's *The Mission of Demythologizing* (2015), a major study of Rudolf Bultmann (1884–1976). During the early 1920s, Barth and Bultmann were generally regarded as theological comrades-in-arms, embracing a common "dialectical" approach to theology and sharing a common aversion to the German liberalism epitomized in the writings of Adolf von Harnack (1851–1930). Yet during the 1920s and 1930s, a chasm opened between them as Barth increasingly aligned himself with the theological orthodoxy of the early church and later

---

401. Vanhoozer, *Remythologizing Theology*, 461. Cf. Holcomb, "Being Bound to God." Holcomb questions whether the Radical Orthodoxy movement has allowed sufficient scope for covenantal motifs, or is too dependent on metaphysical notions of participation.

402. Bayer, *Theologie*, 509, 514, cited in Vanhoozer, *Remythologizing Theology*, 458.

403. Forsyth, *Marriage*, 70; Gunton, *Act and Being*, 127; both cited in Vanhoozer, *Remythologizing Theology*, 429, with n. 167.

404. D. B. Hart, "No Shadow of Turning," 205. Cf. Yocum, "Cry of Dereliction?," 79: "The cry from the cross expresses the suffering of the Son and the non-intervention of the Father, a non-intervention fully and freely embraced by the Son in co-operation and inseparable union with the Father, in order that they might together triumph over the powers and principalities."

Reformed scholasticism, and Bultmann developed a way of thinking—inspired in part by the philosophy of Martin Heidegger (1889–1976)—that sought to reinterpret the Christian message as a call to authentic human existence that did not depend for its validity on the historical facticity or actuality of Jesus of Nazareth.

Describing the intellectual distance between them and their inability to communicate, Barth in a 1952 letter compared Bultmann and himself to an elephant and whale (without specifying who was which animal): "It is clear to you how things are between us—you and me? It seems to me that we are like a whale . . . and an elephant, who have met in boundless astonishment on some oceanic shore. . . . They lack a common key to what each would obviously so much like to say to the other according to its own element and in its language."[405] In *The God Who Saves*, Congdon seeks to bridge this gap and to achieve an elusive synthesis of these two by integrating Bultmann's adamant insistence on the concreteness and historicity of individual human experience with Barth's equally adamant stress on the universal salvific significance of the birth, life, death, and resurrection of Jesus Christ. Whether Congdon has taught the elephant to swim or the whale to walk is an open question, though the effort is instructive.

In his *Church Dogmatics*, Barth distinguishes his own mature theology from that of Bultmann by contrasting his objective approach to salvation—centering on the event of Christ's life—with what Barth saw as Bultmann's subjective standpoint:

> There have been many attempts to make the history of Jesus Christ coincident with that of the believer, and *vice versa*. . . . But we can approve and make common cause with it neither in its earlier forms nor in that authoritatively represented to-day by R. Bultmann. . . . Christian faith takes note of [the history of Jesus Christ], and clings to it and responds to it, without itself being the thing which accomplishes it, without any identity between the redemptive act of God and faith as the free act of man. . . . What takes place in the recognition of the *pro me* of Christian faith is not the redemptive act of God itself, not the death and resurrection of Jesus Christ, not the presentation and repetition of His obedience and sacrifice and victory. . . . It [is] impossible to make what took place *eph' hapax* [Greek "once for all"] in Jesus Christ coincident with what takes place in faith.[406]

Congdon's *The God Who Saves* is based on a premise antithetical to that of Barth in this passage. Rejecting the distinction between objective and subjective

405. Karl Barth, letter to Rudolf Bultmann, December 24, 1952, in Barth and Bultmann, *Briefwechsel*, 192, quoted in Congdon, *Mission of Demythologizing*, 3 (trans. Congdon).
406. Barth, *CD* IV/1, 767.

aspects of salvation, Congdon wants to create, in Barth's terms, an "identity between the redemptive act of God and faith as the free act of man," to make what happened in Christ "coincide" with what happens in faith, and to interpret faith as a "repetition" of Christ's sacrifice.

Congdon states that his "starting point had to be the saving event itself rather than God, and this saving event had to be simultaneously objective and subjective, or rather it had to dispense with the distinction between objective and subjective altogether."[407] For Congdon, "the being of God as an isolated metaphysical entity in itself . . . does not exist." What exists as a topic for theology is "the concrete being of God *for us* . . . which is deity as such."[408] Throughout *The God Who Saves*, the blurring of distinctions between objective reality and subjective experience works consistently in favor of the latter. "Talk of God is always also talk of the human subject and her historical situation," writes Congdon.[409] He rejects any notion of an "essence" or "nature" (Greek *physis*), whether the term is applied to God or to humanity. "With the exclusion of all worldviews goes the exclusion of all talk of permanent natures or essences in theology. 'So-called "deity" can no more be interpreted as a *phusis* than humanity.'"[410] He adds, "Theology is therefore necessarily and thoroughly actualistic . . . because the truth of the Christ-myth, which is the norm for both form and content, is itself an active occurrence and relation."[411]

In describing his own intellectual development, Congdon speaks of his conservative Protestant background and "complicated, often antagonistic, relationship with [his] evangelical heritage." In adopting universalism, he acknowledges the influence of Robin Parry (*DR* 11.4), though he also says that he "never shared MacDonald's [Parry's] particular view" of universalism. On Barth's influence, he comments that "Barth taught [him] to see Christ's saving work as the *actuality* of salvation and not merely its *possibility*."[412] It was "initially quite a shock" for

---

407. Congdon, *God Who Saves*, xv. He writes that "the problem is Barth's sharp distinction between the objective and the subjective, which . . . perpetuates the metaphysical notion that reconciliation applies to us even though it does not concern us existentially" (xv n. 4).

408. Ibid., 24.

409. Ibid., 48.

410. Congdon, *Mission of Demythologizing*, 833, citing Bultmann, "Das christologische Bekenntnis," 258–59.

411. Congdon, *Mission of Mythologizing*, 833.

412. Congdon, *God Who Saves*, ix. While Congdon is largely uncritical of Bultmann, he is perhaps more critical than appreciative of Barth. He writes that "Barth tends to make election a one-time decision in pretemporal eternity, which abstracts election both from the lived historicity of Jesus Christ and the lived historicities of human persons here and now" (xiv). Congdon reinterprets objective realities in terms of human subjectivity, and so too his mediation between Barth and Bultmann reinterprets Barthian universalism in the direction of Bultmannian existentialism, rather than vice versa.

844 The Devil's Redemption

Congdon to encounter Bultmann's 1959 essay "Adam and Christ," which repudiated Barth's claim in *Christ and Adam* of a universal participation of all human
beings in the humanity of Christ (*DR* appendix L). Congdon explains, "The
problem with universalism—as well as any notion of pretemporal election—is
that it makes a judgment about the individual without regard for her particular
historicity and is only, at best, indirectly related to personal existence. Reading Bultmann thus validated an instinct I had inherited from my evangelical
upbringing."[413] He adds that he "would gradually internalize Bultmann's insights
into the historical nature of both God and appropriate talk of God.... The result
was a deep internal tension—a tension between a Bultmannian methodological starting point and a Barthian soteriological conclusion."[414] Congdon is thus
self-aware concerning the tensions within his own theology.[415]

Congdon's argument in *The God Who Saves* is complex and many-sided.
Various lines of reasoning are juxtaposed rather than connected in sequence, so
it may be helpful to unpack a few of his summary statements. In the epilogue
to his work, he says that he presents a "soteriocentric theology . . . arguing . . .
that God acts savingly and definitively in the historical event of Christ's crucifixion . . . [and] that the Spirit of God repeats this event in each new elemental

413. Ibid., x.
414. Ibid., xi. "Christianity is rooted in a concrete historical event. . . . This is the beating heart
of Christianity's rejection of docetism" (35). This statement exists in tension with Congdon's statement that "reconciliation . . . is always a contingent event within each person's concrete history"
(xvi, quoting Congdon, *Mission of Demythologizing*, 833–34).
415. Congdon's theology has varied affinities. Its theological sources lie for the most part in
German-language authors who wrote between 1917 and 1968, apart from the references to Eberhard Jüngel (b. 1934) and to Bruce McCormack, a Barth scholar currently at Princeton Theological
Seminary and one influenced by Jüngel. Congdon comments that his is a "*dialectical* systematic
theology . . . in the consistently actualistic sense represented by a synthetic reading of *inter alia*
Barth, Bultmann, Ebeling, Gollwitzer, and Jüngel" (*God Who Saves*, xviii). We see Congdon's dialectical approach in statements like the following (italicized in the original): "The God who is not an
object of science becomes an object of science without ceasing to be the God who is not an object
of science" (27). "The nonoccurrence of the parousia [i.e., return of Christ] is the fulfillment of the
parousia itself, because the purpose of eschatological expectation is the *unsettling* of the believer"
(127n85). Just as Bultmann prevails over Barth in Congdon's work, so too the Lutheran element
(Bultmann, Jüngel, Gerhard Ebeling, Helmut Gollwitzer) triumphs over Barth's more Calvinistic
influence. Congdon writes of how at Princeton Seminary he learned for the first time of "the
Lutheran theology of the cross," which he says "remains normative for my thought now" (xx).
Yet he does draw from Barth as well as from the German Lutherans. He takes from Barth the key
idea that "faith is not the condition for one's reconciled status before God" (10), which differs from
the position of Bultmann, for whom the human response to God's call is determinative of one's
relation to God. In another side of his thought, Congdon's emphasis on "preflective, unconscious
experience" (189) reminds one of Friedrich Schleiermacher (*DR* 7.3) and Karl Rahner (*DR* 10.2).
Congdon's idea of "unconscious cocrucifixion" with Christ (see below) allows him to affirm the
unconscious affinity of non-Christians with Christ, making them something like "anonymous
Christians" in a Rahnerian sense.

interruption of existence." For Congdon, "each person participates in this event through an unconscious act of cocrucifixion that places us outside ourselves in solidarity with others in the apostolate. Salvation is thus a reality rather than a possibility." He adds, "The result is a version of Christian universalism that has been hermeneutically reconstructed in a dialectical and postmetaphysical way so as to avoid general categories that render salvation abstract and ahistorical." In this way, Congdon "locates salvation in the act of human faith without making it contingent upon a conscious decision of faith—a universalism without universals."[416]

Congdon is highly critical of mainstream theologians who have "wandered off into abstract speculation" on such matters as "the notion of an immanent trinity apart from the economy [of salvation]" and "pointless conundrums regarding problems like predestination and free will, apologetic exercises, and the like."[417] He writes that "the single divine act that elects, justifies, reconciles, redeems, and reveals makes theology *possible* by bringing human beings into an encounter with God."[418] Congdon's "single divine act" of salvation in effect collapses the history of redemption in the world—and God's work in the lives of individuals (traditionally described in the *ordo salutis*)—into a single *divine now* that then becomes identified with the *human now* that occurs within *each individual moment of experience*. "If a person's nature is historical," writes Congdon, "that is, if there is no human essence beyond one's concrete actions and decisions—then *the question of salvation cannot be decided apart from the particular moment in which a person realizes her historical existence*."[419] Congdon's theology is thus centered not on *history* but rather on *historicity*. There is for him no history of redemption as such but rather a God-event impinging on human experience. Congdon seemingly does not make room for a development of salvation in the lives of individuals. Everything is collapsed into a divine now that is also a human now.

Congdon's intention in writing *The God Who Saves*, he says, was "to develop a nonmetaphysical conception of the atoning work of Christ, which means that the ancient substance ontology is done away with entirely," resulting in a "universalism without metaphysics."[420] The definition of "metaphysics" that he uses is pejorative—"a mode of thinking that constrains rational inquiry from

416. Congdon, *God Who Saves*, 260.
417. Ibid., 50–51.
418. Ibid., 50.
419. Ibid., 18; emphasis original. "Reconciliation is not first a transaction of change that occurs 'above us,' so to speak, in relation to some general human substance (a universal *humanum*) in which we all participate; it is always only a contingent event within each person's concrete history" (xvi).
420. Ibid., xiv, 10.

the outset with abstract, ahistorical presuppositions."[421] On this basis, Congdon sees it as useless—and indeed as mistaken or even harmful—to speak of God as "being" or "substance" or to accept the ancient Christology that defined Jesus as "two natures" in "one person." He comments on "the internal incoherence of Chalcedonian christology."[422] Congdon's theology seeks to make a clean sweep of metaphysics, while at the same time intending "to develop an account of participation" that "does not require recourse to a substantival 'logic of assumption.'"[423] Congdon rejects the idea of "human nature," and for this reason his presuppositions will not allow for Christ to "assume" human nature or then to act on behalf of other human beings in the way that was assumed by classical Christian thinkers.[424] In cleansing the gospel from all vestiges of metaphysics, Congdon advocates a theological liberationism that he refers to as a "demetaphysicizing," "detheorizing," "deconstantinizing," "deideologizing," "desacramentalizing," "deinstitutionizing," and "delegalizing" of Christianity.[425]

More, perhaps, as a radical theologian than as a liberal theologian, Congdon shows little interest in hedging or compromising with earlier traditions. His project is a "demythologizing theology [that] attempts to think with and beyond Bultmann."[426] His "demythologizing" includes as a matter of course a repudiation of biblical authority. The Bible cannot serve as the norm of theology but must itself be criticized.[427] Congdon is also a thoroughgoing critic of incarnational Christology. He speaks of himself as among "those of us today seeking a postmetaphysical christology beyond 'the myth of the incarnate Son of God.'"[428]

421. Ibid., 20. "To accept the problem of historicity is to reject the Platonic ontology. . . . Each person is a historical being whose being is thus only ever in becoming" (ibid., 18).

422. Ibid., 105; cf. 107, 110. He writes, "I do not accept the assumption that the ecumenical councils determine what counts as authentically 'Christian,'" adding that these councils "are only authoritative insofar as they embody and bear witness to the norm of the gospel that stands always beyond them" (3n5).

423. Ibid., xiv.

424. Ibid., 207.

425. Congdon, Mission of Demythologizing, 831.

426. Ibid.

427. Congdon reads Scripture as a historical text and not as authoritative: "We must . . . face the fact that the scriptures are thoroughly historical documents of their time. There is nothing directly divine or inspired about the suzerainty treaty. It was simply what the Hebrew tribes knew" (God Who Saves, 161n22). Congdon says he is "refusing to participate altogether in the ongoing attempt to 'normalize' the faith by identifying a particular creaturely artifact (e.g., scriptural text or creedal formula) with God's revelation" (24). "The gospel . . . resists all attempts to turn it into propaganda," and this means that "orthoheterodox multivocality is not opposed to the gospel" (24). Congdon rejects Paul's "heteropatriarchal culture" (230). He uses the German technical term Sachkritik (critique of content) to defend Bultmann and to explain his own methodology (39n39, 40–41n41, 232): "Bultmann interprets all texts in light of the norm that stands beyond every text" (39n39).

428. Ibid., 124, citing Fuchs, "Jesus Christus," 39. "If we dispense with the mythology of a Son in pretemporal eternity who then takes on human flesh in the incarnation, we can interpret Jesus'

He brushes aside as irrelevant the classical christological debates: "Trying to puzzle out how deity and humanity can coincide in a single person is a false metaphysical dilemma. . . . Deity simply *is* his humanity in its eschatologically interruptive mode of existence."[429] As Congdon states in his study of Bultmann, the task of demythologizing requires the theologian to rethink not only certain extraneous or peripheral aspects of the Christian message but also the very concept of God.[430] In the perspective known as "soteriocentrism," Congdon explains that "the starting point had to be the saving event rather than God."[431]

One of the odd elements in Congdon's argumentation lies in his doctrine of "unnature." So strong is he in rejecting substantialist metaphysics and ideas of "being," "substance," and "nature" that Congdon embraces an antithetical notion of "unnature." God did not create a natural world or natural order, but creation itself is "the apocalyptic event of *unnature*."[432] He develops what he calls "a soteriocentric theology of the creature as eccentric, unconscious, and unnatural" and declares that "the apocalyptic event of cocrucifixion puts an end to nature" and that "a faith constituted by the apocalypse is *acosmic*."[433] Such statements are frequently repeated. After a positive reference to Judith Butler's gender theory, Congdon states that "the apocalypse queers the creature," and near the conclusion of *The God Who Saves* he says that "the infinite God is the queer God who unsettles all norms and traditions."[434] Congdon's emphatic affirmation of "unnature" gives a gnostic flavor to his theology. It is as though the universal cocrucifixion with Christ were a hidden reality not known or knowable through this world. But somehow Congdon himself knows it and is able to write about it. In a world of "unnature," without "nature," "being," or "substance," where all that exists is a flux of experience, one

---

statements about coming from the Creator as also eschatological in character: Jesus comes from the Creator in the sense that his existence is divinely authorized and so eschatologically paves the way to the Creator" (*God Who Saves*, 252). This statement might mean that Jesus leads us to God, though Jesus is not God. Consider also the following statement: "The God who saves has no given likeness. . . . This God is utterly hidden from sight, present to us only in absence" (235). Such an unqualified statement of God's absence seems to exclude a doctrine of incarnation. Congdon speaks of Jesus as prophetic rather than messianic: "While the Gospels . . . focus on the person of Jesus, this transition suggests that the Jesus of history was himself focused on the coming reign of God. He was primarily a prophetic rather than messianic figure" (116n41).

429. Ibid., 129.
430. Congdon, *Mission of Demythologizing*, 835.
431. Congdon, *God Who Saves*, xv. On "soteriocentrism" generally, see 21–58. Congdon goes so far as to say that our human experiences are "constitutive" for Christ's identity: "Our concrete experience of abandonment is constitutive of Christ's being as the Abandoned One" (157–58).
432. Ibid., 201.
433. Ibid., 207, 227, 228; cf. 233. "God is a denaturalizing event and the world is the unnatural place of this event" (237). "The apocalypse is the inbreaking of unnature" (248n17).
434. Ibid., 229–30, 258.

wonders what basis there might be for Congdon's affirmation of universal cocrucifixion with Christ.

In his effort "to think with and beyond Bultmann," Congdon's theology is reminiscent of that of Fritz Buri (1907–95), who agreed with Bultmann's initiative but felt that Bultmann himself had not gone far enough. In place of "demythologizing" the gospel (*Entmythologisierung*), Buri called also for "de-kerygmatizing" (*Entkerygmatisierung*), implying that the core or substance of the Christian proclamation (Greek *kerygma*) needed itself to be reinterpreted, and not merely the terms, concepts, or symbols in which the proclamation is made.[435] In the same vein as Buri's work is Charley Hardwick's *Events of Grace* (1996), which argues that "God"-language may be wholly reinterpreted in terms of human experiences of transcendence or transformation.[436] Congdon might resist such a reductive account of his own argument, yet his rejection of a metaphysically substantive "God" raises the question of whether his "God"-language simply denotes elements or aspects of human awareness.[437] The radical theology of *The God Who Saves* might be read as a form of religious naturalism.

Regarding the question of universal salvation, Congdon's answer in short is that all human beings attain salvation because all humans without exception participate—by an "unconscious cocrucifixion"—in Christ's crucifixion, which is itself an experience of abandonment by God.[438] Congdon's theology renews the paradox of the Lutheran theology of the cross, in which the Father's embrace of the suffering Christ is tantamount to abandonment, and the Father's abandonment is a form of embrace. "This death [of Jesus] . . . is saving *because it is a death in God-abandonment.*"[439] In context, the "saving" death Congdon refers to is that of Christ, but in his exposition the distinction between Jesus's death and our own "death"—that is, a comparable experience of abandonment by God—often becomes blurry. This evokes the question of whether human beings are saved by Jesus's death or by their own deathlike experiences. Congdon anticipates this objection and insists that "cocrucifixion is not coredemption. Cocrucifixion occurs where and when our existence corresponds to the cruciform existence

---

435. Buri's works include "Entmythologisierung und Entkerygmatisierung der Theologie" (1952), *Theologie der Existenz* (1954), and *Dogmatik als Selbstverständnis des christlichen Glaubens*, 2 vols. (1956, 1962).

436. See McClymond, review of Hardwick, *Events of Grace*.

437. Congdon professes an affinity for atheism, commenting that "genuine Christian theologians may find that outspoken atheists are actually their strongest and closest allies in the pursuit of truth" (*God Who Saves*, 35n26).

438. The only potential "canon within the canon," for Congdon, that would apply "to all Christian soteriology is Galatians 2:19–20" (ibid., 81).

439. Congdon, *God Who Saves*, 85.

of Jesus."[440] A conundrum in Congdon's argument is that he rejects "magical-mythological belief" in "the efficacy of animal sacrifice" as well as "evangelical crucicentrism," even as he insists on the centrality of Jesus's death as a model of kenotic self-giving.[441] While the argument of *The God Who Saves* is cross-centered, the message seems to be salvation by imitation rather than salvation by representation.

Much like Moltmann (*DR* 9.10–9.11), Congdon views Jesus's death as signifying something eternal in God. Jesus's resurrection therefore does not reverse or counteract suffering but rather extends and intensifies the alienation of the cross: "The resurrection takes death up into the very life of God. Rather than giving assurance of some escape from or end to the offense of the cross, the resurrection instead *intensifies* the offence by eternalizing it [so that] we will always encounter the event of God's own self-distancing in death, which distances us from ourselves and so crucifies us with Christ."[442] Here Congdon's theology approaches the gnostic conception of an inherently suffering God, with its "eternalizing" of "God's own self-distancing in death."

But how is it that everyone is "cocrucified" and shares in Jesus's death in God-abandonment? Congdon's argument "entails locating the saving event of divine action in a prereflective present tense moment—namely, in the *unconscious*."[443] It should be noted that Congdon's idea of the "unconscious" remains rather ambiguous and in need of further clarification. He states, for example, that "Christianity loses sight of the eschatological horizon of the gospel . . . whenever it fails to remain conscious of Christ's interruptive incursion into our unconscious existence."[444] But how is someone supposed to remain *conscious* of that which is said to be *unconscious*?[445] When one reads Congdon's various statements in context, it becomes clear that "unconscious cocrucifixion" with Christ is not divorced from human experience as such and so cannot be unconscious in all respects. Otherwise, Congdon's argument would be much like Barth's doctrine

440. Ibid., 88.
441. Ibid., 52. Congdon writes: "Crucicentrism cannot mean that the crucifixion in itself 'does' something—whether to God or to ourselves. It is not some divine instrument for redeeming the world from sin, any more than slaughtering a goat is really capable of cleansing people from impurity" (53). He rejects the "zero-sum logic that requires the death of one creature in order to gain life for another" and the idea that "blood-shedding has the capacity to propitiate a deity" (64). He speaks of the need to get beyond "a sacrificial mode of thinking" (123–24).
442. Ibid., 128.
443. Ibid., 90. Congdon appeals to Dietrich Bonhoeffer's notion of "unconscious Christianity" (93).
444. Ibid., 176–77.
445. In another passage, Congdon writes of "the notion of unconscious Christianity, in which faith is primarily and normatively an unconscious act of existence" (ibid., 261). The phrase "unconscious act of existence" is not explained, nor is its relation to the exercise of faith.

of universal election, and it would be tantamount to the claim that all human lives are determined by something that lies beyond all human experience (i.e., a divine decision or determination). What Congon seems to mean is that there is a general human experience of "death in God-abandonment," and though it is a conscious experience for all who undergo it, it is generally not understood by most persons as related to Christ, to God, or to religion.[446]

At this point, the argument takes a strange twist, in which an *unconscious connection* to Christ is said to be superior to a *conscious connection*. Congdon comments that "a soteriocentric theology of the creature will prioritize unconsciousness over consciousness as the defining locus of personal identity."[447] In Rahnerian terms (*DR* 10.2), it is as though the anonymous Christian were the true Christian, and the conscious Christian were barely a Christian at all. Congdon follows up his valorization of unconscious Christianity with an attack on conscious, deliberate, professed faith in Christ: "Conscious Christianity is a turning in upon oneself to care for one's own spiritual health and relationship with God. Conscious faith, in other words, is not genuine faith, but rather the objectifying gaze of religion, which turns divine action . . . into an idol."[448] Congdon cites the atheistic novelist Philip Pullman's inverted interpretation of Matthew 25:1–13, in which the wise virgins who go into the feast are actually the outsiders to God's kingdom, while the foolish virgins, who are outside the feast, are insiders to God's kingdom. Congdon writes: "The 'real gospel' . . . is *not* that God's saving apocalypse is available to those who consciously believe, to those who enter the wedding banquet, but rather that the inbreaking of Christ's reign is a reality for those excluded from every banquet and feast."[449] Salvation is for those who, like the foolish virgins, consciously reject Christ. Here Congdon is on the verge of abandoning his own universalism by turning his sheep into goats and his goats into sheep—reversing their roles rather than embracing both groups.

Congdon is critical of the institutional church, though he develops a notion of the "apostolate," which includes those who in some sense bear witness to the reality of death-abandonment by going outside of themselves to identify with and to serve the poor and the marginalized. This "apostolate" is not a

446. "If faith is an act of participating in the crucified Christ, and if this participation occurs in those who are placed outside themselves, then this . . . can be understood in a universalistic way" (ibid., 96n120). "The truth of the gospel is that the apocalypse occurs in the unconscious *actus directus* of being placed outside ourselves [in] kenotic death in God-abandonment" (97).
447. Congdon, *God Who Saves*, 215.
448. Ibid., 96. Later Congdon softens his position: "Conscious Christianity may be, by nature, an exercise in idolatrous unbelief, but it is at least conscious of its idolatry" (99). Another passage states: "Conscious faith is not in itself saving; it is a contextual interpretation of unconscious faith" (261).
449. Ibid., 102, citing Pullman, *Good Man Jesus*, 142.

self-conscious or self-bounded community, since identification with Christ for many or most in this group remains unknown. The "apostolate" must include those who would never imagine themselves as such. Congdon's community serves an ethical aim, by giving individuals the opportunity to serve: "Communal Christian existence, when and where it truly occurs, provides space for people to be placed outside themselves—that is to say, space for ongoing cocrucifixion with Christ."[450] Another line of argument in Congdon's thought pertains to the Holy Spirit, who is said to be the agent who makes effective everyone's participation in Christ.[451] Congdon believes that it is not possible to distinguish Christ from Spirit, and so he collapses these two together into what he calls the "Christ-Spirit."[452]

In one remarkable passage, Congdon specifies more fully how he understands the range of human experience that might be understood in terms of "cocrucifixion" with Christ:

> The eschatological event of salvation thus belongs to those who are placed outside themselves by the powers and principalities of the world—that is, to the poor, the imprisoned, the social invisible, the culturally foreign, those who are vulnerable and disposable. Salvation belongs to them irrespective of their acknowledgement of Christ or their participation in conscious Christian faith. And while the unconscious participation in the apocalypse belongs to them first, we can be confident, based on the logic of the kerygma, that every person has been or will be an unconscious Christian. For some, unconscious faith might only occur in a moment of literal unconsciousness—at birth or at death, where we are placed wholly outside ourselves. Others will encounter eschatological existence in a moment of pure being-for-others, such as at the birth of a child, in the ecstasy . . . of love, or in the ethical encounter with a neighbor in need. Still others will be placed outside themselves through the aesthetic experience of the beautiful. . . . However it occurs, each person will, at some moment, participate in the authentic existence promised by and actualized in the eschatological kerygma. Insofar as they are placed outside themselves, faith recognizes that it is *Christ himself* in whom they are placed.[453]

450. Congdon, *God Who Saves*, 99.

451. For Congdon, "the Spirit is what makes crucifixion into cocrucifixion" (ibid., 142), and this Spirit acts universally: "The eschatological Spirit of this liberation empowers acts of faith and witness that cannot be circumscribed by the tradition, culture, state, policy, or doctrine" (171). The act of the Spirit is the *"nonidentical repetition of interruption"* (249; emphasis original).

452. Congdon writes, "The reconciling work of the Christ-Spirit is already final for each person" (ibid., 263). "The apocalyptic approach to salvation that I am developing here is one that necessarily unites Christ and Spirit in a single event" (66–67n26). On "Christ-Spirit," see also 189, 254. Such language raises the question of whether Congdon has rejected trinitarian theology in favor of some form of modalism.

453. Congdon, *God Who Saves*, 97–98.

A number of things come into focus in this passage. The poor and the marginalized, for Congdon, are closely—though often unconsciously related to God. The wealthy and the privileged must align themselves with the poor in order to share in the poor's spiritually advantaged though materially diminished state. Congdon's theology opens the door to experiences of "unconscious faith" occurring at one's birth as well as at one's death. Aesthetic as well as moral experiences count as participation in Christ. Finally, in truly sweeping terms, Congdon states that "we can be confident, based on the logic of the kerygma, that every person has been or will be an unconscious Christian."

Participation in Christ happens by means of what Congdon calls *"the nonidentical repetition of Christ's death in God-abandonment."*[454] The Holy Spirit functions as the agent of this repetition. On first glance it seems that Congdon's theology simply repeats the Pauline emphasis on cocrucifixion with Christ (Rom. 6:6; Gal. 2:20). Yet Congdon clearly rejects the idea of Christ as a corporate personality representing humanity, which is arguably the position implied in the Pauline texts and in the early church, as well as in Barth. So what significance does Christ's death have for humanity? The term "cocrucifixion" means something more literal for Congdon than is generally the case. It does not mean that individual human beings, by believing in Christ, share in the benefits of his death. It means instead that one has to be crucified too—to undergo some experience of one's own that is comparable to the experience of the cross. One must undergo a personal kenosis, replicating in one's own life what happened in Christ's life. The underlying argument is not a *logic of participation* (despite Congdon's use of that term) but rather a *logic of repetition* (as suggested in the references to Giorgio Agamben and Gilles Deleuze). Congdon's Christ is in no way a representative of humanity but is an exemplar for humanity, and each individual human must suffer as he suffered, in a fashion that Oswald Bayer has aptly termed a "natural theology of the cross."

There is another line of reasoning in *The God Who Saves*—what we might call the apocalyptical-eschatological argument. In short, "the saving event is an existential apocalypse."[455] Congdon attributes to Barth's doctrine of universal election a "protological universalism" and then distinguishes this from his own position, which he calls a "universalism effected by God, but effected *eschatologically*."[456] He believes that his own position "giv[es] greater attention to the subjective or personal dimension as playing some kind of role."[457] Yet his

454. Ibid., 144, emphasis in the original. The key discussion of the theme of repetition is in 143–46, referencing Søren Kierkegaard and Giorgio Agamben.
455. Ibid., 138.
456. Ibid., 11.
457. Ibid., 12.

argument is muddled at this point because Congdon's eschatological universalism is, as he says, "effected by God," just as is any protological universalism (e.g., the universal-election doctrine of Barth). It is not clear what is accomplished if one identifies God's effective action toward humanity as occurring eschatologically rather than protologically. One ends up in either case with the classic theological dilemma of explaining how God's gracious initiative is related to the human response to God, or vice versa.

Congdon understands God's apocalyptic presence in the world as an "inbreaking," "interruption," or "disruption."[458] These are all positive rather than negative terms. God's act both dissolves and reconstitutes the world: "The God who acts is the eschatological God who annuls the world *within* the world and who establishes the new creation *within* the old creation."[459] Following Bultmann and the German liberal tradition generally, Congdon interprets the history of the early church as "the failed parousia," with no return of Christ, thus leaving Christ's followers to "translate the apocalyptic proclamation of Jesus into a sociopolitical message of shalom."[460] So faith itself must become the subjective, inwardized substitute for apocalypse: "The decision of faith is the eschatological event: what Paul still hopes for in the future is now already present to believers. Faith is the ultimate apocalypse."[461] In the New Testament, "both Paul and John . . . interpret the message of the gospel in a way that no longer depends upon a literal return of the Messiah."[462]

Congdon recognizes his own difference from Barth, who wrote of Christ's "future advent" in a way that was "highly minimalist," while he still insisted that it was "essential to the gospel." Yet Barth's "denial of a literal existence beyond death seems to suggest that we should deliteralize the future advent as well." Here Congdon quotes Barth to the effect that the final eschatological moment will be "the eternalizing of our ending life," "nothing further will follow this

---

458. In *The God Who Saves* there are many references to "interrupt" or "interruption"; see 83, 129, 145–47, 155, 185, 196, 210, 212, 234, 238. For "disrupt" or "disruption," see 38, 47, 76, 99, 141, 230, 245. Note the reference (230n16) to Laurie Zoloth's essay "Interrupting Your Life," on interruptive ethics. This stress on "interruption" might help to explain the statement that "*Christ is the divine anarchist*" (Congdon, *God Who Saves*, 187; emphasis in the original).

459. Congdon, *God Who Saves*, 26–27.

460. Ibid., 67n29. Congdon agrees with Ernst Käsemann's view that "this hope [in Jesus's return] proved to be a delusion" (68, citing *New Testament Questions*, 106). He adds that Käsemann shows that "justification is apocalyptic since it proclaims the truth 'that God is only "for us" when God shatters our illusions'" (*God Who Saves*, 70). Congdon revels in the paradox of the nonreturn of Christ that fulfills the promise of Christ's return: "The nonoccurrence of the parousia [i.e., return of Christ] is the fulfillment of the parousia itself, because the purpose of eschatological expectation is the *unsettling* of the believer" (127n85).

461. Congdon, *God Who Saves*, 71.

462. Ibid., 72.

happening," and there is "no continuing into an unending future." Barth himself rejects "pagan dreams of all kinds of good times after death."[463] There is an ironic twist in the epilogue to *The God Who Saves*, because here Congdon acknowledges that his universalism does not embrace the idea of continuing, conscious experience after death. Everyone is said to share the same experience in the present life (i.e., "cocrucifixion" with Christ) but not a common experience beyond this present life.[464] So one is forced to ask: Is Congdon's teaching a form of universalism, if the outcome is the extinction of conscious experience for all persons? Or is it a form of annihilationism?

Congdon summarizes his apocalyptic gospel by saying that "to be crucified with Christ is . . . to share in the cosmos-rupturing incursion that took place in the death of Jesus."[465] There is *apocalypse now*—an eschaton immanentized in each believer:

> The imminent advent of Christ . . . occurs in the existential apprehension of its embarrassing otherness, which is ultimately the otherness of God. . . . Salvation is not salvation from suffering, from oppression, from the final judgment, from eternal torment, from annihilation, from the devil, from mortality—from any of these traditional threats. It is a salvation *from ourselves*. . . . The apocalypse of salvation is, in a sense, *our death*—the death of the existentially secure world that we build around ourselves.[466]

> We cannot and need not sustain belief in a literal cosmic apocalypse in the chronological future. . . . The proper starting point is to see the apocalyptic event in Christ as simultaneously and paradoxically *both* a past occurrence in Jesus *and* a present encounter in the believer. . . . We must say that the apocalypse is *wholly* past, *wholly* present, and *wholly* future. . . . The apocalypse is necessarily existential and paradoxical. . . . We come to participate in the apocalypse through our cocrucifixion in faith.[467]

463. Ibid., 74n45, citing Barth *CD* III/2, 624–25 (translation revised by Congdon).
464. The epilogue (260–74) to *The God Who Saves* is devoted to the question of the afterlife. Congdon maintains that the Christian hope "is not a hope for a conscious existence beyond death." For every New Testament statement "about our creaturely future is a statement about Christ" (270). Congdon favorably quotes (on 273) Jungel's book, *Death*, 120: "Finite life will be *eternalized* as finite. But not through endless extension—there is no immortality of the soul—but rather through participation in God's own life. Our life is *hidden* in God's life. In this sense the briefest form of resurrection hope is the statement: 'God is my beyond.'" Congdon explains that resurrection means "the *eternalizing* of our lived history" and that "God remembers us for eternity" (*God Who Saves*, 273). See *DR*, 623n55, for a discussion of whether Schleiermacher held to personal immortality.
465. Congdon, *God Who Saves*, 82.
466. Ibid., 79–80.
467. Ibid., 85. Congdon's conception of time and eternity is hard to pin down, but might fit into the category of "intensified experience" (see *DR*, 1151–53).

The reference to "faith" at the end of this second quotation is surprising, since Congdon so strongly emphasizes the unconscious rather than the conscious aspects of someone's connection with Christ, and "unconscious faith," though occasionally mentioned, remains unexplained. In the end, Congdon is convinced that "every moment of existence—religious or nonreligious—is potentially the site where God's saving apocalypse invades one's existence."[468]

In one striking passage, Congdon offers his most concrete word picture of what final salvation might mean for the cosmos as a whole. He uses the image of a sun or star flaming outward, in a supernova event, as his model for the coming consummation:

> Creation reaches its end, its *telos*, in the cross, in the undoing of the cosmos. . . . The saving event ripples outwards from the cross deep into the invisible, unconscious underside of history, interrupting all creatures, human and nonhuman alike, in its eschatological wake until the sun, in the ultimate eccentricity, expands beyond itself and consumes the earth in the conflagration of its cosmic communion with the crucified one, offering itself as a final perishable testament to imperishable grace.[469]

Final salvation is tantamount to final destruction. Again, is this universal salvation or universal annihilation?

As an exercise in dialectical theology, *The God Who Saves* is an intriguing work, though its *Sitz im Leben* might be a German theological seminary in 1956 rather than the North American setting in 2016. Congdon's New Testament interpretation seems frozen in time, taking no account of the newer studies of the historical Jesus, of the Jewishness of Jesus and the Gospels, and of Second Temple Judaism as the indispensable context for understanding early Christianity. Congdon's neglect of contemporary biblical scholarship and his existentializing interpretation of the Bible render his work retrograde rather than avant-garde. This book is a time capsule. It embodies an old German tradition—especially associated with Bultmann—of interpreting the Bible without due regard to the geography, customs, society, and history of biblical times.[470]

As an exercise in universalist theology, *The God Who Saves* offers a rather weak argument. Congdon announces his commitment to universalism in the second sentence of the prologue.[471] Yet he fails to present any argument in

468. Ibid., 258.
469. Ibid., 239–40.
470. Bultmann made it his principle not to visit the sites of the Holy Land—in the words of Martin Hengel, "a bad old German tradition with dangerous results" (cited in Ostling, "Who Was Jesus?," 38, quoted in McClymond, *Familiar Stranger*, 159n26).
471. "In 2006 . . . I came to the realization that universal salvation was the only account of Christianity that I could find credible" (Congdon, *God Who Saves*, ix). It is to be expected that this

his book to justify his key assumption that every human being who has ever lived shares a common kenotic, ecstatic, or self-transcending experience that somehow links them to the experience of Christ. As if by fiat, Congdon makes an extraordinary, sweeping, and all-inclusive statement: "We can be confident, based on the logic of the kerygma, that every person has been or will be an unconscious Christian."[472] The critic asks: Why should the Christian gospel be applicable to everyone? And does it make any sense to speak of this applicability as unknowing or unconscious? There seems to be nothing in Scripture or in earlier Christian tradition to support such an idiosyncratic interpretation of the gospel. Beyond this, there is the further question as to why anyone ought to accept the gospel in the first place—an issue brushed aside with a dismissive remark on apologetics.[473] To claim that the Christian message applies to every human being without exception, one must offer some rational or evidential basis for such a claim. Congdon briefly mentions "the uniqueness of Jesus" but does not link this to the church's affirmation of Jesus's sole divinity, and so the significance of the statement remains unclear.[474]

Not least of the problems in *The God Who Saves* is the self-contradiction in its argumentation, which makes a universal claim regarding human cocrucifixion with Christ, while equally asserting that "we cannot speak in general and in the abstract about the particular histories of those who are included objectively

---

initial statement of Congdon's universalism is not explained in his prologue. Yet, after reading the entire book, one still does not know exactly why Congdon believes in universal salvation.

472. Ibid., 97–98.

473. Ibid., 50–51.

474. Ibid., 6. The deeper issue here is a lack of clarity on the question of theological authority. Congdon writes that "heterodoxy is intrinsic to Christian faith. It is an essential dimension of the freedom for which Christ has set us free" (58). He proposes "jettisoning the dichotomy between orthodoxy and heterodoxy by speaking instead of an *orthoheterodoxy*" (24; cf. 57). For Congdon, "the God revealed in Jesus Christ unsettles our assumptions about what is self-evident and disrupts our self-assured attempts to secure our existence" (38). While God is disruptive, the New Testament itself is involved in "protecting and perpetuating a purported orthodoxy," but Congdon does not see this as "some kind of Christian virtue" (55). Citing a number of New Testament passages, he writes that "what we see in these ancient Christian texts is a community deeply concerned about protecting its authority. Here we see a magisterium in the making" (55). "There is . . . something deeply perverse about the way the early Christian community quickly retreated into a fortress mentality" (57). "The norm is not a fixed set of propositional claims but rather an event irrupting into each new situation, calling for new modes of thinking and speaking about God" (57). Congdon says nothing regarding any *continuity* of belief or tradition. His continual stress on discontinuity suggests that for him there is no doctrinal norm properly speaking, though he occasionally speaks of the "gospel"—an undefined norm derived from Scripture but not identified with Scripture. Congdon embraces the idea of a theological plurality of contradictory voices and writes that Pentecost is "not the overturning of Babel . . . but rather the *consecration* of Babel" (57–58). The outcome of all this would seem to be a vacuum of theological authority that just as surely undermines Congdon's affirmation of universal salvation as it would any affirmation of particularist salvation.

in Christ."[475] But what is Congdon's argument if not a "general" or "abstract" claim about what must be the case in the experience of each individual human life? Congdon's rationale for universalism cannot be established unless one presses beyond the flux of individual experience and somehow asserts what is true in human experience-in-general. The effort at a demetaphysicalized and deontologized "universalism without universals" is ultimately a failure, because the argument for universalism requires that Congdon make generalizations about universal human experience that he himself says that no one can make.

The idea of Christ as a universal human representative seems on its face to be less problematic than the notion that all human beings share any specific experience that is common to all. Congdon may be showing that he is aware of this problem when he speaks of many kinds of experience—identifying with the poor, the experience of one's own death or birth, the enjoyment of beauty, experiencing sex, and so forth—as possible links to Christ in cocrucifixion. Yet the argument at this point becomes exceptionally vague. How is watching a beautiful sunset, seeing a baby born, or having sex tantamount to being "cocrucified" with Christ? On this basis, simply living and breathing as a human being would apparently be enough to connect one with Christ. One might as well reintroduce the rejected notion of the Son of God's "assumption" of "human nature" as a way to explain the universal connection between Jesus Christ and all other humans. In any case, it is clear that the idea of a universal experience of cocrucifixion proves untenable. An "unconscious experience" that everyone has, though few if any persons know that they are having, seems implausible. The conscious experiences that human beings generally have at some point in life (i.e., seeing something beautiful, serving a person in need, passing through birth or death, experiencing sex, etc.) are undoubtedly important but have only the most tenuous connection to Christ's crucifixion. Congdon's idea of "cocrucifixion" with Christ has here become so broad and diffuse as to lose its meaning.

9.14. Summary and Conclusions on Barth, Moltmann, and Post-1970s Theologies

The chapter began with a consideration of the last few decades of Barth scholarship. Han-Luen Kantzer Komline speaks of "a fissure opening up in Barth studies between two fundamentally incompatible ways of understanding Barth's own

---

475. Ibid., xv n. 4.

most basic theological commitments." She adds that the Molnar-McCormack interpretive debate "raises the question of whether the schizophrenia from which Barth studies suffers today may be a hereditary disease, lying latent like a recessive trait in some of his modern heirs, but somehow encoded into the very DNA of Barth's own thought."[476] My claim is that the problem *is* in the DNA of Barth's thought. To extend the genetic analogy, one might say that the problem began with a "mutation," which was Barth's introduction of the idea of universal election in *Church Dogmatics* II/2. This alteration brought a great deal of metaphysical mischief in its wake, as we see in the confused state of Barth studies today. This confusion is likely to persist, unless twenty-first-century theologians decide to undo Barth's mistake by returning to some notion of particular election.

Barth's "mutation" brought a cascade of changes in the doctrine of God, as the *God-who-is* (of the early Barth) shifted more and more in the direction of the *God-who-is-for-us* (per Moltmann, Jenson, and McCormack). Recent kenotic-relational onto-theologies (so termed by Kevin Vanhoozer) represent an even more dramatic departure from traditional notions of God's self-sufficiency, freedom, and independence.[477] Today we seem to be coming full circle after a century's passage. Karl Barth's *Epistle to the Romans* (1918) was a protest against the imprisonment of God in the categories of liberal Protestant culture and its human-centered assumptions. Today in the field of academic theology, there is danger of the same sort of imprisonment of God in terms of contemporary categories—whether ontological, anthropomorphic, or relational.

As Barth himself emphasized, his doctrine of universal election in *Church Dogmatics* II/2 was novel. He was breaking with centuries—and indeed with

476. Kantzer Komline, "Friendship and Being," 17, 17n22.

477. In response to Moltmann and other contemporary theologians, Kantzer Komline offers these comments on Barth's frequently expressed notion of God's self-sufficiency:

> Since, for Barth, divine freedom in its primary sense is not possession, but rather something closer to an abundant self-sufficiency defined with reference to God alone, Barth never risks locking divine freedom into the strictures of an inverse relationship with human freedom. . . . Divine and human freedom are not two instances of a general type such that they are realized in the same way or share the same characteristics, being differentiated from one another merely by virtue of the persons to whom they apply univocally. According to Barth, God's freedom is not only unique among all other kinds of freedom; it also refers to that which makes God uniquely God. Therefore the compatibility of divine and human freedom does not require that a mutually *free* relationship between divine and human persons is a *symmetrical* one. For Barth, God's identity as God renders the very idea of such a symmetrical relationship incoherent. Whereas Moltmann contends that Barth's notion of divine lordship as freedom undermines the possibility of human freedom in relationship to God, just the opposite turns out to be the case, given the way Barth develops this notion. For Barth, since human existence itself is a function of an assymetrical exercise of God's lordship, the very possibility of human freedom develops on this asymmetry. . . . [Yet] it is precisely the primary absoluteness of God's freedom which so grates upon Moltmann's theological sensibilities. ("Friendship and Being," 8–9)

millennia—of Christian teaching. In reference to the Hebrew Bible or Old Testament, it becomes clear that Barth was not only breaking with Christian tradition but also with Jewish or Judaic teaching as well, which consistently conceived of election in a particular fashion (i.e., pertaining to Abraham's descendants) rather than in a universalistic fashion. From whatever angle one regards it— exegetically, logically, or metaphysically—Barth's notion of universal election in *Church Dogmatics* II/2 is *weakly argued*, even though it is *relentlessly reasserted* through hundreds of pages of text. Some of Barth's assertions—for example, "Jesus Christ is the electing God"—are hard to understand. The debates among Barth scholars would not have gone on for so long if Barth himself had been clearer in his affirmations.

Critics over the last half century have insisted that Barth in effect subsumed redemption in its concrete, physical, and historical aspects within some notion of divine eternity. This is one of the most consistent criticisms of Barth, voiced by Christian thinkers as diverse as Emil Brunner, G. C. Berkouwer, Gustav Wingren, Robert Jenson, Alister McGrath, and Kathryn Tanner.[478] It is not the objection of one school or party of theologians but rather of a wide cross section of Christian thinkers. This basic claim makes sense when we connect it with Barth's doctrine of eternal Godmanhood, which diminishes the event character of Christ's incarnation and the historicity of Christ's person. Recent theologians stand accused of entangling God in the historical process.[479] In Barth the danger seems to lie in the opposite direction. The problem is not that of immanentizing God or the eschaton but that of eternalizing or transcendentalizing human life and history. If Moltmann represents the left-Hegelian temptation (i.e., of bringing God down to earth), then Barth represents the right-Hegelian problem (i.e., of losing earthly reality in the clouds of heaven). Salvation, on Barth's account, is in danger of turning into *gnosis*—the revelation to human gaze of what is always already the case.

478. Emil Brunner says that on Barth's premises "the Incarnation would no longer be an *Event*" (*Dogmatics*, 1:347). G. C. Berkouwer writes that Barth's theology does not allow conceptual space for the "stepwise" character of God's works, inasmuch as everything has been determined in eternity and history merely reveals what is already the case. For this reason, "the decisiveness of history can no longer be fully honored" (*Triumph of Grace*, 252, 255). Gustav Wingren says that Barth interprets salvation in purely epistemological terms, as a giving of knowledge regarding what already is (*Theology in Conflict*, 24–26). Robert Jenson writes that Barth "puts himself in danger of removing reconciliation itself, the inner reality of Jesus' life, from our history" (*Alpha and Omega*, 85–86, 162–63). So also A. E. McGrath, "Karl Barth als Aufklärer?"; Tanner, "Jesus Christ," esp. 264–68. All here cited in van Driel, *Incarnation Anyway*, 86–87, with n. 20.

479. Paul Molnar (*Divine Freedom*) upbraids any number of modern theologians who have replaced an immanent (or transcendent) Trinity of persons (Father, Son, Spirit) in favor of a purely economic Trinity, fully enmeshed in the human process.

On Barth's assertion of universal election, Stephen N. Williams writes: "The plain reason for disagreeing with him is that to speak of universal election in Christ is to speak of election in a way not only different from but contrary to the way Scripture speaks of it. . . . Election, however we interpret its detailed theological content, is always discriminate in Scripture. Israel or the church or particular individuals are elected." In Barth's treatment of election, one finds, in Williams's words, a "substitution of dogmatic language for biblical theological language [that] amounts to a material alteration of the content of Christian doctrine as it is grounded in Scripture." Along the same lines, Suzanne McDonald summarizes the "utterly withering" response to Barth by biblical scholar James Dunn, who argues that "for Paul there can be absolutely no suggestion of 'all men and women as willy-nilly "in Christ" whether they want to be or not, whether they know or not.'"[480]

To understand Barth's reasoning on the universality of election, one might view *Church Dogmatics* II/2 as focused not so much on *election* as on *union* (i.e., the union of all human individuals with Christ), and this in turn as grounded on an idea of eternal Godmanhood. Perhaps Barth ought to be seen as a Christian Platonist of sorts, who thought of Christ as a form or essence of humanness rather than as a concretely existing human individual.[481] Read in this way, Barth's teaching in *Church Dogmatics* II/2 was at least partially anticipated in the Christ-centered universalism of James Relly (*DR* 6.4), expressed in Relly's major work, *Union; or, A Treatise of Consanguinity and Affinity between Christ and His Church* (1759). Relly did not frame his Christian universalism in terms of an election doctrine, but his reasoning was based on a bedrock conviction—also evident in Barth—of an unbreakable connection between Christ and every human individual. Yet it is just this presumption of Barth and Relly that biblical scholars such as James Dunn say is alien to the Pauline Letters. Little thinkers make little mistakes; great thinkers make great mistakes. Barth's doctrine of

---

480. S. N. Williams, *Election of Grace*, 187, 201, 190–91, citing (on pp. 190–91) McDonald, *Re-Imagining Election*, 68. Even apart from the exegetical issue in Barth, as Williams points out, the conclusion that "all are elect" does not follow theologically from Barth's own premises:

> Jesus Christ as the electing God and Jesus Christ as the elect man do not add up to universal election in Christ. They do not add up, either, to the belief that only the church is elect in Christ. If nothing else is factored in, they actually do not add up to anything with respect to election. If they do add up to anything, it can only be when the limitation which election biblically involves is factored into the sum *from the beginning* in a way that Barth does not. (*Election of Grace*, 201)

481. In Barth, *CD* IV/2, 59, we find the following: "The human nature elected by Him and assumed into unity with His existence is implicitly that of all men. In His being as man God has implicitly assumed the human being of all men. In Him not only we all as *homines*, but our *humanitas* as such—for it is both His and ours—exist in and with God Himself." Might we not see this *humanitas*—"in and with God Himself"—as a Platonic "universal"? See Woozley, "Universals."

universal election is the great mistake of a great thinker. That, at least, might be the conclusion for anyone who has closely examined the biblical and exegetical foundations of Barth's doctrine of universal election. Election in Scripture is particular.

Barth's exegesis of the Old and New Testaments erred by excluding the notion of Israel's partial faithfulness to God under the old covenant. It also blurred the boundaries between God's people and other peoples in the biblical era.[482] In his exegesis of the New Testament, Barth defined the nature, character, and scope of election largely on the basis of a single verse (Eph. 1:4—God "chose us in him," i.e., in Christ) and ignored elements in the Epistle to the Ephesians and other Pauline Letters that point in the direction of particularism rather than universalism. For example, Ephesians 1:13–14 connects salvation with the hearing of God's Word, the human response of faith, and the Holy Spirit's "sealing" of the believer. Barth did not address the numerous New Testament passages (e.g., Matt. 13; John 6) where predestinarian language and ideas emerge as a way of explaining human unbelief and stubbornness, in what was earlier termed the "bottom-up" motif in the New Testament discussion of election. Barth's approach to election was strictly "top-down" and never sought to accommodate this "bottom-up" aspect that appears in Scripture.

Barth showed a tendency toward *illusionism*—that is, regarding sin and evil as unreal or as an "ontological impossibility" (*DR* 12.5)—and, correlatively, toward considering salvation as divine self-manifestation. As God reveals himself, evil vanishes, showing itself to be the illusion that it always was. God's victory over evil is not then a struggle or battle in the full sense but simply a triumph of reality over appearance. Barth's account of "nothingness" (*das Nichtige*) has some affinities with Christian universalist traditions that we examined in earlier chapters. It aligns with the *mē-ontic* "nothing" tradition in such thinkers as Böhme (*DR* 5.3), Schelling (*DR* 7.7), Tillich (*DR* 7.8), and Berdyaev (*DR* 8.5). Barth differs from the Böhmist thinkers generally in not locating *das Nichtige* within God's own being. Yet by identifying nothingness as "neither God nor . . . creature," Barth engendered an ontological conundrum, if not a metaphysical muddle. What sort of thing is it that is neither Creator nor created? In asserting that nothingness is uncreated, Barth assigned a measure of independence to nothingness, and so seems to have moved in the direction of dualism.

In his astute analysis, John Hick points out that Barth considered the only two logical possibilities that he had available and then rejected both of them. Either

---

482. Christopher Wright wryly comments, "Between election in the Hebrew Scriptures of Jesus and election in the formulations of theological systems there sometimes seems to be a great gulf fixed. Few and narrow are the bridges from one to the other" (*Mission of God*, 262).

evil happens by divine permission and is indirectly under God's control or else it happens apart from divine permission and so lies beyond God's control. In rejecting both possibilities, Barth obscured the philosophical choice involved in accounting for the relation between evil and God's will. Barth affirmed God as utterly omnipotent and yet also limited in not being able to prevent evil as a by-product of his own act of creating. While God did not have the power to stop evil from arising, God nonetheless has power to abolish it once it has appeared—and God will do so, or has done so, through Christ. The overall position regarding God's relation to evil thus remains unclear.[483] Barth never explains how or why it is that evil was necessarily involved in God's act of creating the world but is not an enduring hindrance in God's act of redeeming the world. Hick faults Barth for waxing metaphysical about *das Nichtige* while lambasting others for doing the same: "He is thus doing what he has criticized others for doing, namely, going beyond the data of faith and becoming entangled in the dangers of philosophical construction."[484]

In Barth's account of evil—and in contrast to traditional theology—evil does not enter into the world through human (or angelic) sin but in and through God's act of creating. It emerges apart from human choice, and it seems also to be overcome apart from human choice. God himself, says Barth, is the adversary of nothingness, and "the controversy with nothingness, its conquest, removal, and abolition, are primarily and properly God's own affair."[485] If we regard nothingness as a metaphysical principle, and consider that Jesus Christ overcomes nothingness, then we must ask, what does this imply about Christ? Does it not take a metaphysical principle to overcome a metaphysical principle? To say that someone is opposed to nothingness is a very abstract statement—like saying that someone is opposed to entropy. By setting Christ over and against nothingness, Barth runs the risk of making Christ more of a metaphysical principle than a person. There is yet another question to ask regarding *das Nichtige*: Does nothingness or evil cease to exist because of its own inherent ontological deficiency? In that case, it would not be clear why God would have needed to act at all. God might have "waited out" evil and allowed it to collapse of its own accord. Such an approach to evil is suggested in the logic of Gregory of Nyssa (*DR* 3.9). If, to the contrary, evil is *overcome only* through God's decisive intervention, then it seems that evil is not as weak, powerless, or nondangerous

483. Hick, *Evil and the God of Love*, 143–44, 139.
484. Ibid., 136. It is true that Barth interprets *das Nichtige* in light of the biblical phrase *tohu wabohu* (waste and emptiness) in Gen. 1:2. (See Barth, *CD* III/1, 108, 123–24; *CD* III/3, 352–54.) Yet, exegetically, this is a slender thread on which to hang the doctrine of nothingness as Barth has developed it.
485. Barth, *CD* III/3, 354.

as Barth sometimes says it is. Ultimately it remains unclear whether evil must
be defeated by God's action or whether it will fail of itself.

We turn back now to the initial question regarding universalism. Does
the main line of argumentation in Barth's theology *imply* universalism, even
though Barth may not *assert* universalism as such? The answer is yes. While
Barth hedges and affirms some measure of eschatological uncertainty, there
is a problem in so doing. The problem is that Barth plainly asserts that God's
rejection was entirely accomplished or effected at the cross of Christ, when
Christ was displayed as the Rejected One. What rejection then remains? Will
God change his mind, or undo the past, or repudiate the vicarious suffering
that Christ endured for all human beings? Would God be exercising sovereign
freedom if he ignored what Christ had already accomplished? Or would we not
say that God was fickle and inconsistent with himself—that the gracious God
was proving to be ungracious? Barth writes, "Where God has said No, He has
done so and need do so no more; but where he no longer does so[,] that which
he negates no longer exists."[486] If God's "No" is truly final, as Barth says it is,
then the divine rejection of human sin and guilt that occurred at the cross has
dealt forever and dealt decisively with the question of rejection. No rejection,
no damnation, no hell remains as a threat. Emil Brunner, Barth's early interpreter and interlocutor, grasped the nub of the issue better than many of the
later interpreters.[487]

Barth's biographer Eberhard Busch tells of an incident during Barth's last
two or three years of life, while Busch was serving as Barth's assistant. One day
Busch found Barth "very nervous," saying, "I had a very awful dream." Busch
asked, "What have you dreamt?" He said, "I was dreaming that a voice asked
me, 'Would you like to see hell?' And I said, 'Oh, I am very interested to see it
once.'" Busch continues:

> Then a window was opened and he saw an immense desert. It was very cold,
> not hot. In this desert there was only one person sitting, very alone. Barth was
> depressed to see the loneliness. Then the window was closed and the voice said to
> him, "And that threatens you." So Barth was very depressed by this dream. Then
> he said to me, "There are people who say I have forgotten this region. I have

---

486. Barth, *CD* III/3, 362.

487. Jason Goroncy, in "That God May Have Mercy upon All," argues that "Barth's appeal to
God's freedom is . . . inconsistent with Barth's own position regarding God's self-determination to
be Immanuel in Jesus Christ. . . . How can that which has already been overcome in Jesus Christ
[i.e., sin, guilt, condemnation] ever be undone?" (124). Following Matthias Göckel, Goroncy argues
that Schleiermacher may be more consistent than Barth in maintaining the unitary character of
God's decree to bring salvation. For "it cannot be presumed that God in his total freedom will act
other than he has acted in Jesus Christ—full of grace and truth" (127).

not forgotten. I know about it more than others do. But because I know of this, I must speak about Christ. I cannot speak enough about the gospel of Christ."[488]

This episode may help us to understand Barth's ambivalence. He sought always to highlight Christ and the redemption Christ achieved and refused—from as early as 1916—to preach on the theme of hell. Yet he insisted that he had "not forgotten" the sobering truths of divine judgment and of separation from God. He had "not forgotten" the threat to fellowship with God, yet he would not speak or preach of what he had "not forgotten," but would speak only of Christ. It was in the end a deeply dialectical and perhaps an existentially precarious position to take.

To speak in generalities, Barth shifted from an earlier view of a *God-who-is* toward a *God-who-is-for-us*, inaugurated in *Church Dogmatics* II/2 with its affirmation of universal election. Moltmann's theology might be seen as a further movement in this same general direction. Christ's solidarity with those who suffer, for Moltmann, implies not only a *God-who-is-for-us* but also a *God-who-is-for-us-in-suffering* or, one might even say, a *God-who-is-for-us-by-suffering-with-us*. Beginning in the 1960s with an emphasis on eschatological hope, Moltmann in subsequent years developed a complex theology that showed the influence of G. W. F. Hegel (*DR* 7.4–7.6), Ernst Bloch, Karl Barth, the Blumhardts (*DR* 5.8), and Jewish Kabbalah. Our analysis above identified three strands in Moltmann's thinking, corresponding to what Moltmann himself called "christological," "integrative," and "processive," and which we referred to as christological-crucicentric, kabbalistic-cosmological, and trinitarian-processive. Each of the three involves a slightly different yet convergent argument for universalism. The first strand implies that all divine judgment was exhausted in Christ's death. The second suggests that God initially withdrew to create the world (Hebrew *tsimtsum*) but will again expand to fill and to fulfill all things. The third involves a gradual unfolding and emergence of divine life within the world.

Moltmann's opponents—along with some of his defenders—have raised questions about his universalistic theology. He says almost nothing about the biblical themes of sin, repentance, forgiveness, or faith, and his general approach to the Bible seems imprecise and ad hoc. He does not address the motives for believers to live righteously or offer much of a doctrine of sanctification. Critics have charged that Moltmann confuses God's being with that of the world and entangles the former in the latter. The kabbalistic strand, and God's identification with suffering and sufferers, suggests that Moltmann's God cannot escape suffering, but is himself trapped by it and so does not possess freedom

---

488. Busch, "Memories of Karl Barth," 13–14. Cf. Bartholomaeus, "Barth on Hell."

in a true or full sense. In light of the internal tensions and conflicts within Moltmann's God, it might seem that God himself is in need of redemption. Because of a kind of creeping Hegelianism in Moltmann, the historical Jesus seems to be eclipsed by notions of the eschatological Spirit and/or universal spiritual presence. Due perhaps to kabbalistic influence, one reads in Moltmann more about the coming of God than the coming of Christ. Moltmann appears to have a problem with finitude, and it would seem that God's final expansion in the eschaton is more of a threat to finite reality than a promise of its fulfillment. One wonders whether created realities ultimately pass away, as they are displaced by total divine presence—the very problem that plagues Hegel's eschatology too (*DR* 7.6).

Just as Moltmann's theology built on and developed certain themes in Barth, so contemporary kenotic-relational theologians have extended and expanded on themes from Moltmann, including especially the cosmological focus of such writings as his *God in Creation*. Indirectly indebted to Schelling (*DR* 7.7) more than to Hegel (*DR* 7.4–7.6), kenotic-relational thinkers view the creation of the world not as an expression of divine power but rather as a kenotic action of divine self-limiting. In creating, God reduced himself so as to become cor-relative, coextensive, and codeterminate with the world. Once the world comes into being, God—if initially all-powerful—is now no longer so. Because of the inherent ontological bond between God and the world, no creatures could ever truly be separated from God, and so universal salvation seems to be built into the metaphysical premises of kenotic-relational theology.

David Congdon's *The God Who Saves* seeks to mediate Karl Barth's universal-election doctrine and hope for the salvation of all with Rudolf Bultmann's existentialist reading of the New Testament. Generally speaking, Congdon re-interprets Barth's theology in a Bultmannian direction by identifying God's re-demptive work in Christ with the human action of identifying with Christ. In "de-metaphysicizing," "de-ideologizing," "de-theorizing," and "de-constantinizing" the Christian message, Congdon negates all notions of a human or divine nature or essence and rejects the immanent Trinity and Chalcedonian Christology, while seeking a "universalism without universals" that lies beyond "the myth of the incarnate Son of God."[489] Following Bultmann's lead, Congdon's account of the Christian kerygma or message is noncognitivist. There is no intellectual content to be rationally understood or to be accepted in faith. Instead, salvation comes through what Congdon calls "unconscious cocrucifixion with Christ." This personal event is ecstatic, existential, and eschatological. Unconscious identification with the "cosmos-rupturing incursion" of Christ's death may come

---

489. Congdon, *God Who Saves*, 260, 124.

about in various ways—through serving someone in need, through viewing a beautiful object, or in the act of sexual intercourse.

Having rejected trinitarian and christological doctrines, Congdon offers no objective ground for asserting universal salvation or for linking individuals to Christ as their Savior. There seems to be no empirical basis for claiming a universal, salvific experience involving all human beings without exception. Congdon has so broadly defined his terms as to include just about any experience as a form of "cocrucifixion with Christ." Beyond this, there may be a contradiction in the very notion of an unconscious experience. If cocrucifixion is an experience, then does the individual not have to be conscious of it? Or, if it is unconscious, then how can it be regarded as an experience? Furthermore, if cocrucifixion is not an experience and is not a metaphysical reality subsisting outside of individual awareness, then what exactly is it? As an argument for universal salvation, Congdon's *The God Who Saves* would seem to be one of the weakest of any that are treated in this work.

10

Embracing Universal Hope

KARL RAHNER, HANS URS VON BALTHASAR, AND THE INCLUSIVIST, PLUROCENTRIST, AND UNIVERSALIST TURNS IN ROMAN CATHOLICISM

L'esprit est donc désir de Dieu.

—Henri de Lubac[1]

I was tremendously and lastingly attracted by Barth's doctrine of election, that brilliant overcoming of Calvin. It converged with Origen's views and therefore with Adrienne [von Speyr]'s Holy Saturday theology as well.

—Hans Urs von Balthasar[2]

There is a modern tendency . . . to develop a theology of the death of God that . . . seems to me to be gnostic. One can find this in Hans Urs von Balthasar and in Adrienne von Speyr. . . . It also appears in an independent form in Moltmann. To put it crudely, it does not

1. De Lubac, *Surnaturel*, 483 ("Spirit is thus desire for God").
2. Balthasar, *Our Task*, 101.

help me to escape from my mess and mix-up and despair if God is in the same predicament.

—Karl Rahner[3]

Those also can attain to salvation who through no fault of their own do not know the Gospel of Christ or His Church, yet sincerely seek God and moved by grace strive by their deeds to do His will as it is known to them through the dictates of conscience. Nor does Divine Providence deny the helps necessary for salvation to those who, without blame on their part, have not yet arrived at an explicit knowledge of God and with His grace strive to live a good life. Whatever good or truth is found amongst them is looked upon by the Church as a preparation for the Gospel.

—Lumen Gentium[4]

For, since Christ died for all men, and since the ultimate vocation of man is in fact one, and divine, we ought to believe that the Holy Spirit in a manner known only to God offers to every man the possibility of being associated with this paschal mystery.

—Gaudium et Spes[5]

No one can be condemned for ever, because that is not the logic of the Gospel!

—Pope Francis[6]

The catholic tradition—from its postapostolic era, during the Origenist controversies, and guided by such thinkers as Augustine, Anselm, Bonaventure, Aquinas, Bellarmine, and Newman—was consistent through the centuries in teaching a final twofold state of heaven and hell (DR 1.2). The emergence of purgatory as an official Catholic teaching in the High Middle Ages and subsequently did not change this teaching, because purgatory was always understood as a temporary rather than a permanent condition. The eternal state was twofold rather than threefold. Dozens of official Catholic statements either directly proclaimed or else presupposed this final duality, and the

3. Rahner, Karl Rahner in Dialogue, 126.
4. Second Vatican Council, Lumen Gentium, no. 16.
5. Second Vatican Council, Gaudium et Spes, no. 22.
6. Pope Francis, Amoris Laetitia, no. 297. On this text, see DR prologue.

teaching was reaffirmed in the *Catechism of the Catholic Church* (1994) (*DR* 1.2; 1.9). For centuries "universalism" was regarded as a heresy and as a denial of official Catholic teaching. Avery Dulles went even further, speaking of "a virtual consensus among the Fathers of the Church and the Catholic theologians of later ages to the effect that the majority of humankind [would] go to eternal punishment in hell." Yet Dulles noted that "about the middle of the twentieth century, there seems to be a break in the tradition. Since then a number of influential theologians have favored the view that all human beings may or do eventually attain salvation."[7] This chapter explores this recent transition in Catholic thinking about human destiny and those who played a key role in the transition, such as Karl Rahner and Hans Urs von Balthasar.

In the twenty-first-century Roman Catholic Church, among bishops, priests, the consecrated religious, and the lay faithful, there is widespread belief in universal salvation or something closely approaching it—namely, the notion that it is only a small number of exceptionally wicked persons who might conceivably be candidates for damnation (e.g., Hitler and Stalin), while the vast majority of humanity is on its way to an eternity in heaven with God. Richard P. McBrien states that "one of the most important developments in contemporary Catholic theology" is "the shift away from an Augustinian pessimism about salvation to a more hopeful, universalistic outlook." He explains that "the human race is no longer seen as a *massa damnata* [condemned mass] from whom a few are saved to manifest the glory and mercy of God, but as an essentially saved community from whom a few may by the exercise of their own free will, be lost."[8]

The change in Catholic thinking came suddenly. Among Catholic intellectuals during the 1930s through the 1950s—and then in ever-widening circles of Catholics from the 1960s onward—the new ideas on eschatology have spread throughout the church. Many of today's Catholics, according to one Catholic critic, turn on its head Jesus's saying "The gate is wide and the way is broad that leads to destruction, and there are many who enter through it. For the gate is small and the way is narrow that leads to life, and there are few who find it" (Matt. 7:13–14 NASB). Ralph Martin writes that "the words of the gospel have become reversed—and the many headed towards destruction have now become the few, and the few headed to salvation have now become the many."[9] Damnation has become hard to achieve. The ancient Catholic idea of *extra ecclesiam nulla salus est* (outside of the church there is no salvation) has

7. Dulles, "Population of Hell."

8. McBrien, "Church (*Lumen Gentium*)," 90, cited in R. Martin, *Will Many Be Saved?*, 54.

9. R. Martin, *Will Many Be Saved?*, 126. Martin here paraphrases John Henry Newman's sermon "Many Called, Few Chosen": "We do not know what is meant by 'few.' But still the few can never

given way to a position that regards salvation inside the church as an *extraordinary* means of salvation, while salvation outside the church is an *ordinary* means.[10] Proposing that God will give multiple opportunities to each person to embrace the offer of grace—during life, in the hour of death, perhaps after death, perhaps while in purgatory, and perhaps even in hell—some Catholic theologians go further and state that it is not conceivable that anyone can or will finally "say no" to God and so suffer final separation from God.[11] Jesuit author John Sachs in 1991 went so far as to claim that there had been a reversal of the traditional consensus view regarding eschatology: "We have seen that there is a clear consensus among Catholic theologians today in their treatment of the notion of *apocatastasis* and the problem of hell. . . . It may not be said that even one person is already or will in fact be damned. . . . I have tried to show that the presumption that human freedom entails a capacity to reject God definitively and eternally seems questionable."[12]

With more than a billion baptized faithful around the globe today, there is no uniformity among Catholics on questions of final salvation and the afterlife. A spectrum exists. The most stringent views—associated historically with church fathers such as Augustine and Chrysostom, with Thomas Aquinas, and with such moderns as Robert Bellarmine and John Henry Newman—is that there are two final destinations for all human beings (heaven and hell) and that there is good reason to think (from Scripture and from human reason) that the majority of all humans who have ever lived will end up in hell. Purgatory softens this picture by offering a measure of hope for those who died in the Catholic faith but in a condition of venial sin.

A somewhat softer view holds that there are two final destinations and that there will certainly be some who go into the fires of hell (e.g., Judas and Satan) but that we have no idea of the ratio or proportion in the ultimate outcome. A still more open-ended view holds that salvation is *possible* among those who have never heard of Christ or been incorporated into the church through baptism.

---

mean the many" (*Parochial and Plain Sermons*, 1118). Edward Oakes reviews Ralph Martin's book in the essay "Saved from What? On Preaching Hell in the New Evangelization."

10. Theisen, *Ultimate Church and the Promise of Salvation*, 57, cited in R. Martin, *Will Many Be Saved?*, 225–26n15. On salvation outside the church, see Louis Capéran's exhaustive two-volume work, *Le problème de salut des infidèles* (1934); Sullivan, *Salvation outside the Church?*

11. Thomas K. O'Meara writes: "Can a negative decision last into the next life? Can an elected orientation take on an eternal duration? God has created us to share his life, he loves us, and Christ died for us—those realities permeate existence. To say 'no' to them—although possible—is much more difficult than to say 'yes' with one's entire being. . . . One might hope that hell is empty" (*God in the World*, 130). One is reminded of Karl Barth's idea of sin as an "impossible possibility" (*DR* 9.7) and Thomas Talbott's view that no one who truly encounters God will ever reject God (*DR* 11.3).

12. Sachs, "Current Eschatology," 252–53.

Such assertions of *possibility* were not—up to fairly recently—taken as assertions of the *actuality* of salvation for most non-Christians or non-Catholics. Yet since the 1970s the church's teaching on the possibility of salvation for some outside the church has sometimes been taken to imply the actuality of their salvation, and perhaps even as a sanction for the *presumption* that the majority of human beings, if not all, will attain final salvation. The tendency has been toward an ever more open-ended and all-inclusive viewpoint. For those who think that the Catholic Church never changes, here is a change on one of the most momentous points of Christian theology and teaching.[13]

Some contemporary Catholics argue that the existence of hell is official Catholic teaching (*de fide*), but not the idea that anyone is in hell. Not even Judas, the "son of destruction" (John 17:12), is definitely lost, as Hans Urs von Balthasar has argued. The notion that all human beings without exception are finally saved seems plainly to contradict the Catholic Church's historic statements, and so Balthasar and others have suggested that universal salvation ought to be a matter of hope rather than a definite assertion. Balthasar went further by saying that there is properly an *obligation* or *duty* to hope universally for the final salvation of all—an idea discussed below and in the conclusion (*DR* 12.6).

On the one hand, certain passages in the Vatican II documents—especially *Lumen Gentium*, no. 16, and *Gaudium et Spes*, no. 22 (cited as chapter epigraphs)—support an inclusivist perspective on Christian salvation as extending beyond the visible Catholic Church and other Christian communities. On the other hand, one finds in the Vatican II documents no official endorsement of universalism as such. Ralph Martin, in *Will Many Be Saved? What Vatican II Actually Teaches and Its Implications for the New Evangelization* (2012), discusses the popular ideas on salvation that are now current in contemporary Catholicism and their impact on the practice of evangelism and mission. The widespread notion that "everybody is okay" has meant in practice that few Catholics feel a need to engage in verbal evangelism or to call on people to change their

---

13. Per the earlier discussion of annihilationism/conditionalism among British evangelicals (*DR* 1.10), Catholic theologians have historically rejected this view as incompatible with the Catholic faith. Yet this attitude might be changing. Paul Griffiths's *Decreation: The Last Things of All Creatures* (2014) asks whether annihilation is "at least possibly consistent with [Catholic] orthodoxy" (241), on the basis of the Augustinian notion that sinful human beings not only desire sin itself but also the metaphysical fruit of sin, which is the nothingness of death. "The sinner wants to move away from the Lord and toward himself," which implies a "diminution toward nonexistence" (199). De La Noval, in "Fork in the (Final) Road," contrasts Griffiths's eschatology with that of David Bentley Hart. The Catholic thinker Harvey Egan ("Hell," 60), by contrast, maintains that "the annihilation theory . . . cannot be maintained for a number of reasons," since "it overlooks the fact that God alone can annihilate." God could annihilate, but God will not, and Egan thus rejects the notion of self-annihilation.

way of life and to become practicing Catholics. Catholic missiologist Robert J. Schreiter wrote of the perplexity that emerged in the wake of Vatican II. On the one hand, "the Council documents continue to speak of the necessity of the church and membership in the church as the visible side of the fullness of salvation." Yet, on the other hand, the same documents "opened up the question of just how necessary the church was—really—to salvation. Might not conversion to a better life along the lines one's life had already taken be a better task for the missionary rather than insisting upon formal membership in the church?"[14]

Ralph Martin points out that the newer thinking on salvation has affected Catholic views on the parish level. Recent statistics on US Catholics reveal indifference regarding evangelism. In a 2005 survey, when asked whether spreading their faith was a priority in their parishes, 75 percent of conservative Protestant congregations and 57 percent of African American congregations responded affirmatively, whereas only 6 percent of Catholic parishes did the same—which, statistically speaking, marks an order-of-magnitude difference between Catholics and the two other groups. When asked whether they sponsored local evangelistic activities, 39 percent of conservative Protestant and 16 percent of African American congregations responded positively, compared with only 3 percent of Catholic parishes. Sociologist Nancy Ammerman writes, "Converts to Catholicism often report that on their spiritual journey they received little or no encouragement from Catholic clergy whom they consulted. . . . The [Second Vatican] Council has often been interpreted as if it had discouraged evangelization."[15]

After Vatican II, many Catholics and non-Catholics alike viewed the Catholic Church no longer to be preaching a message of otherworldly salvation (i.e., heaven or hell) but of this-worldly enhancement (i.e., "full" versus "partial" experience). In the post–Vatican II milieu, many persons in the Catholic Church believe that they can follow either the Christ-plus-church path or else the spiritual-person-without-church way, and that both paths are acceptable according to official Catholic teaching. In contrast to the spiritual-person-without-church way, the Christ-plus-church path dictates that one does not sleep in on Sunday mornings but instead goes to Mass, supports the church financially, raises one's children in the faith, prays with some regularity, and so on. The latter is thus likely to be a more challenging way of life—even for someone who remains a fairly nominal, though churchgoing, Catholic.

14. Schreiter, "Changes," 114, 118–19, cited in R. Martin, *Will Many Be Saved?*, 228n21.
15. Ammerman, *Pillars of Faith*, 117, 134, cited in R. Martin, "Pastoral Strategy of Vatican II," 142n11.

10.1. Henri de Lubac and Catholic Debates on Nature and Grace

These changes in Catholic thinking on salvation have roots that preceded Vatican II. Especially important were the debates over nature and grace during the 1940s and 1950s in connection with the *nouvelle théologie* (new theology) of this period. In the late nineteenth century, Pope Leo XIII's encyclical *Aeterni Patris* (1879) assigned a central role to Thomas Aquinas in the curricula of Catholic seminaries that trained men for the priesthood. Throughout the eighteenth and the early nineteenth centuries, theological instruction was typically conducted with reference to manuals of theology that set students at arm's length from the primary texts that earlier theologians had written. The first wave of a return to the sources of theology—Scripture, the church fathers, and scholastic authors—took place through a return to the medieval scholastics and especially to St. Thomas. New views began to emerge as thinkers began to see many points of agreement or disagreement between Thomas and later Thomists. Yet this was only the beginning. A deeper and ultimately more far-reaching set of theological changes came as Catholic thinkers began to rediscover the earlier sources of Christian theology—writings whose style and ethos were markedly different from those of medieval and early modern authors. The rereading of the Greek fathers in particular allowed a rising generation of Catholic thinkers during the 1930s and 1940s to approach theological questions in a decidedly nonscholastic way.

Nouvelle théologie and the related word *ressourcement* are general terms for the "new theology" that, paradoxically, took its point of origin from the ancient writings of the church fathers.[16] As sometimes happens in human affairs, the old thing became the new thing. It was the rediscovery of the church fathers that brought a generation of mid-twentieth-century Catholic thinkers to break from neo-scholasticism and to move in some decidedly new directions.[17] Among the thinkers associated with *nouvelle théologie* were Marie-Dominique Chenu (1895–1990), Henri de Lubac (1896–1991), Yves Congar (1904–95), Jean Daniélou (1905–74), and Hans Urs von Balthasar (1905–88). Among them all, it was

16. *Ressourcement* refers to returning to the authentic and authoritative sources of the Christian faith for the purpose of rediscovering their truth and meaning for the present time. It seeks to revitalize the church and to enable the church to meet the critical challenges of the present time.

17. See Boersma, *Nouvelle Théologie and Sacramental Ontology*; Mettepenningen, *Nouvelle Théologie / New Theology*; Flynn and Murray, *Ressourcement*. The name *nouvelle théologie* was originally a pejorative term coined by the Neo-Thomist critique of the emerging movement (Garrigou-Lagrange, "La nouvelle théologie où va-t-elle?"). Yet the label stuck, and over time it was increasingly accepted as a moniker without any negative associations. For an account of the debate from the perspective of Reginald Garrigou-Lagrange, see Peddicord, *Sacred Monster of Thomism*.

arguably Congar whose contributions on ecumenism, ecclesiology, and the role of the laity proved most decisive for the reformulated conception of the church in the Vatican II documents. As far as the question of salvation and its scope is concerned, however, it was de Lubac's rethinking of the doctrine of grace that served as a starting point for much of Rahner's and Balthasar's later reflections.

Catholic manuals of theology in the period before and during the neo-scholastic revival had sharply distinguished "nature" from "grace." The former was understood as a realm of human capacities and possibilities rooted in humanity's creation by God. The latter was set in contrast to the former as a realm of human capacities and possibilities that came about by God's special gift and divine presence. According to one traditional Catholic view, all human beings had by nature (or by creation itself) the power to love. Yet humans did not have by nature the power to love God above all else—a capacity that came only through supernatural grace. There was a tendency in early twentieth-century Catholic thought to divide all aspects of human nature and experience into the antithetical categories of "nature" and "grace," an approach that de Lubac and other critics labeled as "extrinsicism." One common analogy (used by critics of neo-scholasticism) was that of a two-story building. The first story was that of nature; the second was that of grace. The second story completed the first, and yet—since it was built on top of it—these two stories remained separate from one another.

De Lubac's reading of the Greek fathers led him toward a different understanding of human nature. Generally speaking, in the Christian East there was less emphasis than in the Latin and Augustinian West on sin's devastating effect on or corruption of human nature. De Lubac's influential work *Surnaturel* (1946) presented the nature-grace distinction as more of a continuum than a dichotomy.[18] He was concerned that modern Catholic thought had construed "grace" as something against nature or even as unnatural and therefore monstrous. De Lubac depicted the view he disavowed in this way: "The supernatural is certainly not the *abnormal* in the sense that a miracle is. . . . Nor is the supernatural something *adventitious*, something 'superadded' . . . yet it 'dignifies' man much more than these did; it raises him much higher still above the level of his own *essence*, since it is entirely out of proportion with that essence. Finally, the supernatural must not be defined solely by its character of *gratuitousness*."[19]

18. A number of de Lubac's other, related works have been translated into English: *Augustinianism and Modern Theology*, *A Brief Catechesis on Nature and Grace*, and *The Mystery of the Supernatural*.
19. De Lubac, *Surnaturel*, 428, quoted in de Lubac, *Brief Catechesis*, 26. Lawrence Feingold, in *The Natural Desire to See God according to St. Thomas Aquinas and His Interpreters*, summarizes the complex argument of *Surnaturel*:

De Lubac's fundamental concern is to remove an "extrinsicist" view of man's relation to his supernatural end, which he thinks is inherently linked with the theory of the possibility of a state of pure nature, as put forward by Suárez, and with the way the natural desire to see

For de Lubac, creation itself was grace-infused. Nature was understood as *created grace*, and redemption as *further grace*. What is more, the creature in a state of created grace was ordered to the reception of further grace, as de Lubac wrote: "L'esprit est donc désir de Dieu" (Spirit is thus desire for God).[20] One implication that might be drawn—and that some did draw—was that no human being was ever wholly outside of the realm of grace. Everyone had received grace. This new way of thinking had profound implications for Catholic ecclesiology and missiology, since the notion of being either "in a state of grace" or "not in a state of grace" shaped Catholic approaches to pastoral ministry. Another implication was an optimistic view of human responsiveness to God. If everyone by virtue of creation was already within a state of grace, and if this first grace pointed toward further grace, then one might expect a generally positive disposition among people on hearing the good news of God's grace in Christ. De Lubac's rethinking of nature and grace thus created the context for the more positive expectation of the human response to God and the scope of salvation that found expression in the Vatican II documents and in the theologies of Karl Rahner and Hans Urs von Balthasar. In recent years, de Lubac's teaching on nature and grace has itself become controversial. Some scholars have reaffirmed de Lubac's position, others have radicalized it in the direction of overt universalism, and still others have argued that de Lubac was inconsistent with himself.[21]

Thomas Aquinas's theology—a point of departure for de Lubac and most of his interpreters—conceived of human life in Aristotelian terms, defined by the "ends" toward which persons strive. For Aquinas, certain human ends lay beyond the scope of human nature. One such end was the heavenly and blessed vision of God, such as the saints in heaven enjoy. Two things might be said about this end: (1) the blessed vision is the fulfillment of human nature, and human nature is thus directed toward this "end," in some manner; and (2) the blessed vision is an end that lies beyond the power or capacity of human nature apart from grace. Aquinas wrote, "The end to which man is directed by

---

God was interpreted by authors such as Cajetan, Báñez, Suárez, and those who followed them. For de Lubac, the "essential finality" of man is the vision of God. This finality cannot be changed without changing our nature. Man as he is today has only one end that is in harmony with his nature as it now exists—the vision of God. This end, therefore, is "inscribed" or "imprinted" on man's nature as he concretely exists prior to any gift of grace. (297)

20. De Lubac, *Surnaturel*, 483 (my translation).

21. On de Lubac, see Hütter, "*Desiderium Naturale Visionis Dei.*" This intriguing yet complex essay is a five-way conversation, as Hütter interprets John Milbank's reading of de Lubac, who himself interprets Aquinas, while Hütter simultaneously expounds Lawrence Feingold's monograph on Aquinas and sees in it a response to both de Lubac and Milbank. In addition to works by de Lubac, Hütter cites Feingold, *Natural Desire*; Milbank, *Suspended Middle*.

the assistance of divine grace is above human nature. Therefore there needs to be added [*superaddatur*] to man a supernatural form and perfection, by which he may be fittingly ordered to that same end." The point was that grace must be "superadded" to human nature so that it could be ordered to an end that, as Aquinas says, is "above human nature."[22] Aquinas famously declared that "grace does not destroy nature, but perfects it,"[23] a saying that hints at the theological balance that he sought to achieve. On the one hand, grace was something not present in nature alone. On the other hand, grace was not alien to human nature. His teaching on the human acquisition of a *habitus* (i.e., disposition or tendency) through grace—a *habitus* that genuinely belongs to the person in question—shows that he did not think of grace as "extrinsic" in the way that some of his later followers may have done.

Henri de Lubac and Karl Rahner moved in somewhat different directions in their efforts at establishing a more intimate relationship between nature and grace. Rahner's position departed more substantially from that of Aquinas but was generally easier to grasp than that of de Lubac. Rahner recognized that human beings universally—in the Thomistic view—could not be ordered to eternal beatitude and salvation apart from what Aquinas called a "supernatural form," or what others call "the imprinting of supernatural finality" on human nature as such. So Rahner appealed to what he called the "supernatural existential," and some of Rahner's expositors have regarded it as the single most important principle in Rahner's theology (*DR* 10.2).[24] Rahner reasoned that a principle that intrinsically orders us toward a supernatural end must itself be a supernatural principle.[25] While Rahner's argument seems to be self-consistent, his position seems to implant grace within the creature, so that grace is not God's particular gift but belongs to human nature as such. This seeming effacement of the distinction between natural and supernatural prefigures the removal of distinctions between church and nonchurch, or between being in and not being in a state of grace. By redefining nature as grace-filled, Rahner's theology of salvation might be seen as Pelagian or Pelagianizing. His reasoning becomes difficult to follow when he argues that the supernatural existential, present in all persons, leads toward grace but is not itself grace. Human choice

22. Feingold, *Natural Desire*, 318n4, citing Aquinas, *Summa contra Gentiles* III, c. 150, n. 5 (trans. Feingold).

23. Aquinas, *ST* I, q. 1, a. 8.

24. Eamonn Conway emphasizes the importance of Rahner's "supernatural existential" and its pertinence to his famous notion of the "anonymous Christian": "The supernatural existential . . . is Rahner's most important theological concept, and it provides the basis for, and in Rahner's own opinion, has its most important expression in his theory of the anonymous Christian" (*Anonymous Christian*, 10).

25. Feingold, *Natural Desire*, 540n68.

is needed to actualize the supernatural existential so that a particular human being becomes an actual participant in divine grace.

De Lubac followed a different route, perhaps because he desired to remain closer than Rahner did to the main line of the Catholic and Thomistic tradition.[26] He insisted in effect that human nature in and of itself possesses finality toward grace and supernatural beatitude. Yet his reasoning seems contradictory. On the one hand, de Lubac repeats the teaching of Thomas Aquinas that human nature itself *is not ordered* to a supernatural end apart from divine grace. On the other hand, de Lubac argues that human nature itself *is ordered* to a supernatural end apart from divine grace. The two claims cannot both be true. To be logically consistent, de Lubac's position would require that one identify some element or aspect of the natural with the supernatural and vice versa. Yet the notion of a "supernatural nature" would be self-contradictory.[27] By seeking to imprint supernatural finality on created human nature, de Lubac waded into conceptual confusion. Pope Pius XII's encyclical *Humani Generis* (1950) did not specifically name de Lubac but seemed to take issue with de Lubac's recently published *Surnaturel* (1946) when it spoke against "others [who] destroy the gratuity of the supernatural order, since God, they say, cannot create intellectual beings without ordering and calling them to the beatific vision."[28] While John Milbank celebrates de Lubac, and Lawrence Feingold is more critical, they both agree that some of the concerns expressed in *Humani Generis* centered on de Lubac and that de Lubac's way of responding to the encyclical was not wholly satisfying. This is because de Lubac, despite his later caveats and qualifications, never really broke from his earlier insistence that the created human spirit is constituted by a single supernatural end—namely, an *innate natural desire* for the vision of God.[29]

In one of the latest debates on nature and grace, Reinhard Hütter responded to de Lubac as well as to Milbank's interpretation of de Lubac. Hütter rejects Milbank's notion that "the two gifts [i.e., creation and redemption] . . . are to be seen in a continuum, a seamless dynamic of varying intensity, reflecting a fundamental ontological élan drawing the entire cosmos through humanity to beatitude." According to Hütter, Milbank's *The Suspended Middle* (2005)—which

---

26. De Lubac did not wholly reject Rahner's account of nature and grace but wrote of Rahner's "somewhat contorted explanations" (*Brief Catechesis*, 35).

27. Feingold, *Natural Desire*, 523–29.

28. Pope Pius XII, *Humani Generis*, no. 26. Immediately after this reference to the possible destruction of the "gratuity" of grace, there is a reference to mistaken views of original sin. Taken in the larger context of the encyclical, it seems that the Magisterium (i.e., Catholic teaching office) was concerned that de Lubac's new reading of the relationship of nature and grace was part of a many-sided "naturalizing" or "immanentizing" of divine grace.

29. Hütter, "*Desiderium Naturale*," 125. For an intricate analysis of the natural desire to see God, see Rosenberg, *Givenness of Desire*.

Hütter calls a "Bulgakovian radicalization of de Lubac"—is alien to Aquinas and the larger Catholic tradition. This becomes especially clear when one considers Aquinas's teaching on predestination and the way that it "forestalls any attempt to claim his patronage for such a theological project."[30] Hütter concludes. "Where everything is grace all the way down in one and the same way, albeit of infinitely differing intensity, everything that has been brought into being, must have its end in God, by necessary ontological entailment. While undoubtedly a grandiose speculative vision, it, however, is neither the teaching of the Scriptures nor of the Church."[31]

10.2. Karl Rahner's "Anonymous Christians" and Post–Vatican II Theology

Many educated Catholics—including those without theological training—have heard of Karl Rahner's "anonymous Christians." Among laypersons, this is one of the most widely diffused theological notions since Vatican II. Together with Hans Urs von Balthasar's idea of a "hopeful universalism," Karl Rahner's teaching on the "anonymous Christian" has penetrated academic and popular Catholicism alike. Rahner's theology opened the door to an inclusivism that allowed for the salvation of non-Christians yet still required a human act of consent to God and grace that Rahner did not conceive of as necessarily universal. So Rahner is generally categorized as an "inclusivist" rather than "universalist." Balthasar's theology, by contrast, suggested that there is hope

---

30. Ibid., 110. In another passage, Hütter writes, "Aquinas's doctrine of the grace of predestination makes it impossible—despite the very prominent role of the ontological exitus-reditus [outflow and return] scheme in the overall architecture of his thought—to press his theology into the service of an overarching Origenist-Bulgakovian vision of universal *apokatastasis*" (117). Rejection of particular divine election is a common feature among Christian universalists of all times and places—Origenists, Böhmists, Cambridge Platonists, modern Western esotericists, etc. Eastern Orthodox thinkers have typically been highly critical of Augustine's theology of original sin, prevenient grace, and unconditional election. Among Origenists, the antipathy to Augustine runs deep. The bishop of Hippo is almost regarded as the "original sinner" of Christian theologians, the one who for a thousand or more years shackled the Western Church to an utterly pessimistic worldview that stressed sin more than grace. In the Reformation era, the more radical Protestants were happy to disavow Augustine, in part because of his views on church-state relations (the infamous phrase *compelle intrahoro,* "compel them to come in") as well as because of his theology of grace. Jakob Böhme wrote a whole treatise rejecting the Lutheran doctrine of God's unconditional election. Modern Catholics have treaded more carefully, inasmuch as Augustine and Aquinas are too central to historic Catholic teaching to be readily cast aside. Generally speaking, the strategy of twentieth-century Catholic thinkers has been to emphasize Origen and the early Greek fathers, while being cautiously critical of Augustine. In twentieth-century Protestantism, Karl Barth is unique in having attempted a comprehensive reinterpretation of election as universal in scope (*DR* 9.3–9.5), an approach that does not deemphasize election but rather emphasizes it in a nontraditional fashion.

31. Hütter, "*Desiderium Naturale*," 131.

for universal salvation, and Balthasar generally said less than Rahner did about human decision for or against God. So Balthasar is generally categorized as a "hopeful universalist" rather than as an "inclusivist."

Yet when one examines these two figures in a side-by-side comparison, they are not as different from one another as might at first appear. For his part, Rahner seems to move toward a near universalism in which all humanity is saved, with the exception of a few notoriously wicked and intractably unrepentant rebels. What is more, Rahner's writings occasionally comment on the possibility of and hope for universal salvation. Subsequent to Rahner, a number of leading Catholic theologians shifted from cautiously inclusivistic to more pluralistic or universalistic ideas regarding truth and salvation in world religions.[32]

Rahner's writing style is often difficult and obscure, so a fair assessment of his ideas on nature and grace requires that one look *in extenso* at what he has to say. In his observations on the notion of the "anonymous Christian," Rahner explains that "supernatural grace" does not need to be conceived of as an "isolated intervention" by God:

> The supernatural grace of faith and justification offered by God to men does not need to be conceived of as an isolated intervention on God's part at a particular point in a world which is itself profane. On the contrary, it can perfectly well be interpreted on the basis of God's universal will to save as a grace which, as offered, is a constantly present existential of the creature endowed with spiritual faculties and of the world in general, which orients these to the immediacy of God as their final end, though of course in saying this the question still remains wholly open of whether an individual freely gives himself to, or alternately rejects, this existential which constitutes the innermost dynamism of his being and its history, an existential which is and remains continually present. . . . It does this effectively at all times and in all places in the form of the offering and the enabling power of acting in a way that leads to salvation. And even though it is unmerited and "supernatural" in character, it constitutes the innermost *entelecheia* and dynamism of the world considered as the historical dimension of the creature endowed with spiritual faculties.[33]

32. Catholic authors who have recently offered theologies of world religions that are largely pluralistic in character include Paul Knitter, Jacques Dupuis, and Gerald O'Collins. See Knitter, *No Other Name?*; Dupuis, *Toward a Christian Theology of Religious Pluralism*; O'Collins, *Salvation for All*. As a general response to these theological trends, the Congregation for the Doctrine of the Faith (CDF) published the document *Dominus Iesus* ("On the Unicity and Salvific Universality of Jesus Christ") in August 2000. Soon thereafter, the CDF published a "Notification" specifically in response to Jacques Dupuis, calling for a clarification of his views and stating that certain points in Dupuis's book have "no foundation in Catholic theology" (R. Martin, *Will Many Be Saved?*, 55, citing CDF, "Notification").

33. Rahner, "Observations on the Problem of the Anonymous Christian," in *Theological Investigations*, 14:288. See the discussion of these and other passages from Rahner's writings in R. Martin, *Will Many Be Saved?*, 96–105.

Note the phrasing: "at all times and in all places in the form of the offering and the enabling power of acting in a way that leads to salvation." According to Rahner, no one lacks this "enabling power," and so salvation does not require the preaching of the gospel, the presence of the Christian community, or the knowledge of Christ's name or of Israel's God.

In his essay "Anonymous Christians," Rahner speaks of the decision for God as an immanent process within human beings, involving self-acceptance as well as an acceptance of God:

> He also already accepts this revelation whenever he really accepts himself completely, for it already speaks in him. Prior to the explicitness of official ecclesiastical faith this acceptance can be present in an implicit form whereby a person undertakes and lives the duty of each day in the quiet sincerity of patience, in devotion to his material duties and the demands made upon him by the persons under his care. . . . In the acceptance of himself man is accepting Christ.[34]

In his essay "Christianity and the Non-Christian Religions," Rahner suggests that human moral acts can themselves be moments of salvific decision for God:

> We can say quite simply that wherever, and in so far as, the individual makes a moral decision in his life . . . this moral decision can also be thought to measure up to the character of a supernaturally elevated, believing, and thus saving act, and hence to be more in actual fact than merely "natural morality." Hence, if one believes seriously in the universal salvific purpose of God towards all men in Christ, it need not and cannot really be doubted that gratuitous influences of properly Christian supernatural grace are conceivable in the life of all men . . . and that these influences can be presumed to be accepted in spite of the sinful state of men and in spite of their apparent estrangement from God.[35]

One question this raises concerns those who do not overtly or outwardly acknowledge God in any way and so appear to be secular or agnostic in thought and action. Rahner takes a hopeful perspective and states that as long as such a person does not deny God "in his heart," she or he may be thought of as a "believer":

> It is true that it would be wrong to go so far as to declare every man, whether he accepts the grace or not, an "anonymous Christian." . . . Only someone who gives—even if it be ever so confusedly—the glory to *God* should be thus designated. Therefore no matter what a man states in his conceptual, theoretical and

---

34. Rahner, "Anonymous Christians," in *Theological Investigations*, 6:394.
35. Rahner, "Christianity and the Non-Christian Religions," in *Theological Investigations*, 5:125.

religious reflection, anyone who does not say in his heart, "there is no God" (like the "fool" in the psalm) but testifies to him by the radical acceptance of his being, is a believer . . . [and] can be called with every right an "anonymous Christian."[36]

In this way, Rahner defines overt secularity as covert religiosity. Even professed secularism—"what a man states in his conceptual, theoretical and religious reflection"—does not rule out relationship with God.[37]

Rahner further argues that God's universal offer of grace introduces not a mere *possibility* of salvation among non-Christians but its *actuality*:

> If one gives more exact theological thought to this matter, then one cannot regard nature and grace as two phases in the life of the individual that follow each other in time. It is furthermore impossible to think that this offer of supernatural, divinizing grace made to all men on account of the universal salvific purpose of God, should in general (prescinding from the relatively few exceptions) remain ineffective in most cases on account of the personal guilt of the individual. For, as far as the gospel is concerned, we have no really conclusive reason for thinking so pessimistically of men. On the other hand, and contrary to every merely human experience, we do have every reason for thinking optimistically of God and his salvific will which is more powerful than the extremely limited stupidity and evil-mindedness of men. . . . Christ and his salvation are not simply one of two possibilities offering themselves to man's free choice; they are the deed of God that bursts open and redeems the false choice of man by overtaking it. In Christ God not only gives the possibility of salvation, which in that case would still have to be effected by man himself, but the actual salvation itself, however much this includes also the right decision of human freedom which is itself a gift from God.[38]

The post-Christian European intellectual environment formed the locus and context for Rahner's reflections. His expansive theology of salvation for non-Christians arose at least in part out of his pastoral concern over the European situation in his day, where secularism and new ideologies were rapidly replacing Christian faith.[39] Traditional Catholic theology had always regarded deliberate atheism as a serious sin. Yet Rahner's theology mollified this view by suggesting that even some of those who declared themselves atheists were

36. Rahner, "Anonymous Christians," 394–95.

37. Here Rahner's reflections remind one of Paul Tillich (*DR* 7.8), who affirmed that secularity is actually religious at its core, according to Tillich's dictum that "religion is the substance of culture; culture is the form of religion" (Tillich, *Theology of Culture*, 42).

38. Rahner, "Christianity and the Non-Christian Religions," 123–24.

39. Rusty R. Reno suggests that Rahner's approach to nature and grace reflected a "nostalgia for Christendom," thus showing how conservatism and innovation blended within his theology ("Rahner the Restorationist").

in some sense "believers" who had responded positively to God. Ralph Martin writes, "Rahner is attempting to come to grips theologically with the shock of the collapse of Christendom and the ascendency of an aggressive anti-Christian international secular culture in the Christian heartland, as well as the continued existence of vast numbers of people of 'other religions' who show no signs of conversion to Christianity in significant numbers."[40]

Rahner's faith in the implicit faith of secularizing Europeans—based on a "supernatural existential"—seems less plausible today than it might have been in the 1960s or 1970s. It would be difficult to redefine the ever more strident atheists of recent decades as "believers after a fashion." This viewpoint also suffers from a lack of empirical substantiation. If one does not judge people's beliefs on the basis of what they say about themselves, then could one not define the faithful Catholic as an "anonymous Buddhist" or the faithful Hindu as an "anonymous atheist"? In criticizing Rahner, philosophers and theologians point out that the "anonymous Christian" idea attaches labels to persons who do not and would not apply such labels to themselves. A Muslim thinker might attribute "anonymous Muslim" status to whichever Christians, Jews, Buddhists, or secularists that the Muslim might wish honorifically to include in the Islamic community. Religious inclusivism thus appears to be little more than an exercise in religious rebranding in which faith communities apply their labels to anyone whom they wish to acknowledge—notwithstanding the lack of evidence to support their claim. Rahner's critics do not believe that his inclusivist theory is self-consistent or that it offers a meaningful way of construing relations between religious communities.[41] Moreover, this view flies in the face of biblical texts that make public confession of faith the mark of Jesus's genuine disciple: "So everyone who acknowledges me before men, I also will acknowledge before my Father who is in heaven, but whoever denies me before men, I also will deny before my Father who is in heaven" (Matt. 10:32–33).

Rahner's "salvation optimism" did not find much support even in his own life experience, as "Christendom" during his adult life was rapidly dissolving before his eyes. His priesthood (1932–84) began under Nazi rule and continued with half of his native Germany under Soviet Communism. From the environment that he inhabited, it would hardly seem self-evident that almost everyone was saying yes to God. The metaphysical abstractions of Rahner's theology had little to do with flesh-and-blood human beings and the historical events swirling around him. Rahner not only overrated the responsiveness of secular people to God, but he also underrated the importance of proclamation-based

40. R. Martin, *Will Many Be Saved?*, 110.
41. On the problems with Rahnerian inclusivism, see DiNoia, *Diversity of Religions*.

evangelism as a way of winning people to Christianity. From Rahner's writings, one would not guess that the sub-Saharan African Christian population expanded during the twentieth century from about one million to more than four hundred million faithful.[42] It is not clear that Rahner's theology allows for evangelism in the strict sense. Since, as he argues, "nature" and "grace" are not two phases that succeed one another in time, no transition toward or into grace is either necessary or possible, and the Christian preacher need not call for a fundamental conversion or change of life. Since God's grace goes forth "at all times and in all places in the form of the offering and the enabling power of acting in a way that leads to salvation," the evangelist or missionary seemingly becomes redundant. On Rahner's account, the missionary doing traditional evangelism would be like someone trying to sell printed newspapers on a street where every home already has internet access to the very same content.

By universalizing the concept of grace, Rahner's theology ran the risk of eliminating it (*DR* 12.3). By taking the human being in his or her natural condition and asserting that God's gracious offer of salvation is continually present to each one, Rahner redefined "the natural condition" as "a state of grace." When Rahner stated that "a person [who] undertakes and lives . . . in devotion to his material duties" is thereby "accepting Christ," what might this mean, except that solid, decent, law-abiding atheists and agnostics will go to heaven along with faithful Catholics? Rahner failed to substantiate his basic claims in Scripture, and his positions also lacked support in earlier Catholic theology. Gavin D'Costa refers to Rahner's theology as a form of "structural inclusivism" and summarizes Hans Urs von Balthasar's critique that "Rahner's transcendental anthropology is in danger of conflating nature and grace and reducing revelation to a predetermined anthropological system." In Balthasar's analysis, Rahner "minimizes . . . Christ's revelation and the character of sin and tragedy" and leads to "an impoverished theology of the cross."[43]

Rahner's theology of nature and grace and the "supernatural existential" was essentially an exercise in religious renaming or rebranding. "Anonymous Christianity" did not make totalitarian regimes any less brutal, or European churches any less moribund, or Third World poverty any less appalling. Neither the "anonymous Christian" notion nor Rahner's nature-grace theology offered

---

42. The immense expansion of non-European Christianity during the twentieth century hardly seems to have registered in Rahner's European-centered and Christendom-based theology—nor the fact that this expansion was occurring only in small part through the agency of Western missionaries and much more at the initiative of indigenous evangelists in all parts of the globe. For a recent (2016) overview, see Sanneh and McClymond, introduction to *Wiley-Blackwell Companion to World Christianity*, 1–17.

43. D'Costa, in *Christianity and World Religions*, 21. In this summative work, D'Costa surveys Catholic views on salvation (3–33) and analyzes Catholic inclusivism (34–37).

much to the church that was either substantial or lasting. If Rahner's theology engendered a new optimism, this was only because he attached better names to existing phenomena.

10.3. The Ambitious and Ambiguous Cosmology of Teilhard de Chardin

An original and influential figure in Catholic theology since the mid-twentieth century is the renowned Jesuit paleontologist and theologian Pierre Teilhard de Chardin (1881–1955). To most Catholic authorities of the 1930s through the 1950s, Teilhard's theological views were suspect, especially with respect to the church's doctrine of original sin. In consequence, he was encouraged to pursue his scientific interests but banned from publishing his theological works. Because these writings were released after his death, his influence as a theological thinker was greater after his death than before.[44] In the discussion here, we will pass over the question of whether Teilhard's views on biological and cosmic evolution were compatible with evolutionary or Darwinian thinking. While Teilhard's paleontological work was generally respected among scientists, some found fault with his more speculative and theological writings.[45]

The structure of Teilhard's thought pointed toward a final convergence and unification of all created things—each in connection with all the rest and in connection with God. As he said, "Everything that rises must converge."[46] The human race, he believed, was heading toward a radical change of condition—what today's scientists call a "singularity"—that rivals anything yet witnessed during the evolution of the cosmos, and comparable in its significance to the first condensation of energy into matter after the big bang.[47] What Teilhard called

44. Pierre Teilhard de Chardin's works cited here include *Hymn of the Universe; Human Energy; Building the Earth; The Phenomenon of Man; The Future of Man; Activation of Energy*. Secondary works treating Teilhard's eschatology include Corte, *Pierre Teilhard de Chardin*; Safford, "Teilhard de Chardin"; de Lubac, *Teilhard de Chardin*; Mooney, *Teilhard de Chardin*; Pope, "Faith, and the Future"; Berry, "Cosmic Person and the Future of Man"; McCarty, *Teilhard de Chardin*; Trennert-Helwig, "Church as the Axis of Convergence"; Dillon, "Toward the Noosphere."

45. The well-known biologist Theodosius Dobzhansky was more positive in "Teilhard de Chardin and the Orientation of Evolution." McCarty (*Teilhard de Chardin*, 60) notes that the ban on the publication of Teilhard's works during his lifetime unfortunately prevented him from benefiting from constructive criticism: "Teilhard's superiors . . . did not allow him public exposure so that his statements and views could be debated in the public forums of the press, universities and seminaries where he could have explained, clarified or sharpened any of his points."

46. Teilhard, *Building the Earth*, 11. Teilhard's phrase became the title of a collection of short stories by Flannery O'Connor, *Everything That Rises Must Converge*.

47. Safford, "Teilhard de Chardin," 290. Already in 1929, Teilhard expressed his sense that radical change was occurring and was yet to come: "There is now incontrovertible evidence that mankind has just entered upon the greatest period of change the world has ever known. . . . Today

the Omega Point referred to a maximal level of complexity and consciousness toward which the universe was evolving—and which Teilhard identified with Christ. The cosmic process for Teilhard was a great epic, beginning with the emergence of matter itself, then the earth, primitive life forms, humanity, and followed by growth into greater levels of community.

In light of the overall architecture of Teilhard's thought, it may come as a surprise to learn that Teilhard did not affirm universal salvation. In *The Divine Milieu* (1960) Teilhard wrote, "You have told me, O God, to believe in hell," and he added, "O Jesus, . . . closing my eyes to what my human weakness cannot as yet understand and therefore cannot bear—that is to say, to the reality of the damned—I desire at least to make the ever-present threat of damnation a part of my habitual and practical vision of the world."[48] For Teilhard, the existence of hell was a doctrine he affirmed on the basis of church authority—though, as just noted, he wanted this difficult teaching somehow to become part of his "practical vision of the world." Teilhard remained Christ-centered in his philosophy of religion, stating that "the religious gropings of humanity had drawn near to this idea that God, a spirit, could only be reached by spirit," and yet "it is in Christianity alone that the movement achieves its definitive expression and content."[49] At the same time, Teilhard held an open-ended idea of Christianity, which "appears to me today much less as a closed and established whole but rather as an axis of progression and assimilation."[50] While the evolutionary process would converge on the cosmic Christ or Omega Point, the church of the present time did not have complete understanding of Christ's purposes in this process.

Teilhard in general terms was a theologian who believed that it was possible to start with nature, and from nature to discern God's presence and activity. He looked for harmony between faith and reason and between Christ and culture. He was a hopeful thinker and presumed that humanity was "coming of age," or attaining a new kind of maturation.[51] In certain respects Teilhard seems to have been a philosophical idealist. His idea of historical development moves from the material world (geosphere), toward the living world (biosphere), into the ideal world (noosphere), and finally to the divine world (theosphere). His thought moves away from materiality and toward ideality.[52] Yet Teilhard was

---

something is happening to the whole structure of human consciousness" (*Building the Earth*, 19). On the idea of the singularity, see Kurzweil, *Singularity Is Near*.

48. Teilhard, *Divine Milieu*, 147, 149, cited in Ambaum, "An Empty Hell?," 42–43.

49. Teilhard, *Human Energy*, 156.

50. Teilhard, *Lettres intimes*, 137, as translated and cited by Trennert-Helwig, "Church," 82.

51. Pope, "Faith, and the Future," 73–74.

52. There is here some analogy to "spiritualization" in the philosophy of Vladimir Solovyov. See O. Smith, *Vladimir Solovyov and the Spiritualization of Matter*, and *DR*, 226–27, 265–66, 295–96, 416–17, 659.

in no sense a strict Platonist or radical Origenist who had no use for material things. He displayed a "scientist's respect for evidence," and there is an empirical aspect to his thinking that is generally missing from idealist philosophy.[53] Teilhard showed a fascination with matter from his earliest days; in his 1916 essay "La vie cosmique" ("The Cosmic Life"), he wrote of the "fire" that shines in the heart of matter. In this essay he declared, "I have vowed myself to God, the only Origin," yet he professed, "I love the universe, its energies" and "want to vent her my love for matter and life, and to harmonize it, if possible, with the adoration of . . . Divinity."[54] The reconciliation of these two great loves—of God and of matter/energy/life—was the great spiritual and intellectual project of his life. So deep was his love for matter itself that he even wrote a "Hymn to Matter." When, during a geological expedition, this Jesuit Catholic priest found himself in the midst of Mongolia and without any bread to consecrate for the Mass, he offered to God the Gobi Desert.[55]

Without doubt, Teilhard had been influenced in his early life by his reading of the French philosopher Henri Bergson (1859–1941), who sought to bring together science, religion, and philosophy in his philosophy of "creative evolution" and the *élan vital* (creative force).[56] There is much in Teilhard that is not in Bergson, yet the influence of the earlier philosopher is clear. Teilhard's thinking focuses on the *interconnectedness* of everything, as he wrote: "The farther and more deeply we penetrate into matter, by means of increasingly powerful methods, the more we are confounded by the interdependence of its parts. Each element of the cosmos is positively woven from all the others." Individual elements are "subsistent through the apex of an organized whole, and from above through the influence of unities of a higher order which incorporate and dominate it for their own ends."[57] This interconnectedness of the whole is not static but dynamic, and Teilhard's thought shows a strong sense of change and development through time. He even proposed a principle of nonreversibility. This meant that once a certain threshold has been reached, and a new level of reality has been attained, there is no going back. The new reality will remain and serve as the foundation from which all further development occurs.[58]

For Teilhard, matter itself has a "without" in its external relations and also a "within" in its capacity for life and consciousness. In the evolutionary process,

53. Pope, "Faith, and the Future," 75.

54. Teilhard, "La vie cosmique" [1916], *Oeuvres* 12:5, translated and cited in Trennert-Helwig, "Church," 78.

55. See Teilhard, *Hymn of the Universe*, comprising "The Mass on the World" (5–31) and the "Hymn to Matter" (65–69).

56. See Bergson, *Creative Evolution*.

57. Teilhard, *Phenomenon of Man*, 44.

58. McCarty, *Teilhard de Chardin*, 112.

the "within" is at first concealed but then shows itself "without."[59] Teilhard cannot be thought of as a "naturalistic" thinker in the usual sense, because his universe does not unfold according to the naturalistic law of entropy. For him, things do not break down from complex to simple but build themselves up from simple to complex. The rule is complexification rather than simplification, extropy rather than entropy.

At the base of everything was a divine presence—in every thing and every act—and yet Teilhard did not always use the word "God" to describe this presence. Doran McCarty notes some of Teilhard's "pseudonyms for God," which include "love," "spirit," and "Omega Point."[60] Love he identified as an energy that unifies and socializes everything. Spirit was the "withinness" or energy present in all things. "Spirit," wrote Teilhard, "is neither superimposed nor accessory to the cosmos" but is "the stuff of the universe," and so "neither a meta- nor an epi-phenomenon; it is the *phenomenon*."[61] God for Teilhard was not impersonal, but he used the term "hyper-personal."[62] As the Omega Point, God or Christ was like the telos in Aristotelian philosophy—the end toward which all things move. For Teilhard, the Omega Point will not abolish everything preceding it but will be a critical threshold in which everything that has been disparate will be synthesized and brought together.[63]

For Teilhard, the incarnation meant that God has so entered into the universe as to clothe himself with it and that the universe in some sense becomes the body of Christ. The cosmic Christ energizes all things and gives them their purpose and their direction. He wrote that "the essence of Christianity is neither more nor less than a belief in the implication of the world in God by the incarnation."[64] Humanity itself does not exist in a fixed form but will transition and transform into a higher form of existence—a superhumanity, in which humanity and nature will no longer be separated but will exist as one superhuman person. This notion of the superman or the superhuman is nothing like that of Friedrich Nietzsche. It does not involve only a few people who dominate all others but rather involves a collective unity of all human beings.[65] Teilhard used neologisms to describe humanity's and the world's transformation, as "hominization," "totalization," and "planetization." In "planetization," humanity will enclose on itself and form a single entity. To the extent that all humans

59. Pope, "Faith, and the Future," 76.
60. McCarty, *Teilhard de Chardin*, 56–60.
61. Teilhard, *Human Energy*, 94.
62. Teilhard, *Phenomenon of Man*, 254–72.
63. McCarty, *Teilhard de Chardin*, 60.
64. Teilhard, *Human Energy*, 91.
65. McCarty, *Teilhard de Chardin*, 91, 93.

become interconnected, a single, corporate mind of the *noosphere* will emerge (something that Teilhard described in the 1950s but that sounds something like the present-day internet).[66] The key to this coming transformation of humanity lay in what Teilhard referred to as the "Super-Christ." He explained, "By Super-Christ, I most certainly do not mean *another* Christ, a second Christ different from and greater than the first. I mean the same Christ, the Christ of all time, revealing himself to us in a form and in dimensions, with an urgency and area of contact, that are enlarged and given new force."[67]

Anticipating his critics, Teilhard addressed the question of pantheism, making it clear that his view did not abolish the distinctness of each creature from God and from all other creatures:

> A *converging universe*, such as I have delineated, far from being born from the fusion and confusion of the elemental centres it assembles, the universal centre of unification . . . must be conceived as pre-existing and transcendent. A very real "pantheism" if you like (in the etymological meaning of the word) but an absolutely legitimate pantheism—for if, in the last resort, the reflective centres of the world are effectively no more than "one with God," this state is obtained not by identification (God becoming all) but by the differentiation and communicating action of love (God all *in everyone* [1 Cor. 15:28]). And that is essentially orthodox and Christian.[68]

This passage recalls Friedrich Schelling (*DR* 7.7) in his *Stuttgart Seminars*, who, like Teilhard, defended the term "pantheism" and yet defined it as meaning

66. Teilhard wrote, "No one can deny that a network (a world network) of economic and psychic affiliations is being woven at ever increasing speed which envelops and constantly penetrates more deeply within each of us. With every day that passes it becomes a little more impossible for us to act or think otherwise than collectively" (*Future of Man*, 177). At a few points Teilhard spoke of political integration as well: "Man cannot remain in his present, plural, dislocated situation. Irrespective of our wishes, the age of lukewarm pluralisms has gone forever. Either a single nation will succeed in destroying and absorbing all the others: or all nations will come together in one common soul, that so they may be more human" (*Activation of Energy*, 18–19).

67. Teilhard, *Future of Man*, 74. As with other aspects of Teilhard's cosmology and eschatology, the "Super-Christ" is reminiscent of Origen, who referred to different facets of Christ's relationship to creation under the category of *epinoiai* (aspects, concepts). See Origen, *On First Principles* 1.2. Without ceasing to be himself, Christ may manifest himself under different aspects at different times. See R. E. Heine, "*Epinoiai*."

68. Teilhard, *Phenomenon of Man*, 309–10. Cf. Teilhard, *Phenomenon of Man*, 294:
> By a perennial act of communion and sublimation he [i.e., God] aggregates to himself the total psychism of the earth. And when he has gathered everything together and transformed everything, he will close in upon himself. . . . Then as St. Paul tells us *God shall be all in all* [1 Cor. 15:28]. This is indeed a superior form of "pantheism" without trace of the poison of adulteration or annihilation: the expectation of perfect unity, steeped in which each element will reach its consummation at the same time as the universe.

something like "panentheism." Schelling and Teilhard both sound like Origen in their appeal to—or adaptation of—the biblical phrase "God all in all" (1 Cor. 15:28). Schelling, like Origen, understood the final state as a reversal of sin's consequences and so as a state of universal salvation.[69] Teilhard did not, which raises the question: Why not?

Teilhard's writings generally seem to suggest that everyone will be included in the Omega Point and that this is simply how things are. In *The Divine Milieu* (1960), as noted, Teilhard grudgingly admitted that he accepted the reality of hell, though he hoped that hell might have no inhabitants. In *The Phenomenon of Man* (1965), Teilhard included a brief but suggestive passage that suggests that a final separation might occur even at the time of the final convergence:

> Refusal or acceptance of Omega? A conflict may supervene. In that case the noosphere, in the course of and by virtue of the process which draws it together, will, when it reaches its point of unification, split into two zones each attracted to an opposite pole of adoration. Thought has never completely united upon itself here below. Universal love would only vivify and detach finally a fraction of the noosphere so as to consummate it—the part which decided to "cross the threshold," to get outside itself and into the other. *Ramification once again, for the last time.*[70]

From this passage, does it seem, then, that "everything that rises does *not* converge"? Or perhaps that "*not* everything rises" and so "*not* everything converges"? Teilhard called what he wrote here a "supposition." Yet he wrote enough to show that he was not content in affirming universalism as such. The separation—or "ramification," as Teilhard calls it—will be "for the last time" and so seemingly will remain final and irrevocable.

By way of critique, we might ask what God actually does in Teilhard's thinking. Will it work for Teilhard to make God simply a telos or final cause but not

69. Schelling writes:
   It is in these periods of eternity that the restitution [*Wiederbringung*] of evil takes place, which is something we must necessarily believe in. Sin is not eternal, and hence its consequences cannot be so either. This last period within the last is that of the entirely perfect fulfillment—that is, of the complete becoming man of God—the one where the infinite will have become finite without therefore suffering in its infinitude. Then God is in all actuality everything, and pantheism will have become true. (*Stuttgart Seminars*, 243; *Sämtliche Werke*, 7:484)

70. Teilhard, *Phenomenon of Man*, 288–89. Safford comments on the quoted passage: "As a lover of men, he [Teilhard] hopes and prays for the inclusion of all in [the] Omega Point. . . . But he cannot get beyond the possibility of the emerging of two poles of worship: Christ, and His opposite, Antichrist—although Teilhard does not name him. This brings him close to a similar prophecy made by the Russian Christian thinker [Vladimir] Solovyov at the turn of the century" ("Teilhard de Chardin," 297). The Antichrist story has been translated into English as Solovyov, *War, Progress, and the End of History: Including a Short Story of the Anti-Christ* (1915).

an efficient cause? Inevitably there is a question—which also arises in process theology—of whether the outcome of the future is determined or remains contingent. Teilhard seems to be quite assured of the outcome, yet it is unclear how he can be so sure if God is not acting efficaciously to bring the world to the conclusion that God intends. Doran McCarty suggests that Teilhard does not directly "identify spirit with God" because "he is trying to have the advantage of the Divine as a part of withinness without God's involvement and responsibility for all that happens in the world."[71] That is to say, he may have avoided the problem of God's relation to evil by leaving a certain vagueness regarding divine agency. Other questions arise concerning Teilhard's Christology.[72]

One of the most frequent criticisms of Teilhard is that he did not take seriously enough the problem of evil. For him, evil was not something that threatened the accomplishment of God's purposes. Evil was more like an initial stage—and perhaps a necessary one—in the world's progress toward the Omega Point. Teilhard once referred to human suffering as a form of "potential energy"—an identification that could be seen as negating the evilness of evil.[73]

On the Catholic question of nature and grace, it is difficult to pin Teilhard down, and his way of thinking seemed to blur the distinction. Teilhard wrote in his *Hymn of the Universe* that "Christ appears, Christ is born, without any violation of nature's laws, in the heart of the world."[74] In Catholic theological terms, one is bound to ask, does "nature" *need* "grace," or can "nature" *cause* its own "salvation"? And do the categories of "nature" and "grace" make sense within Teilhard's thinking? Along similar lines, one is bound to ask, is there a "heaven" for Teilhard? Or does his vision of the future point to some kind of harmonious condition emerging from the utmost advancement of human capacities and technologies?

Decius Safford presents a different criticism of Teilhard: "Does man live by his brain alone?" Safford concludes that in Teilhard "there is . . . an implication that it is through knowledge that we shall be saved," so that the result is "a dangerously gnostic interpretation."[75] The cognitive focus in Teilhard's vision of the

71. McCarty, *Teilhard de Chardin*, 58.

72. Critics have held that Teilhard's Christ is forever up in the clouds, and McCarty writes that "it is not Jesus of Nazareth who occupied the center of Teilhard's attention but the cosmic Christ" (ibid., 59). "Even the passages which speak of the Incarnation have a strange, non-Galilean ring to them" (58–59). One might find analogies between Teilhard's Christology and those of Eriugena (*DR* 4.10) and Solovyov (*DR* 8.3–8.4).

73. "Human suffering, the sum total of suffering poured out at each moment over the whole earth, is like an immeasurable ocean. But what makes up this immensity? Is it blackness; emptiness, barren waste? No, indeed: it is potential *energy*" (Teilhard, *Hymn of the Universe*, 93).

74. Ibid., 143.

75. Safford, "Teilhard de Chardin," 293, 295–96.

future is a further parallel to Origen, who thought of heaven in intellectualistic terms, as a kind of advanced school for endless learning.[76] The idea of individual minds merging into a Super-Mind is reminiscent of Evagrius and other radical Origenists (*DR* 3.10), who conceived the eschaton as a universal mind meld.[77] While Teilhard insisted that individuality will not be lost, one wonders how one can avoid this outcome if all minds are fully merged with one another.

Finally, there is the issue of freedom and determinism in Teilhard, as Mc-Carty notes: "Believing that the world is heading toward the Omega Point and that this development is irreversible carries with it a significant determinism." While "Teilhard does not wish to deny the reality of human freedom . . . that freedom is a freedom to cooperate with the evolutionary process and to help move it toward its goal."[78] If this is deterministic, then at least it is happy determinism rather than a tragic one.[79]

76. According to Origen, the souls in heaven will ask God why he originally placed each star in one place rather than another—and God will answer them (*On First Principles* 2.11.6–7 [Butterworth, 152–53]).

77. John Dillon writes of Teilhard in terms that sound Evagrian: "The Omega point . . . [culminates], it would seem, in a sort of communal super-consciousness, where we will all think together as one" ("Toward the Noosphere," 16).

78. McCarty, *Teilhard de Chardin*, 102.

79. Because this book is focused on Christian and Christocentric forms of universalism, in turning to consider Balthasar (*DR* 10.4–10.9) we pass over the several forms of nominally Catholic yet functionally pluralistic universalism. A brief yet clear account, focused on Raimundo Panikkar, Hans Küng, and Paul Knitter, appears in L. M. Blanchard, *Will All Be Saved?*, 230–57. A borderline case is that of Jacques Dupuis, whose theology of world religions sought to be both "Christocentric" and in some sense "pluriform" in recognizing non-Christian religions as vehicles of salvation. A sympathetic treatment of Dupuis appears in O'Collins, "Jacques Dupuis." For a more critical account of Dupuis, see D'Costa, *Christianity and World Religions*, 19–23, 180–86; D'Costa, "Pluralist Arguments." D'Costa has argued plausibly for regarding Dupuis as closer to the pluralist Knitter than to Catholic Christocentrists such as Rahner and Balthasar. Dupuis called his own view "inclusivist pluralism." The declaration by the Congregation for the Doctrine of the Faith, *Dominus Iesus* (2000), aimed at excluding Catholic views of salvation (like that of Dupuis) that were tending either implicitly or explicitly in the direction of pluralism:

> To justify the universality of Christian salvation as well as the fact of religious pluralism, it has been proposed that there is an economy of the eternal Word that is valid also outside the Church and is unrelated to her, in addition to an economy of the incarnate Word. The first would have a greater universal value than the second, which is limited to Christians, though God's presence would be more full in the second. These theses are in profound conflict with the Christian faith. . . . Therefore, the theory which would attribute, after the incarnation as well, a salvific activity to the Logos as such in his divinity, exercised "in addition to" or "beyond" the humanity of Christ, is not compatible with the Catholic faith. . . . There are also those who propose the hypothesis of an economy of the Holy Spirit with a more universal breadth than that of the Incarnate Word, crucified and risen. This position also is contrary to the Catholic faith, which, on the contrary, considers the salvific incarnation of the Word as a trinitarian event. In the New Testament, the mystery of Jesus, the Incarnate Word, constitutes the place of the Holy Spirit's presence as well as the principle of the Spirit's effusion on humanity, not only in messianic times . . . but also prior to his coming in history. (nos. 9, 10, 12)

10.4. The Theology of Hans Urs von Balthasar: A General Sketch

During the late 1940s and 1950s, many thinkers associated with the *nouvelle théologie*—such as Marie-Dominique Chenu, Yves Congar, Jean Daniélou, and Karl Rahner—suffered ecclesiastical sanctions of varying severity. Henri de Lubac, for example, lived for about a decade under a cloud of suspicion. The wording of the papal encyclical *Humani Generis* was generally interpreted as a rebuke of de Lubac for having "destroy[ed] the gratuity of the supernatural order." De Lubac's own Jesuit order removed his books from sale and even from the shelves of their libraries. By the 1960s and 1970s, a reversal of fortune took place. During Vatican II, de Lubac played a leading role in drafting documents, and he ended his life as a cardinal. The influence of Congar's theology was especially evident in the Vatican II documents. Yet no reversal of fortune was as spectacular as that of Hans Urs von Balthasar. Following his departure from the Jesuits in 1950, Balthasar was in a profoundly difficult situation. He had to wait longer than others for a rise in his influence and reputation. While hundreds of Catholic theologians played a public role at Vatican II, Balthasar remained at home. Throughout the 1950s and 1960s, he was outside of the theological mainstream of the Catholic Church, and his writings were considered too idiosyncratic to be influential outside of certain small circles.

But when the time came, Balthasar's reputation soared. His polemical book at the close of the Second Vatican Council, *The Moment of Christian Witness* (1966), was a wide-ranging critique of emerging theological ideas, including especially Karl Rahner's notion of the "anonymous Christian."[80] Karen Kilby comments, "For those within Roman Catholicism who worried that the Church was conceding too much to the world, to the secular, to 'the times,' and that it was in danger of losing its identity, Balthasar became a very important figure."[81] Balthasar not only took aim at Rahner's theology for devaluing the institutional church and its sacraments, but he also criticized liberation theology, upheld the value of priestly celibacy, and defended traditional gender roles for men and women. Balthasar soon gained a reputation, especially among those in the Catholic hierarchy, as a reliable conservative. Among Catholic bishops and officials, Balthasar might today be the single most influential twentieth-century theologian.[82] Non-Catholics too found reason to read and appreciate Balthasar.

80. On Balthasar's critique of Rahner, see E. Conway, *Anonymous Christian*.
81. Kilby, *Balthasar*, 37.
82. Despite the conservative labeling, some of Balthasar's theological reasoning was revisionist rather than traditionalist. Thus, in an interview that Balthasar did late in his life with Angelo Scola, he expressed his belief that the Catholic Church would eventually need to revise its doctrine in

While remaining committed to the Catholic tradition, Balthasar had long been in contact with Karl Barth, the leading Protestant thinker of the era, and he wrote a celebrated book on Barth's theology.[83] Balthasar's critique of modernity paralleled certain postmodernist trends in theology.[84] What is more, his use of poetry, literature, and drama to exemplify his own theology was well received by a wide spectrum of readers.[85]

Balthasar is not an easy thinker to grasp, and the problem in reading him does not lie in the individual sentence or paragraph but rather in discerning the overall direction of his thought. Much of what he wrote is expository rather than argumentative in character. Often he simply states his views without presenting an argument as such. Beyond this, the sheer quantity of what Balthasar wrote makes it hard to get a sense of the whole from reading one or another part of his vast corpus. Balthasar rejected the idea that divine revelation is a "system" of ideas. This notion had repelled him during his period of formal seminary training. In his eyes, the reigning neo-scholasticism had first dismembered divine revelation and then rationalistically constructed from the remaining bits and pieces a "system" of doctrines. In contrast to "system" was Balthasar's notion of the "form." While the parts of a "system" could be detached from one another, such was not the case with a "form." A "form" could only be viewed and appreciated in its wholeness and not in terms of its parts.[86] In his mature work *The Glory of the Lord*, Balthasar articulated a conviction that undergirded his theological writings from the start: "For we can be sure of one thing: we can never again recapture the living totality of form once it has been dissected and sawed into pieces, no matter how informative the conclusions which this anatomy may bring to light. Anatomy can be practiced only on a dead body."[87]

As Karen Kilby indicates, there are important consequences that flow from Balthasar's anti-systematic approach to theology. If the "form" is indeed as

light of the teachings of Adrienne von Speyr: "I believe that the Church will gradually have to adopt substantial parts of her doctrine and, perhaps, wonder why these beautiful and enriching things have not been recognized earlier" (Scola, *Test Everything*, 89). The conservative image was based largely on Balthasar's opposition to certain progressivist views rather than a fuller understanding or appreciation of his positive views.

83. Balthasar, *Theology of Karl Barth*.

84. See L. Gardner et al., *Balthasar at the End of Modernity*.

85. Kilby, *Balthasar*, 1, 36–38.

86. Ibid., 2–3, 7, 22.

87. Balthasar, *Glory of the Lord*, 1:31. Balthasar's insistence on holism, his resistance to breaking wholes down into parts, is strongly reminiscent of Romanticism. Compare Balthasar's comment with the lines from the second of William Wordsworth's paired poems "Expostulation and Reply" and "The Tables Turned": "Sweet is the lore which Nature brings; / Our meddling intellect / Mis-shapes the beauteous form of things: / We murder to dissect." Wordsworth, *Poems of William Wordsworth*, 361.

holistic and encompassing as Balthasar says that it is, then the "form" must be seen in its entirety. The only options would be "seeing the form" or else "not seeing the form." The metaphor of "seeing" thus carries with it an all-or-nothing logic. Not to agree with Balthasar is tantamount to not seeing, to being blind, or perhaps to shutting one's eyes.[88] On the basis of these theological premises, it is difficult to see how one may partially agree with and partially disagree with him. The method and ethos of Balthasar's theology present a striking contrast to that of Thomas Aquinas, where individual questions are treated one by one and specific arguments are considered in sequence and then evaluated, accepted, or rejected. The "form" of Thomistic theology gradually takes shape in a bottom-up and part-to-whole fashion. Balthasar's theologizing is the reverse of this—that is, top-to-bottom and whole-to-part.

So striking is Balthasar's insistence on viewing "the form" or the whole that Karen Kilby interprets Balthasar's theology as attempting a "God's eye view" of reality.[89] No clear epistemic boundary exists between what Balthasar knows and does not know, and so "he seems to know too much."[90] His supposed insights into the dramatic, eternal, inner life of the Trinity are a case in point. He tells us that the Son—before he was eternally begotten—gave prior consent to being eternally begotten. He says that the Father had to "strip himself" of his very Godhead so that the Son could come into existence. He states that the Father was surprised by how well the Son turned out and that the persons of the Trinity "worship" one another. The list goes on. But how could he know these things? On the basis of such ideas in his writings, Balthasar's thought has resonances with the theosophical tradition, which likewise purports to provide a "God's eye view" of everything. One factor in shaping Balthasar's thought in this direction was his reliance on the mystical experiences of Adrienne von Speyr as sources for his theological reflections. He knew of God's inner-trinitarian life because von Speyr had so informed him and because he accepted her experiences as genuine. In the final volume of *Theo-drama*, Balthasar often cites von Speyr's writings to illustrate or support his own theology, and such quotations are most frequent in those very passages in which Balthasar is giving an account of God's inner life. *His theology* and *her visions* seem either to stand together or to fall together. It does not seem possible to evaluate Balthasar's theology while sidestepping his relationship with von Speyr, which he himself says was decisive for his writings (*DR* 10.6).

88. Kilby, *Balthasar*, 56. Balthasar's is "a theology which allows little room for argument, little space for a reader to question and disagree" (65).

89. Ibid., 162–64.

90. Ibid., 13–14.

10.5. Balthasar's Roots: Church Fathers, Russian Thinkers, and Karl Barth

Hans Urs von Balthasar is a many-leveled thinker and writer. In reading Balthasar one becomes aware of different strata in his thinking, as though successive levels of influence had been deposited, one on top of another. He had an extraordinary way of absorbing various sources and influences. As Jonathan King and C. Michael Shea argue, he was "famously wide-ranging and peculiar in his use of sources." From any given thinker, Balthasar would simply extract the ideas he regarded as essential and then move on. King and Shea explain that the young Balthasar had a habit of appropriating the thought of a surprisingly wide range of thinkers, many of whom he would later part ways with, though not before incorporating their most crucial insights. "The ferment of his eventual, mature theology is thus remarkably eclectic, a fact which is often obscured by Balthasar's own tendency later to discard such thinkers after he had incorporated what he wished from them."[91] One example is Friedrich Nietzsche, from whom Balthasar assimilated a number of ideas. In later writings, Balthasar mentioned only the problems that he had identified in Nietzsche and not the insights he had gleaned from him.[92]

Many of those who have recently written on Balthasar's hope for universal salvation have begun their reflections with the book that he published during his final decade of life, *Dare We Hope "That All Men Be Saved"?* (1982). Yet the roots of Balthasar's reflections on this theme extend all the way back to his earliest writings. It is difficult to think of any major influence on Balthasar's earlier life and theology that did *not* pull him toward universalism. As he wrote in a late overview of his own theological development:

> The book [*The Theology of*] *Karl Barth* is the fruit of numerous conversations with the man himself. . . . I wanted to get things moving again and clear away some of the chief obstacles in ecumenical dialogue by using ideas from de Lubac's *Surnaturel* [*Supernatural*] and *Sur les chemins de Dieu* [*On the Pathways of God*]. I was tremendously and lastingly attracted by Barth's doctrine of election, that brilliant overcoming of Calvin. It converged with Origen's views and therefore with Adrienne's Holy Saturday theology as well.[93]

91. J. S. King and C. M. Shea, "Role of Nikolai Berdyaev," 253, 232. I wish to thank Jonathan King and Michael Shea for making this essay available to me in its prepublication form.

92. Ibid., 254. In Balthasar's approach to Nietzsche, King and Shea speak of a certain "sleight of hand" as Balthasar "closely engaged the thinker and assimilated all . . . he found valuable," while in his later works he generally referred to Nietzsche "in a negative light" (254). Balthasar throughout his career drew on "unorthodox sources," yet "as a theologian, he seemed to be . . . reticent to publicize his use of such material" (253–54). See the analysis of Balthasar's positive approach to the Western esotericist Valentin Tomberg (1900–1973) in Mongrain, "Rule-Governed Christian Gnosis," 290–91.

93. Balthasar, *Our Task*, 101.

Balthasar here mentions three living persons, Karl Barth (*DR* 9.1–9.9), Henri de Lubac (*DR* 10.1), and Adrienne von Speyr (*DR* 10.6), and one historical figure, Origen (*DR* 3.4–3.8), who all contributed to his theological development. Balthasar mentions them together and speaks of his sense of a convergence between Barth's election doctrine, de Lubac's approach to nature and grace, Origen's theological views, and von Speyr's mystical experiences. Where is the point of convergence? The answer seems clear: Barth taught *universal election* of humanity in Christ; de Lubac proposed a kind of *universal grace* that interpreted nature as grace-oriented or grace-suffused; Origen taught *universal salvation* for all; and von Speyr suggested a *universal reconciliation* of all humanity through Christ's substitutionary sufferings among the departed souls on Holy Saturday. Various influences on Balthasar from the 1930s onward were all drawing him toward universalism.

During his four years of theological study in Lyon, France, beginning in 1932, Balthasar studied under Henri de Lubac, borrowed copies of de Lubac's own books on early Christianity, and received a grounding in the church fathers that he had not gotten during his earlier theological formation in the Jesuit seminary. Balthasar went on to publish works on Origen (an edited anthology), Gregory of Nyssa, and Maximus the Confessor. The published study on Maximus (*Cosmic Liturgy*) may be the most impressive of Balthasar's earlier historical studies, and it laid the conceptual foundation for much of his later writing. Balthasar's slender work *The Theology of Henri de Lubac* is an homage to his revered former teacher.[94] Balthasar correctly interpreted Origen and Gregory of Nyssa (*DR* 3.9) as universalists, while of Maximus the Confessor (*DR* 4.8) Balthasar said that he had maintained an "honorable silence" on the question of *apokatastasis*. The Christocentric themes of Balthasar's patristic studies were manifold: Christ as the focal point of all things, Christ as the nexus between time and eternity, and Christ as the link between divine and human freedom.

An intriguing and yet little-known aspect of the younger Balthasar was his interest in and dependence on Russian thinkers—unusual at that time for a Catholic thinker.[95] The twenty-one-year-old Balthasar commented on his reading of Nicolas Berdyaev (*DR* 8.5) in a letter to a friend in 1927.[96] King

94. These works have been translated into English as *Origen, Spirit, and Fire*; *Presence and Thought*; *Cosmic Liturgy*; and *The Theology of Henri de Lubac*.

95. Jennifer Newsome Martin, "Hans Urs von Balthasar and the Press of Speculative Russian Religious Philosophy," and Brandon Gallaher, *Freedom and Necessity in Modern Trinitarian Theology* (see 167–95, 206, 211–13), both stress Balthasar's debt to Sergius Bulgakov (*DR* 8.6–8.8). J. S. King and C. M. Shea, in "Role of Nikolai Berdyaev," acknowledge the debt to Bulgakov but highlight the earlier and formative influence of Berdyaev.

96. J. S. King and C. M. Shea, "Role of Nikolai Berdyaev," 227, citing Lochbrunner, *Hans Urs von Balthasar und seine Literatenfreunde*, 59.

and Shea—on the basis of their analysis of Balthasar's doctoral dissertation, *Geschichte des eschatologischen Problems in der modernen deutschen Literatur* (*History of the Eschatological Problem in Modern German Literature*) (1930)— conclude that Balthasar at this early stage seemed to be almost like a Russian intellectual transplanted into German-speaking Europe.[97] In a dissertation officially devoted to German literature, there were no less than fifty-one direct references to Russian authors. Berdyaev was referenced eighteen times, Dostoyevsky nine times, and Vladimir Solovyov nine times.[98] Much later, Solovyov (*DR* 8.3–8.4) became the focus of a lengthy chapter in Balthasar's *The Glory of the Lord*.[99] Yet arguably it was Berdyaev rather than Solovyov who became the more long-lasting and pervasive influence on Balthasar's thinking. Balthasar treated Berdyaev in his dissertation chapter "Utopia and Kairos," where he first discussed Martin Heidegger and Paul Tillich (*DR* 7.8) and contrasted both of them unfavorably with Berdyaev. By the standards of later scholarship, this is a surprising judgment, given that Heidegger and Tillich have received vastly more scholarly attention than Berdyaev has since the 1950s. The structure of Balthasar's dissertation followed a pattern laid down in the opening chapter of Berdyaev's *The Meaning of History*. In the dissertation, Balthasar commented, "Berdyaev's astonishingly rich and deep mysticism of history . . . can therefore be considered as the most comprehensive [eschatological] system up to now." While admitting that Berdyaev's system was "not . . . the clearest" and was partially overlaid by "mystical intuitions and speculations," Balthasar judged that Berdyaev's teaching on history and eschatology was essentially sound.[100]

What did Berdyaev do for Balthasar? King and Shea suggest that "Balthasar's reading of Berdyaev remained in the background of his thought as he sought fuller answers from the [church] Fathers."[101] Berdyaev gave Balthasar an approach to history and eschatology that was Christ-centered and that viewed the Logos and the incarnation from the standpoint of myth. Myth, in Berdyaev's sense, was not a false account but a defining narrative that carried symbolic power. Balthasar viewed Berdyaev as a more theologically acceptable alternative to Hegel (*DR* 7.4–7.6), who had dissolved divine and human freedom alike within

97. The relative lack of attention to Balthasar's dissertation in the secondary literature is at least partially due to the fact that Balthasar self-published his dissertation and that copies of the work were hard to obtain until its republication in 1998.

98. J. S. King and C. M. Shea, "Role of Nikolai Berdyaev," 230.

99. Balthasar, *Glory of the Lord*, 3:279–352.

100. J. S. King and C. M. Shea, "Role of Nikolai Berdyaev," 242, citing Balthasar, *Geschichte*, 231 (their translation). King and Shea comment that "the level of praise offered here to Berdyaev is unique" (242).

101. J. S. King and C. M. Shea, "Role of Nikolai Berdyaev," 250.

the realm of the Absolute. Berdyaev's philosophy beckoned because its ethos was personalist (i.e., stressing human agency) rather than necessitarian. At the same time, Balthasar came to criticize Berdyaev for following Böhme and making the *Ungrund* a primal abyss that ontologically preceded and grounded the trinitarian God (*DR* 5.3). Balthasar detected Hegelian or totalizing tendencies that still remained in Berdyaev's philosophy.[102]

In the work that Balthasar wrote during the decade after completing his dissertation, *Apokalypse der deutschen Seele: Studien zur einer Lehre von letzten Haltungen (Apocalypse of the German Soul: Studies toward a Doctrine of the Last Things)* (1937–39), he built on ideas contained in his dissertation yet pursued a more ambitious agenda of cultural criticism. Three volumes, comprising seventeen hundred pages of densely packed prose, treated dozens of major authors and sought to show both the promise and the failure of modern German literature. The overall project of the *Apokalypse* volumes becomes clear only when we refer back to Henri de Lubac and his fundamental notion of a natural human desire for the supernatural. De Lubac's views on nature and grace, as Karen Kilby notes, were "very much absorbed and made his own by Balthasar," and they resulted in a certain worldview that stressed continuity rather than discontinuity between the world's strivings for the transcendent and God's gracious purposes. Kilby writes, "The world as a whole will not fundamentally be conceived as either hostile to or even neutral towards the Church, but as the sphere in which there is necessarily a seeking for what is not yet found, an inchoate, inarticulate desire for the faith, the beginnings and the struggles towards something which cannot be found within the world's own resources."[103] De Lubac's theology thus played a programmatic role in the *Apokalypse* volumes, where Balthasar sought to show that modern German culture embodied certain questions regarding human history and destiny that it could not properly answer without reference to the Christian message. An apologetic program of cultural analysis crystallized

---

102. See J. S. King and C. M. Shea, "Role of Nikolai Berdyaev," 230–31, 252n92. King and Shea state, "The personal character of Berdyaev's thought . . . attracted Balthasar and helped him to begin articulating a fundamentally dramatic understanding of human and divine existence, as opposed to a Hegelian or dialectical understanding of the same" (231). Balthasar's preoccupation with Kierkegaard and Nietzsche, alongside Berdyaev, may have had something to do with their emphasis on freedom. Both were champions of individuality and freedom rather than systematicity and necessity. In later writings, Balthasar upbraided Moltmann for his Hegelianism. In Moltmann, who is "nearer to Hegel" than Rahner was, "God is entangled in the world process and becomes a tragic, mythological God" (Balthasar, *TD* 4:321–22). "Moltmann . . . endeavors to reinterpret Hegel" and yet "has arrived at Hegel's view in his *Phenomenology*" (5:227–28). It comes then as an irony that one recent interpreter argues that Balthasar was Hegelian even against himself. See Quash, *Theology and the Drama of History.*

103. Kilby, *Balthasar*, 21.

out of Balthasar's Lubacian vision of human culture as striving toward the supernatural.[104]

Prior to his encounters with Karl Barth and Adrienne von Speyr, both of whom would have a far-reaching influence, Balthasar by the end of the 1930s had adopted from Berdyaev a Christ-centered model for understanding cosmology, history, and eschatology. His studies of such church fathers as Origen, Gregory of Nyssa, and Maximus the Confessor then allowed him to flesh out some of the basic conceptions of God and the world that he seems originally to have derived from Berdyaev. From de Lubac, Balthasar learned of the natural desire for the supernatural, and this allowed him to engage in an extensive exploration of modern German literature and to interpret its reflections on eschatology and human destiny as embodying an implicit cultural quest for fulfillment—a completion only possible in relation to a Catholic understanding of God, of Christ, and of nature and grace.

At the first stage of his theological development, Balthasar did not think much of Barth. He believed that Barth gave no place to created freedom and human culture, placing it all under the judgment of God's great "No." He regarded Barth's dialectical method in theology as a denial of Christ's full and true incarnation. The God whom Barth's *Epistle to the Romans* had called "wholly Other" could not have a genuine relation to the world. In Balthasar's view, "Berdyaev offered a corrective, which placed Christ at the heart of the world in a primordial sense, thereby offering a lens to interpret the whole of history in more intimately Christological terms."[105] Over time, though, Balthasar's views of Barth began to change. Through reading Barth's *Church Dogmatics*—and especially Barth's account of the divine perfections in *Church Dogmatics* II/1—Balthasar began to believe that Barth had something positive to contribute. By the time that Balthasar published his *Theology of Karl Barth* (1951), a work that Barth regarded as the single best book on his own theology, Balthasar interpreted Barth's theological development as a steady progression away from a dialectical understanding of God-versus-the-world and toward a more "catholic," analogical, and incarnational doctrine of God-with-the-world. Barth's essay "The Humanity of God" (1956) might be cited in support of Balthasar's overall thesis.[106] If Balthasar interpreted Barth correctly

---

104. Given the timing of Balthasar's work in the 1930s, one thinks quite naturally of the "theology of culture" simultaneously being developed by Paul Tillich, who later coined the expression "Religion is the substance of culture, culture is the form of religion" (*Theology of Culture*, 42).

105. J. S. King and C. M. Shea, "Role of Nikolai Berdyaev," 240–41. Balthasar's strictures on Barth appear repeatedly in his 1930 dissertation, *Geschichte*, 201–2, 205, 208.

106. Barth, *Humanity of God*.

on this point, then both Balthasar's view of Barth and Barth's own views shifted over time.[107]

What, then, was Balthasar's relation to Barth? Different interpreters have given different answers. Edward Oakes sees a weak connection, speaking merely of "elective affinities" between the two.[108] In contrast, Fergus Kerr views Balthasar's massive, multivolume *Glory of the Lord* as essentially an elaboration of Barth's view of God's glory in Christ.[109] In this view, Balthasar's reading of Barth's discussion of the divine attributes in *Church Dogmatics* II/1 had a deep and constitutive impact in setting Balthasar's theological-aesthetic agenda. Stephen Wigley in *Karl Barth and Hans Urs von Balthasar* (2007) takes a double-sided approach. On the one hand, Balthasar sometimes reacted against Barth. This was especially the case when Balthasar defended the doctrine of *analogia entis* (analogy of being) as formulated by Balthasar's Jesuit mentor, Erich Przy-wara.[110] In a 1940 letter from Balthasar to Barth, Balthasar vigorously contested Barth's rejection of the *analogia entis*, yet he said that he appreciated the *Church Dogmatics* because he sensed that the form and tone of the work followed the form and tone of revelation itself—something that Balthasar had long wanted to see in theological literature.[111] From this letter it seems that Balthasar was as interested in the formal characteristics of the *Church Dogmatics* as he was in its material content. According to Wigley, when Balthasar was not reacting against Barth, he was often developing theological insights that he had first gleaned from Barth. Both Kerr and Wigley see Barth's influence on Balthasar as far-reaching in scope.[112]

107. Bruce McCormack challenges "the von Balthasarian formula of a 'turn from dialectic to analogy'" and argues instead that "Barth's development . . . did not entail the abandonment or even the weakening of his early commitment to 'dialectical theology.' His mature theology is best understood as a distinctive form of 'dialectical theology' which I will refer to throughout as 'critically realistic dialectical theology.' . . . Where that has not been grasped, virtually the whole of Barth's theology has been read in the wrong light" (*Karl Barth's Critically Realistic Dialectical Theology*, ix–x). McCormack agrees with Ingrid Spieckermann's *Gotteserkenntnis*, according to which Barth's development "after the break with liberal theology" was "a more or less continuous unfolding of a single material insight or intention"—that is, "to ground theology in the objectively real Self-speaking of God in revelation" (McCormack, *Karl Barth's Critically Realistic Dialectical Theology*, 9). On McCormack's general interpretation of Barth, see DR 9.1.

108. Oakes, *Pattern of Redemption*, 48.

109. Kerr, "Assessing This 'Giddy Synthesis,'" 1–5, esp. 10.

110. On the Barth-Balthasar interchange in relation to Przywara, see Betz, "Translator's Introduction."

111. Lochbrunner, *Hans Urs von Balthasar und seine Theologenkollegen*, 269–79, quoted in J. S. King and C. M. Shea, "Role of Nikolai Berdyaev," 241n50.

112. Wigley (*Karl Barth and Hans Urs von Balthasar*, 103–4) notes that the last volume of Balthasar's *Theo-drama* (vol. 5) shows a greater influence of Adrienne von Speyr's visions and experiences. Balthasar remained just as Christocentric as ever, but the interpretation of Christ was largely shaped by von Speyr, who is quoted frequently.

On the other hand, Barth's doctrine of election—alien as it generally was to Balthasar's theological sensibility—does not seem to have influenced Balthasar in the direction of universalism as much as other factors in Balthasar's intellectual background. As noted above, the early influence of the Greek fathers (Origen, Gregory of Nyssa, and Maximus the Confessor), together with Henri de Lubac's revolutionary new understanding of Thomism in terms of a supernatural finality within nature, likely turned Balthasar toward what eventually became his "hopeful universalism." It is striking and surprising to see that Balthasar in *Dare We Hope?* did not cite Barth as an ally in thinking more expansively about salvation. Given Barth's reluctance to assert universal salvation, one might have expected Balthasar to acknowledge Barth as a fellow "hopeful universalist." Instead, in *Dare We Hope?* Balthasar asserted that Barth had gone too far in the direction of *apokatastasis*. Balthasar's objections to Barth sound a bit like those of Emil Brunner and G. C. Berkouwer, two Reformed theologians who had rejected Barth's teaching on universal election (*DR* 9.8). One gets a different impression from Balthasar's statement that he "was tremendously and lastingly attracted by Barth's doctrine of election, that brilliant overcoming of Calvin."[113] In the final volume of *Theo-drama*, Balthasar discussed Barth extensively and appreciatively.[114] For a number of reasons, then, it is remarkable to see how much Balthasar distanced himself from Barth in *Dare We Hope?*[115] This likely had something to do with the polemical responses of Balthasar's fellow Catholic thinkers to his increasingly overt expressions of universalistic belief or hope and to Balthasar's need to show that he was not merely aping the dogmatic theories of a leading Protestant. Yet it also reflected Balthasar's tendency—as we saw with regard to Berdyaev and Nietzsche—of drawing insights from various authors and then distancing himself from them by emphasizing only his points of difference.

---

113. Balthasar, *Our Task*, 101.

114. Balthasar, *TD* 5:236–39, 270–72, 319.

115. The biblical image of two final outcomes, writes Balthasar, "remains a theologically grounded existential statement, and in no way a theoretical-systematic one. It also should not, therefore—as in system-building theses such as those put forward by Karl Barth—be interpreted as meaning that Jesus, as God's chosen One, is rejected in place of all sinners, 'so that, besides him, no one may be lost'" (*Dare We Hope?*, 44–45, citing Barth, *KD* II/1, 551). The problem is that Balthasar's discussion of Holy Saturday in *Mysterium Paschale* and other contexts rests on the same logic of Christ's substitutionary suffering for sinners that Barth also employs. Though focusing on Holy Saturday as much as or more than Good Friday, Balthasar likewise affirms that Christ is "rejected in place of all sinners," and the inference attributed to Barth—"that, besides him, no one may be lost"—is consistent with Balthasar's own reasoning. Balthasar states that Barth's view "comes too close to the doctrine of *apokatastasis*," that "what remains for me an object of hope becomes for him practically a certainty" (*Dare We Hope?*, 197), and that Barth's disavowal of *apokatastasis* is "rhetorical" rather than substantive (94). Yet it is not clear to what extent Balthasar can distinguish his views regarding the salvific outcome of Christ's redemptive work from those of Barth.

10.6. Balthasar's Theological Relation to Adrienne von Speyr

If one takes Balthasar at his word, then it would be difficult to overestimate the importance of his relationship to the Swiss physician Adrienne von Speyr (1902–67).[116] He wrote, "Her work and mine cannot be separated from one another either psychologically or theologically. They are two halves of one whole, with a single foundation at the center."[117] Another quotation is even more intriguing: "On the whole I received far more from her, theologically, than she from me, though, of course, the exact proportion can never be calculated. As her confessor and spiritual director, I observed her interior life most closely, yet in twenty-seven years I never had the least doubt about the authentic mission that was hers." He continues, "I not only made some of the most difficult decisions of my life—including my leaving the Jesuit Order—following her advice, but I also strove to bring my way of looking at Christian revelation into conformity with hers."[118] Von Speyr converted to Catholicism under Balthasar's personal influence. He was, as he states, "her confessor and spiritual director." Yet Balthasar left the Jesuit order "following her advice" and "strove" to interpret Scripture (i.e., "Christian revelation") as von Speyr taught him to read it. So we have to ask, which of the two was spiritually directing, and which was being directed? The answer remains unclear. From his statements, it seems that Balthasar was remarkably receptive, paying close attention to her visions and to their theological implications.

Balthasar learned from von Speyr's experiences, while for her part she declared that he alone was able to understand her. Balthasar spent the latter period of his life living under the same roof with von Speyr and her husband. Balthasar also founded a lay religious community with von Speyr. By any measure, their relationship was extraordinarily close. Karen Kilby writes that "teasing out what influence precisely von Speyr had on him, or indeed which direction the influence worked, would be no easy matter."[119] The problem in seeking to assess this relationship is that we have virtually no access to von Speyr's experiences, ideas, viewpoints, and personality except by means of the books that Balthasar transcribed from her spoken words and published on her behalf. As Balthasar

---

116. See Balthasar, First Glance at Adrienne von Speyr, and Balthasar's account of his common calling and work with von Speyr in Our Task. A sympathetic account of the relationship appears in Roten, "Two Halves of the Moon." Much more critical are Gardiner, "Dubious Adrienne von Speyr"; Mullarkey, "Idolatry of Devout Ideas."

117. Henrici, "Sketch of von Balthasar's Life," 28, quoting Balthasar, Rechenschaft (1965), 35. The "foundation" that Balthasar references in this context may be the Community of St. John that he cofounded with von Speyr.

118. Balthasar, First Glance at Adrienne von Speyr, 13.

119. Kilby, Balthasar, 9.

said, their vocations were fused into one. Yet Balthasar did not merely transcribe von Speyr's words and publish them; he also frequently quoted von Speyr in his own writings. From these quotations alone—without knowing anything else about their relationship—we can trace, at least in general terms, the sort of influence that her writings had on him. Balthasar quite obviously was not dependent on von Speyr for his technical or academic knowledge. Yet when Balthasar discussed the inner life of the Trinity or the psychology of Christ—for example, the relations of Father with Son and Spirit, the primal emptying of the Father to beget the Son (*Urkenosis*), or Jesus's experiences during his descent to the dead—then he seems to have been almost wholly dependent on von Speyr's experiences. This becomes especially evident in volume 5 of *Theo-drama* and in volume 2 of *Theo-logic*, where the quotations from von Speyr increase in number and significance.

Some of von Speyr's reported experiences were rather strange. According to Balthasar's account, she was able to bilocate, so that she could be speaking with Balthasar while being simultaneously in a concentration camp, the papal Curia, a convent, or a confessional. Other ecstatic or paranormal phenomena were also reported in connection with von Speyr. She not only bilocated but also had the stigmata, talked with the Virgin Mary, and visited hell or the realm of the dead each year on Holy Saturday.[120] Supposedly von Speyr overheard dozens if not hundreds of different saints in heaven and so could describe the prayer life of particular saints (e.g., Ignatius of Loyola) because she had heard from the saint in question.[121] The sheer number and variety of unusual phenomena that von Speyr claimed for herself (or that Balthasar claimed for her) ought to give one pause. By Balthasar's account, she had experienced almost everything that the medieval saints and mystics, taken collectively, had experienced. The plethora of reported experiences causes one to wonder whether von Speyr was a great

---

120. Balthasar writes:

> From 1941 onward, year after year—in the interior experiences which she [von Speyr] has described—she was allowed to share in the suffering of Christ. This occurred during the days of Holy Week (and often the whole of Lent was a preparation for it). A landscape of pain and undreamt-of variety was disclosed to me, who was permitted to assist her: how many and diverse were the kinds of fear, at the Mount of Olives and at the Cross, how many kinds of shame, outrage and humiliation, how many forms of Godforsakenness of Christ's relation to the sin of the world, quite apart from the inexhaustible abundance of physical pain. (*First Glance at Adrienne von Speyr*, 64–65)

121. Kilby, *Balthasar*, 27–29. Kilby explains that Balthasar would direct von Speyr to a particular saint: "A short prayer would 'transport' Adrienne into the 'ecstasy of obedience'" (Balthasar, *First Glance at Adrienne von Speyr*, 74, cited in Kilby, *Balthasar*, 28). Then another short prayer would bring her back to this world: "While in this state of ecstasy, she would produce a description of the saint in question, and could, if asked, provide answers to supplementary questions" (Kilby, *Balthasar*, 29).

mystic or else greatly deluded. Von Speyr often commented on Scripture but
said that she avoided rereading the Bible before beginning to comment on it.
She seems to have viewed the actual reading of the Bible as an impediment to
the free flow of her own, God-directed process of commentary: "And since I
started work on the commentaries I have read very little in Scripture. I have to
remain open for God. . . . I do not want to forestall God."[122]

Karen Kilby offers the following reflections regarding von Speyr's influence
on Balthasar:

> If one considers Balthasar's description of the range and extraordinary character
> (even by the standards of previous mystics) of her experiences, as well as the
> enormous effort he put into taking dictation and publishing her work, and again
> the way in which he allowed the requirements she made of him, or that God made
> of him through her, to completely unsettle, indeed to destabilize, the pattern of
> his life, it is hard to avoid the conclusion that she and her visions and other ex-
> periences were of considerable significance in both his life and his thought. It is
> not unheard of for theologians in the Catholic tradition to look to the writings of
> the mystics as a theological source. What the mystics describe is never thought
> to constitute a new revelation, but it can nevertheless be taken as a source of
> possible insight, or a locus to which one might turn to confirm a line of thought.
> Something rather uncommon in Balthasar's case, however, is his *proximity* to his
> theological source. Balthasar is influenced by, and in some cases makes appeal to
> the experiences, not of someone whose visions and writings have been sifted and
> over time received as authentic by the Church, but to someone in whose house
> he lived and with whom he himself was closely involved—as the one who guided
> her into the Church, as spiritual director, as scribe, editor, publisher, co-founder
> of an order, and so on.[123]

This leads into an awkward question: Does the veracity and value of Balthasar's
theology depend on the credibility of von Speyr's visions? To a large extent, the
secondary literature on Balthasar has avoided posing or addressing this question. Judging by Balthasar's own statements, it is hard to see how one can avoid
the question of von Speyr's credibility as a visionary.[124] Von Speyr disclosed to

122. Balthasar, *First Glance at Adrienne von Speyr*, 148.

123. Kilby, *Balthasar*, 30.

124. Might one evaluate von Speyr's theological position *without* appraising the validity or
soundness of her spiritual experiences? The problem is that von Speyr almost never *argues* for a
theological position, but instead *reports* on her encounters in the spiritual world. These accounts
call less for rational analysis than for faith ("Yes, God gave her this experience"), for skepticism, or
for some blend of the two. The same issue appears with regard to a number of universalists who
appealed to paranormal experiences in support of their belief in universalism (see *DR* 12.4). In the
case of reason- and evidence-based argumentation, one wants to avoid the "genetic fallacy," whereby

Balthasar a number of key ideas (e.g., on Holy Saturday and inner-trinitarian relations) that in time became incorporated into the structure of Balthasar's theology and that Balthasar might not have embraced apart from von Speyr's advocacy.[125]

Mysterium Paschale is the work that offers the fullest account of Balthasar's views regarding Holy Saturday. While Christ went to the cross and suffered there, he writes, Christ's agony of separation from the Father did not decrease when he died. At this point, Christ entered what Balthasar in his *Theo-logic* calls the abode of "sin having become already amorphous."[126] In the realm of the dead, the dead Christ became completely passive in his obedient submission to the Father (German *Kadavergehorsam*). His absolute Godforsakenness then "infiltrates" that of sinners.[127] Christ's descent to the dead *precedes* that of sinners in hell, so that Balthasar reverses the time sequence that one would ordinarily expect. Since Christ precedes sinners, they arrive at this place of turning away from God and there confront Christ. The Son catches up with them, and sinners even in the midst of their rebellion against God are confronted by God's loving presence.

---

one seeks to discredit a given belief by giving an unfavorable account of the genesis or origin of the belief in question (e.g., "You only believe *that* because it is politically convenient for you to do so"). In the case of those claiming to receive supernatural guidance or information, the situation is rather different, since the purported source of the information (i.e., a revelatory vision or other God-given experience) is the very basis of someone's claim to be presenting true—though perhaps otherwise unknown—information. In this instance, the character of the experience in which the information was imparted does matter and so needs to be discussed and discerned.

125. Edward Oakes argues that one must "take time" to judge the value of a mystic's utterances and teaching: "Private reflections and personal opinions of a theologian, especially one who bases his works so heavily on the graces of a mystic, take time" (*Pattern of Redemption*, 242). Oakes interprets this "taking time" in Balthasar's favor. Yet two approaches to discernment would be possible. One would be to "take time" and not rush to evaluate Balthasar and von Speyr. The other would be to criticize Balthasar because he himself did not "take time" but based his theology so heavily on the ideas of a mystic who was still living, whose ideas had not been sifted and appraised by the church, and concerning whom Balthasar himself was not objective. Karl Rahner, in his essay "Private Revelations," comments:

> Any given private revelation is always . . . a synthesis in which the character of the recipient, as determined historically . . . and psychologically (or para-psychologically), is fused with the mystical or normal grace given to him in the depths of his existence. Hence one cannot exclude the possibility of illusions, misinterpretations and distortions even where there is genuine private revelation according to the ordinary criteria by which mystical phenomena are judged. . . . The "genuineness" of a private revelation is a very variable quantity. (358)

126. Balthasar, *Theo-logik*, 2:324. The sentence that follows summarizes Lösel, "Murder in the Cathedral," 434–36. The idea of sin as involving formlessness comes up in various contexts in Balthasar's writings. Von Speyr suggested that souls in heaven might have "effigies" existing below in the realm of the dead. It was as though the self could be split, so that one part of the self might experience God's presence, while the other would experience God's absence. For a discussion of this idea, see Balthasar, *Theo-logic*, 2:345–61 (*Theo-Logik*, 2:356–57). The issue is treated in Brotherton, "Possibility of Universal Conversion in Death," 307, 319.

127. Balthasar, *TD* 4:232.

Christ's descent into hell thus becomes God's endgame to bring the final outcome of Balthasar's theo-drama. Without being definitive on the question, Balthasar was hopeful that the encounter of postmortem sinners with a postmortem Christ would avert the tragedy of eternal death for each individual.[128] Summing up his view on Holy Saturday, Balthasar writes, "In Adrienne's new experience and interpretation of hell, this means descent into that reality of sin which the Cross has separated from man and humanity, the thing God has eternally and finally cast out of the world, the thing in which God never, ever, can be."[129]

The idea of a postmortem Christ in the realm of the dead, encountering post-mortem sinners, seeking to bring them to personal conversion, is in multiple respects a theological innovation, without precedent in earlier Catholic tradition on Christ's descent to the realm of the dead (*DR* 1.6). The language cited above regarding sin as a "thing . . . finally cast out of the world" is also quite striking. It suggests a *reification* of sin—no longer a human choice but a thing or entity that God expels from the world.[130] Balthasar's theology of Holy Saturday is thus genuinely novel, and its novelty rests to a large degree on Balthasar's relationship with von Speyr and his theological dependence on von Speyr's experiences.[131]

10.7. Balthasar's *Theo-drama* and the Idea of *Urkenosis*

At the conclusion of the final volume of *Theo-drama*, Balthasar asks his readers to consider eternal damnation from a divine rather than human perspective.

128. Joshua Brotherton, in "Possibility of Universal Conversion in Death," develops a far-reaching interpretation of Balthasar's theology of the human encounter with Christ. Brotherton argues that "the enigmatic relationship between time and eternity is most plausibly the key to interpreting Balthasar's hope for universal salvation" (321). Balthasar's "reflections on Christ's death and descent into hell favor more the notion of an existential opportunity for grace in death, a transformative en-counter with the crucified Christ, than the notion of a post-mortem conversion or the self-annihilative character of condemnation" (324). In Balthasar there is a distinction between "empirical or clinical death and metaphysical death" (324). Brotherton concludes that, in Balthasar, "hope for universal salvation can be none other than hope for universal conversion in death" (324). Brotherton builds on the idea found in Joseph Ratzinger (Pope Benedict XVI) of purgatorial time as an existential moment. See Brotherton, "Balthasar on the Redemptive Descent."

129. Balthasar, *Our Task*, 65.

130. As Matthew Croasmun shows in *The Emergence of Sin: The Cosmic Tyrant in Romans*, there is a biblical basis for such a reification of sin. In Pauline texts, nonetheless, sin is at least as much an individual choice and social reality as it is an impersonal force or agency.

131. Balthasar's doctrinal innovation is a theme in Pitstick, *Light in Darkness*; Pitstick, "Development of Doctrine, or Denial?"; Pitstick and Oakes, "Balthasar, Hell, and Heresy." See also D'Costa, "Descent into Hell"; Oakes, "Internal Logic"; Oakes, "*Descensus* and Development." Against Pitstick's view, Paul Griffiths's "Is There a Doctrine of the Descent into Hell?" argues that Balthasar's Holy Saturday theology did not violate any norm of Catholic teaching or orthodoxy. Cf. Lauber, "Toward a Theology of Holy Saturday."

In that case, the question is not "What do people lose if they lose relationship with God?" but rather "What does God lose?" Nicholas Healy comments, "Now, to pose such a question implies that it is really possible for God to 'lose' something, and that such a loss would be a tragedy for God. According to Balthasar, the *eschaton*, the ultimate destiny of the world, is dramatic not only for creation but also for God."[132] Balthasar's *Theo-drama*, the five-volume work that many see as his finest, is based on a notion of drama not only in the world that God created and is redeeming but also within God's own eternal and trinitarian life. Balthasar describes this intra-divine drama by saying that "it is the drama of the 'emptying' of the Father's heart, in the generation of the Son, that contains and surpasses all possible drama between God and a world."[133]

In *Theo-drama*, Balthasar often uses the analogy of a theatrical performance. In the world-play, God may be regarded alternately as the author, director, and actor.[134] While human beings might not perceive this to be the case, none of us can avoid playing a part in this play. Noninvolvement is impossible. Balthasar comments, "There is no standpoint from which we could observe and portray events as if we were uninvolved narrators of an epic."[135] Notwithstanding Balthasar's portrayal of a theater in which everyone is an actor, Kilby asks, "Is Balthasar himself, in his very construal of the whole of everything as a drama, not taking the role of theater critic—and perhaps also a theorist of drama—rather than that of an actor *within* the drama?"[136]

The theme of kenosis or divine self-giving runs as a leitmotif throughout Balthasar's thinking on the drama of redemption, and indeed throughout his reflections on creation and the inner life of the Godhead as well. The Father, Son, and Spirit set the stage for the drama through the act of creating the world. In the act of creating, the divine persons restrict their freedom in an event that could be considered the first extra-divine kenosis, through sharing their loving communion with other personal beings—that is, creatures.[137] Essential to Balthasar's view of Christ is the notion of "mission" or "sending." Christ's being sent into the world by the Father and his obedience to the Father's call

---

132. Healy, *Eschatology of Hans Urs von Balthasar*, 1.

133. Balthasar, *TD* 4:327.

134. Balthasar, *TD* 1:135–258. Balthasar developed this idea of the "theatre of the world" at least partially through his encounter with the Spanish poet Calderon de la Barca (1600–1681). See *TD* 1:163–77, 361–69.

135. Balthasar, *TD* 2:58.

136. Kilby, *Balthasar*, 65.

137. Lösel, "Murder in the Cathedral," 432. Lösel notes that the idea of creation-as-kenosis—in connection with the Lurianic idea of *tsimtsum*—appears in Moltmann, *Trinity and the Kingdom*, 109–11; Moltmann, *God in Creation*, 86–93. Balthasar critiques the idea of *tsimtsum* in *TD* 2:260–71. See the discussion of kabbalistic theology in *DR* 2.5 and its use by Moltmann in *DR* 9.10–9.11.

give meaning to his life. What is true of Christ in this respect is true of all other human beings. God bestows an individual mission on every individual human being, and it is the particular mission given to each individual that gives that individual his or her ultimate significance.[138]

The event of Christ's death on the cross is the moment when eternity vertically breaks into human history. As Steffen Lösel explains, "The incarnation *per se* is not the focus of Balthasar's interest, but rather its 'perfection' on the cross. The point of the incarnation is not the Son's assumption of creatureliness as such, but rather his assumption of the concrete human condition of suffering and death."[139] Good Friday is the moment in Christ's history that reveals an absolute distance between the Father and the Son. This intra-divine separation constitutes a supreme form of suffering in the Godhead. Yet, as Balthasar states it, "the once-and-for-all, temporal history of Christ is mysteriously rendered present to all times."[140] The trans-temporality of Christ's history is important, since it implies that Christ's suffering does not come to an end on the cross but continues forever. Balthasar states that Christ's "experience of being abandoned on the Cross is timeless," and he quotes approvingly from Pascal, who says that "Jesus' agony lasts until the end of the world."[141] On this point Balthasar's position seems to be closer to that of Russian theologians like Berdyaev (*DR* 8.5) and Bulgakov (*DR* 8.6–8.8) than to that of most fellow Catholic thinkers.

Balthasar's thinking about Christ's cross is rooted in something primordial in God—namely, the kenosis or self-emptying of God the Father in the begetting of God the Son. He presses beyond and away from the historical event of Jesus's crucifixion toward an eternal or transcendent grounding within God for this event. As noted above, Balthasar disavows Moltmann's theology for its Hegelian tendencies. Specifically, he objects to understanding the historical event of Jesus's death as the locus in which God's trinitarian existence first becomes fully actualized. Balthasar objects that Moltmann, like Hegel, draws God downward into the world and thus enmeshes God in the world process. Balthasar's thought generally moves in the opposite or upward direction, asserting that human "suffering," "otherness," and "distance" have an eternal grounding in a "separation" between God the Father and God the Son. This is known as *Urkenosis*, the kenosis before the kenosis—in other words, the

138. Lösel, "Murder in the Cathedral," 430–31, citing Balthasar, *TD* 3:202–30.

139. Lösel, "Murder in the Cathedral," 431, citing Balthasar, *TD* 3:46–56; Balthasar, *Glory of the Lord*, 7:212.

140. Balthasar, *TD* 2:74.

141. Balthasar, *TD* 4:336–37. In another passage Balthasar writes that "the Lord's sufferings were . . . supra-temporal: every moment of his suffering has an 'eternal' intensity, and precisely because of this, it towers far above chronological time. Thus we can say in truth that he suffers until the end of time" (*Grain of Wheat*, 69–70).

kenosis eternally prior to the self-emptying of the Son in the event of becoming incarnate as a human being.

The fourth volume of *Theo-drama* contains one of the clearest expressions of *Urkenosis*: "God the Father can give his divinity away . . . [and] this implies such an incomprehensible and unique 'separation' [*Trennung*] of God from himself that it includes and grounds every other separation—be it never so dark and bitter."[142] This *Urkenosis* is so theologically unconventional that some of Balthasar's interpreters have tried to mollify or modify it. On "God's separation from himself," Healy writes, "It is crucial to note that Balthasar does not mean to suggest that there is negativity in God's inner life. These words must be understood as analogous concepts which point to a positive modality of selfless love."[143] Yet Balthasar affirms what Healy denies, saying expressly that "separation" within God "includes and grounds every other separation—be it never so dark and bitter." In Balthasar's way of thinking, the "separation" within God can "include" or "ground" the "dark and bitter" creaturely "separation," because the "separation" within God is likewise "dark and bitter." *Urkenosis* means that separation and suffering have a place within God. *Urkenosis* derives its fuller meaning from the life history of Jesus, from Jesus's suffering, and perhaps from our own suffering as well.

In expounding his doctrine of *Urkenosis*, Balthasar names Sergius Bulgakov (*DR* 8.6–8.8) as his source: "It is possible to say, with Bulgakov, that the Father's self-utterance in the generation of the Son is an initial 'kenosis' within the Godhead that underpins all subsequent kenosis. For the Father strips himself, without remainder, of his Godhead and hands it over to the Son." He adds that "this divine act that brings forth the Son . . . involves the positing of an absolute, infinite 'distance' that can contain and embrace all the other distances that are possible within the world of finitude, including the distance of sin."[144] Once again, we can see clearly here that *Urkenosis* plays a foundational metaphysical role, since it "underpins all subsequent kenosis." This statement about "subsequent kenosis" says much, since self-emptying, servitude, suffering, and obedience are all fundamental to Balthasar's understanding of Jesus's life and the Christian life too.[145] As Karen Kilby writes, "One finds in his theology . . . a vivid depiction of the inner life of the Trinity which is genuinely *integral* to his presentation of the story of salvation."[146] The explicit reference to Bulgakov

142. Balthasar, *TD* 4:325.

143. Healy, *Eschatology of Hans Urs von Balthasar*, 134.

144. Balthasar, *TD* 4:323.

145. Timothy J. Yoder highlights kenosis as a governing concept in Balthasar's notion of saintliness and the Christian life. See Yoder, "Hans Urs von Balthasar and Kenosis."

146. Kilby, *Balthasar*, 94.

suggests a relation between Balthasar's teaching and the modern Russian theological and sophiological traditions.

Is Balthasar's *Urkenosis* theologically intelligible? What is meant by the Father's eternal act in which he "strips himself, without remainder, of his Godhead" and then "hands it over" to the Son? Balthasar has not left much wiggle room in his verbal formulation. He does not signal in this passage that he is using a metaphor. In ordinary discourse, a person who "strips himself, without remainder" is left with nothing. If I "strip myself" of all my clothing, then I am naked. If I "strip myself" of all my money, then I am destitute. So we are led to ask what Balthasar might mean in speaking of the Father as "stripping himself" of all divinity. Could it be that God the Father, having lost his Godhead, would then *become nothing* or *be nothing*? This sort of *Urkenosis* would mean the death of God the Father to bring life to God the Son.[147] A number of Balthasar's key assertions regarding the *Urkenosis* seem to be not so much false as unintelligible. It is difficult just to decipher what Balthasar means, let alone to defend whatever he means. In placing the *Urkenosis* at the climax of his major work, *Theo-drama*, Balthasar set a question mark above his doctrine of God and his account of the drama of salvation. Karl Rahner went so far as to call Balthasar's viewpoint "a theology of the death of God that . . . seems to me to be gnostic."[148]

What seems "gnostic" here is the implication that suffering is inherent to God as such.[149] Balthasar's frequent identification of love as suffering and suffering as love comes dangerously close to implying that an eternally loving God must be an eternally suffering God. He writes, "The more we come to know God, the more the difference between joy and suffering becomes tenuous . . . [for] love itself becomes painful, and this pain becomes an irreplaceable bliss." In the same context we read that purgatory is "perhaps the deepest but also the most blissful kind of suffering."[150] It seems as though Balthasar is engaged in theodicy, seeking to rationalize the existence of evil by sanctifying, eternalizing, and indeed divinizing, suffering itself. Balthasar lingers over the theme

147. The nearest analogy to this way of speaking about the Father and the Son lies in the radical, Hegelian, Nietzschean, death-of-God theology of Thomas J. J. Altizer. Altizer reinterprets the Christian doctrine of the incarnation as implying a kind of "suicide" by God the Father, which resulted in God's presence within God the Son, followed by a total presence to the world in God the Spirit. See Thomas J. J. Altizer's books *The Gospel of Christian Atheism* (1966); *The Descent into Hell* (1970); *Genesis and Apocalypse* (1990); *The Genesis of God* (1993); *Godhead and the Nothing* (2003); *The Apocalyptic Trinity* (2012).

148. Rahner, *Karl Rahner in Dialogue*, 126.

149. See Koslowski and Hermanni, *Der leidende Gott*, where an inherently suffering God is said to be characteristic of ancient gnosis, Hegelian philosophy, and certain contemporary theological writers.

150. Balthasar, *Grain of Wheat*, 13.

of suffering and emphasizes the magnitude, depth, and immensity of Jesus's agony on the cross and then during his descent into the underworld. In tracing the root of suffering and evil into eternity past and into the Godhead itself, Balthasar's theology shows affinities to the kabbalistic quest for the "root of roots"—that is, the contemplation of an upside-down "tree" of divine emanations (DR 2.5). Beginning with the twigs, continuing to the branches, proceeding to the trunk, one comes at last to the "root of roots"—for Balthasar, the Urkenosis and its implied duality in the Godhead. In this aspect of his theology, Balthasar seems crypto-kabbalistic, finding conflict, division, and suffering not only in God's relation to the world but also in God's inner and eternal nature.

Karen Kilby comments on how Balthasar revises or reverses many traditional ideas regarding the relations of the trinitarian persons in God:

> Where in classic treatments, the closeness, the inseparability, of the Persons tends to be conceived as linked to the fullness of the Fathers's self-gift—because the Father gives everything he is to the Son, there can be no distance between them—in Balthasar's thought this same self-gift of the Father's (though here conceived as self-stripping) leads, it would seem, in precisely the opposite direction: Balthasar's assertion of the infinite difference or separation of the Persons regularly follows references to the Father giving himself away completely to the Son.[151]

For Balthasar, the cross shows us God rejected and alienated from God. God's wrath toward sin is played out between the Father and the Son in such a way that it is taken up into God. Yet, in another sense, the cross is a reflection of what always has been the case—the Urkenosis. Because of what Balthasar calls the "incomprehensible separation" of Father and Son, nothing new or wholly unprecedented is revealed when Jesus dies on the cross. Instead there is a spatial-temporal-material manifestation of the always-already reality of alienation within the Godhead. On the basis of these premises, one wonders what sort of "good news" is conveyed. Karen Kilby writes, "The way in which Balthasar brings together reflection on the immanent Trinity and reflection on the world's horrors involves, in the end, an introduction of . . . elements of darkness into the divine light. The highest love of God and the greatest misery of the world are reconciled in his thought by introducing elements of misery, destruction, and loss into the conception of love itself."[152]

151. Kilby, Balthasar, 100.
152. Ibid., 122. Another esoteric theme in Balthasar lies in his notion of the casta meretrix (virginal whore), a trope that he used to describe the church and her fall and restoration and that he applied to Adrienne von Speyr, who, according to Balthasar, lost her virginity in marital sexuality yet had her "physical virginity" restored. The idea of the fallen and sexualized Sophia, later

Some of what Balthasar wrote on the inner life of the Trinity is hard to comprehend. Balthasar writes, for example, that the Son "antecedently consent[s]" to being begotten by the Father.[153] Antecedence in the sense of temporal priority makes no sense if the Father and the Son are understood in terms of Nicene orthodoxy. Balthasar furthermore states that the Father is grateful to the Son for allowing himself to be begotten, while the Son is grateful to the Father for begetting him. Quoting from von Speyr, Balthasar tells us that "eternal amazement" is part of the life of the Trinity.[154] Thankfulness, worship, and even petitionary prayer exist among Father, Son, and Spirit. Balthasar describes in detail the Trinity's decision-making processes. Assuming that we can make sense of such statements, there is the lingering question: How could he possibly *know*? Balthasar quotes approvingly from von Speyr, saying that "in God everything is full of these loving details which contribute essentially to understanding the Trinity."[155] Here Balthasar seems to place himself, along with the visionary von Speyr, in a privileged place of knowing and understanding God. It is difficult to think of any of the great Catholic saints—for example, Augustine, Thomas Aquinas, Teresa of Ávila, or Ignatius of Loyola—who ever claimed to possess such profound and immediate insight into the *inner life* of the Trinity. No wonder, then, that Ben Quash and Karen Kilby make reference to the "God's eye view" that Balthasar assumes. He purported to know about heaven and God's inner life because it had been *disclosed* to her, she *told* him, and he *believed* her. The notion of *Urkenosis* thus evokes not only substantive questions about Balthasar's conception of God but also methodological issues regarding Balthasar's approach to theology and his claims of knowledge concerning God.

10.8. Balthasar on Eschatology Generally

In his general understanding of eschatology, Balthasar was dependent on Karl Rahner, to whom Balthasar had strongly objected during the 1960s.[156] To his credit, Balthasar acknowledged this debt to Rahner. So we may turn first to

restored to purity, is an ancient gnostic theme (*DR* 2.3, 2.11). Balthasar explores this idea in the lengthy essay "*Casta Meretrix.*"

153. Balthasar, *TD* 5:86.
154. Balthasar, *TD* 5:83.
155. Balthasar, *TD* 5:87; cf. 5:79, 87–89. Karen Kilby notes that these statements about the Trinity are not really out of place within Balthasar's vast oeuvre. His way of thinking about the Trinity was "remarkably consistent from the time that he published *Heart of the World* in 1945 through to the end of his life" (Kilby, *Balthasar*, 114). Cf. Louth, "Place of *Heart of the World.*"
156. The critique of Rahner appears especially in Balthasar, *Moment of Christian Witness.*

Rahner's seminal essay "The Hermeneutics of Eschatological Assertions" and its approach to biblical, eschatological language, and then to the programmatic treatment of eschatology in the opening section of volume 5 of *Theo-drama*. Both Balthasar's appropriation of Rahner's ideas on eschatological language and his distinctive reflections on what he calls "Jewish," "pagan," and "Christian" eschatology—in connection with his notion of "horizontal" and "vertical" dimensions—will set the context for interpreting *Dare We Hope?* and Balthasar's "hopeful universalism."

Rahner's essay on the hermeneutics of eschatological language had far-reaching significance for Rahner and for Balthasar as well. A central aspect of Rahner's argument is his proposal for a christological interpretation of the Bible's eschatological statements: "Christ himself is the hermeneutic principle of all eschatological assertions. Anything that cannot be read and understood as a Christological assertion is not a genuine eschatological assertion. It is soothsaying and apocalyptic, or a form of speech which misunderstands the Christological element, because couched in a style and an imagery borrowed from other sources."[157] Rahner's approach to eschatology in this essay is not only Christocentric but also might be called christologically restrictive. It is not clear how Rahner proposed for Christian theology to interpret the Old Testament prophecies. Throughout church history, Christian interpreters treated passages in the Old Testament (e.g., Ps. 22 and Isa. 53) as predicting the Messiah's coming and even as predicting specific events in connection with the birth, life, and death of the Messiah (e.g., that he would be born in Bethlehem and would be "numbered with transgressors"). Rahner, though, seems to allow no place for predictive prophecy, and the reference to "soothsaying" suggests perhaps that he regards the notion of prediction as pagan. The negative reference to "apocalyptic" apparently rules out present-day predictions regarding future events or Christ's second coming. Rahner's general tendency is thus to "contemporize" or "existentialize" eschatological language in the Bible that might otherwise be taken as having a predictive aspect. For Rahner, such language symbolizes human possibilities or existential choices at the present moment—not impending historical events or future states of affairs. He also denies that the common trope of two ways, two choices, or two outcomes (i.e., receiving God's grace or coming under God's judgment) is properly a New Testament theme at all. It is instead an Old Testament motif that does not carry over into the New Testament. Balthasar echoes Rahner in rejecting what he considers Old Testament or Jewish "dualism" in eschatology and also in applying the Christocentric restriction or reduction to the New Testament.

157. Rahner, "Hermeneutics," 343.

What, then, does Rahner say regarding the severe and sometimes appalling statements in the Old and New Testaments regarding God's judgments on those who reject the way of repentance and who spurn God's mercy? Once again, Rahner's existentializing tendency is apparent. Such language for him falls into the category of "threat discourse," and its purpose is not to point toward future outcomes but rather to provoke individuals who encounter such language to reflect on themselves and their decisions and perhaps to reconsider their overall direction in life.[158] One need not assume that the seeming threats of punishment will be literally fulfilled at some point in the future.[159] Interpreters of Rahner point out that his theology is grounded in a German idealist anthropology and a "transcendental Thomism" that views eschatology as an extrapolation into the future of what has already occurred in human experience. So the question arises: Can Rahner's theology, in principle, allow for radical novelty or newness in a yet-to-be-realized kingdom of God?[160] While Rahner seeks to make Christ the principle by which to judge the Bible's eschatological language, the "turn to the subject" means in practice that Rahner interprets Christ through the grid of human experience. The Christ-centered eschatology in Rahner may thus be in the end an anthropocentric eschatology.

Balthasar presents a more-or-less programmatic account of Christian eschatology in volume 5 of *Theo-drama*.[161] Here he refers approvingly to Rahner's "important article" on the hermeneutics of eschatological assertions, cites the key section regarding Christ as "the hermeneutical principle of all eschatological

158. Phan writes, "Rahner reiterates that eschatological assertions are not 'advance coverage' of the beyond or of what is going to happen at the end of time. The biblical statements about eternal punishment . . . should be interpreted in keeping with their literary genre of 'threat discourse.' That is, they place the hearers before a decision for or against God" ("Eschatology," 186, citing, Rahner, "Hell" [1969], 3).

159. Rahner's interpretation of judgment language as threat and not as prediction, though couched in modern German philosophical categories, is not unlike that of the English archbishop John Tillotson (1630–94), whose sermon "Of the Eternity of Hell Torments" (in *The Works of Dr. John Tillotson*, 3:76–97) expressed a similar view. In response, Jonathan Edwards analyzed the notions of threat, obligation, and truth telling. See Edwards's Miscellany 779 in *The Works of Jonathan Edwards*, 18:434–49. Here he argued that "if God absolutely threatened contrary to what he knew would come to pass, then he absolutely threatened contrary to what he knew to be truth; and how any can speak contrary to what they know to be truth, in declaring, promising, or threatening, or any other way consistent with perfect and inviolable truth, I can't conceive" (445–46). The issue lay in "the truth of the Lawgiver." In the same passage Edwards qualified his argument to make clear that he was only speaking of *unconditional* divine threats and not those that had overt or implied conditions attached to them.

160. See Phan, "Eschatology"; Phan, *Eternity in Time*, 64–76, 205–7; and the discussion in R. Martin, *Will Many Be Saved?*, 140–42.

161. Balthasar, *TD* 5:19–54. The section is entitled "The Idea of a Christian Eschatology."

assertions," and concludes with Rahner's methodological statement that "we can derive from our experience of Christ all that can and may be said objectively in the Catholic theology of eschatology."[162] Yet Balthasar differs from Rahner in that he seems to think of eschatological statements as pertaining not only to personal, existential experience but also to empirical, historical situations. For instance, Balthasar speaks of increasing conflict between good and evil as a characteristic of the ending of history: "The particular internal events expected at the conclusion of the history of the world . . . will be of a qualitatively special kind: they will be characterized by a heightening of the antagonism between the kingdom of Christ . . . and the kingdom of the prince of this world."[163] Certain aspects of Balthasar's discussion do not comport with Rahner's existentialist approach to eschatology. On the whole, though, Balthasar wishes to set aside what he refers to as "Old Testament" eschatology or "the Jewish perspective": "The idea of a disaster-laden end-time (including social and cosmic catastrophes) migrates into New Testament concepts; it is defined with particular clarity in the early Paul's notion of the Antichrist: on his return, Christ will slay his opponent." Balthasar adds that "here the primitive Church seems to have missed the true meaning of Jesus' own 'expectation of the imminent end' and to have directly adopted the Jewish perspective of an end to earthly history."[164] He recognizes the presence of "disaster-laden" or apocalyptic elements in the New Testament, but he regards these features as a relic or residue from Jewish teaching. Setting the Gospel of John above the Synoptic Gospels, Balthasar comments: "Ultimately . . . it is the Johannine, purely christological eschatology that retains its validity."[165]

Even more striking than this bold assertion of the priority of Johannine eschatology is a comment in the same context about how the "exalted Lord" has "taken up the entire content of all history . . . into the supra-temporal realm." The statement is italicized in the original, underscoring its significance:

Apart from unimportant and incidental vestiges of Jewish eschatology, *the New Testament no longer entertains the idea of a self-unfolding horizontal theo-drama; there is only a vertical theo-drama in which every moment of time, insofar as it has christological significance, is directly related to the exalted Lord, who has taken the*

162. Balthasar, *TD* 5:36n3, citing Rahner, "Hermeneutics," 343.

163. Balthasar, *TD* 5:19. Referring back to *TD* 4:15–67, which contains his interpretation of the book of Revelation, Balthasar writes, "There is an ever-intensifying No to the Yes uttered by God in Christ. We saw in the structure of the Book of Revelation that the decisive 'No' (on the part of the anti-Christian pseudo-'trinity') only surfaces after the birth of the Messiah-child" (*TD* 5:22).

164. Balthasar, *TD* 5:44.

165. Balthasar, *TD* 5:48. See also *TD* 5:57: "The Johannine eschatology we have already described will be of central importance in this volume."

entire content of all history—life, death and resurrection—with him into the supra-
temporal realm.[166]

Here we find a remarkably wide-ranging statement—in the final volume of
Balthasar's magnum opus—that declares, by a kind of interpretive fiat, that
New Testament eschatology is something other than Old Testament eschatology. This assertion goes against the grain of most New Testament scholarship
since World War II, which has identified eschatology and the kingdom of God
as central to Jesus's teaching and has repeatedly emphasized the Jewishness
of Jesus and the importance of Second Temple Judaism as the proper locus
for understanding Jesus. N. T. Wright, James Dunn, E. P. Sanders, and many
others have recalibrated New Testament studies along these lines during the
last thirty to forty years. The increased emphasis on the Jewish background
to the New Testament was still unfolding during the years in which Balthasar
was publishing the original German edition of his five-volume *Theo-Drama*
(1973–83). Yet the lack of attention to this development makes his interpretation
of eschatology appear to be out of step with contemporary biblical scholarship.
By subordinating the "horizontal theo-drama" that he associates with Judaism
and Jewishness to what he calls "the supra-temporal realm," Balthasar seems
to sever eschatology from the historical process.

Balthasar distinguishes what he calls "the supra-temporal realm" from the
realm of time and history.[167] More often than words like "supra-temporal,"
Balthasar speaks of the dimensions of the "horizontal" and the "vertical." Of the
three kinds of eschatology that he discusses in *Theo-drama* (Jewish, pagan, and
Christian), Balthasar classifies one of them (Jewish) as being "horizontal" in
character and the other two (pagan and Christian) as being "vertical." Balthasar
thus aligns what he regards as Christian eschatology more closely with paganism than with Judaism.[168]

166. Balthasar, *TD* 5:48.
167. The context does not allow for a discussion of Balthasar's conception of time and eternity. In
Karl Barth's conception of eternity as "God's time," human time is not negated but rather included—
in some fashion—within "God's time." See Hunsinger, "*Mysterium Trinitatis*"; Langdon, "God the
Eternal Contemporary"; *DR* appendix J on time and eternity. In Balthasar, by contrast, one sometimes
gets the impression that the "horizontal" and the "vertical" dimensions compete with one another.
In the passage cited, the "horizontal theo-drama" does not stand on its own but is "taken . . . with
him" (i.e., Christ) into the other "supra-temporal realm." At the same time, Balthasar sometimes
sounds like Barth when he argues that "everything that is understood anthropologically as the doctrine of the 'last things' must be integrated in and subordinated to this trinitarian 'time'" (*TD* 5:57).
168. Balthasar, *TD* 5:50–51. Balthasar states, "Pagan eschatology, if we can consider it such,
seems to have a certain prima facie affinity with Christian eschatology because of its essentially
vertical structure, at least in the mystery cults that . . . share a special interest in dying and rising
divinities" (50). On the next page he speaks of how "the great gnostic systems will deliberately

10.9. Balthasar's *Dare We Hope?* and Universal Salvation

Shortly after the final volume of Balthasar's *Theo-drama* was published (1983), the smaller volume *Dare We Hope?* appeared (1986). The latter was itself a spin-off from controversies that sprang up during 1984–85 over Balthasar's views on eschatology and the possibility of universal salvation.[169] German Catholic critics—whom Balthasar dubbed as "infernalists"—believed that the theologian had contradicted official church tradition and was promoting a thoughtless optimism. The critics argued that Balthasar neglected God's judgment against sin and so encouraged a presumptuousness and laxity about the importance of the church and participation in the sacraments. The opening section of *Dare We Hope?* was written in response to these critics.

When one compares *Dare We Hope?* with Balthasar's earlier publications, it is clear that the later work carries over ideas and convictions previously expressed in *Mysterium Paschale* and *Theo-drama*. *Dare We Hope?* in effect poses and answers the following question: If the redemption of sinful humanity through Christ truly has the timeless grounding in the life of the Trinity that Balthasar says it does (i.e., the *Urkenosis*), and if it also finds expression in the profound sufferings of Christ among the dead on Holy Saturday, then what are the implications for the Christian hope? At this later point in Balthasar's life, he was no longer as isolated as he had been just five or ten years earlier. He was being read more widely than before. Yet he was presenting his views to a Catholic readership that he may have expected to be skeptical. It is no surprise, then, that the controversy over Balthasar came about during the 1980s, even though his views regarding the scope of final salvation may not have shifted very much after the 1950s or 1960s.

By Balthasar's own account, the question of universal salvation lies at the center of the final volume of *Theo-drama*. In summarizing "the subject matter of this volume," Balthasar writes:

> This leaves us . . . with a whole series of open questions, crystallizing around the central question: Can divine freedom, even if it is the freedom of love, simply "overpower" created freedom? On the other hand, if . . . the divine freedom operates "by persuasion, not by force," can it be sure of attaining its goals? In the latter case, surely, may we not have to envisage a final refusal, resulting in a final rejection?[170]

---

develop [their] vertical structure contrary to Christianity" (51). The problem with gnosticism, for Balthasar, is not its "verticality" per se but rather the way that it expresses its verticality.

169. See the brief account of the controversy in Vorgrimler, *Geschichte der Hölle*, 344–45. For a more recent interpretation, see R. Martin, "Balthasar and Salvation: What Does He Really Teach?"

170. Balthasar, *TD* 5:55.

On the one hand, in calling these "open questions," it appears that Balthasar wanted to explore the implications of the different answers that might be given. On the other hand, he shows a tendency in *Dare We Hope?*, as critics note, to declare certain questions to be open but then seemingly to resolve them in the direction of universal rather than particular salvation. When he speaks of the decisive human choice against God, Balthasar appears to regard such sinful choices as preliminary and as reversible, as he says in his essay "On Vicarious Representation": "God gives man the capacity to make a (negative) choice against God that seems *for man* to be definitive, but which need not be taken *by God* as definitive."[171] In this aspect of his theology, Balthasar's position is reminiscent of and perhaps dependent on that of Barth, who spoke of the creature's final, sinful refusal of God as an "impossible possibility" and went so far as to say that a believer in Christ could not regard an unbeliever's lack of faith as a "final fact."[172]

One criticism of *Dare We Hope?* is that Balthasar declares the final outcome of God's judgment to be an open question and yet goes on to argue that we can hope—and indeed must hope—for the salvation of all. Kevin Flannery comments: "It is apparent that Balthasar does not really believe that the two types of passage [i.e., particularist versus universalist] should be left with a 'cleft' between them . . . since he attempts to resolve the tension between them himself. . . . Balthasar closes the gap by giving more weight to the second type of passage (interpreted in a particular way), thereby 'conditionalising' the first type."[173] Geoffrey Wainwright says much the same on how Balthasar rejects the notion of theological "synthesis" but then goes about synthesizing anyway.[174]

171. Balthasar, "On Vicarious Representation," 421.
172. Barth wrote, "For this reason unbelief has become an objective, real and ontological impossibility and faith an objective, real and ontological necessity for all men and every man. In the justification of the sinner which has taken place in Jesus Christ these have both become an event which comprehends all men" (*CD* IV/1, 747). "The believer cannot possibly recognize in the unbelief of others a final fact. How can he even establish it with any certainty as their unbelief? . . . We cannot—essentially—believe against unbelievers but only for them" (*CD* II/2, 327). For further discussion, see *DR* 9.7.
173. Flannery, "How to Think about Hell," 473. The statement in Balthasar about keeping the "cleft" in place appears in *Dare We Hope?*, 23.
174. Wainwright comments:
    Balthasar can hardly do otherwise than abide by his own advice against synthesizing. But he can also hardly leave the matter at mere juxtaposition, otherwise a theologian might as well close up shop, since it is the special task of the theologian to bring the disparate materials of the Christian religion into a coherent vision of the whole. . . . He will offer an account that handles "universalist" interpretations of the complex data *gently* while drawing the *sting* out from the "double outcome" verses, so that he at least risks what in principle he denies as legitimate, namely, the "possibility of subordinating one [series of scriptural texts] to the other." . . . There is no mistaking where Balthasar's sympathies lie. . . . He consistently questions taking the New Testament "extreme warnings as implying the factual existence

Origen and Augustine both come in for criticism because, in Balthasar's view, they both engaged in theological synthesis (even though they did so in opposite ways). To be sure, there are passages in *Dare We Hope?* where Balthasar recommends a kind of agnosticism on the possible outcome of God's final judgment: "I deem it appropriate simply to be content with this existential posture. . . . Let us cast aside what leads to such dead-ends and limit ourselves to the truth that we all stand under God's absolute judgment."[175] Balthasar might have been more consistent with his own argument if he had remained within this sort of eschatological agnosticism. Instead, his book specifies what believers in Christ can and should hope for—and what they indeed are *obligated* to hope for—concerning humanity in general.

Some New Testament passages, including the parables of Jesus, certain passages in Paul's Letters, and the book of Revelation, all seem to support the traditional notion of a final, twofold outcome: eternal union with God in heaven or eternal separation from God in hell. In his reading of Scripture, however, Balthasar is influenced by what we previously labeled the theory of "dual strands," originally developed among German Pietist-Böhmist universalists (*DR* 5.8). A number of midcentury German defenders of universalism taught this idea (e.g., Wilhelm Michaelis, Ethelbert Stauffer, and Ernest Staehelin).[176] Jürgen Moltmann, in *The Coming of God*, embraces it too.[177] So too does Balthasar, when he writes: "In the New Testament there are two series of statements that we cannot bring together into an overall synthesis."[178]

This "dual strands" idea as generally presented focuses especially on the writings of the apostle Paul. Most who hold to this reading of the Bible do not

---

of a populated hell." ("Eschatology," 122–23, citing Balthasar, "Some Points of Eschatology," 267; Balthasar, *Dare We Hope?*, 179)

175. Balthasar, *Dare We Hope?*, 253.

176. See Michaelis, *Versöhnung des Alls*; Stauffer, *New Testament Theology*, 222–25; Staehelin, *Die Wiederbringung aller Dinge*.

177. Moltmann, *Coming of God*, 235–55.

178. Balthasar, *Dare We Hope?*, 177. In another passage he writes, "We shall not try to press these biblically irreconcilable statements into a speculative system" (236). Cf. *Dare We Hope?*, 29. On dual strands in recent scholarship on Paul, see Hillert, *Limited and Universal Salvation*. Yet a differing view appears in Moo, "Paul on Hell," 91–109; I. H. Marshall, "New Testament Does *Not* Teach Universal Salvation"; Francis Chan and Preston Sprinkle, *Erasing Hell*. These authors argue that the Pauline passages that speak of universal reconciliation (e.g., Eph. 1:10; Col. 1:19–20) may be in reference to God's "good pleasure" (Col. 1:19 NASB) or a universal will of salvation that is not necessarily fulfilled. Similarly, the teaching that "every knee will bow" and that "every tongue will confess" (Phil. 2:10–11 NASB) may similarly be in reference to God's will of "good pleasure," or in reference to the subduing of God's enemies, when "God has put all things in subjection" (1 Cor. 15:27). When the apostle Paul wrote of actual outcomes for particular people, he sometimes wrote in a way that cannot be reconciled with final salvation for all: "They will suffer the punishment of eternal destruction, away from the presence of the Lord and from the glory of his might" (2 Thess. 1:9).

attempt to make a case on the basis of the Old Testament, which often distinguishes the differing outcomes of reward for the righteous and punishment for the wicked.[179] Similarly, it seems quite difficult to develop a universalist argument from the sayings and parables of Jesus, which so often point toward a twofold outcome (e.g., the "sheep" and "goats" in Matt. 25), or to make a case for universalism from the book of Revelation.[180] Assuming that one finds both strands of teaching within texts regarded as genuinely Pauline, then one is seemingly required to believe that the apostle Paul himself was of two minds regarding the final outcome of divine judgment and so presented two antithetical teachings.[181] Because of the alleged unclarity of Scripture on eschatology, the Christian believer is permitted to embrace either of the two strands. The German Philadelphian universalists of the eighteenth and nineteenth centuries (*DR* 5.8), foreshadowing both Moltmann and Balthasar, resolved the presumed contradiction in the direction of universalism rather than particularism. In *Dare We Hope?*, Balthasar at one point implies that Jesus's words regarding judgment, since they were spoken prior to Easter, may have a lesser or diminished value—an idea that even Balthasar's defenders have called into question.[182]

179. With the possible exception of passages such as Dan. 12:2–3, it is hard to find the idea of *eternal* reward or *eternal* punishment in the Hebrew scriptures. Yet one can identify in the Hebrew scriptures differing outcomes for the righteous and the wicked—sometimes called the "two ways" motif (in distinction from the "dual strands" of particularism versus universalism). These "two ways" might be seen as a bridge toward the two final or eschatological outcomes presented in New Testament teaching.

180. See the following essays in C. W. Morgan and R. A. Peterson, *Hell under Fire*: Block, "Old Testament on Hell" (43–65); Yarbrough, "Jesus on Hell" (67–90); Beale, "[Book of] Revelation on Hell" (111–34). In the 1970s, Richard Bauckham wrote, "Few would now doubt that many NT texts clearly teach a *final* division of mankind into saved and lost, and the most that universalists now commonly claim is that alongside these texts, there are others which hold out a universal hope (e.g., Eph. 1:10; Col. 1:20)" ("Universalism," 52). Since Bauckham penned these words in the late 1970s, some universalists have made stronger claims to the effect that all biblical texts can be reconciled with universal salvation, thus giving us not "two strands" but "one strand"—i.e., a biblical universalist eschatology but not a biblical particularist eschatology. See *DR* 11.4 on Robin Parry's attempt at a literalist yet universalist reading of the entire Bible.

181. Both the universalistic-sounding passages in 1 Cor. 15 and the text on final destruction in 2 Thess. 1 are regarded by virtually all scholars as genuinely Pauline, while both Ephesians and Colossians are taken by many scholars as deutero-Pauline. The point is that the dual-strand theory cannot be resolved into an issue of Pauline vs. deutero-Pauline texts, since the indubitably Pauline texts include passages that appear to contradict a universalist interpretation.

182. In *Dare We Hope?* Balthasar distinguishes "pre-Easter" from "post-Easter" teachings and says that "the pre-Easter Jesus . . . uses a language and images that were familiar to the Jews of that time" (29)—apparently implying that Jesus's teachings on divine judgment were culturally accommodated to the expectations of his hearers (a familiar idea in liberal Protestant exegesis of the Gospels). Later he states that "the predominantly pre-Easter aspects cannot be merged with the post-Easter ones into a readily comprehensible system" (*Dare We Hope?*, 44). Edward T. Oakes criticizes this pre-/post-Easter distinction, inasmuch as Jesus's parables on judgment were

In *Dare We Hope?*, Balthasar is compelled to treat hard cases—that is, individuals who would appear to be the least likely candidates for heaven. Since universal salvation by definition is thought to include all intelligent creatures, the certain damnation of even one individual would overturn universalism as even a possibility or as a hope. Balthasar says little in *Dare We Hope?* about the possible salvation of fallen angels such as Lucifer.[183] This is definitely a lacuna in his argumentation, inasmuch as Satan's salvation had been a point of debate ever since the time of Origen's ill-fated lecture in Athens when he was reported to have said that Satan might eventually be saved. Regarding Judas, Balthasar argues in *Dare We Hope?* that we have no knowledge of whether Judas is finally saved or finally lost. But if Judas is now experiencing the joys of heaven—or eventually will pass into heaven—it is hard to understand Jesus's saying that "it would have been better for that man if he had not been born" (Matt. 26:24). Why, under these circumstances, would Jesus have made such a statement?[184]

---

included in the Gospels *after* the earliest Christians had experienced the illumination that came in the wake of Christ's resurrection and the outpouring of the Spirit on Pentecost. See Oakes, *Pattern of Redemption*, 311–12.

183. See *Dare We Hope?*, 143–47, where Balthasar questions "to what extent the concept 'person' can still be applied to the satanic being" (145). The devil is better called an "un-person" or "nonperson." Here Balthasar may have been influenced by Karl Barth, who discussed the unfallen angels at length in *Church Dogmatics* III/1 but refused to offer any substantive discussion of Satan or of demons. "Angels and demons are related as creation and chaos, as the free grace of God and nothingness" (Barth, *CD* III/3, 520). "What is the origin and nature of the devil and demons? The only possible answer is that their origin and nature lie in nothingness. . . . Their being is neither that of God nor that of the creature" (*CD* III/3, 522). Barth rejects the idea that Satan and demons are "fallen angels," for "the devil was never an angel" (*CD* III/3, 531).

184. John 17:12 reads, "While I was with them, I kept them in your name, which you have given me. I have guarded them, and not one of them has been lost except the son of destruction, that the Scripture might be fulfilled." The context shows that "son of destruction" refers to Judas and that Judas is here said to be "lost"—a synonym for eternal destruction. Augustine, in his *Tractates on the Gospel of John* (107.7 on John 17:9–13; *NPNF*[1] 7:404), writes that "the betrayer of Christ was called the son of perdition, as foreordained to perdition, according to the Scripture." Pope John Paul II, in *Crossing the Threshold of Hope*, appears to take a Balthasarian position on Judas. He first quotes Matt. 25:46 but then seems to qualify this as follows: "Who will these be [i.e., those who go to hell]? The Church has never made any pronouncement in this regard. This is a mystery, truly inscrutable. . . . The silence of the Church is, therefore, the only appropriate position for Christian faith. Even when Jesus says of Judas, the traitor, 'It would be better for that man if he had never been born' (Matt. 26:24), His words do not allude for certain to eternal damnation" (185–86). But later in the same passage, the pope asks, "Isn't final punishment in some way necessary in order to reestablish moral equilibrium in the complex history of humanity? Is not hell in a certain sense the ultimate safeguard of man's moral conscience?" (186). Regarding Judas, James O'Connor points out that the lack of official or magisterial declarations about certain people being in hell—a "reverse canonization"—does not in itself tell us that the historic church did not believe that such cases existed:

It is undeniably true that the Church has never done the opposite of canonization and consigned any individual human being to hell. This is a fact. Whether this fact has any

Balthasar's *Dare We Hope?* involves an appeal not only to Scripture (or one strand of scriptural teaching) but also to precedents in Catholic history and theology. Augustine clearly is *not* among the theologians whom Balthasar favors on the question of final salvation. On the contrary, Augustine "threw a monstrous shadow across the history of western theology."[185] Balthasar approvingly cites the statements of Henri Rondet and André Manaranche that "Augustine solidified into historical opposites something that was, for Paul, a dialectical opposition" and that "the great Augustine . . . projected the paganly imagined omnipotence of God onto his love."[186] Thomas Aquinas fares little better than Augustine does in Balthasar's presentation because of how Thomas approached the issues of grace, predestination, heaven, and hell. Balthasar does have other authors whom he favors in *Dare We Hope?*; for example, he quotes with approval Maurice Blondel: "Many are enraged by the idea of eternal punishment and do not want to serve so hard a Judge."[187]

Catholic thinking on final salvation has traditionally distinguished the "antecedent will" from the "consequent will" of God. This distinction seems first to appear in the writings of John Chrysostom, who connected the "antecedent will" with the divine "good pleasure" (*eudokia*; Col. 1:19, etc.), and then was echoed later in Maximus the Confessor, in Thomas Aquinas, and throughout the discussions of the Thomists.[188] Balthasar, for his part, gives short shrift to this whole line of thinking in *Dare We Hope?*, speaking of "how outrageous it

significance in the present discussion [i.e., pertaining to universalism], however, is doubtful. The Church's mission is to teach the truth, preach salvation, propose models for living the Christian life well, and warn against those actions and forms of living which will lead to eternal loss. It is to be questioned whether she has been given the knowledge . . . to determine and proclaim the negative results of any individual human life. As a community, that knowledge is reserved to the final judgment. On the other hand, although she does not mention any individual as being among the damned, she, like her Master, does not use the *conditional* but the *future indicative* mode [i.e., tense] when speaking of the outcome of human history in respect to the damnation of some. ("Von Balthasar and Salvation," 18)

185. Vorgrimler cites Balthasar's opinion that Augustine had "einen ungeheuren Schatten auf die Geschichte der westlichen Theologie geworfen" (Vorgrimler, *Geschichte der Hölle*, 344, referencing Balthasar, *Was dürfen wir hoffen?*, 52–58).

186. Rondet, *L'Esprit Saint*, 173–74, and Manaranche, *Le monothéisme chrétien*, 238, respectively, cited in Balthasar, *Dare We Hope?*, 71–72n55.

187. Blondel, *Tagebuch vor Gott*, 322, quoted in Balthasar, *Dare We Hope?*, 120.

188. Torre, "God's Permission of Sin," 35–58. As Torre explains, the antecedent will is the will when not subject to particular conditions. A mother on being asked whether someone might apply a knife to the body of her child, would respond with a vehement "No!" Yet on learning that her child has a tumor, and that the use of a surgical scalpel to remove the tumor will be necessary to preserve the child's life, the mother's "No!" would likely change to a "Yes!" The antecedent will would here be replaced by the consequent will—i.e., the will as particularized within a given set of circumstances. Likewise, God's will may be construed as either independent of circumstances (the antecedent will) or else dependent on circumstances (the consequent will).

is to blunt God's triune will for salvation, which is directed at the entire world."[189] Rather brusquely he states that "eternal damnation with its everlasting pain . . . would frustrate God's universal plan of salvation."[190] A question that Balthasar does not answer is the following: Why should evil exist at all, since the very existence of evil would seemingly "frustrate" God's will?

Another line of argument in *Dare We Hope?* centers on the experiences and writings of the Catholic mystics, whom Balthasar cites as favorable to the idea of universal salvation. But the argument is muddled. Regarding Catherine of Siena, Balthasar admits that "Catherine herself and many other mystics . . . were all convinced, despite everything, that the damnation of many was a fact."[191] Balthasar quotes Teresa of Ávila's *Autobiography*, which describes her anguish at the thought that any soul should spend an eternity in hell. Yet this out-of-context quotation does not negate Teresa's belief that some souls would be lost forever. In fact, Teresa's personal vision of hell suggested to her that God wished for her to become convinced of the utter certainty, reality, and facticity of hell.[192] Balthasar's appeal to the experience of Teresa—now formally acknowledged as a "doctor of the church"—does not strengthen but weakens his argument. Manfred Hauke, who did an analysis of Balthasar's claim of support for his view from the saints, concluded that "the testimony of the saints is decisively unfavorable to the opinion that hell would be empty."[193] Numerous

189. Balthasar, *Dare We Hope?*, 23.

190. Ibid., 237. A number of scholars have judged that Balthasar was shortsighted in the dismissive approach he took in *Dare We Hope?* to earlier Catholic reflections on the will of God. Joshua Brotherton, in "Presuppositions of Balthasar's Universalist Hope," notes that "Balthasar rejects out of hand the setting up of distinctions in the divine will" (729) and judges that "a more adequate understanding of predestination could have prevented Balthasar's universalism" (730). Franklin Hankins, in "The Early Aquinas on the Question of Universal Salvation," notes "how theologically sophisticated and carefully nuanced the early Aquinas was in reading 1 Tim 2.4 [God "desires all people to be saved"], particularly in light of the exegetical tradition he had received" (216). For a systematic Catholic account, see Levering, *Predestination*; Echeverria, *Divine Election*.

191. Balthasar, *Dare We Hope?*, 215–16.

192. The passage in question is Teresa of Ávila, *Life of Teresa of Jesus*, 300–304 (ch. 22). "I found myself . . . plunged right into hell . . . [and] it would be impossible for me to forget it" (300–301). She writes that "the agony of [her] soul . . . accompanied by such hopeless and distressing misery" were such that she could not "too forcibly describe it" (301). Nonetheless, she continues, "This vision was one of the most signal favours which the Lord has bestowed upon me: it has been of the greatest benefit to me, both in taking from me all fear of the tribulations and disappointments of this life and also in strengthening me to suffer them and to give thanks to the Lord" (302). "This vision, too, was the cause of the very deep distress which I experience because of the great number of souls who are bringing damnation on themselves" (303). "This also makes me wish that in so urgent a matter we were not ourselves satisfied with anything short of doing all that we can. Let us leave nothing undone" (303). Teresa's vision of hell was not a transient episode but an experience that continued to engage her more deeply in repentance, prayer, and evangelization.

193. Hauke, "Sperare per tutti?," 219, cited in R. Martin, *Will Many Be Saved?*, 171.

saints over the centuries claimed to have had direct experiences of hell and to have witnessed firsthand the despair of those separated from God and who knew themselves to be separated from God forever.[194]

Balthasar quotes not only from acknowledged and canonized saints of the Catholic tradition but also from other Catholic writers who support his views. He approvingly cites Léon Bloy: "The exclusion of a single soul from the wondrous concert of the world is inconceivable and would pose a threat to the universal harmony."[195] It is perfectly acceptable for Balthasar to use this quotation from Bloy to express his own view, but this statement contradicts the tentative pose that Balthasar had previously adopted in *Dare We Hope?* If Bloy is correct, then believers need not *hope* for universal salvation or *await* the outcome but may *know* in advance what is to come. Any other outcome, as Bloy says, would be "inconceivable." As the preceding paragraphs showed, however, Bloy's position on this question cannot be reconciled with that of such Catholic saints as Catherine of Siena, Teresa of Ávila, and Maria Faustina Kowalska. Logically, there seem to be only two alternatives with regard to what the Catholic saints might teach the Catholic faithful regarding hell. Either the witness of the saints must be regarded as contradictory (e.g., Teresa of Ávila vs. Bloy), or the canonized saints of the Catholic tradition ought to be trusted in what they wrote about hell (Teresa of Ávila, Catherine of Siena) while other Catholic figures—though worthy authors in most respects—were in error in what they wrote on hell (Bloy). Neither of these two interpretations would help Balthasar to advance his case that the witness of the saints supports a hope for universal salvation.

Leo Cardinal Scheffczyk offered a critique of Balthasar's "hopeful universalism" through an analysis of "the supernatural virtue of hope," which Balthasar had not properly construed. "Hope rests upon belief," writes Scheffczyk, while belief in turn "reaches out towards the promises made to it." Without a divine promise, there is no firm theological or Christian basis for hope (*DR* 12.6). Yet "because the belief of the Church does not carry with it the promise of the non-existence of hell, no supernatural hope can arise from it." Thus "only for the believer . . . is the hope for blessedness possible," and that "hope cannot remove the reality of the condition of damnation." While Scheffczyk does not phrase it as such, his argument shows that Balthasar's position is not "hopeful

194. See E. Gardner, *Medieval Visions of Heaven and Hell*. In addition to Saint Teresa of Ávila, consider Saint Maria Faustina Kowalska's description of her experience of hell in Kowalska, *Diary of St. Maria Faustina Kowalska*, no. 741: "I am writing this at the command of God, so that no soul may find an excuse by saying that there is no hell, or that nobody has ever been there, and so no one can say what it is like. . . . I, Sister Faustina, by the order of God, have visited the abysses of hell so that I might tell souls about it and testify to its existence" (quoted in R. Martin, *Will Many Be Saved?*, 277n145).

195. Bloy, *Méditations d'un solitaire en 1916*, 240, quoted in Balthasar, *Dare We Hope?*, 168–69.

universalism" but "wishful universalism": *Wouldn't it be wonderful if no one went to hell?* There are many other such wishful sentiments that one might have: *Wouldn't it be wonderful if there were no poverty? Wouldn't it be wonderful if no one had ever sinned?* There is nothing wrong with wishful thoughts, though positive thoughts, taken by themselves, are powerless to change the world around us. Universalism is only "hopeful"—in other words, "hope-filled"—if it is based on divine promises. Biblical "hope" is not thinking good thoughts but hoping in God's sure promises.[196]

Kevin Flannery, a Jesuit theologian, offered a different response to Balthasar.[197] He notes that Jesus's stark words in Matthew 25 amount to a conditional assertion—namely, "If someone shows no mercy at all to the poor and the needy, then he himself will receive no mercy from God and will go into hell." Logically, this kind of statement—"If P then Q"—does not itself assert Q. The relevant question for the Christian believer concerns not the strength of the P-to-Q connection or inference (which may be presumed by the Christian believer if Jesus is asserting this) but rather the likelihood or unlikelihood that the P-condition will ever be realized. Imagine the statement, "If you crash your helicopter into a building, you will be held liable for damages to that building." Most of us would consider it *extremely unlikely* that we will ever be flying a helicopter or ever at risk of crashing one.[198] When we consider a different case—for example, not showing mercy to the poor—we might ask whether we can be so certain that we ourselves (let alone *all* other persons) will in no case fulfill the P-condition, so that not one single person will be at risk of experiencing Q. This expectation (i.e., that *no one* is unmerciful) indeed seems unreasonable. It appears to be an instance of wishful or utopian thinking. To approach P and Q from a different yet related angle: the definitive teaching of the Catholic Church is that those who die in a state of mortal sin go immediately to hell.[199] But does *no one* ever die in mortal sin? Flannery comments that "our experience is that some persons do go unrepentant to their graves," and so in hoping for the salvation of all, "the basis for this hope . . . must be extremely thin."[200]

Like earlier theologians, Balthasar noted the biblical passages pertaining to God's will to save all humanity alongside other passages that seem to speak of a more limited and yet effectual will to save only some. In *Dare We Hope?* Balthasar initially states that he will allow all these passages to stand together

---

196. Scheffczyk, "Apocatastasis," esp. 394–95.

197. Flannery, "How to Think about Hell." Cameron Surrey, in defense of Balthasar, responded to Flannery and Ralph Martin in "Heaven Attracts and Hell Repels."

198. The helicopter example is not Flannery's but my own, used to illustrate his general argument.

199. For documentation of Catholic teaching regarding mortal sin, see *DR*, 34–35nn32–34.

200. Flannery, "How to Think about Hell," 478.

without minimizing any of them. In the course of his argument, however, he reinterprets the particularist passages in a universalistic way. By doing so, writes Flannery, he "reconciles the two strands of scriptural tradition by an argument for *the fact of universal salvation* and not by an argument for *the possibility of . . . universal salvation.*" In other words, "if Balthasar is right, we need not hope for universal salvation: it could not *not* be." To return, then, to Scheffczyk's critique: Balthasar's argument for "hopefulness" makes little sense unless it is interpreted as *asserting* universal salvation—the very point that he says he is not asserting. Stating that God's "triune will for salvation" may not be "blunted" or "thwarted" by humankind, the conclusion follows that God cannot condemn anyone to hell, lest God violate God's own nature. Balthasar offers an intriguing argument, to be sure, yet it is less an argument for "hopeful universalism" than for actual, assertive, or dogmatic universalism.[201]

Balthasar quotes with evident approval the saying of Hans Jürgen Verweyen: "Whoever reckons with the possibility of even one person's being eternally lost besides himself is unable to love unreservedly." As Flannery notes, in light of Jesus's words in the Gospels, this assertion casts doubt on Jesus's moral character.[202] Another issue to consider is the threat of damnation for oneself. Balthasar in *Dare We Hope?* insists on this point: I as an individual *must reckon* with the possibility that I myself will be in hell. Yet Flannery asks: "If this irrevocable 'No' is a real possibility for me, is it not for others? . . . Or even if condemnation is a possibility just for me, does not this fly in the face of any argument that God cannot condemn a person to hell?"[203] Balthasar's effort to not exclude hell altogether but to give it existential application subverts the main line of argument. The premise that God's love cannot entertain the thought of *anyone* being lost does not allow for the existential application of hell to one's self. The position that Balthasar sets forth in *Dare We Hope?* thus appears to be self-contradictory.

10.10. Summary and Conclusions on Roman Catholicism and Universalism

Roman Catholic theology as recently as the 1950s showed little sign of shifting its teaching on eschatology. According to traditional Catholic teaching,

201. Ibid., 473; emphasis added in the first quotation.

202. Flannery, "How to Think about Hell," 474. Doubts about Jesus's character—based on his preaching on hell—have been expressed, for example, by the atheist Bertrand Russell: "There is one very serious defect to my mind in Christ's moral character, and that is that He believed in hell. I do not myself feel that any person who is really profoundly humane can believe in everlasting punishment" (*Why I Am Not a Christian*, 17).

203. Flannery, "How to Think about Hell," 474.

only those who had received Christian baptism were candidates for heaven, and those practicing Catholics who died without having made satisfaction for their venial sins went first to purgatory, prior to entering heaven. Those persons who died in a state of mortal sin went immediately to hell. Regarding non-Christians, there was little hope for final salvation and perhaps not much hope regarding non-Catholic Christians. The traditional Catholic motif of Christ's descent to the dead (*DR* 1.6) meant that righteous persons who died trusting in Israel's God would join the Christian saints in heaven. Taken more liberally, Christ's descent offered some measure of hope for virtuous non-monotheists.

This interlocking set of traditional eschatological views began to shift decisively among Catholic theologians and laity in the 1970s and 1980s. It was not Vatican II itself but the later development and reception of the council's documents that inaugurated a widespread change of views on final salvation. While the 1970s discussion often centered on Karl Rahner's theology of the "anonymous Christian" and the related idea of inclusive salvation, the 1980s discussion—triggered in part by Hans Urs von Balthasar's *Dare We Hope?*—was directed toward the question of universal salvation. In a generation's time, Catholic teaching and theologizing opened the door to the inclusive salvation of non-Christians and then to the possibility of universal salvation. Certain statements by Pope John Paul II and Pope Francis have suggested that one or both popes have held to "hopeful universalism," as recommended by Balthasar.

Recent changes in Catholic teaching on eschatology are rooted in an altered understanding of the distinction between nature and grace. The theology of Henri de Lubac during the 1940s played a pivotal role in this shift. Karl Rahner intensified the process that started under de Lubac, blurring the distinction between nature and grace in his conception of the "supernatural existential" and implying that human beings might be saved without having believed in Christ or even in God, by inwardly affirming an unrecognized divine call to authentic moral life. Salvation might as well occur outside the church as within the church, through the sacraments or apart from them. The Rahnerian way of thinking has created a dilemma for the Catholic Church and its call for a "new evangelization," since it intimates that the gifts and graces traditionally associated with active participation in the institutional church and in its sacraments are readily available outside the church. Life as a practicing Catholic involves difficulties and disadvantages that are increasingly apparent in global contexts where there is growing secularity or active persecution of Christians.[204]

204. A trio of books published in 2017—two by Catholic authors and one by an Orthodox thinker—stress the inescapable tension between the Christian worldview and ethic and that which

Nonbelievers and half-believers who are drawn to the church's wisdom, ethic, ethos, and aesthetics might find that thinkers like Rahner offer a theological rationale for embracing a nonecclesial Catholicism—a movement of the "nonreligious for [Pope] Francis."

This chapter has traced Balthasar's "hopeful universalism" back to the early influences of Russian sources as well as to the study of the church fathers and to the personal and theological impact of Karl Barth. Balthasar's theological dependence on Adrienne von Speyr for his Holy Saturday theology and for his understanding of God's inner-trinitarian life remains problematic because von Speyr's visionary experiences were never assessed and approved as acknowledged Catholic teaching. Balthasar's concept of *Urkenosis* suggests that elements of division and conflict may exist within the eternal Godhead. On analysis, Balthasar's "hopeful universalism" proves to be largely a form of wishful thinking since it does not rest on any definite divine promise to save everyone. What is more, Balthasar's suggestion that each person must bear in mind the possibility of his or her own damnation does not fit with his general stance of "hopeful universalism," which must include a hopefulness for all persons, including oneself.

Since the existence of hell has been defined through the centuries as an official Catholic doctrine, Balthasar could not deny it without falling into heresy. His idea of a "hope for all" was thus intended to be a middle way or compromise acceptable to the church that neither denied the church's doctrine nor asserted a final twofold state of heaven and hell. Yet, as Alyssa Pitstick has pointed out, the logic of Balthasar's Holy Saturday theology would seem to point in the direction of universal salvation. According to the teaching, Jesus Christ on the cross—and later in Sheol—completely identified himself with all sins and all sinners. In the act of identifying himself with all sins, Jesus expelled them from the realm of existence. Balthasar speaks of "that reality of sin which the Cross has separated from man and humanity, the thing God has eternally and finally cast out of the world, the thing in which God never, ever, can be."[205] Seemingly sin no longer exists, and so there can no longer be separation between God and humanity. Universal salvation thus appears to be assured, despite all the hedges and qualifications that Balthasar attaches to his statements regarding the scope of final salvation.

In the essay "The Final Judgment" in Balthasar's *Explorations in Theology*, we see the substitutionary logic of Holy Saturday and the way in which Balthasar understands the work of Christ as applying to all persons without exception:

prevails in the contemporary secular West. See Archbishop Charles J. Chaput, *Strangers in a Strange Land*; Anthony M. Esolen, *Out of the Ashes*; Rod Dreher, *The Benedict Option*.

205. Balthasar, *Our Task*, 65.

Those who are to be judged do not stand over against either Jesus or the Church as foreigners. Jesus has become their brother, indeed much more: their replacement before God. He has borne their guilt: it is in him. What alienates them from God has now become alien *to them* through Jesus. They are ontically transformed through him to the depths of their being, whether they recognize it and allow it to happen . . . or whether they reject it—if they can—and harden themselves and insist on their guilt as still their own. . . . In any case, the image of two fronts rigidly standing over against each other—Judge and those being judged—is dissolved into a fluid transition. Everyone is basically "in Christ," the judged Judge, through the mystery of the cross.[206]

Balthasar's Holy Saturday thus functions like the Hegelian cross. It is where and how the "negation of the negation" takes place. Given Balthasar's premises, there is no reason to imagine that this reversal or overcoming of evil should not be universal in scope or should not extend to every human being.[207]

Using analytic categories that he ultimately borrowed from the philosophy of Hegel, Balthasar in *Theo-drama* distinguishes what he calls the "epic," the "lyric," and the "dramatic" modes in literature.[208] He is strongly critical of the epic mode and prefers the dramatic. Yet *Mysterium Paschale* together with *Theo-drama* and *Dare We Hope?* would seem be a kind of concealed epic. In Balthasar no less than in Barth, one might speak of a "triumph of grace."[209] Within the pages of *Dare We Hope?*, Balthasar has not established a constitutive place for human choice in accepting or rejecting the person and work of Christ. The references to human choice and willing are perfunctory in comparison with the dramatic account of Holy Saturday. There is a "drama" of Christ's work but,

---

206. Balthasar, "Final Judgment," 452, 454.

207. Nicholas Healy admits that Balthasar's theology gives the impression of being triumphalistic: "Everything said thus far . . . could be taken as a triumphalist undervaluing of the reality of sin and human freedom. After all, if Christ returns to the Father through a radical solidarity with the sinner—and precisely therein effects the ensheltering of the whole world within the divine life—can we seriously maintain that anyone is free to say No to God's offer of salvation?" (*Eschatology*, 204–5). Healy argues that it is a *misconception* to believe that Balthasar held "that all of humanity will be saved by a kind of christocentric automatism" (205). Pitstick is more critical, stating that for Balthasar redemption is "accomplished through . . . the 'physical mechanism' of sin-in-itself entering the Trinity through the Son's being 'literally "made sin."'" . . . In turn, God's absolute freedom coupled with His nature as self-gift (i.e., love) suggests universal salvation as necessary" (*Light in Darkness*, 337). From "the fact that Balthasar's primary argument in support of hope for the salvation of all is that the eternal loss of some implies a defect in God's omnipotence, it would appear that Balthasar's denials of apokatastasis are just as 'rhetorical' as those for which he criticizes Karl Barth" (270). For an argument that Balthasar's theology implies universal salvation, see Pitstick, *Light in Darkness*, 263–74.

208. See the detailed analysis of this point in Quash, *Theology and the Drama of History*, esp. 39–51, 137–55, and 179–95; the second section cited (137–55) deals with Balthasar "as epic reader."

209. See Berkouwer, *Triumph of Grace*.

properly speaking, no "drama" of the human decision regarding Christ. When Balthasar speaks of the cosmic, all-encompassing theo-drama, he states that we all are part of this "play" even if we do not wish to be. What he does not say, but seems to imply, is that there is just one way of participating—namely, through having a positive rather than negative relation to Christ. So we are all sheep rather than goats, whatever we might wish to be. One is reminded of Søren Kierkegaard's critique of Danish Christendom—that it made "Christians" of everyone, whether people wanted to be or not.

One of the striking features of *Dare We Hope?* is the complete absence of reference to mission, evangelism, or proclamation as basic functions of the church. No causal link, in Balthasar's account, connects gospel preaching with human salvation. Nor does he develop the notion of faith as a human choice. Balthasar states that "if we take our faith seriously and respect the words of Scripture, we must resign ourselves to admitting such an ultimate possibility" of rejecting God.[210] Yet this "possibility" is never explained or expounded in *Dare We Hope?* Undoubtedly this had something to do with the fact that Balthasar conceived of humanity in corporate rather than individual terms, and one cannot do justice to human choices without considering the particularites of the lives of individuals.[211] Balthasar's theology is thus fundamentally *unmissional*. It centers on a contemplative practice of "seeing the form" and on a decision to "hope for all," but without a distinctive focus on preaching, mission, or evangelism. It is no wonder, then, that contemporary Catholic leaders find it hard to link Balthasar's theology to the "new evangelization." They do not share the same presuppositions.

During the last decade, the number of Balthasar's critics has significantly increased. What is more, there is a growing convergence among the various lines of criticism. Thomas Dalzell, Karen Kilby, Steffen Lösel, Alyssa Pitstick, and Ben Quash have all viewed Balthasar's theology as problematic, and much of their criticism has centered on the ways in which Balthasar dramatized the inner life of the Trinity.[212] Thomas Dalzell argues that Balthasar's theology

210. Balthasar, *Dare We Hope?*, 237.

211. Balthasar writes elsewhere, "All men are interrelated in a human constellation. One sole human being would be a contradiction in terms, inconceivable even in the abstract, because to be human means to be with others. The God-Man Jesus Christ is no exception" (*Office of Peter*, 136, quoted in Goodall, "Hans Urs von Balthasar," 425). While this emphasis on human relationality has roots in Scripture and in church tradition, the way that Balthasar develops it diminishes the significance of individual human choices. All humanity is so much in solidarity that either all human beings will be saved or else all human beings will be damned.

212. See Lösel, "Unapocalyptic Theology"; Lösel, "Murder in the Cathedral"; Lösel, "Plain Account of Christian Salvation?"; Quash, "'Between the Brutely Given, and the Brutally, Banally Free'"; Quash, *Theology and the Drama of History*; Dalzell, "Lack of Social Drama." Alyssa Pitstick

lacks "social drama" because his idea of theo-drama shifts attention from the creaturely spatiotemporal realm into a non-spatiotemporal and transhistorical realm. Alyssa Pitstick has debated Edward Oakes over Balthasar's theology of Holy Saturday and whether it has a proper foundation within earlier Christian teaching and tradition. Kevin Mongrain examines Balthasar's positive stance toward Valentin Tomberg's *Meditations on the Tarot* (1980), a work of Christian esotericism for which Balthasar wrote an admiring afterword. Mongrain concludes that Balthasar's own work has much in common with Western esotericism.[213] Steffen Lösel recites Balthasar's objections to the theology of Jürgen Moltmann, in which "the Cross is not the privileged . . . locus of the Trinity's self-revelation" but rather "the locus of the Trinity's authentic actualization."[214] Balthasar's criticisms of Moltmann are of a piece with his criticisms of Hegel, who is said to have confused the eternal generation of the Son with the creation of the world.[215] Wishing to escape the danger of an entanglement of God in the world process, Balthasar resorts to a distinctive "two-tiered" interpretation of God, as Lösel explains: "Balthasar's unique strategy for how to think of a passionate God without entangling God into the world process is to present the trinitarian life as a two-tiered course of events: the economic Trinity as a drama on the stage of the world, and the immanent Trinity as an underlying 'primal drama' or *Urdrama*."[216] In this way Lösel's analysis of

---

developed an elaborate critique of Balthasar's Holy Saturday theology in her monograph *Light in Darkness* (2007). What followed was an exchange of essays with Edward Oakes, who took issue with Pitstick's arguments in a series of articles in *First Things* in December 2006 and January 2007 and in the *International Journal of Systematic Theology*: Oakes, "Internal Logic of Holy Saturday"; Pitstick, "Development of Doctrine, or Denial?"; Oakes, "*Descensus* and Development." Paul Griffiths entered the debate in "Is There a Doctrine of the Descent into Hell?"

213. Mongrain, "Rule-Governed Christian Gnosis."

214. Lösel, "Murder in the Cathedral," 428, in reference to Balthasar, *TD* 4:321. Lösel, who dedicated this essay "to Jürgen Moltmann in honor of his seventieth birthday" (427), might be seen as offering a correction of Balthasar's theology in the direction of Moltmann. Balthasar's critique of Moltmann appears in *TD* 4:321-23 (cf. *TD* 1:131; 3:508). On Moltmann, compare Dalferth, "Eschatological Roots of the Doctrine of the Trinity," 151: "At the cross, he [Moltmann] says, God was abandoned by God. He does not merely hold, as Jüngel does, that the cross occasions the distinction between God and God but understands the separation of Father from Son in the dereliction of the cross in a full mythological sense."

215. Balthasar writes regarding Hegel, "The confusion is complete if in the end . . . the inner-divine mystery of the self-outpouring, [and] the 'noughting' of the communicated fullness of being in its non-subsistence . . . are partially or wholly equated; thereby the ultimate theologoumenon is totally shorn of its theological character" (*Glory of the Lord*, 5:629). Hegel's God, for Balthasar, is utterly without mystery and thus opens the door to atheism. Regarding Eckhart, Balthasar is critical of the lack of proper theological analogy: "For Eckhart . . . 'analogy' does not mean *analogia entis* but the purely creative effulgence of Being, which as such endows the creature—which is itself nothing—with a being that is 'borrowed,' not entrusted to it as its own" (*TD* 5:436-37).

216. Lösel, "Murder in the Cathedral," 429.

Balthasar lends support to Dalzell's critique. The human or earthly drama is largely eclipsed by the two great transhistorical, nontemporal dramas: the intratrinitarian *Urkenosis* and Christ's suffering in an otherworldly realm on Holy Saturday.

What, then, of Rahner's and Balthasar's argument that the judgment passages in Scripture refer only to existential possibilities and not to future actualities? As Ralph Martin has noted, the language of the Vatican II dogmatic constitution *Lumen Gentium* would seem to rule this out. The text reads: "It is necessary to keep vigil constantly . . . so that we may not be commanded, like evil and lazy servants, to descend to eternal fire (cf. Matt. 25:41) in the exterior darkness where there will be 'weeping and the gnashing of teeth' (Matt. 22:13 and 25:30)." When one bishop at Vatican II requested that the text of *Lumen Gentium* be amended to make it clear that damnation was not merely a hypothetical outcome, the Theological Commission replied that no emendation was necessary, since "the Lord Himself [in the scriptural text] speaks about the damned in a form which is grammatically future."[217] When the bishops at Vatican II considered and voted on the text of *Lumen Gentium*, it was with the understanding that the references in it to the judgment or punishment of the wicked were "grammatically future" statements and not simply conditional statements about things that might or might not take place.

Rahner's and Balthasar's rejection of dualistic outcomes in judgment conflicts with the past and present teaching of the Catholic Magisterium. General councils of the Catholic Church in 1245 and 1274, the papal bull *Benedictus Deus* (1336), the International Theological Commission's "Letter on Certain Questions concerning Eschatology" (1979), and the *Catechism of the Catholic Church* (1994) all agree in the assertion that those human beings who die in a state of mortal sin go immediately to suffer the pains of hell. The International Theological Commission's letter states that "the Church believes that the definitive state of damnation awaits those who die burdened with grave sin."[218] So the expectation or hope that no one goes into hell is tantamount to the expectation or hope that no one dies in a state of mortal sin. We must ask, then, whether such a hope is consistent with what we ordinarily observe in human life. Unless one speculates—as some Catholic theologians have done—regarding a final encounter of all human beings with God in the moment of their deaths, leading possibly to a final decision for God (*DR* 1.9), then it appears that Catholic Christians must either affirm that some humans go to hell, or set aside the church's

---

217. *Lumen Gentium*, no. 48; Roman Catholic Church, *Acta Synodalia Sacrosancti Concilii Oecumenici Vaticani Secundi*, III/8, 144–45; both quoted in R. Martin, *Will Many Be Saved?*, 153.
218. R. Martin, *Will Many Be Saved?*, 137–38, 151.

teaching on this point.[219] There has recently been some renewed interest in the inclusivist yet not universalist eschatology of Jacques Maritain (1882–1973), which might serve as a Catholic alternative to Balthasar's views.[220]

By positing "distance" in God, Balthasar implies some kind of "fall" within God, which on the face of it seems to imply a gnostic understanding of God. Something in Berdyaev that Balthasar does not accept is the Böhmist notion of the *Ungrund*—a dark, irrational abyss that chronologically or logically precedes the trinitarian persons and from which the trinitarian persons arise. Berdyaev (*DR* 8.5) derived this from his reading of Böhme (*DR* 5.3). For Berdyaev, this *Ungrund*—which is simply a primal longing or desiring that is prior even to the distinction between good and evil—constitutes the source of the divine movement and freedom. Movement here is associated with divine pathos, and so Berdyaev fundamentally challenges any notion of divine impassibility or immovability.[221] In Balthasar's view, Berdyaev's *Ungrund* introduces a fundamentally tragic dimension into freedom itself, and hence evil appears within this system as a kind of tragic necessity. For Balthasar, this problem is not a minor one but is a fundamental error, since it locates the source of all freedom within a realm of primal darkness that is prior even to God himself.[222]

What, then, does Balthasar do with Berdyaev's Böhmist theogony? No longer is there an *Ungrund* of impersonal and primal darkness that precedes God as

219. The idea of a final encounter of each person with God during death finds support in Eminyan, *Theology of Salvation*, as well as in Boros, *Moment of Truth*. Boros's "final decision hypothesis" holds that "death gives man the opportunity of posing his first completely personal act; death is, therefore, by reason of its very being, the moment above all others for the awakening of consciousness, for freedom, for the encounter with God, for the final decision about his eternal destiny" (*Moment of Truth*, viii–ix). Ambaum criticizes Boros's thesis on several fronts: "It is too strongly dependent on Heidegger's mystification of death; that we, in this life, have insufficient means of empirically verifying this hypothesis; that it robs human life of its seriousness and responsibility; and that it speaks about death too restrictively" ("Empy Hell?," 50n42). See also *DR* 1.9.

220. Joshua Brotherton notes that Jacques Maritain's theory of "final limbo" developed very gradually from 1939 up to around 1972 (Brotherton, "Presuppositions," 730)—a theory embodied in Maritain's essay, "Beginning With a Reverie." In Maritain's view, "the damned remain in hell . . . but are transferred from a lower to a higher region" (731). This sounds something like the earlier doctrine of mitigation, which Aquinas rejected but to which Augustine and John Henry Newman gave qualified assent (*DR*, 104, 331). The damned for Maritain have "natural facility," but this falls short of gracious beatitude. Their natural facility comes about as the effects of sin are reversed and they are restored to their original state (734). In this view, the differing intermediate degrees of relationship to God are all manifested in the eschaton. An evangelical view of hell—recently referred to as "reconciliationism," yet anticipated in the nineteenth century by T. R. Birks—has some resemblances to Maritain's view. See Saville, "Reconciliationism," and (on Birks) *DR* 1.8; 1.10.

221. See Berdyaev, *Meaning of History*, 52–59.

222. See Balthasar, *Apokalypse*, 3:428 (cited in J. S. King and C. M. Shea, "Role of Nikolai Berdyaev," 252–53), which concludes that Berdyaev's eschatology fails in the end to be fully Christian.

personal or as tri-personal. Balthasar rejects the sequence that starts with the Abyss and then moves on to the Trinity. Instead, he reverses the sequence: he starts with the Trinity and then moves on to the Abyss. There is indeed something in Balthasar akin to the *Ungrund*. This is the "distance" within God that follows on the "primal kenosis" (*Urkenosis*) that takes shape within God's own being as the Father begets the Son. While Balthasar's doctrine of *Urkenosis* is closer to mainstream Christian teaching than Böhme's *Ungrund*, it is still a questionable notion. There is "distance" within God, and Balthasar does not hesitate to speak also of "tragedy" in God.[223] "Distance" is the precondition for the emergence of evil. The "distance" is not evil per se, but it represents the potentiality or possibility of evil. Balthasar's teaching thus skirts the edges of gnosis without clearly crossing over the line.

In his critique of Balthasar, Karl Rahner speaks of "a Schelling-like projection into God of division, conflict, godlessness, and death." Rahner raises two questions. The first is "What do we know then so precisely about God?"—that is, the epistemological issue of what we can and cannot know about the inner life of God. The second question concerns "consolation," which naturally enough arises for a Jesuit theologian: "What use would that be to me as consolation in the true sense of the word?" Rahner answers his own question by saying, "It is for me a source of consolation to realize that God, when and insofar as he entered into this history as into his own, did it in a different way than I did. From the beginning I am locked into its [i.e., history's] horribleness while God—if this word continues to have any meaning at all—is in a true and authentic and consoling sense the God who does not suffer, the immutable God."[224] Rahner

---

223. Balthasar, *TD* 4:435–36; 5:508. One author important in drawing Balthasar in a "tragic" direction is Gustav Siewerth (1903–63), who is quoted at key points in *TD*. In *TD* 4:436, Balthasar cites Siewerth's 1934 essay "Christentum und Tragik," 299–300, as follows:

> The innermost sanctuary of the divine life . . . could not reveal itself to sinful and finite creatures unless the latter were made ready in the tragic collapse of divine life. . . . For it is only through the love-death of the eternally offered Son that the Creator's love is communicated and expropriated, overflowing onto us. . . . In the Spirit's holy wells of love, all sighing, all suffering of the tragic creature is experienced in painful depth, in order to refine and sanctify the creature and incorporate him as a member of the Lord's holy Body. This love is not something absolutely supra-tragic: it is the creative fashioning and heightening of tragedy itself, making of it the most precious legacy of all eternities in the abyss of divine life.

Siewerth's powerful emphasis on tragedy within God gives a gnostic flavor to his writing. Not only the creature but even God appears to be doomed, fated, compelled, and ultimately unfree. Siewerth's social location in writing this 1934 essay should be considered. In January 1933, Hitler became the German chancellor, and in April 1933, Martin Heidegger—Siewerth's former professor—gave a pro-Nazi address as the new rector of the University of Freiburg. Siewerth's correspondence with Balthasar during Siewerth's latter life has been published in English translation, as Wierciński, *Between Friends*.

224. Rahner, *Karl Rahner in Dialogue*, 126–27.

ultimately came to the same conclusion that Kilby did: that Balthasar introduced "elements of darkness" into the life of God.

Balthasar was a man very much at home in the realm of ideas, and we have already commented on the curious absence of attention to issues of faith, decision, and evangelism in *Dare We Hope?* The question of the ultimate salvation of all persons is generally treated as a speculative problem, not as something pertaining to individual people and their choices. In this sense Ben Quash is correct in saying that Balthasar gives us an *undramatic* picture of human life. We are far removed from the New Testament narratives in which Jesus preaches, heals the sick, calls followers, and provokes some persons to love and others to hatred. In Balthasar's God's-eye perspective, the altitude is so lofty that it is often hard to see the human actors and decisions that are integral to the earthly story of redemption.

11

New Theologies in the New Millennium

THE VARIETY OF CONTEMPORARY UNIVERSALISMS

That God's grace is utterly irrestible over the long run now seems to me the best interpretation. . . . So even though we are indeed free to resist God's grace for a season, perhaps even for a substantial period of time, that very resistance will at some point produce an irresistible means of grace; hence, no one, I argue, is free to resist that grace forever.

—Thomas Talbott[1]

Without realizing it, the "god" we have put our hopes in and portrayed to the world is more like Hitler than Mother Teresa. The god we have unwittingly manufactured has feeble hopes for His own children— hopes that are dependent on human free will, and confined to the length of His children's brief, mortal lifespans.

—Julie Ferwerda[2]

Once upon a time I was a fundamentalist, Southern Baptist and I had God all figured out. I knew it all, and delighted in telling people all about God. Men and women flocked to my Bible study classes. They sold cassette tapes in the church narthex, and people bought

1. Talbott, *Inescapable Love of God* (2nd ed., 2014), xii–xiii.
2. Ferwerda, *Raising Hell*, 60.

them. . . . I knew with absolute certainty how God acted and why. . . .
[Then] a couple of things happened. . . . Two of my children became
very sick with an incurable liver disease, and I went to seminary. All
of a sudden I didn't know everything about God anymore

—Sharon Baker[3]

We are awakening to our True Selves. The false self—under a false
fatherhood of the adversary—has no substance. . . . We are awaking
to our origin—breathed from His very substance, re-created and born
anew in Him—the Lamb of God. . . . He came to awaken humanity to
the truth—that we are a divine race. . . . You are not bound by times
and seasons. Your destiny does not hinge on your natural abilities.
You are eternal, infinite, immortally woven into His own divinity. . . .
Yes, the cosmos has been permanently rewired in the incarnation,
death, and resurrection of Jesus Christ. All things have been forever
united in the Son of God. . . . God included you and absorbed the
entire created order into Himself.

—John Crowder[4]

Universalism has been a hot topic among Christian writers and readers since
the start of the new millennium. The most famous of the recent books
may be Rob Bell's *Love Wins: A Book about Heaven, Hell, and the Fate of Every
Person Who Ever Lived* (2011). Bell's book became a *New York Times* bestseller and
provoked a *Time* magazine cover story during Holy Week that was emblazoned
with the question: "What If There's No Hell?"[5] But Bell's book was not alone.
Over the last twenty years many popular books have addressed the question of
universal salvation. Taking a favorable—or mostly favorable—view of universalism have been the following: Thomas Talbott, *The Inescapable Love of God*
(1999); Randolph Klassen, *What Does the Bible Really Say about Hell?* (2001);
Philip Gulley and James Mulholland, *If Grace Is True: Why God Will Save Every
Person* (2003); Bob Evely, *At the End of the Ages . . . The Abolition of Hell* (2003);
Kalen Fristad, *Destined for Salvation* (2003); Ken Vincent, *The Golden Thread:*

3. Baker, *Executing God*, 1–2.
4. Crowder, *Cosmos Reborn*, 251, 252, 25, 260, and back cover.
5. The *Time* magazine cover (April 25, 2011) read, "What If There's No Hell?—A Popular Pastor's Best-Selling Book Has Stirred Fierce Debate about Sin, Salvation and Judgment," while Jon
Meacham's article (38–43) bore the title and heading "Is Hell Dead? Rogue pastor Rob Bell's argument
about salvation and judgment has Evangelicals in a fury—and a young generation rethinking Jesus."
A study guide to Bell's book appeared in 2011 as *The Love Wins Companion*. For an overview of the
debates in the wake of Bell's book, see John Sanders's 2013 essay "Raising Hell about Razing Hell."

God's Promise of Universal Salvation (2005); Gregory MacDonald, *The Evangelical Universalist* (2006; 2nd ed., 2012); Carlton Pearson, *The Gospel of Inclusion* (2006); Gerry Beauchemin, *Hope beyond Hell* (2007); Boyd C. Purcell, *Spiritual Terrorism: Spiritual Abuse from the Womb to the Tomb* (2008); Bradley Jersak, *Her Gates Will Never Be Shut: Hell, Hope, and the New Jerusalem* (2009); Doug Frank, *A Gentler God* (2010); Sharon Baker, *Razing Hell* (2010); Ted Grimsrud and Michael Hardin, *Compassionate Eschatology* (2011); Charles Gillihan, *Hell No!* (2011); Julie Ferwerda, *Raising Hell: Christianity's Most Controversial Doctrine Put under Fire* (2011); C. Baxter Kruger, *The Shack Revisited* (2012); Heath Bradley, *Flames of Love: Hell and Universal Salvation* (2012); V. Donald Emmel, *Eliminating Satan and Hell: Affirming a Compassionate Creator-God* (2013); Dennis Jensen, *Flirting with Universalism: Resolving the Problem of an Eternal Hell* (2014); Caleb A. Miller, *The Divine Reversal: Recovering the Vision of Jesus Christ as the Last Adam* (2014); Jean Wyatt, *Judge Is the Savior: Towards a Universalist Understanding of Salvation* (2015); Thomas Allin, *Christ Triumphant: Universalism Asserted as the Hope of the Gospel on the Authority of Reason, the Fathers, and Holy Scripture* (2015); Robert Wild and Robin A. Parry, *A Catholic Reading Guide to Universalism* (2015); David Burnfield, *Patristic Universalism: An Alternative to the Traditional View of Divine Judgment* (2016); Ross Marshall, *God's Testimony of All* (2016); Steven Propp, *The Gift of God Is Eternal Life* (2016); and George Hurd, *The Universal Solution* (2017).[6]

Though this listing of recent popular books is not exhaustive, the range of titles suggests a wave of interest among scholars and laypersons alike. The pace at which new titles are appearing seems to be increasing.[7] In response to the literature just cited, a number of authors have suggested that the current support for universalism, in Christian terms, is biblically and theologically mistaken. Appearing about fifteen years ago was Christopher Morgan and Robert Peterson's edited volume *Hell under Fire* (2004). Works responding to Rob Bell and questioning his seeming support for universalism include Mark Galli, *God Wins* (2011); Brian Jones, *Hell Is Real (But I Hate to Admit It)* (2011); Francis Chan and Preston Sprinkle, *Erasing Hell* (2011); Michael Wittmer, *Christ Alone* (2011); and Larry Dixon, *"Farewell, Rob Bell"* (2011). Laurence Malcolm Blanchard's *Will All Be Saved? An Assessment of Universalism in Western Theology* (2015) is one of the few theological surveys that takes a critical stance toward universalism.

---

6. One book suggests that universalism might be true but does not directly assert it: John Noe, *Hell Yes / Hell No* (2011). Two authors support universalism in arguing against atonement theology: Derek Flood, *Healing the Gospel* (2012); Sharon L. Baker, *Executing God* (2013).

7. Also noteworthy is the edited volume by Gregory MacDonald (a pseudonym for British book editor Robin Parry) that explores the historical lineage of universalist thinking from the early church period to the present time: *"All Shall Be Well"* (2011).

There are many schools of fish swimming in the universalist pond. A shared belief in universal salvation does not imply any wider agreement on doctrine.[8] As this chapter demonstrates, universalists themselves are in sharp disagreement on God, the Trinity, Christ, human nature, the nature of salvation, and eschatology. The self-described "evangelical universalist" Robin Parry emphasizes his own Christian orthodoxy, highlights his points of agreement with evangelical Protestantism, and seeks to show that the entire Bible can be interpreted in a universalist way. Yet Parry is an outlier, and most contemporary universalists engage with or appeal to the Bible in a more limited way than he does.

As shown in chapter 6, universalism in nineteenth-century America appeared in multiple and incompatible forms. Something comparable seems to be happening in the new millennium. An unresolved issue left over from the nineteenth century was the dispute between restorationist universalists, who believed in postmortem suffering for sins, and the ultra-universalists, who denied that any such suffering was conceivable. Charismatic teacher John Crowder has repudiated the idea of postmortem purgation or a temporary hell as inconsistent with divine grace: "A god who sovereignly burns someone for a thousand years in a pit of demonic, hellish, molestation is only slightly better than one who does it forever. . . . The main problem with this reasoning is that hell becomes viewed as a *purgatory*. A temporary torture chamber to clean you up. Hell doesn't clean you up. Jesus did."[9] In contrast to this, Robin Parry has argued that "it is legitimate to understand the biblical teaching about hell as compatible with an awful *but temporary* fate from which all can, and ultimately will, be saved."[10] Parry mistakenly suggested that his own idea of a temporary hell was in fact the *only* Christian universalist teaching before the twentieth century.[11] In the twenty-first century, as in the nineteenth century, the purgationist version of universalism has its advocates, as does the "ultra" version. Clearly, both views

8. This claim seems to conflict with statements made in the book introduction (*DR* 0.5) comparing and contrasting esoteric and exoteric versions of Christianity and examining how the beliefs of each of these two are systematically interrelated. This esoteric-exoteric contrast generally works as a theological rule of thumb for the lengthy period from the late second century up to the mid- or late 1900s. From that point onward, and especially during the last two decades, it is difficult to perceive any one theological trend as predominating among universalists, and so one must speak instead of "universalisms," as this chapter should make clear.

9. Crowder, *Cosmos Reborn*, 148.

10. Gregory MacDonald [Parry], *Evangelical Universalist* (2006), 7.

11. Parry, "Evangelical Universalism," 9: "It is commonly claimed by evangelical critics that universalists do not even believe in hell. In fact, this is simply false. Historically, all species of Christian universalism prior to the twentieth century affirmed a doctrine of hell." The earlier discussion (*DR* 6.6; 6.8; 6.9) showed that in the early nineteenth century, many leaders of the Universalist Church in the USA were ultra-universalists who repudiated any notion of postmortem suffering for sins committed during earthly life.

cannot be true. On the basis of past experience, it seems unlikely that any one form of Christian universalism will become so dominant as to displace the others. For the previously regarded "heresy" of universalism to become a new "orthodoxy," one version of universalism would need somehow to establish a consensus in its favor. On the basis of earlier history, this seems improbable.

II.I. Character of the New Millennium Universalist Literature

Popular Christian universalist authors in the new millennium generally come from an evangelical or Pentecostal-Charismatic background. Many of these authors acknowledge that their new universalist faith has taken them beyond the bounds of their earlier faith tradition. Often there is a personal aspect or animus in their writing. For many of these authors, the embrace of universalist theology is a rebellion against fundamentalist religion and an act of personal self-liberation. In *Spiritual Terrorism*, Boyd C. Purcell writes of the "mixed messages of God's love and justice" during his youth.[12] Thomas Talbott, in *The Inescapable Love of God*, begins by describing his "sheltered childhood" and attendance at a "conservative Christian high school" at which "a good Christian was identified as someone who does not smoke, drink, dance (roller skating was 'iffy'), play cards, or attend Hollywood movies."[13] Carlton Pearson grew up as "a Bible-toting, pew-jumping, devil-thumping Pentecostal" and says that prior to his early twenties "the only world [he] ever really knew . . . was the small, sequestered world of the Pentecostal denomination [i.e., Church of God in Christ] in which [his] family has been immersed for four generations." He had a sense of being set apart: "We were proud of being the true citizens of the Kingdom of God."[14]

Doug Frank's *A Gentler God* is a well-written account of the author's experience within the Protestant evangelical (or fundamentalist) subculture, and the author's reaction against what he now takes to be the narrow, intolerant, judgmental, and fear-inducing character of that subculture. Frank's early life experiences are comparable to those of Purcell, Talbott, and Pearson, noted above. Frank mentions many of the same things: a sheltered childhood, a church background characterized by theological rigidity, a sense of being set apart from others, and encounters with non-Christian outsiders only through evangelism.

---

12. Purcell, *Spiritual Terrorism*, 3. Purcell assesses the Bible according to the feelings it evokes in him: "If an interpretation of the Bible is true it will probably cause you to feel loved by God. If, on the other hand, it causes you to feel fearful of God, it probably is not true. Biblical fear of God . . . [is] not morbid fear of eternal torture in literal hellfire. Truth will have a ring of authenticity and will resonate with one's spirit that it is correct—'That just sounds right'" (7).

13. Talbott, *Inescapable Love*, 3.

14. C. Pearson, *Gospel of Inclusion*, 142–43.

Frank says: "I grew up in a pastor's home, had a 'born-again' experience in my childhood, spent most of my discretionary time as a teenager in Christian youth programs, graduated from a well-known evangelical college, and, after a brief time-out in a university graduate school, have spent my life as a history professor in evangelical colleges." As an adult, when Frank drove by a road sign that said simply "Trust Jesus," he mentally added the words "Or Else!"[15] For him, such Christian language connoted *fear and compulsion*—marks of an ex-fundamentalist with a conflicted attitude toward religion, as his book makes clear. The pattern reappearing in these books suggests that the later turn toward universalism had something to do with the sheltered or even suffocating religious culture that many of the authors experienced in their youth.

One might compare Doug Frank's account with the words of Sharon Baker, a professor of theology who is both a universalist and a critic of traditional atonement theology. At the opening of her book *Executing God* (2013), she writes: "Once upon a time I was a fundamentalist, Southern Baptist and I had God all figured out. I knew it all, and delighted in telling people all about God. Men and women flocked to my Bible study classes. They sold cassette tapes in the church narthex, and people bought them. . . . I knew with absolute certainty how God acted and why." The phrase "absolute certainty" bespeaks the rational confidence—or overconfidence—characteristic of fundamentalist Protestantism. Baker goes on to note her faith crisis: "A couple of things happened. . . . Two of my children became very sick with an incurable liver disease, and I went to seminary. All of a sudden I didn't know everything about God anymore." She comments, "I successfully rebuilt my belief system into something new and more forgiving," but "my absolute certainty never returned" and "doubt replaced certainty."[16]

The root-and-branch reevaluation of Christianity that we find among contemporary universalists may also have something to do with the critical voices to which each author is responding. Talbott studied under a college philosophy professor whose argument against an all-powerful and all-loving God triggered a youthful faith crisis. In developing his own arguments, Talbott quotes approvingly from the nineteenth-century skeptic John Stuart Mill and the twentieth-century atheist Bertrand Russell.[17] Universalist author Julie Ferwerda agrees with Bible critic Bart Ehrman that the God of traditional Christianity is a "divine Nazi."[18] Sharon Baker in *Executing God* takes her point of departure from au-

15. Frank, *Gentler God*, 17–18.
16. Baker, *Executing God*, 1–2.
17. Talbott, *Inescapable Love*, 1, 23.
18. Ferwerda, *Raising Hell*, 59–60. After quoting the comment on God as a "divine Nazi" from Bart Ehrman, *Jesus Interrupted*, 276, she comments: "Sadly, I think Bart is right. Without realizing

thors who reject the God of the Old Testament and the notion of substitutionary atonement.[19] Generally speaking, today's proponents of universalism pay much attention to the "cultured despisers of religion" and so seek to mediate between traditional faith and its modern critics.[20]

A scrutiny of recent universalist literature shows that there is more at stake in the current intra-evangelical debates than the final scope of salvation, important as that may be. Under the surface, just about *everything* is up for discussion—for example, what God's character is, how to interpret the Bible, whether the Old Testament is authoritative, what Jesus's death achieved, whether Christians are bound by doctrinal standards, and whether the doctrine of hell is proper Christian teaching or just a fear tactic used to scare people into obeying church leaders. Indeed, some of the universalist literature reads more like earlier deistic or skeptical literature than like traditional evangelical literature. Many universalist authors repudiate the notion that fear plays any appropriate role in Christian experience. Typically they reject the God of the Old Testament and are ready to rethink or reject classic evangelical teachings on substitutionary atonement. Some universalist authors have a love-hate attitude or a one-foot-in-one-foot-out stance toward institutional Christianity in general.

While universalism is most often a private or individual belief among Christians, a few Christian denominations have embraced the teaching. The group today known as Grace Communion International (GCI) was founded by Herbert W. Armstrong in 1934 and originally called the Radio Church of God. It became the Worldwide Church of God in 1968, and in 2009 it changed its named to the present designation. This denomination currently claims some 50,000 members in 900 congregations in some 100 nations. The website states that "the church's message now centers on Trinitarian, Incarnational theology,"

---

it, the 'god' we have put our hopes in and portrayed to the world is more like Hitler than Mother Teresa. The god we have unwittingly manufactured has feeble hopes for His own children—hopes that are dependent on human free will, and confined to the length of His children's brief, mortal lifespans" (*Raising Hell*, 60).

19. Baker's opening citations in her introduction are from Pfau and Blumenthal, "Violence of God"; J. C. Brown, "Divine Child Abuse?"; J. C. Brown and R. Parker, "For God So Loved the World?" The Pfau and Blumenthal essay consists of correspondence between a student and a faculty member centering on the question, "How can you relate to an abusive God in a positive way?" Brown and Parker offer a feminist theology that rejects the idea of Jesus's death as atoning. For analysis of their views, see Guomundsdottir, "Abusive or Abused?"

20. Intellectual *mediation* between traditional beliefs and modern critiques was the hallmark of Protestant liberal theology, beginning with Friedrich Schleiermacher (*DR* 7.3). The phrase "cultured despisers of religion" derives from his epoch-making work, first published in German in 1799, *On Religion: Speeches to Its Cultured Despisers*. In their attention to religion's "cultured despisers," contemporary universalists are akin to the early American universalist Hosea Ballou, whose reading of deist literature (e.g., Thomas Paine, Ethan Allen) shaped his universalist theology (*DR* 6.8).

that the church has "abandoned its former legalistic doctrines, exclusivist teaching," and that "grace lies at the heart of [their] values and mission." The GCI official statement of faith states that all human beings belong to God through Christ and are judged by God so that "they will return to him and live," bringing an "ultimate end of evil":

> God judges all humans through Jesus Christ as those who belong to God through him. Therefore, all humans are, in spite of themselves, loved, forgiven, and included in Jesus Christ, who is their Lord and Savior. God's love will never cease or diminish even for those who, denying the reality of who they are in him, refuse his love and consign themselves to hell; they will not enjoy the fruit of his salvation but rather will experience his love as wrath. God disciplines those he loves so that they will return to him and live; he stands at the door and knocks, urging them to open the door to his everlasting love. God's judgment in Christ means the ultimate end of evil and the renewal of the earth and all creation.[21]

The GCI statement says nothing about unending separation from God and so might be read as endorsing a purgationist form of universalism, in which those in rebellion experience "love as wrath" until such time as they turn to God.

In this chapter it is not possible to examine all the recent popular and semi-popular universalist authors, and so the focus here will lie on a few representative titles: Philip Gulley and James Mulholland, *If Grace Is True: Why God Will Save Every Person* (2003); Carlton Pearson, *The Gospel of Inclusion* (2006); Thomas Talbott, *The Inescapable Love of God* (1999); Gregory MacDonald, *The Evangelical Universalist* (2006); Doug Frank, *A Gentler God* (2010); Rob Bell, *Love Wins* (2011); and C. Baxter Kruger, *The Shack Revisited* (2012). Following the discussion of revisionist evangelicalism, we will turn to the newly emerging Charismatic, antinomian universalism of John Crowder and a few other authors connected with Crowder.

11.2. Liberal and Esoteric Universalism: Gulley, Mulholland, and Pearson

The publisher's cover blurb describes Philip Gulley and James Mulholland's *If Grace Is True: Why God Will Save Every Person* as a "stirring manifesto on the central role of universalism in Christianity." The authors, both members of Quaker congregations, reject the idea of Jesus's unique divinity. They write, "Was God uniquely present in the life of Jesus? I don't think so. Even Jesus

21. See http://www.gci.org/aboutus; http://www.gci.org/aboutus/namechange; http://www.gci.org/aboutus/beliefs.

was uncomfortable with people's attempts to make him unique." The authors come to the "far more wonderful" conclusion that "God was present in Jesus in the same way God wishes to be present in all of us."[22] Gulley and Mulholland's version of universalism is thus evidently unitarian in character. Strictly speaking, there is no mediation of salvation through Jesus. God relates directly to each individual human being, and a deity defined as the God-who-is-love can be expected to bring salvation to everyone.

There is not much theological argumentation in this book, nor does there need to be. The authors' initial premises entail the universalist conclusion. The authors state breezily that they have "a new formula" that is "simple and clear": "I believe God will save every person."[23] They explain, "If grace is true, it is true for everyone. It is really as simple as that."[24] The authors remark that they used to accept a distorted picture of a judging God, and it appears that this was based on the Old Testament: "I knew Jesus loved me because the Bible told me so. The biblical accounts of God's attitude weren't as comforting. Hearing that Jesus was all that stood between me and God's wrath didn't ease my anxiety. God wanted to destroy me, but Jesus had died for me. I found myself wishing that God could be more like Jesus. . . . [Then] I realized he was."[25]

This book does not engage the New Testament passages in which Jesus speaks of judgment. Instead Jesus is simply identified as a principle of love. Ultimately the authors appeal to their own religious experience, which reveals to them a God of "boundless love" rather than "wrath."[26] They have little use for the book of Revelation, which seems to them violent and vindictive.[27] Gulley and Mulholland reject traditional atonement theology in large part because of its link to what they take to be the unworthy image of a God of justice who demands payment. Instead of atonement theology, they teach what we might call "fiat forgiveness": "The forgiveness of sin didn't require the death of Jesus. It only required God's resolve to forgive. Grace isn't about Jesus' paying for our debts."[28]

Gulley and Mulholland admit that the Bible taken as a whole does not support universalism. "I freely admit . . . that my belief [in universalism] is contrary to certain Scriptures." They pose the question, "Can a Christian believe God will save everyone?" which they then proceed to answer: "Obviously if a Christian must believe the Bible is the 'infallible words of God,' the answer is no. There

22. Gulley and Mulholland, *If Grace Is True*, 146.
23. Ibid., 8; italicized in the original.
24. Ibid., 18; first sentence italicized in the original.
25. Ibid., 9.
26. Ibid., 11.
27. Ibid., 78.
28. Ibid., 128.

are too many verses about judgment, hell, and the eternal punishment of the wicked to make such optimism reasonable." The authors uphold what they call "the core message of the Bible," which they arrive at through a process of "weighing scripture" and "discerning which Scriptures accurately reflect God's character."[29] This book is clearly designed for liberally minded Christians or those of Christian background who are ready to accept a viewpoint that the authors themselves admit is contrary to some portions of the Bible.[30]

Carlton Pearson formerly served as a bishop in the Church of God in Christ (COGIC), a predominantly African American Pentecostal denomination. His book *The Gospel of Inclusion* tells of how and why he rejected his earlier theology and instead embraced a version of universalism that he calls "the gospel of inclusion." When he went public with his views regarding universal salvation, his five-thousand-member church in Tulsa lost about 90 percent of its membership, and soon thereafter the church property went up for sale.[31] Pearson's universalism also caused him to be disciplined and removed from the COGIC denomination by his fellow bishops. Pearson differs from other universalists reviewed in this chapter because of his interreligious approach (i.e., the presumption that multiple religions lead to final salvation). One also sees in his writing the influence of New Thought (i.e., human minds as aspects of a single Universal Mind). Pearson repeatedly cites Ralph Waldo Trine's *In Tune with the Infinite* (1897) as well as the anonymous *A Course in Miracles* (1975) and Neale Donald Walsh's *Conversations with God* (1996)—all works that fall into the broad category of New Thought.[32] After leaving COGIC, Pearson took pastoral responsibility in a Chicago-area congregation associated with New Thought.

Pearson sets forth his basic metaphysical system and worldview as follows: "Since we [i.e., human beings] came from God, we are made of the same substance as Divinity. Therefore we remain intrinsically connected to God and to each other. God created us out of Himself, which means that we are innately, internally, and eternally divine. We can experience true peace in this world

29. Ibid., 36, 49, 51. The authors say that they cannot accept God's character as set forth in the Old Testament: "The reported behavior of God in the Bible is erratic at best and nearly double-minded in some instances. God rescues the Jewish people from the oppression of Egypt in one chapter and a few chapters later has to be convinced by Moses not to destroy them" (52). Here Gulley and Mulholland omit a crucial element: the sin of the Israelites with the golden calf, which provoked God's anger against them (Exod. 32).

30. They write, "I believe Abraham, Isaac, and Jacob; Moses, David, and Solomon; Isaiah, Jeremiah, and Ezekiel didn't fully comprehend the character of God. They contributed valuable insights from their experiences with God. . . . [But] I believe in the God of Jesus, the God he called Father" (Gulley and Mulholland, *If Grace Is True*, 54–55). From this passage it seems as though Jesus is not Jewish—or perhaps that he proclaimed a God other than Yahweh, the God of the Old Testament.

31. Sherman, "Too Inclusive," 24.

32. C. Pearson, *Gospel of Inclusion*, 79–80, 243.

only when we reconnect to our Original Source."[33] From this premise, it is not hard to see why Pearson is a universalist. Salvation is not so much a matter of God redeeming or saving anyone but rather a process in which human beings awaken to their own inherent divinity.[34] Pearson says that "everybody is saved already" and that "we are all the chosen people."[35] Why did God create the world? It was because of "God's desire to experience or develop a part of Himself in the aspect of the terrestrial. With humanity, Deity could experience free will . . . evolution, change, and growth in a way no Supreme Being could otherwise." Pearson asks, "Is it not possible that God Himself had to pass through trials and difficulties in distant aeons past, before creation?"[36] Pearson rejects the Christian idea of atonement because it suggests that there is a separation of humanity from God. For Pearson, such separation is an illusion.[37] He leaves open the possibility of hell as "a place of temporary, corrective pain where even the most hardened souls will have their crimes purged away and their spirits renewed through toil, lesson, error, and repetition," but he insists that "there is no horrible eternal inferno."[38]

Pearson has harsh things to say about "religion," his term for institutions that employ fear to control their followers, persuade people that God is their enemy, and offer spurious means for people to protect themselves against God. "Religion," he writes, "is a form of witchcraft" or "the 'plantation' on which many people live as slaves," as religious leaders keep their followers in ignorance. "Christianity seeks to resolve a presumed conflict between a hostile God and His disobedient creation. The Gospel of Inclusion says that the conflict no longer exists, and never really did. Religion manufactured it."[39] Pearson's statement makes sense in light of New Thought teachings. Evil is an illusion; it does not exist. All things are already in harmony with God. Therefore the traditional Christian message about redemption from sin is based on falsehood. Pearson's metaphysical premises lead to far-reaching conclusions. Regarding the Bible, he says that "some of the so-called inspired Word is now 'expired' and

33. Ibid., 44.

34. In ancient gnostic universalism (*DR* 2.3), salvation occurs not so much by theophany (a revelation of God) as by a revelation of the self (egophany). To speak more precisely, salvation occurs through the flash of insight or knowledge (Greek *gnōsis*) in which one sees that one's own true self is a manifestation of the unknown God. Pearson's teaching replicates this gnostic patttern in contemporary vocabulary.

35. C. Pearson, *Gospel of Inclusion*, 4–5.

36. Ibid., 249–50. The idea of an evolving God who needs created reality in order to pass from abstract into concrete existence was a major theme in earlier discussions of Böhme (*DR* 5.3), Hegel (*DR* 7.4–7.6), and Schelling (*DR* 7.7).

37. C. Pearson, *Gospel of Inclusion*, 43.

38. Ibid., 251, 175.

39. Ibid., 7.

irrelevant." It is "not the definitive source of wisdom and command concerning God. No book could be." Pearson writes that "God is not Jesus" and calls himself "pantheistic."[40]

A startling chapter in Pearson's book is called "The Gospel of Evil."[41] Here the author teaches that "there is a beauty and a beast inside each of us." Though "we have been taught that they are enemies," they in fact "complement each other," and so we should be "allowing coexistence of the two." This statement fits in with the gnostic-esoteric idea that the only truly evil thing is *separation*, and the only finally good thing is *unity*. Consequently there is a moral imperative—strange as it sounds—to embrace evil. What God wants for each of us is "to balance the two," which is how Pearson understands the term "atonement or 'at-one-ment.'" "Where there is balance, there is no evil." Atonement means the unification of good with evil, not the overcoming of evil by good. "Evil is just good misunderstood," Pearson writes, and "evil would not exist were it not part of God." Pearson seemingly gives license to do evil when he writes, "You will never know that you are free from sin until you know that you are free to sin and still be loved by God."[42]

11.3. The Philosophical Universalism of Thomas Talbott

Thomas Talbott may be the most influential contemporary Christian philosopher writing in support of universalism.[43] He has published numerous technical articles in philosophical journals that deal with various aspects of universalism, as well as the more accessible book discussed here, *The Inescapable Love of God.*[44]

40. Ibid., 182–84.

41. Ibid., 93–107.

42. Ibid., 100–101, 104, 111. Pearson's blurring of distinctions between good and evil recalls earlier esoteric movements. Jewish Kabbalah displayed antinomian tendencies, which Gershom Scholem called a "doctrine of the holiness of sin." See *DR*, 168–69; see also *DR* appendix F, in connection with Ibn al-'Arabi's philosophy and his comparable antinomian tendency.

43. John Kronen and Eric Reitan have published a major philosophical monograph defending universal salvation, *God's Final Victory* (2011). See the brief comments on Kronen and Reitan in *DR*, 1037n83. Their writing is more technical than Talbott's in *The Inescapable Love of God*, which may limit its popular impact. My thanks to Thomas Talbott for sending me a copy of the second, revised edition of *The Inescapable Love of God*. Where this second edition is referenced, it is noted as such; other citations here are to the first edition.

44. Thomas Talbott's essays include "C. S. Lewis and the Problem of Evil" (1987); "Craig on the Possibility of Eternal Damnation" (1992); "The Doctrine of Everlasting Punishment" (1990); "Freedom, Damnation and the Power to Sin with Impunity" (2001); "The Love of God and the Heresy of Exclusivism" (1999); "Misery and Freedom: Reply to Walls" (2004); "The New Testament and Universal Reconciliation" (1992); "Punishment, Forgiveness, and Divine Justice" (1993); "Universalism and the Greater Good: Reply to Gordon Knight" (1999). In Parry and Partridge, *Universal Salvation?* (2004), Talbott presents his views, and other scholars respond to him.

For Talbott, as for many universalists, the central issue is the character of God. Talbott agrees with the nineteenth-century skeptic John Stuart Mill that we cannot with a straight face say that "God's goodness may be different in kind from man's goodness." This has led Talbott to reconsider his own evangelical faith: "I have felt a need to come to terms with my own heritage, particularly my religious heritage; and though some of the heritage now seems to me limited and defective, I have nonetheless tried to penetrate to the very best within it." Professing open-mindedness, Talbott declares, "I see no reason to begin with the assumption that my religion is better than, or embodies more of the truth than, someone else's religion does."[45]

Talbott writes that his encounter with the problem of evil in his earlier years was a "fundamental assault" on his deepest convictions. What troubled him as much as the philosophical challenge to belief in God was the response of major Christian theologians—Augustine, Aquinas, Luther, Calvin, Jonathan Edwards, and others—who all reflected "the same narrow predestinarian theology, the same exclusivism." He found it a "curious fact" that those with "the most intimate knowledge of the Bible" had the most objectionable theology. "I knew instinctively," he writes, "that I could never worship a God who is less kind, less merciful, less *loving* than my own parents."[46] Talbott came to a new understanding through the writings of George MacDonald. He read MacDonald's *Unspoken Sermons* (1867, 1885, 1889) and found the Scotsman to be a "voice of sanity," someone who "managed to see *everything*, even divine judgment and wrath, as an expression of God's perfecting love, a love that is both all-pervasive and, in the end, inescapable."[47]

Talbott offers a lengthy discussion of "the institutional church" or "imperial church" and his puzzlement that the church as a whole did not embrace universalism: "MacDonald's vision of divine love . . . struck me . . . as so glorious and so powerfully transforming that I began to wonder why the institutional church had so often backed away from it."[48] Talbott's arguments link hell with a sequence of other notions: hell-fear-control-empire-violence. Talbott accepts a line of criticism that is familiar from the eighteenth-century English deists

---

45. Talbott, *Inescapable Love*, 1–2.

46. Ibid., 4–6, 8. Talbott especially took exception to Gordon Clark's *Religion, Reason, and Revelation* (1961). Clark wrote, "God is the sole ultimate cause of everything. There is absolutely nothing independent of him. He alone is the eternal being. He alone is omnipotent. He alone is sovereign" (*Religion, Reason, and Revelation*, 238).

47. Talbott, *Inescapable Love*, 14. The inescapability of God's purifying love, an idea that Talbott took from George MacDonald, found its way into Talbott's book title. Both William Law and George MacDonald influenced Talbott's early development, suggesting that Talbott may have at least some kind of link to the British Böhmist universalists (*DR* 5.9).

48. Talbott, *Inescapable Love*, 15; cf. 15–30, on the imperial politics of hell.

and Enlightenment philosophes—namely, that church leaders used hell to keep rank-and-file members in line.[49] Talbott places no confidence in the pronouncements of the historic church and feels no need to reconcile his views with those of the early church councils. He reasons that the doctrine of hell has had negative effects and so must be false: "Since certain doctrines have consistently led to violence in God's name, the doctrine must be suspect."[50] Talbott concludes that "the vibrant faith of the early Christians had congealed into an organized religion with its own orthodoxy and political intrigues," and "the organized Christian church had simply lost its prophetic edge."[51]

Talbott's philosophical argument for universalism is a variation on the ancient problem of evil, propounded as early as the time of Epicurus in the third to fourth centuries BCE. Talbott presents the age-old paradox in three propositions. His revised version is focused not on evil in general but on the *specific evil* of sinners who remain forever unreconciled to God. (1) It is God's redemptive purpose for the world (and therefore his will) to reconcile all sinners to himself. (2) It is within God's power to achieve his redemptive purpose for the world. (3) Some sinners will never be reconciled to God, and God will therefore either consign them to a place of eternal punishment, from which there will be no hope of escape, or put them out of existence altogether.[52] Talbott notes correctly that Calvinists have qualified their assertion of proposition 1—God's purpose of salvation for all—by affirming a doctrine of the unconditional election of some but not all for salvation. Arminians have tended instead to qualify proposition 2, affirming that God's original gift of freedom to creatures brings a limitation of God's power to achieve his redemptive purpose. Proposition 3, says Talbott, does not seem to be compatible with the other two statements if propositions 1 and 2 are both fully affirmed.

49. Talbott writes:
> It is hardly surprising that a church under the control of such an emperor [i.e., Justinian], who is famous for his anathemata and his persecutions, should have rejected the doctrine of universal reconciliation. For insofar as fear of eternal damnation and the power of excommunication, backed by the coercive power of the state, had become the Emperor's primary means of social control, he could hardly tolerate a doctrine that would seem to undermine that power altogether. Justinian thus illustrates an important historical truth. Many religious doctrines serve, among other things, a sociological function, and over the centuries the traditional understanding of hell has served one function especially well: It has enabled religious and political leaders to cultivate fear and to employ fear as a means of social control. That more than anything else explains, I believe, why the imperial church came to regard the idea of universal reconciliation as a threat not only to social stability, but to its own power and authority as well. (ibid., 21–22)

50. Ibid., 24.

51. Ibid., 32–33.

52. Ibid., 43. This paradox of three propositions appears also in Gregory MacDonald [Parry], *Evangelical Universalist* (2006), 38–39.

He wonders why there have not been more evangelical Christians who have resolved the logical paradox by denying proposition 3 rather than by denying or qualifying proposition 1 or 2. As Talbott sees it, evangelical Christians have long been caught between Calvinism and Arminianism, while ignoring the third option of universalism.[53]

The answer to Talbott's puzzlement seems clear enough. The Bible offers a complex, nuanced picture of God's "will" or "purpose" for the world. In many passages of Scripture, there seems to be a primary purpose and will of God that is gracious, while this gracious will is opposed by human sin and rebellion against God. The idea that God always gets what God wants is an oversimplification. If God *always* got what God wanted, then evil would never have come to exist at all.[54] Moreover, the New Testament clearly presents the idea that "some sinners will never be reconciled to God." Literal interpreters of the Bible will not doubt that proposition 3 finds support in Scripture. So it is not surprising that evangelical Protestants since the mid-eighteenth century have oscillated between Calvinistic and Arminian views. Nor is it surprising that Calvinists and Arminians, despite their disagreements, generally regard one another as fellow brothers and sisters in Christ, while they regard universalists as seriously mistaken.[55] Many Calvinist and Arminian evangelicals admit the obscurity of the exegetical and philosophical questions regarding divine predestination and human free will, yet consider the doctrine of eternal punishment to be indubitably taught in the Bible.[56]

To return to the paradox of the three propositions, we may be suspicious of Talbott's argument for universalism because the argument *proves too*

---

53. Talbott, *Inescapable Love*, 44–54.

54. Talbott expands his analysis of the dilemma of the three propositions in *Inescapable Love* (2nd ed., 2014), 41–48, where he argues that "there is at least some *prima facie* biblical support" (42) for each of the three propositions. For this reason, he argues, those who profess to follow biblical teaching *must reject* one of the three biblically supported propositions. His choice is to reject proposition 3, which limits the scope of final salvation. My response is that Talbott's framing of the dilemma is flawed and that the problem concerns proposition 1. The Augustinian, Thomist, and Calvinist traditions have all observed that the New Testament texts present "the will of God" in a manifold and nuanced way rather than in a simple and unitary fashion. This much can be established through a lexical analysis of New Testament language regarding the divine will, which is itself manifold and nuanced (*boulē*, *thelēma*, *eudokia*, *horizō*, *proorizō*, etc.). In the Greek New Testament, it is definitely not the case that "the will of God" has a singular or simplistic meaning. The Augustinian tradition is thus not splitting hairs in distinguishing different senses of the divine will, but instead is paying close attention to the biblical texts. For historical references regarding "the will of God," see *DR*, 922–23.

55. Jerry Walls notes that the idea that "some sinners will never be redeemed" is "a matter of consensus among orthodox Christians" ("Philosophical Critique," 107–8).

56. On Wesleyan-Arminian views, see Ellison, *John Wesley and Universalism*, and Jerry Walls's works.

much—that is, more than Talbott might wish. To make the difficulty apparent, let us revise the argument slightly, without changing its basic format, as follows. (1) An all-loving God wills for there to be no sin, evil, or suffering in the universe he has created. (2) An all-powerful God is able to prevent any sin, evil, or suffering from existing in the universe he has created. (3) Sin, evil, and suffering exist in the universe that God has created. From the three revised propositions we might draw the conclusion that an all-loving, all-powerful God does not exist. The original form of this argument—as allegedly presented by Epicurus and reported by the later Christian author Lactantius—entailed this conclusion that there is no loving, omnipotent God.[57] If we take Talbott's argument seriously, then it is necessary to consider not only the possibility of sinners who are finally unreconciled to God but also the larger question of why evil exists at all in a world created by a loving God. Talbott seems to assume that a universalist "happy ending" to the universe will answer the age-old problem of evil. But is it so? In terms of the logic of the argument, it might not matter if all sinners are finally reconciled to God or if some are not finally reconciled to God. The question is this: Has God allowed evil to exist in the universe? The answer to this is yes.[58] On the basis of the three-proposition argument, Talbott could just as well go the way of Epicurus into a denial of any loving and omnipotent God. Talbott's argument for universalism and against particular salvation might equally function as an argument against the existence of the biblical God.[59]

The Inescapable Love of God includes at least as much biblical exegesis as philosophical discussion. Talbott claims that "the universalism of the New

---

57. Known as "the Epicurean paradox," the argument may be presented as follows: "Is God willing to prevent evil, but not able? Then he is not omnipotent. Is he able, but not willing? Then he is malevolent. Is he both able and willing? Then whence cometh evil? Is he neither able nor willing? Then why call him God?" (Hospers, *Introduction to Philosophical Analysis*, 310). While Epicurus himself left no written form of this argument, the Christian author Lactantius (ca. 250–ca. 325) in *Treatise on the Anger of God* presents this argument and offers a critique. As Lactantius presents Epicurus's argument, the conclusion drawn is that an all-powerful, all-good God does not exist and that the gods are distant and uninvolved in human affairs.

58. The only philosophical position denying that evil exists would be illusionism, which is not a viewpoint that Talbott entertains or endorses.

59. In a lecture given at the University of Notre Dame (Notre Dame, IN) in summer 2015, David Bentley Hart argued that universal salvation follows necessarily from God's moral character in combination with the doctrine of divine creation. As Creator, God is responsible for the ethical choices of creatures, and so is responsible for saving all sinful creatures. If damnation is the final outcome for *any* creatures, then God's moral goodness is called into question. The objection applied above to Talbott's argument might apply also to Hart's argument. Even if all intelligent creatures were to be finally saved, a God who is directly responsible for all sinful acts of all creatures can hardly be regarded as blameless, but must be faulted for every wrong ever done. Why did evil come to be? And how, on Hart's premises, could God not be faulted for it? See D. B. Hart, "God, Creation, and Evil."

Testament is not only all pervasive, but clear and obvious as well."[60] Yet Talbott uses some far-fetched exegesis to support his views. Interpreting the Pauline statement on "eternal destruction" in 2 Thessalonians 1:9, Talbott reads this passage as a *destructive salvation*, whereby the old self is destroyed and a new self is born. He writes, "The [biblical] writer may describe one side of the redemptive process as divine judgment upon a sinner and the destruction of the old person (perhaps even in hell), or the writer may describe the other side as the birth of a new person."[61] So when Paul wrote the words "eternal destruction," he meant "eternal salvation." Along these lines Talbott writes, "The destruction of the false self is clearly a good thing; it is liberation, salvation itself."[62]

In Talbott's account of salvation, the historical Jesus and the atoning death of Jesus recede in importance while salvation itself is equated with the human individual's self-willed purification. The chapter on punishment in *The Inescapable Love of God* states that some people are finally saved even though God never forgives them. Instead of being forgiven, they make full payment for their sins through personal suffering: "They will experience his love as a consuming fire. . . . So in that sense, *they will literally pay for their sin*; and God will never—not in this age and not in the age to come—forgive (or set aside) the final payment they owe."[63] Talbott thus arrives at an ironic conclusion. In his effort to extend grace to everyone, Talbott ends up denying the necessity of grace. Some are saved by grace, while others are saved apart from grace. Through what Talbott calls an "alternative strategy," some people pay the price on their own—in other words, they atone or compensate for their own sins.[64]

Other problems arise in relation to Talbott's idea of human freedom and his notion that all intelligent creatures will finally submit voluntarily to God. Jerry Walls has offered an incisive critique of Talbott on this point.[65] For Talbott, the final bowing of the knee to Christ (Phil. 2:10) must be a glad and voluntary surrender and not a grudging acknowledgment of Jesus as Lord: "If they [those who

60. Talbott, *Inescapable Love*, 55.
61. Ibid., 97.
62. Ibid., 102.
63. Ibid., 106 (emphasis added).
64. Talbott's salvation through the destruction of the old self is reminiscent of Immanuel Kant's rationalist reinterpretation of Christianity in *Religion within the Limits of Reason Alone* (1793). Here Kant argues that each individual makes atonement for his or her own sins. Christ's atonement fades in importance because every person accomplishes atonement in the very process of conversion from the old self to the new self (Kant, *Religion within the Limits of Reason Alone*, 66–68). On the antecedents to Kant's self-atonement, see Ritschl, *Critical History*, 320–86. Here Ritschl shows how objective atonement by Jesus on the cross gradually gave way among Germany's eighteenth-century rationalist theologians to a subjective notion of salvation through moral improvement.
65. Walls, "Philosophical Critique."

bow the knee] are forced to make obeisance against their will, then their actions are merely fraudulent and bring no glory to God; a Hitler may take pleasure in forcing his defeated enemies to make obeisance against their will, but a God who honors the truth could not possibly participate in such a fraud."[66] Talbott will not accept the idea of a powerful God who triumphs over his adversaries. Instead he accepts only a persuasive model for God's interaction with creatures. As we will see below, Talbott himself seems to have compromised his own idea that God works only through persuasion.

A basically optimistic view of human nature pervades Talbott's account of salvation. He presumes that no one who truly and fully understands who God is—and the grace that God offers—would ever reject God or God's grace. Talbott allows no place for willful, defiant, or inexplicable rebellion against goodness. It is only a lack of full information or education, Talbott argues, that leads some people temporarily to reject God. Once someone comes truly to know God, Talbott asks, "What possible motive might remain for embracing such eternal misery [i.e., hell] freely?"[67] Some common answers are pride, stupidity, folly, orneriness, stubbornness, and so on. Human experience shows that people make foolish decisions and often stick by them, regardless of mounting evidence that they have made a self-destructive choice and that they are experiencing self-imposed misery because of their choice. The pharaoh of the book of Exodus is the poster boy for such willfulness—a stubbornness without a reasonable motive. It is not just that Pharaoh persistently resists and refuses God's call to the bitter end. It is also that the Old Testament describes God as glorified among the nations through Pharaoh's refusal.[68] On Talbott's universalist premises, such a thing is impossible. God is glorified only in the *persuasive exercise* of mercy and never through the *coercive imposition* of judgment.

God's goodness is Talbott's basic premise in arguing for universalism. And human goodness is a second postulate, not so much proven as presupposed. Talbott's optimistic anthropology—embodied in the Socratic maxim that "to know the good is to do the good"—is both the driving principle and the Achilles'

66. Talbott, *Inescapable Love*, 69. There is a forceful statement by Talbott in his essay "Christ Victorious": "For so long as a single will remains in a state of rebellion against Christ, so long as a single person is able to cling to his or her hatred of God, at least one power in the universe—namely, the power of that person's will—is not yet in subjection to Christ" (23).

67. Talbott, "Freedom, Damnation," 423. Much like Thomas Talbott, David Bentley Hart writes that "no one can *freely* will the evil as evil" (Hart, "God, Creation, and Evil," 10). Describing Hart's position, De La Noval writes that "God would *not* be respecting the freedom of the damned by letting them undo themselves eschatologically, for they have not actually freely chosen their fate" ("Fork in the [Final] Road," 317).

68. In Exod. 9:16, God speaks to Pharaoh through Moses in these words: "But for this purpose I have raised you up, to show you my power, so that my name may be proclaimed in all the earth."

heel of his universalism. If one admits that there is such a thing as blind, willful, or senseless resistance to goodness, then it becomes apparent that not everyone can be counted on to make correct choices. Unlike such thinkers as Karl Barth (DR 9.1–9.9) or Hans Urs von Balthasar (DR 10.4–10.9), Talbott is primarily an *anthropocentric* universalist, who suspends his hopes for final salvation on the slender thread of correct human choices. If this thread breaks, then all is lost.

The problem with Talbott's account of human choice runs even deeper, as Jerry Walls has noted. It is not only excessively optimistic but also self-contradictory. Talbott writes that "if separation from God can bring only greater and greater misery into a life, as Christians have traditionally believed, then the very idea of . . . freely embracing a destiny apart from God seems to break down altogether."[69] Talbott holds that the forcibly imposed misery of hell will eventually cause even the most resistant and recalcitrant sinners to repent and choose instead to be with God. Hell is God's forcibly imposed punishment on the disobedient and rebellious, and God increases the misery to ever-higher levels, until at last the human sufferer finally submits to God. Yet how could such a submission ever count, on Talbott's own premises, as a *genuinely free choice?*

Walls comments on both the unfree character of choices made under duress and the morally dubious value of such choices:

There are serious problems with his [i.e., Talbott's] claim that persons who repent under forcibly imposed punishment are free in the libertarian sense. . . . The notion of ever increasing misery, misery without a distinct limit, destroys the very notion of a free choice. The reason for this is that finite beings like ourselves are simply not constituted in such a way that we can absorb ever increasing misery. At some point, we would either be coerced to submit, or we would go insane, or we would perish. We have neither the power nor the psychological ability to withstand constantly increasing misery. . . . For punishment to elicit a free choice

---

69. Talbott, "Freedom, Damnation," 420. Eric Reitan holds a view like that of Talbott, to the effect that the notion of freely chosen damnation is incoherent or self-contradictory. See Reitan, "Human Freedom." Self-chosen damnation may indeed be incoherent *and yet happen anyway,* as Jerry Walls explains:

The view that hell can be preferred to heaven obviously requires a profound illusion. Those who remain in hell because they take it in some way to be better than heaven are deeply self-deceived. . . . It is the ability to deceive ourselves that finally makes intelligible the choice of eternal hell. . . . What the damned want is to be happy on their own terms. However, that is impossible. The only possible way we can truly be happy is on God's terms. So the damned choose what they *can* have on their own terms, namely, a distorted sense of satisfaction that is a perverted mirror image of the real thing. At some level they know this. Self-deception is not a matter of being unaware of truth, but of choosing not to attend to it, of turning our eyes away from it and acting as if it is not true. A person who is doing this cannot experience a deep sense of unity and integrity. There will inevitably be a deep sense of unease and unhappiness. ("Philosophical Critique," 120–22)

that is morally significant, the person receiving the punishment must come to see the truth about himself and his actions and genuinely want to change. He must achieve moral insight in the process and willingly desire to act on that insight. He must want to change because of the truth he has seen, not merely to escape or avoid the punishment that is being forced on him.[70]

Talbott's account of the postmortem conversion process thus seems self-contradictory. At one point he rejects the idea that human beings make "obeisance against their will" to God and says that only "a Hitler" would "take pleasure in forcing his defeated enemies" to acknowledge him. Yet Talbott's idea of hell as ever-increasing misery looks like the very thing that he says he rejects.

Talbott offers a disturbing picture of the process involved in postmortem salvation. With the best of motives, God employs the postmortem equivalent of waterboarding or electroshock, at ever-increasing levels of intensity, until the poor sufferer finally "cries uncle" and surrenders to God's demand to be recognized. Though Talbott speaks of love, this seems more like torture. Somehow this picture is supposed to be compatible with an unimpeded, libertarian freedom of the human will. The pains he describes do not purify the soul or pay the price for sins. They are designed simply to drive the sufferer to yield to God.[71]

From our examination of Talbott's universalism, we have shown that his position contains a number of tensions, if not contradictions. In an ironic way, the effort to extend grace to all undermines the principle of grace. To assert that salvation comes through the spiritual purification of the human self (per Talbott's interpretation of 2 Thess. 1:9) sounds like moralism rather than a gospel of grace. Just as troubling is the insistence that every creature will finally submit to God as God inflicts ever-increasing measures of pain in the afterlife to bring rebellious creatures into submission. Talbott's universalism is thus unevangelical. Neither Scripture, nor tradition, nor philosophical reasoning supports the theories that he offers as a replacement for traditional Christian teachings on the afterlife.

11.4. The Evangelical Universalism of Robin Parry

Robin Parry is one of the most influential advocates for Christian universalism today. Alone among contemporary universalists, Parry uses multiple lines of

70. Walls, "Philosophical Critique," 111–12.
71. Talbott presents postmortem suffering in different ways. In *Inescapable Love*, 81–106, postmortem suffering permits people to pay the penalty for their own sins (106). Yet in Talbott's essay "Freedom, Damnation, and the Power to Sin with Impunity," hell as "ever-increasing misery" aims at bringing sufferers to submit to God. Talbott seemingly cannot decide whether postmortem suffering expiates the guilt of sins or leads people—amid their pain—to cry out for God's mercy.

argument—philosophical reasoning, biblical exegesis, and historical tradition—in his books and essays in favor of universalism. Speaking broadly, we might identify three of his books as embodying these three appeals. The coedited *Universal Salvation? The Current Debate* (2004) deals primarily (though not exclusively) with philosophical argumentation for universalism. The pseudony mously published *The Evangelical Universalist* (2006) is mostly devoted to biblical exegesis.[72] The edited volume *"All Shall Be Well": Explorations in Universal Salvation and Christian Theology from Origen to Moltmann* (2011) examines historical precedents for Christian universalism.[73] Much to his credit, Parry readily entertains counterarguments opposing his own position. This becomes apparent in the inclusion of pro- and anti-universalist authors in *Universal Salvation?*; in the postings at his personal website, Theological Scribbles; and in the section "Responses to (Some of) My Critics" in the second edition of *The Evangelical Universalist* (2012).[74]

Parry's story is interesting on a human level. While serving as an editor at a British evangelical publishing house, Parry published the first edition of *The Evangelical Universalist* (2006) under the pseudonym Gregory MacDonald. At his blog, Parry said this decision was the result of his wish to spare his publisher the unfavorable publicity that might result from having an editor associated with the "heresy" of universalism. When Parry came out publicly in 2009 as "the Evangelical Universalist," he commented that attitudes toward universalism in conservative Protestant churches had become more open and accepting in a few years' time. "We're not there yet," he wrote, "but we are closer than we were a few years back, so I thought, 'It's going to come out some time—better to reveal my identity than be 'exposed.'"[75]

72. Gregory MacDonald's [Parry's] *The Evangelical Universalist* has appeared in two editions (2006, 2012), and the content of the two differs. The second edition includes a new preface and appendices. Unless otherwise indicated, all citations are to the first or 2006 edition. The discussion here will also draw on an archive of Parry's online postings at http://theologicalscribbles.blogspot.com.

73. Robin Parry's pseudonymous books (i.e., books published under the name "Gregory Mac-Donald") in favor of universalism are *The Evangelical Universalist* and *"All Shall Be Well."* The work that Parry coedited under his own name with Christopher Partridge is *Universal Salvation?* Thomas Talbott wrote four of the twelve chapters in the last-mentioned work, while other contributors interact with Talbott. Parry's views cannot simply be assimilated to those of Talbott, though the two have much in common, and Parry attributes his turn toward universalism as due in part to his reading of Talbott's *The Inescapable Love of God.* See also Parry, "Evangelical Universalism: Oxymoron?" (2012).

74. Gregory MacDonald [Parry], *Evangelical Universalist*, 2nd ed., 199–221.

75. Parry's "coming out" blog post ("I Am the Evangelical Universalist") was published on August 29, 2009 at http://theologicalscribbles.blogspot.com/2009/08/I-am-evangelical-universalist .html. During the years in which he was concealing his identity as author of *The Evangelical Universalist*, Parry did an interview for the London-based Premier Radio with his voice "disguised to sound like Darth Vader in order to hide my identity" (MacDonald [Parry], *Evangelical Universalist*, 2nd ed.,

Later we will return to the issue of Parry's relationship to evangelicalism, since this is a central issue for understanding his motivations and intentions in writing. In his 2012 essay "Evangelical Universalism. Oxymoron?," Parry set aside the question of the truth or falsity of universalism and focused instead on defining "evangelical" so as to make it possible to combine it with "universalist." "The question I wish to address is not whether universalism is true or not," he wrote, but "whether one can be *both* an evangelical *and* a universalist."[76] Unlike many other contemporary universalists surveyed in this chapter, Parry positions himself as an evangelical—not as an *ex*-evangelical— and indicates that he would like universalism to become a live option for other self-professing evangelicals.[77] Universalism versus particularism ought, he thinks, to be a question on which disagreements are allowable without breaking the bonds of evangelical fellowship—much like Calvinism versus Arminianism, paedobaptism versus adult baptism, or premillennialism versus amillennialism. Parry's writings on universalism seek to expand the range of acceptable evangelical opinions.

There is some ambiguity regarding Parry's view in *The Evangelical Universalist*, since he ends his book with the words "I am a Christian universalist," though early on in the book he says, "I am a hopeful dogmatic universalist." On analysis, Parry does not seem to be merely a "hopeful universalist," since in the course of his argument he disavows the "hopeful" label and prefers instead to call himself an assertive or dogmatic universalist.[78] To distinguish

---

xvi). The link to the interview with "Gregory MacDonald" (with disguised voice), is dated March 15, 2008, and appears at https://www.premierchristianradio.com/Shows/Saturday/Unbelievable /Episodes/17-Oct-2009-The-Evangelical-Universalist-is-revealed.

76. Parry, "Evangelical Universalism," 3.

77. The authors treated in this chapter might be arranged in terms of their stance vis-à-vis the Protestant evangelical tradition. On such a spectrum, Parry might be the most affirmative toward evangelicalism, followed by Bell and Talbott (both of whom are ambivalent), and Pearson on the other end (as clearly ex-evangelical). The Charismatic authors (Crowder, Dunn, du Toit, Rabe) also display varying degreees of ambivalence toward the Charismatic tradition that they embrace and yet question.

78. Gregory MacDonald [Parry], *Evangelical Universalist*, 177, 4. The elaboration on "hopeful dogmatic" is murky. He writes that "hopeful universalism" is "*not* my position." "Dogmatic universalists," he writes, "argue that it is certain that God will save all. I agree but with a qualification. The theology outlined in this book is one that espouses a dogmatic universalism, but I must confess to not being 100% certain that it is correct. Thus I am a hopeful dogmatic universalist, a non-dogmatic dogmatic universalist" (4). The "hopeful" aspect drops away in the course of Parry's exposition, and the "dogmatic" side of universalism predominates. In *The Evangelical Universalist*, 2nd ed., Parry finds fault with Rob Bell in *Love Wins* for being a "hopeful universalist," and he adds: "Most critics of [Rob] Bell think that he goes too far. It will come as no surprise to learn that I, on the contrary, think that *he does not go far enough*. . . . To the extent that any individual fails to achieve love's desires for her or him, love has not won." So he worries about Bell's measure of "agnosticism" about universal salvation (197–98; emphasis in the original).

his own position from other forms of universalism, Parry notes that Christian universalism ought not to be confused with the idea that "all roads lead to God" and that ultimate salvation can take place either through Christ or apart from Christ. Such a pluralistic perspective represents one form of universalism, but this is not the *Christian universalism* to which Parry adheres. Parry argues that his version of universalism does not imply any disparagement of Christ's atoning death, nor a denial of the doctrine of the Trinity, nor even a denial of hell, since he interprets hell as a temporary place of purgation or purification.

Parry indicates that his universalist belief arose from the crucible of a faith crisis that centered on the question of God's character. Was God truly worthy of worship? Or, as Parry puts it, "Could I love a God who could rescue everyone but chose not to?"[79] He explains further what he experienced in the opening words to the second edition of *The Evangelical Universalist*:

> Have you ever felt that soul-sickening feeling when you know that you cannot worship God with sincerity any longer? Have you ever experienced the painful knowledge that the noble words of praise coming from your lips are hollow? I can recall one Sunday morning when I had to stop singing for I was no longer sure whether I believed that God deserved worship. For a believer, that is a moment of despair. Ever since I had been a Christian, I had never wavered in my conviction that God loved people, but on that Sunday I didn't know if I could believe that anymore.[80]

In the same context, Parry writes of reading William Lane Craig's philosophical treatise on divine foreknowledge, *The Only Wise God* (1987), the doubts that Craig's work raised in his mind, and the powerful impact on him of his later reading of Thomas Talbott's *The Inescapable Love of God* (1999). He also mentions reading an essay on universalism by the philosopher Keith DeRose.[81] This immersion into contemporary philosophical debates caused Parry to begin to doubt God's goodness.[82]

This is not an irrelevant biographical datum. What it suggests is that, despite Parry's later effort at defending universalism on a biblical basis, the trigger that led him into universalist belief was not exegetical but philosophical. Parry's autobiographical reflections suggest that his journey into universalism began

79. Gregory MacDonald [Parry], *Evangelical Universalist*, 2nd ed., 3.

80. Ibid., 1.

81. Ibid., 2–3. Keith DeRose, "Universalism and the Bible: The *Really* Good News" (1998); online at http://campuspress.yale.edu/keithderose/1129-2/.

82. Craig and Talbott debated universalism in a series of articles: Craig, "Talbott's Universalism"; Talbott, "Craig on the Possibility of Eternal Damnation"; Craig, "Talbott's Universalism Once More."

with a revised concept of God that was itself defined primarily by rational or philosophical argumentation.[83] What Parry came to embrace was a purgationist universalism centering on the claim that "one's eternal destiny is not fixed at death" and that "those in hell can repent and throw themselves upon the mercy of God in Christ and thus be saved."[84] Hell is thus "an awful *but temporary* fate from which all can, and ultimately will, be saved."[85] Parry's *The Evangelical Universalist* reinterprets the whole of Scripture in light of this central idea that there is postmortem suffering for sins—a temporary rather than eternal "hell"—and that everyone who enters this state will eventually find their way out of it and into heaven.

The Evangelical Universalist is an exceptionally detailed work of biblical exegesis. Considered strictly as a *universalist exegete*, Parry may rival and surpass all of his predecessors, including Origen and the modern eighteenth- through twentieth-century authors. To his credit, he seems never deliberately to have dodged a difficult question. No one has striven as doggedly as Parry has to identify and to defeat every exegetical objection against universalism. What is more, Parry has eschewed the tendency of earlier universalist exegetes to rely on allegorical or symbolic readings of texts that, taken literally, do not seem to support universalism. Most universalists gave up on the book of Revelation, a rather unpromising book for universalist interpretation. Not so with "Gregory MacDonald," who is undaunted in reinterpreting the final book of the Christian Bible, along with all the rest, in a more or less literal way.

In comparison with the New Testament, the Old Testament does not contain much clear teaching on the afterlife, and yet there is a definite doctrine of divine election. This doctrine of election involves two correlative elements—namely, that Israel is the chosen nation and that other nations are not so chosen. Such a line of demarcation within humanity might suggest that salvation should be conceived of as particular rather than as universal. Parry resists this conclusion, arguing that "in the Old Testament, election is corporate" and does not focus on individuals per se. Applied to the New Testament, Parry's account of election means that "God calls individuals to participate in a corporate election

---

83. In Parry's "Responses to (Some of) My Critics," the first objection that he addresses is that he is guilty of "making God fit human reason" (Gregory MacDonald [Parry], *Evangelical Universalist*, 2nd ed., 199). Parry states, "Any interpretation of Genhenna [sic] must be compatible with the claim that God is love and would never act in a way towards a person that was not ultimately compatible with what is best for that person. Any interpretation of Gehenna as a punishment must be compatible with the claim that divine punishment . . . has a corrective intention" (Gregory MacDonald [Parry], *Evangelical Universalist*, 148). This statement suggests that Parry's presuppositions have shaped his exegesis of particular passages.

84. Gregory MacDonald [Parry], *Evangelical Universalist*, 6.

85. Ibid., 7.

in Christ." In this way "the set of 'the elect' is an expanding set."[86] For Parry, election becomes a divine invitation that may or may not meet with human acceptance. A difficulty with Parry's notion of an expandable election comes in the New Testament phrase "Lamb's book of life," since the names of those in the book are said to have been "written before the foundation of the world" (Rev. 13:8; cf. 3:5; 17:8; 20:12, 15; 21:27). Quite rightly, Parry notes that "the universalist needs a [book of life] with flexible contents—one in which names can be deleted and, more importantly, added."[87] Yet it is hard to imagine Revelation's "book of life" as flexible in this way—like a cell phone listing with add and delete functions. Parry uses Talbott's suggestion that people may have two different names written in the "book of life," one of which reflects their new birth in Christ and the other which does not. Supplementary hypotheses—like this one regarding the two names—are occasionally required to reconcile the biblical texts with Parry's version of universalism.

In approaching the New Testament Gospels, Parry makes the revealing statement, "I am not trying to show that Jesus taught universalism nor that he taught that those in Gehenna could or would be saved, for he did neither." At first blush, this looks like an admission of failure, since Parry is acknowledging that Jesus *did not teach* what he himself teaches. His aim, he writes, is the "more modest one of showing that what [Jesus] did teach does not formally contradict universalist claims."[88] In this way Parry applies what we might call a lawyerly approach to the Bible. As long as Jesus's words do not "formally contradict" universalism, then universalist belief remains admissible.

Parry admits, "I may be offering ways of reading the texts that go beyond what their authors had in mind," and the arguments in *The Evangelical Universalist* bear this out.[89] The parable of the rich man and Lazarus contains the simple statement that "a great chasm has been fixed" between the realm of the blessed and that of the lost (Luke 16:26). Parry interprets this to mean that "the chasm may be fixed up to the Day of Judgment but not necessarily afterward"—thus importing into the text a distinction that it never suggests.[90] The effort to discover what Parry calls "post-damnation salvation" leads to some unusual interpretations.[91] Parry quotes Mark 9:45–48, in which Jesus says that "the fire is not quenched" (Mark 9:48), but then in a complicated note he claims that "Jesus . . . legitimates limiting the temporal duration of the fires," thus inverting

86. Gregory MacDonald [Parry], *Evangelical Universalist* (2nd ed.), 236, 238.
87. Gregory MacDonald [Parry], *Evangelical Universalist*, 192.
88. Ibid., 144–45.
89. Ibid., 140.
90. Ibid., 146.
91. Ibid., 120.

the literal sense of Jesus's words.[92] In one passage Parry suggests that God allowed "misunderstandings about hell" to result from Jesus's teaching, since any "clarification would have undermined the rhetorical force of his message."[93] Here he makes it sound as though Jesus's teaching on hell was a pious fraud.

The interpretations of Paul's Letters in *The Evangelical Universalist* are equally problematic. Parry calls 2 Thessalonians 1:9 "a problem text for universalists" and fails to reconcile Paul's reference to "eternal destruction" with his general universalist reading of Paul.[94] Like many other universalists, Parry interprets Romans 5:12–21 out of context. Not only does he fail to connect this passage with the rest of Paul's Letters, but he also ignores the immediate context in Romans 5:1–11, which begins with the words, "Therefore, since we have been justified by faith, we have peace with God through our Lord Jesus Christ" (Rom. 5:1). Sound hermeneutical practice would suggest that "for all men" in Romans 5:18 should be read alongside "justified by faith" in 5:1. Parry does not adequately take into account the alternating terms in the passage ("many" versus "all"), the possible qualifying phrase in 5:17 ("those who receive the abundance of grace"), nor the reasonable surmise of N. T. Wright that the "all" of Romans 5:18 refers to "all nations" (or gentiles) and not Jews only.[95]

With regard to 1 Corinthians 15, Parry's case is even weaker than with regard to Romans 5. The "all" who "shall . . . be made alive" are those who are "in Christ" (1 Cor. 15:22), and the following reference to "those who belong to Christ" (1 Cor. 15:23) delimits the scope of Paul's "all" statement.[96] References in the Pauline Letters to the neutralization or subjugation of hostile, demonic powers to God and God's kingdom (1 Cor. 15:24–28; Col. 2:13–15) cannot be equated with the notion of a free, glad, or voluntary submission of Satan and demons. Understanding

92. Ibid., 143, with n. 21. In an email to me on March 25, 2017, Parry wrote in response to the passage above: "My core argument is the same as that of the annihilationists: that an unquenchable fire is not the same thing as a never-ending fire (it is simply a fire that cannot be put out). Like other unquenchable fires in the Bible, it need not last forever. So I do not see the claim that the fire is temporary as in any way an *inversion* of what Jesus says, as in my view he does not say anything about the duration of the fire."

93. Ibid., 149.

94. Ibid., 154. Thomas Talbott's reading of 2 Thess. 1 has been discussed above (*DR*, 952–53), and Parry seems to be unwilling to follow Talbott's exegetical lead vis-à-vis this text.

95. Ibid., 81, citing N. T. Wright, "Towards a Biblical View of Universalism." Parry appeals (*Evangelical Universalist*, 84) to Martinus de Boer's comment that, in any non-universalist reading of Rom. 5, "death is then given the last word over the vast majority of human beings and God's regrasping of the world for His sovereignty becomes a limited affair" (de Boer, *Defeat of Death*, ch. 5, n. 89). De Boer's statement shows how the universalist exegesis of Rom. 5 and other Pauline passages is often driven by philosophical or theological presumptions, not by Greek grammar, syntax, or semantics. See *DR* appendix L for a discussion of Christ's union with humanity in Barth's and Bultmann's exegesis of Rom. 5.

96. Gregory MacDonald [Parry], *Evangelical Universalist*, 84–86.

this point gives us a context for interpreting "every knee should bow" and "every tongue confess" in Philippians 2:10–11. The Philippians reference to those "under the earth" is most likely to demonic powers, and every indication we have in the Pauline Letters is that these powers are coerced into submission and not persuaded to abandon their hostility to God. Demons do not become angels—or at least not in the Old and New Testaments.[97]

Parry's interpretation of the book of Revelation is one of the more problematic aspects of *The Evangelical Universalist*. Already we noted Parry's inability to account for the "Lamb's book of life," but this is just one of a number of exegetical problems. Parry misses the representative universalism of the book of Revelation, where we never read that God saves "every nation" but saves people "from every nation" (Rev. 7:9; cf. 5:9). Not all nations, but some persons *from* all nations, will finally receive salvation.[98] Parry asserts that "there is a continuous flow from outside the City (clearly the lake of fire) . . . into the [heavenly] City."[99] He suggests that "someone in the lake of fire could wash their robes in the blood of the Lamb and thus be added into the book of life."[100] Along these same lines, Parry interprets the final invitations from "the Spirit" and "the Bride" to "come" (Rev. 22:17) as directed not to the readers of the book of Revelation but rather to those cast into the lake of fire—that is, that they should come out of the fire and enter the new Jerusalem.[101]

A number of problems arise from Parry's notion of "post-damnation salvation."[102] Regarding the devil's damnation, Parry is not sure what to say, but he suggests that either the devil is "non-personal" or else that "the devil is punished forever" even though "Lucifer will ultimately be saved." He explains that "it would still be possible to speak of the devil being tormented forever and ever to symbolize this defeat even though no actual being is still in the lake of fire."[103] Likewise, with regard to the human beings in Revelation 14 who bear "the mark of the beast" and are said to be tormented forever, Parry suggests "that the damned are indeed justly sentenced to suffer eternal conscious torment but that none of them serve

97. Ibid., 45–48, 88–89, 97, 191. In an email to me on March 25, 2017, Parry clarified his position on this passage: "I do not see 'those under the earth' as demons, so I do not even try to make that case in this context. You may wish to make clear . . . that I work with the idea that 'those under the earth' are the dead."

98. Parry correctly says that "the saints are never identified with the nations" (*Evangelical Universalist*, 111) and cites the phrase *"from* every nation" (Rev. 5:9; 7:9) (111n12), yet he fails to see that this phrase supports particularism rather than universalism.

99. Ibid., 115.
100. Ibid., 117.
101. Ibid., 118–19.
102. Ibid., 120.
103. Ibid., 131.

out the full term of their sentence." Struggling with Revelation 14 and the clear statement that "the smoke of their torment goes up forever and ever" (Rev. 14:11), Parry proposes another novel idea to the effect that "the *smoke* will rise forever as a memorial *long after the punishment itself has ceased*."[104] We end up then with two different kinds of smoke: punishment smoke and memorial smoke.

The Evangelical Universalist shows more clearly than perhaps any recent work the perils—and indeed the absurdities—of universalist interpretations of the New Testament. The exegesis of *The Evangelical Universalist* preserves universalism by adding ancillary hypotheses to the reading of the texts. To use a scientific analogy, the process reminds one of premodern astronomy. The earth-centered system of Ptolemy was able to achieve the same result as Copernican astronomy and "save the appearances," but only by adding innumerable epicycles to the cycles of planetary motion.[105] By contrast, the sun-centered system of Copernicus was clear, elegant, and straightforward. If one initially assumes particular salvation in reading the New Testament, then one does not have to force artificial interpretations on the relevant biblical texts. Conversely, if one assumes universal salvation at the outset, then there seems to be no limit of "problem passages" that tax the exegetical ingenuity of even the cleverest interpreter. Because of its thoroughness in identifying the exegetical difficulties in the case for universalism, *The Evangelical Universalist* is rather effective at establishing a counterargument. Particularism was never so exegetically secure until Parry attempted to disprove it.

What, then, is Parry up to with his "evangelical universalism"? Is he aiming to redefine the evangelical tradition? Historically speaking, there has been decided opposition to universalism among evangelicals in Britain and North America for about two hundred and fifty years. Early nineteenth-century evangelicals regarded universalist theology as logically incoherent and morally corrosive. A 1790 treatise claimed that the universalist "doctrines and preaching, have abundantly more tendency to do mischief and propagate libertinism and corruptness, than any other in the whole world; and consequently call for the strongest resistance."[106] A typical evangelical polemic in 1838 typified universalism as incoherent: "When he [the author] commenced his investigation, he was not aware of the astonishing absurdity of a system so extensively received [i.e.,

104. Ibid., 130n53; emphasis in the original.

105. The idea of "saving the appearances" (or "saving the phenomena") comes from Simplicius's sixth-century CE commentary on Aristotle's *De Caelo* (*On the Heavens*) and Simplicius's attribution of the phrase to Plato. The phrase suggests that hypotheses that explain the existing appearances are not necessarily true. Two contradictory hypotheses might both be able to explain (i.e., "save") the appearances, as in the case of the competing Ptolemaic and Copernican conceptions of the cosmos. See Goldstein, "Saving the Phenomena," 1–11.

106. A Youth of the City [pseud.], *Thoughts on the Doctrine of Universal Salvation*, 13.

universalism]. When compared with . . . the statements of the Bible, it is a mass of intolerable nonsense."[107] Another wrote in 1848 that universalist "doctrines are so palatable, so much in accordance with the taste of our depraved natures, that, unless well guarded by Divine grace, we are in danger of being seduced by its allurements."[108] Another spoke of universalism as "a system, false in all its leading features, and more dangerous in its tendencies than all other errors put together."[109] Since the late eighteenth century, the total number of evangelical anti-universalist books has been sizable.[110]

Only historical amnesia on the part of twenty-first-century evangelicals would cause them to forget these past debates. From the 1780s onward, one of Anglo-American evangelicalism's defining traits has been its anti-universalism.[111] If

107. McClure, *Lectures on Ultra-Universalism*, v.

108. Anonymous, *Universalism Tested by Reason and Revelation*, preface, 3.

109. Strickland, introduction to *Universalism against Itself*, 15.

110. An incomplete list up to 1900 (in chronological order) would include Andrew Croswell, *Mr. Murray Unmask'd* (1775); Isaac Backus, *The Doctrine of Universal Salvation Examined and Refuted* (1782); Joseph Eckley, *Divine Glory Brought to View* (1782); William Gordon, *Universal Salvation Examined* (1783); Jonathan Edwards Jr., *Brief Observations on the Doctrine of Universal Salvation* (1784); Samuel Peters, *A Letter to the Rev. John Tyler* (1785); Nathanael Emmons, *A Discourse concerning . . . the General Judgment* (1791); Samuel Shepard, *Universal Salvation* (1793); Josiah Spaulding, *Universalism Confounds and Destroys Itself* (1805); Daniel Isaac, *Universal Restoration Examined and Refuted* (1808); Seth Crowell, *Strictures on the Doctrine of Universal Salvation* (1821); James Sabine, *Universal Salvation Indefensible* (1825); W. L. M'Calla, *Discussion of Universalism* (1825); George Peck, *Universal Salvation Considered* (1827); John Tripp, *Strictures on . . . Universal Reconciliation* (1829); Timothy Merritt and Wilbur Fisk, *A Discussion on Universal Salvation* (1832); Parsons Cooke, *Modern Universalism Exposed* (1834); Lewis Todd, *Renunciation of Universalism* (1834); Luther Lee, *Universalism Examined and Refuted* (1836); James M. Davis, *Universalism Unmasked, or the Spurious Gospel Exposed* (1837); Stephen Remington, *Anti-Universalism* (1837); Alexander W. McLeod, *Universalism in Its Ancient and Modern Form . . . Unscriptural* (1837); A. Wilson McClure, *Lectures on Ultra-Universalism* (1838); Alexander Campbell and Dolphus Skinner, *Discussion of the Doctrine of Endless Misery and Universal Salvation* (1840); Matthew Hale Smith, *Universalism Examined* (1842); E. M. Pingree and N. L. Rice, *A Debate on the Doctrine of Universal Salvation* (1845); Nicholas Van Alstine, *Modern Universalism at War with the Bible and Reason* (1847); John Borland, *Observations on the Moral Agency of Man* (1848); A. B. Winfield, *Antidote to the Errors of Universalism* (1850); Archibald Alexander, *Universalism False and Unscriptural* (1851); Thomas Jefferson Sawyer and Isaac Wescott, *A Discussion on the Doctrine of Universal Salvation* (1854); Samuel C. Bartlett, *Lectures on Modern Universalism* (1856); N. D. George, *Universalism Not of the Bible* (1856); H. M. Dexter, *The Reasonableness of the Doctrine of Future Eternal Punishment* (1858); J. Litch and Miles Grant, *The Doctrine of Everlasting Punishment* (1859); Joseph Parrish Thompson, *Love and Penalty* (1860); B. F. Foster and J. H. Lozier, *Theological Discussion on Universalism* (1867); E. Manford and T. S. Sweeney, *Universal Salvation* (1870); Marshall Randles, *For Ever!* (1873); Thomas Wood, *Annihilation and Universalism* (1877); Nehemiah Adams, *Endless Punishment* (1878); J. R. Graves and John C. Burruss, *A Discussion on the Doctrine of Endless Punishment* (1880); Junius Reimensnyder, *Doom Eternal* (1880); Thomas Powell, *The Larger Hope* (1881); Alexander Wilford Hall, *Universalism against Itself* (1883); William G. T. Shedd, *Endless Punishment* (1886).

111. In *"All Shall Be Well"* (1–13), Parry suggests that universalism is a "theologoumenon" that is neither orthodox nor heretical but stands somewhere "between heresy and dogma" (see

anti-universalist literature was less extensive during the early twentieth century than previously, then this was likely because universalism from the 1890s
onward found a place in mainline Protestant liberal churches and became
identified as a distinctive liberal or modernist tenet. The universalist debate was
folded into the larger fundamentalist-modernist controversy rather than being
conducted as a separate dispute. Since the 1940s, however, anti-universalism
has been an almost continuous preoccupation among self-professed evangelical authors.[112] Those taking aim against universalism include such evangelical
figures as C. S. Lewis, Leon Morris, J. I. Packer, Paul Helm, and N. T. Wright.

There are numerous other problems with Parry's "evangelical universalism."
Parry does not seem to acknowledge the existence or pervasiveness of Christian

---

DR, 192n222). Richard Cherok, in "We Fraternize with None," notes that the nineteenth-century
Stone-Campbell movement leader Alexander Campbell (1788–1866), prior to about 1830, regarded
belief in universal salvation as simply a matter of personal opinion, but he changed his views after
he began publicly debating universalists (7). Campbell began to see the long-term consequences
of universalist belief, and that some universalists were becoming atheists (19). "What he [Camp-
bell] once saw as a tolerable personal opinion he gradually came to see as a dangerous heretical
idea" (15–16). Especially crucial was Campbell's debate with Jesse Babcock Ferguson (1819–70).
Campbell rejected "Ferguson's claim that his post-mortem gospel [of salvation after death] was
nothing more than an opinion, or a nonbinding idea to which he believed he was entitled to
adhere" (19). Campbell's experience might suggest that Parry's proposal—i.e., to allow universalism as a permitted but nonbinding doctrine among evangelical Protestants—has already been
tried and found wanting.

112. A partial listing of late twentieth-century and early twenty-first-century evangelical polemics
against universalism would include E. J. Carnell, "Hell Is Irrational" (1948); T. F. Torrance, "Uni-
versalism or Election?" (1949); H. G. Jones, "Universalism and Morals" (1950); R. V. G. Tasker,
The Biblical Doctrine of the Wrath of God (1951); D. G. Barnhouse, "Hell in Norway" (1954); G. C.
Berkouwer, "Universalism" (1957); L. Morris, The Biblical Doctrine of Judgment (1960); H. Lindsell,
"Universalism Today" (1964–65); J. A. Motyer, After Death (1965); N. T. Wright, "Towards a Biblical
View of Universalism" (1979); L. A. King, "Hell—The Painful Refuge" (1979); E. A. Blum, "Shall
You Not Surely Die?" (1979); J. E. Braun, Whatever Happened to Hell? (1979); J. Gerstner, Jonathan
Edwards on Heaven and Hell (1980); V. C. Grounds, "The Final State of the Wicked" (1981); J. R.
Blue, "Untold Billions: Are They Really Lost?" (1981); A. Fernando, A Universal Homecoming?
(1983); P. Helm, "Universalism and the Threat of Hell" (1983); R. Nicole, "Will Everyone Be Saved?"
(1987); H. Brown, "Will Everyone Be Saved?" (1987); N. M. de S. Cameron, "Universalism and the
Logic of Revelation" (1987); K. S. Kantzer and C. F. H. Henry, Evangelical Affirmations (1990); J. I.
Packer, "The Problem of Eternal Punishment" (1990); H. Brown, "Will the Lost Suffer Forever?"
(1990); W. Crockett, "Will God Save Everyone in the End?" (1991); W. Crockett, "Wrath That En-
dures Forever" (1991); W. L. Craig, "Talbott's Universalism" (1991); E. W. Davies, An Angry God?
(1991); A. Fernando, Crucial Questions about Hell (1991); L. Morris, "The Dreadful Harvest" (1991);
L. Dixon, The Other Side of the Good News (1992); J. Walls, Hell: The Logic of Damnation (1992);
L. Lacy, "Talbott on Paul as a Universalist" (1992); J. Kvanvig, The Problem of Hell (1993); W. L. Craig,
"Talbott's Universalism Once More" (1993); J. Blanchard, Whatever Happened to Hell? (1993); J. I.
Packer, "The Problem of Universalism Today" (1998); C. Townsend, Hell: A Difficult Doctrine We
Dare Not Ignore (1999); D. Hilborn and P. Johnston, The Nature of Hell (2000); J. Colwell, "The
Glory of God's Justice and the Glory of God's Grace" (2000); C. W. Morgan and R. A. Peterson, Hell
under Fire (2004); A. M. Climenhaga, "Mission and Neo-Universalism" (2004).

esotericist universalism (see esp. *DR* 2; 5), and he generally ignores the historical overlap between universalism and unitarianism (*DR* 6). Moreover, Parry tends to neglect the ultra-universalism that represented no small or insignificant movement. Europe's most influential contemporary Protestant thinker, Jürgen Moltmann, seems to affirm a version of ultra-universalism, since his eschatology affirms there is no more place for hell after Jesus's suffering on the cross.[113] Parry states that "all species of Christian universalism prior to the twentieth century affirmed a doctrine of hell"—by which he means a "hell" of temporary suffering.[114] This is not so. Parry has glossed over the purgationist versus non-purgationist rift (*DR* 6.8) so as to give the appearance of a cohesive universalist movement. To establish continuity between universalism and evangelicalism, Parry minimizes those versions of universalism that are heterodox not only with regard to eschatology but also with regard to other important doctrines. It appears, then, that "evangelical universalism" does not exist, except as an ink-and-paper construct. It has no ecclesial existence as the official position of a particular church community.

11.5. Evangelical Revisionism in Frank, Bell, and Kruger

We turn now to three more evangelical authors who are all concerned with revising traditional evangelical theology while at the same time retaining what they see as the strong points in this tradition.

As implied in the title of Doug Frank's book, *A Gentler God: Breaking Free of the Almighty in the Company of the Human Jesus*, the author has a bone to pick with common Christian conceptions of God.[115] He criticizes a hell-obsessed evangelicalism and seeks to exorcize the ghost of sermons past, with most of his examples taken from the late 1940s and early 1950s.[116] Frank holds that "the spirit of Jesus is continually present in every human heart, and thus the

---

113. On Moltmann, see *DR* 9.10–9.11. Parry acknowledges that Moltmann leaves no place for postmortem suffering and affirms that "hell is exhausted at Golgotha" (*Evangelical Universalist*, 139). By affirming that many people experience a temporary hell, Parry sets himself against Moltmann's universalism. The powerful rhetoric that Christ did everything on the cross seems appropriate for Barth and Moltmann but inappropriate for Parry and Talbott, who advocate a purgationist universalism.

114. Parry, "Evangelical Universalism," 9.

115. Rob Bell endorses the book by saying that it will "help lots of people find liberation from the malevolent Being they never believed in in the first place" (Frank, *Gentler God*, 4).

116. To find objectionable hellfire preaching, Frank goes back to the very early Billy Graham and to the preachers Percy Crawford and Jack Wyrtzen (ibid., 34–39). Yet the "evangelical God"—at least in the United States—has been getting progressively gentler for the last sixty years, and Frank's critique hardly engages the twenty-first-century milieu.

good news is always somewhere inside all of us." Yet the "bad news associated with the conventional evangelical God" too easily drowns this out.[117] Frank is encouraged to see that "the bad-news God of evangelicalism" is "undergoing a crisis of credibility" and that "younger evangelicals . . . seem less interested in wooden, literalistic readings of the Bible." He does not use the term "universalism," but he cites the names of Rob Bell, Jan Bonda, Philip Gulley, and James Mulholland, while commending the "voices courageous enough to entertain the possibility that God's love may be truly unconditional and never-ending."[118] He rejects what he calls the "two-pronged formula" to the effect that "God so *loves you* that he graciously offers you eternal life" and yet "God is so *angry with you* that he will punish you for ever and ever if you refuse his gracious offer." Frank finds this portrait of God to be "emotionally incoherent." He also raises a number of standard, early modern objections to an eternal hell.[119] Like most universalists, he holds that "fear never motivates genuine love."[120]

In his exposition, Frank questions and then rejects "substitutionary atonement," noting that even when the doctrine is presented in its most attractive form—for example, in John Stott's *The Cross of Christ*—God seems to be "trapped by his holiness," yearning in compassion for sinners but unable to "condone their sin." He sees the emphasis on sin as a reflection of human self-hatred. Frank affirms a form of purgationism when he writes that "hell . . . is a metaphor for the kindness of God, who cannot bring us to ourselves except through suffering." Words like "forever" and "eternal" have a qualitative rather than quantitative meaning, "connoting a peculiar existential experience whose intensity, if only for a moment, feels infinite." Universal salvation seems to be necessary, because "God and 'the saints in heaven' will in some sense also be in 'hell' until the last human being is brought to eternal life. . . . If there are no tears in heaven . . . perhaps this is because there are no sufferers left in hell."[121]

One striking aspect of Frank's book lies in his reflections on God's weakness. An earlier generation of evangelicals in the mid-twentieth century described God as "powerful world-maker," "master molder," "self-sufficient deity," "previous prime cause," "hater of sin," and "demanding judge."[122] Yet Frank looks at the biblical Jesus and concludes, "God is *not* the Almighty. . . . I see in Jesus

117. Frank, *Gentler God*, 20.
118. Ibid., 26, with n. 8.
119. Ibid., 41, 43. "Why does God decide that the proportionate punishment for a finite disobedience is an infinite agony?" "Why does God decide that the moment of death is our final deadline?" (48).
120. Ibid., 53.
121. Ibid., 118–19, 125–26, 296, 305, 301n16. On eternity as a form of intensified experience, see *DR*, 1151–53.
122. Ibid., 81–83.

a God whose hands are tied." He quotes Jürgen Moltmann: "If Christ is weak and humble on earth, then God is weak and humble in heaven." Though the "defenseless God" at first left him "feeling betrayed and a bit resentful," this realization "reveal[ed] hidden aspects of [his] own motivations."[123] Frank writes of God's utter inability to change or reform the evil world, except by his "whisper" to evildoers:

> When we [human beings] ignore the call of love, God can do nothing at all about it—except, of course, continue to whisper, continue to call, continue to touch, continue to be present in the silence. This is the meaning of "God is love." If God cannot straightforwardly micromanage human events so as to rescue the abused child, the tortured prisoner, the cancer victim, neither can God rescue God's very own self, incarnated in Jesus. God can and will continue to whisper—to the killers as well as the killed, to the mourners as well as the mockers. God can and will hang on the gibbet in utter solidarity with the son, helplessly receiving the cruel blows rained down on the naked, dying flesh of the beloved.[124]

Here Jesus's crucifixion is not treated as one moment within a larger narrative of human redemption or God's victory over the forces of evil. Instead, the moment of suffering is ontologized and eternalized: Jesus remains on the cross forever. Neither the glorious Son in eternal preexistence with the Father nor the glorious Christ of the second coming are anywhere in view. Unsurprisingly, Frank balks at affirming Christ's bodily resurrection.[125] His assumptions about God exclude a glorious resurrection, let alone a coming kingdom in which God's enemies suffer a decisive defeat. His "gentler God" bears little relationship with the biblical God, so often described as "rock," "refuge," "tower," "strength," and "deliverer," and with other words and images connoting power and protectiveness.[126]

Rob Bell's *Love Wins* (2011) is the slenderest book of those surveyed in this chapter, more an evocative prose poem than an in-depth analysis of the afterlife. Bell's book avoids answering any number of difficult questions that might be posed regarding his own views. The author toys with competing ideas without definitely committing himself. Theological differences among reviewers became

---

123. Ibid., 205 (with n. 28), 185, 206n29. Frank cites Moltmann, *Trinity and the Kingdom*, 31. On the "weakness of God," Frank also cites Caputo, *Weakness of God*, and Dietrich Bonhoeffer, who wrote that "the Bible directs man to God's powerlessness and suffering; only the suffering God can help" (*Letters and Papers from Prison*, 361).

124. Frank, *Gentler God*, 209–10.

125. Ibid., 369.

126. Frank also rejects creation from nothing—which, again, one might expect from his notion of divine weakness. Instead, he suggests that creation implies a divine activation of preexisting elements (ibid., 210n35).

obvious in the polarized reactions to the book.[127] Eugene Peterson in his cover endorsement praised the book's "thoroughly biblical imagination," while Greg Boyd called it a "bold, prophetic, and poetic masterpiece." Peter Marty declared that "the triumph of Bell's book is the absence of triumphalism," and he did not view Bell as a universalist: "He simply refuses to limit how far Christ's redemptive love can reach. He makes an argument that easily frustrates those who inhabit a world of theological certainty."[128] In contrast, Kevin DeYoung was scathing in his rejection: "The theology is heterodox. The history is inaccurate. . . . The use of Scripture is indefensible."[129]

Much of the book is devoted to the posing of one question after another—a total of 350 questions in less than 200 pages, according to DeYoung's estimate.[130] The sole thing that Bell seems dogmatic about is the mistaken character of traditional Christian teaching on heaven and hell. Bell offers this summary of orthodox evangelicalism: "God offers us everlasting life by grace, freely, through no merit on our part. Unless you do not respond the right way. Then God will torture you forever." He adds that "Jesus's story is first and foremost about the love of God for every single one of us," though this story "has been hijacked by a number of other stories."[131] Edward Oakes criticizes *Love Wins* for not presenting an argument to the reader: "Bell doesn't really argue his case. Rather, he hurls a set of disjointed statements to see what sticks. . . . Logical gaps in the argument (of which there are many) are rhetorically obscured by a vigorous self-confidence."[132]

Bell appeals to what he presents as long-standing Christian tradition in favor of his own views: "Nothing in this book hasn't been taught, suggested, or celebrated by many before me. . . . That's the beauty of the historic, orthodox Christian faith. It's a deep, wide, diverse stream that's been flowing for thousands of years, carrying a staggering variety of voices, perspectives, and experiences."[133]

127. For critical responses, see DeYoung, "God Is Still Holy"; Loane, "Evangelically Flawed Theological Method." More appreciative were Marty, "Betting on a Generous God"; Paul Jones, "Hopeful Universalism." Oakes, in "Bell's Present Heaven," offered an intriguing response from a Catholic scholar of Balthasar's theology.

128. Marty, "Betting on a Generous God," 23–24.

129. DeYoung, "God Is Still Holy." DeYoung objected to the aesthetic validation of the book (i.e., as a piece of artful writing), insisting that such evaluations miss the point: "This book is not a poem. . . . This is a theological book by a pastor trying to impart a different way of looking at heaven and hell. . . . If Bell is inconsistent, unclear, or inaccurate, claiming the 'artist' mantle is no help."

130. Ibid.

131. R. Bell, *Love Wins*, vii.

132. Oakes, "Bell's Present Heaven," 24.

133. R. Bell, *Love Wins*, x–xi. Bell does not back up his historical claims with any footnotes or citations, so it is not possible to evaluate the basis for his claims. In citing Scripture, he rarely indicates chapter and verse.

The words "historic" and "orthodox" show that Bell claims that his position on the afterlife agrees with what has been defined and held in the major churches. Yet in the same preface he states that "torment and punishment in hell with no chance for anything better . . . is misguided and toxic and ultimately subverts the contagious spread of Jesus's message of love, peace, forgiveness, and joy."[134] On the one hand, Bell presents himself as open-minded, committed to dialogue, and willing to consider multiple points of view. On the other hand, the reference in the book's preface to the traditional hell as "toxic" gives a different impression. Bell anathematizes the traditional Christian perspective before he has offered any arguments or presented an alternative view.

While Bell does not embrace the "universalist" label, his reasoning tends in that direction. The preface shows that he rejects an eternal hell, and the book's arguments are almost all adopted from earlier universalist authors. He challenges the idea of eternal punishment and interprets the Greek word *aiōn* as meaning "age-long": "*Aion* . . . doesn't mean forever as we think of forever." Instead the word primarily refers to a "period of time with a beginning and an end."[135] "Hell" refers to a garbage dump outside of Jerusalem—a place for burning trash.[136] Among universalists, these are old chestnuts. Bell asks, "Does God punish people for thousands of years with infinite, eternal torment for things they did in their few finite years of life?"[137] At one point, Bell speaks of "flames in heaven," adding that "Jesus makes no promise that in the blink of an eye we will suddenly become totally different people who have vastly different tastes, attitudes, and perspectives."[138] From this it seems that Bell entertains the notion of postmortem purgation—or at least that he flirts with the idea, as he does with many other ideas in the course of his presentation. At another point, Bell sounds Barthian, asking whether God is all-powerful in accomplishing salvation: "Does God get what God wants?"[139] He casts doubt on whether eternal salvation depends on what human beings say or do: "Accepting, confessing,

---

134. Ibid., viii.

135. Ibid., 31. Elsewhere in the book, Bell suggests that *aiōn* can also refer to "a particular intensity of experience that transcends time" (57). As is typical in this book, Bell proposes antithetical points of view—a temporal and durative versus nontemporal and nondurative notion of *aiōn*—but does not commit himself to either view. He insists that it is Jesus himself who "blurs the lines" between concepts of "heaven" as lying in the future or present, or as simply designating God himself (59). For further discussion, see *DR* appendix J.

136. R. Bell, *Love Wins*, 68. Bell gives the misleading impression that Christian belief about eternal punishment is solely based on the biblical references to gehenna (69), thereby ignoring such expressions as "lake of fire," "outer darkness," "worm that devours," "eternal destruction," "eternal fire," "eternal punishment," and so forth.

137. Ibid., 2.

138. Ibid., 50.

139. Ibid., 95.

believing—those are things that we do. Does that mean, then, that going to heaven is dependent on something I do?"[140] He asks, "Which is stronger and more powerful, the hardness of the human heart or God's unrelenting, infinite, expansive love?"[141] From the phrasing and context, it seems obvious which answer Bell is expecting. He speaks of some teachers (i.e., universalists) who say that "given enough time, everybody will turn to God and find themselves in the joy and peace of God's presence. The love of God will melt every hard heart, and even the most 'depraved sinners' will eventually give up their resistance and turn to God."[142]

Despite all these assertions and implications in the book, Bell refrains from an unambiguous affirmation of universal salvation. He sounds hopeful rather than assertive, stating that "it is fitting, proper, and Christian to long for it [i.e., salvation for all]."[143] He speaks of human choice and the seeming possibility of wrongful choices: "God gives us what we want, and if that's hell, we can have it. We have that kind of freedom, that kind of choice. We are that free."[144] In another passage he writes, "Love demands freedom. . . . We are free to resist, reject, and rebel against God's ways for us. We can have all the hell we want."[145] Oakes offers the astute observation that Bell's "central thesis [is that] heaven and hell are already present on earth, and Christians are specifically called to spread the reality of God's heaven to the hellish realities of earth."[146] The suggestion here is that Bell's larger project is one of immanentizing the eschaton—and linking God's kingdom to a call for social amelioration. If this is a fair characterization of *Love Wins*, it might imply that Bell's this-worldly rereading of biblical eschatology has much in common with the Protestant liberal theology of the late 1800s and early 1900s.

In the one passage where Bell most clearly poses the central question, he refuses to answer it: "Will everybody be saved, or will some perish apart from God forever because of their choices? Those are questions, or more accurately, those are tensions we are free to leave fully intact."[147] The irony is that Bell, near the start of his book, says that "this isn't a book of questions" but "a book of responses to . . . questions."[148] By the end, Bell's book is just what he said that it was not: a book of questions. The author is more interested in raising

140. Ibid., 11.
141. Ibid., 109.
142. Ibid., 107.
143. Ibid., 111.
144. Ibid., 72.
145. Ibid., 113.
146. Oakes, "Bell's Present Heaven," 24.
147. R. Bell, *Love Wins*, 115.
148. Ibid., 19.

questions than in finding answers. The most contradictory aspect of the book lies in the author's profession of open-mindedness combined with a decisive rejection of traditional views of God and hell as "toxic."[149]

C. Baxter Kruger's *The Shack Revisited* (2012) is unusual in being not a straightforward theological exposition but a book that interacts with the religiously themed novel *The Shack* (2007). The novel was a surprise bestseller, with some ten million copies sold by 2009. The novel's author, William Paul Young, disavows the labels "universalist" and "ultimate reconciliation," though he admits that he had been influenced by such views.[150] Kruger calls himself "a son of the Bible belt."[151] He seeks to step beyond "the same old distant, untouchable, legalistic god who scans the universe with his disapproving heart."[152] He mentions Jonathan Edwards's sermon "Sinners in the Hands of an Angry God," and though he acknowledges that "this [sermon] is not the full picture of Edwards's vision," he sees the God-concept in this text as especially

---

149. For some persons today, *not* finding answers to ultimate questions—a blend of faith and agnosticism—might be a preferred or deliberately chosen stance. Kevin DeYoung suggests that Rob Bell's viewpoint could be "the last rung for evangelicals falling off the ladder into liberalism or unbelief" ("God Is Still Holy"). Since publishing his book, Bell's further shifts away from evangelical faith might support DeYoung's interpretation. The book that Bell coauthored with his wife—*The Zimzum of Love* (2014)—develops an understanding of marriage based less on the Bible than on Kabbalah. In *What Is the Bible?* (2017), Bell speaks of the Bible as "a book about what it means to be human" (4) that reflects its ancient context: "Remember, this story [in Acts 5] was written in the first century. People had a much more magical and mythical worldview" (238). As compared with other texts, the Bible is not uniquely inspired (267); one might say that "the Bible is inspired in much the same way that you are inspired" (287). Bell rejects the idea that God ever commanded or required sacrifice: "God didn't set up the sacrificial system. People did. . . . God didn't need the blood of sacrifices. People did" (244). Bell stresses the here-and-now character of the scriptural message: "That's why the Bible is not a book about going to heaven. The action is here. The life is here. The point is here. It's a library of books about the healing and restoring and reconciling and renewing of this world" (53).

150. The website associated with the publisher of *The Shack* has a Q&A section regarding whether the novel contains "heresy."
> *Does the book promote universalism?* Some people can find a universalist under every bush. This book flatly states that all roads do not lead to Jesus, while it affirms that Jesus can find his followers wherever they may have wandered into sin or false beliefs. Just because he can find followers in the most unlikely places, does not validate those places. . . . People will quote portions out of that context and draw a false conclusion. . . . *Does The Shack promote Ultimate Reconciliation (UR)?* It does not. While some of that was in earlier versions because of the author's partiality at the time to some aspects of what people call UR, I made it clear at the outset that I didn't embrace UR as sound teaching and didn't want to be involved in a project that promoted it. In my view UR is an extrapolation of Scripture to humanistic conclusions about our Father's love that has to be forced on the biblical text. http://tentmaker.org/forum/christian-life/the-shack-9064/5/?wap2.

Young wrote an appreciative foreword to Kruger's *The Shack Revisited* (ix–xiii), which appears to teach universalism.

151. Kruger, *Shack Revisited*, 55.

152. Ibid., 2.

galling.[153] It was his reading of Athanasius that reshaped his thinking: "This was . . . a different God from that of the Calvinism of my youth. The sheer love of Athanasius's God captured my imagination."[154] In *The Shack Revisited*, Kruger often returns to Athanasius, especially as interpreted by Thomas Torrance. And Karl Barth is excerpted in the book's appendix.[155] Somewhat surprisingly, Kruger cites passages from Augustine and Calvin and develops some of his arguments from their writings.[156] In building his universalist theology on past Christian teachers—Athanasius, Augustine, Calvin, and Torrance—Kruger does not divorce himself from the historical church as Talbott, Gulley, and Pearson seem to do.[157]

Kruger situates the trinitarian love of Father and Son in the Holy Spirit at the center of his theology. This love is eternal: "Before the creation of the world the Father, Son, and Spirit set their love upon us, and dreamed of the day when we could be included in . . . the unbridled delight that they share together from all eternity."[158] He often states that "we"—that is, human beings in general—are included in God's eternal love: "The mutual indwelling of the blessed Trinity now includes us! In Jesus, the human race has been gathered into the Holy Spirit's world. Adam's fallen race has been embraced by Jesus' Father and made his children forever."[159] Kruger does not use the term "universalism," but he does not need to do so. His wording indicates that every human being without exception will be saved: "The hope of the human race is that we belong to the Father, Son, and Holy Spirit; we always have, and always will."[160]

153. Ibid., 53–54.

154. Ibid., 56.

155. Ibid., 157n12: "Barth's treatment of 'the election of Jesus Christ' is one of the greatest contributions to Christian thought."

156. Ibid., 101–5, 138–39, 197.

157. With the possible exception of Karl Barth (a complicated case; see *DR* 9.1–9.9), *none* of the major theologians that Kruger cites—e.g., Athanasius, Augustine, Calvin, and Torrance—were universalists. Archibald Robertson writes that "the subject of eschatology is nowhere dealt with in full by Athanasius . . . [yet] there is also no reason to think that he held with the Universalism of Origen, Gregory of Nyssa and others" (introduction to the *Treatise on the Incarnation of the Word*, 33). Athanasius seems to reject Origen's opinion on final salvation in his exegetical writings (*Fragmenta in Matthaeum*, PG 27:1384A; *Fragmenta in Lucam*, PG 1404A). Thomas F. Torrance, who is most often cited by Kruger, stated that "the Catholic Church . . . throughout all ages has consistently judged universalism as a heresy for faith and a menace to the Gospel" ("Universalism or Election?," 310). On Torrance's view of universalism, see *DR* 9.8.

158. Kruger, *Shack Revisited*, 56. The statement that "God dreamed" or "dreams" appears several times (42, 56, 155). This seems to be Kruger's alternative (like that of Douglas Frank) to an all-powerful or controlling God. But it raises the question of how we can know—without affirming God's power—that this "dream" will become reality.

159. Ibid., 141. "Adoption is the way things really are, now and forever" (195).

160. Ibid., 247.

Like other universalists, Kruger does not understand Jesus's cross as traditional Protestants do: "Jesus did not come to suffer punishment inflicted by his Father."[161] Instead, the rejection that Jesus suffered came simply from the human side: "It was the human race, not the Father, who rejected his beloved Son and killed him."[162] Jesus did not die to satisfy divine justice. Kruger mentions a radio sermon he heard regarding the call to "receive" Jesus, and this leads him to ask, "When did any of us pray to receive our parents into our lives[?] . . . The gospel is not the news that we can receive Jesus in our lives. The gospel is the news that Jesus has received us in his."[163] Here Kruger seems to reject the biblical terminology regarding "receiving" Christ.[164] In response to the question of why believe and repent at all, he writes, "We must repent and believe, *not* in order to be accepted and loved and included, but to *live in that reality*."[165]

Kruger regards *The Shack's* symbolization of the Holy Spirit as the female figure Sarayu to be the book's "finest contribution to Christian thought."[166] Quoting William Paul Young, Kruger writes that she is "a *free* Spirit" and "*way* out there," and he explains, "From the day of Pentecost on, the Spirit is everywhere and into everything, but never visible and always completely unpredictable." The Spirit of God "works within the root systems of the gardens of our souls."[167] To his credit, Kruger makes a greater effort than most other universalists to be fully trinitarian (rather than binitarian) and to account for the role of the Holy Spirit in salvation. Yet the day of Pentecost as a distinct, historical coming of the Spirit does not fit well into Kruger's Christ-centered account of redemption. Nor is Kruger able to show that the Spirit indwells the church in a way that distinguishes the church from the nonchurch. Instead the Holy Spirit becomes a universal divine presence that continually aims at overcoming dichotomies: the Spirit's "passion is fellowship: she loves to connect people. She is the 'Overcomer of the Gap' and the 'Space Between.'"[168] Kruger writes, "Pentecost is the inevitable fruit of Jesus' ascension, and of ours in him. Embracing us in our darkness, Jesus was also including us in his own anointing with the Holy Spirit."[169]

161. Ibid., 130. For Kruger, God's wrath may refer to purification from sin: "Wrath is the love of the triune God in passionate action, saying 'NO!' It is love's fiery opposition to our destruction" (128).

162. Ibid., 185. To explain atonement, Kruger recommends Jersak and Hardin, *Stricken by God?*

163. Kruger, *Shack Revisited*, 142.

164. The radio preacher's terminology follows a scriptural precedent: "But to all who did receive him, who believed in his name, he gave the right to become children of God" (John 1:12).

165. Kruger, *Shack Revisited*, 243.

166. Ibid., 88.

167. Ibid., 87.

168. Ibid., 90.

169. Ibid., 230.

11.6. Charismatic Preachers of Grace: Dunn, du Toit, Rabe, and Crowder

A development of the last decade is the lilt toward universalism among certain Pentecostal-Charismatic preachers and teachers. These speakers and authors include John Crowder, Benjamin Dunn, Francois du Toit, and Andre Rabe.[170] The justification for treating these authors as a group derives not only from their parallel teachings but also from their intertwining ministries. Often they have partnered with one another in ministry around the world, and they promote one another's work.[171] While there are variations in their teachings, they all reflect what is popularly called the "the grace message." Nevertheless, I attempt to distinguish these figures from one another in what follows. Despite resemblances, one cannot presume that the teachings of one author are found in all the others.[172] The question of "grace" versus "hyper-grace" or "cheap grace" has been a matter of dispute throughout Protestant history. Historic debates invoked the term "antinomianism," understood as the teaching that Christians have no moral obligations to fulfill because faith alone is necessary for salvation. Some of Kruger's and Crowder's teachings—for example, that human beings were already accepted or saved by God before anyone fell into

170. All of these figures promote their ministries through websites and YouTube videos. Key texts include the following: Crowder, *Miracle Workers*; Crowder, *Ecstasy of Loving God*; Crowder, *Mystical Union*; Crowder, *Cosmos Reborn*; du Toit, *Logic of His Love*; du Toit, *Divine Embrace*; du Toit, *Mirror Bible*; Dunn, *Happy Gospel!*; Rabe, *Imagine*.

171. John Crowder wrote an endorsement for Benjamin Dunn's *The Happy Gospel!* and there mentioned how they have "partnered closely in ministry." Crowder dedicated his book *Mystical Union* to Dunne. Francois du Toit wrote the foreword to Crowder's most recent book, *Cosmos Reborn*, and the final chapter of *Cosmos Reborn*, "The Divinity of Man," summarizes many of du Toit's themes. Both Andre Rabe and C. Baxter Kruger (whom Crowder regularly cites) wrote endorsements for *Cosmos Reborn*. Francois du Toit wrote the foreword to the second edition of Rabe's *Imagine*. John Crowder wrote an endorsement for du Toit's *Mirror Bible*, as did Mary-Anne Rabe (Andre Rabe's spouse) and C. Baxter Kruger. John Crowder founded a school for ministry, Cana New Wine Seminary, which offered its first classes in summer 2014. The teaching is said to focus on "Finished work of the Cross, Trinitarian Theology, New Covenant Grace, Mystical Christianity, Contemplative Spirituality, [and] Supernatural Experience." The scheduled speakers for 2014 included C. Baxter Kruger, Francois du Toit, Benjamin Dunne, Andre Rabe, and John Crowder. In keeping with Crowder's over-the-top rhetoric, the school is called a "unique seminary for wild-eyed wonder junkies" that "offers a unique marriage of life-transforming, happy theology woven seamlessly with the intoxicating practice of the presence of God. A place where you will find doctorate level theologians and mystical ecstatics sharing the same platform. Cana is a drunken seminary" (https://www.youtube.com/watch?v=wR7HEL_phMo).

172. The Singapore-based megachurch pastor Joseph Prince offers teachings on grace that are analogous to these other figures. Prince leads New Creation Church, with a reported attendance of 31,000 (as of 2014), and is author of *Destined to Reign: The Secret to Effortless Success, Wholeness and Victorious Living* (2007). See Sahat Sinaga's essay, "Is Joseph Prince's Radical Grace Teaching Biblical?"; Michael Brown, *Hyper-Grace*, with a prompt rebuttal from Paul Ellis, *Hyper-Grace Gospel*.

sin—are reminiscent of arguments presented in English Protestantism during the seventeenth century.[173]

The "grace message" should be seen in light of recent developments in the independent Charismatic churches. Since the 1990s, the global Charismatic movement has often emphasized *dominionism*—an aggressive spiritual and cultural movement to advance Christian social influence, fueled by intense prayer and fasting, bold strategies of evangelism, and practices of spiritual warfare against evil spirits.[174] Rejecting the eschatological pessimism of premillennialism and the gloomy presumption that things must get worse before Jesus returns again, many Charismatics embraced postmillennialism and the vision of a restored or "glorious church."[175] Some insist that Christ's earthly reign will be exercised through an elite corps of disciples, led by superapostles whose authority will exceed that of the first-century apostles.[176] Others, like C. Peter Wagner, have offered less grandiose visions for the future and yet insist that the church must seek to influence all "seven mountains" of human life—namely, business, government, media, arts and entertainment, education, the family, and religion.[177] The "grace message" may be seen as a backlash against this activist mentality in favor of a more quietistic stance. Some in the younger generation of Charismatics are less ready to do battle against the devil and more inclined to rest in the full enjoyment of divine grace.

The stress on grace is associated with joy, happiness, and celebration rather than a lugubrious stress on sin, repentance, and the evils of modern society. Benjamin Dunn quotes selectively from Martin Luther—"The gospel is nothing else but laughter and joy"—and he appeals to wine, drinking, and inebriation as symbols of Christian experience.[178] The language of "drunkenness," "inebriation," and "ecstasy" appears often in the writings of Dunn and Crowder, who are contending with what they take to be legalistic attitudes, moralistic

173. The resemblance is specifically to Tobias Crisp (1600–1643), John Saltmarsh (d. 1647), John Eaton (1575–ca. 1631), and other seventeenth-century Calvinist antinomians. Crisp taught "eternal justification," and his teaching on grace seemed to undercut all moral exertion. See Parnham, "Humbling of 'High Presumption'"; Parnham, "Covenantal Quietism of Tobias Crisp"; Parnham, "Motions of Law and Grace"; Parnham, "John Saltmarsh."

174. See McClymond, "Charismatic Renewal and Neo-Pentecostalism," 43.

175. See Althouse and Waddell, *Perspectives in Pentecostal Eschatologies*.

176. Paul Cain and other 1980s "Kansas City" prophets expressed such ideas, as recounted in Mike Bickle's audio memoir, *Encountering Jesus*.

177. Wagner, *Dominion!*

178. Dunn, *Happy Gospel!*, 39. "Wine is the only thing that can communicate the intense joy and inebriation that fills the heart when salvation's cup is drunk" (44). Dunn's reference is to Luther as cited in C. H. Spurgeon's commentary on Ps. 126, in Spurgeon, *Treasury of David*, 3b:68–82. Dunn's appeal to Luther is one-sided, since Luther insisted on preaching God's law as a way of making sinners aware of their guilt.

heavy-handedness, and institutional rigidity in the church. In the rhetoric of
many contemporary Charismatics, the word "religion" connotes everything that
is wrong with the church and that causes it to be somber, lifeless, and stultifying.
While "religion offers dull, sedative, boring theories," says Georgie Banov, "the
real Gospel can be nothing less than a radical affectionate enjoyment."[179] Benjamin Dunn's definition of "religion" is wholly pejorative: "External ordinances
and disciplines; a form of godliness that does not come from within the heart."[180]
By definition, there can be no such thing as "true religion." Religion is always
bad. Religion's ordinances, forms, disciplines, and structures are unnecessary
and unhelpful. There is a deeply embedded anti-institutionalism in much of
the Pentecostal-Charismatic world, and the teachers of the "grace message" are
generally more strident than others in their utter rejection of and contempt for
what they call "religion."

The "grace message"—as we find it in Dunn and Crowder—is that the church
must accept the once-for-all and finished work of Christ on the cross. The
grace teachers might accurately be described as antinomian in the sense that
they deny that Christians today live under an obligation to obey the moral law.[181]
Commandments that must be obeyed reflect "religion" rather than "grace."
Dunn writes that "the Gospel gives us a life that is no longer stuck in the orbit
of moral law."[182] "Law" implies failure, falling short, and guilt, and in contrast
to this the Christian believer is liberated from concern with laws and rules. A
related motif is usually termed "quietism." The distinctive quietist teaching

179. Georgie and Winnie Banov, book endorsement, in Dunn, Happy Gospel!, 7.
180. Dunn, Happy Gospel!, 33.
181. Sixteenth-century Lutherans debated the so-called third use of the law. The question was
whether Old Testament law had a role not only in civil legislation ("first use") and in revealing our
need as sinners for God's grace ("second use") but also in living the Christian life ("third use").
Calvinists generally answered yes to the "third use." While some Lutherans denied the "third use,"
the Epitome of the Formula of Concord (6.2–3) accepted it in the following terms:

We believe, teach, and confess that the preaching of the Law should be urged not only upon
those who have not faith in Christ, and do not yet repent, but also upon those who truly
believe in Christ, are truly converted to God, and regenerated and are justified by faith. For,
although they are regenerate and renewed in the spirit of their mind, yet this regeneration
and renewal is in this life not absolutely complete, but only begun. And they that believe
according to the spirit of their mind have perpetually to struggle with their flesh, that is,
with corrupt nature, which inheres in us even till death. (Schaff, Creeds of Christendom, 1:132)

The Formula of Concord thus justified preaching God's law to Christians on the basis of the continuing presence of the fallen nature or "flesh" in believers, an idea that John Crowder specifically
repudiates. During the 1980s, the North American evangelical debate over "Lordship salvation"
renewed the discussion on law and grace. The grace emphasis appeared in Charles C. Ryrie, So
Great Salvation (1989), and Zane C. Hodges, Absolutely Free! (1989), while John F. MacArthur's The
Gospel according to Jesus (1989) argued that Jesus in the believer's life is always both Savior (who
gives grace) and Lord (who commands obedience).
182. Dunn, Happy Gospel!, 63.

is that human efforts get in the way of one's relationship with God. Christian quietists call for a kind of holy passivity. As Dunn says, "We can only be the dependent, passive recipients of the Gospel. It can only be drunk down and received as a gift."[183] Any summons to exertion or effort in the spiritual life is thus mistaken. Our efforts are the problem, not the answer. Du Toit states, "Any form of striving to become more like Jesus through personal devotion and diligence, no matter how sincere, bears the same fruit of failure and guilt."[184] The implication is that *striving and effort* play no part in the Christian life. Dunn writes, "I realized that not only are our efforts unnecessary, they are not allowed. . . . We must yield to the ease and effortlessness of the Gospel."[185] Fasting from food is something difficult to do, and accordingly Crowder denies that fasting has value.[186] This teaching may be shocking to Charismatics, many of whom (especially during the last decade or two) have gone on ten-, twenty-one-, and even forty-day fasts, partaking only of juice and other liquids, and sometimes water only. For Crowder, though, there is no need to "seek God," because grace is immediate and total. There are no "means of grace," because grace already *is*. As he states in one of his chapters, "sanctification is not a process."[187]

Crowder and du Toit operate with an implicit canon within the canon in reading the Bible, in which the Old Testament is neglected in favor of the New Testament, and the Pauline Epistles are the crown or apex of divine revelation. Crowder says that Matthew, Mark, Luke, and John are not "the gospel." It is the letters of the apostle Paul that convey the message of grace. Crowder's marginalization of Jesus's moral instruction in the Gospels might raise the question of whether Jesus himself falls short of Crowder's idea of grace—that is, whether Jesus himself was a legalist. It is telling that Francois du Toit's *Mirror Bible* not only leaves out the Old Testament but also omits all of Matthew, Mark, Luke, and John, except for parts of the prologue in John 1:1–18. This "Bible" consists almost exclusively of heavily paraphrased and reinterpreted portions of the Pauline Letters and some of the General Epistles. Like the Synoptic Gospels,

183. Ibid., 127.
184. Du Toit, *Mirror Bible*, 10.
185. Dunn, *Happy Gospel!*, 142.
186. Crowder, *Mystical Union*, 142: "Although it is promoted on some of the fanciest web sites and largest conferences today, fasting is two clicks shy of outright gnosticism for a New Testament believer. Fasting does not draw you closer to God." Dunn, like Crowder, is anti-ascetic, and he says that "Christianity is not a fast; it is a festival" (*Happy Gospel!*, 157). Christian penitence is ruled out: "Fasting seems almost always synonymous with sadness and mourning. It implies want and longing. This can in no way be the true expression of Christianity" (160). Crowder and Dunn seemingly have no choice but to reject Old Testament texts (e.g., the books of Nehemiah, Ezra, and Daniel) that made fasting and mourning over sin a deliberate means of spiritual revitalization.
187. Crowder, *Mystical Union*, 57–96.

the book of Revelation is entirely absent from the *Mirror Bible*, at least in the present version of this Bible paraphrase.

Among the Charismatic grace teachers, Benjamin Dunn is one who embodies the grace message and yet does not indicate a belief in universal salvation. Like the others, his emphasis is on salvation as a present-time experience rather than as something that believers still await. He defines the word "salvation" as "the spiritual and eternal deliverance granted immediately by God to those who accept His conditions of repentance and faith in the Lord Jesus."[188] The word "immediately" is determinative. Dunn—like the others—does not speak of waiting for final salvation at Christ's return. Salvation is *here and now*, not *there and then*. Dunn writes, "In the New Creation language, you won't find longing and wanting. You will find endless praises declaring that the waiting and wanting is over. It's a language and song of blissful fulfillment and ecstatic satisfaction."[189]

Since "the waiting and wanting is over," Dunn seems to be in heaven already. His eschatology is *overrealized* in the sense that he thinks of the kingdom of God as already present in its full and final form: "The realm people enter then, when they become Christians, is a realm that is no longer merely human. They are lifted out of their corrupted condition and into a divine one. They are raised into the humanity that God had in mind when He created us."[190] The new self *replaces* the old self. The sinner is gone, and someone else is present: "We are new in quality and in kind, and superior to what we were in our fallen state."[191] The stress on "already" rather than "not yet" affects the way in which Dunn construes holiness. He defines "sanctification" as both "Christ Himself" and "the divine act preceding the acceptance of the Gospel by the individual."[192] Sanctification is already accomplished and completed in Christ prior to any human decision or act of faith. Dunn rejects fear as a motive in the Christian life, saying that "the Gospel leads people to repentance, not because of the fear of eternal punishment, but because of the promise of eternal bliss."[193] Union with Christ is not only a doctrine but also an experience: "This is the ecstasy that the Gospel announces. It declares your new reality of mystical oneness with Christ."[194]

188. Dunn, *Happy Gospel!*, 31.
189. Ibid., 128.
190. Ibid., 62–63.
191. Ibid., 64. "Everything that we were 'in Adam' has been shattered and destroyed! We have been completely disconnected from the Fall of humanity and its curse. . . . We are not new creatures still under the curse and Fall of man. We are in a new, divinely-lifted condition" (66).
192. Ibid., 33.
193. Ibid., 41.
194. Ibid., 57.

Dunn promotes a doctrine of perfectionism—namely, that believers can cease from sin during the present life. For Dunn, mainstream and nonperfectionist Christians have adopted a distorted, or even gnostic, view of the body as something evil. He writes, "Following the idea that the body is evil is the belief that Christians will never be free from sin until they die. . . . If death delivers us from what Christ could not, then death, not Christ, becomes our savior."[195] Salvation cannot be "process-based," because this would lead to "a multi-tiered Christianity, with some holier than others," which is "obviously not the gospel." Instead Dunn insists that "sanctification" or "holiness" is "available freely once for all at the moment of salvation."[196] By implication, there is no process of development in holiness in the Christian life. What is more, Dunn's denial that some believers might be holier than others undercuts the biblical teaching on *imitation*, wherein believers are called to follow the example of eminent fellow believers—and above all to follow and imitate Christ (1 Cor. 4:16; 11:1; Phil. 2–3; 1 Thess. 1:6; Heb. 13:7). In general, the grace teachers minimize the idea of *imitatio Christi* (the imitation of Christ).[197] Dunn defines "the offense of the cross" as "the preaching of instantaneous righteousness and union through Christ's cross." He denies that "Christianity is a struggle" and says that "the true stumbling block is the ease of the Gospel."[198] This is so because most people "are striving for something that is simply a gift."[199]

Francois du Toit states that "every human life is . . . represented in Christ" and "equally included in God's economy of grace"—a theme in Kruger and Crowder too. In du Toit's reasoning, though, it is not easy to tell whether Christ represents humanity or humanity represents Christ. His appeal to the image of the mirror functions in both ways. Christ "gives . . . reference to our being as in a mirror, not as an example for us, but of us."[200] Du Toit diminishes the

195. Ibid., 74. For Dunn and Crowder, "gnosticism" is a term that applies not to their own opinions but rather to mainstream Christianity in denying that believers attain perfection during the present life.

196. Ibid., 80.

197. In *Happy Gospel!*, Dunn's exposition becomes confusing, because he recognizes the imitation of Christ theme in Scripture yet cannot reconcile it with his notion of radical grace:

The view of Christ for many is that He was a template after whom we should order our lives. They view His work on the cross as their highest example . . . which they should follow. . . . Yes, of course He is the perfect example of holy living, but His purpose was not to show us how to live, but to live it out for us—in us and through us. . . . Everything Jesus said and did in His life . . . should be seen in light of His death. His death on the cross wasn't just a part of His purpose—it was His purpose. (91–92)

This passage raises questions: Why did Jesus preach and teach over several years? Does his earthly life, prior to his death, have enduring significance?

198. Ibid., 86–87.

199. Ibid., 99.

200. Du Toit, *Divine Embrace*, 12, 161.

distance between Christ and humanity in his teaching that "man pre-existed in the Logic of God."[201] Not only did Christ eternally preexist with God the Father, but so did every human being. Christ's coming functions as a manifestation to us of our own eternal and divine nature. The flesh-and-blood Jesus fades from view. Jesus is less an individual human being and more a reflection of corporate or collective humanity. In rhapsodic language, du Toit stresses the manifestation to humanity of its own true selfhood: "Jesus . . . did not come as an example for us but of us. . . . He is introduced to us not as Christ in history, or Christ in outer space, nor even as Christ in a future event, but as Christ in you. . . . Jesus is what God believes about you! Jesus is God's mind made up about the human race! Awake to innocence, awake to oneness!"[202] God acted not because of humanity's sin-ridden state but because of humanity's essential worth: "The lost coin never lost its original value."[203]

The paraphrasing in du Toit's *Mirror Bible* often shifts the meanings in the biblical texts. In the English Standard Version, John 1:12 reads: "But to all who did receive him, who believed in his name, he gave the right to become children of God." In the *Mirror Bible*, this same verse is rendered as: "Everyone who realizes their association in him, convinced that he is their original life and that his name defines them, in them he endorses the fact that they are indeed his offspring, begotten of him; he sanctions the legitimacy of their sonship."[204] One notices that the word "faith" has dropped away in the *Mirror Bible* and is replaced by "realizes." Rather than faith in Jesus, there is salvation by intellectual realization. This paraphrase also changes the historical Jesus into a Christ who is the "original life" of human beings. Christ as Primal Man is a representation of original, eternal humanity. In du Toit's teaching, Christ's function is to reveal myself to me. Self-discovery and God-discovery seem to be essentially the same thing: "To discover yourself in the mirror is the key that unlocks the door to divine encounter."[205] The *Mirror Bible*'s rendering of 2 Corinthians 3:18 makes this clear: "In gazing with wonder at the blueprint likeness of God displayed in human form [i.e., in Jesus], we suddenly realize that we are looking at ourselves! Every feature of his image is mirrored in us! . . . We are led from an inferior mind-set to the revealed endorsement of our authentic identity. Mankind is his glory!"[206]

201. Ibid., 13. "Man began in God; we are not the invention of our parents" (15).
202. Ibid., 6.
203. Ibid., 7.
204. Du Toit, *Mirror Bible*, 17.
205. Ibid., 11.
206. Ibid., 123 (paraphrase of 2 Cor. 3:18). For another striking change of meaning in paraphrasing, compare the English Standard Version of Rom. 9:18 with du Toit's version: "So then he has mercy on whomever he wills, and he hardens whoever he wills" (ESV); "The same act of mercy that

Du Toit's themes are paralleled in the literature of ancient gnosis, wherein theophany or christophany gives way to egophany, the manifestation of the self.[207] Du Toit lays out his theory of humanity's "lost and found" identity as follows:

> Man began in God! . . . The unveiling of mankind's redemption also reveals our true genesis. . . . We are *anothen*, from above. We are perfect and complete and lacking in nothing . . . our natural birth is not our beginning! We come from above! If man did not come from above, the heavenly realm would offer no attraction to him. In our make-up we are the god-kind with an appetite for more than what bread and the senses could satisfy us with.[208]

This teaching is bona fide esotericism. Human beings come from another spiritual realm but are marooned temporarily within the realm of flesh. Our supernal origin causes us to look toward the sky and pine for our return there once again. Translated into Coptic, written on a papyrus scroll, and buried in the Egyptian sands, du Toit's sayings might be mistaken for a missing portion of an ancient gnostic library. Du Toit quotes with approval the saying, "The only difference between Christ and us was his understanding of who he was."[209] It is not clear whether du Toit believes that Jesus was uniquely divine or whether Jesus simply revealed the divine nature of all humans.[210]

---

he willingly bestows on everyone may bless the one and harden the heart of the other" (du Toit, *Mirror Bible*, 46). Ephesians 2:1 (ESV), "You were dead in the trespasses and sins," becomes "We were in a death trap of an inferior lifestyle, constantly living below the blueprint measure of our lives" (du Toit, *Mirror Bible*, 151). Colossians 2:10 (ESV), "You have been filled in him [i.e., Christ]," is paraphrased as "Jesus mirrors our completeness and endorses our true identity" (du Toit, *Mirror Bible*, 186).

207. For ancient and modern gnostics, salvation occurs through knowledge (Greek *gnōsis*), and the key transition occurs with the self's realization of its own identity—a moment tantamount to rebirth. Marvin C. Meyer states, "The insight that awakens us is within us . . . and the knowledge that saves us is self-knowledge. In order to be saved we need to remember, understand, and know our true selves . . . that is the gospel of gnosis" (*Gnostic Discoveries*, 166). Cyril O'Regan quotes Eric Voegelin's remark that gnosticism centers on "egophany" (*Gnostic Return in Modernity*, 250n24).

208. Du Toit, *Mirror Bible*, 245.

209. Du Toit, *Logic of His Love*, 31. Du Toit attributes this saying to the early Pentecostal leader John G. Lake (1870–1935).

210. The emergence of gnostic-esoteric thinking among Pentecostal-Charismatic Christians seems to be a recent development, perhaps less than a decade old. Yet Thomas Weinandy finds a gnostic subtext among late twentieth-century authors such as John Macquarrie, John Hick, Roger Haight, and David Griffin, for whom "Jesus differs from us only in degree and not in kind in that he manifests to a greater degree than we the ever-present God" ("Gnosticism and Contemporary Soteriology," 258). This means that "Jesus does not establish an entirely new relationship between God and man but makes it possible for the God-man relation, which always was[,] to become more fully actualized" (261). Such views of Jesus are reminiscent of the "Gnostic Redeemer" who "does not change the cosmic blueprint" but "rather makes known what has always been the case" (257). Though these authors differ from the ancient gnostics in not viewing matter as evil, "salvation

In the final chapter of his book *Divine Embrace*, du Toit addresses the question of hell. The final page states that everyone is already redeemed, and for this reason "the greatest hell that anyone can face in any age is the torment of the ignorance of their true, redeemed identity revealed in Christ as in a mirror."[211] Du Toit interprets hell in a subjective way, yet he makes no explicit statement about whether people do or do not come out of their state of ignorance.

Much like du Toit, the Charismatic preacher and teacher Andre Rabe offers a version of Christian universalism that shows resemblances to the universalism of ancient gnosis (*DR* 2.3). Rabe tells his readers, "You have your origin in Him. . . . Your identity, as God imagined it long before you were born, is displayed in all its purity and beauty by this Word,"[212] for "Jesus . . . is not ashamed to call you brother because we all have the same origin."[213] This statement raises a question regarding Christ's eternal preexistence: Is every human being eternal and preexistent with God in the same way that the Son of God is said to be? Rabe saves his most telling statements for the final chapter of *Imagine* (2013), "The Incarnation Continues," which suggests that all human beings are an extension of Christ's incarnation:

> The same logos [word] that John wrote of—the logos that was in the beginning with God, the logos that became flesh in the person of Christ Jesus—this is the same logos with which we have been enriched. He has enriched us with all of Himself! Not just a portion or a fragment, but everything He is has been deposited in you. *The same logos that became flesh in Christ, now becomes flesh in you!* . . . God sees no reason to expect any lesser manifestation of His life in you than in Jesus.[214]

Later we will return to this theme and reconsider Rabe's language regarding "the same logos."

The idea of God as transcendent, writes Rabe, is a reflection of "our natural mind and reasoning," for "a people who are alienated and confused about God . . . develop philosophies about His unknowability—or 'transcendence' for the theologically minded."[215] Unlike the God of the Bible and Christian tradition, Rabe's God seems to be wholly immanent. The meaning of "Christ" also hangs in doubt, since Rabe speaks of Jesus's earthly life as the "manifestation of an

---

within these soteriologies similarly consists in coming to know the 'eternally' established and unchanging (and unchangeable) cosmological order," so that "salvation is reduced to and identified with cosmology" (262).

211. Du Toit, *Divine Embrace*, 164.
212. Rabe, *Imagine*, 15.
213. Ibid., 16.
214. Ibid., 138–39; emphasis added.
215. Ibid., 15.

eternal event": "The life, death and resurrection of Jesus Christ happened within our time, but it was a manifestation of an eternal event. His appearance revealed what has always been true—the mystery hidden for ages and generations was finally made known in our dimension of time and space."[216] But is Jesus eternally born in Bethlehem and forever crucified at Golgotha?

In Rabe's teaching, God's will toward humanity did not change because of Jesus's coming in the flesh. The divine disposition regarding humanity was settled from all eternity. The benefit of Jesus's coming was purely subjective—that is, it changed human attitudes toward God: "Jesus did not come to change the heart and mind of God concerning man, but to change our minds about God. He came to reveal the truth about God and about us and in so doing make us true—genuinely ourselves."[217] Rabe refers to evil as something that "has no substance in itself, no eternal significance," and he adds that "evil is the potential by-product of creation—it is everything that God did not create."[218]

For Rabe, God was never alienated from humanity, though human beings may have thought so. Here Rabe's reasoning resembles that of New Thought, which regards evil as illusory and as rooted in false thinking about God and self (see *DR* 11.2, on Carlton Pearson). Once one's thinking is rectified, then evil disappears, since evil has always been an illusion due to distorted thinking. Regarding Christ's atonement, Rabe stresses God's restorative and not vindictive justice: "God's justice is not the selfish desire to satisfy His own offense. God's justice is restorative and healing."[219] More sharply he states, "We continue to subject ourselves to mythical deception when we view the cross of Jesus as the punishment that satisfies God's anger; when we speak of the blood of Jesus that magically satisfies God's blood lust. These are the very fallacies that the cross came to expose."[220] Humanity, not God, was responsible for Jesus's

216. Ibid., 26–27.

217. Ibid., 56.

218. Ibid., 35. Rabe's language at this point echoes that of Karl Barth. On God's noncreation of evil, compare the elaborate account of evil as *das Nichtige* (Nothingness) in Barth, *CD* III/1, 289–368. For Barth, evil-as-nothingness is neither Creator nor created—and is thus a metaphysical anomaly (*DR* 9.7).

219. Rabe, *Imagine*, 79.

220. Ibid., 99–100. Rabe seems to be following René Girard (1923–2015) when he writes, "The cross . . . exposes the violence of societies build [sic] upon sacrificial systems. The principalities and powers of this world, of every culture, began in false accusation escalating to murder. Human societies have violent and deceptive beginnings. . . . Let's first say this: if the cross is the event that God required to satisfy his need for retribution, then it has no revelatory power. That is the story that mythology has always told" (102–3). As Girard argues, in the New Testament writings, one finds a divine victim (i.e., Jesus) lynched by a mob, as in many ancient myths. Yet the biblical recognition of the sufferer's innocence lays a basis for a destruction of the entire sacrificial order. See

death: "Man is responsible for the death of Jesus, God is responsible for the resurrection of Jesus."[221]

In one of his most revealing passages, Rabe writes, "Man is God's idea. And so when God became man it was the original, authentic idea of man that manifested in the person of Christ—the perfect man. What God always knew to be true of man suddenly burst upon the stage of human history."[222] This statement points to a possible parallel between du Toit's and Rabe's teachings and such early Christian thinkers as Gregory of Nyssa and Maximus the Confessor. Human preexistence within the eternal Son or Word of God is a theme in early Greek Christian authors. For Gregory and Maximus (*DR* 3.9; 4.8), the "ideal" preexistence of human individuals—that is, as ideas or ideals in the divine mind or intention—was a modification of early Origenism, away from a doctrine of preexisting souls as intelligent, volitional agents. Yet missing from preexistent humanity as du Toit and Rabe conceive it are the ethical and teleological elements that one finds in the Greek fathers. For Gregory and Maximus, Christ in his coming shows us *what human beings are called to be.* For du Toit and Rabe, it would seem that Christ in his coming shows us *what human beings simply are.* Without the idea of moral and spiritual striving, so prominent in Gregory and Maximus, any parallel to the Greek fathers is limited in scope. The logic of du Toit's and Rabe's theologies appears to be more gnostic than patristic. The human problem for them is not ethical but cognitive—that many or most people do not know of their own identity in Christ.

On Rabe's premises, it does not seem that anyone can be damned, lost, or separated from God, except to the extent that someone might cling to a false and untrue identity. Rabe states, "To recognize the Lordship of Jesus Christ cannot be separated from recognizing His image and likeness within you. You belong to Him because He made you."[223] Relationship to Christ is grounded in God's creation of us rather than in Christ's redemptive work. To be human is already to be connected to God. Our calling is to discover ourselves and to discover God: "Awake to His reality[,] awake to His likeness in you!"[224]

Girard, *Things Hidden.* On Girard's relation to contemporary Christian theology, see Kaplan, *René Girard, Unlikely Apologist.*

221. Rabe, *Imagine*, 108.

222. Ibid., 59.

223. Ibid., 132–33. Other passages likewise emphasize humanity's universal acceptance in Christ. "Receiving Christ is based on the truth that he already 'received,' embraced and reconciled you" (133). "The ascension is the glorification of man to the place and position that He prepared for us—permanent union with Him. All this is of God, He accomplished it without our help and without our permission! It is truth whether we acknowledge it or not" (123).

224. Ibid. On Jesus's divinity, Rabe states: "Jesus not only represents God, He is God. What He says, God says; what He does, God does" (54). Yet other statements to the effect that other persons

We turn finally to John Crowder, a self-appointed spiritual troublemaker. He writes that "in every generation, the Lord appoints a few troublers of Israel to challenge the status quo and awaken His people to the authentic Gospel."[225] Reflecting the wilder, untamed side of the independent Charismatic movement, Crowder was earlier associated with Todd Bentley, a fiery young evangelist who, prior to his preaching ministry, had been a juvenile offender. In his writings Bentley reported paranormal experiences, including visions of heaven and encounters with an angel.[226] A 2008 local revival at a church in Lakeland, Florida, led by Bentley, involved reports of miraculous healings and drew the attention of Charismatic Christians around the globe. Crowder expresses high regard for Bentley.[227]

Subsequently, Crowder became known for conducting worship services that drew participants into a kind of spiritual intoxication, not induced by alcohol or drug use but by what Crowder calls "God's drunken glory." Crowder's "Sloshfest" has been held in various locations and was described in 2010 in the British press.[228] His first two books—*Miracle Workers, Reformers, and the New Mystics* (2006) and *The Ecstasy of Loving God* (2009)—recount many of the most unusual miracles from church history. Included are Catholic saints levitating, Francis of Assisi conversing with animals, and missing limbs being supernaturally restored. Crowder embraces the miraculous phenomena associated with Catholic and Orthodox saints but rejects the spiritual disciplines (e.g., fasting and monastic routine) generally regarded as integral to the lives of the saints.[229]

---

are not a "lesser manifestation" of the Logos than Jesus was (138–39) suggest that Jesus might be divine but not uniquely so.

225. Crowder, book endorsement, in Dunn, *Happy Gospel!*, 10.

226. Todd Bentley claims to have visited heaven, seen the apostle Paul, and encountered an angel he called "Emma." His books include *The Journey into the Miraculous*, *The Reality of the Supernatural World*, and *Kingdom Rising*.

227. Crowder refers to Bentley as "a modern-day miracle worker" and says that he personally witnessed Bentley healing the sick: "I have seen Todd . . . work all manner of healings under the power of the Lord both on the mission field and in conferences in the United States and Canada" (*Miracle Workers*, 228–29).

228. The UK press account reads:

With sweaty clothes clinging to their backs, some people even pass out. While this could easily be mistaken for a dodgy booze and drug-fuelled party, there is something very different about Sloshfest. The revellers are party loving Christians who don't drink or take drugs—but say their euphoria is down [sic] to the power of God and their seeming drunkenness due to "God-ka" and the "yum rum of Heaven." Last weekend around 600 people attended the annual rave-like event—where no alcohol or drugs are available—at the dowdy Dolphin Club in Barry Island, South Wales. Now in its fourth year, it attracts visitors from alternative churches around the UK. (Lowe, "Ravers Who Get High on God")

229. In Catholic teaching, the higher state of union with God generally comes only after a prolonged process of purification. This led to a distinction between "ascetic theology" and "mystical theology":

Crowder's teaching has evolved during the last decade. His first two books were less theological than the more recent *Mystical Union* (2010) and *Cosmos Reborn* (2013). *Cosmos Reborn* cites C. Baxter Kruger and Thomas Torrance and is the first of Crowder's books to raise explicitly the issue of universal salvation. The final chapter in *Cosmos Reborn* seems to move in a new direction, affirming that human beings are "a divine race" and that "there is a very real eternal aspect" to all of us.[230] Crowder's arguments weave together multiple strands, including a trinitarian inclusion of all humanity in Christ (per Karl Barth, Thomas Torrance, and C. Baxter Kruger) and the esoteric motif of humanity's divine origin and divine nature (per Andre Rabe and Francois du Toit).

Crowder addresses universalism in *Cosmos Reborn* (2013) as well as a ninety-minute online video.[231] Sometimes it is difficult to follow his argument, because he begins with strong, bold statements of his position, followed by a series of qualifications. The video states that he intends to "bring more clarity" to the discussion on hell yet adds that he will present no "clean, tidy, theological system." The teaching on hell is tied to "the grace message" or "the finished work of the cross." He sees today a "massive exodus" of "people coming out of the shallow, stagnant, uncreative waters of religion and into the depths of this glorious grace message." Miracles, joy, and God's "benefits package" come from realizing that Christ has already accomplished everything.[232]

Regarding hell, Crowder says that "two seemingly opposite things" appear as a "paradox in scripture." One is "the existence of hell," which Crowder affirms. The other side is "a very real universal scope of work accomplished on the cross of Jesus Christ."[233] Crowder takes up the theme of predestination, rejects both Calvinist and Arminian views, and favorably cites Karl Barth's teaching on this topic. Crowder emphasizes God's sovereignty in electing everyone, stating

---

Ascetical Theology . . . is called the *science of the Saints*, and rightly so, because *it comes to us from the Saints*, who have taught it more by their life than by word of mouth. . . . The word "*ascetical*" comes from the Greek *askesis* (exercise, effort) and means any arduous task connected with man's education, physical or moral. Christian perfection, then, implies those efforts that St. Paul himself compares to the training undergone by athletes with the purpose of obtaining the victory [1 Cor. 9:24–27]. (Tanquerey, *Spiritual Life*, 2–3)

Mystical experiences derive from supernatural graces that cannot be produced by human striving alone. Yet a deeper prayer life or union with God requires effort (*askēsis*). Unusual phenomena among the mystics, in Catholic thought, are merely epiphenomenal or surface-level manifestations of an underlying process of theosis or progressive union with God. As noted above, Crowder repudiates the idea that union with God is a process or progress and instead maintains that union is total and immediate for all Christian believers.

230. Crowder, *Cosmos Reborn*, 252, 242.

231. Crowder, "Hell Revisited"; Crowder, *Cosmos Reborn*, 155–66. From August 2012 to February 2016, Crowder's YouTube video on hell drew some 38,000 hits.

232. Crowder, "Hell Revisited," 1–2 mins. into the video.

233. Ibid., 4–5 mins. into the video.

that "there is no freedom outside of his [God's] will." Human beings have no independent or self-willed existence. Crowder repudiates what he calls the "demonic" and "disgusting idea" of "double predestination, which makes God "much worse than Hitler." Sounding like a number of earlier universalists (e.g., Isaac of Syria, William Law, George MacDonald [*DR* 4.9; 5.9]), he says that for God "there is no such thing as hatred apart from love," since God's "wrath is an extension of . . . love." Wrath is God's opposition to what destroys human beings, and so "his wrath has always been for you, never truly against you."[234]

Taking a cue from Barth, Crowder states that "it is time we put Jesus Christ right back in the middle of this whole equation." In eternity, God did not make an "arbitrary choice." Jesus Christ is "the elect one . . . he is the choice of the Father." Election "has always been about the Father's choice for Jesus, and therefore the Father's choice for us." Crowder quotes Barth's summary statement that "election is the sum of the gospel." This implies that Jesus was "the vessel of honor who was also the vessel of wrath" (Rom. 9:22–23) and that "the reconciliation already happened two thousand years ago."[235] He cites 1 Corinthians 15:22—"In Christ all will be made alive"—and states that "all means all." He says, "I am not a universalist," yet he concedes, "I do have a strong hope in the salvation of all mankind," for Christ "has become our human response to God."[236]

After stating his "strong hope" for universal salvation, Crowder backtracks by admitting, "I just don't know." "This hope in the salvation of all man[kind] is not just permitted, it is commanded," while at the same time "hope cannot verge into dogmatism." Crowder finds the basis for his double-sided attitude in what he takes to be the double-sidedness of Scripture. Since "scripture is fluid," one can make a "solid, scriptural case" for "rigid infernalism" and yet also for universalism. The Bible shows an "open-ended tension." He states that salvation must come through Christ—"Jesus is the only door"—and so distinguishes himself from religiously pluralistic universalism. He says that he identifies with trinitarians like Karl Barth and Thomas F. Torrance, who teach "the inclusion of humanity in the work of Christ." For this reason Crowder does not "vilify Christian universalists as . . . heretics."[237]

Drawing on Eastern Christian writers, Crowder states that hell is "not separation from God." Instead "heaven" and "hell" are human terms for what it is like to be in God's presence in two radically different ways. Since there is no escape from God's presence, human beings will necessarily experience either torment

234. Ibid., 7–8, 12, 14–19 mins. into the video.
235. Ibid., 20–25 mins. into the video, quoting Barth, *CD* II/2, 13: "The election of grace is the sum of the Gospel—we must put it as pointedly as that."
236. Crowder, "Hell Revisited," 34, 79 mins. into the video.
237. Ibid., 33–44 mins. into the video.

or joy. Paradise and hell do not exist from God's standpoint but only from a human point of view. God is paradise for saints, but God is hell for sinners. Nowhere in Scripture do we find that God needed to be reconciled to humanity; instead we find that humanity needed to be reconciled to God. Christ did not cause God to begin to love us, for God always loved us and God has never been opposed to us. Crowder quotes from Isaac of Nineveh (*DR* 4.9), who wrote that sins against love would bring the greatest torment to sinners. Those in hell continue to be the objects of God's love—but are tormented by this love.[238]

Jesus's death is a "black hole" in which all sins and condemnation have vanished. Though there may be torment for those who do not accept Christ, hell is not outside the realm of God's grace. Crowder notes that his views have caused him to look on his fellow human beings in a new way: "Everybody is included in the finished work of the cross. Even unbelievers are included in a hidden way. We can't really use terms any more like outsider versus insider." Crowder now avoids such terms as "saved" and "unsaved" and prefers to speak of "believer" versus "unbeliever." The former group differs from the latter in *realizing* what Christ has already done for them. Christians may "see unbelievers as insiders who haven't realized their inclusion yet by faith." The "personal encounter" with God, or "altar-call moment," is not crucial for Crowder, and he says, "I was born again two thousand years ago." Unbelievers "are burning"—in the present tense—so long as they do not recognize what God has done for them. In the end, he writes, "we can reject God all we want but you can't make him stop including you." Crowder distinguishes inclusion into Christ (involving everyone) from faith in Christ (involving only believers). Believing in Christ accomplishes nothing as far as inclusion into Christ is concerned.[239]

Crowder rejects purgationism, stating that "hell doesn't clean you up or purge you. Jesus did." Instead he identifies with Calvinists (e.g., Karl Barth and Thomas Torrance) who reject postmortem suffering or purification as a precondition for heaven. In interpreting Romans 9, Crowder sees Jacob, Esau, Moses, and Pharaoh less as historical figures and more as symbols of human possibilities. Each one of us *was* Esau, he says, but we *can be* Jacob. We *were* Pharaoh but *can be* Moses. When we read in Scripture that God loved Jacob and hated Esau (Mal. 1:2–3; Rom. 9:13), this means that "God hates that false self." The vessels of honor and dishonor (Rom. 9:22–23) are not separate individuals but "two identities, one true and one false," and so "Jacob represents the true self."[240] This argument shifts in a new direction, since

238. Ibid., 67–73 mins. into the video.
239. Ibid., 33–44 mins. into the video.
240. Ibid., 72–76 mins. into the video.

Crowder earlier insisted that salvation is entirely accomplished for everyone in the person of Christ. In distinguishing a "true self" from a "false self" and ascribing this difference to human faith or decision, Crowder adopts a more human-centered standpoint. His position becomes more moralistic and less grace-based, since individuals face antithetical options and must choose to be "Jacob" rather than "Esau."

Always the provocateur, Crowder opens his book *Mystical Union* with the query, "When you think of the cross, do you think of *fun*? If the answer is 'no' then you have not been taught the cross aright." Because Christ has already done everything, there is a "happy, effortless Christianity" that may "sound scandalous" but is in fact "*the gospel.*"[241] Crowder accepts "the wildest miracles" reported by mystics of the past, though he rejects the spiritual disciplines that mystics practiced: "Ascetic disciplines do not bring us into union."[242] Crowder repudiates the phrase "seeking God," because, he writes, "we are no longer seeking," and "*seeking* is a pre-Christ action." Instead there is "enjoyment of the Promise Land [*sic*] that we have entered."[243] In another passage he insists, "Your attempts to get closer to God are the very things that alienate you from grace."[244] He states that believers in Christ are *not* to model themselves on Christ.[245]

Crowder takes issue not only with Catholic ascetic and mystical teachings but also with the Protestant Reformation, which to his mind did not go far enough in rejecting the Catholic emphasis on good works in the Christian life. Early Protestantism, he argues, went astray in asserting that Christian believers continue to struggle with aspects or remnants of the flesh or "indwelling sin." Crowder declares that "the reformation is not finished" until Christians abolish this notion of the flesh or indwelling sin.[246] He labels Reformation theology

241. Crowder, *Mystical Union*, 9.

242. He explains further: "Much of traditional mysticism has been marked by thinly veiled 'works' righteousness. . . . Its focus was often on ascetic practice, prayer and annihilation of self through meditation or other means to gain reception into God. . . . Let us not drag up any vestiges of that kind of mysticism. In fact, the point of this book is to help you renounce all your own endeavors to find favor with your Father" (ibid., 14–15).

243. Ibid., 117–19.

244. Ibid., 133. Crowder also does not believe that marriage takes effort: "I don't believe the religious lies that tell me marriage is hard work" (183). At the end, he states, "Our union is effortless. This does not mean we become idle" (207). There may be *activity* but apparently no *exertion*.

245. Ibid., 164: "Jesus . . . did not bring a formula or model for you to repeat. He stepped into your place and bore the bullet that was yours to take."

246. Ibid., 17. He says, "It is a myth that Christians must overcome their flesh" (56). On p. 51, Crowder especially blames Puritan theologian John Owen (1616–83), author of the influential treatises *Of the Mortification of Sin in Believers* (1656) and *Nature, Power, Deceit, and Prevelancy of the Remainders of Indwelling Sin in Believers* (1667). A recent edition of these treatises was published as Owen, *Overcoming Sin and Temptation*.

as heterodox: "The heresy is this: it is the idea that you, as a believer, still have a *sinful nature*."[247] That the apostle Paul had "an internal war going on within himself" is "unbiblical hogwash" and "demonic rhetoric."[248] Throughout *Mystical Union*, Crowder insists that the entire Christian life is an exercise of faith in one's already achieved union with Christ.[249] "Your union with Christ," he writes, "is an effortless state of being. It takes no more work for me than being a natural born citizen of America. . . . The moment you decide to do something to be holy, you have trusted in yourself, instead of Christ, for salvation."[250] Not only does Crowder negate the Ten Commandments and Old Testament laws, but he also ignores Jesus's instructions in the Gospels on discipleship.[251] Crowder has to ignore much of the apostle Paul's teaching, since Paul often spoke of exertion in the Christian life and compared the Christian life to the running of a race that required training and self-discipline so that one might run well (1 Cor. 9:24–27).

Crowder's most recent work, *Cosmos Reborn* (2013), exhibits many of the same themes as Kruger. Sounding a bit like Barth, Crowder here says, "I am and I am not a universalist."[252] As in his video presentation, Crowder states that "all are included in Christ" and that "it is now impossible to see insiders or outsiders," for "God has clearly reconciled, redeemed and unified all of humanity in Himself," and "even the unbeliever is included in Christ in a hidden way."[253] All of humanity thus becomes "church," and telling everyone that they are already included in Christ is the new definition of "evangelism." He reaffirms his rejection of a purgative hell.[254] Such a view would clearly conflict

247. Crowder, *Mystical Union*, 24.
248. Ibid., 43.
249. On the question of how or why a Christian believer might still sin, Crowder suggests that "maybe you're an unbeliever," or "maybe no one ever told you any of this [i.e., the truth that one is no longer a sinner]" (ibid., 40–41). The proper response to every manifestation of sin is *faith*—i.e., believing that one is not a sinner. "Believe you're a sinner; you'll have sin" (41).
250. Ibid., 42.
251. Crowder states: "The *gospel* is not Matthew, Mark, Luke and John. The gospel is the good news of Christ's sacrifice for the removal of sinfulness. It is most clearly articulated through the epistles of Paul. . . . Does this sound too Pauline for you? Still want to mix your grace with law? Law and grace don't mix. Put them together and you get law. . . . Most of the church is still eating a leftover form of Judaism" (*Mystical Union*, 80–81). Quoting Robert Capon, Crowder states that "the Gospels . . . were written for the sake of the Epistles, not the other way around" (98, citing Capon, *Health, Money, and Love and Why We Don't Enjoy Them*, 32).
252. Crowder, *Cosmos Reborn*, 17. Compare Barth's comparable statement, used as an epigraph to *DR* 9: "I do not teach it, but I also do not not teach it" (*DR*, 749).
253. Ibid., 116–17.
254. "A god who sovereignly burns someone for a thousand years in a pit of demonic, hellish, molestation is only slightly better than one who does it forever. . . . The main problem with this reasoning is that hell becomes viewed as a *purgatory*. A temporary torture chamber to clean you

with his radical-grace teaching, in which everything pertaining to salvation has already been accomplished in Christ. Yet *Cosmos Reborn* fails to present a clear-cut position. After commending universalism, he says, "I am a hopeful *agnostic*" and "I am okay not knowing all the answers."[255] His book recalls Rob Bell's *Love Wins* (DR 11.5) in combining expressions of agnosticism regarding the afterlife with rejections of traditional Christian views.[256] Confronting the story of the sheep and goats (Matt. 25:31–46), he asks, "Can a goat become a sheep?" His answer is that "we don't really know." He suggests that perhaps "sheep" and "goat" are symbols of two aspects of the human self, so that "the separation of sheep and goats" would be "the separation of individuals from what is false into what is true."[257]

Crowder's motif of two selves moves in the direction of an esoteric rather than a Christocentric version of universalism. In this account, salvation comes as human individuals realize their true rather than false selves. In the final chapter of *Cosmos Reborn*, "The Divinity of Man," Crowder's argument approximates that of Francois du Toit. As human beings, "we pre-existed invisibly in the heart and imagination of God," so "there is a very real eternal aspect about you that goes eternally forward and backward," and "Adam was breathed from the very divine substance." If "dogs produce dogs," he reasons, "what does God produce?" Thus "we are a mirror image of God himself."[258]

Crowder concludes *Cosmos Reborn* with a quasi-gnostic evocation of humanity's awakening knowledge of its eternal origin in God, its divine nature, and its final calling to be eternally united to God:

We are awakening to our True Selves. The false self—under a false fatherhood of the adversary—has no substance. . . . We are awaking to our origin—breathed from His very substance, re-created and born anew in Him—the Lamb of God. . . . He came to awaken humanity to the truth—that we are a divine race. . . . You are not bound by times and seasons. Your destiny does not hinge on your natural abilities. You are eternal, infinite, immortally woven into His own divinity. . . . The entire cosmos has been restored and reconciled to its divine origin. . . . God is not simply bound up in Christ. But rather through Christ, He has bound himself up to the entire created order. . . . Yes, the cosmos has been permanently rewired

up. Hell doesn't clean you up. Jesus did" (ibid., 148). Strictly interpreted, this passage implies ultra-universalism—i.e., that everyone enters heaven immediately after death (DR 6.8–6.9).

255. Ibid., 147.
256. Crowder asks, "Is it possible that our concept of a hell-mongering deity is the chief underlying idol of our churches today? Is our Western version of 'Christianity' more akin to Molech worship with a fish on the bumper?" (*Cosmos Reborn*, 127).
257. Ibid., 157–58.
258. Ibid., 241–42.

in the incarnation, death, and resurrection of Jesus Christ. All things have been forever united in the Son of God. . . . God included you and absorbed the entire created order into Himself.[259]

In this peroration, Crowder's agnostic and hopeful statements about final salvation give way to an assertive universalism of the gnostic-esoteric variety.

11.7. Summary and Conclusions on Contemporary Universalisms

This chapter has displayed the wide variations that exist among contemporary Christian universalist authors. Popular books in support of universalism may agree on final salvation for all, but not agree on much else. The authors diverge in their assessment of Jesus of Nazareth, with Gulley and Mulholland denying Jesus's unique divinity, and other authors like Robin Parry and C. Baxter Kruger remaining clearly committed to this central Christian affirmation. Carlton Pearson is akin to Gulley and Mulholland in the minimal role that he assigns to Jesus, and this may be one reason that his universalism is multi- or interreligious. For Pearson there are many paths to God, and Jesus is only one of the ways. In contrast to this, C. Baxter Kruger is deeply Christocentric, as is John Crowder. The authors diverge also in their assessments of church history and Christian tradition. Talbott seems profoundly suspicious of the institutional church, and he seeks to build his universalist theology from the text of the Bible, shorn of past interpretations, together with his own philosophical reasoning from an a priori notion of divine love. C. Baxter Kruger operates in a different realm, appealing to Augustine, Calvin, Barth, and Torrance and situating his universalist theology in relation to a number of great Christian thinkers of the past.

We also find major differences among contemporary universalists in their interpretations of the Bible. Gulley and Mulholland largely follow a "canon within the canon" approach, finding fault with the God of the Old Testament and arguing that Jesus embodies a principle of divine love and mercy that offers a key to interpreting the entire Bible. Contrasting with this is John Crowder's exegesis, which diminishes the importance of the New Testament Gospels and instead exalts the Letters of Paul. The four Gospels are "not the gospel" as Crowder sees it, and only the Pauline message of free grace through faith alone is the "gospel." Benjamin Dunn agrees with Crowder in his basic approach to the Bible, which we might call a Pauline antinomianism.

Rob Bell is prone to spiritualizing or allegorical readings of Scripture. In the parable of the prodigal son (Luke 15:11–32), the elder brother represents the

---

259. Ibid., 251, 252, 25, 260, and back cover.

particularist who wishes to limit salvation to just a few and so refuses to enter the party and rejoice with the father and the once-erring yet now-returned younger brother. Allegorical exegesis on behalf of universalism goes back to the time of Origen and is prominent in nineteenth-century Anglo-American universalism, and so Bell follows a long line of nonliteralist universalist exegetes. Wholly different is the approach to the Bible taken by Robin Parry (a.k.a. Gregory Mac-Donald), who seeks to base his universalist conclusions on the Old Testament as well as the New Testament, all literally interpreted. As we showed above, Parry's exegetical arguments break down at many places, but the point here is that Parry's hermeneutical principles diverge from those of Crowder, or Bell, or Gulley and Mulholland. Francois du Toit, in his *Mirror Bible* paraphrase, differs radically from Parry's literal exegesis, as du Toit systematically reinterprets the Bible in what might be considered a gnostic-esoteric interpretation.

Another point of divergence among contemporary universalist authors centers on the contrast between esoteric and Christocentric versions of universalism. Esoteric thought highlights the self's discovery of its own true nature. In coming to conscious realization of its divine origin or nature, the human self is "saved." The difference between those who are "saved" and those "yet to be saved" lies wholly on the intellectual or cognitive plane. In the Christocentric universalism of such thinkers as Barth (*DR* 9.3–9.7) and Balthasar (*DR* 10.4–10.9), there is a partial parallel to esoteric universalism: everyone without exception, whether they realize it or not, is already included in Christ and in all that Christ has accomplished. So the "saved"/"unsaved" distinction might be construed as a cognitive difference. Yet for the Christocentric universalist, the salvific truth to be understood and realized is not fundamentally a truth about the human self as such but is a truth about Christ—or, perhaps one might say, a truth about the human self in relation to Christ. Kruger is plainly Christocentric, as Crowder was in his earlier writings. By contrast, Francois du Toit's reasoning floats between esoteric and Christocentric motifs without ever clearly resolving itself. Am I saved because of *who Christ is* or because of *who I am*—revealed to me by Christ? On the basis of du Toit's and Rabe's writings, it is almost impossible to give a definite answer to this question. Crowder in his later writings shifts away from Barth's and Kruger's views and moves in the direction of du Toit's and Rabe's esotericism. How Crowder's theology will continue to develop, only time will tell.

A crucial yet unresolved question in contemporary universalism is the issue that was never resolved during the nineteenth century—namely, whether postmortem punishment or purgation is necessary for at least some people before going to heaven. Talbott's and Parry's versions of universalism hinge on postmortem suffering. Parry sees this postmortem suffering as *purgative*. He looks to

Elhanan Winchester and the nineteenth-century Anglo-American restorationists rather than the ultra-universalists as his theological progenitors. Parry also cites Moltmann, asserting that hell was taken away at the cross, although this line of argument is at odds with Parry's consistent emphasis on postmortem suffering as a preparation for the presence of God. Talbott's view on postmortem suffering diverges from Parry's, since Talbott argues that God will use increasing levels of pain to bring every human individual finally to make some kind of decision to submit to God. For Talbott, it is not clear if postmortem suffering is simply purgative, or if its point is to force rebel souls to submit themselves to God.

Many more points of contrast might be drawn between the authors surveyed above. As far as theological arguments for universalism are concerned, the only thing that these various "universalisms" have in common with one another is the conclusion that all human beings will finally be saved. The theological positions presented here differ on the following: the nature of God, the doctrine of the Trinity, the proper principles of biblical exegesis, the person of Jesus, the nature of good and evil, the origin and nature of humans, the role of human free will, the significance of Jesus's death on the cross, faith versus effort in the Christian life, and the question of postmortem suffering for sins. Someone today who professes to be a Christian universalist might be asked, "What sort of universalist are you?," since the various types of universalism start from disparate assumptions, offer different arguments, and seem to have little in common with one another.

Today's "evangelical universalists," led by Robin Parry, seek to support their views from the text of the New Testament. Yet the problems with any biblically based univeralism are legion, and they commence with Jesus's attributed teachings in the Gospels. Jesus repeatedly warned of the danger of refusing God's offer of grace and the peril of delaying one's response. Germain Grisez and Peter F. Ryan note that "Jesus would have been dishonest had he tried to motivate people by warnings that were not truthful information about their prospects if they failed to heed his warnings."[260] In response to Parry's *The Evangelical Universalist*, Graham Watts disputes the claim "that universalism offers greater theological coherence" than traditional evangelical theology. It may present "a form of logical coherence," but this is "quite different from being *theologically* coherent."[261]

Derek Tidball offers a number of incisive comments on Robin Parry's views. So-called evangelical universalism, Tidball argues, is "at best . . . an argument from silence, since scripture nowhere positively states several crucial elements in

260. Grisez and Ryan, "Hell and Hope for Salvation," 612–13.
261. Watts, "Is Universalism Theologically Coherent?," 46.

universalism." He notes that "the accent of the New Testament teaching falls on the significance of this life and the decisions made here, with no hint of a second chance, post-mortem, or of re-education in a hell prior to release in heaven." Moreoever, "there is no reason to believe that those who were impenitent on earth will become penitent in hell. This is pure supposition. Hell may, indeed, have the reverse effect and harden its residents against God." Regarding the final outcome of God's work, "the triumph of God and the reconciliation of 'all things' are adequately explained in terms of the destruction of evil and of all that opposes him." For this reason, "to say that the reconciliation cannot take place unless enemies are persuaded by re-education to agree with God puts a particular contemporary cultural spin on what we believe must happen."[262] Finally, Tidball inquires into the contemporary Western context and asks whether universalist theology is not a Christian cultural accommodation to the current Zeitgeist: "We must ask if the embrace of universalism is not a further example of evangelicals seeking to be civil and of stretching doctrine to accommodate as comfortably as possible to contemporary culture."[263] In light of the ideas presented in this chapter, this question seems apt.

---

262. Tidball, "Can Evangelicals Be Universalists?," 29–30. Tidball uses the analogy of a cancer sufferer who is saved not by the "reconciliation" of the cancerous cells to the rest of his body but by their "destruction" (30).

263. Ibid., 32. On the contemporary evangelical impetus toward civility, see Hunter, *American Evangelicalism*, 87–89. In another book, *Evangelicalism: The Coming Generation*, Hunter speaks of a "normative ethic of civility" (47; cf. 33–34, 150–53, 183), according to which the foremost imperative is *not to offend*—a principle that might help to explain the desire on the part of some evangelicals to downplay or to deny the traditional doctrine of eternal punishment.

12

The Eclipse of Grace

AN APPRAISAL OF CHRISTIAN UNIVERSALISM

Of course [Origen's universalism] was rejected. It would make non-sense of everything else. If what we do now is to make no difference in the end, then all the seriousness of life is done away with.

—Ludwig Wittgenstein[1]

God whose being is love preserves our human freedom, for freedom is the condition of love. Although God's love goes, and has gone, to the uttermost, plumbing the depths of hell, the possibility remains for each human being of a final rejection of God, and so of eternal life.

—Doctrine Commission of the Church of England (1995)[2]

Though I used to complain about the indecency of the idea of God's wrath, I came to think that I would have to rebel against a God who *wasn't* wrathful at the sight of the world's evil. God isn't wrathful in spite of being love. God is wrathful *because* God is love.

—Miroslav Volf[3]

1. Rees, *Recollections of Wittgenstein*, 161.
2. Doctrine Commission of the Church of England, *Mystery of Salvation*, 198, cited in Molt-mann, "Logic of Hell," 44.
3. Volf, *Free of Charge*, 139.

The great mystery is, not that evil has no end, but that it had a
beginning.

—John Henry Newman[4]

Heaven will solve our problems, but not, I think by showing us subtle
reconciliations between all our apparently contradictory notions. The
notions will all be knocked from under our feet. We shall see that
there never was any problem.

—C. S. Lewis[5]

I f one were to ask most modern Christian universalists why they believe that
everyone will finally be saved, the most likely one-word answer would be
"love." Universalists view themselves as affirming God's love, mercy, or grace,
while particularists, in their view, offer a theology that is seriously deficient in
this respect. In defending the traditional views of heaven and hell, Christian
particularists have often gone along with the universalists' understanding of
their own position, invoking God's "justice" as a balancing consideration to
be set over against God's "love." Yet, as this chapter will argue, a particularist
response to universalism might take a different and better course. On close
inspection, the idea of "love" or "grace" as interpreted in univeralism proves
to be suspect. The irony is that universalist theology in its varied forms has
often negated the doctrine of divine grace. As we will show below, the effort to
extend grace to *all* undermines grace to *any*.

A one-word explanation for universalism might be not "love" but "metaphysics." Whenever universal salvation has been expounded as part of a larger
theological system—as in Origen, Gregory of Nyssa, Eriugena, Bulgakov, or
Moltmann—its metaphysical underpinnings have often become evident. Universalist theologizing rests on assumptions about the nature of God, the nature of
humanity, or the nature of good and evil that are neither taught in Scripture nor
embodied in the larger Christian tradition. Because of the incomplete character
of much universalist theology, this fact is not generally recognized. As the earlier
chapters have shown, it is easy to affirm salvation for all without considering the
full consequences of that affirmation. Universalism throughout the centuries
found its strongest support in gnostic, kabbalistic, and esoteric versions of Christianity. This is why, as we have seen, universalism has generally flourished not
in the vital center but at the outer fringes of the Christian tradition. That many

4. Newman, *Grammar of Assent*, 422, cited from Flannery, "How to Think about Hell," 476.
5. C. S. Lewis, *Grief Observed*, 83.

recent Christian thinkers have embraced universalism is not a hopeful sign for the contemporary church, since it suggests that metaphysical speculations with little or no support in Scripture or tradition have become almost as acceptable as doctrines that have strong scriptural and traditional backing.

It should be apparent from the earlier chapters that there have been different forms of universalism, different lines of argument, and different ideas about when, or how, or why all intelligent creatures—fallen human beings and perhaps fallen angels too—will come to final salvation. Yet each of the preceding chapters pointed toward a single conclusion—namely, that Christian universalism has been theologically problematic in each of its successive historical forms. We may now survey the argument thus far to see how the pieces fit together with respect to three major problems: *theological, soteriological,* and *epistemic.* These will be labeled as *the problem of God, the problem of grace,* and *the problem of belief.* These three problems correspond to three questions: What sort of God is the universalist God? What role or place is there for divine grace (i.e., God's unmerited favor) in universalist teaching? And what ground or rationale is there for believing that all will finally be saved? The claim presented below, that universalism generally abolishes grace, is counterintuitive and will require explanation (*DR* 12.3). But first we begin with some comments regarding the problem of God in universalism (cf. *DR* 12.2).

The analysis offered in this book shows that universalism raises issues pertaining not only to salvation and human freedom but also to the character of God. Karl Barth noted that assertive or dogmatic universalism, which he generally referred to as *apokatastasis,* is a threat to the freedom and self-sufficiency of God as presented in the Bible. Barth wrote, "It is His concern what is to be the final extent of the circle [of salvation]. If we are to respect the freedom of divine grace, we cannot venture . . . the doctrine of the so-called *apokatastasis.* No such right or necessity can legitimately be deduced. Just as the gracious God does not need to elect or call any single man, so He does not need to elect or call all mankind."[6] Assertive universalism, as Barth saw it, is based on anthropocentric premises: "It is from an optimistic estimate of man in conjunction with this postulate of the infinite potentiality of the divine being that the assertion of a final redemption of each and all, known as the doctrine of the *apokatastasis,* usually draws its inspiration and power. [The apostle] Paul does not start from this point."[7]

On the one hand, Barth affirmed that God is God and that God is free. God does not need us, yet we need God. On the other hand, Barth's advocacy of a

6. Barth, *CD* II/2, 417.
7. Barth, *CD* II/2, 295.

doctrine of universal election—beginning with the 1942 publication of *Church Dogmatics* II/2—pressed in a different direction. No longer, as in Barth's earlier writings, was there simply a *God-who-is*, but now there was a *God-who-is-for-us*. The final volumes of the *Church Dogmatics* whipsaw back and forth between these competing pictures of God. Unsurprisingly, Barth's interpreters have become divided in recent decades in attempting to sort out a basic metaphysical problem or paradox evoked by the *Church Dogmatics*: Does God become the God he is only in and through the decision to be "for us," or is God who he is independent of any such decision or self-determination?

If the later writings of Barth show a certain unclarity regarding God, then many later theologians influenced by Barth—Jürgen Moltmann, Hans Urs von Balthasar, Robert Jenson, Bruce McCormack, and others—clearly opted against the God-who-is and for the God-who-is-for-us. The latter construal of God, as Bruce Marshall has argued, implies a reconceptualization of salvation itself, so that it is at least in part an *intra-divine* as well as *extra-divine* process: "Conceived in this way, the reconciliation of the world to God seems to put God in need of reconciliation with himself. God reconciles the world to himself by making the world's sin and death, even its Godforsakenness, his own in the Person of the Son."[8] Here one begins to see an analogy between twentieth-century and earlier gnostic or esoteric theologies of the suffering God, whose inner crisis brought about the fashioning of the human and material worlds, and whose self-reconciling process will restore God's original wholeness and accomplish final salvation for all.

Universalist theology creates problems for the Christian doctrine of God and doctrine of grace. It does so by limiting the independence and self-sufficiency of God and imperiling the freedom and graciousness of grace. It thus becomes clear why Paul Molnar speaks of universalism as "a problem grounded in the doctrine of God."[9] Not content with salvation for everyone as merely a possible or a contingent result, universalist thinkers have sought to identify some basis in the very nature of God that guarantees the universalist outcome. Alfred North Whitehead wrote that "Christianity . . . has always been a religion seeking a metaphysic." All the more, one might say that universalism has been a doctrine "seeking a metaphysic."[10] With the recent arrival of kenotic-relational theologies since the 1990s, the quest for a universalist "metaphysic" has now ripened into a picture of God as "essentially kenotic"—a view that renders the

8. B. Marshall, "Absolute and the Trinity," 159.

9. Molnar, "Thomas F. Torrance," 167. In context, Molnar is referring to John A. T. Robinson's attempt to link eschatology with the doctrine of God, but the point could be broadened to cover many other theological authors of the last sixty to seventy years.

10. Whitehead, *Religion in the Making*, 39.

Creator as inherently limited alongside the creatures God has fashioned. It is as though God made a rock so big that he cannot lift it.[11]

Such a depotentiated God would be not only unwilling but also unable to exercise divine judgment against creatures—sending Lucifer into the lake of fire or excluding unrepentant sinners from heaven. One might compare this "essentially kenotic" God with a high school teacher, not allowed to expel anyone, who faces unruly or even criminal behavior in the classroom. She might give students a time-out yet find herself compelled to readmit even the worst offenders, regardless of what they have done, because "relationality" with each student requires her to remain forever linked as teacher to each individual student. Though the troublemakers kindle a fire at the back of the classroom, they remain students in good standing. This way of thinking about God has little in common with the biblical picture of a holy and majestic God who created all things from nothing and is rightly referred to as Lord, Master, and King. Such a diminished view of God does not sufficiently distinguish creation from redemption. Neither does it allow for the fact that creatures' self-chosen sinning is profoundly offensive to God and threatens to establish a deep rift between a holy God and sinful creatures. While a gracious God loves all that he has made, a holy God is provoked by creatures' sin. Small though it might appear in our own sight, sin is no small thing in God's sight. The thinking underlying the diminished view of God is anthropocentric. Baldly stated, it is the idea that God will save everyone because God needs to save everyone, and that God needs to save everyone because God needs everyone. Every creature matters, and I matter. God needs me to be God. Without me God cannot be God. The Brethren of the Free Spirit said these sorts of things—that they had cocreated the world with God (DR 4.12). Some contemporary theologians likewise speak of being cocreators with God.[12] Many more people carry such things in their hearts, mentally raising themselves to God's level or lowering God to their own.

Not every Christian who considers or embraces universalism will be aware of the long-term theological consequences of affirming this doctrine. In arguing for "evangelical universalism," Robin Parry urges contemporary evangelical Christians to add belief in universal salvation to their repertoire of beliefs, without however altering what they already believe regarding the character of God, the Trinity, Christ's humanity and divinity, the atonement, the nature of salvation,

---

11. Thomas Jay Oord, in *The Uncontrolling Love of God*, argues that God is not only "voluntarily kenotic" (i.e., self-emptying) but is also "essentially kenotic." See DR, 683–84n311.

12. In the Hebrew Bible, the verb *bara'* (to create) appears with God as its subject in all cases, and the same is true of the Greek New Testament and the verb *ktizō*. The exegetical implication is that creating is purely and exclusively a divine prerogative. The contemporary language about human beings as God's "cocreators" is at odds with the biblical representation.

and so on (*DR* 11.4).[13] Yet the chapter on Anglo-American universalism (*DR* 6) showed what happened two centuries ago when one group of evangelicals accepted universalism. The outcome was ironic. The theology of these evangelicals turned-universalists shifted profoundly, leading ultimately to an official rejection of Jesus's divinity and the acceptance of unitarianism. What began as a well-intentioned impulse to expand grace to everyone—and to argue that Christ's death would save not only believers but everyone—ended up as the very opposite. What tasted sweet in the mouth was bitter in the stomach. Universalist thinkers deduced the conclusion that Christ's death accomplished nothing. Beginning with Hosea Ballou's *Treatise on Atonement* (1805), American universalists began to jettison all forms of atonement theology. Once it had omitted the crucial doctrine of Christ's atoning death, the all-grace teaching ended up as a no-grace teaching, and universalist theology drifted toward moralism. During the nineteenth century, many universalists continued to believe in postmortem preparation for heaven. By the early twentieth century, belief in the afterlife among many universalists became hazy and indefinite. Teachings on human sin and divine grace gave way to a message of moral uplift through individual, ethical striving.

To explain the relationship of the doctrine of universal salvation to the other Christian doctrines, one might use the analogy of a chess game. In chess, every move of a piece on the board has implications for the status of the other pieces. The position of a lowly pawn might determine whether more important pieces like the king and the queen are safe or in danger and whether a state of check or checkmate occurs. What is more, each move has implications that may become apparent not immediately but only several moves ahead. Indeed, the mark of the chess grand master lies in his or her ability to foresee many moves ahead the ultimate implications of each move of a chess piece, and so to choose moves that are advantageous over the long term and to reject moves that might be game-ending. In a comparable way, the doctrine of universal salvation, though initially appealing, seems to be a game-ending move that ends up undoing other doctrines such as the doctrine of the atonement and perhaps also the doctrine of Jesus's divinity.

12.1. The Cumulative Argument: A Survey of Preceding Chapters

Chapter 1 showed that the Christian church through the centuries—Catholic, Orthodox, Protestant, evangelical, or Pentecostal—has consistently taught a final, twofold state of heaven and hell. Universalism has nearly always been

13. For an argument along these lines, see Parry, "Evangelical Universalism."

regarded as a serious mistake, if not a heresy, both false in itself and productive of other theological mistakes. Historically speaking, tolerance for universalism was greatest in the Orthodox Church, where at least a few respected figures (e.g., Gregory of Nyssa) were universalists. Yet the tolerance was just that and no more. While universalism was allowable as a private opinion of individual thinkers, it never became official teaching in any of the Orthodox churches, nor did these churches allow it to be taught publicly as Orthodox doctrine. In Western Christianity, universalism was likewise never an officially sanctioned teaching, except in the very small universalist societies (e.g., Jane Lead's Philadelphian Society) and then in a Universalist Church that once had a sizable membership in the United States. From a historical standpoint, the upsurge of interest in and adherence to universalism among Christian academics since the 1960s and 1970s—and among increasing numbers of Christian laypersons since the 1980s and 1990s—is unprecedented in the history of the church. The Christian church in each of its major, historical branches previously held to a particularist, not universalist, view of salvation.

Chapter 2 traced the origin of Christian universalism to a period some decades prior to Origen, the best-known Christian universalist of the early church or indeed of any epoch. As far as the evidence allows one to say, the first religious teachers to insist that every human being is destined for heaven were the second-century Christian gnostics associated with Alexandria, Egypt—for example, Basilides, the school of Valentinus, and the Carpocratians. The Nag Hammadi documents suggest the same conclusion. The complex and contradictory movement known as "gnosis" included an idea of comprehensive *apokatastasis*, or restoration of fallen spirits to God. Gnostic teachers generally portrayed the story of salvation according to a threefold schema of *unity-diversity-unity*: a primal spiritual unity with God, a lapse into diversity (understood as evil), and a final return to unity with God. Origen's *On First Principles* embodied the same schema. Origen did not invent, but sought to amend, improve, and "biblicize" an already existing gnostic theory of salvation. The innumerable debates over Origen's ideas from the third and fourth centuries (e.g., Bishop Peter of Alexandria, Methodius of Olympus, Epiphanius) up to the seventeenth century (e.g., Samuel Parker, Jean Leclerc, Pierre Bayle) are eloquent testimony to the difficulties inherent in Origen's theological project of biblicizing a gnostic theory.

Chapter 2 also showed that the history of Christian universalism is neither coextensive nor coterminous with the history of Origenism. The problem is that historians and theologians have looked for universalism in the wrong places and neglected authors who belonged to what Cyril O'Regan has called a "third kind" of Western religious thought, neither conservative-traditional nor liberal-revisionist but gnostic-kabbalist-esoteric.[14] The second- and third-century gnostics, Stephen bar Sudaili, John Scotus Eriugena, the Cathars, Pico della Mirandola, Guillaume Postel, the early Jewish Kabbalists, Isaac Aboab, and such Islamic universalists as Ibn 'Arabi and Jalal al-Din Rumi attest the existence of a gnostic-kabbalist-esoteric universalism stretching from the second century to the modern era and manifesting itself in Jewish, Christian, and Islamic contexts. According to the general teaching here, the human self at its inmost level is a "spark of the divine," originating with God, prior to its entry into the human body, and thus is destined finally to return to God. The interreligious comparison of Jewish and Islamic universalism with Christian universalism demonstrates the strong association of universalism with esotericism rather than with Christianity as such. From about 1700 onward, the dominant forms of Christian universalism are to a surprising extent linked to the teachings, writings, and legacy of Jakob Böhme.

Chapters 3 and 4 examined the long and tortuous history of "Origenism," which was never a unified or well-integrated set of ideas but rather a cluster of related teachings. This is not to say that Origen himself failed to be a unified and well-integrated thinker. Yet Origen's explicit or implicit followers faced a dilemma. The cosmic narrative and salvation story contained in Origen's *On First Principles* was conceptually tight and theologically appealing, especially in the way in which it justified the existence of evil in the world, explained how and why God desires and wills only good for everyone, and anticipated a final restoration (*apokatastasis*) of all fallen spiritual beings, including Satan and the evil spirits. The problem was that this Origenian "system" included elements that clearly went beyond the bounds of official church teaching and the clear teaching of Scripture (e.g., preexistent souls, the earthly body as secondary to the human spirit, and the salvation of Satan). So the dilemma among Origen's followers was whether to cleave tightly to the "system," with its great self-consistency and intellectual cogency, or else to revise Origen's teaching to make it more compatible with church tradition and a more literal exegesis of the Bible. The Origenists themselves could never resolve the difficulties endemic to Origenism, and this may be one reason why the movement gradually died out during the early modern period. By the early 1800s, there was a residue of Origenism among German and English Romantic poets (e.g., Novalis and Wordsworth). We are born into this world, wrote William Wordsworth, "trailing clouds of glory."[15] Yet belief in preexistent souls, wrote Samuel Taylor Coleridge,

---

14. Cyril O'Regan speaks of "a band of ostensibly Christian discourses in the post-Reformation period, which are neither orthodox nor liberal, but of a genuinely third kind" (*Gnostic Return in Modernity*, 1–2).

15. Wordsworth, "Ode: Intimations of Immortality from Recollections of Early Childhood," lines 59–66: "Our birth is but a sleep and a forgetting: / The Soul that rises with us, our life's Star, / Hath had

while "very intelligible poetry," was "very wild philosophy."[16] By the nineteenth century, Origenism as a serious theological option had more or less vanished.

Chapters 3 and 4 showed that many of the church's leading thinkers through the early centuries were anti-Origenists, including Theophilus of Alexandria, the later Jerome, Shenoute of Atripe, Augustine, Severus of Antioch, Philoxenus of Mabbug, Jacob of Sarug, Barsanuphius, Maximus the Confessor, Simon the Persecuted, and Thomas Aquinas. Of these early Christian anti-Origenists, there were three figures—Augustine, Maximus the Confessor, and Thomas Aquinas—who presented powerful philosophical critiques of Origen centered on one or another aspect of Origen's complex, many-sided theology. Augustine objected to Origen's Platonic metaphysics of the soul and to his idea of freedom. Along Platonic lines, Origen reasoned that the soul, having an endless future life with God, must have had an endless past life with God. Augustine objected, insisting that the human soul, like the human body, had a beginning in time, and yet, in the state of salvation, both the soul and the resurrected and transformed body would never have an ending in time. Regarding freedom, Augustine objected that Origen's idea that the will is always free to turn either toward or away from God meant that there could be no final stability, even among the saints with God in heaven. Maximus objected that Origen's threefold schema implied a transition from stasis to movement and back to stasis. In Maximus's metaphysically subtle argument, to be a creature is to be in movement, and this meant that Origen's theory of an original state of all souls in quiescent enjoyment of God was mistaken. Thomas Aquinas, in an equally subtle and far-reaching argument, held that Origen erred by presuming that all souls were at first equal with one another, fell into inequality, and would finally be restored to equality. God had created the world from the first as a place of diversity and distinction, argued Aquinas, and such diversity and distinction among creatures was not something evil but was a positive good.

In differing ways, Augustine, Maximus, and Aquinas all argued in effect that Origen had not allowed the creature to be a creature, for God to be God, and for these two to be fully distinct from each other. Origen mixed up earth with heaven, eternalizing and divinizing the human soul and so making the soul's final destiny with God an inevitable outcome. The anti-Origenist arguments of the monk Barsanuphius were less metaphysical and more pragmatic in character. He viewed Origenism as a dangerous teaching because it distracted

---

elsewhere its setting, / And cometh from afar: / Not in entire forgetfulness, / And not in utter nakedness, / But trailing clouds of glory do we come / From God, who is our home" (https://www.poetryfoun dation.org/poems/45536/ode-intimations-of-immortality-from-recollections-of-early-childhood).

16. Rowell, *Hell and the Victorians*, 64, citing E. L. Griggs, ed., *Collected Letters of Samuel Taylor Coleridge* (1956–59), 1:278 (letter dated December 17, 1796).

attention from the pressing tasks of prayer, self-denial, and Christian service, teaching its devotees to rely on their own reasoning and to cast off an appropriate attitude of intellectual humility and respect for the mysteries of God's love, justice, and power.

Chapter 5 traced the modern resurgence of universalism, with its roots in the religious thought of Jakob Böhme, but emerging first among Böhme's followers in London, England. While Origenist universalism (ca. 200–ca. 1700) offered variations on *a basic theme of preexistent, fallen, and restored souls*, Böhmist universalism (ca. 1700–ca. 1950) centered on *a dialectic of divine self-differentiation and divine self-reconciliation*. The roots of Böhme's picture of a conflicted God lay in Jewish Kabbalah and its modifications within Christian Cabala. Adaptations of Böhmist thought appeared later in the German idealist philosophies of Hegel and Schelling as well as in certain twentieth-century theologies that were in some way affiliated with Hegel (e.g., Moltmann) or with Schelling (e.g., Tillich). Though Böhme himself was not a universalist, Böhme's ideas helped to spawn universalist theologies not only in England but also in Germany, the German-American colonies, France, and Russia. Hans Martensen, the Danish Lutheran bishop who bore the brunt of Søren Kierkegaard's criticism, was himself a Böhmist after a fashion.

Chapter 6 examined the rise and fall of Anglo-American universalism, showing that its earliest American expressions drew on German, Pietist, and Böhmist currents rather than on the better-known Calvinist-trinitarian universalism of James Relly in England and that of Relly's disciple John Murray in the American colonies. The first universalist book published in the colonies, Paul Siegvolck's *The Everlasting Gospel* (1753), was the English translation of a German, Böhmist, universalist treatise. In early America there were at least three types of universalism (epitomized by Caleb Rich, John Murray, and Elhanan Winchester), and these three types were mutually inconsistent. Internal arguments among the universalists generated many of the same arguments that external debates with anti-universalists had presented. To a large extent, the Anglo-American universalist movement became self-defeating. The bitter and protracted "Restorationist Controversy" (over postmortem punishment) was never resolved, with so-called ultra-universalists arguing that salvation comes immediately to everyone at the moment of death, and so-called restorationists arguing that wicked behavior in the present life had to be linked to some form of punishment in the next life. This issue remains unresolved among Christian universalists to the present time.

Chapter 7 treated German thinkers: Kant, Müller, Schleiermacher, Hegel, Schelling, and Tillich. The critical philosophy of the later Kant (which launched the German idealist tradition) flowed from reflection on the nature of human moral agency and included a pivotal notion of "transcendental selfhood." Such a "transcendental self" was not limited by the spatial, temporal, or material restrictions of the earthly, embodied self. One possible implication of Kant's reasoning was that the present moral condition of each person was a consequence of choices made by the "transcendental self." The parallel between Kant and Origen is clear. Both thinkers sought to justify and to rationalize the inequities of the present world in terms of choices made beyond the boundaries of the present world. In Julius Müller, Kant's reasoning led into an unusual non-universalistic Origenism. Each one merited his or her present condition on the basis of one's transcendental choices, and this served as a rationale for the obvious inequalities of human life. Everyone had either to choose or to reject God, and hell might last forever.

Schleiermacher's idea of human solidarity in sin and in redemption tended toward universalism, and his unitary election doctrine had a major influence on Barth. Hegel's philosophical interpretation of Jesus's cross culminated in a universal divine presence and an equally universal community of the Spirit. Schelling's cosmocentric—rather than cross-centered—version of idealism led into a final, universal restoration of creatures to the Creator. Schelling's disciple, Tillich, exhibited the same pattern, though Tillich preserved much of Plato's story of the fall and restoration of souls in a "half-way demythologized" form.

Chapter 8 examined a series of Russian thinkers—Solovyov, Berdyaev, Florovsky, and Bulgakov—against the backdrop of Russian church and intellectual history. On the basis of an analysis of his sources as well as his esoteric arguments and occultic practices, Solovyov appears to be a figure in the Western esoteric lineage. This may be one of the underlying reasons for the murkiness and lack of clear definition in Russian Sophiology from its earlier phases onward. Moreover, this also helps to explain why Solovyov speaks much of "Christ" as a spiritual principle but little of "Jesus" as a historical figure. Florovsky was highly critical of Solovyov and regarded him as a "gnostic," despite Bulgakov's appreciation of Solovyov. Solovyov affirmed a final *apokatastasis*, yet the relation of the eschaton to the progress of history remains unclear, a problem that Solovyov shares with Moltmann (*DR* 9.10–9.11). Berdyaev closely followed one aspect of Böhme's thought by making the chaotic freedom of the *Ungrund* foundational. Berdyaev denounced the doctrine of an eternal hell as diabolical. Yet he had few disciples. Not many were ready to accept Berdyaev's notion that the principle of chaotic freedom had metaphysical priority over the personal or trinitarian God. Bulgakov in *The Bride of the Lamb* (1944) offered what may be the most ambitious and systematic attempt ever to defend Christian universalism and to address the many doctrinal issues evoked by this teaching. Ultimately, Bulgakov's teaching removes the principle of grace by insisting that every individual "expiates" all his or her own sins through purgatorial and penitential suffering. Neither a pure heaven nor a pure hell exists, according to Bulgakov. Heaven becomes somewhat hellish, because everyone bound for heaven still contains some bit of hell within themselves. Hell in turn becomes rather heavenly, since the infernal denizens are ultimately on their way out of hell and into heaven. Bulgakov's universalism comes at a heavy price: the loss of grace. And he is only able to defend his views exegetically by taking liberties with the biblical text.

Chapter 9 included an analysis of Karl Barth's theology, especially his doctrine of universal election. As Barth himself noted, his doctrine of universal election was novel. He was breaking with centuries, and indeed with more than a millennium, of Christian teaching. In our analysis of Barth's approach to the Hebrew Bible or Old Testament, it became clear that Barth was setting aside not only Christian tradition but also Jewish teaching, which has always conceived of election in a particularistic fashion (i.e., pertaining to Abraham's descendants). Yet from whatever angle one regards it—exegetically, logically, or metaphysically—Barth's notion of universal election in *Church Dogmatics* II/2 is weakly argued and poorly supported. Some of Barth's assertions—for example, "Jesus Christ is the electing God"—made his position on election not only weak but also perhaps incoherent. The ongoing debates among Barth scholars would not have gone on for so long if Barth himself had been clear and consistent in his affirmations.

Barth's doctrine of an eternal Godmanhood leads us back to a common objection to Barth's theology for over half a century. Critics insist that Barth shortchanges redemption in its concrete, physical, and historical aspects by subsuming it into the realm of eternity. Christian thinkers as diverse as Emil Brunner, G. C. Berkouwer, Gustav Wingren, Robert Jenson, Alister McGrath, and Kathryn Tanner have all voiced this objection. The "mutation" that Barth introduced into the twentieth-century theological genome (i.e., by introducing the innovative idea of universal election) brought many further changes, as the God-who-is (of the early Barth) shifted more and more in the direction of the God-who-is-for-us (of Moltmann, Jenson, and McCormack). The recent kenotic-relational onto-theologies (so termed by Kevin Vanhoozer) represent an even more dramatic departure from traditional notions of God's self-sufficiency, freedom, and independence. Barth's universal election doctrine seems to be one of the roots of this problem. David Congdon's effort to mediate between Barth's hope for universal salvation and Bultmann's existentialist reading of the Bible focuses on a supposedly universal experience of "unconscious cocrucifixion with Christ." Yet there seems to be no empirical basis for Congdon's assertion, and the experience in question is defined so broadly as to evacuate the notion of "cocrucifixion" of any clear or distinct meaning.

Chapter 10 dealt with Roman Catholic theology, which as recently as the 1950s showed little sign of shifting its teaching on eschatology. According to the traditional Catholic teaching, only those having received Christian baptism were candidates for heaven, and those practicing Catholics who died without having made satisfaction for their venial sins went first to purgatory, prior to entering heaven. Those persons who died in a state of mortal sin went immediately to hell. Regarding non-Christians, there was little hope for final salvation, and perhaps not much hope regarding non-Catholic Christians. The traditional Catholic motif of Christ's descent to the dead (DR 1.6) meant that righteous persons who died trusting in Israel's God would join the Christian saints in heaven. Taken more liberally, Christ's descent offered some measure of hope for virtuous non-monotheists. This general set of traditional eschatological views began to shift decisively among Catholic theologians and laity beginning in the 1970s and 1980s. It was not Vatican II itself but the later development and reception of the council's documents that marked the change of views on final salvation. While the discussions in the 1970s often centered on Karl Rahner's theology of the "anonymous Christian" and the related motif of *inclusive salvation*, the discussions in the 1980s—as inaugurated by Hans Urs von Balthasar's *Dare We Hope?* (1986)—were directed toward the question of *universal salvation*. In a generation's time, Catholic teaching and theologizing opened the door to the inclusive salvation of some non-Christians and then to the possibility of salvation for all persons. Certain statements by Pope John Paul II and Pope Francis have suggested that one or both popes have held to "hopeful universalism," as it had earlier been suggested by Balthasar.

Chapter 10 traced the root of recent changes in Catholic teaching on eschatology to an altered understanding of the distinction between nature and grace in the theology of Henri de Lubac. Karl Rahner intensified the process that started with de Lubac, blurring the distinction between nature and grace in his conception of the "supernatural existential" and implying that human beings might be saved without having believed in Christ or even in God, by inwardly affirming an unrecognized divine call to authentic moral life. Salvation might as well occur outside the church as within the church, through the sacraments or apart from them. This Rahnerian teaching has created a dilemma for the Catholic Church and its call for a "new evangelization."

The "hopeful universalism" of Hans Urs von Balthasar was a major focus in chapter 10, which traced Balthasar's thought back to Russian sources as well as to the study of the church fathers and the personal and theological influences of Henri de Lubac and Karl Barth. Balthasar's theological dependence on Adrienne von Speyr for his "Holy Saturday theology" and his understanding of God's inner-trinitarian life remains problematic, because von Speyr's visionary experiences were never assessed and approved as acknowledged Catholic teaching. Balthasar's notion of *Urkenosis* suggests that elements of division and conflict may lie within God himself. On analysis, Balthasar's "hopeful universalism" proves to be largely a form of wishful thinking, since it does not rest on any firm divine promise to save everyone. What is more, Balthasar's suggestion that each person must bear in mind the possibility of his or her own damnation does not fit well with his general stance of "hopeful universalism," which must include a hopefulness for all persons, including oneself.

Chapter 11 treated contemporary universalists, divided into various groups on the basis of their arguments, associations, and affinities. These included universalists of the liberal, unitarian, esoteric, evangelical, and Pentecostal types. Most contemporary universalists express dissatisfaction with historic Christianity and the historic church, and to a surprising extent their arguments overlap with those of "new atheists" or secular apologists who argue against belief in the Christian God. This suggests that the recent turn toward universalism may be linked to an apologetic interest in making Christianity credible to an increasingly secular and even hostile world. Robin Parry's effort to provide an exegetical foundation for universalism in a literal reading of the Bible is intriguing but ultimately unpersuasive. His reading of the New Testament Gospels and the book of Revelation strains credulity. Thomas Talbott too has difficulty in showing the compatibility of universalism with the text of the New Testament. One of the surprising developments is the new Pentecostal-Charismatic universalism, which is strongly antinomian (i.e., by rejecting any notion that Christians are bound to the moral law) and conforming more and more to esoteric versions of universalism (i.e., by regarding the human self as eternal and akin to God). The various forms of popular Christian universalism since the year 2000 use differing and conflicting arguments in favor of universalism. The Christian universalisms of the new millennium are like those of the nineteenth century (*DR* 6) in offering a smorgasbord of theological options but no single, coherent, or cohesive theology of universalism.

The appendices supplement and support various parts of the overall argument. Appendix B, on Zoroastrian eschatology, is devoted to showing that early second-century Christian gnostic universalism in Alexandria and its environs most likely antedated the appearance of Zoroastrian universalism. In this case, the direction of influence is more likely to have been from Egypt to Persia than from Persia to Egypt. Appendix F treats the little-known phenomenon of Islamic universalism, which appears in connection with Sufism or Islamic esotericism. Unlike Jewish Kabbalah, which had a direct influence on the history of Christian universalism, Islamic Sufi universalism ought to be seen as a development parallel to the Jewish and Christian forms of universalism.

Islamic universalism is important because it helps to confirm a basic claim in this book regarding the link between universalism and gnostic-esoteric religions. In each of the three Abrahamic religions, one commonly finds universalism not in the exoteric forms of faith—based on more or less literal readings of the sacred texts—but rather in the esoteric manifestations of each religion: Kabbalah, Sufism, and Western (Christian-based) esotericism.

12.2. The Problem of God in Christian Universalism

In most of the forms of Christian universalism treated in this volume, a primal or divine drama must be played out in order for all creatures to come to salvation.[17] In second-century gnosis, there is a crisis within God or the divine Pleroma caused by the fall of Sophia, who lapses yet is later restored to the divine realm. In Origen and in later Origenism, the preexistent souls, at first in union with God, fall out of harmony, enter into physical bodies, pass through a learning process, and are finally brought back to their primal unity with God. In Jewish Kabbalah—particularly in its Lurianic version—the "vessels" made by God are unable to contain the light that God pours into them, and then the primal catastrophe of "the shattering of the vessels" causes the scattering of the light particles and the emergence of the physical universe. As in the rest of these grand narratives, the divine drama involves the particles of light returning to the source from which they emerged.

The term "primal drama" might be more apt as a generic designation than "divine drama." For certain thinkers, the drama is in the strictest sense intradivine, especially as focused on the relation between God the Father and God the Son (so Hegel, Barth, and Balthasar). Yet, in other cases, there is a multiplicity of nondivine or quasi-divine entities that in some way participate in the drama of world creation or divine self-fashioning. In second- and third-century gnosis, the *plērōma* was understood as a pluralized divine realm, with hierarchical ordering, so that some aeons were of lower or ambiguously divine status. This is why Sophia falls from the divine realm and must be restored. Böhme presented competing versions of a primal drama, some involving the *Ungrund*, others with Lucifer (a brother to Christ) as protagonist, and so forth. The Sophiological thought of Solovyov and Bulgakov centers on the ambiguous divine/nondivine Sophia. Schelling's account of world origin through the self-limitation of God as Absolute involves the emerging cosmos as the Other, against which God's being is both defined and delimited. So Schelling's primal

17. On Mormon cosmology, see *DR* appendix K.

drama involves the world itself as partner or counterpart in an emergent God-world relationship. French Martinism (*DR* 5.11–5.12) and Mormon theology present complex versions of a primal drama tied to a universal (or near universal) return of spirits to God.

In the thought of Jakob Böhme, the Christian or trinitarian God only comes to exist in the midst of a struggle with the chaos and negativity of the *Ungrund*. In another variation of the primal myth, Böhme depicted Lucifer's struggle against Christ or the Father as "God against God," and his theosophy evolved from this starting point. A succession of British Böhmists, including Jane Lead, William Law, Thomas Erskine of Linlathen, and George MacDonald, adopted aspects of Böhme's theology, while generally moderating its dualistic aspects and modifying it in the direction of universalism. Much the same can be said of German-American Böhmists such as George de Benneville and Elhanan Winchester and the German Philadelphian universalists Johann and Johanna Petersen. In the French esotericist Martines de Pasqually, one finds an idiosyncratic theory of divine emanation and a hierarchical universe of angels, demons, and humans, in connection with a theory of reintegration and reunion with God. Pasqually's disciple Louis-Claude de Saint-Martin sought to wed Pasqually's theories with Böhme's theology, while maintaining Pasqually's universalism.

Islamic universalism includes both an Origenist-type fall and restoration of souls (in Jalal al-Din Rumi) and a Böhmist-type dialectic of divine self-differentiation and self-reconciliation (in Ibn 'Arabi). There is divine or primal drama in Islamic universalism as in Christian universalism.

In the German philosopher G. W. F. Hegel there appears a new kind of divine drama, centered less on any primal state and more on Jesus's life and death, wherein the self-alienation and self-reconciliation of *Geist* (Spirit, Mind) is accomplished. One might say that Hegel "Christocentrized" and "crucicentrized" the dialectic of divine self-alienation and self-reconciliation that he had inherited from Böhme. Hegel's dramatic, death-of-God theology of the cross has been highly influential in Christian theology since the 1960s. In the philosophy of Friedrich Schelling, one finds a more cosmocentric and less Christocentric understanding of the divine drama. Not only at the cross but also in the act of creating, God must become kenotic, self-limiting, or self-relativizing. God as the Absolute must become self-limited, so that God may enter into a mutually conditioning relation to the created world, with the final result that the world attains its *apokatastasis* and "God may be all in all." This Schellingian divine drama had an impact on the thought of Vladimir Solovyov and Sergius Bulgakov as well as on certain contemporary kenotic-relational theologians, such as Philip Clayton. In Russian Sophiology, divine drama became Sophia's struggle. At first divided against herself, Sophia will undergo self-integration and final union with God.

In Karl Barth's theology, there is a denial in principle of divine drama (i.e., in Barth's insistence on God's freedom and independence), while nonetheless divine drama comes in the back door through Barth's dramatic reconceptualization of the doctrine of election. Because Barth's doctrine of election absorbs into itself, so to speak, the earthly drama of Christ's rejection, crucifixion, suffering, resurrection, and vindication, the human conflict of good versus evil gets imported into the eternal and intra-trinitarian life of God. The dramatic history of Jesus's life, rejection, and death migrates from an earthly context into the primal, primordial realm of God's self-determination. Jesus's cross is relocated above, in the atmosphere, rather than on terra firma.[18] Robert Jenson's and Bruce McCormack's "historicized christology" (per Paul Molnar) picks up the drama embedded in Barth's election doctrine and further amplifies it. Jürgen Moltmann, influenced as much by Hegel and Kabbalah as by Barth, not only emphasizes the drama of Jesus's death but also interprets it in terms of an inherently, eternally suffering God. In Hans Urs von Balthasar, divine drama appears in the doctrine of *Urkenosis*, in which God the Father must "utterly strip himself" to engender God the Son, so that "infinite distance" enters into the intra-trinitarian life. God himself is at risk, as Balthasar himself states. Another enactment of divine drama occurs in connection with Balthasar's theology of Holy Saturday. In this Holy Week analogue to the *Urkenosis*, it is now God the Son who risks all in his utter identification with sinners and his absolute, "cadaver-like obedience" (German *Kadavergehorsam*) to God the Father.[19]

There are forms of Christian universalism that do not readily fit this pattern of divine or primal drama. This would include especially the high-Calvinist universalists such as James Relly and John Murray, whose belief in universal salvation was a deduction from their strong doctrine of divine sovereignty. Yet, historically speaking, this particular form of universalism was a minor development. Late in life, Murray said that he knew of only one minister in the United States who adhered to his own version of universalism. The later acclamation of John Murray as the "father" of American universalism seems to derive from the Unitarian side of the merged Unitarian Universalist movement. This may be because Murray's theology was much closer to that of the American Unitarians than that of Elhanan Winchester, with its German Böhmist undertones. The historical evidence in any case does not support the idea that Relly's or Murray's high-Calvinist universalism was attractive to any more than a few Calvinistic intellectuals. What we might call the mainstream of Christian universalism—in its

18. The mental image evoked for me by Barth's doctrine of election is Salvador Dali's renowned painting "Christ of St. John of the Cross" (1951)—an image of the crucified Jesus floating in the atmosphere.
19. Balthasar, *TD* 4:232.

Origenist, Böhmist, and twentieth-century expressions—affirmed that all will be saved in connection with some sort of primal, divine, or intra-trinitarian drama.

One response to these ideas regarding divine drama is *methodological*. The objection is that affirmations of divine drama are suspect in violating the appropriate apophatic reserve that every Christian theologian should use in speaking of God. On the Father's eternal begetting of the Son, Gregory of Nazianzus wrote:

> The begetting of God must be honored in silence. It is a great thing for you to learn that he was begotten. But the manner of his generation we will not admit that even angels can conceive, much less you. Shall I tell you how it was? It was in a manner known to the Father who begot, and to the Son who was begotten. Anything more than this is hidden by a cloud, and escapes your dim sight.[20]

In the same vein, Kevin Vanhoozer suggests that Balthasar, in his account of the intra-trinitarian relation of Father and Son, was attempting to say more than can properly be said: "To respond to Balthasar: theologians should proceed most carefully (i.e., non-speculatively) where even angels fear to tread. While it is possible to infer certain things about the inner life of God on the basis of its outward expression in history, one looks in vain for biblical evidence that the eternal generation of the Son should be construed in terms of the Father's kenosis, the condition for the possibility of divine suffering." Vanhoozer adds that "Balthasar introduces a non-biblical complication into the drama when he speaks of the 'risk' the Father takes in begetting the Son, a risk that blossoms into divine possibility."[21] One may conclude that Christian theology in the twenty-first century needs to recover a sense of its boundaries and to apply an apophatic reserve at the proper point—namely, in speaking of God's inner-trinitarian relations. To borrow a phrase from Ludwig Wittgenstein, "philosophical problems arise when language goes on holiday."[22] Theological reflection becomes not only unguarded and risky but also unprofitable and jejune when it fails to recognize its own inherent limitations.

Another response to divine drama is *substantive*. The fundamental problem with primal or divine drama is that it conflicts with the biblical picture of God and the classical theological tradition of the Christian church. In the teaching of the Old and New Testaments, there simply is no division, conflict, or tragedy in God.[23]

20. Gregory of Nazianzus, *Theological Orations* 3.8, in Hardy and Richardson, *Christology of the Later Fathers*, 165.

21. Vanhoozer, *Remythologizing Theology*, 243.

22. Wittgenstein, *Philosophical Investigations*, sec. 38.

23. Neither is there tragedy—in the proper sense—within the created realm as presented in the Bible. Tragedy implies some kind of fatal necessity that gradually unspools itself—like the thread of life, in Greek mythology, spun by the three Fates and then suddenly cut off. Instead, in

To oversimplify, the classical Christian tradition shows us an *undramatic* God—Father, Son, and Spirit—but a *dramatic* picture on earth, where there is risk, uncertainty, conflict, contingency, and evil.[24] Jesus's life is dramatic. During the final week of his earthly existence, Jesus enters Jerusalem. How will the Jewish leaders respond? What will be the outcome? He is killed! Is this the end? So it seems. Yet the answer proves to be no, it is not the end. Jesus rises again, having triumphed over sin, Satan, and death. The life of Jesus is a dramatic unfolding of humanly contingent events, just as is the proclamation of the gospel to nations, families, and individuals, calling on each person to repent of sins and to believe in Christ. In contrast to this general picture, the message of ancient, medieval, modern, and contemporary universalism is quite different. In the inverted theology of universalism, it is within heaven or God's realm that one finds risk, uncertainty, contingency, and perhaps even evil (or the potential for evil). The placid realm of the eternal Trinity becomes turbulent. As if to compensate for the stormy skies above, the earthly realm now becomes strangely serene. Earthly life is no longer a place of risk and contingency, because the final outcome of the still-unfolding heavenly conflict is declared in advance, known in advance, and carries with it an assurance of final salvation for all fallen creatures.[25]

In this universalist teaching, something is amiss. God is God. God is. God is not at risk of perishing, ceasing to exist, or becoming divided against himself. Evil does not threaten God. On the other hand, evil most certainly threatens us, and the great and eternal threat to me is my own sin, according to the prayer said to be Augustine's: "O Lord, save me from that wicked man—myself!" The inverted theology noted above places risk, danger, and contingency in the wrong place (i.e., within God) while at least implicitly removing risk, danger, and contingency from where it actually lies (i.e., within the human sphere). Properly speaking, the drama is not "up there" but "down here." Christian thinkers in

---

the biblical narrative evil arises in the realm of created freedom, not by necessity but by creaturely choice. Gnostic and kabbalistic notions of tragedy, whether in God or even in the created world, are alien to the biblical or Christian message and worldview. For recent discussion, see Taylor and Waller, *Christian Theology and Tragedy*.

24. In speaking of an "undramatic God," the assertion is not that God is uninvolved with the world and creatures, as in the Aristotelian notion of God as "thought thinking itself." Instead the point is that the drama is enacted, so to speak, *between* God and creatures rather than *within* God. On God and drama, see Vanhoozer, *Drama of Doctrine*.

25. Someone might argue that traditional doctrines of divine predestination likewise remove the element of risk and contingency from human affairs. Yet the unconditional Augustinian-Calvinist and the conditional Molinist-Arminian versions of divine election both maintain that the outcome of election remains a mystery insofar as it pertains to particular persons. Even if determinate for God, individual outcomes remain indeterminate on the human level. Precisely for this reason, the public preaching and teaching of divine election is consistent with a pastoral and missiological posture of openness and uncertainty.

the twenty-first century need to recover the *undramatic God* of the Bible and the classical tradition and conversely to recover the *dramatic episode* that is human life in this world, with all of its opportunities and threats. When lived in the light of eternity as presented in the Bible, human life is an epic call to adventure, prayer, danger, and exertion, for one's own salvation and for the salvation of others.

Christian thinkers of the classical tradition have consistently held that God in himself is wholly free and independent of the world, having created all things from nothing. Following the rise of German idealist philosophy in the nineteenth century, the Catholic Church at the First Vatican Council reaffirmed its commitment to such an understanding of God. Canon 3 rejected the notion that "the substance and essence of God and all things is one and the same," while canon 4 argued against the notion that "finite beings, the corporeal as well as the spiritual, or at least the spiritual ones, have emanated from the divine substance; or that the divine essence becomes all things by self-manifestation or self-evolution; or lastly that God is the universal or indefinite being which, by self determination, constitutes the universality of beings, differentiated in genera, species, and individuals." Hegelian or Schellingian motifs lie in the background of these Catholic magisterial assertions. Canon 5 took issue with those who hold "that God created, not by an act of will free from all necessity, but with the same necessity by which he necessarily loves himself."[26]

During the twentieth century, Karl Barth's theology reiterated this Catholic and classical Christian theme of God's freedom, self-sufficiency, aseity, and independence. In his *Church Dogmatics*, Barth wrote that "in His Word becoming flesh, God acts with inward freedom and not in fulfillment of a law to which He is supposedly subject. His Word will still be His Word apart from this becoming, just as Father, Son and Holy Spirit would be none the less eternal God, if no world had been created."[27] Here he links the freedom of God in creating with the freedom of God in becoming incarnate. Both are expressions of God's essential independence from all constraints that might be imposed on him by the created world. Much later in his theological career, Barth asked: "Why should God not also be able, as eternal Love, to be sufficient unto himself? In His life as Father, Son, and Holy Spirit He would in truth be no lonesome, no egotistical God even without man, yes, even without the whole created universe."[28] Again Barth writes that God "could have remained satisfied with the fullness of His own being. If He had willed and decided in this way, He would not have

26. First Vatican Council (1869–70), Dogmatic Constitution *Dei Filius* on the Catholic Faith, Canons 3–5, in Denzinger, *Compendium*, 607 (nos. 3023–25).

27. Barth, *CD* I/2, 135.

28. Barth, *Humanity of God*, 50. For this reference—and those that follow from Barth, Torrance, and Webster—I am indebted to Molnar, *Faith, Freedom, and the Spirit*.

suffered any lack. He would still be eternal love and freedom. But . . . He has willed and decided otherwise."[29]

Thomas Torrance comments that "the world needs God to be what it is, but God does not need the world to be what he is. . . . The Creator was free not to create."[30] This means that "the Fatherhood of God is in no way dependent on or constituted by relation to what he has created outwith himself."[31] Regarding God's freedom and independence from the world, Torrance writes, "We do not say that God is Father, Son and Holy Spirit, because he becomes Father, Son and Holy Spirit to us. . . . He only becomes Father, Son, and Holy Spirit to us precisely because he is first and eternally Father, Son, and Holy Spirit in himself alone."[32] Torrance again writes, "The incarnation must be regarded as something 'new' even for God, for the Son was not eternally man any more than the Father was eternally Creator."[33] Along the same lines, John Webster argues that the world is not necessary to God but exists only contingently: "We do not understand the [divine] economy unless we take time to consider God who is, though creatures might not have been."[34]

Summarizing this classical Christian tradition regarding God, Bruce Marshall writes, "As gifts, creation and reconciliation must be free acts of the Triune God, and as free acts they must be contingent. Creation and reconciliation are free, and so contingent, not only as to whether they happen but as to how they happen. The Triune God might not have created a world, and having created one might not have reconciled it to himself when it fell away from him."[35] Marshall argues that "it seems impossible that the identities of the divine persons could be

---

29. Barth, *CD* III/1, 69. Compare the following statements: "The Word of God is properly understood only as a word which has truth and glory in itself and not just spoken to us. It would be no less God's eternal Word if it were not spoken to us" (*CD* I/1, 171–72). "'God for us' does not arise as a matter of course out of the 'God in Himself.' . . . It is true as an act of God, a step which God takes towards man" (*CD* I/1, 172). "The Word is what He is even before and apart from His being flesh. Even as incarnate He derives His being to all eternity from the Father and from Himself, and not from the flesh" (*CD* I/2, 136). "[God] could be everything only for Himself (and His life would not on that account be pointless, motionless and unmotivated, nor would it be any less majestic or any less the life of love)" (*CD* II/1, 280–81). "The divine essence does not, of course, need any actualization. On the contrary, it is the creative ground of all other, i.e., creaturely actualizations. Even as the divine essence of the Son it did not need his incarnation, his existence as man . . . to become actual" (*CD* IV/2, 113). "God loves, and to do so He does not need any being distinct from His own as the object of His love. If He loves the world and us, this is a free overflowing of the love in which He is and is God and with which he is not content, although He might be, since neither the world nor ourselves are indispensable to His love and therefore to His being" (*CD* IV/2, 755).
30. Torrance, *Divine and Contingent Order*, 34.
31. Torrance, *Christian Doctrine of God*, 207.
32. Torrance, *Doctrine of Jesus Christ*, 107.
33. Torrance, *Trinitarian Faith*, 155.
34. Webster, "Trinity and Creation," 7.
35. B. Marshall, "Absolute and the Trinity," 162–63.

contingent," because God is dependent on no one and nothing. Each person of the Trinity "would be the person he is, the person with whom we are allowed to become acquainted in time, even if there were no creatures." Since the Council of Nicaea, says Marshall, Christian theologians have "uniformly insisted" that "the identities of the three divine persons who freely give themselves to us in creation, redemption, and consummation are the same as they would be even if the three had not decided to create and give themselves to us."[36]

The patristic and medieval tradition—followed for the most part by Luther and Calvin—taught that suffering and death were properly ascribed to God the Son because of, and only because of, the human nature he freely assumed. Suffering and death were not in any sense ascribed to the divine nature that God the Son possesses from all eternity. This teaching of course required a *differentiation* of the divine and human natures—not, to be sure, a *separation* in Christ's person (in Nestorian fashion), but a recognition of the two natures' *distinctness* (in Chalcedonian fashion), as was characteristic of classical Christian reflection on the person of Christ.[37]

In contrast to this classical Christian doctrine of God, Bruce Marshall notes that "several basic theses endorsed by much modern Trinitarian theology seem to originate chiefly with Hegel," even though Hegel's influence has been "not merely indirect but subterranean" among those who were "almost always openly critical of him." According to Marshall, Hegelian motifs have been "variously articulated by (for example) Barth, Moltmann, Jüngel, and Balthasar, that in the suffering and death of Jesus[,] death, sin, and even divine rejection and God-forsakenness enter into the very being of God."[38] In *The Crucified God* (1972), Moltmann asserted that "only if all disaster, forsakenness by God, absolute death, the infinite curse of damnation and sinking into nothingness is in God himself, is community with this God [the source of] eternal salvation, infinite joy." This means for Moltmann that "in the death of the Son he suffers the death of his own being as Father."[39] Yet, as Marshall notes, by failing to mark "what belongs to God incarnate in virtue of his human nature and what belongs to him in virtue of his divine nature," Moltmann and other contemporary theologians

36. B. Marshall, *Trinity and Truth*, 262–64.
37. B. Marshall ("Absolute and the Trinity," 155) and Molnar (*Faith, Freedom, and the Spirit*, 293, 304, 307) both argue that much of contemporary theology, while not officially or overtly rejecting the two-natures doctrine, has made this doctrine functionally irrelevant. The eternalizing of Christ's humanity and the temporalizing of Christ's divinity, both characteristic of the newer "historicized christology," make it difficult to see how the dictum of the Council of Chalcedon (451 CE) that the divine and human natures are joined in Christ "without change" (*atreptos*) and "without confusion" (*asynchytos*) is currently being acknowledged and given full weight.
38. B. Marshall, "Absolute and the Trinity," 147–48, 153.
39. Moltmann, *Crucified God*, 246, 243.

have overseen "a massive expansion in the properties the divine nature is said to include, a vast catalogue of distinctively human characteristics . . . [so that] suffering, death, sin, and abandonment all enter into the divine nature itself."[40] The Son's human nature becomes an occasion for the introduction of further properties into the divine nature.[41]

Those advocating the dramatic conception of God, in Marshall's words, claim that "we must be bold enough . . . to see that on the cross what seems to be most foreign to God actually belongs to God's own nature." Yet "this is just the thought that structures the whole of Hegel's philosophy of religion." The dramatic view "appears to open up an abyss of separation and distance within God's Trinitarian life," and so "it is not immediately clear how these antidivine properties can belong to one possessor of the divine nature, namely the Son."[42] Marshall writes, "One might, perhaps, expect theologians to be wary of a Trinitarian claim that attributes . . . diastatis and opposition to the divine Persons. On the contrary, however, an exuberant embrace of this idea is now common in Trinitarian theology."[43] For example, Hans Urs von Balthasar argues that in his descent into hell, Jesus underwent the "second death" that the book of Revelation reserves for those who are finally rejected by God. In believing in Christ's incarnation, says Balthasar, we must see that "it is really God who takes upon himself what is, at all events, opposed to God and eternally rejected by God, in the form of the Son's obedience to the Father all the way to the end."[44] Marshall writes that "conceived in this way, the reconciliation of the world to God seems to put God in need of reconciliation with himself. God reconciles

40. B. Marshall, "Absolute and the Trinity," 154–55. "The human nature of Christ . . . is now merely the locus of manifestation, the place where properties the Son already has in primordial form—self-emptying, obedience, distance from the Father, and so forth—are actualized or made present to us" (155).

41. The doctrine of the *communicatio idiomatum*, as presented in traditional Lutheranism, raised questions about how one ought to conceptualize the distinction between the divine and human natures, once the Son of God had become incarnate. Yet traditional Lutheranism presupposed an eternal, divine Son of God who was distinct from humanity prior to the assumption of human nature. See Haga, *Was There a Lutheran Metaphysics?* In contrast to this, the newer "historicized Christology" goes much further (see n. 37 above) in its suggestion that there never was a time in which the divinity of God's eternal Son was properly distinct from the humanity of God's Son.

42. B. Marshall, "Absolute and the Trinity," 155, 157. The Son's utter abandonment by the Father also seems problematic to Marshall: "The Son of God . . . could not undergo divine abandonment because he could not cease to be divine" (156). But on the premises of esoteric thought, with its "coincidence of opposites," it is possible simultaneously to attribute both divine and antidivine properties to God. In esoteric reasoning, it belongs to God's perfection or absoluteness to combine contradictory traits or predicates, thus combining and including everything and its opposite within himself.

43. Ibid., 158.

44. Ibid., citing Balthasar, *Mysterium Paschale*, 52.

the world to himself by making the world's sin and death, even its Godforsakenness, his own in the Person of the Son." In "introducing the world's alienation
and Godforsakenness into the divine nature . . . there is something stirringly
dramatic here. God loves us even to the point of putting his own unity, and
with that his very existence, at hazard for our sake. Ultimately, the reconciliation that must take place for the world's deliverance from evil is not that of
the world to God, but of the Father and the Son to one another, at the heart of
God's Trinitarian life."[45]

The upshot of Marshall's analysis of the dramatic view of God is that "the
unity of God is in the final analysis a temporal event, the climax of the historical and dramatic separation and reconciliation of the divine Persons across the
abyss of evil, death, and nothingness." For this reason, the Trinity cannot be
conceptualized at all, or at least not as an immanent reality existing *in se*. In
Hegelian terms, God as Trinity can only be narrated as the climax of a drama of
alienation and reconciliation. God exists as Trinity only at the final, eschatological
stage. Apart from God's relationship to the world in general and humanity in
particular, the Trinity remains only an "abstract" idea that is empty of content.
The dramatic view asserts that the unity of Father, Son, and Spirit must be
"enacted and sustained in the face of everything that opposes it."[46]

To a surprising extent, then, contemporary Christian theologians have
adopted a largely Hegelian conception of God's relation to the world. This
current Hegelianizing is also an esotericizing of God. The God who must
be enacted and sustained in the face of opposition is the Böhmist deity. For
Böhme, God is not God apart from struggling against negativity in the form
of the *Ungrund*. From the analysis offered in the earlier chapters, it should not
be surprising that the shift toward a conflictual or Böhmist conception of God
should also involve a shift in the direction of universalism.

Connected with the dramatic view of God that we are criticizing is the common use of the language of "kenosis" in ways not supported by Scripture or by
church tradition. The brief, biblical mention of kenosis—that Christ "emptied
himself" (Phil. 2:7)—has nothing to do with God's creating of the world. The

45. B. Marshall, "Absolute and the Trinity," 159. On this scenario of separation within God
(Father vs. Son), it is normal to posit the resurrection as the point at which God's ruptured unity
is once again restored (159). Alternatively, it may be the Spirit who restores the unity of Father
and Son. Robert Jenson writes that the Spirit "liberates the Father and Son to love each other"
(*Systematic Theology*, 1:156).
46. B. Marshall, "Absolute and the Trinity," 160–61. "Post-Hegelian theology had made it seem
as though the unity of the three Persons somehow depends on what comes to pass in creation
or the saving economy, but if the temporal acts of the Triune God are genuinely contingent, the
opposite is the case: what happens in creation and reconciliation wholly depends on the unity of
the divine Persons" (163). Cf. B. Marshall, "Unity of the Triune God."

context in Paul's Epistle to the Philippians has to do with God's eternal Son and his assumption of the human form (Greek *morphē*) or human nature. Though it is possible that an idea like kenosis might have legitimate application in some extended sense, the burden of proof lies on those who would seek to extend and broaden the idea. To affirm without any careful delimitation of meaning that God's creation of the world is "kenotic" is like my saying that my coworkers are "trinitarian" in their relations or that "I am God's incarnation." These terms—"trinitarian," "incarnation," and "kenotic"—have distinct meanings through their connection with the narrative grammar of the trinitarian, redemptive story, but only indistinct significance once they are disjoined from these contexts and used in other circumstances and with altered meanings.

Creation-as-kenosis—the subtitle of a book edited by physicist-cum-theologian John Polkinghorne—may rest on a category mistake.[47] Plainly stated, God the Father in creating the world did not "empty himself and take the form of a servant." If someone believes in creation-as-kenosis, then the basis for doing so will not be the biblical text or classical, incarnational Christology. The intellectual ancestry of creation-as-kenosis lies in Jewish Kabbalah and the thought of Jakob Böhme and Friedrich Schelling. For these thinkers, God as Absolute remained abstract and characterless until God delimited and defined himself by fashioning an Other. The idea that God in creating the world must depotentiate himself and become self-limited is an inversion of the biblical doctrine of creation, according to which God's act of creating is not a renunciation of divine power but a preeminent expression of power, majesty, and dominion. As Martin Luther argued, God's creating and God's commanding are equivalent.[48]

Bulgakov's and Balthasar's alternative reinterpretation of kenosis—namely, the primal self-emptying (*Urkenosis*) of the Father that makes possible the begetting or existence of the Son—is just as problematic as the creation-as-kenosis idea. Underlying this idea of *Urkenosis* is a logic of deficiency. Imagine two glasses of water. If I pour half the water of the first glass into the second, then there is less water in the first and more in the second. The second glass is filled only by emptying the first. But to project onto God's own being this logic of deficiency is a serious mistake. The limitations of the creaturely realm ought not to be applied to God, for otherwise one will have endless difficulties from the outset in affirming creation from nothing or the Son's eternal generation. It hardly seems fitting to say, as Balthasar does, that the Father "must" utterly "strip himself" of all his being to beget the Son. How would Balthasar know this? And why would or should a Catholic theologian think this?

47. Polkinghorne, *Work of Love.*
48. Althaus, *Theology of Luther,* 109.

Rather than adopting a logic of deficiency and lack, Christian thinkers in approaching God might instead be guided by a logic of plenitude and suffi-ciency. It may be better to cease speaking about the *kenotic* God—except in the specific sense of Philippians 2.7—and begin to speak instead of the *plerotic* God. In a "plerotic" view, the stress would lie not on metaphysical deficiency but on the fullness, completeness, and overflow of the Father's existence in the existence of the Son and of the Spirit.[49] Within the intra-trinitarian life of God—so far as we understand it—there is no competition, no give-and-take, no fixed sum of available deity. The language of the Nicene Creed might suggest a plerotic interpretation: "The only Son of God, eternally begotten of the Father, God from God, Light from Light, true God from true God, begotten, not made." Where here is the tug-of-war? Where is the competitive relation of Father and Son? These are non-Nicene notions of God. Do we not instead see in the creed a beautiful picture of the Son as the overflow or fullness (*plērōma*) of the Father's being? "For in him the whole fullness [*plērōma*] of deity dwells bodily" (Col. 2:9).

12.3. The Problem of Grace in Christian Universalism

One of the ironies of Christian universalism lies in what we might call an eclipse of grace.[50] Time and again in the history of universalism, the effort to extend grace to all has ended up compromising the notion of grace. What seemed to be all-grace turned out on inspection to be no-grace. This problem of grace will be discussed below in relation to four assertions: "I am saved because I am divine," "I am saved because I am human," "I am saved because I suffer," and "I am saved because God so wills it." To lay a foundation for discussing grace, we begin by considering some of the biblical and linguistic data concerning the Hebrew words and cognates (*hen, hesed*) and the Greek word (*charis*) often translated into English as "grace."[51]

In ancient secular Greek, the term *charis* referred to "demonstrations of a ruler's favor," which were often recorded in inscriptions. It could denote both the "gracious disposition" of the ruler as well as the specific demonstration of this disposition.[52] In ancient Hebrew, *hen* referred to "the kind turning of one

49. Needless to say, such a "plerotic" view is not aligned with the ancient gnostic idea of the Pleroma, which involved a non-trinitarian deity and a multiplicity of divine aeons.

50. The phrase was suggested by the recent book by Nicholas Adams, *The Eclipse of Grace: Divine and Human Action in Hegel* (2013).

51. The discussion here is based on the extensive analysis in Conzelmann and Zimmerli, "χαίρω κτλ."

52. Ibid., 375–76.

person to another as expressed in an act of assistance." Yet it never denoted an outer act "detached from the inner mood." Instead it referred to "the attitude of a person in its direction to another in a specific gracious action." The Hebrew term thus implied interpersonal relationship, inner disposition, and specificity in action—"a heart-felt movement of the one who acts to the one acted upon."[53] It was applied to a gift given to the poor, to the leniency shown to the defenseless captives of warfare, and to Queen Esther when she appealed to the king to spare her life.[54] When the term was applied to God in the Hebrew Bible, writes Walther Zimmerli, "this graciousness is always God's free gift, as is said with almost offensive severity in the word to Moses . . . 'I am gracious to whom I am gracious, and have mercy on whom I have mercy' (Exod. 33:19)."[55] No less than seventy times in the Hebrew Bible one finds the phrase, "to find grace [hen] in the eyes" of another person.

The related Hebrew term hesed (loving-kindness, grace) originally referred to "the individual good act." The good act in this case "always contains an element of spontaneous freedom in the demonstration of goodness or in kindly conduct and it cannot be reduced to what is owed or to a duty." While hesed in the Hebrew Bible is associated with the theme of covenant (berith), one ought not to assert "too narrow a connection . . . with a fixed covenant," because of the freedom and spontaneity connected with hesed.[56] Within the book of Psalms, there are 127 uses of hesed. In only three instances does the word refer to relations between human beings (Pss. 109:12, 16; 141:5), and in all other cases it denotes God's relation to humans. In the Psalms, hesed is never a "mere, self-evident obligation of the covenant," as Zimmerli says, since it is connected with miracles (Ps. 107:8, 15, 21, 31) or a request for a miracle (Pss. 17:7; 31:21), and because joy (Pss. 31:7; 90:14; 101:1) and praise (Ps. 138:2) arise as a result of God's display of loving-kindness.[57] Though Yahweh's hesed remains stable or reliable, it remains surprising and even unpredictable.

In the New Testament, the term charis (grace) appears only rarely in the Gospel of John and the Johannine Epistles. In the prologue to John's Gospel, the word is used to express an antithesis of grace and law: "For the law was given through Moses; grace and truth came through Jesus Christ" (John 1:17).[58] While the Gospel of John does not develop this contrast, in the Pauline Epistles "charis is a central concept that most clearly expresses his understanding of

53. Ibid., 377.
54. Ibid., 377, 379.
55. Ibid., 378.
56. Ibid., 382.
57. Ibid., 384.
58. Ibid., 399.

the salvation event."[59] Hans Conzelmann notes that *charis* in Paul's Letters carries the nuances of the Hebrew *hen/hesed*. It means the "showing [of] free, unmerited grace," and "the element of freedom in giving is constitutive." *Charis* also means "making glad by gifts." Paul sets "grace" in opposition to "law" (Rom. 6:14; Gal. 2:21; 5:4), and he sometimes sets both "grace" and "faith" in opposition to "law" (Rom. 4:14–16).[60] Grace is actualized in the cross of Christ (1 Cor. 2:2; Gal. 2:20–21), though "grace" can also denote a state—"this grace in which we stand" (Rom. 5:2). Conzelmann comments that grace "does not come in the form of destiny" but represents "free election" or "the exception" that breaks the rule. In this sense, Paul spoke of his own apostleship as a matter of "grace" received from God (Rom. 1:5).[61] Conzelmann notes that "*charis* is not a basic term" in ancient gnosis. In gnostic texts, *charis* is interpreted as a "power of illumination," or else it is hypostasized as a distinct person.[62] The ancient gnostics did not understand *charis* as the apostle Paul did.

We may summarize the biblical data by saying that grace is a gift of God's undeserved favor, freely conferred by God and received by human beings. Grace thus has a *gift* character or *unmerited* character, a *freedom* character (i.e., resting on God's freedom in giving), a *relational* character (i.e., implying a human relation to God), and a *reception* character (i.e., as something that humans receive).

Turning to the various forms of Christian universalism, one finds that almost all of them either overtly or subtly undermine the graciousness of grace. A first option, concisely stated, is as follows: "*I am saved because I am divine.*" According to this view, I cannot finally be damned, because in my inmost self I am part and parcel of God, and God cannot be fully or finally divided against himself. This "spark of the divine" theology is characteristic of ancient gnosis during the second and third centuries and appeared among the Cathars, in Western esotericism generally, in Böhme and many Böhmists, in Lady Anne Conway, in Sadhu Sundar Singh, and in Bulgakov. Many Origen scholars would not attribute this view to Origen himself, though Jerome in the ancient church and the seventeenth-century Pierre-Daniel Huet and nineteenth-century Gottfried Thomasius held that Origen conceived of the human self as either divine or quasi-divine.

The link between the "spark of the divine" theology and universal salvation is apparent. The human self, if somehow divine, could hardly be subject to eternal rejection. How could God reject God? Conversely, the self's divinity might mean that the self will finally save itself—that is, the self's inherently good and positive aspects will at last triumph over any evil and negativity. One might picture

59. Ibid., 393.
60. Ibid., 394.
61. Ibid., 396.
62. Ibid., 401.

the divine self as like a helium balloon trapped in one's chest. As soon as one dies, the balloon is released and ascends heavenward, back to its natural resting place in God. Missing from such an account of universal salvation is any notion of salvation as God's gift, as freely chosen by God, as unmerited, or as something received from God and implying some relation to God. Each of the four key elements in the biblical theology of grace (as noted above) is missing. A strict interpretation of the "divine spark" theology would make Jesus Christ unnecessary. There would be no point in the incarnation itself—in Jesus's life, death, resurrection, and coming again—if each person's eternal destiny with God is already built into the very nature of the human self as such.

Another universalist option that is almost as antithetical to the biblical notion of grace is the view that *"I am saved because I am human."* According to this view, I cannot finally be damned, because I am part of humanity, and humanity is eternally conjoined to God through the eternal God-man. This idea appears, or is at least hinted at, in the theology of Gregory of Nyssa, though Maximus the Confessor (as we saw in *DR* 4.8) avoided the universalist outcome. It also clearly appears in Jewish Kabbalah, in the concept of *Adam Qadmon* and the related notion of a "tree of souls" from which individual human beings are separated. In Friedrich Schleiermacher's doctrine of election, Christ is the original image or archetype (*Urbild*) for all humanity. Schleiermacher shows a Platonic sensibility, according to which Christ as archetype incorporates each human individual. Not all of Schleiermacher's followers subscribed to his distinction between the archetypal (*urbildlich*) Christ and the historical (*historisch*) Christ, but many embraced his notion of human solidarity in salvation. Salvation for one meant salvation for all, and if even one human individual were not included in the final salvation, then no one would truly be saved. Both Barth and Balthasar were in agreement with Schleiermacher on this point. In his account of divine election, Barth never ceased from insisting that what Christ accomplished in his life and death was for all humanity, applied to all humanity, and affected all humanity. While Barth's *Church Dogmatics* II/2 is generally interpreted as an account of *divine election*, it is at least as much a treatise on *divine-human union* (*DR* appendix L). It was Barth's assertion of a purportedly unbreakable bond between Christ and every human being that pointed toward universal salvation as the only conceivable outcome. In *Dare We Hope?*, Balthasar suggested that God's plan of salvation will fail if even one human being is finally separated from God. Universal solidarity in human salvation was thus a basic principle in Schleiermacher, Barth, and Balthasar, and in each thinker the foundational principle of solidarity was christological.

This idea of Christ's inviolable human solidarity with all humanity implies that to be human is to be saved. What Barth wrote in seeking to protect the freedom of God in salvation, to make universal salvation a hope and not a given, and to deny any "right" or "necessity" of an *apokatastasis*, ultimately fails to offset Barth's teaching on an always-already completed and realized union of Christ with each person. Whatever my state of faith or unbelief, whatever my character in terms of virtue or vice, the human solidarity idea expresses the notion that I am already and forever conjoined with the Savior, Jesus Christ, and for this reason "I am saved because I am human."

This second line of universalist theology fails to do justice to the biblical teaching on grace, just like the "spark of God" theology. If human solidarity with Christ is contingent on the historical fact of the incarnation of God's Son, then this way of reasoning preserves at least some element of God's freedom in conferring salvation. Yet in previous chapters, we saw how Barth's election doctrine eternalizes the God-man, and also how Balthasar's notion of *Urkenosis* implies that Christ's salvific identification with all humanity is grounded in an eternal event transpiring between God the Father and God the Son. The gifted-ness, freeness, and unmeritedness of grace, as taught in Scripture, is difficult to discern in Barth's and Balthasar's accounts of human solidarity with Christ. Examined from the human side, grace does not seem to be something "received." Compared with Barth and Balthasar, the idea of an eternal Godmanhood in Kabbalah is perhaps even less compatible with the biblical teaching on grace, and the same is likely true of Schleiermacher's Platonic, archetypal interpretation of Christ. Some interpreters of Gregory of Nyssa insist that baptism, faith, and obedience play a key role in Gregory's idea of the individual's participation in Christ, though it is not clear how individual choice or action offsets the strong focus on Christ's corporate humanity and its all-inclusive character.

A third viewpoint that affirms universal salvation yet compromises grace is *"I am saved because I suffer."* According to this view, I cannot finally be damned, because I myself will suffer to make sufficient expiation or satisfaction for my own sins in a temporary purgatorial fire or cleansing process. As we saw above, this theory of the cleansing purgatorial fire became prominent in Christian literature through the writings of Clement of Alexandria and Origen (*DR* 3.3; 3.7), though it had earlier appeared in ancient classical literature (e.g., Plato) and about the time of Clement in gnostic literature on the "wise fire" that purges the wicked of their evil but does not harm the righteous who need no cleansing. The idea of a postmortem cleansing or purgatorial process is extremely common in Christian universalist literature. Uncharacteristically for a Lutheran of his era, Böhme was open to the idea of purgatory, stating that there was truth as well as falsehood in the Catholic doctrine. Almost all later Böhmist universalists—for example, Jane Lead, William Law, Johann and Johanna Petersen, Louis-Claude de Saint-Martin, Thomas Erskine of Linlathen, George MacDonald, and Andrew

Jukes—affirmed postmortem purgation in preparation for heaven. The Russian universalists—for example, Vladimir Solovyov, Nicolas Berdyaev, and Sergius Bulgakov—accepted this idea as well. So too did Elhanan Winchester and the many American and British followers who adhered to Winchester's "restorationist" version of universalism. Leading contemporary universalists, such as Thomas Talbott and Robin Parry, are also purgationists. Parry emphasizes that all sin carries consequences and that forgiveness from God does not remove the necessity of purifying sufferings.

In response to this third line of universalist theology, it should be noted that Barth, Balthasar, and Moltmann have little in common with purgationism. The idea that "I am saved because I suffer" finds no place in Barth's theology and contradicts Moltmann's affirmation that hell's fury and God's judgment were fully expressed and exhausted when Jesus died. This theological Good Friday focus conflicts with any belief in the necessity of postmortem suffering. This is an important point in light of the many contemporary universalists who hold to purgationism and yet appeal to thinkers like Barth and Moltmann in support of their universalist beliefs. Barth's and Moltmann's theologies of the cross contradict purgationism, and so someone committed to universalism has to make a choice—much like the nineteenth-century American universalists, who fell into two theological camps. Eternal Godmanhood, if true, might serve as a basis for believing in universal salvation. Everything-happening-at-the-cross theology—that is, the overcoming of hell and judgment when Jesus died—also might lead to an internally coherent theology of universalism. Postmortem purgation is likewise self-consistent as a universalist theory. What does not make sense is to attempt a combination of eternal Godmanhood with purgationism. If every human being is eternally and necessarily joined to God, then why would anyone need to suffer after death? Likewise, it makes no sense for purgationists to appeal to Barth as favoring their universalist theology. Barth was no friend, but rather an enemy, to anyone claiming that salvation comes as a result of his or her own sufferings or through self-expiation for sins.

Within the Böhmist lineage of universalists, purgationists have been inconsistent in their attitude toward divine law and divine justice. William Law, George MacDonald, and Sergius Bulgakov all denounced the idea that God's justice dictated that Jesus had to die on the cross for sinners. They repudiated the idea of penal, vicarious, or substitutionary atonement as utterly unworthy of the character of a good and loving God. At the same time, however, these thinkers insisted that individual sinners must pay the price for their own transgressions in postmortem, purgatorial sufferings. Bulgakov demonstrates the theological problem quite clearly. Because he did not accept the notion that Christ bore the penalty or responsibility for human sins, Bulgakov seemingly had no choice except to say either that God simply set aside any punishment for sins, or that there will be some kind of self-satisfaction for one's sins. The abrogation of divine punishment was to him a horrifying idea, and so he opted for a doctrine of self-satisfaction, which he described with the terminology of "expiation." He rejected any notion of "simple forgiveness" as "sentimental" and perhaps as naive or simpleminded: "One must reject every pusillanimous, sentimental hope that the evil committed by a human being and therefore present in him can simply be forgiven, as if ignored at the tribunal of justice." To make the point yet clearer, he added, "God does not tolerate sin, and its simple forgiveness is ontologically impossible. Acceptance of sin would not accord with God's holiness and justice. Once committed[,] a sin must be lived through to the end, and the entire mercilessness of God's justice must pierce our being."[63]

Here we see the flip side of the purgationist rejection of legal or justice-based reasoning on the atonement. The exorcised demon of juridicism came back to haunt Bulgakov's theology. By rejecting Christ's vicarious or substitutionary self-offering for sinners, Bulgakov placed the entire burden of "expiation" on the backs of sinners themselves. Astonishingly, he spoke of "the entire mercilessness of God's justice." Divine justice was thus wholly severed from divine mercy. While most Christians believe that their Savior bore responsibility for their sins and in sheer grace forgives them, Bulgakov in accord with his purgationist view would not allow this. Bulgakov's theology is thus a stark reminder of how purgationist universalism contrasts with the message of salvation by grace. If I am saved because I suffer, then, in all consistency, it is not clear how or why Christ needed to suffer for me. Implicitly or explicitly, the message of salvation by grace is obscured in purgationist universalism.

None of the three forms of universalism just discussed are compatible with the biblical way of thinking. So we must ask, is there no form of universalism that does not deny grace?

The version of universalism that affirms grace in some way is so-called ultra-universalism, according to which God simply reverses all possible consequences of sin at the time of death, so that everyone without exception passes immediately into heaven. One might also call this "fiat forgiveness" or "fiat universalism." It might be summarized in the statement *"I am saved because God so wills it."* Historically speaking, it has never been a widely popular view, in large part because it seems to trivialize sin, to minimize the moral and spiritual life, and to evacuate salvation itself of its meaning. Though some intellectual leaders in nineteenth-century America tried to promote it, the rank-and-file

63. Bulgakov, *Bride of the Lamb*, 475–76.

members of the Universalist Church viewed it as antinomian and held that it destroyed what they called the "moral nexus" between this life and the next. It is not clear how one could justify ultra-universalism in relation to the Bible, since Sacred Scripture contains so many energetic exhortations to moral and spiritual striving.

If one were to assume that when human beings enter the postmortem condition, God simply overrides and reverses the effect of every wrongful decision made during the present life (as ultra-universalists presume), then we might call this grace, but the present human life would then be emptied of its intrinsic moral or spiritual meaning. Michael J. Murray argues "that [ultra-]universalism offers no explanation for the fact that God puts human creatures through the earthly life, and that if there is no such reason then the earthly life and the evil it contains are both gratuitous."[64] Centuries earlier, Jerome raised essentially the same issue: "Will Gabriel be like the devil? Will the apostles be the same as demons? Prophets and false prophets? Martyrs and persecutors?"[65] The renowned twentieth-century philosopher Ludwig Wittgenstein, on hearing one of his students express regret that the early church rejected Origen's universalism, commented: "Of course it was rejected. It would make nonsense of everything else. If what we do now is to make no difference in the end, then all the seriousness of life is done away with."[66] Jerome, Wittgenstein, and Murray all agreed on one point: an identical (or nearly identical) postmortem outcome to every human life—independent of the particular choices that people make—would evacuate earthly choices of their significance. This objection to ultra-universalism has recurred throughout history, and there seems to be no adequate universalist response.

To sum up the argument regarding grace, an analysis of the biblical idea of grace allows us to assess four different ways of thinking about salvation that universalists have offered: *"I am saved because I am divine," "I am saved because I am human," "I am saved because I suffer,"* and *"I am saved because God so wills it."* Of these four views, it is only the last—that of ultra-universalism—that preserves something like the biblical teaching on grace. Yet this last view is antinomian in its implications, and it wholly disjoins salvation from faith, repentance, obedience, and moral striving. Ultra-universalism cannot make sense of biblical teachings on spiritual exertion or of the rich literature of ethical exhortation and spiritual instruction in church history, which has always linked salvation in the life beyond to one's way of acting in the here and now. The

64. M. Murray, "Three Versions of Universalism," 55.

65. Jerome, *Commentary on Jonah* 3:6–9; Adriaen, *Jerome . . . Commentarii in prophetas minors,* 407–8.

66. Rees, *Recollections of Wittgenstein,* 161.

general conclusion is that Christian universalism has notably failed to preserve the principle of salvation by grace and to express the basic biblical insight that *"I am saved because of God's free, unconditional, unmerited love."*

The universalist problem with grace is intimately connected to the universalist problem with God, discussed above (*DR* 12.2). Philosophers Leszak Kolakowski and William Desmond both distinguished "erotic" from "agapeic" conceptions of God. Kolakowski captures the basic idea and the basic problem of an "erotic" deity in this way: "God brought the Universe into being so that He might grow in its body. . . . He needs His alienated creatures to complete His perfection. The growth of the universe . . . involves God himself in the historical process. Consequently God himself becomes historical. At the culmination of cosmic evolution He is not what He was 'in the beginning.' He creates the world and in reabsorbing it enriches Himself."[67] When God is conceived of "erotically" rather than "agapeistically," God remains in what a psychologist might call a codependent relationship with the world. For this reason God cannot love in a free, full, or independent way. Grace in the biblical sense becomes impossible, not because of an impediment on the human side but because of an inherent limitation or flaw within God.[68]

According to the "erotic" model, God is initially deficient in himself and then seeks to complete what is lacking in himself. The emergence and development of the cosmos is a process in which God is developing toward completion, so that the world fulfills God just as God fulfills the world. One might call this a philosophical *hieros gamos* (sacred marriage). God and the world are "married." The God-concept in Böhme, Hegel, Whitehead, process thought, and much of current kenotic-relational theology is based on the "erotic" rather than the "agapeic" model. God needs the world. God becomes complete through relating to the world. But the biblical idea of free grace is ruled out in erotic conceptions of God. The God-concept of historic Christianity, which is "agapeic," holds that God created the world out of a sufficiency or even a surplus of being, happiness, and goodness.[69] As Augustine wrote, "We exist because God is good."[70] The

---

67. Kolakowski, "Can the Devil Be Saved?," 77–78. Kolakowski links the evolving God to belief in a final reconciliation of all reality: "The implication of this belief is that cosmic history leaves no rubbish behind; everything is finally digested, everything incorporated, in the triumphal progress of the spirit. In the ultimate balance, all is justified, each element and event. Struggle and contradiction will appear as an individual contribution to the same work of salvation" (77–78).

68. William Desmond is among the world's leading Hegel scholars, and he breaks with Hegel over this issue of "erotic" versus "apapeic" conceptions of God in his book *Hegel's God*. See also Desmond, *God and the Between*.

69. The argument above suggested a "plerotic" rather than "kenotic" idea of God (*DR* 12.2), and in that context the emphasis was on the intra-trinitarian fullness and sufficiency of God.

70. Augustine, *De doctrina christiana* 1.31, as quoted in Maurer, *Medieval Philosophy*, 161.

world is an overflow of divine goodness, yet God does not "need" the world. This "apapeic" viewpoint, connected with the foundational Christian teaching on creation from nothing, makes it possible to conceive that God is genuinely gracious and that God loves the world freely and unconditionally.

12.4. The Problem of Belief in Christian Universalism

Earlier (*DR* 1.8), we noted H. B. Wilson's proposal—controversial when expressed in 1860—of a hope for universal salvation based on the progress of all souls in a postmortem state:

> We must rather entertain a hope that there shall be found, after the great adjudication, receptacles suitable for those who shall be infants, not as to years of terrestrial life, but as to spiritual development—nurseries as it were and seed-grounds, where the undeveloped may grow up under new conditions—the stunted may become strong, and the perverted restored. And when the Christian Church, in all its branches shall have fulfilled its sublunary office, and its Founder shall have surrendered His kingdom to the Great Father—all, both small and great, shall find a refuge in the bosom of the Universal Parent, to repose, or be quickened into higher life, in the ages to come, according to His Will.[71]

The eloquent words convey an awe-inspiring picture of the future. In contrast to traditional Christian notions of the finality of death, and the urgency of moral and spiritual preparation prior to death, Wilson offers the panorama of an endless progress of souls, in which the present life is merely a "nursery" or "seed-ground" for spiritual beings still in "infancy" and thus destined for further development so that "the stunted may become strong, and the perverted restored." Beautiful as these words may be, they raise an epistemic question: How does Wilson know this?

As compelling and attractive as their visions of the future might be, Wilson and other universalist authors assert alternative eschatologies that are generally not grounded on biblical teaching or precedents in church tradition. Often their projections of the future manifest a dreamlike or visionary quality. In that sense, their words and ideas are *utopian*—like the modern books describing a world without war, a world without conflict between nations or individuals, a world without poverty or want, or a world without painful toil.[72] Science fiction extrapolates

---

71. H. B. Wilson, "Séances Historiques," 205–6, quoted in Rowell, *Hell and the Victorians*, 116–17.

72. See Sargent, *Utopianism*. A utopian strand runs through Western post-Enlightenment politics. Karl Marx (1818–83) and Friedrich Engels (1820–95) took thousands of pages in their many books to critique modern capitalism, but only a handful of pages to describe their imagined final

from present-day or anticipated technologies into realms of future possibilities. Wilson's words have themselves a science-fiction character. He built a world on theory. Origen likewise began from certain rational presuppositions—for example, that God treats everyone according to merit—and projected backward in time (thus reversing the futuristic, science-fiction paradigm) to hypothesize a world preceding our own world (i.e., the realm of preexistent souls) that provided an explanation for all the inequities and disparities of the present life. Origen too built a world on theory. Wilson and Origen were both utopians. Moreover, utopian thinking, whether of the theological or the political kind, will primarily appeal to intellectuals for whom a world built on theory is the only sort of world they wish to believe in. Universalism is the opiate of the theologians.[73]

Many of the Christian universalist thinkers treated in the preceding chapters were *speculators*: Origen, Gregory of Nyssa, Evagrius, bar Sudaili, Eriugena, Guillaume Postel, Jakob Böhme, Jane Lead, William Law, Vladimir Solovyov, Sergius Bulgakov, Paul Tillich, Jürgen Moltmann, and (in some measure) both Karl Barth and Hans Urs von Balthasar.[74] Alongside this lineage we might set another groups of thinkers, whom we might designate as *antispeculators*, including Irenaeus, Athanasius, Augustine, Aquinas, Luther, Calvin, Jonathan Edwards (for the most part), John Henry Newman, Georges Florovsky, Dumitru Stăniloae, Yves Congar, Thomas Torrance, Pope John Paul II, and Pope Emeritus Benedict XVI. The latter group holds that God's intra-trinitarian life is only known and knowable in part, through hints and glimmerings contained in biblical revelation. Human destiny and the future of the universe, too, are

---

condition of "the withering away of the State." Engels, in *Anti-Dühring*, stated that the political state will not be abolished, but over time becomes "superfluous" and so "withers away of itself" (387). Cf. Lefebvre, "Withering Away of the State." Marx and Engels believed that the overthrow of the capitalist system would allow a radically new state of affairs to spring up spontaneously, as it were, from the soil on which the oppressive capitalistic factories had formerly stood. A parallel to Christian universalist utopianism may be closer in the case of Jean-Jacques Rousseau, whose *Discourse on the Origin and Basis of Inequality among Men* (1755) suggested that human beings existed in a natural state of equality with one another, had fallen into inequality, but might be restored to their primal equality. The three-stage pattern recalls Origen's *On First Principles*, which postulated that all souls were originally equal to one another, had fallen into inequality, but would be restored to final equality. Origen's radical or Evagrian followers were called "iso-Christs" because they held that they and everyone else in the eschaton would be equal to Christ himself—something like a political promise that everyone in the future will become a millionaire.

73. Secular thinkers will likely say that *all forms* of Christian eschatology are utopian, whether universalist or particularist. One response would be to say that Christian beliefs regarding the future are wholly based on God's promise as given in revelation and that there is no other basis on which to claim that Christ will return again, that evil will be defeated, or that death and suffering will be abolished. The eschatological claim stands or falls with the larger, revelational claim—i.e., that God has spoken and has promised certain things regarding the future.

74. Anyone who denies that Barth engaged in metaphysical speculation should reread his stunning account of evil as *das Nichtige* in *CD* III/3. See the discussion in *DR* 9.7.

knowable only insofar as God reveals them to us. The antispeculators generally understand theology as a practical enterprise, rooted in the life of the church, and aimed at cultivating that human knowledge of God that leads ultimately toward heavenly union with God and beatitude in God.[75]

To understand the significance of Christian universalism, it is necessary to consider not only the doctrine itself but also its spirit and ethos. Albert Camus, in *The Rebel* (1951), offered an interesting discussion of what he called "metaphysical revolt." Camus argued that modern people revolt not only against particular political systems or forms of enslavement but also against the very nature of reality itself. Sir Herbert Read, in his preface to the book, wrote that "it is no longer the revolt of the slave against the master, nor even the revolt of the poor against the rich; it is a metaphysical revolt, the revolt of man against the conditions of life, against creation itself."[76] Of course, this description sounds much like ancient gnosis. "Metaphysical rebellion is the movement by which man protests against his condition and against the whole of creation." Camus writes that "the metaphysical rebel . . . is frustrated by the universe."[77] Such a revolt against the way things are is linked not only to the logic of political utopianism and but also to theological universalism. Here there is a rejection of the givenness of the conditions of human life, the fact of sin, and the way of salvation offered by God.[78] Why should God become incarnate? Why should atonement for sins be necessary? *Why?* The "metaphysical rebel" rejects the universe as it is in favor of the universe as he or she prefers it to be.

This mind-set pervades much of universalist argumentation. One does not become a universalist without a thorough rethinking of received Christian ideas regarding God, Christ, the self, and the nature of salvation. In ancient times,

75. In reference to early church Christology, Thomas Weinandy writes: "The task of theology and the defining of doctrine is not to solve theological problems but to clarify exactly what the mysteries of the faith are. Heresy always solves what is considered to be a theological problem and in so doing renders the mystery of faith completely comprehensible and so depriving it of its very mystery" ("Terrence Tilley's Christological Impasses," 249). Schulz, in "Universalism: The Urgency of Christian Witness," 90, argues for an antispeculative posture on the question of our own salvation and that of others: "We are . . . not to engage in abstract speculation but to find assurance of our salvation by turning to the revealed Word of God, to our baptism and the visible means of grace, so that we may find and receive through them the assurance that we have been called."

76. Read, preface to *The Rebel*, viii.

77. Camus, *The Rebel*, 23.

78. Camus writes, "The metaphysical rebel . . . attacks a shattered world in order to demand unity from it. He opposes the principle of justice which he finds in himself to the principle of injustice which he sees being applied in the world" (ibid., 23–24). "Metaphysical rebellion . . . is motivated by the concept of a complete unity" (24). "The [metaphysical] rebel refuses to recognize the power that compels him to live in this condition. The metaphysical rebel is therefore not definitely an atheist, as one might think him, but he is inevitably a blasphemer. Quite simply, he blasphemes primarily in the name of order, denouncing God as the father of death and as the supreme outrage" (24).

the issue of divine justice or injustice lay at the heart of the "metaphysical rebellion" that occurred in ancient gnosis. Gnosticism was a radical rejection of the world as it appears to us and an imaginative reconstrual or counterconstrual of reality. This rebellion against the status quo, and the Judeo-Christian God, gave rise for the first time to the teaching on universal salvation (*DR* 2.3). Gnostic writers developed elaborate mythologies of alternate universes, invisible to the unaided eye. Yet far from seeing this enterprise as fanciful or as irrelevant, the great twentieth-century esotericist Carl Gustav Jung wrote in praise of the gnostics' mythmaking imagination.[79]

The Claims of Reason and the Issue of Abstract Rationality

To the question of why one should believe in universalism, there are four possible sources for Christian theological affirmations: Scripture, tradition, reason, and experience. Since much of this book has dealt already with the question of Christian tradition (see esp. *DR* 1), the focus here will lie on just three: reason, experience, and Scripture, in that order.

Universalist reasoning is often abstractly rational or a priori. On a popular level, many have argued that if God is love, then everyone must be saved. Rob Bell asked simply, "Does God get what God wants?"[80] This question can be taken in more than one way, because the notion of God "wanting" might have more than one meaning.[81] If sin and evildoing is "not what God wants"—that is, contrary to God's moral will—then the answer has to be no. As soon as any creature rebels against God, then God is not "getting what God wants." Of course, Bell probably wanted to pose a different question—namely, whether God could have any purposes that remain indefinitely or eternally unfulfilled. Yet even so, we have to consider the question not in a purely abstract way but in relation to the world in which we are actually living—in other words, not in relation to possible worlds that we might imagine but that do not exist in any empirical sense (e.g., the world in which there are free beings who freely follow God without sinning at all). John Henry Newman wrote that "the great mystery is, not that evil has no end, but that it had a beginning."[82] From the

---

79. Jung wrote, "In Gnosticism we see man's unconscious psychology in full flower, almost perverse in its luxuriance; it contained the very thing that most strongly resisted the *regula fidei* [rule of faith]: Promethean and creative spirit which will bow only to the individual soul and to no collective ruling. Although in crude form, we find in Gnosticism what was lacking in the centuries that followed: a belief in the efficacy of individual revelation and individual knowledge" (*Collected Works*, 6:241–42, cited in O'Regan, *Gnostic Return in Modernity*, 250n23).

80. R. Bell, *Love Wins*, 95.

81. See *DR*, 922–23, 951, for further discussion of God's will.

82. Newman, *Grammar of Assent*, 422, cited from Flannery, "How to Think about Hell," 476.

standpoint of someone like Newman, the very existence of evil is and remains a mystery, and such would in principle be the case even if universalism were true. The final salvation of all would still not answer the irreducible question of why evil ever entered the universe in the first place.

An abstractly rational approach to God will likely start with God's attribute of love—a theological tenet known from Scripture—and detach this tenet from its scriptural context (i.e., the connection with justice, the Old Testament, the life of Jesus, the cross, the preaching of the good news, and so forth) and draw conclusions from this single theological tenet.[83] On this basis one might argue simply, "For God so loved the world that to all he gave eternal life." This is an abbreviated version of what may be the best-known verse in the Bible, John 3:16. The rationalistic mind regards God's love as an abstract principle and is willing to skip over the middle part of the verse—"that he gave" (the Father's gift of the Son) "his only Son" (the internal differentiation in the trinitarian God, as Father and Son), "that whoever believes in him" (the necessity of faith, linking individual human beings to God) "should not perish" (the threat of destruction apart from God's salvation) "but have eternal life" (eternity in fellowship with God as God's gift).

Exegetically speaking, a striking thing in this verse is that the first thing mentioned after God's love is the gift of the Son. God so loved the world that *he gave his Son.* Jesus Christ *is* the concrete, historical, personal expression of the Father's love, and no one enters into the Father's love apart from Jesus Christ (John 14:6). In contrast to this, the abstractly rational mind will start from divine love and then proceed without further ado to the salvation of all persons, considering everything pertaining to the mediation of Jesus Christ as messy and cumbersome—if not unnecessary. We see this in unitarianism, which has a far simpler theology than that implied in the Gospel of John.[84] God

83. A philosophically sophisticated discussion and defense of universalism appears in Kronen and Reitan, *God's Final Victory,* which employs the logic of possible worlds to discuss what God might, could, or should do in providing salvation to the creatures God has made. Yet the argument is based on a form of abstract theism in neglect of Christ's incarnation and resurrection, and with attention to Christ's death only as a payment making forgiveness possible (178–79). The authors argue that "if He [God] limited His forgiveness only to those who *accepted* Christ . . . then He would be failing to attribute to Christ's Atonement its full worth" (121). They further claim that "it is hard to imagine *why* God would be incapable of attributing Christ's merit to the unfaithful" (122). The reasoning here is theologically counterfactual in making assumptions (e.g., the non-essential character of faith) that run counter to Scripture and to Christian tradition. The book is thus philosophically intriguing yet not all that illuminating for Christian theology.

84. Gulley and Mulholland's *If Grace Is True,* discussed previously (*DR* 11.2), expresses a simple, unitarian theology of universal salvation: God loves everyone; Jesus is not God and does not mediate salvation, but taught us that God loves us; and the loving God, as Jesus taught, patiently awaits each human self to turn to him.

exists, and so do human selves. Humans need salvation, and therefore God, being loving, saves them. It is rather easy to see why universalists should often be unitarians and why unitarians should generally be universalists. As soon as one introduces a historical Savior, things become complicated.

An irony appears in unitarian forms of universalism. Unitarian-universalists need the Bible and yet they must reject the Bible. They rely on the Bible's depiction of God's love for sinners and gracious care for the undeserving. All the same, they are generally horrified by the Old Testament with its sacrifice of animals, its strict insistence that God is holy and punishes sin, and its anticipation of the later doctrine of Jesus's atoning death on the cross. Unitarians reject the idea of *mediatory* salvation. Neither the blood of bulls and goats nor the blood of Christ has significance for unitarians, except in the limited sense that Jesus's death might serve as an inspiring moral example of a person dying for his principles (like Socrates drinking the hemlock). The unitarian standpoint vis-à-vis the Bible remains ambiguous. It is like a geometrician, who extracted from Euclid's *Elements* the parallel postulate as a starting point but then shut the book and evolved a whole system of non-Euclidean geometry starting from this one postulate. Unitarian-universalism extracts the principle of divine love from Scripture but then turns it against the rest of Scripture.

Abstract reasoning about God leads inevitably to the question of "fiat forgiveness": Could God forgive all sins by simply deciding and announcing that all sins are forgiven? Richard Roach, in *The Imperial Standard of Messiah Triumphant* (1727), proposed what he called a "General Amnesty." God will announce a comprehensive forgiveness of sins for all creatures. All alienated human beings and fallen angels will be restored to the relationship they had with God before they sinned (*DR* 5.7). Among contemporary authors, Sharon Baker embraces what seems to be "fiat forgiveness" when she writes, "If God has the authority as the sovereign creator of the universe to make the rules [then] God can also take away the threat of damnation and hell by simply forgiving sin."[85] This issue goes deep into the history of Christian thought, and it seems to have been Athanasius who first explicitly raised the question in *On the Incarnation of the Word.*[86] Once the world had fallen into sin, why didn't God at that point simply declare that everyone was forgiven? In other words, why wasn't there "fiat forgiveness"? Here Athanasius was questioning the reason for the incarnation of God's eternal Son—not the reason for the Son's death on the cross—yet the "fiat

85. Baker, *Executing God*, 67.
86. Athanasius, in *On the Incarnation of the Word* 44 (NPNF² 4:60; PG 25:173–75), describes the objection to his own incarnational theology as follows: "They will choose to say that God, if He wished to reform and save mankind, ought to have done so by a mere fiat, without His word taking a body, in just the same way as He did formerly, when He produced them out of nothing."

forgiveness" idea would call both into question. If forgiveness happens simply by divine fiat, then the usual arguments regarding the necessity of Christ's incarnation or death on the cross would no longer apply.

The Italian jurist Faustus Socinus (1539–1604) posed the seemingly straightforward question, if God is all-powerful, then could not God forgive sins without Jesus having to die on the cross? Following the publication of Socinus's *De Jesu Christo Servatore* (*Concerning Jesus Christ the Savior*) in 1594, there was a prolonged theological controversy that stretched over more than two centuries. One scholar estimates that Socinus's original publication evoked around seven hundred critical responses prior to 1800. Though Socinus is little known today, the theological movement he initiated ranks as one of the most influential in the modern era. The lines of influence may be traced from the Socinians to the later deists, Enlightenment critics of Christianity, and secular rationalists. The best-known line of influence is from Socinianism to Unitarianism.[87] Socinus and his followers concluded that Jesus's death was not an act of atonement that paid a penalty or debt of sin. They objected that it would be cruel and immoral for God to punish an innocent man in place of the guilty. Jesus therefore died simply as a moral example. What the historical record on Socinianism suggests is that the acceptance of "fiat forgiveness" led over time to a downgrading of Christ's religious status and ultimately to a rejection of the doctrine of Christ's divinity.

Though not directly inspired by Socinus and his idea of "fiat forgiveness," many contemporary Christian universalists reject the idea of divine punishment. Their governing assumption is that God does not *punish* sinners but *reforms* them. They set aside retributive justice in favor of some notion of reformatory, rehabilitative, or restorative justice. During the nineteenth century, the philosopher and social reformer Jeremy Bentham expressed such a view: "All punishment is mischief, all punishment in itself is evil."[88] Some today cite the saying attributed to Mohandas Gandhi: "An eye for an eye for an eye for an eye . . . ends in making everybody blind."[89] Friedrich Nietzsche

---

87. See Wilbur, *Socinianism and Its Antecedents*; McLachlan, *Socinianism in Seventeenth-Century England*; Godbey, "Study of Faustus Socinus' *De Jesu Christo Servatore*"; Reedy, "Socinians"; Gomes, "*De Jesu Christo Servatore*"; Gomes, "Some Observations." Reedy's essay shows a close link between Socinianism and early modern rationalism in its various forms. Gomes notes the 700 responses to Socinus from 1595 to 1797 and adds that "Socinianism is not . . . a dispute about a particular doctrine or set of doctrines, but represents instead a reconstruction and reinvention of the entire Christian edifice" ("Some Observations," 50, with n. 2). The same might be said of Christian universalism.

88. Bentham, *Principles of Morals and Legislation*, 13.2, cited in Gorringe, *God's Just Vengeance*, 241.

89. Though the saying encapsulates a viewpoint that is consistent with Gandhi's philosophy, there seems to be no direct evidence that Gandhi actually said this. See Shapiro, *Yale Book of Quotations*, 269–70. One version of the saying derives from a member of Parliament in Canada in 1914 (*Official Report of the Debates of the House of Commons of the Dominion of Canada*, 496).

argued that punishment does not bring moral improvement to those being punished.[90] This stigmatization of retribution as immoral requires a rejection of the traditional doctrine of hell. According to the standard account, people in hell are not morally improved but are paying the price for sins committed during their earthly lives.[91] Hell seems to make sense only in connection with some idea of retributive justice.

The currently prevailing views of justice make the doctrine of a retributive hell implausible to many people, and also impinge on attitudes toward the doctrine of the atonement. The doctrine of Christ's substitutionary death and the doctrine of hell are systematically interrelated. This correlation is in evidence today, inasmuch as nearly everyone who favors the doctrine of universal salvation also rejects the doctrine of Christ's substitutionary or vicarious atonement, and vice versa.[92] C. S. Lewis saw retributive justice and the notion of deserved punishment as foundational to the exercise of criminal justice. Punishment, as generally practiced, is only sensible or humane on the basis of the theory that the offender *deserves* punishment. What Lewis called "the humanitarian theory of punishment" proves ultimately to be inhumane, because it denies offenders their own freedom, agency, and responsibility and instead places them at the mercy of the supposed higher wisdom of the lawgiver and law enforcer, who together know what is good for offenders better than offenders know themselves. Lewis writes:

> There is no sense in talking about a "just deterrent" or "just cure." We demand of a deterrent not whether it is just but whether it will deter. We demand of a cure not whether it is just but whether it succeeds. Thus when we cease to consider what the criminal deserves and consider only what will cure him or deter others, we have tacitly removed him from the sphere of justice altogether; instead of a person, a subject of rights, we now have a mere object, a patient, a "case."[93]

90. Punishment, wrote Nietzsche, was the very last thing to awaken "the sting of conscience." He added, "Generally speaking, punishment makes men hard and cold; it concentrates; it sharpens the feeling of alienation; it strengthens the power of resistance. . . . Punishment tames men, but it does not make them 'better'" (*Genealogy of Morals*, 2.14, cited in Gorringe, *God's Just Vengeance*, 241).

91. Some hold that those who are in hell *continue to sin and to incur guilt*—perhaps through sins of blasphemies and curses uttered against God and hatred in the heart toward God. In this view, people in hell are punished for sins committed not only prior to their death but also after their death.

92. See Jersak and Hardin, *Stricken By God?* Jersak's introductory essay (18–53) rejects the category of "substitution" and proposes instead a weaker notion of "identification." His view recapitulates earlier Abelardian, subjectivist, and exemplarist theories of atonement: "We repent by choosing to identify instead with Christ in his commitment to actively resist the powers, but in his way (nonviolently and with forgiveness)" (32). Christ's suffering is here more an example for imitation than a basis for salvation.

93. C. S. Lewis, "Humanitarian Theory of Punishment," 496–97.

To apply Lewis's insight to the sphere of postmortem punishment, one would have to say that God treats human beings with so much dignity that God allows them to make choices and then to bear the consequences of those choices.

The Claims of Experience and the Phenomena of the Paranormal

A person of a secular or skeptical bent may wonder what the fuss regarding Christian universalism is all about. Why should anyone believe in an afterlife at all, let alone in the biblical idea of heaven or hell? Who could ever know *anything* regarding an afterlife?

A passage in Bede's *Ecclesiastical History of the English People*, dating from the eighth century CE, emphasizes the limitations of human knowledge concerning our origins and possible destiny. The speaker, addressing the king, compares the individual human life to the flight of a sparrow passing into a building from outside and then passing outside once again. The bird is visible only while it flits about in the mead hall, and no one in the hall can see where it has come from or where it is going:

> Your Majesty, when we compare the present life of man on earth with that time of which we have no knowledge, it seems to me like the swift flight of a single sparrow through the banqueting-hall where you are sitting at dinner on a winter's day with your thegns [sic] and counselors. In the midst there is a comforting fire to warm the hall; outside, the storms of winter rain or snow are raging. This sparrow flies swiftly in and through one door of the hall, and out through another. While he is inside, he is safe from the winter storms; but after a few moments of comfort, he vanishes from sight into the wintry world from which he came. Even so, man appears on earth for a little while; but what went before this life or of what follows, we know nothing.

These words in Bede's account purportedly sum up the advice given to Edwin, king of Northumbria, by one of his leading men at a meeting at which the king had proposed that he and his subjects should convert to Christianity. The speech ends with the words: "If this new teaching has brought any more certain knowledge [i.e., of the afterlife], it seems only right that we should follow it."[94]

It should be obvious that if one understands heaven and hell in traditional terms as postmortem states of existence, then the question of their possible existence and nature are not open to ordinary, empirical investigation. One can ask, "What does the inside of *that building* look like?" and then answer the question by going inside to investigate. Yet one cannot ask, "What does the inside

94. See Bede, *Ecclesiastical History*, 129–30 (bk. 2, ch. 13).

of heaven, or of hell, look like?" and investigate through one's own exploration.
The recent bestselling book *Heaven Is for Real* (later made into a Hollywood
movie) centered not on everyday perceptions but on a visionary experience that a
small child claimed to have had in seeing Jesus and in experiencing heaven—at
least in some sort of anticipatory way.[95] The reaction of the secular psychology
professor in the film showed the multiple ways that the boy's experience could
be interpreted. In the film, both parents were initially skeptical about their
son's reported experiences, and some members of the Christian congregation
remained skeptical to the end. Christians, who are believers in certain respects,
can be skeptics in other respects. Those who claim to have seen or to know what
lies on the other side of death are likely to face hard questions from religious
believers and nonbelievers alike.

A hard-nosed empiricist need not conclude that heaven and hell do not
exist. Instead, a more appropriate conclusion could be agnostic: I don't know.
In legal jargon, this is the verdict of *non liquet* (it is not clear)—in effect a kind
of nonverdict, indicating that the matter is not decided (and perhaps cannot be
decided). Christians believe in heaven as something divinely revealed. This is
why even the greatest of Christian literature on the afterlife, including Dante
Alighieri's *Divine Comedy* and John Milton's *Paradise Lost*, is often surpass-
ingly odd. Both Dante and Milton had no choice but to invent innumerable
details of the afterlife, since biblical representations were sketchy and later
church tradition and reflection were also incomplete. Milton's depiction of
battles between angels and the weaponry used is a case in point. He had to
make it up. Christians who affirm an afterlife—whether or not a *universalist*
afterlife—are utterly dependent on divine revelation for everything that they
might say on this topic. Moreover, there is only so much that can be said on
this topic on the basis of Scripture. It is quite easy to say more than Scripture
says or to look to sources other than Scripture to support one's beliefs regarding the afterlife.

The Lutheran theologian Ehregott Daniel Colberg, in *Das platonische-
hermetische Christentum* (1710), took issue with the esoteric thinkers of his
day, some of whom in his view were influenced less by the Bible than they
were by alchemy, astrology, and books of magic. Colberg did not affirm that the
Bible was the only source of knowledge. Instead he affirmed that the "philosophical arts and sciences" may be a "hearty gift of God" when used in "civil
[*bürgerlich*] life." The problem, he thought, lay in an inappropriate attempt to
use philosophical reasoning to explain God's mysteries: "When they [i.e., the
philosophical arts and sciences] are applied to divinely revealed mysteries,

and overstep the bounds of reason, they create manifold confusion. From this come all manner of sects and errors." Colberg added that "Paul does not reject philosophy itself but rather condemns its shameful misuse, when it climbs above the clouds, and arrives at a premature judgment concerning the divine things that it does not know according to its principles. . . . This unauthorized presumption in taking on the office of judge is the mother of all mistakes in theology."[96]

Universalists throughout history have had visionary or paranormal experiences in which they saw everyone receiving salvation. They *knew* it was so because they *saw* it to be so.[97] Regarding Origen, no one knows what experiential basis there might or might not have been for his inventive theologizing. A better case can be made regarding the ancient Syrian universalist Stephen bar Sudaili, who was said to have had visions and to have come to the conclusion that "all things are consubstantial with God" (*DR* 4.5). In the year 1600, Jakob Böhme experienced his "central vision" (*Zentralschau*), in which he saw the sunlight reflecting off a pewter dish, which revealed to him the inner structure of all reality. A number of Böhme's leading second- and third-generation followers—including Johann Georg Gichtel, John Pordage, and Jane Lead—were visionaries, as Böhme was. They claimed to have seen angels, demons, heaven, or hell. All of them, except for Gichtel, became universalists. And even he was convinced that escape from hell was possible for some (*DR* 5.6).

The modern universalist movement began in London, in connection with the visionary Jane Lead, leader of the Philadelphian Society and a former disciple of John Pordage, of whom Richard Baxter had written, "Dr. Pordage and his Family . . . live together in Community, and pretend to hold visible and sensible Communion with Angels."[98] The stories of their paranormal experiences were known throughout the surrounding community. Jane Lead believed in universal salvation not primarily because of a logical argument but because she reportedly saw things in the spirit world that convinced her (*DR* 5.7). In Germany, the earlier spread of universalism was linked to the Lutheran-Böhmist pastor Johann Petersen, who had been called in to interview a young visionary, Rosamunde Juliane von der Asseburg, and to ascertain whether or not her visions were genuinely God-given. Bringing his wife Johanna with him, he was favorably impressed and invited the young visionary to stay in his home. He even published a treatise defending the idea of continuing, postbiblical revelation, which

96. Colberg, *Das platonische-hermetische Christentum*, 2–3 (my translation).

97. On the spiritual evaluation or discernment of visionary experiences, in relation to the so-called genetic fallacy, see *DR*, 904–5n124.

98. Baxter, *Reliquiae Baxterianae*, 77, cited in Thune, *Behmenists and the Philadelphians*, 14–15.

did much to undermine his reputation among his fellow Lutherans (*DR* 5.8). Shortly thereafter, the Petersens emerged as the leading German proponents of universalism, publishing dozens of works and millions of words in defense of what they called "the eternal gospel" of salvation for all.[99]

In the American colonial era, George de Benneville presented a striking case of universalism based on paranormal experiences. Before departing from Germany for America in 1741, de Benneville underwent a second life-changing experience. A brief, firsthand account reports a trance state, lasting forty-two hours, in which de Benneville visited and witnessed "the Regions of Misery and Happiness." In the trance, he was taken to a region where spirit beings "clothed in garments as white as snow" proclaimed to him the good news of "the restoration of all of the human species without exception." After saying farewell to his earthly friends, he felt himself "die by degrees" and sensed his spirit departing from his body. While in hell, he "had great compassion toward the sufferers." One of the spirits then comforted him with a vision of universal salvation. He heard voices shouting, "an eternal and everlasting deliverance, an eternal and everlasting restoration, an universal and everlasting restitution of all things."[100] Forty-two hours after being pronounced dead, de Benneville awoke inside a coffin. Once he came back to the land of the living, he committed himself to preaching universalism with renewed vigor. The German-speaking colonists known as the Ephrata Community were also "quite familiar with spiritual trances, visions, strange dreams, 'signs,' and other parapsychological phenomena." The "spirits" made their appearance with them around 1759. De Benneville probably introduced universalism into this community, and the Ephrata Community not only believed in universalism but also promoted it by publishing universalist literature.[101]

In France during the late 1700s, the Martinist universalists employed theurgical practices to invoke spirit beings among them. Martines de Pasqually's Élus Coëns (Elect priests) in performing their rituals were said to have witnessed what they called "passes," glowing symbols or "luminous glyphs" that appeared in the chamber of their theurgical operation and that signaled the presence of an angel. Such manifestations were not the purpose of the rituals, according to Martinist teaching, but were visible signs to indicate that the process of "reintegration" (i.e., the salvation of all creatures) was steadily advancing. The invocation of spirits and the doctrine of universal salvation, or Martinist practice and Martinist doctrine, were closely integrated. Through

---

99. On Asseburg, see Matthias, *Johann Wilhelm und Johanna Eleonora Petersen*; Trippenbach, "Rosamunde Juliane von der Asseburg."

100. De Benneville, *A True and Most Remarkable Account*, title page, 23–24, 27–28.

101. Alderfer, *Ephrata Commune*, 99, 147–48, 170.

their ritual practice, Pasqually taught, even Satan and the fallen angels would finally be saved.

In colonial America, the universalist pioneer Caleb Rich came to his universalist beliefs and his vocation to preach those beliefs through visionary experiences. Rich had two visionary experiences around 1773. From the first vision he learned not to fear "the torments of hell or future judgment," which cannot help anyone to live a God-pleasing life. Through this experience he felt an overwhelming sense of love for all humanity, which he interpreted as an experience of Christ's universal love. From the second vision, a spiritual guide instructed him to "follow no man any further . . . tho' they follow Christ," adding that "if you continue so doing you will soon . . . again be lost in the wilderness." In Massachusetts, Rich promoted the idea of disbelief in hell, and in 1778 he had yet another set of visions that gave a final shape to his theology. From his visions he learned the dual nature of human beings. The earthly and sinful part of each person would be wholly destroyed at death, while the spiritual part would survive and go immediately to join God in heaven. Another vision featured Jesus holding out corn to him and telling him to "feed my sheep and lambs" (cf. John 21:15–17). From this point onward Rich not only held to universalism but also felt a call to preach the message to others.[102]

Vladimir Solovyov had a range of paranormal experiences during 1875–78 that shaped his later universalist philosophy. Journeying to London, specifically to study gnostic, kabbalistic, and esoteric literature in the British Museum, Solovyov had a vision of Sophia while in the reading room. This led him to an ill-fated trip to the Egyptian desert at Sophia's beckoning (a trip that almost cost him his life), to attendance at séances in London and Cairo, and to communication with the spirit world, including an alleged message from a deceased professor of his. Most important of all, Solovyov received what he took to be a message from Sophia herself: that he had a great mission to fulfill at her behest. During this period, Solovyov was often engaged in the practice of automatic or trance writing. For Solovyov, no less than for the earlier Böhmists, Martinists, and colonial American universalists, belief in the final salvation of all went hand in hand with paranormal or visionary experiences.

So, too, the truth of universalism became apparent to the evangelical spiritual writer Hannah Whitall Smith (1832–1911) as a visionary experience: "The vividness with which all this came to me can never be expressed. I did not think it, or imagine it, or suppose it. I *saw* it. It was a revelation of the *real* nature of things."[103] Sadhu Sundar Singh (*DR* 2.10)—who in India made multiple

---

102. The quotations in this paragraph are drawn from Peter Hughes, "Caleb Rich."
103. H. W. Smith, *Unselfishness of God*, 205.

journeys into the spirit world during the 1910s and 1920s—said that he had
many encounters with the deceased spirit of Emanuel Swedenborg. In the aftermath of these paranormal experiences, Singh became a convinced universalist.
Balthasar's less rigid yet still "hopeful" universalism is linked to the reported
mystical or visionary experiences of Adrienne von Speyr. Balthasar believed
that he knew of God's inner-trinitarian life because von Speyr had so informed
him and because he accepted her experiences as genuine. In the final volume
of *Theo-drama* Balthasar often cites von Speyr's writings. Balthasar's theology
of Holy Saturday, according to which Christ continued to suffer for sinners
after his death, was largely based on von Speyr's visions. The Holy Saturday
teaching undergirded and supported Balthasar's "hopeful universalism," and
so the theological teaching at this point is intertwined with von Speyr's unusual
or paranormal experiences.

This phenomenon of universalism based on visionary experiences continues
into the present time—as, for example, in the literature of those purporting to
have near-death experiences (NDEs). Betty Eadie's *Embraced by the Light* (1992)
and several of her later books present a universalist message on the basis of
what she saw and heard in a visionary state of mind. Eadie claims in 1973 to
have left her hospital bed and traveled into the world beyond, where she met
multiple spirit beings, including Jesus. In her otherworldly journeys she discovered that spirits preexist their human bodies (see *DR* 3.5), and she even saw
one spirit trying to get a man and woman (i.e., the parents) to come together
so that a certain man would be able to enter a body. She learned that human
spirits helped God in the beginning to create the world, that every human being
is naturally divine, that there is no eternal hell, and that all souls will finally be
saved. The various religions in the world, she learned, are all valuable, and each
is designed to help a different sort of spirit being. From the spirits she learned
that Jesus is "a God" but is not equal in divinity to God the Father.[104]

It should be obvious that someone's response to Eadie's teachings will depend on whether one accepts her visions as valid. Since the mainstream of the
Christian church has always insisted that visionary experiences must be tested
for their congruity with church teaching, a visionary experience does not stand
on its own as an independent basis for faith, nor can it contradict whatever is
already known clearly from biblical teaching or from the authoritative teaching
of the church.[105]

---

104. See Eadie, *Embraced by the Light;* http://www.embracedbythelight.com. For analysis, see
Introvigne, "Embraced by the Church?," esp. 107–8; R. Wise, "Embraced by the Light of Deception."
105. For an analysis from a Catholic standpoint, see Hvidt, *Christian Prophecy,* 3–21; Congar,
"La crédibilité." It might be objected that many of the church's mystics had visions too and that
sometimes they based certain teachings on their visionary experiences. The point is debatable,

At first glance, visionary reasons for accepting universalism would seem to have little in common with rationalist arguments. Yet mystical movements have often evolved into rationalism.[106] Böhmism, as embodied in Johann Dippel, offered a strident criticism of Lutheran teachings on predestination, justification by faith, and Christ's atoning death. Dippel's arguments anticipated those of the German "Neologians," whose rationalism was much like that of English deists and found a later echo in the arguments of Immanuel Kant's *Religion within the Bounds of Reason Alone*.[107] The historical pattern seems to be as follows: first the mystic, then the rationalist.

The Claims of Scripture and the Issue of Universalist Hermeneutics

Biblical interpretation has been pivotal in the development of universalism since the time of Origen, who was largely responsible for introducing into mainstream Christian discourse a number of ideas supporting universalism. These included the notion of a purifying fire that burns away sin or guilt (and prepares people for heaven), the teaching that all God's punishments are remedial or reformatory in character, the idea of the soul's preexistence, the notion of a succession of world ages (in which all souls might return to God), and the idea of a final restoration or *apokatastasis* in which all intelligent creatures (human or angelic) willingly subject themselves to Christ. Certain verses of Scripture, especially in the Pauline Letters, were of paramount importance for Origen and later Origenists—for example, Romans 5 on justification for "all," 1 Corinthians 3 on purifying fire, 1 Corinthians 15 on universal subjection to Christ, and Philippians 2 on "every knee" bowing to Christ.[108] Book 21 of

---

yet generally the acknowledged Catholic mystics did not purport to teach any wholly new doctrine based on their otherworldly experiences, which is what seems to have happened in the cases of Jakob Böhme, Jane Lead, and Betty Eadie.

106. Briggs, "Mysticism and Rationalism."

107. On Dippel as an early theological rationalist, see *DR*, 490–91. As a practicing alchemist and a rationalist critic of Lutheran theology, Dippel shows how mysticism and rationalism could be combined in the same person. Isaac Newton, who dabbled in alchemy and esoteric literature as he made natural philosophy (i.e., physics) his primary endeavor, might be another instance.

108. Regarding Paul's "all" language in Rom. 5:18 and 1 Cor. 15:22, Douglas J. Moo comments: "That 'all' does not always mean 'every single human being' is clear from many passages, it often being clearly limited in context (cf. Rom. 8:32; 12:17, 18; 14:2; 16:19)" (*Epistle to the Romans*, 343–44). See, e.g., Rom. 16:19: "For your obedience [that of the Roman Christians] is known to all, so that I rejoice over you." "Repay no one evil for evil, but give thought to do what is honorable in the sight of all. . . . Live peaceably with all" (Rom. 12:17–18). These instances are pertinent to the interpretation of Rom. 5:18, since they come from the same Pauline letter. Moreover, the text of Rom. 5:12–21 comes immediately after Rom. 5:1–11, which speaks not of the "justification" of all persons but of the "justification" occurring "by faith" (Rom. 5:1). Universalist interpretation of Paul requires a decontextualized reading of Rom. 5:12–21 *against* Rom. 5:1–11. See *DR* appendix L for a discussion

Augustine's *City of God* was an especially important effort to overturn universalist interpretations of Scripture. Particularists have often appealed to Jesus's teaching on the sheep and the goats (Matt. 25) and to the book of Revelation in their opposition to universalism.

Christian universalist exegesis is a topic that would require a large book—or perhaps a series of books—to canvass adequately. Generally speaking, most universalists through most of church history have relied on nonliteral, typological, and allegorical approaches to the Bible to support their views. They interpret the "fire" that threatens human beings in the New Testament Gospels not as threatening but as purifying and healing. The "lake of fire" in the book of Revelation, argues Robin Parry, is not an eternal or endless punishment but represents God himself cleansing and preparing people for heavenly bliss. Even though Parry is one of the most biblically literalistic of recent Christian universalists, in this case his interpretation becomes quite nonliteralistic (*DR* 11.4).[109] In some cases, the interpretations of Scripture in support of universalism seem quite arbitrary, as when, for example, John Murray appealed to the Old Testament passage on Aaron's priestly garments (Exod. 28:2), and from this elaborated an argument for universal salvation (*DR* 6.5). Many other examples of universalist exegesis might be supplied.[110]

---

of Christ's union with humanity in Barth's and Bultmann's exegesis of Rom. 5. I. H. Marshall takes issue with Thomas Talbott's argument that God's final supremacy in Phil. 2 and 1 Cor. 15 is necessarily due to the creatures' happy and willing self-submission to God:

> Talbott rejects the idea of "subjugation" on the grounds that God's victory is incomplete so long as anybody can cling to their hatred of God. But the New Testament plainly uses the language of judgement and destruction to describe what God will do. This is clear from 1 Corinthians 15:24–28, where the vocabulary of destruction and subjugation is used. . . . Talbott's suggestion that the subjugation here is like that of Christ to the Father ignores the mention of destruction. The willing subordination of Christ is different from the destruction of hostile powers. (I. H. Marshall, "New Testament Does *Not* Teach Universal Salvation," 69)

109. So too John Noe writes, "The lake of fire is God himself in some way" (*Hell Yes / Hell No*, 92). Catholic teachings on purgatory likewise involve nonliteral interpretation. Pope Benedict XVI describes the "fire" of 1 Cor. 3 that burns up the wood, hay, and stubble as equivalent to Christ himself: "The fire which both burns and saves is Christ himself, the Judge and Savior." This equation of "fire" with "Christ" is not obvious from the texts. See Pope Benedict XVI, *Spe Salvi*, no. 47. Cf. Ratzinger, *Eschatology*, 230: "Encounter with the Lord *is* this transformation. It is the fire that burns away our dross and re-forms us to be vessels of eternal joy."

110. Recent literature that seeks to offer biblical support for universalism includes especially Talbott, *Inescapable Love*, esp. 43–129; Gregory MacDonald [Parry], *Evangelical Universalist*. Also worth noting for universalist interpretation of Scripture are Bonda, *One Purpose of God*; Jersak, *Her Gates Will Never Be Shut*. A popular work favorable to universalism but with an ambiguous conclusion is Noe, *Hell Yes / Hell No*. Exegetical arguments favoring universalism also appear in Beauchemin, *Hope beyond Hell*. Recent works opposing universalist biblical interpretations include C. W. Morgan and R. A. Peterson, *Hell under Fire*, which includes Block, "Old Testament on Hell" (43–65); Yarbrough, "Jesus on Hell" (67–90); Moo, "Paul on Hell" (91–109); Beale,

During the modern period, universalists have used a number of exegetical strategies in interpreting the Bible. In addition to spiritual, allegorical, or non-literal interpretation of the biblical text—which has continued in the modern era as in the premodern period—a common strategy has been two-strand or dual-strand interpretation. This idea, which seemingly began among the German Philadelphian universalists just after 1700 (*DR* 5.8), holds that the New Testament (and especially the Pauline literature) contains both particularist and universalist motifs.[111] Neither strand of biblical teaching has ultimate priority over the other. So it lies with the interpreter to choose which strand to highlight. Some contemporary exegetes favor this idea of two strands in the Pauline Letters, while others oppose the idea.[112] The dual-strand interpretation requires that one believe that the Bible is at odds with itself in its teaching on eschatology and perhaps that the apostle Paul was himself of two minds on the question. A variation on this dual-strand view is what we might call the paradoxical interpretation, which emphasizes the Bible's plurality of views, the tension between divergent teachings in the Bible, and the undecidability of interpretive questions.[113] In light of the undecidability of biblical teaching, one must either affirm all the different strands or else choose one strand over the rest.

A different approach to the Bible—often in support of universalism—lies in existentialist interpretation. According to this view, the eschatological language

---

"[Book of] Revelation on Hell" (111–34). A concise account of anti-universalist exegesis appears in I. H. Marshall, "New Testament Does *Not* Teach Universal Salvation." Francis Chan and Preston Sprinkle's *Erasing Hell* contains biblical analysis in opposition to universalism. Other exegetical anti-universalist works are listed in *DR*, 965–67nn110–12. Surprisingly comprehensive in assessing universalist exegesis, despite its age, is Lampe, *Theological Dissertations* (1796). N. T. Wright is among the biblical scholars today who do not support universalist interpretations of the Gospels and the other New Testament texts. Wright's opposition to a universalist reading of the Pauline Letters was evident in his early essay "Towards a Biblical View of Universalism." He later commented that Jesus "went along with the normal first-century Jewish perception" that "there really are some who finally reject God and, as it were, have that rejection ratified" (*Surprised by Hope*, 176–77). With the release of his major two-volume work *Paul and the Faithfulness of God*, Wright addressed nearly one thousand scholars at the Society of Biblical Literature meeting in Baltimore in November 2013, and, on being asked if Paul was a universalist, said—in one word—"No."

111. See Groth, *Die "Wiederbringung aller Dinge,"* 14–17. The dual-strand interpretation might antedate the German Philadelphians of the early eighteenth century, though I have no evidence to this effect.

112. In general support of the two-strands idea, see R. H. Bell, "Rom. 5:18–19 and Universal Salvation"; de Boer, *Defeat of Death*; Hillert, *Limited and Universal Salvation*. For a critique, see Gundry-Volf, "Universalism"; Pegler, "Nature of Paul's Universal Salvation Language in Romans."

113. "In computability theory and computational complexity theory, an undecidable problem is a decision problem for which it is known to be impossible to construct a single algorithm that always leads to a correct yes-or-no answer" (https://en.wikipedia.org/wiki/Undecidable_problem).

of the Bible is said to be concerned not with future states of existence or with something "out there" in the objective world but with alternate human possibilities. Prominent instances of existential interpretation would include writings by Rudolf Bultmann, John A. T. Robinson, and Karl Rahner.[114] Though Bultmann and Robinson preceded Rahner, it may be Rahner's works that did the most since the 1960s to give currency to existentialist readings of biblical eschatological language. Balthasar was among those influenced by Rahner's approach to eschatology (*DR* 10.8). Alongside the existentializing approach are various forms of reductive reading, whereby some part of the Bible—not the whole Bible—functions as a norm for Christian belief. This would include canon-within-the-canon interpretation, based on the Bible's purported plurality of views, calling for a nonharmonious reading whereby the interpreter decides to embrace one part of the written text as having priority or authority over other parts. In reduced-canon interpretation, one part of the Bible is flatly rejected in favor of other parts of the Bible. In thematic interpretation of the Bible, one theme in the Bible—for example, the teaching of Jesus, as reconstructed by the interpreter—has priority or authority for the interpretation of the whole of the Bible.[115] The terminology used to describe these different interpretive techniques is not standardized by any means, and the literature on biblical hermeneutics is both vast and complex. The varied interpretive strategies often merge into one another and are not wholly distinct.[116]

Existentialist interpretation of the Bible, which first appeared only in the twentieth century, shows certain similarities to the ancient allegorical reading of Scripture, in that it insists that the literal reading of the biblical text must be, as it were, translated into some different mode to be interpreted and unpacked. Existentialist interpretation of the Bible is anthropological or anthropocentric in the sense that it finds the referents for biblical language in contemporary human life and experience. Karl Rahner wrote: "The metaphors in which Jesus describes the eternal perdition of man as a possibility which threatens him . . . [fire, worm, darkness, etc.] . . . all mean the same thing, the possibility of man being finally lost and estranged from God in all the dimensions of his existence. . . . Suchlike words are metaphorical expressions for something radically not

114. Rahner, "Hermeneutics of Eschatological Assertions"; John A. T. Robinson, *In the End, God*; Bultmann, *Jesus and the Word*. David Congdon (see *DR* 9.13) might also be seen as holding to an *existentialist* interpretation of biblical eschatological language—though his defense of universal salvation, his affirmation that all persons have analogous "ecstatic" experiences, and his partial embrace of Barthian theology would seem to point in a different direction.

115. Ellen F. Davis proposes a thematic or partial reading of the Bible in "Critical Traditioning."

116. Some of the recent literature addresses parts of the Bible regarded as morally problematic. See Collins, "Zeal of Phineas"; Cosgrove, *Appealing to Scripture in Moral Debate*; E. W. Davies, "Morally Dubious Passages of the Hebrew Bible."

of this world . . . [that] can only be spoken of 'in images.'"[117] Rahner used the expression "threat discourse" to signify that biblical language might seem to be speaking of some unfortunate, future state of existence but in actuality has to do with one's present life choices.[118] John A. T. Robinson's existentialist hermeneutics was perhaps even more complex than Rahner's. Robinson insisted that the seemingly twofold outcome of the "sheep" and the "goats" in Jesus's parable refers to alternative human possibilities that each apply to each individual. Both heaven and hell are true as human possibilities, even though only one of these possibilities—salvation rather than damnation—will ever be realized. Robinson commented, "To the man in decision—and that means to all men, always, right up to the last hour—hell is in every way as real a destination as heaven. Only the man who has genuinely been confronted with both alternatives can be saved."[119]

Paradoxical interpretation of the Bible is especially characteristic of German scholarship, perhaps because of the dialectical character of Lutheran thought, which is structured around contrasting principles or ideas (e.g., law vs. gospel). Paul Althaus in *Die letzten Dingen* argues that the question of a dual outcome (i.e., heaven and hell) versus a single outcome (i.e., universalism) cannot be resolved but must remain an open question. For Althaus, the necessary tension between law and gospel requires that the question remain open. The one who affirms universalism abolishes the law, while the one who affirms the twofold outcome abolishes the gospel. Paradoxically, then, it would seem that Christian thinkers, preachers, and laypersons must affirm both positions at the same time. At first blush, Jürgen Moltmann in *The Coming of God* (1996) would seem to fit with this common German approach. Moltmann affirms that there are two strands in the biblical teaching, standing in tension with one another. Yet Moltmann then rejects the biblical passages that suggest a twofold outcome in favor of those he takes in support of universalism.[120] Moltmann's hermeneutic is thus more reductive than synthetic or paradoxical, since it involves the setting

117. Rahner, "Hell" [1975], 603.

118. As Peter C. Phan explains, Karl Rahner denied that the New Testament language provides any "'advance coverage' of the beyond" or information about the future. Taking the biblical language as "threat discourse" means that it has to do with human decision in the here and now. "Because biblical statements on hell are not factual descriptions but a summons to personal decision for God, it is not possible to know from them whether there are people in hell" ("Eschatology," 186, citing Rahner, "Hell" [1969], 7).

119. John A. T. Robinson, *In the End, God*, 118; cf. 123. I. H. Marshall finds "logical difficulties" in insisting on the "subjective reality" of Jesus's statements on final judgment but their "objective emptiness" ("New Testament Does *Not* Teach Universal Salvation," 74n9). On Robinson's dialectical approach to universalism, see K. S. Harmon, "Finally Excluded from God?," 133–218; T. Hart, "Universalism."

120. Moltmann, *Coming of God*, 240–43.

aside of particularist passages. A recent instance of paradoxical interpretation appears in Bradley Jersak's *Her Gates Will Never Be Shut* (2009). Jersak speaks of the Bible's teaching as "richly polyphonic on the topic of hell and judgment" and contends that there are three different and irreconcilable strands of biblical teaching on the subject of hell: infernalist, annihilationist, and universalist. He explains, "These three types of passages . . . cannot be integrated easily into a cogent dogmatic system. In fact, my argument for hope over presumption is just this: the Bible doesn't allow us to settle easily into any of these as 'isms.' Perhaps that's because humankind needs all of these voices."[121]

Thematic or canon-within-the-canon interpretation of the Bible has been increasingly common among authors in support of Christian universalism. Sharon Baker's *Razing Hell* (2010) starts from the assumption that the Old Testament offers us a morally problematic picture of God: "We receive most of our images of God as violent and retributive from the Old Testament, whereas the New Testament typically portrays God as peace-loving and reconciling. In fact, the character of God described in the Old Testament seems quite different from the one drawn for us in the New Testament."[122] Baker enjoins, "To harmonize or not to harmonize—that is the question." She answers her own question by stating, on the one hand, that "we just can't reconcile the differences between a God who exacts justice through violence and a God of peace," while, on the other hand, "we can still decide which texts we will focus upon, which image of God we will use as a basis for our own behavior." There are two conflicting gods in the Bible and one must choose. Baker's approach lies in "determining the main message" through "the lens of Jesus." "Interpreting divine justice through the lens of Jesus, his life, teachings, death, and resurrection," she writes, "challenges retribution and paints a picture of justice that reconciles and restores people to God."[123] Along similar lines, Rob Bell in *What Is the Bible?* (2017) comments, "I don't read the Bible like a flat line. I don't see all of the passages in the Bible sitting equally side by side."[124] In *God's Final Victory* (2013), John Kronen and Eric Reitan argue for universalism chiefly on philosophical grounds, yet they also argue from a canon-within-the-canon perspective, denying that "every passage of the Bible has the same kind of revelatory significance," and suggesting that it is

121. Jersak, *Her Gates Will Never Be Shut*, 6–7.

122. Baker, *Razing Hell*, 21.

123. Ibid., 56–57, 89.

124. R. Bell, *What Is the Bible?*, 116. "These things people wrote down [in Scripture] reflected the world at their time in their context. . . . And right there in the midst of those stories, you often see growth and maturing and expanding perspectives" (117). In Bell's evolutionary interpretation of the Bible, "new ideas sit side by side with old ideas," and alongside the "violent stories" there are "radically new ideas about freedom, equality, justice, compassion, and love" (123).

possible that "God inspired some biblical authors to express mistaken cultural biases."[125]

Generally speaking, universalist exegetes have always had a hard time with the Old Testament and the book of Revelation, which both speak of fierce judgments and punishments inflicted by God. Some contemporary universalists are ready to jettison the Old Testament and the book of Revelation as reflecting a judgmental or vindictive God. Such an argument, however, is almost never used with regard to Jesus himself. Wanting to maintain a connection to Jesus, universalists must use a different hermeneutical strategy vis-à-vis the passages on hell and judgment that appear in the Synoptic Gospels. With regard to Paul, much of the same situation exists. Most universalists cling to certain verses in Paul's Letters as offering hope for a universal restoration, and few universalists are ready to give up on Paul. Even if the Old Testament has been abandoned, and the book of Revelation is treated as a text filled with enigmatic symbols, universalist exegetes will generally look for support for their views in the text of the New Testament Gospels and in the Pauline Letters.

The various hermeneutical approaches used by Christian universalists in reading the Bible involve, on some level, a hermeneutics of diminishment. In each case the surface-level meanings of the biblical text disappear and are replaced by something else. In the symbolic and allegorical reading of the Bible, the threatening "fire" as spoken of by Jesus becomes a cleansing and purifying "fire" that removes my wickedness, or the "fire" of my own self-lacerating conscience. The "lake of fire" in the book of Revelation is sometimes said to be God himself, thus contradicting the text of the Bible, which identifies the "lake" with "the second death" (Rev. 20:14). (Or is God himself "the second death"?) In the existentialist reading of the Bible, the "shut door" in Jesus's parable that allows no one to enter the feast (Matt. 25:10) has nothing to do with any future situation or circumstance. These words instead, in Rahner's terms, belong to the genre of "threat discourse," challenging me to make rightful decisions here and now. By emptying biblical language of its future reference, Rahner's existential interpretation—like that of Bultmann and Robinson—evacuates Jesus's teaching of its spiritual force and its terrible urgency.

The thematic or canon-within-the-canon approaches to the Bible are even less satisfactory than allegorical or existentialist interpretations for those who receive the Bible as divinely revealed. A New Testament interpretation that begins by rejecting the Old Testament is ipso facto a non-Christian interpretation. Such approaches to the Bible are alien to the church's historic position, which has always been to see itself and its teaching as founded on the Old Testament

---

125. Kronen and Reitan, *God's Final Victory*, 59–60.

no less than the New Testament. Those who accept only some of the Gospels, or only certain passages in Paul, or the New Testament minus the book of Revelation, are hardly in a better position. The most ambitious attempt at a complete, canonical reading of the Bible—interpreted literally and consistent with universalist premises—is that of Robin Parry in *The Evangelical Universalist* (2006). Yet this attempt, as shown earlier, is exegetically unsuccessful (*DR* 11.4). Seemingly the only options for Christian universalism lie in either rejecting one or more parts of the Bible or else interpreting it implausibly.

12.5. Christian Universalism and the Challenge of Evil

In the ancient, cultured, and multicultural city of Alexandria, Egypt, Christian teachers were under tremendous pressure to justify the biblical God in the eyes of pagan philosophers: Could God be considered good if God created a world filled with evil and suffering? And was the Old Testament God a worthy being, since this God so often was represented as wrathful and punishing? Many early Christian gnostics distinguished the God of the Old Testament from the God of the New Testament. They insisted that the earthly, physical, material world was not created by the highest God but rather by lesser spiritual powers (*DR* 2.3). But there were other tendencies at work among the gnostics. Some of them responded to the challenge of evil by taking a page from Plato's philosophy and proposing that earthly life was merely a temporary sojourn for the soul. The souls originally with God would all finally return to God. Salvation would be universal. This was a genuinely new teaching, since Plato in his dialogues had stated that a few souls were so wicked that even the fiery punishments of the afterlife would not bring them salvation. Such souls were incorrigibly and impenitently evil (*DR* 2.1).

From this brief recounting, one begins to see where, how, and why Origen may have developed his idea of universal salvation. Fundamentally it was a response to the problem of evil.[126] The argument worked in both directions—backward and forward in time. The sufferings of this present life could be reconciled with God's goodness, said Origen, because every person in the present life got the degree of happiness or unhappiness he or she deserved on the basis of past choices as a preexistent and premortal soul with God. Regarding the forward-looking aspect, Origen concurred with earlier gnostic Christians on a final *apokatastasis*—an ultimate happy ending for all—that made the sufferings of the present time fade into insignificance. Evil and suffering were not

126. See M. S. M. Scott, *Journey Back to God*.

merely theoretical issues for Origen. His life was overshadowed by the Christian martyrdom of his father at the hands of the pagan Romans and the sufferings endured by his family after his father's death. The authorities confiscated his family's land and wealth. Origen became financially responsible for his widowed mother and a large household. Early church scholar Mark Scott judges that this event during Origen's teen years shaped his entire life.[127]

The modern revival of universalism took place among the followers of Jakob Böhme (1575–1624). The Thirty Years' War in Germany (1618–48) was the backdrop for the publication of Böhme's major works during the final years of his life. Up to a third of the German population perished in a generation's time. Böhme's quest for the "root" of all things, good and evil alike, might have something to do with his tumultuous and disconcerting social context. Likewise, the Böhmist movement in England took root during the English conflicts of the mid-seventeenth century, and universalism found its first modern advocate in the English language in Gerrard Winstanley's *The Mysterie of God* (1648), a work published during the English Civil War and just before the 1649 execution of King Charles I by Puritan radicals (*DR* 5.7). In the New World, universalist ideas spread rapidly during the trials and tribulations of the American Revolution (1770s–1780s).

The two leading Anglo-American universalists of the eighteenth century, Elhanan Winchester (1751–97) and John Murray (1741–1815), both had unusually tragic lives. As a boy, Winchester lost his mother at age nine. As a younger man, he married five times over a period of seven years because each of his first four wives died in succession. All but one of the children deriving from these marriages died in childbirth. The one child that survived childbirth died before the age of two. His fifth and final marriage proved to be an unhappy one. He left America for London without his wife, whom he said had made his life miserable for more than nine years.[128] The life of John Murray was almost as full of loss as that of Winchester. Married in 1760, he passed through a period of profound suffering prior to his departure from England to America in 1770. According to

127. Scott writes: "After the execution of his father, the family's property was confiscated by the imperial treasury. Bereavement was thus compounded by impoverishment. As the eldest son, the responsibility to provide for the family fell on his shoulders. . . . Persecution, loss, and hardship during his formative years would leave an indelible impression on him. For the rest of his days, he would live in the shadow of his father's martyrdom. It would set him on an intellectual and spiritual journey to make sense of and ultimately overcome the evil and suffering of the world [as he] delineated the first systematic Christian theodicy" (ibid., 1–2).

128. Peter Hughes, "Elhanan Winchester": "In 1769 he [i.e., Winchester] married Alice Rogers (at first secretly, it has been said, and without legal ceremony). Alice, the first of his five wives, died in 1776. In 1776 he married Sarah Peck (d. 1777), in 1778 Sarah Luke (d. 1779), in 1781 Mary Morgan (d. 1783), and in 1784 or 1785 Maria Knowles."

one biographer, "There followed a period in which Murray experienced a series of personal losses that drove him to the brink of despair. His only son died in infancy. His wife also died and, soon after that, he learned of the deaths of four of his siblings. He was thrown into debtor's prison." The biographer adds, "Although he was rescued by his brother-in-law and eventually paid his debts, he remained too depressed to engage in the preaching . . . urged upon him. At that time he wished 'to pass through life, unheard, unseen, unknown to all, as though I ne'er had been.'" In 1770 Murray came to America without ever intending to preach the universalist message. He had "resolved to quit his life in the old world and start afresh in the new."[129] Out of this set of tragic experiences, though, Murray came to believe that he had a vocation to preach the final salvation of all.

It is striking also to see that Karl Barth's influential treatise on universal election, *Church Dogmatics* II/2, appeared originally in German in 1942, during the Nazi occupation of Europe and an exceedingly dispiriting time for the Allied forces opposed to Germany and the Axis powers. Could there have been any darker hour in Europe in which to proclaim the good news that everyone is chosen for salvation in Christ? What is more, the Russian universalists Nicolas Berdyaev and Sergius Bulgakov were both living as exiles in France when they wrote their major works. From a Russian Orthodox standpoint, World War I and the war's aftermath in the Russian Revolution were a historical catastrophe that called for reflection on the nature of good and evil and God's historical and eschatological purposes.

The historical pattern thus shows that Christian universalism often emerged in conflicted and chaotic periods of history. It hardly seems an accident that a hope for universal salvation often burned brightest in the darkest hour. Universalism appeared again and again in contexts that evoked the question of theodicy—that is, an ultimate explanation for the reality of evil and suffering. Generally the human quest for an explanation has taken the form of narrative, a story that helps us to make sense of disconnected, painful, and random aspects of our experience. Sociologist Max Weber (1864–1920) pointed to theodicy as one of the fundamental and defining features of world religions. Suffering becomes endurable, argued Weber, if and when it fits within some larger framework that makes it comprehensible to us. Suffering becomes unendurable if and when there is no way to comprehend it.[130]

In the historical debates over Christian universalism, we may distinguish four broad tendencies, each of which is associated with a differing response to

---

129. Peter Hughes, "John Murray."
130. Weber, "Theodicy, Salvation, and Rebirth." On evil, and making sense of everything, see also Frankl, *Man's Search for Meaning.*

the problem of evil. We term these tendencies as *pedagogical, dualist, illusionist,* and *voluntarist.* The *pedagogical* view holds that evil and suffering are intended to teach someone (or everyone) a lesson. Connected with the pedagogical view is the presumption that people learn lessons from their experiences and that eventually everyone, including the slowest learner or most recalcitrant evildoer, will come around to understanding goodness and choose to act in accord with goodness. In contrast to this, the *dualistic* approach holds that good and evil are irreducible features of the world that we live in and that they have always been in conflict with one another and will always be so. For the dualist, we live in a world where people do evil things, and it would be foolish to expect otherwise.

A quite different approach to evil is *illusionist*—that is, claiming that what we call evil is only an appearance. So-called evil may very well seem to be all bad, yet when one looks more deeply or reflects on it more comprehensively, the evilness of evil disappears, and so apparent evil proves to be a form of disguised good. Finally, there is the approach to evil that one might call *voluntarist,* affirming the reality of evil, denying that everyone finally learns their lesson, and yet also denying that evil is inherent in reality as such or is simply the way things are. The voluntarist sees evil as rooted in the evil will, which may prove to be baffling, nonrational, and hence inexplicable. Simply put, the cause of the evil will is the evil will. One cannot go further than this in searching for an explanation, but must allow that evil is genuinely evil and that it takes shape in the volition of the one who chooses it. Broadly speaking, Origen serves as an example of the *pedagogical,* Böhme of the *dualistic,* Barth of the *illusionist,* and Augustine of the *voluntarist* approach.

Origen approached evil in terms of the pedagogical perspective, according to which everyone finally learns their lesson, with the outcome of universal salvation. In Origen's theology, there is ultimately no way of explaining the preexistent, heavenly spirits' falling away from God. Evil emerges, so to speak, *ex nihilo*—an objection that is often lodged against Augustine's theology as well. Moreover, Origen has other problems of his own making. In propounding a fall into sin that seemingly took place prior to the story of Adam and Eve in the garden of Eden, the problem of evil's origin is shifted backward in time. So we might well ask how the positing of a preexistent fall offers a better explanation of the origin of sin and evil than the story of Adam and Eve in Genesis.

Origen's pedagogical theology faces a challenge in light of general human experience, which suggests that some people learn from experience and improve as a result of the opportunities afforded to them while others do not. Even if, rather optimistically, we declare that the vast majority of human beings are learners rather than laggers, it seems impossible on the basis of collective life experience to make a universal claim to the effect that everyone will eventually learn their lesson. Some people seem bent on self-destruction. Folly and stubbornness in wrongdoing are enduring human traits, at least when we collectively consider large numbers of people. If the theologians and philosophers have forgotten this fact, then the poets and novelists have not. The great authors—Dante, Cervantes, Shakespeare, Milton, Melville, Dostoyevsky—attest to the realities of human folly and hardness of heart.[131]

In the face of evil, Jakob Böhme adopted a dualistic perspective and so followed a pattern set in Jewish Kabbalah, in which evil first emerges not within creation but within God himself. In Kabbalah, good and evil are aspects or dimensions of God's being, the "emanations of the right" alongside the "emanations of the left." What results in Kabbalah and in Böhme's philosophy is thus an essentializing of evil. Lucifer and Christ—whom Böhme called brothers to one another—are both expressions of the divine nature. While there might be an ultimate unity in God beyond the dualism of good and evil, this unity remains abstract in Böhme's philosophy. All concrete, describable existence or experience is ethically dualistic. In even the sticks and stones, wrote Böhme, good and evil strive against one another. Even the trinitarian God of Father, Son, and Spirit is dualistically divided against himself. F. C. Baur compared Böhme's thought to Manichaeism, a classically dualistic religion. The problems with dualism are manifold from the standpoint of Christian theology, which has consistently maintained that "God is light, and in him is no darkness at all" (1 John 1:5).[132] The attribution of the origin of evil to God breaks the basic grammar of biblical discourse and classical Christian theology. It would also seem to be a counsel of despair, since dualism suggests that evil and good remain forever locked in conflict with one another. It is intriguing to see that Böhme's own disciples (excepting Johann Gichtel) abandoned his unremitting dualism in favor of a theology in which good overcame evil (DR 5.4). In this way, the Böhmists came to approximate Origen's pedagogical rather than Böhme's dualistic approach to evil.

Karl Barth tended toward an *illusionist* account of evil. At various points in his vast corpus Barth toyed with a kind of dualism—that is, an uncreated and

---

131. Literary approaches to the theme of hardness of heart include W. Moore, "'Dom Juan' Reconsidered"; McCullum and Guilds, "Unpardonable Sin in Hawthorne"; D. G. Cunningham, "Macbeth"; G. H. Cox, "Marlowe's *Doctor Faustus.*"

132. Balthasar, in a more limited way than Böhme, arguably adopted a dualistic view regarding the origin and nature of evil. In proposing his doctrine of "primal self-emptying" (*Urkenosis*) within God, Balthasar stated that a pretemporal "separation" (*Trennung*) between the Father and the Son constituted the "precondition" for evil (DR 10.7). From an Augustinian standpoint, the problem with this line of argument lies at the starting point. Evil requires no precondition. The will chooses evil because the will chooses evil.

yet nondivine form of evil that he called "nothingness" (*das Nichtige*). But for the most part Barth moved toward illusionism, declaring that Christ's coming had now rendered sin an "ontological impossibility." The sinful person, he asserted, had been altogether abolished at Christ's coming. This created an empirical problem for Barth's theology, because even the most cursory glance at the daily news shows us that the sinful person is still very much with us. Barth's illusionist tendencies might help to explain his decision in the *Church Dogmatics* to write extensively on the subject of the unfallen or holy angels yet not to discuss Satan or the fallen angels. Barth asserted that Satan had never been an angel at all, rendering the ontological status of "Satan" wholly ambiguous, like that of *das Nichtige*, which was said to be neither Creator nor created. In general, sin and evil simply do not have the full weight of reality in Barth's theology. Of the various approaches to the problem of evil, illusionism may be the most problematic, since it conflicts with the profound seriousness regarding sin and evil that one finds in Scripture and Christian tradition. So far from being unreal, sin and evil are so real that they require God's intervention through the incarnation, life, crucifixion, resurrection, and return of Christ. Illusionism conflicts with the Christian redemptive narrative, since sin and evil, if unreal, would not require God to act as he has acted in Christ.

These four divergent approaches to theodicy all involve an appeal to mystery and yet they locate mystery in different places. The illusionist approach locates the mystery of evil in the realm of appearances. The problem regarding evil is why anyone should see a problem regarding evil. The dualistic approach finds evil to be rooted in the character of God. Evil is firmly rooted in mundane reality because it is rooted in God's own reality. The mystery for the dualist is that God should be both things—evil as well as good. How could this be? And would the ambiguously good-evil deity be worthy of worship? The pedagogical approach must confront the mystery of folly and irrationality in human behavior. Because some people demonstrably fail to learn their life lessons or to improve in any conspicuous fashion, it remains unclear how or why anyone should agree with the pedagogical claim that "people learn." The Augustinian approach, as noted already, locates the mystery of evil within the evil will itself. This view seems for a number of reasons to be more congruent with Scripture and Christian tradition than the other three views.

Augustine is known for appealing to creatures' freedom as an "answer" to evil. God gave to angels and to human beings the gift of free will. They could choose.[133] Augustine is also known for several other intellectual moves, including the idea of a final harmony at the end, or what has been called teleological

---

133. See M. T. Clark, *Augustine, Philosopher of Freedom*.

justification.[134] His idea of the *privatio boni*—that evil is a "privation of good" and therefore not a separately existing thing in the created universe—is sometimes viewed as a form of illusionism. This interpretation is not quite fair to Augustine, who regarded evil as very real and very painful to those encountering it. The point in Augustine's metaphysics of evil as privation was to deny the dualistic tenet of the Manichaeans—to whom Augustine himself had once belonged—to the effect that evil was a "thing" existing alongside goodness and perhaps an eternally self-subsisting entity or substance.[135] Augustine's more perceptive critics faulted him for different reasons, and they relentlessly posed the following questions: How does one explain the evil will itself? Where does it come from? How does it arise? Why? Augustine's detractors claimed that he made evil originate *ex nihilo*, without a sufficient cause or ground of any kind.

Why do humans spurn and reject God despite God's love and goodness? There is no rational answer. If evil is irrational, then perhaps it does not admit of a rational explanation. Despite these Augustinian nonanswers to any number of questions about the evilness of the evil will, the Augustinian approach to evil has positive value in ruling out answers to the problem of evil that ultimately prove to be much more theologically problematic and dangerous than Augustine's stress on the evil will. On Augustinian premises, one is not allowed in Christian theological terms to say that there is a mystery of appearances and that evil is not ultimately real (the illusionist mistake). Nor is one permitted to affirm a mystery of light and darkness mingled within God's own being or ranged against each other as separate phenomena, principles, or deities (the dualist mistake). Nor is one allowed to put one's confidence in human educability and perfectibility (the pedagogic mistake), since this hope has so often throughout history proved to be delusory. In Augustine's account, some of God's creatures do not learn their lessons because that is simply the nature of the evil will—stubborn, perverse, and irrational. Traditional theology affirmed that Lucifer was created as the most intelligent and gifted of the angels. Yet this creature of supreme intelligence undertook the most idiotic course of action ever conceived, by seeking to topple and to replace God. What could be more foolish? As the traditional theological saying goes, *corruptio optima pessima est* (the worst things arise through the corruption of the best). In summary, then,

134. One of the best accounts of Augustine's theodicy, demonstrating its multiple dimensions, is Hick, "The Augustinian Type of Theodicy," in *Evil and the God of Love*, 38–114.

135. At times Augustine refers to a sort of cosmic balance of good and evil, like light and shadow that equally play their part and contribute to the overall beauty of some vast picture. In my view, this is a minor motif in Augustine's reflection on evil. In any case, this line of thinking, when followed to its logical conclusion, tends in the direction of the dualism that Augustine once embraced and later rejected.

we see that Augustine's voluntaristic approach to the question of evil and his particularist theology of salvation make sense of the problem of evil better than the alternative theologies just noted.

In Augustine's view, evil originates in the wrongful will. The worst of situations is when the creature's will becomes fixed or steadfast in willing and accomplishing evil. Origenist thought takes the speculative position that since evil is not human nature per se but is contrary to nature, there cannot in principle be any habituation in evil, though there can be habituation in good. The biblical texts point in the other direction, presupposing and demonstrating that habituation in evil is possible.[136] In the book of Exodus, Pharaoh in Egypt receives no less than nine chances (after each of the first nine of the ten plagues) to humble himself and to consent to Moses, who speaks for God in telling Pharaoh to "let my people go" (Exod. 5:1; 7:16; 8:1, 20–21; 9:1, 13; 10:3–4). Pharaoh refuses to listen.[137] As a result of this hardness of heart, Pharaoh and the Egyptian people suffer dire consequences.[138] Origen in *On First Principles* felt the need to discuss Pharaoh's hardness of heart at great length, because the biblical narrative of Pharaoh's rebellion against God seemed on its face to conflict with his pedagogical theory that Pharaoh, like everyone else, will gradually learn his lesson, once given opportunity to do so.[139]

The Hebrew prophets also touched on the theme of hardness of heart. Hosea wrote, "The more they were called, the more they went away; they kept sacrificing to the Baals and burning offerings to idols" (Hosea 11:2). The book of Jeremiah, as much as any text in the Bible, shows how God repeatedly gave opportunities for repentance while God's people went further and further away. "Can . . . the leopard [change] his spots? Then also you can do good who are accustomed to do evil" (Jer. 13:23). This theme continues into the New Testament Gospels, where in Matthew 13 Jesus appeals to Isaiah 6 with its theme of the hardened heart. Hardness of heart reappears in the book of Revelation. Revelation 2

136. On the hardening of the heart as a general biblical theme, see Meadors, *Idolatry and the Hardening of the Heart*.

137. On Pharaoh's hardness of heart, see R. R. Wilson, "Hardening of Pharaoh's Heart"; Beale, "Hardening of Pharaoh's Heart"; Coover-Cox, "Hardening of Pharaoh's Heart."

138. The Islamic universalist Ibn 'Arabi claimed that Pharaoh was saved. He suggested that Pharaoh repented at the Red Sea, commenting that "Allah accepted his sincere belief and Allah does not accept someone's belief unless he will surely reward him." Pharaoh's faith did not begin at the moment of his death, said Ibn 'Arabi, but rather when he saw the waters of the Red Sea miraculously divided in two. When someone comes from idolatry into Islam, he receives a ritual bath, and so Ibn 'Arabi wrote that "Pharaoh's drowning was his ritual bathing" (*Futuhat al-Makkiyah*, ch. 9 [In the Remembrance of God], 12th Oneness, trans. al-Muatasim Said al-Maawali). On Ibn 'Arabi's account of Pharaoh, see *DR* appendix F.

139. On Pharaoh's hardness of heart, see Origen, *On First Principles* 3.1.7–17 (*PA* 481–531; Butterworth, 166–95).

speaks of the false prophetess who is given the name Jezebel. Here God says, "I gave her time to repent, but she refuses to repent of her sexual immorality" (2.21). God's judgments in Revelation 16 do not bring sinners to repentance but instead cause them to blaspheme God. Having deceived the nations and having led them into rebellion against God, Satan in Revelation 20 is confined for a thousand years. Having been released, he returns immediately to his rebellion against God. Only at this point is Satan seized and thrown into the lake of fire. In the biblical presentation there is such a thing as habituation in evil, in contradiction to Origen's pedagogical assumption.[140]

12.6. Christian Particularism and the Call to Hope

According to the apostle Paul's teaching in Romans 5, the gift of God's grace overshadows, overpowers, and eclipses the reality of Adam's sin. Human life and history are not defined primarily by the fact of sin but by the fact of God's grace in Christ. While Paul is not arguing in this passage for universal salvation, his stress on the disproportion between God's grace and human sin suggests that those with a sin-dominated worldview should exchange it for a perspective that is more grace-dominated. Paul in this passage expresses wonderment at the presence and power of divine grace that so completely cancels out the negative effects of sin and brings full salvation for those who receive it. We must read Romans 5:12–21 in light of Romans 5:1–11. The many-sidedness of God's salvation in Christ (5:1–11) underlies Paul's declaration of the greatness of grace in comparison with the paltriness of sin (5:12–21). Romans 8:1–39 testifies even more fully than Romans 5:1–11 to Paul's extraordinary range of ideas and thoughts on the many-sidedness of salvation. The qualitative as well as quantitative aspects of salvation ought to be considered.

The apostle Paul did not seem to think that saved humanity is a tiny speck in a vast ocean of wickedness and final doom. Instead he presumed that justified humanity, the heirs of God and fellow heirs with Christ (Rom. 8:17), is an imposing multitude of people, drawn from every nation and united with the Savior and with one another through faith in him. Paul's point of view on humanity in Adam and in Christ is striking when we consider that the apostle did not write retrospectively—looking back on two millennia of church

140. For philosophical views on hardness of heart, see the Walls-Talbott exchange: Walls, "Hell and Human Freedom," in *Hell*, 113–38; Talbott, "Freedom, Damnation and the Power to Sin with Impunity"; Walls, "Hell of a Choice"; Walls, "Hell of a Dilemma." See also Kretzmann, "God among the Causes of Moral Evil"; Stump, "Sanctification"; Schatz, "Freedom, Repentance and Hardening of the Hearts."

history—but prospectively, seeing around him only the tiny, struggling congregations of Christian believers in his own day, which he had done so much to establish. Nonetheless, Paul saw in this seedbed of renewed humanity a vast multitude taking shape and finally entering into God's eternal grace. Christian philosopher-theologian Oliver Crisp calls himself an "optimistic particularist," and such a perspective would find broad support in the arguments presented in this study.[141]

Paul wrote as an apostle of hope, his message was a gospel of hope, and he viewed the Christian community as a people of hope. Nonetheless, it is possible for true hope to be so extended, or rather overextended, that it turns into a false hope—that is, a hope that deceives and disappoints those who share in it. False hopes have the tendency to undermine the possibility of true hope. For this reason, false or excessive hope is not too much of a good thing but something other than a good thing. Universalism represents a well-meaning but unfortunate form of false hope—overshooting the mark, going too far, and thus subverting the biblical optimism of grace.

Many arguments against hell have been based on metaphysical or aesthetic criteria, if not personal predispositions. In the minds of its opponents, hell is not only morally questionable but also a kind of philosophical blasphemy or metaphysical obscenity. It throws the entire universe out of whack by disallowing a final harmony. Such harmony or coherence is deeply satisfying to a certain sort of mind, which might well regard it as indispensable.[142] According to the standard doctrine of hell, all intelligent creatures are made by God, yet not all intelligent creatures return to God. For some people, the immediate reaction to this idea is "No!" Hell rubs against the grain. Hell severs the seamless ontology.

The modernist project of post-Enlightenment Europe seeks closure, coherence, consistency, and explanatory totality. The doctrine of hell is discontinuous, disruptive, and so—in an ironic way—it may be closer to what is sometimes called the postmodernist view than to a modernist standpoint. It is interesting to trace the appearance of the Greek word *phōnē* (voice) in the book of Revelation. One hears in the text the voice of angels, the voice speaking "from the throne," the voice of the martyrs crying for justice, and the voice of the heavenly faithful agreeing with God's judgments. Then, rather surprisingly, there is the voice of the wicked. They ask, "Who is like the beast?" (Rev. 13:4). Evil entrances

141. Crisp, *Saving Calvinism*, 87–107. Crisp explains that "the optimistic particularist is someone who is hopeful about the scope of salvation but who believes that God will finally damn some small remnant of fallen humanity to hell" (88).

142. Consider, e.g., Hohyun Sohn's aesthetically based rejection of the traditional doctrine of hell in "The Beauty of Hell?": "God's beautiful justice will not tolerate the eternal frustration of hell" (47).

them. They say, "Fall on us!" asking the mountains to shield them from the fearful scrutiny and impending judgment of God (Rev. 6:16–17). When they fall under judgment, they blaspheme God; and though their actual words of blasphemy are not rendered in the biblical text, their blasphemous voices are not expunged from the narrative.

Christian universalism would seek to smooth this out and to silence the conflicting voices, so that we end up with something more concordant than discordant, more unitary than manifold. The universalist position seems more "totalizing" and thus more Hegelian, as it were, than the text of the book of Revelation. If there is alienation, then for the Hegelian it somehow has to be overcome and sublated. Alienation cannot endure. So both the alienation and the overcoming of alienation are announced in advance together, and one ends up not with a genuine drama of salvation history but a bloodless ballet of pure concepts. But what if reality is not smoothly shaped? What if it is more like a jagged shard of glass? Søren Kierkegaard commented, "That God could create beings free over against himself is the cross which philosophy could not bear but upon which it has remained hanging."[143]

It is perfectly possible to wish for all kinds of things that one does not expect to happen. Some wishes are based on counterfactual premises. A man might say to himself, "I wish I had proposed to Ellen before she left for Vancouver. Then she might not have gotten involved with Eric, and she might have married me instead." Other wishes are based on idealistic aspirations for a state of affairs that is not impossible but seems very unlikely: "I wish that all the governments with nuclear weapons would dismantle them." Or, "I wish that reliable cures for all forms of cancer existed." What these wishful or wistful desires have in common with one another is a lack of any definite expectation that the desire will be fulfilled. In contrast, the biblical notion of hope includes a sense of definite and confident expectation. So "hopeful universalism" seems to be in this vein: "I wish that all people would receive eternal salvation." Barthian and Balthasarian "hopeful universalism" seems more wishful than hopeful.

Christian hope is not mere wishfulness. Christian hope is not utopian. It is instead a joyful and confident expectation for the future that is grounded on God's promise. Christian hope does not rest on a human capacity for imagining alternate futures, however important a trait that may be in certain contexts. On the contrary, Christian hope is founded on what God has already done in the life, death, and resurrection of Jesus Christ, and it looks to the completion and fulfillment of that work that has already begun. Because Christian universalism fails to identify a divine promise on which it may rest, it migrates away from

143. Kierkegaard, *Journals and Papers*, 2:1237.

hope and in the direction of wishfulness. When the Christian church embraces a message and an attitude of *wishfulness*, then the genuine, reliable, well-founded Christian hope will be progressively weakened and eventually lost.

Connected with wishfulness is the reliance on what we earlier called abstract rationality. "God is love, therefore. . . ." The universalist fills in the blank with the idea that "all will be saved": "God is love, therefore all will be saved." But the human mind is endlessly inventive. I might think to myself, "God is love, therefore I will get the new job that I just applied for." It is no more silly or arbitrary to begin with the premise that "God is love" and then to infer consequences for myself during the next twenty-four hours than to infer consequences for the entire universe for the next twenty-four million years. An abstractly rational way of reasoning about God reflects an inflated human confidence in our ability to figure things out—not only with respect to everyday affairs but also with respect to God's ultimate purposes and intentions.

What, then, is the alternative to universalism, or at least the universalistic *hope-for-all*? It is an antispeculative, earthbound, practically engaged, particularistic *hope-for-each*. There's a saying: "I love all humanity—it's just people I can't stand." None of us are obligated to hope for all humanity any more than we are obligated to love all humanity. Humanity-in-general is simply too massive, too abstract, and too mentally intimidating for any of us seriously to ponder, and so the paralysis of analysis soon sets in. Rather than doing what we can, we end up doing nothing. Jesus focused attention on loving the neighbor rather than loving humanity, perhaps because the project of loving everyone leads us so easily into impossible ethical conundrums: "Does the beggar in front of me matter more than the beggar across the ocean? To whom should I give?" The expert in Jewish law whom Jesus encountered (Luke 10:25–37) was preoccupied with the speculative issue of "Who is my neighbor?" rather than the practical question—to which Jesus directed him—of "being a neighbor" to the person next to him.

Applying this insight to Christian hope, *hope-for-each* rather than hope-for-all means that Jesus's follower must begin from the standpoint of God's gracious purpose toward each individual person without exception. *That person* is loved by God. *This person* is also loved by God. Augustine's notion of "loving the neighbor in God" might be helpful here. For Augustine, love is the ambience of the Christian life. In light of God's gracious purpose toward the particular person near us, Jesus's followers seek to align themselves with what God may be purposing and effecting in each specific situation. In this way they set their sights toward the highest good for everyone—including especially the aim of final beatitude in God. This means acts of loving service, devotion to prayer, words of encouragement, efforts in evangelism, and so forth. Spiritual discernment is part of this process, because God is in the business of dealing with different people differently.[144]

For the person engaged in love of neighbor, the speculative question of what will finally happen to all rational souls may prove distracting. We might consider how Jesus responds when the apostle Peter becomes too curious about the future prospects of the beloved disciple (John 21:20–21). The Teacher redirects Peter's attention with the words "Follow me!" (21:22). And Peter is merely inquiring about one person, not the destiny of humanity-in-general! Elsewhere in the Gospels, the question is posed to Jesus: "Lord, will those who are saved be few?" Jesus responds, "Strive to enter through the narrow door. For many, I tell you, will seek to enter and will not be able" (Luke 13:23–24). The response does not gratify the itch to know, surmise, or calculate the number of the saved. Peter and this unknown interlocutor are redirected and reoriented by Jesus: "Follow me!" "Strive to enter!" Such biblical texts do not make sense on the presumption of a universalistic hope-for-all, but they make perfect sense in light of a particularistic hope-for-each.

---

144. The hope-for-each, as recommended here, may find support in Thomas Aquinas. Trabbic argues in "Can Aquinas Hope 'That All May Be Saved'?" that Aquinas offers not only the possibility but also the duty of hoping for others besides oneself. Yet, for Aquinas's eschatology to be coherent, "this duty to hope for all has to be reconciled with his doctrine of reprobation" (352). Trabbic ends up with what he calls a hope for a "non-universal all" (352), which is something like what I am calling a hope-for-each. Grisez and Ryan, "Hell and Hope for Salvation," argue that Christians should not be universalists but "should also believe that no one still alive and able to repent need end in hell" (613). "Every Christian," they say, "should make every reasonable effort to promote their own and others' salvation" (613).

Appendix A

Gnosis and Western Esotericism: Definitions and Lineages

Generally speaking, "esotericism" represents a wisdom tradition that is philosophical in character and seeks to illumine the human mind with a true understanding of the human condition, the character of the spiritual or divine world, and hidden pathways to the soul's liberation. It is difficult to give any precise definition of the term "esotericism." While there is no one accepted definition, Arthur Versluis has pointed to six general traits of "Christian theosophy," regarded as a branch of "Western esotericism," and one or more of these six traits appear in many of the "esoteric" groups or teachings surveyed in this book on Christian universalism: (1) a focus on the figure of divine Wisdom or Sophia, the "mirror of God," generally conceived as feminine; (2) an insistence on direct spiritual experience or cognition, meaning both insight into the divine nature of the cosmos and metaphysical or transcendent gnosis; (3) nonsectarianism and self-identification with the theosophic current; (4) a spiritual leader who guides his or her spiritual circle through letters and spiritual advice; (5) reference to the works and thought of Jakob Böhme; and (6) visionary insight into nature and nonphysical realms (though no. 6 is a subset of no. 2). Versluis states that all of the Christian theosophical figures he has studied display at least four of the first five traits.[1]

1. Versluis, "What Is Esoteric?," 1. Cf. Versluis, *Wisdom's Book*, 10–14. Antoine Faivre, the well-known scholar of Western esotericism, points to his own six general characteristics of Western

"Western Esotericism" as a Field of Study

Wouter J. Hanegraaff's *Dictionary of Gnosis and Western Esotericism* has helped to define the academic field of "Western esotericism," linked to the better-established and better-known study of ancient gnosis or gnosticism.[2] The world's largest organization for professional scholars of religion, the American Academy of Religion (AAR), has had a subgroup on "Western Esotericism" for some twenty years now. One of the more significant publication series in this field in the English language is the SUNY (State University of New York) Series in Western Esoteric Traditions. Many academic works have appeared in French, German, Dutch, and Italian on these themes, some of which have been translated into English. Among the authors and texts generally regarded as "gnostic" or "esoteric" are leading teachers of ancient gnosis (Basilides, the Carpocratians, Valentinus); the Nag Hammadi corpus; *Corpus Hermeticum*; the early classics of Jewish mysticism *Sefer Yetsirah*, *Sefer ha-Bahir*, and the *Zohar*, and authors in the tradition of Lurianic Kabbalah; Giovanni Pico della Mirandola; Paracelsus (Philippus Aureolus Theophrastus Bombastus von Hohenheim); Jakob Böhme; Francis Mercury van Helmont; Lady Anne Conway; William Blake and Johann Wolfgang von Goethe; the initiatic Freemasonry of Martines de Pasqually and Louis-Claude de Saint Martin; Emanuel Swedenborg; and such twentieth-century figures as Carl Gustav Jung, the Eranos Conference participants (Mircea Eliade, Ernst Benz, Henri Corbin, Gershom Scholem), and Valentin Tomberg.

Multiple Lineages in Esotericism

It is possible to identify several different lineages in esotericism. (1) A *Platonic-Neoplatonic* lineage includes Plato, Plotinus, Origen, Iamblichus, Proclus, Pseudo-Dionysius, and Eriugena. (2) A *kabbalistic* lineage stretches from the

esotericism: (1) correspondences and interdependence, (2) living nature, (3) imagination, (4) transmutation, (5) praxis of concordance, and (6) transmission (*Access to Western Esotericism*, cited in Versluis, "What Is Esoteric?," 1). The problem with Faivre's traits is their high level of generality, which is one of the common problems that emerge when scholars attempt a comprehensive definition of "Western esotericism."

2. In addition to Hanegraaff's *Dictionary*, the more important works connecting ancient gnosis with modern Western esotericism include Yates, *Giordano Bruno and the Hermetic Tradition*; Filoramo, *History of Gnosticism*; Faivre, *Access to Western Esotericism*; Faivre, *Theosophy, Imagination, Tradition*; Hanratty, *Studies in Gnosticism and in the Philosophy of Religion*; Versluis, *Wisdom's Children*; Koslowski, *Philosophien der Offenbarung*; Schmidt-Biggemann, *Philosophia Perennis*; DeConick, *Religion: Secret Religion*, 1–262; and the three-volume contribution by Cyril O'Regan on the "gnostic return" in modern times: *Heterodox Hegel*; *Gnostic Return in Modernity*; *Gnostic Apocalypse*. O'Regan drew inspiration from the major nineteenth-century work by F. C. Baur, *Die christliche Gnosis*.

Sefer ha-Bahir to the *Zohar*, Lurianic teaching, and the Christian Cabala of Pico della Mirandola, Jakob Böhme, Francis Mercury van Helmont, and Lady Anne Conway. (3) An *alchemical* lineage extends from ancient times to Paracelsus, Jakob Böhme, Goethe, and C. G. Jung, the latter of whom is generally regarded as a psychologist and yet devoted much of his effort to studying alchemy. (4) A *Böhmist* lineage starts from Böhme and then extends toward Germany (Johann Gichtel, Johann Petersen), German-Americans (George de Benneville), France (Louis-Claude de Saint-Martin), and Russia (Vladimir Solovyov, Nicolas Berdyaev).

Complicating the picture is the fact that the lineages listed above are not entirely distinct from one another. Jung, for example, while primarily identified with alchemy, used the name of the ancient gnostic teacher Basilides as his pseudonym in writing his *Seven Sermons to the Dead* (1916). Ficino, Pico, and many Christian esotericists were Platonic or Neoplatonic, while being kabbalistic as well. Böhme is perhaps the most important bridging figure in the early modern period, since he might be placed into all four genealogies—as Neoplatonic, kabbalistic, and alchemical, as well as the founder of a new lineage of his own. So far as Christian universalism is concerned, Böhme is an exceptionally important figure, as the argument in this book makes clear.

Common Esoteric Teachings

A number of ideas or teachings appear frequently in the writings generally identified as "Western esoteric." Here we go beyond Arthur Versluis's six general traits of Christian theosophy (see above) and note some of the more specific teachings.

First, there are traits that pertain to *the nature of God or the Godhead*: (1) crisis within the Godhead; (2) evil within the Godhead; (3) plurality within the Godhead; (4) temporality or process within the Godhead; (5) inherent or intrinsic suffering within the Godhead; (6) a divine feminine principle or heavenly Sophia; (7) radical apophaticism concerning God (though sometimes combined with affirmations of divine immanence); and (8) the principle of *coincidentia oppositorum* (coincidence of opposites).

A second set of traits pertains to *God's relationship with the world or the cosmos regarded in itself*: (9) rejection of creation from nothing; (10) nothingness or chaos as a constitutive principle (*mē-ontic* rather than *ouk-ontic* nothingness);[3]

---

3. "Nothing" in the *ouk*-ontic sense refers to an absolute void that wholly lacks existence, has no metaphysical status, and is entirely passive. "Nothing" in the *mē*-ontic sense denotes an active or creative void—a realm of possibilities that might engender change, drive existence forward, or

(11) "spiritual corporeality" (i.e., the materiality of spiritual things and the spirituality of material things); (12) panvitalism or panpsychism (i.e., all things have "life"), (13) the material universe as ontologically inferior (but not necessarily evil per se); (14) the material universe as generated by human desire and imagination; and (15) the doctrine of correspondences ("as above, so below").

A third set of traits relates to *humanity, human nature, and Christ*: (16) the idea of the primal God-Man or human-shaped heaven; (17) the myth of the androgyne (male-female polarity on the divine or human levels); (18) docetic Christology (i.e., that Christ merely *seems* to be physical or to have an earthly body); (19) Christ understood as Teacher rather than Savior per se; (20) rejection of the doctrine of Christ's atonement for sins; (21) an exalted view of humanity as divine or as having godlike powers; (22) positive valuation of the imagination, as having the power to create reality; (23) a positive (or at least tolerant) stance toward magic, divination, and astrology; (24) the doctrine of reincarnation or transmigration of souls; and (25) a purgatorial process in this life or in a realm beyond (God's purifying "fire" to remove sin or guilt).

A fourth set of traits captures other, broader *aspects of the esoteric ethos*: (26) spiritual elitism; (27) antijuridicism—stressing love, not law, or identifying strict justice with evil or the demonic realm; (28) salvation understood as self-knowledge, self-realization, or self-integration; (29) an emphasis on gnosis rather than on faith; (30) nonliteral readings of Scripture—allegorical interpretation, symbolic reading, and "arcanization" of Scripture; and (31) authoritative religious claims based on visions, dreams, or supernatural encounters.[4]

The figure who might be the twentieth century's greatest Christian esotericist—Valentin Tomberg, who wrote *Meditations on the Tarot* (1980)—speaks of a "Hermetic" or "esoteric" lineage in which he situates his own writing. This lineage, for Tomberg, includes Pythagoras, Plato, the early gnostics, Plotinus, Hermes Trimegistus, Clement of Alexandria, Plotinus, Origen, Iamblichus, Proclus, Pseudo-Dionysius, the Jewish and Christian Kabbalah, Jakob Böhme, Martines de Pasqually, Johann Wolfgang von Goethe, Louis-Claude de Saint-Martin, Eliphas Lévi (pseudonym for Alphonse Louis Constant), Papus (pseudonym for Gérard Encausse), Nicolas Berdyaev, Pierre Teilhard de Chardin, and Carl

---

else threaten it with diminishment. See Tsambassis, "Evil and the 'Abysmal Nature' of God in the Thought of Brightman, Berdyaev, and Tillich"; Armitage, "Heidegger's Contributions to Philosophy"; O'Regan, "Žižek's Meontology."

4. Many thinkers not regarded as esoteric offered allegorical readings of Scripture (e.g., Ambrose, Augustine, medieval exegetes, etc.). Taken singly, this trait is less definitive of esotericism than most of the others. Some esoteric thinkers go deep into symbolic interpretation, engaging in what Moshe Idel calls "hyposemantic arcanization," in which the individual letters of words as well as numbers carry hidden meanings.

Gustav Jung.[5] Esotericism is very much a living tradition today, as evidenced by the fanfare surrounding the 2009 publication of Jung's *Red Book* (1914–30), a visionary notebook of jottings and drawings that proved to be foundational for the whole of Jung's massive oeuvre.

"Oriental Esotericism" and Occultism

For the sake of clarity, it is necessary to distinguish Western esotericism from so-called Oriental esotericism. During the late nineteenth century, Western esoteric currents of thought were increasingly "orientalized" through the inclusion of ideas derived from the historic religions of Asia, such as Hinduism, Buddhism, and Taoism. New concepts and practices received emphasis, such as karma, yoga, yogis, gurus, mantras, mandalas, and reincarnation. While many of these had Western analogues that extended back to ancient times, the replacement of Western with Eastern (i.e., Asian) terminology and practices altered the character of esotericism. The founding of the Theosophical Society in New York City in 1875 by Helena Petrovna (Madame) Blavatsky and Colonel Henry Steel Olcott marked a turning point.[6] To some extent, the Western esoteric tradition from the Renaissance onward always had a religiously eclectic dimension. Pico della Mirandola in his *Nine Hundred Theses* sought not only to prove "the divinity of Christ" through appeal to Jewish Kabbalah, but, even more ambitiously, to reconcile all differences among all religions (*DR* 4.12). Yet it was only during the nineteenth century that the incursion of Asian religious ideas was so pronounced that one needs to speak of "Oriental esotericism" in distinction from "Western esotericism."

Another distinction may be drawn between esotericism and occultism. Whereas esotericism, as noted, is a wisdom tradition, occultism by contrast is more pragmatic and results oriented. It offers hidden techniques to allow the practitioner to obtain the results that he or she wishes, whether that be causing spirits to appear on command (theurgy), turning lead to gold (alchemy), or accomplishing other physical or personal transformations (magic). Yet it is difficult to draw hard and fast distinctions between esotericism and occultism. Tomberg's *Meditations* frequently cites the writings of Eliphaz Levi and Papus, two practitioners of ceremonial magic in nineteenth-century France, and so

---

5. [Tomberg], *Meditations on the Tarot*, esp. 26, 474, and 503 regarding this lineage. The Russian-born Tomberg, who later lived in various European countries and wrote in French, viewed his own work as a summation and continuation of what he termed either "Hermeticism" or "esotericism."

6. See Prothero, *White Buddhist*; Goodrick-Clarke, *Helena Blavatsky*; G. Lachman, *Madame Blavatsky*.

Tomberg's work seems to straddle the divide between esotericism and occultism. The ancient *Corpus Hermeticum* is philosophical in its content, and yet
other ancient Egyptian texts connected with it— and often ignored by modern
scholars—consist of spells, charms, and incantations. Alchemy always had
not only a magical-occultic dimension but also a philosophical and religious
aspect concerned with a "lead-to-gold" transmutation of the soul into a new
and perfected state. One of the most famous of all esoteric texts, known as *The
Emerald Tablet*, yokes together esoteric theory and magical practice: "That which
is above is like to that which is below, and that which is below is like to that
which is above, *to accomplish the miracles* of (the) one thing."[7] The knowledge
of correspondences—as above, so below—is for working "miracles." This text
suggests that only a soft distinction may be drawn between esotericism and
occultism.

"Hermetism" and "Hermeticism"

Other words crop up often in connection with esotericism, including especially
"Hermetism" and "Hermeticism." The former term as used by academics refers to persons, texts, ideas, and practices that are directly linked to the *Corpus
Hermeticum*, a relatively small body of texts that appeared most likely in Egypt
during the second or third centuries CE.[8] "Hermetism" is used in this fashion
by Frances Yates in her pathbreaking book, and its meaning has not varied much
over recent decades.[9] Yet "Hermeticism" is often used in a wider way to refer
to the general style of thinking that one finds in the *Corpus Hermeticum* and
other works of ancient gnosis, alchemy, Kabbalah, and so forth. "Hermeticism"
sometimes functions as a synonym for "esotericism." The adjective "Hermetic"
is ambiguous, since it can refer either to "Hermetism" or to "Hermeticism."

"Panentheism" and "Dialectical Theism"

In considering the Western esoteric tradition in terms of the God-world relationship, one encounters the term "panentheism" and what John Macquarrie
calls "dialectical theism." John W. Cooper writes that "panentheism" does not
directly identify God and world but asserts that "the world is 'in' God ontologically." He maintains that "panentheism" in this sense is "largely the history of

7. Steele and Singer, "Emerald Table," 42 (*Tabula Smaragdina* [*Emerald Tablet*], 2), quoted in
[Tomberg], *Meditations*, 22 (emphasis added).
8. For an excellent, newer translation with extensive notes, see Copenhaver, *Hermetica*.
9. Yates, *Giordano Bruno and the Hermetic Tradition*, ix–x.

Neoplatonism." Macquarrie defends panentheism by arguing that "the pantheist and the classical theist really share the same fundamental error, though they have developed it in opposite directions," and the error lies in "one-sidedness." He refers to this position as "dialectical theism" to stress that this view is closer to theism than to pantheism.[10]

10. J. W. Cooper, *Panentheism*, 18–19; Macquarrie, *In Search of Deity*, 53–54.

Appendix B

Zoroastrian Eschatology

The only ancient stream of thought other than Egyptian gnosis that has been claimed as a possible source of universalism is the Iranian or Persian religion of Zoroastrianism. So the question arises: Were the second-century gnostics of the Mediterranean region influenced by the Zoroastrians of Persia, particularly with respect to the doctrine of universal salvation? Some seventy to one hundred years ago, there was a school of opinion, led by Wilhelm Bossuet (1865–1920) and Richard Reitzenstein (1861–1931), that held that there was a single, definable "gnostic myth" that originated in Persia and was later adapted and modified by the gnostics of Palestine, Egypt, and the Roman Empire. Their so-called history of religions school (German *Religionsgeschichtliche Schule*) tended toward pan-Persianism—that is, seeing many ancient religions as influenced by Persia. Reitzenstein even suggested that Plato, centuries before the gnostics, had been under Iranian influence. The New Testament scholar Rudolf Bultmann (1884–1976) adhered to at least some theories of the history of religions school. Today nearly all scholars have rejected these earlier views and maintain that no single gnostic myth ever existed.[1]

To answer the question about possible Zoroastrian influence on the second-century Egyptian gnostics, we need first to take into account the complexity of the Zoroastrian scriptures. The little-known founding figure, Zoroaster, may have lived in the seventh or sixth century BCE, though there is no certainty about this.

---

1. An exposition and critique of the school appears in K. L. King, "History of Religions School," in *What Is Gnosticism?*, 71–109.

The dates suggested for the life of Zoroaster vary from 1500 to 400 BCE. From a literary standpoint, the principal sources for the study of Zoroastrianism are the *Avesta* and the Pahlavi books. Achaemenid and Sassanian inscriptions also shed some light on the history of the religion. Some Greek sources, especially Herodotus, Strabo, Plutarch, and Agathias, provide additional information. The Zoroastrian canon of scripture falls into multiple parts. While the Zoroastrians attribute to Zoroaster the *Gathas*—the hymns that are the foundational layer of their scriptures—even the first part of the scriptural canon took centuries to be completed. Because of Alexander the Great's invasion of Persia, followed by the Seleucid and Parthian periods, we have essentially no knowledge of what may have happened within the Zoroastrian tradition before the second and third centuries CE. Many of the sacred texts were said to have been destroyed at the time of Alexander the Great. According to the traditional account of the origin of the scriptures, the first portion of the canon, the *Avesta*, began to be compiled under the royal patronage of a series of rulers, beginning with King Valakhsh (ca. 51–79 CE), who ordered a search for and collection of all the parts of the scriptures that remained. This process was continued under later kings during the third and fourth centuries. It was only under the Sassanid ruler King Shahpur II (309–80 CE) that a canonical text, consisting of a fixed number of books, was established. The first or foundational layer of the Zoroastrian scriptures did not reach a canonical or fixed form until the late fourth century CE.[2]

What is more, the Arab conquest of Iran in the seventh century likely brought far more damage to the Zoroastrian scriptures than either the ravages of Alexander the Great or the neglect of the priests in the succeeding centuries. Small communities of Zoroastrians in Iran and in India were able to preserve a few texts. S. A. Nigosian writes that these texts "were recopied from time to time and constitute the *Avesta* in its present form." Given that the *Avesta* in its surviving form dates from some 1,000 to 1,200 years after the time of Zoroaster, this textual history makes it very difficult to say exactly what may have been written when. The oldest of the manuscripts preserved by the Zoroastrians in India date from the thirteenth century CE, while those from the Zoroastrians in Iran are not earlier than the seventeenth century CE. It seems likely that the *Gathas* reflect an earlier tradition, while other parts of the *Avesta* may derive from a period as late as the time of the Sassanid kings. The preservation of these texts was determined by liturgical interests. Those texts that were not used in ritual may have ceased to have been copied and so may have disappeared over time. The *Avesta* in its present form likely represents only a small portion of the original writings. In addition to the *Avesta*, there are various writings in the

---

2. Nigosian, *Zoroastrian Faith*, 16, 46–47, 32–33; Zaehner, *Dawn and Twilight of Zoroastrianism*, 27.

Pahlavi language that Zoroastrians regard as scriptural and that date from the third to the eleventh centuries CE. R. C. Zaehner, an Oxford historian of Zoroastrianism, claims that the Pahlavi books "in their present form . . . were mostly written in the ninth century AD," though they reflect the theological views of an earlier period.[3]

One of the basic principles of the Zoroastrian religion is cosmic dualism—that is, that evil is separate from and independent of good. Ahriman (the evil god or principle) did not originate from Ahura Mazda or Ohrmazd (the good god or principle), nor vice versa. Both were equally primordial and primeval. Ahriman was not even aware of the existence of Ahura Mazda until Ahriman arose from his eternal place in the abyss. At the end, Ahriman will preside over a large host of evil spirits that will all be defeated eventually in a decisive battle. In the present world, the struggle of Ahura Mazda and Ahriman extends throughout the seen and unseen world. The universe is a battleground in which these conflicting principles combat each other. In every situation demanding a decision, human beings must choose between these two. Yet final victory will come to Ahura Mazda or the good principle. Ahriman will mobilize a vast army for the great and final battle. There will be so much slaughter that the rivers of blood will reach the horses' girths.[4] The final result will be the triumph of Ahura Mazda.

Because of their fundamental commitment to original dualism, the Zoroastrians rejected as heresy the so-called Zurvanite teaching that the Godhead had originally been unified. The Zurvanites maintained that a single divine primordial being, Zurvan, was the father of two sons, Ahura Mazda and Ahriman. This revised view resolved cosmic dualism into an original unity. The Zurvanite view might be seen as a gnosticization of Zoroastrianism, an effort to overcome dualism by an affirmation of original unity.[5]

On the theme of individual judgment, the *Gathas* teach that each person must come to the Bridge of the Separator (the Account-Keeper's Bridge, or Chinvat Bridge). The process of judgment is not described in detail in the *Gathas*, and only the later texts spell this out. At death, each one comes to the bridge, and this crossing can lead either to the House of Song (heaven) or to the House of Lies (hell). In some texts, wicked persons, when crossing the bridge, will find that the bridge contracts beneath them, sending them tumbling into hell. The founding teacher, Zoroaster, seems to have believed that this separation is

---

3. Nigosian, *Zoroastrian Faith*, 47–48, 61; Zaehner, *Dawn and Twilight of Zoroastrianism*, 27.

4. This detail regarding the blood reaching the horses' bridles may have been taken from the book of Revelation (14:20).

5. Nigosian, *Zoroastrian Faith*, 84–85, 88–89. The Zurvanite teaching might be seen as a form of "mitigated dualism," such as one finds in the Cathars (*DR*, 155n91) and Böhme (*DR*, 467–68).

final and irrevocable. Those who worshiped false gods will be punished. One text says, "When they reach the Account-keeper's Bridge their own soul(s) and their own religious view(s) will make them tremble, and they will be guests in the house of deceit for all time." Zoroastrian scholar Peter Clark notes that the phrasing "for all time" does not seem to allow for any escape from punishment. The prophet Zoroaster states elsewhere that the trial of souls by molten metal will not be purgative but final. Yet, in the later scriptures of Zoroastrianism, the House of Song (heaven) and the House of Lies (hell) begin to be described as temporary places where men and women wait in bliss or agony until the arrival of the final judgment. In Zoroaster's day, though, this development had not taken root. For him, only the *saoshyant-ashavans* (faithful followers), who have helped to bring about the *frashokereti* (world's refreshment), will be able to experience the cosmic renewal. Zoroaster's eschatology displays a finality that is in keeping with his strict, unrelenting sense of justice.[6]

While later Zoroastrianism spoke of multiple saviors that were to appear throughout history, this idea is foreign to the *Gathas*. Here we find no evidence that Zoroaster believed in future prophet-like figures who were to take over and continue his task, generations or even centuries after his own death. Zoroaster's teaching shows an urgency that impelled him to gather as many people as he could into a family of coworkers so that the hostile spirit might be defeated and the *frashokereti* brought about speedily. It may have been the failure of this hope to materialize that led to the notion that there would be a succession of religious leaders—of which Zoroaster was the first—who over succeeding millennia would be born of virgins from among Zoroaster's descendants. At some point the number of *saoshyants* (prophets) was set at three. The Pahlavi text known as the *Bundahishn* outlines a 12,000-year period from the beginnings of the creation to the consummation and to Ahirman's final defeat. The last three thousand years are the period of greatest conflict. The final three millennia were named for the *saoshyants* who appeared in them.[7]

6. P. Clark, *Zoroastrianism*, 63–64, citing *Yasht* 46:11 and *Yasht* 51:9. Along the same lines, Jal Dastur Cursetji Pavry summarizes Zoroastrian teaching without saying anything about a hope beyond the judgment at Chinvat Bridge:

> Step by step we have traced the fate of the soul from death to the individual judgment where its lot, for weal or woe, is assigned. . . . The ordeal which each must undergo in the assize over which stern judges preside is a test filled with awe for just and unjust alike. This is the accounting at which all life's records are impartially weighed in the balance before the soul can attempt to cross the Chinvat Bridge, that span over which all must go. . . . Through its own evil thoughts (*dusmata*), evil words (*duzuxta*), and evil deeds (*duzvarsta*), the soul of the damned sinks lower and lower into Hell. . . . Suffering anguish and crying words of woe, the wicked soul is plunged into still greater terror and misery to be endured for ages to come. (*Zoroastrian Doctrine*, 112–13)

7. P. Clark, *Zoroastrianism*, 65–66.

By the time the *Bundahishn* received its final redaction (perhaps during the ninth century CE), the strictness of Zoroaster's original message had given way to a more moderate eschatology. Zoroaster had taught that the trial by molten metal would result either in salvation or in destruction—depending on one's accumulation of either good or bad deeds—and that this judgment was final. Yet the *Bundahishn* tilts toward leniency. For fifty-seven years the souls of all human beings will be recalled from the House of Lies or the House of Song and will be reunited with their bodies. When people pass through molten metal as a phase of the judgment, the righteous will be unaffected, while the wicked will experience purification, and after this ordeal all people will "come together with the greatest affection." The wicked will join their fellow humans in the perfection of Ahura Mazda's good dominion. "Not one human must be lost when the restoration takes place," writes Peter Clark, "for if that happens the completeness of creation will also be lost."[8] Eventually, all evil will cease.

In the end, the molten metal that had been used to purge evil from human hearts will be used to purge the cosmos itself. Evil will be locked in the inner depths of the earth from where it can never again wield influence.[9] Mary Boyce speaks of an "annihilation of evil" in the Zoroastrian eschatology. The fiery river of molten metal will pour down into hell, burning away its horrors and forever sealing off its once-dreaded entrance. Boyce comments that "hell will thus cease to exist, with all its demonic inhabitants, including the Evil Spirit."[10]

The Pahlavi texts repeatedly state that hell is not eternal, and subsequently this doctrinal point was recognized as a key difference between Zoroastrianism and Islam.[11] The shift away from a doctrine of eternal punishment apparently took place during the period of King Shapur II (309–79 CE). Boyce, a historian of Zoroastrianism, writes:

> Only one modification is known of a teaching of Zoroaster's which became a part of standard belief, apparently from this time [i.e., the 300s CE]. This concerns the doctrine that sinners will perish, body and soul, in the molten metal of the

---

8. Ibid., 71.

9. Ibid., 73–74.

10. Boyce, *Zoroastrianism*, 77.

11. Expounding the later Pahlavi text *Dadestan-i-Denig* (31.4–5; 36.95; 31.10), Zaehner writes that hell is not a permanent state, since the soul at last understands reality as it is, understands the wickedness of Ahriman (who mocks those who suffer) and the goodness of Ohrmazd whom it has betrayed. Hell is thus like purgatory. "When the final Rehabilitation comes to pass . . . the souls of the damned will be made to pass through a river of molten metal, and this will purify them of all remaining taint of sin. Sanctified they will join the souls of the saved and all will live in perfect harmony for evermore" (Zaehner, *Dawn and Twilight of Zoroastrianism*, 308). In the final conflict, the evil that had coexisted with good from all eternity is brought to helplessness by its own incoherence and discord, and Ahriman appeals to Ohrmazd for mercy (314–15).

river at Judgment Day. Instead, it came to be held that they will experience only excruciating pangs through that immersion, and be purged thereby of their wickedness, and so be able to enter into the kingdom of Ohrmazd together with the righteous. This softening of the prophet's teachings, over a millennium and a half after he lived, can be compared with the modern abandonment by various branches of the Christian church of the stern Gospel teaching of everlasting hell-fire for sinners.[12]

While "the stern old doctrine" of eternal punishment is attested during the Seleucid-Parthian period, a more lenient view is found in various passages.[13] A seventeenth-century European traveler to Persia, on meeting with Zoroastrians, commented, "They also say that God will have pity upon the damn'd, and that they shall go into Paradise as having suffer'd enough."[14] Boyce notes that there may have been theological rather than simply humanitarian reasons for this shift away from belief in hell, since the "theologians of the Sasanian period may have come to think that Ahriman could not be allowed the lasting triumph of having diminished the creation of God."[15]

Regarding the fate of Ahriman, the Evil One, there are texts that speak of him as "reduced to a never ending unconsciousness" and others that speak of him as "'as it were' slain." Zaehner says that Ahriman's end—even though he is a spirit—is like the physical death of a human being, in which the faculties are dissipated or dispersed. This is "annihilation" in the sense that "Ahriman as an active force utterly ceases to be." When finally cornered at the end of the last battle, Ahriman appeals for mercy. Yet Ahura Mazda knows that Ahriman is incapable of improving or reforming and so must pass out of existence.

12. Boyce, *Zoroastrianism*, 143. She adds a helpful note (81–82n72) pointing out that some translations of the *Avesta* speak of the wicked as suffering forever, but in *Yasht* 46:11 and *Yasht* 31:20, the phrase "for all [their] lifetime" might mean "for all the remainder of their existence—that is, until the Last Judgment."

13. Regarding the "stern doctrine," see Boyce, *Zoroastrianism*, 148n99, citing Boyce, *History of Zoroastrianism*, 1:243; 3:393–94. The more lenient view appears in the *Greater Bundahishn* 34:19; *Pahlavi Rivayat* accompanying the *Dadestan-i-Denig* 48:70, cited in Boyce, *Zoroastrianism*, 148n100. The *Greater Bundahishn* preserves a reference to the earlier and sterner view in *Pahlavi Rivayat* accompanying the *Dadestan-i-Denig* 32:5, where we read of how Ahriman and the demons seek to triumph over a man "when they make his soul wicked and annihilate it" (148n100). In Boyce's view, this seems to be not universalism but rather annihilation of the wicked. Boyce later refers to "Zoroaster's doctrine of the annihilation of sinners" (169).

14. Boyce, *Zoroastrianism*, 169, citing Tavernier, *Collections of Travels*, 1:164–65.

15. Boyce, *Zoroastrianism*, 170. Boyce adds: "The idea of a gradation according to virtue among the inhabitants of God's kingdom is plainly linked with this modification, since it would be a discouragement to goodness to think that sinners would in the end be entirely equal with the righteous." This teaching on a gradation in reward is "first found in a ninth-century book" (ibid., citing *Dadestan-i-Denig*, Purs, 31.10–13, in F. M. Müller, *Sacred Books of the East*, 18:73–74, as 32.12–16).

While the later (i.e., Pahlavi) Zoroastrian texts present an eschatology in which all human beings are saved, this is not true of Ahriman.[16]

We return to the original question: Is there evidence that the second-century gnostics of the Mediterranean region, in affirming universal salvation, were influenced by Zoroastrian texts or ideas? The short answer is no; there is no convincing evidence for this assertion. In fact there are multiple reasons not to believe in a Zoroastrian influence on the gnostics. The leading scholars of Zoroastrianism argue that the shift from a strict eschatology of an eternal hell in the direction of something like universalism did not likely take place until sometime during the fourth century CE. The later Pahlavi texts documenting this transition draw on earlier ideas and materials, but these texts do not reach their final form, according to Zaehner, until the ninth century CE. This is some seven centuries after the first intimations of universal salvation among the gnostics. Even if we could account for how the Zoroastrian ideas found their way into the Mediterranean cultural sphere, the sequence of historical events makes it far more likely that gnostic texts influenced Zoroastrian texts rather than the reverse.[17] We have already noted that one of the details in the Zoroastrian eschatology, the blood up to the horses' bridles, may come from the book of Revelation, which suggests that the Pahlavi texts were in part dependent on the New Testament. One of the claims made in chapter 2 (*DR* 2.1–2.3) thus seems to hold true: the idea of universal salvation is first attested among the second-century gnostics, and especially among those associated with Alexandria, Egypt.

---

16. "Ohrmazd . . . whose nature is always to show mercy, knows that here there can be no mercy, for his enemy is utterly and irretrievably depraved, evil in essence and beyond all redemption; therefore he must be once and for all destroyed" (Zaehner, *Dawn and Twilight of Zoroastrianism*, 314–15).

17. On the question of Zoroastrian or Persian influences on ancient Israel and ancient Christianity, see P. D. Hanson, *Dawn of Apocalyptic*, 4–5; Barr, "Question of Religious Influence."

Appendix C

Anti-Origenist Declarations in the Early Church

FROM ALEXANDRIA, JERUSALEM, ROME, AND CONSTANTINOPLE

Synodical Letter of Theophilus to the Bishops of Palestine and of Cyprus (400 CE)[1]

The synodical letter of the council held at Alexandria in 400 AD to condemn Origenism. Written originally in Greek it was translated into Latin by Jerome.

This letter has been sent in identical terms to the Bishops of Palestine and to those of Cyprus. We reproduce the headings of both copies. That to the Bishops of Palestine commences thus: To the well-beloved lords, brothers, and fellow-bishops, Eulogius, John, Zebianus, Auxentius, Dionysius, Gennadius, Zeno, Theodosius, Dicterius, Porphyry, Saturninus, Alan, Paul, Ammonius, Helianus, Eusebius, the other Paul, and to all the Catholic bishops gathered together at the dedication festival of Ælid [i.e., Jerusalem], Theophilus [sends] greeting in the Lord.

The Cyprians he addresses thus: To the well-beloved lords, brothers, and fellow-bishops, Epiphanius, Marcianus, Agapetus, Boethius, Helpidius, Entasius,

---

1. The texts of the synodical letter of Theophilus and the synodical letter from Jerusalem are taken from *NPNF*[2] 6:185–86. These documents were translated into Latin by Jerome and appear as Letters 92 and 93 in his collection.

Norbanus, Macedonius, Aristo, Zeno, Asiaticus, Heraclides, the other Zeno, Cyri-
acus, and Aphroditus, Theophilus [sends] greeting in the Lord.

The scope of the letter is as follows:

We have personally visited the monasteries of Nitria and find that the Origenistic heresy has made great ravages among them. It is accompanied by a strange
fanaticism: men even maim themselves or cut out their tongues to show how
they despise the body. I find that some men of this kind have gone from Egypt
into Syria and other countries where they speak against us and [against] the truth.

The books of Origen have been read before a council of bishops and unani-
mously condemned. The following are his chief errors, mainly found in the *Peri
archōn* [*On First Principles*].

1. The Son compared with us is truth, but compared with the Father he is
   falsehood.
2. Christ's kingdom will one day come to an end.
3. We ought to pray to the Father alone, not to the Son.
4. Our bodies after the resurrection will be corruptible and mortal.
5. There is nothing perfect even in heaven; the angels themselves are faulty,
   and some of them feed on the Jewish sacrifices.
6. The stars are conscious of their own movements, and the demons know
   the future by their courses.
7. Magic, if real, is not evil.
8. Christ suffered once for men; he will suffer again for the demons.

The Origenists have tried to coerce me; they have even stirred up the heathen
by denouncing the destruction of the Serapeum; and have sought to withdraw
from the ecclesiastical jurisdiction two persons accused of grave crimes. One of
these is the woman who was wrongly placed on the list of widows by Isidore, the
other Isidore himself. He is the standard-bearer of the heretical faction, and his
wealth supplies them with unbounded resources for their violent enterprises. They
have tried to murder me; they seized the monastery church at Nitria, and for a
time prevented the bishops from entering and the offices from being performed.
Now, like Zebul (Beelzebub) they go to and fro on the earth.

I have done them no harm; I have even protected them. But I would not let
an old friendship (with Isidore) impair our faith and discipline. I implore you
to oppose them wherever they come, and to prevent them from unsettling the
brethren committed to you.

Synodical Letter of the Council of Jerusalem (ca. 400 CE)

This letter was sent to Theophilus in reply to his synodical letter from Alexandria
(see above). The translation as before was due to Jerome. The following is an
epitome of the synodical letter from the Council of Jerusalem:

We have done all that you wished, and Palestine is almost wholly free from the taint of heresy. . . . Origenism does not exist among us. The doctrines you describe are never heard here. We anathematize those who hold such doctrines, and also those of Apollinaris, and shall not receive anyone whom you excommunicate.

Letter of Pope Anastasius (Bishop of Rome) to Bishop John of Jerusalem (401 CE)[2]

As for Origen . . . the impression which I have received is this—and it has been brought out clearly by the reading of parts of Origen's works by the people of our city [i.e., Rome], and by the sort of mist of blindness which it threw over them—that his object was to disintegrate our faith, which is that of the apostles, and has been confirmed by the tradition of the fathers, by leading us into tortuous paths. I want to know what is the meaning of the translation of this work [i.e., Origen's *On First Principles*] into the Roman tongue [i.e., Latin]. If the translator [Rufinus of Aquileia] intends by it to put the author in the wrong, and to denounce to the world his execrable deeds, well and good. In that case he will expose to well-merited hatred one who has long laboured under the adverse weight of public opinion [i.e., Origen]. But if by translating all these evil things he means to give his assent to them, and in that sense gives them to the world to read, then the edifice that he has reared at the expense of so much labour serves for nothing else than to make the guilt the act of his own will, and to give the sanction of his unlooked for support to the overthrow of all that is of prime importance in the true faith as held by Catholic Christians from the time of the apostles till now. Far be such teaching from the catholic system of the Church of Rome. It can never by any possibility come to pass that we should accept as reasonable things which we condemn.

The Ten Anathemas of 543 CE[3]

1. Whoever maintains that the souls of human beings preexisted, in that they had been beforehand spirits and holy powers, but that they became weary (sated) of divine contemplation, that they made themselves worse, were thus cooled (*psychō*) in the love of God, and for this reason are called souls (*psychē*) and were sent for punishment in[to] bodies—let him be anathema!

2. The text below comes from *NPNF*[2] 3:433.
3. The text of the ten anathemas and of the fifteen anathemas comes from Luke Dysinger's webposting of the Greek text with his translation: http://www.ldysinger.com/@magist/0543-53_an -orig/03_anath_543-53.htm. The Greek text and a German translation of the 543 and 553 condemnations appear in Herwig Görgemanns and Heinrich Karpp, eds. and trans., *Origenes vier Bücher von den Prinzipien* (Darmstadt: Wissenschaftliche Buchgesellschaft, 1976), 822–31 (appendix).

2. Whoever maintains that the soul of the Lord had preexisted and was united to God the Word before the incarnation and birth from the Virgin Mary—let him be anathema!

3. Whoever maintains that the body of Our Lord Jesus Christ was first formed in the womb of the blessed Virgin Mary and thereafter was united to God the Word and the soul that had existed beforehand—let him be anathema!

4. Whoever maintains that the Word of God became similar to all heavenly orders, in that he became a cherub to the cherubim and a seraph to the seraphim, in brief in that he became to all the superior powers—let him be anathema!

5. Whoever maintains that in the resurrection the bodies of human beings will be awakened [in] spherical [form] and does not acknowledge that we will be properly resurrected—let him be anathema!

6. Whoever maintains that the heaven, the sun, the moon, the stars, and the waters above the heavens are some kind of ensouled and reasoning [material] powers—let him be anathema!

7. Whoever maintains that the Lord Christ, as [he was] for human beings, will in the world to come also be crucified for the demons—let him be anathema!

8. Whoever maintains either that the power of God is limited and that he has created as much as he can comprehend and think, or that the creation is equally as eternal as God—let him be anathema!

9. Whoever maintains that the punishment[s] of the demons and godless human beings are temporal[ly limited], and that after a specified time they will have an end, that is to say there will be a restoration [*apokatastasis*] of demons or godless human beings—let him be anathema!

10. Anathema to Origen also called Adamantius, who set forth these opinions together with his nefarious and execrable and wicked doctrine and to whomsoever there is who thinks thus, or defends these opinions, or in any way hereafter at any time shall presume to protect them.

The Fifteen Anathemas of 553 CE

1. If anyone maintains the mythical preexistence of souls and the monstrous *apokatastasis* that follows [from] it—let him be anathema!

2. If anyone says that the totality of all the reasoning beings was immaterial and incorporeal intellects, without either number or name, with the result that they all formed a *henad* [i.e., unity] by the identity of essence, power and energy and by the union to the Word-God and knowledge; that they have had enough of divine contemplation, have turned to the bad, each in proportion to its inclination, have taken subtler or thicker bodies and have received a name, considering that the powers on high have differences of

names as well as bodies; and that from there they have become and have been named, some Cherubim, others Seraphim, others Principalities, Powers, Dominations, Thrones, Angels, and all the other celestial orders which exist—let him be anathema!

3. If someone says that the sun, the moon and stars are part of the same *henad* [unity] of reasoning beings; and that they have become what they are as a result of their deviation to the bad—let him be anathema!

4. If anyone says that the reasoning beings that have cooled in divine love have been joined to thicker bodies, [i.e.,] those we possess, and had been designated men, and that those who attained the height of wickedness have been joined to dark and cold bodies, and have been called demons or spirits of perversity—let him be anathema!

5. If anyone says that a "psychic" [i.e., soul-ish or ensouled] state can arise from an angelic or archangelic state, and furthermore that from the soul can arise the demonic and the human [state], and that from the human [state] there can again arise angels and demons; and that each rank of the celestial powers is constituted entirely of either those [from] above or below [it], or of [those] from below and above [it]—let him be anathema!

6. If anyone says that the species of demons appears to be twofold, being composed of human souls and superior spirits fallen into this state; that a solitary intellect [alone] of all the *henad* [unity] of reasoning beings had remained immutable with regard to divine contemplation and [divine] love, which [having] become Christ and king of all reasoning beings, directs all the corporeal nature, the heaven, the earth and what is in between [them]; that the world, when it was born had the subsistent elements older than its own existence of the dry, moist, the hot and the cold, and the form according to which it was shaped; and that it is not the all-holy and consubstantial Trinity that made the world . . . but [rather] the intellect, as they say, the demiurge [who] existed before the world and supplied the being of the world he himself has created—let him be anathema!

7. If anyone says that the Christ [who] is said to have existed in the form of God and who has been united before all ages to the divine Word has emptied himself in the human state, having had pity, as they say, when the fall occurred to those belonging to the same *henad*, that, willing to return them, he has traversed everywhere, has clothed himself in different bodies and has received different names, and that, having been made all for all, Angel for Angels, Power for Powers, and similarly for the other orders or species of reasoning beings, he has taken a form adapted to each; that he has then participated, like us, in flesh and blood and has also become human for human beings, and if he does not confess that it is the divine Word who emptied himself and became man—let him be anathema!

8. If someone says that the divine Word consubstantial with God, with the Father and with the Holy Spirit, who was incarnate and become [*sic*] man,

one with the Holy Trinity, properly Christ, but fully so because, as they say, of the *nous* [mind or intellect] emptying out upon him as if uniting him to the divine Word, and [only then] properly said to be Christ, and [further] that the latter because of the former is Christ and the former because of the latter is God—let him be anathema!

9. If someone says that it is not the Word of God who, being incarnated in flesh animated by an intelligent and reasoning soul, has descended into Hell and is ascended the same into heaven, but that which is called by them intellect which, in their impiety, they [claim] is properly said to be the Christ, rendered such by knowledge of the unity—let him be anathema!

10. If anyone says that the body of the Lord after the resurrection was ethereal and spherical in form; that so also will be the bodies of all others after the resurrection; and the Lord himself having first laid aside his body, all will then do likewise, [and] the nature of body will go into nonexistence—let him be anathema!

11. If anyone says that the judgment to come means the complete suppression of bodies, that at the end of the myth there is the immaterial nature, and that in the world to come it will not subsist of any material beings, rather that the intellect will be naked—let him be anathema!

12. If anyone says that the celestial powers, all human beings, the devil and the spirits of perversity will be united to the divine Word in exactly the same way as the intellect itself which by them is called "Christ," which exists in the form of God and which is, as they say, "outpoured," and that there will be an end to the kingship of Christ—let him be anathema!

13. If anyone says that there will be absolutely no difference between Christ and any of the reasoning beings, neither by essence, nor by knowledge, neither by power over all, nor by energy; but that all will be at the right [hand] of God, as Christ is said by them to be—let him be anathema!

14. If anyone says that all the reasoning beings form a sole *henad* [unity], persons and numbers being suppressed with bodies, that the knowledge concerning the reasoning beings . . . follows the destruction of worlds, the deposition of bodies and the abolition of names, [and that] that there will be identity of knowledge as also identity of substances, and that in the mythical *apokatastasis* there will be only naked intellects as they . . . were in the preexistence, the object of their gibberish—let him be anathema!

15. If anyone says that the condition of intellects will be the same as that which they previously had when they had not yet descended or fallen, considering that the beginning is identical to the end and that the end is the measure of the beginning—let him be anathema!

Appendix D

Ilaria Ramelli's *The Christian Doctrine of* Apokatastasis (2013)

hristian universalism has been a hot topic since the start of the new millennium (*DR* 11). During the last fifteen years, a wide range of popular or semipopular books have addressed the question, mostly defending the idea of universal salvation and arguing that it should be regarded as an acceptable Christian belief or teaching. Recent titles suggest a wave of interest among Christian laity, pastors and priests, and scholars alike. Against this backdrop of surging popular and scholarly interest, the appearance of a major academic book on the theme of universal salvation by an acknowledged and well-published scholar of early Christianity, surveying no less than nine centuries over nine hundred pages, is a publishing event of some significance. Before examining Ilaria Ramelli's tome, however, let me set a context by saying something about the church's historical and twentieth-century reception of Origen, the central figure in Ramelli's narrative.

Shifting Views of Origen over the Last Century

From his own lifetime up through the past nineteen centuries, Origen's reputation was mixed. Later writers often borrowed from Origen's biblical exegesis, though the source of the ideas or quotations was usually not credited. The medieval author Peter Comestor (d. 1178) laid down the principle "*Non credas*

Origeni dogmatizanti."[1] This Latin tag is interesting not only because of what it says but also because of what it implies (in brackets): "[I learn from Origen's biblical interpretations and spiritual writings, but] don't believe Origen when he theologizes!" Such a stipulation of distrust made sense only if there was some situation where one might trust Origen. Where in his writings was Origen "dogmatizing"? The saying applied above all to Origen's *Peri archōn* (*On First Principles*), and particularly to the speculations in that work regarding preexistent souls, the nature of the resurrected body, the reconciliation of Satan and demons, multiple lives, and the possibility of universal salvation. It was not Origen's exegesis so much as his "dogmatizing"—and that of his followers—that stirred controversy for over a century and a half in the early church (390s–550s CE).

During the last century, Origen's theological reputation has steadily advanced, as one can see by comparing works by Eugène de Faye (1926), Jean Daniélou (1955), and Henri Crouzel (1989).[2] De Faye was generally wary of Origen, whom he accused of presenting Platonic or gnostic ideas in Christian dress. Purportedly imbued with Platonic and Neoplatonic notions of the soul's gradual self-purification and ascent to its divine source, Origen made Christ all but irrelevant to the process of salvation. At the same time, de Faye believed that Origen deserved further scholarly scrutiny.

Some thirty years later, Daniélou offered a different assessment. In connection with the *nouvelle théologie* and its recovery of the ancient Christian heritage, Origen came into his own, no longer a dubious figure at the periphery of church tradition, but now a central figure in his own right. Nonetheless, Daniélou's verdict on Origen's theology remained mixed. Daniélou argued that Origen's interpretation of the Bible was often subjective and arbitrary, and that it sometimes paralleled ancient gnostic interpretations of events in the Gospels in terms of a cosmic drama of the fall and restoration of souls. While Daniélou made no effort to defend Origen's teaching on universalism, he argued that Origen's biblical interpretation contained valuable insights that enriched church tradition. For Daniélou, when reading Origen one needs to separate the gold from the dross, and it is especially in the field of spirituality that the treasure is hidden.

---

1. *Et non credas Origeni dogmatizanti, quia in aeternum non irascetur Dominus, imo etiam daemonum quandoque miserebitar* (Do not trust Origen when he dogmatizes, since [he says that] God will not be angry forever, indeed when he [i.e., God] will show mercy even on the demons) (Peter Comestor, *Historia scholastica* [PL 198:1764d]). Hildebert of Lavardin (d. 1133 or 1134) uses the same Latin expression in his writings (PL 171:429a), as does Pierre of Blois (ca. 1130–ca. 1211) in "In Hebdomada Poenosa, Sermo XVI," in *Opera*, 354.

2. The publication years listed above apply to the English translations, all from French: de Faye, *Origen and His Work*; Daniélou, *Origen*; Crouzel, *Origen*.

Crouzel offered an account of Origen that was much more positive than either de Faye's or Daniélou's. Crouzel offered no substantive critique of Origen's ideas. When he confronted aspects of Origen's thought that seemed at odds with church teaching, he argued that Origen, properly understood, was indeed orthodox. Crouzel occupied himself not only with Origen but also with later Origenism, and published a book on the Renaissance debate centered on Pico della Mirandola and his argument for Origen's salvation. In sum, Crouzel strove in a number of books and articles to vindicate Origen's reputation.[3]

Ramelli's Book in Overview

Ramelli's advocacy of Origen makes Crouzel's look tepid by comparison. Her book offers what one might call an "Origen-centric" account of the history of Christian theology during the church's first millennium. What Origen's previous defenders regarded as a liability—namely, his universalism—Ramelli treats as an asset:

> Although Origen is credited with being the founder of this doctrine [*apokatastasis*] in Christianity, I shall argue that he had several antecedents. I shall also argue that this doctrine was abundantly received throughout the Patristic era, up to the one who can be regarded as the last of the Fathers: John Eriugena. (1)[4]

Ramelli argues that Christian universalism has roots in the New Testament and that Origen was not influenced by gnosticism but was resolutely anti-gnostic (*pace* de Faye and Daniélou). She describes her own volume as "the result of almost fifteen years of scholarly research" (ix). Her wide reading in the primary and secondary sources is evident. The ambitious scope of her inquiry appears in the summary statement offered at the outset: "My analysis will extend to the whole of the Patristic age, from the New Testament—and indeed the whole

3. Henri Crouzel offered his own assessment of scholarship on Origen in "Current Theology." In "Origène est-il un systématique?," he denied that Origen can be regarded as a "systematic" thinker in the usual sense. Crouzel dealt with Origen's eschatology in "Letter from Origen 'To Friends in Alexandria'"; several of his essays on Origen's eschatology appear in *Les fins dernières selon Origène*. The Renaissance debate over the possibility of Origen's salvation is the theme of Crouzel's *Une controverse sur Origène*.

4. Numbers in parentheses after quotations are page references in Ramelli's book. Her assessment of Eriugena as a "Father" or acknowledged Catholic author needs a supporting argument, given that Pope Honorius III in a 1225 letter judged Eriugena's major work, the *Periphyseon*, to be "'swarming with worms of heretical perversity'" and called for all copies of the book to be destroyed. See Pope Honorius III, "Letter of January 23, 1225," as quoted by Potter, "John the Scot, and His Background," xxiii. On Pope Honorius's censure of Eriugena, see Cappuyns, *Jean Scot Erigène*, 248.

of the Bible, which is the basis for any Patristic speculation—to John the Scot Eriugena, whose thought was nourished by the best of Greek Patristics" (2).

The idea that Origen's universalism drew from earlier gnostic universalism— which existed in Alexandria prior to Origen's lifetime among the Carpocratians, Basilideans, and Valentinians—deserves more attention than the three pages Ramelli devotes to it (87–89). In her presentation, she ignores Holger Strutwolf's *Gnosis als System* (1993), which argues convincingly for continuities between Origen and second-century gnosticism.[5] Because Ramelli defines "gnosticism" in terms of soteriological elitism and determinism, she sees Origen's stress on free will and universal salvation as marking him as "anti-gnostic." Yet she overlooks the larger patterns, highlighted by Strutwolf, of the fall-and-restoration-of-souls motif as found among the Nag Hammadi community, the Valentinians, Plotinus and the Neoplatonists, and Origen's *Peri archōn* (see *DR* 2.3; 3.4–3.6). Moreover, Ramelli's reduction of gnosticism to soteriological determinism is out of step with recent scholarship and does not take account of M. A. Williams's argument in *Rethinking "Gnosticism"* (1996). Ramelli's essay "Apokatastasis in Coptic Gnostic Texts from Nag Hammadi and Clement's and Origen's Apokatastasis" denies that "Coptic Gnostic texts" teach "universal salvation," but the sources she cites do not allow for any such definitive conclusion. Her larger strategy of differentiating Origen from his second- and third-century context leaves us with a decontextualized Origen.

Throughout her book, Ramelli reveals her ambition to vindicate the doctrine of *apokatastasis* as a Christian and Catholic teaching that does not violate either the teachings of Scripture or the decisions of church councils. For this reason, one must take with a grain of salt her claim that "the present study is not primarily concerned about 'orthodoxy' and 'heresy'" (2n3). Her book is more than a dispassionate analysis of ancient texts. On the very same page where she claims to disavow the categories of "orthodoxy" and "heresy," she argues for the salience of ancient discussions of universalism by appealing to pro-universalist statements by contemporary African-American Pentecostal bishop Carlton Pearson, by Christian Orthodox scholars such as Bishop Hilarion Alfeyev of Vienna and Bishop Kallistos Ware, and by the Roman Catholic archbishop of Westminster, Murphy O'Connor, and Pope John Paul II (2–3n6).[6] To assess the

5. A major scholar of gnosis in the twentieth century, Hans Jonas, arrived independently at a view like that of Strutwolf, linking Origen to his second- and third-century gnostic context. See Jonas's "Origen's Metaphysics."

6. In favorably citing Carlton Pearson, Ramelli may not be aware of Pearson's arguments for universalism based on claims that human beings are divine by nature and that evil is "part of God" (see *DR* 11.2). In *The Gospel of Inclusion*, Pearson states that "we [humans] are made of the same substance as Divinity. . . . God created us out of Himself, which means that we are innately, internally, and eternally divine" (44). Pearson comments, "Evil would not exist were it not part of God" (104).

work, one must regard it in terms not only of its historical analysis but also of its implied theological arguments.

Broadly speaking, Ramelli offers revisionist theological history and a new paradigm for understanding the church's first millennium. She rarely engages the second millennium, though there are a few ad hoc comments toward the end of the book (820–26). Throughout the book she intersperses footnoted references to recent debates over universalism. Repeatedly Ramelli returns to two figures, Origen and Gregory of Nyssa, who, taken together, seem to offer the touchstone for her theological analysis.

Some of Ramelli's claims may raise eyebrows. For example, she states that Augustine in his earlier years "espoused Origen's *apokatastasis* doctrine" (659; see also 659–76).[7] This assertion regarding Augustine is touted on the book's back cover as among the "surprises [that] await readers of this book." What is more, Ramelli states that the anathema naming Origen (anathema 11) in the official acts of the Fifth Ecumenical Council (553 CE) was likely interpolated into the text. This assertion allows Ramelli to state plainly: "Origen was never formally condemned by any Christian ecumenical council" (737). To her mind, Origen's fall from ecclesial favor rests on a mistake—an error lasting fifteen centuries.[8]

Ramelli also states that Basil of Caesarea's statements on everlasting punishment are likewise not original but probably were interpolated into the texts (354–58). Her claims of interpolation are designed to uphold Origen's reputation and minimize disagreements between Origen and other ancient

7. The text on which Ramelli bases her conclusion regarding Augustine is taken from *On the Morals of the Manichaeans* 2.7.9, where Augustine writes: "Dei bonitas . . . omnia deficientia sic ordinat . . . donec ad id recurrent unde defecerunt" (cited in Ramelli, *Christian Doctrine of* Apokatastasis, 663). Ramelli renders the passage into English—without ellipses—on the following page: "The goodness of God orders and leads all the beings that have fallen until they return/are restored to the condition from which they had fallen" (664). The verb is *ordinat*, which translates as "orders" and not as "orders and leads." There is no second verb alongside *ordinat*. Moreover, Augustine's statement that creatures are *ordered* toward restoration does not imply that all will attain it. In *Retractations* 1.6, Augustine discusses this very passage—a point Ramelli fails to mention. He disavows the idea of creatures' returning to God "as it seemed to Origen," indicates that the statement applies only "to all those things that return," and adds that the wicked "are most suitably in a place of punishment" (Augustine, *Retractations*, 26–27). Since Augustine's *Retractations* are often clarifications of his originally intended meanings, it does not follow that the presence of the text cited above in the *Retractations* means that Augustine had changed his mind or had once agreed with Origen.

8. One indication of Origen's reputation as a heretic during late antiquity and the early medieval period is found in the wholesale destruction of most of his writings. If, as Ramelli suggests, the anathematizing of Origen—in the last place in anathema 11—was not original, then the interpolation must have been added so quickly to the original text that no one recognized it as an interpolation. But then how is Ramelli—almost 1,500 years later—able to identify an interpolation when no one before her seems to have done so?

Christian authors. Those acquainted with early Christian history will recall Origen's pro-Nicene defender, Rufinus of Aquileia (*DR* 3.11–3.13), who argued that the apparent unorthodoxies of Origen's writings were due to widespread interpolations into his texts "by heretics and evilly disposed persons."[9] While modern scholars have not embraced Rufinus's interpolation theory, Ramelli exemplifies a certain "Rufinian" quality in her many-sided effort to vindicate Origen and Origenism—through biblical exegesis, claims of interpolations into ancient texts, and her own philosophical argumentation.[10]

The book's chapter and section titles do not give clear indications of their contents. While almost eighty pages are devoted to Origen (137–221), there is no chapter on Origen per se; rather, the discussion of Origen is incorporated into a megachapter on "The Roots of the Doctrine of *Apokatastasis*" (1–221), which includes a discussion of New Testament texts (10–62). The blurred boundaries between biblical and patristic evidence may reflect Ramelli's desire to establish historical continuities in the teaching of *apokatastasis*, but the chapters' arrangement is likely to confuse readers. Another sort of blurring takes place by inserting quotations from Origen and Gregory of Nyssa outside their respective sections. This is apparent, for instance, in the section on Isaac of Syria (or Isaac of Nineveh) (758–66). As a result of such blended citations, legitimate distinctions between Isaac and both Origen and Gregory are consistently obscured. This problem is not limited to the section on Isaac; it occurs throughout the book.

In Ramelli's account, almost everyone, from the first-century New Testament authors to the ninth-century Eriugena, concurred with Origen's views.[11] If Ramelli is correct, then patristic and medieval scholars have long labored

---

9. In the preface to his bowdlerized translation of Origen's *Peri archōn*, Rufinus of Aquileia wrote that Origen's writings

> are known to contain in the original a good many statements likely to cause offense, [but Jerome] so smoothed over and emended these in his translation, that a Latin reader would find in them nothing out of harmony with our faith. His example, therefore, I am following to the best of my ability . . . taking care not to reproduce such passages from the books of Origen as are found to be inconsistent with and contrary to his true teaching. The cause of these variations . . . [is] that these have been corrupted in many places by heretics and evilly disposed persons. (Rufinus of Aquileia, "Preface of Rufinus," in Butterworth, *"On First Principles,"* lxiii)

Rufinus's letter on the corruption of Origen's works has been translated in Scheck, *St. Pamphilus.*

10. Ramelli commends "the perspicacious Rufinus" (211) and writes that "Rufinus was a faithful Origenian for the whole of his life" (656), who sought "to show directly from the evidence of the texts Origen's greatness and orthodoxy against his detractors" (636). Yet it should be noted that Rufinus tampered with the textual evidence and saddled later scholars and readers with a skewed, inaccurate Latin rendering of *Peri archōn* (*DR* 3.2).

11. According to the book's table of contents (vii), ch. 2 covers Origen's "First 'Detractors,'" but the word "detractors" is set in scare quotes, as if to imply that the "detractors" were perhaps not detractors at all—just mistaken in their reading and interpretation of Origen.

under the misapprehension that there was a diversity of views in the early church on the scope of final salvation. One searches this book in vain to find a single case in which Ramelli admits that someone understood Origen and then disagreed with him. Dissent from Origen, as she says again and again, was due to misunderstanding—by Augustine, Emperor Justinian, and others. Not even the Fifth Ecumenical Council is justified in its dissent, for Ramelli's claim here is that "Origen was never formally condemned by any Christian ecumenical council" (737). Nor is Augustine permitted to dissent. Instead he appears as a sort of Origenist manqué who earlier in his life attained a blessed vision of universal salvation but then fell away. The bishop of Hippo failed to understand Origen.[12] In every ancient contest of ideas, Origen always wins, even when he apparently loses. Where ancient authors express ideas like Origen's, Ramelli often attributes to the author in question the other ideas that she associates with Origen.[13]

Of all the authors treated in this book, Ramelli assigns the most space to Origen (137–221), Gregory of Nyssa (372–440), and John Scotus Eriugena (773–815). Conspicuously missing from her expositions of Origen and Gregory are acknowledgments of differences between these two thinkers. Without prior knowledge of early Christian literature, a reader of Ramelli's book would not surmise that Gregory deviated from Origen in basic ways and repudiated Origen's teaching on preexistent (or premortal) souls.[14] Gregory also rejected the idea of the eschaton as the restoration of a primal condition of stasis. In Gregory's mature theological teaching, the final state is one of continuous change and development, a conception that contradicts Origen's *apokatastasis*. In fact, Gregory, Maximus the Confessor, and Eriugena all rejected Origen's static afterlife. In this sense, Origen's *apokatastasis* had no sequel or successor. It was a teaching that began and ended with Origen. In several ways Ramelli glosses over differences, and sameness prevails throughout her exposition.

12. Ramelli speaks of "how distorted Origen's thought was in Augustine's reports" (670). The implication seems to be that Augustine did not reject Origen's theology but misunderstood it. With more justification, Ramelli claims that Origen was misunderstood by Emperor Justinian and others in the sixth century (724–38), yet this point was already well established half a century ago in Guillaumont, *Les 'Kephalaia gnostica'* (1962).

13. Irenaeus gives us "a notion [of eschatology] that is close to Origen's own idea" (105). Athanasius gives us "an Origenian idea" (245). The theology of the image is "the same in Origen, in Methodius here . . . and in Gregory of Nyssa" (267). Ephrem's teaching is "clearly the same position as Origen's" (337).

14. Ramelli admits that Gregory rejected the preexistence of souls, yet she insists that his argument to this effect was *not against Origen* (729), a position that makes no sense in light of Gregory's statement that his argument against preexistent souls had to do with "those before our time who have dealt with the question of 'principles'"—an obvious reference to Origen (*On the Making of Man* 28.1; *NPNF²* 5:78).

Moderate followers of Origen (e.g., Gregory) rejected the idea of a primal fall of souls, followed by embodiment and a final restoration to God. It was only Origen's more radical followers (e.g., Evagrius of Pontus, and Stephen bar Sudaili, presumed author of the *Book of the Holy Hierotheos*) who maintained the fall-and-restoration-of-souls motif that was essential to Origen's *Peri archōn*. On the other hand, the vision of the eschaton in Evagrius's *Great Letter*—and even more obviously in Stephen bar Sudaili—involved a pantheistic or pantheizing dissolution of the Creator-creature distinction (*DR* 3.10; 4.5).[15] Stephen was even more radical than Evagrius, claiming that even the names "Father," "Son," and "Spirit" would pass away in an eschatological state of oneness. While the point may be disputed, Evagrius and Stephen seem to have affirmed the final unity of creatures with their Creator in a way that Origen did not (or not explicitly).[16] For this basic reason, it is difficult, if not impossible, to claim a common tradition of Christian *apokatastasis* when Christian thinkers construed the eschaton in differing and even contradictory ways. The differences between the eschatological teachings of Origen, Gregory, Evagrius, Maximus, and Eriugena are perhaps as striking as their similarities.

In a brief section entitled "The Syriac Heritage" (690–94), Ramelli treats Evagrius of Pontus, Stephen bar Sudaili, and the *Book of the Holy Hierotheos*. The terse treatment of these important and influential thinkers belies the fact that Evagrius and bar Sudaili both clearly taught universal salvation, and both were widely read and debated figures in early Christian literature. Since most scholars regard Evagrius and especially Stephen bar Sudaili as representatives of a gnosticizing or pantheizing version of *apokatastasis*, Ramelli's failure to deal more fully with these writers gives the appearance that she is slighting the evidence that does not fit her Origen-centered interpretation of the history of Christian teachings on *apokatastasis*.

In her opening pages, Ramelli seeks to show that the Bible supports universalism. Yet one of the oddest aspects of this book is the attempt to clinch a biblical or exegetical argument by appealing to early translations, sometimes *against* the Hebrew or Greek texts. She appeals to the Vulgate when its rendering supports her scriptural interpretations (14, 23, 45, 47, 51n122).[17] She also cites

15. According to Augustine Cassiday, Evagrius's eschaton is nonpantheistic. Compare Parmentier, "Evagrius of Pontus' 'Letter to Melania'"; Konstantinovsky, "Last Things," in *Evagrius Ponticus*, 153–78; with Casiday, "Universal Restoration."

16. Jerome, in his *Letter* 124 (*ad Avitum*), and the early modern Jesuit Pierre-Daniel Huet, in *Origenis in Sacras Scripturas Commentaria* (1668), held that Origen's theology made the human spirit or mind consubstantial with God. On this reading, such Origenists as Evagrius were merely making explicit what was already implicit in Origen's thought—namely, a final merging or nondistinction of creatures and the Creator. See *DR*, 267n141, 421, 619n40.

17. There is one case where Ramelli cites the Vulgate and rejects its rendering (32).

Syriac (12, 48) and Coptic (47–48) versions of the Bible. For example, in her discussion of Matthew 17:11, "Elijah will indeed come and restore all things," Ramelli objects to the seeming implication in this verse that Elijah is one who will "restore all" (*apokatastēsei panta*). She insists instead that "God is the agent of the eschatological universal restoration" (13). She then proceeds to find an early translation that uses a passive construction in the second part of the verse. The Syriac Harklean reads (in her translation): "Elijah will indeed come first, and all beings / everything will be restored" (13). The problem here is not with the rendering of this verse but rather with the methodological assumptions that allow Ramelli to reject the New Testament Greek text in favor of a Syriac translation of it. The evidence has been forced to fit certain preconceptions—in this case, the assumption that God must in all cases be the subject of the phrase "restore all" (*apokatastēsei panta*).

Daley versus Ramelli: *The Hope of the Early Church* (1991) and *The Christian Doctrine of* Apokatastasis (2013)

Scientific researchers try to avoid what is sometimes known as "selection bias." Hypotheses that would not find support from a randomly selected data set might become plausible—and seem to be provable—if one uses a skewed data set. One question to be posed regarding Ramelli's book is whether the whole idea of an early Christian doctrine and tradition of *apokatastasis* is based on "selection bias" in the choices of authors and texts to consider.

To evaluate Ramelli's presentation of her evidence, it may be instructive to juxtapose her book with Brian Daley's *The Hope of the Early Church* (1991), one of the most carefully argued and copiously documented guides to early Christian eschatological views. Daley's work is widely acknowledged and regarded as a model of careful reading and scrupulous attention to detail. In his analysis, a large number of authors or texts affirmed the idea of everlasting punishment and so should be regarded as anti-universalist. I list them here in roughly chronological order: 1 *Clement*, 2 *Clement*, *Epistle of Barnabas*, the *Shepherd of Hermas*, Ignatius of Antioch, *Sibylline Oracles* (apart from one passage), *Epistula Apostolorum*, Aristides, Athenagoras, Justin Martyr, *Martyrdom of Polycarp*, Theophilus of Antioch, Irenaeus, Tertullian, Minucius Felix, Hippolytus, Cyprian, Victorinus of Pettau, Lactantius, *Apophthegmata Patrum*, Aphrahat, Ephrem (in Daley's analysis), Cyril of Jerusalem, Apollinaris of Laodicea, Basil, Epiphanius, Firmicus Maternus, Hilary of Poitiers, Zeno of Verona, John Chrysostom, Cyril of Alexandria, Theodore of Mopsuestia (in Daley's analysis), Theodoret of Cyrus, Hesychius of Jerusalem, the Pseudo-Macarian *Homilies*, *Apocalypse of Paul*,

Gaudentius of Brescia, Maximus of Turin, Hilarianus, Tyconius, Augustine, Evodius of Uzala (or whoever wrote the *Dialogue of Zaccheus*), Orosius, *Liber de Promissionibus*, Salvian of Marseilles, Pope Leo the Great, Aurelius Prudentius Clemens, Paulinus of Nola, Orientius, Commodian, Peter Chrysologus, Agathangelos, Shenoute of Atripe, Narsai, Jacob of Sarug, Oecumenius, Pseudo-Dionysius (in Daley's analysis), Severus of Antioch, Leontinus of Byzantium (in Daley's analysis), Cyril of Scythopolis, Barsanuphius, John of Gaza, Aeneas of Gaza, Cosmas Indicopleustes, Andrew of Caesarea, Romanos the Melodist, Maximus the Confessor (in Daley's analysis), and John of Damascus.

Other authors and texts are difficult to interpret on the question of universalism. In Daley's analysis these include Clement of Alexandria, *Apocalypse of Peter*, *Sibylline Oracles* (in one passage), Eusebius, Gregory of Nazianzus, Ambrose (who seems to oscillate), and Jerome (who seems to oscillate, both before and after 394 CE). Another eschatological position might be labeled as pantheistic or pantheizing and ought therefore to be distinguished from universalism in an Origenian sense. Stephen bar Sudaili and Evagrius of Pontus would both likely fall into this category.

The list of figures clearly teaching or asserting universalism in an Origenian way includes Origen (though a few scholars disagree), Gregory of Nyssa (also with some dissenters), Didymus the Blind, and Isaac the Syrian (in all likelihood).[18] Marcellus of Ancyra seems to have held to a non-Origenist version of universalism. The data that Daley has carefully sifted show sixty-eight authors and texts that clearly affirm the eternal punishment of the wicked, while seven authors are unclear, two teach something like eschatological pantheism, and perhaps four authors appear to be universalists in the Origenian sense.

To summarize the early Christian data, the support for universalism is paltry in comparison with opposition to it. There is not much of a universalist tradition during the first centuries of the Christian church. The sixty-eight non-universalist authors come from each of the centuries surveyed, from both East and West, and wrote in Greek, Latin, Coptic, Syriac, and Armenian. From Daley's analysis, one can see the distortion involved in claiming a "universalist East" versus an "infernalist West." The Coptic, Syriac, and Armenian opposition to Origenism is little known and yet clear-cut. Also very striking is that there are no unambiguous cases of Christian universalist teaching after the days of the apostles and before the writings of Origen. This observation undercuts Ramelli's claim that Origen was not an innovator in his eschatology and that

18. The essays by Giulio Maspero ("Apocatastasis") and Lucas Francisco Mateo-Seco ("Eschatology") in *The Brill Dictionary of Gregory of Nyssa* each acknowledge evidence in Gregory that contradicts universalism as well as evidence that supports it. Mario Baghos ("Reconsidering *Apokatastasis*") challenges the majority view of Gregory as a universalist.

universalism was either implicitly or explicitly maintained from the first century up to the early third century when Origen wrote *Peri archōn*. Even if one were to agree with Ramelli that the New Testament teaches universal salvation, then second-century Christian literature represents a perhaps insuperable problem for her historical reconstruction. To the extent that second-century authors agreed in teaching everlasting punishment, the claim of an unbroken tradition of Christian universalism from the time of the apostles onward is called into question.[19] Daley's analysis might support a counterthesis to Ramelli—namely, that early Christian writing on eschatology, from as early as the third century, could be seen as *an extended argument against Origen*.

Is Ramelli guilty, then, of "selection bias"? To be fair, she does not claim to offer a comprehensive account of early Christian eschatology, as Daley does. Because she seeks to give an account of Christian teaching on the *apokatastasis*, her choice of authors and texts is necessarily selective. Yet one of the biggest problems lies in the book's homogenizing tendencies. Despite their many differences, Origen, Bardaisan, Gregory of Nyssa, Isaac of Syria, and Eriugena all go into the blender and come out looking alike. Attentiveness to non-universalists and anti-universalists might have added more color to Ramelli's narrative. In largely omitting the anti-Origenists, Ramelli's presentation becomes less engaging and less intelligible. If one were to imagine the early Christian debate over Origen as a telephone conference call with six, eight, or ten or more voices, then how well might one discern the flow of conversation if one could hear only one or two voices? Much of the contextual information on the Origenist debates is not included; the voices of the anti-Origenist authors are rarely heard, and their absence gives the book a hollowed-out or fragmentary structure.

Concluding Assessment

The Christian Doctrine of Apokatastasis contains a number of philosophical as well as historical arguments.[20] To appraise the larger sweep of Ramelli's historical

19. Admittedly, Christian literature is less abundant in the second century than in the third or fourth century. Yet the absence of second-century Christian universalist texts—except among Carpocratians, Basilideans, Valentinians, or other "gnostics"—lends support to the idea that Origen's universalism was innovative in the context of early third-century mainstream or catholic Christianity.

20. Ramelli develops at some length the familiar argument that *aiōnios* in ancient sources need not mean "eternal" in the absolute, unqualified sense—a point that has some merit. Yet she claims, mistakenly, that in the New Testament *aidios* means "absolutely eternal" and so "*never* refers to punishment . . . in the other world" (26 [emphasis original]; see also 33), even though the word occurs in reference to the fallen angels' "eternal chains" (Jude 6). Another of Ramelli's arguments (based on Origen and Gregory) is that evil was not created by God and is ontologically weak or deficient, so that it cannot endure forever. She speaks of "the ontological non-existence of evil and

reconstruction, we have to ask, what exactly is "the doctrine of *apokatastasis*" that was supposedly passed from Origen to his successors through the centuries?

Origen himself stressed the parallel between cosmic beginnings and endings: "For the end is always like the beginning."[21] *Apokatastasis*, in this sense, is a restoration and return of a state of affairs that previously existed. Gregory of Nyssa, for his part, rejected the idea of souls existing outside of mortal bodies, and so he offered a teaching on *apokatastasis* no longer consonant with Origen's. On the one hand, if one interprets *apokatastasis* to mean not "the restoration of fallen souls to their original condition" but simply "universal salvation," then one might link Origen to Gregory. On the other hand, Origen and Gregory held differing conceptions of salvation: a static condition versus a continuously changing one.

The effort to extend the idea of "universal salvation" to Eriugena creates yet another problem. As Willemien Otten has demonstrated, Eriugena's notion of the eschaton involved a universal return of souls to God, according to Jesus's saying, "in my Father's house are many rooms" (John 14:2). Yet for Eriugena not all souls will be happy in their final state with God, and some seemingly will be stuck within the hurtful, misleading, and even hellish fantasies that captivated them during their earthly lives. The heavenly saints will enjoy no shared beatific vision. On the contrary, those in the afterlife might be compared to people placed into private video booths, each staring at a separate screen.[22] If Origen's *apokatastasis* is a state in which all souls share in blessed contemplation of God, then Eriugena in that sense did not follow Origen.

The deceptively simple question of whether a particular Christian thinker taught the *apokatastasis* proves to be more complex than it first appears to be. Instead we must ask a series of questions: Was there a preexistent state of souls to which all souls will finally return (Origen)? Will all souls enter into a static heaven (Origen), or into a heaven that is constantly changing and dynamic (Gregory of Nyssa and Maximus)? Will souls in returning to God retain their individuality (Origen and most of his followers)? Or will the soul be changed into God's nature, like water flowing into the ocean (Evagrius)? Will God himself cease to be trinitarian and enter a post-trinitarian state of ultimate oneness

---

its eventual disappearance in *apokatastasis*" (210; cf. 51, 142–48). But this argument might prove too much—namely, that evil will defeat itself, apart from divine agency. See *DR* 3.9; 4.3.

21. Origen, *On First Principles* 1.6.2 (Butterworth, 53); Origen, *PA* 216: *Semper enim similis est finis initiis.*

22. See W. Otten, "Dialectic of Return in Eriugena's *Periphyseon*." In Eriugena's eschaton, "these theophanies [i.e., divine manifestations] are said to be manifold . . . since each saint will have his or her own theophany. . . . A clear, unimpaired vision of God appears not to be reached" (418). Eriugena writes that "all . . . shall return into Paradise, but not all shall enjoy the Tree of Life—or rather . . . not all equally" (*Periphyseon* 1015A [Sheldon-Williams and O'Meara, 705–6]).

(bar Sudaili)? Will all souls returning to God be truly happy with God, or might some souls be unhappy in God's presence (Eriugena)?

In arguing for a "Christian doctrine of *apokatastasis*," Ramelli glosses over the disparities and contradictions that appeared during nine centuries of Christian teaching and debate over *apokatastasis*. Her book is large and abundantly documented yet oversimplified. Because of the blurred distinctions between Origen and Gregory, neither author is accurately rendered. Ramelli downplays differences between Origen and Gregory to make Origen seem more like Gregory, who may be the hidden hero in this book. A certain "Nyssification" and homogenization of early Christian teachings occurs. As a guide to the diversity of early Christian eschatological teachings, Brian Daley's *The Hope of the Early Church* is much more reliable. As a "critical assessment" of early Christian teaching on *apokatastasis*, Ramelli's book comes up short. Further research and writing in this area will need to engage the wealth of material presented here. Yet it will also need to reconsider and reevaluate the arguments and claims offered in this book.

Appendix E

The *Sefiroth*

A Kabbalistic Diagram

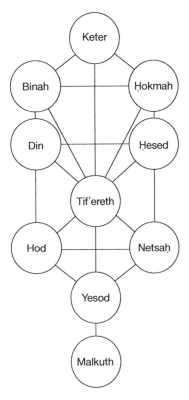

Keter = Crown; *Binah* = Understanding; *Ḥokmah* = Wisdom; *Din* (or *Gevurah*) = Judgment; *Ḥesed* = Loving-kindness or Mercy; *Tif'ereth* = Beauty; *Hod* = Hand; *Netsaḥ* = Victory; *Yesod* = Foundation; *Malkuth* = Kingdom (figure from Gershom Scholem, *On the Mystical Shape of the Godhead*, 44).

Appendix F

Universal Salvation in Islamic Teaching

Islam is well known for teaching that all human beings are destined to go either to heaven (paradise) or else to hell (the fire).[1] What is more, mainstream Islamic teaching insists not only on the eternity of heaven but also on the eternity of hell. Jon Hoover speaks of "the deeply held classical consensus that the Fire [i.e., hell] will definitely remain forever."[2] What is not so well known is that some of the best-known representatives of Islamic mysticism or Sufism presented teachings on the afterlife that significantly departed from this consensus view. The greatest philosophical mind among the Sufis, Ibn al-'Arabi (or Ibn 'Arabi; 1165–1240), held an esoteric doctrine in which God is manifested in all existing things, including phenomena that human beings judge to be evil.[3] Satan as well as Gabriel, the idolater as well as the Muslim, the prostitute as well as the virgin, are all manifestations of God. Ibn al-'Arabi's notion that everything not-God will be finally reconciled to God implied what William Chittick, an authority on Islamic mysticism, called "the ontological roots of hell's impermanence."[4]

1. Sources on Muslim eschatology include J. I. Smith and Y. Y. Haddad, *Islamic Understanding of Death and Resurrection*; Abrahamov, "Creation and Duration of Paradise in Hell in Islamic Theology"; Bijlefeld, "Eschatology"; Chittick, "Muslim Eschatology"; Hoover, "Islamic Universalism"; Khalil, *Islam and the Fate of Others*; Rizvi, review of *Islam and the Fate of Others*; Hoover, review of *Islam and the Fate of Others*.
2. Hoover, "Islamic Universalism," 197.
3. Ibn al-'Arabi is also known as Shaykh Al-Akbar ("the Great Master"), while his full name is Abū 'Abd Allāh Muhammad ibn 'Alī ibn Muhammad ibn 'Arabī al-Ḥātimī aṭ-Ṭā'ī.
4. Chittick, *Imaginal Worlds*, 113.

Hell as a state of purification must be a temporary state, because God's mercy has ultimate priority over God's wrath. Hell will eventually cease to be unpleasant, according to Ibn al-'Arabi. Those in hell will enjoy their condition there and thank God that they are not in heaven. For Jalāl ad-Dīn Muhammad Rūmī (or simply Rumi; 1207–73), the soul originates in a nonbodily realm, in God's presence, and after its sojourn in the body it will return again to God. Rumi, like Ibn al-'Arabi, teaches a form of Islamic universalism.

Islamic teachings on eschatology recall various Jewish and Christian teachings that were treated above. Ibn al-'Arabi's notion that hell purges people of sin, guilt, or ignorance is reminiscent of Origen, along with the corollary that hell's sufferings must finally come to an end (DR 3.6–3.7). Ibn al-'Arabi's idea of the imaginal world as the sphere of heavenly reward or hellish punishment is reminiscent of John Scotus Eriugena. In Eriugena's teaching, all human beings will finally return to God, and heaven and hell consist in images that correspond to the respective soul state of each person (DR 4.10). The Sufi principle of the priority of mercy over wrath reminds one of Jewish Kabbalah (DR 2.6), emerging in southern France at about the same time that Ibn al-'Arabi lived in Catalonia (i.e., Spain). As we will see below, the foremost Sufi poet, Rumi, offered an even closer parallel to Origenism in his teaching on the preexistence of the soul, its entrance into the body, and its return back to the divine realm from which it came.

From the Islamic data, a general conclusion emerges. In Islam, no less than in Judaism and Christianity, it is the esoteric doctrine of God, the soul, and salvation that offers a foundation for belief in universal salvation. To be sure, there are a number of important Islamic thinkers who definitely held to the possible or actual salvation of non-Muslims. The list of Islamic "inclusivists" includes al-Ghazali, Ibn al-'Arabi, Ibn Taymiyya, Ibn Qayyim, and Rashid Rida.[5] Furthermore, there are universalist tendencies and arguments in the writings of Ibn Taymiyya and Ibn Qayyim (see below). Yet Ibn Taymiyya seems finally to back off from the implications of some of his own arguments and from inferring final salvation for all. His considered position might be described as a pious agnosticism in recognizing that "verily, your Lord is the doer of what He wills" (Qur'an 11:107).[6] Allah will decide. Ibn Taymiyya's leading disciple, Ibn Qayyim, published a number of works dealing with the question of postmortem punishment and gradually moved in the direction of universalism. Ibn Qayyim in the end, though, seems also to have backed off from his earlier statement of

5. In *Islam and the Fate of Others*, Khalil discusses in depth al-Ghazali, Ibn al-'Arabi, Ibn Taymiyya, and Rashid Rida.

6. All qur'anic quotations are taken from www.quran.com. While this first quotation is from Muhsin Khan's translation, Yusuf Ali's translation will be used in all following quotations.

a universalist position.[7] It is the Islamic esotericists such as Ibn al-'Arabi and Rumi who consistently affirmed the doctrine of universal salvation.

Islamic Eschatology and Qur'anic Teaching

Muhammad's preaching during the first period of his preaching in Mecca involved a detailed description of paradise and hell—the places of final reward and punishment respectively, often referred to under the figures of the "garden" and the "fire." In fact, the Qur'an speaks more often of death, the end of the world, and the resurrection than any other scripture of a major religious tradition. The hadith, or set of prophetic sayings, follows suit, as does the larger Islamic tradition. The broad pattern of Islamic eschatology was not original but followed earlier precedents in Judaism and Christianity. On the other hand, the descriptions of heaven and hell in the Qur'an and in classic Islamic literature were exceptional in their concreteness and specificity, as Chittick notes:

> The Koran is especially graphic when describing the terrors of hell. People are overcome by flames, and clothed in garments of tar. Every time they scream and shriek, boiling water is poured down their throats, melting away their organs. As often as their skin and organs are burned away, God replaces them. Their bodies are pierced by iron rods and torn apart by beasts and demons. . . . There is a strong current in the [traditional] accounts, however, that suggests that hell is in fact a purgatory for many, if not most, of those who go there. The descriptions of paradise are no less graphic. The garden is watered by rivers of water, milk, honey, and wine, and its inhabitants have everything their hearts desire: every sort of beautiful flower, bird, and scent; food and drink of unimaginable variety; luxurious clothing and peerless jewelry; marvelous companions (including their family and friends from this world); perfect spouses; and all the joys and delights of human intimacy, not least the sexual.[8]

The Qur'an contains numerous passages that speak of God's wrath on sinners.[9] The circumstance mentioned most often as the occasion of God's

---

7. Here I follow Jon Hoover's meticulous analysis of both Ibn Taymiyya and Ibn Qayyim in "Islamic Universalism." The reviews of Khalil's *Islam and the Fate of Others* by Sajjad Rizvi and Jon Hoover intimate that Khalil may have overstated his case for a universalist strand in pre-twentieth-century Islamic literature, though both Rizvi and Hoover agree that Ibn al-'Arabi's position might accurately be described as universalistic. I am indebted to Professor David Thomas, my former colleague at the University of Birmingham (UK), for directing me to the work of Jon Hoover, one of Professor Thomas's former doctoral advisees.

8. Chittick, "Muslim Eschatology," 134.

9. God's "wrath" is mentioned specifically in Qur'an (trans. Yusuf Ali) 1:7; 3:112; 3:162; 5:60; 5:80; 6:147; 7:152; 16:26; 16:106; 16:113; 17:15; 20:81; 25:65; 54:39.

wrath and indignation is the deliberate rejection of God's messengers and God's signs. "They draw on themselves wrath from Allah. . . . This because they rejected the Signs of Allah, and slew the prophets in defiance of right; this because they rebelled and transgressed beyond bounds" (Qur'an 3:112). "But those who disobey Allah and His Messenger and transgress His limits will be admitted to a Fire, to abide therein: And they shall have a humiliating punishment" (Qur'an 4:14). "And there came to them a Messenger from among themselves, but they falsely rejected him; so the Wrath seized them even in the midst of their iniquities" (Qur'an 16:113; cf. 29:23; 34:5; 45:11). The Qur'an also describes various expressions of God's wrath: "He flingeth the loud-voiced thunder-bolts, and therewith He striketh whomsoever He will" (Qur'an 13:13). God manifests his indignation in unexpected ways: "Allah took their structures from their foundations, and the roof fell down on them from above; and the Wrath seized them from directions they did not perceive" (Qu'ran 16:16). In one passage we read of "those who incurred the curse of Allah and His wrath, those of whom some He transformed into apes and swine, those who worshipped evil" (Qur'an 5:60).

Those who offer false religious teachings will experience God's opposition: "Those who took the calf (for worship) will indeed be overwhelmed with wrath from their Lord, and with shame in this life: thus do We recompense those who invent (falsehoods)" (Qur'an 7:152).[10] Those who reject the Islamic faith after having accepted it will also suffer: "Any one who, after accepting faith in Allah, utters Unbelief, except under compulsion, his heart remaining firm in Faith—but such as open their breast to Unbelief, on them is Wrath from Allah, and theirs will be a dreadful Penalty" (Qur'an 16:106). A number of passages suggest that the punishment of the wicked lasts forever, and this is the consensus view as it developed among authoritative Islamic authors. "Evil indeed are (the works) which their souls have sent forward before them (with the result), that Allah's wrath is on them, and in torment will they abide" (Qur'an 5:80). Another text states that "from people in guilt never will His wrath be turned back" (Qur'an 6:147). Still another says that "never will be warded off our punishment from those who are in sin" (Qur'an 12:110).

The eleventh surah contains a passage that seems to set the eternity of heaven alongside an eternity of punishment and suffering:

> Those who are wretched shall be in the Fire: There will be for them therein (nothing but) the heaving of sighs and sobs: They will dwell therein for all

10. In Islamic interpretation, a first-person plural statement by Allah in the Qur'an must not be taken as implying plurality within God but is to be understood instead as the plural of majesty.

the time that the heavens and the earth endure, except as thy Lord willeth: for thy Lord is the (sure) accomplisher of what He planneth. And those who are blessed shall be in the Garden: They will dwell therein for all the time that the heavens and the earth endure, except as thy Lord willeth: a gift without break. (Qur'an 11:106–8)

Other passages seem likewise to say that heaven is eternal and so is hell. "But give glad tidings to those who believe and work righteousness, that their portion is Gardens, beneath which rivers flow . . . and they have therein companions pure (and holy); and they abide therein (for ever)" (Qur'an 2:25). "Those who reject Faith and do wrong, Allah will not forgive them nor guide them to any way except the way of Hell, to dwell therein for ever" (Qur'an 4:168–69).

Islamic discussions about the salvation of evildoers have sometimes focused on Pharaoh, who opposed Moses and God's good purposes for the children of Israel. One text in the Qur'an states that Pharaoh believed in Allah when he with his charioteers was about to perish in the Red Sea:

We took the Children of Israel across the sea: Pharaoh and his hosts followed them in insolence and spite. At length, when overwhelmed with the flood, he said: "I believe that there is no god except Him Whom the Children of Israel believe in: I am of those who submit (to Allah in Islam)." (It was said to him): "Ah now!—But a little while before, wast thou in rebellion!—and thou didst mischief (and violence)! This day shall We save thee in the body, that thou mayest be a sign to those who come after thee! but verily, many among mankind are heedless of Our Signs!" (Qur'an 10:90–92)

Taken in isolation, this text might suggest that Pharaoh believed rightly in Allah—"I believe that there is no god except Him"—and so repented of the idolatrous religion he had previously embraced. Yet the very next surah states that on the day of judgment, Pharaoh will continue to lead his people but will lead them away from salvation:

They [i.e., the Egyptians] followed the command of Pharaoh and the command of Pharaoh was no right (guide). He will go before his people on the Day of Judgment, and lead them into the Fire (as cattle are led to water): But woeful indeed will be the place to which they are led! (Qur'an 11:97–98)

The consensus view of these two passages is that God, in speaking to Pharaoh in 10:90–92, is not saying that Pharaoh's faith was acceptable to him but rather the opposite. What Pharaoh manifested in the way of faith and repentance came too late. No repentance is possible once Allah has already begun, at the moment of death, to remove one's soul from one's body. Ibn al-ʿArabi took another view and held that God approved Pharaoh's faith and repentance at the Red Sea.[11]

One sobering passage in the Qur'an states that evildoers would not repent even if they were given another chance:

> If thou couldst but see when they are confronted with the Fire! They will say: "Would that we were but sent back! Then would we not reject the signs of our Lord, but would be amongst those who believe!" Yea, in their own (eyes) will become manifest what before they concealed. But if they were returned, they would certainly relapse to the things they were forbidden, for they are indeed liars. (Qur'an 6:27–28)

This passage suggests that at least some evildoers become increasingly recalcitrant and resistant to repentance.[12]

Certain texts in the Qur'an soften the picture just presented. Muslims stressing God's mercy often cite the following text: "He said: 'With My punishment I visit whom I will; but My mercy extendeth to all things'" (Qur'an 7:156). The implication seems to be that mercy is more fundamental than wrath. While wrath and punishment arise in particular situations, God's mercy endures always. Another passage says, "O my servants who have transgressed against their souls! Despair not of the mercy of Allah: for Allah forgives all sins: for He is often-forgiving, Most Merciful" (Qur'an 39:53). The statement that "Allah forgives all sins" sounds like a prooftext for universalism—though it has to be read out of context to carry that meaning. Another passage notes that God never visits his wrath on anyone who has not been forewarned by a messenger sent by God: "Nor would We visit with Our Wrath until We had sent a messenger (to give warning)" (Qur'an 17:15). Finally, there is the text much beloved of Sufis stating that "whithersoever ye turn, there is the presence of Allah. For Allah is all-Pervading" (Qur'an 2:115).

---

11. Ibn al-ʿArabi suggested that Pharaoh repented at the Red Sea, commenting that "Allah accepted his sincere belief and Allah does not accept someone's belief unless he will surely reward him." Ibn al-ʿArabi argued that Pharaoh's faith began not at the moment of his death but rather when he saw the waters of the Red Sea miraculously divided in two. When someone comes from idolatry into Islam, he is to receive a ritual bath, and so Ibn al-ʿArabi writes that "Pharaoh's drowning was his ritual bathing" (*Futuhat al-Makkiyah*, ch. 9 [In the Remembrance of God], 12th Oneness, trans. al-Muatasim Said al-Maawali). I am indebted to al-Maawali, a Muslim educator at Sultan Qaboos University in Oman, for providing this reference to the Arabic text and for translating it for me.
12. See the discussion of this text in Abrahamov, "Creation and Duration," 96. This qur'anic passage recalls the argument of Severus of Antioch, Jacob of Sarug, Gregory the Great, and Thomas Aquinas that inveterate sinners—if spared divine judgment and given another chance in life—would simply return to their sinful ways (*DR*, 351, 357–58 with n. 138).

Philosophical Foundations in Ibn al-'Arabi

The "return" to God is one of the basic ideas of Islam. "To Allah we belong, and to Him is our return" (Qur'an 2:156). Yet this return takes place in one of two ways: compulsorily or voluntarily. The wicked and righteous alike must die, and this event brings about the compulsory return. The voluntary return to God applies to those who consciously turn themselves toward Allah in the present life, believe in his messenger, and submit to his rule.

In some Sufi authors, the notion of the "return" to God has a more literal meaning. Rumi, as we will see below, offers a robust doctrine of the soul's pre-existence prior to its entrance into the present bodily state. Chittick notes that "every evolution . . . is preceded by a devolution" and "as the Sufis like to put it, the ascending arc of reality curves back on the initial point of the descending arc, thus completing the circle of being and consciousness."[13] Along the same lines, Sajjad Rizvi comments that in Islam "the beginning of humans is a good and positive place in the presence of the divine, and hence the end desired is a return to that primordial place."[14]

We turn now to consider the complex theology and eschatology of Ibn al-'Arabi.[15] Often called "the Greatest Shaykh," he is considered the leading Sufi or Islamic mystical philosopher of all time. There are said to be 856 separate works by Ibn al-'Arabi. His major work, the *Meccan Openings* or *Meccan Revelations* (*Futuhat al-Makkiyah*), runs to 15,000 pages in its original Arabic edition. Only portions of it have appeared in English. Many of Ibn al-'Arabi's works have never appeared in a critical edition, nor have they been the focus of academic study and analysis. A brief summary of his philosophy appears in *The Bezels of Wisdom* (*Fusus al-Hikam*), on which Muslim thinkers have published some one hundred commentaries.[16] Broadly speaking, Ibn al-'Arabi's worldview revolves around two pivotal ideas. The first idea is his notion of God, the Real, or the Absolute—unknown and unknowable in its essential nature and yet endlessly

---

13. Chittick, "Muslim Eschatology," 144. Chittick continues in his description of the general Sufi view regarding the liberation of the soul from the body:

> As long as we are hindered by corporeal restraints, the invisible realms can only be accessed imperfectly. The soul needs to be freed from its fetters in order to spread its wings. . . . Death allows the infinite potential of the soul to achieve an invisible visibility through imaginal embodiment in realms of becoming that lie beyond physical possibility. Once the body is shucked off, the soul has direct access to the in-between realms that lead on to the divine spirit. Ibn 'Arabi tells us that death internalizes everything that had been outward, visible, and physical in our own individual nature. . . . Not that the body was simply the soul's hindrance, quite the contrary. The body is necessary for the development of the soul's faculties. (145)

14. Rizvi, review of *Islam and the Fate of Others*, 536.

15. The exposition of Ibn al-'Arabi here is largely based on Izutsu, *Sufism and Taoism*; Chittick, *Imaginal Worlds*. For a brief account, see Chittick, "Ibn 'Arabi."

16. One English version is Ibn al-'Arabi, *Seals of Wisdom*.

manifesting itself in everything perceived in the world. Like the endlessly toss-
ing waves of the ocean, which appear and disappear again, so all creatures are
manifestations of the divine that soon cease and dissolve back into the source
whence they sprang. The second idea is that of the Perfect Man, who undergoes
ontological descent and ascent.[17]

For Ibn al-'Arabi, the sense world is not real but dreamlike. It does not have
being or existence (*wujud*). He writes:

> The world is an illusion; it has no real existence. And this is what is meant by
> "imagination" (*khayal*). For you just imagine that it (i.e., the world) is an au-
> tonomous reality quite different from and independent of the absolute Reality,
> while in truth it is nothing of the sort. Know that you yourself are an imagina-
> tion. And everything that you perceive and say to yourself, "this is not me," is
> also an imagination. So that the whole world of existence is imagination within
> imagination.[18]

The task, then, is to take these imaginal forms back to their original or true
status. The phrase "to die and wake up" refers not to physical death but to the
spiritual event in which a human being throws off the shackles of sense and
reason, stepping from the phenomenal world into the beyond. This is the
mystical experience of self-annihilation, called *fana'*.[19]

For Ibn al-'Arabi, God per se is entirely inconceivable. As the Absolute, God
transcends all names and all distinctions, and this means that God is "the
most indeterminate of all indeterminates" (*ankar al-nakirat*).[20] It is impossible for the Absolute to manifest itself in its absoluteness. God considered
in himself is "absolute mystery" (*ghayb mutlaq*). God existing on the level of
"unity" (*ahadiyah*) is not yet self-revealed (*tajalli*). Having started with this
notion of God's utter transcendence, Ibn al-'Arabi then turns to speak of God's
immanence. Everything without exception is a mirror or self-manifestation
of God. The problem is that we see them only in an outward fashion and do
not penetrate to their interior and so experience the divine life that is pulsating within them.[21]

Ibn al-'Arabi distinguishes "Allah" from "Lord" (*Rabb*). "Allah" is the Absolute
manifested according to the divine names, while the "Lord" is the particular

17. Izutsu, *Sufism and Taoism*, 2–4, with 4n3.
18. Ibid., 7–8, citing Ibn al-'Arabi, *Fusus al-Hikam*, 103–4. All later citations of the Arabic *Fusus*
refer to this edition.
19. Izutsu, *Sufism and Taoism*, 8.
20. Ibid., 23, citing Ibn al-'Arabi, *Fusus al-Hikam*, 188. For a comparison of Sufism with contemporary deconstructionism (esp. vis-à-vis Jacques Derrida), see I. Almond, "Shackles of Reason."
21. Izutsu, *Sufism and Taoism*, 24, 32, 39.

manifestation of the Absolute through a particular divine name.[22] In Ibn al-'Arabi's thought, each individual being or thing expresses only one of many of the measureless divine names. Divine revelation, on this account, is partial and relative according to its very nature. Within the everyday or sense world, there can be no final or complete revelation of God. The Absolute existing on the level of ultimate oneness is a synthesis of all names. While individual entities may manifest one name, none can manifest all the names together. The exception lies in the Perfect Man, who contains all names but cannot be actualized bodily or materially.[23]

One implication of Ibn al-'Arabi's philosophy is an antinomian tendency, inasmuch as the distinction between good and evil is relativized along with all other distinctions on the creaturely or material plane of existence.[24] In traditional Islamic interpretation, the prophet Noah before the time of the flood preached against the rampant idolatry of his era. In Ibn al-'Arabi's view, Noah represents a quest for purity—associated with reason—in distinguishing God from every-thing that is not-God. Yet Ibn al-'Arabi does not give unqualified assent to Noah's rejection of idolatry. He takes the novel view that Noah, while outwardly condemning his contemporaries, was inwardly praising them.[25] Commenting

22. Ibn al-'Arabi's distinction between *Allah* and *Rabb* is reminiscent of the kabbalistic distinc-tion of *En Sof* from *Sefiroth* (*DR* 2.5)—the former term in each pair unnameable and ineffable, and the latter knowable yet manifesting only one aspect of the former.

23. Izutsu, *Sufism and Taoism*, 110, 112. In the Christian context, this line of reasoning leads to docetism. While a Perfect Man might exist on the immaterial, nonbodily plane, this spiritual arche-type or perfect synthesis of opposites could never exist in a bodily fashion. The Islamic esotericist Henri Corbin offers a defense of docetism in his *Creative Imagination*: "An Incarnation of 'God in person' in empirical history and, consequently, the historical consciousness which goes hand in hand with it, are unknown to the traditional Orient . . . [which] was fundamentally . . . 'docetic'" (84). He continues: "All esotericism in Islam . . . recognizes a divine anthropomorphosis, a divine Manifestation in human form; this anthropomorphosis is essential to the Godhead, but it takes place 'in heaven,' on the plane of the angelic universes. The celestial Anthropos is not 'incarnated' on earth; he is manifested on earth in theophanic figures which draw his followers, those who rec-ognize him, toward their celestial assumption." Corbin suggests that Shiite imamology and gnostic Christology both diverge from Pauline Christology and Christian orthodoxy: "The theophanism of Ibn 'Arabi will show us why no history, or philosophy of history, can be made with theophanies. Their time does not coincide with historical time. God has no need of coming down to earth" (84).

24. Fazlur Rahman notes the ethical problem in Sufism generally and Ibn al-'Arabi specifically: "The more insidious effect . . . was that the position of the Shari'a and its visible pillar, the law, was gravely endangered. A thoroughly monistic system, no matter how pious and conscientious it may claim to be, cannot, by its very nature, take seriously the objective validity of moral standards. 'All is He' . . . was the inevitable conclusion" (*Islam*, 146). Rumi wrote: "Good and evil are a single thing and cannot be separated. . . . Everything is good and perfect in relation to God, but not in relation to us. Fornication and purity, abandonment of the daily prayers and praying, unbelief and Islam, idolatry and the profession of God's Unity—all are good in relation to God" (Chittick, *Sufi Path of Love*, 54, citing Rumi, *Fihi ma fihi*, 213–4/221 and 31/42–3).

25. Izutsu, *Sufism and Taoism*, 49–61, esp. 59.

on Ibn al-ʿArabi, A. E. Affifi writes, "Those who are admonished, whatever their religion and whatever the object they worship, are in reality worshipping nothing other than God. . . , The idols are so many self-manifestations of God."[26] In some sense, all theologies are idolatries, because all involve limiting concepts of one kind or another as applied to God. It follows then that the distinction between monotheism and idolatry is relative and not absolute. The verse that says, "Thy Lord hath decreed that ye worship none but Him" (Qur'an 17:23), is therefore *not* a command to worship only God. Instead, for Ibn al-ʿArabi it means that whatever one worships, one is not actually worshiping anything other than Allah. The danger of idolatry lies not in the veneration given to an image or physical object but rather in the state of mind in which one fails to see a given object as a manifested form of God.[27]

Ibn al-ʿArabi sharply distinguishes the human spirit from the body, stating that "bodies are the sepulchers and tombs of the spirits . . . [that] veil the spirits from witnessing." A clear vision of spiritual reality is not possible until the spirit severs its link to the body. He also draws a basic distinction between God as the Universal Spirit and the partial, human spirits that are blown into living things by God. God's Spirit is the root of every spirit. In Ibn al-ʿArabi's reading of the Qur'an, God himself is the "one Spirit" (*nafs wahida*) from which Adam, Eve, and all their descendants were created (cf. Qur'an 4:1; 6:98; 39:6). Each human being manifests the properties of the divine Spirit to the extent of his or her "preparedness." Human beings are partial spirits that reflect a part of God, while the divine Spirit is universal. What divides the divine Spirit are bodies, just as windows divide the light of the sun. Elsewhere in the *Meccan Openings*, Ibn al-ʿArabi uses another analogy, comparing created

26. Ibid., 59, citing Affifi, in *Fusus al-Hikam*, by Ibn al-ʿArabi, 39.
27. Izutsu, *Sufism and Taoism*, 59–61. Izutsu speaks of Ibn al-ʿArabi's ontology as "beyond good and evil," since "everything is a self-manifestation of the Absolute . . . and there is no distinction at this stage between good and evil" (123). Ibn al-ʿArabi writes: "It is clear, then, that everybody walking on the earth is on the straight Way of the Lord. From this point of view nobody is of 'those upon whom is God's wrath' nor of 'those who go astray' [Q 1:7]. Both 'wrath' and 'going astray' come into being only secondarily. Everything goes ultimately back to the Mercy which is universal and which precedes [all distinctions]" (Izutsu, *Sufism and Taoism*, 123, citing Ibn al-ʿArabi, *Fusus al-Hikam*, 106). The implication is that whatever exists is good. It is only from the human, subjective, and relative point of view that one can speak of a distinction between good and evil (Izutsu, *Sufism and Taoism*, 124). Ibn al-ʿArabi offers a creative interpretation of Moses's staff that turned into a serpent and devoured the serpents made by the wise men of Egypt. In this way evil is swallowed up by goodness (125–26). Everything that happens reflects the will of God (127). Izutsu writes that "this standpoint is totally different from that of the Sacred Law [in Islam] which approves of this and disapproves of that" (127). According to Ibn al-ʿArabi, the evil man never in fact goes against the divine will (127). We thus find an overt antinomianism in Ibn al-ʿArabi.

intellects to lamp wicks lighted from God, who is the First Lamp.[28] The continuity between God and other spirits is stressed. Yet the human spirit even in its final, future state will preserve its individuality: "They [human spirits] never cease to be distinct for all eternity. They never return to their original state of being one entity."[29]

Of all the names of God, the greatest and most powerful for Ibn al-'Arabi is "merciful" (rahman).[30] Toshihiko Izutsu comments that in Ibn al-'Arabi "mercy" is not "an essentially emotive attitude" but is "rather an ontological fact." By nature, God overflows with bounteousness and so gives existence to everything. Even the archetypes that have no actual existence are said to be desirous of existence, and God's mercy extends to them and so brings them into being. Mercy means the bestowal of existence. Ibn al-'Arabi writes that "God's Mercy . . . covers every existence." To be sure, Ibn al-'Arabi admits wrath (ghadab) as well as mercy in God. Yet this too has an ontological character and exists in subordination to divine mercy. He comments that "the very existence of Wrath originates from the Mercy of God." Like the Neoplatonists, Ibn al-'Arabi thought that nondivine realities had different capacities to receive the divine presence. Wherever the divine is not received, there one sees wrath, and yet this wrath is due to God's nonpresence rather than God's presence. The objects of God's wrath are, as Izutsu says, "philosophically speaking, the things that properly cannot have existence." As nonexistent to begin with—or destined for nonexistence—the objects of wrath cannot endure. As they disappear, so will the divine wrath disappear.[31]

One of Ibn al-'Arabi's boldest ideas is that of the "mutual constraint" of God and world—in other words, the notion that the world "constrains" God just as God "constrains" the world.[32] What he means is that the so-called preparedness

28. Chittick, Self-Disclosure of God, 364, 271–73, citing Ibn al-'Arabi, Futuhat al-Makkiyah, III.388.33; III.187.22; II.66.33.

29. Chittick, Imaginal Worlds, 99, citing Ibn al-'Arabi, Futuhat al-Makkiyah, III.188.1.

30. Izutsu, Sufism and Taoism, 107. On mercy in Ibn al-'Arabi, see Izutsu's chapter on "Ontological Mercy," 116–40.

31. Izutsu, Sufism and Taoism, 116–18, citing Ibn al-'Arabi, Fusus al-Hikam, 177. Al-Qashani in his explanation of Ibn al-'Arabi writes: "Wrath . . . is not of the essence of the Absolute. On the contrary, it is simply a negative property that arises from the absence of receptivity on the part of some of the things for a perfect manifestation [of God]. . . . The absence of receptivity in some of the things for Mercy entails the non-appearance of Mercy . . . whether in this world or the Hereafter" (quoted in Izutsu, Sufism and Taoism, 117).

32. Panentheism in its various forms typically teaches some kind of "mutual constraint." The kenoticist teaching of Schelling (DR 7.7) and his recent successors (DR 9.12) comes to mind. Compare Alfred North Whitehead's famous statement: "It is as true to say that God transcends the World, as that the World transcends God. It is as true to say that God creates the World, as that the World creates God" (Process and Reality, 348).

of each thing, in accordance with the requirements of the archetype, determines the self-manifestation of the Absolute. The idea of *taskhir*, "constraint," applies throughout Ibn al-'Arabi's philosophy. In each case, the natural capacities of individual existents determine God's self-manifestation. As water has no color of its own but takes on the color of the vessels that contain it, so God takes on a defined character only in relation to the finite entities that manifest God.[33]

In Ibn al-'Arabi's thought, humanity exists on differing levels. On a cosmic level, there is what he calls the Perfect Man, which he describes as part of his cosmogonic narrative.[34] On the individual level, not many persons deserve the title of the Perfect Man. The designation applies only to a few. Adam was in some sense the Perfect Man, and Ibn al-'Arabi writes that "God has brought to light . . . various degrees [of existence] in him [i.e., Adam]." Because God taught Adam the names of all things (Qur'an 2:31), humanity itself actualizes all of the divine names. Humanity stands higher than the angels, since the angels are simply spiritual, while humanity is both spiritual and bodily and so more metaphysically comprehensive.[35]

Another of Ibn al-'Arabi's central concepts is "the Reality of Muhammad" (*haqiqah Muhammad*), which is simply another aspect of the problem of the Perfect Man. For Ibn al-'Arabi, Muhammad as a cosmic being existed eternally and so represents the permanent archetypes. This is something like the early church doctrine of Jesus as the eternal Logos (John 1:1–3) that contains the ideas or archetypes of all other, nondivine things. Yet the Reality of Muhammad is not simply the sum of the archetypes but is also the active principle making them effective in God's own creativity. The Reality of Muhammad was also the Light of Muhammad, existing before anything was created. Successive prophets manifested aspects of this light. Muhammad, writes Ibn al-'Arabi, was "the most perfect being of the human species" and existed when Adam was not yet created.[36]

33. Izutsu, *Sufism and Taoism*, 182, 186.
34. See Chittick, *Self-Disclosure of God*, 366, citing Ibn al-'Arabi, *Futuhat al-Makkiyah*, III.390.6: Since the intended goal of the cosmos was the perfect human being, the animal human being—who is similar to the perfect human being in the natural configuration—is also found in the cosmos. The realities that were brought together by the human being were disseminated throughout the cosmos. The Real summoned them from the whole cosmos, and they came together. The human being came to be from their coming together, so he was their storehouse. The faces of the cosmos turned toward this human storehouse to see what would become manifest from God's summoning all these realities. They saw a form standing erect, moving straight, and designated in directions. No one in the cosmos had ever seen the like of this human form.
35. Izutsu, *Sufism and Taoism*, 247, 229, 230–31, citing Ibn al-'Arabi, *Fusus al-Hikam*, 56.
36. Izutsu, *Sufism and Taoism*, 236–38, citing Ibn al-'Arabi, *Fusus al-Hikam*, 214. Izutsu writes, "Divine Consciousness is reflected most faithfully by the self-consciousness of the Perfect Man. The Perfect Man, in this sense, is the outwardly manifested Consciousness of God" (*Sufism and*

Hell's Cooling and Final Salvation in Ibn al-'Arabi

In dealing with questions of eschatology, Ibn al-'Arabi did not reject the teaching of the Qur'an, contrary to what some critics of Sufism have maintained. Nevertheless, in interpreting the Qur'an in Ibn al-'Arabi's fashion, one has to bear in mind the "ontological referents of the passages in question."[37] In its return to God, the human spirit retains its primordial constitution (Arabic *fitra*) that inclines it toward God.[38] The resurrected body, according to Ibn al-'Arabi, will be markedly different from the present human body. The body of the present time does not manifest the underlying reality of the soul within it. Citing the text "Now We have removed the veil, and sharp is thy sight this day!" (Qur'an 50:22), Ibn al-'Arabi argues that the body to come will truly show forth the character of its corresponding soul. What is now inward and hidden will become outward and conspicuous, so that the moral and spiritual character of each person will be apparent.[39] This means that the divine element hidden in each human being will show itself. Ibn al-'Arabi writes, "In this world, He wears your form, but in the next world, you wear His form."[40]

In paradise, each soul determines its situation by its own desires. In effect, human beings by willing or desiring construct their own paradises. They replicate, on a lesser level, what is said of God: "For to anything which We have willed, We but say the word, 'Be,' and it is" (Qur'an 16:40). The state of paradise is so subtle that people can exist in one form while also existing in other forms. A person may be in several places at the same time.[41] Not only do people construct heavens for themselves, but they also construct their own hells. Ibn al-'Arabi conceives of hell as a subjective state of awareness that derives from the dreadful thoughts of those within it: "The People of the Fire conceive no dreadful thought of a chastisement . . . without that chastisement coming into existence within them and for them; the chastisement is identical with the actualization of the thought."[42] Why does anyone suffer such chastisement? Ibn al-'Arabi affirms that "the Fire seeks only those human beings whose divine form has not become manifest, outwardly and inwardly." Yet even hell's fire is rooted in God's mercy, and its goal is to purify (*tathir*) those who enter

---

Taoism, 236). Izutsu sees an analogy between the "Reality of Muhammad" and the *Nous* (mind) in the philosophy of Plotinus (237).

37. Chittick, *Imaginal Worlds*, 97–98.

38. Ibid., 99.

39. Ibid., 103–6. Emanuel Swedenborg taught something similar regarding the future body (*DR* 2.9).

40. Chittick, *Imaginal Worlds*, 108, citing Ibn al-'Arabi, *Futuhat al-Makkiyah*, III.502.24.

41. Chittick, *Imaginal Worlds*, 108, citing Ibn al-'Arabi, *Futuhat al-Makkiyah*, I.318.26.

42. Chittick, *Imaginal Worlds*, 109, citing Ibn al-'Arabi, *Futuhat al-Makkiyah*, I.259.30.

it. The process of purification burns away from each human being everything inconsistent with their *fitra* or God-given nature.[43]

Divine mercy has priority over divine wrath in Ibn al-'Arabi. The Throne of God, he writes, is sheer mercy and has nothing to do with wrath. Wrath enters the picture only at the second level of sensory experience, which he designates as "the Footstool." While mercy is in God as God's essential attribute, the same is not true of wrath. In fact, wrath does not exist "in" God but only "in" relation to certain creatures: "Nothing makes the Real wrathful except what He has created. Were it not for the creatures, the Real would not have become wrathful." Only at the level of the Footstool—or what lies below it—can one speak of wrath. As creatures return to God, they pass beyond God's wrath and into God's mercy.[44]

For Ibn al-'Arabi, pure wrath cannot exist apart from mercy, and punishment cannot last forever. While the qur'anic texts say that sinners will forever remain in hell or the fire, this does not mean that chastisement will last forever. Hell's punishment must come to an end, he argues, because mercy must finally display its precedence over wrath. "Wretchedness derives from the divine wrath," he writes, "but wrath will be cut off." Every existing thing must finally return to the root from which it came, which is God's mercy and goodness. Evil, unbelief, and wrath all lie within the sphere of unreality, which is destined to pass away, while the Real remains. Chittick writes, "What keeps human beings away from reality is simply unreality. The unreal is annihilated and the Real subsists . . . which points to the ontological roots of hell's impermanence."[45] The unreality that causes unbelief will pass away, and, with the passing away of unreality, punishment and wretchedness will also disappear.

One of Ibn al-'Arabi's most novel ideas is that hell will never cease but will become pleasurable rather than miserable. The Day of Resurrection—which, he surmises, lasts fifty thousand years, like the angelic day (Qur'an 70:4)—is the maximum time period for God's punishments.[46] He writes:

After the expiration of this time period, the ruling property [in God] returns to the All-merciful, the All-compassionate. . . . Through mercy He abases [wrath] and holds back its reality. Hence the property of mutual contradictoriness of the names subsists in the relationships, but the creatures are drowned in mercy.

43. Chittick, *Imaginal Worlds*, 109, citing Ibn al-'Arabi, *Futuhat al-Makkiyah*, III.387.10.
44. Chittick, *Imaginal Worlds*, 109, citing Ibn al-'Arabi, *Futuhat al-Makkiyah*, III.386.1.
45. Chittick, *Imaginal Worlds*, 113, citing Ibn al-'Arabi, *Futuhat al-Makkiyah*, III.382.35.
46. As noted in the introduction (*DR* 0.2), the period of 50,000 years (as a maximum period for a world-age and its attendant sufferings) is mentioned not only in the Qur'an and Ibn al-'Arabi's speculations but also in kabbalistic sources and in modern universalists such as Johann Petersen in Germany and Elhanan Winchester in the United States and England.

The property of mutual contradictoriness remains forever in the names, but not in us.[47]

This passage is one of the clearest expressions of Ibn al-'Arabi's universalism. The Qur'an and the hadith speak of fierce angels and wild animals inflicting pain on those in hell. Ibn al-'Arabi cites the text "Whithersoever ye turn, there is the presence of Allah" (Qur'an 2:115) and argues that the activity of these angels and animals eventually will bring pleasure rather than pain. "The People of the Fire find pleasure in that [i.e., animal assaults], just as the serpent and the Fire find pleasure in taking vengeance for God, because . . . mercy has exercised its ruling property over them."[48]

Though hell will approximate heaven, one distinction will remain, and that is the veil that keeps the inhabitants of hell from seeing God as those in heaven do. For if hell's inhabitants could see God, then it would increase their sense of shame and their suffering. Ibn al-'Arabi in the end identifies blessedness in the afterlife with whatever is agreeable to one's own particular nature. This helps us to understand how the "People of the Fire" can enjoy being in the fire and how they can be aware of those in paradise while still enjoying their own lot in the afterlife:

After mercy has embraced them, the people of the Fire will find their joy from being in the Fire, and they will praise God for their not being in the Garden. That is because of what is demanded by their constitution in that state: If they were to enter the Garden with that constitution, pain would overcome them and they would suffer. So—if you have understood—bliss is nothing but the agreeable, and chastisement is nothing but the disagreeable, whatever it might be. So be wherever you are! . . . The abodes have been made lovable to their inhabitants.[49]

The Universalistic Theology of Jalal al-Din Rumi

Just as Ibn al-'Arabi is the leading philosopher of Sufism, Jalal al-Din Muhammad Rumī (1207–73) is regarded as the leading poet. Annemarie Schimmel calls Rumi's writings "the pinnacle in the achievements of Persian mystical poetry."[50] Rumi was Ibn al-'Arabi's younger contemporary, and we know that Rumi met him and was friends with one of Ibn al-'Arabi's friends. As Chittick insists, though, one must not reduce Rumi's poetry to Ibn al-'Arabi's concepts. While

47. Chittick, Imaginal Worlds, 115, citing Ibn al-'Arabi, Futuhat al-Makkiyah, III.346.14.
48. Chittick, Imaginal Worlds, 115, citing Ibn al-'Arabi, Futuhat al-Makkiyah, III.411.15.
49. Chittick, Imaginal Worlds, 117–18, citing Ibn al-'Arabi, Futuhat al-Makkiyah, IV.14.34.
50. Schimmel, Mystical Dimensions of Islam, 279.

there are similarities, these two wrote in differing genres. Rumi's down-to-earth analogies have enabled him to engage readers who have been unable to comprehend Ibn al-'Arabi's philosophy.[51]

A common idea in Islamic mysticism is that soul and body are separable and have differing destinies and differing origins. Mulla Sadra, for example, wrote that the human body was like a net, while the human soul was like a bird. The net is needed to catch the bird, but once the bird is caught, the net may be discarded.[52] Rumi taught the soul's pre-bodily and premortal existence in the divine realm, followed by its entrance into the body and its later return to God. Chittick comments on Rumi, "Originally, man's spirit dwelt with God in a state of oneness with all other spirits and the angels. Having accepted the Trust [i.e., the so-called Covenant of Alast], man's spirit was given a body in this world."[53] He adds that "in one respect the body is utterly opposed to the spirit, but in another respect it is the spirit's reflection or shadow. . . . Hence Rumi calls the body 'the shadow of the shadow of the shadow of the heart.'"[54]

In his doctrine of the soul's preexistence, Rumi is part of a rich and complex Islamic tradition regarding a "mystery of Alast" or "Covenant of Alast" in which Allah entered into an agreement with human souls prior to their entrance into the body. Both Sunni and Shiite authors developed this tradition, and it found later expression among the Baha'i. Farshid Kazemi speaks of "one of the more important and dramatic scenes which informs the whole spectrum of Islamic thought, namely the Primordial Covenant of Qur'an 7:171–72. It is there, in what seems to be preexistence, that God addresses humanity in the form of particles or seeds (*dharr*) saying 'Am I not your Lord?' (*alastu bi-rabbikum*) while the archetype or potential of all future generations of humanity responds with the loving reply, 'Yes' (*bala*)."[55] The meaning of the qur'anic passage becomes clear from the context, as cited by Kazemi:

And when thy Lord took from the Children of Adam, From their loins, their seed [*dhurriyyatahum*], And made them testify concerning themselves, 'Am I

51. See Chittick, "Rumi and the Mawlawiyyah," esp. 113–17.
52. Chittick, "Muslim Eschatology," 146.
53. The term "Alast" comes from a reported Arabic question, as posed by God: "Am I not [alast] your Lord?" When human beings existed with God before their earthly creation, God asked them this question, and they all replied and testified in the affirmative, thus committing themselves in advance to being servants of God. At the resurrection, human beings will be assessed to see if they were faithful to their original affirmation and testimony. See Kazemi, "Mysteries of *Alast*."
54. Chittick, *Sufi Path of Love*, 69, citing Rumi, *Mathnawi*, book 5, verses 2123–26.
55. Kazemi, "Mysteries of *Alast*," 39. Chittick concurs with the preexistence interpretation, writing that "the 'Covenant of Alast,' took place before man entered into the world, when he existed as a disembodied spirit in proximity to God" (*Sufi Path of Love*, 68).

not your Lord?' [*alastu bi-rabbikum*] They replied, 'Yes, we bear witness' [*bala shahadna*].[56]

In this preexistent realm, not only the covenant between God and humanity but also the prophethood of Muhammad was determined. The designation "Day of Alast" appears especially among the Persian poets, such as Attar of Nishapur (ca. 1145–ca. 1221), Hafez (ca. 1326–ca. 1390), and Rumi. There are numerous variations on the term: "Covenant of Alast," "Day of Alast," "Call of Alast," "Song of Alast," and "Wine of Alast." Sahl al-Tustari (818–96) may have been the first Sufi author to link this passage in the Qur'an with the recollection of knowledge from the soul's timeless state prior to embodiment.[57] Some see the Alast idea as rooted in Neoplatonism.[58] In one passage Plato suggested that human souls agreed to enter human (or animal) bodies before their coming into this world.[59]

Rumi's idea of the descent and ascent of the spirit is based on traditional Islamic cosmology, according to which the world consists of nine concentric spheres that surround the earth at the center. Everything that happens on the

56. Qur'an 7:171–72, as cited in Kazemi, "Mysteries of *Alast*," 40.

57. Kazemi, "Mysteries of *Alast*," 39–40, with n. 5. On the remembrance (*dhikr*) of God as a recollection of preexistent knowledge, see Böwering, *Mystical Vision of Existence in Classical Islam*, 45–49, 201–7; Böwering, "Ideas of Time in Persian Sufism." The Sufi author Dhu'l-Nun al-Misri (d. ca. 861) speaks of the recollection of preexistent knowledge and is cited in this connection by Ibn al-'Arabi. See Chittick, *Sufi Path of Knowledge*, 155–56, 399.

58. Philip Irving Mitchell states that "the Day of Alast" was "when God created all souls before the world as sparks of himself." This implies that "all Muslims are to be reunited to God through renunciation and meditation. This doctrine has strong, neo-Platonic elements" (http://www3.dbu .edu/Mitchell/rumiprin.htm).

59. The so-called Myth of Er in Plato's *Republic* describes how disembodied souls in their interim state—i.e., in between their successive embodiments—are allowed to choose their new lot in life yet then must drink the waters of forgetfulness so that they forget everything that happened before their reembodiment (*Republic* 614b–621d; Hamilton and Cairns, *Plato*, 839–44). In this way, writes Plato, "the blame is his who chooses; God is blameless" (*Republic* 617e; Hamilton and Cairns, *Plato*, 841). Three teachings on preexisting souls—Plato's idea of souls that choose their lot in life, Origen's speculations on preexisting souls that loved God but cooled off in their love (*DR* 3.5–3.6), and the Islamic teaching on the "Day of Alast"—all imply that human selves are connected to God and responsible to God even before the time that they enter material bodies. Sergius Bulgakov moved in a quite different direction by affirming that everyone created by God gave advance permission to God to be created. In *The Bride of the Lamb*, Bulgakov called "creation itself a divine-human creative act" (95) and explained: "This self-witness of our consciousness . . . proclaims with certainty that, in the creation of I, I itself was *asked* to agree to be, and this agreement was I's self-positing . . . the witness of its own belonging to itself. From the emptiness . . . there resounds this *yes of the creature* that is asked whether it consents to exist" (88; emphasis in the original). Setting aside the logical incoherence (i.e., creatures agreeing to exist while as yet nonexistent), Bulgakov's reasoning minimizes God's power in creating and highlights creaturely autonomy, while the context in *The Bride of the Lamb*—with references to "I" and the "Not-I"—suggests that Bulgakov was influenced by Fichte and German egoist or *Ich*-philosophy.

material plane of existence derives from the heavens, representing the higher ontological levels of reality. According to Rumi's teaching, the spirit must travel through all the descending levels of the universe in its journey from the abode of Alast to its manifestation in this present world as a body. From another point of view, the spirit retains its status as a spirit in the realm of light, while outwardly becoming manifested through a series of ever-darkening shadows, until the darkest shadow of all—that is, the physical body—becomes manifest. Rumi asserts that the spirit must manifest itself on every level of reality: the four elements and the three kingdoms (vegetable, animal, and human).

The journey upward begins as the spirit takes the form of a mineral and then progresses to the plant, animal, and human levels. Once the spirit assumes the human form, it begins to disengage itself from the material world. Even as a human being, its consciousness at first will be on an animal level. Spiritual discipline, however, aims at the spirit's release from the prison of the body and the process of the homeward or return journey. Symbolically, the journey is represented as an ascent by means of the ladder of the heavens. Chittick explains: "Having transcended all the levels of physical and spiritual existence, the spirit rejoins the divine Command from which it arose. But now it has actualized and maintains a conscious awareness of every stage and degree of the descending and ascending levels of existence."[60]

Rumi's thought is universalistic in its basic structure. Preexistent spirits descend to become embodied in material reality. Yet Rumi's metaphysical principle dictates that each spirit, however low its present level of existence (e.g., mineral), must pass to and through all levels of reality, culminating in union with God. The cycle or circle has to be completed. While Rumi's thought differs in many respects from Ibn al-'Arabi's, both authors hold to final salvation for all spiritual beings.[61]

60. Chittick, *Sufi Path of Love*, 75. Regarding the undescended spirit, outside of embodiment (in one sense) while also embodied (in another sense), Chittick says, "Even when Rumi says that the spirit 'enters into' the world of the elements, this is only a manner of speaking. The spirit is always transcendent, dwelling in its original home" (74). John Dillon writes of a Greek philosophical "concept of an aspect of the individual person that is 'above,' and some degree separable, from the 'normal' human soul" ("Plutarch, Plotinus and the Zoroastrian Concept of the *Fravashi*," 1). Since the *Fravashi* is a Zoroastrian concept that seems to be equivalent to Rumi's undescended spirit, and Rumi himself wrote in Persia, it might be possible to see a Zoroastrian influence on Rumi at this point.

61. To delimit the discussion here, we omit any treatment of the doctrine of the Perfect Man, which is a major teaching in Ibn al-'Arabi, Rumi, and other Sufi authors. Seyyed Hossain Nasr describes the core idea: "The reality of this archetypal human being, who is called by Ibn 'Arabi the Universal or Perfect Man (*al-insan al-kamil*), is contained potentially in every human being but is actualized only within the being of prophets and the greatest saints" (*Garden of Truth*, 216). Cf. Nicholson, "Perfect Man." Here Nicholson expounds al-Jili ('Abdu 'l-Karim ibn Ibrahim al-Jili;

The Jurist Ibn Taymiyya and His Pupil Ibn Qayyim

In the mainstream or classical Sunni tradition, the dominant view is that unbelievers and those who who worship anyone or anything other than Allah (i.e., *mushrikun*, or those who "associate" partners with God) will spend an eternity in hellfire. But this prevailing opinion is officially based less on the actual text of the Qur'an than on the consensus (*ijma'*) of acknowledged Muslim scholars. According to the general Sunni theory, once a point of view has been defined and then accepted by consensus, it is no longer open to discussion. As Jon Hoover explains, the most forthright challenge to the apparent Sunni consensus on the eternality of punishment in hell for unbelievers is found in the writings of Ibn Taymiyya (1263–1328) and his leading student, Ibn Qayyim al-Jawziyya (1292–1350).[62] Ibn Taymiyya is well known for his polemic against Ibn al-'Arabi as well as the Neoplatonic philosophy of Ibn Sina (Avicenna) and the Kalam theologies of the Ash'aris and Mu'tazilis.[63] In the eyes of some critics, the Islamic juristic and legal tradition militates against any genuine religious knowledge at all, other than the knowledge of one's duty. God is not to be known but simply to be obeyed. On the character of God, one ends up in pious agnosticism.[64] Yet, as Jon Hoover has argued, "there is more to the shaykh [i.e., Ibn Taymiyya] than polemics and unyielding literalism." Perhaps surprisingly, Ibn Taymiyya shares with Ibn al-'Arabi "a similar stance on . . . theodicy" and takes the optimistic view that God created the present world as the best of all possible worlds.[65] What is more, Ibn Qayyim goes further in affirming the goodness of God's punishments than Ibn Taymiyya does. "Unprecedented in their thoroughness and length," Ibn Qayyim's writings on hell propose that "the Fire no longer functions retributively to punish as in

1366–1424), author of *al-Insanu 'l-kamil fi ma'rifati 'l-awakhir wa 'l-awa'il* (*The Man Perfect in Knowledge of the First and Last Things*). The Sufi Perfect Man teaching has obvious parallels with gnostic notions of the Primal Man, and in both cases the teaching often was allied with universalism (*DR* 2.11). Primal Man, once dismembered, will be at last reintegrated.

    62. Hoover, "Islamic Universalism," 181.

    63. Schimmel, in *Mystical Dimensions of Islam*, notes that "the orthodox [Muslims] have never ceased attacking him [i.e., Ibn 'Arabi]" (263). Ibn Taymiyya "claimed that he [Ibn 'Arabi] made no distinction between the *wujud* [i.e., existence] of God and the *wujud* of the cosmos" (Chittick, "Ibn 'Arabi," 504). Ibn Taymiyya thus charged Ibn 'Arabi with pantheism. Chittick continues: "In fact, it is easy to pick out passages from the *Futuhat* [*Meccan Openings*] that support this claim. But from what has already been said about the pivotal nature of the dialectic between *tanzih* and *tashbih* [i.e., incomparability and similarity] in Ibn 'Arabi's writings, it should be clear that passages identifying the *wujud* of God with that of the cosmos represent the perspective of *tashbih* [similarity]" (504; cf. 501–2).

    64. Lory, "Henry Corbin," esp. 1151.

    65. Hoover, *Ibn Taymiyya's Theodicy of Perpetual Optimism*, 1.

the classical doctrine but therapeutically to cleanse from sins, even the sins of unbelief (*kufr*) and associationism (*shirk*)."[66]

In an autobiographical passage, Ibn Qayyim tells of how he asked Ibn Taymiyya about everlasting chastisement in hell, and Ibn Taymiyya said, "This issue is very great," yet then "gave no reply." Raising doubt in Ibn Qayyim's mind were certain traditional sayings (i.e., hadith) attributed to companions of Muhammad that supported the notion of a temporary hell. 'Umar was reported to have said, "Even if the People of the Fire stayed in the Fire like the amount of sand of 'Alij [a tract of sand near Mecca], they would have, despite that, a day in which they would come out." Another saying, attributed to Abu Huraya, was that "there will come to Hell a day when no one will remain in it." Muhammad's companion, Ibn 'Abbas, is reported to have said, "It is not necessary for anyone to judge God with respect to His creatures or to assign them to a garden or a fire."[67]

Despite reports in some early sources that Ibn Taymiyya held that hell is not eternal, modern scholars have been hard pressed to identify any direct statements in Ibn Taymiyya's acknowledged writings to this effect. On this basis, a Saudi scholar in 1990 asserted that Ibn Taymiyya never said that the fire will pass away.[68] Yet Hoover notes the existence of a treatise just published in 1995 and reliably attributed to Ibn Taymiyya, given the title *Response to Whoever Says That the Garden and the Fire Will Pass Away*. Ibn Taymiyya's *Response* seems to be the last work that he wrote before his death. This writing considers the arguments for the passing away of heaven (the Garden) and hell (the Fire).

Ibn Taymiyya argues that time spent by the wicked in hell is contingent on both the existence of this world and God's will. He also suggests that the residents of hell will remain there only as long as their chastisement lasts. God's mercy implies that heaven will remain. While heaven is a direct expression of God's attributes, the same is not true of hell. Chastisement in hell is the result of creatures and their sin and does not follow necessarily from God's character. Ibn Taymiyya argues that God's mercy encompasses all things and that God has "written mercy for himself" (Qur'an 6:120). He cites the hadith in which God says, "My mercy overcomes my anger." On this basis, God's mercy appears to rule out chastisement without end. What is more, God has a wise purpose in everything that God does. It is not possible to imagine God as having any wise purpose in eternal punishment, but there is a wise purpose in punishment for the sake of purification and cleansing from sin.[69]

66. Hoover, "Islamic Universalism," 181–82.
67. Citations from ibid., 182–83.
68. 'Ali ibn 'Ali Jabir al-Harbi, *Kashf al-astar* . . . (Mecca: Dar tayyiba, 1410/1990), 77–78, cited in Hoover, "Islamic Universalism," 184.
69. Hoover, "Islamic Universalism," 186, 188–89.

Regarding the supposed consensus (*ijma'*) on the perpetuity of the fire, Ibn Taymiyya argues that no consensus exists on this question. In making this claim, Ibn Taymiyya employs (like Ibn Qayyim after him) a Salafi hermeneutic that sets him at odds with most Sunni teachers.[70] The only consensus Ibn Taymiyya acknowledges is that of the Salaf, which only includes the first three generations of Muslims at most. Taqi al-Din al-Subki (d. 1355), who wrote in opposition to Ibn Taymiyya, insisted that the eternity of hell is a matter of consensus among Muslims and that to deny this is to fall directly into unbelief. Al-Subki's position reflects the dominant Sunni position rather than, as noted, a Salafi interpretation. If there had been an expression of a "clear difference" of views on the issue, writes al-Subki, then one might question whether consensus had been attained. Yet no such divergence of views is apparent in the tradition as it emerged over time. In Sunni thought, while there may be divergences of view in the earliest authors, the main line of tradition becomes increasingly clear over time. This way of reading the tradition does not allow one to cite early or obscure sayings in support of a position that goes against the majority view that eventually emerged.[71]

Ibn Qayyim built on and extended Ibn Taymiyya's arguments. He insists that God did not create some people from the outset with the intention that they should be punished forever. There is no unbelief that God cannot remove. Everyone can be made fit for the Garden, and so Ibn Qayyim's teaching has a strong therapeutic orientation. He writes that "trial and punishment are the remedies appointed to remove maladies. They are not removed by any other means. And the Fire is the Great Remedy." Everlasting punishment would serve no purpose, according to Ibn Qayyim: "It is not in the divine wise purpose that evils remain perpetually without end and without interruption forever such that [evils] and goods would be equivalent."[72]

A number of scholars (e.g., Abrahamov, Khalil) have interpreted Ibn Taymiyya and Ibn Qayyim as universalists. As Hoover notes, though, while Ibn Taymiyya's

70. The adjective "Salafi" and noun "Salafist" are today sometimes used for any strict theories of Islam and Islamic law. In this sense, the terms may be synonymous with "Wahhabi" and "Wahhabist." Applied to Ibn Taymiyya, though, the words carry a more specific meaning, implying the rejection of later Islamic legal theories and seeking a return to the Islamic practices of Muhammad himself and the "pious forefathers" (*al-salaf al-salih*) of the first two or three generations of Islam.

71. Hoover, "Islamic Universalism," 187–88. Al-Ashqar argues for a consensus among Sunnis on the eternity of hell, commenting that Ibn Taymiyya and Ibn Qayyim are wrong on this question yet should not be censured as unbelievers (188, citing al-Ashqar, *Paradise and Hell*, 57). One might compare this Sunni idea of consensus (*ijma'*) with Roman Catholic and Orthodox Christianity, which builds its views on the early Christian consensus, as reflected in the ecumenical councils of the church, rather than the sayings or opinions of individual authors.

72. Hoover, "Islamic Universalism," 189–90.

Response presents arguments for the non-eternality of hell, it "never states categorically . . . that the Fire and its chastisement will pass away. While Ibn Qayyim's arguments against an eternal hell seem even stronger than Ibn Taymiyya's, Ibn Qayyim qualifies his overall conclusion with the qur'anic text, "Surely your Lord does whatever He wills" (Qur'an 11:107). Ibn Qayyim's final position therefore seems to be a pious agnosticism on the question of the eternality or non-eternality of hell. Ultimately God will determine whether hell comes to an end. Ibn Qayyim writes in another passage: "And [I] follow the doctrine of Ibn Zayd where he says, 'God has informed us what He wills for the People of the Garden.' He said, 'A gift never cut off' (Q. 11:108). He did not inform us what he wills for the People of the Fire." Once again, Ibn Qayyim's stated view is agnostic.[73]

On the basis of Hoover's thorough analysis of Ibn Taymiyya's and Ibn Qayyim's writings, Islamic universalism has only a tenuous or ambiguous place in their thinking. It is only in the context of Islamic esotericism that universalism seems definitely to have attained a foothold.[74]

---

73. Ibid., 190–91, 193. A late writing of Ibn Qayyim's, *The Thunderbolts Sent Out*, presents the strongest case this author ever made for universalism (193–96). Here Ibn Qayyim "abandons his reserve and follows the theological argument from God's mercy to its logical conclusion that chastisement will come to an end for all" (197). Yet Hoover's 2013 review of Khalil's *Islam and the Fate of Others* questions Khalil's judgment that Ibn Qayyim remained "a univeralist to the very end." "A very late work" by Ibn Qayyim states that "when an associationist (*mushrik*) is . . . foul in essence, the Fire does not cleanse his foulness. . . . If he were to come out of it, he would return as foul as he was [before]." This assertion undermines the idea that the Fire can or will prepare everyone for eventual entrance into paradise. Hoover adds, "I am on record interpreting this to mean that Ibn al-Qayyim affirmed eternal punishment for unbelievers" (review of *Islam and the Fate of Others*, 79).

74. Along similar lines, Sajjad Rizvi notes that al-Ghazali, Ibn Taymiyya, and Ibn al-ʿArabi all had stern things to say regarding Shiites. In light of what they wrote against their fellow Muslims, writes Rizvi, "one wonders in what sense one can safely describe them as Universalists" (review of *Islam and the Fate of Others*, 538).

Appendix G

Types of Christian Universalism

In the universalists' house there are many dwelling places. Christian universalists today might not be aware of the full variety of viewpoints—the universalisms—that have taken shape over the last two millennia, many of which still exist today. When anyone speaks of Christian universalism, a first question ought to be, what *sort* of Christian universalism? What follows below is a brief attempt at a taxonomy. There have been a couple of earlier efforts—by Robin Parry and Laurence Blanchard—to map out different forms of universalism.[1] While Parry focuses on universalism of a decidedly Christian sort, Blanchard's typology includes not only Christocentric but also plurocentric forms of universalism. In the typology of Christian universalism offered here, I have only briefly touched on plurocentric (or interreligious) universalism, which is not a major focus in this study and which raises a different set of theological questions than those treated here.[2] Certain early modern figures (e.g., Pico della Mirandola) seem to be on the cusp that separates Christian universalism from plurocentric universalism. More recent universalist authors generally seem to be either clearly Christocentric (e.g., Jürgen Moltmann) or else definitely plurocentric (e.g., John Hick). Gnostic-esoteric universalists include some who have self-identified as Christian, even though they may be regarded as marginal or heterodox according to earlier or later standards of Christian orthodoxy. For

---

1. See the introduction to Gregory MacDonald [Parry], *"All Shall Be Well,"* 13–20; and the conclusion to L. M. Blanchard, *Will All Be Saved?*, 258–66.

2. Unlike the various forms of Christocentric universalism—which affirm the uniqueness and the universal salvific role of Jesus Christ—interreligious universalism begins with a different set of preliminary assumptions and so would require a different sort of analysis.

these universalists, it is *the nature of the human soul or self* that largely dictates the doctrine of universal salvation. In the words of the early twentieth-century Christian mystic Sadhu Sundar Singh: "If this divine spark or element cannot be destroyed, then we can never be hopeless for any sinner. . . . And even though many wander and go astray[,] in the end, they will return to Him in Whose image they have been created; for this is their final destination. . . . Since God has created man for His own fellowship, therefore he cannot remain eternally separate from Him."[3] Gnostic-esoteric thinkers conceive the soul, spirit, or inmost human self as having an inherent kinship with God, and in some cases one might say a quasi-divine status.

The second major lineage of universalism is that of the Origenists, who might have some affinity with the gnostic-esoteric lineage and yet are distinct from them. In part as a reaction against certain aspects of second-century gnostic theologies, Origen offered a version of Christian universalism that stressed God's loving, gracious, and patient character. God would not give up on or abandon any soul, until at long last it responded to grace. Yet Origen's universalism also rested on a speculative theory of preexistent souls, which established an attractive symmetry between the origin of all things and the end of all things. When we speak of an Origenist lineage, this does not imply that Origen's followers all agreed with Origen in all respects but simply that Origen's ideas were influential or even determinative for many later Christian universalists.

The Böhmist lineage, like the Origenist, is based on the prevailing influence of one decisive thinker, Jakob Böhme. Böhme's cosmology was more involved than Origen's. Before the world existed, and even before God existed, there was a primal *Ungrund* (unground or abyss) of chaos and indeterminacy. As *Ungrund*, the blind primordial will did not even know itself, argued Böhme, and yet in struggle and agony it gave birth to God. Böhme himself was not a universalist. Yet the majority of Böhme's disciples after around 1700 resolved his tension-laden philosophy in the direction of universalism—a final restoration in which light triumphed over darkness. From the early eighteenth century up through the early twentieth century, Böhmist universalism made its appearance in Britain, Germany, the German-speaking American colonies, France, and Russia.

In using the term "Christocentric" below, I intend to distinguish many modern universalists from ancient and modern Origenists. What distinguishes the modern Christocentric universalists from earlier Origenists is an intense focus on Jesus that derives from modern Protestant and evangelical piety. Christo-centrists believe that in telling the story of Jesus, and especially the story of his atoning death on the cross, they are narrating a story of universal salvation.

3. Singh, *Meditations*, 57–59.

Fundamental to Christocentric universalism is the notion that all human beings without exception are incorporated into Christ, who has represented all, died for all, rose for all, and redeemed all. This all-encompassing redemption might or might not include the necessity of an individual response to the gospel or personal faith in Christ. Christocentric universalists generally base their idea of salvation on a principle of substitution. Karl Barth and Hans Urs von Balthasar both wrote of how Christ died in our place and how he represented all humanity.

Another important distinction lies between the purgationist and non-purgationist forms of univeralism. The non-purgationists or so-called ultra-universalists took the idea of Christ's universal substitutionary death to imply that all divine punishment, judgment, and wrath were wholly swallowed up and forever abolished when Jesus died on the cross. From this point onward, punishment for anyone was inconceivable. Purgationists presented a counter-argument. The "ultra" position, they held, undermined moral effort and ethical exertion by severing the "moral connection" between present-day actions and future rewards or punishments.

Another category in the list of authors below is set aside for interreligious universalists. This group includes universalists who may self-identify as Christian and yet believe that many different religions lead people to heaven or to final human fulfillment (nirvana, nibbana, paradise, and so forth).

Certain universalists do not fit into any of the existing categories, because their thinking is eclectic, idiosyncratic, or, in some cases, hard to pin down. They are listed as "miscellaneous universalists."

What follows is a list of universalist authors who have contributed to Christian universalist literature in some significant way, with some indication of their particular lineage.[4] The listing includes annotations, with the letter *K* indicating "kabbalistic Christian," *Pn* referring to a "pantheistic" conception of the soul's final union with God, and an asterisk (*) denoting those authors who are indefinite or ambiguous in affirming universalism.

Gnostic-Esoteric Universalists

Basilides (early second century)
School of Carpocrates (early second century)

4. Famous Christian universalists would include such figures as Hans Christian Anderson, P. T. Barnum, Clara Barton, Helen Keller, Madeleine L'Engle, Florence Nightingale, and "Peanuts" cartoonist Charles Schulz (before reportedly becoming secular). The following list is not intended to identify well-known persons who were universalists but rather to indicate some of the authors who have made substantial contributions to the theology or literature of Christian universalism.

School of Valentinus (mid-second century)*

Nag Hammadi texts (mid- to late second century)*

Stephen bar Sudaili, *The Book of the Holy Hierotheos* (early sixth century) [Pn]

Medieval "dualists": Bogomils, Albigensians, Cathars (seventh to fourteenth centuries)

John Scotus Eriugena, *Periphyseon* (ca. 860)

Amalric of Bène and the Brethren of the Free Spirit (thirteenth to sixteenth centuries) [Pn]

Pico della Mirandola, *Nine Hundred Theses* (1486) [K]

Guillaume Postel, *De orbis terrae concordia* (*On Worldwide Concord*) (1544) [K; also interreligious]

Christian Knorr von Rosenroth, *Kabbalah Denudata* (1677–78) [K]

Franciscus Mercurius van Helmont, *Seder Olam* (1693) [K]

Anne Conway, *Principle of the Most Ancient and Modern Philosophy* (1690) [K]

Sadhu Sundar Singh, *The Search after Reality* (1925); *Visions of the Spiritual World* (1926)

Valentin Tomberg, *Meditations on the Tarot* (1980)

Betty Eadie, *Embraced by the Light* (1992)

Andre Rabe, *Imagine* (2011)

Francis DuToit, *The Mirror Bible* (2012)

Origenist Universalists

Clement of Alexandria, *Stromateis* (ca. 200)*

Origen, *On First Principles* (ca. 210)

Didymus the Blind (mid-300s)

Gregory of Nyssa, *Catechetical Oration* (ca. 370s); *On the Soul and the Resurrection* (ca. 370s)

Evagrius Ponticus, *Kephalaia gnōstika* (late fourth century) [Pn]

Isaac of Nineveh (seventh century)

Hans Denck, *Von der wahren Liebe* (*On True Love*) (1527)*

Jakob Kautz (Cucius), *Seven Theses* (1527)

George Rust, *A Resolution concerning Origen* (1660)

Jean Le Clerc, *Parrhasiana* (1700)*

Sergei Bulgakov, *The Orthodox Church* (1935)*; *Apocatastasis and Transfiguration* (1930s)

Kallistos Ware, *The Inner Kingdom* (2000)*

Ilaria Ramelli, *The Christian Doctrine of* Apokatastasis (2013)

Böhmist Universalists

Gerard Winstanley, *The Mysterie of God* (1648)

Jane Lead, *Enochian Walks with God* (1696)

Johann Wilhelm Petersen, *Das ewige Evangelium der allgemeinen Wiederbringung aller Creaturen* (*The Eternal Gospel of the Universal Return of All Creatures*) (1698)

Ernst Christoph Hochmann von Hochenau, *Glaubens-Bekenntnis* (*Confession of Faith*) (1702)

Jeremiah White, *The Restitution of All Things* (1712)

Johanna Petersen, *Leben* (autobiography) (1719)

Berlenburg Bibel (multivolume German Bible with universalist annotations) (1726–42)

Ludwig Gerhard, *Systema Apokatastaseos* (1727)

William Law, *Spirit of Prayer* (1749); *Spirit of Love* (1758)

Friedrich Christian Oetinger, *Theologia ex idea vitae deducta* (*Theology Derived from the Idea of Life*) (1765)

Martines de Pasqually, *Traité de reintegration* (written in the 1770s; published in 1899)

George de Benneville, *Life and Trance of Dr. George de Benneville* (1800)

Louis-Claude de Saint-Martin, *Le ministère de l'homme esprit* (*Man: His Ministry*) (1802)

Friedrich Joseph von Schelling, *Stuttgart Seminars* (1810)

Johann Heinrich Jung-Stilling, *Siegsgeschichte der christlichen Religion* (*Victorious History of the Christian Religion*) (1814)

Georg Wilhelm Friedrich Hegel, *Lectures on the Philosophy of Religion* (1830s)*

Thomas Erskine (of Linlathen), *The Brazen Serpent* (1831); *The Spiritual Order and Other Papers* (1871); *Letters* (1877); *The Fatherhood of God* (1885)

Johann Michael Hahn, *Briefe von der ersten Offenbarung* (1835)

Franz von Baader, *Sämtliche Werke* (1850–60)

Hans Martensen, *Christian Dogmatics* (1856–66?)*; *Jacob Boehme* (1885)

Andrew Jukes, *The Second Death and the Restitution of All Things* (1867)

George MacDonald, *Unspoken Sermons*, 3 vols. (1867–89)

Vladimir Solovyov, *Lectures on Divine Humanity* (1878)

Nicolas Berdyaev, *The Destiny of Man* (1937)

Paul Tillich, *Systematic Theology*, vol. 3 (1963)

Christocentric Non-Purgationist Universalists ("Ultra"-Universalism)

James Relly, *Union; or, Consanguity with Christ* (1759)

Joseph Huntington, *Calvinism Improved* (1796)

John Murray, *Universalism Vindicated* (1798)

Hosea Ballou I, *A Treatise on Atonement* (1805); *Future Retribution* (1834)

Friedrich Schleiermacher, *The Christian Faith*, 2nd ed. (1830–31); *On the Doctrine of Election* (1836)

Alexander Schweizer, *Glaubenslehre* (*Christian Doctrine*) (1844–47)

Johann Christoph Blumhardt, *Blätter aus Bad Boll* (*Papers from Bad Boll*) (1873–77)

John G. Lake, "The Habitation of God" and "The Second Crowning" (1920s–1930s)

Karl Barth, *Church Dogmatics* II/2 (1942 German)*

Wilhelm Michaelis, *Versöhnung des Alles* (1950)

John A. T. Robinson, *In the End, God* (1950)

J. Preston Eby, *Christ the Savior Series* (1970s)

Hans Urs von Balthasar, *Dürfen wir Hoffen?* (*Dare We Hope "That All Men Be Saved"?*) (1986)*

Jan Bonda, *The One Purpose of God* (1989 Dutch; 1998 English)

Jacques Ellul, *What I Believe* (1989)

Jürgen Moltmann, *The Coming of God* (1996)

John Crowder, *Cosmos Reborn* (2013)

Christocentric Purgationist Universalists

Charles Chauncy, *Salvation for All Men* (1782)

Elhanan Winchester, *Universal Restoration* (1788)

John Tyler, *Universal Damnation and Salvation* (1798)

Samuel Cox, *Salvator Mundi* (1877); *The Larger Hope* (1883)

John Wesley Hanson, *A Cloud of Witnesses* (1880); *The Bible Hell* (1888); *Universalism, the Prevailing Doctrine of the Early Church* (1899)

Thomas Allin, *Universalism Asserted* (1891)

William Barclay, *A Spiritual Autobiography* (1975)

Robin Parry [pseudonym: Gregory MacDonald], *The Evangelical Universalist* (2006)

Interreligious Universalists

Pico della Mirandola, *Nine Hundred Theses* (1486) [K]

Guillaume Postel, *De orbis terrae concordia* (*On Worldwide Concord*) (1544) [K]

Ernst Troeltsch, *The Place of Christianity among the World Religions* (1923)

Paul Tillich, *Christianity and the Encounter of the World Religions* (1963)

Stanley Samartha, *Living Faiths and Ultimate Goals* (1974); *One Christ, Many Religions* (1991)

John Hick, *An Interpretation of Religion* (1989)

Paul Knitter, *The Myth of Religious Superiority* (2005); *Without Buddha I Could Not Be a Christian* (2009)

Gerald O'Collins, *Salvation for All* (2008)

Miscellaneous Christian Universalists

Richard Coppin, *Divine Teachings in Three Parts* (1649)

Joseph Alford, *The Christian Triumphant* (1649)

Marie Huber, *The World Unmask'd* (1736)

Andrew Michael (Chevalier) Ramsay, *Philosophical Principles of Natural and Revealed Religion* (1748–49)

David Hartley, *Observations on Man* (1749)

Frederick Denison Maurice, *Theological Essays* (1853)*

Henry Bristow Wilson, "Seances Historiques," in *Essays and Reviews* (1860)*

T. R. Birks, *Victory of Divine Goodness* (1867)*

Frederic Farrar, *Eternal Hope* (1878)*

Edward Hayes Plumptre, *The Spirits in Prison* (1884)*

Hannah Whitall Smith, *The Unselfishness of God* (1903)

Giovanni Papini, *Il Diavolo* (*The Devil*) (1953)

Rob Bell, *Love Wins* (2011)*

Gary Amirault, tentmaker.org

Appendix H

The Cosmic Saga

AN ESOTERIC VIEW

Wilhelm Schmidt-Biggemann, in *Philosophia Perennis: Historical Outlines of Western Spirituality in Ancient, Medieval and Early Modern Thought* (Dordrecht, Neth.: Springer, 2004), offers a synthetic summary of the grand narrative that one commonly finds in Western esoteric sources (pp. 445–47). This summary helps to show how universal salvation fits into a comprehensive story regarding God and the cosmos.

Philosophy of Spirituality. The spirit is recognized as being original; it is conscious of its own originality and therefore of its absolute status. The moment of beginning is characterised by an initially undetermined beginning becoming defined in a process of original separation. This definition allows for a perception of the beginning, the original separation, and the connection of both moments in the continuity of a Trinitarian self-relation. Thus the first, self-cognizant moment of being has the character of trinitarian self-constitution. The primordial world: The trinitarian self-sufficiency of the original beginning transcends itself in a subsequent fourth movement. This is the moment of Sophia. Now the thinking, trinitarian God no longer thinks only himself but beyond himself. These thoughts transcending the divine realm constitute the preconceived primordial world that precedes the creation of the extended world.

The Emergence of the Extended World. The extended world is characterised by its status as ectype of the archetypical, primordial world. . . . One essential element of spiritualist physics consists in the explanation of this extension. There are two complementary models: The first is the (Neoplatonic) model of the bursting point, which expands from non-extension into the three dimensions of space and fills the universe as God's spirit. The second is the (Neopythagorean) model, where a potential space is already conceived as opening up in God's original Christological separation from the undefined One to the defined two. It is common to both models that neither time nor space is absolute, but only emerges with development and movement.

The Phases of Becoming. The description of theogony and cosmogony in perennial philosophy is oriented toward the process of becoming. The basic pattern of becoming is the (Aristotelian) model of life. In the pulsating of an active impulse and a passive reception, a being develops. It is in this being that the development of life appears as contraction (systole) and expansion (diastole). This movement of becoming is defined as the life of every being. The life of theogony and cosmogony develops in the three phases that characterise every becoming: theogony, the creation of a primordial world, and the creation of the extended world. These phases of creation are not historical periods but modal steps that mark the various states of dependency and independency. While the absolute constitutes itself in the process of theogony, the defined eternal essences constitute a primordial world that is reflected in the extended, contingent world.

Eschatology. Every life and essence that stems from the absolute yearns to regain the absolute state of its beginning. It is characteristic of this philosophy of becoming that it employs the concept of separation. Separation generates yearning as a sign of love for the absolute One. This is why every development urges towards its end. This paradoxical situation shows itself for instance in music, where the melody is always longing for its end. It is similar with the course of nature, which on earth appears as eternal becoming and decaying, but always longing for its perfection. This perfection is the eternal remaining in blossom and fruit, the *apokatastasis*, the eternal restitution of all beings. This central moment of Origenistic eschatology holds sway over the philosophy of history in perennial philosophy. The time of perennial philosophy longs, from within the mourning of earthly separation and unfinished development, for the glory of eternal and final redemption. This glory cannot derive from the created beings, but comes to the present from the future.

Appendix I

Ultra-Dispensational Universalism

U ltra-dispensational universalism" (also sometimes called "ultra-dispensationalist" or "hyper-dispensational/ist") refers to Christian universalist literature that interprets the New Testament or church history as falling into a series of distinct, nonoverlapping "ages" or "dispensations" in which some subgroup of humanity will receive salvation. As universalists, these ultra-dispensationalists believe that all human beings without exception will finally be with God in heaven, but distinctive to their view is the notion that this final outcome will occur in stages.

A possible ancient source feeding into ultra-dispensationalism is the theology of Origen, who in *On First Principles* argued that "after the dissolution of this world there will be another one," and so too "there were others [i.e., other worlds] before this one existed."[1] Origen's speculation about multiple world ages was important in the development of Christian universalism, because it suggested that even if certain people were in fact shut out from heaven (as a literal interpretation of the Gospels might suggest), such exclusion did not have to endure eternally but might last only for one or more ages of time. A proximate source for twentieth-century ultra-dispensational universalism may be German Philadelphian theology, as classically expressed by Johann and Johanna Petersen. One of the "dispensational" teachings presented in the Petersens' many books circulating just after 1700 was the notion of 144,000 persons (see Rev. 14:1–5) who will be the first persons to receive full and final salvation from God, while

1. Origen, *On First Principles* 3.5.3 (Butterworth, 238–39).

other humans enter heaven at a later stage, and Satan and the fallen spirits are ultimately included as well (*DR* 5.8).[2]

Ultra-dispensational universalist authors over the last century have included Adolph Ernst Knoch (1875–1965), Adlai Loudy (1893–1984), and their contemporary follower Martin Zender, whose writings are the focus here.[3] Martin Zender connects his case for universalism with the claim that the Bible has been mistranslated and that many key terms must be reconstrued so that the texts communicate their true meanings. Like many other biblically oriented universalists, Zender insists that the New Testament Greek word *aiōnios* ought not to be translated with the English word "eternal." In fact, Zender argues that the word *never* means "eternal" but only refers to an age or time duration that is limited.[4] Regarding these biblical mistranslations, Zender claims that "God purposely sends deception into the world—even in the form of mistranslated Scripture—to separate truth lovers from the lovers of injustice."[5] This assertion is part of Zender's general polemic against traditional Christianity, its clergy, and its theological teachings. He states that "the religious majority is always wrong . . . not some time, but every time."[6] The debate over eternal hell, he suggests, calls attention to those teachers who should be believed and adhered to and those who should not.

Zender's universalism is a highly modified form of dispensational millennialism that revolves around the nation of Israel and the thousand-year-reign of Christ that is mentioned in the book of Revelation (Rev. 20:4). He claims that "understanding the time aspect of Jesus' earthly ministry is the key to understanding the entire New Testament."[7] Laurence Blanchard explains that "by construing all references to the kingdom to be speaking of the millennial reign, Zender is able to compress all discussion of the kingdom, including the threats made referring to nonparticipation, into that limited time frame."[8] Jesus came only to reach "the lost sheep of the house of Israel" (Matt. 15:24), and everything that Jesus said must be understood in the context of Jesus's

2. The idea of an initial 144,000 who are saved—followed by other persons later on—is an official teaching of the Watchtower Society, better known as the Jehovah's Witnesses. See *DR*, 113n326.

3. See Loudy, *God's Eonian Purpose*; Knoch, *Unveiling of Jesus Christ*; Knoch, *All in All*; Knoch, *Concordant Commentary on the New Testament*; Zender, *Martin Zender Goes to Hell*. For Zender, see also http://www.martinzender.com. My account of ultra-dispensational universalism closely follows that of L. M. Blanchard, *Will All Be Saved?*, 144–51. My thanks are due to Dr. Blanchard, both for his published monograph and for a helpful conversation with him as I was preparing my own book manuscript for publication.

4. Zender, *Martin Zender Goes to Hell*, 48.

5. Ibid., 18; cf. 19–23, 35–37, 42, 73.

6. Ibid., 91.

7. Ibid., 55.

8. L. M. Blanchard, *Will All Be Saved?*, 145.

dialogue and debate with Jewish leaders. Because the New Testament's threats of exclusion apply to a millennialist context, these threats have only limited application. Zender holds that the biblical language regarding the unquenchable fire, the devouring worm, the outer darkness, and so on applies *exclusively* to those who are barred from entering the *millennial* kingdom, which is itself limited in duration. Biblical references to "gehenna" pertain to the Valley of Hinnom outside Jerusalem, while "hades" denotes a place where people are "unseen." The judgment of "nations" in Matthew 25:31–46 implies that each nation will be judged according to how they have treated the people of Israel.[9]

In Zender's eschatology, no human beings will ever experience hell. There is no postmortem suffering or purgatory-like state to prepare anyone for heaven. Zender's position is thus a form of ultra-universalism (*DR* 6.8–6.9). All people are elected to salvation, and all will come to personal faith at the time that God confers on each the gift of that faith. At whatever point God wills it to be so, salvation will occur instantaneously. Three nonhuman creatures will suffer in the "lake of fire"—Satan, the beast, and the false prophet—as specifically mentioned in the book of Revelation (19:20; 20:10). Yet even these three will eventually find salvation, for "Satan shall be delivered from the Lake of Fire with a changed heart, to be granted an eternity of praising God at his Creator's throne."[10]

Zender's interpretation of the New Testament—though contrary to generally accepted biblical and hermeneutical principles—in Blanchard's words "contains within itself an ingenious sort of internal consistency." Yet it fails to account for Jesus's affirmative interactions with individual gentiles, as noted in the Gospels, and—most notably—his imperative for the apostles to preach the gospel throughout "the nations."[11]

9. L. M. Blanchard (ibid., 146n98) comments that "the Parable of the Rich Man and Lazarus found in Luke 16:19–30 poses a particular difficulty for Zender's view," since it seems plainly to speak of the judgment of individuals qua individuals rather than as members of nations. Zender concludes simply that this passage of Scripture is a parable that does not directly describe the afterlife (*Martin Zender Goes to Hell*, 68–71).

10. Zender, *Martin Zender Goes to Hell*, 85.

11. L. M. Blanchard, *Will All Be Saved?*, 148–50.

Appendix J

Words and Concepts for Time and Eternity

What is meant by the biblical words—and especially the New Testament words—rendered in most English Bibles as "eternal" or "everlasting" (Greek *aiōnios, aidios*)? The answer to this seemingly straightforward question proves to be quite complex, inasmuch as the linguistic data on the use of the terms does not resolve the underlying conceptual issue of how one is to think about the nature of time, or the idea of eternity, as either an extension of ordinary time or as some kind of alternative to it.

In a recent critical review of Ilaria Ramelli and David Konstan's *Terms for Eternity* (2007), Jan van der Watt notes that "as . . . with concepts of eternity," so too "the conception of time is fundamental to any worldview." The task of interpretation becomes challenging, though, when one realizes that "the notion of eternity has multiple senses, often involving a high level of philosophical abstraction." This means that "frequently the sense in which eternity is applied is not immediately self-evident," and "it may bear senses ranging from 'a very long time' to 'endless' or even not being subject to time at all." Further complicating the picture is the issue of semantic field, whereby a given term may have a wide range of uses and can denote many things (e.g., the encompassing English term "love" versus the more specific Greek terms *agapē, philos, erōs, storgē*). With regard to the term *aiōnios*, van der Watt comments, "The same word (e.g., *aiōnios*) can be used with different meanings, while different words can be used within the same semantic field with basically the same meaning."[1] For many reasons, then, the literary context in which a term appears is often indispensable in determining its originally intended meaning.

The two most important terms for "eternal" or "eternity" in biblical Greek (i.e., the New Testament together with the Septuagint) are *aiōnios* and *aidios*. Ramelli and Konstan's monograph, *Terms for Eternity*, is devoted to an analysis of the use of these two terms in the history of ancient Greek literature. The study, as Ramelli notes, was motivated by her concern with *apokatastasis*, which she defines as the idea that "the wicked are not condemned to eternal punishment, but will eventually, in accord with divine mercy, be included among the saved."[2] In *Terms for Eternity*, as in *The Christian Doctrine of* Apokatastasis, Ramelli claims that in the New Testament *aidios* means "absolutely eternal" and so "*never* refers to punishment . . . in the other world."[3] But since *aidios* only appears twice in the New Testament, there are really not enough uses to allow it to be clearly defined over and against *aiōnios*, as Ramelli seeks to do. Still more damaging to Ramelli's linguistic argument is that *aidios* in the New Testament refers to the "eternal chains" (*desmois aidiois*; Jude 6) in which the disobedient angels are bound, and so the term—in one of the two New Testament uses—does indeed make reference to God's punishment.[4]

Ramelli and Konstan attempt to distinguish sharply the meanings of these two terms (*aidios* and *aiōnios*) as a way of arguing for universal salvation. Because of the rarity of *aidios* in biblical Greek, Ramelli makes her case for distinguishing the two terms on the basis of patristic Greek. But patristic usage cannot be definitive and determinative for Christian belief. Moreover, Ramelli is looking at detached words in patristic texts without considering the contexts in which they appear or the arguments that the authors are presenting. As all Greek scholars will admit, *aiōnios* in biblical Greek sometimes refers to entities that are not strictly eternal (e.g., the "everlasting hills," or *thinōn aenaōn* in the Septuagint version of Gen. 49:26). All the same, *aiōnios* is also often used in biblical texts as an adjective for God. Thus, one can only determine the meaning of *aiōnios* by a close reading of the word in its literary context. Such an approach is quite different from that taken by Ramelli and Konstan, in examining texts removed

---

1. Van der Watt, review of Ramelli and Konstan, *Terms for Eternity*.

2. Ramelli and Konstan, *Terms for Eternity*, 4.

3. Ramelli, *Christian Doctrine of* Apokatastasis, 26; cf. 33.

4. The other New Testament occurrence of *aidios* is in Rom. 1:20, where it refers to the "eternal attributes" of God. Heleen Keizer, in her review of *Terms for Eternity*, finds a "potentially misleading generalization" in Ramelli's reflections on the meaning of *aidios*, since its biblical use is confined to only four cases (4 Macc. 10:15; Wis. 7:25; Rom. 1:20; Jude 6). In contrast to this, there are no fewer than 70 occurrences of *aiōnios* in the New Testament and 222 in the New Testament together with the Septuagint (Keizer, review of Ramelli and Konstan, *Terms for Eternity*, 205–6).

from the historical and linguistic context of the New Testament writings and drawing fixed conclusions about what certain words must mean wherever or whenever they appear in ancient Greek literature.[5]

Another issue is more directly relevant to the question of universalism than to the meaning of the Greek words for eternity—namely, that there are New Testament words or phrases other than *aiōnios* and *aidios* that speak of the duration and perhaps the endlessness of God's punishments in the afterlife. These words are in Mark 9:44, 46, 48 (a thrice-repeated verse in some manuscripts): "where their worm does not die and the fire is not quenched." To address the question of the duration of divine punishment in the New Testament, one would need not only to parse the Greek words *aiōnios* and *aidios* but also give some convincing account of how to interpret the "undying worm" and the "unquenchable fire" (cf. Matt. 3:12; Mark 9:43; Luke 3:17)—two phrases that, at least on the surface, seem to suggest endless duration.

The discussion below probes the differing ways in which the language of "eternal" and "eternity" is used by the authors surveyed in the present work. Five broad categories are considered, with certain influential authors (e.g., Plato,

5. Jan G. van der Watt and Heleen Keizer, in their reviews of *Terms for Eternity*, both note the unexamined assumptions and questionable arguments of the book. Van der Watt states regarding *Terms for Eternity*: "What is offered seems to me to be at most impressionistic or intuitive. The word is not considered within the literary and semantic context of the particular document, neither is the philosophical framework of the ancient author taken into account. It goes without saying that this way of semantic analysis is not really convincing" (review of Ramelli and Konstan). He adds: "It amazed me that one of the major concepts that forms part of every discussion of eschatology . . . namely, that of eternal life and its relation to the present and future, is not really considered in any detail at all. . . . In the very brief and superficial remarks made about the use [of *aiōnios*] in Johannine literature, the authors only point out that *aiōnios* points to the *aiōn* to come. Not all the cases of *aiōnios* in the Gospel [of John] (and Letters) are considered. The theological meaning of the *aiōn* in the Johannine literature is not determined; the semantic content of 'eternal life' does not come into focus." So van der Watt found "disappointment" in the "lack of theoretical finesse" in the book. The lack of interest in "eternal life" in this volume might reflect the authors' agenda to build a case for punishment as non-eternal. If one gives full consideration to "eternal life," then the question of the duration of "eternal punishment" alongside of "eternal life" (mentioned in parallel in Matt. 25:41, 46) inevitably comes into focus. It is possible that Ramelli and Konstan wanted to avoid this line of inquiry. Heleen Keizer adds further criticisms of *Terms for Eternity*. The book "nowhere provides us with unequivocal definitions of the various senses of 'eternity' that are distinguished throughout the book." So "we are often left in the dark as to whether the eternity the authors . . . are speaking about is supposed to be of a temporal (durational and endless) or supra-temporal nature" (review of Ramelli and Konstan, 202). Keizer shows that in a certain passage of Philo, the term *aiōnios*, applied to God, denotes not God's being but God's doing—an insight that Ramelli's and Konstan's interpretive frameworks will not allow them to perceive and consider (ibid., 203–4). Keizer concludes that "weakness of method, a leaning on unwarranted assumptions, an equivocal formulation of outcomes, and numerous erroneous details unfortunately make it [*Terms for Eternity*] an unreliable guide" (ibid., 206).

Origen, Barth) included in more than one category.[6] We conclude with some remarks pertaining to the question of universalism.

"Eternity" as Endless Duration

If asked what they thought was meant by "eternity," many people would likely describe it as an endless duration of time—something like present life or experience but stretched out without limit. The best known of modern Christian hymns, "Amazing Grace" (1779), contains a commonly sung verse that aptly captures this popular religious notion of eternity:

> When we've been there ten thousand years,
> Bright shining as the sun,
> We've no less days to sing God's praise,
> Than when we first begun.

This verse was not part of the hymn as originally written by John Newton (1725–1807) and was first put into printed form as part of Newton's hymn in the renowned novel *Uncle Tom's Cabin* (1852) by Harriet Beecher Stowe. For at least half a century, the black church orally transmitted this verse prior to its inscription by Stowe. As an oral tradition linked to a famous hymn, it is thus an expression of the popular spirituality of the black church.[7] What is heaven? In popular terms, it is life with God, life that endures endlessly. What is hell? In popular terms, it is the converse: a state of being separated from God and continuing to suffer endlessly because of this separation.

Not only popular spirituality but also philosophical argumentation may be marshaled in support of the idea that "eternity" should be conceptualized as endlessly durative. In *Man's Conception of Eternity* (1854), H. L. Mansel took issue with F. D. Maurice's idea (see below) of "eternity" as a qualitative, nonsuccessive state of being rather than a quantitative and successive condition. Mansel argued that "eternity," understood in this way, is almost

---

6. For further discussion of the nature of time and eternity, see (among many other works) Baillie, *And the Life Everlasting*; S. Davis, *After We Die*; Eire, *Very Brief History of Eternity*; Horvath, *Eternity and Eternal Life*; Hoye, *Emergence of Eternal Life*; Küng, *Eternal Life?*; Padgett, *God, Eternity, and the Nature of Time*; Pike, *God and Timelessness*; Salmond, *Christian Doctrine of Immortality*; Streeter, *Immortality*; Hügel, *Eternal Life*.

7. The words "When we've been there . . . ," were one of between fifty to seventy verses of a song titled "Jerusalem, My Happy Home," which first appeared in Broaddus and Broaddus, *Collection of Sacred Ballads* (1790). See https://en.wikipedia.org/wiki/Amazing_Grace. The published version of "Amazing Grace" appears in Stowe, *Uncle Tom's Cabin*, 417 (ch. 38: "The Victory"). Cf. Aitken, *John Newton*, 235; J. Watson, *Annotated Anthology of Hymns*, 216.

certainly *incompatible* with human personhood. If "eternity" is nonsuccessive, then whatever is eternal simply *is*. It would be more logically consistent to think of those entering eternity as effectively frozen, fixed, or static.[8] If the very concept of life requires some notion of development or progress, then there seems to be a problem with nonsuccessive or nondurative views of the afterlife. Gregory of Nyssa posited an eternal progress in heaven (DR 3.9), as did Jonathan Edwards, and so both of these thinkers might lend credence to an endlessly durative idea of eternity.[9]

Some have sought to distinguish the durative and nondurative senses of eternity as a contrast between Hebrew thought (durative) and Greek thought (nondurative). Yet the distinction is inaccurate as a way of typifying Hebrew in contrast to Greek literature. To be sure, Plato's writings contain what Heleen Keizer calls the "supra-temporal idea of durationless time all-in-one"—the notion that most people have in mind in speaking of a "Platonic" view of eternity.[10] But Plato's writings clearly contain the idea of an endlessly durative eternity as well. Plato even believed in endless punishment, at least for a few. The incurably wicked, put on display to others, served as a warning and a deterrent to others who arrived in the place of punishment and were still curable.[11]

Perhaps the most famous invocation of eternity as endless duration appeared in Augustine's *City of God*. After citing Matthew 25:46, "And these will go away into eternal punishment, but the righteous into eternal life," Augustine argues:

> If both destinies are "eternal," then we must either understand both as long-continued but at last terminating, or both as endless. For they are correlative—on the one hand, punishment eternal, on the other hand, life eternal. And to say in one and the same sense, life eternal shall be endless, punishment eternal shall come to an end, is the height of absurdity. Wherefore, as the eternal life of the saints shall be endless, so too the eternal punishment of those who are doomed to it shall have no end.[12]

The same argument from the use of the word "eternal" in Matthew 25 appeared also in some eastern Christian authors, including Severus of Antioch in his *Letter* 98 (DR 4.7). This argument is not unique to Augustine.

8. Mansel, *Man's Conception of Eternity* (1854), 22–23, cited in Rowell, *Hell and the Victorians*, 86.
9. On Nyssa's view of progress in heaven, see DR 3.9; on Jonathan Edwards, see P. Ramsey, "Appendix III."
10. Keizer, review of Ramelli and Konstan, *Terms for Eternity*, 202.
11. Plato's view, as Alan Bernstein states, amounted to "eternal punishment for the incorrigibly evil." See Plato, *Gorgias* 523a–526c (Hamilton and Cairns, *Plato*, 303–6); Bernstein, *Formation of Hell*, 57.
12. Augustine, *City of God* 21.23 (NPNF¹ 2:469; PL 41:736). On Augustine generally, see DR 4.3.

Some later authoritative statements regarding "*eternal* punishment" interpret this phrase as meaning "*endless or unending* punishment." From the phrasing we see that a durative idea of "eternal punishment" is clearly in view. Among the Anathemas of 543 CE against Origen is the statement: "Whoever maintains that the punishment[s] of the demons and godless human beings are temporal[ly limited], and that after a specified time they will have an end, that is to say there will be a restoration [*apokatastasis*] of demons or godless human beings—let him be anathema!"[13] George Scholarios, a patriarch of Constantinople, spoke against Origen for being "the father of Arianism, and [who] worst of all, said that *hellfire would not last forever*."[14] The sixteenth-century Lutheran Augsburg Confession states that "Christ . . . will give pious men eternal life and perpetual joy, but He will condemn impious men and devils to *torture without end*." The Augsburg Confession also "condemn[s] the Anabaptists, who hold that *there will be an end to the punishments of the damned and of devils*."[15] In all these texts it is clear that hell or eternal punishment is understood as an endless duration that "lasts forever." In none of these cases does any assertion regarding postmortem punishment depend on the meaning or interpretation of the word *aiōnios*. This Greek word is just one of the terms or phrases used to denote the endless character of final punishment.[16]

"Eternity" as Age-Long Duration

An alternative to the notion of eternity as endless duration is the idea of eternity as "age-long," often building on the possible rendering of the Greek *aiōn* as "age" or "epoch." This understanding has roots in the writings of Origen (also associated with eternity as timelessness) and became a major feature of Philadelphian universalism, eighteenth- and nineteenth-century Anglo-American universalism, popular universalist arguments, and the hyper-dispensational universalism of Martin Zender (*DR* appendix I). In *On First Principles*, Origen argued that "after the dissolution of this world there will be another one," and

13. See *DR* appendix C and anathema 9 of the "Ten Anathemas of 543 CE."

14. Vaticanus Gr. 1742, fol. I^r, translated and quoted in Chadwick, *Early Christian Thought*, 95 (emphasis added).

15. Augsburg Confession, art. 17 (emphasis added), quoted in Walker, *Decline of Hell*, 22.

16. There is a further complexity that we will pass over here, discussed earlier (*DR* 4.3) in connection with Augustine and Gregory of Nazianzus, who both rejected the Platonic argument (accepted by Origen and Gregory of Nyssa) that whatever begins in time must come to an end in time. Augustine and Gregory of Nazianzus both argue that the blessedness of the saints begins in time (i.e., when they attain heaven) but never ends in time. An endlessly durative notion of eternity is implied here, while the damned are seen as the reverse case—i.e., those whose suffering begins in time but never ends in time and so endures endlessly.

so too "there were others [i.e., other worlds] before this one existed."[17] Origen's speculation about multiple world ages proved to be crucial for the development of Christian universalism, because it suggested that even if certain people were shut out from heaven at one point in time (as a literal interpretation of the Gospels might suggest), such exclusion did not have to endure eternally but might last only for one or more ages of time and then come to an end.

George Rust, a seventeenth-century defender of Origen, argued that all God's punishments aim at restoration and that the word "eternal" need not refer to a state of existence that is strictly unending. Only "Scholastick Definitions" of terms assert this to be so, according to Rust. He endorses what he takes to be Origen's viewpoint: "That after long *periods* of time the damned shall be delivered from their torments, and try their fortunes again in such regions of the world as their Nature fits them for."[18] Mormon founder Joseph Smith held that the term "eternal" in the phrase "eternal punishment" did not imply endless separation from God. In a revelation Smith is said to have received in 1830, he learned that phrases such as "endless punishment" and "eternal life" have qualitative as well as quantitative implications. Smith says that God used the term "endless" in Scripture because of its psychological impact on readers: "that it might work upon the hearts of the children of men." In the same passage we read: "Eternal punishment is God's punishment. Endless punishment is God's punishment."[19] In a comparable way, "eternal life" also has a qualitative aspect and so denotes a quality of life that is like that of God.[20] In interpreting eternity, Smith's position seems to be indistinguishable from that of his nineteenth-century universalist contemporaries.

Rob Bell, in *Love Wins*, interprets *aiōn* as meaning "age-long," stating that "*aion* . . . doesn't mean forever as we think of forever." Instead the word primarily refers to a "period of time with a beginning and an end."[21] Elsewhere in the book, Bell suggests that *aiōn* can also refer to "a particular intensity of experience that transcends time." Here Bell proposes antithetical points of view—a temporal and durative versus a nontemporal and nondurative notion of *aiōn*—and yet does not commit himself to either view. It is Jesus himself, writes Bell, who "blurs the lines" between concepts of "heaven" as lying in the future or the present or as simply a designation for God himself.[22] Martin Zender argues more straightforwardly than Bell does that *aiōnios* in no case

17. Origen, *On First Principles* 3.5.3 (Butterworth, 238–39).
18. [Rust], *Letter*, 131, 14.
19. *Doctrine and Covenants*, 19:7, 11–12.
20. A. Bassett, "Endless and Eternal," 454.
21. R. Bell, *Love Wins*, 31.
22. Ibid., 57, 59.

means eternal in the sense of endless duration but only refers to an age or time that is limited in duration.[23]

Both views considered thus far conceive of eternity in durative terms, but the difference is that the first regards it as *unlimited* in duration while the second considers it to be *limited*. Although the view of eternity as "age-long" is frequently brought forward as an argument for universal salvation, it fails to provide an effective riposte to Augustine's well-known exegesis of Matthew 25. There is no effective universalist response to the argument that *aiōnios*, if referring to a time period of limited duration, would in Matthew 25 imply that heaven as well as hell must come to an end.[24] William Whiston (1667–1752) seems to have been one of the few authors to follow out this logic rigorously, by denying the endlessness of heaven and hell alike.

"Eternity" as Timelessness

A different view, common among those influenced by Plato or the Neoplatonists, regards eternity as—in the words of Heleen Keizer—the "supra-temporal idea of durationless time all-in-one." This idea of eternity differs from the first two views in rejecting the idea of duration. It appears in Origen, in Western esotericism generally, in F. D. Maurice, in Paul Tillich, and arguably in the early Barth. Origen taught that all creatures existed eternally, and so he rejected the idea of a temporal creation, implying something "non-existent at first but coming into existence afterwards."[25] George Rust and Anne Conway both later affirmed Origen's position that all creatures existed from all eternity. In saying that creatures are eternal, Origen did not intend to say that creatures are divine, although his theology seems to diminish the metaphysical distance between Creator and creatures. Some later Western thinkers would say that all spirits were created *ex Deo* or from God's own substance or essence (e.g., Böhme, Bulgakov). In contrast, Christian thinkers who began with the sense of a metaphysical chasm between Creator and creature have generally interpreted the creature's eternity as endless duration. Timeless or durationless eternity, on their view, applies only to God and is something that human beings might not even be able to comprehend.

23. Zender, *Martin Zender Goes to Hell*, 48.
24. D. P. Walker explains that, in Matt. 25:34, 41, 46, "Christ is clearly drawing a parallel between the eternity of bliss awaiting the sheep and the eternity of misery awaiting the goats. It [i.e., the non-eternity of hell] can only stand if one also denies eternal life to the saved; only the ruthlessly honest and literal-minded Whiston dared to take this step" (*Decline of Hell*, 20, citing Whiston, *Eternity of Hell Torments Considered*, 63–64, 106).
25. Origen, *On First Principles* 1.2.9 (*PA* 142–44; Butterworth, 23); cf. *On First Principles* 1.4.3 (*PA* 188; Butterworth, 42).

In one of Origen's more interesting and elusive comments, he wrote of an "eternal gospel" that somehow corresponds to the earthly events of Christ's life but exists on a higher plane.[26] In the nineteenth century, Julius Müller spoke of humanity's "primitive state in the eternal ideas," and he suggested a twofold life of humanity. One level was that of earthly life, and the other was not a preexistence prior to earthly life but a transcendental existence, determinative of present human life yet not locatable as occurring before, during, or after our earthly lifetime.[27]

Another proponent of eternity as timelessness, F. D. Maurice, asked in his *Theological Essays*, "What, then, is Death Eternal, but to be without God?" Maurice added, "What other can equal this? Mix up with this, the consideration of days and years and millenniums, you add nothing either to my comfort or my fears."[28] The New Testament word for "eternal" (*aiōnios*), argued Maurice, does not denote endless time but has qualitative rather than quantitative significance, so that "eternal life" means "life in God eternal." Maurice raised the question, if "Eternity in relation to God has nothing to do with time or duration, are we not bound to say that also in reference to life or to punishment, it has nothing to do with time or duration?"[29]

In response to Maurice's arguments, H. L. Mansel argued that one precondition for personhood is memory. Yet memory itself is necessarily linked with some notion of temporal succession. This means that if Maurice's nonsuccessive, nondurative "eternity" truly existed, then human persons would be unable to participate in it. Mansel also took Maurice to task for applying the early church idea of divine eternity to human beings. While the patristic authors thought of God as unbounded by time, they thought of humans as creatures of time. God's relation to time, as the infinite Creator, was simply different from that of finite creatures. Mansel concluded that Maurice's position was "incompatible with the conception of the next life as a continuation and development of the present" or with any "state of progress and increasing knowledge." What Maurice offered was only "the vague . . . intimation of some possible state of existence under no conditions which we can figure to ourselves of human consciousness, or human personality."[30]

---

26. Origen, *Commentary on John* 1.40, explains: "And that which John calls an eternal gospel, which would properly be called a spiritual gospel, clearly presents both the mysteries presented by Christ's words and the things of which his acts were symbols, to those who consider 'things face to face' concerning the Son of God himself" (R. E. Heine, *Origen: Commentary on the Gospel according to John, Books 1–10*, 42).

27. J. Müller, *Christian Doctrine of Sin*, 2:425.

28. Maurice, *Theological Essays*, 437.

29. Ibid., 446–50.

30. H. L. Mansel, *Man's Conception of Eternity*, 22–23, cited in Rowell, *Hell and the Victorians*, 86.

The idea of eternity-as-timelessness does not support the doctrine of universalism as clearly as some of its supporters have thought. Passing from the present human life into a durationless postmortem state might be a matter of becoming fixed or getting stuck—like a fly forever frozen in ancient amber. If this is the case, then any separation from God that occurred during one's earthly life could become locked in for all time. It is not clear that Maurice's defense of timeless eternity serves the cause of universalism. Maurice's contemporary, F. J. A. Hort, agreed with Maurice that the notion of eternity was not tied to that of duration. Yet Hort regretted Maurice's unequivocal rejection of purgatory, and hoped that there might be opportunity for postmortem repentance.[31] Such hopes for spiritual improvement after death are clearly tied to ideas of temporal succession—a further occasion for decision, for acting, or for being acted on. Some universalists embrace "eternal life" as a state of durationless eternity, while also insisting that the afterlife allows for continuing spiritual development. This viewpoint would seem to be an inconsistent hybrid of eternity-as-endless-duration with eternity-as-timelessness.

During his later years, Karl Barth acknowledged what he called the philosophical Kantian and Platonic conceptions in both the first and the second editions of his commentary on Romans. Barth's positing of "eternity" against "time" had a Platonic aspect to it and suggests a law-gospel dialectic in which God's eternity is the judgment of human time and the works of time-bound humanity.[32] In his maturity, Barth developed a different view of time and eternity (see below).

Paul Tillich maintained an idea of eternity-as-timelessness throughout his career. He wrote, "The eternal is not a future state of things. It is always present, not only in man (who is aware of it), but also in everything that has being."[33] Tillich called his theology a "Platonizing answer" to the question of eternity: "Being, elevated into eternity, involves a return to what a thing essentially is; this is what Schelling has called 'essentialization.'"[34] "Eternal Life . . . includes the positive content of history, liberated from its negative distortions." "Since eternal life is participation in the divine life, every finite happening is significant for God."[35] So too "an immanent judgment . . . is always going on in history."[36] Tillich's thought contains a strong "vertical" dimension, as though salvation involves an escape from the "horizontal" passage of time. This "vertical" aspect is common among thinkers who conceive of eternity-as-timelessness.

31. Rowell, *Hell and the Victorians*, 83.
32. Berkouwer, *Triumph of Grace*, 21n29, 26.
33. Tillich, *Systematic Theology*, 3:400.
34. Ibid.
35. Ibid., 3:397–98.
36. Ibid., 2:164.

For some contemporary Christian universalists, earthly happenings are manifestations of eternal events. André Rabe in *Imagine* speaks of Jesus's earthly life as the "manifestation of an eternal event": "The life, death and resurrection of Jesus Christ happened within our time, but it was a manifestation of an eternal event. His appearance revealed what has always been true—the mystery hidden for ages and generations was finally made known in our dimension of time and space."[37] Rabe here seems to be more an esoteric than a Platonic thinker, and the "vertical" dimension noted with regard to Tillich suggests some kind of escape from this present, time-bound world. Such an esoteric understanding of Christianity inevitably creates difficulties for the doctrine of incarnation, as noted in the earlier discussion (*DR* 11.6).

"Eternity" as Intensified Experience

The fourth and fifth views of eternity are somewhat more elusive than the first three. The idea of eternity as intensified experience is arguably present in Meister Eckhart, John A. T. Robinson, Nicolas Berdyaev, Karl Rahner, Jürgen Moltmann, Hans Urs von Balthasar, and Rob Bell. For Meister Eckhart, in the language of Cyril O'Regan, "the vision of the mystic is God's own vision," and this "has to be understood in nondurational terms." So Eckhart "suggests . . . a definition of eternity as the transcendence of time and not . . . as indefinite temporal extension, i.e., everlastingness." This means that "the Eckhartian vision of mystical union and vision" implies a "subversion of [the] temporalizing tendency of popular religious imagination."[38] O'Regan's analysis of Eckhart might place him in the third category, as holding to eternity-as-timelessness. Yet Eckhart presented a strongly experiential account of the breakthrough experience in which the mystic came into full awareness of union with God. There is thus a kind of eschatological mysticism or mystical eschatology in Eckhart, involving a heightening of human experience as eternal reality impinges on the temporal moment.

For Karl Rahner, the biblical language of eternity must be interpreted in terms of present-day experience. He wrote: "The metaphors in which Jesus describes the eternal perdition of man as a possibility which threatens him . . . [fire, worm, darkness, etc.] . . . all mean the same thing, the possibility of man being finally lost and estranged from God in all the dimensions of his existence. . . . Suchlike words are metaphorical expressions for something radically not

37. Rabe, *Imagine*, 26–27.
38. O'Regan, *Heterodox Hegel*, 256–57.

of this world . . . [that] can only be spoken of 'in images.'"[39] Peter Phan writes: "Rahner reiterates that eschatological assertions are not 'advance coverage' of the beyond or of what is going to happen at the end of time. The biblical statements about eternal punishment . . . should be interpreted in keeping with their literary genre of 'threat discourse.' That is, they place the hearers before a decision for or against God."[40]

Laudislaus Boros placed the experiential encounter with eternity in the moment of death. His "final decision hypothesis" holds that "death gives man the opportunity of posing his first completely personal act; death is, therefore, by reason of its very being, the moment above all others for the awakening of consciousness, for freedom, for the encounter with God, for the final decision about his eternal destiny."[41]

Balthasar situated the intensified experience of eternity in Christ's own life and also in the universal human encounter with Christ in death or in the underworld. He explicitly linked the word "eternal" with the word "intensity," commenting that "the Lord's sufferings were . . . supra-temporal: every moment of his suffering has an 'eternal' intensity, and precisely because of this, it towers far above chronological time. Thus we can say in truth that he suffers until the end of time."[42] Balthasar even seems to have embraced Gustav Siewerth's notion of God's eternal suffering: "For it is only through the love-death of the eternally offered Son that the Creator's love is communicated and expropriated, overflowing onto us."[43] In some sense there is an intensified experience of eternity within the intra-trinitarian life of God, which cascades into human life as well.

Joshua Brotherton argues that "the enigmatic relationship between time and eternity is most plausibly the key to interpreting Balthasar's hope for universal salvation." Balthasar's "reflections on Christ's death and descent into hell favor more the notion of an existential opportunity for grace in death, a transformative encounter with the crucified Christ, than the notion of a post-mortem conversion or the self-annihilative character of condemnation."[44] In Balthasar's theology, the "horizontal" and the "vertical" dimensions of time sometimes seem to compete with each other. The "horizontal theo-drama" does not stand on its own but is "taken . . . with him [i.e., Christ]" into the other "supra-temporal realm."[45] In his writings on eschatology, prior to and after becoming pontiff, Pope Emeritus

39. Rahner, "Hell" [1975], 603.
40. Phan, "Eschatology," 186, citing, Rahner, "Hell" [1969], 3.
41. Boros, Moment of Truth, viii–ix.
42. Balthasar, Grain of Wheat, 69–70.
43. Balthasar, TD 4:436, cites Gustav Siewerth's 1934 essay "Christentum und Tragik," 299–300.
44. Brotherton, "Possibility," 321, 324.
45. Balthasar, TD 5:57.

Benedict XVI identifies the eschatological encounter with God as an intensification of experience. "Encounter with the Lord is this transformation. It is the fire that burns away our dross and re-forms us to be vessels of eternal joy."[46]

Moltmann sometimes speaks in terms that suggest a notion of eternity as intensified experience. In "The Logic of Hell," he quotes Luther's "Sermon on Preparing for Death" (1519) and claims that "for Luther, hell is not a place in the next world, the underworld: it is an experience of God." He quotes Luther's own words: "Thou must look upon hell and the eternity of torments, not in themselves, not in those who are damned. . . . Look upon the heavenly picture of Christ who for thy sake descended into hell and was forsaken by God as one eternally damned. . . . See in that picture thy hell is conquered and thy uncertain election made sure."[47]

Finally, mention may be made of the currently growing interest in annihilationist or conditionalist eschatology. In 1995 the Doctrinal Commission of the Church of England in a formal statement suggested that persons who reject God thereby diminish themselves and so tend in the direction of nothingness or nonbeing: "Hell is not eternal torment, but it is the final and irrevocable choosing of that which is opposed to God so completely and so absolutely that the only end is total non-being."[48] In this case, intensified experience might be a process of diminishment, not augmenting but subtracting from human existence.[49]

"Eternity" as the Eternalizing-of-Temporality or Temporalizing-of-Eternity

The fifth and last perspective on eternity may be the most difficult to explain. At core, this viewpoint holds that time and eternity are not distinct from each other—or at least that they do not remain distinct. There is thus either an *eternalizing of time* (perhaps Barth, Jüngel, Congdon), or, alternatively, a *temporalizing of eternity* (perhaps Schelling, Jüngel, Jenson, McCormack). It is not always easy to distinguish these two motifs. Bruce McCormack interprets the later Barth's theology and Christology as a temporalizing of eternity, even though this view arguably finds more overt support in German idealism than in Barth's own writings.

46. Ratzinger [Pope Benedict XVI], *Eschatology*, 230 (emphasis added).
47. Moltmann, "Logic of Hell," 46.
48. Doctrine Commission of the Church of England, *Mystery of Salvation*, 198, cited in Moltmann, "Logic of Hell," 43.
49. Nicolas Berdyaev had much to say regarding the experience of hell, and yet his position is hard to categorize. "The experience of unending torments is that of being unable to escape from one's self-centred agony. There is no hell anywhere except in the illusory and utterly unreal sphere of egocentric subjectivity powerless to enter eternity. Hell is not eternity at all but endless duration in time" (Berdyaev, "Hell," 268–69). His idea of endless duration in time would seem to put him in the first of our five categories, and yet he is insistent that an eternal hell does not exist.

One sees hints of this fifth notion of eternity in Schelling's *Stuttgart Seminars*. He writes:

> It is in these periods of eternity that the restitution [*Wiederbringung*] of evil takes place, which is something we must necessarily believe in. Sin is not eternal, and hence its consequences cannot be so either. This last period within the last is that of the entirely perfect fulfillment—that is, of the complete becoming man of God—the one where the infinite will have become finite without therefore suffering in its infinitude. Then God is in all actuality everything, and pantheism will have become true.[50]

One of the striking phrases here is "periods of eternity," a phrase that cannot be identified with any of the previous viewpoints. Schelling is not speaking of eternity as endless duration, or as timelessness, or as an age-long duration, or as intensified experience. There is something within eternity—even within God's eternity—that is somehow analogous to "periods" or epochs or ages on the level of ordinary human time.

Karl Barth picks up and develops a similar conception of eternity as "God's time." For Barth, human time is not negated but is included—in some fashion—within "God's time."[51] The idea of eternity as an endless duration resembling the present life is clearly not acceptable to him. Barth took a minimalist approach to Christ's second advent, though he still insisted that this teaching was doctrinally essential.[52] The final eschatological moment, writes Barth, will be "the eternalizing of our ending life," and "nothing further will follow this happening," and there is "no continuing into an unending future." For this reason, Barth rejects "pagan dreams of all kinds of good times after death."[53] Eberhard Jüngel takes a position like that of Barth: "Finite life will be *eternalized* as finite. But not through endless extension—there is no immortality of the soul—but rather through participation in God's own life. Our life is *hidden* in God's life. In this sense the briefest form of resurrection hope is the statement: 'God is my beyond.'"[54] David Congdon adds his voice to these others, explaining that resurrection means "the *eternalizing* of our lived history" and that "God remembers us for eternity."[55]

50. Schelling, *Stuttgart Seminars*, 243; Schelling, *Sämtliche Werke*, 7:484.

51. See Hunsinger, "Mysterium Trinitatis"; Langdon, "God the Eternal Contemporary." Balthasar sounds like Barth when he argues that "everything that is understood anthropologically as the doctrine of the 'last things' must be integrated in and subordinated to this trinitarian 'time'" (*TD* 5:57).

52. Congdon, *God Who Saves*, 74n45.

53. Barth, *CD* III/2, 624–25 (translation revised).

54. Jüngel, *Death*, 120.

55. Congdon, *God Who Saves*, 273.

Such an eternalizing of the temporal seems somewhat Platonic—an affirmation of temporal reality becoming atemporal or of the time-bound becoming timeless. There is a coming together of the eternal and the temporal, but this means that the temporal is adapted to the eternal. In contrast to this, what Paul Molnar calls "historicized christology" inverts the prioritization of the eternal over the temporal. Bruce McCormack states: "There is no such thing as an 'eternal Son' in the abstract. The 'eternal Son' has a name and his name is Jesus Christ." Just as boldly, he comments that "the immanent Trinity is already, in eternity, what it will become in time."[56] These statements might be taken as a metaphysical claim that the eternal must be understood from the standpoint of the temporal. Along similar lines, Robert Jenson views the Trinity in eternity as determined eschatologically, by what will happen in history: "Truly, the Trinity is simply the Father and the man Jesus and their Spirit as the Spirit of the believing community. This 'economic' Trinity is eschatologically God 'himself,' an 'immanent' Trinity. And that assertion is no problem, for God is himself only eschatologically, since he is Spirit."[57] In a later work, Jenson writes: "In that Christ's Sonship comes 'from' his Resurrection, it comes from God's future into which he is raised," for "the way in which the triune God is eternal, is by the events of Jesus' death and resurrection," so that "his individuality is constitutive of the true God's infinity."[58]

In conclusion, it should be noted that only the second of the five views of eternity considered here—eternity as age-long duration—is clearly and directly supportive of the universalist claim that God's punishment in the afterlife will not last forever. At the same time, this idea of the age-long duration of divine punishment is vulnerable to the objections articulated long ago by Augustine and Severus of Antioch, on the basis of their exegesis of Matthew 25. If punishment in hell is not strictly endless but is simply "age-long," then why would one not say that same thing regarding heaven? The first view considered (eternity as endless duration) is clearly not favorable to universalism, while the third viewpoint (eternity as timelessness) might favor an interpretation of postmortem punishment as endless separation from God rather than as separation for a limited period of time (as argued above). Strictly speaking, if human beings at death enter into eternity, and if eternity means timelessness, then we ought to speak of bliss or suffering neither as beginning nor as ending. The understanding of eternity as intensified experience is compatible either with the view of such experience as endless or else as limited in duration. Just as one might

56. McCormack, "Doctrine of the Trinity after Barth," 111.
57. Jenson, *Triune Identity*, 141.
58. Jenson, *Systematic Theology*, 1:142.

become "stuck" or "fixed" in a timeless eternity, one could also get "stuck" in some experiential state as well. The issue remains ambiguous. So too there is ambiguity in the fifth and final viewpoint, in which there is an eternalizing-of-temporality or temporalizing-of-eternity. If eternity itself involves successiveness in time, and so either is, or has become, temporalized, then one might expect such a temporalized eternity to be something like the interpretation of eternity as endless duration. So the last view considered, like all but one of the others, seems to be aligned with an idea of endless duration or unbroken continuity in the afterlife.

Appendix K

Mormon Teachings on God, Cosmos, and Salvation

The Church of Jesus Christ of Latter-day Saints—popularly known as the Mormon Church—presents a set of complex teachings on the character of God, the nature of the spiritual and material universes, and the plan of salvation. These teachings differ significantly from the doctrines taught in most Christian traditions or denominations and so require special treatment in this appendix. The earlier discussion of Mormon universalism or near universalism (*DR* 2.9) dealt only with the question of final salvation, and not with the larger, interlocking set of Mormon teachings that is the focus here.[1]

A suitable starting point for discussion might be the "King Follett Discourse," one of the best-known public addresses of the Prophet Joseph Smith Jr., delivered in Nauvoo, Illinois, on April 7, 1844. Smith delivered this comprehensive statement of his teaching less than three months before his death, to an audience of several thousand.[2] In the address, Smith declared that the human spirit is eternal. God the Father is who he presently is because of the eternities of progress he has already made. All of God's children are embryonic gods or goddesses, undergoing a perfecting progress that proceeds from one small

1. For a reliable account of the teachings of the Church of Jesus Christ of Latter-day Saints (here generally referred to as Mormonism), I have relied principally on essays in D. H. Ludlow, *Encyclopedia of Mormonism*, 4 vols. (1992), along with references to the Mormon scriptures and other authoritative Mormon texts.
2. D. Cannon, "King Follett Discourse," 791.

degree to another. In one of the most remarkable statements made on this occasion, Smith affirmed a basic continuity between God the Father and humanity, stating, "God himself was once as we are now, and is an exalted man, and
sits enthroned in yonder heavens! That is the great secret. If the veil were rent
today . . . you would see him like a man in form—like yourselves."[3] According
to Smith's teaching in this discourse, everyone will finally be saved, except for
those committing the "unpardonable sin."[4]

Metaphysical Assumptions

Mormonism's theological teachings rest on a number of metaphysical assumptions. According to the authoritative Mormon text known as *Doctrine and
Covenants*, matter and spirit are not distinct from one another; rather, spirit
is itself a form of matter: "All spirit is matter, but it is more fine or pure" than
physical matter.[5] The Prophet Joseph Smith said that "the spirit is a substance, that it is material, but that it is more pure, elastic and refined matter
than the body, that it existed before the body . . . and will exist separate from
the body."[6] The implication is that the elements from which all things exist

3. K. C. Carter, "Godhood," 554–55, citing Joseph Smith Jr., *Teachings of the Prophet Joseph Smith*,
345. S. E. Robinson writes, "Latter-day Saints perceive the Father as an exalted Man in the most
literal, anthropomorphic terms. They do not view the language of Genesis as allegorical; human
beings are created in the form and image of a God who has a physical form and image" ("God
the Father," 548).
4. D. Cannon, "King Follett Discourse," 791, citing Joseph Smith Jr., *Teachings of the Prophet
Joseph Smith*, 357.
5. *Doctrine and Covenants*, 131:7–8, cited in J. Jensen, "Spirit," 1404.
6. Joseph Smith Jr., *Teachings of the Prophet Joseph Smith*, 207, cited in J. Jensen, "Spirit," 1404.
The idea that spirit is a form of refined matter was characteristic of ancient Stoic philosophy,
and this view exerted influence in the earlier history of Christian thought. Tertullian considered
both God and the human soul to be corporeal in some sense, writing, *Quis enim negabit deum
corpus esse, esti deus spiritus est?* (For who will deny that God is body, although God is a spirit?).
See Tertullian, *Against Praxeas* 7.7–9, quoted in Colish, *Stoic Tradition*, 2:22 (cf. 2:19–25). Baltzly,
in "Stoicism," writes:
> The Stoics accept . . . that only bodies can act or be acted upon. Thus, only bodies exist. . . .
> Moreover, all existent things are particular. . . . In accord with this ontology, the Stoics . . .
> make God a corporeal entity, though not (as with the Epicureans) one made of everyday
> matter. . . . The Stoic God is immanent throughout the whole of creation and directs its
> development down to the smallest detail. . . . Because pneuma acts, it must be a body and
> it appears that the Stoics stressed the fact that its blending with matter is "through and
> through." . . . Perhaps [on one view of the Stoics] . . . pneuma is the matter of a body at a
> different level of description. Pneuma comes in gradations and endows the bodies which
> it pervades with different qualities as a result.
Ancient Stoicism and modern Mormonism share a materialistic idea of God and of the human
soul. Yet the top-down element of divine providence or control over the world in Stoicism finds no
clear analogue in Mormonism, which emphasizes individual free will and self-determination. The

were not created or made by God *ex nihilo,* as traditionally taught in Christian theology.[7] The spirit, intelligence, or light that is central to human existence has always existed, being coeternal with God. Spirit is a self-existent principle, and this applies to human, angelic, animal, and plant spirits, no less than to God. Mormon scripture in the Book of Moses states that every plant of the field was created "in heaven" before it was on earth.[8] Spirit can be organized or reorganized, but it is neither created nor destroyed. Every living thing had a pre-earthly or premortal existence in the realm of the spirit. All the spirits that have ever existed are susceptible of enlargement. Human spirits are, literally speaking, the offspring of perfect and exalted parents—a heavenly Father and a heavenly Mother.[9]

The Mormon teaching on the eternity of spirits and the spirit world might make Mormonism sound something like ancient Platonism or Origenism. Yet there is a decisive difference: Mormonism regards matter and body as fundamental to all reality and so shows itself on this point to be anti-Platonic. Mormonism teaches that a material body is necessary for happiness. The devil's punishment consists in the fact that he lacks a body. The evil spirits, in seeking to possess or infest human beings, display their own awareness that they are deficient and that they need a body to inhabit.[10] This focus on materiality extends to God himself: God the Father and Jesus Christ are exalted beings with glorified bodies of flesh and bones.[11] The official teaching in *Doctrine and Covenants* is that the Father and Son—but not the Holy Spirit—are bodily and tangible: "The Father has a body of flesh and bones as tangible as man's; the Son also; but the Holy Ghost has not a body of flesh and bones, but is a personage of Spirit."[12] This teaching is as firmly established as any Mormon doctrine, since it came as an integral part of Joseph Smith's original vision.[13]

Mormon worldview involves less unity and more plurality than Stoic philosophy, and Mormonism teaches an endless spiritual progression, in contrast with Stoic ideas of world cycles and cosmic repetition.

7. Mormonism recognizes creation, but considers it "as organization of preexisting materials, and not as an ex nihilo event (creation from nothing)" (Nielsen and Ricks, "Creation," 340). In developing their doctrine of origins, Mormons look not only to the book of Genesis but also to other texts they regard as canonical, including the Book of Abraham and the Book of Moses.

8. Book of Moses 3:5–7, cited in J. Jensen, "Spirit," 1405.

9. J. Jensen, "Spirit," 1404. Cf. Joseph Smith Jr., *Teachings of the Prophet Joseph Smith,* 351–54.

10. Joseph Smith Jr., *Teachings of the Prophet Joseph Smith,* 181; cf. 297–98.

11. J. Jensen, "Spirit," 1405, citing *Doctrine and Covenants,* 130:22.

12. *Doctrine and Covenants,* 130:22, cited in S. E. Robinson, "God the Father: Overview," 548.

13. It was the very first visionary experience of the prophet Joseph Smith that established the Mormon doctrine of God. "Here, Joseph Smith saw for himself that the Father and the Son were two separate and distinct beings, each possessing a body in whose image and likeness mortals are created" (S. E. Robinson, "God the Father: Overview," 548). No later theological or philosophical reflection can override the implications of this first vision of the prophet.

Another basic principle in Mormon thought is termed "agency," which denotes the capacity of human beings to act for themselves and to be held accountable for their actions.[14] The principle of agency implies that no one is compelled either to act virtuously or to sin. In Mormon theology, agency is a defining feature of premortal human existence as well as mortal human life.[15] The war in heaven that broke out prior to life on earth (see below) occurred because Satan—in the words of the Book of Moses—"sought to destroy the agency of man."[16] Because of the reality of agency, humans not only can but must choose and cannot remain in neutrality regarding good and evil.

God, Gods, and Gods-in-the-Making; The Father God

The Mormon idea of God is not singular or unitary but pluralistic. By 1842, Joseph Smith had come to the conclusion that the word "Elohim" in the Hebrew Bible should be rendered in the plural as "Gods" in the creation account. It is so rendered throughout the account of creation in the Book of Abraham. So in one passage of the Book of Abraham we read: "And the Gods came down . . . in the day that the Gods formed the earth and the heavens."[17] Despite this emphasis on divine plurality, Mormonism does not hold to the traditional Christian doctrine of the Trinity. In the words of Joseph Smith, the Father, the Son, and the Spirit are "three Gods." Three gods form the Godhead, and each one is an independent personage. The three gods are united in their thoughts, purposes, and actions, but they are not one in being or substance. In Joseph Smith's last Sunday sermon before his death in 1844, he declared that he had taught, over the preceding fifteen years, the doctrine of "the plurality of Gods."[18]

The Father God achieved his exalted, heavenly rank by progressing over time, just as human beings must progress. God may even be described as a perfected and exalted man, as Joseph Smith declared in the King Follett Discourse. In Mormon theology, Jesus is the way-shower and the example. In attaining his own godhood, Jesus Christ marked a path for others to become exalted divine beings, through following after him.[19] All of God's spirit children have seemingly

---

14. C. T. Warner, "Agency," 26. Cf. 2 Nephi 2:26; *Doctrine and Covenants*, 93:30–32.

15. The principle of agency and of noncoercion is foundational in Mormon theology, and it leads Mormons to reject divine predestination: "The Father will never violate individual agency by forcing his children to exaltation and happiness. Coercion in any degree, even in the form of predestination to the celestial kingdom, is abhorrent to the nature of the Father" (S. E. Robinson, "God the Father: Overview," 550).

16. Book of Moses 4:3, cited in C. T. Warner, "Agency," 26.

17. Book of Abraham 5:4–5, cited in Nielsen and Ricks, "Creation," 341–42.

18. Joseph Smith Jr., *Teachings of the Prophet Joseph Smith*, 370, cited in P. Dahl, "Godhead," 552.

19. P. Dahl, "Godhead," 553.

boundless potential. The human potential to become divine is not an abstract possibility but is part of the plan of salvation (see below) set in place before the physical universe existed. As Mormon scholar K. Codell Carter writes, "All resurrected and perfected mortals become gods. . . . They will dwell again with God the Father, and live and act like him in endless worlds of happiness, power, love, glory, and knowledge; above all, they will have the power of procreating endless lives."[20] Joseph Smith wrote, "You have got to learn how to be Gods yourselves . . . by going from one small degree to another . . . from grace to grace, from exaltation to exaltation, until you . . . sit in glory, as do those who sit enthroned in everlasting power."[21] Becoming like God means that one gains the power to create life and to create and reign over worlds. Joseph Smith said, "Every man who reigns in celestial glory is a God to his dominions."[22]

Mormon teaching on God's begetting of spirits implies that preexisting human spirits were made, so to speak, out of "God-stuff." They were begotten from and out of God, not created from or out of nothing. Stephen E. Robinson explains, "Gods and humans represent a single divine lineage, the same species of being, although they and he are at different stages of progress. This doctrine is stated concisely in a well-known couplet by President Lorenzo Snow: 'As man now is, God once was; as God now is, man may be.'" Robinson continues, "Thus, the Father became the Father at some time before 'the beginning' as humans know it, by experiencing a mortality similar to that experienced on earth." The heavenly Father and heavenly Mother serve as the heavenly pattern and example of what mortal human beings can become if they are obedient to the gospel. The Mormons' religious motivation is derived in no small part from this consideration.[23]

Jesus Christ; Mother in Heaven; and Angels

Mormon teachings on God and the spiritual world will likely be confusing to the uninitiated because of their nonstandard use of biblical terminology. Jesus Christ, for example, is said in Mormon scriptures to be both "Father" and "Son." Christ states, "I am the Father and the Son" (Ether 3:14). Another Mormon scriptural passage refers to the Lamb of God as "the Eternal Father" (1 Nephi 11:21). In yet another passage, we read that the Messiah will be "the Father . . . and the Son" (Moses 15:3). The difficulty is how to reconcile this

20. K. C. Carter, "Godhood," 553.
21. Ibid., 554, citing Joseph Smith Jr., *Teachings of the Prophet Joseph Smith*, 346–47.
22. K. C. Carter, "Godhood," 554, citing Joseph Smith Jr., *Teachings of the Prophet Joseph Smith*, 374.
23. S. E. Robinson, "God the Father: Overview," 549.

phraseology with the Mormon teaching of a Godhead with three distinct beings.[24] More difficulties arise when we consider that Jesus Christ *in his premortal state is Jehovah*. That is, the "Jehovah" of the Old Testament became the "Jesus Christ" of the New Testament once he was born into a mortal state.[25] Stephen Robinson states that "with few exceptions, scriptural references to God, or even to the Father, have Jesus Christ as the actual subject, for the Father is represented by his Son."[26]

The Latter-day Saints teach that there is a Heavenly Mother as well as a Heavenly Father—though this teaching on the Heavenly Mother is a rudimentary and undeveloped area of Mormon doctrine.[27] Parenthood as a concept requires both Father and Mother, whether in the creation of spirits in the premortal life or in the fashioning of physical tabernacles for earthly, mortal existence. Elaine Cannon writes that the Heavenly Mother "is like him [i.e., God the Father] in glory, perfection, compassion, wisdom, and holiness."[28] The concept of an eternal family is not merely a Mormon belief but also governs the Mormon way of life. Mormon leader Joseph F. Smith, in the first presidency, stated that "all men and women are in the similitude of the universal Father and Mother, and are literally sons and daughters of Deity."[29]

The Mormon teaching on angels includes some distinctive ideas. Angels who appear on earth do not simply arise from some nonearthly locality, which is their proper home. Instead, the Mormon teaching is that angels who appear on earth in some sense belong to it and have been assigned to it. In *Doctrine and Covenants* it is said, "There are no angels who minister to this earth but those who do belong or have belonged to it."[30] Some angels may be spirit children of the Eternal Father who have not yet been born on the earth but who are intended in time to share in the state of earthly mortality. There is here an analogy with Origen and Origenism, in which angels and humans transition back and forth between these two states. In ancient times, certain mortal human beings were "translated" from earth, including the biblical figures of Enoch and Elijah. Such

24. Millet, "Jesus Christ, Fatherhood and Sonship of," 739.

25. J. C. Giles, "Jesus Christ, Firstborn in the Spirit," 728.

26. S. E. Robinson, "God the Father: Overview," 549.

27. Elaine Cannon speaks of the belief as more implicit than explicit: "Belief in a living Mother in Heaven is implicit in Latter-day Saint thought" ("Mother in Heaven," 961).

28. Ibid.

29. Cited in ibid. The origin of humanity as engendered by a heavenly Father and Mother is stated in the following official statement from 1909: "Man as a spirit was begotten and born of heavenly parents, and reared to maturity in the eternal mansions of the Father, prior to coming upon the earth in a temporal body" (First Presidency, "The Origin of Man," November 1909 Appendix, cited in Nielsen and Ricks, "Creation," 341).

30. *Doctrine and Covenants*, 130:5, cited in O. McConkie, "Angels," 40.

"translated beings," in the words of the prophet Joseph Smith, "are designed for future missions" and so function as angels.[31] Another sort of angel is a person who has completed his mortal life but continues to labor in the spirit world prior to the resurrection of his body. Since the time that Jesus rose again, some angels are said in *Doctrine and Covenants* to be "resurrected personages, having bodies of flesh and bones." Moses, Elijah, Elisha, John the Baptist, Peter, and James were all "resurrected angels" in this sense.[32] Still another use of the word "angel" refers to those who did not keep God's new and everlasting marriage covenant. They will not qualify for exaltation (i.e., in a postmortem married state) but will remain single and separate as ministering angels. In Mormon teaching—as in mainstream Christian teaching—a fall occurred in the spirit world, with the result that some of the Father's spirit children fell and became demons (see below, under "Council in Heaven; War in Heaven").[33]

Preexistent or Premortal Spirits

As noted already, human beings were originally born as spirit sons and spirit daughters of the Heavenly Father and Heavenly Mother before any of them were born as mortals to earthly parents. A spirit creation preceded physical creation on earth: "I, the Lord God, created all things . . . spiritually, before they were naturally upon the face of the earth . . . for in heaven created I them; and there was not yet flesh upon the earth, neither in the water, neither in the air."[34] The souls or spirits of individual humans were not created *ex nihilo*. How, then, did the begetting of these spirit children occur? The begetting took place out of "preexisting intelligence."[35] The term "intelligence" in Mormon thought stands on the highest metaphysical level, from which "spirit" emerges at a level below. The intelligence that indwells each human person is coeternal with God, having always existed and having never been created. In *Doctrine and Covenants* we read that "man was also in the beginning with

31. Joseph Smith Jr., *Teachings of the Prophet Joseph Smith*, 191, cited in O. McConkie, "Angels," 40–41. "Translated" beings are defined as those "changed from a mortal state to one in which they are temporarily not subject to death" (M. McConkie, "Translated Beings," 1485). All such translated beings will eventually die or else be changed suddenly, without dying, into the resurrected state. Resurrection is thus a step beyond translation. Yet translated beings are given special ministries among mortals on earth (1486).

32. *Doctrine and Covenants*, 129:1, cited in O. McConkie, "Angels," 41. See also *Doctrine and Covenants*, 13; 27:12–13.

33. O. McConkie, "Angels," 41.

34. Book of Moses 3:5, cited in Nielsen and Ricks, "Creation," 341. Cf. "I [God] made the world and men before they were in the flesh" (Book of Moses 6:51, cited in G. O. Brown, "Premortal Life," 1124).

35. S. E. Robinson, "God the Father: Overview," 549.

God. Intelligence, or the light of truth, was not created or made, neither indeed can be."[36] Here there is an analogy with Origen, who held that each "rational nature"—something like the "intelligence" in Mormonism—had always existed with God. In contrast to Mormonism, though, Origen insisted that the "rational natures," though eternal, were nonetheless *created* (i.e., eternally or beginninglessly). In asserting human intelligence to be *uncreated* as well as eternal, Mormonism assigns a degree of metaphysical independence to the human intelligence that Origen did not.

After the emergence of spirit from intelligence, the spirit body emerges as a second stage, as a vehicle for spirit. All living things had spirit existence prior to material existence. Even inanimate entities—such as the earth itself—had spirit existence before physical existence. Joseph Fielding Smith wrote that "the spirits that possess the bodies of the animals are in the similitude of their bodies."[37] Mormonism teaches that the character of one's premortal life in the spirit world likely has influence on one's disposition and desires during the present, mortal life—another point of contact between Mormonism and Origenism. Failure to remember one's premortal life does not alter its actuality or facticity.[38]

Many Worlds; The Plan of Salvation; The Fall of Adam and Eve

Mormonism teaches the existence of many worlds. The physical universe as known and understood by human beings is not the totality of God's creative work. The Mormon scriptural text, the Book of Moses, states: "And worlds without number have I created . . . for mine own purpose. . . . And as one earth shall pass away, and the heavens thereof even so shall another come; and there is no end to my works."[39] The earth that humans inhabit is just one part of a larger universe of multiple worlds. As Kent Nielsen and Stephen Ricks explain, "The Creation is placed in a much larger context of ongoing creations of innumerable inhabited earths with their respective heavens (in all of which Christ played a central role)."[40] What Moses received from God and recorded in the book of Genesis was knowledge only of the present heaven and present earth, not of the many others.[41]

36. *Doctrine and Covenants*, 93:29; a revelation given through Joseph Smith the Prophet, at Kirtland, Ohio, May 6, 1833, cited in G. O. Brown, "Premortal Life," 1123–24.
37. G. O. Brown, "Premortal Life," 1124, citing Joseph Fielding Smith, *Doctrines of Salvation*, 1:63–64.
38. G. O. Brown, "Premortal Life," 1125.
39. Book of Moses 1:33, 38, cited in Nielsen and Ricks, "Creation," 340–41.
40. Nielsen and Ricks, "Creation," 340.
41. Ibid., 341. The Mormon idea of multiple worlds is reminiscent of Origen and Origenism.

The Book of Abraham reveals that both the empty space where the earth came to be and the earth's material existed prior to its creation—that is, the organizing of its elements into their present form. This book also describes a structured cosmos of many disparate levels, with eternally existing spirits that are ranked in order of intelligence, ascending to the level of the Lord God, who is "more intelligent than they all" (Abraham 3:19). In this text, one member of the premortal assembly speaks to others with the words, "We will go down . . . and we will make an earth whereon these may dwell; and we will prove them herewith, to see if they will do all things whatsoever the Lord their God shall command them."[42] This text makes it clear that the purpose of God in fashioning the earth—and of earthly, mortal bodies—is probation or testing in obedience.

What Mormonism calls a plan of salvation or plan of redemption—in relation to the known human world—emerged as the answer to a problem among God's spirit children. In the premortal life, also known as the first estate, these spirit children could not readily make spiritual progress. They required physical bodies, so as to be placed in an environment where, by the exercise of their own free agency, they could demonstrate their willingness to keep God's commandments.[43]

After Adam and Eve entered the garden of Eden in their physical bodies, there was still a problem—namely, there was no opposition and so there could be no progression. One Mormon scriptural text says that "there must needs be an opposition in all things."[44] Another problem in Eden was that Adam and Eve, as they were originally constituted, would have had no children.[45] The reason that Satan and the fallen angels were given access to the earth and to the garden of Eden was so that everyone would be enticed both by good and by evil.[46] Gerald Lund writes that "the Fall [of humanity] was part of God's plan for mankind and came as no surprise." So far from being blamed for sinning in the garden of Eden, Adam and Eve should therefore be acknowledged and appreciated for the legacy they gave to their posterity. The Mormon scriptures give a positive spin to the fall of Adam and Eve, stating, "Adam fell that men might be" (2 Nephi 2:25). Another scriptural text says, "Because that Adam fell, we are" (Book of Moses 6:48).

Once the fall had happened, Adam and Eve and their posterity entered a world with new possibilities for spiritual advancement.[47] The Book of Moses

42. Nielsen and Ricks, "Creation," 341, citing Book of Abraham 3:19, 24–25.
43. G. N. Lund, "Plan of Salvation, Plan of Redemption," 1088.
44. 2 Nephi 2:11, cited in G. N. Lund, "Plan of Salvation, Plan of Redemption," 1089.
45. "Without the Fall, Adam and Eve would have had no children. . . . Hence, the human family would not have come into existence upon this earth under the conditions and circumstances in the garden" (Matthews, "Fall of Adam," 485).
46. 2 Nephi 2:22–23 and 2:16, cited in G. N. Lund, "Plan of Salvation, Plan of Redemption," 1089.
47. G. N. Lund, "Plan of Salvation, Plan of Redemption," 1090–91.

recounts that Adam and Eve rejoiced at the opportunities that came to them because of the fall into disobedience.[48] After his sinning against God, Adam blessed God, saying, "Because of my transgression my eyes are opened, and in this life I shall have joy" (Moses 5:10). Eve was equally glad, saying, "Were it not for our transgression we never should have had seed [i.e., posterity], and never should have known good and evil, and the joy of our redemption, and the eternal life" (Moses 5:11). Robert Matthews comments: "The Fall was not an accident, not an obstruction to God's plan, and not a wrong turn in the course of humanity. . . . Since Adam and Eve would have had no children in their Edenic condition, the Fall was a benefit to mankind. It was part of the Father's plan."[49]

Council in Heaven; War in Heaven

God's plan of salvation was not simply imposed on God's spirit children. Mormonism teaches instead that the spirit children deliberated with God prior to entrance into mortal life, as part of a Heavenly Council or Council in Heaven—also known as the Grand Council. This council consisted in a meeting of God the Father with his spirit sons and daughters to discuss the terms and conditions under which these spirit children would come to earth as physical beings. Although the terms "Council in Heaven" and "Grand Council" are not used in the Mormon scriptures, the idea appears in a number of places.[50] During this council meeting, the Father presented his plan of salvation and proposed that an earth be created on which his spirit children might dwell, with each spirit child in a physical body, and in a probationary state, to be tested to see if they would obey God. The two principal associates of God the Father in this Heavenly Council were the premortal Jesus (also known as Jehovah) and the premortal Adam (also known as Michael; see below).[51] At this time God gave an explanation in advance to his spirit children concerning the plan for the creation, fall, mortality, atonement, resurrection, and final judgment. At this meeting, all the Father's spirit children had a choice about whether to accept this plan and all that it entailed.[52] One sees a definite parallel here between the

48. Ibid., 1089; Book of Moses 5:10–11.

49. R. Matthews, "Fall of Adam," 485.

50. Authoritative Mormon texts supporting the doctrine include Alma 13:3–9; *Doctrine and Covenants*, 29:36–38; 76:25–29; Book of Moses 4:1–4; Book of Abraham 3:23–28; Joseph Smith Jr., *Teachings of the Prophet Joseph Smith*, 348–49, 357, 365; all cited in J. L. Lund, "Council in Heaven," 328.

51. Holland, "Atonement of Jesus Christ," 83.

52. J. L. Lund, "Council in Heaven," 328–29. Nielson and Ricks not only state that the Father's spirit children consented to the plan of salvation but add that there is "an active role for God's spirit children in the Creation" ("Creation," 340). The spirit children were in some sense

Mormon idea of the Heavenly Council and the idea of the "Covenant of Alast" in esoteric Islam (*DR* appendix F), in which all human souls, prior to their physical embodiment, acknowledged Allah as God and consented to their own entrance into physical, mortal life, as Allah's servants.

This Heavenly Council not only set the terms and conditions for the plan of salvation but also established the particular vocation and calling of particular persons. John Lund comments, "Many spirits were foreordained to specific roles and missions during their mortal experience, conditional upon their willingness and faithfulness in the premortal sphere and their promised continued faithfulness upon the earth."[53] Joseph Smith once stated that he believed that his own prophetic role had been foreordained in that council: "Every man who has a calling to minister to the inhabitants of the world was ordained to that very purpose in the Grand Council of heaven before this world was. I suppose I was ordained to this very office in that Grand Council."[54] Jesus and the prophets were foreordained in this way. Jesus Christ was then known as "the great I AM" and as "Jehovah," and he volunteered for his redemptive mission. The Heavenly Council may have involved multiple meetings at which business was transacted.

During the Heavenly Council a problem emerged, because Christ was not the only volunteer to serve as humanity's redeemer. Lucifer also volunteered, as rival to Christ. Jehovah (i.e., Jesus) had already volunteered, when the Father asked, "Whom shall I send?" (Book of Abraham 3:27), and at this point Lucifer offered himself instead. Lucifer's plan involved a way of salvation for everyone. According to the Book of Moses, Lucifer said, "I will redeem all mankind, that one soul shall not be lost, and surely I will do it" (Book of Moses 4:1). Yet Lucifer's plan would not have allowed persons to make their own choices regarding God. Joseph Smith's account of the Heavenly Council states that "Jesus said that there would be certain souls that would not be saved; and the devil said that he could save them all, and laid his plans before the grand council, who gave their vote in favor of Jesus Christ."[55] This text is bit obscure, though the general idea is that Lucifer promised to save everyone while in some way forcing people into relationship with God. God the Father and the Father's spirit children—who all had a "vote"—rejected Lucifer's proposal.

---

cocreators of the world along with the Heavenly Father, the Heavenly Mother, Jesus Christ, and other divine beings.

53. J. L. Lund, "Council in Heaven," 329.

54. Joseph Smith Jr., *Teachings of the Prophet Joseph Smith*, 365, cited in J. L. Lund, "Council in Heaven," 329.

55. Joseph Smith Jr., *Teachings of the Prophet Joseph Smith*, 357, cited in J. L. Lund, "Council in Heaven," 329.

As one might have expected, the Heavenly Council's rejection of Lucifer's proposal was not the ending but only the beginning of Lucifer's rebellion. Mormons use the phrase "war in heaven" to refer to the conflict in the premortal life that began when Lucifer sought to overthrow God the Father and Jesus Christ. As a result of this rebellion, Lucifer and his followers were cast out of heaven.[56]

Puzzles over Adam

Just as Mormon theology identifies Jesus in his premortal state with Jehovah, so too the figure of Adam is interpreted in an unusual way and said to be equivalent in his premortal state to the archangel Michael. Adam is identified with the titles "Michael," "archangel," and "Ancient of Days."[57] It was Adam in the form of Michael who led the battle against Satan in the heavenly realm (cf. Rev. 12:7–9).[58] In the teaching of Joseph Smith, Adam shared in the creation of the earth and occupied a position of authority next to Jesus Christ.[59] At the end of the millennium, Adam as Michael will again lead the righteous in battle against the devil, as he earlier led the battle against the devil in which the devil was cast from heaven. Adam will then sound the trumpet, the graves will be opened, and Adam will preside eternally over his posterity—subject to the Father and to Christ.[60]

Mormonism assigns divine prerogatives to Adam. In 1852 Brigham Young stated that Adam "is our Father and our God, and the only God with whom we have to do."[61] Young later claimed that Joseph Smith had privately spoken to him regarding this Adam-God doctrine. Later in the same speech by Brigham Young, as Arthur Bailey notes, Young said that there were three distinct persons who organized (i.e., created) the earth—namely, "Eloheim," "Yabovah," and "Michael." This statement makes it seem that one cannot simply identify Adam with God without further qualification.[62] Brigham Young's teaching may have implied a doctrine of divine investiture, according to which the essential keys, titles, and dominions possessed by the Father were conferred on Adam.[63] Scholars of Mormonism have debated the Adam-God doctrine as presented by

56. Top, "War in Heaven," 1546.
57. "Michael" in *Doctrine and Covenants*, 27:11; 29:26; "archangel" in *Doctrine and Covenants*, 88:112; and "Ancient of Days" in *Doctrine and Covenants*, 138:38.
58. Top, "War in Heaven," 1546.
59. A. Bailey, "Adam," 15, citing Joseph Smith Jr., *Teachings of the Prophet Joseph Smith*, 158.
60. A. Bailey, "Adam," 15–16.
61. B. Young et al., *Journal of Discourses*, 1:50, cited in A. Bailey, "Adam," 17.
62. A. Bailey, "Adam," 17.
63. *Doctrine and Covenants*, 84:38; 88:107.

Brigham Young. The Church of Jesus Christ of Latter-day Saints does not accept this doctrine as part of its official teaching at the present time.

Grace, Atonement, and Salvation

The intention of God the Father is to make all human beings as happy as they can be.[64] Yet the Father's love cannot make all creatures happy if they are not willing to follow the plan of salvation. As noted already, Mormonism stresses individual free will and self-determination. The choice to act rightly belongs to individual persons, as we read in *Doctrine and Covenants*: "Men should . . . bring to pass much righteousness. For the power is in them, wherein they are agents unto themselves" (58:28). Bruce Hafen explains that Mormonism does not teach salvation by grace alone. Instead "the LDS doctrine [is] that salvation requires *both* grace and works."[65]

Mormonism teaches that Christ came to earth to accomplish redemption from sin: "Adam fell that men might be. . . . And the Messiah cometh in the fulness of time, that he may redeem the children of men from the fall" (2 Nephi 2:25–26). Latter-day Saints teach that this atonement is universal in extent. It opens the way for the redemption of all mankind—for non-Christians as well as for Christians, for the godless as well as for the god-fearing.[66] Somehow Jesus's death made it possible for human beings to obey God, as Jesus did, and thereby to attain their own godhood. Latter-day Saints believe that Jesus after his death went to the underworld, so that departed humans would also have opportunity for salvation.[67] In contrast to the teaching of most of the early church authors (*DR* 1.6), Mormonism affirms that Christ in his descent to the dead offered new spiritual opportunity to those who had ended their earthly lives without reaching salvation. Mormonism highlights the access or opportunity that God gives to all persons without exception to hear and to respond to the gospel. Larry Dahl writes that "everyone will hear the gospel of Jesus Christ, either on earth on in the postearthly spirit world."[68]

As noted in the earlier discussion (*DR* 2.9), Mormonism teaches that heaven exists on three levels and that nearly all persons attain to one of these three final

---

64. S. E. Robinson, "God the Father: Overview," 549.

65. Hafen, "Grace," 560.

66. Holland, "Atonement of Jesus Christ," 84.

67. "Jesus Christ went to the postmortal spirit world while his body lay in the tomb to preach the gospel to them . . . so that those spirits in the postmortal spirit world could hear and accept or reject the gospel" (G. N. Lund, "Plan of Salvation, Plan of Redemption," 1091, citing *Doctrine and Covenants*, 138:11–27). "Since baptism, the gift of the Holy Ghost, temple endowment, and sealing are earthly ordinances, Latter-day Saints perform the ordinances vicariously for the dead in their temples" (1091).

68. L. Dahl, "Degrees of Glory," 369, citing *Doctrine and Covenants*, 137–38.

states: "celestial" (the highest), "terrestrial" (intermediate), or "telestial" (lower).[69] Only a small number of persistently disobedient and recalcitrant persons, known collectively as the "sons of perdition," will be finally and fully lost and not enter into one of the three heavens. The Mormon doctrine of spiritual progression and its essentially dynamic rather than static understanding of the cosmos—and even of the divine nature itself—makes it difficult to affirm that anyone would ever be stuck in a spiritual state from which there is no possibility of escape.

Joseph Smith held that the term "eternal" in the phrase "eternal punishment" did not imply a state of separation from God that was literally endless. In a revelation in 1830, he learned that phrases such as "endless punishment" and "eternal life" have qualitative as well as quantitative implications. In his writings, Smith uses arguments pertaining to the New Testament word "eternal" (Greek *aiōnios*) very similar to those used previously by eighteenth- and early nineteenth-century universalists (*DR* appendix J). Smith says that God used the term "endless" in Scripture because of its psychological impact on readers: "that it might work upon the hearts of the children of men" (*Doctrine and Covenants*, 19:7). In the same passage we read: "Eternal punishment is God's punishment. Endless punishment is God's punishment" (*Doctrine and Covenants*, 19:11–12). In a comparable way, "eternal life" also has a qualitative aspect and so denotes a quality of life that is like that of God.[70] In interpreting the term "eternal," Smith's position seems indistinguishable from that of his nineteenth-century universalist contemporaries.

As we have noted already, Mormonism in the sweep of its cosmology and its doctrine of salvation shows broad similarities to Origenism (*DR* 3.4–3.8). Each of these theologies teaches that all spiritual beings have existed forever. They each assert that the specific character of one's earthly existence depends on one's pre-earthly state. The mortal, earthly life of each spiritual being offers opportunity for spiritual advancement. Earthly existence is a time of learning, in which disobedient persons learn to be obedient. Once one makes adjustments for the distinctive Mormon notion that spirit itself is a form of matter (see above under "Metaphysical Assumptions"), one finds Mormonism and Origenism to be roughly analogous. Some Mormon authors have appealed to Origen as anticipating later Mormon theology.[71] For Origenism and Mormon-

---

69. L. Dahl, "Degrees of Glory," 367–69. Cf. *Doctrine and Covenants*, 76:50–70; 84:33–39; 132:19–25.

70. A. Bassett, "Endless and Eternal," 454.

71. Mormon authors Kent Nielsen and Stephen Ricks connect the Mormon teaching on "individual premortal existence" to Origen, *De principiis* 1.7; 2.8; 4.1, as well as to Philo's *De mutatione nominum* 39; *De opificio mundi* 51; *De cherubim* 32; and the deuterocanonical Wisdom of Solomon 8:19–20; 15:3. See Nielsen and Ricks, "Creation, Creation Accounts," 343. See also the appreciative history of the idea of preexistent souls by a Mormon author in Givens, *When Souls Had Wings*.

ism, all human beings originally come forth from God and will finally return
to God. There is an essential optimism built into each theology. The idea of a
human origin as "spirit children" orients Origenism and Mormonism toward
the notion of universal return and universal salvation. Moreover, Origenism
and Mormonism are strikingly meritocratic in outlook. Every person has full
moral and spiritual freedom to act independently (which Mormonism calls
"agency"); all persons are held accountable for their actions, and in each case
they get what they deserve.[72]

Mormon scholar Stephen Robinson calls the Mormon doctrine of God "sub-
ordinationist." He comments: "God the Father is not one in substance with the
Son or the Holy Spirit, but is a separate being. The Father existed prior to the
Son and the Holy Ghost and is the source of their divinity. In classical terms,
LDS [Latter-day Saint] theology is subordinationist."[73] This is also one way of
reading Origen's doctrine of God—or at least the interpretation of Origen's
trinitarianism that prevailed among Origen's fourth-century Arian followers.
There is a built-in subordinationism in the way that Mormonism depicts its
multileveled afterlife. Those in the lowest heaven receive the influence of the
Holy Spirit but not the presence of the Father or the Son.[74] In Origen's theology—
and more clearly in the radical Origenism of Evagrius and the Evagrians (DR
3.10)—the individual, preexistent rational natures (logoi or noes) find their model
for spiritual life and for salvation in the preexistent Christ (Logos or Nous). The
Evagrian Origenists and the Mormons present what seems to be an exemplarist
Christology—that is, a doctrine according to which salvation is the outcome
of a human effort to follow after and to imitate Christ. Joseph Smith's promise
that human beings would finally become gods was anticipated among ancient
Evagrians who believed that their souls would finally progress to become equal
to the soul of Christ (Greek isochristos). If Christ in certain respects is subordinated in Origenist and Mormon teaching, then human spirits are elevated and
exalted to an unexpected degree.

The Mormon doctrine of a Heavenly Council at which all God's spirit children (with the exception of Lucifer and his followers) gave advance consent to

72. One feature of Origen and Origenism (and many other forms of universalism) but seemingly absent from Mormonism is a doctrine of purification through suffering. Mormonism stresses
obedience as the pathway to God, while Origen also emphasizes the cleansing fire of conscience
(DR 3.7).

73. S. E. Robinson, "God the Father: Overview," 548.

74. Those in the telestial state (the lowest of the three heavens) will forever be servants of God
but not in the presence of God, for "where God and Christ dwell they cannot come, worlds without
end" (Doctrine and Covenants, 76:112; L. Dahl, "Degrees of Glory," 369). They do, however, receive
"of the Holy Spirit through the ministrations of the terrestrial" (Doctrine and Covenants, 76:86;
L. Dahl, "Degrees of Glory," 368).

God's plan of salvation is certainly unusual but is not wholly unprecedented. The closest parallel may be in the Islamic idea of the Covenant of Alast, as presented by Jalal al-Din Rumi and other Sufi teachers (*DR* appendix F). The Arabic term "Alast" comes from a reported question, as posed by God: "Am I not [alast] your Lord?" According to the idea of the Covenant of Alast, when human beings existed with God prior to their earthly creation, God posed this question to them, and they all replied in the affirmative, thus committing themselves in advance to being servants of Allah. At the resurrection, each human being will be assessed to see whether he or she was faithful to this original commitment.[75] It should be clear that this idea of a preexisting covenant or agreement between God and humanity—agreed to before any human soul ever entered a physical body—serves to accentuate everyone's responsibility before God. As humans, we are not only creatures who owe God our lives, but we are contractees who owe God the specific obedience that we agreed to render. The Qur'anic-Islamic version of humanity's premortal deal with God is not quite as democratic as the Mormon-American version. In the former case, Allah tells the unborn souls how things will be, and they agree to this; in the latter case, everyone actually votes to say yes to God's plan of salvation.

At certain points the Mormon doctrines of God, the soul, and salvation appear to be closer to Böhmism than to Origenism. The doctrine that the eternal human spirit is made out of "God-stuff" is a version of the *creatio ex Deo* idea, previously encountered in Böhme (*DR* 5.3), Jane Lead (*DR* 5.7), Sergius Bulgakov (*DR* 8.6; 8.8), and some others. Some of Origen's interpreters (e.g., Jerome, Pierre-Daniel Huet, Gottfried Thomasius) held that Origen taught the essential divinity of the human soul, but this is more a matter of inference from Origen's known statements, while it is a matter of direct affirmation in Mormonism as well as in Böhme and Böhmism.[76] The Mormon teaching on a premundane conflict in the heavenly realm between Christ and Lucifer is also reminiscent of Böhme. Mormon authors Nielsen and Ricks speak of a "divine victory over the opposing powers of chaos" as a generalized feature of the mythology of the ancient Near East, thus linking Mormonism with these ancient cultures.[77] Yet in the *specific form* of the conflict and the victory (i.e., Christ defeating Lucifer in premundane battle), Mormonism much more closely resembles Böhmism than the mythologies of ancient Mesopotamia.

In its strikingly positive view of Adam and Eve's original sin and its necessity for humanity's spiritual progress, Mormon theology most closely resembles the

75. See Kazemi, "Mysteries of *Alast*." Cf. Qur'an 7:171–72.

76. For documentation and discussion of this question of Origen's view of the human self, see *DR*, 267n141, 421, 619n40.

77. Nielsen and Ricks, "Creation," 342.

philosophy of Hegel (*DR* 7.4–7.7). In each case, the fall is in some sense a "fall upward" or transition into new possibilities of spiritual progress and advancement. It is interesting to see that Hegel's interpretation of Genesis 3:22—"Then the LORD God said, 'Behold, the man has become like one of us in knowing good and evil'"—is much like that of Mormonism. For Hegel, God is not speaking ironically but literally, and it is humanity's sin that allows for the man and the woman to be or to become "like one of us." There is an obvious paradox here. In Hegel, this is the paradox that advancement toward God (i.e., the elevation of finite spirit to the infinite) requires an initial step of alienation from God (i.e., partaking of the forbidden fruit). In Mormonism, there is a related paradox: that to fulfill God's plan (i.e., to be physically fruitful and to multiply on earth), Adam and Eve had to violate what seemed to be God's plan (i.e., the command for them not to eat). Mormon author Arthur Bailey captures the contradiction when he writes, "In order to obey the command of God to multiply and people the earth, Adam and Eve transgressed the law."[78] To obey, they had to disobey.

In conclusion, we see that Mormon teachings on God, human selves, angels, sin, righteousness, spiritual progress, and final salvation show many points of contact with prior systems of thought, including those of Origen and Origenism, Böhme and Böhmism, the speculative thought of Hegel, and the Islamic idea of the Covenant of Alast. Despite these resemblances, it is also clear that Mormonism includes many innovative features and is a creative system with elements that are all its own.

78. A. Bailey, "Adam," 16.

Appendix L

Barth and Bultmann on Romans 5

The discussion of Karl Barth in chapter 9 argued that Barth's doctrine of election was as much a doctrine of *union with Christ* as it was a doctrine of *election by or with Christ*. One passage of Scripture that held great importance for Barth's interpretation of humanity is Romans 5:12–21, and Barth published a separate monograph focused on just these verses, *Christ and Adam: Man and Humanity in Romans 5* (1956). In this work Barth asserts that Adam does not *precede* Christ either chronologically or logically. Although Scripture calls Christ "the last Adam" (1 Cor. 15:45), Barth reverses the sequence so that Christ comes first rather than second. In this way, it is not Adam but only Christ who defines humanness.

In *Christ and Adam*, Barth writes that "man's nature in Adam is not, as is usually assumed, his true and original nature; it is only truly human at all in so far as it reflects and corresponds to essential human nature as it is found in Christ."[1] This means that "Adam is subordinate, because he can only be the forerunner, the witness, the preliminary shadow . . . of the Christ who is to come. . . . For Christ who seems to come second, really comes first, and Adam who seems to come first really comes second. . . . Our relationship to Adam depends for its reality on our relationship to Christ."[2] Barth's argument has far-reaching theological implications, in that Adam's eclipse by Christ implies the erasure of the created order by the work of redemption, as Barth

1. Barth, *Christ and Adam*, 43.
2. Ibid., 24.

interprets it. Redemption, then, is not so much a re-creation of the world as it is a first creation, wholly determined and defined by Christ. Conversely, the figure of Adam becomes almost as shadowy and unreal as Barth's doctrine of nothingness (DR 9.7). "The guilt and punishment we incur in Adam have no independent reality of their own," writes Barth, "but are only the dark shadows of the grace and life we find in Christ."[3] Basic to Barth's exegesis in *Christ and Adam* is the denial that Adam is in any sense a corporate head over humanity. Barth comments that "Adam . . . as man can represent humanity—but only as one among others. Thus he can represent all the others only in the same way that each of them can represent him. Adam has no essential priority of status over other men. He cannot be their lord and head; he cannot determine their life and destiny."[4]

Barth's *Christ and Adam* evoked a powerful retort from Rudolf Bultmann in the essay "Adam and Christ" (1962), which can be appreciated as a work of exegetical polemics even by those unpersuaded by other aspects of Bultmann's theology. "Since he himself [i.e., Barth] asserted that theological issues ought to be settled on the basis of exegesis, it seems appropriate to test critically his exegesis of Romans 5."[5] On Barth's exegesis of Romans 5:1–11, Bultmann comments: "Barth . . . does not interpret the section in the context of the letter [to the Romans] and thus not under the dominant question of the presence of salvation, or life. What interests him is the relationship between man and Christ, and he maintains that he must take from the text the thought that Christ as human individual at the same time includes in himself all other men."[6] Bultmann quotes from Barth's essay: "In believing in Him they are acknowledging that when He died and rose again, they, too, died and rose again in Him, and that, from now on, their life, in its essentials, can only be a copy and image of His." For "He is in them and they in Him—and that happens quite independently of any prior love towards God from their side."[7]

After citing this passage, Bultmann goes on to raise a number of critical questions. "One would like to know how, according to Barth, this 'being in' [Christ] is to be understood."[8] Bultmann claims that Barth's interpretation sub-

---

3. Ibid., 11.
4. Ibid., 45. Barth seems to forget his own strictures about Adam not being a "head" over humanity, since Barth affirms a reciprocal representative relation between Adam and Israel: "The history of Israel is the story of God's dealings with Adam—and of Adam's dealings with God—expanded so that it covers the continuing life of a whole people; the story of Adam is the history of Israel contracted into the life story of a single man" (25).
5. Bultmann, "Adam and Christ," 143.
6. Ibid., 150.
7. Ibid., citing Barth, *Christ and Adam*, 4.
8. Bultmann, "Adam and Christ," 150.

ordinates Romans 5:1–11 to 5:12–21 and that Barth interprets Romans 5:1–11 as he does "because he already has 5:12–21 in view, where that Christology [i.e., of humanity being "in Christ"] actually is present."[9] The experiential dimensions of Romans 5:1–11, which Barth passes over, become a focus in Bultmann's reading of the chapter. Paul's argument in 5:5 is that "we are certain of the divine love" and that "this certainty includes the certainty of the completion of our salvation in the future [and] is identical with the knowledge of the reception of the Spirit."[10] This bottom-up rather than top-down understanding of salvation in Romans 5:1–11 begins with the believer's experience of faith, in the power of the Holy Spirit, rather than with christological assertions regarding Jesus and his inclusive humanness. Bultmann shows that the experiential aspects of Romans 5:1–11, centering on the Holy Spirit, should not be neglected in favor of the unitive and representative themes of 5:12–21, centering on Christ. Thus Bultmann argues that there are two distinct christological strands in Romans 5 and that Barth pays attention only to one of them. "In 5:1–11 the substitutionary, or sacrificial, conception prevails [and] is formulated with the help of cultic, juristic conceptions of the Jewish tradition." In Romans 5:12–21, by contrast, "the Christology . . . is actually Gnostic"—Bultmann's term for the Pauline idea of being "in Christ." The exegetical problem is that "Barth apparently does not see this difference."[11]

Bultmann presents his overall construal of Romans 5:12–21, which he reads in a non-universalistic way:

> There is a basic difference between Adam and Christ. . . . For Adamic mankind there was no choice between death and life, but all were doomed to death. According to logical consequence all men after Christ should receive life. Of course Paul does not mean that; instead all men now face the decision whether they wish to belong to "those who have received [Rom. 5:17]," provided that the word of proclamation has already reached them. While Adam, then, brought death to all men after him without a possibility of escape, Christ brought for all the possibility (of life). One thing, however, is clear now: just as the fate of Adamic mankind is predestined by the trespass of Adam, so, to be sure, the *fate* of mankind after Christ is not predestined by the obedience of Christ, for this depends upon the decision of faith 'to receive.' However the fate of 'those who receive' is determined. . . . For them life is certain.[12]

9. Ibid. After mentioning Rom. 5:1–11, Barth adds that "in vv. 12–21 Paul does not limit his context to Christ's relationship to believers but gives fundamentally the same account of his relationship to all men" (*Christ and Adam*, 41–42). But Barth does not justify or explain this key assertion.

10. Bultmann, "Adam and Christ," 147.

11. Ibid., 150–51.

12. Ibid., 158.

Here is a reading that makes better sense of the text and its flow, in general terms, than Barth's reading.

Barth's difficulty in *Christ and Adam*, according to Bultmann, is that he interprets the text "without regarding the context of the Epistle and the leading question." Romans 5:12–21, in Barth's eyes, deals with "the secret and truth of *human nature* as such."[13] To make sense of the chapter as a whole, Barth must therefore insert an inferential relationship that is not actually stated in the text. In interpreting the relation of Romans 5:12–21 to 5:1–11, Barth "adds a 'because' . . . which is to apply to the entire section 5.12–21."[14] The effect of this is to make 5:12–21 the foundation for all that is said in 5:1–11. Barth might have read the text the other way, so that 5:1–11 is the foundation for 5:12–21. Alternatively, he might have read 5:1–11 and 5:12–21 as independent though perhaps complementary accounts of salvation in Christ. Instead, Barth's presuppositions require him to minimize the first half of the chapter and subordinate it to the latter half. Reading the chapter without Barth's presuppositions in mind and with emphasis on "those who receive" (5:17), it is possible to construe the relation of the two sections of Paul's chapter in a different way, and to see the theme of union with Christ in 5:1–11 as the ground of the statements of what Christ has accomplished for "those who receive" (5:17). With his focus on a preexisting union of Christ with all humanity without exception, Barth seems to have reversed the relationship between the two parts of Romans 5, according to Bultmann.

Barth does not accept that there is in Romans 5 an idea of a human existence apart from Christ, including in the period prior to Christ's coming. Barth's argument is that "our former existence outside Christ, rightly understood, was already a real, though still hidden, existence in Him." In the period prior to Christ's coming, "the same Jesus Christ, then, is already present there."[15] On this point, Bultmann writes: "Of that I am not able to see anything in the text. Paul says nothing about whether the Adamic mankind stood within the rule of Christ. Instead he sets the periods before and after Christ against each other purely as contrasts."[16] Barth seems to be engaged in eisegesis in finding a reign of Jesus Christ over humanity that somehow exists prior to Christ's earthly life. The biblical interpretation becomes detached from history as Christ's life and work become effectively eternalized.

Barth asserts that the essence or nature of humanity in Romans 5:12–21 is not determined with reference to Adam but rather in relation to Christ. The

13. Ibid., 162. Cf. Barth, *Christ and Adam*, 41: "Jesus Christ is the secret truth about the essential nature of man."
14. Bultmann, "Adam and Christ," 162.
15. Ibid.
16. Ibid.

humanity of Christ is the secret to humanity as such. Barth writes that "the relationship that existed between Adam and us is, according to verse 12, the relationship that exists originally and essentially between Christ and us."[17] So we have to understand Adam from Christ and not Christ from Adam. Adam is only in appearance the head of humanity. The seemingly second figure is truly the first, and the seemingly first figure is actually the second. Despite the opposing line of argument throughout Romans 5:12–21, Barth states that Adam is just one human being among others.[18]

Bultmann comments that, "in designating Adam in verse 14 as 'the prototype of the coming [one],'" Paul "asserts the contrary" of what Barth asserts. Likewise in 1 Corinthians 15:45–47, Paul "distinguishes . . . between Adam and Christ as the first and the second man and expressly rejects the reverse order." In short, in Romans "Paul does not reflect upon an original mankind whose head was Christ."[19] In Pauline thought, writes Bultmann, "grace . . . became an event" when Christ came into the world, and this was "in contrast to a grace from creation, if one can speak of such; which Paul certainly does not." "Something new (II Cor. 5.17) . . . was established [in] the rule of Christ under which the sinful Adamic mankind did not yet stand. Precisely this is veiled through Barth's exegesis."[20] Bultmann is thus questioning whether Barth does justice to the historicity and event-character of God's grace in Jesus Christ. Is grace the always-already state of all humanity as such, or is it something that comes by a decisive, historical work of God?

Bultmann notes too that Barth's idea that gospel precedes law means that "the purpose of the law in salvation history is not grasped." Barth has trouble with the phrase in Romans "that the transgression might increase" (Rom. 5:20), and he argues that this means that the gentiles were spared from their transgressions becoming apparent. The phrase "is not reckoned" (Rom. 5:13) also causes Barth trouble, and he applies it to the pagan and gentile worlds rather than to the span of time between Adam and Moses, which is clearly Paul's meaning in the context of Romans 5.[21]

Bultmann concludes his critique of Barth's exegesis by noting its implausibility and the way that it ultimately undoes itself:

> If for him [Barth] Adam is not the head of pre-Christian mankind but "one among others," who as such represents mankind, then Adam has become actually the idea

17. Ibid., citing Barth, *Christ and Adam*, 7.
18. Bultmann, "Adam and Christ," 163. "As man he [Adam] can represent humanity—but only as one among others" (Barth, *Christ and Adam*, 45).
19. Bultmann, "Adam and Christ," 163.
20. Ibid., 164.
21. Ibid.

of man, after all. . . . As the figure of Adam is changed into an idea, so Christ also seems to become an idea. If, according to Barth, he is "true man" as such, then he is nevertheless not the concrete historical man but the idea of "true" man. Since, according to Barth, now the unity of man and mankind belongs to the true human nature, it follows that "the sinful man also, whom we alone know, with respect to this unity of human nature reflects the human nature of Christ and thus has not ceased to be the true man and to show us the image of the true man." How one can read this out of Romans 5 is incomprehensible to me.[22]

In Barth's exegesis of Romans 5, Adam and Christ have both turned into ideas or idealizations of humanity, and neither of them touches the terra firma of fact and history.

---

22. Ibid., 165, citing Barth, *Christ and Adam*, 94.

Bibliography

Abrahamov, Binyamin. "The Creation and Duration of Paradise and Hell in Islamic Theology." *Der Islam* 79 (2002): 87–102.

Abrams, M. H. *Natural Supernaturalism: Tradition and Revolution in Romantic Literature.* New York: Norton, 1971.

Adam, Jens. *Paulus und die Versöhnung aller: Eine Studie zum paulinischen Heilsuniversalismus.* Neukirchen-Vluyn: Neukirchener Verlag, 2009.

Adam, Karl. "Zum Problem der Apokatastasis." *Theologische Quartalschrift* 131 (1951): 129–38.

Adams, John Coleman. "The Universalists." In *The Religious History of New England: King's Chapel Lectures,* by John Winthrop Platner et al., 295–321. Cambridge, MA: Harvard University Press, 1917.

Adams, Marilyn McCord. "Hell and the God of Justice." *Religious Studies* 11 (1975): 433–47.

Adams, Nehemiah. *Endless Punishment.* Boston: D. Lothrop & Co., 1878.

Adams, Nicholas. *The Eclipse of Grace: Divine and Human Action in Hegel.* Malden, MA: Wiley, 2013.

Adriaen, Marc, ed. *Jerome: Opera, Pars I, Exegetica 6, Commentarii in prophetas minores.* CCSL 76. Turnhout: Brepols, 1969.

Aitken, Jonathan. *John Newton: From Disgrace to Amazing Grace.* Wheaton: Crossway, 2007.

al-Ashqar, 'Umar Sulayman. *Paradise and Hell in the Light of the Qur'an and Sunnah.* Translated by Nasiruddin al-Khattab. 1986. Reprint, Riyadh: International Islamic Publishing House, 2002.

Alderfer, E. Gordon. *The Ephrata Commune: An Early American Counterculture.* Pittsburgh: University of Pittsburgh Press, 1985.

Aldwinckle, Russell. *Death in the Secular City: Life after Death in Contemporary Theology and Philosophy.* Grand Rapids: Eerdmans, 1974.

Aleksandr I. "O misticheskoi slovesnosti." In *Perepiska imperatora Aleksandra I s sestroi, Velikoi kniaginei Ekaterinoi Pavlovnoi.* Saint Petersburg: Velikii kniaz' Nikolai Mikhailovich, 1910.

Alexakis, Alexander. "Was There Life beyond the Life Beyond? Byzantine Ideas on Reincarnation and Final Restoration." *Dumbarton Oaks Papers* 55 (2001): 155–77.

Alexander, Archibald. *Universalism False and Unscriptural: An Essay on the Duration and Intensity of Future Punishment.* Philadelphia: Presbyterian Board of Publication, 1851.

Alexander, James. "Universalism and the Early Brethren." *Brethren Life and Thought* 32 (1987): 25–32.

Alfeyev, Hilarion. *Christ the Conqueror of Hell: The Descent into Hades from an Orthodox Perspective.* Crestwood, NY: St. Vladimir's Seminary Press, 2009.

———. *The Spiritual World of Isaac the Syrian.* Kalamazoo, MI: Cistercian Publications, 2000.

Alighieri, Dante. *The Comedy of Dante Alighieri the Florentine; Cantica 1: Hell.* Translated by Dorothy L. Sayers. London: Penguin, 1949.

Allen, Ethan. *Reason the Only Oracle of Man, or a Compenduous System of Natural Religion; Alternatively Adorned with Confutations of a Variety of Doctrines Incompatible to It; Deduced from the Most Exalted Ideas Which We Are Able to Form of the Divine and Human Characters, and from the Universe in General.* Bennington, VT: Haswell & Russell, 1784.

Allen, Joseph Henry, and Richard Eddy. *A History of the Unitarians and the Universalists in the United States.* New York: The Christian Literature Company, 1894.

Allen, Percy Stafford, ed. *Opus Epistolarum Des. Erasmi Roterdami.* 12 vols. Oxford: Clarendon, 1905–58.

Allen, Richard C. *David Hartley on Human Nature.* Albany: State University of New York Press, 1999.

Allin, Thomas. *The Question of Questions: Is Christ Indeed the Saviour of the World?* London: T. Fisher Unwin, 1885. 2nd ed., *Universalism Asserted.* London, 1887. Reprint, *Christ Triumphant: Universalism Asserted as the Hope of the Gospel on the Authority of Reason, the Fathers, and Holy Scripture.* Annotations by Robin Parry and Thomas B. Talbott. Eugene, OR: Wipf & Stock, 2015.

Allison, Henry E. *Lessing and the Enlightenment: His Philosophy of Religion and Its Relationship to Eighteenth-Century Thought.* Ann Arbor: University of Michigan Press, 1966.

Almond, Ian. "The Shackles of Reason: Sufi/ Deconstructive Opposition to Rational Thought." *Philosophy East and West* 53 (2003): 22–38.

Almond, Philip. *Heaven and Hell in Enlightenment England.* Cambridge: Cambridge University Press, 1994.

Althaus, Paul. *Die letzten Dinge.* 6th ed. Gütersloh: Bertelsmann, 1956.

———. *The Theology of Martin Luther.* Philadelphia: Fortress, 1966.

Althouse, Peter, and Robby Waddell, eds. *Perspectives in Pentecostal Eschatologies. World without End.* Eugene, OR: Pickwick, 2010.

Altizer, Thomas J. J. *The Apocalyptic Trinity.* New York: Palgrave Macmillan, 2012.

———. *The Descent into Hell: A Study of the Radical Reversal of the Christian Consciousness.* Philadelphia: Lippincott, 1970.

———. *Genesis and Apocalypse: A Theological Voyage toward Authentic Christianity.* Louisville: Westminster John Knox, 1990.

———. *The Genesis of God: A Theological Genealogy.* Louisville: Westminster John Knox, 1993.

———. *Godhead and the Nothing.* Albany: State University of New York Press, 2003.

———. *The Gospel of Christian Atheism.* Philadelphia: Westminster, 1966.

Altmann, Alexander. "Eternality of Punishment: A Theological Controversy within the Amsterdam Rabbinate in the Thirties of the Seventeenth Century." *Proceedings of the American Academy for Jewish Research* 40 (1972): 1–88.

———. "The Motif of 'Shells' (*Qelipoth*) in 'Azriel of Gerona." *Journal of Jewish Studies* 9 (1958): 73–80.

Alvarado, José Tomás, et al. "The Apostolic Exhortation *Amoris Laetitiae*: A Theological Critique." https://www.catholicculture.org /culture/library/view.cfm?recnum=11324.

———. "Letter to Cardinal Angelo Sodano, Dean of the College of Cardinals." June 29, 2016. https://www.catholicculture.org /culture/library/view.cfm?recnum=11324.

Amadou, Robert. *Louis-Claude de Saint-Martin et le Martinisme.* Paris: Éditions du griffon d'or, 1946.

Ambaum, Jan. "An Empty Hell? The Restoration of All Things? Balthasar's Concept of Hope for Salvation." *Communio* 18 (1991): 35–52.

Ambrosiaster. *Ambrosiaster: Commentaries on Romans and 1–2 Corinthians.* Edited by Gerald L. Bray. Downers Grove, IL: InterVarsity, 2009.

———. *In Epistola ad Romanos.* In *Ambrosiastri qui dicitur commentarius in epistulas Paulinas: Pars I.* Edited by Heinrich J.

Vogels. CSEL 81/1. Vienna: Hoelder-Pichler-Tempsky, 1966.

Ammerman, Nancy T. *Pillars of Faith: American Congregations and Their Partners*. Berkeley: University of California Press, 2005.

Anastasius. *Letter* 1 [to John of Jerusalem concerning Rufinus]. PL 20:68–73.

Andelson, Jonathan G. "The Community of True Inspiration from Germany to Amana Colonies." In *America's Communal Utopias*, edited by Donald E. Pitzer, 181–201. Chapel Hill: University of North Carolina Press, 1997.

Anderson, Gary A. "Is Purgatory Biblical? The Scriptural Structure of Purgatory." *First Things* 218 (November 2011): 39–44.

Anderson, Raymond Kemp. "Barth on Tillich: Neo-Gnosticism?" *Christian Century* 87 (1970): 1477–81.

Anderson, Wilson K. "Spirit Body." In D. H. Ludlow, *Encyclopedia of Mormonism*, 3:1405–6.

Andrews, C. F. *Sadhu Sundar Singh: A Personal Memoir*. London: Hodder & Stoughton, 1934.

Androutsos, Chrestos. *Dogmatikē tēs Orthodoxou Anatolikēs Ekklēsias*. Athens: Kratous, 1907.

Anklesaria, B. T., trans. *The Pahlavi Rivayat of Aturfarnbag and Farnbag-Sros*. Bombay: Published by P. K. Anklesaria at M. F. Cama Athornan Institute, 1969.

———, trans. and ed. *Zand-Akasih: Iranian or Greater Bundahishn*. Bombay: Rahnumae Mazdayasnan Sabha, 1956.

Anonymous. *A Course in Miracles*. 3 vols. N.p.: Foundation for Inner Peace, 1975.

———. "Everlasting Punishment." *Dublin Review* 88 (1881): 117–45.

———. Review of *Purgatory and the Means to Avoid It*, by Martin Jugie. *Orate Fratres* 24 (1950): 333–35.

———. "Rosamunde Juliane von Asseburg." In *Cyclopedia of Biblical, Theological, and Ecclesiastical Literature, Supplement*. Vol. 2, *Co–Z*, edited by John McClintock and James Strong, 1046. New York: Harper & Brothers, 1887.

———. *Universalism Tested by Reason and Revelation*. Philadelphia: Clayton, 1848.

Anrich, Gustav. "Clemens und Origenes als Begründer der Lehre vom Fegfeuer." In *Theologische Abhandlungen: Eine Festgabe zum 17. Mai 1902 für Heinrich Julius Holtzmann*, edited by Wilhelm Nowack et al., 97–120. Tübingen: J. C. B. Mohr, 1902.

Ansell, Nicholas. "The Annihilation of Hell and the Perfection of Freedom: Universal Salvation in the Theology of Jürgen Moltmann." In MacDonald [Parry], *"All Shall Be Well,"* 417–39.

———. *The Annihilation of Hell: Universal Salvation and the Redemption of Time in the Eschatology of Jürgen Moltmann*. Eugene, OR: Cascade, 2013.

Aphrahat. *Demonstratio XXII: De Morte et Novissimis Temporibus (Of Death and the Latter Times)*. In *Patrologia Syriaca*, edited by R. Graffin, 1:991–1050. Paris: Firmin-Didot, 1894. ET: *NPNF²* 13:402–12.

"Apokatastasis: The Doctrine of Reintegration." The Eleazar Institute. http://www.ordrereauxcroix.org.

Apophthegmata Patrum. In PG 65:71–441.

Aquinas, Thomas. *See* Thomas Aquinas

Argárate, Pablo. "Maximus Confessor's Criticism of Origenism: The Role of Movement within Ontology." In Perrone, *Origeniana Octava*, 1037–41.

Aristophanes. *The Frogs*. In *Aristophanes IV*, translated by Jeffrey Henderson, 3–236. LCL 180. Cambridge, MA: Harvard University Press, 2002.

Arjakovsky, Antoine. "The Sophiology of Father Sergius Bulgakov and Contemporary Western Theology." *St. Vladimir's Theological Quarterly* 49 (2005): 219–35.

Arkin, Marc M. "Song of Himself: Harold Bloom on God." *New Criterion* 10, no. 9 (1992). https://www.newcriterion.com/issues/1992/5/song-of-himself-harold-bloom-on-god.

Armitage, Duane. "Heidegger's Contributions to Philosophy: Pauline Meontology and Lutheran Irony." *Heythrop Journal* 55 (2014): 576–83.

Arnobius. *Arnobii Adversus Nationes, Libri VII.* Edited by Augustus Reifferscheid. CSEL 4. Vienna: C. Geroldi, 1875. ET: *ANF* 6:405–571.

Arnold, Gottfried. *Die Abwege oder Irrungen und Versuchungen gutwilliger und frommer Menschen, aus Beystimmung des gottseeligen Alterthums.* Frankfurt am Main, 1708.

———. *Gottfried Arnolds Gedoppelter Lebenslauf.* Lebenslauf: Campe, 1716.

———. *Wahre Abbildung des inwendiges Christentum.* Frankfurt am Main: Fritsch, 1709.

Asbill, Brian D. *The Freedom of God for Us: Karl Barth's Doctrine of Divine Aseity.* London: Bloomsbury T&T Clark, 2015.

Ashwin-Siejowski, Piotr. *Clement of Alexandria on Trial: The Evidence of 'Heresy' From Photius' Bibliotheca.* Leiden: Brill, 2010.

Augustine. *City of God.* Translated by Henry Bettenson. Harmondsworth, UK: Penguin, 1972.

———. *City of God.* Vol. 7, *Books 21–22.* Translated by William M. Green. LCL 417. Cambridge, MA: Harvard University Press, 1972.

———. *De baptismo contra Donatistas.* In CSEL 51, edited by M. Petschenig, 143–375. Vienna: F. Tempsky, 1908. ET: *NPNF*¹ 4:407–514.

———. *De civitate Dei [City of God].* In PL 41. ET: *NPNF*¹ 2:1–511.

———. *De Genesi contra Manichaeos.* In *S. Aur. Augustini Hipponensis Episcopi Opera Omnia,* 1:1046–1106. Paris: Beau, 1836.

———. *Enarrationes in Psalmos, I–L,* edited by E. Dekkers and J. Fraipont. CCSL 38. Turnhout: Brepols, 1990.

———. "The Enchiridion, Addressed to Laurentius; Being a Treatise on Faith, Hope, and Love." *NPNF*¹ 3:229–76.

———. *Enchiridion ad Laurentium, sive de Fide, Spe et Charitate.* In PL 40:231–90.

———. "Faith, Hope and Charity," in *Augustine: Christian Instruction; Admonition and Grace; The Christian Combat; Faith, Hope and Charity,* translated by Bernard M. Peebles, 369–472. FC 2. Washington, DC: Catholic University of America Press, 1947.

———. *On Genesis: Two Books on Genesis against the Manichees.* Translated by Roland J. Teske, 45–142. Washington, DC: Catholic University of America Press, 1990.

———. *Quaestiones Evangeliorum.* In *Aurelii Augustini Opera, Pars XIII.3.* Edited by Almut Mutzenbecher. CCSL 44B. Turnhout, Brepols, 1980.

———. *The Retractations.* Translated by Mary Inez Bogan. FC 60. Washington, DC: Catholic University of America Press, 1968.

———. *Sermon 113B.* In *Patrologia Latina Supplementum,* edited by E. Hamman, 2:446–49. 5 vols. Paris: Garnier, 1958–74.

Avens, Robert. "Re-visioning Resurrection: St. Paul and Swedenborg." *Journal of Religion and Health* 23 (1984): 299–316.

Baader, Franz von. *Franz von Baader's Sämmtliche Werke: systematisch Geordnete, durch reiche Erläuterungen von der Hand des Verfassers bedeutend vermehrte, vollständige Ausgabe der gedruckten Schriften sammt dem Nachlasse, der Biographie und dem Briefwechsel / hrsg. durch einen Verein von Freunden des Verewigten.* Edited by Franz Hoffmann et al. 16 vols. Leipzig: Bethmann, 1850–60.

———. *Vorlesungen über Jacob Boehmes Theologumena und Philosopheme.* In *Werke,* vol. 3. Leipzig, 1852.

———. *Vorlesungen und Erläuterungen über J. Boehmes Lehre.* In *Werke,* vol. 13. Leipzig, 1855.

Babcock, H. E. "Origen's Anti-Gnostic Polemic and the Doctrine of Universalism." *Unitarian Universalist Christian* 38 (1983): 53–59.

Backus, Isaac. *The Doctrine of Universal Salvation Examined and Refuted.* Providence: printed by John Carter, 1782.

Badcock, Gary. "Hegel, Lutheranism, and Contemporary Theology." *Animus* 5 (2000): 144–58.

Baghos, Mario. "Reconsidering *Apokatastasis* in St. Gregory of Nyssa's *On the Soul and Resurrection* and the *Catechetical Oration.*" *Phronema* 27 (2012): 125–62.

Bailey, Arthur A. "Adam." In D. H. Ludlow, *Encyclopedia of Mormonism,* 1:15–17.

Bailey, Margaret Lewis. *Milton and Jakob Boehme: A Study of German Mysticism in Seventeenth-Century England*. New York: Oxford University Press, 1914.

Baillie, John. *And the Life Everlasting*. London: Oxford University Press, 1934.

Baker, Sharon L. *Executing God: Rethinking Everything You've Been Taught about Salvation and the Cross*. Louisville: Westminster John Knox, 2013.

———. *Razing Hell: Rethinking Everything You've Been Taught about God's Wrath and Judgment*. Louisville: Westminster John Knox, 2010.

Bakewell, Sarah. *At the Existentialist Café: Freedom, Being, and Apricot Cocktails*. New York: Other Press, 2016.

Balas, David L. "*Plenitudo Humanitatis*: The Unity of Human Nature in the Theology of Gregory of Nyssa." In *Disciplina Nostra: Essays in Memory of Robert F. Evans*, edited by Donald F. Winslow, 115–31. Philadelphia: Philadelphia Patristic Foundation, 1979.

Ballou, Hosea. *The Ancient History of Universalism, from the Time of the Apostles, to Its Condemnation in the Fifth General Council, A.D. 553*. Boston: Marsh & Capen, 1829.

———. "Dogmatic and Religious History of Universalism in America." *Universalist Quarterly* 5 (1848): 81–83.

———. "Effect of Our Present Conduct on Our Future State." *Universalist Quarterly* 2 (1845): 39–51.

———. *An Examination of the Doctrine of Future Retribution, on the Principles of Morals, Analogy and the Scriptures*. Boston: Trumpet Office, 1834.

———. "Relation of Our Present Character to the Future." *Universalist Quarterly* 2 (1845): 312–20.

———. *A Treatise on Atonement*. Portsmouth, NH: Charles Pierce, 1812.

Ballou, Hosea, II. "Analogy between the Present State and the Future." *Universalist Quarterly* 4 (1847): 113–28.

———. *Counsel and Encouragement: Discourses on the Conduct of Life*. Boston: Universalist Publishing House, 1866.

Balthasar, Hans Urs von. *Apokalypse der deutschen Seele: Studien zur einer Lehre von letzten Haltungen*. 3 vols. Salzburg: Pustet, 1937–39. Reprint, Einsiedeln: Johannes, 1998.

———. "*Casta Meretrix*." In *Spouse of the Word*, vol. 2 of *Explorations in Theology*, 193–288. San Francisco: Ignatius, 1991.

———. "Christliche Universalismus." In *Verbum Caro*, vol. 1 of *Skizzen zur Theologie*, 260–75. Einsiedeln: Johannes, 1960.

———. *Cosmic Liturgy: The Universe according to Maximus the Confessor*. Translated by Brian E. Daley. San Francisco: Ignatius, 2003.

———. *Dare We Hope "That All Men Be Saved"? With a Short Discourse on Hell*. Translated by David Kipp and Lothar Krauth. San Francisco: Ignatius, 1988. Originally published as *Was dürfen wir hoffen?* (Einsiedeln: Johannes, 1986).

———. "The Final Judgment." In Balthasar, *Spirit and Institution*, 444–57.

———. *First Glance at Adrienne von Speyr*. Translated by Antje Lawry and Sergia Englund. San Francisco: Ignatius, 1981.

———. Foreword to *Méditations sur les 22 arcanes majeurs du Tarot*, by Valentin Tomberg, 7–16. Paris: Aubier Montaigne, 1980.

———. *Geschichte des eschatologischen Problems in der modernen deutschen Literatur*. 1930. Reprint, Einsiedeln: Johannes, 1998.

———. *The Glory of the Lord: A Theological Aesthetics*. 7 vols. San Francisco: Ignatius, 1984–91.

———. *The Grain of Wheat: Aphorisms*. Translated by Erasmo Leiva-Merikakis. San Francisco: Ignatius, 1995.

———. "The Metaphysics and Mystical Theology of Evagrius." *Monastic Studies* 3 (1965): 183–95.

———. *The Moment of Christian Witness*. Translated by Richard Beckley. Glen Rock, NJ: Newman, 1969.

———. *Mysterium Paschale: The Mystery of Easter*. Translated by Aidan Nichols. Edinburgh: T&T Clark, 1990. Reprint, San Francisco: Ignatius, 2000.

————. *The Office of Peter and the Structure of the Church*. Translated by Anree Emery. San Francisco: Ignatius, 1986.

————, "On Vicarious Representation." In Balthasar, *Spirit and Institution*, 415–22.

————, ed. *Origen: Spirit and Fire; A Thematic Anthology of His Writings*. Translated by Robert J. Daly. Washington, DC: Catholic University of America Press, 1984.

————. *Our Task: A Report and a Plan*. Translated by John Saward. San Francisco: Ignatius, 1994. Originally published as *Unser Auftrag: Bericht und Entwurf* (Einsiedeln: Johannes, 1984).

————. *Presence and Thought: An Essay on the Religious Philosophy of Gregory of Nyssa*. Translated by Mark Sebanc. San Francisco: Ignatius, 1995. Originally published as *Présence et pensée: Essai sur la philosophie religieuse de Grégoire de Nysse* (Paris: Beauchesne, 1942, 1988).

————. "Soloviev." In *Studies in Theological Styles, Lay Styles*, vol. 3 of *The Glory of the Lord: A Theological Aesthetics*, 279–352. Translated by Andrew Louth et al. San Francisco: Ignatius, 1986.

————. "Some Points of Eschatology." In *The Word Made Flesh*, vol. 1 of *Explorations in Theology*, 255–77. Translated by A. V. Littledale with Alexander Dru. San Francisco: Ignatius, 1989.

————. *Spirit and Institution*. Vol. 4 of *Explorations in Theology*. Translated by Edward T. Oakes. San Francisco: Ignatius, 1995.

————. *Theo-drama: Theological Dramatic Theory*. 5 vols. San Francisco: Ignatius, 1988–98. Originally published as *Theodramatik* (Einsiedeln: Johannes, 1973–83).

————. *Theo-logic: Theological Logical Theory*. 3 vols. San Francisco: Ignatius, 2000–2005. Originally published as *Theologik*, 3 vols. (Einsiedeln: Johannes, 1985–87).

————. *The Theology of Henri de Lubac: An Overview*. Translated by Joseph Fessio and Michael M. Waldstein. San Francisco: Ignatius, 1991.

————. *The Theology of Karl Barth: Exposition and Interpretation*. Translated by Edward T. Oakes. San Francisco: Ignatius, 1992.

Baltzly, Dirk. "Stoicism." In *The Stanford Encyclopedia of Philosophy*, edited by Edward N. Zalta. https://plato.stanford.edu/entries/stoicism. First published April 15, 1996; substantive revision December 6, 2013.

Balz, Horst Robert, Gerhard Krause, and Gerhard Müller, eds. *Theologische Realenzyklopädie*. Berlin: de Gruyter, 1977.

Balzac, Honoré de. *Séraphita*. Translated by Katherine Prescott Wormeley. Freeport, NY: Books for Libraries, 1970.

Bammel, Ernst. "Die Zitate aus den Apokryphen bei Origenes." In Daly, *Origeniana Quinta*, 131–36.

Barclay, Robert. *An Apology for the True Christian Divinity: Being an Explanation and Vindication of the Principles and Doctrines of the People Called Quakers*. 8th ed. London: J. Phillips, 1780.

Bardy, Gustave. "Rufin d'Aquilée." In *Dictionnaire de théologie catholique*, edited by A. Vacant, E. Mangenot, et al., 14/1:153–60. Paris: Letouzey, 1939.

Barhebraei, Gregorii. *Chronicon Ecclesiasticum*. Vol. 1. Edited by Johannes Baptista Abbeloos and Thomas Josephus Lamy. Louvain: Peeters, 1872.

————. "Extracts from the 'Book of Excerpts' and Other Writings of Gregory Bar-Hebraeus." In Marsh, *Book of the Holy Hierotheos*, 173–82.

bar Hiyya, Abraham (Savasorda). *Sefer Megilath ha-Megaleh*. Berlin: Hevrat Mekitse Nirdamim, 1924.

Barnard, Justin D. "Purgatory and the Dilemma of Sanctification." *Faith and Philosophy* 24 (2007): 311–30.

Barnhouse, Donald G. "Hell in Norway." *Eternity* (July 6, 1954): 11–13.

Barnstone, Willis, and Marvin Meyer, eds. *The Gnostic Bible*. Rev. ed. Boston: Shambala, 2009.

Barr, James. "The Question of Religious Influence: The Case of Zoroastrianism, Judaism, and Christianity." *Journal of the American Academy of Religion* 53 (1985): 201–35.

Barsanuphius. *Doctrina circa opiniones Origenis, Evagrii et Didymi*. In PG 86/1:891–900.

Barth, Karl. *Die Botschaft von der freien Gnade Gottes*. Zollikon-Zürich: n.p., 1947.

———. *Christ and Adam: Man and Humanity in Romans 5* Translated by T. A. Smail. Edinburgh: Oliver & Boyd, 1956.

———. *Church Dogmatics*. 14 vols. Edited by G. W. Bromiley and T. F. Torrance. 1942–68. Reprint, Edinburgh: T&T Clark, 1956–69.

———. *Credo: A Presentation of the Chief Problems of Dogmatics with Reference to the Apostles' Creed*. New York: Scribner's Sons, 1936. Originally published as *Credo: Die Hauptprobleme der Dogmatik dargestellt im Anschluss an das apostolische Glaubensbekenntnis* (Munich: Kaiser, 1935).

———. *The Epistle to the Romans*. Translated by Edwyn C. Hoskyns. London: Oxford University Press, 1933.

———. *Ethics*. Edited by Dietrich Braun. Translated by Geoffrey Bromiley. New York: Seabury, 1981.

———. "Fragebeantwortung bei der Konferenz des 'Weltbundes Christlicher Studenten' [1960]: 3: Über die Realität des Bösen und der Hölle." In *Karl Barth: Gesamtausgabe; Gespräche, 1959–1962*, edited by Eberhard Busch, 4:108–14. Zürich: Theologischer Verlag, 1995.

———. *Gesamtausgabe*. 47 vols. Zürich: Theologischer Verlag, 1971–2011.

———. "Gospel and Law." In *Community, State, and Church: Three Essays*, edited by David Haddorff, 71–100. Eugene, OR: Wipf & Stock, 2004. Originally published as *Evangelium und Gesetz* (Munich: Kaiser, 1935).

———. *Gottes Gnadenwahl*. Zürich: EVZ-Verlag, 1936.

———. *The Humanity of God*. Translated by Thomas Wieser and John Newton Thomas. Richmond: John Knox, 1960.

———. *Kirchliche Dogmatik*. 13 vols. Munich: Kaiser, 1932; Zürich: EVZ-Verlag, 1938–65.

———. *Protestant Theology in the Nineteenth Century: Its Background and History*. Translated by Brian Cozens and John Bowden. London: SCM, 1959, 1972, 2001. New ed., Grand Rapids: Eerdmans, 2002.

———. *The Theology of Schleiermacher*. Edited by Dietrich Ritschl. Translated by Geoffrey W. Bromiley. Grand Rapids: Eerdmans, 1982.

———. *The Word of God and the Word of Man: Lectures 1916–1924*. Translated by Douglas Horton. London: Hodder & Stoughton, 1928. Reprint, Gloucester, MA: Peter Smith, 1978.

Barth, Karl, and Rudolf Bultmann. *Briefwechsel, 1911–1966*. Edited by Bernd Jaspert. 2nd ed. *Karl Barth Gesamtausgabe* 5. Zürich: Theologischer Verlag, 1994.

Bartholomaeus, Michael. "Barth on Hell." *Reformed Theological Review* 74 (2015): 176–90.

Bartlett, Samuel C. *Lectures on Modern Universalism*. Manchester, NH: Fisk & Gage, 1856.

Bassett, Arthur R. "Endless and Eternal." In D. H. Ludlow, *Encyclopedia of Mormonism*, 2:454.

Bauckham, Richard. "Eschatology in *The Coming of God*." In Bauckham, *God Will Be All in All*, 1–34.

———. *The Fate of the Dead: Studies on the Jewish and Christian Apocalypses*. Supplements to Novum Testamentum 93. Leiden: Brill, 1998.

———. Foreword to *The Fire That Consumes: A Biblical and Historical Study of the Doctrine of Final Punishment*, by Edward W. Fudge, ix–x. 3rd ed. Eugene, OR: Cascade, 2011.

———, ed. *God Will Be All in All: The Eschatology of Jürgen Moltmann*. Edinburgh: T&T Clark, 1999.

———. *The Theology of Jürgen Moltmann*. Edinburgh: T&T Clark, 1995.

———. "Time and Eternity." In Bauckham, *God Will Be All in All*, 155–226.

———. "Universalism: An Historical Survey." *Themelios* 4 (1978): 47–54.

Baur, Ferdinand Christian. *Die christliche Gnosis; oder, Die christliche Religions-Philosophie in ihrer geschichtlichen Entwicklung*. Tübingen: Osiander, 1835.

Bawulski, Shawn. "Reconciliationism, a Better View of Hell: Reconciliationism and Eternal Punishment." *Journal of the Evangelical Theological Society* 56 (2013): 123–38.

Baxter, Richard. *Reliquiae Baxterianae; or, Mr. Richard Baxter's Narrative of the Most Memorable Passages of His Life and Times. Faithfully Published from His Own Original Manuscripts by Matthew Sylvester.* London, 1696.

Bayer, Oswald. *Theologie.* Gütersloh: Gütersloher Verlagshaus, 1994.

Bayle, Pierre. "Origen." In *The Dictionary Historical and Critical of Mr. Peter Bayle,* edited by Des Maizeaux, 4:412–22. 2nd ed. 5 vols. London: Midwinter, 1737.

Beale, G. K. "An Exegetical and Theological Consideration of the Hardening of Pharaoh's Heart in Exodus 4–14 and Romans 9." *Trinity Journal* 5 (1984): 129–54.

———. "The [Book of] Revelation on Hell." In Morgan and Peterson, *Hell under Fire,* 111–34.

Beatrice, Pier Franco. *The Transmission of Sin: Augustine and the Pre-Augustinian Sources.* Translated by Adam Kamesar. New York: Oxford University Press, 2013.

Beauchemin, Gerry. *Hope beyond Hell: The Righteous Purpose of God's Judgment.* Olmito, TX: Malista, 2007.

Becker, Matthew L. *The Self-Giving God and Salvation History: The Trinitarian Theology of Johannes von Hofmann.* New York: T&T Clark, 2004.

Beckwith, Clarence Augustine. "Apocatastasis." In *New Schaff-Herzog Encyclopedia of Religious Knowledge,* edited by Samuel Macauley Jackson, 1:211. New York: Funk & Wagnalls, 1908.

Becq, Annie. "Les traditions ésotériques en France de la Révolution à la Restauration." In *Manuel d'histoire littéraire de la France,* IV/1:274–301. Paris: Éditions sociales, 1972.

Bede. *Ecclesiastical History of the English People.* Rev. ed. London: Penguin, 1990.

Bedjan, Paul, ed. *Homiliae selectae Mar Jacobi Sarugensis.* 5 vols. Paris: Harrassowitz, 1905–10.

———. *Homiliae S. Isaaci: Syri Antiocheni.* Paris: Otto Harrassowitz, 1903.

———. *Mar Isaacus Ninevita, De perfectione religiosa.* Paris: Otto Harrassowitz, 1909.

Beeke, Joel R. *The Quest for Full Assurance: The Legacy of Calvin and His Successors.* Edinburgh: Banner of Truth, 1999.

Bell, Albert D. *The Life and Times of Dr. George de Benneville, 1703–1793.* Boston: Department of Publications of the Universalist Church of America, 1953.

Bell, Richard H. "Rom. 5:18–19 and Universal Salvation." *New Testament Studies* 48 (2002): 417–32.

Bell, Rob. *Love Wins: A Book about Heaven, Hell, and the Fate of Every Person Who Ever Lived.* New York: HarperOne, 2011.

———. *The Love Wins Companion: A Study Guide for Those Who Want to Go Deeper.* Edited by David Vanderveen. New York: HarperOne, 2011.

———. *What Is the Bible? How An Ancient Library of Poems, Letters, and Stories Can Transform the Way You Think and Feel about Everything.* New York: HarperOne, 2017.

Bell, Rob, and Kristen Bell. *The Zimzum of Love: A New Way of Understanding Marriage.* New York: HarperOne, 2014.

Bellarmino [Bellarmine], Roberto Francesco Romolo. *De Christo capite totius Ecclesiae, libri iv, De Christi Anima.* In *Disputationes de controversiis christianae fidei,* edited by Josephum Giuliano, 1:265–88. Neapoli, 1856.

———. *Disputationes Roberti Bellarmini e Societate Iesu, de controuersijs Christianae fidei, aduersus huius temporis haereticos: tribus tomis comprehensae.* 3 vols. Ingolstadt: Adami Sartorij, 1593–97.

Bender, Kimlyn J., and Bruce L. McCormack. *Theology as Conversation: The Significance of Dialogue in Historical and Contemporary Theology.* Grand Rapids: Eerdmans 2009.

Benedict XVI. *Encyclical Letter Spe Salvi of the Supreme Pontiff Benedict XVI to the Bishops, Priests and Deacons, Men and Women Religious and All the Lay Faithful on Christian Hope.* Ottawa: CCCB Publications Service, 2007.

Ben-Sasson, Haim Hillel, Raphael Jospe, and Dov Schwartz. "Maimonidean Controversy." In *Encyclopaedia Judaica,* edited by Michael Berenbaum and Fred Skolnik, 13:371–81. 2nd ed. New York: Macmillan, 2007.

Bente, Friedrich. "Controversy on Christ's Descent into Hell." http://bookofconcord.org/historical-19.php.

———. *Historical Introductions to the Book of Concord*. St. Louis: Concordia, 1965.

Bentham, Jeremy. *An Introduction to the Principles of Morals and Legislation*. London: Payne, 1789. Reprint, New York: Hafner, 1948.

Bentley, Todd. *The Journey into the Miraculous*. Shippensburg, PA: Destiny Image, 2008.

———. *Kingdom Rising: Making the Kingdom Real in Your Life*. Shippensburg, PA: Destiny Image, 2008.

———. *The Reality of the Supernatural World: Exploring Heavenly Realms and Prophetic Experiences*. Shippensburg, PA: Destiny Image, 2008.

Benz, Ernst. *Adam, der Mythus vom Urmenschen*. Munich: O. W. Barth, 1955.

———. "Der Mensch und die Sympathie aller Dinge am Ende der Zeiten (nach Jacob Boehme und seiner Schule)." In *Eranos-Jahrbuch 1955, Band XXIV*, edited by Olga Fröbe-Kapteyn, 132–97. Zürich: Rhein, 1956.

———. *The Mystical Sources of German Romantic Philosophy*. Translated by Blair R. Reynolds and Eunice M. Paul. Allison Park, PA: Pickwick, 1983. Originally published as *Les sources mystiques de la philosophie romantique allemande* (Paris: Vrin, 1968).

———. *Der Prophet J. Boehme*. Wiesbaden: Akademie, 1959.

———. "Theogony and the Transformation of Man in Friedrich Wilhelm Joseph Schelling." In *Man and Transformation: Papers from the Eranos Yearbooks*, edited by Joseph Campbell and translated by Ralph Manheim, 203–49. New York: Pantheon, 1964.

Berchman, Robert M. *Porphyry: Against the Christians*. Leiden: Brill, 2005.

Berdyaev, Nicolas. *The Beginning and the End*. Translated by R. M. French. New York: Harper, 1952.

———. *The Destiny of Man*. Translated by Natalie Duddington. London: Geoffrey Bles, 1937.

———. *The Divine and the Human*. Translated by R. M. French. London: Geoffrey Bles, 1949.

———. Introduction to *Six Theosophic Points and Other Writings*, by Jacob Böhme, v–xxxvii. Translated by John Rolleston Earle. Ann Arbor: University of Michigan Press, 1958.

———. *The Meaning of History*. Translated by George Reavey. New York: Scribner's, 1936.

———. "Mutnye liki" (1923). In *Filosofiia tvorchesvta, kul'tury i iskusstva*, 447–55. Moscow: Mir, 1994.

———. "Quenchers of the Spirit (Gasiteli Dukha) (1913)." Translated by Fr. Stephen Janos. http://www.chebucto.ns.ca/Philosophy/Sui-Generis/Berdyaev/essays/gasiteli.htm.

———. *Sobranie sochinenii*. 5 vols. Paris: YMCA Press, 1983–97.

———. "Studies concerning Jacob Boehme: Etude I; The Teaching about the Ungrund and Freedom." *Journal Put'* 20 (1930): 47–79. http://www.berdyaev.com/berdiaev/berd_lib/1930_349.html.

———. "Studies concerning Jacob Boehme: Etude II; The Teaching about Sophia and the Androgyne." *Journal Put'* 21 (1930): 34–62. http://www.berdyaev.com/berdiaev/berd_lib/1930_351.html.

Beresford Hope, A. J. B. "Future Punishment: The Present State of the Question, Considered in a Series of Papers on Canon Farrar's New Book." *Contemporary Review* 32 (1878): 545–50.

Bergara, Gary James. "The Orson Pratt–Brigham Young Controversies: Conflict within the Quorums, 1853–1868." *Dialogue: A Journal of Mormon Thought* 13 (1980): 7–49.

Bergjan, Silke-Petra. "Clement of Alexandria on God's Providence and the Gnostic's Life Choice: The Concept of *Pronoia* in the *Stromateis*, Book VII (with Appendix: Fragments from Clement of Alexandria, *Peri pronoias*)." In *The Seventh Book of the "Stromateis": Proceedings of the Colloquium on Clement of Alexandria (Olomouc, October 21–23, 2010)*, edited by Matyáš Havrda, Vít Hušek, and Jana Plátová, 63–92. Leiden: Brill, 2012.

Bergson, Henri. *Creative Evolution.* Translated by Arthur Mitchell. New York: Holt, 1913

Berkouwer, Gerrit Cornelis. *The Triumph of Grace in the Theology of Karl Barth.* Grand Rapids: Eerdmans, 1956.

———. "Universalism." *Christianity Today* 1, no. 16 (1957): 5–6.

Bernstein, Alan E. *The Formation of Hell: Death and Retribution in the Ancient and Early Christian Worlds.* Ithaca, NY: Cornell University Press, 1993.

Berry, Thomas. "Cosmic Person and the Future of Man." *Anima* 3 (1975): 20–29.

Bettis, Joseph D. "Is Karl Barth a Universalist?" *Scottish Journal of Theology* 20 (1967): 423–36.

Betz, John. "Translator's Introduction." In *Analogia Entis: Metaphysics; Original Structure and Universal Rhythm,* by Erich Przywara, 1–116. Translated by John R. Betz and David Bentley Hart. Grand Rapids: Eerdmans, 2014.

Bianchi, Ugo. "Origen's Treatment of the Soul and the Debate over Metensomatosis." In Lies, *Origeniana Quarta,* 270–81.

Bickell, Gustav, ed. *S. Ephraemi Syri Carmina Nisibena.* Leipzig: Brockhaus, 1866.

Bickle, Mike. *Encountering Jesus: Visions, Revelations, and Angelic Activity from IHOP-KC's Prophetic History.* Audio memoir. 2009. http://mikebickle.org/resources/series/38.

Bienert, Wolfgang A. "Zur Entstehung des Antiorigenismus im 3./4. Jahrhundert." In Perrone, *Origeniana Octava,* 829–42.

Bienert, Wolfgang A., and U. Kühneweg, eds. *Origeniana Septima.* Louvain: Peeters, 1999.

Bigg, Charles. *The Christian Platonists of Alexandria.* Oxford: Clarendon, 1886.

Bijlefeld, J. W. "Eschatology: Some Muslim and Christian Data." *Islam and Christian-Muslim Relations* 15 (2004): 35–54.

Binet, Étienne. *Du salut d'Origène.* Paris: Chez Sebastien Cramoisy, 1629.

Binns, John. Introduction to *Lives of the Monks of Palestine,* by Cyril of Scythopolis. Translated by R. M. Price. Kalamazoo, MI: Cistercian Publications, 1991.

Birks, Thomas Rawson. *The Difficulties of Belief in Connection with the Creation and the Fall, Redemption and Judgment.* 2nd ed. London: Macmillan, 1876.

———. *The Victory of Divine Goodness.* London: Rivingtons, 1867.

Bitton-Ashkelony, Brouria. "The Limit of the Mind (ΝΟΥΣ): Pure Prayer according to Evagrius Ponticus and Isaac of Nineveh." *Zeitschrift für antikes Christentum* 15 (2011): 291–321.

Blake, William. *Jerusalem: The Emanation of the Giant Albion; The Illuminated Books, Volume 1,* edited by Morton D. Paley. Princeton: Princeton University Press / William Blake Trust, 1991.

———. *The Marriage of Heaven and Hell.* New York: Oxford University Press, 1975.

Blakney, Raymond. *Meister Eckhart.* New York: Harper, 1941.

Blanchard, John. *Whatever Happened to Hell?* Durham, UK: Evangelical Press, 1993.

Blanchard, Laurence Malcolm. *Will All Be Saved? An Assessment of Universalism in Western Theology.* Milton Keynes, UK: Paternoster, 2015.

Bloch, Ernst. *Das Prinzip Hoffnung.* 2 vols. Frankfurt: Suhrkamp, 1959.

Blocher, Henri. "Everlasting Punishment and the Problem of Evil." In Cameron, *Universalism and the Doctrine of Hell,* 283–312.

Block, Daniel I. "The Old Testament on Hell." In Morgan and Peterson, *Hell under Fire,* 59–65.

Bloesch, Donald G. *Jesus Is Victor! Karl Barth's Doctrine of Salvation.* Nashville: Abingdon, 1976.

Blondel, Maurice. *Tagebuch vor Gott.* Einsiedeln, Switzerland: Johannesverlag, 1964.

Bloom, Harold. *The American Religion: The Emergence of the Post-Christian Nation.* New York: Simon & Schuster, 1992.

———. Foreword to *Absorbing Perfections: Kabbalah and Interpretation,* by Moshe Idel, ix–xiv. New Haven: Yale University Press, 2002.

Blosser, Benjamin P. *Become like the Angels: Origen's Doctrine of the Soul.* Washington,

DC: Catholic University of America Press, 2012.

Blowers, Paul M. "The Logology of Maximus the Confessor in His Criticism of Origenism." In Daly, *Origeniana Quinta*, 570–75.

Bloy, Léon. *Méditations d'un solitaire en 1916.* Vol. 9 of *Oeuvres.* Paris: Mercure de France, 1917.

Blue, J. Ronald. "Untold Billions: Are They Really Lost?" *Bibliotheca Sacra* 138 (1981): 338–50.

Blum, Edwin A. "Shall You Not Surely Die?" *Themelios* 4 (1979): 58–62.

Bobrov, E. *Literatura i prosveshchenie v Rosii XIX v. Materialy, issledovaniia i zametki.* 4 vols. Kazan: Tipo-lit. imp. Unta, 1901–2.

Boer, Charles, trans. *The Homeric Hymns.* Dallas: Spring, 1980.

Boersma, Hans. *Nouvelle Théologie and Sacramental Ontology: A Return to Mystery.* Oxford: Oxford University Press, 2009.

Bogaard, Milko. "Manifestations of the Martinist Order." http://omeganexusonline.net/rcmo/martinistorders.htm.

Bogdanov, A. P. *Russkie patriarkhi (1589–1700).* 2 vols. Moscow: Respublika, 1999.

Böhme, Jakob. *De electione gratia and Quaestiones theosophicae.* Edited by John Rolleston Earle. London: Constable, 1930.

———. *Signatura Rerum, Das ist: Von der Gebuhrt und Bezeichnung aller Wesen.* Amsterdam, 1682.

———. *Six Theosophical Points, and Other Writings.* Translated by John Rolleston Earle. London, 1919.

———. *Theosophische Sendbriefe.* 2 vols. Freiburg: Aurum-Verlag, 1979.

———. *The Works of Jacob Behmen, the Teutonic Philosopher.* Edited by William Law. 4 vols. London, 1764–81.

Bonaventura. *Opera omnia S. Bonaventurae,* vol. 4, *Commentarius in quatuor libros Sententiarum Petri Lombardi.* Claras Aquas (Quaracchi): Collegium S. Bonaventurae, 1887.

Bonda, Jan. *The One Purpose of God: An Answer to the Doctrine of Eternal Punishment.*

Translated by Reinder Bruinsma. Grand Rapids: Eerdmans, 1998.

Bonhoeffer, Dietrich. *The Communion of Saints: A Dogmatic Inquiry into the Sociology of the Church.* New York: Harper & Row, 1963.

———. *Letters and Papers from Prison.* Edited by Eberhard Bethge. London: SCM, 1967.

Bonner, Gerald. *St. Augustine of Hippo: Life and Controversies.* Philadelphia: Westminster, 1963. Reprint, Norwich, UK: Canterbury, 1989.

Borghesi, Francesco, Michael Papio, and Massimo Riva, eds. *Pico della Mirandola: "Oration on the Dignity of Man"; A New Translation and Commentary.* Cambridge: Cambridge University Press, 2012.

Borland, John. *Observations on the Moral Agency of Man.* Sherbrooke, QC: J. S. Walton, 1848.

Bornkamm, Heinrich. *Luther und Böhme.* Bonn: A. Marcus and E. Weber, 1925.

Boros, Ladislaus. *The Moment of Truth: Mysterium Mortis.* London: Search Press, 1972. Published earlier as *Mysterium Mortis: Der Mensch in der letzten Entscheidung,* 9th ed. (Freiburg: Olten, 1971).

Bostock, Gerald. "Origen and the Pythagoreanism of Alexandria." In Perrone, *Origeniana Octava,* 465–78.

———. "Origen: The Alternative to Augustine?" *Expository Times* 114 (2003): 327–32.

———. "Satan—Origen's Forgotten Doctrine." In Kaczmarek and Pietras, *Origeniana Decima,* 109–23.

———. "The Sources of Origen's Doctrine of Pre-Existence." In Lies, *Origeniana Quarta,* 259–64.

Boulanger, Nicolas-Antoine [a possible false authorial ascription for Baron d'Holbach = Paul Henri Thiry, 1723–89; and/or Denis Diderot, 1713–84]. *L'antiquité dévoilée par ses usages; ou Examen critique des principales, opinions, cérémonies & institutions religieuses & politiques des différens peuples de la terre.* Amsterdam: Chez Marc Michel Rey, 1766.

Boulton, David. "Militant Seedbeds of Early Quakerism: Winstanley and Friends." *Quaker Universalist Voice,* March 2005.

https://universalistfriends.org/library /militant-seedbeds-of-early-quakerism.

Bouwsma, William. *Concordia Mundi: The Career and Thought of Guillaume Postel.* Cambridge, MA: Harvard University Press, 1957.

Böwering, Gerhard. "Ideas of Time in Persian Sufism." In *Classical Persian Sufism from Its Origins to Rumi (700–1300),* vol. 1, *The Heritage of Sufism,* edited by Leonard Lewisohn, 199–233. 2nd ed. Oxford: Oneworld, 1999.

———. *The Mystical Vision of Existence in Classical Islam.* Berlin: de Gruyter, 1980.

Bowman, Paul Frank. "Illuminism, Utopia, Mythology." In *The French Romantics,* edited by D. G. Charlton, 1:76–112. 2 vols. Cambridge: Cambridge University Press, 1984.

Boyce, Mary. *History of Zoroastrianism.* 3 vols. Leiden: Brill, 1975–91.

———. *Zoroastrianism: Its Antiquity and Constant Vigour.* Costa Mesa, CA: Mazda Publishers in association with Bibliotheca Persica, 1992.

Boyer, Blanche B., and Richard McKeon, eds. *Peter Abailard, "Sic et Non": A Critical Edition.* Chicago: University of Chicago Press, 1977.

Brach, Jean-Pierre, and Wouter J. Hanegraaff. "Correspondences." In Hanegraaff et al., *Dictionary of Gnosis and Western Esotericism,* 275–79.

Bradley, Andrew Cecil. *A Commentary on Tennyson's "In Memoriam."* London: Macmillan, 1901.

Bradshaw, David. Review of *Apophasis and Pseudonymity in Dionysius the Areopagite: "No Longer I,"* by Charles Stang. *Modern Theology* 30 (2014): 159–61.

Brakke, David. *The Gnostics: Myth, Ritual, and Diversity in Early Christianity.* Cambridge, MA: Harvard University Press, 2010.

———. "A New Fragment of Athanasius's Thirty-Ninth *Festal Letter*: Heresy, Apocrypha, and the Canon." *Harvard Theological Review* 103 (2010): 47–66.

Brandt, Richard B. *The Philosophy of Schleiermacher.* New York: Harper & Brothers, 1941.

Braude, Ann. *Radical Spirits: Spiritualism and Women's Rights in Nineteenth-Century America.* 2nd ed. Bloomington: Indiana University Press, 2001.

Braun, Jon E. *Whatever Happened to Hell?* Nashville: Nelson, 1979.

Braund, Susanna Morton, trans. *Juvenal and Persius.* LCL 91. Cambridge, MA: Harvard University Press, 2004.

Bray, Gerald L., ed. *Ambrosiaster: Commentaries on Romans and 1–2 Corinthians.* Downers Grove, IL: InterVarsity, 2009.

———. *Documents of the English Reformation, 1526–1701.* 1994. Corrected reprint, Cambridge: James Clarke, 2004.

———. "Hell: Eternal Punishment or Total Annihilation?" *Evangel* (Summer 1992): 19–24.

Brecht, Martin. "Die Berleburger Bibel: Hinweise zu ihrem Verständnis." *Pietismus und Neuzeit* 8 (1982): 162–200.

Bregman, Jay. *Synesius of Cyrene.* Berkeley: University of California Press, 1982.

Breidert, Martin. *Die kenotische Christologie des 19. Jahrhunderts.* Gütersloh: Gütersloher Verlagshaus Mohn, 1977.

Breitman, Richard. *The Architect of Genocide: Himmler and the Final Solution.* New York: Knopf, 1991.

Bremond, Louis. *La conception catholique de l'enfer.* Paris: Librarie Bloud, 1904.

Bressler, Ann Lee. *The Universalist Movement in America, 1770–1880.* New York: Oxford University Press, 2001.

Briggs, E. R. "Mysticism and Rationalism in the Debate upon Eternal Punishment." *Studies on Voltaire and the Eighteenth Century* 24 (1986): 241–54.

Brinton, Howard H. *The Mystic Will: Based on a Study of the Philosophy of Jacob Boehme.* London: Allen & Unwin, 1931.

Brito, Emilio. "Création et eschatologie chez Schelling." *Laval théologique et philosophique* 42 (1986): 247–67.

———. "Création et temps dans la philosophie de Schelling." *Revue philosophique de Louvain* 84 (1986): 362–84.

———. *Hegel et la tâche actuelle de la christologie.* Paris: Lethielleux, 1979.

Broaddus, Richard, and Andrew Broaddus, eds. *Collection of Sacred Ballads*. Caroline County, VA, 1790.

Brock, Sebastian. Introduction to *Hymns on Paradise*, by Ephrem the Syrian, 7–75. Translated by Sebastian Brock. Crestwood, NY: St. Vladimir's Seminary Press, 1990.

Broderick, Carl, Jr. "Another Look at Adam-God." *Dialogue: A Journal of Mormon Thought* 16 (1983): 4–7.

Broer, Ingo. "Fegfeuer II: Biblischer Befund." In *Lexikon für Theologie und Kirche*, edited by Walter Kasper et al., 3:1204–5. 3rd ed. Freiburg: Herder, 1993–2001.

Bromiley, Geoffrey W. *An Introduction to the Theology of Karl Barth*. Grand Rapids: Eerdmans, 1979.

Bromley, Thomas. *The Way to the Sabbath of Rest. Or, the Souls Progresse in the Work of Regeneration; Being a Brief Experimental Discourse of the New-Birth. In which Many of the Serpents Wiles Are Detected: the Mysteries of the Crosse Unvailed: the Death of the Old Man, the Life of the New Man, the Angelicall Dispensation, with the Entrance into the Divine; Clearly Layed Open, and Discovered*. London: printed by John Streater, 1655.

Brooke, John L. *The Refiner's Fire: The Making of Mormon Cosmology, 1644–1844*. Cambridge: Cambridge University Press, 1996.

Brotherton, Joshua R. "Hans Urs von Balthasar on the Redemptive Descent." *Pro Ecclesia* 22 (2013): 167–88.

———. "The Possibility of Universal Conversion in Death: Temporality, Annihilation, and Grace." *Modern Theology* 32 (2016): 307–24.

———. "Presuppositions of Balthasar's Universalist Hope and Maritain's Alternative Eschatological Proposal." *Theological Studies* 76 (2015): 718–47.

———. "Universalism and Predestinarianism: A Critique of the Theological Anthropology That Undergirds Catholic Universalist Eschatology." *Theological Studies* 77 (2016): 603–26.

Brown, Dan. *The Da Vinci Code*. New York: Doubleday, 2003.

Brown, David. "No Heaven without Purgatory." *Religious Studies* 21 (1985): 447–56.

Brown, Gayle Oblad. "Premortal Life." In D. H. Ludlow, *Encyclopedia of Mormonism*, 3:1123–25.

Brown, Harold O. J. "Will Everyone Be Saved?" *Pastoral Renewal* 1 (1987): 1, 12–16.

———. "Will the Lost Suffer Forever?" *Criswell Theological Review* 4 (1990): 261–78.

Brown, Joanne Carlson. "Divine Child Abuse?" *Daughters of Sarah* (Summer 1992): 25–28.

Brown, Joanne Carlson, and Rebecca Parker. "For God So Loved the World?" In *Christianity, Patriarchy, and Abuse: A Feminist Critique*, edited by Joanne Carlson Brown and Carole R. Bohn, 1–30. New York: Pilgrim, 1989.

Brown, Louise Fargo. *The Political Activities of the Baptists and Fifth Monarchy Men in England during the Interregnum*. Washington, DC: American Historical Association, 1912.

Brown, Michael. *Hyper-Grace: Exposing the Dangers of the Modern Grace Message*. Lake Mary, FL: Charisma House, 2014.

Brown, Robert F. *The Later Philosophy of Schelling: The Influence of Boehme on the Works of 1809–1815*. Lewisburg, PA: Bucknell University Press; London: Associated University Presses, 1977.

———. "The Transcendental Fall in Kant and Schelling." *Idealistic Studies* 14 (1984): 49–66.

Browning, Christopher R. *The Origins of the Final Solution*. London: Heinemann, 2004.

Brunner, Emil. *The Christian Doctrine of Church, Faith, and the Consummation*. Vol. 3 of *Dogmatics*. Translated by David Cairns in collaboration with T. H. L. Parker. Philadelphia: Westminster; London: Lutterworth, 1962.

———. *The Christian Doctrine of God*. Vol. 1 of *Dogmatics*. Translated by Olive Wyon. Philadelphia: Westminster; London: Lutterworth, 1949. Originally published as *Die christliche Lehre von Gott* (Zurich: Zwingli-Verlag, 1946).

———. *Eternal Hope*. Translated by Harold Knight. London: Lutterworth, 1954.

Bruno, Giordano. *The Expulsion of the Triumphant Beast* Translated by Arthur D. Imerti. Lincoln: University of Nebraska Press, 2004 (first published in 1584).

Bruns, Hans. *Jakob Vetter: Der Gründer der Zeltmission*. Giessen: Brunnen Verlag, 1954.

Bryson, Michael. *The Tyranny of Heaven: Milton's Rejection of God as King*. Newark: University of Delaware Press, 2004.

Buckareff, Andrei A., and Allen Plug. "Escaping Hell: Divine Motivation and the Problem of Hell." *Religious Studies* 41 (2005): 39–54.

Bucur, Bogdan G. *Angelomorphic Pneumatology: Clement of Alexandria and Other Early Christian Witnesses*. Leiden: Brill, 2009.

———. "The Other Clement of Alexandria: Cosmic Hierarchy and Interiorized Apocalypticism." *Vigiliae Christianae* 60 (2006): 251–68.

Buehrens, John A. *Universalists and Unitarians in America: A People's History*. Boston: Skinner House, 2011.

Buenting, Joel, ed. *The Problem of Hell: A Philosophical Anthology*. Burlington, VT: Ashgate, 2010.

Buerger, David John. "The Adam-God Doctrine." *Dialogue: A Journal of Mormon Thought* 15 (1982): 14–58.

Buis, Harry. *The Doctrine of Eternal Punishment*. Grand Rapids: Baker, 1957.

Bulgakov, Sergei. *Agnets Bozhii* [*The Lamb of God*]. Moscow: Obshchedostupnyi Pravoslavnyi Universitet, 2000.

———. *The Bride of the Lamb*. Translated by Boris Jakim. Grand Rapids: Eerdmans, 2002. Originally published as *Neviesta agntsa* (Farnborough: Gregg, 1945).

———. *The Comforter*. Translated by Boris Jakim. Grand Rapids: Eerdmans, 2004.

———. "On the Question of the Apocatastasis of the Fallen Spirits." In *Sergius Bulgakov: Apocatastasis and Transfiguration*, 7–30. Translated and edited by Boris Jakim. New Haven: Variable Press, 1995.

———. *The Orthodox Church*. Crestwood, NY: St. Vladimir's Seminary Press, 1988.

———. *The Philosophy of Economy: The World as Household*. Translated by Catherine Evtuhov. New Haven: Yale University Press, 2000. Originally published as *Filosofiia khoziaistva* (Moscow, 1912).

———. "Piat' Let." In *S. N. Bulgakov: Pro et Contra*. St. Petersburg: Ruskii Khristianskii Gumanitarnyi Universitet, 2003.

———. "Po povodu vykhoda v svet shestogo toma sobraniia sochinenii Vladimira Sergeevicha Solov'eva." *Voprosy zhizni* 2 (1905): 361–68.

———. *Unfading Light: Contemplations and Speculations*. Edited and translated by Thomas Allan Smith. Grand Rapids: Eerdmans, 2012. Originally published as *Svet nevechernii: Sozertsaniia i umozreniia* (Moscow, 1917).

Bultema, Harry. "Emanuel Swedenborg." *Bibliotheca Sacra* 96 (1939): 319–34.

Bultmann, Rudolf. "Adam and Christ according to Romans 5." In *Current Issues in New Testament Interpretation: Essays in Honor of Otto A. Piper*, edited by William Klassen and Graydon F. Snyder, 143–65. New York: Harper & Brothers, 1962.

———. "Das christologische Bekenntnis des Ökumenischen Rates [1951]." In *Glauben under Verstehen: Gesammelte Aufsätze*, 2:246–61. 4 vols. Tübingen: Mohr, 1933–65.

———. *Jesus and the Word*. Translated by Louise Pettibone Smith and Erminie Huntress Lantero. New York: Scribner's Sons, 1958.

———. "Science and Existence [1955]." In *New Testament Mythology and Other Basic Writings*, edited by Schubert Ogden, 131–44. Philadelphia: Fortress, 1984.

Bundy, David. "The Philosophical Structures of Origenism: The Case of the Expurgated Syriac Version (S1) of the *Kephalaia gnostica* of Evagrius." In Daly, *Origeniana Quinta*, 577–84.

Bunge, Gabriel. "Origenismus-Gnostizismus, zum geistesgeschichtlichen Standort des Evagrios Pontikos." *Vigiliae Christianae* 40 (1986): 24–54.

Burci, Salvo. *Liber supra stella.* In *Beiträge zur Sektengeschichte des Mittelalters,* edited by J. J. Ignaz von Döllinger, 2:52–84. Münich, 1890.

Burfeind, Peter M. *Gnostic America: A Reading of Contemporary American Culture and Religion according to Christianity's Oldest Heresy.* Toledo, OH: Pax Domini, 2014.

———. "The Harrowing of Hell." *Logia* 18 (2009): 5–14.

Buri, Fritz. *Dogmatik als Selbstverständnis des christlichen Glaubens.* 3 vols. Bern: Paul Haupt, 1956–78.

———. "Entmythologisierung oder Entkerygmatisierung der Theologie." In *Kerygma und Mythos,* edited by H.-W. Bartsch, 2:85–101. Hamburg: Herbert Reich, 1952.

———. *Theologie der Existenz.* Bern: Paul Haupt, 1954.

Burmistrov, Konstantin. "Christian Orthodoxy and Jewish Kabbalah: Russian Mystics in the Search for Perennial Wisdom." In *Polemical Encounters: Esoteric Discourse and Its Others,* edited by Olav Hammer and Kocku Von Stuckrad, 25–54. Leiden: Brill, 2007.

———. "The Place of Kabbalah in the Doctrine of the Russian Freemasons." *Aries* 4 (2004): 27–68.

Burnet, Thomas. *De Statu Mortuorum et Resurgentium.* London: A. Bettesworth and C. Hitch, 1733.

Burnfield, David. *Patristic Universalism: An Alternative to the Traditional View of Divine Judgment.* 2nd ed. Charleston, SC: Create Space, 2016.

Burns, Norman T. *Christian Mortalism from Tyndale to Milton.* Cambridge, MA: Harvard University Press, 1972.

Burpo, Todd. *Heaven Is for Real: A Little Boy's Astounding Story of His Trip to Heaven and Back.* Nashville: Nelson, 2010.

Burton, Bryan. "Universalism." In *The Westminster Handbook to Karl Barth,* edited by Richard E. Burnett, 217–18. Louisville: Westminster John Knox, 2013.

Burton, John. "Abrogation." In *Encyclopedia of the Qur'ān.* Vol. 1, A–D, edited by Jane Dammen McAuliffe, 11–19. Brill: Leiden, 2001.

Burton, Rulon T. *We Believe: Doctrines and Principles of the Church of Jesus Christ of Latter-Day Saints.* Draper, UT: Tabernacle, 2004.

Busch, Eberhard. *Karl Barth: His Life from Letters and Autobiographical Texts.* Philadelphia: Fortress, 1976.

———. "Memories of Karl Barth." In *How Karl Barth Changed My Mind,* edited by Donald K. McKim, 9–14. Grand Rapids: Eerdmans, 1986. Reprint, Eugene, OR: Wipf & Stock, 1998.

Bushman, Richard Lyman. *Joseph Smith: Rough Stone Rolling.* New York: Knopf, 2005.

Butterworth, G. W., trans. *"On First Principles": Being Koetschau's Text of the "De principiis" Translated into English, Together with an Introduction and Notes,* by Origen. 1966. Reprint, Gloucester, MA: Peter Smith, 1973.

Byrne, Brendan. "Christ's Pre-Existence in Pauline Soteriology." *Theological Studies* 58 (1997): 308–30.

Cain, James. "On the Problem of Hell." *Religious Studies* 38 (2002): 355–62.

Calian, Carnegie Samuel. *The Significance of Eschatology in the Thought of Nicolas Berdyaev.* Leiden: Brill, 1965.

Calvin, John. *Institutes of the Christian Religion.* 2 vols. Edited by John T. McNeill. Translated by Ford Lewis Battles. London: SCM, 1961.

———. "Psychopannychia; or, The Soul's Imaginary Sleep between Death and Judgement." *Tracts Relating to the Reformation,* 3:413–90. Translated by Henry Beveridge. Edinburgh: Calvin Translation Society, 1851.

———. *Vivere apud Christum non dormire animis sanctos, qui in fide Christi decedunt: assertio [Psychopannychia].* Argentorati: Per Wendelinum Rihelium, 1542.

Cameron, Nigel M. de S., ed. *Universalism and the Doctrine of Hell: Papers Presented at the Fourth Edinburgh Conference on Christian Dogmatics, 1991.* Carlisle, UK: Paternoster; Grand Rapids: Baker, 1992.

———. "Universalism and the Logic of Revelation." *Evangelical Review of Theology* 11 (1987): 311–35.

Campbell, Alexander, and Dolphus Skinner. *Discussion of the Doctrine of Endless Misery and Universal Salvation.* Utica, NY: C. C. P. Grosh, 1840.

Campbell, Donald, ed. *Memorials of John McLeod Campbell, D.D., Being Selections from His Correspondence.* 2 vols. London: Macmillan, 1877.

Campbell, Joseph. *The Masks of God: Creative Mythology.* New York: Viking, 1968.

Camplani, Alberto. "Per la cronologia di testi valentiniani: *Il Trattato Tripartito* e la crisa ariana." *Cassiodorus* 1 (1995): 171–95.

Camus, Albert. *The Rebel: An Essay on Man in Revolt.* Translated by Anthony Bower. New York: Knopf, 1956.

Cannon, Donald Q. "King Follett Discourse." In D. H. Ludlow, *Encyclopedia of Mormonism*, 2:791–92.

Cannon, Elaine Anderson. "Mother in Heaven." In D. H. Ludlow, *Encyclopedia of Mormonism*, 2:961.

Capéran, Louis. *Le problème de salut des infidèles.* 2 vols. Toulouse: Grand Séminaire, 1934.

Capon, Robert. *Health, Money and Love . . . and Why We Don't Enjoy Them.* Grand Rapids: Eerdmans, 1990.

Capp, B. S. *The Fifth Monarchy Men: A Study in Seventeenth-Century English Millenarianism.* London: Faber, 1972.

Cappuyns, Maïeul. *Jean Scot Erigène, sa vie, son œuvre, sa pensée.* Bruxelles: Culture et Civilisation, 1964.

Caputo, John D. *The Weakness of God: A Theology of the Event.* Bloomington: Indiana University Press, 2006.

Carlson, Maria. "Fashionable Occultism: Spiritualism, Theosophy, Freemasonry, and Hermeticism in *Fin de Siècle* Russia." In *The Occult in Russian and Soviet Culture*, edited by Bernice Glatzer Rosenthal, 135–52. Ithaca, NY: Cornell University Press, 1997.

———. "Gnostic Elements in the Cosmogony of Vladimir Solovyov." In *Russian Religious Thought*, edited by Judith Deutsch Kornblatt and Richard F. Gustafson, 49–67. Madison: University of Wisconsin Press, 1996.

Carnell, E. J. "Hell Is Irrational." In *An Introduction to Christian Apologetics*, 349–50. Grand Rapids: Eerdmans, 1948.

Carpenter, Lant. *An Examination of the Charges Made against Unitarians and Unitarianism . . . by the Rt. Rev. Dr. Magee, Bishop of Raphoe.* Bristol, UK: T. J. Manchee, 1820.

Carrouges, Michel, et al. *L'enfer.* Foi vivante. Paris: Les Éditions de la Revue des Jeunes, 1950.

Carson, Donald A. *Divine Sovereignty and Human Responsibility: Biblical Perspectives in Tension.* Atlanta: John Knox, 1981.

Carter, K. Codell. "Godhood." In D. H. Ludlow, *Encyclopedia of Mormonism*, 2:553–55.

Casey, John. *After Lives: A Guide to Heaven, Hell, and Purgatory.* Oxford University Press, 2009.

Casey, Robert P. "Clement of Alexandria and the Beginnings of Christian Platonism." *Harvard Theological Review* 18 (1925): 39–101.

Casiday, Augustine, ed. and trans. *Evagrius Ponticus.* New York: Routledge, 2006.

———. *Reconstructing the Theology of Evagrius Ponticus: Beyond Heresy.* Cambridge: Cambridge University Press, 2013.

———. "Universal Restoration in Evagrius Ponticus' 'Great Letter.'" In *Studia Patristica*, vol. 47, edited by J. Baun, A. Cameron, M. Edwards, and M. Vinzent, 223–38. Leuven: Peeters, 2010.

Cassara, Ernest. "Hosea Ballou." http://uudb .org/articles/hoseaballou.html.

———. *Hosea Ballou: The Challenge to Orthodoxy.* Boston: Beacon, 1961.

———. *Universalism in America: A Documentary History.* Boston: Beacon, 1971.

Cassidy, James J. "Election and Trinity." *Westminster Theological Journal* 71 (2009): 53–81.

Cassiodorus. *De institutione divinarum litterarum.* In PL 70:1105–50.

Castellano, Daniel J. "Origen and Origenism." Arcane Knowledge. http://www .arcaneknowledge.org/catholic/origen.htm.

Catechism of the Catholic Church. New York: Doubleday, 1994.

Catherine of Genoa. *Purgation and Purgatory; The Spiritual Dialogue.* Translated by Serge Hughes. Classics of Western Spirituality. New York: Paulist Press, 1979.

Cazier, Pierre, ed. *Isodorus Hispalensis Sententiae.* CCSL 111. Turnhout: Brepols, 1998.

Chaadaev, Peter. "First Philosophical Letter [1836]." In *Philosophical Works of Peter Chaadaev,* edited by Raymond T. McNally and Richard Tempest. Boston: Kluwer Academic, 1991.

Chadwick, Henry, trans. *Contra Celsum,* by Origen. Cambridge: Cambridge University Press, 1980.

———. *Early Christian Thought and the Classical Tradition.* Oxford: Oxford University Press, 1966.

Chan, Francis, and Preston M. Sprinkle. *Erasing Hell: What God Said about Eternity, and the Things We Made Up.* Colorado Springs: David C. Cook, 2011.

Chaplin, Geoff. Review of *Gnostic Apocalyse,* by Cyril O'Regan. *Journal of Religion* 85 (2005): 115–17.

Chaput, Charles J. *Strangers in a Strange Land: Living the Catholic Faith in a Post-Christian World.* New York: Henry Holt, 2017.

Charles, R. H., ed. *The Ascension of Isaiah, Translated from the Ethiopic Version, Which, Together with the New Greek Fragment, the Latin Version and the Latin Translation of the Slavonic, Is Here Published in Full.* London: Adam and Charles Black, 1900.

———. *The Book of Enoch the Prophet.* 1912. Reprint, San Francisco: Weiser, 2012.

Charlesworth, James H., ed. *The Old Testament Pseudepigrapha.* 2 vols. New York: Doubleday, 1983–85.

Chauncy, Charles. *The Mystery Hid from Ages and Generations: Made Manifest by the Gospel-Revelation: or, the Salvation of All Men the Grand Thing Aimed at in the Scheme of God.* London: printed for Charles Dilly, 1784.

———. *Salvation for All Men, Illustrated and Vindicated as a Scripture Doctrine: In Numerous Extracts from a Variety of Pious and Learned Men, Who Have Purposely Writ upon the Subject: Together with Their Answer to the Objections Urged against It.* Boston: printed and sold by T. and J. Fleet, 1782.

Cherok, Richard J. "'We Fraternize With None': Alexander Campbell and the Question of Universalism." *Discipliana* 67 (2008): 5–22.

Chittick, William C. "Ibn 'Arabi." In *History of Islamic Philosophy,* edited by Seyyed Hossein Nasr and Oliver Leaman, 1:497–509. London: Routledge, 1996.

———. *Imaginal Worlds: Ibn al-'Arabi and the Problem of Religious Diversity.* Albany: State University of New York Press, 1994.

———. "Muslim Eschatology." In *The Oxford Handbook to Eschatology,* edited by Jerry L. Walls, 132–50. New York: Oxford University Press, 2007.

———. "Rumi and the Mawlawiyyah." In *Islamic Spirituality: Manifestations,* edited by Seyyed Hossein Nasr, 105–26. New York: Crossroad, 1991.

———. *The Self-Disclosure of God: Principles of Ibn al-'Arabi's Cosmology.* Albany: State University of New York Press, 1998.

———. *The Sufi Path of Knowledge.* Albany: State University of New York Press, 1989.

———. *The Sufi Path of Love: The Spiritual Teachings of Rumi.* Albany: State University of New York Press, 1994.

Cho, Dongsun. *St. Augustine's Doctrine of Eternal Punishment: His Biblical and Theological Argument.* Lewiston, NY: Edwin Mellen, 2010.

Choufrine, Arkadi. *Gnosis, Theophany, Theosis: Studies in Clement of Alexandria's Appropriation of His Background.* New York: Lang, 2001.

Chretien, Claire. "Full Text of 45 Theologians' Appeal to Correct *Amoris Laetitia*'s Errors Revealed." Lifesite News, July 28, 2016. https://www.lifesitenews.com/news/full-text-of-45-theologians-appeal-to-correct-amoris-laetitias-errors-revea.

Chryssavgis, John, trans. *Barsanuphius and John: Letters.* 2 vols. FC 113–14. Washington, DC: Catholic University of America Press, 2006–7.

Church of England. *The Thirty-Nine Articles, and the Constitutions and Canons, of the Church of England: Together with Several Acts of Parliament and Proclamations*. London: printed by Charles Eyre and William Strahan, 1773.

Church of England, Archbishop's Commission on Doctrine. *Doctrine in the Church of England: The Report of the Commission on Christian Doctrine Appointed by the Archbishop of Canterbury and York in 1922*. New York: Macmillan, 1938.

Church of Jesus Christ of Latter-Day Saints. *The Book of Mormon, the Doctrine and Covenants, the Pearl of Great Price*. Salt Lake City: Church of Jesus Christ of Latter-Day Saints, 1981.

———. *Messages of the First Presidency*, 5 vols. Edited by J. Clark. Salt Lake City: Bookcraft, 1965–75.

Churton, Tobias. *Gnostic Philosophy: From Ancient Persia to Modern Times*. Rochester, VT: Inner Traditions, 2005.

———. "Jacob Böhme's Theosophic Cosmos." In Churton, *Gnostic Philosophy*, 234–59.

Clark, Elizabeth A. "John Chrysostom and the 'Subintroductae.'" *Church History* 46 (1977): 171–85.

———. *The Origenist Controversy: The Cultural Construction of an Early Christian Debate*. Princeton: Princeton University Press, 1992.

———. "The Place of Jerome's Commentary on Ephesians in the Origenist Controversy: The *Apokatastasis* and Ascetic Ideals." *Vigiliae Christianae* 41 (1987): 154–71.

Clark, Gordon. *Religion, Reason, and Revelation*. Philadelphia: P&R, 1961.

Clark, Mary T. *Augustine, Philosopher of Freedom: A Study in Comparative Philosophy*. New York: Desclée, 1958.

Clark, Peter. *Zoroastrianism: An Introduction to an Ancient Faith*. Brighton, UK: Sussex Academic, 1998.

Clarke, Oliver Fielding. *Introduction to Berdyaev*. London: Geoffrey Bles, 1950.

Clarke, R. F. "On the Mitigation of Punishment in Hell." *Irish Theological Record* 14 (1893): 481–97.

Clarkson, George E. *The Mysticism of William Law*. New York: Lang, 1992.

Clayton, Philip. *Adventures in the Spirit: God, World, Divine Action*. Edited by Zachary Simpson. Minneapolis: Fortress, 2008.

———. "Panentheist Internalism: Living within the Presence of the Trinitarian God." *Dialog: A Journal of Theology* 40 (2001): 208–15.

———. *The Problem of God in Modern Thought*. Grand Rapids: Eerdmans, 2000.

Clayton, Philip, and Arthur Peacocke, eds. *In Whom We Live and Move and Have Our Being: Panentheistic Reflections on God's Presence in a Scientific World*. Grand Rapids: Eerdmans, 2004.

Clement of Alexandria. *Stromata I–VI*. Edited by O. Stählin. 3rd ed. GCS 52. Berlin: Akademie Verlag, 1972. ET: *ANF* 2:299–567.

Climenhaga, Arthur M. "Mission and Neo-Universalism." *Evangelical Review of Theology* 28 (2004): 1–20.

Clymer, Wayne K. "The Life and Thought of James Relly." *Church History* 11 (1942): 193–216.

Coakley, Sarah. "Introduction: Re-thinking Dionysius the Areopagite." *Modern Theology* 24 (2008): 531–40.

Coakley, Sarah, and Charles M. Stang, eds. *Re-thinking Dionysius the Areopagite*. Oxford: Blackwell, 2009.

Cohen, Martin Samuel. *The Shi'ur Qomah: Liturgy and Theurgy in Pre-Kabbalistic Jewish Mysticism*. Lanham, MD: University Press of America, 1983.

Cohn, Norman. *The Pursuit of the Millennium: Revolutionary Millenarians and Mystical Anarchists of the Middle Ages*. Rev. ed. New York: Oxford University Press, 1970.

Colberg, Ehregott Daniel. *Das platonisch-hermetisches Christenthum*. Leipzig: Gleditsch, 1710.

Coleridge, Samuel Taylor. *Aids to Reflection in the Formation of a Manly Character on the Several Grounds of Prudence, Morality, and Religion*. London: printed for Taylor and Hessey, 1825.

———. *Biographia Literaria; or, Biographical Sketches of My Life and Opinions.* 2nd ed. 2 vols. in 3. London: William Pickering, 1847.

———. *Collected Letters of Samuel Taylor Coleridge.* Edited by Earl Leslie Griggs. 6 vols. Oxford: Clarendon, 1956–71.

———. *The Literary Remains of Samuel Taylor Coleridge.* Edited by Henry Nelson Coleridge. 4 vols. London: William Pickering, 1836–39.

———. *Specimens of the Table Talk of the Late Samuel Taylor Coleridge.* 2 vols. London: John Murray, 1835.

Colish, Marcia L. *The Stoic Tradition from Antiquity to the Early Middle Ages.* 2 vols. Studies in the History of Christian Thought 24–25. Leiden: Brill, 1985.

Collins, John J. "The Zeal of Phineas: The Bible and the Legitimation of Violence." *Journal of Biblical Literature* 122 (2003): 3–21.

Collins Winn, Christian T. *"Jesus Is Victor!": The Significance of the Blumhardts for the Theology of Karl Barth.* Eugene, OR: Pickwick, 2009.

Collins Winn, Christian T., and Peter Goodwin Heltzel. "'Before Bloch There Was Blumhardt': A Thesis on the Origins of the Theology of Hope." *Scottish Journal of Theology* 62 (2009): 26–39.

Colwell, John. "The Contemporaneity of the Divine Decision: Reflections on Barth's Denial of Universalism." In Cameron, *Universalism and the Doctrine of Hell,* 139–60.

———. "The Glory of God's Justice and the Glory of God's Grace: Contemporary Reflections on the Doctrine of Hell in the Teachings of Jonathan Edwards." In *Called to One Hope: Perspectives on the Life to Come,* edited by J. Colwell, 113–29. Carlisle, UK: Paternoster, 2000.

Comoth, Katharina. "*Hegemonikon*: Meister Eckharts Rückgriff auf Origenes." In Lies, *Origeniana Quarta,* 265–69.

Congar, Yves. "La crédibilité des révélations privées." *Supplément de la vie spirituelle* 53 (1937): 29–48.

Congdon, David W. *The God Who Saves: A Dogmatic Sketch.* Eugene, OR: Cascade, 2016.

———. *The Mission of Demythologizing: Rudolf Bultmann's Dialectical Theology.* Minneapolis: Fortress, 2015.

Congregation for the Doctrine of the Faith. *Dominus Iesus* (On the Unicity and Salvific Universality of Jesus Christ). Vatican website. August 6, 2000. http://www.vatican.va/roman_curia/congregations/cfaith/documents/rc_con_cfaith_doc_20000806_dominus-iesus_en.html.

———. "Notification on the Book *Toward a Christian Theology of Religious Pluralism* . . . by Father Jacques Dupuis, S.J." Vatican website. January 24, 2001. http://www.vatican.va/roman_curia/congregations/cfaith/documents/rc_con_cfaith_doc_20010124_dupuis_en.html.

Connell, Francis. "Again the Doctrine of Hell." *Homiletic and Pastoral Review* 35 (January 1935): 368–83.

———. "Is the Fire of Hell Eternal and Real?" *Homiletic and Pastoral Review* 34 (September 1934): 1250–60.

Conquest, Robert. *The Great Terror: Stalin's Purge of the Thirties.* Rev. ed. New York: Collier, 1975.

———. *The Harvest of Sorrow: Soviet Collectivization and the Terror-Famine.* New York: Oxford University Press, 1986.

Constable, Henry. *Hades; or, The Intermediate State of Man.* 2nd ed. London: Kellaway, 1875.

Constas, Nicholas. Introduction to *On Difficulties in the Church Fathers: The Ambigua,* by Maximus the Confessor, 1:vii–xxxii. Translated by Nicholas Constas. 2 vols. Dumbarton Oaks Medieval Library. Cambridge, MA: Harvard University Press, 2014.

[Conway, Anne]. *The Principles of the Most Ancient and Modern Philosophy.* London, 1692.

Conway, Eamonn. *The Anonymous Christian: A Relativised Christianity? An Evaluation of Hans Urs von Balthasar's Criticisms of Karl Rahner's Theory of the Anonymous Christian.* Frankfurt am Main: Lang, 1993.

Conzelmann, Hans, and Walther Zimmerli. "χαίρω κτλ." In *Theological Dictionary of the New Testament*, edited by Gerhard Kittel and Gerhard Friedrich, 9:359–415. Translated by Geoffrey Bromiley. Grand Rapids: Eerdmans, 1974.

Cooke, Parsons. *Modern Universalism Exposed*. Lowell, MA: Asa Rand, 1834.

Cooper, Brian. "Festival Play Poses Faith Questions." *Church of England Newspaper*, August 21, 2015. http://www.churchnews paper.com/wp-content/uploads/2015/08 /coen_17-08-2015.pdf.

Cooper, John W. *Panentheism: The Other God of the Philosophers—From Plato to the Present*. Grand Rapids: Baker Academic, 2006.

Coover-Cox, Dorian G. "The Hardening of Pharaoh's Heart in Its Literary and Cultural Context." *Bibliotheca Sacra* 163 (2006): 292–311.

Cope, Jackson I. *Joseph Glanvill: Anglican Apologist*. St. Louis: Committee on Publications, Washington University, 1956.

Copenhaver, Brian P., trans. *Hermetica: The Greek "Corpus Hermeticum" and the Latin "Asclepius" in a New English Translation*. Cambridge: Cambridge University Press, 1992.

Copleston, Frederick C. "Hegel and the Rationalization of Mysticism." In *New Studies in Hegel's Philosophy*, edited by Warren E. Steinkraus, 187–200. New York: Holt, Rinehart & Winston, 1971.

———. *Russian Religious Philosophy: Selected Aspects*. Notre Dame, IN: University of Notre Dame Press, 1988.

Corbin, Henri. *Creative Imagination in the Sufism of Ibn 'Arabi*. Translated by Ralph Manheim. Princeton: Princeton University Press, 1969.

———. *Swedenborg and Esoteric Islam*. Translated by Leonard Fox. West Chester, PA: Swedenborgian Foundation, 1995.

Cornélis, Humbert-Marie. "Les fondements cosmologiques de l'eschatologie d'Origène." *Revue des sciences philosophiques et théologiques* 43 (1959): 32–80, 201–47.

Corte, Nicolas. *Pierre Teilhard de Chardin*. Translated by Martin Jarrett-Kerr. New York: Macmillan, 1960.

Cosgrove, Charles H. *Appealing to Scripture in Moral Debate: Five Hermeneutical Rules*. Grand Rapids: Eerdmans, 2002.

Cottier, Georges M.-M. *L'athéisme du jeune Marx: Ses origines hégéliennes*. Paris: Vrin, 1969.

Cottle, Joseph. *Essays on Socinianism*. London: Longman, Brown, Green, & Longmans, 1850.

Coudert, Allison P. *The Impact of the Kabbalah in the Seventeenth Century: The Life and Thought of Francis Mercury van Helmont (1614–1698)*. Leiden: Brill, 1999.

Cox, Gerard H., III. "Marlowe's *Doctor Faustus* and 'Sin against the Holy Ghost.'" *Huntington Library Quarterly* 36 (1973): 119–37.

Cox, Harvey. *The Secular City: Secularization and Urbanization in Theological Perspective*. New York: Macmillan, 1965.

Cox, Samuel. "Future Punishment: The Present State of the Question, Considered in a Series of Papers on Canon Farrar's New Book." *Contemporary Review* 32 (1878): 364–70.

———. *The Larger Hope: A Sequel to "Salvator Mundi."* London: Kegan Paul, Trench, 1883.

———. *Salvator Mundi; or, Is Christ the Saviour of All Men?* London: Henry S. King, 1877.

Craig, William Lane. "Talbott's Universalism." *Religious Studies* 27 (1991): 297–308.

———. "Talbott's Universalism Once More." *Religious Studies* 29 (1993): 497–518.

Craven, William G. *Giovanni Pico della Mirandola—Symbol of His Age: Modern Interpretations of a Renaissance Philosopher*. Genève: Librairie Droz, 1981.

Crisp, Oliver. "'I Do Teach It, but I Also Do Not Teach It': The Universalism of Karl Barth." In MacDonald [Parry], *"All Shall Be Well,"* 305–24.

———. "On Barth's Denial of Universalism." *Themelios* 29 (2003): 18–29.

———. *Saving Calvinism: Expanding the Reformed Tradition*. Downers Grove, IL: IVP Academic, 2016.

Cristea, Hans-Joachim, trans. *Schenute von Atripe: Contra Origenistas.* Tübingen: Mohr Siebeck, 2011.

Croasmun, Matthew. *The Emergence of Sin: The Cosmic Tyrant in Romans.* New York: Oxford University Press, 2017.

Crockett, William. "Will God Save Everyone in the End?" In Crockett and Sigountos, *Through No Fault of Their Own,* 159–66.

———. "Wrath That Endures Forever." *Journal of the Evangelical Theological Society* 34 (1991): 195–202.

Crockett, William V., and James G. Sigountos, eds. *Through No Fault of Their Own: The Fate of Those Who Have Never Heard.* Grand Rapids: Baker, 1991.

Croswell, Andrew. *Mr. Murray Unmask'd.* Boston: J. Kneeland, 1775.

Crouse, Moses Corliss. "A Study of the Doctrine of Conditional Immortality in Nineteenth-Century America with Special Reference to the Contributions of Charles F. Hudson and John H. Pettingell." PhD diss., Northwestern University, 1953.

Crouzel, Henri. "Current Theology: The Literature on Origen 1970–1988." *Theological Studies* 49 (1988): 499–516.

———. "L'apocatastase chez Origène." In Lies, *Origeniana Quarta,* 282–90.

———. *Les fins dernières selon Origène.* Brookfield, VT: Gower, 1990.

———. "A Letter from Origen 'To Friends in Alexandria.'" In *The Heritage of the Early Church: Essays in Honor of Georges Vasilievich Florovsky,* edited by David Neiman and Margaret Schatkin, 135–50. Rome: Pontificum Institutum Studiorum Orientalium, 1973.

———. "Origène est-il un systématique?" *Bulletin de littérature ecclésiastique* 10 (1961): 81–116.

———. *Origen: The Life and Thought of the First Great Theologian.* Translated by A. S. Worrall. San Francisco: Harper & Row, 1989.

———, ed. and trans. *Une controverse sur Origène à la Renaissance: Jean Pic de la Mirandole et Pierre Garcia.* Paris: J. Vrin, 1977.

Crowder, John. *Cosmos Reborn: Happy Theology on the New Creation.* Portland, OR: Sons of Thunder, 2013.

———. *The Ecstasy of Loving God: Trances, Raptures, and the Supernatural Pleasures of Jesus Christ.* Shippensburg, PA: Destiny Image, 2009.

———. "Hell Revisited—The Jesus Trip." YouTube, August 16, 2012. http://www.youtube.com/watch?v=afloDCTwluY.

———. *Miracle Workers, Reformers, and the New Mystics.* Shippensburg, PA: Destiny Image, 2006.

———. *Mystical Union.* Santa Cruz, CA: Sons of Thunder, 2010.

Crowell, Seth. *Strictures on the Doctrine of Universal Salvation.* New York: Hoyt & Bolmore, 1821.

Cudworth, Ralph. *A Treatise concerning Eternal and Immutable Morality.* London: James and John Knapton, 1731.

Culianu, Ioan P. *The Tree of Gnosis: Gnostic Mythology from Early Christianity to Modern Nihilism.* Translated by H. S. Wiesner and Ioan P. Culianu. San Francisco: HarperSanFrancisco, 1992.

Culp, John. "Panentheism." In *The Stanford Encyclopedia of Philosophy,* edited by Edward N. Zalta. https://plato.stanford.edu/entries/panentheism/. First published December 4, 2008; substantive revision February 5, 2013.

Cumming, Richard Paul. "The Problem of Universal Salvation in the Theology of Emil Brunner." *Union Seminary Quarterly Review* 65 (2014): 74–95.

Cunningham, David. "Participation as a Trinitarian Virtue: Challenging the Current 'Relational' Consensus." *Toronto Journal of Theology* 14 (1998): 7–25.

Cunningham, Delora G. "Macbeth: The Tragedy of the Hardened Heart." *Shakespeare Quarterly* 14 (1963): 39–47.

Cupitt, Don. "The Language of Eschatology: F. D. Maurice's Treatment of Heaven and Hell." *Anglican Theological Review* 54 (1972): 305–17.

Cyril of Alexandria. *Homilia Pascalis* 7. In PG 77:535–54.

Dabney, D. Lyle. *Die Kenosis des Geistes: Kontinuität zwischen Schöpfung und Erlösung im Werk des Heiligen Geistes*. Neukirchen-Vluyn: Neukirchener Verlag, 1997.

Dahl, Larry E. "Degrees of Glory." In D. H. Ludlow, *Encyclopedia of Mormonism*, 1:367–69.

Dahl, Paul E. "Godhead." In D. H. Ludlow, *Encyclopedia of Mormonism*, 2:552–53.

Dahlke, Benjamin. *Karl Barth, Catholic Renewal, and Vatican II*. London: T&T Clark, 2012.

Daley, Brian E. "Apokatastasis and 'Honorable Silence' in the Eschatology of Maximus the Confessor." In *Maximus Confessor: Actes du symposium sur Maxime le Confesseur, Fribourg, 2–5 Septembre 1980*, edited by Felix Heinzer and Christoph Schönborn, 309–39. Fribourg: Editions Universitaires, 1982.

———. *The Hope of the Early Church: A Handbook of Patristic Eschatology*. New York: Cambridge University Press, 1991. Reprint, Peabody, MA: Hendrickson, 2003.

———. "What Did Origenism Mean in the Sixth Century?" In Dorival and Le Boulluec, *Origeniana Sexta*, 627–38.

Dalferth, Ingolf U. "The Eschatological Roots of the Doctrine of the Trinity." In *Trinitarian Theology Today*, edited by Christoph Schwöbel, 147–70. Edinburgh: T&T Clark, 1995.

Dalton, W. J. *Christ's Proclamation to the Spirits: A Study of 1 Peter 3:18–4:6*. Rome: Pontifical Biblical Institute, 1965.

Daly, Robert J., ed. *Origeniana Quinta: Historica, Text and Method, Biblica, Philosophica, Theologica, Origenism and Later Developments; Papers of the 5th International Origen Congress, Boston College, 14–18 August 1989*. Leuven: Peeters, 1992.

Dalzell, Thomas G. "Lack of Social Drama in Balthasar's Theological Dramatics." *Theological Studies* 60 (1999): 457–75.

Dan, Joseph. "Menasseh Ben Israel: Attitude towards the Zohar and Lurianic Kabbalah." In *Menasseh Ben Israel and His World*, edited by Yosef Kaplan, Henry Méchoulan, and Richard H. Popkin, 199–206. Leiden: Brill, 1989.

Daniel, E. Randolph. *Abbot Joachim of Fiore and Joachimism*. Variorum Collected Studies. Aldershot, UK: Ashgate, 2011.

Daniélou, Jean. *Essai sur le mystère de l'histoire*. Paris: Seuil, 1953.

———. "L'apocatastase chez Saint Grégoire de Nysse." *Revue des sciences religieuses* 30 (1940): 328–47.

———. *Origen*. Translated by Walter Mitchell. New York: Sheed & Ward, 1955.

———. *The Theology of Jewish Christianity*. Edited and translated by John A. Baker. London: Darton, Longman & Todd, 1964.

Darby, John Nelson. "Examination of the Book Entitled 'The Restitution of All Things.'" In *Collected Writings of John Nelson Darby*. https://bibletruthpublishers.com/examination-of-the-book-entitled-the-restitution-of-all-things/john-nelson-darby-jnd/collected-writings-of-j-n-darby/la63121.

Date, Christopher M., and Ron Highfield, eds. *A Consuming Passion: Essays on Hell and Immortality in Honor of Edward Fudge*. Eugene, OR: Pickwick, 2015.

Date, Christopher M., Gregory G. Stump, and Joshua W. Anderson, eds. *Rethinking Hell: Readings in Evangelical Conditionalism*. Eugene, OR: Cascade, 2014.

David, N. E. *Karma and Reincarnation in Israelitism*. Karachi, Pakistan: L. Solomon, 1923.

David, Zdenek V. "The Influence of Jacob Boehme on Russian Religious Thought." *Slavic Review* 21 (1962): 43–64.

Davies, Eryl W. *An Angry God? The Biblical Doctrine of Wrath, Final Judgment, and Hell*. Bridgend: Evangelical Press of Wales, 1991.

———. "The Morally Dubious Passages of the Hebrew Bible: An Examination of Some Proposed Solutions." *Currents in Biblical Research* 3 (2005): 197–228.

Davies, W. Merlin. *An Introduction to F. D. Maurice's Theology*. London: SPCK, 1964.

Davis, Ellen F. "Critical Traditioning: Seeking an Inner Biblical Hermeneutic." *Anglican Theological Review* 82 (2000): 733–51.

Davis, James M. *Universalism Unmasked, or the Spurious Gospel Exposed*. Philadelphia: I. Ashmead & Co., 1837.

Davis, Stephen T. *After We Die: Theology, Philosophy, and the Question of Life after Death.* Waco: Baylor University Press, 2015.

———. "Universalism, Hell, and the Fate of the Ignorant." *Modern Theology* 6 (1990): 173–86.

Dawson, David. *Allegorical Readers and Cultural Revision in Ancient Alexandria.* Berkeley: University of California Press, 1992.

D'Costa, Gavin. *Christianity and World Religions: Disputed Questions in the Theology of Religions.* Oxford: Wiley-Blackwell, 2009.

———. "The Descent into Hell as a Solution for the Problem of the Fate of Unevangelized Non-Christians: Balthasar's Hell, the Limbo of the Fathers, and Purgatory." *International Journal of Systematic Theology* 11 (2009): 146–71.

———. "Pluralist Arguments." In *Catholic Engagements with World Religions: A Comprehensive Survey*, edited by Karl J. Becker and Ilaria Morali, 329–44. Maryknoll, NY: Orbis, 2010.

Deak, Esteban. "Apokatastasis: The Problem of Universal Salvation in the Twentieth Century." PhD diss., University of St. Michael's College, Toronto, 1977.

de Benneville, George. "The Life and Trance of Dr. George de Benneville." Edited by Ernest Cassara. *Journal of the Universalist Historical Society* 2 (1960–61): 71–87.

———. *A True and Most Remarkable Account of Some Passages in the Life of Mr. George de Benneville.* Translated by Elhanan Winchester. London, 1791.

de Boer, Martinus C. *The Defeat of Death: Apocalyptic Eschatology in 1 Corinthians 15 and Romans 5.* Sheffield: Sheffield Academic, 1988.

Debus, Allen G. *The English Paracelsians.* New York: Franklin Watts, 1966.

Dechow, Jon F. *Dogma and Mysticism in Early Christianity: Epiphanius of Cyprus and the Legacy of Origen.* Macon, GA: Mercer University Press, 1988.

———. "Origen and Corporeality: The Case of Methodius' *On the Resurrection.*" In Daly, *Origeniana Quinta*, 509–18.

———. "Origen's 'Heresy': From Eustathius to Epiphanius." In Lies, *Origeniana Quarta*, 405–9.

———. "Origen's Shadow over the Erasmus/Luther Debate." In Dorival and Le Boulluec, *Origeniana Sexta*, 739–57.

———. "Pseudo-Jerome's Anti-Origenist Anathemas." In Kaczmarek and Pietras, *Origeniana Decima*, 955–65.

———. "Seminar II: The Heresy Charges against Origen." In Lies, *Origeniana Quarta*, 112–22.

Declève, Henri. "Schöpfung, Trinität und Modernität bei Hegel." *Zeitschrift für katholische Theologie* 108 (1985): 187–98.

DeConick, April D., ed. *The Gnostic New Age: How a Countercultural Spirituality Revolutionized Religion from Antiquity to Today.* New York: Columbia University Press, 2016.

———. *Religion: Secret Religion.* Macmillan Interdisciplinary Handbooks. Farmington Hills, MI: Gale Cengage Learning, 2016.

de Courten, Manon. *History, Sophia and the Russian Nation.* Bern: Lang, 2004.

de Faye, Eugène. "De l'influence du gnosticisme sur Origène." *Revue de l'histoire des religions* 44 (1923): 181–235.

———. *Origen and His Work.* Translated by Fred Rothwell. London: Allen & Unwin, 1926.

Deghaye, Pierre. "Jacob Boehme and His Followers." In *Modern Esoteric Spirituality*, edited by Antoine Faivre and Jacob Needleman, 201–47. New York: Crossroad, 1992.

de Halleux, A. *Philoxène de Mabbog: Sa vie, ses écrits, sa théologie.* Louvain: Imprimerie orientaliste, 1963.

De La Noval, Roberto. "The Fork in the (Final) Road: Universalist and Annihilationist Eschatologies—and What Ultimately Divides Them." *Pro Ecclesia* 25 (2016): 315–20.

DeLeón-Jones, Karen Silvia. *Giordano Bruno and the Kabbalah: Prophets, Magicians, and Rabbis.* New Haven: Yale University Press, 1997.

de Lubac, Henri. *Augustinianism and Modern Theology.* Translated by Lancelot Sheppard. New York: Crossroad, 2000.

————. *A Brief Catechesis on Nature and Grace*. Translated by Richard Arnandez. San Francisco: Ignatius, 1984.

————, Introduction to *On First Principles*, by Origen. Translated by G. W. Butterworth. Gloucester, MA: Smith, 1973.

————. *La postérité spirituelle de Joachim de Fiore*. 2 vols. Paris: Lethielleux; Namur: Culture et vérité, 1979–81.

————. *Medieval Exegesis: The Four Senses of Scripture*. Translated by Mark Sebanc et al. 3 vols. Grand Rapids: Eerdmans, 1998–2009.

————. *Pic de la Mirandole: Études de discussions*. Paris: Aubier Montaigne, 1974.

————. *Surnaturel: Études historiques*. Paris: Aubier, 1946. Translated by Rosemary Sheed as *The Mystery of the Supernatural* (New York: Crossroad, 1998).

————. *Teilhard de Chardin: The Man and His Meaning*. New York: Hawthorn, 1965.

Dempsey, Michael T., ed. *Trinity and Election in Contemporary Theology*. Grand Rapids: Eerdmans, 2011.

Denis, John. "The Editor's Preface." In *The Restoration of All Things: Or, a Vindication of the Goodness and Grace of God, to Be Manifested at Last, in the Recovery of His Whole Creation out of Their Fall*, by Jeremiah Wright, xxxi–xlii. London, 1712. 3rd ed. London: John Denis & Son, 1779.

Denisenko, Gennady. "Solovyov's Syzygy." PhD diss., University of Virginia, 2010.

Denzinger, Heinrich. *Compendium of Creeds, Definitions, and Declarations on Matters of Faith and Morals*. 43rd ed. Edited by Peter Hünermann, Robert Fastiggi, and Anne Englund Nash. San Francisco: Ignatius, 2012.

————. *The Sources of Catholic Dogma*. Translated by Roy J. Deferrari. St. Louis: Herder, 1957. Translation of *Enchiridion Symbolorum*, 30th edition.

de Regnon, Théodore. *La métaphysique des causes d'après Saint Thomas et Albert le Grand*. Paris: Retaux-Bray, 1886.

DeRose, Keith. "Universalism and the Bible: The *Really* Good News" (1998). http://campuspress.yale.edu/keithderose/1129-2/.

Derrida, Jacques. "From Restricted to General Economy: A Hegelianism without Reserve." In *Writing and Difference*, 317–50. Translated by Alan Bass. London: Routledge, 1978. Originally published as *l'écriture et la différence* (Paris: Seuil, 1967).

Desmond, William. *God and the Between*. Malden, MA: Blackwell, 2008.

————. *Hegel's God: A Counterfeit Double?* Aldershot, UK: Ashgate, 2003.

Dexter, H. M. *The Reasonableness of the Doctrine of Future Eternal Punishment*. Boston: John P. Jewett & Co., 1858.

DeYoung, Kevin. "God Is Still Holy and What You Learned in Sunday School Is Still True." Review of *Love Wins*, by Rob Bell. Gospel Coalition, March 14, 2011. http://thegospelcoalition.org/blogs/kevindeyoung/2011/03/14/rob-bell-love-wins-review/.

d'Hondt, Jacques. *Hegel secret: Recherches sur les sources cachées de la pensée de Hegel*. Paris: Presses Universitaires de France, 1968.

Dibb, Andrew M. T. *Servetus, Swedenborg, and the Nature of God*. Lanham, MD: University Press of America, 2005.

Diekamp, Franz. *Die origenistischen Streitigkeiten im sechsten Jahrhundert und das fünfte allgemeine Concil*. Münster: Aschendorff, 1899.

Diels, H., and W. Kranz. *Die Fragmente der Vorsokratiker*. 6th ed. Berlin: Weidmann, 1951–52.

Dillon, John. "The Descent of the Soul in Middle Platonic and Gnostic Thought." In *The Rediscovery of Gnosticism*, edited by Bentley Layton, 1:357–64. 2 vols. Leiden: Brill, 1980.

————. *The Middle Platonists: A Study of Platonism 80 BC to AD 220*. Ithaca, NY: Cornell University Press, 1996.

————. "Origen and Plotinus: The Platonic Influence on Early Christianity." In *The Relationship between Neoplatonism and Christianity*, edited by Thomas Finan and Vincent Twomey, 7–26. Dublin: Four Courts, 1992.

————. "*Pleroma* and Noetic Cosmos: A Comparative Study." In *Neoplatonism and Gnosticism*, edited by Richard Wallis and Jay Bregman, 99–110. Albany: State University of New York Press, 1992.

———. "Plutarch, Plotinus, and the Zoroastrian Concept of the *Fravashi*." https://www.academia.edu/4368314/Fravashi_and_Un descended_Soul.

———. "Saving Plato: Ficino on Plato's Doctrine of the Soul's Eternity and Reincarnation in Context." In *The Rebirth of Platonic Theology: Proceedings of a Conference Held at the Harvard University Center for Italian Renaissance Studies (Villa I Tatti) and the Istituto Nazionale di Studi sul Rinascimento (Florence, 26–27 April 2007)*, edited by James Hankins and Fabrizio Meroi, 191–202. Firenze: Casa Editrice Leo S. Olschki, 2013. https://tcd.academia.edu/JohnDillon/Papers.

———. "Towards the Noosphere: Plotinus, Origen, Teilhard de Chardin, and the Striving for a Rational World." In *Towards the Noosphere*, edited by John Dillon and Stephen R. L. Clark. Dilton Marsh, UK: Prometheus Trust, 2013. http://www.academia.edu/5432305/Towrds_the_Noosphere.

DiNoia, Joseph Augustine. *The Diversity of Religions: A Christian Perspective*. Washington, DC: Catholic University of America Press, 1992.

Dionysius Petavius. *De Angelis*. In *Dionysii Petauii Aurelianensis e Societate Jesus de Theologicis Dogmatibus*, edited by F. A. Zaccaria, 3:1–112. Venice: Andreæ Poleti, 1745.

Dioscorus of Alexandria. "Letter to Shenoute concerning an Origenist Monk." Translated by Herbert Thompson as "Dioscorus and Shenoute," in *Recueil d'études égyptologiques dédiées à la mémoire de Jean-François Champollion*, 367–76. Paris: Librairie Ancienne Honoré Champion, 1922. http://www.tertullian.org/fathers/dioscorus_of_alexandria_let ter_to_shenoute.htm.

Dixon, Larry. *"Farewell, Rob Bell": A Biblical Response to "Love Wins."* Columbia, SC: Theomedian Resources, 2011.

———. *The Other Side of the Good News: Confronting the Contemporary Challenge to Jesus' Teaching on Hell*. Wheaton: Victor, 1992.

Dobzhansky, Theodosius. "Teilhard de Chardin and the Orientation of Evolution." *Zygon* 3 (1968): 242–58.

Dockrill, D. W. "The Fathers and the Theology of the Cambridge Platonists." *Studia Patristica* 17 (1982): 427–39.

———. "The Heritage of Patristic Platonism in Seventeenth-Century English Philosophical Theology." In *The Cambridge Platonists in Philosophical Context: Politics, Metaphysics, and Religion*, edited by G. A. J. Rogers et al., 55–77. Dordrecht: Kluwer Academic, 1997.

Doctrine Commission of the Church of England. *The Mystery of Salvation: The Story of God's Gift*. London: Church Publishing House, 1995.

Döllinger, Ignaz von. "Die Schelling'sche Philosophie und die christliche Theologie." *Historisch-politische Blätter für das katholische Deutschland* 11 (1843): 585–601.

Dombart, Bernardus, and Alphonsus Kalb, eds. *Augustine: De civitate dei; Aurelii Augustini Opera, Pars XIV, 1–2*. CCL 47–48. Turnhout: Brepols, 1955.

Donmeh West: The Neo-Sabbatian Collective of the Internet. http://www.donmeh-west.com/index.shtml.

Doody, John, Kari Kloos, and Kim Paffenroth, eds. *Augustine and Apocalyptic*. Lanham, MD: Lexington, 2013.

Doolan, A. "Is Hell Unending? Is There Anybody in Hell? St. Thomas's Teaching." *Irish Ecclesiastical Review* 95 (1961): 39–44.

Dorgan, Howard. *In the Hands of a Happy God: The "No-Hellers" of Central Appalachia*. Knoxville: University of Tennessee Press, 1997.

Dorival, Gilles. "Origène a-t-il enseigné le transmigration des âmes dans les corps d'animaux? (A propos de *PArch* 1.8.4)." In *Origeniana Secunda*, edited by Henri Crouzel and Antonio Quacquarelli, 11–32. Bari, It.: Edizioni dell'Ateneo, 1980.

Dorival, Gilles, and Alain Le Boulluec, eds. *Origeniana Sexta: Origène et la Bible = Origen and the Bible; Actes du Colloquium Origenianum Sextum, Chantilly, 30 Août–3 Septembre 1993*. In collaboration with Monique Alexandre et al. Leuven: Peeters, 1995.

Dorner, Isaak August. *History of the Development of the Doctrine of the Person of Christ*.

Translated by Rev. D. W. Simon. 5 vols. Edinburgh: T&T Clark, 1861.

Dornseiff, Franz. *Buchstabenmystik*. Leipzig: Teubner, 1916

Dorrien, Gary J. *The Barthian Revolt in Modern Theology: Theology without Weapons*. Louisville: Westminster John Knox, 2000.

————. *Kantian Reason and Hegelian Spirit: The Idealistic Logic of Modern Theology*. Maldon, MA: Wiley-Blackwell, 2015.

Dostoyevsky, Fyodor. *The Brothers Karamazov*. Translated by Richard Pevear and Larissa Volokhonsky. New York: Farrar, Straus and Giroux, 1990.

Doucin, Louis, SJ. *Histoire des mouvemens arrivez dans l'Eglise au sujet d'Origène et de sa doctrine*. Paris: Nicolas Le Clerc, 1700.

Dougherty, Trent, and Ted Poston. "Hell, Vagueness, and Justice: A Reply to Sider." *Faith and Philosophy* 25 (2008): 322–28.

Dreher, Rod. *The Benedict Option: A Strategy for Christians in a Post-Christian Nation*. New York: Sentinel, 2017.

Drewery, Benjamin. "The Condemnation of Origen: Should It Be Reversed?" In Hanson and Crouzel, *Origeniana Tertia*, 271–77.

Driel, Edwin Chr. van. *Incarnation Anyway: Arguments for Supralapsarian Christology*. New York: Oxford University Press, 2008.

————. "Karl Barth on the Eternal Existence of Jesus Christ." *Scottish Journal of Theology* 60 (2007): 45–61.

————. "Schleiermacher's Supralapsarian Christology." *Scottish Journal of Theology* 60 (2007): 251–70.

Drury, Maurice. "Some Notes on Conversations with Wittgenstein." In *Recollections of Wittgenstein*, edited by Rush Rhees, 76–171. Oxford: Oxford University Press, 1984.

Duclow, Donald F. *Masters of Learned Ignorance: Eriugena, Eckhart, Cusanus*. Variorum Collected Studies. Burlington, VT: Ashgate, 2006.

————. "Nothingness and Self-Creation in John Scotus Eriugena." *Journal of Religion* 57 (1977): 109–23.

Duclow, Donald F., and Paul A. Dietrich. "Hell and Damnation in Eriugena." In Duclow, *Masters of Learned Ignorance*, 121–38.

Dulles, Avery Cardinal. "The Population of Hell." *First Things* 133 (2003). https.//www.firstthings.com/article/2003/05/the-population-of-hell.

Dulles, Avery Cardinal, et al. "Responses to 'Balthasar, Hell, and Heresy.'" *First Things* 171 (March 2007): 5–14.

Dunn, Benjamin. *The Happy Gospel! Effortless Union with a Happy God*. Shippensburg, PA: Destiny Image, 2011.

Dupuis, Jacques. *Toward a Christian Theology of Religious Pluralism*. Maryknoll, NY: Orbis, 1997.

Durnbaugh, Donald F. "Jane Ward Leade (1624–1704) and the Philadelphians." In *The Pietist Theologians: An Introduction to Theology in the Seventeenth and Eighteenth Centuries*, edited by Carter Lindberg, 128–46. Oxford: Blackwell, 2005.

du Toit, Francois. *Divine Embrace*. Hermanus, South Africa: Mirror Word, 2012.

————. *The Logic of His Love*. Hermanus, South Africa: Mirror Word, 2007.

————. *Mirror Bible*. Hermanus, South Africa: Mirror Word, 2012.

Duvernoy, Jean. *Le Catharisme*. Vol. 1, *La religion des Cathares*. Toulouse: Éditions privat, 1976.

————. *Le Catharisme*. Vol. 2, *L'histoire des Cathares*. Toulouse: Éditions privat, 1979.

————. *Le registre d'inquisition de Jacques Fournier, évêque de Pamiers (1318–1325); Manuscrit no. Vat. Latin 4030 de la Bibliothèque vaticane*. 3 vols. 1965. Reprint, Toulouse, France: Éditions privat, 1973.

Dweck, Yaacob. *The Scandal of Kabbalah: Leon Modena, Jewish Mysticism, Early Modern Venice*. Princeton: Princeton University Press, 2011.

Dysinger, Luke, trans. *Kephalaia Gnostica*, by Evagrius Ponticus. http://www.ldysinger.com/Evagrius/02_Gno-Keph/00a_start.htm.

Eadie, Betty J. *Embraced by the Light*. Placerville, CA: Gold Leaf, 1992.

Ebeling, Florian. *The Secret History of Hermes Trismegistus: Hermeticism from Ancient to Modern Times*. Ithaca, NY: Cornell University Press, 2007.

Echeverria, Eduardo J. *Divine Election: A Catholic Orientation in Dogmatic and Ecumenical Perspective*. Eugene, OR: Pickwick, 2016.

Eckert, Georg. "*True, Noble, Christian Free-thinking": Leben und Werk Andrew Michaels Ramsays (1686–1743)*. Munster, Germany: Aschendorff, 2009.

Eckhart, Meister. *Die deutschen Werke*. Edited by Josef Quint, Georg Steer, Heidemarie Vogl, and Max Pahnde. 5 vols. Stuttgart: Kohlhammer, 1958–76.

————. *The Essential Sermons, Commentaries, Treatises, and Defense*. Translated by Edmund Colledge and Bernard McGinn. Classics of Western Spirituality. New York: Paulist Press, 1981.

————. *Meister Eckhart: Teacher and Preacher*. Edited by Bernard McGinn, with Frank J. Tobin and Elvira Borgstadt. Mahwah, NJ: Paulist Press, 1986.

Eckley, Joseph. *Divine Glory Brought to View*. Boston: Robert Hodge, 1782.

Eddy, Richard. *Universalism in America: A History*. 2 vols. Boston: Universalist Publishing House, 1884.

Edelheit, Amos. *Ficino, Pico, and Savonarola: The Evolution of Humanist Theology 1461/2–1498*. Leiden: Brill, 2008.

Edie, James M., James P. Scanlan, and Mary-Barbara Zeldin, eds. *Russian Philosophy*. With the collaboration of George L. Kline. 3 vols. Chicago: Quadrangle, 1965.

Edighoffer, Roland. "Rosicrucianism, I: First Half of the 17th Century." In Hanegraaff et al., *Dictionary of Gnosis and Western Esotericism*, 1009–14.

Edwards, David L., and John Stott. *Essentials*. London: Hodder & Stoughton, 1988.

Edwards, Denis. "A Relational and Evolving Universe Unfolding with the Dynamism of the Divine Communion." In Clayton and Peacocke, *In Whom We Live*, 199–210.

Edwards, Graham Robert. "Purgatory: 'Birth' or Evolution?" Review of *The Birth of Purgatory*, by Jacques Le Goff. *Journal of Ecclesiastical History* 36 (1985): 634–46.

Edwards, Jonathan. *The Works of Jonathan Edwards*. 73 vols. New Haven: Yale University Press, 1957–2011. All 73 vols. online at http://edwards.yale.edu.

————. *The Works of President Edwards*. Edited by Edward Hickman. 2 vols. 1834.

Reprint, Edinburgh: Banner of Truth, 1984.

Edwards, Jonathan, Jr. *Brief Observations on the Doctrine of Universal Salvation*. New Haven: Meigs, Bowen, and Dana, 1784.

Edwards, Mark J. "The Fate of the Devil in Origen." *Ephemerides Theologicae Lovanienses* 86 (2010): 163–70.

————. *Origen against Plato*. Aldershot, UK: Ashgate, 2002.

————. "Origen No Gnostic; or, On the Corporeality of Man." *Journal of Theological Studies* 43 (1992): 23–37.

Egan, Harvey D. "Hell: The Mystery of Eternal Love and Eternal Obduracy." *Theological Studies* 75 (2014): 52–73.

————. "In Purgatory We Shall All Be Mystics." *Theological Studies* 73 (2012): 870–89.

Ehmer, Hermann. "Johann Albrecht Bengel (1687–1752)." In *The Pietist Theologians: An Introduction to Theology in the Seventeenth and Eighteenth Centuries*, edited by Carter Lindberg, 224–37. Malden, MA: Blackwell, 2005.

Ehrman, Bart D., ed. and trans. *The Apostolic Fathers I and II*. LCL. Cambridge, MA: Harvard University Press, 2003.

————. *Jesus, Interrupted: Revealing the Hidden Contradictions in the Bible (and Why We Don't Know About Them)*. New York: HarperCollins, 2009.

Eire, Carlos. *A Very Brief History of Eternity*. Princeton: Princeton University Press, 2010.

Eisenbeis, Walter. *The Key Ideas of Paul Tillich's Systematic Theology*. Washington, DC: University Press of America, 1983.

Eliade, Mircea. *The Forge and the Crucible: The Origins and Structures of Alchemy*. 2nd ed. Chicago: University of Chicago Press, 1978.

————. *Mephistopheles and the Androgyne: Studies in Religious Myth and Symbol*. New York: Sheed & Ward, 1965.

Ellard, G. A., SJ. Review of *The Divine Crucible of Purgatory*, by Mother Mary of St. Austin. *Theological Studies* 2 (1941): 596–98.

Elliott, J. K., ed. *The Apocryphal New Testament: A Collection of Apocryphal Christian*

Literature in an English Translation based on M. R. James. 1993. Reprint. Oxford: Clarendon, 2005.

Ellis, E. Earle. "New Testament Teaching on Hell." In "The Reader Must Understand": Eschatology in the Bible and Theology, edited by K. E. Brower and M. W. Elliott, 199–219. Leicester, UK: Apollos, 1997.

Ellis, Paul. The Hyper-Grace Gospel: A Response to Michael Brown and Those Opposed to the Modern Grace Message. N.p.: Kingspress, 2014.

Ellison, James E. John Wesley and Universalism. N.p.: CreateSpace, 2014.

Ellul, Jacques. What I Believe. Translated by Geoffrey W. Bromiley. Grand Rapids: Eerdmans, 1989.

Emerson, Ralph Waldo. "Compensation." In The Essential Writings of Ralph Waldo Emerson, 49–68. New York: Modern Library, 2000.

Emery, Gilles. "Essentialism or Personalism in the Treatise on God in Saint Thomas Aquinas?" Thomist 64 (2000): 521–64.

Eminyan, Maurice. The Theology of Salvation. Boston: St. Paul Editions, 1960.

Emlyn-Jones, Chris, and William Preddy, eds. and trans. Plato: Republic Books 1–5. LCL 237. Cambridge, MA: Harvard University Press, 2013.

Emmel, V. Donald. Eliminating Satan and Hell: Affirming a Compassionate Creator-God. Eugene, OR: Wipf & Stock, 2013.

Emmons, Nathanael. A Discourse concerning . . . the General Judgment. Philadelphia: William Young, 1791.

Endean, J. Russell. What Is the Eternal Hope of Canon Farrar? London: Kirby & Endean, 1878.

Engels, Frederick. Anti-Dühring: Herr Eugen Dühring's Revolution in Science. Moscow: Foreign Languages Publishing House, 1959.

Ensign, David Chauncey. "Radical German Pietism (c. 1675–c. 1760)." PhD diss., Boston University, 1955.

Ephrem the Syrian. Carmina Nisibena 36. S. Ephraemi Syri Carmina Nisibena, edited by Gustav Bickell, 146–49. Leipzig: Brockhaus, 1866. ET: NPNF² 13:196–98.

————. Hymns on Paradise. Translated by Sebastian Brock. Crestwood, NY: St. Vladimir's Seminary Press, 1990.

Epiphanius [bishop of Constantia in Cyprus]. Ancoratus und Panarion II, Haer. 34–64, edited by K. Holl. GCS 31. Leipzig: J. C. Hinrichs, 1922.

————. The Panarion of Epiphanius of Salamis. Translated by Frank Williams. 3 vols. Leiden: Brill, 1987, 1994, 2014.

Epistula Apostolorum [The Epistle of the Apostles]. In Gespräche Jesu mit seinen Jüngen nach der Auferstehung. Edited by C. Schmidt. Leipzig, 1919. ET in Elliott, Apocryphal New Testament, 555–90.

Erb, Peter. Introduction to Jacob Boehme: The Way to Christ, 1–26. Classics of Western Spirituality. New York: Paulist Press, 1978.

Erickson, Millard J. How Shall They Be Saved? The Destiny of Those Who Have Not Heard of Jesus. Grand Rapids: Baker, 1996.

Eriugena, John Scotus. Homilia in Prologum S. Evangelii Secundum Joannem. In PL 122:283–96.

————. Periphyseon (The Division of Nature). Translated by I. P. Sheldon-Williams. Revised by John J. O'Meara. Montreal: Bellarmin; Washington, DC: Dumbarton Oaks, 1987.

————. Treatise on Divine Predestination. Translated by Mary Brennan. Notre Dame, IN: University of Notre Dame Press, 1998.

Erskine, Thomas. The Brazen Serpent; or, Life Coming through Death. Edinburgh: Waugh & Innes, 1831.

————. The Doctrine of Election. London: James Duncan, 1837.

————. Extracts of Letters to a Christian Friend, by a Lady, with an Introductory Essay by Thomas Erskine. Greenock: R. B. Lusk, 1830.

————. "Introductory Essay" (1825). In Letters of the Rev. Samuel Rutherford, Late Professor of Divinity at St. Andrews, v–xxvii. Edinburgh: David Douglas, 1878.

————. Letters of Thomas Erskine of Linlathen. Edited by William Hanna. 2 vols. Edinburgh: David Douglas, 1877.

———. *The Spiritual Order and Other Papers Selected from the Manuscripts of the Late Thomas Erskine of Linlathen.* 3rd ed. Edinburgh: David Douglas, 1877.

———. *The Unconditional Freeness of the Gospel.* 2nd ed. Edinburgh: Waugh & Innes, 1828.

Esolen, Anthony M. *Out of the Ashes: Rebuilding American Culture.* Washington, DC: Regnery, 2017.

Essary, Kirk. "Origen's Doctrine of the Soul: Platonist or Christian?" MA thesis, Texas Technical University, 2008.

Eusebius. *The Ecclesiastical History.* In *NPNF²* 1:81–403.

———. *Ecclesiastical History, Volume II: Books 6–10.* Translated by J. E. L. Oulton. LCL 265. Cambridge, MA: Harvard University Press, 1932.

Evagrius. *Epistula Fidei* = Basil. *Letter* 8. In *Basil: Letters 1–58.* Translated by Roy J. Deferrari, 46–93. LCL 190. Cambridge, MA: Harvard University Press, 1926.

———. *Évagre le Pontique Scholies à l'Ecclésiaste [Scholia on Ecclesiastes].* Edited by P. Géhin. SC 397. Paris: Cerf, 1993.

———. *Évagre le Pontique Scholies aux Proverbs.* Edited by P. Géhin. SC 340. Paris: Cerf, 1987.

———. *Kephalaia Gnostica.* Edited by A. Guillaumont. PO 28/1. Paris: Firmin-Didot, 1958.

———. *Scholia on Psalms.* In Origen, *Selecta in Psalmos,* PG 12:1053–686.

Evangelical Alliance Commission on Unity and Truth among Evangelicals. *The Nature of Hell: A Report by the Evangelical Alliance Commission on Unity and Truth among Evangelicals* [ACUTE]. London: Evangelical Alliance, 2000.

Evans, C. Stephen, ed. *Exploring Kenotic Christology: The Self-Emptying of God.* New York: Oxford University Press, 2006.

Evans, Gillian R. "Origen in the Twelfth Century." In Hanson and Crouzel, *Origeniana Tertia,* 279–85.

Evely, Bob. *At the End of the Ages . . . the Abolition of Hell.* Bloomington, IN: First Books Library, 2003.

Evtuhov, Catherine. *The Cross and the Sickle: Sergei Bulgakov and the Fate of Russian Religious Philosophy.* Ithaca, NY: Cornell University Press, 1997.

Fairclough, H. Ruston, trans. *Virgil: Eclogues, Georgics, Aeneid 1–6.* LCL 63. Cambridge, MA: Harvard University Press, 1916.

Fairhurst, Alan M. "'Dare We Hope . . .': From C. F. D. Moule (1953) to Jürgen Moltmann (1996)." *Expository Times* 111 (2000): 373–76.

Fairweather, Eugene R., ed. and trans. *A Scholastic Miscellany: Anselm to Ockham.* Library of Christian Classics 10. Philadelphia: Westminster, 1956.

Faivre, Antoine. *Access to Western Esotericism.* Albany: State University of New York Press, 1994.

———. "Love and Androgyny in Franz von Baader." In Faivre, *Access to Western Esotericism,* 201–74.

———. *Theosophy, Imagination, Tradition: Studies in Western Esotericism.* Translated by Christine Rhone. Albany: State University of New York Press, 2000.

Falke, Robert. *Die Lehre von der ewigen Verdammnis; mit besonderer Berücksichtigung des Conditionalismus, der Apokatastasis, und der Seelenwanderung.* Eisenach: Wilckens, 1892.

Falla, Claire. *L'apologie d'Origène par Pierre Halloix (1648).* Paris: Société d'Édition "Les Belle Lettres," 1983.

Farley, Edward. *Divine Empathy: A Theology of God.* Minneapolis: Fortress, 1996.

Farley, Wendy. *Tragic Vision and Divine Compassion: A Contemporary Theodicy.* Louisville: Westminster John Knox, 1990.

Farmer, S. A. *Syncretism in the West: Pico's 900 Theses (1486); The Evolution of Traditional Religious and Philosophical Systems.* Tempe, AZ: Medieval and Renaissance Texts and Studies, 1998.

Farrar, Frederic William. *Eternal Hope.* London: Macmillan, 1878.

———. *Mercy and Judgment: A Few Last Words on Christian Eschatology with Reference to Dr. Pusey's "What Is of Faith?"* London: Macmillan, 1881.

Farrow, Douglas B. "In the End Is the Beginning: A Review of Jürgen Moltmann's Systematic Contributions." *Modern Theology* 14 (1998): 425–47.

Feingold, Lawrence. *The Natural Desire to See God according to St. Thomas Aquinas and His Interpreters.* 2nd ed. Ave Maria, FL: Sapientia Press of Ave Maria University, 2010.

Feld, Edward. "Spinoza the Jew." *Modern Judaism* 9 (1989): 101–19.

Fernando, Ajith. *Crucial Questions about Hell.* Eastbourne, UK: Kingsway, 1991.

———. *A Universal Homecoming? An Examination of the Case for Universalism.* Madras, India: Evangelical Literature Service, 1983.

Ferrarin, Alfredo. *Hegel and Aristotle.* Cambridge: Cambridge University Press, 2004.

Ferwerda, Julie. *Raising Hell: Christianity's Most Controversial Doctrine Put under Fire.* Lander, WY: Vagabond Group, 2011.

Fesko, John V. *Diversity within the Reformed Tradition: Supra- and Infralapsarianism in Calvin, Dort, and Westminster.* Greenville, SC: Reformed Academic, 2001.

Feuerbach, Ludwig. *The Essence of Christianity.* Translated by George Eliot. 1841. Reprint, London: Trübner, 1843.

———. *Sämtliche Werke.* 10 vols. Leipzig: Otto Wigand, 1846–66.

Feuerstein, Otto. *Gibt es eine ewige Verdammnis?* Lorch: Rohm, 1914.

Fichte, J. G. *Die Anweisung zum seligen Leben.* In *Sämtliche Werke,* edited by I. H. Fichte, 5:397–574. Berlin: Veit, 1845–46.

Ficino, Marsilio. *De Religione Christiana.* Bremen: Typis Thomae Villeriani, 1617.

———. "Epistola de salute philosophorum." In *Opera,* 1:806. Basel, 1561.

———. *Marsilii Ficini Florentini, insignis philosophi Platonici, medici, atque theologi clarissimi, Opera.* 2 vols. Basileae [Basel]: [Heinrich Petri], 1561.

Fiddes, Paul S. *The Creative Suffering of God.* Oxford: Clarendon, 1988.

Fiedler, Leslie A. Introduction to *Waiting for God,* by Simone Weil, 3–39. Translated by Emma Craufurd. 1951. Reprint, New York: Harper & Row, 1973.

Filoramo, Giovanni. *A History of Gnosticism.* Translated by Anthony Alcock. Cambridge, MA: Blackwell, 1990.

Fine, Lawrence, trans. *Safed Spirituality: "Rules of Mystical Piety," "The Beginning of Wisdom."* New York: Paulist Press, 1984.

Finkel, Stuart. "Nikolai Berdiaev and the Philosophical Tasks of the Emigration." In *A History of Russian Philosophy, 1830–1930,* edited by G. M. Hamburg and Randall Poole, 346–62. Cambridge: Cambridge University Press, 2010.

Finn, Nathan A. "The Making of a Baptist Universalist: The Curious Case of Elhanan Winchester." *Baptist History and Heritage* 47 (2012): 6–18.

Finnis, John, and Germain Grisez. "The Misuse of *Amoris Laetitia* to Support Errors against the Catholic Faith: A Letter to the Supreme Pontiff Francis, to All Bishops in Communion with Him, and to the Rest of the Christian Faithful." November 21, 2016; Notre Dame, Indiana, USA. https://www .firstthings.com/uploads/resource_584ae0 6685216.pdf.

Fiori, Emiliano. "The Impossibility of the *Apokatastasis* in Dionysius the Areopagite." In Kaczmarek and Pietras, *Origeniana Decima,* 831–43.

———. "Mystique et liturgie: Entre Denys l'Aréopagite et le Livre de Hiérothée; Aux origines de la mystagogie syro-occidentale." In *Les mystiques syriaques,* edited by Alain Desreumaux, 27–44. Paris: Geuthner, 2011.

———. "The Topic of Mixture as a Philosophical Key to the Understanding of the *Divine Names*: Dionysius and the Origenist Monk Stephen bar Sudaili." In *Nomina Divina: Proceedings of the Colloquium Dionysiacum Held in Prague, 30–31 October 2009,* edited by L. Karfikova and M. Havrda, 71–88. Fribourg: Academic Press, 2011.

Flannery, Kevin L. "How to Think about Hell." *New Blackfriars* 72 (1991): 469–81.

Flood, Derek. *Healing the Gospel: A Radical Vision for Grace, Justice, and the Cross.* Eugene, OR: Wipf & Stock, 2012.

Florensky, Pavel. *The Pillar and Ground of the Truth: An Essay in Orthodox Theodicy in Twelve Lectures.* Translated by Boris Jakim.

Princeton: Princeton University Press, 1997. Originally published as *Stolp i utverzhdenie istiny* (Moscow: Put', 1914).

Florovsky, Georges. "The Seductive Path of Vladimir Solov'ev." In *The Ways of Russian Theology, Part 2*. Vol. 6 of *The Collected Works of Georges Florovsky*, 243–51. Belmont, MA: Nordland, 1987.

———. "V mire iskanii i bluzdanii" [In the World of Searches and Wanderings]. In *Iz proshlogo russkoi mysli* [From the Heritage of Russian Thought]. Moscow: Agraf, 1998. Originally published in *Russkaia mysl'* [Russian thought] 43 (1923): 120–46 and 44 (1924): 210–31.

Florschütz, Gottlieb. *Swedenborg and Kant: Emanuel Swedenborg's Mystical View of Humankind and the Dual Nature of Humankind in Immanuel Kant*. West Chester, PA: Swedenborg Foundation, 1993.

Flynn, Gabriel, and Paul D. Murray, eds. *Ressourcement: A Movement for Renewal in Twentieth-Century Catholic Theology*. New York: Oxford University Press, 2012.

Ford, Clyde D. "The Book of Mormon, the Early Nineteenth-Century Debates over Universalism, and the Development of the Novel Mormon Doctrines of Ultimate Rewards and Punishments." *Dialogue: A Journal of Mormon Thought* 47 (2014): 1–23.

Forster, Michael. "Friedrich Daniel Ernst Schleiermacher." In *The Stanford Encyclopedia of Philosophy*, edited by Edward N. Zalta. http://plato.stanford.edu/archives/sum2015/entries/schleiermacher.

Forsyth, P. T. *Marriage: Its Ethics and Religion*. London: Hodder & Stoughton, 1912.

Foster, B. F., and J. H. Lozier. *Theological Discussion on Universalism*. Indianapolis: B. F. Foster, 1867.

Foster, Ryan J. "The Creativity of Nature: The Genesis of Schelling's *Naturphilosophie*, 1775–1799." PhD diss., Rice University, 2008.

Fournié, Abbé Pierre. *Ce que nous avons été, ce que nous sommes, ce que nous deviendrons* [What we have been, are, and shall become]. Londres: Chez A. Dulau, 1801.

Foussard, Jean-Claude. "Apparence et apparition: La notion de 'phantasia' chez Jean Scot." In *Jean Scot Érigène et l'histoire de philosophie*, edited by René Roques, 337–48. Paris: Ed. du Centre national de la recherche scientifique, 1977.

Fowler, Harold North, trans. *Plato: Cratylus, Parmenides, Greater Hippias, Lesser Hippias*. LCL 167. Cambridge, MA: Harvard University Press, 1926.

———. *Plato: Euthyphro, Apology, Crito, Phaedo, Phaedrus*. LCL 36. Cambridge, MA: Harvard University Press, 1914.

Fox, George. *The Journal of George Fox*. Rev. ed. by John L. Nickalls. Cambridge: Cambridge University Press, 1952.

Francis, Pope. *Amoris Laetitia*: Post-Synodal Apostolic Exhortation of the Holy Father. Vatican website. March 19, 2016. https://w2.vatican.va/content/dam/francesco/pdf/apost_exhortations/documents/papa-francesco_esortazione-ap_20160319_amoris-laetitia_en.pdf.

Frank, Doug. *A Gentler God: Breaking Free of the Almighty in the Company of the Human Jesus*. Menangle, NSW, Australia: Albatross, 2010.

Frankl, Viktor E. *Man's Search for Meaning: An Introduction to Logotherapy*. 4th ed. Boston: Beacon, 1992.

Frei, Hans. *Types of Christian Theology*. New Haven: Yale University Press, 1992.

Fretheim, Terence E. *The Suffering of God: An Old Testament Perspective*. Overtures to Biblical Theology. Philadelphia: Fortress, 1984.

Freud, Sigmund. *The Joke and Its Relation to the Unconscious*. Translated by Joyce Crick. London: Penguin, 2002.

Freyd, Christophe. "Gott als die universale Wahrheit von Mensch und Welt: Die Versöhnungslehre Karl Barths im Lichte der Religionsphilosophie Hegels." PhD diss., University of Hamburg, 1978.

Frik, Johann. *Herrn M. Johann Friken . . . Gründliche Untersuchung Jacob Böhmens vornehmster Irrthümer*. Ulm: Ferdinand Mauch, 1697.

Fristad, Kalen. *Destined for Salvation: God's Promise to Save Everyone.* Kearney, NE: Morris, 2003.

Froome, Leroy E. *The Conditionalist Faith of Our Forefathers.* 2 vols. Washington, DC: Review & Herald, 1966.

Frothingham, A. L., Jr. *Stephen Bar Sudaili, the Syrian Mystic, and the Book of Hierotheos.* Leiden: Brill, 1886.

Fuchs, Ernst. "Jesus Christus in Person: Zum Problem der Geschichtlichkeit der Offenbarung" [1944]. In *Zur Frage nach dem historischen Jesus,* 21–54. Tübingen: Mohr, 1960.

Fudge, Edward W. "The Final End of the Wicked." *Journal of the Evangelical Theological Society* 27 (1984): 325–34.

———. *The Fire That Consumes: A Biblical and Historical Study of the Doctrine of Final Punishment.* 1982. 3rd ed. Eugene, OR: Cascade, 2011.

Fudge, Edward W., and Robert A. Peterson. *Two Views of Hell: A Biblical and Theological Dialogue.* Downers Grove, IL: InterVarsity, 2000.

Fukuyama, Francis. *The End of History and the Last Man.* New York: Free Press, 1992.

Fulford, Tim. "Coleridge, Böhme, and the Language of Nature." *Modern Language Quarterly* 52 (1991): 37–52.

Fünning, Albert. *Das feste, prophetische Wort: Arbeiten über Prophetie, über Israel, über die Gemeinde Jesu Christi, über die Endgerichte und über die Vollendung aller Dinge.* Fellbach-Stuttgart: Geugelin, 1950.

Fürst, Alfons. "Autonomie und Menschenwürde: Die origeneische Tradition." In *Autonomie und Menschenwürde: Origenes in der Philosophie der Neuzeit,* edited by Alfons Fürst and Christian Hengstermann, 9–46. Münster: Aschendorff Verlag, 2012.

———, ed. *Origenes und sein Erbe in Orient und Okzident.* Adamantiana 1. Münster: Aschendorff, 2011.

———. *Von Origenes und Hieronymus zu Augustinus: Studien zur antiken Theologiegeschichte.* Berlin: de Gruyter, 2011.

Fürst, Alfons, and Christian Hengstermann, eds. *Autonomie und Menschenwürde: Origenes in der Philosophie der Neuzeit.* Adamantiana 2. Münster: Aschendorff, 2012.

———. *Die Cambridge Origenists: George Rusts "Letter of Resolution concerning Origen and the Chief of His Opinions"; Zeugnisse des Cambridger Origenismus.* Adamantiana 4. Münster: Aschendorff, 2013.

Gallaher, Brandon. "Antinomism, Trinity, and the Challenge of Solov'evean Pantheism in the Thought of Sergij Bulgakov." *Studies in Eastern European Thought* 64 (2012): 205–25.

———. "The Christological Focus of Vladimir Solov'ev's Sophiology." *Modern Theology* 25 (2009): 617–46.

———. *Freedom and Necessity in Modern Trinitarian Theology.* Oxford: Oxford University Press, 2016.

Gallaher, Brandon, and Irina Kukota. "Protopresbyter Sergii Bulgakov: Hypostasis and Hypostasicity; Scholia to *The Unfading Light.*" *St. Vladimir's Theological Quarterly* 49 (2005): 5–46.

Galli, Mark. *God Wins: Heaven, Hell, and Why the Good News Is Better than "Love Wins."* Carol Stream, IL: Tyndale, 2011.

Gamaleia, S. N. *Pis'ma.* 3 vols. Moscow: Mosk. Univ. tip., 1832–39.

Gaon, Saadia. *Commentaire sur Séfer Yesira; ou, Livre de la creation par Gaon Saadya de Fayyoum.* Edited by Mayer Lambert. Paris: Bibliothèque de l'École pratique des hautes études, 1891.

Gardiner, Anne Barbeau. "The Dubious Adrienne von Speyr." *New Oxford Review* 69 (2002): 31–36.

Gardner, Alice. "Scotus as Optimist." In *Studies in John the Scot (Erigena): A Philosopher of the Dark Ages,* 97–114. London: Henry Frowde / Oxford University Press, 1900.

Gardner, Clinton C. "Vladimir Solov'ëv: From Theism to Panentheism." In van den Bercken, de Courten, and van der Zweerde, *Vladimir Solov'ëv,* 107–17.

Gardner, Eileen. *Medieval Visions of Heaven and Hell: A Sourcebook.* New York: Garland, 1993.

Gardner, Lucy, David Moss, Benjamin Quash, and Graham Ward. *Balthasar at the End of Modernity*. Edinburgh: T&T Clark, 1999.

Garrigou-Lagrange, Reginald. *Dieu, son existence et sa nature: solution thomiste des antinomies agnostique*. Paris: Beauchesne, 1914.

———. "La nouvelle théologie où va-t-elle?" *Angelicum* 23 (1946): 126–45. Translated by Suzanne Rinni as "Where Is the New Theology Leading Us?" *Catholic Family News Reprint Series #309* (August 1998). https://archive.org/stream/Garrigou-LagrangeEnglish.

———. *Life Everlasting*. Translated by Patrick Cummin. London: Herder, 1952.

Gatti, Hilary. *Essays on Giordano Bruno*. Princeton: Princeton University Press, 2011.

Gavin, Frank. *Some Aspects of Contemporary Greek Orthodox Thought*. Milwaukee: Mowbray, 1923.

Gavrilyuk, Paul. *Georges Florovsky and the Russian Religious Renaissance*. Oxford: Oxford University Press, 2014.

———. "The Kenotic Theology of Sergius Bulgakov." *Scottish Journal of Theology* 58 (2005): 251–69.

———. "The Reception of Dionysius in Twentieth-Century Eastern Orthodoxy." *Modern Theology* 24 (2008): 707–23.

———. "Universal Salvation in the Eschatology of Sergius Bulgakov." *Journal of Theological Studies* 57 (2006): 111–32.

Gay, Peter. *The Enlightenment: An Interpretation; The Science of Freedom*. New York: Knopf, 1969.

Geels, Antoon. "Sacred Sexuality: From the Ancient Sumerians to Contemporary Esalen." *Studies in Spirituality* 20 (2010): 355–79.

Geffert, Bryn. "The Charges of Heresy against Sergii Bulgakov." *St. Vladimir's Theological Quarterly* 49 (2005): 47–66.

Géhin, Paul, ed. *Évagre le Pontique Scholies à l'Ecclésiaste*. SC 397. Paris: Cerf, 1993.

———. *Évagre le Pontique Scholies aux Proverbs*. SC 340. Paris: Cerf, 1987.

Geiger, Abraham. *Leon da Modena*. Breslau: Verlag von Joh. Urban Kern, 1856.

Generchak, Christopher M. *The Sunday of the Negative: Reading Bataille Reading Hegel*. Albany: State University of New York Press, 2003.

George, N. D. *Universalism Not of the Bible*. New York: Carlton & Phillips, 1856.

George, Robert P. "Gnostic Liberalism." *First Things* 268 (December 2016): 33–38.

Gerhard, Ludwig. *Systema apokatastaseos d.i. ein vollständiger Lehrbegriff des ewigen Evangelii von der Wiederbringung aller Dinge*. Hamburg: Herold, 1727.

Gerrish, Brian. *Tradition and the Modern World: Reformed Theology in the Nineteenth Century*. Chicago: University of Chicago Press, 1978.

Gersh, Stephen. *From Iamblichus to Eriugena: An Investigation of the Prehistory and Evolution of the Pseudo-Dionysian Tradition*. Leiden: Brill, 1978.

Gerstner, John. *Jonathan Edwards on Heaven and Hell*. Grand Rapids: Baker, 1980.

Geyer, Karl. *Ewiges Gericht und Allversöhnung*. Neuhof: Deutrich, 1932.

Gibbons, Brian J. *Gender in Mystical and Occult Thought: Behmenism and Its Development in England*. Cambridge: Cambridge University Press, 1996.

Gichtel, Johann Georg. *Awakening to Divine Wisdom*. Translated by Arthur Versluis. St. Paul: New Grail, 2004.

———. *Theosophia practica: Halten und Kämpfen ob dem h. Glauben bis ans Ende . . .* 7 vols. 3rd ed. Leiden, 1722.

Gignoux, Philippe. "Les doctrines eschatologiques de Narsai [Part 3]." *L'Orient Syrien* 12 (1967): 23–54.

Gil, Thomas. "Zeitkonstruktion als Kampf- und Protestmittel: Reflexionen über Joachim von Fiores trinitätstheologische Geschichtskonstruktion und deren Wirkungsgeschichte." In *Constructions of Time in the Late Middle Ages*, edited by Carol Poster and Richard Utz, 35–49. Evanston, IL: Northwestern University Press, 1997.

Giles, Jerry C. "Jesus Christ, Firstborn in the Spirit." In D. H. Ludlow, *Encyclopedia of Mormonism*, 2:728.

Giles, Kevin. *The Eternal Generation of the Son: Maintaining Orthodoxy in Trinitarian Theology*. Downers Grove, IL: IVP Academic, 2012.

Gill, Michael. "The Religious Rationalism of Benjamin Whichcote." *Journal of the History of Philosophy* 37 (1999): 271–300.

Gillihan, Charles. *Hell No! A Fundamentalist Preacher Rejects Eternal Torment*. Santa Barbara, CA: Praeger, 2011.

Gilson, Étienne. *A History of Christian Philosophy in the Middle Ages*. New York: Random House, 1955.

———. *The Spirit of Medieval Philosophy*. New York: Scribner's, 1940.

Ginzberg, Louis. "Elisha ben Abuyah." In *The Jewish Encyclopedia*, edited by Isidore Singer, 5:138–39. 12 vols. New York: Funk & Wagnalls, 1901–6.

Girard, René. *Things Hidden since the Foundation of the World*. Stanford, CA: Stanford University Press, 1987.

Givens, Terryl L. *By the Hand of Mormon: The American Scripture That Launched a New World Religion*. New York: Oxford University Press, 2002.

———. *When Souls Had Wings: Pre-mortal Existence in Western Thought*. New York: Oxford University Press, 2010.

Gladstone, William Ewart. *Studies Subsidiary to the Works of Bishop Butler*. Oxford: Clarendon, 1896.

Glanvill, Joseph. *Lux Orientalis*. In *Two Choice and Useful Treatises: The One Lux Orientalis; or, An Enquiry into the Opinion of the Eastern Sages concerning the Præexistence of Souls, Being a Key to Unlock the Grand Mysteries of Providence. The Other, a Discourse of Truth*, edited by George Rust, 1–151. London: James Collins, 1662.

———. *The Vanity of Dogmatizing; or, Confidence in Opinions Manifested in a Discourse of the Shortness and Uncertainty of Our Knowledge, and Its Causes*. London, 1661.

Gnilka, Joachim. "Fegfeuer II: Lehre der Schrift im Neuen Testament." In *Lexikon für Theologie und Kirche*, edited by Walter Kasper et al., 10:50–51. 3rd ed. Freiburg: Herder, 1993–2001.

Göckel, Matthias. *Barth and Schleiermacher on the Doctrine of Election: A Systematic Theological Comparison*. Oxford: Oxford University Press, 2006.

Godbey, John Charles. "A Study of Faustus Socinus' *De Jesu Christo Servatore*." PhD diss., University of Chicago, 1968.

Godfrey, Kenneth W. "Freemasonry and the Temple." In D. H. Ludlow, *Encyclopedia of Mormonism*, 2:528–29.

———. "Freemasonry in Nauvoo." In D. H. Ludlow, *Encyclopedia of Mormonism*, 2:527–28.

Godin, André. *Erasme: Lecteur d'Origène*. Geneva: Droz, 1982.

Godsey, John D., ed. *Karl Barth's Table Talk*. Richmond: John Knox, 1963.

Goldish, Matt. "Halakhah, Kabbalah, and Heresy: A Controversy in Early Eighteenth-Century Amsterdam." *Jewish Quarterly Review* 84 (1993–94): 153–76.

Goldstein, Bernard R. "Saving the Phenomena: The Background to Ptolemy's Planetary Theory." *Journal for the History of Astronomy* 28 (1997): 1–11.

Gomes, Alan W. "*De Jesu Christo Servatore*: Faustus Socinus on the Satisfaction of Christ." *Westminster Theological Journal* 55 (1993): 209–31.

———. "Some Observations on the Theological Method of Faustus Socinus (1539–1604)." *Westminster Theological Journal* 70 (2008): 49–71.

Goodall, Lawrence D. "Hans Urs von Balthasar: A Respectful Critique." *Pro Ecclesia* 8 (1999): 423–36.

Goodrick-Clarke, Nicholas. *Helena Blavatsky*. Berkeley: North Atlantic, 2004.

Gordon, William. *Universal Salvation Examined*. Boston: T. and J. Fleet, 1783.

Görgemanns, Herwig, and Heinrich Karpp, eds. and trans. *Origenes vier Bücher von den Prinzipien*. Darmstadt: Wissenschaftliche Buchgesellschaft, 1976.

Gorodetzky, Nadejda. *The Humiliated Christ*. New York: Macmillan, 1938.

Goroncy, Jason. "'That God May Have Mercy upon All': A Review Essay on Matthias Göckel's *Barth and Schleiermacher on the*

Doctrine of Election." *Journal of Reformed Theology* 2 (2008): 113–30.

Gorringe, Timothy. *God's Just Vengeance: Crime, Violence, and the Rhetoric of Salvation.* Cambridge: Cambridge University Press, 1996.

Goshen-Gottstein, Alon. *The Sinner and the Amnesiac: The Rabbinic Invention of Elisha ben Abuya and Eleazar ben Arach.* Stanford, CA: Stanford University Press, 2000.

Goudriaan, Aza, and Fred van Lieburg, eds. *Revisiting the Synod of Dordt (1618–1619).* Leiden: Brill, 2010.

Grace Communion International. "The GCI Statement of Beliefs." http://www.gci.org /aboutus/beliefs.

———. "Our Story." http://www.gci.org/about us.

———. "Worldwide Church of God Announces Name Change." April 15, 2009. http://www.gci.org/aboutus/namechange.

Graetz, Heinrich. *Gnosticismus und Judenthum.* Krotoschin: B. L. Monasch, 1846.

Grafton, Anthony. "Protestant versus Prophet: Isaac Casaubon on Hermes Trismegistus." *Journal of the Warburg and Courtauld Institutes* 46 (1983): 78–93.

Graves, J. R., and John C. Burruss. *A Discussion on the Doctrine of Endless Punishment.* Atlanta: J. O. Perkins & Co., 1880.

Gray, Ronald D. *Goethe the Alchemist.* Cambridge: Cambridge University Press, 1952.

Green, Michael. *Evangelism through the Local Church.* London: Hodder & Stoughton, 1990.

Greenberg, Shoshana. "Lucas Hnath, a Humana Festival Staple." *Culturadar,* March 6, 2014. http://www.culturadar.com/blog/201 4/03/06/Lucas-Hnath-a-Humana-Festival -staple.html.

Greene, Murray. *Hegel on the Soul: A Speculative Anthropology.* The Hague: Nijhof, 1972.

Greer, Rowan. *Evagrius Ponticus: The Gnostic Chapters; A Translation of the Two Syriac Versions with an Introduction.* Unpublished manuscript, 2006.

Greggs, Tom. *Barth, Origen, and Universal Salvation: Restoring Particularity.* Oxford: Oxford University Press, 2009.

———. "'Jesus Is Victor': Passing the Impasse of Barth on Universalism." *Scottish Journal of Theology* 60 (2007): 196–212.

———. "Pessimistic Universalism: Rethinking the Wider Hope with Bonhoeffer and Barth." *Modern Theology* 26 (2010): 495–510.

Gregory, Alan. "'No New Truths in Religion': William Law's Appropriation of Jacob Boehme." In Hessayon and Apetrai, *Introduction to Jacob Boehme,* 142–61.

Gregory of Nyssa. *The Catechetical Oration.* Translated by J. H. Strawley. London: SPCK, 1917.

———. *Dialogus de Anima et Resurrectione.* Edited by J. G. Krabinger. Leipzig: In Libraria Gustavi Wuttigii, 1837. ET: *NPNF*[2] 5:428–68.

Grenz, Stanley. *The Social God and the Relational Self.* Louisville: Westminster John Knox, 2001.

Greshake, Gisbert. *Stärker als der Tod: Zukunft, Tod, Auferstehung, Himmel, Hölle, Fegfeuer.* Mainz: Matthias-Grünewald, 1976.

Griffin, Edward M. *Old Brick: Charles Chauncy of Boston, 1705–1787.* Minneapolis: University of Minnesota Press, 1980.

Griffiths, Paul J. *Decreation: The Last Things of All Creatures.* Waco: Baylor University Press, 2014.

———. "Is There a Doctrine of the Descent into Hell?" *Pro Ecclesia* 17 (2008): 257–68.

———. "Purgatory." In *The Oxford Handbook of Eschatology,* edited by Jerry Walls, 427–45. New York: Oxford University Press, 2008.

Grillmeier, Aloys. *Christ in Christian Tradition.* Translated by J. S. Bowden. New York: Sheed & Ward, 1965.

———. "La 'Peste d'Origène': Soucis du patriarché d'Alexandrie dus à l'apparition d'origénistes en Haute Egypt (444–451)." In *Alexandrina, hellénisme, judaisme et christianisme d'Alexandrie: Mélanges offerts au P. Claude Mondésert,* 221–37. Paris, 1987.

Grimsrud, Ted, and Michael Hardin, eds. *Compassionate Eschatology: The Future as Friend.* Eugene, OR: Cascade, 2011.

Grisez, Germain, and Peter F. Ryan. "Hell and Hope for Salvation." *New Blackfriars* 95 (2014): 606–15.

Groeschel, Benedict. Introduction to *Purgation and Purgatory; The Spiritual Dialogue*, by Catherine of Genoa, 1–45. Translated by Serge Hughes. New York: Paulist Press, 1979.

Groth, Friedhelm. "'Bebel- und auch Bibelfest': Eschatologischer Universalismus und Engagement für den Sozialismus in der Reich-Gottes-Hoffnung des jüngeren Blumhardt. Eine Hoffnung und ihre Nachwirkungen." Stuttgart: Württembergische Landesbibliothek, 1999. http://www.pastoerchen.de/BlumhardtuWiederbringung.pdf.

———. "Chiliasmus und Apokatastasishoffnung in der Reich-Gottes-Verkündigung der beiden Blumhardts." *Pietismus und Neuzeit* 9 (1983): 56–116.

———. "Petersen (Jean Guillaume)." In *Dictionnaire de spiritualité ascétique et mystique: Doctrine et histoire*, edited by Marcel Viller, 12:1195–97. Paris: Beauchesne, 1937–95.

———. *Die "Wiederbringung aller Dinge" im württembergischen Pietismus: Theologiegeschichtliche Studien zum eschatologischen Heilsuniversalismus württembergischer Pietisten des 18. Jahrhunderts*. Arbeiten zur Geschichte des Pietismus 21. Göttingen: Vandenhoeck & Ruprecht, 1984.

Grounds, Vernon C. "The Final State of the Wicked." *Journal of the Evangelical Theological Society* 24 (1981): 211–20.

Grützmacher, Georg. *Hieronymus: Eine biographische Studie zur alten Kirchengeschichte*. 3 vols. 1906. Reprint, Aalen: Scientia Verlag, 1969.

Grützmacher, H. *Hieronymus: Eine biographische Studie zur alten Kirchengeschichte*. 3 vols. Leipzig: Dieterich; Berlin: Trowitzsch und Sohn, 1901–8.

———. "Die Lehre von der Apokatastasis." *Evangelische Kirchenzeitung* 75 (1901): 673ff.

Guardini, Romano. *The Last Things*. Translated by Charlotte Forsyth and Grace Branham. New York: Pantheon, 1954.

Guillaumont, Antoine. "Évagre et les anathématismes antiorigénistes de 553." In *Studia Patristica*, vol. 3, edited by F. L. Cross, 219–26. Berlin: Akademie Verlag, 1961.

———. "Gnose et monachisme: exposé introductive." In *Gnosticisme et monde hellénistique: Actes du Colloque de Louvain-la-Neuve*, edited by Julien Ries, 301–10. Louvain-la-Neuve: Institut orientaliste, 1982.

———. *Les 'Kephalaia gnostica' d'Évagre le Pontique et l'histoire de l'Origenisme chez les Grecs et chex les Syriens*. Paris: Éditions du Seuil, 1962.

———, ed. *Les Six Centuries des 'Kephalaia gnostica' d'Évagre le Pontique*. PO 28/1. Paris: Firmin-Didot, 1958.

Guinan, Michael Damon. "The Eschatology of James of Sarug." PhD diss., Catholic University of America, 1972.

Gulley, Philip, and James Mulholland. *If Grace Is True: Why God Will Save Every Person*. New York: HarperOne, 2003.

Guly, Sebastian. "The Salvation of the Devil and the Kingdom of God in Origen's Letter *To Certain Close Friends in Alexandria*." In Kaczmarek and Pietras, *Origeniana Decima*, 197–220.

Gundry-Volf, Judith M. "Universalism." In *Dictionary of Paul and His Letters*, edited by Gerald F. Hawthorne, Ralph P. Martin, and Daniel G. Reid, 956–61. Downers Grove, IL: InterVarsity, 1993.

Gunther, John J. *St. Paul's Opponents and Their Background: A Study of Apocalyptic and Jewish Sectarian Teachings*. Leiden: Brill, 1973.

Gunton, Colin E. *Act and Being: Towards a Theology of the Divine Attributes*. London: SCM, 2002.

———. *Yesterday and Today: A Study of Continuities in Christology*. Grand Rapids: Eerdmans, 1983.

Guomundsdottir, Arnfriour. "Abusive or Abused? Theology of the Cross from a Feminist Critical Perspective." *Journal of the European Society of Women in Theological Research* 15 (2007): 37–54.

Gustafson, Richard F. "Solovyov's Doctrine of Salvation." In Kornblatt and Gustafson, *Russian Religious Thought*, 31–48.

Hafen, Bruce C. "Grace." In D. H. Ludlow, *Encyclopedia of Mormonism*, 2:560 63.

Haga, Joar. *Was There a Lutheran Metaphysics? The Interpretation of* Communicatio Idiomatum *in Early Modern Lutheranism.* Göttingen: Vandenhoeck & Ruprecht, 2012.

Hagan, Annette J. *Eternal Blessedness for All? A Historical-Systematic Examination of Friedrich Schleiermacher's Reinterpretation of Predestination.* Eugene, OR: Pickwick, 2013.

Hahn, Johann Michael. *Briefe von der ersten Offenbarung Gottes: durch die ganze Schöpfung bis an das Ziel aller Dinge.* Tübingen: L. F. Fues, 1825.

Hall, Alexander Wilford. *Universalism against Itself.* Rev. ed. New York: Hall & Company, 1883.

Hallamish, Moshe. *An Introduction to the Kabbalah.* Translated by Ruth Bar-Ilan and Ora Wiskind-Elper. Albany: State University of New York Press, 1999.

Hallesby, Ole Christian. *Himmel, Tod und Hölle.* Wuppertal: Brockhaus, 1958.

Hamberger, Julius. *Die Lehre des deutschen Philosophen Jacob Boehme.* Munich, 1844.

———. *Zur tieferen Würdigung der Lehre Jacob Boehme's.* Leipzig, 1855.

Hamilton, Edith, and Huntington Cairns, eds. *Plato: Collected Dialogues.* Princeton: Princeton University Press, 1961.

Hanegraaff, Wouter J. *Swedenborg, Oetinger, Kant: Three Perspectives on the Secrets of Heaven.* West Chester, PA: Swedenborg Foundation, 2007.

Hanegraaff, Wouter J., ed., with A. Faivre, R. van den Broek, and J.-P. Brach. *Dictionary of Gnosis and Western Esotericism.* 2 vols. Leiden: Brill, 2005. One-volume edition, Leiden: Brill, 2006.

Hankins, Franklin T. "The Early Aquinas on the Question of Universal Salvation, or How a Knight May Choose Not to Ride His Horse." *New Blackfriars* 95 (2014): 208–17.

Hannak, Kristine. "Boehme and German Romanticism." In Hessayon and Apetrai, *Introduction to Jacob Boehme*, 162–79.

———. "Boehme and the Early English Romantics." In Hessayon and Apetrai, *Introduction to Jacob Boehme*, 180–95.

Hanratty, Gerald. "The Gnostic Synthesis of G. W. F. Hegel." In Hanratty, *Studies in Gnosticism and in the Philosophy of Religion*, 81–116.

———. *Studies in Gnosticism and in the Philosophy of Religion.* Portland, OR: Four Courts, 1997.

Hanson, Paul D. *The Dawn of Apocalyptic.* Philadelphia: Fortress, 1975.

Hanson, R. P. C. *Allegory and Event: A Study of the Sources and Significance of Origen's Interpretation of Scripture.* London: SCM, 1959.

Hanson, R. P. C., and Henri Crouzel, eds. *Origeniana Tertia.* Rome: Edizioni dell'Ateneo, 1985.

Hardin, James N., and Christoph E. Schweitzer. *German Writers in the Age of Goethe: Sturm und Drang to Classicism.* Detroit: Gale Research, 1990.

Hardwick, Charley D. *Events of Grace: Naturalism, Existentialism, and Theology.* New York: Cambridge University Press, 1996.

Hardy, Edward Rochie, and Cyril C. Richardson, eds. *Christology of the Later Fathers.* Philadelphia: Westminster, 1954.

Harl, Marguerite. *Origène et la fonction révélatrice de verbe incarné.* Paris: Éditions du Seuil, 1958.

———. "La préexistence des âmes dans l'oeuvre d'Origène." In Lies, *Origeniana Quarta*, 238–58.

———. "Structure et cohérence du *Peri Archon*." In *Origeniana: Premier colloque international des études origèniennes*, edited by Henri Crouzel, Gennaro Lomiento, and Josep Rius-Camps, 11–32. Bari, It.: Istituto di letteratura Cristiana antiqua, 1975.

Härle, Wilfried. *Sein und Gnade: Die Ontologie in Karl Barths Kirchlicher Dogmatik.* Berlin: de Gruyter, 1975.

Harmon, Kendall S. "Finally Excluded from God? Some Twentieth-Century Theological Explorations of the Problem of Hell and Universalism with Reference to the Historical Development of These Docrines." PhD diss., Oxford University, 1993.

Harmon, Steven. "*Apokatastasis* and Exegesis: A Comparative Analysis of the Use of Scripture in the Eschatological Universalism of Clement of Alexandria, Origen, and

Gregory of Nyssa." PhD diss., Southwestern Baptist Theological Seminary (Fort Worth, TX), 1997.

———. "The Subjection of All Things In Christ: The Christocentric Universalism of Gregory of Nyssa (331/340–c. 395)." In MacDonald [Parry], *All Shall Be Well,*" 47–65.

Harnack, Adolf von. *Lehrbuch der Dogmengeschichte.* 3 vols. 5th ed. Tübingen, 1931.

Harris, H. S. *Hegel's Development: Night Thoughts (Jena 1801–1806).* Oxford: Clarendon, 1983.

Hart, David Bentley. "God, Creation, and Evil: The Moral Meaning of *Creatio Ex Nihilo.*" *Radical Orthodoxy: Theology, Philosophy, Politics* 3 (2015): 1–17.

———. "No Shadow of Turning: On Divine Impassibility." *Pro Ecclesia* 11 (2002): 184–206.

Hart, John W. *Karl Barth vs. Emil Brunner: The Formation and Dissolution of a Theological Alliance, 1916–1936.* New York: Lang, 2001.

Hart, Ray L. *God Being Nothing.* Chicago: University of Chicago Press, 2016.

Hart, Trevor. Foreword to *Laws of the Spiritual Order: Innovation and Reconstruction in the Soteriology of Thomas Erskine of Linlathen,* by Don Horrocks, xiii–xiv. Carlisle, UK: Paternoster, 2004.

———. *"In the End, God . . . :* The Christian Universalism of J. A. T. Robinson (1919–1983)." In MacDonald [Parry], *All Shall Be Well,"* 355–81.

———. "Universalism: Two Distinct Types." In Cameron, *Universalism and the Doctrine of Hell,* 1–34.

Hartley, David. "The Correspondence of David Hartley and John Lister [March 1736–January 1737]." Calderdale Archives, Calderdale Central Library, Halifax, Great Britain.

———. *Observations on Man . . . in Two Parts.* 2 vols. in 1. London, 1749. Facsimile reproduction. Gainsville, FL: Scholars' Facsimiles & Reprints, 1966.

———. *Various Conjectures on the Perception, Motion, and Generation of Ideas (1746).* Translated by Robert E. A. Palmer. The Augustan Reprint Society. Los Angeles:

William Andrews Clark Memorial Library, University of California, 1959.

Hartman, Klaus. "Hegel: A Non-Metaphysical View." In *Hegel: A Collection of Critical Essays,* edited by Alasdair MacIntyre, 101–24. Notre Dame, IN: University of Notre Dame Press, 1972.

Hartmann, Frank. *Johann Heinrich Horb (1645–1695): Leben und Werk bis zum Beginn der Hamburger pietistischen Streitigkeiten 1693.* Halle: Verlag der Franckeschen Stiftungen; Tübingen: Niemeyer, 2004.

Hartshorne, Charles, and William L. Reese, eds. *Philosophers Speak of God.* Chicago: University of Chicago Press, 1953.

Hartwell, Herbert. *The Theology of Karl Barth: An Introduction.* Philadelphia: Westminster, 1964.

Hatch, Edwin. *The Influence of Greek Ideas on Christianity.* New York: Harper & Brothers, 1957.

Haug, Johann Heinrich, et al., trans. *Die Heilige Schrift Altes und Neues Testaments: nach dem Grund-Text aufs neue übersehen und übersetzet: nebst einiger Erklärung des buchstäblichen Sinnes, wie auch der fürnehmsten Fürbildern und Weissagungen von Christo und seinem Reich, und zugleich einigen Lehren die auf den Zustand der Kirchen in unseren letzten Zeiten gerichtet sind: welchem allem noch untermängt eine Erklärung die den inneren Zustand des geistlichen Lebens, oder die Wege und Wirckungen Gottes in der Seelen . . . zu erkennen gibt.* 8 vols. Berlenburg, 1726–42.

Hauke, Manfred. "Sperare per tutti? Il ricorso all'esperienza dei santi nell'ultima grande controversia di Hans Urs von Balthasar." *Rivista Teologico di Lugano* 6 (2001): 195–220.

Hausherr, Irénée. "L'influence du 'Livre de Saint Hiérothée.'" In *Études de spiritualité orientale,* 23–58. Rome: Pontificum Institutum Studiorum Orientalium, 1969.

Havelaar, Henriette W., ed. *The Coptic Apocalypse of Peter (Nag-Hammadi Codex VII, 3).* Berlin: Akademie Verlag, 1999.

Hayes, Stephen Andrew. "Emil Brunner's Criticism of Karl Barth's Doctrine of Election." PhD diss., McGill University, 1970.

Hayes, Thomas Wilson. *Winstanley the Digger: A Literary Analysis of Radical Ideas in the English Revolution.* Cambridge, MA: Harvard University Press, 1979.

Hayes, Zachary. "The Purgatorial View." In *Four Views on Hell*, edited by William Crockett, 91–118. Grand Rapids: Zondervan, 1996.

Haynes, Renee. *The Society for Psychical Research, 1882–1982: A History.* London: MacDonald, 1982.

Hayward, Deirdre. "George MacDonald and Jacob Boehme: Lilith and the Seven-fold Pattern of Existence." *Seven* 16 (1999): 55–72.

Healy, Nicholas. *The Eschatology of Hans Urs von Balthasar.* Oxford: Oxford University Press, 2005.

Hector, Kevin W. "Actualism and Incarnation: The High Christology of Friedrich Schleiermacher." *International Journal of Systematic Theology* 8 (2006): 307–22.

———. "God's Triunity and Self-Determination: A Conversation with Karl Barth, Bruce McCormack and Paul Molnar." *International Journal of Systematic Theology* 7 (2005): 246–61.

———. "Immutability, Necessity, and Triunity: Towards a Resolution of the Trinity and Election Controversy." *Scottish Journal of Theology* 65 (2012): 64–81.

Heer, Friedrich. *Abschied von Himmeln und Höllen.* Munich: Bechtle, 1970.

Hege, Christian. "Kautz, Jakob (1500–1532?)." In *Global Anabaptist Mennonite Encyclopedia Online.* http://gameo.org.

Hegel, G. W. F. *The Difference between Fichte's and Schelling's System of Philosophy.* Translated by Walter Cerf and H. S. Harris. Albany: State University of New York Press, 1976.

———. *Faith and Knowledge.* Translated by Walter Cerf and H. S. Harris. Albany: State University of New York Press, 1977.

———. *Hegel's Philosophy of Mind.* Translated with revisions and commentary by W. Wallace, A. V. Miller, and M. J. Inwood. Oxford: Clarendon, 2007.

———. *Hegel's Philosophy of Mind . . . Translated from the Encyclopedia of the Philosophical Sciences, with Five Introductory Essays.* Translated by William Wallace. Oxford: Clarendon, 1894.

———. *Hegels theologische Jugendschriften.* Edited by H. Nohl. Tübingen: J. C. B. Mohr, 1907.

———. *Lectures on the History of Philosophy.* 3 vols. Translated by E. S. Haldane and F. H. Simson. 1892–96. Reprint, London: Routledge & Kegan Paul, 1955–63.

———. *Lectures on the Philosophy of History.* Translated by J. Sibree. 1899. Reprint, New York: Dover, 1956.

———. *Lectures on the Philosophy of Religion.* Translated and edited by R. F. Brown, Peter C. Hodgson, and J. M. Stewart. 3 vols. Berkeley: University of California Press, 1984, 1985, 1987.

———. *Letters.* Translated by Clark Butler and Christiane Seiler. Bloomington: Indiana University Press, 1984.

———. *Logic: The First Part of the Encyclopedia of the Philosophical Sciences in Outline.* 2nd ed. Translated by William Wallace. Oxford: Clarendon, 1892.

———. *On Christianity: Early Theological Writings of Friedrich Hegel.* Translated by G. T. M. Knox. New York: Harper & Row, 1961.

———. *Phenomenology of Spirit.* Translated by A. V. Miller. Oxford: Oxford University Press, 1977.

———. *Philosophy of Mind: Encyclopedia of the Philosophical Sciences, Part Three (1830).* Translated by A. V. Miller. Oxford: Clarendon, 1971.

———. *Philosophy of Nature: Encyclopedia of the Philosophical Sciences, Part Two (1830).* Translated by A. V. Miller. Oxford: Clarendon, 1970.

———. *Philosophy of Right.* Translated by T. M. Knox. 1952. Reprint, Oxford: Oxford University Press, 1967.

———. *Reason in History: A General Introduction to the Philosophy of History.* Translated by Robert S. Hartman. Indianapolis: Bobbs-Merrill, 1953.

———. *Science of Logic.* Translated by A. V. Miller. New York: Humanities Press, 1969.

Heiler, Friedrich. *The Gospel of Sadhu Sundar Singh.* New York: Oxford University Press, 1927.

Heimbach, Werner. "Das Urteil des Görlitzer Oberpfarrers Richter über Jakob Böhme." *Herbergen der Christenheit* 9 (1973–74): 97–151.

Heine, Heinrich. *Historisch-kritische Gesamtausgabe der Werke.* Edited by Manfred Windfuhr. 16 vols. Hamburg: Hoffmann und Campe, 1973–97.

Heine, Ronald E., trans. *The Commentaries of Origen and Jerome on St. Paul's Epistle to the Ephesians.* Oxford: Oxford University Press, 2002.

———. "*Epinoiai.*" In *The Westminster Handbook to Origen,* edited by John Anthony McGuckin, 93–95. Louisville: Westminster John Knox, 2004.

———. *Origen: Commentary on the Gospel according to John, Books 1–10.* FC 80. Washington, DC: Catholic University of America Press, 1989.

———. *Origen: Commentary on the Gospel according to John, Books 13–32.* FC 89. Washington, DC: Catholic University of America Press, 1993.

Helleman, Wendy. "The World Soul and Sophia in the Early Work of Solov'ëv." In van den Bercken, de Courten, and van der Zweerde, *Vladimir Solov'ëv,* 164–84.

Helm, Paul. "Eternity." In *The Stanford Encyclopedia of Philosophy,* edited by Edward N. Zalta. http://plato.stanford.edu/entries/eternity.

———. "Universalism and the Threat of Hell." *Trinity Journal* 4 (1983): 35–43.

Helmbold, A. K. "Gnostic Elements in the 'Ascension of Isaiah.'" *New Testament Studies* 18 (1972): 222–27.

Heltzel, Peter Goodwin, and Christian T. Collins Winn. "Karl Barth, Reconciliation, and the Triune God." In *The Cambridge Companion to the Trinity,* edited by Peter C. Phan, 171–91. Cambridge: Cambridge University Press, 2011.

Henderson, Jeffrey, trans. *Aristophanes IV.* LCL 180. Cambridge, MA: Harvard University Press, 2002.

Hengstermann, Christian. "The Neoplatonism of Origen in the First Two Books of His *Commentary on John.*" In Kaczmarek and Pietras, *Origeniana Decima,* 75–87.

Henrici, Peter. "A Sketch of von Balthasar's Life." In Schindler, *Hans Urs von Balthasar,* 7–43.

Heppe, Heinrich. *Geschichte der quietistische Mystik in der katholischen Kirche.* Berlin, 1875.

Héring, Jean. *Étude sur la doctrine de la chute et de la préexistence des âmes chez Clément d'Alexandrie.* Paris: E. Leroux, 1923.

Hermes, Gerhard. "Ist die Hölle leer?" *Der Fels* 15 (1984): 350–56.

Herodotus. *Herodoti Historiae* [The histories]. Edited by N. G. Wilson. Oxford: Clarendon, 2015.

Hessayon, Ariel. "Jacob Boehme's Writings during the English Revolution and Afterwards: Their Publication, Dissemination, and Influence." In Hessayon and Apetrai, *Introduction to Jacob Boehme,* 77–97.

Hessayon, Ariel, and Sarah Apetrai, eds. *An Introduction to Jacob Boehme.* London: Routledge, 2014.

Hewett, Philip. "Samuel Taylor Coleridge." In *Dictionary of Unitarian and Universalist Biography.* http://uudb.org/articles/samueltaylorcoleridge.html.

Hick, John. *Death and Eternal Life.* 1976. Reprint, Louisville: Westminster John Knox, 1994.

———. *Evil and the God of Love.* London: Macmillan, 1966. Rev. ed. New York: Harper & Row, 1978. Reprint, New York: Palgrave Macmillan, 2010.

———, ed. *The Myth of God Incarnate.* London: SCM, 1977.

Hilberg, Isidor, ed. *Jerome: Opera Epistularum Pars I.* CSEL 54. Vienna: F. Tempsky, 1910.

———. *Jerome: Opera Epistularum Pars II.* CSEL 55. Vienna: F. Tempsky, 1912.

———. *Jerome: Opera Epistularum Pars III.* CSEL 56. Vienna: F. Tempsky, 1918.

Hilberg, Raul. *The Destruction of the European Jews*. New York: Holmes & Meier, 1985.

Hilborn, David, and Don Horrocks. "Universalistic Trends in the Evangelical Tradition: An Historical Perspective." In Parry and Partridge, *Universal Salvation?*, 219–44.

Hilborn, David, and P. Johnston, eds. *The Nature of Hell*. Carlisle, UK: Paternoster, 2000.

Hill, Andrew. "James Relly." *Dictionary of Unitarian and Universalist Biography*. http://uudb.org/articles/jamesrelly.html.

———. "Winchester, Elhanan." In *Dictionary of National Biography*, vol. 62. 1900. http://onlinebooks.library.upenn.edu/webbin/metabook?id=dnb.

Hill, Charles E. *Regnum Caelorum: Patterns of Millennial Thought in Early Christianity*. Grand Rapids: Eerdmans, 2001.

Hill, Robert C., trans. *Didymus the Blind; Commentary on Zechariah*. FC 111. Washington, DC: Catholic University of America Press, 2006.

Hillert, Sven. *Limited and Universal Salvation: A Text-Oriented and Hermeneutical Study of Two Perspectives in Paul*. Stockholm: Almqvist & Wiksell, 1999.

Hilton, Boyd. *The Age of Atonement: The Influence of Evangelicalism on Social and Economic Thought, 1785–1865*. Oxford: Clarendon, 1991.

Hippolytus of Rome. *De Antichristo*. Edited by Enrico Norelli. Florence: Nardini, 1987.

———. *Kommentar zu Daniel*. Edited by George Nathanael Bonwetsch and Marcel Richard. 2nd ed. Berlin: Akadamie Verlag, 2000.

Hirsch, Emanuel. *Geschichte der neueren evangelischen Theologie*. 5 vols. Gütersloh: Bertelsmann, 1951.

Hirst, Julie. *Jane Leade: Biography of a Seventeenth-Century Mystic*. Burlington, VT: Ashgate, 2005.

Hobhouse, Stephen, ed. *Selected Mystical Writings of William Law. Edited with Notes and Twenty-Four Studies in the Mystical Theology of William Law and Jacob Boehme and an Inquiry into the Influence of Jacob Boehme on Isaac Newton*. 2nd ed. New York: Harper, 1948.

Hochhuth, W. C. "Geschichte und Entwicklung der Philadelphischen Gemeinden." *Zeitschrift für die historische Theologie* 29 (1865): 171–290.

Hodges, Zane C. *Absolutely Free! A Biblical Response to Lordship Salvation*. Grand Rapids: Zondervan, 1989.

Hofmann, Martin. *Theologie und Exegese der Berleburger Bibel (1726–42)*. Gütersloh: Bertelsmann, 1937.

Hoheisel, Karl. "Das frühe Christentum und die Seelenwanderung." *Jahrbüch für Antike und Christentum* 27–28 (1984–85): 24–46.

Holcomb, Justin S. "Being Bound to God: Participation and Covenant Revisited." In *Radical Orthodoxy and the Reformed Tradition: Creation, Covenant, and Participation*, edited by James K. A. Smith and James H. Olthuis, 243–62. Grand Rapids: Baker Academic, 2005.

Holifield, E. Brooks. *Theology in America: Christian Thought from the Age of the Puritans to the Civil War*. New Haven: Yale University Press, 2003.

Holl, Karl. *Epiphanius I: Ancoratus und Panarion Haer. 1–33*. GCS 25. Leipzig: J. C. Hinrichs, 1915.

———. *Epiphanius II: Panarion II, Haer. 34–64*. GCS 31. Leipzig: J. C. Hinrichs, 1922.

Holland, Jeffrey R. "Atonement of Jesus Christ." In D. H. Ludlow, *Encyclopedia of Mormonism*, 1:82–86.

Holliday, Lisa R. "Will Satan Be Saved? Reconsidering Origen's Theory of Volition in *Peri Archon*." *Vigiliae Christianae* 63 (2009): 1–23.

Holtmann, Stefan. *Karl Barth als Theologe der Neuzeit: Studien zur kritischen Deutung seiner Theologie*. Göttingen: Vandenhoeck & Ruprecht, 2007.

Holzapfel, Richard Neitzel. "Damnation." In D. H. Ludlow, *Encyclopedia of Mormonism*, 1:353–54.

Hombergen, Daniel. *The Second Origenist Controversy: A New Perspective on Cyril of Scythopolis' Monastic Biographies as Historical Sources for Sixth-Century Origenism*. Rome: Pontificio Ateneo S. Anselmo, 2001.

Homer. *Odyssey, Volume 1.* Translated by A. T. Murray. LCL 104. Cambridge, MA: Harvard University Press, 1995.

Hoover, Jon. *Ibn Taymiyya's Theodicy of Perpetual Optimism.* Leiden: Brill, 2007.

———. "Islamic Universalism: Ibn Qayyim al-Jawziyya's Salafi Deliberations on the Duration of Hell-Fire." *Muslim World* 99 (2009): 181–201.

———. Review of *Islam and the Fate of Others,* by Mohammed Hassan Khalil. *Review of Middle East Studies Association* 47 (2013): 78–79.

Hopkins, Jasper. *Nicholas of Cusa on God as Not-Other: A Translation and an Appraisal of De li non aliud.* Minneapolis: University of Minnesota Press, 1979.

Horb, Johann Heinrich. *Joannis Henrici Horbii Historia Origeniana.* Frankfurt, 1670.

———. *Mystische und Profetische Bibel.* 1712. 2nd ed. Reprint, Marburg: Philipp Casimir Müller, 1733.

Horn, Arne, ed. *The Gospel of Nicodemus.* Paramaribo, Suriname: Nova Foederis Vulgata Apostolicam, 2014.

Horn, H. J. "*Ignis Aeternus*: Une interprétation morale du feu éternel chez Origène." *Revue des études grecques* 82 (1969): 76–88.

Horrocks, Don. *Laws of the Spiritual Order: Innovation and Reconstruction in the Soteriology of Thomas Erskine of Linlathen.* Carlisle, UK: Paternoster, 2004.

———. "Postmortem Education: Universal Salvation in Thomas Erskine (1788–1870)." In MacDonald [Parry], *"All Shall Be Well,"* 198–218.

Horvath, Tibor. *Eternity and Eternal Life: Speculative Theology and Science in Discourse.* Waterloo, ON: Wilfred Laurier University Press, 1993.

Hospers, John. *An Introduction to Philosophical Analysis.* 3rd ed. New York: Routledge, 1990.

Hotham, Charles. *An Introduction to the Teutonick Philosophie: Being a Determination concerning the Original of the Soul, viz., Whether It Be Immediately Created [by] God and Infus'd into the Body, or Transmitted from the Parent.* London, 1650.

Howe, Charles A. "British Universalism, 1787–1825: Elhanan Winchester, William Vidler and the Gospel of Universal Restoration." *Unitarian Historical Society Transactions* 17 (1979): 1–14.

Howey, Matthew S. "Karl Barth's Unnatural Exegesis: An Inquiry into Barth's Biblical Interpretation with Special Reference to *Christ and Adam.*" PhD diss., University of Nottingham (UK), 2004.

Hoye, William J. *The Emergence of Eternal Life.* Cambridge: Cambridge University Press, 2013.

Hryniewicz, Waclaw. "Das Geheimnis der Gehenna in den Meditationen des hl. Isaak des Syrers." *Östkirchliche Studien* 53 (2004): 28–44.

Huber, Wolfgang. "Die Kabbala als Quelle zum Gottesbegriff Jakob Böhmes." Diss. Theol., Salzburg, 1964.

———. "Die Kabbala als Quelle zur Anthropologie J. Böhmes." *Kairos: Zeitschrift für Religionswissenschaft und Theologie,* neue Folge, 13 (1971): 131–50.

Hübner, Reinhard M. *Die Einheit des Leibes Christi bei Gregor von Nyssa: Untersuchungen zum Ursprung der 'physischen Erlösungslehre.'* Leiden: Brill, 1974.

Hudson, Charles. *A Series of Letters Addressed to Rev. Hosea Ballou . . . Being a Vindication of the Doctrine of Future Retribution.* Woodstock, VT: David Watson, 1827.

Huet, Pierre-Daniel. *Against Cartesian Philosophy (Censura Philosophiae Cartesianae).* Translated and edited by Thomas M. Lennon. Amherst, NY: Humanity Books, 2003.

———. *Origenis in Sacras Scripturas Commentaria.* Rotterdam: Ioannis Berthelini, 1668.

Hügel, Friedrich von. *Eternal Life: A Study of Its Implications and Applications.* 1912. Reprint, Edinburgh: T&T Clark, 1948.

———. "What Do We Mean by Heaven? And What Do We Mean by Hell?" In *Essays and Addresses on the Philosophy of Religion,* 195–224. London: J. M. Dent, 1921.

Hughes, Peter. "Caleb Rich." *Dictionary of Unitarian and Universalist Biography.* http://uudb.org/articles/calebrich.html.

———. "Elhanan Winchester." *Dictionary of Unitarian and Universalist Biography*. http://uudb.org/articles/elhananwinchester.html.

———. "John Murray." *Dictionary of Unitarian and Universalist Biography*. http://uudb.org/articles/johnmurray.html.

———. "The Origins of New England Universalism: Religion without a Founder." *Journal of Unitarian Universalist History* 24 (1997): 31–63.

———. "The Restorationist Controversy." *Dictionary of Unitarian and Universalist Biography*. http://uudb.org/articles/restorationist.html.

———. "Some Problems in the Chronology of Early American Universalism." *Unitarian Universalist Christian* 60 (2005): 24–51.

Hughes, Philip E. *The True Image: The Origin and Destiny of Man in Christ*. Leicester, UK: Inter-Varsity, 1989.

Hugo, Victor. *La fin de Satan*. 11th ed. Paris: J. Hetzel; A. Quantin, 1887.

Huguelet, Theodore L. "Introduction." In *Observations on Man [. . .] in Two Parts*, by David Hartley, v–xxvii. London: S. Richardson for James Leake and Wm. Frederick, Booksellers in Bath, 1749. 2 vols. in 1. Facsimile reproduction. Gainesville, FL: Scholars' Facsimiles & Reprints, 1966.

Hunsinger, George. "Election and the Trinity: Twenty-Five Theses on the Theology of Karl Barth." *Modern Theology* 24 (2008): 179–98.

———. *How to Read Karl Barth: The Shape of His Theology*. Oxford: Oxford University Press, 1991.

———. "*Mysterium Trinitatis*: Karl Barth's Conception of Eternity." In *Disruptive Grace: Studies in the Theology of Karl Barth*, 186–209. Grand Rapids: Eerdmans, 2000.

———. Review of *The Trinity and the Kingdom*, by Jürgen Moltmann. *The Thomist* 47 (1983): 129–39.

———. "Robert Jenson's *Systematic Theology*: A Review Essay." *Scottish Journal of Theology* 55 (2002): 161–200.

Hunter, James Davison. *American Evangelicalism: Conservative Religion and the Quandary of Modernity*. New Brunswick, NJ: Rutgers University Press, 1983.

———. *Evangelicalism: The Coming Generation*. Chicago: University of Chicago Press, 1987.

Huntington, William. *Advocates for Devils Refuted, and the Hope of the Damned Demolished; or, an Everlasting Task for Winchester and All His Confederates*. London, 1794.

Hurd, George Sidney. *The Universal Solution: Presenting Biblical Universalism as the Solution to the Debate between Calvinists and Arminians*. N.p.: TriumphofMercy.com, 2017.

Hurst, D., and Marc Adriaen, eds. *Hieronymi [Jerome]: Opera Exegetica, 7; Commentariorum in Matheum libri IV*. CCSL 77. Turnhout: Brepols, 1969.

Hurth, Elisabeth. "The 'Cures for Atheism': Emerson and Jakob Böhme." In *Between Faith and Unbelief: American Transcendentalists and the Challenge of Atheism*, 149–72. Leiden: Brill, 2007.

Husson, Pierre, and Pierre Nautin, trans. and eds. *Origène: Homélies sur Jérémie*. 2 vols. SC 232, 238. Paris: Cerf, 1976, 1977.

Hutin, Serge. *Les disciples anglais de Jacob Boehme aux XIIe et XIIIe siècles*. Paris: Éditions Denoël, 1960.

Hütter, Reinhard. "*Desiderium Naturale Visionis Dei—Est autem duplex hominis beatitudo sive felicitas*: Some Observations about Lawrence Feingold's and John Milbank's Recent Interventions in the Debate over the Natural Desire to See God." *Nova et Vetera* [English ed.] 5 (2007): 81–132.

Hutton, Sarah. *Anne Conway: A Woman Philosopher*. Cambridge: Cambridge University Press, 2004.

Hvidt, Niels Christian. *Christian Prophecy: The Post-Biblical Tradition*. New York: Oxford University Press, 2007.

Ibekwe, Linus. *The Universality of Salvation in Jesus Christ in the Thought of Karl Rahner: A Chronological and Systematic Investigation*. Würzberg: Echter, 2006.

Ibn al-'Arabi. *Fusus al-Hikam*, ed. A. E. Affifi. Beirut: Dar al-Kutub al-'Arabi, 1946.

———. *The Meccan Revelations*. Translated by Michel Chodkiewicz et al. 2 vols. New York: Pir Press, 2002–4.

———. *The Seals of Wisdom*. Norwich, UK: Diwan Press, 1980.

Idel, Moshe. *Absorbing Perfections: Kabbalah and Interpretation*. New Haven: Yale University Press, 2002.

———. "Kabbalah, Platonism, and Prisca Theologia: The Case of R. Menasseh Ben Israel." In *Menasseh Ben Israel and His World*, edited by Yosef Kaplan, Henry Méchoulan, and Richard H. Popkin, 207–19. Leiden: Brill, 1989.

Ignatius of Antioch. "To the Magnesians." In *The Apostolic Fathers I*, edited by Bart D. Ehrman, 241–55. LCL 24. Cambridge, MA: Harvard University Press, 2003.

———. "To the Trallians." In *The Apostolic Fathers I*, edited by Bart D. Ehrman, 257–69. LCL 24. Cambridge, MA: Harvard University Press, 2003.

Inge, W. R., et al. *What Is the Real Hell?* London: Harper, 1930.

Insole, Christopher. "The Irreducible Importance of the Religious Hope in Kant's Conception of the Highest Good." *Philosophy* 83 (2008): 333–51.

———. "Kant and the Creation of Freedom: A Response to Terry Godlove." *International Journal for Philosophy of Religion* 76 (2014): 111–28.

———. *Kant and the Creation of Freedom: A Theological Problem*. Oxford: Oxford University Press, 2013.

———. "Kant's Transcendental Idealism, Freedom, and the Divine Mind." *Modern Theology* 27 (2011): 608–38.

———. "A Thomistic Reading of Kant's *Groundwork of the Metaphysics of Morals*: Searching for the Unconditioned." *Moral Theology* 31 (2015): 284–311.

International Theological Commission. "Some Current Questions in Eschatology." *Irish Theological Quarterly* 58 (1992): 209–43.

Introvigne, Massimo. "Embraced by the Church? Betty Eadie, Near-Death Experiences, and Mormonism." *Dialogue: A Journal of Mormon Thought* 29 (1996): 99–119.

Irenaeus of Lyon. *Adversus Haereses*. Edited by Norbert Brox. Fontes Christiani 8/1–4. Freiburg: Herder, 1993–95. ET: *ANF* 1:315–567.

———. *Libros quinque adversus haereses*. Edited by W. Wigan Harvey. 2 vols. Cantabrigiae: Typis Academics, 1857.

Irwin, Charlotte. "Pietist Origins of American Universalism." MA thesis, Tufts University, 1966.

Isaac, Daniel. *Universal Restoration Examined and Refuted*. London: Donference-Office, North-Green, 1808.

Isaac the Syrian. *The Ascetical Homilies of Saint Isaac the Syrian*. Translated by D. Miller. Boston: Holy Transfiguration Monastery, 1984.

———. *Homiliae S. Isaaci Syri Antiocheni*. Vol. 1. Edited by Paul Bedjan. Paris: Harrassowitz, 1903.

———. *Mystic Treatises by Isaac of Nineveh, Translated from Bedjan's Syriac Text with an Introduction*. Translated by Arent Jan Wensinck. 1923. Reprint, Wiesbaden: M. Sändig, 1969.

———. "The Second Part," Chapters IV–XLI. Corpus Scriptorum Christianorum Orientalium 555. Scriptores Syri 225. Translated by Sebastian Brock. Louvain: Peeters, 1995.

Islam, Kazi Nurul. "The Qur'anic Message of Universalism and Religious Pluralism." *Dialogue and Alliance* 27 (2013): 101–12.

Itter, Andrew. *Esoteric Teaching in the "Stromateis" of Clement of Alexandria*. Leiden: Brill, 2009.

———. "The Restoration of the Elect: Clement of Alexandria's Doctrine of *Apokatastasis*." In *Studia Patristica*, edited by F. Young, M. Edwards, and P. Parvis, 41:169–74. Leuven: Peeters, 2006.

Iverson, I. "Debate on Hell in Norway." *Lutheran Quarterly* 6 (May 1954): 165–67.

Izmirlieva, Valentina. *All the Names of the Lord: Lists, Mysticism, Magic*. Chicago: University of Chicago Press, 2008.

Izutsu, Toshihiko. *Sufism and Taoism: A Comparative Study of Key Philosophical Concepts*. Berkeley: University of California Press, 1984.

Jackson, Samuel Macauley, ed. *Selected Works of Huldreich Zwingli*. Philadelphia: University of Pennsylvania Press, 1901.

Jacobsen, Anders Lund. "Genesis 1–3 as Source for the Anthropology of Origen." *Vigiliae Christianae* 62 (2008): 213–32.

———. "Origen on the Human Body." In Perrone, *Origeniana Octava*, 649–56.

Jakim, Boris. "Translator's Introduction." In Bulgakov, *Bride of the Lamb*, ix–xvi.

Jeauneau, Édouard. "Le division des sexes chez Grégoire de Nysse et chez Jean Scot Érigène." In *Études Érigéniennes*, edited by Édouard Jeauneau, 1:343–65. 2 vols. Paris: Études Augustiniennes, 1987.

———, ed. *Periphyseon: Editionem nouam a suppositiciis quidem additamentis purgatam, ditatam uero appendice in qua uicissitudines operis synoptice exhibentur I–V*. Corpus Christianorum Continuatio Mediaevalis 161–65. Turnhout: Brepols, 1996–2003.

———. "Le theme du retour." In *Études Érigéniennes*, edited by Édouard Jeauneau, 2:367–94. 2 vols. Paris: Études Augustiniennes, 1987.

Jecht, Richard, and Curt Adler. *Jakob Böhme: Gedenkgabe der Stadt Görlitz zu seinem 300 jährigen Todestage*. Görlitz, Ger.: Selbstverlag des Magistrats der Stadt Görlitz, für den Buchhandel E. Remer, 1924.

Jensen, Dennis. *Flirting with Universalism: Resolving the Problem of an Eternal Hell*. Eugene, OR: Resource Publications, 2014.

Jensen, Jay E. "Spirit." In D. H. Ludlow, *Encyclopedia of Mormonism*, 3:1403–5.

Jensen, Paul T. "Intolerable but Moral? Thinking about Hell." *Faith and Philosophy* 10 (1993): 235–41.

Jenson, Robert W. *Alpha and Omega: A Study in the Theology of Karl Barth*. Edinburgh: Thomas Nelson, 1963.

———. *Systematic Theology*. Vol. 1, *The Triune God*. New York: Oxford University Press, 1997.

———. *The Triune Identity: God according to the Gospel*. Philadelphia: Fortress, 1982.

Jerome. *Apology for Himself against the Books of Rufinus*. In *NPNF²* 3:482–541.

———. "The Letters of St. Jerome." In *NPNF²* 6:1–295.

Jersak, Bradley. *Her Gates Will Never Be Shut: Hell, Hope, and the New Jerusalem*. Eugene, OR: Wipf & Stock, 2009.

Jersak, Bradley, and Michael Hardin, eds. *Stricken by God? Nonviolent Identification and the Victory of Christ*. Grand Rapids: Eerdmans, 2007.

John Chrysostom. "Homily XXXVI (on Matthew 11:1)." In *PG* 57:500–510. ET: *NPNF¹* 10:233–37.

John of Damascus. *Expositio Fidei*. In *Die Schriften des Johannes von Damaskos*, edited by B. Kotter, 2:3–239. Patristische Texte und Studien 12. Berlin: de Gruyter, 1973. ET: *NPNF²* 9:1–101.

John Paul II [Karol Wojtyła]. *Crossing the Threshold of Hope*. Edited by Vittorio Messori. New York: Knopf, 1997.

———. *Sign of Contradiction*. Translated by Mary Smith. London: Hodder & Stoughton, 1979.

Johnson, David A. "George de Benneville and the Heritage of the Radical Reformation." *Journal of the Universalist Historical Society* 8 (1969–70): 25–43.

Johnson, Merwyn S. "Gospel and Law." In *The Westminster Handbook to Karl Barth*, edited by Richard E. Burnett, 85–87. Louisville: Westminster John Knox, 2013.

Johnston, Charles. "Conditional Immortality." *Atlantic Monthly* 143 (1929): 476–83.

Johnston, John Octavius, ed. *Life and Letters of Henry Parry Liddon*. London: Longmans, Green & Co., 1904.

Jonas, Hans. "Origen's Metaphysics of Free Will, Fall, and Salvation: A 'Divine Comedy' of the Universe." *Journal of the Universalist Historical Society* 8 (1969–70): 3–24.

Jones, Brian. *Hell Is Real (But I Hate to Admit It)*. Colorado Springs: David C. Cook, 2011.

Jones, David Albert. *The Soul of the Embryo: An Enquiry into the Status of the Human Embryo in the Christian Tradition*. New York: Continuum, 2004.

Jones, Herbert Gresford. "Universalism and Morals." *Scottish Journal of Theology* 3 (1950): 27–32.

Jones, Paul Dafydd. "A Hopeful Universalism: Why We Can Hope Everyone Will Be Saved." *Christian Century* 129 (2012): 22–27. http://www.christiancentury.org/reviews/2012-06/hopeful-universalism.

———. *The Humanity of Christ: Christology in Karl Barth's "Church Dogmatics."* New York: T&T Clark, 2008.

Jones, Rufus M. *Spiritual Reformers in the 16th and 17th Centuries.* London: Macmillan, 1914.

Jorgenson, James. "The Debate over the Patristic Texts on Purgatory at the Council of Ferrara-Florence, 1438." *St. Vladimir's Theological Quarterly* 30 (1986): 309–34.

Josephus. *The Life; Against Apion.* Translated by H. St. J. Thackeray. LCL 186. Cambridge, MA: Harvard University Press, 1926.

Jouhandeau, Marcel. *Monsieur Godeau intime.* Paris: Librairie Gallimard; Éditions de la Nouvelle revue française, 1926.

Journet, Charles. "Le mystère de l'enfer." *Nova et Vetera* 34 (1959): 264–87.

Jugie, Martin. *Purgatory and the Means to Avoid It.* Translated by Malachy G. Carroll. Westminster, MD: Newman, 1949.

Juhász, Gergely M. *Translating Resurrection: The Debate between William Tyndale and George Joye.* Leiden: Brill, 2014.

Jukes, Andrew. *The Restitution of All Things.* 3rd ed. London: Longmans, Green, 1873.

———. *The Second Death and the Restitution of All Things, with Some Preliminary Remarks on the Nature and Inspiration of Holy Scripture.* London: Longmans, Green, 1867.

Julian of Norwich. *Revelations of Divine Love.* Translated by Clifton Wolters. London: Penguin, 1966.

———. *Revelations of Divine Love (Short and Long Text).* Translated by Elizabeth Spearing. Introduction and notes by A. C. Spearing. New York: Penguin, 1998.

———. *Showings.* Translated by Edmund Colledge and James Walsh. Classics of Western Spirituality. New York: Paulist Press, 1978.

Jundt, Auguste. *Histoire du panthéisme populaire au moyen âge et au seizième siècle.* Paris: Sandoz et Fischbacher, 1875.

Jung, Carl Gustav. *Collected Works*, vol. 6, *Psychological Types.* Edited and translated by Gerhard Adler and R. F. C. Hull. Princeton: Princeton University Press, 1971.

———. *The Red Book: Liber Novus.* Edited by Sonu Shamdasani. Translated by Mark Kyburz and John Peck. New York: Norton, 2009.

Jung [Jung-Stilling], Johann Heinrich. *Apologie der Theorie der Geisterkunde.* New edition. Nürnberg: Verlag der Kaw'schen Buchhandlung, 1833.

———. *Johann Heinrich Jung's (genannt Stilling) ausgewählte Werke.* 4 vols. Stuttgart: Scheible, Rieger & Sattler, 1842.

———. *Johann Heinrich Jung's (genannt Stilling) Lebensgeschichte.* Calw and Stuttgart: Verlag der Vereinsbuchhandlung, 1899.

———. *Sämtliche Werke.* 12 vols. Stuttgart: Scheible, Rieger & Sattler, 1841–43.

Jung, Martin H. "Johanna Eleonora Petersen (1644–1724)." In *The Pietist Theologians: An Introduction to Theology in the Seventeenth and Eighteenth Centuries,* edited by Carter Lindberg, 147–60. Malden, MA: Blackwell, 2005.

Jüngel, Eberhard. *Death: The Riddle and the Mystery.* Translated by Iain and Ute Nicol. Philadelphia: Westminster, 1975.

———. *The Doctrine of the Trinity: God's Being Is in Becoming.* Translated by Horton Harris. Grand Rapids: Eerdmans, 1976.

———. *God's Being Is in Becoming: The Trinitarian Being of God in the Theology of Karl Barth.* Translated by John Webster. Grand Rapids: Eerdmans, 2001.

———. *Karl Barth: A Theological Legacy.* Translated by Garrett E. Paul. Philadelphia: Westminster, 1986.

———. "The Last Judgment as an Act of Grace." *Louvain Studies* 15 (1990): 389–405.

Junod, E. "Controverses autour de l'héritage origénien aux deux extrémités de 4ième siècle: Pamphile et Rufin." In Bienert and Kühneweg, *Origeniana Septima,* 215–23.

Justinian. *Epistle to Mennas.* In *Acta conciliorum oecumenicorum,* Tomus III, *Collectio Sabbaitica contra Acephalos et Origeniastas destinata, insunt acta Synodorum*

Constantinopolitanae et Hierosolymitanae, a. 536. Edited by Eduard Schwartz. Berlin: de Gruyter, 1927.

Justin Martyr. *Dialogue avec Tryphon* [Dialogue with Trypho]. Edited by Philippe Bobichon. 2 vols. Fribourg: Academic Press Fribourg, 2003.

——. "Dialogue with Trypho." In *Writings of Saint Justin Martyr*, edited by Thomas B. Falls, 139–366. FC 6. Washington, DC: Catholic University of America Press, 1948.

Juvenal. *Satire 6.* In *Juvenal and Persius*, edited and translated by Susanna Morton Braund, 230–95. LCL 91. Cambridge, MA: Harvard University Press, 2004.

Kaczmarek, Sylwia, and Henryk Pietras, eds. *Origeniana Decima: Origen as Writer; Papers of the 10th International Origen Congress.* Leuven: Peeters, 2011.

Kannengiesser, Charles. "Origen, Systematician in the De Principiis." In Daly, *Origeniana Quinta,* 395–405.

Kant, Immanuel. "Beantwortung der Frage: Was ist Aufklärung?" *Berlinische Monatsschrift* 12 (1784): 481–94.

——. *Critique of Practical Reason.* Edited and translated by Mary Gregory. Cambridge: Cambridge University Press, 2004.

——. *Critique of Pure Reason.* Edited and translated by Paul Guyer and Allen W. Wood. Cambridge: Cambridge University Press, 2007.

——. *Immanuel Kant's "Critique of Pure Reason."* Translated by Norman Kemp Smith. 1933. Reprint, London: Macmillan, 1978.

——. *Kant's gesammelte Schriften.* Berlin: de Gruyter, 1902–.

——. *Lectures on Metaphysics.* Edited and translated by Karl Ameriks and Steve Naragon. Cambridge: Cambridge University Press, 1997.

——. *Religion within the Limits of Reason Alone.* Translated by Theodore M. Greene and Hoyt H. Hudson. 1934. Reprint, New York: Harper Torchbooks, 1960.

——. *Theoretical Philosophy, 1755–1770.* Edited and translated by David Walford and Ralf Meerbote. Cambridge: Cambridge University Press, 2003.

——. *Träume eines Geistersehers.* 1766. Translated as *Dreams of a Spirit-Seer Illustrated by Dreams of Metaphysics.* London: Swan Sonnenschein; New York: Macmillan, 1899.

——. "What Is Enlightenment?" In *"Foundations of the Metaphysics of Morals" and "What Is Enlightenment?,"* 85–91. Translated by Lewis White Beck. New York: Macmillan, 1959.

Kantzer, Kenneth S., and Carl F. H. Henry, eds. *Evangelical Affirmations.* Grand Rapids: Zondervan, 1990.

Kantzer Komline, Han-Luen. "Friendship and Being: Election and Trinitarian Freedom in Moltmann and Barth." *Modern Theology* 29 (2013): 1–17.

Kaplan, Grant. *Answering the Enlightenment: The Catholic Recovery of Historical Revelation.* New York: Crossroad, 2006.

——. *René Girard, Unlikely Apologist: Mimetic Theory and Fundamental Theology.* Notre Dame, IN: University of Notre Dame Press, 2016.

Karl, Christian. *Rudolf Steiner Handbook,* 2011–15. http://www.rudolf-steiner-handbuch.de.

Käsemann, Ernst. *New Testament Questions of Today.* Philadelphia: Fortress, 1969.

Kazemi, Farshid. "Mysteries of *Alast*: The Realm of Subtle Entities (*'Alam-I dharr*) and the Primordial Covenant in the Babi-Baha'i Writings." *Baha'i Studies Review* 15 (2009): 39–66.

Keith, Graham. "Patristic Views on Hell." *Evangelical Quarterly* 71 (1999): 217–32, 291–310.

Keizer, Heleen J. Review of *Terms for Eternity: Aiônios and Aïdios in Classical and Christian Texts,* by Ilaria Ramelli and David Konstan. *Studia Philonica Annual* 23 (2011): 200–206.

Keller, Catherine. *Apocalypse Now and Then: A Feminist Guide to the End of the World.* Boston: Beacon, 1996.

Keller, Timothy, et al. *Is Hell for Real or Does Everyone Go to Heaven?* Grand Rapids: Zondervan, 2011.

Kelly, David M. "Origen: Heretic or Victim? The 'Apocatastasis' Revisited." *Patristic and Byzantine Review* 18–19 (2000–2001): 273–86.

———. "The Treatment of Universalism in Anglican Thought from George MacDonald (1824–1905) to C. S. Lewis (1898–1963)." PhD diss., University of Ottawa, 1989.

Kelly, J. N. D. *Jerome: His Life, Writings, and Controversies.* New York: Harper & Row, 1975.

Kentish, John. *The Moral Tendency of the Genuine Christian Doctrine.* London: J. Johnson, 1796.

Kerr, Fergus. "Assessing This 'Giddy Synthesis.'" In Gardner, Moss, Quash, and Ward, *Balthasar at the End of Modernity*, 1–14.

Keyserling, Hermann Graf. "Dauer und Ewigkeit." In *Unsterblichkeit: Eine Kritik der Beziehungen zwischen Naturgeschehen und menschlicher Volstellungswelt*, 133–60. Zweite Auflage. München: J. F. Lehmanns, 1911.

Khalil, Mohammed Hassan. *Islam and the Fate of Others: The Salvation Question.* New York: Oxford University Press, 2012.

Kielholz, A. *J. Boehme: Ein pathographischer Beitrag zur Psychologie der Mystik.* Leipzig and Vienna: Franz Deuticke, 1919.

Kierkegaard, Søren. *The Concept of Anxiety.* Translated by Reidar Thomte with Albert B. Anderson. Princeton: Princeton University Press, 1980.

———. *Journals and Papers.* Edited and translated by Howard V. Hong and Edna H. Hong. 7 vols. Bloomington: Indiana University Press, 1967–78.

———. *Philosophical Fragments.* Edited and translated by Howard V. Hong and Edna H. Hong. Princeton: Princeton University Press, 1985.

———. *Sickness unto Death.* Translated by Howard V. Hong and Edna H. Hong. Princeton: Princeton University Press, 1980.

———. *Training in Christianity.* Translated by Walter Lowrie. Princeton: Princeton University Press, 1941.

Kilby, Karen. *Balthasar: A (Very) Critical Introduction.* Grand Rapids: Eerdmans, 2012.

King, Jonathan S., and C. Michael Shea. "The Role of Nikolai Berdyaev in the Early Writings of Hans Urs von Balthasar: A Contribution to the Question of Balthasar's Appropriation of Sources." *Journal for the History of Modern Theology / Zeitschrift für neuere Theologiegeschichte* 20 (2013): 226–57.

King, Karen L., ed. *Images of the Feminine in Gnosticism.* Harrisburg, PA: Trinity Press International, 2000.

———. *What Is Gnosticism?* Cambridge, MA: Harvard University Press, 2005.

King, L. A. "Hell—The Painful Refuge." *Eternity* 30 (1979): 27–28, 30.

Klassen, Randolph J. *What Does the Bible Really Say about Hell? Wrestling with the Traditional View.* Telford, PA: Pandora, 2001.

Klassen, William. "Was Hans Denck a Universalist?" *Mennonite Quarterly Review* 39 (1965): 152–54.

Klimhoff, Alexis. "Georges Florovsky and the Sophiological Controversy." *St. Vladimir's Theological Quarterly* 49 (2005): 67–100.

Klostermann, Erich. *Origenes Werke, III.* Edited by P. Nautin. 2nd ed. GCS. Berlin: Akademie-Verlag, 1983.

Knauber, Adolf. "Die patrologische Schätzung des Clemens von Alexandrien bis zu seinem neuerlichen Bekanntwerden durch die ersten Druckeditionen des 16. Jahrhunderts." In *Kyriakon: Festschrift für Johannes Quasten*, edited by Patrick Granfield and Josef A. Jungmann, 1:289–308. München: Aschendorff, 1970.

Knepper, Timothy D. "Ranks Are Not Bypassed, Rituals Are Not Negated: The Dionysian Corpus on Return." *Modern Theology* 30 (2014): 66–95.

Knitter, Paul. *No Other Name? A Critical Survey of Christian Attitudes toward the World Religions.* Maryknoll, NY: Orbis, 1985.

Knoch, Albert Ernst. *All in All: The Goal of the Universe.* Canyon Country, CA: Concordant Publishing Concern, 1978.

———. *Concordant Commentary on the New Testament.* Canyon Country, CA: Concordant Publishing Concern, n.d.

———. *The Unveiling of Jesus Christ.* Canyon Country, CA: Concordant Publishing Concern, 1935.

Köberle, Adolf. *Universalismus der christlichen Botschaft: Gesammelte Aufsätze und Vorträge.* Darmstadt: Wissenschaftliche Buchgesellschaft, 1978.

Koch, Hal. *Pronoia und Paideusis: Studien über Origenes und sein Verhältnis zum Platonismus.* Berlin: de Gruyter, 1932.

Koetschau, Paul. *Die Textüberlieferung der Bücher des Origenes Gegen Celsus in den Handschriften dieses Werkes und der Philokalia; Prolegomena zu einer kritischen Ausgabe.* Leipzig: Hinrichs, 1889.

Kohler, Kaufmann, and Henry Malther. "Shabbethai Zebi ben Mordecai." *Jewish Encyclopedia.* http://www.jewishencyclopedia.com /articles/13480-shabbethai-zebi-b-mordecai.

Kojève, Alexandre. *Introduction to the Reading of Hegel: Lectures on the "Phenomenology of Spirit."* Assembled by Raymond Queneau. Edited by Allan Bloom. Translated by James H. Nichols Jr. New York: Basic, 1969. Originally published as *Introduction à la lecture de Hegel leçons sur la Phénoménologie de l'esprit.* Paris: Gallimard, 1947.

Kolakowski, Leszak. "Can the Devil Be Saved?" In *Modernity on Endless Trial,* 75–85. Chicago: University of Chicago Press, 1997.

———. "Ernst Bloch: Marxism as a Futuristic Gnosis." In *Main Currents of Marxism,* 3:421–49.

———. *Main Currents of Marxism.* Translated by P. S. Falla. 3 vols. in 1. 1976. Reprint, New York: Norton, 2005.

Kolb, David. *Critique of Pure Modernity: Hegel, Heidegger, and After.* Chicago: University of Chicago Press, 1986.

Konstantinovsky, Julia. *Evagrius Ponticus: The Making of a Gnostic.* Farnham, UK: Ashgate, 2009.

Kornblatt, Judith Deutsch. *Divine Sophia: The Wisdom Writings of Vladimir Solovyov.* Ithaca, NY: Cornell University Press, 2009.

———. "Spirits, Spiritualism, and the Spirit: 'Evenings in Cairo' by V. S. Solovyov and D. N. Tsertelev." In *Russian Literature and the West: A Tribute for David M. Bethea,* edited by Alexander Dolinin, Lazar Fleischman, and Leo Livak, 1:336–58. 2 vols. Stanford, CA: Stanford Department of Slavic Studies; Oakland: Berkeley Slavic Specialties, 2008.

———. "Who Is Sophia and Why Is She Writing My Manuscript? Vladimir Solov'ev and the Channeling of Divine Wisdom." *Journal of Eastern Christian Studies* 59 (2007): 213–44.

Kornblatt, Judith Deutsch, and Richard F. Gustafson, eds. *Russian Religious Thought.* Madison: University of Wisconsin Press, 1996.

Koslowski, Peter. "Hegel—'der Philosoph der Trinität'?—Zur Kontroverse um seine Trinitätlehre." *Theologische Quartalschrift* 162 (1982): 105–31.

———. "Der leidende Gott als Problem der spekulativen Philosophie und Theologie: Statt einer Einleitung." In Koslowski and Hermanni, *Der leidende Gott,* 11–27.

———. *Philosophien der Offenbarung: Antiker Gnostizismus, Franz von Baader, Schelling.* Paderborn: Schöningh, 2001.

Koslowski, Peter, and Friedrich Hermanni, eds. *Der leidende Gott: Eine philosophische und theologische Kritik.* Munich: Fink, 2001.

Kovacs, Judith L. "Introduction; Clement as Scriptural Exegete: Overview and History of Research." In *Clement's Biblical Exegesis: Proceedings of the Second Colloquium on Clement of Alexandria (Olomouc, May 29–31, 2014),* edited by Veronika Cernuskova, Judith L. Kovacs, and Jana Platova, 1–37. Leiden: Brill, 2014.

Koval'kov, A. I. *Mysli o mistike I pisateliakh eia.* Orel: Gubernskaia tipografia, 1815.

Kowalska, Saint Maria Faustina. *Diary of St. Maria Faustina Kowalska: Divine Mercy in My Soul.* Stockbridge, MA: Marian Press, 2009.

Koyré, Alexandre. *La philosophie de Jacob Boehme.* 1929. Reprint, Paris: Librarie Philosophique Vrin, 1971.

Kraevich, N. A. *Luch blagodati ili pisaniia N.A.K.* Moscow, 1804.

Kreck, Walter. *Die Zukunft des Gekommenen.* Münich: Kaiser, 1961.

Kretmann, Norman. "God among the Causes of Moral Evil: Hardening of Hearts and Spiritual Blinding." *Philosophical Topics* 16 (1988): 189–214.

Kronen, John D. "The Idea of Hell and the Classical Doctrine of God." *Modern Schoolman* 77 (1999): 13–24.

Kronen, John, and Eric Reitan. *God's Final Victory: A Comparative Philosophical Case for Universalism.* New York: Continuum, 2011.

Krötke, Wolf. *Sin and Nothingness in the Theology of Karl Barth.* Translated and edited by Phillip G. Ziegler and Christiana-Maria Bammel. Princeton: Princeton Theological Seminary, 2005.

Kruger, C. Baxter. *The Shack Revisited: There Is More Going on Here than You Ever Dared to Dream.* Foreword by William Paul Young. New York: FaithWords, 2012.

Krüger, Paul. "Gehenna und Scheol in dem Schriftum unter dem Namen des Isaak von Antiochen." *Östkirchliche Studien* 2 (1953): 270–79.

Kuhn, Johannes. "Die Schelling'sche Philosophie und ihr Verhältnis zum Christentum, 3: *Die Philosophie der Offenbarung.*" *Theologische Quartalschrift* 27 (1845): 3–39.

Küng, Hans. *Eternal Life? Life after Death as a Medical, Philosophical, and Theological Problem.* Translated by Edward Quinn. Garden City, NY: Doubleday, 1984.

———. *Justification: The Doctrine of Karl Barth and a Catholic Reflection.* New York: Nelson, 1964.

Kunz, Marion. *Guillaume Postel: Prophet of the Restitution of All Things; His Life and Thought.* The Hague: Nijhoff, 1981.

Kurzweil, Ray. *The Singularity Is Near: When Humans Transcend Biology.* New York: Viking, 2005.

Kvanvig, Jonathan L. *The Problem of Hell.* New York: Oxford University Press, 1993.

Lachman, David C. *The Marrow Controversy: An Historical and Theological Analysis.* Edinburgh: Rutherford House, 1988.

Lachman, Gary. *Madame Blavatsky: The Mother of Modern Spirituality.* New York: Tarcher, 2012.

———. *Swedenborg: An Introduction to His Life and Ideas.* New York: Tarcher, 2012.

Lachower, Fischel, and Isaiah Tishby, trans. and eds. *The Wisdom of the Zohar: An Anthology of Texts, Systematically Arranged and Rendered into Hebrew.* Translated by David Goldstein. 3 vols. New York: Oxford University Press, 1989.

Lacy, Larry. "Talbott on Paul as a Universalist." *Christian Scholar's Review* 21 (1992): 395–407.

Lamb, W. R. M., trans. *Plato: Laches, Protagoras, Meno, Euthydemus.* LCL 165. Cambridge, MA: Harvard University Press, 1924.

Lamm, Julia. *The Living God: Schleiermacher's Theological Appropriation of Spinoza.* University Park: Pennsylvania State University Press, 1996.

Lampe, Frederick Adolphus. *Theological Dissertations concerning the Endless Duration of Punishment.* Translated by Joseph Robertson. Edinburgh, 1796.

Lang, Bernhard. "The Sexual Life of the Saints: Towards an Anthropology of Christian Heaven." *Religion* 17 (1987): 149–71.

Langdon, Adrian E. V. "God the Eternal Contemporary: Trinity, Eternity, and Time in Karl Barth's *Church Dogmatics.*" PhD diss., McGill University, 2008.

Lardet, P., ed. *Jerome: Opera Pars III, Opera Polemica I, Contra Rufinum.* CCL 79. Turnhout: Brepols, 1982.

Lauber, David Edward. "Toward a Theology of Holy Saturday: Karl Barth and Hans Urs von Balthasar on the *Descensus ad Inferna.*" PhD diss., Princeton Theological Seminary, 1999.

Laufer, Catherine Ella. *Hell's Destruction: An Exploration of Christ's Descent to the Dead.* Farnham, UK: Ashgate, 2013.

Law, David L. "Kenotic Christology." In *The Blackwell Companion to Nineteenth-Century Theology,* edited by David Fergusson, 251–79. Malden, MA: Blackwell, 2010.

———. *Kierkegaard's Kenotic Christology*. Oxford: Oxford University Press, 2013.

Law, William. *An Appeal to All That Doubt*. London: W. Innys and J. Richardson, 1740.

———. *Earnest and Serious Answer to Dr. Trapp*. London: W. Innys and J. Richardson, 1740.

———. *Selected Mystical Writings of William Law*. Edited by Stephen Hobhouse. London: C. W. Daniel, 1938.

———. *"The Spirit of Prayer" and "The Spirit of Love."* Edited with notes by Sidney Spencer. Cambridge: James Clarke, 1969.

———. *The Works of the Reverend William Law*. 9 vols. 1762. Reprint, London: G. Moreton, 1893.

Lead, Jane. *Eine Offenbarung der Bottshafft des ewigen Evangelii*. Amsterdam, 1697.

———. *The Enochian Walks with God*. 2nd ed. London: J. Bradford, 1702.

———. *A Revelation of the Everlasting Gospel-Message*. London, 1697.

———. *Sechs unschätzbare durch göttliche Offenbarung und Befehl ans Licht gebrachte mystiche Tractätlein*. Amsterdam, 1696.

———. *The Wonders of God's Creation Manifested*. London, 1695.

Le Clerc, Jean [Parrhasi, pseud.]. "A Vindication of Providence from the Objections of the Manichees." In *Parrhasiana; or, Thoughts upon Several Subjects; as Criticism, History, Morality, and Politics*, 217–25. London: A. and J. Churchil, 1700.

Lee, Francis. *The History of Montanism*. Printed in George Hickes, *The Spirit of Enthusiasm Exorcised*. London: Share, 1709.

Lee, Luther. *Universalism Examined and Refuted*. Watertown, NY: Knowlton & Rice, 1836.

Lefebvre, Henri. "The Withering Away of the State." In *State, Space, World: Selected Essays*, edited by Neil Brenner and Stuart Elden, 69–94. Minneapolis: University of Minnesota Press, 2009.

Leff, Gordon. *Heresy in the Later Middle Ages*. 2 vols. Manchester, UK: Manchester University Press, 1967.

Le Goff, Jacques. *The Birth of Purgatory*. Translated by Arthur Goldhammer. Chicago: University of Chicago Press, 1984.

Leibniz, Gottfried Wilhelm. *Lettres et opuscules inédits*. Edited by Louis-Alexandre Foucher de Careil Hildesheim. New York: Olms, 1975. English translation by Lloyd Strickland. http://www.leibniz-translations.com/origen.htm.

———. *Theodicy: Essays on the Goodness of God, the Freedom of Man, and the Origin of Evil*. Translated by E. M. Huggard. London: Routledge & Kegan Paul, 1952. Originally published in French as *Essais de Théodicée sur la bonté de Dieu, la liberté de l'homme et l'origine du mal* (Amsterdam: Chez Isaac Troyel, 1710).

Leloir, Louis. "Infiltrations dualistes chez les pères du désert." In *Gnosticisme et monde hellénistique: Actes du Colloque de Louvain-ila-Neuve*, edited by Julien Ries, 326–36. Louvain-la-Neuve: Institut orientaliste, 1982.

Lenin, Vladimir. *Filosofskie tetrad*. Moscow: Izd.-vo TsK VKP, 1965.

Lennon, Thomas M., and Michael Hickson. "Pierre Bayle." In *The Stanford Encyclopedia of Philosophy*, edited by Edward N. Zalta. Winter 2013 ed. http://plato.stanford.edu/archives/win2013/entries/bayle/.

Lerner, Robert E. *The Heresy of the Free Spirit in the Later Middle Ages*. Berkeley: University of California Press, 1972.

Levering, Matthew. *Predestination: Biblical and Theological Paths*. New York: Oxford University Press, 2011.

———. *Scripture and Metaphysics: Aquinas and the Renewal of Trinitarian Theology*. Malden, MA: Blackwell, 2004.

Lewis, C. S., ed. *George MacDonald: An Anthology*. London: Geoffrey Bles, 1946.

———. "The Humanitarian Theory of Punishment." In *The Collected Works of C. S. Lewis: The Pilgrim's Regress, Christian Reflections, God in the Dock*, 496–504. New York: Inspirational Press, n.d.

———. *Letters to Malcolm: Chiefly on Prayer*. New York: Harcourt, Brace, 1964.

———. *The Problem of Pain*. 1940. Reprint, Glasgow: William Collins, 1978.

———. *Surprised by Joy*. London: Collins Fontana, 1959.

———. *The Voyage of the Dawn Treader*. Vol. 5 of *The Chronicles of Narnia*. New York: HarperCollins, 2008.

Lewis, Rhodri. "Of 'Origenian Platonisme': Joseph Glanvill on the Pre-Existence of Souls." *Huntington Library Quarterly* 69 (2006): 267–300.

Lialine, Dom C. "Le débat sophiologique." *Irénikon* 13 (1936): 168–205, 328–29, 704–5.

Liddell, Henry George, and Robert Scott. *A Greek-English Lexicon*. Revised by Sir Henry Smart Jones. 1843. Reprint, Oxford: Clarendon, 1940.

Liddon, Henry Parry. *Life and Letters of Henry Parry Liddon*. Edited by J. O. Johnston. London: Longmans, Green & Co., 1904.

Lies, Lothar. "Die 'Gottes Würdige' Schriftauslegung nach Origenes." In Dorival and Le Boulluec, *Origeniana Sexta*, 365–72.

———. "Origenes und Reinkarnation." *Zeitschrift für katholische Theologie* 121 (1999): 139–58, 249–68.

———, ed. *Origeniana Quarta: Die Referate des 4. Internationalen Origeneskongresses; Innsbruck, 2–6 September 1985*. Innsbruck-Vienna: Tyrolia Verlag, 1987.

Lilla, Salvatore R. C. *Clement of Alexandria: A Study in Christian Platonism and Gnosticism*. London: Oxford University Press, 1971.

Lindbeck, George. "*Fides ex auditu* and the Salvation of Non-Christians: Contemporary Catholic and Protestant Positions." In *The Gospel and the Ambiguity of the Church*, edited by V. Vajta, 92–133. Minneapolis: Fortress, 1974.

Lindsell, Harold. "Universalism Today." *Bibliotheca Sacra* 121 (1964): 209–17; 122 (1965): 31–40.

Lippy, Charles H. *The Christadelphians in North America*. Studies in American Religion 43. Lewiston, NY: Edwin Mellen, 1989.

Lister, John. "The Correspondence of David Hartley and John Lister." Calderdale Archives, Calderdale Central Library, Halifax, Great Britain.

Litch, J., and Miles Grant. *The Doctrine of Everlasting Punishment: A Discussion of the Question "Do the Scriptures Teach the Doctrine of the Eternal Conscious Suffering of the Wicked?"* Boston: Damrell & Moore, 1859.

Lloyd, Genevieve. *Providence Lost*. Cambridge, MA: Harvard University Press, 2008.

Loane, Edward. "An Evangelically Flawed Theological Method: A Response to Robin Parry's *The Evangelical Universalist*." *Churchman* 130 (2016): 349–60.

Lochbrunner, Manfred, ed. *Hans Urs von Balthasar und seine Literatenfreunde: Neun Korrespondenzen*. Würzburg: Echter, 2007.

———. *Hans Urs von Balthasar und seine Theologenkollegen: Sechs Beziehungsgeschichten*. Würzburg: Echter, 2009.

Lohr, Joel N. "Taming the Untamable: Christian Attempts to Make Israel's Election Universal." *Horizons in Biblical Theology* 33 (2011): 24–33.

Loncar, Samuel. "German Idealism's Long Shadow: The Fall and Divine-Human Agency in Tillich's *Systematic Theology*." *Neue Zeitschrift für systematische Theologie und Religionsphilosophie* 54 (2012): 95–118.

Long, D. Stephen. *Saving Karl Barth: Hans Urs von Balthasar's Preoccupation*. Minneapolis: Fortress, 2014.

Lory, Pierre. "Henry Corbin: His Work and Influence." In *History of Islamic Philosophy, Part II*, edited by Seyyed Hossein Nasr and Oliver Leaman, 1149–55. London: Routledge, 1996.

Lösel, Steffen. "Murder in the Cathedral: Hans Urs von Balthasar's New Dramatization of the Doctrine of the Trinity." *Pro Ecclesia* 5 (1996): 427–39.

———. "A Plain Account of Christian Salvation? Balthasar on Sacrifice, Solidarity, and Substitution." *Pro Ecclesia* 13 (2004): 141–71.

———. "Unapocalyptic Theology: History and Eschatology in Balthasar's Theo-Drama." *Modern Theology* 17 (2001): 201–25.

Lossky, Vladimir. *In the Image and Likeness of God*. Edited by John H. Erickson and Thomas E. Bird. Crestwood, NY: St. Vladimir's Seminary Press, 2001.

———. *The Mystical Theology of the Eastern Church*. London: James Clarke, 1957.

Loudy, Adlai. *God's Eonian Purpose.* Los Angeles: Concordant Publishing Concern, 1929.

Louth, Andrew. "The Collectio Sabbaitica and Sixth-Century Origenism." In Perrone, *Origeniana Octava,* 1167–75.

———. "The Place of *Heart of the World* in the Theology of Hans Urs von Balthasar." In *The Analogy of Beauty: The Theology of Hans Urs von Balthasar,* edited by John Riches, 147–63. Edinburgh: T&T Clark, 1986.

———. "The Reception of Dionysius in the Byzantine World: Maximus to Palamas." *Modern Theology* 24 (2008): 585–99.

———. "The Reception of Dionysius up to Maximus the Confessor." *Modern Theology* 24 (2008): 573–83.

———. Review of *Pseudo-Dionysius: A Commentary on the Text and an Introduction to Their Influence,* by Paul Rorem. *Modern Theology* 10 (1994): 427–28.

Love, William DeLoss. "Clement of Alexandria Not an After-Death Probationist or Universalist." *Bibliotheca Sacra* 45 (1888): 608–28.

Lovejoy, Arthur O. *The Great Chain of Being: A Study of the History of an Idea; The William James Lectures Delivered at Harvard University, 1933.* Cambridge, MA: Harvard University Press, 1964.

Lowe, David. "The Ravers Who Get High on God." *The Sun,* January 21, 2010. http://www.goldminemedia.eu/WP/2011/11/the-ravers-who-get-high-on-god/.

Ludlow, Daniel H., ed. *Encyclopedia of Mormonism.* 4 vols. New York: Macmillan, 1992.

Ludlow, Morwenna. "Universalism in the History of Christianity." In Parry and Partridge, *Universal Salvation?,* 191–246.

———. *Universal Salvation: Eschatology in the Thought of Gregory of Nyssa and Karl Rahner.* Oxford: Oxford University Press, 2000.

———. "Why Was Hans Denck Thought to Be a Universalist?" *Journal of Ecclesiastical History* 55 (2004): 257–74.

Luft, Stefan. *Leben und Schreiben für den Pietismus: Der Kampf des pietistischen Ehepaares Johanna Eleonora und Johann Wilhelm Petersen gegen die lutherische Orthodoxie.* Hertzberg: Traugott Bautz, 1994.

Luibheid, Colm, trans. *Pseudo-Dionysius: The Complete Works.* New York: Paulist Press, 1987.

Lund, Gerald N. "Plan of Salvation, Plan of Redemption." In D. H. Ludlow, *Encyclopedia of Mormonism,* 3:1088–91.

Lund, John L. "Council in Heaven." In D. H. Ludlow, *Encyclopedia of Mormonism,* 1:328–29.

Lundhaug, Hugo. "Origenism in Fifth-Century Upper Egypt: Shenoute of Atripe and the Nag Hammadi Codices." In *Studia Patristica,* vol. 64, edited by Markus Vinzent, 217–28. Leuven: Peeters, 2013.

———. "Shenoute's Heresiological Polemics and Its Context(s)." In *Invention, Rewriting, Usurpation: Discursive Fights over Religious Traditions in Antiquity,* edited by Jörg Ulrich, Anders-Christian Jacobsen, and David Brakke, 239–61. Frankfurt: Lang, 2012.

———. "'Tell Me What Shall Arise': Conflicting Notions of the Resurrection Body in Fourth- and Fifth-Century Egypt." In *Coming Back to Life: The Permeability of Past and Present, Mortality and Immortality, Death and Life in the Ancient Mediterranean,* edited by Frederick S. Tappenden and Carly Daniel-Hughes, 215–36. Montreal: McGill University Library, 2017.

Lutaud, Olivier. *Winstanley: Socialisme et Christianisme sous Cromwell.* Paris: Didier-Erudition, 1976.

Luther, Martin. *Against the Heavenly Prophets in the Matter of Images and Sacraments.* In *Luther's Works,* vol. 40, *Church and Ministry II,* edited by Conrad Bergendoff, 73–224. Translated by Bernhard Erling and Conrad Bergendoff. Philadelphia: Muhlenberg, 1958.

———. *D. Martin Luthers Werke: kritische Gesamtausgabe.* 136 vols. Weimar: Hermann Böhlau, 1883–2009.

———. *Lectures on Romans.* Vol. 25 of *Luther's Works.* Edited by Hilton C. Oswald. St. Louis: Concordia, 1972.

———. *Sendbrief über die Frage, ob auch jemand, ohne Glauben verstorben, selig werden möge* (to Hans v. Rechenberg, 1522). In *D. Martin Luthers Werke: kritische Gesamtausgabe*, 10/2:318–26. Weimar: Hermann Böhlaus Nachfolger, 1907.

———. *Works of Martin Luther*. Philadelphia Edition. Philadelphia: Muhlenberg, 1915–43.

Lüthi, Kurt. "Die Erörterung des Allversöhnungslehre durch des pietische Ehepaar Johann und Johanna Eleonora Petersen." *Theologische Zeitschrift* 12 (1956): 362–77.

———. *Gott und das Böse: Eine biblisch-theologische und systematische These zur Lehre vom Bösen, entworfen in Auseinandersetzung mit Schelling und Karl Barth*. Zurich: Zwingli-Verlag, 1961.

Lyman, Rebecca. "Marcellus of Ancyra." In *Encyclopedia of Early Christianity*, edited by Everett Ferguson, 713–14. 2nd ed. London: Routledge, 1999.

Lyotard, Jean-François. *The Postmodern Condition: A Report on Knowledge*. Translated by Geoff Bennington and Brian Massumi. Minneapolis: University of Minnesota Press, 1984.

MacArthur, John F. *The Gospel according to Jesus*. Grand Rapids: Zondervan, 1989.

Macchia, Frank D. *Spirituality and Social Liberation: The Message of the Blumhardts in the Light of Wuerttemberg Pietism*. Metuchen, NJ: Scarecrow, 1993.

MacCullough, J. A. *The Harrowing of Hell: A Comparative Study of an Early Christian Doctrine*. Edinburgh: T&T Clark, 1930.

MacDonald, George. *God's Words to His Children: Sermons Spoken and Unspoken*. New York: Funk & Wagnalls, 1887.

———. *Phantastes*. 1858. Reprint, Grand Rapids: Eerdmans, 2000.

———, trans. *Twelve of the Spiritual Songs of Novalis*. Arundel, 1851.

———. *Unspoken Sermons: Series I, II, and III in One Volume*. Whitethorn, CA: Johannesen, 1997. Series 1, 2, and 3 originally published in 1867, 1885, and 1889, respectively.

MacDonald, Gregory [Robin Parry], ed. *"All Shall Be Well": Explorations in Universal Salvation and Christian Theology from Origen*

to Moltmann. Eugene, OR: Wipf & Stock, 2011.

———. *The Evangelical Universalist*. 1st ed. Eugene, OR: Wipf & Stock, 2006.

———. *The Evangelical Universalist*. 2nd ed. Eugene, OR: Wipf & Stock, 2012.

MacGregor Mathers, S. L., trans. *Kabbala Denudata: The Kabbalah Unveiled; Translated into English from the Latin of Knorr von Rosenroth*. New York: Theosophical Publishing Company, 1912.

Macken, John. *The Autonomy Theme in the Church Dogmatics: Karl Barth and His Critics*. Cambridge: Cambridge University Press, 1990.

Mackintosh, Hugh Ross. *Types of Modern Theology: Schleiermacher to Barth*. London: Nisbet, 1937.

MacMullen, Ramsey. *Christianizing the Roman Empire (A.D. 100–400)*. New Haven: Yale University Press, 1984.

Macquarrie, John. *In Search of Deity: An Essay in Dialectical Theism; The Gifford Lectures, 1983–1984*. London: SCM, 1984.

———. *Jesus Christ in Modern Thought*. London: SCM, 1990.

Madec, Goulven, ed. *Iohannis Scotti "De divina praedestinatione liber."* Corpus Christianorum Continuatio Mediaevalis 50. Turnhout: Brepols, 1978.

Magee, Glenn Alexander. *Hegel and the Hermetic Tradition*. Ithaca, NY: Cornell University Press, 2001.

———. "Hegel's Reception of Jacob Boehme." In Hessayon and Apetrai, *Introduction to Jacob Boehme*, 224–43.

Maitland, Samuel Roffey. *Facts and Documents Illustrative of the History, Doctrine, and Rites of the Ancient Albigenses and Waldenses*. London: Rivington, 1832.

Manaranche, André. *Le monothéisme chrétien*. Paris: Cerf, 1985.

Mandelbrote, Scott. "Ramsay, Andrew Michael [Jacobite Sir Andrew Ramsay, baronet] (1686–1743)." In *Oxford Dictionary of National Biography*. Edited by Lawrence Goldman. Online ed. Oxford: Oxford University Press, 2004. http://www.oxforddnb.com/view/article/23077.

Manford, E., and T. S. Sweeney. *Universal Salvation*. Chicago: Rand McNally, 1870.

Mansel, H. L. *Man's Conception of Eternity: An Examination of Mr. Maurice's Theory of a Fixed State Out of Time*. London: John Henry Parker, 1854.

Mansukhani, Gobind Singh. *Introduction to Sikhism*. New Delhi: Helmkunt, 1977.

Manuel, Frank Edwards, and Fritzie P. Manuel. *Utopian Thought in the Western World*. Cambridge, MA: Harvard University Press, 1979.

Marcus, Ralph, trans. *Philo: Questions on Genesis*. LCL 380. Cambridge, MA: Harvard University Press, 1953.

Marcus Aurelius. *The Meditations of the Emperor Marcus Aurelius Antoninus*. Translated by George Long. London: The Chesterfield Society, 1890.

Marini, Stephen. *Radical Sects of Revolutionary New England*. Cambridge, MA: Harvard University Press, 1982.

Maritain, Jacques. "Beginning with a Reverie." In *Untrammeled Approaches*. Vol. 20 of the Collected Works of Jacques Maritain, 3–26. Notre Dame, IN: University of Notre Dame Press, 1997.

Markley, Lucy Whitney. "Conceptions of Future Punishment as Developed among the Universalists." PhD diss., University of Chicago Divinity School, 1925.

Marsay, Charles-Hectore de Saint George. *Nouveaux discours spirituels sur diverses matiéres de la vie intérieure & des dogmes de la religion chrétienne, ou Témoignage d'un enfant de la vérité & droiture des voyes de l'esprit pour l'encouragement & avertissement des autres enfants ses compagnons*. 3 vols. Berleburg, Ger.: Christoph Michel Regelain, 1738–40.

———. *Témoignage d'un enfant de la vérité & droiture des voyes de l'esprit, demontré dans la vie de Saints Patriarches, ou des XXIV. Anciens, etc.* Berleburg, Ger.: Christoph Michel Regelain, 1740.

———. *Témoignage d'un enfant de la vérité & droiture des voyes de l'esprit, ou Abrégé de l'essence de la vraie religion chrétienne par*

demandes & réponces. Berleburg, Ger.: Christoph Michel Regelain, 1740.

———. *Témoignage d'un enfant de la verité & droiture des voyes de l'esprit, ou explication mystique et litérale de l'Fpître aux Hébreux*. Berleburg, Ger.: Christoph Michel Regelain, 1740.

———. *Témoignage d'un enfant de la vérité et droiture des voyes de l'esprit, ou Explication mystique et litérale de l'Epître aux Romains*. Berleburg, Ger.: Christoph Michel Regelain, 1739.

———. *Témoignage d'un enfant de la vérité & droiture des voyes de l'esprit, ou explication mystique & literale de l'Apocalipse de Jesus Christ revélée à S. Jean Apôtre*. Berleburg, Ger.: Christoph Michel Regelain, 1739.

———. *Témoignage d'un enfant de la vérité et droiture des voies de l'esprit, ou l'on traite de la Magie Divine, Angelique, Naturelle, et Charnelle*. Berleburg, Ger.: Christoph Michel Regelain, 1739.

———. *Témoignage d'un enfant de la verité & droiture de voyes de l'esprit, ou, Explication des trois premiers chapitres de la Genese, ou, L'on traité de plusieurs merveilles & mysteres de la Création*. Berleburg, Ger.: Christoph Michel Regelain, 1731.

———. *Témoignage d'un enfant de la verité & droiture de voyes de l'esprit, ou, Résponse à la question, Quel est l'esprit de l'inspiration d'aujourd'hui? c'est à dire l'esprit qui meur les hommes par des gestes extraordinaires & mouvemens singuliers & les pouff à prononcer*. Berleburg, Ger.: Christoph Michel Regelein, 1738.

Marsh, F. S., trans. and ed. *The Book of the Holy Hierotheos*. London: published for the Text and Translation Society by Williams and Norgate, 1927.

Marsh, Robert. "The Second Part of [David] Hartley's System." *Journal of the History of Ideas* 20 (1959): 264–73.

Marshall, Bruce D. "The Absolute and the Trinity." *Pro Ecclesia* 23 (2014): 147–64.

———. *Trinity and Truth*. Cambridge: Cambridge University Press, 2000.

———. "The Unity of the Triune God: Reviving an Ancient Question." *Thomist* 74 (2010): 1–32.

Marshall, I. Howard. "The New Testament
Does *Not* Teach Universal Salvation." In
Parry and Partridge, *Universal Salvation?,*
55–76.

Marshall, Ross S. *God's Testimony of All: The
Greatest Promise Ever Made.* Charleston, SC:
CreateSpace, 2016.

Martens, Peter W. *Origen and Scripture: The
Contours of the Exegetical Life.* New York:
Oxford University Press, 2012.

———. "Origen's Doctrine of Pre-Existence
and the Opening Chapter of Genesis."
Zeitschrift für Antikes Christentum 16 (2013):
516–49.

Martensen, Hans L. *Jacob Boehme: Studies in
His Life and Teaching.* Translated by T. Rhys
Evans. London: Hodder & Stoughton, 1885.
Rev. ed. with notes by Stephen Hobhouse.
London: Salisbury Square, 1949.

Martin, James Perry. *The Last Judgment:
In Protestant Theology from Orthodoxy to
Ritschl.* Grand Rapids: Eerdmans, 1963.

Martin, Jennifer Newsome. "Hans Urs von
Balthasar and the Press of Speculative
Russian Religious Philosophy." PhD diss.,
University of Notre Dame, 2012. Published
as *Hans Urs von Balthasar and the Critical
Appropriation of Russian Religious Thought.*
Notre Dame, IN: University of Notre Dame
Press, 2015.

Martin, Ralph. "Balthasar and Salvation: What
Does He Really Teach?" *Josephinum Journal
of Theology* 21 (2014): 313–41.

———. "The Pastoral Strategy of Vatican II:
Time for an Adjustment?" In *The Second
Vatican Council: Celebrating Its Achievements
and the Future,* edited by Gavin D'Costa
and Emma Jane Harris, 137–64. London:
Bloomsbury T&T Clark, 2013.

———. *Will Many Be Saved? What Vatican II
Actually Teaches and Its Implications for the
New Evangelization.* Grand Rapids: Eerd-
mans, 2012.

Marty, Peter. "Betting on a Generous God."
Christian Century, May 17, 2011, 22–25.

Marx, Alexander. "Texts by and about Maimonides." *Jewish Quarterly Review* 25
(1934/35): 406–28.

Maspero, Giulio. "Apocatastasis." In *The Brill
Dictionary of Gregory of Nyssa,* edited by
Lucas Francisco Mateo Seco and Giulio
Maspero, 55–64. Translated by Seth Cher-
ney. Leiden: Brill, 2010.

Mateo-Seco, Lucas Francisco. "Eschatology."
In *The Brill Dictionary of Gregory of Nyssa,*
edited by Lucas Francisco Mateo-Seco and
Giulio Maspero, 275–88. Translated by Seth
Cherney. Leiden: Brill, 2010.

Matt, Daniel C. "*Ayin*: The Concept of Nothingness in Jewish Mysticism." In *Essential
Papers of Kabbalah,* edited by Lawrence
Fine, 67–108. New York: New York University Press, 1995.

———. *The Essential Kabbalah.* New York:
Quality Paperback Book Club, 1998.

Matthews, Robert J. "Fall of Adam." In
D. H. Ludlow, *Encyclopedia of Mormonism,*
2:485–86.

Matthias, Markus. *Johann Wilhelm und Johanna Eleonora Petersen: Eine Biographie bis
zur Amtsenthebung Petersens im Jahre 1692.*
Göttingen: Vandenhoeck & Ruprecht,
1993.

Maurer, Armand A. *Medieval Philosophy.* 1962.
2nd ed. Toronto: Pontifical Institute of Medieval Studies, 1982.

Maurice, Frederick Denison. *Theological Essays.* 2nd ed. Cambridge: Macmillan, 1853.

———. *The Word "Eternal" and the Punishment of the Wicked.* Cambridge, UK: Macmillan, 1854.

Maximus the Confessor. *Maximus Confessor:
Selected Writings.* Translated by George C.
Berthold. New York: Paulist Press, 1985.

———. *On Difficulties in the Church Fathers:
The Ambigua.* Translated by Nicholas Constas. 2 vols. Dumbarton Oaks Medieval Library. Cambridge, MA: Harvard University
Press, 2014.

———. *On the Cosmic Mystery of Jesus Christ:
Selected Writings from Maximus the Confessor.* Translated by Paul M. Blowers and Robert Wilken. Crestwood, NY: St. Vladimir's
Seminary Press, 2003.

———. *St. Maximus the Confessor's Questions and Doubts.* Translated by Despina D.

Prassas. DeKalb: Northern Illinois University Press, 2010.

Mayer, Paola. *Jena Romanticism and Its Appropriation of Jakob Böhme: Theosophy—Hagiography—Literature.* Montreal: McGill-Queen's University Press, 1999.

Mazzotti, José Antonio. "El Inca Garcilaso Translates León Hebreo: The *Dialogues of Love,* the Cabala, and Andean Mythology." In *Beyond Books and Borders: Garcilaso de la Vega and La Florida del Inca,* edited by Raquel Chang-Rodríguez, 99–118. Cranbury, NY: Associated University Presses, 2006.

M'Calla, W. L. *Discussion of Universalism.* Philadelphia: John Young, 1825.

McBrien, Richard. "The Church (*Lumen Gentium*)." In *Modern Catholicism: Vatican II and After,* edited by Adrian Hastings, 84–95. New York: Oxford University Press, 1991.

McCalla, Arthur. "Saint-Martin, Louis-Claude de." In Hanegraaff et al., *Dictionary of Gnosis and Western Esotericism,* 1024–31.

McCambley, Casimir, trans. "When (the Father) Will Subject All Things to (the Son), Then (the Son) Himself Will Be Subjected to Him (the Father) Who Subjects All Things to Him (the Son): A Treatise on First Corinthians 15.28 by Saint Gregory of Nyssa." *Greek Orthodox Theological Review* 28 (1983): 1–25.

McCarty, Doran. *Teilhard de Chardin.* Makers of the Modern Theological Mind. Waco: Word, 1976.

McClure, A. Wilson. *Lectures on Ultra-Universalism.* 4th ed. Boston: Crocker & Brewster, 1838.

McClymond, Michael J. "Charismatic Renewal and Neo-Pentecostalism: From American Origins to Global Permutations." In *The Cambridge Companion to Pentecostalism,* edited by Cecil M. Robeck and Amos Yong, 31–51. Cambridge: Cambridge University Press, 2014.

———. "Christian Mysticism—Help or Hindrance for Godly Love? A Case Study of Madame Guyon." In *Godly Love: Impediments and Possibilities,* edited by Matthew T. Lee

and Amos Yong, 195–224. Dekalb: Northern Illinois University Press, 2012.

———, ed. *Encyclopedia of Religious Revivals in America.* 2 vols. Westport, CT: Greenwood, 2007.

———. *Familiar Stranger: An Introduction to Jesus of Nazareth.* Grand Rapids: Eerdmans, 2004.

———. Review of *Events of Grace: Naturalism, Existentialism, and Theology,* by Charley D. Hardwick. *Theological Studies* 58 (1997): 14–16.

McClymond, Michael J., and Gerald R. McDermott. *The Theology of Jonathan Edwards.* New York: Oxford University Press, 2012.

McConkie, Mark L. "Translated Beings." In D. H. Ludlow, *Encyclopedia of Mormonism,* 4:1485–86.

McConkie, Oscar W. "Angels." In D. H. Ludlow, *Encyclopedia of Mormonism,* 1:40–41.

McCormack, Bruce L. "The Doctrine of the Trinity after Barth: An Attempt to Reconstruct Barth's Doctrine in the Light of His Later Christology." In *Trinitarian Theology after Barth,* edited by Myk Habets and Philip Tolliday, 87–118. Eugene, OR: Pickwick, 2011.

———. "Election and the Trinity: Theses in Response to George Hunsinger." *Scottish Journal of Theology* 63 (2010): 203–24.

———. "God *Is* His Decision: The Jüngel-Gollwitzer 'Debate' Revisited." In *Theology as Conversation: The Significance of Dialogue in Historical and Contemporary Theology,* edited by Kimlyn J. Bender and Bruce L. McCormack, 48–66. Grand Rapids: Eerdmans 2009.

———. "Grace and Being: The Role of God's Gracious Election in Karl Barth's Theological Ontology." In *The Cambridge Companion to Karl Barth,* edited by John Webster, 92–110. Cambridge: Cambridge University Press, 2000.

———. *Karl Barth's Critically Realistic Dialectical Theology: Its Genesis and Development, 1909–1936.* Oxford: Clarendon, 1995.

———. "Let's Speak Plainly: A Response to Paul Molnar." *Theology Today* 67 (2010): 57–65.

———. *Orthodox and Modern: Studies in the Theology of Karl Barth*. Grand Rapids: Baker Academic, 2008.

———, "Seek God Where He May Be Found. A Response to Edwin Chr. van Driel." *Scottish Journal of Theology* 60 (2007): 62–79.

———. "So That He May Be Merciful to All: Karl Barth and the Problem of Universalism." In *Karl Barth and American Universalism*, edited by Bruce L. McCormack and Clifford B. Anderson, 227–49. Grand Rapids: Eerdmans, 2011.

McCullum, Joseph T., and John C. Guilds. "The Unpardonable Sin in Hawthorne: A Re-Examination." *Nineteenth-Century Fiction* 15 (1960): 221–37.

McDannell, Colleen, and Bernhard Lang. *Heaven: A History*. 2nd ed. New Haven: Yale Nota Bene, 2001.

McDermott, Gerald R. *Jonathan Edwards Confronts the Gods: Christian Theology, Enlightenment Religion, and Non-Christian Faiths*. New York: Oxford University Press, 2000.

McDonald, Suzanne. "Calvin's Theology of Election: Modern Reception and Contemporary Possibilities." In *Calvin's Theology and Its Reception*, edited by J. Todd Billings and I. John Hesselink, 121–39. Louisville: Westminster John Knox, 2012.

———. *Re-Imagining Election: Divine Election as Representing God to Others and Others to God*. Grand Rapids: Eerdmans, 2010.

McDowell, J. C. "Learning Where to Place One's Hope: The Eschatological Significance of Election in Barth." *Scottish Journal of Theology* 53 (2000): 326–38.

———. "Much Ado about Nothingness: Karl Barth's Being Unable to Do Nothing about Nothingness." *International Journal of Systematic Theology* 4 (2002): 319–35.

McDowell, Paula. "Enlightenment Enthusiasms and the Spectacular Failure of the Philadelphian Society." *Eighteenth-Century Studies* 35 (2002): 515–33.

McFarland, Ian A. *From Nothing: A Theology of Creation*. Louisville: Westminster John Knox, 2014.

McGehee, Charles White. "Elhanan Winchester: A Decision for Universal Restoration." *Journal of the Universalist Historical Society* 1 (1959): 45–58.

McGiffert, Arthur. "Modern Ideas of God." *Harvard Theological Review* 1 (1908): 10–27.

McGinn, Bernard. "The Spiritual Heritage of Origen in the West: Aspects of the History of Origen's Influence in the Middle Ages." In *Origene: Maestro di vita spirituale*, edited by Luigi F. Pizzolato and Marco Rizzi, 263–89. Milan: Vita e Pensiero, 2001.

———. *The Varieties of Vernacular Mysticism, 1350–1550*. Vol. 5 of *The Presence of God: A History of Christian Mysticism*. New York: Crossroad, 2012.

McGlasson, Paul. *Jesus and Judas: Biblical Exegesis in Barth*. Atlanta: Scholars Press, 1991.

McGrath, Alister E. "The Doctrine of the Trinity: An Evangelical Reflection." In *God the Holy Trinity: Reflections on Christian Faith and Practice*, edited by Timothy George, 17–35. Grand Rapids: Baker Academic, 2006.

———. "Karl Barth als Aufklärer? Der Zusammenhang seiner Lehre vom Werke Christi mit der Erwählungslehre." *Kerygma und Dogma* 30 (1984): 273–83.

———. "Karl Barth's Doctrine of Justification from an Evangelical Perspective." In *Karl Barth and Evangelical Theology*, edited by Sung Wook Chung, 172–90. Milton Keynes, UK: Paternoster; Grand Rapids: Baker Academic, 2006.

McGrath, S. J. "Boehme, Hegel, Schelling and the Hermetic Theology of Evil." *Philosophy and Theology* 18 (2006): 257–86.

McGuckin, John Anthony, ed. *The Westminster Handbook to Origen*. Louisville: Westminster John Knox, 2004.

McIntosh, Christopher. *Eliphas Lévi and the French Occult Revival*. 1972. Reprint, Albany: State University of New York Press, 2011.

McKanan, Daniel. "Unitarianism, Universalism, and Unitarian Universalism." *Religion Compass* 7 (2013): 15–24.

McKeating, Colm. *Eschatology in the Anglican Sermons of John Henry Newman.* Lewiston, NY: Mellen Research University Press, 1992.

McLachlan, H. J. *Socinianism in Seventeenth-Century England.* Oxford: Oxford University Press, 1951.

McLeod, Alexander W. *Universalism in Its Ancient and Modern Form . . . Unscriptural.* Halifax, NS: William Cunnabell, 1837.

McNeill, John T., ed. *John Calvin: Institutes of the Christian Religion.* Translated by Ford Lewis Battles. 2 vols. London: SCM, 1961.

Meacham, Jon. "What If There's No Hell? A Popular Pastor's Best-Selling Book Has Stirred Fierce Debate about Sin, Salvation and Judgment." *Time,* April 20, 2011, 38–43.

Mead, George Herbert. *Movements of Thought in the Nineteenth Century.* Chicago: University of Chicago Press, 1936.

Meadors, Edward P. *Idolatry and the Hardening of the Heart: A Study in Biblical Theology.* New York: T&T Clark, 2007.

Meeks, M. Douglas. *Origins of the Theology of Hope.* Philadelphia: Fortress, 1974.

Méhat, André. "'Apocatastase': Origène, Clément d'Alexandrie, Acts 3, 21." *Vigiliae Christianae* 10 (1956): 196–214.

Meier, Marcus. "Horch und Petersen: Die Hintergründe des Streits um die Apokatastasis im radikalen Pietismus." *Pietismus und Neuzeit* 32 (2006): 157–74.

Melzer, Arthur M. *Philosophy between the Lines: The Lost History of Esoteric Writing.* Chicago: University of Chicago Press, 2014.

Menke, Karl-Heinz. *Stellvertretung: Schüsselbegriff christlichen Lebens und theologische Grundkategorie.* Einsiedeln: Johannes, 1991.

Menke-Peitzmeyer, Michael. *Subjektivität und Selbstinterpretation des dreifaltigen Gottes: Eine Studie zur Genese und Explikation des Paradigmas "Selbstoffenbarung Gottes" in der Theologie Karl Barths.* Münster: Aschendorff, 2002.

Merkle, John C. "Heschel's Theology of Divine Pathos." In *Abraham Joshua Heschel: Exploring His Life and Thought,* edited by John C. Merkle, 66–83. New York: Macmillan, 1985.

Merritt, Timothy, and Wilbur Fisk. *A Discussion on Universal Salvation: In Three Lectures and Five Answers against That Doctrine.* New York: B. Waugh & T. Mason, 1832.

Merx, Adalbert. *Idee und Grundlinien einer allgemeinen Geschichte der Mystik.* Heidelberg: Universitäts-Buchdruckerei von J. Hörning, 1893.

Messina Colloquium [on gnosticism]. "Proposal for a Terminological and Conceptual Agreement with Regard to the Theme of the Colloquium." In *The Origins of Gnosticism, Colloquium of Messina, 13–18 April 1966,* edited by Ugo Bianchi, xxvi–xxix. Leiden: Brill, 1967.

Mettepenningen, Jürgen. *Nouvelle Théologie / New Theology: Inheritor of Modernism, Precursor of Vatican II.* London: T&T Clark, 2010.

Meyendorff, John. "Creation in the History of Orthodox Theology." *St. Vladimir's Theological Quarterly* 27 (1983): 27–37.

Meyer, Marvin. Epilogue to Meyer, *Nag Hammadi Scriptures,* 777–98.

———. *The Gnostic Discoveries: The Impact of the Nag Hammadi Library.* San Francisco: HarperSanFrancisco, 2005.

———, ed. *The Nag Hammadi Scriptures: The International Edition.* New York: HarperOne, 2007.

Meyers, Mary Ann. "Death in Swedenborgian and Mormon Eschatology." *Dialogue: A Journal of Mormon Thought* 14 (1981): 58–64.

Michaelis, Wilhelm. *Versöhnung des Alls: Die frohe Botschaft von der Gnade Gottes.* Gümlingen: Siloah, 1950.

Michel, A. "Purgatoire." In *Dictionnaire de théologie catholique,* edited by A. Vacant, E. Mangenot, et al., 13:1163–326. Paris: Letouzey, 1936.

Milbank, John. *The Suspended Middle: Henri de Lubac and the Debate concerning the Supernatural.* Grand Rapids: Eerdmans, 2005.

Mill, John Stuart. *An Examination of Sir William Hamilton's Philosophy, and of the Principal Philosophical Questions Discussed in his Writings.* London: Longmans, Green & Co., 1865.

———. *The Utility of Religion, and Theism [Three Essays on Religion].* 2nd ed. London: Longmans, Green, Reader, and Dyer, 1874.

Miller, Allen O., and Donald E. Arther. *Paul Tillich's Systematic Theology.* St. Louis: Eden Publishing House, 1975.

Miller, Caleb A. *The Divine Reversal: Recovering the Vision of Jesus Christ as the Last Adam.* N.p.: Father's House Press, 2014.

Miller, Perry. *The New England Mind: From Colony to Province.* Cambridge, MA: The Belknap Press of Harvard University, 1953.

Miller, Russell E. *The Large Hope.* 2 vols. Boston: Unitarian Universalist Association, 1979, 1985.

Millet, Robert L. "Jesus Christ, Fatherhood and Sonship of." In D. H. Ludlow, *Encyclopedia of Mormonism*, 2:739–40.

Milton, John. *Paradise Lost.* Edited by Scott Elledge. 2nd ed. New York: Norton, 1993. Originally published in 1674.

Min, Anselm K. "The Trinity and the Incarnation: Hegel and Classical Approaches." *Journal of Religion* 66 (1986): 177–95.

Mitchell, Philip Irving. "Introduction to Sufism and Rumi." www3.dbu.edu/Mitchell/rumiprin.htm.

Mitscherling, Jeff. "The Identity of the Human and the Divine in the Logic of Speculative Philosophy." In *Hegel and the Tradition: Essays in Honor of H. S. Harris*, edited by Michael Baur and John Russon, 143–61. Toronto: University of Toronto Press, 1997.

Molnar, Paul D. "Can Jesus' Divinity Be Recognized as 'Definitive, Authentic and Essential' If It Is Grounded in Election? Just How Far Did the Later Barth Historicize Christology?" *Neue Zeitschrift für systematische Theologie und Religionsphilosophie* 52 (2010): 40–81.

———. "Can the Electing God Be God without Us? Some Implications of Bruce McCormack's Understanding of Barth's Doctrine of Election for the Doctrine of the Trinity." *Neue Zeitschrift für systematische Theologie und Religionsphilosophie* 49 (2007): 199–222.

———. *Divine Freedom and the Doctrine of the Immanent Trinity: In Dialogue with Karl Barth and Contemporary Theology.* 2002. Reprint, London: T&T Clark, 2005.

———. *Faith, Freedom, and the Spirit: The Economic Trinity in Barth, Torrance, and Contemporary Theology.* Downers Grove, IL: IVP Academic, 2015.

———. "The Function of the Trinity in Moltmann's Ecological Doctrine of Creation." *Theological Studies* 51 (1990): 673–97.

———. "A Response: Beyond Hegel with Karl Barth and T. F. Torrance." *Pro Ecclesia* 23 (2014): 165–73.

———. "Thomas F. Torrance and the Problem of Universalism." *Scottish Journal of Theology* 68 (2015): 164–86.

———. "The Trinity, Election and God's Ontological Freedom: A Response to Kevin W. Hector." *International Journal of Systematic Theology* 8 (2006): 294–306.

Moltmann, Jürgen. *The Church in the Power of the Spirit: A Contribution to Messianic Ecclesiology.* Translated by Margaret Kohl. London: SCM, 1977.

———. *The Coming of God: Christian Eschatology.* Translated by Margaret Kohl. Minneapolis: Fortress, 1996.

———. *The Crucified God: The Cross of Christ as the Foundation and Criticism of Christian Theology.* Translated by R. A. Wilson and John Bowden. New York: Harper & Row, 1974. Reprint, Minneapolis: Fortress, 1993.

———. *The Future of Creation.* Translated by Margaret Kohl. Philadelphia: Fortress, 1979.

———. *God in Creation: A New Theology of Creation and the Spirit of God; The Gifford Lectures, 1984–1985.* Translated by Margaret Kohl. San Francisco: Harper & Row, 1985.

———. *History and the Triune God: Contributions to Trinitarian Theology.* Translated by John Bowden. New York: Crossroad; London: SCM, 1991.

———. *Jesus Christ for Today's World.* London: SCM, 1994.

———. "The Logic of Hell." In Bauckham, *God Will Be All in All*, 42–47.

———. *The Open Church: Invitation to a Messianic Lifestyle.* Translated by M. Douglas Meeks. London: SCM, 1978.

———. *Perspektiven der Theologie: Gesammelte Aufsätze.* Munich: Kaiser; Mainz: Grünewald, 1968.

———. "Politics and the Practice of Hope." *Christian Century* 87 (1970): 288–91.

———. "The Presence of God's Future: The Risen Christ." *Anglican Theological Review* 89 (2007): 577–88.

———. *The Spirit of Life: A Universal Affirmation.* Minneapolis: Fortress, 1992.

———. *Sun of Righteousness, Arise! God's Future for Humanity and the Earth.* Translated by Margaret Kohl. Minneapolis: Fortress, 2010.

———. *Theology of Hope: On the Ground and the Implications of a Christian Eschatology.* New York: Harper & Row, 1967. Originally published as *Theologie der Hoffnung: Untersuchungen zur Begründung und zu den Konsequenzen einer christlichen Eschatologie* (Munich: Kaiser, 1965).

———. *The Trinity and the Kingdom: The Doctrine of God.* Translated by Margaret Kohl. San Francisco: Harper & Row, 1981. Reprint, Minneapolis: Fortress, 1993.

———. *The Way of Jesus Christ: Christology in Messianic Dimensions.* London: SCM, 1990. Reprint, San Francisco: Harper, 1993.

———. "The World in God or God in the World? Response to Richard Bauckham." In Bauckham, *God Will Be All in All*, 35–41.

Monahan, Michael. *Heinrich Heine.* New York: Mitchell Kennerly, 1911.

Mongrain, Kevin. "Rule-Governed Christian Gnosis: Hans Urs von Balthasar on Valentin Tomberg's *Meditations on the Tarot*." *Modern Theology* 25 (2009): 285–314.

Monnerjahn, Engelbert. *Giovanni Pico della Mirandola: Ein Betrag zur philosophischen Theologie des italienischen Humanismus.* Wiesbaden: Steiner, 1960.

Moo, Douglas. *The Epistle to the Romans.* Grand Rapids: Eerdmans, 1996.

———. "Paul on Hell." In Morgan and Peterson, *Hell under Fire*, 92–109.

Mooney, Christopher F. *Teilhard de Chardin and the Mystery of Christ.* Garden City, NJ: Image, 1968.

Moore, David George. *The Battle for Hell: A Survey and Evaluation of Evangelicals' Growing Attraction to the Doctrine of Annihilationism.* Lanham, MD: University Press of America, 1995.

Moore, Will G. "'Dom Juan' Reconsidered." *Modern Language Review* 52 (1957): 510–17.

Moore, William, and Henry Austin Wilson. "The Life and Writings of Gregory of Nyssa." In *NPNF*[2] 5:1–29.

Moran, Dermot. "John Scottus Eriugena." In *The Stanford Encyclopedia of Philosophy*, edited by Edward N. Zalta. Fall 2008 ed. http://plato.stanford.edu/archives/fall2008/entries/scottus-eriugena/.

———. "Origen and Eriugena: Aspects of Christian Gnosis." In *The Relationship between Neoplatonism and Christianity*, edited by Thomas Finan and Vincent Twomey, 27–53. Dublin: Four Courts, 1992.

———. *The Philosophy of John Scottus Eriugena: A Study of Idealism in the Middle Ages.* Cambridge: Cambridge University Press, 1989.

More, Henry. *Conjectura Cabbalistica; or, A Conjectural Essay of Interpreting the Minde of Moses, according to a Threefold Cabbala: viz. Literal, Philosophical, Mystical, or, Divinely Moral.* London, 1653.

———. *The Immortality of the Soul, So Farre Forth as It Is Demonstrable from the Knowledge of Nature and the Light of Reason.* London, 1659.

———. *Philosophicall Poems.* London, 1647.

Moreira, Isabel. *Heaven's Purge: Purgatory in Late Antiquity.* New York: Oxford University Press, 2010.

Morgan, Christopher W., and Robert A. Peterson, eds. *Hell under Fire: Modern Scholarship Reinvents Eternal Punishment.* Grand Rapids: Zondervan, 2004.

Morgan, John C., and Nelson C. Simonson. "George de Benneville." *Dictionary of Unitarian and Universalist Biography.* http://uudb.org/articles/georgedebenneville.html.

Morgan, Robert. *The Nature of New Testament Theology: The Contribution of Wilhelm Wrede and Adolf Schlatter.* 1973. Reprint, Eugene, OR: Wipf & Stock, 2009.

Morris, K. R. "The Puritan Roots of American Universalism." *Scottish Journal of Theology* 44 (1991): 457–87.

Morris, Leon. *The Biblical Doctrine of Judgment*. Grand Rapids: Eerdmans, 1960.

———. "The Dreadful Harvest." *Christianity Today* 35 (1991): 34–38.

Morrison, Roy. "Paul Tillich's Appropriation of Jacob Boehme." In *Tillich Studies: Papers Prepared for the Second North American Consultation on Paul Tillich Studies*, edited by John J. Carey, 14–25. Tallahassee: Florida State University Department of Religion, 1975.

Mosshammer, Alden A. "Historical Time and the Apokatastasis according to Gregory of Nyssa." In *Studia Patristica*, vol. 27, edited by Elizabeth A. Livingstone, 70–93. Leuven: Peeters, 1993.

Motyer, J. A. *After Death*. Philadelphia: Westminster, 1965.

Moule, C. F. D. *The Meaning of Hope*. London: Highway Press, 1953.

Mozley, John Kenneth. *Some Tendencies in British Theology from the Publication of "Lux Mundi" to the Present Day*. London: SPCK, 1951.

Mühlenberg, E., ed. "Great Catechism." In GNO III.iv. Leiden: Brill, 1996. ET in *The Catechetical Oration*. Translated by J. H. Strawley. London: SPCK, 1917.

Mulder, David. *The Alchemy of Revolution: Gerrard Winstanley's Occultism and Seventeenth-Century English Communism*. New York: Lang, 1990.

Mulder, Jack, Jr. *Kierkegaaard and the Catholic Tradition: Conflict and Dialogue*. Bloomington: Indiana University Press, 2010.

———. "Must All Be Saved? A Kierkegaardian Response to Theological Universalism." *International Journal for Philosophy of Religion* 59 (2006): 1–24.

Mullarkey, Maureen. "The Idolatry of Devout Ideas." *Studio Matters* (blog), September 3, 2013. http://studiomatters.com/idolatry-of-devout-ideas.

Müller, F. Max. *The Sacred Books of the East*. 50 vols. Delhi: Motilal Banarsidass, 1962–66.

Müller, Gotthold. *Apokatastasis Panton: A Bibliography*. Basel: Basler Missionsbuchhandlung, 1969.

——— "The Idea of an Apokatastasis ton Panton (Universal Salvation) in European Theology from Schleiemacher to Barth." *Journal of the Universalist Historical Society* 6 (1966): 47–64.

Müller, Julius. *The Christian Doctrine of Sin*. 2 vols. Edinburgh: T&T Clark, 1852–53.

Müller-Fahrenholz, Geiko. *Phantasie für das Reich Gottes: Die Theologie Jürgen Moltmanns; Eine Einführung*. Gütersloh: Gütersloher Verlagshaus, 2000.

Mullett, Charles F. "A Letter by Joseph Glanvill on the Future State." *Huntington Library Quarterly* 1 (1938): 447–56.

Murphy, Francis X. *Rufinus of Aquileia (345–411): His Life and Works*. Washington, DC: Catholic University of America Press, 1945.

Murray, A. T., trans. *Odyssey, Volume 1*. LCL 104. Cambridge, MA: Harvard University Press, 1995.

Murray, John. *The Life of Rev. John Murray*. Boston: published at the Trumpet Office, 1833.

———. *The Life of the Rev. John Murray*. Boston: Universalist Publishing House, 1882.

———. *Records of the Life of the Rev. John Murray . . . Written by Himself*. Boston: Munroe and Francis, 1816.

Murray, Michael J. "Three Versions of Universalism." *Faith and Philosophy* 16 (1999): 55–68.

Musurillo, Herbert. "The Recent Revival of Origen Studies." *Theological Studies* 24 (1963): 250–63.

Myers, Benjamin. "Election, Trinity, and the History of Jesus: Reading Barth with Rowan Williams." In *Trinitarian Theology after Barth*, edited by Myk Habets and Philip Tolliday, 121–37. Eugene, OR: Pickwick, 2011.

Nasr, Seyyed Hossain. *The Garden of Truth: The Vision and Promise of Sufism, Islam's Mystical Tradition*. New York: HarperCollins, 2007.

Nautin, Pierre, trans. *Didyme L'Aveugle: Sur la Genèse*. Vol. 1. Paris: Cerf, 1976.

Neff, Christian, and Walter Fellmann. "Denck, Hans (ca. 1500–1527)." In *Global Anabaptist Mennonite Encyclopedia Online*. http://gameo.org.

Nesteruk, Alexei V. "The Universe as Hypostatic Inherence in the Logos of God." In Clayton and Peacocke, *In Whom We Live*, 169–83.

Neusner, Jacob. *The Mishnah: A New Translation*. New Haven: Yale University Press, 1988.

Newman, John Henry. *Grammar of Assent*. London: Longmans, Green, 1930.

———. "On the Introduction of Rationalistic Principles into Revealed Religion" [Tract 73]. In *Essays Critical and History*, 1:30–101. London: Longmans, Green & Co., 1901. http://www.newmanreader.org/works/essays/volume1/rationalism/section1.html.

———. *Parochial and Plain Sermons*. San Francisco: Ignatius, 1987.

———. *Prose and Poetry*. Edited by G. Tillotson. Cambridge, MA: Harvard University Press, 1957.

Neyt, François, and Paula de Angelis-Noah, eds. *Barsunuphe et Jean de Gaza, Correspondance*. Translated by Lucien Regnault. 5 vols. SC 426, 427, 450, 451, 468. Paris: Cerf, 2001.

Nicholas of Cusa. *De docta ignorantia, Liber tertius*. Edited by Raymundus Klibansky. Hamburg: Felix Meiner, 1999.

———. *Nicholas of Cusa: Selected Spiritual Writings*. Translated by H. Lawrence Bond. New York: Paulist Press, 1997.

Nicholson, Reynolds A. "The Perfect Man." In *Studies in Islamic Mysticism*, 77–142. 1921. Reprint, Cambridge: Cambridge University Press, 1978.

Nicol, Iain G., and Allen G. Jorgenson. Introduction to *On the Doctrine of Election, with Special Reference to the Aphorisms of Dr. Bretschneider*, by Friedrich Schleiermacher, 1–20. Translated by Iain G. Nicol and Allen G. Jorgenson. Louisville: Westminster John Knox, 2012.

Nicole, Roger. "Will Everyone Be Saved?" *Christianity Today* 31 (1987): 31–45.

Nicolin, Günther, ed. *Hegel in Berichten seiner Zeitgenossen*. Hamburg: Felix Meiner, 1970.

Nielsen, F. Kent, and Stephen D. Ricks. "Creation, Creation Accounts." In D. H. Ludlow, *Encyclopedia of Mormonism*, 1:340–43

Nietzsche, Friedrich. *The Anti-Christ, Ecce Homo, Twilight of the Idols, and Other Writings*. Edited by Aaron Ridley and Judith Norman. Translated by Judith Norman. Cambridge Texts in the History of Philosophy. Cambridge: Cambridge University Press, 2005.

———. *The Genealogy of Morals*. Translated by Walter Kaufmann. New York: Random House, 1969.

Nigosian, S. A. *The Zoroastrian Faith: Tradition and Modern Research*. Montreal: McGill-Queen's University Press, 1993.

Noack, Ludwig. *Die christliche Mystik seit dem Reformationszeitalter*. Königsberg: Gebrüder Bornträger, 1853.

Noe, John. *Hell Yes / Hell No*. Indianapolis: East2West, 2011.

Noll, Mark. *The Rise of Evangelicalism: The Age of Edwards, Whitefield, and the Wesleys*. Downers Grove, IL: InterVarsity, 2004.

Nordmann, Walter. "Die Eschatologie des Ehepaares Petersen: ihre Entwicklung und Auflösung." *Zeitschrift des Verein für Kirchengeschichte der Provinz Sachsen und des Freistaates Anhalt* 26/27 (1930/31): 1–19, 83–108.

———. "Die theologische Gedankenwelt des pietistischen Ehepaares Petersen." PhD diss., Berlin University, 1929.

Norelli, Enrico, ed. *Ippolito* [Hippolytus of Rome]: *L'anticristo (De antichristo)*. Florence: Nardini, 1987.

Norris, Frederick W. "Universal Salvation in Origen and Maximus." In Cameron, *Universalism and the Doctrine of Hell*, 35–72.

Norwood, Donald W. *Reforming Rome: Karl Barth and Vatican II*. Grand Rapids: Eerdmans, 2015.

Nurbakhsh, Javid. *The Great Satan 'Eblis.'* London: Khaniqahi-Nimatullahi Publications, 1986.

Oakes, Edward T. "Bell's Present Heaven." *First Things* (October 2011): 23–25.

————. "*Descensus* and Development: A Response to Recent Rejoinders." *International Journal of Systematic Theology* 13 (2011): 3–24.

————. "The Internal Logic of Holy Saturday in the Theology of Hans Urs von Balthasar." *International Journal of Systematic Theology* 9 (2007): 184–99.

————. *The Pattern of Redemption: The Theology of Hans Urs von Balthasar.* Corrected reprint, New York: Continuum, 1997.

————. "Saved from What? On Preaching Hell in the New Evangelization: A Review of Ralph Martin, *Will Many Be Saved?* (2012)." *Pro Ecclesia* 22 (2013): 378–94.

O'Brien, John A. "Are Lost Souls Eternally Tortured?" *Homiletic and Pastoral Review* 35 (March 1935): 599–611.

————. "Are Lost Souls Eternally Tortured?" (concluded). *Homiletic and Pastoral Review* 35 (April 1935): 703–14.

————. "Father Connell's Ideas of Hell." *Homiletic and Pastoral Review* 34 (October 1934): 31–44.

————. "A Sane Treatment of Hell." *Homiletic and Pastoral Review* 34 (June 1934): 966–69.

————. "Statement." *Homiletic and Pastoral Review* 35 (August 1935): 1129.

Obst, Helmut. "Zum 'Verhör' Jakob Böhmes in Dresden." *Pietismus und Neuzeit* (1974): 25–31.

O'Collins, Gerald. "Jacques Dupuis: The Ongoing Debate." *Theological Studies* 74 (2013): 632–54.

————. *Salvation for All: God's Other Peoples.* New York: Oxford University Press, 2008.

O'Connor, Flannery. *The Correspondence of Flannery O'Connor and the Brainard Cheneys.* Edited by C. Ralph Stephens. Jackson: University of Mississippi Press, 1986.

————. *Everything That Rises Must Converge.* New York: Farrar, Straus & Giroux, 1965.

O'Connor, James T. "Von Balthasar and Salvation." *Homiletic and Pastoral Review* 89 (1989): 10–21.

Oetinger, Friedrich Christoph. *Sämtliche Schriften.* Edited by Karl Chr. Eberh. Ehmann. Stuttgart: Steinkopf, 1858–64.

————. *Theologia ex idea vitae deducta.* 2 vols. Edited by Konrad Ohly. Berlin: de Gruyter, 1979.

————. *Theologia ex idea vitae. Deducta in sex locos redacata, quorum quilibet: I. Secundum sensum communem; II. Secundum mysteria scripturae; III. Secundum formulas theticas, nova et expermentali methodo pertractatur.* Francofurti et Lipsiae: Apud Aug. Lebr. Stettin, 1765.

Official Report of the Debates of the House of Commons of the Dominion of Canada. Third Session—Twelfth Parliament. Vol. XCIII. Ottawa: J. de La Taché, 1914.

Okely, Francis, trans. *Memoirs of the Life, Death, Burial, and Wonderful Writings, of Jacob Behmen: Now First Done at Large into English.* Northampton, England: Thomas Dicey, 1780.

O'Laughlin, Michael. "New Questions concerning the Origenism of Evagrius." In Daly, *Origeniana Quinta,* 528–34.

Olin, John C. *Six Essays on Erasmus, and a Translation of Erasmus' Letter to Carondolet, 1523.* New York: Fordham University Press, 1979.

O'Meara, Thomas K. *God in the World: A Guide to Karl Rahner's Theology.* Collegeville, MN: Liturgical Press, 2007.

O'Neil, Michael. "Karl Barth's Doctrine of Election." *Evangelical Quarterly* 76 (2004): 311–26.

Oord, Thomas Jay, ed. *Theologies of Creation: Creatio ex Nihilo and Its New Rivals.* London: Routledge, 2015.

————. *The Uncontrolling Love of God: An Open and Relational Account of Providence.* Downers Grove, IL: IVP Academic, 2015.

O'Regan, Cyril. *Gnostic Apocalypse: Jacob Boehme's Haunted Narrative.* Albany: State University of New York Press, 2002.

————. *Gnostic Return in Modernity.* Albany: State University of New York Press, 2001.

————. *The Heterodox Hegel.* Albany: State University of New York Press, 1994.

————. "Žižek's Meontology: An Inflected Hegel and the Possibility of Theology." *Modern Theology* 30 (2014): 600–611.

Origen. *Contra Celsum*. Translated by Henry Chadwick. Cambridge: Cambridge University Press, 1980.

———. *"On First Principles": Being Koetschau's Text of the "De Principiis" Translated into English, Together with an Introduction and Notes*. Translated by G. W. Butterworth. 1966. Reprint, Gloucester, MA: Peter Smith, 1973.

———. *"Origen against Celsus": Translated from the Original into English by James Bellamy*. London: B. Mills, 1660.

———. *Origenes: Contra Celsum libri viii*, edited by M. Marcovich. Supplements to Vigiliae Christianae 54. Leiden: Brill, 2001. ET: ANF 4:395–670.

———. *Origenes kata Kelsou*. Edited by William Spencer. Cambridge, 1658.

———. *Origen: Homilies on Leviticus 1–16*. Translated by Gary Wayne Barkley. FC 83. Washington, DC: Catholic University of America Press, 1990.

———. *Peri archōn* [*De principiis*]. PG 11. *Vier Bücher von den Prinzipien*. Edited by Herwig Görgemanns and Heinrich Karpp. Darmstadt: Wissenschaftliche Buchgesellschaft, 1985.

Orlandi, Tito. "A Catechesis against Apocryphal Texts by Shenute and the Gnostic Texts of Nag Hammadi." *Harvard Theological Review* 75 (1982): 85–95.

———, trans. and ed. *Shenute contra Origenistas: Testo con Introduzione e Traduzione*. Rome: Corpus del Manoscritti Copti Letterari, 1985.

Orwell, George. *Nineteen Eighty-Four*. 1949. Reprint, London: Secker and Warburg, 1987.

Osborn, Eric. "Clement and Platonism." In Perrone, *Origeniana Octava*, 419–27.

———. *Clement of Alexandria*. Cambridge: Cambridge University Press, 2005.

———. "Origen: The Twentieth Century Quarrel and Its Recovery." In Daly, *Origeniana Quinta*, 26–39.

Ostling, Richard. "Who Was Jesus?" *Time*, August 15, 1988, 37–42.

Ott, Heinrich. *Eschatologie: Versuch eines dogmatischen Grundrisses*. Zollikon: Evangelische Verlag, 1958.

Otten, Bernard J. *A Manual of the History of Dogmas*. St. Louis: Herder, 1917.

Otten, Willemien. "The Dialectic of Return in Eriugena's *Periphyseon*." *Harvard Theological Review* 84 (1991): 399–421.

Otto, Randall E. *The God of Hope: The Trinitarian Vision of Jürgen Moltmann*. Lanham, MD: University Press of America, 1991.

———. "The Use and Abuse of Perichoresis in Recent Theology." *Scottish Journal of Theology* 54 (2001): 368–72.

Oulton, J. E. L., trans. *Eusebius: Ecclesiastical History, Volume II: Books 6–10*. LCL 265. Cambridge, MA: Harvard University Press, 1932.

Ouspensky [Uspenskiĭ], P. D. *A New Model of the Universe*. 2nd ed. New York: Knopf, 1969.

———. *Tertium Organum: The Third Canon of Thought; A Key to the Enigmas of the World*. 1950. Translated by Nicholas Bessaraboff and Claude Bragdon. Reprint, New York: Vintage, 1970.

Overton, John H. *William Law, Nonjuror and Mystic*. London: Longmans, Green, 1881.

Owen, John. *Overcoming Sin and Temptation*. Edited by Kelly M. Kapic and Justin Taylor. Wheaton: Crossway, 2006.

Owens, Lance S. "Joseph Smith: America's Hermetic Prophet." In *The Prophet Puzzle: Interpretive Essays on Joseph Smith*, edited by Bryan Waterman, 155–71. Salt Lake City: Signature, 1999.

———. "Joseph Smith and Kabbalah: The Occult Connection." *Dialogue: A Journal of Mormon Thought* 27 (1994): 117–94.

———. Review of *The Refiner's Fire*, by John L. Brooke. *Dialogue: A Journal of Mormon Thought* 27 (1994): 187–91.

Oxenham, Henry Nutcombe. *Catholic Eschatology and Universalism: An Essay on the Doctrine of Future Retribution*. London: Basil, Montague, Pickering, 1876.

———. *What Is the Truth as to Everlasting Punishment?* London: Kegan Paul, Trench, 1882.

Packer, J. I. "The Problem of Eternal Punishment." *Crux* 26 (1990): 18–25.

————. "The Problem of Universalism Today." In *Celebrating the Saving Work of God*, 169 78. Carlisle, UK: Paternoster, 1998.

Packull, Werner O. "Denck's Alleged Baptism by Hubmaier: Its Significance for the Origin of South German-Austrian Anabaptism." *Mennonite Quarterly Review* 47 (1973): 327–38.

Padgett, Alan G. *God, Eternity, and the Nature of Time*. New York: St. Martin's Press, 1992.

Pagels, Elaine. *The Johannine Gospel in Gnostic Exegesis*. Nashville: Abingdon, 1973.

Palmer, Grant H. *An Insider's View of Mormon Origins*. Salt Lake City: Signature, 2002.

Pältz, Eberhard H. "Böhme, Jacob." In *Theologische Realenzyklopädie*, edited by Horst Robert Balz et al., 6:748–54. Berlin: de Gruyter, 1980.

————. "Jacob Boehmes Hermeneutik, Geschichtsverständis und Sozialethik." Habilitationsschrift, Jena, 1962.

Pangritz, Andreas. *Karl Barth in the Theology of Dietrich Bonhoeffer*. Translated by Barbara and Martin Rumscheidt. Grand Rapids: Eerdmans, 2000.

Pannenberg, Wolfhart. "Subjectivité de Dieu et doctrine trinitaire." In *Hegel et la théologie contemporaine: L'absolu dans l'histoire?*, by Louis Rumpf et al., 171–87. Neuchâtel: Delachaux & Niestlé, 1977.

————. *Systematic Theology*. Translated by Geoffrey W. Bromiley. 3 vols. Grand Rapids: Eerdmans, 1991–98.

Papadopoulos, Iōannēs A. *Epitomos Dogmatikē tēs Orthodoxou Anatolikēs Ekklēsias*. 1932. 2nd ed. New York: n.p., 1955.

Parker, Samuel. *A Free and Impartial Censure of the Platonick Philosophie*. Oxford: W. Hall, 1666.

Parmentier, M. "Evagrius of Pontus' 'Letter to Melania.'" *Bijdragen tijdschrift voor filosofie en theologie* 46 (1985): 2–38.

Parnham, David. "The Covenantal Quietism of Tobias Crisp." *Church History* 75 (2006): 511–43.

————. "The Humbling of 'High Presumption': Tobias Crisp Dismantles the Puritan *Ordo Salutis*." *Journal of Ecclesiastical History* 56 (2005): 50 74.

————. "John Saltmarsh and the Mystery of Redemption." *Harvard Theological Review* 104 (2011): 265–98.

————. "Motions of Law and Grace: The Puritan in the Antinomian." *Westminster Theological Journal* 70 (2008): 73–104.

Parry, Robin. "Between Calvinism and Arminianism: The Evangelical Universalism of Elhanan Winchester (1751–1797)." In MacDonald [Parry], *"All Shall Be Well,"* 141–70.

————. "Evangelical Universalism: Oxymoron?" *Evangelical Quarterly* 84 (2012): 3–18.

————. "I Am the Evangelical Universalist." August 29, 2009. http://theologicalscrib bles.blogspot.com/2009/08/i-am-evangeli cal-universalist.html.

————. "Introduction to Thomas Allin (1838–1909)." In *Christ Triumphant: Universalism Asserted as the Hope of the Gospel on the Authority of Reason, the Fathers, and Holy Scripture*, by Thomas Allin, ix–xxxvii. Annotations by Robin Parry and Thomas B. Talbott. Eugene, OR: Wipf & Stock, 2015.

Parry, Robin A., and Christopher H. Partridge, eds. *Universal Salvation? The Current Debate*. Grand Rapids: Eerdmans, 2004.

Patterson, L. G. "*Pleroma*: The Human Plenitude, from Irenaeus to Gregory of Nyssa." In *Studia Patristica*, vol. 34, edited by M. F. Wiles and E. J. Yarnold, 529–40. Leuven: Peeters, 2001.

Pattison, George. "H. L. Martensen on Jacob Boehme." In Hessayon and Apetrai, *Introduction to Jacob Boehme*, 244–61.

Patton, Kimberley C. "Can Evil Be Redeemed? Unorthodox Tensions in Eastern Orthodox Theology." In *Deliver Us from Evil*, edited by M. David Eckel and Bradley L. Herling, 186–206. New York: Continuum, 2008.

Patuzzi, Giovanni Vincenzo. *De futuro impiorum statu libri tres ubi aduers. deistas, nuperos origenistas, aliosque nouatores ecclesiae catholicae doctrina de poenarum inferni veritate, qualitate, et aeternitate asseritur et illustratur. Authore p.f. Io. Vincentio*

Patuzzi. Editio secunda ab authore recognita, & pluribus additamentis locupletata. 2nd ed. Venetiis: ex Typographia Remondiniana, 1764.

Paulson, Michael. "Lucas Hnath's 'The Christians' Tackles a Schism among the Flock." *New York Times*, September 3, 2015. http://www.nytimes.com/2015/09/06/theater/lucas-hnaths-the-christians-tackles-a-schism-among-the-flock.html.

Pavry, Jal Dastur Cursetji. *The Zoroastrian Doctrine of a Future Life.* 1929. 2nd ed. New York: AMS, 1965.

Pawson, David. *The Road to Hell.* London: Hodder & Stoughton, 1992.

Peacocke, Arthur. "The Cost of New Life." In *The Work of Love: Creation as Kenosis*, edited by John Polkinghorne, 32–42. Grand Rapids: Eerdmans, 2001.

Pearson, Birger A. *Ancient Gnosticism: Traditions and Literature.* Minneapolis: Fortress, 2007.

Pearson, Carlton. *The Gospel of Inclusion: Reaching beyond Religious Fundamentalism to the True Love of God and Self.* New York: Atria, 2006.

Peck, George. *Universal Salvation Considered.* Wilkesbarre, PA: S. D. Lewis, 1827.

Peddicord, Richard. *The Sacred Monster of Thomism: An Introduction to the Life and Legacy of Reginald Garrigou-Lagrange.* South Bend, IN: St. Augustine's Press, 2005.

Pedersen, Daniel. "Eternal Life in Schleiermacher's *The Christian Faith*." *International Journal of Systematic Theology* 13 (2011): 340–57.

Pegler, Stephen. "The Nature of Paul's Universal Salvation Language in Romans." PhD diss., Trinity International University, 2002.

Pelikan, Jaroslav. *The Christian Tradition: A History of the Development of Doctrine.* 5 vols. Chicago: University of Chicago Press, 1971–89.

———. "The Odyssey of Dionysian Spirituality." In *Pseudo-Dionysius: The Complete Works*, 11–24. Translated by Colm Luibheid, with the assistance of Paul Rorem. New York: Paulist Press, 1987.

Pelikan, Jaroslav, and Valerie Hotchkiss, eds. *Creeds and Confessions of Faith in the Christian Tradition.* 4 vols. New Haven: Yale University Press, 2003.

Penman, Leigh T. J. "Boehme's Intellectual Networks and the Heterodox Milieu of His Theosophy, 1600–1624." In Hessayon and Apetrai, *Introduction to Jacob Boehme*, 57–76.

Penton, M. James. *Apocalypse Delayed: The Story of Jehovah's Witnesses.* 2nd ed. Toronto: University of Toronto Press, 1997.

Percesepe, Gary John. *Future(s) of Philosophy: The Marginal Thinking of Jacques Derrida.* New York: Lang, 1989.

Perczel, István. "The Earliest Syriac Reception of Dionysius." *Modern Theology* 24 (2008): 557–71.

———. "God as Monad and Henad: Dionysius the Areopagite and the *Peri Archon*." In Perrone, *Origeniana Octava*, 1193–209.

———. "Pseudo-Dionysius and Palestinian Origenism." In *The Sabaite Heritage in the Orthodox Church from the Fifth Century to the Present*, edited by Joseph Patrich, 261–82. Louvain: Peeters, 2001.

Perkins, Pheme. *The Gnostic Dialogue.* New York: Paulist Press, 1980.

Perl, Eric D. "Metaphysics and Christology in Maximus Confessor and Eriugena." In *Eriugena East and West: Papers of the Eighth International Colloquium of the Society for the Promotion of Eriugenian Studies*, edited by Bernard McGinn and Willemien Otten, 253–70. Notre Dame, IN: University of Notre Dame Press, 1991.

Perrone, Lorenzo, ed. *Origeniana Octava: Origen and the Alexandrian Tradition = Origene e la tradizione alessandrina; Papers of the 8th International Origen Congress, Pisa, 27–31 August 2001.* 2 vols. In collaboration with P. Bernardino and D. Marchini. Leuven: Peeters, 2003.

———. "Origenism." In *Religion Past and Present: Encyclopedia of Theology and Religion*, edited by Hans Dieter Betz, Don S. Browning, Bernd Janowski, and Eberhard Jüngel, 9:376–78. 4th ed. Leiden: Brill, 2010.

―――. "Palestinian Monasticism, the Bible, and Theology in the Wake of the Second Origenist Controversy." In *The Sabaite Heritage in the Orthodox Church from the Fifth Century to the Present*, edited by Joseph Patrich, 245–59. Louvain: Peeters, 2001.

Pétau, Denis [Petavius, Dionysius]. "De Angelis." In *Dionysii Petauii Aurelianensis e Societate Jesus de Theologicis Dogmatibus*, 3:1–112. Venice: Andreæ Poleti, 1745.

Peter, Ralph V. "*Descendit ad inferos*: Medieval Views on Christ's Descent into Hell and the Salvation of the Just." *Journal of the History of Ideas* 27 (1966): 173–94.

Peters, Samuel. *A Letter to the Rev. John Tyler*. London, 1785.

Peters, Ted. *God as Trinity: Relationality and Temporality in the Divine Life*. Louisville: Westminster John Knox, 1993.

Petersen, Johanna Eleonora. *The Life of Lady Johanna Eleonora Petersen, Written by Herself: Pietism and Women's Autobiography in Seventeenth-Century Germany*. Edited and translated by Barbara Becker-Cantarino. Chicago: University of Chicago Press, 2005.

Petersen, Johann Wilhelm. *A Letter to Some Divines concerning the Question, Whether God since Christ's Ascension, Doth Any More Reveal Himself to Mankind by the Means of Divine Apparitions? With an Exact Account of What God Hath Bestowed upon a Noble Maid, from Her Seventh Year, until Now, MDCXCI*. London: John Whitlock, 1695.

―――. *Mysterion Apokatastaseos panton; Das ist, Das Geheimniss der Wiederbringung aller Dinge*. 3 vols. Pamphilia [Offenbach, Ger.]: n.p., 1700, 1703, 1710.

―――. *Petachia, oder die neu-geöffnete Bibel*. Frankfurt-am-Main: Johann Maximillian von Sand, 1765.

―――. *Send-Schreiben an einige Theologos und Gottes-Gelehrte; Betreffend die Frage Ob Gott nach der Auffahrt Christi nicht mehr heutiges Tages durch göttliche Erscheinung den Menschenkindern sich offenbahren wolle und sich dessen gantz begeben habe? Sampt einer erzehlten Specie Facti Von einem Adelichen Fräulein / was ihr vom siebenden Jahr ihres Alters biß hieher von Gott gegeben ist*. N.p.: 1691.

Peterson, Daniel J. "Jacob Boehme and Paul Tillich: A Reassessment of the Mystical Philosopher and Systematic Theologian." *Religious Studies* 42 (2006): 225–34.

Peterson, Robert A. *Hell on Trial: The Case for Eternal Punishment*. Phillipsburg, NJ: P&R, 1995.

Petschenig, Michael, ed. *Johannis Cassiani Opera*. CSEL 13. Vienna: F. Tempsky, 1886.

Peukert, Will-Erich. *Pansophie*. 2nd ed. Berlin: E. Schmidt, 1956.

Pfau, Julie Shoshana, and David R. Blumenthal. "Violence of God: Dialogic Fragments." *Cross Currents* 51 (2001): 177–200.

Pfister, Oskar. *Die Legende Sundar Singhs: Eine auf enthüllungen protestantischer Augenzeugen in Indien gegründete religionspsychologische Untersuchung*. Bern/Leipzig: P. Haupt, 1926.

Pfizenmaier, Martin. *Mit Vernunft glauben: Fides ratione formata; die Unformung der Rechfertigungslehre in der Theologie der deutschen Aufklärung, dargestellct am Werk J. G. Töllners (1724–1774)*. Stuttgart: Calwer, 1986.

Phan, Peter. "Eschatology." In *The Cambridge Companion to Karl Rahner*, edited by Declan Marmion and Mary E. Hines, 174–92. New York: Cambridge University Press, 2005.

―――. *Eternity in Time: A Study of Karl Rahner's Eschatology*. Cranbury, NJ: Associated University Presses, 1988.

Pico della Mirandola, Giovanni Francesco. *Of Being and Unity (De ente et uno)*. Translated by Victor Michael Hamm. Milwaukee: Marquette University Press, 1943.

―――. *Opera omnia Ioannis Pici Mirandulae concordiaeque comitis, theologorum et philosophorum, sine controversia, principis: viri, siue linguarum, siue rerum & humanarum, & diuinarum, cognitionem spectes, doctrina et ingenio admirando*. 2 vols. Basel: Ex officina Henricpetrina, 1572–73.

Pierre, Marie-Joseph, trans. *Aphraate le Sage Persan*. SC 349. Paris: Cerf, 1988.

Pierre of Blois. "In Hebdomada Poenosa, Sermo XVI." In *Opera Petri Blesensis*, 354–57. Mainz: Typographia Ioannis Albini, 1600.

Pike, Nelson. *God and Timelessness*. New York: Schocken, 1970.

Pinggéra, Karl. *All-Erlösung und All-Einheit: Studien zum "Buch des heiligen Hierotheos" und seiner Rezeption in der syrisch-orthodoxen Theologie*. Wiesbaden: Reichert, 2002.

Pingree, E. M., and N. L. Rice. *A Debate on the Doctrine of Universal Salvation*. Cincinnati: J. A. James, 1845.

Pinkard, Terry. *German Philosophy, 1760–1860: The Legacy of Idealism*. Cambridge: Cambridge University Press, 2002.

———. *Hegel: A Biography*. Cambridge: Cambridge University Press, 2000.

Pinnock, Clark H. "The Conditional View [of Hell]." In *Four Views on Hell*, edited by William Crockett, 135–66. Grand Rapids: Zondervan, 1996.

———. "The Destruction of the Finally Impenitent." *Criswell Theological Review* 4 (1990): 243–59.

Pinnock, Clark H., and Robert C. Brow. *Unbounded Love: A Good News Theology for the Twenty-First Century*. Carlisle, PA: Paternoster, 1994.

Pirard, M., ed. *Abba Isaak tou Syrou Logoi Asketikoi: Kritiki ekdosi*. Mount Athos: Moni Iviron, 2012.

Pitstick, Alyssa Lyra. "Development of Doctrine, or Denial? Balthasar's Holy Saturday and Newman's Essay." *International Journal of Systematic Theology* 11 (2009): 129–45.

———. *Light in Darkness: Hans Urs von Balthasar and the Catholic Doctrine of Christ's Descent into Hell*. Grand Rapids: Eerdmans, 2007.

Pitstick, Alyssa Lyra, and Edward Oakes. "Balthasar, Hell, and Heresy: An Exchange." *First Things* 168 (December 2006): 25–32. https://www.firstthings.com/article/2006/12/balthasar-hell-and-heresy-an-exchange.

———. "More on Balthasar, Hell, and Heresy." *First Things* 169 (January 2007): 16–19. https://www.firstthings.com/article/2007/01/003-more-on-balthasar-hell-and-heresy.

Pius XII. *Humani Generis* (Concerning Some False Opinions Threatening to Undermine the Foundations of Catholic Doctrine). 1950. http://w2.vatican.va/content/pius-xii/en/encyclicals/documents/hf_p-xii_enc_12081950_humani-generis.html.

Plato. *Collected Dialogues*. Edited by Edith Hamilton and Huntington Cairns. Princeton: Princeton University Press, 1961.

———. *Laws, Volume II: Books 7–12*. Translated by R. G. Bury. LCL 192. Cambridge, MA: Harvard University Press, 1926.

———. *Plato: Euthyphro, Apology, Crito, Phaedo, Phaedrus*. Translated by Harold North Fowler. LCL 36. Cambridge, MA: Harvard University Press, 1914.

———. *Plato: Laws, Volume II: Books 7–12*. Translated by R. G.Bury. LCL 192. Cambridge, MA: Harvard University Press, 1926.

———. *Plato V: Republic Books 1–5*. Edited and translated by Chris Emlyn-Jones and William Preddy. LCL 237. Cambridge, MA: Harvard University Press, 2013.

Platon, Metropolitan of Moscow. *The Orthodox Doctrine of the Apostolic Eastern Church; or, A Compendium of Christian Theology, Translated from the Greek*. New York: AMS, 1969.

Plotinus. *Enneads, Volume II*. Translated by A. H. Armstrong. LCL 441. Cambridge, MA: Harvard University Press, 1966.

Plumptre, Edward Hayes. *The Spirits in Prison and Other Studies on the Life after Death*. London: William Isbister, 1884.

Pohle, Joseph. *Eschatology; or, The Catholic Doctrine of the Last Things*. 7th ed. St. Louis: Herder, 1937.

Pohle, Joseph, and Arthur Preuss. *Eschatology; or, The Catholic Doctrine of the Last Things*. St. Louis: Herder, 1917.

Polkinghorne, John, ed. *The Work of Love: Creation as Kenosis*. Grand Rapids: Eerdmans, 2001.

Poncé, Charles. *Kabbalah: An Introduction and Illumination for the World Today*. San Francisco: Straight Arrow, 1973.

Pontifex, Mark. "The Doctrine of Hell." *Downside Review* 71 (1953): 135–52.

Pope, Richard Martin. "Faith, and the Future: An Introduction to Teilhard de Chardin." *Lexington Theological Quarterly* 6 (1971): 71–80.

Popkin, Richard H. *The History of Scepticism: From Savonarola to Bayle.* 2nd ed. New York: Oxford University Press, 2003.

———. "The New Sceptics: Simon Foucher and Pierre-Daniel Huet." In Popkin, *History of Scepticism,* 274–82.

Popp, Karl Robert. *Jakob Böhme und Isaac Newton.* Leipzig: Hirzel, 1935.

———. "Über den Ursprung der Gravitationslehre: J. Böhme, H. More, I. Newton." *Die Drei* 34 (1964): 313–40.

Popper, Hans. "Jacob Boehme's Doctrine of a Natural Language ('Natursprache'): With Special Reference to Its Influence on Novalis and Others." PhD diss., University of Bristol, 1958.

Pordage, John. *Innocencie Appearing through the Dark Mists of Pretended Guilt.* Cornhill: Blunden, 1654.

———. *Sophia: Dass ist, Die Holdselige ewige Jungfrau der Göttlichen Weisheit.* Amsterdam: n.p., 1699.

———. *Theologia Mystica; or, The Mystic Divinitie of the Aeternal Invisibles, viz., the Archetypous Globe, or the Original Globe, or World of all Globes, Worlds, Essences, Centres, Elements, Principles and Creations Whatsoever.* London: n.p., 1683.

Porete, Marguerite. *The Mirror of Simple Souls.* Translated by Ellen L. Babinsky. Classics of Western Spirituality. Mahwah, NJ: Paulist Press, 1993.

Postel, Guillaume. "La nouvelle Eve." In *Guillaume Postel: Apologies et rétractions; Manuscrits inédits publiés avec une introduction et notes,* edited by François Secret, 9–54. Nieuwkoop: B. de Graaf, 1972.

———. *Panthenosia: compositio omnivm dissidiorum circa æternam ueritatem aut uerisimilitudinem uerfantium, quæ non solum inter eos qui hodie infidelium, Iudæorum, hæreticorum & catholicorum nomine uocantur, orta sunt & uigent, sed iam ab admissis per peccatum circa nostrum intellectu tenebris fuere inter ecclesiæ peculiaris & communis membra.* [Basel]: n.p., 1547.

Potter, Jean A. "John the Scot, and His Background." Introduction to *Periphyseon: On the Division of Nature,* by John Scotus Eriugena, ix–xli. Translated by Myra Uhlfelder. 1976. Reprint, Eugene, OR: Wipf & Stock, 2011.

Pourrat, Pierre. *Christian Spirituality.* 4 vols. Translated by Donald Attwater. Westminster, MD: Newman, 1955.

Powell, Thomas. *The Larger Hope.* London: Kerby & Endean, 1881.

Powys, David J. *"Hell": A Hard Look at a Hard Question.* Carlisle, UK: Paternoster, 1998.

———. "The Nineteenth and Twentieth Century Debates about Hell and Universalism." In Cameron, *Universalism and the Doctrine of Hell,* 93–138.

Prager, L. *Die Lehre von der Vollendung aller Dinge aus der heiligen Schrift begründet und verteidigt.* Leipzig, 1904.

Pratt, Orson. "The Increased Powers and Capacities of Man in the Future Estate." In *The Vision; or, The Degrees of Glory,* edited by Ned B. Lundwall. Independence, MO: Zion Printing and Publishing, 1945.

Preger, Wilhelm. *Geschichte der deutschen Mystik im Mittelalter. Nach den Quellen untersucht und dargestellt.* 3 vols. Leipzig: Dörfling und Franke, 1874, 1881, 1893.

Premier Christian Radio. "Unbelievable? 15 Mar 2008: Christian Universalism—Will All Be Saved?" Premier Christian Radio, March 15, 2008. http://www.premierchristianradio.com/Shows/Saturday/Unbelievable/Episodes/Unbelievable-15-Mar-2008-Christian-Universalism-will-all-be-saved.

Price, Richard, trans. *The Acts of the Council of Constantinople of 553; With Related Texts on the Three Chapters Controversy.* Texts Translated for Historians 51. Liverpool, UK: Liverpool University Press, 2009.

Pridmore, John. "George MacDonald and the Languages of Liberal Spirituality." *Modern Believing* 39 (1998): 28–36.

Priestley, Joseph. *Hartley's Theory of the Human Mind, on the Principle of the Association of Ideas; With Essays Relating to the Subject of It.* London, 1775.

———. *Memoirs of Dr. Joseph Priestley, to the Year 1795, Written by Himself, with a Continuation, to the Time of His Decease by His Son Joseph Priestley.* London, 1806.

———. *Unitarianism Explained and Defended, in a Discourse Delivered at the Church of the Universalists, at Philadelphia, 1796.* Philadelphia, 1796.

Prince, Joseph. *Destined to Reign: The Secret to Effortless Success, Wholeness, and Victorious Living.* Tulsa: Harrison House, 2007.

Prinzivalli, E. "The Controversy about Origen before Epiphanius." In Bienert and Kühneweg, *Origeniana Septima*, 195–213.

Proclus. *The Elements of Theology.* Translated by E. R. Dodds. 2nd ed. Oxford: Clarendon, 1963.

Procter, Everett. *Christian Controversy in Alexandria: Clement's Polemic against the Basilideans and Valentinians.* New York: Lang, 1995.

Propp, Steven H. *The Gift of God Is Eternal Life: A Novel about Universalism.* Bloomington, IN: iUniverse, 2016.

Prothero, Stephen. *The White Buddhist: The Asian Odyssey of Henry Steel Olcott.* Bloomington: Indiana University Press, 2010.

Prudentius of Troyes. *De Praedestinatione contra Joannem Scotum cognomento Erigenam.* In PL 122:1009–366.

Pullman, Philip. *The Good Man Jesus and the Scoundrel Christ.* Edinburgh: Canongate, 2010.

Purcell, Boyd C. *Spiritual Terrorism: Spiritual Abuse from the Womb to the Tomb.* Bloomington, IN: AuthorHouse, 2008.

Pusey, E. B. *What Is of Faith as to Everlasting Punishment? In Reply to Dr. Farrar's Challenge in His "Eternal Hope," 1879.* 3rd ed. Oxford: James Parker & Co., 1880.

Quantin, Jean-Louis. "The Fathers in Seventeenth-Century Anglican Theology." In *The Reception of the Church Fathers in the West: From the Carolingians to the Maurists*, edited by Irena Backus, 2:987–1008. 2 vols. Leiden: Brill, 1997.

Quash, Ben. "'Between the Brutely Given, and the Brutally, Banally Free': Von Balthasar's Theology of Drama in Dialogue with Hegel." *Modern Theology* 13 (1997): 293–318.

———. *Theology and the Drama of History.* New York: Cambridge University Press, 2005.

Quilliet, H. "Descente de Jésus aux enfers." In *Dictionnaire de théologie catholique*, edited by A. Vacant, E. Mangenot, et al., 4:565–619. Paris: Letouzey, 1903–72.

Quinn, D. Michael. *Early Mormonism and the Magic World View.* Salt Lake City: Signature, 1987.

Quispel, Gilles. "Origen and the Valentinian Gnosis." *Vigiliae Christianae* 28 (1974): 29–42.

R. R. "Salvation Is from the Jews: An Assessment and Critique of Karl Barth on Judaism and the Jewish People." *Kesher: A Journal of Messianic Judaism.* http://www.kesherjournal.com/index.php?option=com_content&view=article&id=144&Itemid=.

Rabe, Andre. *Imagine.* 2nd ed. N.p.: Andre Rabe, 2013.

Rabil, Albert, Jr. *Erasmus and the New Testament: The Mind of a Christian Humanist.* Lanham, MD: University Press of America, 1993.

Rabinowitz, Celia E. "Apokatastasis and Suntelia: Eschatological and Soteriological Speculation in Origen." PhD diss., Fordham University, 1989.

———. "Personal and Cosmic Salvation in Origen." *Vigiliae Christianae* 38 (1984): 319–29.

Rahman, Fazlur. *Islam.* 2nd ed. Chicago: University of Chicago Press, 1979.

Rahner, Karl, ed. *Encyclopedia of Theology: The Concise "Sacramentum Mundi."* New York: Continuum, 1975.

———. "Hell [1969]." In Rahner, *Sacramentum Mundi: An Encyclopedia of Theology*, 3:7–9.

———. "Hell [1975]." In Rahner, *Encyclopedia of Theology: The Concise "Sacramentum Mundi*," 603.

———. "The Hermeneutics of Eschatological Assertions." In *More Recent Writings*, vol. 4 of *Theological Investigations*, translated by Kevin Smyth, 323–46. Baltimore: Helicon, 1966.

———. *Karl Rahner in Dialogue: Conversations and Interviews, 1965–1982.* Edited by Paul Imhof and Hubert Biallowons. Translated by Harvey D. Egan. New York: Crossroad, 1986.

———. *On the Theology of Death.* Translated by Charles H. Henkey. Freiburg: Herder; Edinburgh: Nelson, 1961.

———. "Penance." In Rahner, *Encyclopedia of Theology: The Concise "Sacramentum Mundi,"* 1187–204.

———. "Private Revelations." In Rahner, *Sacramentum Mundi: An Encyclopedia of Theology,* 5:358.

———. *Sacramentum Mundi: An Encyclopedia of Theology.* Edited by Karl Rahner et al. 6 vols. New York: Herder & Herder, 1968–70.

———. *Theological Investigations.* 23 vols. Baltimore: Helicon, 1961–79.

Rahner, Karl, and Herbert Vorgrimler. "Penalties of Sin." In *Dictionary of Theology,* 2nd ed., 369–70. Translated by Richard Strachan et al. New York: Crossroad, 1981.

———. "Satisfaction." In *Dictionary of Theology,* 2nd ed., 461. Translated by Richard Strachan et al. New York: Crossroad, 1981.

Ramelli, Ilaria L. E. "Apokatastasis in Coptic Gnostic Texts from Nag Hammadi and Clement's and Origen's Apokatastasis: Toward an Assessment of the Origin of the Doctrine of Universal Restoration." *Journal of Coptic Studies* 14 (2012): 33–45.

———. *The Christian Doctrine of* Apokatastasis. Leiden: Brill, 2013.

———. "Origen, Bardaisan, and the Origin of Universal Salvation." *Harvard Theological Review* 102 (2009): 135–68.

———. "Origen's Doctrine of Apokatastasis: A Reassessment." In Kaczmarek and Pietras, *Origeniana Decima,* 649–70.

Ramelli, Ilaria, and David Konstan. *Terms for Eternity: Aiônios and Aïdios in Classical and Christian Texts.* Piscataway, NJ: Gorgias, 2007.

Ramsay, Andrew Michael. *The Philosophical Principles of Natural and Revealed Religion Unfolded in Geometrical Order.* 2 vols. Glasgow: Robert Foulis, 1748–49.

———. *The Travels of Cyrus to Which Is Annexe'd a Discourse upon the Theology and Mythology of the Pagans.* London, 1728.

Ramsey, Boniface, ed. *John Cassian: The Conferences.* New York: Newman, 1997.

Ramsey, Ian T. *Models and Mystery.* London: Oxford University Press, 1964.

Ramsey, Paul. "Appendix III." In *Ethical Writings,* vol. 8 of *The Works of Jonathan Edwards,* 706–38. New Haven: Yale University Press, 1989.

Randles, Marshall. *For Ever! An Essay on Eternal Punishment.* London: Wesleyan Conference Office, 1873.

Rashdall, Hastings. *The Idea of the Atonement in Christian Theology.* London: Macmillan, 1919.

Rashkovsky, Evgeny. "Three Justifications: Some Pivotal Themes in the Last Decade of Solov'ëv's Christian Philosophy." In van den Bercken, de Courten, and van der Zweerde, *Vladimir Solov'ëv,* 29–38.

Rattanasi, Piyo, and Antonio Clericuzio, eds. *Alchemy and Chemistry in the 16th and 17th Centuries.* Boston: Kluwer, 1994.

Ratzinger, Joseph. *Eschatology: Death and Eternal Life.* 2nd ed. Translated by Michael Waldstein. Translation edited by Aidan Nichols. Washington, DC: Catholic University of America Press, 1988.

Recinova, Monika. "Clement's Angelological Doctrines: Between Jewish Models and Philosophic-Religious Streams of Late Antiquity." In *The Seventh Book of the "Stromateis": Proceedings of the Colloquium on Clement of Alexandria (Olomouc, October 21–23, 2010),* edited by Matyáš Havrda, Vít Hušek, and Jana Plátová, 93–111. Leiden: Brill, 2012.

Reed, David. *"In Jesus' Name": The History and Beliefs of Oneness Pentecostals.* Blandford Forum Dorset, UK: Deo Publishing, 2008.

Reedy, Gerard. "Socinians, John Toland, and the Anglican Rationalists." *Harvard Theological Review* 70 (1977): 285–304.

Reimensnyder, Junius. *Doom Eternal.* Philadelphia: Nelson S. Quiney, 1880.

Reinink, Gerrit J. "'Origenism' in Thirteenth-Century Northern Iraq." In *After Bardaisan: Studies on Continuity and Change in Syriac Christianity in Honour of Professor Han J. W. Drijvers,* edited by Gerrit J. Reinink and

Alex C. Klugkist, 237–52. Louvain: Peeters, 1999.

———. "The Quotations from the Lost Works of Theodoret of Cyrus and Theodore of Mopsuestia in an Unpublished East Syrian Work on Christology." In *Studia Patristica*, vol. 33, *Augustine and His Opponents, Jerome, Other Latin Fathers after Nicaea, Orientalia; Papers Presented at the Twelfth International Patristic Conference, Held at Oxford University 1995*, edited by Elizabeth A. Livingstone, 562–67. Louvain: Peeters, 1997.

Reitan, Eric. "Human Freedom and the Impossibility of Eternal Damnation." In Parry and Partridge, *Universal Salvation?*, 125–42.

Relly, James. *Christian Liberty; or, The Liberty wherewith Christ Hath Made Us Free*. London: M. Lewis, 1775.

———. *Epistles; or, The Great Salvation Contemplated: In a Series of Letters to a Christian Society*. London, 1776.

———. *The Sadducee Detected and Refuted: In Remarks on the Works of Richard Coppin*. London: M. Lewis, 1764.

———. *Salt of the Sacrifice; or, The True Christian Baptism Delineated according to Reason and Spirit: As Gathered from Sundry Discourses on That Subject*. London, 1762.

———. *Union; or, A Treatise of Consanguinity and Affinity between Christ and His Church*. 1759.

———. *Written on Hearing of the Much-Lamented Death of the Rev. Mr. George Whitefield*. London, 1770.

Remington, Stephen. *Anti-Universalism*. New York: Harper & Brothers, 1837.

Rendtorff, Trutz. *Theorie des Christentums: historisch-theologische Studien zu seiner neuzeitlichen Verfassung*. Gütersloh: Gütersloher Verlagshaus G. Mohn, 1972.

———, ed. *Die Realisierung der Freiheit: Beiträge zur Kritik der Theologie Karl Barths*. Gütersloh: Mohn, 1975.

Renkewitz, Heinz. *Hochmann von Hochenau (1670–1721): Quellenstudien zur Geschichte des Pietismus*. Breslau: Maruschke & Berendt, 1935.

Reno, R. R. "Rahner the Restorationist: Karl Rahner's Time Has Passed." *First Things* 233 (2013): 45–51. http://www.firstthings.com/article/2013/05/rahner-the-restorationist.

Reynolds, A. G., ed. *Life and Death: A Study of the Christian Hope*. London: Lutterworth, 1960.

Reynolds, Roger E. "*Virgines subintroductae* in Celtic Christianity." *Harvard Theological Review* 61 (1968): 547–66.

Riemann, Otto. *Die Lehre von der Apokatastasis*. 2nd ed. Magdeburg: Heinrichshofen's Verlag, 1897. 3rd ed., *Die Lehre von der Wiederbringung und schliesslichen Beseligung aller (Apokatastasis)*. 1889. Reprint, Chemnitz: Wernigerode, G. Koezle, 1918.

Ritschl, Albrecht. *A Critical History of the Christian Doctrine of Reconciliation and Justification*. Translated by John S. Black. Edinburgh: Edmonston & Douglas, 1872.

Rivers, Isabel. "Law, William." In *Dictionary of National Biography*. Oxford Dictionary of National Biography Online. http://www.oxforddnb.com.

Rix, Robert W. "'In Infernal Love and Faith': William Blake's *The Marriage of Heaven and Hell*." *Literature and Theology* 20 (2006): 107–25.

Rizvi, Sajjad. Review of *Islam and the Fate of Others*, by Mohammed Hassan Khalil. *Islam and Christian-Muslim Relations* 24 (2013): 536–38.

Roach, R. [Richard]. *The Imperial Standard of Messiah Triumphant: Coming Now in the Power and Kingdom of His Father to Reign with His Saints on Earth*. London: N. Blanford, 1727.

Robb, Nesca A. *Neoplatonism of the Italian Renaissance*. 1935. Reprint, New York: Octagon, 1968.

Roberts, B. H., ed. *History of the Church of Jesus Christ of Latter-Day Saints*. Vol. 4. Salt Lake City: Deseret News, 1908.

Robertson, Archibald. Introduction to the *Treatise on the Incarnation of the Word*, by Athanasius. In *NPNF*[2] 4:31–34.

Robinson, John A. T. *In the End, God: A Study of the Christian Doctrine of the Last Things*. London: James Clarke, 1950.

———. "Universalism: A Reply." *Scottish Journal of Theology* 2 (1949): 378–80.

———. "Universalism: Is It Heretical?" *Scottish Journal of Theology* 2 (1949): 139–55.

Robinson, Stephen E. "God the Father: Overview." In D. H. Ludlow, *Encyclopedia of Mormonism*, 2:548–50.

Roche, Charles R. "Eternal Punishment." *Irish Theological Quarterly* 5 (1910): 64–79.

Rodin, S. *Evil and Theodicy in the Theology of Karl Barth.* New York: Lang, 1997.

Roman Catholic Church. *Acta Synodalia Sacrosancti Concilii Oecumenici Vaticani Secundi.* 35 vols. Rome: Typis Polyglottis Vaticanis, 1970–86.

———. *Catechismus ex decrete Concilii Tridentini ad parochos.* Ratisbonae [Regensburg]: Sumptibus et typis Friderici Pustetis, 1907.

Romanowsky, John. "Sexual-Spousal Love in the Theological Anthropology of V. S. Soloviev." PhD diss., Catholic University of America, 2011.

Rondet, Henri. *L'Esprit Saint et l'Eglise.* Paris: Fayard, 1969.

———. "Les peines de l'enfer." *La nouvelle revue théologique* 67 (1940): 397–427.

Röper, Anita, ed. *The Anonymous Christian.* New York: Sheed & Ward, 1966.

Roper, Lyndal. "Sexual Utopianism in the German Reformation." *Journal of Ecclesiastical History* 42 (1991): 394–418.

Roques, René. *L'univers dionysien.* Paris, 1954.

———. Preface to *Pseudo-Dionysius: The Complete Works.* Translated by Colm Luibheid, in collaboration with Paul Rorem. New York: Paulist Press, 1987.

Rorem, Paul. Foreword to *Pseudo-Dionysius: The Complete Works.* Translated by Colm Luibheid, in collaboration with Paul Rorem. New York: Paulist Press, 1987.

Rorty, Richard. *Essays on Heidegger and Others: Philosophical Papers.* Cambridge: Cambridge University Press, 1991.

Rosenberg, Randall S. *The Givenness of Desire: Concrete Subjectivity and the Natural Desire to See God.* Toronto: University of Toronto Press, 2017.

Rosenbloom, Noah H. "Menasseh Ben Israel and the Eternality of Punishment Issue."

Proceedings of the American Academy for Jewish Research 60 (1994): 241–62.

Rosenkranz, Karl. *Georg Wilhelm Friedrich Hegels Leben.* Berlin: Verlag von Duncker und Humblot, 1844.

———. *Hegel: Sendschreiben an . . . Dr. Carl Friedrich Bachmann in Jena von Dr. Karl Rosenkranz.* Königsberg: Wilhelm Unzer, 1834.

———. "Hegels ursprüngliches System 1798–1806." *Literarhistorisches Taschenbuch* 2 (1844): 153–242.

———. *Schelling: Vorlesungen, gehalten im Sommer 1842 an der Universität zu Königsberg.* Danzig, 1843.

Rosenroth, Christian Knorr von. *Kabbala denudata, seu, Doctrina hebræorum transcendentalis et metaphysica atqve theologica opus antiquissimæ philosophiæ barbaricæ variis speciminibus refertissimum.* 4 vols. Sulzbach, Ger.: Typis Abrahami Lichtenthaleri, 1677–84.

Rotelle, John E., ed. *Sermons on the New Testament.* The Works of Saint Augustine. Brooklyn, NY: New City Press, 1992.

Roten, Johann. "The Two Halves of the Moon: Marian Anthropological Dimensions in the Common Mission of Adrienne von Speyr and Hans Urs von Balthasar." In Schindler, *Hans Urs von Balthasar,* 65–86.

Roth, Cecil, ed. *Encyclopedia Judaica.* 16 vols. Jerusalem: Encyclopedia Judaica; New York: Macmillan, 1971–72.

Rousseau, Jean-Jacques. *Discourse on the Origins of Inequality (Second Discourse); Polemics and Political Economy.* Hanover, NH: University Press of New England, 1992.

———. "Profession of Faith of a Savoyard Vicar" (1782), in *Émile.* In *French and English Philosophers: Descartes, Rousseau, Voltaire, Hobbes.* New York: Collier, 1910. https://legacy.fordham.edu/halsall/mod/1782rousseau-savoyard.asp.

Rowe, J. N. "The Eventual Reconciling of Human Beings to the Father by Christ, and His Consequent Subjugation to the Father." In Hanson and Crouzel, *Origeniana Tertia,* 139–50.

Rowell, Geoffrey. *Hell and the Victorians: A Study of the Nineteenth-Century Theological Controversies concerning Eternal Punishment and the Future Life.* Oxford: Clarendon, 1974.

———. "The Origins and History of Universalist Societies in Britain, 1750–1850." *Journal of Ecclesiastical History* 22 (1971): 35–56.

Rowland, Ingrid D. *Giordano Bruno: Philosopher / Heretic.* Chicago: University of Chicago Press, 2009.

Rudolph, Erwin Paul. *William Law.* Boston: Twayne, 1980.

Rufinus of Aquileia. "Preface of Rufinus." In *On First Principles,* by Origen, lxii–lxiv. Translated by G. W. Butterworth. Gloucester, MA: Peter Smith, 1973.

Runia, David T. "Philo and Origen: A Preliminary Survey." In Daly, *Origeniana Quinta,* 333–39.

Russell, Bertrand. *The Theory and Practice of Bolshevism.* London: George Allen, 1920.

———. *Why I Am Not a Christian.* New York: Simon & Schuster, 1957.

Russell, Norman. *Theophilus of Alexandria.* London: Routledge, 2007.

Russell, Robert P., trans. *Augustine: The Teacher; The Free Choice of the Will; Grace and Free Will.* FC 59. Washington, DC: Catholic University of America Press, 1968.

Russian Orthodox Church Outside Russia (ROCOR). "On the Decision of the Council . . . on the New Doctrine of Archpriest Sergius Bulgakov concerning Sophia, the Wisdom of God [Oct. 1935]." *Living Orthodoxy* 17 (1995): 23–34.

[Rust, George]. *A Letter of Resolution concerning Origen and the Chief of His Opinions Written to the Learned and Most Ingenious C. L., Esquire, and by Him Published.* London: C. L., 1661.

Ryrie, Charles C. *So Great Salvation: What It Means to Believe in Jesus Christ.* 1989. Reprint, Chicago: Moody Press, 1997.

Sabine, James. *Universal Salvation Indefensible.* Boston: Ezra Lincoln, 1825.

Sachs, John R. "Apocatastasis in Patristic Theology." *Theological Studies* 54 (1993): 617–40.

———. "Current Eschatology: Universal Salvation and the Problem of Hell." *Theological Studies* 52 (1991): 227–54.

Sachse, Julius Friedrich. *The German Pietists of Provincial Pennsylvania, 1694 1708.* Philadelphia, 1895.

———. *The German Sectarians of Pennsylvania: A Critical and Legendary History of the Ephrata Cloister and the Dunkers.* 2 vols. Philadelphia, 1899–1900.

Safford, Decius Wade. "Teilhard de Chardin: A Vision of the Past and of the Future." *Anglican Theological Review* 46 (1964): 286–97.

Sagnard, F., ed. *Extraits de Théodote.* SC 23. Paris: Cerf, 1970.

Salkeld, Brett. *Can Catholics and Evangelicals Agree about Purgatory and the Last Judgment?* New York: Paulist Press, 2011.

Salmond, Stewart D. F. *The Christian Doctrine of Immortality.* 3rd ed. Edinburgh: T&T Clark, 1897.

Salvey, Courtney. "Riddled with Evil: Fantasy as Theodicy in George MacDonald's *Phantastes* and *Lilith.*" *North Wind* 27 (2008): 16–34.

Sanders, J. Oswald. *What of the Unevangelized?* London: OMF, 1966.

Sanders, John. *No Other Name: An Investigation into the Destiny of the Unevangelized.* Grand Rapids: Eerdmans, 1992.

———. "Raising Hell about Razing Hell." *Perspectives in Religious Studies* 40 (2013): 267–81.

Sanneh, Lamin, and Michael J. McClymond. "Introduction." In *The Wiley-Blackwell Companion to World Christianity,* edited by Lamin Sanneh and Michael J. McClymond, 1–17. Oxford: Wiley-Blackwell, 2016.

Santayana, George. *Egotism in German Philosophy.* London: J. M. Dent, 1916.

Sargent, Lyman Tower. *Utopianism: A Very Short Introduction.* Oxford: Oxford University Press, 2010.

Sartory, Thomas, and Gertrude Sartory. *In der Hölle brennt kein Feuer.* Munich: Kindler, 1968.

Sasse, Hermann. "*aiōn, aiōnios.*" In *Theological Dictionary of the New Testament,* edited by Gerhard Kittel, 1:197–209. Translated by Geoffrey Bromiley. Grand Rapids: Eerdmans, 1964.

Satran, David. "The Salvation of the Devil: Origen and Origenism in Jerome's Biblical Commentaries." In *Studia Patristica*, vol. 23, edited by Elizabeth A. Livingstone, 171–77. Leuven: Peeters, 1989.

Sauter, Gerhard. *Die Theologie des Reiches Gottes beim älteren und jüngeren Blumhardt*. Zurich: Zwingli Verlag, 1962.

Saville, Andy. "Hell without Sin: A Renewed View of a Disputed Doctrine." *Churchman* 119 (2005): 243–61.

———. "Reconciliationism: A Forgotten Evangelical Doctrine of Hell." *Evangelical Quarterly* 79 (2007): 35–51.

Sawyer, Thomas Jefferson, and Isaac Wescott. *A Discussion on the Doctrine of Universal Salvation*. New York: Henry Lyon, 1854.

Schaff, Philip, and David S. Schaff, eds. *The Creeds of Christendom: With a History and Critical Notes*. 3 vols. 1931. Reprint, Grand Rapids: Baker, 1983.

Schär, Max. *Das Nachleben des Origenes im Zeitalter des Humanismus*. Basel: Helbing & Lichtenhahn, 1979.

Schatz, David. "Freedom, Repentance, and Hardening of the Hearts: Albo vs. Maimonides." *Faith and Philosophy* 14 (1997): 478–509.

Schauer, Friedrich, ed. *Was ist es um die Hölle? Dokumente aus dem norwegischen Kirchenstreit*. Stuttgart: Evangelische Verlagswerk, 1956.

Schauf, Heribert. "Die ewige Verwerfung in neueren und älteren kirchlichen Verlautbarungen." *Theologisches* 178 (1985): 6253–58.

Scheck, Thomas P., trans. *Jerome: Commentary on Matthew*. Washington, DC: Catholic University of America Press, 2008.

———. *Origen: Commentary on the Epistle to the Romans, Books 1–5*. FC 103. Washington, DC: Catholic University of America Press, 2001.

———. *St. Pamphilus: Apology for Origen, with the Letter of Rufinus on the Falsification of the Books of Origen*. FC 120. Washington, DC: Catholic University of America Press, 2010.

Scheffczyk, Leo. "Apocatastasis: Fascination and Paradox." *Communio* 12 (1985): 385–97.

Scheinerman, Amy. "Is There Life after Death?" http://scheinerman.net/judaism/Ideas/afterlife.html.

Schelling, Friedrich. *The Ages of the World (Fragment) from the Handwritten Remains, Third Version (ca. 1815) by Friedrich Wilhelm Joseph Schelling*. Translated by Jason M. Wirth. Albany: State University of New York Press, 2000.

———. "Exegetischer Nachweiss aus Phil. 2,6–8." In *Fünfundzwanzigste Vorlesung (Lecture Twenty-Five)*, 39–50. *Sämtliche Werke*. Pt. 2, vol. 4. Stuttgart: Cotta'scher Verlag, 1858.

———. *Idealism and the Endgame of Theory: Three Essays by F. W. J. Schelling*. Edited and translated by Thomas Pfau. Albany: State University of New York Press, 1994.

———. *Initia Philosophiae Universae: F. W. J. Schelling's Erlanger Lectures (1821)*. Translated by Adam Arola. http://www.academia.edu/11513755/Initia_Philosophiae_Universae_F.W.J_Schelling_s_Erlanger_Lectures.

———. *Of Human Freedom*. Translated by James Gutman. Chicago: Open Court, 1936.

———. *Sämtliche Werke*. Edited by K. F. A. Schelling. 14 vols. Stuttgart and Augsburg: Cotta, 1856–61.

———. *Stuttgart Seminars*. In *Idealism and the Endgame of Theory: Three Essays by F. W. J. Schelling*, edited and translated by Thomas Pfau, 195–243, 261–68. Albany: State University of New York Press, 1994.

———. *System of Transcendental Idealism*. Translated by P. Heath. Charlottesville: University Press of Virginia, 1978. Originally published as *System des transcendentalen Idealismus* (Tübingen: J. G. Cotta'schen Buchhandlung, 1800).

———. *Urfassung der Philosophie der Offenbarung*. Edited by Walter E. Ehrhardt. 2 vols. Hamburg: F. Meiner, 1992.

Scheuers, Timothy. "An Evaluation of Some Aspects of Karl Barth's Doctrine of Election." *Mid-America Journal of Theology* 22 (2011): 161–73.

Schimmel, Annemarie. *Mystical Dimensions of Islam.* Chapel Hill: University of North Carolina Press, 1975.

Schindler, David L., ed. *Hans Urs von Balthasar: His Life and Work.* San Francisco: Ignatius, 1991.

Schleiermacher, Friedrich. *Aus Schleiermacher's Leben; in Briefen / 4 Schleiermachers Briefe an Brinckmann, Briefwechsel mit seinen Freunden von seiner Uebersiedlung nach Halle bis zu seinem Tode, Denkschriften, Dialog über das Anständige, Recensionen.* Edited by Ludwig Jonas and Wilhelm Dilthey. Berlin: Reimer, 1863.

———. *The Christian Faith.* Translated by H. R. Mackintosh and J. S. Steward. 1928. Reprint, Edinburgh: T&T Clark, 1989. Originally published as *Der christliche Glaube,* 2nd ed. (Berlin: G. Reimer, 1830–31).

———. *Dialectic; or, The Art of Doing Philosophy: A Study Edition of the 1811 Notes.* Edited and translated by Terrence N. Tice. Atlanta: Scholars Press, 1996.

———. *Friedrich Schleiermachers Dialektik.* Edited by Rudolf Odebrecht. Leipzig: Hinrichs, 1942.

———. *On Religion: Speeches to Its Cultured Despisers.* Edited and translated by Richard Crouter. Cambridge: Cambridge University Press, 1996.

———. *On the Doctrine of Election, with Special Reference to the Aphorisms of Dr. Bretschneider.* Translated by Iain G. Nicol and Allen G. Jorgenson. Louisville: Westminster John Knox, 2012.

Schmidt-Biggemann, Wilhelm. *Philosophia Perennis: Historical Outlines of Western Spirituality in Ancient, Medieval, and Early Modern Thought.* Dordrecht, Neth.: Springer, 2004.

Schnackenberg, Rudolf. "Prädestination I: Aussagen der Schrift." In *Lexikon für Theologie und Kirche,* edited by Josef Höfer and Karl Rahner, 8:661–62. 2nd ed. Freiburg: Herder, 1957–67.

Schneider, Hans. *German Radical Pietism.* Translated by Gerald T. MacDonald. Lanham, MD: Scarecrow, 2007.

Schneider, Robert. *Schellings und Hegels schwäbische Geistesahnen.* Würzburg-Aumühle: Konrad-Trilsch, 1938.

Scholem, Gershom. "Gilgul." In Roth, *Encyclopedia Judaica,* 7:573–77.

———. *Kabbalah.* New York: New American Library, 1974.

———. "Kabbalah." In Roth, *Encyclopedia Judaica,* 10:490–653.

———. *Major Trends in Jewish Mysticism.* 3rd rev. ed. New York: Schocken, 1961.

———. *The Messianic Idea in Judaism.* New York: Schocken, 1971.

———. *On the Kabbalah and Its Symbolism.* Translated by Ralph Manheim. 1965. Reprint, New York: Schocken, 1996.

———. *On the Mystical Shape of the Godhead: Basic Concepts in the Kabbalah.* Translated by Joachim Neugroschel. New York: Schocken / Pantheon, 1991.

———. *Origins of the Kabbalah.* Edited by R. J. Zvi Werblowsky. Translated by Allan Arkush. Princeton: Princeton University Press; New York: Jewish Publication Society, 1987.

———. *Sabbatai Sevi: The Mystical Messiah; 1626–1676.* London: Routledge Kegan Paul, 1973.

Schopenhauer, Arthur. "On Authorship and Style." In *Essays,* 1–27. London: Walter Scott, 1903.

Schouppe, F. X. *Hell: The Dogma of Hell, Illustrated by Facts Taken from Profane and Sacred History.* Rockford, IL: TAN, 1989.

Schrader, Hans-Jürgen. *Literaturproduktion und Büchermarkt des radikalen Pietismus.* Göttingen: Vandenhoeck & Ruprecht, 1989.

Schrader, Otto. *Die Lehre von der Apokatastasis oder der endliche Beseligung aller.* Berlin: Boll, 1901.

Schreiter, Robert J. "Changes in Roman Catholic Attitudes toward Proselytism and Mission." In *New Directions in Mission and Evangelization 2: Theological Foundations,* edited by James A. Scherer and Stephen B. Bevans, 113–25. Maryknoll, NY: Orbis, 1994.

Schulz, Klaus Detler. "Universalism: The Urgency of Christian Witness." *Missio Apostolica* 14 (2006): 86–96.

Schulze, Wilhelm August. "Jakob Böhme und die Kabbala." *Zeitschrift für philosophische Forschung* 9 (1955): 447–60.

Schumacher, Heinz. *Das biblische Zeugnis von der Versöhnung des Alls.* Stuttgart: Paulus Verlag Karl Geyer, 1959.

Schüssler Fiorenza, Francis. "Systematic Theology: Tasks and Methods." In *Systematic Theology: Roman Catholic Perspectives,* edited by Francis Schüssler Fiorenza and John P. Galvin, 1–78. 2nd ed. Minneapolis: Fortress, 2011.

Schwartz, Eduard, ed. *Acta conciliorum oecumenicorum, Tomus III; Collectio Sabbaitica contra Acephalos et Origeniastas destinata, insunt acta Synodorum Constantinopolitanae et Hierosolymitanae.* Berlin: de Gruyter, 1927.

Schwartz, Hillel. *The French Prophets: The History of a Millenarian Group in Eighteenth-Century England.* Berkeley: University of California Press, 1980.

Scola, Angelo. *Test Everything, Hold Fast to What Is Good: An Interview with Hans Urs von Balthasar.* Translated by Maria Shrady. San Francisco: Ignatius, 1989.

Scott, Alan. *Origen and the Life of the Stars: A History of an Idea.* Oxford Early Christian Studies. Oxford: Clarendon, 1994.

Scott, Clinton Lee. *The Universalist Church in America.* Boston: Universalist Historical Society, 1957.

Scott, Mark S. M. "Guarding the Mysteries of Salvation: The Pastoral Pedagogy of Origen's Universalism." *Journal of Early Christian Studies* 18 (2010): 347–68.

———. *Journey Back to God: Origen on the Problem of Evil.* New York: Oxford University Press, 2012.

———. "Suffering and Soul-Making: Rethinking John Hick's Theodicy." *Journal of Religion* 90 (2010): 313–34.

Seaburg, Alan. "Recent Scholarship in American Universalism: A Bibliographical Essay." *Church History* 41 (1972): 513–23.

Second Vatican Council. Dogmatic Constitution on the Church *Lumen Gentium.* Vatican website. November 21, 1964. http://www .vatican.va/archive/hist_councils/ii_vatican _council/documents/vat-ii_const_19641121 _lumen-gentium_en.html.

———. Pastoral Constitution on the Church in the Modern World *Gaudium et Spes.* Vatican website. December 7, 1965. http://www .vatican.va/archive/hist_councils/ii_vatican _council/documents/vat-ii_const_19651207 _gaudium-et-spes_en.html.

Secret, François. *Les Kabbalistes chrétiens de la Renaissance.* Paris: Dunod, 1964.

———. "L'herméneutique de Guillaume Postel." *Archivio di Filosofia: Umanesimo e Ermeneutica* 3 (1963): 91–145.

———, ed. *Postelliana.* Nieuwkoop: B. de Graaf, 1981.

Seeberg, Reinhold. *Christliche Dogmatik.* Vol. 2. Leipzig: Deichert, 1925.

Seiling, Jonathan R. "From Antinomy to Sophiology: Modern Russian Religious Consciousness and Sergei N. Bulgakov's Critical Appropriation of German Idealism." PhD diss., University of St. Michael's College, Toronto, 2008.

Severus of Antioch. *A Collection of Letters from Numerous Syriac Manuscripts (1915).* Edited and translated by E. W. Brooks. PO. http:// www.tertullian.org/fathers/severus_coll_3 _letters.htm.

Seymour, Charles. *A Theodicy of Hell.* Boston: Kluwer Academic, 2000.

Shapiro, Fred R., ed. *The Yale Book of Quotations.* New Haven: Yale University Press, 2006.

Sharpe, Eric J. "The Legacy of Sadhu Sundar Singh." *International Bulletin of Missionary Research* 14 (1990): 161–67.

Shedd, William G. T. *Endless Punishment.* New York: Scribner's Sons, 1886.

Sheldon-Williams, I. P. "The Ps.-Dionysius and the Holy Hierotheos." In *Studia Patristica,* vol. 8, edited by F. L. Cross, 108–17. Berlin: Akademie Verlag, 1966.

Shelford, April G. *Transforming the Republic of Letters: Pierre-Daniel Huet and European Intellectual Life, 1650–1720.* Rochester: University of Rochester Press, 2007.

Shepard, Samuel. *Universal Salvation.* Exeter, NH, 1798.

Shepherd of Hermas. "Parable IX." In *The Apostolic Fathers II*, edited by Bart D. Ehrman, 387–465. LCL 25. Cambridge, MA: Harvard University Press, 2003.

Sherman, Bill. "'Too Inclusive: Church Loses Building after Members Flee Pastor's Universalism." *Christianity Today* 50, no. 3 (2006): 24. http://www.christianitytoday .com/ct/2006/march/4.25.html.

Sherwood, Polycarp. *The Earlier Ambigua of Maximus the Confessor and His Refutation of Origenism*. Studia Anselmiana 36. Rome: Orbis Catholicus / Herder, 1955.

Sider, Ted. "Hell and Vagueness." *Faith and Philosophy* 19 (2002): 58–68.

Siegvolck, Paul. *The Everlasting Gospel, Commanded and Preached by Jesus Christ*. 1753. Reprint, London: Gillet, 1792.

Siewerth, Gustav. "Christentum und Tragik." In *Grundfragen der Philosophie im Horizont der Seinsdifferenz: Gesammelte Aufsätze zur Philosophie*, 295–300. Düsseldorf: Schwann, 1963.

Simmons, Michael Bland. "Porphyrian Universalism: A Tripartite Soteriology and Eusebius's Response." *Harvard Theological Review* 102 (2009): 169–92.

Simonetti, Manlius, ed. *Tyrannii Rufini, Opera*. CCSL 20. Turnhout: Brepols, 1961.

Simut, Corneliu C. *F. C. Baur's Synthesis of Böhme and Hegel: Redefining Christian Theology as a Gnostic Philosophy of Religion*. Leiden: Brill, 2015.

Sinaga, Sahat. "Is Joseph Prince's Radical Grace Teaching Biblical?" https://independ ent.academia.edu/SinagaS.

Singer, Dorothea Waley. *Giordano Bruno: His Life and Thought; With Annotated Translation of His Work, "On the Infinite Universe and Worlds."* 1950. Reprint, New York: Greenwood, 1968.

Singh, Sadhu Sundar. *Meditations on Various Aspects of the Spiritual Life*. London: Macmillan, 1926.

———. *The Search after Reality: Thoughts on Hinduism, Buddhism, Muhammadanism, and Christianity*. London: Macmillan, 1925.

Sinsart, Dom. *Défense du dogme catholique sur l'éternité des peines*. Strasbourg, 1748.

Slaveva-Griffin, Svetla. "Trial by Fire: An Ontological Reading of *Katharsis*." In *Gnosticism, Platonism, and the Late Ancient World*, edited by Kevin Corrigan and Tuomas Rasimus, 525–42. Leiden: Brill, 2013.

Slesinski, Robert. "Toward an Understanding of V. S. Solovyov's 'Gnosticism.'" *Diakonia* 31 (1998): 77–88.

Smart, James D., trans. *Revolutionary Theology in the Making: The Barth-Thurneysen Correspondence, 1914–1925*. Richmond: John Knox, 1964.

Smith, Aaron T. "God's Self-Specification: His Being Is His Electing." *Scottish Journal of Theology* 62 (2009): 1–25.

Smith, Christian, and Melinda Lundquist Denton. *Soul Searching: The Religious and Spiritual Lives of American Teenagers*. New York: Oxford University Press, 2005.

Smith, Hannah Whitall. *The Unselfishness of God and How I Discovered It*. New York: Revell, 1903.

Smith, James. "Papus the Misogynist: Honor, Gender, and the Occult in Fin-de-Siècle France." In *Confronting Modernity in Fin-de-Siècle France: Bodies, Minds, and Gender*, edited by Christopher E. Forth and Elinor Accampo, 112–30. New York: Palgrave Macmillan, 2010.

Smith, Jane Idelman, and Yvonne Yazbeck Haddad. *The Islamic Understanding of Death and Resurrection*. Albany: State University of New York Press, 1981.

Smith, John Clark, trans. *Origen: Homilies on Jeremiah, Homily on 1 Kings 28*. FC 97. Washington, DC: Catholic University of America Press, 1998.

Smith, Joseph. "King Follett Discourse." In *Improvement Era, Volume 12*, edited by Joseph Smith and Edward Anderson, 160–91. Salt Lake City: Heber Grant, 1909.

Smith, Joseph, Jr. *Teachings of the Prophet Joseph Smith*. Edited by Joseph Fielding Smith. Salt Lake City: Deseret News, 1938.

Smith, Joseph Fielding. *Doctrines of Salvation: Sermons and Writings of Joseph Fielding Smith*. 3 vols. Salt Lake City: Bookcraft, 1954–56.

———. "Funeral Services . . . An Age of Visitation and Revelation" (April 11, 1878). In *Journal of Discourses by President Brigham Young, His Counselors, and the Twelve Apostles*, 19:258–65. Liverpool: William Budge, 1878.

Smith, Matthew Hale. *Universalism Examined.*
12th ed. Boston: Tappan & Dennet, 1844.

Smith, Nigel. "Did Anyone Understand
Boehme?" In Hessayon and Apetrai, *Introduction to Jacob Boehme,* 98–119.

Smith, Oliver. "The Russian Boehme." In
Hessayon and Apetrai, *Introduction to Jacob
Boehme,* 196–223.

———. *Vladimir Solovyov and the Spiritualization of Matter.* Boston: Academic Studies
Press, 2010.

Snyder, Alice D. "Coleridge on Böhme." *Publication of the Modern Languages Association*
45 (1930): 616–18.

Sohn, Hohyun. "The Beauty of Hell? Augustine's Aesthetic Theodicy and Its Critics."
Theology Today 64 (2007): 47–57.

Solomon, Robert C. *In the Spirit of Hegel.* New
York: Oxford University Press, 1983.

Solovyov, Vladimir. *Collected Works.* 15 vols.
Moscow: Nauka, 2000.

———. *Divine Sophia: The Wisdom Writings of
Vladimir Solovyov.* Edited by Judith Deutsch
Kornblatt, including annotated translations
by Boris Jakim, Judith Kornblatt, and Laury
Magnus. Ithaca, NY: Cornell University
Press, 2009.

———. *Lectures on Divine Humanity.* Translated by Boris Jakim. Hudson, NY: Lindisfarne, 1995.

———. *Russia and the Universal Church.*
Translated by Herbert Rees. London: Geoffrey Bles / Centenary Press, 1948.

———. *La Russie et l'église universelle.* Edited
by Albert Savine. Paris: Nouvelle Librairie
Parisienne, 1889.

———. *La Sophia et les autres écrits français.*
Edited by François Rouleau. Lausanne: La
Cité / L'Age d'Homme, 1978.

———. *War, Progress, and the End of History:
Including a Short Story of the Anti-Christ.*
Translated by Alexander Bakshy. London:
Hodder & Stoughton, 1915.

Sonderegger, Katherine. *That Jesus Christ Was
Born a Jew: Karl Barth's "Doctrine of Israel."*
University Park: Pennsylvania State University Press, 1992.

Soumet, Alexandre. *La Divine Épopée.* Paris:
H.-L. Delloye, 1841.

Spaulding, Josiah. *Universalism Confounds and
Destroys Itself.* Northampton, MA: Andrew
Wright, 1805.

Speidell, Todd H. "A Trinitarian Ontology
of Persons in Society." *Scottish Journal of
Theology* 47 (1994): 283–300.

Spence, Brian John. "Von Balthasar and
Moltmann: Two Responses to Hegel on the
Subject of the Incarnation and the 'Death of
God.'" PhD diss., University of St. Michael's
College, Toronto, 1995.

Spencer, Sidney. Introduction to *"The Spirit
of Prayer" and "The Spirit of Love,"* by William Law, 9–11. Cambridge: James Clarke,
1969.

Spieckermann, Ingrid. *Gotteserkenntnis: Ein
Beitrag zur Grundfrage der neuen Theologie
Karl Barths.* Munich: Kaiser, 1985.

Spinka, Matthew. "Berdyaev and Origen: A
Comparison." *Church History* 16 (1947):
3–21.

Spira, Andreas, ed. "On the Soul and Resurrection." In GNO III.iii. Leiden: Brill,
2014.

Spurgeon, Charles. *The Treasury of David.*
3 vols. Grand Rapids: Zondervan, 1966.

Stackhouse, John, Jr. "The Hard Work of
Holiness." *Christian Century* 131 (2014):
26–29.

Stafford, Decius Wade. "Teilhard de Chardin:
A Vision of the Past and of the Future."
Anglican Theological Review 46 (1964):
286–97.

Stähelin, Ernest. *Die Wiederbringung aller
Dinge: Rektoratsrede.* Basel: Helbing & Lichtenbahn, 1960.

Stählin, Otto. *Clemens Alexandrinus, Volume
3: "Stromata" Buch VII und VIII, Excerpta
ex Theodoto, Eclogae propheticae, Quis dives
salvatur, Fragmente.* GCS 17, Pt. 2. Leipzig:
J. C. Hinrichs, 1909.

Stang, Charles M. *Apophasis and Pseudonymity
in Dionysius the Areopagite: "No Longer I."*
Oxford: Oxford University Press, 2012.

———. "Dionysius, Paul, and the Significance of the Pseudonym." *Modern Theology*
24 (2008): 541–55.

Stăniloae, Dumitru. *The Experience Of God.*
2 vols. Translated by Ioan Ioniță and Robert

Barringer. Brookline, MA: Holy Cross Orthodox Press, 1994.

Stauffer, Ethelbert. *New Testament Theology.* London: SCM, 1955.

Steel, Carlos. "The Return of the Body into Soul: Philosophical Musings on the Resurrection." In *History and Eschatology in John Scottus Eriugena and His Time,* edited by J. McEvoy and M. Dunne, 581–609. Leuven: Peeters, 2002.

Steele, Robert, and Dorothea Waley Singer. "The Emerald Table." *Proceedings of the Royal Society of Medicine* 21 (1928): 41–57.

Stein, Stephen J. *The Shaker Experience in America: A History of the United Society of Believers.* New Haven: Yale University Press, 1992.

Steinberg, Justin. "Dante's Justice? A Reappraisal of the *Contrapasso.*" *L'Alighieri* 44 (2014): 59–74.

Steiner, Rudolf. "Salt, Mercury, Sulphur." *Anthroposophy: A Quarterly Review of Spiritual Science* 6 (1931): 1–17.

Stengel, Friedemann, ed. *Kant und Swedenborg: Zugänge zu einem umstrittenen Verhältnis.* Tübingen: Niemeyer, 2008.

Stewart, J. S. "The Godhead." *Latter Day Saints' Millennial Star* 49 (1887): 785–89.

Stiglmayr, Joseph. "Der Neuplatoniker Proclus also Vorlage des sogen: Dionysius Areopagita in der Lehre vom Übel." *Historisches Jahrbuch* 16 (1895): 253–73, 721–48.

———. "Der sogenannte Dionysius Areopagita und Severus von Antiochien." *Scholastik* 3 (1928): 1–27, 161–89.

Stirner, Max. *The Ego and Its Own.* Cambridge: Cambridge University Press, 1995. Originally published as *Einzige und sein Eigentum* (Leipzig: Wigand, 1845).

Stonhouse, James. *Universal Restitution a Scripture Doctrine. This Prov'd in Several Letters Wrote on the Nature and Extent of Christ's Kingdom: Wherein the Scripture Passages, Falsly Alleged in Proof of the Eternity of Hell Torments, Are Truly Translated and Explained.* London, 1761.

Stoudt, John Joseph. *Sunrise to Eternity.* Philadelphia: University of Pennsylvania Press, 1957.

Stowe, Harriet Beecher. *Uncle Tom's Cabin, or Life among the Lowly.* New York: R. F. Fenno & Company, 1899.

Strange, David. *The Possibility of Salvation among the Unevangelized: An Analysis of Inclusivism in Recent Evangelical Theology.* Carlisle, UK: Paternoster, 2002.

Strauss, Leo. *Persecution and the Art of Writing.* Glencoe, IL: Free Press, 1952.

Streeter, B. H., and A. J. Appasamy. *The Sadhu: A Study in Mysticism and Practical Religion.* London: Macmillan, 1921.

Streeter, B. H., A. Clutton-Brock, C. W. Emmet, and J. A. Hadfield. *Immortality: An Essay in Discovery; Co-ordinating Scientific, Psychical, and Biblical Research.* New York: Macmillan, 1922.

Strickland, W. P. Introduction to *Universalism against Itself,* by Alexander Wilford Hall. New York: Hall & Co., 1883.

Ströter, Ernst Ferdinand. *Das Evangelium Gottes von der Allversöhnung in Christus.* Chemnitz: G. Koezle, 1915.

———. *Die Herrlichkeit des Leibes Christi: Der Epheserbrief.* Neumünster: G. Ihloff, 1910. Translated as *The Glory of the Body of Christ: An Opening Up of the Epistle to the Ephesians* (London: Morgan & Scott, 1909).

———. *Die Judenfrage und ihre göttliche Lösung nach Römer Kapitel 11.* Kassel: Röttger, 1903.

———. *Das Königreich Jesu Christi: Ein Gang durch die alttestamentlichen Verheissungen.* Gotha: Verlag der Missionsbuchhandlung P. Ott, 1909.

Strousma, Guy G. "Clement, Origen, and Jewish Esoteric Tradition." In *Schleier und Schwelle,* vol. 2, *Geheimnis und Offenbarung,* edited by Theo Sundermeier, 123–42. Münich: Wilhelm Fink, 1998.

Strutwolf, Holger. *Gnosis als System: Zur Rezeption der valentinianischen Gnosis bei Origenes.* Göttingen: Vandenhoeck & Ruprecht, 1993.

Stump, Eleonore. "Dante's Hell, Aquinas's Moral Theory, and the Love of God." *Canadian Journal of Philosophy* 16 (1986): 181–98.

———. "Sanctification, Hardening of the Heart, and Frankfurt's Concept of Free

Will." *Journal of Philosophy* 85 (1988): 395–420.

Sullivan, Francis. *Salvation outside the Church? Tracing the History of the Catholic Response.* 1992. Reprint, Eugene, OR: Wipf & Stock, 2002.

Surrey, Cameron. "Heaven Attracts and Hell Repels: Dynamic Interpretation of Balthasar's *Dare We Hope "That All Men Be Saved"? Pro Ecclesia* 25 (2016): 321–36.

Swedenborg, Emanuel. *Arcana Cœlestia, quae in Scriptura Sacra seu Verbo Domini sunt, detecta.* 8 vols. N.p., 1749–56.

Sweeny, Joseph. "Elhanan Winchester and the Universal Baptists." PhD diss., University of Pennsylvania, 1969.

Swinburne, Richard. "A Theodicy of Heaven and Hell." In *The Existence and Nature of God,* edited by Alfred J. Freddoso, 37–54. Notre Dame, IN: University of Notre Dame Press, 1983.

Swinden, Tobias. *An Enquiry into the Nature and Place of Hell: Shewing I. The Reasonableness of a Future State. II. The Punishments of the Next Life. III. The Several Opinions concerning the Place of Hell. IV. That the Fire of Hell Is Not Metaphorical, but Real. V. The Improbability of That Fire's Being in, or about the Center of the Earth. VI. The Probability of the Sun's Being the Local Hell, with Reasons for This Conjecture, and the Objections from Atheism, Philosophy, and the Holy Scriptures.* 2nd ed. London, 1727.

Takahashi, Hidemi. *Barhebraeus: A Bio-Bibliography.* Piscataway, NJ: Gorgias, 2005.

Talbott, Thomas. "Christ Victorious." In Parry and Partridge, *Universal Salvation?,* 15–31.

———. "Craig on the Possibility of Eternal Damnation." *Religious Studies* 28 (1992): 495–510.

———. "C. S. Lewis and the Problem of Evil." *Christian Scholar's Review* 17 (1987): 36–51.

———. "The Doctrine of Everlasting Punishment." *Faith and Philosophy* 7 (1990): 19–42.

———. "Freedom, Damnation and the Power to Sin with Impunity." *Religious Studies* 37 (2001): 417–34.

———. *The Inescapable Love of God.* Salem, OR: Universalist Publishers, 1999.

———. *The Inescapable Love of God.* 2nd ed. Eugene, OR: Cascade, 2014.

———. "The Just Mercy of God: Universal Salvation in George MacDonald (1824–1905)." In MacDonald [Parry], *"All Shall Be Well,"* 219–46.

———. "The Love of God and the Heresy of Exclusivism." *Christian Scholar's Review* 27 (1999): 99–112.

———. "Misery and Freedom: Reply to Walls." *Religious Studies* 40 (2004): 217–24.

———. "The New Testament and Universal Reconciliation." *Christian Scholar's Review* 21 (1992): 376–94.

———. "Punishment, Forgiveness, and Divine Justice." *Religious Studies* 29 (1993): 151–68.

———. "Universalism and the Greater Good: Reply to Gordon Knight." *Faith and Philosophy* 16 (1999): 102–5.

Talmage, James. *The Articles of Faith . . . of the Church of Jesus Christ of the Latter-Day Saints.* Salt Lake City: Deseret News, 1899.

Tanner, Kathryn. "Jesus Christ." In *The Cambridge Companion to Christian Doctrine,* edited by Colin Gunton, 245–72. Cambridge: Cambridge University Press, 1997.

Tanquerey, Adolphe. *The Spiritual Life: A Treatise on Ascetical and Mystical Theology.* Translated by Herman Branderis. 2nd ed. New York: Desclée, 1930.

Tardieu, Michel. *Écrits gnostiques: Codex de Berlin; Sources gnostiques et manichéennes.* Paris: Cerf, 1984.

Tasker, R. V. G. *The Biblical Doctrine of the Wrath of God.* London: Tyndale, 1951.

Tavernier, J. B. *Collections of Travels through Turkey into Persia and the East-Indies . . . The Travels of Monsieur Tavernier, Bernier, and Other Great Men.* 2 vols. London, 1684.

Taylor, Kevin, and Giles Waller, eds. *Christian Theology and Tragedy: Theologians, Tragic Literature, and Tragic Theory.* Burlington, VT: Ashgate, 2011.

Teilhard de Chardin, Pierre. *Activation of Energy.* Translated by Rene Hague. New York: Harcourt Brace, 1971.

———. *Building the Earth*. Translated by Nöel Lindsay. London: Geoffrey Chapman, 1965.

———. *The Divine Milieu*. Translated by Bernard Wall. New York: Harper, 1960.

———. *The Future of Man*. Translated by Norman Denny. 1959. Reprint, New York: Harper, 1964.

———. *Human Energy*. Translated by J. M. Cohen. New York: Harcourt Brace Jovanovich, 1962.

———. *Hymn of the Universe*. Translated by Gerald Vann. New York: Harper & Row, 1965.

———. *Lettres intimes à August Valensin, Bruno de Solages, Henri de Lubac, 1919–1955*. Paris: Aubier Montaigne, 1976.

———. *Oeuvres de Pierre Teilhard de Chardin*. 13 vols. Paris: Éditions du Seuil, 1955–76.

———. *The Phenomenon of Man*. Translated by Bernard Wall. 2nd ed. New York: Harper & Brothers, 1965.

Temple, Frederick, et al. *Essays and Reviews*. London: John W. Parker and Son, 1860.

Tennyson, Hallam. *Alfred Lord Tennyson: A Memoir by His Son*. 2 vols. London, Macmillan, 1897.

Teresa of Ávila. *The Life of Teresa of Jesus: The Autobiography of St. Teresa of Ávila*. Translated by E. Allison Peers. Garden City, NY: Image / Doubleday, 1960.

Ternovskii, F. "Materialy po istorii mistitsizma v Rossii. Zapiski K. A. Lohkvitskogo." *Trudy Kievskoi dukhovnoi akademii* 11 (1863).

Tertullian. *Quinti Septimi Florentis Tertulliani De Anima*, edited by J. H. Waszink. Supplements to Vigiliae Christianae 100. Leiden: Brill, 2010.

Teske, Roland J., trans. *On Genesis: Two Books on Genesis against the Manichees* [by Augustine]. Washington, DC: Catholic University of America Press, 1990.

Thackeray, H. St. J., trans. *Philo: The Life; Against Apion*. LCL 186. Cambridge, MA: Harvard University Press, 1926.

Thandeka. *The Embodied Self: Friedrich Schleiermacher's Solution to Kant's Problem of the Empirical Self*. Albany: State University of New York Press, 1995.

———. "Schleiermacher's *Dialektik*: The Discovery of the Self That Kant Lost." *Harvard Theological Review* 85 (1992): 433–52.

Theisen, Jerome. *The Ultimate Church and the Promise of Salvation*. Collegeville, MN: St. John's University Press, 1976.

Theodosius, Patriarch of Antioch. "Extracts from the Prolegomena and Commentary Attributed to Theodosius of Antioch." In Marsh, *Book of the Holy Hierotheos*, 143–72.

Theodotus. "*Excerpta ex Theodoto*; from the writings of Clement of Alexandria." http://gnosis.org/library/excr.htm. Online version of Robert Pierce Casey, *The Excerpta ex Theodoto of Clement of Alexandria*, 40–91. London: Christophers, 1934.

Theophilus of Antioch. *Ad Autolycum*. Edited and translated by Robert M. Grant. Oxford: Oxford University Press, 1970.

Thérèse of Lisieux. *The Poetry of St. Thérèse of Lisieux*. Translated by Donald Kinney. Washington, DC: Institute of Carmelite Studies, 1996.

Thiel, John E. "Time, Judgment, and Competitive Spirituality: A Reading of the Development of the Doctrine of Purgatory." *Theological Studies* 69 (2008): 741–85.

Thijssen, J. M. M. H. *Censure and Heresy at the University of Paris, 1200–1400*. Philadelphia: University of Pennsylvania Press, 1998.

Thomas, Mark. "Revival Language in the Book of Mormon." *Sunstone* 8 (May–June 1983): 19–25.

Thomas à Kempis. *The Imitation of Christ*. Translated by Aloysius Croft and Harold Bolton. Milwaukee: Bruce Publishing Co., 1940.

Thomas Aquinas. *Summa contra Gentiles: Book Three; Providence, Part II*. Translated by Vernon J. Bourke. Notre Dame, IN: University of Notre Dame Press, 1975.

———. *Summa Theologica*. Translated by Fathers of the English Dominican Province. New York: Benzinger, 1947.

Thomasius, Gottfried. *Origenes: Ein Beytrag zur Dogmengeschichte*. Nürnberg: Leonhard Schrag, 1837.

Thomassen, Einar. Introduction to *The Gospel of Truth*. In Meyer, *Nag Hammadi Scriptures*, 31–35.

———. Introduction to *The Treatise on Resurrection*. In Meyer, *Nag Hammadi Scriptures*, 49–51.

———. Introduction to *The Tripartite Tractate*. In Meyer, *Nag Hammadi Scriptures*, 57–58.

———. *The Spiritual Seed: The Church of the "Valentinians."* Leiden: Brill, 2008.

———. "The Valentinian School of Gnostic Thought." In Meyer, *Nag Hammadi Scriptures*, 790–94.

Thompson, Herbert. "Dioscorus and Shenoute." In *Recueil d'études égyptologiques dédiées à la mémoire de Jean-François Champollion*, 367–76. Paris: Librairie Ancienne Honoré Champion, 1922.

Thompson, Joseph Parrish. *Love and Penalty*. New York: Sheldon & Co., 1860.

Thompson, Thomas R. "Nineteenth-Century Kenotic Christology: The Waxing, Waning, and Weighing of a Quest for a Coherent Orthodoxy." In *Exploring Kenotic Christology: The Self-Emptying of God*, edited by C. Stephen Evans, 74–111. New York: Oxford University Press, 2006.

Thune, Nils. *The Behmenists and the Philadelphians: A Contribution to the Study of English Mysticism in the 17th and 18th Centuries*. Uppsala: Almqvist & Wiksell, 1948.

Tidball, Derek. "Can Evangelicals Be Universalists?" *Evangelical Quarterly* 84 (2012): 19–32.

Tillich, Paul. *The Construction of the History of Religion in Schelling's Positive Philosophy: Its Presuppositions and Principles*. Translated by Victor Nuovo. Lewisburg, PA: Bucknell University Press, 1974. Originally published as *Die religionsgeschichtliche Konstruktion in Schellings positiver Philosophie: Ihre Voraussetzungen und Prinzipien* (Breslau: H. Fleischmann, 1910).

———. *The Courage to Be*. 1952. Reprint, New Haven: Yale University Press, 2000.

———. *The Eternal Now*. New York: Scribner's Sons, 1963.

———. Foreword to *Jacob Boehme: His Life and Thought*, by John Stoudt, 7–8. New York: Seabury, 1957.

———. *A History of Christian Thought: From Its Judaic and Hellenistic Origins to Existentialism*. Edited by Carl E. Braaten. New York: Simon & Schuster, 1968.

———. *Mysticism and Guilt-Consciousness in Schelling's Philosophical Development*. Translated by Victor Nuovo. Lewisburg, PA: Bucknell University Press, 1974. Originally published as *Mystik und Schuldbewusstsein in Schellings philosophischer Entwicklung* (Gütersloh: Bertelsmann, 1912).

———. *Perspectives on 19th and 20th Century Protestant Theology*. New York: Harper & Row, 1967.

———. Preface to *Sunrise to Eternity: A Study of Jacob Boehme's Life and Thought*, by John Joseph Stoudt. Philadelphia: University of Pennsylvania Press, 1957.

———. "Schelling und die Anfänge des existentialistischen Protestes." *Zeitschift für philosophische Forschung* 9 (1955): 197–208.

———. *Systematic Theology*. 3 vols. Chicago: University of Chicago Press, 1951, 1957, 1963.

———. *Theology of Culture*. Edited by Robert C. Kimball. New York: Oxford University Press, 1959.

Tilliette, Xavier. *Schelling: Une philosophie en devenir*. Paris, 1970.

Tillotson, John. "Of the Eternity of Hell Torments." In *The Works of Dr. John Tillotson*, 3:76–97. 10 vols. London: J. F. Dove, 1820.

———. *A Sermon Preach'd before the Queen at White-Hall, March 7th, 1689–90*. London: Brabazon Aylmer, 1690.

———. *The Works of Dr. John Tillotson*. 10 vols. London: J. F. Dove, 1820.

Tirosh-Samuelson, Hava. "Engaging Transhumanism." In *H±: Transhumanism and Its Critics*, edited by Gregory R. Hansell and William Grassie, 19–52. Philadelphia: Metanexus Institute, 2011.

Tischendorf, Constantinus, ed. *Evangelia Apocrypha*. Lipsiae: Hermann Mendelssohn, 1876.

Tishby, Isaiah. "Gnostic Doctrines in Sixteenth-Century Jewish Mysticism." *Journal of Jewish Studies* 6 (1955): 146–52.

Todd, Lewis. *A Defense, Containing the Author's Renunciation of Universalism.* Erie, PA: O. Spafford, 1834.

[Tomberg, Valentin]. *Meditations on the Tarot.* Translated by Robert A. Powell. Afterword by Cardinal Hans Urs von Balthasar. Amity, NY: Amity House, 1985. Reprint, New York: Tarcher / Putnam, 2002. Published in French as *Méditations sur les 22 arcanes majeures du tarot* (Paris: Aubier / Montaigne, 1980).

Top, Brent L. "War in Heaven." In D. H. Ludlow, *Encyclopedia of Mormonism,* 4:1546–47.

Torrance, Thomas F. *The Atonement: The Person and Work of Christ.* Edited by Robert T. Walker. Downers Grove, IL: InterVarsity, 2009.

———. "The Atonement, the Singularity of Christ, and the Finality of the Cross: The Atonement and the Moral Order." In Cameron, *Universalism and the Doctrine of Hell,* 225–56.

———. *The Christian Doctrine of God: One Being Three Persons.* Edinburgh: T&T Clark, 1996.

———. *Divine and Contingent Order.* Edinburgh: T&T Clark, 1998.

———. *The Doctrine of Jesus Christ.* Eugene, OR: Wipf & Stock, 2002.

———. *Karl Barth: An Introduction to His Early Theology, 1910–1931.* London: SCM, 1962.

———. *Karl Barth: Biblical and Evangelical Theologian.* Edinburgh: T&T Clark, 1990.

———. *The Trinitarian Faith: The Evangelical Theology of the Ancient Catholic Church.* Edinburgh: T&T Clark, 1988.

———. "Universalism or Election?" *Scottish Journal of Theology* 2 (1949): 310–18.

Torre, Michael Durham. "God's Permission of Sin: Negative or Conditional Decree? A Defense of the Doctrine of F. Marin Sola, O.P., Based on the Principles of Thomas Aquinas." PhD diss., Graduate Theological Union, 1983.

Townsend, Anne Bradford. "The Cathars of Languedoc as Heretics: From the Perspectives of Five Contemporary Scholars." PhD diss., Union Institute and University, 2008.

Townsend, C. *Hell: A Difficult Doctrine We Dare Not Ignore.* Cambridge: Cambridge Papers, 1999.

Trabbic, Joseph G. "Can Aquinas Hope 'That All May be Saved'?" *Heythrop Journal* 57 (2016): 337–58.

Trennert-Helwig, Matthias. "The Church as the Axis of Convergence in Teilhard's Theology and Life." *Zygon* 30 (1995): 73–89.

Trigg, Joseph W. "The Charismatic Intellectual: Origen's Understanding of Religious Leadership." *Church History* 50 (1981): 5–19.

———. "A Decade of Origen Studies." *Religious Studies Review* 7 (1981): 21–27.

Trine, Ralph Waldo. *In Tune with the Infinite; or, Fullness of Peace, Power, and Plenty.* New York: Crowell, 1897.

Tripolitis, Antonia. "Return to the Divine: Salvation in the Thought of Plotinus and Origen." In *Disciplina Nostra: Essays in Memory of Robert F. Evans,* edited by Donald F. Winslow, 171–78. Philadelphia: Philadelphia Patristic Foundation, 1979.

Tripp, John. *Strictures on . . . Universal Reconciliation.* Portland: Shirley & Hyde, 1829.

Trippenbach, Max. "Rosamunde Juliane von der Asseburg: Die Prophetin und Heilige des Pietismus." In *Asseburger Familiengeschichte: Nachrichten über das Geschlecht Wolfenbüttel-Asseburg und seine Besitzungen,* 304–29. Hanover: Hahn, 1915.

Trumblower, Jeffrey A. *Rescue for the Dead: The Posthumous Salvation of Non-Christians in Early Christianity.* New York: Oxford University Press, 2001.

Tsambassis, Alexander Nicholas. "Evil and the 'Abysmal Nature' of God in the Thought of Brightman, Berdyaev, and Tillich." PhD diss., Northwestern University, 1957.

Tsirpanlis, Constantinos N. "The Concept of Universal Salvation in Saint Gregory of Nyssa." *Patristic and Byzantine Review* 28 (2010): 79–94.

Tugwell, Simon. *Human Immortality and the Redemption of Death*. Springfield, IL: Templegate, 1991.

Tulloch, John. *Pascal*. Edinburgh: William Blackwood, 1878.

Turner, Alice K. *The History of Hell*. New York: Harcourt Brace, 1993.

Turner, Denys. "Dionysius and Some Late Medieval Mystical Theologians of Northern Europe." *Modern Theology* 24 (2008): 651–65.

———. *Julian of Norwich, Theologian*. New Haven: Yale University Press, 2011.

———. "'Sin Is Behovely' in Julian of Norwich's *Revelations of Divine Love*." *Modern Theology* 20 (2004): 407–22.

Turner, H. E. W. *The Pattern of Christian Truth: A Study in the Relations between Orthodoxy and Heresy in the Early Church*. Bampton Lectures 1954. Eugene, OR: Wipf & Stock, 2004.

Turner, John D. Introduction to *The Thought of Norea*. In Meyer, *Nag Hammadi Scriptures*, 607–9.

Tyerman, Luke. *The Life and Times of the Rev. John Wesley, M.A., Founder of the Methodists*. 3 vols. New York: Harper & Bros., 1872.

———. *The Life of the Rev. George Whitefield*. New York, 1877.

Tyler, John. *Universal Damnation and Salvation, Clearly Proved by the Scriptures of the New and Old Testament*. Boston: B. Edes, 1798.

Ulrich, Hans G. "Adiaphora." In *The Encyclopedia of Christianity*, edited by E. Fahlbusch et al., 1:16–17. 6 vols. Grand Rapids: Eerdmans; Leiden: Brill, 1999.

Underhill, Evelyn. *Ruysbroeck*. London: G. Bell and Sons, 1915.

Urbach, Ephraim. *The Sages: Their Concepts and Beliefs*. Translated by Israel Abrahams. Cambridge, MA: Harvard University Press, 1987.

Valliere, Paul. *Modern Russian Theology: Bukharev, Soloviev, Bulgakov; Orthodox Theology in a New Key*. Edinburgh: T&T Clark, 2000.

———. "Solov'ëv and Schelling's Philosophy of Revelation." In van den Bercken, de Courten, and van der Zweerde, *Vladimir Solov'ëv*, 119–29.

Van Alstine, Nicholas. *Modern Universalism at War with the Bible and Reason*. Baltimore: Publication Rooms of the Evangelical Luther Church, 1847.

van den Bercken, Wil. "The Macrochristianity of Vladimir Solov'ëv." In van den Bercken, de Courten, and van der Zweerde, *Vladimir Solov'ëv*, 63–84.

van den Bercken, Wil, Manon de Courten, and Evert van der Zweerde, eds. *Vladimir Solov'ëv: Reconciler and Polemicist*. Leuven: Peeters, 2000.

van den Berg, Jan. "Menasseh Ben Israel, Henry More, and Johannes Hoornbeck on the Pre-Existence of Souls." In *Menasseh Ben Israel and His World*, edited by Yosef Kaplan, H. Méchoulan, and Richard H. Popkin, 98–116. Leiden: Brill, 1989.

van den Hoek, Annewies. "Clement and Origen as Sources on 'Noncanonical' Scriptural Traditions." In Dorival and Le Boulluec, *Origeniana Sexta*, 93–113.

———. "Origen and the Intellectual Heritage of Alexandria: Continuity or Disjunction?" In Daly, *Origeniana Quinta*, 40–50.

Vander Laan, David. "The Sanctification Argument for Purgatory." *Faith and Philosophy* 24 (2007): 331–39.

van der Sypt, Liesbeth. "A Practical Solution to Late Antique Asceticism: Syneisaktism." In *Studia Patristica* 72, edited by A. Brent, M. Ludlow, and M. Vinzent, 211–17. Leuven: Peeters, 2014.

van der Watt, Jan. Review of *Terms for Eternity: Aiônios and Aïdios in Classical and Christian Texts*, by Ilaria Ramelli and David Konstan. Piscataway, NJ: Gorgias, 2007. *Review of Biblical Literature* (September 2009). http://www.bookreviews.org.

van der Zweerde, Evert. "Deconstruction and Normalization: Towards an Assessment of the Philosophical Heritage of Vladimir Solov'ëv." In van den Bercken, de Courten, and van der Zweerde, *Vladimir Solov'ëv*, 39–62.

VanDoodewaard, William. *The Marrow Controversy and Seceder Tradition.* Grand Rapids: Reformation Heritage, 2011.

van Holten, Wilko. "Hell and the Goodness of God." *Religious Studies* 35 (1999): 37–55.

Vanhoozer, Kevin J. *The Drama of Doctrine: A Canonical-Linguistic Approach to Christian Theology.* Louisville: Westminster John Knox, 2005.

———. *Remythologizing Theology: Divine Action, Passion, and Authorship.* Cambridge: Cambridge University Press, 2010.

———, ed. *The Trinity in a Pluralistic Age: Theological Essays on Culture and Religion.* Grand Rapids: Eerdmans, 1997.

van Laak, Werner. *Allversöhnung: Die Lehre von der Apokatastasis; Ihre Grundlegung durch Origenes und ihre Bewertung in der gegenwärtigen Theologie bei Karl Barth und Hans Urs von Balthasar.* Sinzig: Sankt Meinrad Verlag für Theologie Christine Maria Esser, 1990.

van Unnik, W. C. "The 'Wise Fire' in a Gnostic Eschatological Vision." In *Kyriakon: Festschrift Johannes Quasten,* edited by Patrick Granfield and Josef A. Jungmann, 1:277–88. 2 vols. Münster: Aschendorff, 1970.

Var, Jean-François. "Martinism: First Period." In Hanegraaff et al., *Dictionary of Gnosis and Western Esotericism,* 770–79.

———. "Pasqually, Martines de." In Hanegraaff et al., *Dictionary of Gnosis and Western Esotericism,* 931–36.

Venn, Henry. *The Complete Duty of Man.* Edinburgh: J. Ogle, M. Ogle; Glasgow / London: R. Ogle and T. Hamilton, 1812.

———. "The Poetry of Death." *Tait's Magazine* 22 (1855): 157–59.

Versluis, Arthur. "The Mystery of Böhme's 'Ungrund.'" *Studies in Spirituality* 11 (2001): 205–11.

———. "What Is Esoteric? Methods in the Study of Western Esotericism." *Esoterica* 4 (2002): 1–15.

———. *Wisdom's Book: The Sophia Anthology.* St. Paul: Paragon House, 2000.

———. *Wisdom's Children: A Christian Esoteric Tradition.* Albany: State University of New York Press, 1999.

Vetter, Jakob. *Warum ich die Lehre von der Wiederbringung aller Dinge ablehne.* Geisweid: Deutsche Zeltmission, 1911. Reprinted in *Warum ich die Lehre der Allversöhnung verwerfen,* by Daniel Werner. Privately published, 1978.

Viatte, Auguste. *Les sources occultes du romantisme.* 2 vols. Paris: Champion, 1928.

Victoria, Queen of Great Britain. *The Letters of Queen Victoria.* 2nd series. *A Selection from Her Majesty's Correspondence and Journal between the Years 1862 and 1878.* 3 vols. Edited by George Earle Buckle. London: John Murray, 1926–28.

Vincent, Ken. *The Golden Thread: God's Promise of Universal Salvation.* New York: iUniverse, 2005.

Voegelin, Eric. "On Hegel: A Study in Sorcery." In *Published Essays, 1966–1985,* edited by Ellis Sandoz, 213–55. Vol. 12 of *The Collected Works of Eric Voegelin.* Baton Rouge: Louisiana State University Press, 1990.

Vogel, Dan. "Anti-Universalist Rhetoric in the Book of Mormon." In *New Approaches to the Book of Mormon,* edited by Brent Lee Metcalfe, 21–52. Salt Lake City: Signature, 1993.

Vogl, August. "Die Scheolvorstellungen Afrahats." *Östkirchliche Studien* 27 (1978): 46–48.

Volf, Miroslav. "After Moltmann: Reflections on the Future of Eschatology." In Bauckham, *God Will Be All in All,* 233–57.

———. *After Our Likeness: The Church as the Image of the Trinity.* Grand Rapids: Eerdmans, 1998.

———. *Exclusion and Embrace: A Theological Exploration of Identity, Otherness, and Reconciliation.* Nashville: Abingdon, 1996.

———. *Free of Charge: Giving and Forgiving in a Culture Stripped of Grace.* Grand Rapids: Zondervan, 2006.

Vööbus, Arthur. "Pneumatism." In *History of Asceticism in the Syrian Orient: A Contribution to the History of Culture in the Near East,* 2:307–15. 3 vols. Louvain: Secretariat du Corpus SCO, 1958–88.

Vorgrimler, Herbert. *Geschichte der Hölle.* Munich: Wilhelm Fink, 1993.

Wachter, Johann George. *Der Spinozismus im Judentum.* Amsterdam: Johann Wolters, 1699.

Wagner, C. Peter. *Dominion! How Kingdom Action Can Change the World.* Grand Rapids: Chosen, 2008.

Wainwright, Geoffrey. "Eschatology." In *The Cambridge Companion to Hans Urs von Balthasar,* edited by Edward T. Oakes and David Moss, 113–30. Cambridge: Cambridge University Press, 2004.

Waldrop, Charles T. *Karl Barth's Christology: Its Basic Alexandrian Character.* Berlin: de Gruyter, 1984.

Walker, Daniel Pickering. *The Decline of Hell: Seventeenth-Century Discussions of Eternal Torment.* Chicago: University of Chicago Press, 1964.

Walls, Jerry L. *Heaven, Hell, and Purgatory: Rethinking the Things That Matter Most.* Grand Rapids: Brazos, 2015.

———. "A Hell of a Choice: Reply to Talbott." *Religious Studies* 40 (2004): 203–16.

———. "A Hell of a Dilemma: Rejoinder to Talbott." *Religious Studies* 40 (2004): 225–27.

———. *Hell: The Logic of Damnation.* Notre Dame, IN: University of Notre Dame Press, 1992.

———. "A Philosophical Critique of Talbott's Universalism." In Parry and Partridge, *Universal Salvation?,* 105–24.

———. "Purgatory for Everyone." *First Things* 122 (April 2002): 26–30. https://www.firstthings.com/article/2002/04/purgatory-for-everyone.

———. *Purgatory: The Logic of Total Transformation.* New York: Oxford University Press, 2012.

Walsh, David. *The Mysticism of Innerworldly Fulfillment: A Study of Jacob Boehme.* Gainesville: University Presses of Florida, 1983.

Walsh, Maureen L. "Re-Imagining Redemption: Universal Salvation in the Theology of Julian of Norwich." *Horizons* 39 (2012): 189–207.

Walsh, Neale Donald. *Conversations with God.* New York: Putnam, 1996.

[Walton, Christopher]. *Notes and Materials for an Adequate Biography of the Celebrated Divine and Theosopher, William Law.* London, 1854.

Walvoord, John F. "The Literal View [of Hell]." In *Four Views on Hell,* edited by William V. Crockett, 11–28. Grand Rapids: Zondervan, 1996.

Wapler, Paul. "Die Theologie Hofmanns in ihrem Verhältnis zu Schellings positive Philosophie." *Neue kirchliche Zeitschrift* 16 (1905): 699–718.

Ware, Kallistos. *The Inner Kingdom.* Crestwood, NY: St. Vladimir's Seminary Press, 2000.

Warner, C. Terry. "Agency." In D. H. Ludlow, *Encyclopedia of Mormonism,* 1:26–27.

Warner, Rebecca. *Original Letters, from Richard Baxter, Matthew Prior, Lord Bolingbroke, Alexander Pope, Dr. Cheyne, Dr. Hartley, Dr. Samuel Johnson, Mrs. Montague, Rev. William Gilpin, Rev. John Newton, George Lord Lyttleton, Rev. Claudius Buchanan, etc., etc.* Bath: Richard Cruttwell; London: Longman, Hurst, Rees, Orme, and Brown, 1817.

Warren, Edward. *No Praeexistence; or, A Brief Dissertation against the Hypothesis of Humane Souls, Living in a State Antecedaneous to This.* London, 1667.

Warren, Samuel M., ed. *A Compendium of the Theological Writings of Emanuel Swedenborg.* 1875. Reprint, New York: Swedenborg Foundation, 1979.

Warton, John. *Death-bed Scenes and Pastoral Conversations.* 3 vols. London: C. & J. Rivington / John Murray, 1826–28.

Wasserstrom, Steven. "Uses of the Androgyne in the History of Religions." *Studies in Religion / Sciences Religieuses* 27 (1998): 437–53.

Watson, J. R., ed. *An Annotated Anthology of Hymns.* New York: Oxford University Press, 2002.

Watson, Nicholas, and Jacqueline Jenkins, eds. *A Revelation of Love: The Writings of Julian of Norwich.* University Park: Pennsylvania State University Press, 2006.

Watts, Graham H. "Is Universalism Theologically Coherent? The Contrasting Views of

P. T. Forsyth and T. F. Torrance." *Evangelical Quarterly* 84 (2012): 40–46.

Webb, Stephen. *Jesus Christ, Eternal God: Heavenly Flesh and the Metaphysics of Matter.* New York: Oxford University Press, 2012.

———. *Re-figuring Theology: The Rhetoric of Karl Barth.* Albany: State University of New York Press, 1991.

Weber, Max. "Theodicy, Salvation, and Rebirth." In *Economy and Society: An Outline of Interpretive Sociology,* edited by Guenther Roth and Claus Wittich, 1:518–29. 2 vols. Berkeley: University of California Press, 1978.

Webster, John. "'Love Is Also a Lover of Life': *Creatio ex Nihilo* and Creaturely Goodness." *Modern Theology* 29 (2013): 156–71.

———. "Trinity and Creation." *International Journal of Systematic Theology* 12 (2010): 4–19.

Weeks, Andrew. *Boehme: An Intellectual Biography of the Seventeenth-Century Philosopher and Mystic.* Albany: State University of New York Press, 1991.

Weil, Simone. *Waiting for God.* 1951. Translated by Emma Craufurd. Reprint, New York: Harper & Row, 1973.

Weinandy, Thomas. *Does God Suffer?* Notre Dame, IN: University of Notre Dame Press, 2000.

———. "Gnosticism and Contemporary Soteriology." In *Jesus: Essays in Christology,* 256–65. Ave Maria, FL: Sapientia, 2014.

———. "Terrence Tilley's Christological Impasses: The Demise of the Doctrine of the Incarnation." In *Jesus: Essays in Christology,* 243–55. Ave Maria, FL: Sapientia, 2014.

Weiss, Frederick G. *Beyond Epistemology: New Studies in the Philosophy of Hegel.* The Hague: Martinus Nijhoff, 1974.

Wenham, John W. "The Case for Conditional Immortality." In Cameron, *Universalism and the Doctrine of Hell,* 161–91.

———. *Facing Hell: An Autobiography, 1913–1996.* Carlisle, PA: Paternoster, 1998.

———. *The Goodness of God.* Leicester, UK: Inter-Varsity, 1974. Republished as *The Enigma of Evil* (Leicester, UK: Inter-Varsity, 1985).

Wensinck, A. J., trans. *Bar Hebraeus's "The Book of the Dove."* Leiden: Brill, 1919.

Wenz, Gunther. *Geschichte der Versöhnungslehre in der evangelischen Theologie der Neuzeit.* München: Kaiser, 1984.

Wesley, John. *John Wesley's Journal.* Edited by N. Curnock. 8 vols. London: Epworth, 1938.

West, E. W., trans. *Dadestan i denig.* Vol. 18 of *Sacred Books of the East.* Oxford: Oxford University Press, 1880.

Weyer-Menkhoff, Martin. "Friedrich Christoph Oetinger." In *The Pietist Theologians: An Introduction to Theology in the Seventeenth and Eighteenth Centuries,* edited by Carter Lindberg, 239–55. Malden, MA: Blackwell, 2004.

Whiston, William. *The Eternity of Hell Torments Considered; or, A Collection of Texts of Scripture, and Testimonies of the Three First Centuries, Relating to Them.* London, 1740.

White, Carol Wayne. *The Legacy of Anne Conway (1631–1679): Reverberations from a Mystical Naturalism.* Albany: State University of New York Press, 2008.

White, Edward. *Life in Christ.* London: E. Stock, 1878.

White, Jeremiah. *The Restoration of All Things.* London: N. Cliff and D. Jackson, 1712.

Whitehead, Alfred North. *Process and Reality: An Essay in Cosmology.* Edited by David Ray Griffin and Donald W. Sherburne. Corrected ed. New York: Free Press, 1978.

———. *Religion in the Making: The Lowell Lectures, 1926.* Cambridge: Cambridge University Press, 1927.

Widmer, Kurt. *Mormonism and the Nature of God: A Theological Evolution, 1830–1915.* Jefferson, NC: McFarland, 2000.

Widtsoe, John Andreas. *Joseph Smith: Seeker after Truth, Prophet of God.* Salt Lake City: Deseret News, 1951.

Wierciński, Andrzej, ed. *Between Friends: The Hans Urs von Balthasar and Gustav Siewerth Correspondence, 1954–1963.* Constance, Ger.: Gustav Siewerth Gesellschaft, 2005.

Wigley, Stephen D. *Karl Barth and Hans Urs von Balthasar: A Critical Engagement.* Edinburgh: T&T Clark, 2007.

Wikipedia. "Jehovah's Witnesses and Salvation." https://en.wikipedia.org/wiki/Jehovah ʼsʼuWitnesses_and_salvation.

Wilbur, Earl Morse. Socinianism and Its Antecedents. Vol. 1 of A History of Unitarianism. Cambridge, MA: Harvard University Press, 1947.

Wild, Robert, and Robin A. Parry. A Catholic Reading Guide to Universalism. Eugene, OR: Resource Publications, 2015.

Williams, Frank, trans. The Panarion of Epiphanius of Salamis Books II and III. De Fide. Leiden: Brill, 2013.

Williams, George Hunston. American Universalism: A Bicentennial Historical Essay. N.p.: Universalist Historical Society, 1971.

———. The Radical Reformation. 3rd ed. Kirksville, MO: Truman State University Press, 2000.

Williams, Mariam. "No Hell? That's an Unnerving Thought." National Catholic Reporter, March 24, 2014. https://www.ncron line.org/blogs/intersection/no-hell-thats-un nerving-thought.

Williams, Michael Allen. Rethinking "Gnosticism": An Argument for Dismantling a Dubious Category. Princeton: Princeton University Press, 1996.

Williams, Rowan. "Barth on the Triune God." In Karl Barth: Studies of His Theological Method, edited by S. W. Sykes, 147–93. Oxford: Clarendon, 1979.

———. "Does It Make Sense to Speak of Pre-Nicene Orthodoxy?" In The Making of Orthodoxy: Essays in Honour of Henry Chadwick, edited by Rowan Williams, 1–23. Cambridge: Cambridge University Press, 1989.

———, ed. Sergii Bulgakov: Towards a Russian Political Theology. Edinburgh: T&T Clark, 1999.

———. Wrestling with Angels: Conversations in Modern Theology. Edited by Mike Higton. Grand Rapids: Eerdmans, 2007.

Williams, Stephen N. The Election of Grace: A Riddle without a Resolution? Grand Rapids: Eerdmans, 2015.

———. "The Question of Hell and Salvation: Is There a Fourth View?" Tyndale Bulletin 57 (2006): 263–83.

Williams-Hogan, Jane. Review of Servetus, Swedenborg, and the Nature of God, by Andrew Dibb. Journal of Religious History 30 (2008): 374–75.

———. "Swedenborg, Emanuel." In Hanegraaff, Dictionary of Gnosis and Western Esotericism, 1096–105. 2 vols. Leiden: Brill, 2005. One-volume edition, Leiden: Brill, 2006.

Wilson, H. B. "Séances Historiques de Genève: The National Church." In Essays and Reviews: The 1860 Text and Its Reading, edited by Victor Shea and William Whitla, 275–344. Charlottesville: University Press of Virginia, 2000.

Wilson, N. G., ed. Herodoti Historiae. Oxford: Clarendon, 2015.

Wilson, Robert R. "The Hardening of Pharaoh's Heart." Catholic Biblical Quarterly 41 (1979): 18–36.

Wilson, Walter. The History and Antiquities of the Dissenting Churches and Meeting Houses in London, Westminster, and Southwark. 4 vols. London, 1808–14.

Winchester, Elhanan. "The Life and Trance of Dr. George de Benneville." With an introductory note by Ernest Cassara. Journal of the Universalist Historical Society 2 (1960–61): 71–87.

———. The Reigning Abominations, Especially the Slave Trade. London: H. Trapp, 1788.

———. A True and Remarkable Account of the Life and Trance of Dr. George de Benneville . . . Including What He Saw and Heard, during a Trance of Forty-Two Hours Both in the Regions of Happiness and Misery . . . To Which Is Prefixed a Recommendation Preface by the Rev. E[lhanan] Winchester. Norristown: David Sower, 1800.

Wind, Edgar. "The Revival of Origen." In Studies in Art and Literature for Belle da Costa Greene, edited by D. Miner, 412–24. Princeton: Princeton University Press, 1954.

Winfield, A. B. Antidote to the Errors of Universalism. Auburn, NY: Derby, Miller & Co., 1850.

Wingren, Gustav. Theology in Conflict: Nygren, Barth, Bultmann. Edinburgh: Oliver & Boyd, 1958.

Winstanley, Gerrard. *The Complete Works of Gerrard Winstanley*, edited by Thomas N. Corns et al. 2 vols. Oxford: Oxford University Press, 2009.

———. *The Law of Freedom and Other Writings*. Edited by Christopher Hill. Harmondsworth, UK: Penguin, 1973.

———. *The Works of Gerrard Winstanley*. Edited by G. Sabine. Ithaca, NY: Cornell University Press, 1959.

Wise, Joshua. "The Role of Hell in Various Universalistic Theologies with Special Reference to the Theology of George MacDonald." PhD diss., Catholic University of America, 2016.

Wise, Russ. "Embraced by the Light of Deception." Review article. http://www.leaderu.com/orgs/probe/docs/eadie.html.

Wisse, Frederick. "Gnosticism and Early Monasticism in Egypt." In *Gnosis: Festschrift für Hans Jonas*, edited by B. Aland, 431–40. Göttingen: Vandenhoeck & Ruprecht, 1978.

———. Introduction to *The Apocryphon of John*. In *The Nag Hammadi Library in English*, edited by James M. Robinson, 98–116. New York: Harper & Row, 1977.

Wittgenstein, Ludwig. *Philosophical Investigations*. Translated by G. E. M. Anscombe. Oxford: Basil Blackwell, 1953.

Wittmer, Michael. *Christ Alone: An Evangelical Response to Rob Bell's "Love Wins."* Grand Rapids: Edenridge, 2011.

Wolfson, Elliot R. *"Tiqqun ha-Shekhinah*: Redemption and the Overcoming of Gender Dimorphism in the Messianic Kabbalah of Mose hayyim Luzzatto." *History of Religions* 36 (1997): 289–332.

Wolterstorff, Nicholas. "Barth on Evil." *Faith and Philosophy* 13 (1996): 584–608.

Wood, Thomas. *Annihilation and Universalism*. London: Wesleyan Conference Office, 1877.

———. *The Doctrines of Annihilation and Universalism Viewed in the Light of Reason, Analogy, and Revelation: With Critical Notes and a Review of "Salvator Mundi."* London: Wesleyan Conference Office, 1881.

Woozley, A. D. "Universals." In *The Encyclopedia of Philosophy*, edited by Paul Edwards, 8:194–206. 8 vols. New York: Macmillan, 1967.

Wordsworth, William. *The Poems of William Wordsworth*. London: Edward Moxon, 1858.

Wormhoudt, Arthur. "Newton's Natural Philosophy in the Behmenist Works of William Law." *Journal of the History of Ideas* 10 (1949): 411–29.

Wright, Christopher. *The Mission of God: Unlocking the Bible's Grand Narrative*. Nottingham, UK: Inter-Varsity, 2006.

Wright, N. T. *Paul and His Recent Interpreters: Some Contemporary Debates*. Minneapolis: Fortress, 2015.

———. *Paul and the Faithfulness of God*. 2 vols. Minneapolis: Fortress, 2013.

———. *The Resurrection of the Son of God*. Vol. 3 of *Christian Origins and the Question of God*. Minneapolis: Fortress, 2003.

———. *Surprised by Hope: Rethinking Heaven, the Resurrection, and the Mission of the Church*. New York: HarperOne, 2008.

———. "Towards a Biblical View of Universalism." *Themelios* 4 (1979): 54–61.

Wright, Nigel G. *The Radical Evangelical: Seeking a Place to Stand*. London: SPCK, 1996.

———. "Universalism in the Theology of Jürgen Moltmann." *Evangelical Quarterly* 84 (2012): 33–39.

Wright, Richard. *The Eternity of Hell Torments Indefensible: Being an Examination of Several Passages in Dr. Ryland's Sermon, Intitled 'The First Lye Refuted'; in a Series of Letters to a Friend*. London: William Burton, n.d. [ca. 1800].

Wuthnow, Robert. *Boundless Faith: The Global Outreach of American Churches*. Berkeley: University of California Press, 2010.

Wyatt, Jean. *Judge Is the Savior: Towards a Universalist Understanding of Salvation*. Eugene, OR: Resource Publications, 2015.

Wyschogrod, Michael. "Why Was and Is the Theology of Karl Barth of Interest to a Jewish Theologian?" In *Abraham's Promise: Judaism and Jewish-Christian Relations*, edited by R. Kendall Soulen, 211–24. Grand Rapids: Eerdmans, 2004.

Yandell, Keith E. "The Doctrine of Hell and Moral Philosophy." *Religious Studies* 28 (1992): 75–90.

Yarbrough, Robert W. "Jesus on Hell." In Morgan and Peterson, *Hell under Fire*, 67–90.

Yates, Frances A. *Giordano Bruno and the Hermetic Tradition.* 1964. Reprint, Chicago: University of Chicago Press, 1991.

Yocum, John. "A Cry of Dereliction?" *International Journal of Systematic Theology* 7 (2005): 72–80.

Yoder, Timothy J. "Hans Urs von Balthasar and Kenosis: The Pathway to Human Agency." PhD diss., Loyola University, 2013.

Young, Brigham. "Adam, Our Father and Our God" (April 9, 1852). In *Journal of Discourses by Brigham Young . . . and Others*, edited by G. D. Watt, 1:46–53. Liverpool, UK: F. D. and S. W. Richards, 1854.

———. *Journal of Discourses.* 26 vols. Edited by G. D. Watt. Liverpool, UK: F. D. Richards, 1854–86.

———. "To Know God Is Eternal Life" (February 8, 1857). In *Journal of Discourses*, vol. 4. http://jod.mrm.org/4/215.

Young, George M. *The Russian Cosmists: The Esoteric Futurism of Nikolai Fedorov and His Followers.* New York: Oxford University Press, 2012.

Young, William Paul. *The Shack.* Newbury Park, CA: Windblown Media, 2011.

Youth of the City, A [pseud.]. *Thoughts on the Doctrine of Universal Salvation.* Philadelphia: Prichard & Hall, 1790.

Zaehner, R. C. *The Dawn and Twilight of Zoroastrianism.* New York: Putnam's Sons, 1961.

Zalitis, Emma. "Stock, Bud, and Flowers: A Comparative Study of Mysticism in Böhme, Blake, and Coleridge." PhD diss., Purdue University, 1981.

Zander, Lev. *Bog i mir: mirosozertsanie ottsa Sergiia Bulgakova.* 2 vols. Paris: YMCA Press, 1948.

Zender, Martin. *Martin Zender Goes to Hell: A Critical Look at an Un-Criticized Doctrine.* Canton, OH: Starke & Hartman, 2004.

Zen'kovskiĭ, V. V. *A History of Russian Philosophy.* Translated by George L. Kline. New York: Columbia University Press, 1953.

Zernov, Nicholas. *The Russian Religious Renaissance of the Twentieth Century.* New York: Harper & Row, 1963.

Ziegler, Clement. *Elsass I: Strasbourg, 1522–1532.* Edited by Manfred Krebs and Jean-George Rott. Gütersloh: Gerd Mohn, 1959.

Zoloth, Laurie. "Interrupting Your Life: An Ethics for the Coming Storm." 2014 AAR [American Academy of Religion] Presidential Address. *Journal of the American Academy of Religion* 84 (2016): 3–24.

Zwingli, Ulrich. *Huldreich Zwinglis sämtliche Werke.* Edited by Emil Egli et al. Berlin: C. A. Schwetschke und Sohn, 1905–.

Index of Ancient Sources

Index of Names and Subjects

Geels, Antoon, 540n384
Geffert, Bryn, 690n16, 713n101, 725n157
Oehli, Paul, a panaaG
Geiger, Abraham, 191n217
Generchak, Christopher M., 640–41n124
George, N. D., 965n110
Gerhard, Ludwig, 514, 566, 1131
Gerrish, Brian, 627
Gersh, Stephen, 226n369
Gerstner, John, 966n112
Geyer, Karl, 809
Gibbons, Brian J., 406n305, 476n128,
    499n207
Gichtel, Johann Georg, 225, 442, 475n128,
    483–84, 487–90, 492, 497n203, 498–500,
    553, 577n20, 696n42, 697, 1043, 1058,
    1069
Gignoux, Philippe, 332n49
Gil, Thomas, 49n79, 657n191
Giles, Jerry C., 1162n25
Giles, Kevin, 784n152
Gill, Michael, 81n193
Gillihan, Charles, 939
Gilson, Étienne, 276n174
Ginzberg, Louis, 183n196
Girard, René, 985n220
Givens, Terryl L., 212n319, 222n349, 251n77,
    252n80, 253, 406n303, 618n36, 1170n71
Gladstone, William Ewart, 96
Glanvill, Joseph, 405, 411–12
Gnilka, Joachim, 74
gnosis and/or gnosticism, 3, 215, 392, 413,
    444, 668–70, 910
  and Islamic Sufism, 3, 1013
  as precedent for universalism, 3, 1005
  and Western esoteric universalism, 3, 9,
    127–28, 158, 218–34, 444, 543–44, 557,
    944–48, 995, 1006, 1127
Göckel, Matthias, 30n12, 624nn56–57,
    627n71, 629n83, 777n121, 863n487
God, 200–207, 222, 348, 354, 365–66, 607,
    681, 1003, 1013–24
  "agapeistic" vs. "erotic" conceptions of,
    12–13, 25, 459, 655, 1032
  becoming/evolving of, 128, 210, 325, 375,
    454, 459n69, 463–65, 624–25, 640–41,
    654, 659–60, 720, 829–31, 947, 1032
  death of, 646–47, 867, 910, 1014
  as event, 784
  Father of all, 90, 98, 569, 597
  goodness of, 949, 959
  immutability of, 371, 519, 934

knowability, 160, 444, 566, 641–42, 715,
    810, 1034, 1111
  love of, xxii, xxiii, 11, 22, 32–33, 36–78,
    70–71, 78, 85–86, 106–8, 218, 262, 282,
    371–74, 396, 423, 426–27, 432, 436, 480,
    491, 508, 511–12, 519–20, 524, 529–30,
    570–72, 622–23, 678, 709–10, 716, 730,
    821, 831, 837, 911, 926, 941, 968–72, 990,
    1000, 1008, 1037–38, 1060, 1085
  Mormon ideas of, 207–15, 1160–61
  names of, 11–12, 344, 349, 435, 887, 1112
  nonbeing and, 375–76, 461
  omnipotence of, 36–37, 421, 425–26, 532,
    683, 821, 952
  "plerotic" vs. "kenotic," 1029
  providence of, 12, 154, 246–47, 254, 317–19,
    343, 492, 558, 836, 922–23
  rejection of, xxii, 373, 736, 870, 999, 1009,
    1060, 1153
  self-revelation of, 642, 658, 682, 715–18, 745,
    756, 767, 784, 838
  theophanies and manifestations of, 11–12,
    158–59, 230, 342, 379–83, 461–62, 544,
    579, 661–62
  transcendence/immanence of, 11–14, 160–
    62, 349, 375–77, 438, 625, 654–55, 665,
    834, 984–85
  will of, 452–53n41, 683–84n311, 783, 950–52,
    1003n11, 1057, 1061
  wrath of, 33, 60–61, 111, 164n123, 467,
    478–81, 522, 535, 566, 599, 677, 975n161,
    989, 1106–10
Godbey, John Charles, 1039n87
Godin, André, 404n396
Goldish, Matt, 188n211, 189n214
Goldstein, Bernard R., 964n105
Gomes, Alan W., 1039n87
Goodall, Lawrence D., 930n211
Goodrick-Clarke, Nicholas, 107n6
Gordon, William, 965n110
Gorodetzky, Nadejda, 713n101
Goroncy, Jason, 863n487
Gorringe, Timothy, 1039n88, 1040n90
Goshen-Gottstein, Alon, 183n196
gospel, xxii, 20, 89, 846–48, 989n235
  eternal gospel, 176, 269, 270n152, 489, 567,
    1044, 1149
  preaching of, 45, 278, 930
  substance of the, 525, 877, 977–83, 987–89,
    991
  See also universalism: "gospel" of
Goudriaan, Aza, 768n77

Peters, Samuel, 965n110
Peters, Ted, 831
Petersen, Johanna Eleonora, 8, 23, 128, 175,
    442, 486–87, 492, 509–16, 564, 1014,
    1028, 1131, 1137
Petersen, Johann Wilhelm, 6, 8, 23, 128,
    174–75, 178n183, 372, 442, 486–87, 492,
    509–16, 534n349, 564, 1014, 1028, 1043,
    1069, 1118n46, 1131, 1137
Peterson, Daniel J., 665
Peterson, Eugene, 970
Peterson, Robert A., 109, 920n180, 966n112,
    1048n110
Peukert, Will-Erich, 452n37
Pfau, Julie Shoshana, 943n19
Pfister, Oskar, 216n334
Pfizenmaier, Martin, 491n168
Phan, Peter, 37n39, 914, 1051–52
Pharaoh (biblical and qur'anic figure), 130,
    273n165, 286, 773, 777–79, 781, 954, 990,
    1061, 1109–10
Pharisees, 144, 594, 603, 606
Philoxenus of Mabbug, 275, 278, 333n50, 344–
    45, 347n102, 349–51, 354, 356, 435, 1007
Pico della Mirandola, Giovanni Francesco, 12,
    59–60, 168, 176–78, 340n73, 390, 397–
    400, 414, 439, 450n29, 634, 649, 691n22,
    696, 718n121, 1006, 1068–69, 1071, 1091,
    1127, 1130, 1133
Pierre of Blois, 236n13, 1090n1
Pike, Nelson, 1144n6
Pindar, 133–34
Pinggéra, Karl, 344n88
Pingree, E. M., 965n110
Pinkard, Terry, 611n6, 639n117
Pinnock, Clark H., 45, 46n68, 109n307, 114,
    114n328, 123
Pitstick, Alyssa Lyra, 37n42, 62, 906n131,
    928–31
Pius XII (pope), 877
Plato, 133–40, 222, 247, 251–53, 272, 281, 316,
    334, 337, 374n190, 397, 407, 410, 413–14,
    434, 619, 653, 669, 671, 679n305, 718–19,
    964n105, 1028, 1054, 1068, 1070, 1075,
    1121, 1143–45, 1148
Platon (metropolitan of Moscow), 43, 561
Platonism, 112, 129, 141, 245, 267n141, 272,
    325, 334–38, 397, 412–14, 439, 528–29,
    678–79, 701, 718, 860, 1159
    Cambridge Platonists, 80–81, 405–7,
    878n30

Plotinus, 151, 156n95, 245, 249–51, 317,
    336n60, 341 42n79, 374n190, 397, 407,
    409, 413n341, 421n383, 434, 456–57, 621,
    703n67, 1068, 1070, 1092, 1116–17n36,
    1122n60
Plugg, Allen, 102n282
Plumptre, Edward Hayes, 31, 93n244, 1133
Plutarch, 138–39, 1076
pneumatology, 469–70, 814, 820
Pocquet, Anthony, 400–401
poena damni vs. poena sensus, 102
Pohle, Joseph, 34n32, 67n147, 67n149, 68,
    68n152
Polkinghorne, John, 1023
polytheism, 170, 183, 376n197, 721
Poncé, Charles, 158n107, 167n139, 222n351,
    224n359
Pontifex, Mark, 34n32
Pope, Richard Martin, 884–87
Popkin, Richard H., 404n299, 419n375
Popp, Karl Robert, 418n371, 442n7
Popper, Hans, 452n37
Pordage, John, 178n183, 414, 442, 491–94,
    497–500, 503n217, 553, 564, 696–97, 1043
Porete, Marguerite, 391, 392, 392nn246–47
Porphyry, 245, 247, 268n144, 334, 337–38,
    374n190, 397
Postel, Guillaume, 176–80, 228, 230, 397,
    439, 696n41, 1006, 1034, 1130, 1133
Poston, Ted, 432n430
Potter, Jean A., 376n198, 390n242, 109n4
Pourrat, Pierre, 72n165
Powell, Thomas, 965n110
Powys, David J., 77n181, 109n307
Prager, L., 32n23
Pratt, Orson, 207n300, 209, 209n307, 211
prayer, 36, 65–69, 107–8, 121, 142, 161–62,
    217, 241, 272, 278, 293, 305, 424, 434, 488,
    494, 517, 549, 666, 698–99, 724, 903,
    912, 979, 1008, 1018, 1065
prayers for the dead. See suffrages
predestination, 12–14, 188, 283, 374n189, 377,
    380, 404, 480, 509, 523n298, 526, 566,
    572, 626, 766, 779–82, 791–92, 807, 845,
    878, 922, 923n190, 951, 988–89, 1017n25,
    1027, 1047, 1160n15
Preger, Wilhelm, 393n252
Premier Christian Radio, 957n75
premillennialism, 958, 977. See also
    millennialism
Preuss, Arthur, 67n147, 67n149, 68n152